Cases and Materials
on Michigan Criminal Law

Cases and Materials
on Michigan Criminal Law

Project Director and Editor
Donald A. Calkins
Associate Professor, Wayne State University
Criminal Justice and Law Enforcement Program

Consultant
James H. Brickley
Lieutenant Governor, State of Michigan

Volume II
Wayne State University Press, Detroit, 1974

Library of Congress Cataloging in Publication Data

Calkins, Donald A
    Cases and materials on Michigan criminal law.
    Published in 1970 under title: Cases and materials
on Michigan criminal law for the police.
    1. Criminal law—Michigan—Cases. I. Title.
KFM4761.A7C34 1974   345′.774   74–12490
ISBN 0–8143–1538–0 (V. 2)

*The research was funded by a grant from the National Institute of Law
Enforcement and Criminal Justice, Law Enforcement Assistance Administration, United States Department of Justice. The fact that the National Institute
of Law Enforcement and Criminal Justice furnished financial support to the
activity described in this publication does not necessarily indicate the concurrence of the Institute in the statements or conclusions contained herein.*

TABLE OF CONTENTS

PART II

SUBSTANTIVE CRIMINAL LAW - SPECIFIC CRIMES

CHAPTER V

HOMICIDAL OFFENSES

CHAPTER VI

ASSAULTS, EXTORTION AND RELATED OFFENSES

CHAPTER VII

SEXUAL OFFENSES

CHAPTER VIII

ABDUCTION, FALSE IMPRISONMENT, AND KIDNAPPING

iv

CHAPTER IX

OFFENSES INVOLVING THEFT

v

CHAPTER X

BURGLARY AND POSSESSION OF BURGLAR'S TOOLS

CHAPTER XI

ROBBERY

CHAPTER XII

FORGERY, COUNTERFEITING, AND FRAUD

PART II

SUBSTANTIVE CRIMINAL LAW - SPECIFIC CRIMES

CHAPTER V

HOMICIDAL OFFENSES

A. Murder

    1. Michigan Compiled Laws (1948)

750.316 First degree murder

    Sec. 316. FIRST DEGREE MURDER - All murder which shall be perpetrated by means of poison, or lying in wait, or any other kind of wilful, deliberate and premeditated killing, or which shall be committed in the perpetration, or attempt to perpetrate any arson, rape, robbery, burglary, larceny of any kind, extortion or kidnapping, shall be murder of the first degree, and shall be punished by solitary confinement at hard labor in the state prison for life.

750.317 Second degree murder

    Sec. 317. SECOND DEGREE MURDER - All other kinds of murder shall be murder of the second degree, and shall be punished by imprisonment in the state prison for life, or any term of years, in the discretion of the court trying the same.

750.319 Death as result of fighting a duel

    Sec. 319. DEATH AS RESULT OF FIGHTING A DUEL - Any person, being an inhabitant or resident of this state, who shall, by previous appointment or engagement made within the same, fight a duel without the jurisdiction of this state, or who shall fight a duel within this state, and in so doing shall inflict a mortal wound upon any person, whereof the person so injured shall afterwards die within this state, shall be guilty of murder of the first degree within this state, and may be indicted, tried and convicted in the county where such death shall happen.

750.320 Seconds in duels resulting in death

    Sec. 320. SECONDS IN DUELS RESULTING IN DEATH - Any person, being an inhabitant or resident of this state, who shall be the second of either party in such duel as is mentioned in the next preceding section,[1] and shall be present as a second when such mortal wound is inflicted, whereof death shall ensue within this state, shall be deemed to be an accessory before the fact to the crime of murder in this state, and may be indicted, tried and convicted in the county where the death shall happen, or in which such wound shall have been inflicted.

Footnote

1. Section 750.319

750.327 Death due to explosives

Sec. 327. DEATH DUE TO EXPLOSIVES - No person shall order, send, take or carry, or attempt to order, send, take or carry dynamite, nitro-glycerine or any other explosive substance which explodes by concussion or friction, concealed in any bag, satchel, valise, trunk, box or in any other manner, either as freight or baggage, on any passenger boat or vessel, or any railroad car or train of cars, street car, motor bus, stage or other vehicle used wholly or partly for carrying passengers.

In case any person violates any of the provisions of this section, he, and any consignee to whom any such dynamite, nitro-glycerine, or other explosive substance has been consigned by his procurement in violation of any of the provisions hereof, shall be guilty of a felony, punishable by imprisonment in the state prison for life or any term of years, in case such dynamite, nitro-glycerine or other explosive substance explodes and destroys human life while in possession of any carrier or on any boat, vessel, railroad car, street car, motor bus, stage or other vehicle contrary to any of the provisions hereof.

750.328 Death due to explosives; placed with intent to destroy building or object

Sec. 328. DEATH FROM EXPLOSIVES PLACED WITH INTENT TO DESTROY, ETC., BUILDING OR OBJECT - Any person who with intent to destroy, throw down or injure the whole or any part of any building or object, places or causes to be placed in, upon, under, against or near such building or object any gun powder or other explosive substance which upon explosion causes the death of any person, shall be guilty of a felony, punishable by imprisonment in the state prison for life or any term of years.

2. Definitions and Construction of Statutes

People v. Austin
221 Mich. 635

SHARPE, J. The defendants, 19 and 16 years of age respectively, tried together, review their conviction of murder in the first degree on writ of error. It is clearly established by the proofs that Paul DeLisle died at his home in Flint on December 10, 1921, and that his death re-

659

sulted from poison by carbolic acid taken by him in a drink of whisky. The defendants were arrested, charged with the crime, and, as the prosecution claims, on December 11th made a voluntary confession of their guilt. . . .

The prosecution relies on the statute (3 Comp. Laws 1915, Sec. 15192):

"All murder which shall be perpetrated by means of poison, or lying in wait, or any other kind of wilful, deliberate and premeditated killing, or which shall be committed in the perpetration, or attempt to perpetrate any arson, rape, robbery or burglary, shall be deemed murder of the first degree, and shall be punished by solitary confinement at hard labor in the State prison for life."

Attention is also called to the following language from the opinion in People v. Hall, 48 Mich. 482, 484 (42 Am. Rep. 477):

"Murder by poison, under the statute, is always murder in the first degree, and the jury should have been so charged."

Reliance is also placed on People v. Repke, 103 Mich. 459, wherein this court held that when murder is committed and "there is no fact or circumstance that would reduce it below the first degree," the jury should be so instructed.

"Murder is where a person of sound memory and discretion unlawfully kills any reasonable creature in being, in the peace of the State, with malice prepense or aforethought, either express or implied." Tiffany's Criminal Law (How. 4th Ed.), p. 952.

"Manslaughter is the unlawful and felonious killing of another without malice, either express or implied." Id 972.

In 13 R. C. L. p. 784, involuntary manslaughter is defined as follows:

"The crime is defined by the common law as the killing of one person of another person, in doing some unlawful act not amounting to a felony, nor likely to endanger life and without an intention to kill; or where one kills another while doing a lawful act in an unlawful manner."

Neither murder nor manslaughter is defined in our statutes. The section above quoted simply classifies a murder perpetrated in a particular manner as murder in the first degree. It has no application until a murder has been established. Then, if the proofs show that it was perpetrated by means of poison, lying in wait, etc., the jury should be instructed that it is deemed murder in the first degree. Homicide is the killing of a human being by a human being. It may, or may not, be felonious. If felonious, it is either murder or manslaughter, dependent upon

the facts and circumstances surrounding the killing. To
constitute murder, the killing must have been perpetrated
with malice aforethought, either express or implied. The
intent to kill will be implied when death results from poison intentionally administered. If it appears that the
poison was not administered with intent to take life, but
to aid in the perpetration of another crime, or in order
to accomplish an unlawful act, it is no less murder. But
where it is not so administered, and where death as a result is so remote a contingency that no reasonably person
could have taken it into consideration when administering
the poison and could not have contemplated that death would
result therefrom, the homicide is manslaughter only. The
statute classifies all murders perpetrated "by means of poison, or lying in wait, or any other kind of wilful, deliberate and premeditated killing" as murder in the first degree.
Murder by poison is so included because it results from a
wilful, deliberate and premeditated act. Administering poison with intent to kill is necessarily so. That the intent
with which the poisonous substance is administered is material to the issue presented on such a charge was clearly recognized in People v. Thacker, 108 Mich. 652 and People v. Mac-
Gregor, 178 Mich. 436. In each of these cases this court
held that the prosecution might show that the defendant,
about the same time, was giving poison to another inmate
of the household, as bearing upon the intent with which it
was administered to the deceased person. The reasoning in
Wellar v. People, 30 Mich. 16, and in People v. Droste, 160
Mich. 66, is instructive on the general rule that where there is
testimony from which the jury might find the absence of such
a felonious intent as is necessary to constitute murder, an
instruction that they might convict of manslaughter should
be given. On the record here presented, the jury should have
been so instructed. . . .

The judgment of the court is set aside and a new trial
granted. The defendants will be returned to the custody
of the sheriff of Genesee county to await such trial.

WIEST, C. J., and FELLOWS, McDONALD, BIRD, MOORE, and
STEERE, JJ., concurred. CLARK, J., did not sit.

People v. Potter
5 Mich. 1

On exception from Wayne Circuit.
The prisoner was indicted for the murder of Michael
Walsh and convicted of murder of the first degree.
It was proved, on the trial, that Walsh and the prisoner
had been working together for some time before the 25th of
October, 1857, and were on friendly terms; that, on the
evening of October 24th, the prisoner and Walsh went to the
theatre in Detroit, and left about ten o'clock, in company

with *two or three other persons; that they had been drinking some in the course of the evening, and immediately
after leaving the theater drank together three times, each
treating the other in turn, and were soon badly intoxicated;
and that, in company with others, they went up Third street
to a public-house. The prosecution then offered to show, by
persons who accompanied them from the theater to the public-
house, that when the prisoner was passing along Third street
he said he had been reading "Jack Rand," and he should not
be surprised if he should turn highwayman sometime, for he
had struggled with poverty long enough; and that, at the
time he said this, he had an open dirk-knife in his hand,
and said if any man piled on to him, he would stick him. To
the introduction of which evidence the counsel for the prisoner objected that it did not tend to show that the prisoner
committed the offense for which he was then being tried,but
only a general disposition to commit crime. The court overruled the objection, and permitted the evidence to be given;
and defendant's counsel excepted.

It appears from the evidence, that, immediately after this
statement, the prisoner handed his knife to one of the witnesses, who shut it, and handed it back to the prisoner, and
prisoner then put it in his pocket; that, up to this time,
there had been no difficulty or unkind words between prisoner
and the deceased; that the prisoner did not threaten Walsh,
or any one else, when he flourished his knife; that, after
arriving at the public-house, Walsh treated, the prisoner
drinking with him; that Walsh and the prisoner left the public-
house about a quarter before twelve that night, alone, up to
which time there had been no difficulty between them, and
they seemed to be fast friends; that the prisoner returned
to the public-house about one o'clock, and stayed all night;
and that Walsh was found next morning, a short distance from
said public-house, badly cut, and died soon after. It was
proved by the government that the prisoner said the next day
he had killed Walsh; that Walsh seized him, twitched him a-
round, *threw him down, and got him by the throat, and that
he thought one or the other must die, and when Walsh had
him down, holding him by the throat, he stabbed him and killed him in self-defense. The evidence showed Walsh to have
been a much larger man than the prisoner. There was no other
testimony to show under what circumstances the act was done,
and no proof tending to show that the prisoner had any other
motive to kill the deceased.

The counsel for the prisoner asked the court to charge
the jury that, to constitute murder of the first degree,
under the statute, something more was necessary than was
necessary to constitute murder at the common law; that, to
constitute murder of the first degree, the murder must be
preceded or attended by facts and circumstances not necessarily an ingredient of murder at the common law; that, if the
government sought to have the jury convict the prisoner of
murder of the first degree, the burden of proof was on the

662

government, to show that the murder was committed in the perpetration, or in the attempt to perpetrate, arson, rape, robbery, or burglary, or by poison, or by lying in wait; or to prove such facts in addition to the act of killing as made the killing murder of the first degree. The court refused so to charge, but did charge the jury that if the act of killing was proved, the presumption of law was that it was done with malice aforethought; that the burden of proving that the killing was not done with malice aforethought rested upon the prisoner; that, unless it appeared by testimony introduced by the prosecution, the prisoner, to overcome the presumption of law, must either introduce sufficient testimony to satisfy the jury that the act of killing was not done with malice aforethought, or he must make a sufficient showing to raise a reasonable doubt in the mind of the jury as to whether the act was done with malice aforethought or not; that it was not necessary that a premeditated design to kill should have existed any particular length of time before the act of killing; that, if the jury believed that Walsh first assaulted the prisoner, twitched him around, threw *him down, and clinched him by the throat, and the prisoner believed, and had good reason to believe, that Walsh was about to take his life, or to do him some great bodily harm, and he struck the fatal blow to save his own life, or to prevent Walsh doing him some great bodily harm, it would be a case of excusable homicide; but the burden of proof was upon the defendant to show that it was done in self-defense. To which refusal of the court to charge as requested, and to the charge as given, defendant's counsel excepted. . . .

The request of the counsel for the prisoner, that the court should charge the jury that to constitute murder in the first degree, under our statute, something more was necessary than would be <u>necessary</u> to constitute murder at common law; that to constitute murder in the first degree, the murder must be preceded or attended by facts and circumstances not necessarily an ingredient of murder at common law; and that, if the government sought to have the jury convict the prisoner of *murder in the first degree, the burden of proof was upon the government to show that the murder was committed in the perpetration, or attempt to perpetrate, arson, rape, robbery, or burglary; or by poison, or lying in wait; or to prove such facts, in addition to the act of killing, as made such act murder in the first degree; although somewhat obscurely expressed, was substantially correct.

Murder is where a person of sound memory and discretion unlawfully kills any reasonable creature in being, in the peace of the state, with malice prepense or aforethought, either express or implied. This, the common law definition, is still retained in our statute. It speaks of the offense as one already ascertained and defined, and divides it into degrees, by providing that all murder which shall be perpetrated

663

by means of poison, or lying in wait, or any other kind
of willful, deliberate, and premeditated killing, or which
shall be committed in the perpetration, or attempt to perpetrate, any arson, rape, robbery, or burglary, shall be
deemed murder in the first degree; and that all other kinds
of murder shall be deemed murder in the second degree; and
requires the jury, in case of a trial, to find, by their
verdict, the degree of the crime; and the court, in case of
a confession of guilt, to ascertain the same from evidence.
This division of the crime had its origin in Pennsylvania,
where death was the penalty for murder, as early as the year
1794, and its object was "to diminish the area of cases to
which the penalty of death is applicable." Accordingly,
amongst other things recited in the preamble of that law,
is the following: "And, whereas, the several offenses
which are included under the general denomination of murder differ so greatly from each other in the degree of
atrociousness that it is unjust to involve them in the same
punishment, all murder," etc. Of this act ours is a substantial copy. Mr. Wharton, in his "American Law of Homicide" (in which, and in his "Criminal Law," this subject
is fully discussed, and of which I have made liberal use),
in commenting upon this law, says: "The principle upon
which rests this statutory distinction, is that of the *lex
talionis, and took its origin from the admitted harshness
of inflicting death for a homicide, when death was not intended." "No objection was taken to the common law distinctions. The general feeling was, that it was proper
that they should remain. The question was one of punishment, not of definition. It was felt that there was a
large class of cases falling under the general head of
murder, in which a jury ought to be allowed to say whether
there was an intent to take life or not, and where no such
intent was found, that it was proper that a sentence lighter
than death should be inflicted. And it was to meet this
class of cases that legislative action was involved."
    Now, at the common law, if a mortal blow was malicious,
although not given with intent to kill, or if death ensued from an act accompanying an unlawful collateral act,
or under circumstances which showed general malice, such
as a reckless disregard of the safety or lives of others,
the killing would be murder, and would be punishable in
the same manner as though perpetrated with the deliberate
design of taking the life of the victim. It was to mitigate the punishment for this class of murders, and to leave
it to the discretion of the court, to a considerable extent, that our statute was passed; while for murder perpetrated willfully, or in the perpetration, or attempt to
perpetrate, either of the four felonies mentioned, the punishment is inflexibly fixed by the law. Hence, in defining the first degree of murder, the statute specifies two
instances in which willfulness, deliberation, and premeditation are most strongly indicated, viz, the use of poison,

664

and lying in wait; and then provides that all other willful, deliberate, and premeditated killing, should also be murder in the same degree. The more atrocious crime is separated from the general class of murder; and, it would seem to follow that to establish murder in the first degree, more proof is necessary than of the single fact of malicious homicide, and that it must be shown that the killing was willful, and with design to take the life of the victim, or in some one of the ways pointed out in the *statute. When the intent is specially made by the statute an ingredient in the crime, or where it is made essential to enable a court or jury to determine its degree, and to fix the character and amount of the punishment with which its commission is to be visited, such intent must be affirmatively shown, and can not be established by those ordinary legal inferences which were sufficient at the common law to establish the general crime, but at which the statute, by dividing the crime into degrees, especially aimed. Sometimes this intent is established by evidence of hostile feelings, of previously uttered threats, of previous attempts to do bodily injury, or of deliberate preparation. In some instances, the proof of the intent is furnished by the manner of killing; as when the murder is shown to have been committed with a lethal weapon, in an unequivocal manner. Here, "the inquiring mind can come to no other conclusion than that the death of the victim was intended. Thus, if one man shoot another through the head with a musket or pistol-ball, or if he stab him in a vital part with a sword or dagger, if he cleave his skull with an axe, or the like, it is almost impossible for a reflecting and intelligent mind to come to any other conclusion than that the perpetrators of such acts of deadly violence intended to kill:" Am. Law of Hom., 473. In such case, the law presumes every person to intend the usual consequences which accompany the use of the means employed in the manner employed, and casts upon the accused, as much as in the case of avowed malice, the burden of showing that the intention in using the weapon was harmless, or not murderous. The mere proof of the murder, then, without other proof deduced from the manner of the killing, or from other evidence tending to establish a design to take the life of the victim, would not establish the higher degree of the crime, but would only authorize a verdict of murder in the second degree.

We think the court erred, therefore, in refusing to charge as requested, and in omitting to define clearly to the jury the degrees of murder as established by law. . . .

The charge of the court, we think, had a tendency to mislead the jury. The proposition submitted to them, and which was to be their guide in ascertaining the degree of the crime, was, whether there was proof of malice aforethought, or not. Now, it is true, as charged, that if the act of killing was proved, the presumption of law is that it was done with malice aforethought; but this rule only

665

obtains where there is an entire absence of qualifying or
explanatory evidence involved in, or deducible from, the
manner of the killing. But, malice aforethought is as much
an essential ingredient of murder in the second degree, as
in that of the first. Without this, the killing would be
only manslaughter, if criminal at all. Now, malice aforethought is either express or implied, and there can be no
case of murder in the first degree, except when committed
in the perpetration, or attempt to perpetrate, arson, rape,
robbery, burglary, or when there does not exist express
malice; while, in case of murder in the second degree, the
malice is generally, if not universally, implied.
     The rule of the common law in respect to malice is in
no degree changed; the statute only relates to its application by the jury in determining the degree of guilt. It
is also true that the burden of disproving malice is in all
cases of murder cast upon the prisoner, unless the case
made by the prosecution *shows it to be absent; and this
rule now applies with special force to the second degree
of murder, if not entirely to it. While, therefore, as
a common law propósition, the charge of the court below
was correct, yet it falls far short, in our apprehension,
of an illustration of the statute, and tended to mislead
the jury in the discharge of their duty.
     The other justices concurred.

                                   New trial directed.*

* On a second trial, the prisoner was convicted of murder
of the second degree.

                    People v. Scott
                    6 Mich. 287

     On exceptions from the Recorder's Court of the city of
Detroit.
     The prisoner was tried at the December term of said
court, on an information for assault with intent to murder
one McDonald. Several witnesses were examined, as well for
the government as for the prisoner, whose testimony established the following facts:
     The prisoner and McDonald are both sailors, and met for
the first time on the dock, where their respective vessels
were lying, on the night of the assault. They had both
*been drinking, and the latter was very much intoxicated.
The prisoner was visiting the captain of the schooner Swan,
and while on board this vessel, and at about the hour of 9
o'clock P.M., McDonald came alongside on the dock, and, in
a loud and threatening tone, dared the persons on board to
come off and fight him, saying, among other things, with an
oath, that he could whip any of them. The captain of the
Swan and McDonald had some talk about fighting, but the

                          666

captain finally refused to fight, when McDonald took up a
board, three or four feet long, and three or four inches
wide, and said it would be a good thing to knock his brains
out with, attempting at the same time to get on board the
vessel. His friends now came up and took him on board his
own schooner, a short distance off. McDonald's manner was
such as to induce the captain to anticipate further trouble
during the night, and at his request the prisoner remained
on board. About 12 o'clock, McDonald came back to the Swan,
and, in a wild and threatening manner, boarded her. So far
as appeared by the evidence, he was unarmed at the time, but
was warned by the captain not to come on board. The prisoner
and the captain were forward of the main mast when McDonald
came on board the vessel. The prisoner had a double-barrel
gun in his hand, with which he shot McDonald in the face.
The ball entered the left cheek, cutting the tongue nearly
off, and passed out on the right side. The only injury done
was the hole in the cheeks and wound on the tongue. The
cook of the vessel swore he was in the cabin below deck, and
that the prisoner called to him to hand up the gun, which he
did. The gun was loaded, and the cook so informed the prisoner when he gave it to him, telling him at the same time
he had better let it alone. The captain also testified that,
before the prisoner fired the gun, he advised him to put it
away, and that the latter replied, "Mind your own business;"
at the same time cocking both barrels. The prisoner, after
cocking the gun, pointed it at *McDonald, and said to the
captain, "Louis, give the word of command;" at the same instant firing. He was within a few feet of McDonald at this
time. McDonald fell, and the witness supposed he was killed.
The testimony and argument of counsel being closed, the
recorder proceeded to charge the jury, and, after commenting
on the evidence, proceeded as follows: "At the common law,
all killing was either murder, manslaughter, or excusable or
justifiable homicide; but the humanity of modern legislation
has subdivided the first into murder in the first degree and
murder in the second degree. This is the subdivision under
our statute; and were you trying the prisoner for the crime
of murder, it would be your duty to ascertain in your verdict of which, if either of these, the prisoner was guilty.
The statute under which the prisoner is informed against,
reads as follows: 'If any person shall assault another with
intent to commit the crime of murder, every such offender
shall be punished by imprisonment in the state prison for
life, or any number of years. My view of the proper construction of this section, and of the duty of a jury in
finding a verdict under it, makes it necessary that I should
briefly define what constitutes murder, in either of the degrees, under our statute.

"Murder in the first degree is where one reasonable being
willfully, deliberately, and premeditatedly, kills another,
in the peace of the state; murder in the second degree is the

intentional, unlawful killing of any reasonable being by another, without deliberation and premeditation; manslaughter is where one person unintentionally, but unlawfully, kills another; justifiable or excusable homicide is where the killing is necessary for self-defense, or by accident, under circumstances furnishing a reasonable excuse.

"An intent to kill is a necessary ingredient in murder, either of the first or second degree, but is excluded from the crime of manslaughter.

"In order to convict the prisoner of an assault with *intent to murder, you must be satisfied, beyond a reasonable doubt, that had death ensued, it would have been murder either of the first or second degree. If you find that the prisoner committed the assault willfully, deliberately, and premeditatedly, intending to take McDonald's life, then, had death ensued, it would have been murder in the first degree; if you find that the prisoner intended to kill McDonald unlawfully, but without deliberation and premeditation, then, had death ensued, it would have been murder in the second degree. Therefore, if you shall find, from the evidence, beyond any reasonable doubt, that had death ensued, it would have been murder either of the first or second degree, then it will be your duty to find the prisoner guilty as charged in the information; otherwise you must acquit of the main charge, but may bring him in guilty of an assault." To this charge, the counsel for the prisoner excepted.

They requested the recorder to charge the jury that, in order to convict the prisoner of the crime charged in the information, they must find that, had death ensued, it would have been murder in the first degree; and if they do not so find, the prisoner must be acquitted.

The recorder refused so to charge, and the counsel for the prisoner also excepted to this refusal.

The substance of all the evidence in the case was set forth in the bill of exceptions, and there was no controversy respecting it. . . .

CAMPBELL, J.:

The respondent, having been convicted of an assault with intent to commit the crime of murder, alleged exceptions before sentence, and these are certified up for our opinion under the statute.

The first exception was taken to so much of the charge of the court as defines the various classes of homicide, and instructs the jury what facts must exist to render the accused guilty of the offense charged.

As abstract definitions, we are of opinion that the definitions given are wanting in preciseness, and would not, in many cases, be as accurate as they should be to guide a jury. But it would be very unsafe, in practice, to construe the language of a charge without reference to the facts upon which it is given. In this case, the bill of exceptions sets forth the whole facts; and in determining the legal

propriety of the charge, we must bear these in mind. If
the whole facts were not before us, it might perhaps be
necessary to look solely at the general correctness of the
rules laid down, as universal propositions.

The facts show that there was no evidence in any way
tending to prove that if death had ensued, the homicide
would have been either excusable or justifiable. Neither
do they tend to show that it would have come within the
terms of voluntary manslaughter, for there are none of the
elements in the case which would reduce an intentional
killing to that *grade. Involuntary manslaughter was excluded, because the charge expressly informed the jury
that an intention to take life was a necessary ingredient
of the offense charged. The facts relating entirely to a
case which, if death had ensued, would have constituted
murder, there was no error in the charge given which could
in any way prejudice the respondent, or mislead the jury
to his damage, unless it was in so much of it as authorized
a conviction where the intent was to commit murder in the
second degree. This seems to have been the real ground of
the exceptions appearing of record, as taken to the charge
given; and it was in reference to this that a specific charge
was asked, the refusal of which is the ground of the second
exception.

We are somewhat at a loss to perceive the exact point of
the objection to the charge of the recorder on this subject.
He had already laid it down very distinctly that in order
to constitute the offense there must be an express intent
to destroy life. If we should hold that murder in the second
degree is always an unintentional killing, the refusal to
charge as requested could do no harm, because the instructions
actually given would prevent a verdict without proof of the
more aggravated offense. The jury could not, under the
charge, convict of any unintentional offense. But the
language of the statute is entirely too plain for controversy.
Whenever a man assaults another, intending to commit murder,
the crime is complete. The intention to take life under
any circumstances which would not render the killing manslaughter or justifiable or excusable homicide, constitutes
the offense under the statute. As the questions presented
seem to be founded on a misapprehension of the views expressed by this court in the case of The People v. Potter,
5 Mich., 6, we deem it proper to repeat the explanation
given on that occasion, and to define the different degrees
of murder under our statute.

Murder at the common law, embraced all unlawful killing
done with malice aforethought. Murder under our statute
*embraces every offense which would have been murder at
common law, and it embraces no other crime. But murder is
not always attended with the same degree of wicked design,
or, to speak more accurately, with the same degree of malice.
It may be committed on a sudden impulse of passion, where
the intent is formed and executed in the heat of blood,

669

without any sufficient provocation to extenuate the degree
of the offense to manslaughter. In both of these instances,
and in the intermediate cases where the design is of greater
or less duration, there is the actual intent to take life.
Other cases exist, where, in the attempt to commit some
other offense which is _malum in se_ and not merely _malum pro-
hibitum_, human life is taken with an express design to take
it, and yet the crime is held to be murder, because resulting
from the same species of depravity or maliciousness which
characterizes that offense when committed designedly.

The statute, recognizing the propriety of continuing to
embrace within the same class all cases of malicious killing,
has, nevertheless, divided these offenses into different
grades for the purposes of punishment, visiting those which
manifest deep malignity with the heaviest penalties known
to our law, and punishing all the rest according to a sliding scale, reaching, in the discretion of the court, from a
very moderate imprisonment to nearly the same degree of severity prescribed for those convicted of murder in the first degree. Each grade of murder embraces some cases where there
is a direct intent to take life, and each grade also embraces
offenses where the direct intent was to commit some other
crime. As the law names all of the offenses, an attempt to
commit which renders the person who takes life guilty of
murder in the first degree, no difficulty can arise in defining the degree of any murder committed, without the actual
design either of taking life or of doing bodily harm to the
person assailed.

*Except in the cases expressly named in the statute,
muder in the first degree requires the existence of a deliberate intention to take life; and any slaying in which
a jury should find either the absence of deliberation, or
that the intent was to commit another and a lesser injury,
must be either murder in the second degree, or one of the
lighter grades of homicide. Accordingly, in the case of
Potter, where the court below had held that the jury could
convict of murder in the first degree upon any proof which
would establish murder at common law, we reversed the decision, and held that murder in the first degree, except in
the specified cases, could only be made out by proof of express malice, and a deliberate design against life itself.
We were not called upon in that case to go any further into
definitions, and we accordingly abstained from so doing.

The common law having made no distinction in the offense
or its punishment, it is not to be wondered at that text
writers should differ in their views of the exact boundaries
between express and implied malice; and the terms are not
such as would give a modern jury any very clear idea, without explanation. We think the language of the statute itself, taken in connection with its context, affords to persons in our times a very fair means of judgment. And the
best modern writers have had the good sense to convey their
ideas in such terms as are generally intelligible.

When, therefore, following the statute, we hold murder in

the first degree to be that which is willful, deliberate, and premeditated, and all other murders to be murder in the second degree, we should be undertaking a task which, if possible, would be exceedingly dangerous to undertake, to enumerate what facts constitute deliberation, and what exclude it. Practically, a jury could rarely find much difficulty in applying the test. Where there is positive proof of previous threats, ill-will, or preparation, and all of such a nature as to lead naturally and clearly to a fatal crime, questions seldom arise. It is where surrounding circumstances are not clearly proven, and where the offense has no established antecedents, that difficulties have arisen in defining it.

In all these cases the circumstances proven must be taken into the account, and the jury must, from the whole facts, determine the intent and the deliberation. Voluntary manslaughter often involves a direct intent to kill, but the law reduces the grade of the offense because, looking at the frailty of human nature, it considers great provocations sufficient to excite the passions beyond the control of reason. But provocations often arise which are of less intensity, and are not in law regarded as sufficient to reduce the crime to manslaughter. If it appears that murder is committed upon a heat of passion engendered entirely by such provocations, and suddenly conceived, such a murder can not properly be called deliberate. But whenever murder is intentionally committed without serious provocation, and under circumstances which do not reasonably account for such an excitement of passion as naturally deprives men of deliberation, common experience teaches us that such an act is wanton, and its perpetrator responsible for it, as in other cases of cold-blooded crime. The time within which a wicked purpose is formed is immaterial, provided it is formed without disturbing excitement. The question of deliberation, when all the circumstances appear, is one of plain common sense, and an intelligent jury can seldom be at a loss to determine it. No sane man acts without some cause for his action; and it is not difficult, in most cases of murder, to determine whether the cause was a sudden heat or not. The recorder, although not precisely accurate in confining all murder in the second degree to intentional homicide, presented very intelligibly the difference in intent between the two degrees.

As murder in the second degree, like voluntary manslaughter, does embrace some cases of intentional killing, he was entirely correct in refusing the instructions prayed for, which would confine the statutory assault with intent to *commit murder to the offense which involves a deliberate intent. The intent to kill must undoubtedly be established, as an inference of fact, to the satisfaction of the jury; but they may draw that inference, as they draw all other inferences, from any fact in evidence which, to their minds, fairly proves its existence. Intentions can only be proved

671

by acts, as juries can not look into the breast of the
criminal. And where any act is knowingly committed which
naturally and usually leads to certain consequences, a
jury certainly has the right, in the exercise of ordinary
sagacity, to draw the inference that such results are intended.

There is no error in the proceedings, and a new trial is
denied. Let it be certified accordingly.

CHRISTIANCY J.:

I concur, with my brethren, in the opinion of my brother
Campbell. The recorder properly refused to charge as requested by the defendant's counsel. Under this information,
the question of the degrees of murder was wholly immaterial.
The statute has not altered the common law definition of
murder; but, recognizing it, has simply divided it into classes,
or degrees of enormity, for the purpose of apportioning the
punishment; and this only when the prosecution is for murder,
eo nomine. Both classes or degrees are equally murder, and
if the defendant committed the assault with the intent to
kill, under circumstances where the killing would have been
murder in the second degree, he is equally guilty of an assault with intent to murder, as if the intent had been to
kill under circumstances which would have made the killing
murder in the first degree.

Perhaps the more appropriate charge, because the more
simple, less difficult, and more easily intelligible, would
have been to give the jury a definition of murder at common
law, and to have instructed them that if they should find
the prisoner committed the assault with intent to kill, and
that the circumstances were such that, if death had ensued,
the killing *would have constituted murder under this common law definition, they should find him guilty, otherwise,
not guilty.

But such a charge would be equally faultless, in point of
law, if, instead of defining murder at common law, it should
accurately define what constituted the two degrees of murder
under the statute; because these two degrees must, together,
include all cases of murder at common law.

The recorder chose the latter course; but, in defining
the degrees, his attention being probably drawn only to the
points on which he was requested to charge - which, I infer
from the case, were the only points discussed before him -
and confining his attention to the statute, which, instead
of defining murder, only divides it into degrees, he inadvertently, it would seem, neglected to include in the first
degree the ingredient of "malice aforethought." But no
specific objection was made to the charge on this account,
which, in fairness to the court, ought to have been made,
and doubtless would have been made had the defendant's
counsel supposed the omission likely to prejudice his client.
Had the attention of the recorder been called to the point,
I can not doubt it would have been at once corrected. Though

the definition given by the recorder, of murder in the second degree, may not have been technically correct, as an abstract definition, yet it was sufficiently so when taken in connection with that part of the charge which had reference to the intent, and could not possibly mislead the jury to the injury of the prisoner.

The only remaining question is (admitting the general exception to the charge sufficient to raise the question), should a new trial be granted on account of the inaccurate definition of murder in the first degree? If the error be one which might have misled the jury to the prejudice of the defendant, a new trial should be granted. If the nature of the transaction were doubtful, or the evidence of it conflicting, so that without weighing the evidence we could not determine whether the defendant might not have been prejudiced by the charge; or if the whole substance of the evidence bearing on the transaction *were not before us, we might not, without usurping the province of the jury, be able to say that they had not been misled. But as we have all the testimony, and the case states it to have been undisputed, and from the whole transaction we can clearly see that, under any proper charge, the jury could not, without a violation of their oaths, fail to find the defendant guilty, it must be obvious that the defendant has not been injured by the charge, that a new trial would be of no avail, and that it ought therefore to be denied.

The other justices concurred in the foregoing opinions.

People v. Case
7 Mich. App. 217

HOLBROOK, P. J. . . .
First-degree murder has been defined in our statute as:

"All murder which shall be perpetrated by means of poison, or lying in wait, or any other kind of wilful, deliberate and premeditated killing, or which shall be committed in the perpetration, or attempt to perpetrate any arson, rape, robbery or burglary, shall be murder of the first degree." CL 1948, Sec. 750.316 (Stat Ann 1954 Rev Sec. 28.548).

Second-degree murder has been defined as: "All other kinds of murder shall be murder of the second degree." CL 1948, Sec. 750.317 (Stat Ann 1954 Rev Sec. 28.549).

In People v. Dunn (1925), 233 Mich 185, 196, murder in the first degree was differentiated from murder in the second degree in the following manner:

"The difference between murder in the first degree and murder in the second degree is that in murder of the first degree there must be premeditation and deliberation and such a lapse of time as will give the mind time to calculate the purpose and intent of the killing."

673

The trial judge in the case at hand had before him the following as to the physical facts and circumstances surrounding the death of Leonard Reed and the manner in which he was killed: the defendant entered the Howard residence, and from what he said and with the brevity of his stay, he was interested only in making arrangements to see Leonard Reed; shortly after defendant's departure, Leonard Reed, with his sister, also left; the defendant parked alongside a country road in the dark, waiting for the Reed car to come along; the defendant said to Leonard that he wanted to talk to him and after Leonard left his car to talk to defendant, the murder took place in an extraordinarily brutal and vicious manner - i.e., severe and repeated blows upon the head of the victim with a tire iron; the record made on preliminary examination; the exhibits; the testimony of Detective Olepa relating the defendant's "story" of the crime as set forth, supra; and finally, that the defendant after killing Leonard Reed beat Naomi Reed in a similar manner after she left the car to find out what happened to her brother.

In the case of People v. Van Camp (1959), 356 Mich 593, the homicide took place without the use of any weapon and the trial judge submitted to the jury the question of defendant's guilt as to first-degree murder. Mr. Justice EDWARDS stated on pp 600,601 as follows:

"Nor do we think the charge was in error in submitting to the jury the question of first-degree murder. We note the absence of any weapon. But we entertain no doubt that kicking a man to death can constitute first-degree murder if the clear intent to kill is present." People v. Collins (1942), 303 Mich 34.

The facts in the instant case are more forceful in that the murder was committed with a lethal weapon, to wit, a tire iron. A clear intent to kill was present and malice can be inferred from the type of weapon used and the way in which the crime was committed.

We conclude under the testimony and evidence presented at the statutory hearing the necessary elements to a finding of first-degree murder of "lying in wait" or "any other kind of wilful, deliberate and premeditated killing"* were present. The trial judge was justified in determining defendant's guilt as being first-degree murder and in rendering judgment accordingly.

Affirmed.

FITZGERALD and J. H. GILLIS, JJ., concurred.

Footnote

* People v. Sutic (1953), 41 Cal 2d 483 (261 P2d 241).

3. Intent

Wellar v. People
30 Mich. 16

CAMPBELL, J.:

Plaintiff in error was convicted of the murder of Margaret Campbell by personal violence committed on July 25, 1873. They had lived together for several months, and on the occasion of her death she had been out on an errand of her own in the neighborhood, and on coming back into the house entered the front door of the bar-room, and fell, or was knocked down upon the floor. While on the floor there was evidence tending to show that Wellar ordered her to get up, and kicked her, and that he drew her from the bar-room through the dining-room into a bed room, where he left her, and where she afterwards died. The injury of which she died was inflicted on her left temple, and the evidence does not seem to have been clear how she received it or at what specific time. It was claimed by the prosecution to have been inflicted by a blow when she first came in, and if not, then by a blow or kick afterwards. All of the testimony is not returned, and the principal questions arise out of rulings which depend on the assumption that the jury might find that her death was caused by some violent act of Wellar's; which, they must done(sic) to convict him. There can be no question but that, if she so came to her death, he was guilty of either murder or manslaughter. The complaint made against the *charge is, that a theory was put to the jury on which they were instructed to find as murder what would, or at least might be, manslaughter.

There was no proof tending to show the use of any weapon, and, if we may judge from the charge, the prosecution claimed the fatal injury came from a blow of Wellar's fist, given as she entered the house. The judge seems to have regarded it as shown by a preponderance of proof, that the injury was visible when she was in the bar-room, and that the principal dispute was as to how it was caused, whether by a blow, or kick, or by accident. It also appears that, if inflicted in that room, it did not produce insensibility at the time, if inflicted before the prisoner dragged her into the bed room. It does not appear from the case at what hour she died.

It may be proper to remark that while it is not desirable to introduce all the testimony into a bill of exceptions in a criminal case, it is important to indicate in some way the whole chain of facts which the evidence tends to prove. Without this we cannot fully appreciate the relations of many of the rulings, or know what instructions may be necessary to be sent down to the court below. The bill before us is full upon some things, but leaves out some things which it would have been better to include.

Upon any of the theories presented, there is no difficulty in seeing that if Wellar killed the deceased, and if he distinctly intended to kill her, his crime was murder. It is not claimed on his behalf that there was any proof which could reduce the act to manslaughter if there was a specific design to take life. Upon this the charge was full and pointed, and is not complained of. There was no claim that he had been provoked in such a way or to such an extent as to mitigate

675

intentional slaying to anything below one of the degrees of
murder.

But it is claimed that, although the injury given was
fatal, yet, if not intended to produce any such results, it
was of such a character that the jury might, and properly*
should, have considered it as resting on different grounds
from those which determine responsibility for acts done with
deadly weapons used in a way likely to produce dangersous
consequences. But the charge of the court did not permit
them to take that view.

It will be found by careful inspection of the charge,
that the court specifically instructed the jury, that if
Wellar committed the homicide at all, it would be murder,
and not manslaughter, unless it was committed under such extreme provocation as is recognized in the authorities as sufficient to reduce intentional and voluntary homicide commited
with a deadly weapon to that degree of crime. And in this
connection the charge further given that if the intent of
the respondent was to commit bodily harm, he was responsible
for the result, because he acted willfully and maliciously
in doing the injury necessarily led to a conviction of murder, because there was no pretense of any provocation of that
kind.

Manslaughter is a very serious felony, and may be punished
severly. The discretionary punishment for murder in the second degree comes considerably short of the maximum punishment
for manslaughter. But the distinction is a vital one, resting chiefly on the greater disregard of human life shown in
the higher crime. And in determining whether a person who
has killed another without meaning to kill him is guilty of
murder or manslaughter, the nature and extent of the injury
or wrong which was actually intended, must usually be of controlling importance.

It is not necessary in all cases that one held for murder
must have intended to take the life of the person he slays
by his wrongful act. It is not always necessary that he
must have intended a personal injury to such person. But
it is necessary that the intent with which he acted shall
be equivalent in legal character to a criminal purpose aimed
against life. Generally that intent must have been to commit either a specific felony, or at least an act involving
all the wickedness of a felony. And if the intent be *directly to produce a bodily injury, it must be such an injury
as may be expected to involve serious consequences, either
periling life or leading to great bodily harm. There is no
rule recognized as authority which will allow a conviction
of murder where a fatal result was not intended, unless the
injury intended was one of a very serious character which
might naturally and commonly involve loss of life, or grievous mischief. Every assault involves bodily harm. But
any doctrine which would hold every assailant as a murderer
where death follows his act, would be barbarous and unreasonable.

The language used in most of the statutes on felonious assaults, is, an intent to do "grievous bodily harm:" Carr. Sup. p. 237. And even such an assault, though "unlawfully and maliciously" made, is recognized as one where, if death followed, the result would not necessarily have been murder: Ibid. Our own statutes have made no provision for rendering assaults felonious unless committed with a dangerous weapon, or with an intent to commit some felony: Comp. L., ch. 244.

In general, it has been held that where the assault is not committed with a deadly weapon, the intent must be clearly felonious, or the death will subject only to the charge of manslaughter. The presumption arising from the character of the instrument of violence, is not conclusive in either way, but where such weapons are used as do not usually kill, the deadly intent ought to be left in no doubt. There are cases on record where death by beating and kicking has been held to warrant a verdict of murder, the murderous intent being found. But where there was no such intent the ruling has been otherwise. In State v. McNab, 20 N. H., 160, it is held that unless the unlawful act of violence intended was felonious, the offense was manslaughter. The same doctrine is laid down in State v. Smith, 32 Maine, 369. That is the statutory rule in New York and in some other states.

The willful use of a deadly weapon, without excuse or *provocation, in such a manner as to imperil life, is almost universally recognized as showing a felonious intent: See 2 Bish. Cr. L., Sec. 680,681. But where the weapon or implement used is not one likely to kill or to maim, the killing is held to be manslaughter, unless there is an actual intent which shows a felonious purpose: See Turner's case, 1 Raym, 144, where a servant was hit on the head with a clog; State v. Jarrott, 1 Ired, 76, where the blow was with a hickory stick; Holly v. State, 10 Humph, 141, where a boy threw a stone; Rex V. Kelley, 1 Moody, C. C., 113, where it was uncertain whether a person was killed by a blow with the fist, which threw him on a brick, or by a blow from a brick, and the court held it a clear case of manslaughter. In Darry v. People 10 N.Y., 120, the distinctions are mentioned and relied upon, and in the opinion of Parker J. there are some remarks very applicable. In the case of Com. v. Webster, 5 Cush. R., 295, the rulings of which have been regarded as going beyond law in severity, this question, is dealt with in accordance with the same views, and quotations are given from East to the same purport.

The case of death in a prize fight is one of the commonest illustrations of manslaughter, where there is a deliberate arrangement to fight, and where great violence is always to be expected from the strength of the parties and the purpose of fighting till one or the other is unable to continue the contest. A duel with deadly weapons renders every killing murder; but a fight without weapons, or with weapons not deadly, leads only to manslaughter, unless death is intended: 1 East, P.C. 270; Murphy's case, 6 C. & P., 103; Hargrave's

677

case, 5 C. & P., 170.

The case of Commonwealth v. Fox, 7 Gray, 585, is one resembling the present in several respects, in which the offense was held to be manslaughter.

The jury was sufficiently and rightly charged upon the extent of the respondent's liability for any intended killing. And if respondent willfully and violently kicked the deceased* in such a way as he must have known would endanger her life, and her life was destroyed in that way, an actual intention of killing would not be necessary, as in such case the death would have been a result he might fairly be held to regard as likely. But it was certainly open to him to claim that, whatever may have been the cause of death, he did nothing which was designed to produce any serious or fatal mischief, and that the injury from which the deceased came to her death was not intentionally aimed at a vital spot, or one where the consequences would be probably or manifestly dangerous. We have no right to say that there was no room for a verdict of manslaughter, and the effect of the charge was to deny this. . . .

The judgment must be reversed, and a new trial granted. The respondent to be remanded to the custody of the sheriff of Saginaw county.

COOLEY and CHRISTIANCY, JJ., concurred.
GRAVES, CH. J., did not sit in this case.

People v. Palmer
105 Mich. 568

Respondent was convicted of murder in the second degree, and sentenced to imprisonment in the State prison at Jackson for 25 years. Judgment affirmed. The facts are stated in the opinion.

GRANT, J. . . .
. . . It is next argued that the court erred in giving the following instruction:

"Now, if, after he entered the saloon, he became aware that his brother Albert was there, and he then formed the intent to take his brother Albert's life, taking into account whatever may have been in his mind as to their past relations, their quarrels, or anything that he may have heard about Albert having a pistol, and if he became aware that Albert was in the back part of the saloon, surrounded by his friends, if he then, even though but a moment before he fired the fatal shot, formed in his mind the purpose of taking his brother's life, and pursuant to that purpose he shot and killed him, that would constitute the crime of murder."

The precise point urged is that there was no evidence to support such a theory, and that neither the prosecution nor

678

the defense conducted the trial with reference to it. We cannot tell what the argument was to the jury. If there is any testimony upon which to base the charge of the court, the charge must be sustained. The respondent claimed that he had no murderous intent at any time. There was evidence that, when he entered the saloon, he appeared in his usual manner, and there was evidence that, when he raised the gun, his countenance changed. Whether this was because he saw his brother, or saw the pistol pointed at him, and whether it was necessary for him then to shoot in self-defense, were all questions for the jury, and made competent the charge complained of, which was given in connection with instructions covering the respondent's theories. The entire instructions covering this point were as follows:

"Now, if after carefully considering all the evidence in the case introduced upon both sides, and after carefully considering all the facts and circumstances surrounding the tragedy, and the relations of the accused and the deceased prior to the tragedy, and taking into account previously uttered threats, if any there were by either, and taking into consideration any quarrels that may have been between the brothers, if any, and also taking into account whether the parties became reconciled and were friends before this fatal day, and whether they were friends, then, I say, taking into consideration all of those facts and circumstances, it would be a subject for the jury to inquire into as to the intent with which this act was done, - whether it was an act committed in malice, whether it was an act committed in passion, or whether it was an act committed under the impulse of fear; and if, after a careful examination of all those facts that I have called your attention to, if each juror, looking into his conscience, could say that he has an abiding conviction, to a moral certainty, of the defendant's guilt, it would be his duty to convict, because that would be proving the case by evidence beyond a reasonable doubt, as defined by the law.

"As has been said, the killing may have constituted manslaughter, or it may be entirely excusable, according to the circumstances, and according to the state of mind with which the act was committed; and the principal inquiry in this case must be limited finally to the question of the intent with which this act was done. At the danger of repeating, I say that the principal inquiry in this case must be limited finally to the question as to the intent with which William Palmer fired that gun on the day of the shooting. If, at any time before the shot from the revolver was fired, William Palmer had formed the intent and purpose in his own mind, with malice aforethought, to take the life of Albert Palmer, then the mere fact that, while he was engaged in issuing this challenge, his brother, knowing of the danger, was able to first pull a revolver and to discharge it, would not affect the guilt of the defendant. That implies the forming

in his mind, before the firing of the fatal shot, of the
intent to take his brother's life; and that would be so because the firing in that case upon his part is immediately
connected with the previous malicious and willful intent to
take his life; and if Albert, seeing his danger, or knowing
that William Palmer was coming in his direction, armed with
the fatal weapon, and with the challenge upon his lips, was
able first to draw his pistol and fire, that act would not
affect the guilt of William Palmer.

"If the jury should find beyond a reasonable doubt that,
before he fired the fatal shot, William Palmer had formed a
settled, premeditated, preconceived, or deliberately formed
purpose to take his brother's life, and that in pursuance of
that purpose he procured the gun and the cartridges, and
loaded the gun, and carried it to the place where the shooting occurred, with the previously formed purpose, with malice
aforethought, to there make use of that gun for the purpose
of taking his brother's life, that would constitute the crime
of murder, and you would be justified and it would be your
duty to find the respondent guilty of murder in the second
degree. Or if you should find the fact to be beyond a reasonable doubt that in the first intention William Palmer procured this gun for an entirely innocent purpose, and that he
loaded it with an innocent purpose, and intended to go hunting an eagle, as testified to by him, but that any time after
procuring the gun, or at any time after entering the saloon,
he formed a settled, deliberate purpose and intention with
malice aforethought, to take his brother's life, by shooting
him with that gun, that would constitute the crime of murder;
for if, at the time the shooting occurred, there was present in the mind of William Palmer this malicious purpose
and intent to take Albert Palmer's life, then, no matter how
quickly it was formed, or how immediately before the shooting it was formed, if it existed in the mind of William
Palmer when he fired that shot, and if it was the actuating,
moving cause that impelled him to fire that shot, and if you
believe from the evidence, beyond a reasonable doubt, giving
the respondent at all times the benefit of this presumption
of innocence which I have defined, but, notwithstanding that,
you found him so guilty, it would be your duty to find him
guilty of murder in the second degree. In other words, the
state of facts I have defined would constitute the crime of
murder, and you would be justified in bringing a verdict of
murder in the second degree.

"In the next place, if, after a consideration of all of
this evidence you do not find from the testimony in this case
beyond a reasonable doubt the existence of all the ingredients
constituting the crime of murder in the second degree, as I
have defined it to you, you should then direct your attention
to the investigation of the evidence in the case to see if a
crime of lesser degree had been committed by this respondent,
and you should endeavor to ascertain and determine if the
crime of manslaughter was committed, for the crime of manslaughter,as before stated and defined to you, is an unlawful

and felonious killing of another without malice expressed and implied. When one man suddenly kills another in the heat of passion, but without malice, and without a previously settled and deliberately formed purpose to do so, if no such purpose or wicked intent existed at the time in his mind, and in the heat of blood, and inflamed with passion, he suddenly strikes the fatal blow or fires the fatal shot which causes the death of another, if the jury should find the existence of such a state of facts beyond a reasonable doubt, they would be justified in finding the accused guilty of the crime of manslaughter. Manslaughter is perfectly distinguishable from murder, in this: That though the act that causes death be unlawful or willful, though attended with fatal results, yet malice, either expressed or implied, which is the very essence of murder, is to be presumed to be wanting in manslaughter.

"If the jury should reject this evidence, but should find beyond a reasonable doubt, in accordance with the theory of the respondent and his witness, that he procured this gun with the innocent purpose of hunting near Green Point, or hunting for an eagle that he had ascertained was there, that he did not know at the time where his brother was, and that there existed at the time in his mind no intent to do his brother harm, but that, pursuant to his purpose to hunt for this eagle, he went to the saloon of Jerry Noel after the rubber boots and the cartridges and some liquor, and that he was intending, as soon as he had performed his errand there, to proceed upon his hunt, let us see what situation that would present. That assumed that, at the time he entered that saloon, there was no criminal intention in his mind. Now, if, after he entered the saloon, he became aware that his brother Albert was there, and he then formed the intent to take his brother Albert's life, taking into account whatever may have been in his mind as to their past relations, their quarrels, or anything that he may have heard about Albert having a pistol, and if he became aware that Albert was in the back part of the saloon, surrounded by his friends, if he then, even though but a moment before he fired the fatal shot, formed in his mind the purpose of taking his brother's life, and pursuant to that purpose he shot and killed him, that would constitute the crime of murder. If, however, he did not form any such purpose, but if, seeing the other parties in the saloon, he raised the gun in his hand in the spirit of banter only, and said, 'Where is the man that wants to shoot me? Come up, come up,' and approached the party, and if, while he was doing that in friendliness and in play, he saw his brother, and saw the revolver in his hand, and if that aroused his blood or any rancor that might have existed in his heart or angered him, and in that anger and passion, if he raised his gun and shot his brother, - if you should find the existence of those facts beyond a reasonable doubt, - that would constitute the crime of manslaughter. But if, putting both of those aside, there was no intention in the heart of William Palmer when he entered there to kill his brother, if he was going upon this hunt, and had no thought of malice or ill will towards his brother, and no intent to do him harm, but entered the saloon for the purpose that he said he did, and passed to the opening in the screen door, and when he was in front of the door, and but a short distance from the door, if he suddenly saw a hand extended with a revolver pointing towards him, and if at the time he was impelled by fear and apprehended at the time, as appeared to him, that he was in danger of losing his own life or in danger of great bodily harm, and if he raised his gun under those circumstances, and discharged it, and his brother's death was caused thereby, that would be excusable homicide; and the matter is to be viewed from the standpoint of William Palmer at that time when he saw that deadly weapon confronting him.

"The jury are to pass on the weight of all the evidence tending to establish any one of these different theories. But, before you can convict the respondent, you must find him guilty beyond a reasonable doubt."

. . . After the first difficulty in the saloon between the two brothers, and about an hour before the tragedy, Albert went out of the saloon, and had a conversation with one Bruce and one Poquette. The conversation related to the trouble in the saloon. The respondent stood on the sidewalk, 150 or 200 feet from him. Bruce testified that Albert said: "I won't be beat and bruised up by that bully. He is too big for me. I am not able to fight him, and, furthermore, I don't have to. I got something to aid me;" showing a box of cartridges. Albert then said to Poquette, in Bruce's presence: "What did you people up in that saloon mean by letting that man abuse me? He is too big for me. I don't want to fight him, and don't intend to. I have got something to protect myself with;" taking a revolver out of his pocket. Poquette replied: "I haven't anything to do with your troubles, Al. Didn't I take him to Bay City yesterday to keep him away from you?" Complaint is made only of the admission of the statement of Poquette, who was not produced as a witness, although upon the trial the objection was to the entire conversation. Certainly, the statements of the deceased were competent, and were favorable to the respondent, in that they showed a hostile feeling on the part of the deceased and an express threat. It was not only the right but the duty of the prosecution to place this conversation before the jury in so far as it showed the state of mind and disposition towards the respondent. The objection to its admission was raised when the testimony was offered. The judge, in admitting it, stated that he received it as a part of the res gestae, and confined it to such conversation as involved the relations of the brothers on the day of the homicide. This ruling is sustained by the following

authorities: <u>People v. Potter</u>, <u>5</u> <u>Mich</u>. <u>5</u>; <u>Brown v. People</u>,
<u>17 Id</u>. <u>433</u>; <u>Patten v. People</u>, <u>18 Id</u>. <u>327</u>; <u>1 Greenl. Ev. Sec</u>.
<u>108</u>. Greenleaf says:

"Upon an inquiry as to the state of mind, sentiments, or
disposition of a person at any particular period, his declarations and conversations are admissible."

The admission of the statement of Poquette to the deceased
is more doubtful. The general rule is, however, that the entire conversation is admissible. It all related to the trouble existing between the two brothers. They had just had a
quarrel in a saloon at which Poquette was present. It is not
the rule to include that portion of a conversation which is
favorable to a party, and exclude that which may be against
him. The entire conversation is admissible, and a jury may
well be trusted with its consideration. We think no error
was committed in admitting it. . . .

The judgment is affirmed.

LONG and HOOKER, JJ., concurred with GRANT, J.
(Concurring opinion of MONTGOMERY, J. and dissenting
opinion of McGRATH, C. J., omitted.)

People v. Collins
303 Mich. 34

BOYLES, J. Defendant was tried by jury in Jackson
county on an information charging murder of the first degree, with count for manslaughter, committed against one
Elmer Parker. For reversal, defendant claims that the
verdict was against the great weight of the evidence, and
that the court was in error in his charge to the jury in
several particulars.

The defendant, about 8 o'clock in the evening of April
18, 1941, met in the vicinity of the Hayes hotel in the
city of Jackson a Miss Kearney with whom he had been keeping
company. During the day he had consumed a considerable
quantity of intoxicating liquor and was then somewhat intoxicated. The two proceeded to a restaurant in Jackson
where they remained until about 10 o'clock and from there
went to a tavern where they both drank beer. While there,
both of them had occasion to leave the table at which they
were seated and when they returned they found seated there
one Elmer Parker and his lady companion, both of whom were
previously unknown to them. Parker apologized and prevailed upon them to sit down, and thereafter they all talked together and drank more beer. Somewhere around 1 o'clock
in the morning they all went outside the tavern and while defendant and his companion were waiting for a taxicab to arrive, Parker offered to take them anywhere in his automobile;
there was some discussion about defendant and his companion

683

desiring to go home; they all got into Parker's car and
proceeded to defendant's home but the defendant and his
companion did not stop there; someone suggested that they
go to a certain other tavern which they proceeded to do.
They remained there for some time drinking more beer, the
defendant, however, insisting he didn't need any more.
While there, some confusion arose about paying for the beer.
The men were slow about paying so Miss Kearney took a dollar
bill from her purse and placed it on the table. Parker also
laid a dollar bill on the table. The waitress took one of
the bills, made change and in some way the other dollar bill
fell to the floor, the waitress picked it up, Parker took
it and put it in his pocket. They all left this tavern in
Parker's car about 2 o'clock in the morning. Parker's companion drove, Parker sat at her right in the front seat, the
defendant was seated behind him in the back seat, and defendant's companion, Miss Kearney, was seated behind the driver.
Someone suggested they go to the Regent restaurant and while
on the way there, defendant (according to his own testimony)
discovered Parker trying to feel Miss Kearney's legs, reached over and pushed Parker's hand away and said, "Just what
is the trouble? What is the matter with you? Are you
crazy?" It appears that about that time Parker handed Miss
Kearney the dollar bill that had previously been picked up
by him; that the defendant said to Miss Kearney "That man
has insulted you," and she said, "Now, never mind. He has
not." Defendant testified that during the rest of the time
until they got downtown, he and Miss Kearney were arguing
about whether Parker had insulted her. The party finally
arrived in front of the post-office in the city of Jackson,
on the opposite side of the street from the Regent restaurant. The car was there parked parallel with the curb. Parker and his companion went into the restaurant, leaving the
defendant and Miss Kearney seated in the rear seat of Parker's car. Looking out the window of the restaurant, Parker's companion saw the defendant get out of the car once
and testified that defendant was in his shirtsleeves, with
his coat off. Shortly afterward Parker left his companion
in the restaurant, walked across the street to his automobile
in which the defendant and his companion were then seated.
Exactly what occurred next is in dispute. The defendant testified that Parker pulled open the door of the car, grabbed
at defendant's ankle, and that:

"When he did that, I withdrew my ankle from him and I
took my topcoat in the right hand and I started to get out
of the car. As I started out the door, Mr. Parker partly
withdrew from the door. He moved, it seemed to me, toward
the front of the car but not far. Then when I got both
feet on the sidewalk, I stood there and looked at him, and
he mumbled something more and then lifted his arm like this
(indicating) high, like with his clenched fist, and I rea-
lized he was about to deliver a blow, and I, in self-defense,
hit him with my left hand, and it seems to me that I threw

my topcoat away with my right hand, and then I hit him in
the face with my right hand. I hit him with my left hand
in the body some place, and in the face. I hit him in the
front of the body, he was facing me at all times.

"I did not see him fall down. The next thing I remembered -
I was shocked and surprised. There he lay before me, very
close to me, and my - I am sure when I saw him he was lying
there face upwards, and I thought: Well, I do not believe
he is knocked out. I believe he is just shamming." . . .

(Other witnesses testified that Collins stomped Parker
as he lay on the sidewalk.)

. . .The defendant ran down the street and either ran
into or was hit by another automobile, rolled over, got up,
refused the assistance offered by the driver, and hurried
on down the street. He was apprehended at his home later
the same morning. In the meantime, Parker died in the am-
bulance on the way to the hospital. On post mortem examination, the autopsy disclosed that death was caused by a
traumatic hemorrhage at the base of the brain, an injury
due to a blow. There was a bruise or contusion under the
scalp and over the medulla oblongata - definitely a vital
part of the brain. Except for superficial abrasions or
bruises on Parker's face, there were no other indication of
injury. . . .

Defendant claims the court erred in failing to take from
the consideration of the jury the charges of murder in the
first degree and murder in the second degree, as requested,
and in refusing to submit the case to the jury solely as a
charge of manslaughter. The record before us, including
defendant's own testimony and admissions, justified the
court in submitting to the jury the question whether the
killing was wilful, deliberate, premeditated, and malicious.
In Wellar v. People, 30 Mich. 16, 19, 21, the defendant was
convicted of murder by kicking the deceased while on the
floor after she had fallen or been knocked down. There was
no proof tending to show the use of a weapon. The issue
was whether death resulted from a blow of the defendant's
fist, a kick, or by accident. The court said:

"In determining whether a person who has killed another
without meaning to kill him is guilty of murder or manslaughter, the nature and extent of the injury or wrong which was
actually intended, must usually be of controlling importance.

"It is not necessary in all cases that one held for murder must have intended to take the life of the person he
slays by his wrongful act. It is not always necessary that
he must have intended a personal injury to such person. But
it is necessary that the intent with which he acted shall be
equivalent in legal character to a criminal purpose aimed
against life. . . .

"The jury were sufficiently and rightly charged upon the
extent of the respondent's liability for any intended killing. And if respondent willfully and violently kicked the

deceased in such a way as he must have known would endanger her life, and her life was destroyed in that way, an actual intention of killing would not be necessary, as in such case the death would have been a result he might fairly be held to regard as likely." . . .

It was the province of the jury, and not of the court, to decide whether there was much or little testimony which would reduce the crime from murder to manslaughter. While there may be little testimony to reduce the crime to manslaughter, it was for the jury to measure the quantity of proof. People v. Toner, 217 Mich. 640 (23 A.L.R. 433).

"It will suffice to say that the testimony justified submitting the case to the jury on the charge of murder, and whether the testimony bearing on that charge was much or little was for the jury and not for the court." People v. Vanderhoof, 234 Mich. 419.

The court was not in error in submitting to the jury the issue as to whether defendant was guilty of murder or manslaughter. . . .

After fully explaining the necessary elements to prove first degree murder, second degree murder, and manslaughter, and explaining what constitutes wilfulness, motive, malice, and premeditation, the court charged the jury as follows:

"I also instruct you, members of the jury, in a case of an offense such as the one charged, committed during a period of intoxication, the law presumes the defendant to have intended the obscuration and perversion of his faculties, which followed his voluntary intoxication. He must be held to have purposely blinded his moral perception and set his will free from the control or reason, to have suppressed the guards and invited the mutiny, and should therefore be held responsible as well for the vicious excesses of the will thus set free as for the acts done by its prompting. In other words, it is well-settled law in this State that voluntary drunkenness is not a defense to crime. A man who puts himself in a position to have no control over his actions must be held to intend the consequences. The safety of the community requires this rule. Intoxication is so easily counterfeited and, when real, is so often resorted to as a means of nerving a person up to the commission of some deliberate act and, withal, is so inexcusable in itself, that the law has never recognized it as an excuse for crime. But, in this connection, I instruct you further, members of the jury, that voluntary intoxication though being no excuse for the commission of a crime and will not relieve a person committing a crime from the penalty of the law, still, in a case of this kind, if there is evidence introduced that the defendant was intoxicated at the time it was alleged he committed the crime, it should be considered by you for the purpose of determining whether the accused at the time of the alleged killing was capable of forming a wilful, deliberate, and premeditated purpose to take life. And if in this case, although you believe from the evidence, beyond a reasonable doubt, that the defendant killed the deceased in manner and form as charged in the information, still, if you further believe from the evidence that at the time he inflicted the fatal injuries he was so deeply intoxicated as to be incapable of forming in his mind a design deliberately and premeditatedly to do the killing, or if you entertain a reasonable doubt as to these things, then such killing would be only at most murder in the second degree or manslaughter."

This has heretofore had the approval of this court and was proper under the facts and circumstances of this case. People v. Garbutt, 17 Mich. 9 (97 Am. Dec. 162); Roberts v. People, 19 Mich. 400; People v. Toner, supra.

We have examined the charge as a whole, in connection with defendant's assignments of error for failure to give defendant's requests to charge. The requests were adequately covered by the court.

Conviction and sentence affirmed.

CHANDLER, C. J., and NORTH, STARR, BUTZEL, BUSHNELL, and SHARPE, JJ., concurred. WIEST, J., did not sit.

People v. Carl
11 Mich. App. 226

BURNS, J. Defendant appeals from an order denying defendant's motion to withdraw his plea of guilty to murder in the second degree,[1] vacate sentence and grant a new trial.

The record indicates that at about 3:00 a.m. or 3:30 a.m., October 11, 1966, the defendant, who had been drinking heavily, entered a house in St. Louis, Michigan, through a kitchen window. Inside he killed Mrs. Emily Housel (whom he had never seen before this time) with a knife which he took from the kitchen sink. Defendant then went to the garage and drove the Housel automobile to Tallahassee, Florida. Later he was apprehended and charged with murder in the first degree.[2] With the advice of assigned counsel defendant pleaded guilty to second degree murder and was sentenced to life imprisonment. Different counsel was appointed to assist in defendant's unsuccessful attempt to withdraw his plea of guilty.

Defendant first contends that the arraigning circuit judge should have taken testimony to determine the degree of the crime pursuant to CL 1948, Sec. 750.318 (Stat Ann 1954 Rev Sec. 28.550). Defendant specifically pleaded guilty to second-degree murder, and therefore no hearing was necessary to determine the degree of the crime. See People v. Grillo (1948), 319 Mich 586.

The question remains, however, whether the court erred in accepting defendant's guilty plea after it learned that the

687

defendant went into a house which was unfamiliar to him, did not know where he was or why he was there and had no intention of committing any crime therein. It appears that the arraigning court's recognition of defendant's claimed lack of awareness of his surroundings caused the court to extensively interrogate Carl regarding his sensibilities at the time of the stabbing:

"The Court: Well, did you cut her throat?
"Mr. Carl: Yes.
"The Court: Did you know that in doing this is would kill her?
"Mr. Carl: Yes.
"The Court: That's what I am getting at. Did you know what you did would result in her death?
"Mr. Carl: Yes.
"The Court: You knew that? No question about that, is there?
"Mr. Carl: No.
"The Court: I wasn't asking you whether you had planned this. I was asking what you actually did at the time; whether you knew what you were doing would result in her death.
"Mr. Carl: Yes.
"The Court: You knew that?
"Mr. Carl: Yes."

Defendant's admissions manifest a second-degree murder intent which has been described in People v. Hansen (1962), 368 Mich 344, 350, as an "intent to cause the very harm that results." Furthermore:

"If a person voluntarily or willfully does an act which has a direct tendency to destroy another's life, the natural and necessary conclusion from the act is that he intended so to destroy such person's life." 40 CJS, Homicide, Sec. 17, p 864.

Defendant's acknowledgment that he knew death would result from his acts justifies the court's acceptance of the plea as against defendant's claim that he formed no intent to kill. . . .
. . . From carefully reading the transcript of that hearing (69 pages) and the transcript of the arraignment (15 pages) this Court finds that the trial judge did not abuse his discretion in refusing permission to withdraw defendant's plea.
Affirmed.

J. W. FITZGERALD, P. J., and NEAL E. FITZGERALD, J., concurred.

Footnotes

1. CL 1948, Sec. 750.317 (Stat Ann 1954 Rev Sec. 28.549).
2. CL 1948, Sec. 750.316 (Stat Ann 1954 Rev Sec. 28.548).

3. "After sentence the withdrawal of a plea rests within the sound discretion of the court. People v. Williams (1923), 225 Mich 133; People v. Kobrzycki (1928), 242 Mich 44; People v. Skropski (1940), 292 Mich 461; People v. Vasquez (1942), 303 Mich 340; People v. Kearns (1965), 2 Mich App 60." People v. Wilkins (1966), 3 Mich App 56,58.

4. Transferred Intent

People v. Hodges
196 Mich. 546

The information in this case charged respondent with an assault upon one Edward L. Merritt with intent to kill and murder said Merritt. The facts out of which the prosecution grew were briefly as follows: In the afternoon of August 2, 1913, respondent had sold to one Green, a farmer, a team of horses. It appears that after the trade was complete Green asked the opinion of one Honsinger, a blacksmith, about the horses. Honsinger made some disparaging remarks about the horses, and likewise said that respondent Hodges was a horse trader and dishonest. Resenting the acts and language of Honsinger, respondent and Honsinger shortly came to blows. A violent and somewhat protracted fight ensued in which Honsinger seems to have inflicted more punishment upon respondent, Hodges, than he received from Hodges. The men were finally separated, and did not meet again until several hours later. About seven o'clock in the evening respondent entered Schneider's saloon. Several men were in the barroom, and among them Honsinger and Merritt. Shortly after entering the saloon, respondent drew a revolver and pointed it toward Honsinger, who at the time was walking toward respondent. Respondent pulled the trigger, but no explosion followed, because the particular chamber in apposition proved to be unloaded. Almost immediately respondent pulled a second time, when an explosion followed. The bullet entirely missed Honsinger, at whom it was aimed,but lodged in the shoulder of Merritt, passing nearly through his body. It is undisputed that respondent had never seen Merritt before the moment of the shooting and bore him no ill will. Respondent pleaded not guilty to the information. At the conclusion of the case made by the people respondent, through his counsel, made a motion. This motion was understood by the trial court to be for a directed verdict upon the ground:

"That the evidence shows, if this man committed an offense at all, it was an assault upon Honsinger with intent to murder Honsinger, and it appears beyond dispute at this stage of the case that he hit and wounded Merritt when he fired the shot which was intended for Honsinger."

Counsel for defendant corrected the court, saying:

"It is my opinion, even if that were true, that the

689

information would not necessarily or entirely fail. I
think from the facts there might be a case still on this
information for assault and battery, because there are
some text-books which hold intent is not necessary in an
assault."

In this court counsel for respondent treats his motion
as one for leave to enter a plea of guilty to the charge
of assault and battery. The motion, whatever it was, was
denied by the court, and respondent took the stand in his
own behalf. It was his claim that he drew the revolver and
pointed it at Honsinger under the belief that it was unloaded and with the idea of intimidating Honsinger. He did not
claim to have fired the shot in self-defense. The court
charged the jury in part as follows:

"The information does not mention Mr. Honsinger, and it
has been claimed here for that reason, inasmuch as all the
proof on the part of the people is that the real purpose was
to hit and kill or wound Honsinger, that the jury cannot
consider the case. But it is the duty of the jury to take
the law from the court, and I conceive it my duty, in the
absence of a decision that is squarely in point in this
State, to say to you that, even if his purpose in shooting
was to hit Honsinger, if he did hit Merritt, doing an unlawful act in that way, he may be considered as intending the
natural and probable results of his shooting, and if there
was intent to kill Honsinger, but he hit Merritt, that unlawful purpose, design, or intent entertained against Honsinger will pass over and to characterize the act in shooting and hitting Merritt. Therefore you should not acquit
because it is charged that he intended to kill Merritt, although the proof shows that his primary purpose, if he had
any such intent at all was to either kill or hit and hurt
Honsinger. . . .
"I have already said, perhaps, in almost the same language, and I will repeat, that the charge is on its face an
intent to murder Honsinger, but the pistol ball hit Merritt
as a matter of fact. Merritt was in company of others.
Honsinger was in company of others. They were practically
in the company of each other, and there were other men there.
Now, if in shooting at Honsinger and hitting Merritt, Hodges
was seeking to kill or inflict great bodily harm on Honsinger,
he was committing a felony, and if others stood around there,
and one, not Honsinger, was hit, and, shooting in that way,
it was likely and probable he might hit some of the others
instead of the one he wanted to hit, then the intent to hit
Honsinger, if it was the intent to kill him or do him great
bodily harm less than murder, the intent passes right over
to Merritt, because the jury has a right to infer that if a
man does an act of that kind with a weapon of that kind he
does intend whatever happens. He takes his chances whether
he will hit the right fellow or not."

A single request to charge was presented on behalf of

respondent as follows:

"I charge you, gentlemen, that the people cannot sustain a conviction for attempt of murder under their information; that the people's information charges Hodges with intent to murder Merritt, and the proof shows that the injuries received by him were entirely accidental; therefore Hodges cannot be convicted under this information with any offense with which an intent is coupled. Under the proofs as they now stand under the information, your verdict must be not guilty."

The jury brought in a verdict finding respondent guilty of assault with intent to do great bodily harm less than the crime of murder, under which verdict respondent was sentenced to State's prison for a maximum period of ten years and a minimum period of five years and a recommended maximum period of seven years.

The sole question raised upon this record is whether respondent under an information charging an assault with intent to kill and murder Merritt is properly convicted of the included offense of which he is found guilty, when the evidence conclusively shows that when he fired the shot which took effect in Merritt's body, if he had any intent, it was an intent to kill or wound Honsinger.

BROOKE, J. (after stating the facts). The jury evidently disbelieved the claim of respondent that he pointed the revolver at Honsinger and snapped it twice with the purpose merely of intimidating Honsinger and under the belief that it was unloaded. Under the evidence in the case and the verdict found by the jury it cannot be doubted that, had Merritt died from the effect of the wound, respondent would have been guilty of murder. Maher v. People, 10 Mich. 212 (81 Am. Dec. 781); People v. Garbutt, 17 Mich. 9 (97 Am. Dec. 162); Roberts v. People, 19 Mich. 401; Wilson v. People, 24 Mich. 410; People v. Lilley, 43 Mich. 521 (5 N.W. 982). Indeed, that this would be true is admitted by counsel for respondent. The rule touching the question involved is laid down in volume 1 of McClain on Criminal Law, Sec. 126 as follows:

"From the rule above stated with reference to inferring the intent from the act, it follows that, where a specific intent is required, it may be inferred from the doing of an unlawful act implying such intent, even though the actual intent was different. Thus, if the charge is of shooting with intent to kill A., the crime will be made out by proof of unlawfully shooting and injuring A., and it will be immaterial that defendant actually intended to kill B. and hit A. by mistake."

See, also, section 276 Id.
We are of opinion that the case at bar is governed in principle by People v. Raher, 92 Mich. 165 (52 N.W. 625, 31 Am. St. Rep. 575). There the respondent was convicted

691

of an assault with intent to do great bodily harm less than the crime of murder upon the person of one John Peterson. Other persons besides Peterson were standing near when the respondent fired a revolver wounding Peterson in the head. The court was requested to instruct the jury that they must find the specific intent to assault Peterson. This request was refused, and the court instructed them that, if respondent shot into the crowd with the intention to wound any of them, he might be convicted, notwithstanding he had no specific intent against Peterson. This court affirmed the conviction. The law presumes every person to intend the usual consequences which accompany the use of the means employed in the manner employed. People v. Potter, 5 Mich. 1 (71 Am. Dec. 763); People v. Getchell, 6 Mich. 496. A case very similar to the one at bar is Dunaway v. People, 110 Ill. 333 (51 Am. Rep. 686). There the court said:

"The charge is, defendant assaulted Hendrickson with intent to commit murder, and the insistence is, no such intent is shown, because the intent was to murder Hartwell. The reasoning on this branch of the case is too subtle to be adopted with safety. Undoubtedly there are cases that hold the doctrine contended for, and so many of the early text-writers wrote, but the better and more modern doctrine is against the position taken. Conceding, as is done, had the shot fired by defendant killed Hendrickson, it would have been murder, the proposition the severe wounding by the same shot would not have been done with intent to commit murder - that is, to commit the greater crime that might have been the result - finds no sanction either in reason or the analogies of the law."

See, also, State v. Meadows, 18 W. Va. 658; Callahan v. State, 21 Ohio St. 306; and 21 Cyc. p. 786.
The judgment is affirmed.

KUHN, C. J., and STONE, OSTRANDER, BIRD, MOORE, and STEERE, JJ., concurred. FELLOWS, J., did not sit.

5. Felony - Murder Rule - Inferred Intent
(a) Introduction

Note
43 U. Det. L. J. 118

CRIMINAL LAW - Homicide - Felony-Murder - Felon Convicted for the Death of Co-Felon During Commission of Robbery. People v. Washington, 62 Cal. 2d - , 44 Cal. Rptr 442, 401 P.2d 130 (1965). The defendant, Washington, and a partner, Ball, attempted to rob a service station. While the defendant was emptying a safe in one room, Ball, with his gun drawn, entered the station's office, and was thereupon shot and killed by the owner. Washington was later tried for first degree murder under the California felony-murder statute,[1] which makes murder, during the commission of a robbery, murder in the first degree. He was convicted, and later appealed to the California Court of Appeals,[2] which affirmed the conviction on the basis of the application of the proximate cause rule to the felony-murder doctrine, in People v. Harrison.[3] In Harrison it was held that a felon is responsible for all the foreseeable consequences of his felonious acts, whether the results flow directly or indirectly from his hand.[4] Held, conviction reversed.

The California Supreme Court rejected the incorporation of the proximate cause rule into the felony-murder doctrine[5]. It refused to hold a felon responsible for an act which he did not actually or constructively commit.[6]

Introduction

This note will discuss the significance of People v. Washington[7] within the framework of the recent history of the felony-murder doctrine. More specifically, this holding will be examined as the culmination of a reverse trend in the area of criminal law. Inherent in this discussion will be a treatment of the modern trend which had evolved whereby a felon had been held responsible for killings, accidentally committed by others, who were not felons[8] but which did occur during the commission of a robbery.[9] Almost as soon as this trend began, those jurisdictions[9] which had adopted the rule began to have reservations about its further extension. It is the rise and fall of the extension of the felony-murder rule, through the use of the proximate cause doctrine with which this note will be concerned.

History of the Doctrine

A brief resume[10] of the history of the felony-murder doctrine is necessary for a complete understanding of its present status.

The common law definition of the doctrine may be stated quite simply: "If a man intends to do another a felony, and undesignedly kills a man, this is murder."[11] Although the early common law treated killings arising from all felonies alike[12] - as murder - the doctrine was later restricted in its application to only those killings which arose out of those acts which were considered inherently dangerous to life or "malum in se."[13]

As the law developed, the number of felonies, during the commission of which a killing is deemed murder, has steadily diminished. The common law definition, while remaining the same in substance, has been greatly restricted in its application by statutory enactments in forty-seven states.[14] Three states[15] still have no statutory limitation of the felony-murder rule. The overwhelming majority[16] of states demand that the killing occur during the commission of one

of the following felonies in order to apply the rule:
robbery, rape, arson, and burglary.

The unmistakable trend from the early common law down
to the twentieth century, then, has been a lessening of
the area in which the felony-murder rule could be applied.

Elements of the Doctrine

There are four essential elements which constitute the
substance of the felony-murder doctrine: there must be a
killing; there must be a felony out of which the killing
arises; there must be legal malice on the part of the felon;
the felon must have caused the death.

First, there must be a killing. Without a homicide un-
excused and unjustifiable, there can obviously be no cause
for the application of rules relating to responsibility for
murder.

Secondly, there must be the commission of, or attempted
commission of, a felony.[17] The killing must take place
during the commission of the felonious act, must be _causally
related_ to it, and not merely a coincidence thereof.[18] It
is essential that the felon not merely provide the occasion
for a killing, but that _because_ of the felonious act a killing ensued. For example, an officer who is mortally wounded
when coming to the aid of a rape victim would be held to be
a killing "arising out of the felony." However, if the same
officer, attempting to arrest the same felon days afterward,
is killed, then this would not be a killing "arising out of
a felony." The crime was, at most, an occasion for the arrest.[19]

Third, there must be malice on the part of the felon.
Legal malice may be defined as "that man-endangering state-
of-mind,"[20] the intent to do another harm.[21] In a killing
occuring during the commission of a felony, however, there
may be no specific intent to do another harm; the killing
may be entirely accidental, in fact, it may be the farthest
thing from the felon's mind. In cases of this sort, the
constructive malice doctrine is invoked. This doctrine
states that where a homicide occurs during, and arises out
of a felony, the legal malice necessary for a first degree
murder conviction is imputed[22] to the felon. The malice
inherent in the commission of the felony is implied in the
act of killing. The malice of the initial felonious act
flows to all consequential acts.[23] The constructive malice
doctrine, employed in the application of the felony-murder
doctrine may be summarized as follows: "The theory of the
common law was that anyone who commits a . . .felony, possessed the legal malice; and where a killing . . .results therein
or therefrom . . .the legal malice is carried over from the
original felony, and the original felon is guilty of murder."[24]

Fourthly, and most important for the purpose of this note,
is the requirement that the felon must cause the death. To
be held responsible for any wrong, civil or criminal, one

must have caused it.[25]   In every criminal proceeding, the
trier of fact must find that the accused was the cause of
the specific criminal result.[26]   In the area of felony-murder, the felon must cause the death by his own hand, or by
that of one of his accomplices.[27]

Although these four elements have long been recognized
as necessary for a first degree murder conviction, under
the various felony-murder statutes, there has been considerable variation in the manner in which the last-mentioned
element has been applied to situations[28] where the felon did
not kill by his own hand, either actually or constructively.
It is upon such situations that focus will be brought.

At this point, a distinction must be drawn and observed
between the terms "cause" and "proximate cause." "Cause"
here means that the felon did the killing himself or
through an accomplice. "Proximate cause" here means that
a third person, not a part of the felonious conspiracy, did
the killing, by violently resisting the felon. His act of
killing is imputed to the felon. To "proximately cause" a
death, one need only set in motion the events which gave
rise to the death. These are the two theories under which
a felon is held guilty by the application of the felony-
murder rule. One deems it necessary for the felon to fire
the fatal shot. The other deems it necessary only that the
felon make someone else fire the fatal shot. It is the close
examination of these polar theories, and their embodiment in
case law, which is of present concern.

The Expansion of the Doctrine

The essence of the felony-murder rule, both at the common law and under statute has been the killing of another
human being by the felon. Since 1935, however, some jurisdictions[29] began to expand the felon's responsibility in
cases where violent resistance was called forth in response
to the felony, and in which a non-felon did the killing, with
the non-felon's action thus attributed to the felon. The
felon has been found guilty of first degree murder when a
victim, or one coming to the aid of a victim, has accidentally killed another potential victim,[30] thus raising an
issue similar to that in the instant case.

The leading authority for the incorporation of the proximate cause rule into the felony-murder doctrine is Commonwealth v. Almeida.[34]   In this Pennsylvania case, a robber
was found guilty of murder in the death of an off-duty policeman, who was killed in a crossfire between the felons and
policemen. There was conflicting evidence as to who fired
the fatal shot. The trial judge stated it mattered not who
fired the fatal shot.[35]   The supreme court approved this
charge; it continued, setting down what has become the definitive statements of the proximate cause rule in felony-
murder:

If one or more persons set in motion a chain of circum-

stances out of which death ensues, those persons will be
held responsible for any death which by direct, almost inevitable sequence results from such unusual criminal act. . . .
So, if the death . . . was the inevitable consequence of the
unlawful act, . . . or the continuation of the unlawful act
. . . if the unlawful act be robbery, and if the result of
that act is a killing . . . that killing is murder.[36]

Under the ruling in Almeida, the felon did not have to
"cause" the death by firing the fatal shot. It was sufficient if the felon called forth the violent resistance to
the robbery out of which the killing arose. The initiation of the robbery, inherently dangerous to life, was "the
proximate cause of another's death . . ."[37] The majority
opinion asserts that robbers who arm themselves with weapons show their expectation of resistance and their desire
to overcome that resistance.[38] Therefore, when a robbery
is committed, and since the felons are charged with the
knowledge that violent resistance will ensue, a killing resulting from such resistance is, as to them, first degree
murder.[39]

The robbery was the cause of the resistance. The resistance was the cause of the death. The felons are, thus, the
cause of the cause of the death. As such they are guilty
of murder.

Under Almeida[40] the ancient application of the felony-
murder rule applies only to those situations in which the
felon killed by his own hand, or the hand of a felon, was
greatly expanded. The felon now need only cause another
to kill while resisting the felon.

Six years later, Pennsylvania further extended its novel[41]
application of the rule in Commonwealth v. Thomas.[42] This
case was considered to be a "logical" extension of Almeida.
Here Thomas and a partner committed a robbery, during which
the partner was killed by the potential victim. The supreme court affirmed the conviction of murder. The reasoning differs not at all from Almeida, which the majority
adopts without hesitation. In the concurring opinion it is
said that Almeida, and therefore the proximate cause rule,
"clearly and directly rules the instant case"[43] (although
the factual situations were drastically different as were
the relationships between the defendant and the deceased).[44]

There was no distinction drawn between the killing of an
innocent non-participant in Almeida and the killing of a
felon in Thomas. To the majority, it made no difference
who the person killed might be,[45] as long as the death was
proximately caused by the initiation of the felonious act.

Pennsylvania, while it may have been the first to extend the felony-murder rule to the above situations, was
not the last. Michigan, in People v. Podolski,[46] in 1952,
and California, in People v. Harrison,[47] in 1959, applied
the Almeida rule of proximate cause to situations in which
a non-participant accidentally killed another non-participant

696

while resisting the felon.

In Podolski, the defendant was convicted for the murder of a policeman in attempting to capture defendant and two partners who were fleeing the scene of the robbery. The Michigan Supreme Court did not cite Almeida directly (though this case followed Almeida by three years)[48] However, the court did rely upon Commonwealth v. Moyer[48] which was the seed from which Almeida grew and from which Almeida drew much of the language in support of its decision. The Michigan court[49] quoted with approval the same sections of Moyer which Almeida had quoted.[50]

The Podolski decision was based on the incorporation of the proximate cause rule into the felony-murder doctrine. Justice Reid, writing for the court, declared that "when a felon's attempt to commit a robbery . . . sets in motion a chain of events which were or should have been within his contemplation when the motion was initiated, he should be held responsible"[51] for any killing which arises out of those events.

The reasoning is similar in Harrison, the California case. The accused was convicted of the murder of an employer accidentally shot by an employee, while he was resisting the felon's attempted robbery. The California court, in affirming, said it thought "the better reasoning is that of the authorities to which we have referred, (i.e., Podolski and Almeida, and others) to the effect that the doctrine of proximate cause is applicable"[52] to the facts of the case. The California Appellate Court went on to say that where one creates a situation which involuntarily exposes another to the danger of death, "the creation of such (a) situation is the proximate cause of the death."[53] (Emphasis added.)

The appellate court went one step further when it affirmed Washington's conviction of murder for the death of his co-felon shot by the robbery victim.[54] Not only did the appellate court approve Almeida, but it also approved Commonwealth v. Thomas[55] which had already been expressly overruled by Commonwealth v. Redline.[56] Redline had also restricted Almeida to its facts, implicitly disapproved its holding, and left its future in serious doubt.[57]

Justice Ford, speaking for the majority, refused to accept the reasoning of Redline and rejected any distinction between Harrison and the case before him, based on factual differences. He stated that responsibility is placed on defendant Washington by the doctrine of proximate cause as expressed in the Harrison case which was a complete adherent to the Almeida ruling.

This is the case for the proponents of the incorporation of the proximate cause rule into the felony-murder doctrine. By means of this incorporation, the courts had been able to extend the application of the doctrine, to hold a felon guilty of murder in cases in which a non-felon kills while resisting a felon's criminal act. The felon need not kill by his own hand or that of an accomplice. It suffices that

the accused, charged with the knowledge that violent resistance
would be called forth and that a probable result of such resistance would be death, commit a named felony out of which
a death arose. Under these circumstances the felon was the
cause of the cause. The felon "proximately caused" the death
and therefore is guilty of murder.

A Delimitation of the Proximate Cause Rule

The opponents of the felony-murder rule's extension rely
upon various theories. The opinions refusing to expand the
doctrine present a steady progression. They continually
erode the underpinnings of the extension.[58]
Redline, People v. Austin,[58] as well as the dissent to the
appellate court's decision in its review of the instant case,
seem to avoid confronting the issue of the desirability of
the proximate cause rule's incorporation into the felony-
murder doctrine. The California Supreme Court, in the instant case, appears to have faced the issue squarely. Because of Washington's importance as the final step away from
the expansion of the felony-murder doctrine, it will be discussed last.
The cases which typify the state courts' rejection of the
expansion (except for Washington) seek to restrict the widen-
ing application of the rule on the following bases: first,
on statutory definition of felony-murder; secondly, on the
nature of the homicide committed; and third, on the absence
of malice on the part of the felon. The greatest reliance
is on the first two closely related arguments.
The first argument advanced is a constitutional, or more
precisely, a separation of powers argument. Various opinions[59]
state that the extension of the rule is invalid as an unwarranted usurpation of legislative prerogatives. This contention is founded on the supposed intent of the respective[60]
state legislatures which drafted the felony-murder statues.
Justice Jones, for the majority in Redline, believes that
"the only constitutional power competent to define crimes
and prescribe punishment . . . is the legislature, and courts
would do well to leave the promulgation of police regulations
to the people's chosen legislative representatives."[61]
Redline's reasoning is that only "murder" committed during
the felony is included under the Pennsylvania statute, not
all "killing," and that the court in Almeida unjustifiably
changed the intent of the legislature when it interpreted
the statute to mean all "killing." Murder, says Redline, is
the actual or constructive killing of one human being by
another - the definition known to the common law. The killing of the felon, it asserts, was not murder as to either
the policeman or the accused. The majority declared that
if this were deemed the necessary public policy, the legislature, not the courts by judicial pronouncement, should
make the required change.[62]
Lending authority to the holding that the extension of

698

the felony-murder rule in <u>Almeida</u> was wrong, the <u>Redline</u>
majority observes that prior to <u>Almeida</u>, the Pennsylvania[64]
court,[63] as well as the other United States jurisdictions,
applied the felony-murder doctrine only in those instances
in which the felon actually or constructively killed someone.

The reasoning is similar in <u>Austin</u>. Here the Michigan
Supreme Court refused to extend its holding in <u>People v.
Podolski</u>[65] to a situation in which one of the robbers was
killed by a potential victim. The majority approved the
holding of the trial court that conviction of Austin "would
be an unwarranted extension of the policy of felony-murder...."[66]

Justice Kelley, speaking for the majority, supports the
<u>Redline</u> reasoning that any extension of the rule must come
from the state legislature by amending the felony-murder
statute.[67] The extension of the rule by the courts would,
it was flatly stated, "infringe upon legislative prerogatives."[68]

Implicit in the courts' discussion of constitutional
powers is the second argument employed to thwart the extension of the rule - the object of the exercise of those powers -[69]
the felony-murder statutes of the respective states.

<u>Redline</u>, and <u>Austin</u> as well, attempt to distinguish the
word "murder" as used in the statutes from the word "killing."
Both the Michigan and Pennsylvania court had previously interpreted the statutes as saying "killing" not "murder."[70]
It is necessary to call attention to the misinterpretation
of the statutes, by the courts applying the proximate cause
rule to felony-murder to draw the distinction between two
different types of homicide. <u>Redline</u> and <u>Austin</u> reason that
a killing which is justifiable homicide as to the actual
killer cannot be murder as to the felon. If the actual killer
is free from all legal and moral guilt, they say, it is difficult to comprehend how a felon, who did no act which killed
anyone, can be found to have any greater culpability - especially first degree murder culpability - than the actual
killer has.

In <u>Austin</u> it is stated that the "killing . . . by the intended holdup victim was not murder but a justifiable homicide (both as to the actual killer as well as to the felon)."[71]
Justice Files' dissent (in the California Court of Appeals)[72]
in <u>Washington</u> echoes this opinion.

Finally, the courts have employed the argument that there
is an absence of malice on the part of the felon when a
third party, not a felon, does the actual killing, and therefore the felon cannot be guilty of murder.[73] As already
stated,[74] malice is a necessary element of murder, one of
the elements which distinguishes it from all other forms of
himicide.[75]

While <u>Redline</u> admits that malice may be imputed to a
felon where he did not actually or constructively kill, to
do so would border on the absurd.[76] The classic mens rea
of murder <u>is</u> malice, and, it is argued, this requisite malice
is absent <u>as</u> between two felons co-operating to achieve a
common criminal end. (This argument, it seems, may be used

somewhat less effectively in cases in which a non-felon is killed.) Prior to _Almeida_ only where a felon killed actually or constructively was malice implied,[77] and therefore only then was the felony-murder rule invoked.

Justice Files, in his dissent to the appellate court decision in _Washington_ believes the absence of malice to have been the controlling factor. He says "there is no logical basis for saying that the attempt to commit a felony implies malice between the two felons. . . ."[78]

The above arguments were those urged by the opponents of the extension of the felony-murder rule, prior to the decision in the instant case. However, this opposition has not cut to the core of the problem, which is the incorporation of the proximate cause rule, absent other considerations, into the felony-murder doctrine. It has concentrated its force on the periphery of the issue. The proximate cause doctrine has not been completely abandoned in Michigan or Pennsylvania. These two jurisdictions have merely refused to hold a felon responsible for the death of a co-felon killed by a third person.

Washington's Rejection of the Proximate Cause Rule

Turning to the instant case, it is submitted that Justice Traynor, speaking for a divided court, has dealt the coup de grace to the relatively modern extension of the felony-murder doctrine in California. There are some very important distinctions between the instant case's reasoning and that in _Redline_ and _Austin._

First, this opinion directly and unequivocally rejects completely the incorporation of the proximate cause rule into the felony murder rule. Justice Traynor declares:

When a killing is not committed by a robber or by his accomplice but by his victim . . . the killing is not committed by him in the perpetration or attempt to perpetrate robbery. It is not enough that the killing was a risk reasonably to be foreseen and that the robbery might therefore be regarded as a proximate cause of the killing.[79] (Emphasis added.)

And later, Traynor again states that proximate cause, as applied to felony-murder, is no longer a relevant consideration in determining a felon's first degree murder guilt, because "for a defendant to be guilty of murder under the felony murder rule the act of killing must be committed by the defendant. . . ."[80] (Emphasis added.)

Secondly, the California court goes further than either the Michigan or Pennsylvania courts have gone in limiting the felony-murder rule. Its rejection of the proximate cause rule is not limited to the facts of the instant case. As the issue[81] is framed by the majority, and later resolved, California's rejection of the rule includes its rejection in those cases in which a non-felon accidentally kills another

700

non-felon while resisting the felonious attack. After stating its views on the felony-murder rule as applied to the
facts, the majority emasculated the last vestiges of the
proximate cause rule in California by stating: "language in
People v. Harrison (citation omitted) inconsistent with this
holding is disapproved."[82]

In People v. Washington, then, the supreme court of a
state which had hitherto employed the proximate cause rule
in felony-murder cases, abandons it completely. This is
the strongest action yet taken by any of the jurisdictions
which have had similar cases, under similar statutes, presented to them for review.

Pennsylvania and Michigan, as discussed above, have rejected the extension of the felony-murder rule to those cases
in which a felon was killed by a non-participant, but left
as law, albeit uncertain, their decisions supporting first
degree murder convictions where a non-participant accidentally kills another non-participant in repulsing the felon.[83]

Redline intimates that the decision in Almeida will be
overruled when a similar case presents itself.[84] Austin provides no such direct implication that Podolski will be overruled, for the majority did not deem it necessary to expressly disapprove its holding in that case,[85] because of the
great factual differences between the cases. However, the
Michigan Supreme Court's strict interpretation of the state's
felony-murder statute,[86] as well as its great reliance on,
and approval of Redline's reasoning and enunciation of public
policy, leaves little room for doubt that Podolski will be
overruled as soon as the opportunity presents itself.

There are also important differences between the manner
in which the Michigan and Pennsylvania courts, on the one
hand, the the California court on the other refused to accept the extension of the felony-murder rule.

Michigan and Pennsylvania skirted the central issue of
the incorporation of the proximate cause rule into the felony-murder doctrine. These courts concentrated on the periphery, and limited the felony-murder doctrine mainly by statutory interpretation.

California faced the issue squarely, continuing where
Michigan and Pennsylvania stopped. Where California utterly
refused to accept the directives of the proximate cause rule
in felony-murder cases, Pennsylvania and Michigan merely
avoided applying it to the factual situation before them.
Where these courts had feared to tread, the California court
proceeded without hesitation to consummate a reverse trend
in criminal law.

In summary, the California Supreme Court decision in Washington may be seen as the final step in a long process beginning with the Almeida holding. Prior to Almeida only where
a felon had actually or constructively killed during the perpetration, or attempted perpetration of a named felony, could
he be found guilty of first degree murder. This was true
both at common law and under statute.

701

Almeida stated that an actual or constructive killing by
the felon was not necessary. It was sufficient that a felon
cause one to resist the felonious attempt. If, as a result
of that resistance, a non-participant was accidentally killed
by another non-participant, that killing was attributable to
the felon. He was guilty of murder. The initiation of the
felony was the proximate cause of death. This ruling was
followed in _Harrison_ and _Podolski_.

The holding was further extended in _Thomas_ and in the appellate court decision in _Washington_. In both those cases,
a surviving felon was found responsible for the death of a
co-felon killed by one resisting the robbery. The same reasoning that was employed in _Almeida_ was employed in these
clearly distinguishable cases. All the felon need do was
cause violent resistance to the felony. If death resulted
he was responsible, for he caused the cause of death.

While _Redline_ (which overruled _Thomas_) and _Austin_ did not
apply the proximate cause rule to the facts of the case before them, it was not, it would seem, from any gross dis-
pleasure with the rule itself. Rather these courts relied
upon strict interpretation of their respective felony-murder
statutes to avoid application of the felony-murder rule.

Finally in _Washington_, the court completely rejected the
proximate cause rule. The reasoning buttressing the rule,
it declared, was unsound, and therefore the rule should not
be invoked to increase criminal responsibility beyond its
common law limits.

Conclusion

Thus, within a period of less than twenty years, the
felony-murder doctrine has undergone a complete metamorphosis.
From the ancient common law manner of application, the rule
was extended to include killings not done by a felon or a
co-felon. However, this extension was short-lived. By 1965,
of the three states which had used the proximate cause rule
in determining felony-murder responsibility, California has
completely rejected it; Michigan and Pennsylvania have refused to expand it further, and have intimated its rejection
for such cases wherein it may be applied. There have been
no cases decided by a state's highest court, since 1959,
which have deemed the proximate cause rule applicable in regard to felony-murder cases.

The rule is definitely on the wane, and as soon as Michigan and Pennsylvania act, the felony murder doctrine shall
be restored to its historic limits: it will be employed only
where a felon actually or constructively kills while perpetrating, or attempting to perpetrate, a named felony.

J. Thomas Carroll, Jr.

Footnotes

1. Cal. Pen. Code, Sec. 189 (1955)

All murder which is perpetrated by means of poison, or lying in wait, torture, or by any other kind of wilful, deliberate, and premeditated killing, <u>or which is committed in the per-</u> <u>petration or attempt to perpetrate arson, rape, robbery,</u> <u>burglary, mayhem, or any act punishable under Section 288 is</u> <u>murder in the first degree</u>; all other kinds of murder are of the second degree. (Emphasis added.)

2. People v. Washington, 230 Cal. App. 2d 351. 40 Cal. Rptr 791 (1964).

3. 176 Cal. App. 2d 330, 1 Cal. Rptr. 414 (1959). Defendant was convicted of first degree murder in the death of a storeowner who was accidentally killed by an employee, the latter resisting the felons. The court said that the doctrine of proximate cause was applicable in criminal proceedings.

4. People v. Washington, 230 Cal. App. 2d 351, 40 Cal. Rptr. 791, 793 (1964).

5. People v. Washington, 62 Cal. 2d - , 44 Cal. Rptr. 442, 445, 402 P.2d 130, 133 (1965).

6. Id. at 0 44 Cal. Rptr. at 446.

7. People v. Washington, 62 Cal. 2d - 44 Cal. Rptr. 442, 402, P.2d 130 (1965).

8. All cases which treated the issue of a felon's responsibility for killings committed by third parties involved robberies.

9. California, Michigan and Pennsylvania.

10. See generally Maesel, <u>A Survey of Felony-murder</u>, 28 Temp. L.Q. 453 (1955), for an extended and thorough discussion of the history of the felony-murder doctrine.

11. Blackstone, Commentaries 200.

12. Maesel, <u>supra</u> note 10, at 453.

13. Id. at 454.

14. 5 Ala. Code tit. 14, Sec. 314 (1940); Alaska Stat. Sec. 11.15.010 (1962); 5 Ariz. Rev. Stat. Ann. Sec. 13-452 (1956); 4 Ark. Stat. Ann. Sec. 4102205 (1964); Cal. Pen. Code, Sec. 189 (1955); 3 Colo Rev. Stat. Ann. Sec. 40-23 (1964); 28 Conn. Gen. Stat. Ann. Sec. 53-9 (1960); 7 Del Code Ann. Sec. 571 (1953); 22 Fla. Stat. Ann. Sec. 782.04 (1944 ; 10 Ga. Code Ann. Sec. 26.1009 (1933). The Georgia statute makes a killing during the felony involuntary manslaughter; 2 Hawaii Rev. Law. Sec. 247-2 (1955); 4 Idaho Code Ann. Sec. 18-4003 (1947); Ill Rev. Stat. Chap. 33, Sec. 9-1 (1961); 4 Ind. Ann. Stat. Sec. 10-3401 (1956); 2 Iowa Code Sec. 690.2 (1962); Kansas Stat. Ann. Sec. 21-401 (1949); 2 La. Rev. Stat. Sec. 30 (1950); 3 Md. Ann. Code Act. 27 Sec. 408-10 (1957); 9 Mass Ann. Laws Ch. 265 Sec. 1 (1956); Mich. Comp. Laws Sec. 750.316 (1948); 40A Minn.Stat. Ann. Sec. 609.185

(1964); 2A Miss. Code Ann. Sec. 2215 (1956); 3 Mo. Rev. Stat. Sec. 559.010 (1959); 8 Mont. Rev. Codes Ann. Sec. 94-2503 (1949); 2 Neb. Rev. Stat. Sec. 28-401 (1948); 2 Nev. Rev. Stat. Sec. 200-030 (1957); 5 N.H. Rev. Stat. Ann. Sec. 585-1 (1955); 2A N.J. Stat. Ann. Sec. 113-1 (1953); 6 N.M. Stat. Ann. Sec. 40A-2-1 (1953); N.Y. Pen. Sec. 1044 (1944); 18 N.C. Gen.Stat. Sec. 14-17 (1953); 2 N.D. Cent. Code Sec. 12-27-12 (1960); Ohio Rev. Code Ann. Sec. 2901-01 (1964); 1 Okla Stat. tit. 21 Sec. 21 - 70 (1961); 1 Ore. Rev. Stat. Sec. 163.010 (1954); Pa. Stat. Ann. tit. 18, Sec. 4701 (1963); 3 R.I. Gen. Law. Ann. Sec.11-23-1 (1956); 1 S.D. Code Sec. 13.2007 (1939); 7 Tenn Code Ann. Sec. 39.2402 (1955); Tex. Pen. Code Acts. 1241, 1256 (1948); 8 Utah Code Ann. Sec. 76-30-3 (1953); 5 Vt. Stat. Ann. tit. 13 Sec. 2301 (1959); 4 Va. Code Ann. Sec. 18-1-21 (1950); 1 Wash. Rev. Code Sec. 9.48.030 (1951); W. Va. Ann. Code Sec. 5916 (1961); Wisc. Stat. Ann. Sec. 940.03 (1958). In Wisconsin the offense of felony-murder is only third degree murder. 3 Wyo. Stat. Ann. Sec. 6-54 (1959).

15. Kentucky, Maine, and South Carolina. South Carolina retains much of the spirit of the early common law. A death caused during the commission of another offense (not necessarily a felony) may constitute murder. State v. Coleman, 85 S.C. 237 (1875).

16. Thirty-one states require that murder occurring during the commission of one of these felonies is murder in the first degree. The typical statute reads as does the California statute in note 1.

17. State v. Adams, 339 Mo. 926, 98 S.W. 2d 632 (1936); Commonwealth v. Thomas 382 Pa. 639, 117 A.2d 204 (1955).

18. State v. Leopold, 110 Comm. 55 147 Atl. 118 (1929) Commonwealth v. Doris, 287 Pa. 547, 135 Atl. 313 (1926).

19. See Commonwealth v. Bolish, 381 Pa. 500 -, 113 A.2d 462, 470 471 (1958), wherein it is states "malice is . . . the criterion, the absolutely essential ingredient of murder."

20. Miesel, supra note 10, at 454.

21. Commonwealth v. Bolish, 381 Pa. 500 -, 113 A2d 464, 480 (1955).

22. Commonwealth v. Guida, 341 Pa. 305, 19 A2d 98 (1941).

23. See Perkins, A Re-examination of Malice Aforethought, 43 Yale L.J. 537 (1934).

24. Commonwealth v. Bolish, 381 Pa. 500 -, 113 A.2d 464, 470 (1955).

25. Green, The Rationale of Proximate Cause, 132-33 (1927).

26. State v. Glover, 330 Mo. 709, 50 S.W. 2d 1049 (1949).

27. People v. Washington, 62 Cal. 2d -, 44 Cal. Rptr 442, 446, 402 P.2d 130,134 (1965).

28. There are several distinct factual situations which have arisen and which are pertinent to this note: The potential victim may accidentally kill another potential victim, People v. Harrison, 176 Cal. App. 2d 330, 1 Cal. Rptr. 414 (1959). A policeman may kill an innocent bystander, Commonwealth v. Almeida, 362 Pa. 596, 68 A2d 595 (1949). A potential victim may kill one of the felons, People v. Washington, 230 Cal. App. 2d 351, 40 Cal. Rptr 791 (1964); Commonwealth v. Thomas, 382 Pa. 639, 117 A2d 204 (1955). A policeman may kill an escaping felon, Commonwealth v. Redline, 391 Pa. 486, 137 A2d 472 (1958). A policeman shoots another policeman, People v. Podolski, 332 Mich. 508, 52 N.W. 2d 201 (1952). See generally Hitchler, The Killer and His Potential Victim in Felony-Murder Cases, 53 Dick. L. Rev. 3 (1948), for a review of the myriad factual situations in which the felony-murder rule has been applied.

29. California, Michigan and Pennsylvania.

30. People v. Harrison, 176 Cal. App. 2d 330, 1 Cal. Rptr. 414 (1959).

31. Commonwealth v. Almeida, 362 Pa. 596, 68 A.2d 595 (1949).

32. People v. Podolski, 332 Mich. 508, 52 N.W. 2d 201 (1952).

33. Commonwealth v. Thomas, 382 Pa. 639, 117 A2d 204 (1955); People v. Washington, 230 Cal. App. 2d 351, 40 Cal. Rptr. 791 (1964). It is noteworthy that neither Thomas nor Washington suffered. The Thomas case upon remand was never retried. The decision in Thomas was later expressly overruled by Commonwealth v. Redline, 391 Pa. 500, 137 A2d 472 (1958) and the appellate court decision in Washington was overruled by the instant case. Both Thomas and Washington thus escaped the death penalty.

34. 362 Pa. 596, 68 A.2d 595 (1949).

35. Commonwealth v. Almeida, 362 Pa. 596, -, 68 A.2d 595, 598 (1949).

36. Ibid.

37. Id. at -, 68 A.2d at 599.

38. Id. at -, 68 A.2d at 614.

39. Ibid.

40. It should be pointed out here that the cases relied upon by the majority in Almeida, as support for its reasoning, are clearly distinguishable from Almeida, and therefore, are poor authority for its ultimate decision. For an extensive discussion of these distinguishing features see Morris, The Felon's Responsibility For the Lethal Acts of Others, 105 U.Pa. L. Rev. 52, 62-67 (1956).

41. Commonwealth v. Almeida, 362 Pa. 596, -, 68 A.2d 595, 611 (1949).

42. 382 Pa. 369, 117 A.2d 204 (1955), later overruled by

Commonwealth v. Redline, 391 Pa. 486, 137 A.2d 472 (1958).

43. Commonwealth v. Thomas, 382 Pa. 639, -, 117 A.2d 204, 212 (1955).

44. In Almeida, a felon was held responsible for the death of an innocent person, involuntarily placed in danger. In Thomas a felon was held responsible for the death of a criminal who voluntarily placed himself in danger, and who, in fact, set in motion the events which caused his own death.

45. Commonwealth v. Thomas, 382 Pa. 639, -, 117 A.2d 204, 208 (1955).

46. 332 Mich. 508, 52 N.W. 2d 201 (1952).

47. 176 Cal. App. 2d 330, 1 Cal. Rptr 414 (1959). The reasoning in this case was expressly disapproved in the instant case.

48. 357 Pa. 181, 53 A.2d 736 (1947).

49. People v. Podolski, 332 Mich. 508, 516, 52 N.W. 2d 201, 204 (1952).

50. Commonwealth v. Almeida, 362 Pa. 596, -, 68 A.2d 595, 599 (1949).

51. People v. Podolski, 332 Mich. 508, 516, 52 N.W. 2d 201, 204 (1952); Commonwealth v. Moyer, 357 Pa. 181, -, 53 A.2d 736, 741 (1947).

52. People v. Harrison, 176 Cal. App. 2d 330, 1 Cal. Rptr. 414, 425 (1959).

53. Ibid.

54. People v. Washington, 230 Cal. App. 2d 351, 40 Cal. Rptr. 791 (1964).

55. 382 Pa. 639, 117 A.2d 204 (1955).

56. 391 Pa. 486, 137 A.2d 472 (1958).

57. Id. at -, 137 A.2d at 483. Justice Moxey commented on Almeida: "The limitation which we place on the decision in the Almeida case renders unnecessary any present reconsideration of the extended holding in that case. It will be time enough for action in such regard if and when a conviction based on (similar facts) . . . should again come before this court." (Emphasis added.)

58. 370 Mich. 12, 120 N.W. 2d 766 (1962). It should be noted that here, only the information was being appealed. There was no trial on the merits.

59. People v. Austin, 370 Mich. 12, 120 N.W. 2d 766 (1962).

60. The Michigan statute is as follows: "All murder . . . which shall be committed in the perpetration or attempt to perpetrate any arson, rape, robbery, or burglary, shall be murder of the first degree . . . ." Pa. Stat. Ann. tit. 18

Sec. 4701 (1963). (Emphasis added.) Thirty-one states have similar statutes.

61. Commonwealth v. Redline, 391 Pa. 486 -, 137 A.2d 472, 473-74 (1958).

62. Id. at -, 137 A.2d at 474: "If predominant present-day thinking should deem it necessary to the public's safety and security that felons be made chargeable with murder for all deaths occurring in and about the perpetration of their felonies - regardless of how or by whom such fatalities come - the legislature should be looked to for competent exercise of the State's sovereign police power to that end which has never been legislatively ordained." (Footnote omitted.)

63. Id. at -, 137 A.2d at 476-77. See the extensive citation of cases which buttresses this statement and reasoning of the court. Cf. the careful distinguishing of the cases, cited in note 40 supra, relied upon by the majority in Almeida.

64. Id. at 137 -, 137 A.2d at 477.

65. People v. Podolski, 332 Mich. 508, 52 N.W. 2d 201 (1952).

66. People v. Austin, 370 Mich. 12, 32, 120 N.W. 2d 766 (1962).

67. Mich. Comp. Laws Sec. 750.316 (1948).

68. People v. Austin, 370 Mich. 12, 24, 120 N.W. 2d 766, 771 (1962).

69. See statutes cited in note 60 supra.

70. The courts seem to give this interpretation when they apply the proximate cause rule as in Almeida and Podolski, because according to the common law rules of murder, and Michigan, Pennsylvania and California are all common law jurisdictions in this regard, a killing by one is justifiable as to the killer, so it could hardly be murder as to a felon who did not do the actual killing. Therefore, since it could not be murder, the court "mentally substitutes" the word "killing" for"murder"-either that or completely changes the common law definition of murder.

71. People v. Austin, 370 Mich. 12, 31-32, 120 N.W. 2d 766 (1962).

72. People v. Washington, 230 Cal. App. 351, -, 40 Cal. Rptr. 791, 795 (1964).

73. The same sort of reasoning may be used in cases where the non-felon kills another non-felon in resisting the felon. Here again, the killing is accidental, "per accidens," and thus justifiable. The killer's innocence could just as easily be imputed in this situation as in the case where a non-felon purposely kills an attacking felon.

74. See generally Perkins, supra note 23.

75. State v. Glover, 330 Mo. 709, 50 S.W. 2d 1049 (1942);

Commonwealth v. Bolish, 381 Pa. 500, 113 A.2d 462 (1958);
Commonwealth v. Guida, 341 Pa. 305, 19 A.2d 98 (1941);
Green, supra note 25; Maesel, supra note 10; Perkins supra
note 23.

76. Commonwealth v. Redline, 391 Pa. 486, -, 137 A.2d 472,
476, 477 (1958).

77. Commonwealth v. Thomas, 382 Pa. 639, -, 117 A.2d 204,
215 (1955).

78. People v. Washington, 230 Cal. App. 2d 351, -, 40 Cal.
Rptr. 791, 795 (1964).

79. People v. Washington, 62 Cal. 2d -, -, 44 Cal. Rptr.
442, 446, 402 P.2d 130, 133 (1965).

80. Ibid

81. Id. at -, 44 Cal. Rptr. at 445, 402 P.2d at 133.

82. Id. at -, 44 Cal. Rptr. at 446-47, 402 P.2d at 134-35.

83. People v. Podolski, 332 Mich. 508, 52 N.W. 2d 201 (1952);
and Commonwealth v. Almeida, 362 Pa. 596, 68 A.2d 595 (1949).

84. 391 Pa. 486, -, 137 A.2d 472, 483 (1958).

85. People v. Austin, 370 Mich. 12, 32, 120 N.W. 2d 766,
775 (1962).

86. Mich. Comp. Laws, Sec. 750.316 (1948).

(b) Case Law

People v. Gordon
100 Mich. 518

HOOKER, J. The respondent was convicted of murder in
the first degree, upon a trial. The victim was his own
child, and respondent testified that he accidentally shot
the child in attempting to shoot one Robinson, of whom he
was jealous, and who at the time was a boarder in the house,
and whom respondent supposed to be intimate with his wife.
He further stated that he obtained the weapon some hours
before, for the purpose of shooting him the first time that
he crossed his path. He did not state that he intended to
kill Robinson. It further appeared from his testimony that
the shooting was preceded by an altercation between the two
men. . . .
    . . .He admits that he procured a revolver for the purpose
of shooting Robinson, and that he did shoot him, after becoming enraged in a controversy with him. Had he killed him,
and the prosecution been upon the charge of murdering him,
the degree of the offense would have been for the jury, who,
under the evidence, might have found him guilty of murder
in the second degree or manslaughter, and in such case the

708

cause would have to be reversed for the error mentioned; and, as it was, the prisoner was entitled to have the degree of the offense, to say the least, determined by the jury, upon competent evidence. It was for the jury to say whether there was an attempt to kill Robinson. The respondent said he bought the pistol to shoot him under certain circumstances, not to kill him. He did not shoot him on sight, but only after a quarrel. Hence it does not appear, as matter of law, that the child was killed in the attempt to take the life of another under circumstances that would have made such killing murder in the first degree.

Under the rule that "if a person, whilst doing or attempting to do another act, undesignedly kill a man, if the act intended or attempted were a felony, the killing is murder," such homicide might or might not be murder in the first degree (see How. Stat. Sec. 9075); and in the present case that would be a question for the jury, if indeed, it cannot be said that it could not be murder in the first degree, because not within the language of that section. We cannot say, then, that the testimony was equivalent to a plea of guilty of murder, upon which the court might, from the testimony given, determine the degree, the respondent having a right to the verdict of the jury upon that subject.

The judgment must be reversed, and a new trial ordered.

The other justices concurred.

People v. Koharski
177 Mich. 194

(For the opinion in this case see page 518 , supra.)

People v. Peranio
225 Mich. 125

STEERE, J. . . . .
"In a private interview, respondent stated that he and Louis Martin and Tom Corbey had had a conversation in which the other two men told him that they were going to hold up a man. Respondent claimed he didn't know his name, but knew he kept a store; that respondent let Martin have his loaded 38-caliber revolver for the purpose of the hold-up; that he knew they were going to stick up this man and rob him, but didn't know they were going to kill anybody; that if he had he would not have gone. Respondent admits that he took the two men in question in his automobile on the Saturday night in question, about 11 o'clock and drove them out on Milwaukee street, not far from where the attempted robbery was committed; that there they got out of the car, and he remained with the car to wait for them; that he waited

about twenty minutes; that he heard no shots, but that during the time he was there a freight train came by and made a lot of noise, including whistling; that shortly Martin came back, and said, 'let's go;' that Martin was some excited, and said that Corbey was not coming; that he had gone away alone; that Martin told him that he had shot Woloshen three times, but did not know if he had killed him; that Martin said that Woloshen tried to grab his gun, and also started to holler and that he shot him; repondent and Martin went home to 804 Railroad street, and that this was all he had to do with the crime."

In the court's opinion denying a new trial it is said in part:

"One of the reasons urged for a new trial is that the respondent was not given an opportunity to consult with relatives and friends and had no opportunity to be represented by counsel in said case. The affidavit in support of this motion does not allege that the respondent was denied the right to see his relatives and friends or denied the right to have an attorney. There is no showing made that he requested either one. . . . The court had no difficulty in conversing in English with this respondent. While he does not speak English perfectly, it is apparent from the interview which the court had with him privately and from the stenographic transcript of the conversation with the prosecuting attorney, that he is capable of using the English language with little difficulty, and that he understands the same without any particular difficulty. There can be no doubt as a matter of law, that if the respondent's confession is true, that he was aiding and assisting in the hold-up of Woloshen for the purpose of robbery, and was equally guilty of murder with the party who fired the fatal shot. The court sees no foundation for the claim that respondent's confession was not voluntary and uninfluenced by fear or promises. . . . In fact he made substantially the same statement to the court in the private interview which the court had with him relative to his plea. The principal points of such confession are embodied in the record in the judge's statement filed in the case, as required by law. The court is therefore of the opinion that the respondent understood the proceedings; that he made his confession freely and voluntarily, without any influence of any kind; that he was treated fairly by the officers, and the court believes his confession to be true."

While in this proceeding the views and findings of fact of the trial judge are not legally conclusive as in case of return to certiorari, they are official, convincing and well supported by the record. . . .

By statute all murder committed in the perpetration or attempt to perpetrate any robbery is deemed murder in the first degree, and all parties knowingly aiding, abetting or participating in a robbery so resulting are equally guilty.

710

As twice related by defendant, his knowledge of and participation in this hold-up, in perpetration of which a murder
was committed, would constitute the crime of which he pleaded
guilty.

The conviction and sentence will stand affirmed.

WIEST, C. J., and FELLOWS, McDONALD, CLARK, BIRD,
SHARPE, and MOORE, JJ., concurred.

People v. Arnett
239 Mich. 123

(For the opinion of the Court in this case see page 402, supra.)

People v. Crandell
270 Mich. 124

WIEST, J. Defendant, a boy between 15 and 16 years of
age, was convicted of murder of the first degree and sentenced to life imprisonment.

The day he was arrested, and without counsel or knowledge
of his father, the juvenile division of the probate court
waived its jurisdiction, he was arraigned in the police court,
waived examination, was arraigned in the superior court and
pleaded guilty to an information charging him with the crime
of murder. After sentence the court was petitioned to set
the sentence and conviction aside and accord defendant a trial
with the assistance of counsel. The court refused to do so
and, upon application, we allowed an appeal. The murder was
clearly established by evidence, and the degree thereof was
confessed by defendant and verified by other evidence as a
killing in an attempt to perpetrate a robbery. This constituted murder of the first degree. Act. No. 328, Sec. 316,
Pub. Acts 1931.

Defendant loaded his father's revolver, placed a mask
over his face, went into the house of a neighbor, demanded
money from Ima Brewer and, when she called him by his given
name and started to get a broom stick he shot and killed her.
Defendant then went home, burned the mask, replaced his
father's revolver and, the next day, attended school and
was there arrested.

The fact that in the confession defendant stated an unintentional firing of the revolver did not reduce the degree of murder. People v. Roberts, 211 Mich. 187 (13 A.L.R.
1253).

As stated in People v. Lytton, 257 N.Y. 310, 316 (178 N.
E. 290, 79 A.L.R. 503):

"The court did not err in charging the jury in effect

711

that the discharge of a pistol by a defendant who is holding it in his hand in furtherance of an attempt to rob, will
lay the basis for a verdict of murder in the first degree,
though the discharge was not intended, an accident induced
by the terror or nervousness or excitement of the robber." . . .

We find no reversible error and the conviction is affirmed.

POTTER, C. J., and NELSON SHARPE, NORTH, FEAD, BUTZEL,
and EDWARD M. SHARPE, JJ., concurred with WIEST, J.

(Dissenting opinion of Justice BUSHNELL omitted.)

People v. Wright
315 Mich. 81

NORTH, J. Donald L. Wright on trial by jury was convicted in the recorder's court of Detroit of murder in the
first degree. He was sentenced to life imprisonment. His
motion for a new trial was denied. . . .
The people's claim is that on January 13, 1944, in a
holdup of a gasoline station appellant shot and killed the
attendant, Arthur Wilkie. At the trial the prosecution's
proof made a case for jury determination. The defendant
testified in his own defense, and it is the examination of
defendant that has given rise to the two questions above
noted.
Shortly after the shooting third parties calling at the
gasoline station discovered the dead attendant on the floor
in a sitting position leaning against some oil cans. Appellant had left the scene and was not taken into custody
until the early morning of February 5th, 23 days after the
date of the alleged offense. The arrest seems to have occurred because police authorites were notified about 10:30
the evening of February 4th of a holdup which had just occurred. Following this information police officers went
to the home of defendant's mother, and remained there until
defendant came home in an automobile about 5:30 a.m. when
defendant was arrested. A search of his person, his car,
and the basement where he slept was made, but nothing incriminating was found. Upon being interrogated by the officers defendant stated the automobile he was driving belonged to his mother, that he had been to a dance and after
the dance had gone down town.
At the time of his arrest defendant was 21 years of age.
He was married in 1941, but was separated from his wife at
the time of his arrest, and had gone to live with his mother.
He was awaiting induction into the merchant marine service
and in the meantime was employed at a part-time job with
the Fenkell Auto Service. Within the two days following
defendant's arrest, according to the testimony, he made
confessions. Seemingly in the first instance, defendant's
confessions or admissions were made to police officers and
were not reduced to writing; but on the afternoon of the

712

day he was arrested his statement or confession in the form of question and answer was taken at the prosecutor's office by an assistant prosecutor; and again in the evening of the following day defendant made another confession or statement at the prosecutor's office which was stenographically taken in the form of questions and answers. In these confessions defendant not only admitted that he committed the offense of which he was convicted in the instant case, but also he admitted he committed like holdups on four occasions shortly prior to the one in the instant case and on two subsequent occasions. Defendant claims the alleged confessions were obtained by means of promises of official cooperation in securing lenient disposition of his case, continuous and prolonged questioning following his arrest, depriving defendant of sleep and food, threats to arrest defendant's mother and involve other members of his family, and assaults upon defendant by the police officers. There was denial by the officers of the extent of the questioning, the claimed assaults upon defendant, as well as denial of threats or promises which defendant asserted were made to him. As to defendant's being deprived of food, one officer testified defendant "was served food," but others testified they did not know since feeding prisoners was not part of their duties. In substance in the alleged confessions made defendant said that on the date of the alleged offense between 9 and 10 p.m. he went to the gasoline statione in question, held it up, took about $50, and escaped in his car which was parked near by. That he had a .32 caliber revolver, that he did not intend to hurt anyone, but when he stated to the attendant in the gasoline station "This is a holdup," the attendant said "No punk kid is going to stick me up," and thereupon the attendant with his right hand "grabbed" defendant by the neck and with his left hand "grabbed the right arm in which he had the revolver;" that defendant did not remember pulling the trigger but he knew that the gun went off and the attendant fell.

The testimony on direct examination given by defendant in his own behalf was of very different purport than the statements in his confessions. In his direct testimony he stated on the date of the alleged offense defendant drove with an automobile to see an uncle about 6 o'clock in the afternoon, that after leaving the uncle's place defendant stopped at a beer garden and from there he went to the gasoline station where the shooting occurred, that he asked the attendant to use the telephone which was a side wall pay phone, and defendant continued with the following testimony:

"During the time I was making my telephone call, I heard a buzzing on the phone when I tried to make another phone call, after I had finished my first one, so I took the receiver cap apart, that is the cap of the receiver, and Mr. Wilkie walked in as I was at the phone, and walked over and we got into an argument, he grabbed me around the neck from behind and he must have either felt or seen the gun in my pocket because he made a grab for the gun, and the gun went

713

off. He was struck. He did not fall. I helped him to the floor. I offered to assist him. I did not deliberately fire the gun. I say there was a scuffle. I believe I had an overcoat on. The gun (offered in evidence) was in my overcoat pocket. . . . I had to have the gun as I carried it in the car, because I carried large sums of money at times for Mr. Connor (defendant's employer) to and from the bank. When I entered that gas station I did not intend to commit the crime of robbery armed. . . . I did not take anything of value."

Obviously it was essential to the prosecution's case to meet the very material discrepancy between defendant's confessions wherein he had admitted the holdup and taking money incident to which the fatal shooting occurred; whereas the purport of his direct examination was that defendant neither comtemplated nor perpetrated a robbery and that the fatal shooting was accidental. Clearly the foregoing condition of the record raised as an essential issue the matter of defendant's intent. It is the people's claim that under the circumstances defendant's confessions, if voluntarily made, as to his having committed other like offenses within a reasonable time either before or after that charged in the instant case, became competent, relevant and material testimony in the instant case. . . .

. . . In the brief for appellant it is stated: "it (the prosecution) was from the beginning to the end of the trial burdened with the onus of proving a specific intent to rob. Proof of such intent was a necessary element of its primary case." Admittedly the homicide in the instant case would not constitute murder in the first degree unless defendant was at the scene of the alleged crime either with intent to rob or in the actual act of robbing. Act. No. 328, Sec. 316, Pub. Acts 1931 (Comp. Laws Supp. 1940, Sec. 17115-316, Stat. Ann. Sec. 28.548). In consequence thereof appellant's contention as stated in his brief is as follows:

"It is, we think, therefore, obvious that the required proof of the commission of the offense charged must carry with it an implication or presumption of the necessary criminal intent - in this case the specific intent to rob.

"Under these circumstances, proof of other like offenses is never admissible, and no such case is an exception to the general rule that excludes proof of other offenses."

We are not in accord with the foregoing contention. By statute it is provided:

"In any criminal case where the defendant's motive, intent, the absence of, mistake or accident on his part, or the defendant's scheme, plan or system in doing an act, is material, any like acts or other acts of the defendant which may tend to show his motive, intent, the absence of, mistake or accident on his part, or the defendant's scheme, plan or system in doing the act, in question, may be proved,

714

whether they are contemporaneous with or prior or subsequent thereto; notwithstanding that such proof may show or tend to show the commission of another or prior or subsequent crime by the defendant." 3 Comp. Laws 1929, Sec. 17320 (Stat. Ann. Sec. 28.1050).

Appellant cites and quotes from a large number of our decisions in an attempt to sustain his contention that since intent to rob was an essential element in establishing the prosecution's main case, it was error to receive in evidence, incident to rebutting defendant's testimony, his admissions or confessions of having committed other offenses involving a like intent. We shall not extend our opinion to the undue length which would be necessitated by detailing the manner in which each of such cases is distinguishable from the case at bar. In none of them were the attendant circumstances at the trial comparable to those in the instant case. In some of the cited cases the defendant did not testify in his own behalf, in some the defense was an alibi or complete disavowal of any connection with the offense charged, and as a result intent was not the crux of the prosecution as in the instant case. In some of the cases cited by appellant we expressly held there was lacking the requisite of a similar intent, and in some intent was not an element of the offense charged, as in manslaughter cases.

The instant case is materially different. Here the defendant admitted everything essential to the people's case, except his intent to rob. In appellant's reply brief it is stated: "The defense was negation of intent to rob the gasoline station." After defendant testified the only controverted issue was that of intent, which defendant denied, and in negativing intent claimed the homicide was an accident. The prosecuting attorney could not and did not know that the prosecution of the case would take on that aspect until defendant had testified. Thereupon it was proper for the prosecutor in rebuttal of defendant's testimony to show intent by cross-examination or any other competent testimony, including defendant's admissions or confessions, if lawfully obtained. Under the circumstances of this case, the fact, stressed by appellant, that from the inception of and throughout the trial the prosecution had the burden of proving defendant committed a robbery or had the intent to rob, did not deprive the prosecution of its right to rebut defendant's testimony. We are in accord with the State's contention in this particular, as stated in its brief:

"Defendant . . . states that the only proof necessary and admissible in the case at bar was proof of the robbery, and that such proof carries with it an implication or presumption of the necessary criminal intent, and, therefore, we are barred from offering proof of similar crimes. This theory is partially true. . . . But, when defendant took the

715

stand and admitted the killing but denied the robbery and stated the killing was accidental, we were then permitted to rebut his theory of accident to show criminal intent by his admissions that he has committed other similar crimes. At this point, our statutes (above quoted) permit the introduction of evidence of similar offenses."

As a witness in his own behalf defendant was subject to cross-examination as to any material fact or circumstance (People v. Roxborough, 307 Mich. 575); and it was competent as a part of his cross-examination to confront him with and to disclose to the jury any lawfully-obtained confession or admission of the defendant tending to prove his intent to rob. That it is competent in proving intent to take testimony disclosing other like offenses committed by the accused has long been the law in this State. It was so held in People v. MacGregor, 178 Mich. 436. We quote a paragraph from the headnotes:

"On a trial for homicide, evidence that a brother of deceased had died of poisoning while he was under the care of respondent physician, and from the same drug, was properly received in evidence as having a bearing on the issue of intent, absence of mistake or accident and the identity of the guilty person. . . . Nor was the prosecution precluded from showing actual intent or malice because the law would imply intent to kill from the giving of a poisonous drug."

Under the circumstances of the instant case the trial court was not in error in admitting in evidence on cross-examination of defendant his admissions or confessions, if lawfully obtained, which admissions or confessions tended to prove that defendant committed other like offenses a relatively short time before or after the commission of the alleged offense for which he was on trial. Under our decisions and the statute above quoted such testimony was competent to prove an intent on the part of defendant, which he had denied on his direct examination.

"The court did not err in permitting testimony to be introduced in reference to other 'intent' transactions. Such testimony is in accordance with the provisions of 3 Comp. Laws 1929, Sec. 17320. People v. Armstrong, 256 Mich. 191; People v. Dixon, 259 Mich. 229, and People v. Kolowich, 262 Mich. 137, and see other authorities therein cited." People v. Hopper, 274 Mich. 418, 426.

We are of the opinion that the purpose or object of the statute was correctly stated by Justice POTTER:

"The object of the statute above quoted was to make testimony relevant which might otherwise not be so; to broaden the scope of inquiry as to similar transactions; to make relevant evidence of transactions which in the absence of the statute would not be relevant. Ordinarily a witness may not be impeached upon questions relating to a separate and distinct offense at another time and place. A witness may not

716

be impeached upon a collateral issue. Mills v. Warner, 167 Mich. 619. But the purpose and object of the statute above quoted was to do away with the rule as to proof of other offenses and permit the introduction of such testimony even though it might show or tend to show the commission of another prior or subsequent offense by the defendant." People v. Rose, 268 Mich. 529, 535.

. . . The verdict and judgment entered in the circuit court are affirmed.

BUTZEL, C. J., and CARR, SHARPE, BOYLES, REID, and STARR, JJ., concurred. BUSHNELL, J., took no part in the decision of this case.

People v. Podolski
332 Mich. 508

REID, J. Upon leave granted, defendant appealed December 11, 1950, from a conviction and sentence, September 4, 1925, for murder of the first degree committed in the robbery of a bank at the corner of Chene and Harper in the city of Detroit. The offence is charged as committed on June 13, 1925.

Anthony Machus and Walter Filipowski were charged as accomplices with Podolski in an information filed June 22, 1925, on which day defendants Machus and Filipowski were arraigned, and each pleaded guilty to murder of the first degree committed in said robbery and each was given a life sentence on June 22, 1925. . . .

The trial of defendant Podolski before court and jury began on August 28, 1925, and ended with a verdict of guilty on September 2, 1925. . . .

The principal ground relied on for reversal seems to be that the fatal bullet came from the revolver of a fellow officer and was not fired by any one of the robbers. On this phase of the appeal, one statement of the prosecution's theory may be made as follows: The defendant began the hold-up by holding a gun at the teller, witness Wasnik, directing him to raise his hands. The robbers proceeded with the robbery of the bank, and were about to escape when the police officers arrived; in the ensuing gun battle, officer Kliezewski was killed by a bullet, it now seems, from the gun of a fellow officer, at a point in the immediate vicinity of the bank. Under the testimony, the jury had a right to consider that defendant had the murderous intent that any innocent resisting person should die as a result of resistance, and the resultant death of office Kliezewski was within the murderous intent of defendant in the holdup. When a defendant deliberately engenders an affray, deliberately using therein a lethal weapon, it must be considered to be within his intent that death should result from the affray

717

as a natural and probable consequence of his acts, where
the death is directly attributable to the affray and not
resulting from some independent intervening cause.

Defendant cites People v. Elder, 100 Mich. 515, in which
defendant who was a bartender, got into an altercation with
deceased, and struck and knocked deceased down, whereupon a
bystander Nixon kicked deceased, from which kick the death
resulted. There was no testimony to indicate that defendant
Elder intended the death or that defendant intended or expected any intervention by any third person or that the forces
used by Elder would normally be expected to result in death.
The intent of defendant Elder in the Elder Case is clearly
distinguishable from the defendant's intention in the instant case.

On the question of homicide in commission of a felony
where the killing was the act of one not a participant in
the felony, see 12 ALR2d 210 et seq.

There are not a sufficient number of cases on the point
to establish with finality the weight of authority. Defendant cites cases from Illinois, Butler v. People, 125
Ill 641 (18 NE 338, 1 LRA 211, 8 Am St Rep 423); Massachusetts, Commonwealth v. Campbell, 89 Mass 541 (83 Am Dec 705);
Kentucky, Commonwealth v. Moore, 121 Ky 97 (88 SW 1085, 2
LRA NS 719, 123 Am St Rep 189); and Missouri, State v. Majors,
237 SW 486.

We think the better reasoning appears in a Pennsylvania
case, Commonwealth v. Moyer, 357 Pa 181 (53 A2d 736). See,
also, a Texas case, Taylor v. State, 63 SW 330, and Arkansas,
Wilson v. State, 188 Ark 846 (68 SW2d 100).

The court in Commonwealth v. Moyer, supra, says:

"It is . . . consistent with reason and sound public
policy to hold that when a felon's attempt to commit robbery or burglary sets in motion a chain of events which were
or should have been within his contemplation when the motion
was initiated, he should be held responsible for any death
which by direct and almost inevitable sequence results from
the initial criminal act. . . . Every robber or burglar knows
that a likely later act in the chain of events he inaugurates
will be the use of deadly force against him on the part of
the selected victim. For whatever results follow from that
natural and legal use of retaliating force, the felon must
be held responsible. For Earl Shank, the proprietor of a
gas station . . . which . . . was being attacked by armed
robbers, to return the fire of these robbers with a pistol
which he had at hand was as proper and as inevitable as it
was for the American forces at Pearl Harbor . . . to return
the fire of the Japanese invaders. . . . If in fact 1 of the
bullets fired by Earl Shank in self-defense killed Harvey
Zerbe (a gasoline station attendant), the responsibility
for that killing rests on Moyer and his co-conspirator Byron,
who had armed themselves with deadly weapons for the purpose
of carrying out their plan to rob Shank and whose murderous
attack made Shank's firing at them in self-defense essential

718

to the protection of himself and his employees and his property."

We adopt the above-quoted reasoning as far as applicable to the instant case.

Plaintiff cites 4 Blackstone (Lewis), pp 195-197, as follows:

"Murder is, therefore, now thus defined . . . by Sir Edward Coke: 'When a person of sound memory and discretion unlawfully killeth any reasonable creature in being, and under the king's peace, with malice aforethought, either express or implied.' . . .

"Next, it happens when a person of such sound discretion unlawfully killeth. The unlawfulness arises from the killing without warrant or excuse; and there must also be an actual killing to constitute murder; for a bare assault, with intent to kill, is only a great misdemeanor, though formerly it was held to be murder. The killing may be by poisoning, striking, starving, drowning, and a thousand other forms of death by which human nature may be overcome. . . .

"If a man however does such an act of which the probable consequence may be, and eventually is death; such killing may be murder, although no stroke be struck by himself, and no killing may be primarily intended: As was the case of the unnatural son who exposed his sick father to the air, against his will, by reason whereof he died; of the harlot who laid her child under the leaves in an orchard where a kite struck it and killed it; and the parish-officer who shifted a child from parish to parish, till it died for want of care and sustenance. So too, if a man hath a beast that is used to mischief; and he knowing it, suffers it to go abroad and it kills a man, even this is manslaughter in the owner; but if he had purposely turned it loose, though barely to frighten people and make what is called sport it is with us (as in the Jewish law) as much murder, as if he had incited a bear or dog to worry them."

The conviction of defendant as guilty of murder under the circumstances of the instant case can be considered to be within the principles of the common law, notwithstanding the fact that the fatal bullet was fired by an officer.

The trial judge correctly charged the jury that if the fatal bullet had been fired by an officer, such fact would not preclude the jury from finding the defendant guilty of murder.

On the question whether the homicide in the instant case was committed during the perpetration of the robbery, plaintiff cites Wharton, Law of Homicide (3d ed), p 186:

"Where a homicide is committed within the res gestae of a felony, however, it is committed in the perpetration of, or attempt to perpetrate, a felony within the meaning of such statutes. That the attempt to commit the felony was not far advanced does not lessen the offense. And a burglar

719

who breaks into a building, or who shoots a person who discovers him in an effort to escape, cannot avoid punishment for murder in the first degree, upon the theory that the burglary consisted in breaking in, and was consummated before the killing. A burglar may be said to be engaged in the commission of the crime of burglary while making away with the plunder, and while engaged in securing it. So, a robbery within the meaning of a rule that a homicide committed in the perpetration of a robbery is murder in the first degree is not necessarily concluded by the removal of the goods from the presence of the owner; and it is not necessary that the homicide should be committed at the precise time and place of the robbery. As in the case of burglary, the robber may be said to be engaged in the commission of the crime while he is endeavoring to escape and make away with the goods taken. And a homicide committed immediately after a robbery, apparently for the purpose of preventing detection, is within the rule". . . .

We think the verdict should be upheld as supported by the testimony. Judgment and denial of motion for new trial affirmed.

NORTH, C. J., and DETHMERS, CARR, BUSHNELL, SHARPE, and BOYLES, JJ., concurred. BUTZEL, J., did not sit.

People v. Austin
370 Mich. 12

DETHMERS, J. (dissenting). The stipulated facts for purposes of this appeal are as follows: The 2 defendants and George Rowe agreed to commit an armed robbery together. While they were attempting to perpetrate it Rowe was shot and killed by the intended robbery victim. Defendants were charged with first-degree murder of Rowe. The examining magistrate bound them over to the recorder's court for the city of Detroit for trial. That court granted their motions to quash the information on the ground that the killing of 1 of the robbers by the victim during the robbery does not render the co-robbers guilty of murder in the first degree. The people appeal here.

It is not disputed that if defendants are guilty of any crime for the killing of their co-robber it is murder in the first degree. CL 1948, Sec. 750.316 (Stat Ann Sec. 28.548), provides that murder committed in the attempt to perpetrate a robbery shall be murder in the first degree.

The essence of the trial court's opinion and of defendants' theory is that the killing of the would-be robber by the intended robbery victim was a justifiable homicide, not murder, and, hence, no murder having been committed, defendants cannot be charged therewith.

Defendants' theory seems to fall into 2 parts. The first is, as stated by the recorder's court judge, "that a killing

720

during the perpetration or attempted perpetration of a felony is not a murder if the person killed is a co-felon". This is reminiscent of the old story about a justice of an appellate court who, in explaining its operations, stated that, in reviewing convictions in murder cases, "the first thing we decide is 'should the deceased have went'". In Commonwealth v. Thomas, 382 Pa 639 (117 A2d 204), the court's majority, after referring to cases in which first-degree murder convictions against those engaged in perpetrating a felony were upheld for the killing of robbery victims, police-men or bystanders, whether by accomplices or by others, dur-ing perpetration of the felony, went on to say (p 645): "We can see no sound reason for distinction merely because the one killed was a co-felon." With that we agree. It is not the law that police officers or victims of robberies may inflict the death penalty upon robbers without benefit of judicial proceedings or court sentence. Indeed, capital punishment for robbery does not exist here. Robbers are not, legally and per se, the fair prey of every passing marksman. Accordingly, it may not be said that the killing of a person, which otherwise would be unlawful, becomes lawful for the sole reason that he is a robber, a felon. The shooting of a robber may be justifiable, however, not because he is a robber, a bad fellow who ought to be dead anyhow, but only because it may lawfully be done for the purpose of prevent-ing robbery or the escape of robbers. Such purpose is hardly to be ascribed to the defendants here. However, lawful or laudable the motive or purpose of the robbery victim who fired the shot may have been, it was not shared by defend-ants. If accepted criminal jurisprudence permits and sound legal reasoning leads to the conclusion, as we shall later see, that, under certain circumstances, robbers may be held for murder in the first degree for the killing by another of an innocent person during and arising out of the perpe-tration of the robbery, such reasoning permits of no other conclusion merely because the person killed happened to be one of the robbers.

The second part of defendants' theory seems to be that although a killing during and arising out of the perpetration of a robbery can render the robbers guilty of murder in the first degree, even when the killing was not specifically in-tended or done by them but perhaps by the robbery victim or a policeman or some other person, if the killing was acci-dental, that cannot be so if the killing by that same person was done purposefully, in an effort to prevent the robbery or escape of the robbers, because then it would be a justi-fiable homicide. This acknowledgment of criminal liability in the accidental killing situation is undoubtedly in de-ference to our holding in People v. Podolski, 332 Mich. 508. In that case police officers came upon the scene of a bank robbery just perpetrated by defendant and others who were about to escape. A gun battle ensued between the robbers and police officers. In the course of the shooting 1 officer was accidentally shot and killed by a bullet from the gun of a fellow officer. In affirming defendant's conviction of murder in the first degree, this Court, in effect, said that the jury had a right to consider that the armed robbers had the murderous intent that any innocent resisting person should die as a result of resistance and the resultant death of the policeman was within that murderous intent, even though the bullet came from another officer's gun; that when a robber deliberately engenders an affray, using a lethal weapon, it must be considered to be within his intent that death should result from the affray as a natural and probable consequence of his acts. This Court then said, in Podolski, that it approved the reasoning in Commonwealth v. Moyer, 357 Pa 181 (53 A2d 736), a 1947 case, in which the Pennsylvania court affirmed convictions of 2 robbers for murder for the killing, during the robbery, of a gasoline station attendant, saying that they were guilty regardless of whether the fatal bullet came from the gun of his employer who was shooting at the robbers, or the gun of 1 of defendants. This Court (pp 515, 516) adopted from the Pennsylvania opinion (pp 190, 191) the following:

"'It is . . . consistent with reason and sound public policy to hold that when a felon's attempt to commit robbery or burglary sets in motion a chain of events which were or should have been within his contemplation when the motion was initiated, he should be held responsible for any death which by direct and almost inevitable sequence results from the initial criminal act. . . . Every robber or burglar knows that a likely later act in the chain of events he inaugurates will be the use of deadly force against him on the part of the selected victim. For whatever results follow from that natural and legal use of retaliating force, the felon must be held responsible.'"

The court in Moyer also said (p 189), with respect to the Pennsylvania statute which makes murder committed during perpetration of a robbery murder in the first degree (from which Michigan's CL 1948, Sec. 750.316 (Stat Ann Sec. 28.548), was copied) the following:

"The numerous States which have copied this Pennsylvania statute (including the States of Massachusetts, New York, Connecticut, New Jersey and Michigan) all use in their respective statutes the word 'murder' instead of the word 'homicide' for the reason that a killer in the malicious perpetration of 1 of the specified felonies has committed common-law murder. The felon obviously possesses that 'wickedness of disposition, hardness of heart, cruelty and recklessness of consequences and a mind regardless of social duty' (Commonwealth v. Drum, 58 Pa 9) which constitutes malice."

The latter aptly answers defendants' argument here that upholding a charge of murder against them under the cited

722

statute which makes "murder" during a robbery murder in the
first degree, would amount to judicial legislation, that is,
an amending of the statute so as to change the word "murder"
therein to "homicide", because here the killing was not murder but justifiable homicide by the intended robbery victim.
Moyer was followed by Commonwealth v. Almeida (1949), 362
Pa 596 (68 A2d 595, 12 ALR2d 183), certiorari denied 339 US
924 (70 S Ct 614, 94 L ed 1346), rehearing on certiorari
denied 339 US 950 (70 S Ct 798, 94 L ed 1364), in which the
court upheld a first-degree murder conviction of a robber
where an innocent person was killed during the robbery, even
though the shot was fired by a policeman.

In 1955, after this Court had decided Podolski, the Pennsylvania court had before it the case of Commonwealth v.
Thomas, 382 Pa 639 (117 A2d 204). There the facts were as
here; 1 of the robbers was shot and killed by the robbery
victim. A majority of the court held the surviving robber
guilty of murder in the first degree for that killing,
through an extension, as defendants view it, of the doctrine of the Moyer and Almeida decisions. In that case
the Pennsylvania court said, inter alia (pp 642, 643):

"If the defendant sets in motion the physical power of
another, he is liable for its result. 'Acts should be
judged by their tendency under the known circumstances, not
by the actual intent which accompanies them . . ."the law
requires (men) at their peril to know the teachings of common experience, just as it requires them to know the law . . . .
the test of murder is the degree of danger attending the act under the known circumstances of the case."'. . .
'"He whose act causes in any way, directly or indirectly,
the death of another, kills him, within the meaning of the
law of felonious homicide. It is a rule both of reason
and the law that whenever one's will contributes to impel
a physical force, whether another's, his own, or a combined
force, proceeding from whatever different sources, he is
responsible for the result, the same as though his hand,
unaided, had produced it."' . . . 'There can be no doubt
about the "justice" of holding that felon guilty of murder in the first degree who engages in a robbery or burglary and thereby inevitably calls into action defensive
forces against him, the activity of which forces result in
the death of a human being': Commonwealth v. Almeida, 362
Pa 596, 605, 629 (68 A2d 595, 12 ALR2d 183).
"As has been said many times, such a rule is equally consistent with reason and sound public policy, and is essential to the protection of human life. The felon's robbery
set in motion a chain of events which were or should have
been within his contemplation when the motion was initiated.
He therefore should be held responsible for any death which
by direct and almost inevitable sequence results from the
initial criminal act.
"'For any individual forcibly to defend himself or his
family or his property from criminal aggression is a primal

723

human instinct. It is the right and duty of both individuals and nations to meet criminal aggression with effective counter-measures. Every robber or burglar knows when he attempts to commit his crime that he is inviting dangerous resistance . . . . knows that a likely later act in the chain of events he inaugurates will be the use of deadly force against him on the part of the selected victim. For whatever results follow from that natural and legal use of retaliating force, the felon must be held responsible': Commonwealth v. Moyer, 357 Pa 181, 191 (53 A2d 736). (Italics supplied.)"

Defendants point out, however, that the majority decision in Thomas was overruled by a majority of the court in Commonwealth v. Redline (1958), 391 Pa 486 (137 A2d 472), and urge that fact as a reason why we should not extend Podolski, as they say, and thus follow Thomas here. The reasoning of the majority in Redline is essentially that of the trial court and defendants in this case, that the killing of the robber by a policeman in that case (robbery victim here) was justifiable homicide as to the one who shot him and hence could not be murder as to anyone else. The majority in Redline, nonetheless, continued adherence to the doctrine that robbers may be held guilty of murder for the killing, by another, of an innocent person so long as it was accidental, not justifiable; hence, while overruling Thomas, they did not overrule Commonwealth v. Moyer, supra, or Commonwealth v. Almeida, supra. In fact, the majority, in Redline, sought to distinguish Almeida by saying (p 509):

"In short, the Almeida Case was concerned with the killing, during the perpetration of a felony, of an innocent and law-abiding person by someone other than the felons or ones acting in aid of their criminal conspiracy. The evidence warranted a finding that it was an accidental killing by an officer of the law, but the felons were held accountable nonetheless on the basis of proximate causation regardless of who fired the fatal shot. In the present instance, the victim of the homicide was one of the robbers who, while resisting apprehension in his effort to escape, was shot and killed by a policeman in the performance of his duty. Thus, the homicide was justifiable and, obviously, could not be availed of, on any rational legal theory, to support a charge of murder. How can anyone, no matter how much of an outlaw he may be, have a criminal charge lodged against him for the consequences of the lawful conduct of another person? The mere statement of the question carries with it its own answer."

To this Mr. Justice Bell (now Chief Justice), in a dissenting opinion, responded (pp 515, 519):

"In order to free Redline of murder
"(1) the present majority has to expressly overrule the very important and controlling recent felony murder decisions of this court namely Commonwealth v. Almeida, 362 Pa 596. . . .
"The killing of the co-robber by a policeman was a justifiable killing qua the policeman, but not qua the robber who

set in motion the felonious forces which he knew would likely cause death to his co-felon or to a policeman or the proposed victim or an innocent bystander."

We see no profit in an empty exercise in semantics. Certainly it must not be permitted to be controlling of legal responsibilities. Regardless of what has happened in Pennsylvania or any of the few other jurisdictions from which defendants are able to cite cases, in this State the law still is as announced in Podolski. There, this Court held robbers guilty of murder in the first degree when, during a robbery and ensuing gun battle between them and officers, a policeman is accidentally killed by a bullet from a fellow officer's gun. Defendants do not urge that this should be overruled. Yet, the only difference between that case and this is that there the person killed was 1 of the policemen while here it was 1 of the robbers, and that there the killing was accidentally done by a policeman and here purposely by the robbery victim. It is said that these differences present an accidental or, as it is sometimes termed, excusable killing in Podolski and a justifiable homicide in the instant case. This points up the vagaries of the semantical contest. Suppose the intended robbery victim here, in seeking to prevent robbery or escape, had shot the robber accidentally instead of by design. Would that have altered or improved the case for defendants? Despite the interesting differences there may be between the meanings of the 2 words "excusable" and "justifiable", neither legal principle or reasoning nor considerations of public policy are persuasive of a legal result different in the one case than in the other. In the one the deceased is just as dead and the robber just as much a moving cause and as responsible, as a matter of fact, for the occurrence of the death as in the other. No more guilt attached to the act, if excusable, of the policeman who fired the fatal shot in Podolski than to that of the intended robbery victim who shot in this case. Neither had a criminal intent. Both were prompted by the desire to halt the robbery or robbers. As for the robbers in the 2 cases, they were equally possessed of the "wickedness of disposition, hardness of heart, cruelty and recklessness of consequences and a mind regardless of social duty . . . which constitutes malice" (Commonwealth v. Moyer, supra, 189, 190) which, coupled with actions resulting in a killing, make the offense murder. Of both sets of robbers it must be said, as we did of the one in Podolski, that they deliberately engendered an affray, deliberately using lethal weapons and that it must be considered to have been within their intent that death should result from the affray as a natural and probable consequence of these acts. The death here was a direct consequence of their deliberate acts as certainly as if they themselves had fired the fatal shot. In point is the following from Justice Bell's concurring opinion in Commonwealth v. Thomas, supra (p 647):

725

"Justice Jones states: 'I am at a loss to understand how anyone can be guilty of murder at common law for . . . a justifiable homicide.' We might fairly ask the analogous question: If Justice Jones is correct, 'How can anyone be guilty of murder (as _all_ authorities agree they can) for an accidental or an unintentional homicide?' How is it possible to draw a logical or realistic or sound or legal distinction - so far as the crime of murder is concerned - between an unintentional or accidental killing in the perpetration of a robbery and (what the minority calls) a justifiable killing in the perpetration of a robbery? Another point overlooked by the minority is that the killing of a robber may be (and usually is) a justifiable killing so far as the intended victim or a police officer is concerned, but that does not make it a justifiable killing qua the co-felon who caused the shooting."

The order quashing the information and discharging defendants should be reversed and the cause remanded for trial of defendants on the charge of murder in the first degree.

CARR, C. J., concurred with DETHMERS, J.

KELLY, J. This court's 1952 _Podolski_ opinion (_People v. Podolski_, _332_ Mich _508_) called attention to decisions in other States that were contrary to Pennsylvania and concluded (p 515) "there are not a sufficient number of cases on the point to establish with finality the weight of authority", but "we think the better reasoning appears in a Pennsylvania case, _Commonwealth v. Moyer_, _357_ Pa _181_ (_53_ A2d _736_)." Thus, in deciding _Podolski_, this Court adopted _Moyer_.

Justice DETHMERS' opinion (hereinafter referred to as the "opinion") quotes with approval Pennsylvania's _Moyer_ and _Thomas_ (_Commonwealth v. Thomas_, _382_ Pa _639_ (_117_ A2d _204_)) decisions, but refuses to accept Pennsylvania's _Redline_ decision (_Commonwealth v. Redline_, _391_ Pa _486_ (_137_ A2d _472_)) repudiating _Thomas_ and condemning as "dicta" important parts of _Moyer_.
The "opinion" admits that the facts in _Thomas_ and _Redline_ are identical with the facts in this appeal and that: "The reasoning of the majority in _Redline_ is essentially that of the trial court and defendants in this case."
I dissent to the "opinion" because I believe that the Pennsylvania supreme court's reasoning in _Redline_ is sound; because no state in the union has approved a policy such as is advocated in the "opinion"; and, finally, because the "opinion" infringes upon legislative prerogatives.
The "opinion" seems to discredit _Redline_ and holds onto _Thomas_ because _Redline_ "while overruling _Thomas_, they did not overrule _Commonwealth v. Moyer_, supra, or _Commonwealth v. Almeida_, _362_ Pa _596_ (_68_ A2d _595_, _12_ ALR2d _183_)."
To understand _Redline's_ appraisal of Almeida, we add the following from _Redline_ (pp 508-510), which immediately precedes and follows the _Redline_ quotation as contained in the

726

"opinion" (underscoring denotes portion quoted in Justice
DETHMERS' opinion):

"The instant appeal affords an appropriate occasion for
the repudiation of Commonwealth v. Thomas, supra, which we
now expressly overrule as an unwarranted judicial extension
of the felony-murder rule. Fortunately, no one has suffered
any penalty as a result of the holding in that case. Following our remand of the record in the Thomas Case, the district attorney moved the trial court for leave to nol pros
the murder indictment. The court approved the motion, and
a nolle prosequi was duly entered. At the same time, the
court accepted the defendant's plea of guilty to an indictment charging him with armed robbery of which he was unques-
tionably guilty and for which he was immediately sentenced
and committed to the penitentiary where he is now serving
his sentence. Since we herewith overrule Commonwealth v.
Thomas, it follows that the present appellant's conviction
of murder cannot be sustained on the basis of the decision
in that case.

"The Commonwealth contends, however, that, entirely a-
part from the Thomas Case, the appellant's conviction of
murder can be upheld on the rationale of Commonwealth v.
Almeida. As already indicated, Almeida was, itself an extension of the felony-murder doctrine by judicial decision
and is not to be extended in its application beyond facts
such as those to which it was applied. In short, the Almeida Case was concerned with the killing, during the perpetration of a felony, of an innocent and law-abiding person by someone other than the felons or ones acting in aid
of their criminal conspiracy. The evidence warranted a
finding that it was an accidental killing by an officer of
the law, but the felons were held accountable nonetheless
on the basis of proximate causation regardless of who fired
the fatal shot. In the present instance, the victim of the
homicide was one of the robbers who, while resisting apprehension in his effort to escape, was shot and killed by a
policeman in the performance of his duty. Thus, the homicide was justifiable and, obviously, could not be availed
of, on any rational legal theory, to support a charge of
murder. How can anyone, no matter how much of an outlaw he
may be, have a criminal charge lodged against him for the
consequences of the lawful conduct of another person? The
mere statement of the question carries with it its own
answer.

"It is, of course, true that the distinction thus drawn
between Almeida and the instant case on the basis of the
difference in the character of the victims of the homicide
is more incidental than legally significant so far as relevancy to the felony-murder rule is concerned: cf. Morris, op.
cit., supra, at p 56.⁷ In other words, if a felon can be
held murder for a killing occurring during the course of a
felony, even though the death was not inflicted by 1 of the
felons but by someone acting in hostility to them, it should
make no difference to the crime of murder who the victim of

the homicide happened to be. However, the factual difference, so noted, admits of a recognizable distinction with respect to a felon's responsibility for an incidental killing (which another has committed), depending upon whether the homicide was justifiable or excusable, and such distinction serves the useful purpose of thwarting further extension of the rule enunciated in Commonwealth v. Almeida that it is immaterial who fires the fatal shot so long as the accused was engaged in a felony.

"The limitation which we thus place on the decision in the Almeida Case renders unnecessary any present reconsideration of the extended holding in that case. It will be time enough for action in such regard if and when a conviction for murder based on facts similar to those presented by the Almeida Case (both as to the performer of the lethal act and the status of its victim) should again come before this court."

Redline (p 505) refers to the "dicta" in Moyer and brands the statement in Moyer (p 189) that "'A man or men engaged in the commission of such a felony as robbery can be convicted of murder in the first degree if the bullet which causes death was fired not by the felon but by the intended victim in repelling the aggressions of the felon or felons'" as a "palpable gratuity," and then proceeds to prove this point by an examination of the trial record in Moyer, stating (pp 505, 506):

"In its general charge, the court submitted the Moyer and Byron Case on the basis that, in order to convict, the jury would have to find, beyond a reasonable doubt, that either one or the other of the defendants fired the bullet which killed the innocent gasoline station attendant whose death was the subject-matter of the indictment. And, in addition, the court affirmed without qualification the defendants' second point for charge as follows: 'The defendant is entitled to an acquittal unless the commonwealth has produced evidence of such a quality as to prove beyond a reasonable doubt that the bullet causing the death of the deceased was fired from the gun of either of the defendants.' Furthermore, at the conclusion of the charge and after reading to the jury the above-mentioned point as affirmed, the trial judge, at the insistence of counsel for the defendants, repeated to the jury verbatim this same requested instruction. Naturally, neither Moyer nor Byron charged the trial judge with any error in regard to his instructions on the law concerning what was necessary for the the (sic) jury to find, relative to who fired the fatal shot, before the defendants could be convicted of murder. Nor did the district attorney at any time argue or even intimate that the trial judge had charged the jury more favorably to the defendants than he should have. The indisputable fact is that the contention that it was immaterial who fired the fatal shot was never raised in the court below in the Moyer and Byron Case. Consequently, the point required no discussion by this court. What was said in the Moyer and Byron opinion in such connection was, therefore, no more than an expression of the opinion writer's individual view concerning a matter coram non judice. In the light of the trial court's charge, the jury's verdict in that case cannot be taken to mean otherwise than that the fatal bullet was fired by one of the felons in furtherance of their criminal conspiracy.

"It follows that the decision in the Moyer and Byron Case was in no sense authority for the ruling in Almeida."

The "opinion" quotes with apparent approval the statement in Moyer that Michigan, Massachusetts, and New York "all use in their respective statutes the word 'murder' instead of the word 'homicide' for the reason that a killer in the malicious perpetration of 1 of the specified felonies has committed common-law murder" (emphasis ours), and the "opinion" states this "aptly answers defendants."

Redline, commenting on the fact that the common law did not recognize degrees of murder but did recognize classes of homicide, states (pp 492-494):

"Although degrees of murder were, and still are, unknown to the common law, 3 classes of homicide are there recognized, the term 'homicide' being generic and embracing every killing of a human being by another: 1 Warren, Homicide (Perm Ed), Sec. 54; 4 Blackstone, Commentaries, Sec 177. The classifications of homicide at common law are (1) justifiable, (2) excusable and (3) felonious. 'The first has no share of guilt at all; the second very little; but the third is the highest crime against the law of nature that man is capable of committing': 4 Blackstone, Commentaries, Sec. 178. A justifiable homicide is such as is committed either by command or, at least, with the permission of the law, e.g., execution of a convicted criminal, apprehension of an escaping felon, et cetera; an excusable homicide is such as is committed either per infortunium (i.e., accidentally) or se defendendo (i.e., in self defense): 4 Blackstone Commentaries, Sec. 178-186; and a felonious homicide (i.e., murder) occurs when a person of sound memory and discretion unlawfully and feloniously kills any human being in the peace of the sovereign with malice prepense or aforethought, express or implied: see 4 Blackstone, Commentaries, Sec. 195; 1 Warren, Homicide, Sec. 63; 1 Wharton, Criminal Law (12th ed), Sec. 419. . . .

"Malice is the 'grand criterion which now distinguishes murder from other killing': 4 Blackstone, Commentaries, Sec. 198. . . .

"Thus, 'if one intends to do another felony, and undesignedly kills a man, this is also murder': 4 Blackstone, Commentaries, Sec. 200-201."

The "opinion" does not refer to decisions of other States to support its conclusion and this dissent[4] will not review decisions in other jurisdictions opposite to the "opinion" but will answer Moyer's grouping of Michigan statutes with Massachusetts by stating that Massachusetts took an opposite position to Moyer at the time we adopted Moyer, and this dissent,[5] in an effort to eliminate the confusion caused by Moyer's reference to New York, calls attention to the New York statute and the recent decision of New York's court of last resort, namely People v. Wood, 8 NY2d 48[6] (167 NE2d 736), decided May 10, 1960. The New York statute provides:

"The killing of a human being, unless it is excusable or justifiable, is murder in the first degree, when committed . . . by a person engaged in the commission of, or in an attempt to commit a felony, either upon or affecting the person killed or otherwise."

People v. Wood, supra, decides contra to the "opinion" and refers to our Podolski decision and to Pennsylvania's Almeida, Thomas, and Redline decisions, as is disclosed by the following (pp 50-53):

"It is the people's contention that the statutory phrase, 'a person engaged in the commission of, or in an attempt to commit, a felony', was intended to include, in addition to the felon and accomplices, 'all persons involved', e.g., the victim of the felony and those assisting him. They contend, therefore, that, since the deaths of Lee and Moses were the foreseeable consequence of this assault, the defendant should be held criminally responsible for felony murder. We do not so construe the statute. We shall not vindicate the wrong by a strained interpretation of this legislative codification of the common law. Penal responsibility, unlike moral responsibility, cannot be extended beyond the fair scope of the statutory mandate. . . .
"In other words, in order for a felon to be guilty of the homicide, the act (as in agency) must be 'either actually or constructively his, and it cannot be his act in either sense unless committed by his own hand or by some one acting in concert with him or in furtherance of a common object or purpose.' (Commonwealth v. Campbell, 89 Mass 541, 544 (rioter not guilty of a murder for accidental killing of an innocent person by those suppressing the riot); Butler v. People, 125 Ill 641 (18 NE 338, 1 LRA 211) (felon not guilty where unknown person killed his accomplice during course of a robbery); Commonwealth v. Moore, 121 Ky 97 (88 SW 1085, 2 LRA NS 719, 123 Am St Rep 189) (felon not guilty where victim of robbery accidentally killed a bystander); State v. Oxendine, 187 NC 658 (122 SE 568) (felon not guilty where victim of assault killed a bystander).) Where, however, the felon kills someone during the felony, but in a separate and distinct act and to satisfy his own end, his accomplice in the felony is not guilty of murder in the first degree (People v. Sobieskoda, 235 NY 411, 416 (139 NE 558). If the lethal act is in furtherance of their common purpose, the accomplice is guilty even though there was an express agreement not to kill, and even if he actually attempts to prevent the homicide (People v. Friedman, 205

NY 161 (98 NE 471, 45 LRA NS 55)). . . .

"Although several jurisdictions (People v. Wilburn (Cal App), 314 P2d 590 affirmed 49 Cal 2d 714 (321 P2d 452); People v. Podolski, 332 Mich 508; cf. People v. Cabalter, 31 Cal App 2d 52 (87 P2d 364)) would, by application of the proximate cause theory, hold a felon responsible for a homicide committed, by someone other than a coconspirator, during the commission of a felony, at least 1 jurisdiction has repudiated its former position as an 'unwarranted judicial extension of the felony-murder rule'. (Commonwealth v. Redline, 391 Pa 486, 508 (137 A2d 472).) Formerly the leading decision in that jurisdiction (Commonwealth v. Almeida, 362 Pa 596 (68 A2d 595, 12 ALR2d 183)) held the defendant liable for the killing of an innocent bystander by a police officer, because it was defendant's act which set in motion the chain of events which resulted in the homicide. This far-reaching extension was carried to its logical conclusion in Commonwealth v. Thomas (382 Pa 639 (117 A2d 204)) wherein the court found that a felon could be liable for the justifiable slaying of his accomplice by the robbery victim. The Redline Case (supra) expressly overruled the Thomas decision, and, in limiting the Almeida Case to its facts, cast serious doubt as to its rationale."

In our Michigan penal code, PA 1931, No 328, in chapter 45, entitled "Homicide", we find section 316, relative to the crime of murder in the first degree, which provides:

"All murder which shall be perpetrated by means of poison, or lying in wait, or any other kind of wilful, deliberate and premeditated killing, or which shall be committed in the perpetration, or attempt to perpetrate any arson, rape, robbery or burglary, shall be murder of the first degree, and shall be punished by solitary confinement at hard labor in the State prison for life." CL 1948, Sec. 750.316 (Stat Ann 1954 Rev. Sec. 28.548).

Defendants call attention to our Michigan statutes as follows:

"We must not lose sight of the fact that although given a common-law name, the crime herein involved is a product of the legislature. The pertinent statute CL 1948, 750.316, (Stat Ann 1954 Rev Sec. 28.548), commences 'all murder which' and therein lies our answer. If the legislature had used the term 'homicide' instead of 'murder,' the people's position in this case might be stronger. . . . Apparently the intent of the legislature was to make a murder committed during the perpetration of 1 of the 4 enumerated felonies, first-degree murder whether there was in fact, premeditation. If it is murder, there is only 1 possible degree but here, in our case, the killing of Rowe by the intended holdup victim, was not murder, but a justifiable homicide."

The trial judge did not repudiate Podolski in deciding to quash the indictment that charged appellees with murder. He drew a distinction between the Podolski accidental shooting

731

of 1 police officer by another police officer during Podolski's attempt to escape the scene of a bank robbery and the present case where the shooting of felon Rowe was by the intended victim. The trial court concluded, as did Redline, that it would be an unwarranted extension of the policy of felony-murder in Podolski to rule Rowe's accomplices, defendants Austin and Gell, accountable for murder of Rowe.

The writer of this opinion was not a member of this Court when the Podolski decision was handed down.

This is not a rehearing of People v. Podolski, 332 Mich 508. We are deciding 1 important question, namely: Did the trial court err in refusing the people the right to try defendants Austin and Bell for the crime of murder?

It is not necessary to overrule Podolski to hold that the trial court did not commit error in quashing the indictment.

No killing under circumstances such as the instant case has ever been declared murder in this State. This opinion has repeatedly referred to and quoted from Redline because of the belief that the decision in Redline more completely supports the trial court in this instant appeal than Moyer supported our opinion in Podolski.

In support of the previous statement that the "'opinion' infringes upon legislative prerogatives" there is set forth a final quote from Redline (p 490):

"If predominant present-day thinking should deem it necessary to the public's safety and security that felons be made chargeable with murder for all deaths occurring in and about the perpetration of their felonies - regardless of how or by whom such fatalities came - the legislature should be looked to for competent exercise of the State's sovereign police power to that end which has never yet been legislatively ordained."

Affirmed.

BLACK, KAVANAGH, SOURIS, and SMITH, JJ., concurred with KELLY, J.

O'HARA, J., took no part in the decision of this case.

Footnotes

1. Butler v. People, 125 Ill 641 (18 NE 338, 1 LRA 211, 8 Am St Rep 423); Commonwealth v. Campbell, 89 Mass 541 (83 Am Dec 705); Commonwealth v. Moore, 121 Ky 97 (88 SW 1085, 2 LRA NS 719, 123 Am St Rep 189); State v. Majors (Mo), 237 SW 486.

2. Justice KELLY'S opinion in this case is the majority opinion. - Reporter.

3. Morris, The Felon's Responsibility for the Lethal Acts of Others, 105 U of Pa L Rev 50 - Reporter.

4. Justice KELLY'S opinion is the majority opinion in this case. - Reporter.

5. Justice KELLY"S opinion is the majority opinion in this

case. - Reporter.

6. McKinney's Consolidated Laws of New York, Penal Code Sec. 1044. - Reporter.

7. The California supreme court affirmed on a factual question of who fired the fatal shot and held immaterial the question discussed by the court of appeals. The Pacific Reporter contains the notation, "Opinion, 314 P2d 590, vacated." Reporter.

People v. Hearn
354 Mich. 468

Kelly, J. While perpetrating a robbery at a Ferndale gasoline station defendant Hearn beat, stabbed and mortally wounded the station attendant. A jury found defendant, and 3 others who participated in the robbery, guilty of first-degree murder.* This is defendant Hearn's separate appeal, and the other defendants are not appealing.

The information contained one count, alleging that defendant feloniously, wilfully and with malice aforethought did kill and murder one Alfred Jones (the gasoline station attendant). Only one question is presented in this appeal: "Did not the court err in refusing to charge as to included offenses, as orally requested, and in excluding consideration of the lesser offenses from the jury?"

Defendant did not deny that his acts of beating and stabbing caused the attendant's death, but relied upon the defense of temporary insanity, claiming he did not know what he was doing because of his consumption of alcohol and marijuana. Conflicting testimony on this question included medical testimony.

An examination of the court's charge to the jury discloses that the jury was completely and properly instructed and defendant fully protected, as shown by the following instruction:

"Now, the defense in this case is marijuana and alcohol, either one or both, or a combination. The defense claims that because of its use that the respondents in this case did not know what they were doing or why they were doing it and consequently could not form an intent to rob and didn't know the difference between right and wrong. Now, these are questions for you to decide upon after you reach the jury room. . . .

"If their mental faculties were so far overcome by the use of marijuana and liquor that they were not conscious of what they were doing, or if they knew what they were doing but did not know why they were doing it, or that their actions and the means they were using were naturally adapted to produce death, then they had not the capacity to entertain the intent and, in such case, intent could not be

733

inferred from their actions. . . . This question of intent and common purpose to rob a gasoline station is a question of fact for you to determine after considering the acts before the commission of the crime and afterwards, and bearing upon the question of whether or not they knew what they were doing. Take into consideration all the testimony bearing upon that question. . . .

"You cannot convict unless you find intent to commit the crime of robbery. You don't have to find intent to kill, but you do have to find intent to commit the crime of robbery. If you don't find that intent, of course the respondents are not guilty. If you do find it, then there is another question for you to pass on. You must find intent to commit the crime of robbery, felonious intent, before you can convict of first-degree murder."

Appellant claims the jurors should have had the right to select between first and second-degree murder and manslaughter.

This Court passed upon a similar claim in People v. Utter, 217 Mich 74, where the defendant was charged with statutory murder committed in the perpetration of a robbery and where the defendant claimed the trial judge erred in instructing the jury that their verdict should be murder in the first degree or not guilty. At pages 87, 88, the Court stated:

"In State v. Zeller, 77 NJL 619 (73 A 498) defendant was charged with murder while perpetrating robbery under a like statute with ours. A statute of that State also provided as here that if the jury found the accused guilty of murder they should ascertain the degree. In a well-reasoned opinion it was held that the latter provision did not give a defendant the right to have the court leave it to the jury to find him guilty of a lesser degree if there was no reasonable ground for such verdict in the evidence, saying in part (p 621):

"'Our statute declares that murder committed in the perpetration or attempt to perpetrate a robbery is murder in the first degree. All the evidence that tended to implicate Zeller in the murder of William Read (including Zeller's own confession" tended to show that the murder was committed in the perpetration of a robbery. All the circumstances of the homicide bore a similar import as to the character of the crime. If under the evidence, Zeller was guilty at all, he was guilty of a murder committed in the perpetration of a robbery. The charge of the trial judge upon this question was therefore entirely proper.'

"In People v. Schleiman, 197 NY 383 (90 NE 950, 27 LRA NS 1075, 18 Ann Cas 588), defendant was convicted, under a similar statute, of murder while perpetrating burglary. The court there held (p 390) that under such a statutory charge, with the proofs limited to it, -

"'There was no room for the exercise of a power to find the defendant guilty of a lesser degree of felonious homicide

734

depending upon the existence or nonexistence of deliberation and premeditation. Hence, the learned trial judge committed no error in refusing to charge in reference to the various degrees of crime in this case or in instructing the jury that they must find the defendant guilty of murder in the first degree, or not guilty.'

"In Essery v. State, 72 Tex Crim 414, 418 (163 SW 17), the proposition is tritely stated as follows:

"'When the code said that murder committed in a certain way was murder of the first degree, the law so makes it, and the jury by their verdict could not find otherwise.'

"While the authorities in other jurisdictions are not entirely harmonious upon this question we think sound reasoning supports the foregoing views, to which this court is in effect committed. Defendant was charged with statutory murder, committed by acts and under circumstances declared by statutory definition to constitute murder in the first degree, to which the testimony was confined with no evidence from which a reasonable inference of any other degree could be drawn. He was entitled to acquittal if the charged murder in the first degree was not proven to the satisfaction of the jury. Under the testimony in this case the court committed no error in instructing the jury that their verdict should be murder in the first degree, or not guilty."

In People v. Andrus, 331 Mich 535, 542, 547, this Court said:

"On behalf of defendants it is contended that the court erred in permitting the jury to return a verdict of guilty of manslaughter, on the theory that the proofs indicated that the homicide was, under the statute, murder in the first degree because committed in the perpetration or attempt to perpetrate a robbery. It is argued, in substance, that the jury should have been instructed to return a verdict of either murder in the first degree or not guilty. . . . On the factual situation presented it cannot be said that the verdict of the jury was rendered without a proper basis therefor. See People v. Droste, 160 Mich 66. Appellants' claim that the verdict and sentences should be vacated for such reason is without merit."

In People v. Droste, 160 Mich 66, this Court held that the trial court properly refused to charge that the respondent must be found guilty of murder or was innocent, when the evidence supported the theory that the crime may have been committed in the heat of passion while respondent was under the influence of liquor, and constituted manslaughter.

We are in accord with appellant's contention that this Court can and should reverse when the charge to the jury omits a legally essential ingredient, even though no request to charge was made by defendant. See People v. Guillett, 342 Mich 1.

The fact that defendant's request to instruct was orally

made and not in writing is not of any controlling importance to this Court in this appeal.

Appellant claims that because the court declined to charge on a very important issue in the case "an injustice may very well have resulted." Appellant cannot charge that an injustice resulted, because it is apparent that the jury which found defendant guilty of first-degree murder could also have refused to reduce the crime to second-degree or manslaughter, even though the court had granted that privilege to the jury. The record does not sustain appellant's contention that "there was ample ground for the jury to find the defendant guilty on one of the included offenses."

There were no reasonable grounds for the jury to find defendant guilty of a lesser degree, and there was a total absence of evidence to support the theory that defendant was guilty of the included offenses rather than murder in the first degree.

Affirmed.

DETHMERS, C. J., and CARR, SMITH, BLACK, and VOELKER, JJ., concurred.

EDWARDS and KAVANAGH, JJ., did not sit.

Footnote

* See CL 1948, Sec. 750.316 (Stat Ann 1954 Rev Sec. 28.548). - Reporter.

People v. Bowen
12 Mich. App. 438

FITZGERALD, P. J. The "felony-murder" rule in Michigan is found at <u>CL 1948</u>, Sec. <u>750.316</u> (<u>Stat Ann 1954</u>, Sec. <u>28.548</u>). It reads as follows:

"All murder which shall be perpetrated by means of poison, or lying in wait, or any other kind of wilful, deliberate and premeditated killing, or <u>which shall be committed in the perpetration, or attempt to perpetrate any arson, rape, robbery, or burglary, shall be murder of the first degree</u>, and shall be punished by solitary confinement at hard labor in the state prison for life." (Emphasis supplied).

The rule supports a conviction of first degree murder against an accomplice of the murderer, if the accomplice entered into the felony with the contemplation, actual or implied, that resistance from citizens or police officers could be expected. See <u>People v. Podolski</u> (<u>1952</u>), <u>332 Mich 508</u>.*

Defendant was convicted of first-degree murder by a patent application of the felony-murder rule to him as an accomplice as the result of the fatal shooting of a police officer by his partner when the 2 men were attempting to escape from a

736

bank in Benton Harbor where they had just committed a robbery. The murder took place inside the bank. However, defendant urges this Court to accept the claimed fact that the felons had discussed the matter of shooting while planning to rob the bank and that they had agreed not to injure anyone, thus negating any intent on the part of the defendant to participate in bloodshed. The theory advanced is that the act of the murderer was separate and independent of any action by the defendant. It is also alleged that the statute does not apply to defendant for the robbery was not being perpetrated, being fully "consummated" prior to any shooting. We are not concerned here with defendant's plea of lack of intent to murder. If he intends to commit a robbery, and clearly contemplates a violent reaction by him to any resistance by a victim, then the rule will apply to him if a murder occurs at the hands of his accomplice. See People v. Podolski, supra; People v. Utter,(1921), 217 Mich. 74; 12 ALR2d 210. The exact contemplations of this defendant are best shown by the testimony of witnesses in the bank who heard him urge his partner to "shoot", and by his own use of a lethal weapon, in wounding another police office. In any case, all that is necessary is that the defendant undertook the robbery with the intent to commit a felony, not necessarily to commit murder. Defendant's claim that the robbery was not being perpetrated at the time of the shooting is also without merit. The definition of "perpetrate", as given in Webster's 3rd New International Dictionary, p 1684, is: "1a. To be guilty of (as a crime, an offense); . . . b. To carry through."

Defendant, by his own admission, was guilty of the crime of robbery, and since the defendant and his partner were still in the bank it cannot be said that the entire contemplated robbery, which would include escape, was as yet carried through.

Affirmed.

J. H. GILLIS and McGREGOR, JJ., concurred.

Footnote

* The defendant bank robber was convicted of first-degree murder when a police officer accidentally was killed by the bullet of another officer, since the defendant, by engaging in a dangerous felony with a dangerous weapon, contemplated resistance. Also, see People v. Austin(1963), 370 Mich 12, on convicting an accomplice of murder where his partner was justifiably killed by the victim of the crime. The felony-murder rule was not applied despite the vigorous dissent of Justice DETHMERS. Nevertheless, the basic rule applies to the case at bar where the act was clearly one of "murder".

6. Malice

People v. Hansen
368 Mich. 344

737

(For the opinion of the court in this case see page 77, supra.)

People v. Nye
35 Mich. 16

CAMPBELL, J.:

Nye was charged with the murder of Robert Molyneaux, and was convicted of murder in the first degree. Many questions arose on the trial, but the objections urged in this court are confined to such as bear on the quality of the offense as murder or manslaughter.

The homicide occurred in a sudden affray. Nye and his co-defendant, Betts, were playing cards with an elderly man named Chambers when Molyneaux interfered in a somewhat offensive way on a claim, according to some of testimony, that they were imposing on, or likely to ill-treat the old man. There was nothing to indicate that they were doing so, and we have found nothing to indicate very clearly that Molyneaux had any reason to think so. His interference provoked Nye and Betts, and after some harsh language, Molyneaux and Betts proceeded to take off their coats for a scuffle. Betts struck at Molyneaux, who was a powerful man, and who knocked him a considerable distance. He also knocked Nye down in the same way, Nye having, according to most of the witnesses, struck at him first. Nye then stabbed him with a knife which he had in his *pocket, and which was apparently one calculated to be used as a weapon.

The court, among other things, told the jury that if Nye and Betts, or if Betts alone, began the attack, the offense would be murder.

The court also, in defining malice, defined it as including "anger, hatred, revenge, and every other unlawful and unjustifiable motive." And the jury were also instructed that while murder in the first degree in ordinary cases required a willful, deliberate, premeditated design to take life, that design might be formed an instant before the act.

The record indicates that the trial took place under much excitement, and we do not think it desirable to enlarge upon the many points which are presented. Upon the facts it was legally competent for the jury to have found a verdict of manslaughter or of murder in the second degree, according to the view they took of some inconsistent testimony.

It was error to hold that Nye must be held guilty of murder if Betts began the assault. Without discussing under what circumstances the first assailant may be guilty of no higher crime than manslaughter, it cannot certainly be claimed that a man who makes no assault until he is struck first himself must necessarily be responsible for the misdoings of his companions. It was not within the province of the court to decide as a matter of fact the Nye was a party to any assault made by Betts if he made none himself.

738

The definition of malice given in this case would remove manslaughter from the catalogue of homicide. Every crime must be attended with an unlawful and unjustifiable motive. Malice includes those which are more wicked, but it does not include them all. There are many unlawful and unjustifiable motives which have never been classed as malicious. Manslaughter may in some cases be intentional. In such a case it differs from murder because it is *provoked. It is not justifiable to take life under provocation, and yet the provocation may be serious enough to deprive the intentional killing of its malicious character, so that it is neither murder on the one hand nor justifiable or excusable on the other. It is a very serious crime, though not reckoned as done with malice.

The instruction concerning the degrees of murder was also erroneous. There is much learning and some subtlety in the older books upon the question whether a sudden homicide could be properly classed as murder, because that requires malice aforethought. The courts decided that the real test of malice in such cases was to be found in the presence or absence of adequate cause or provocation to account for the violence, and that an unprovoked homicide, however suddenly conceived, might be malicious. In other words, malice aforethought did not mean deliberate and calculating malice, but only malice existing at any time before the act so as to be its moving cause or concomitant.

In dividing murder into degrees, its common-law qualities are not changed, but (except in special cases) the division is chiefly between cases where the malice aforethought is deliberate and where it is not. It was rightly considered that what is done against life deliberately indicates a much more depraved character and purpose than what is done hastily or without contrivance. But it is a perversion of terms to apply the term deliberate to any act which is done on a sudden impulse.

In the record before us there is no testimony whatever upon which a verdict of murder in the first degree could properly have been rendered, and the charge given must have misled the jury. That alternative should not have been left open to them.

The judgment must be reversed, and a new trial granted, and the plaintiff in error must be delivered by the keeper of the state prison into the custody of the sheriff of Calhoun county to be dealt with according to law.

The other justices concurred.

People v. Vinunzo
212 Mich. 472

BROOKE, J. Defendant is now undergoing a life sentence in solitary confinement, at hard labor, as punishment for

739

the commission of the crime of murder in the first degree. The evidence introduced on behalf of the people tended to show that about the hour of half-past seven p.m. on March 27, 1918, defendant, in company with one James H. Blair, was walking west of Hamilton boulevard on Banner avenue in the village of Highland Park; that when they had arrived at the alley first west of Hamilton defendant reached around behind Blair and fired a revolver shot into the back of his head; that Blair fell to the ground, whereupon defendant shot three or four other bullets into Blair's body and immediately ran up the alley. He was pursued and in a very short time was overtaken and placed under arrest.

He took the stand and testified in his own behalf. He admitted being within four or five paces of Blair at the time of the shooting, but claimed that the shots were fired by another man. He further admitted that he ran up the alley immediately after the shooting, but claimed that he did so being impelled by fear.

The one assignment of error discussed in the brief of counsel for defendant deals with the contention of counsel that express malice, under the statutes of Michigan, is an essential element of the crime of murder in the first degree, and that there is no evidence in this case of express malice within the meaning of the statute. The statute (3 Comp. Laws 1915, Sec. 15192) is as follows:

"All murder which shall be perpetrated by means of poison, or lying in wait, or any other kind of willful, deliberate and premeditated killing, or which shall be committed in the perpetration, or attempt to perpetrate any arson, rape, robbery or burglary shall be deemed murder of the first degree, and shall be punished by solitary confinement at hard labor in the State prison for life."

It is argued by counsel for defendant that because the words "or any other kind of willful, deliberate and premeditated killing" follow the language "all murder which shall be perpetrated by means of poison or lying in wait," the doctrine of ejusdem generis should be applied and the words "or any other kind of willful, deliberate and premeditated killing" should be construed as applicable to acts only of the same general nature or class as those enumerated, i.e., killing by means of poison or lying in wait. Counsel say: (sic)

"The statute makes the crime more explicit by requiring that the murder shall be perpetrated by willful, deliberate and premeditated killing. It seems to counsel that the character of willfulness, deliberation and premeditation meant is that of the character evidenced by killing by poison, lying in wait or in the perpetration of some of the crimes mentioned."

We are of the opinion that this question is definitely settled by our own decisions contrary to defendant's con-

740

tention. The doctrine was announced in this State in the early case of People v. Potter, 5 Mich. 1 (71 Am. Dec. 763), and is correctly summarized in the brief of counsel for the people as follows:

"The use of a lethal weapon is not in itself sufficient evidence to warrant a verdict of murder in the first degree but in addition to this there must be evidence in the case, as to circumstances surrounding the killing or the manner in which the weapon is used, from which a logical inference may be drawn that there was willfulness, deliberation and pre-meditation."

In the case of People v. Wolf, 95 Mich. 625, it is said:

"The learned counsel for respondent contends that there was no evidence to sustain the verdict because there was no proof of previous deliberation or premeditation. This would result in holding that deliberation and premeditation can-not be inferred from the character of the weapon used, the wounds inflicted upon vital parts, the circumstances sur-rounding the killing, the acts, conduct and language of the accused before and after the killing and the improbability of the story told by him."

See, also, People v. Jackzo, 206 Mich. 183, where the doctrine announced in these two cases is affirmed.

Evidence introduced on the part of the people indicated that powder marks and burns were found on the cheek of Blair, the deceased, indicating that the weapon had been fired at very close range. Defendant's evidence was to the effect that the man who did the killing stood at a distance of some 15 or 20 feet from Blair at the time of the shooting. This fact, together with the defendant's evidence as to his flight and the reasons therefor indicate the improbability of the story told by him. Aside from this, the evidence of the people's witnesses shows that the killing was willful, deliberate, and premeditated. There was no sudden affray nor was the homicide preceded by any altercation, according to the evidence of eyewitnesses.

We are of the opinion that the verdict and judgment are fully justified by the evidence. The judgment is affirmed.

MOORE, C. J., and STEERE, FELLOWS, STONE, CLARK, BIRD, and SHARPE, JJ., concurred.

7. Final Draft - Michigan Revised Criminal Code

PART II: SPECIFIC OFFENSES

TITLE A: OFFENSES INVOLVING DANGER TO
THE PERSON

Chapter 20. Homicide

(Definition of Terms)

741

Sec. 2001. The following definitions are applicable in this chapter unless the context otherwise requires:

(a) "Homicide" means conduct which causes the death of a person under circumstances constituting murder in the first or second degree, manslaughter, or criminally negligent homicide.

(b) "Persons",when referring to the victim of a homicide, means a human being who had been born and was alive at the time of the homicidal act.

Committee Commentary

Section 2001 defines terms only. It is adapted from New York Revised Penal Law, Sec. 125.00 and 125.05 (1).

(Murder in the First Degree)

Sec. 2005. (1) A person commits the crime of murder in the first degree if:

(a) With intent to cause the death of a person other than himself, he causes the death of that person or of another person; or

(b) Acting either alone or with one or more persons, he commits or attempts to commit arson in the first degree, burglary in the first or second degree, escape in the first degree, kidnapping in the first degree, rape in the first degree, robbery in any degree, or sodomy in the first degree, and in the course of and in furtherance of the crime that he is committing or attempting to commit, or of immediate flight therefrom, he, or another participant if there be any, causes the death of a person other than one of the participants.

(2) A person does not commit murder in the first degree under subsection (1) (a) or murder in the second degree under section 2006 if he acts under the influence of extreme mental or emotional disturbance for which there is a reasonable explanation or excuse. The reasonableness of the explanation or excuse shall be determined from the viewpoint of a person in the actor's situation under the circumstances as he believes them to be. The burden of injecting the issue of extreme mental or emotional disturbance is on the defendant, but this does not shift the burden of proof. This subsection does not apply to a prosecution for or preclude a conviction of manslaughter or any other lesser crime.

(3) A person does not commit murder in the first degree under subsection (1) (a) if his conduct consists of causing or aiding, without the use of duress or deception, another person to commit suicide. The burden of injecting the issue is on the defendant, but this does not shift the burden of proof.

(4) It is an affirmative defense to a charge of violating subparagraph (1) (b) that the defendant:

(a) Was not the only participant in the underlying crime; and
(b) Did not commit the homicidal act or in any way solicit, request, command, importune, cause, or aid the commission thereof; and
(c) Was not armed with a deadly weapon, or any instrument, article or substance readily capable of causing death or serious physical injury and of a sort not ordinarily carried in public places by law-abiding persons; and
(d) Had no reasonable ground to believe that any other participant was armed with such a weapon, instrument, article or substance; and
(e) Had no reasonable ground to believe that any other participant intended to engage in conduct likely to result in death or serious physical injury.

(5) Murder in the first degree is punishable by imprisonment not less than ten years to life.

Committee Commentary

A. Summary

Section 2005 preserves the core of what has been murder under common law and existing Michigan statutes. However, it eliminates the degree distinction, and limits the scope of murder to intentional killings and a qualified version of the felony-murder rule. The punishment provision authorizes, but does not require, life imprisonment

B. Derivation

The section is unique, but incorporates elements from New York Revised Penal Law, Sec. 125.25 and Model Penal Code Sec. 210.2.

C. Relationship to Existing Law

Michigan with most other states, makes no effort to define or redefine murder. Instead, following the example of the early Pennsylvania murder degree statute, it singles out some forms of common-law murder as first-degree murder and decrees mandatory life imprisonment for them, and imposes discretionary terms of imprisonment for the rest under the label of second-degree murder.

The common law classified as murder: (a) intentional killings; (b) deaths resulting from injuries inflicted with the intent to produce great bodily harm; (c) deaths resulting from acts done with knowledge of their highly dangerous propensities but without a specific intent to kill or inflict grave bodily injuries - usually denominated murder through disregard of known dangerous consequences; (d) deaths occurring in the course of some, and perhaps all, felonies - the "felony-murder rule"; and (e), according to a modest amount of case authority outside Michigan, "negligent murder" when the defendant, though in fact ignorant of the

highly dangerous potential of his projected activity, was
held to what he should have known on the basis of the reasonable man standard. (In general on these points, see
Moreland, The Law of Homicide, ch. 4, 5, 6 (1952); Model
Penal Code, Tent. Draft No. 9, pp 28-40 (1959).)

Under the Michigan first-degree murder provision (C.L.
1948, Sec. 750.316), murder as defined at common law is
first degree if it is "perpetrated by means of poison, or
lying in wait, or any other kind of wilful, deliberate and
premeditated killing" or if it is "committed in the perpetration, or attempt to perpetrate any arson, rape, robbery or
burglary". The original purpose was to single out the most
dangerous kinds of offenders for visitation of mandatory
life terms. In part, however, this effort was frustrated
by over-broad judicial interpretation. The phrase "or any
other kind of wilful, deliberate and premeditated killing"
was probably intended as an ejusdem generis clause for calculated killings, like ambush killings, which require advance planning. But judicial interpretation holds that any
intent to kill amounts to wilfulness, deliberation and premeditation, which renders the specific examples superfluous
(see People v. Palmer, 105 Mich. 568, 63 N.W. 656 (1895)).
The use of poison as such has been held enough to constitute the killing murder in the first degree if there was
the expectation that death would result (People v. Roberts,
211 Mich. 187, 178 N.W. 690 (1920)), at least provided there
was enough mens rea in the picture to qualify under some definition of murder at common law (People v. Austin, 221 Mich.
635, 192 N.W. 590 (1923)). Felony-murder was not first-degree murder unless the underlying felony was one of the four
felonies listed.

All common-law murder not singled out for first-degree
penalties is second degree murder (C.L. 1948, Sec. 750.317).
Before there can be murder there must be an intent to kill
(People v. Marshall, 366 Mich. 498, 115 N.W.2d 309 (1962);
People v. Andrus, 331 Mich. 535, 50 N.W.2d 310 (1951)) or
an intent to inflict serious bodily injury. Whether the
Michigan cases contemplate a "negligent murder" is not clear.
Language in Wellar v. People (30 Mich. 16, 21 (1874)), to
the effect that "if respondent willfully and violently
kicked the deceased in such a way as he must have known
would endanger her life, and her life was destroyed in that
way, an actual intention of killing would not be necessary,
as in such case the death would have been a result he might
fairly be held to regard as likely", sounds as if an objective test is being applied. However this language could
as well go to a credibility test applied to the defendant's
testimony. Later cases seem not to state clearly that the
defendant is held to what he ought to have known (cf. People v. Collins, 303 Mich. 34, 5 N.W.2d 556 (1942); People
v. Austin, 221 Mich. 635, 192 N.W. 590 (1923)).

Whether the felony-murder rule applies to all felonies
is likewise not clear. One leading Michigan case (People

v. Pavlic, 227 Mich. 562, 199 N.W. 373 (1924)) seems to say
that the felony must be one dangerous to life, and in fact
the reported decisions all involve these serious felonies.
At least one decision suggests that the jury can consider
the actual intent and find manslaughter when there was clearly no intent to kill (People v. Andrus, 331 Mich. 535, 50
N.W.2d 310 (1951)), but where intoxication was an issue in
a felony-murder case the court held that the only intent required was the intent sufficient to commit the underlying
felony (People v. Hearn, 354 Mich. 468, 93 N.W.2d 302 (1958)).

Felony-murder is sometimes asserted to include any killing which on a "but-for" test occurs in the course of a
felony, i.e., any death resulting from violence when the
nature of the felony makes violence to be expected. The Michigan Supreme Court, however, has taken the position that the
death of one of the criminal participants cannot constitute
felony-murder so far as the remaining criminals are concerned
(People v. Austin, 370 Mich. 12, 120 N.W.2d 766 (1963)). But,
if anyone else dies, even though not at the hand of one of
the criminal participants, it is still felony-murder (People
v. Podolski, 322 Mich. 508, 52 N.W.2d 201 (1952)). The felony
transaction includes the stages of attempt, perpetration and
escape from the scene of the felony, according to the Podolski decision.

A killing done intentionally may nonetheless not constitute murder if it was committed under heat of passion under
circumstances in which "ordinary men, of fair average disposition" would be "liable to act rashly or without due deliberation, or reflection, and from passion, rather than
judgment" (People v. Bucske, 241 Mich. 1, 216 N.W. 372 (1927)),
provided that a "reasonable" cooling time had not elapsed by
the time of the killing (People v. Milhem, 350 Mich. 497, 87
N.W.2d 151 (1957)). Under these circumstances the killing
is manslaughter (C.L. 1948, Sec. 750.321).

There are certain special circumstances in which killings
are either denominated murder or punished at a level corresponding to murder: death inflicted in the course of fighting a duel (C.L. 1948, Sec. 750.320); death due to explosives
carried on passenger vehicle (C.L. 1948, Sec. 750.327; punishable by life or any term of years); death from explosives
placed with intent to destroy building or object (C.L. 1948,
Sec. 750.328) and sabotage resulting in death (C.L. 1948,
Sec. 752.326; punishable by life or any term of years). Attempted murder through poison, drowning or strangling, or
by means not constituting assault with intent to murder is
punishable by imprisonment for life or any term of years (C.
L. 1948, Sec. 750.91).

* * *

The Draft takes a somewhat different position than existing law on several points. Under the Draft, murder in the
first degree under Sec. 2005(1)(a) can be committed by one
who has the intent to kill someone other than himself and
succeeds in killing someone else. In requiring that the

745

victim be someone other than the actor, the Draft reinforces the idea that attempted suicide is not a crime in Michigan ((1943 - 1944) Ops. Mich. Att'y Gen. 342 (1943)). The Draft language continues in effect the doctrine of "transferred intent" which has been held by dictum to pertain in Michigan (People v. Hodge, 196 Mich. 546, 162 N.W. 966 (1917)).

The felony-murder rule is preserved in Sec. 2005(1)(b) of the Draft, but with the same limitation set down in the Austin case that the victim must be a non-criminal participant. The definition also makes it explicit that the killing must be in the course of and in furtherance of the perpetration of one of the enumerated felonies or immediate flight thereafter. This probably restates the posture of Michigan case law, particularly the Podolski case. To a degree the motivation of the actual killer is taken account of in deciding whether the killing falls within subparagraph (b) as "in the course of and in furtherance of" the felony. It should also be noted that the felony-murder doctrine is available only in the instance of the listed dangerous felonies. Decision on the bracketed degrees should turn on how much inherent dangerousness to life the underlying felony must embody, which is determined from its particular definition. If the felony listing is to be expanded, it must be done through adding other names of crimes.

Having defined the three general categories of murder, the Draft then sets out three circumstances under which the killing may be taken out of the murder concept.

The first, under Sec. 2005 (2), is a restatement of the basic thrust of the voluntary manslaughter concept at common law. However, the key factor that precludes a conviction of either degree of murder under the Draft is that the defendant is "under the influence of extreme mental or emotional disturbance" when he acts. Instead of perpetuating the difficult concept of "reasonable cooling time," etc., the test is whether "there is a reasonable explanation or excuse" for the defendant's act, determined on the basis of the circumstances as the actor believes them to be. This reinforces the general "diminished responsibility" provisions of Sec. 710 (impaired mental condition). The burden of injecting the issue is on the defendant, but this does not shift the burden on the state to prove that the extreme mental or emotional disturbance did not exist. If there is a reasonable doubt, the appropriate verdict is manslaughter under Sec. 2010(1)(d).

Second, under Sec. 2005(3) a person does not commit murder if he causes or aids another to commit suicide, without utilizing duress or deception in the process. This is aimed specifically at the holding in People v. Roberts, 211 Mich. 187, 178 N.W. 690 (1920), in which the defendant was held guilty of first-degree murder when at the request of his wife, a terminal multiple sclerosis victim, he mixed arsenic and placed it within her reach. The trend is away from treating a euthanasia case as first-degree murder.

Subsection (3) does not embody a judgment that the actor
should go free, but only that the circumstances suggest a
less stringent form of punishment. The burden of injecting the issue is placed on the defendant, but the burden
of proving intent or recklessness remains always on the
state. This approximates what is now done in the administration of the so-called "presumption of malice" in murder
cases (cf. People v. Collins, 216 Mich. 541, 185 N.W. 850
(1921)).

Third, the existing felony-murder doctrine produces in-
equity when it is coupled with the doctrine of accomplice
responsibility to make co-felons guilty of murder if they
were accomplices in the underlying felony, even though they
may have had no idea that force was to be used. No very
strong basis supporting continuation of the doctrine has
appeared other than pure convenience to the prosecution.
Whether penalites for the underlying felony or for first-
or second-degree murder are imposed against a particular
accomplice turns on the purely fortuitous question of
whether someone (other than a criminal participant) happens
to be killed. This does not make much functional sense
even within the classical deterrence theory, and even less
sense if the emphasis switches to segregation or rehabilitation. However, whether a particular criminal participant
actually contemplated the use of violence is something that
cannot readily be determined from the objectively viewable
circumstances surrounding the killing. Therefore, Sec.
2005 (4) adopts the device in the New York Revised Penal
Law that puts the burden on a non-acting accomplice to
show that he did not aid or bring about the homicide as
such in any way, that he was not armed and that he had
no reasonable ground to believe that any of the other participants were armed and intended to use the weapons with
which they were armed. A dangerous weapon for the purposes
of Sec. 2005 (4) (c) does not include something a person
might ordinarily carry in public if he is law-abiding. This
is to prevent an ordinary pocket knife or a tire iron in an
automobile from being classed as the dangerous weapon about
which the defendant is to be ignorant and which he cannot
have under his control. If the non-acting defendant establishes these five elements by a preponderance, he is not
guilty of criminal homicide in any of its forms, and can
only be convicted of the underlying felony in the commission
of which he participated. The same protection does not extend to the actor himself. This should impose no serious
hardship in the usual felony-murder case because the actor
almost always acts either with intent to kill or recklessly
as defined in subparagraph (1) (b). There is also less urgency in the matter so long as there is no mandatory life
penalty attached to murder.

There is no division of murder into degrees on the basis
of "premeditation" or "deliberation". The reason is a belief that no single factor or list of factors can satisfactorily form the basis of treatment distinctions. A man

who lies in wait to kill his wife's lover may not in fact
be as dangerous to society as a man who on impulse selects
a random victim and kills. A man who administers poison may
under some circumstances[vide (sic)Roberts'] be less a matter
of concern than one who makes use of an automobile to kill
(cf. People v. Jackson, 1 Mich. App. 207, 135 N.W.2d 557
(1965) (wife placed baby behind wheels of the family car and
the husband backed the car anyway in the apparent expectation that the wife would remove the child; this was manslaughter as a matter of law, but query as to dangerousness).
The Model Penal Code (Sec. 210.6 (3)) sets out a specific
list of aggravating factors, including the fact that the defendant is already a convict, or has been convicted of a
previous murder or felony involving violence, or committed
more than one murder on the occasion in question, or was
resisting arrest or escaping, or committed the crime for
pecuniary gain, or used especially cruel or heinous means.
But this is used in the Model Penal Code to determine whether
the death penalty is to be inflicted, a matter of no legal
concern in this state because of the constitutional prohibition against infliction of the death penalty (Mich. Const.
(1963) art. IV, Sec. 46). Moreover, this listing is likely
to produce its share of inequities in administration,as does
any listing which permits a trial court to inflict a fixed
punishment without possibility of relief other than pardon
or commutation.

The Draft does not use a felony classification for first-
degree murder, but instead indicates a punishment range of
from ten years to life. Though now there is in form an absolute requirement that the first-degree murder convict
spend the rest of his life in solitary confinement, in fact
most such sentences are commuted by the Governor at a much
earlier time, and currently at about the fifteen-year mark.
To fix a flexible sentencing provision, therefore, is to
bring out into the open what in fact takes place now in
disguised form.

<u>Note on causation, defenses and insanity</u>: Matters of
excuse, justification, mental condition and causation are
provided for in the general part of the Draft, and qualify
all specific offenses in the special part. For the relationship that Draft provisions on these points bear to
existing law, see the several commentaries.

(Murder in the Second Degree)

Sec. 2006. (1) A person commits the crime of murder
in the second degree if:

(a) With intent to cause serious physical injury to a
person other than himself, he causes the death of that person or of another person; or

(b) Under circumstances manifesting extreme indifference
to the value of human life, he recklessly engages in conduct
which creates a grave risk of death to a person other than

748

himself, and thereby causes the death of another person.

(2) Murder in the second degree is a Class A felony.

Committee Commentary

Section 2006 contains elements from New York Revised Penal Law Sec. 125.25 and 125.30. Its relationship to existing law is discussed in the Commentary to Sec. 2006 to 2015.

B. Manslaughter

    1. Michigan Compiled Laws (1948)

750.321 Manslaughter

Sec. 321. Manslaughter - Any person who shall commit the crime of manslaughter shall be guilty of a felony punishable by imprisonment in the state prison, not more than 15 years or by fine of not more than 7,500 dollars, or both, at the discretion of the court.

750.322 Same; wilful killing of unborn quick child

Sec. 322. Wilful killing of unborn quick child - The wilful killing of an unborn quick child by any injury to the mother of such child, which would be murder if it resulted in the death of such mother, shall be deemed manslaughter.

750.323 Same; death of a quick child or mother from use of medicine or instrument

Sec. 323. Death of quick child or mother from use of medicine, etc. with intent to destroy such child - Any person who shall administer to any woman pregnant with a quick child any medicine, drug or substance whatever, or shall use or employ any instrument or other means, with intent thereby to destroy such child, unless the same shall have been necessary to preserve the life of such mother, shall, in case the death of such child or of such mother be thereby produced, be guilty of manslaughter.

In any prosecution under this section, it shall not be necessary for the prosecution to prove that no such necessity existed.

750.329 Death, firearm pointed intentionally, but without malice

Sec. 329. Death from wound, etc., from firearm pointed intentionally, but without malice - Any person who shall wound, maim or injure any other person by the discharge of any firearm, pointed or aimed, intentionally but without malice, at any such person, shall, if death ensue from such wounding, maiming or injury, be deemed guilty of the crime of manslaughter.

750.14 Miscarriage, administering with intent to procure

Sec. 14. Administering drugs, etc., with intent to procure miscarriage - Any person who shall wilfully administer to any pregnant woman any medicine, drug, substance or thing whatever, or shall employ any instrument or other means whatever, with intent thereby to procure the miscarriage of any such woman, unless the same shall have been necessary to preserve the life of such woman, shall be guilty of a felony, and in the case the death of such pregnant woman be thereby produced, the offense shall be deemed manslaughter.

In any prosecution under this section, it shall not be necessary for the prosecution to prove that no such necessity existed.

750.236 Spring gun, trap or device, setting

Sec. 236. Setting spring guns, etc. - Any person who shall set any spring or other gun, or any trap or device operating by the firing or explosion of gunpowder or any other explosive, and shall leave or permit the same to be left, except in the immediate presence of some competent person, shall be guilty of a misdemeanor, punishable by imprisonment in the county jail not more than 1 year, or by a fine of not more then 500 dollars, and the killing of any person by the firing of a gun or device so set shall be manslaughter.

2. Definitions and General Elements of the Offense

(a) Voluntary Manslaughter

People v. Lilley
43 Mich. 521

MARSTON, C. J. The respondent was tried upon an information which charged him with having made an assault upon one Horace McKenzie, with intent then and there etc. to kill and murder him. Under instructions the respondent was found guilty of an assault with intent to commit manslaughter. . . .

A difficulty had arisen between the person claimed to have been assaulted and the father of respondent as to the proper division of certain wheat then being threshed, and which led to blows. It appears the respondent was struck on the head by McKenzie, and that he thereupon "retreated" or walked towards the straw-stack some ten or twelve feet distant. There is some conflict in the evidence as to what thereupon took place, but as respondent was entitled as a matter of right to have the case submitted to the jury under instructions applicable to the evidence, favorable as well as unfavorable to him, we must for the present purpose consider the charge as given and the refusals in view of the evidence most favorable to the accused.

After respondent reached the straw-stack, he turned around, took a knife out of his pocket, made some threat and advanced towards McKenzie. After he had advanced one or two steps he was caught by a bystander, and there is some question as to whether the knife at this time was open or not, and witnesses testified that he was then ten to fifteen feet distant from McKenzie - the person assaulted, and that respondent then put the knife in his pocket. This practically ended the matter. . . .

In a case of this character we have only to deal with voluntary manslaughter. This "often involves a direct intent to kill, but the law reduces the grade of the offense because, looking at the frailty of human nature, it considers great provocations sufficient to excite the passions beyond the control of reason." People v. Scott, supra. "Manslaughter, when voluntary, arises from the sudden heat of the passions; murder, from the wickedness of the heart." Manslaughter is "the unlawful killing of another without malice, either express or implied." 4 Bl. Com. 191; 3 Greenl. Ev. Sec. 119. The offense is one that is committed without malice and without premeditation; the "result of temporary excitement, by which the control of the reason was disturbed, rather than of any wickedness of heart, or cruelty or recklessness of dispostion." The true general rule is "that reason should, at the time of the act, be disturbed or obscured by passion to an extent which might render ordinary men, of fair average disposition, liable to act rashly or without due deliberation or reflection, and from passion, rather than judgment." Maher v. The People, 10 Mich. 220. Where the provocation falls short of this, or if there was time for the passion to subside and the blood to cool, or if there is evidence of actual malice, or if the provocation be resented in a brutal and ferocious manner, evincing a malignant disposition, in all such cases, if death ensue the offense would be murder. To reduce the offense to manslaughter all these things must be wanting, and the act must be done while reason is obscured by passion, so that the party acts rashly and without reflection. As was said in Nye v. People 35 Mich. 19 it would be a perversion of terms to apply the term 'deliberate' to any act which is done on a sudden impulse," under such circumstances.

Is then an intent thus formed, without malice, deliberation or reflection, but rashly, and while the reason is obscured by passion caused by a sufficient provocation, such as the law contemplates in cases of assault with intent to commit a felony?

An examination of our statutes will show that a punishment is provided for those who shall maim or disfigure another in a certain manner, as well as those privy to such intent. Comp. L. Sec. 7520. Also any person who shall assault another with intent to maim or disfigure in any of the ways mentioned. Sec. 7521. Attempts to commit the crime of murder and assaults with like intent are provided for. Sec. 7522-3. Assaults made in connection with robbing, stealing and taking from the person, such robber being armed with a dangerous weapon, with intent, if resisted, to kill or maim, or being so armed shall assault another with intent to rob. So assaults with like intent, where not so armed, are provided for by Sec. 7524-5-7. Malicious threats with intent to extort money or any pecuniary advantage, or with intent to compel the person threatened to do any act against his will; assaults with intent to commit the crime of rape; kidnapping with intent to sell, etc.; poisoning food with intent to kill or injure any person, or willfully placing poison in a well, etc., with like intent; enticing away a child with intent to detain or conceal; administering medicines to any woman pregnant with a quick child, with intent thereby to destroy such child; administering stupefying drugs with intent, while such person is under the influence thereof, to induce him to enlist, are all provided for in the same chapter, 244 of the Compiled Laws.

In each and every of these cases it will be seen the intent is a deliberate one. So in the section 7537, under which it is claimed this case come, "if any person shall assault another, with intent to commit any burglary, or any other felony " - here the assault with intent to commit the burglary, - the intent is a deliberate one. In none of these cases can the intent be one formed under such circumstances as would reduce a voluntary homicide to manslaughter. When, therefore, in a chapter and section devoted entirely, in so far as it speaks of offenses committed with a particular intent, such intent is a deliberate one, must not the general language, referring to assaults with intent to commit any other felony, in like manner have reference to cases of deliberate intent? McDade v. People 29 Mich. 50.

Had the assault been committed in this case and death had ensued, the intent might have been inferred from all the circumstances. The homicide, if not excusable, would have furnished evidence of the intent. In cases of assault with intent to commit a felony, a specific intent must be found to exist, and it is very difficult to imagine how such a specific intent can be found to exist in the absence of reflection and deliberation. When once it appears that the assault was made with intent to take life, under circumstances where the killing would not be lawful or excusable, then, if under such circumstances death should ensue, the party would be guilty of murder. It seems like a contradiction of terms to say that a person can assault another with intent to commit manslaughter. See also Wright v. People 33 Mich. 301.

As this case now stands the respondent may be convicted of an assault, and a new trial must therefore be ordered.

The other Justices concurred.

People v. Poole
159 Mich. 350

BROOKE, J. Respondent was convicted of murder in the
first degree. He was, at the time of the commission of
the act for which he was prosecuted, a man 33 years of age,
had been married 12 years, and lived with his wife and
seven children in the city of Ypsilanti. The eldest child
(born out of wedlock) was 14 years old. The youngest were
twins about one year old. On the evening of April 28, 1909,
respondent went home from work at the usual time. His wife
was present and prepared the evening meal. She, however,
did not eat it with the family, but left the house, going
to a house about three blocks distant, in which one Henry
Martin was living. At about 9 o'clock in the evening, respondent's wife not having returned, he went out to look
for her. Not finding her at the home of an immediate
neighbor, he went to the house of a Mrs. Hamilton, who was
a second cousin of his own, and stepmother to Henry Martin.
Respondent did not find his wife at the Hamilton home, so
returned to his own home, and from there tracked his wife,
in the new fallen snow, to the door of Henry Martin's house.
He knocked, but got no response, and, after waiting around
for a short time, again returned to his own home. At about
5 o'clock the next morning he again visited Mrs. Hamilton
and told her his wife had stayed away all night. Mrs. Hamilton thereupon told him that an undue intimacy existed between
his wife and Henry Martin, and that his wife had told her
that Martin intended to marry her, and that she would go
away with him and take the twins. Respondent then returned
to the Martin house, gained admission, but did not find his
wife there. Passing through the house, however, he opened
the back door, and there saw fresh tracks in the snow. Following these for about four blocks, he overtook his wife,
and, after walking with her a short distance and holding a
brief conversation with her, he drew a razor and instantly
killed her by cutting her throat. Respondent admitted the
homicide, so that the sole question for the determination
of the jury was whether respondent was guilty of murder in
the first degree, murder in the second degree, or manslaughter.

There are 67 assignments of error. We will consider first
those relating to the charge of the court. After properly
defining the various crimes of any one of which the respondent might be convicted, the learned circuit judge proceeded
as follows:

"The crime which you are now considering was not committed
in secret or in the dark. This awful deed was committed in

753

the broad light of day in the open streets of the city of Ypsilanti, in bold and wicked defiance of all human and divine law. You have heard the story of this crime from the lips of the prisoner and from others who were eyewitnesses thereto. You have been told what occurred at the time and the statements of the prisoner at the time. It is for you to bear in your minds and memory all of these facts and circumstances. So far as we know, on this April morning life was as sweet and precious to this poor wife and mother as it was to the prisoner. A more horrible or brutal death can scarcely be conceived. It shocked the senses of the entire community. There remains but little that you or I can do. We cannot restore life to this stricken woman; but we may do our share towards the guarding and the protecting of human life hereafter.

"It appears without dispute that this prisoner, on the discovery of his wife, that she had left the Martin residence, followed her tracks along the streets of Ypsilanti for several blocks, and he finally overtook her, walked with her some distance, and after some altercation drew his razor from his pocket and sent her instantly into eternity. He is here now pleading for mercy. If from the evidence in this case you find that he was in a state of such excitement that his reason was dethroned, that he was driven along by an uncontrollable and irresistible impulse so that he was no longer morally or legally accountable for his conduct, so that he did not realize his crime or what he was doing or where he was, and had gone some distance from this scene before he was able to recover himself and his senses, then, under such circumstances, the defendant in this case is guilty of no higher crime than manslaughter; but, gentlemen of the jury, if under the evidence in this case, you find that when this prisoner committed this deed there was anger, hatred, and malice in his heart, that he wickedly and wilfully applied this weapon of death to the throat of his wife intending to take her life, and that he did it deliberately knowing just what he was doing, and doing it because he wished to do it, then the defendant is guilty of murder.

"Now, gentlemen, under the evidence in this case, if you find the prisoner guilty, you can find him guilty of murder in the first degree, or murder in the second degree, or guilty of manslaughter, and it will be your duty, if you find him guilty, to find in your verdict the crime of which you find him guilty. In your deliberations there will be, I am sure, no hesitation or false sentimentality. To your sober and mature judgment are committed the rights of the people of this State, as well as the rights of the defendant.

It is urged on behalf of respondent that the portion of the charge above quoted is erroneous: (1) In that it tended to inflame the minds of the jury; and (2) that it improperly defined a condition of mind which would render respondent guilty of manslaughter only. With reference to the first point, it is sufficient to say that we think the charge is open to the objection urged. Touching the second, it is clear that that portion of the charge of the court, above quoted, in which he defines a condition of mind at the time of the homicide which would justify the jury in bringing in a verdict for manslaughter only, is entirely at variance with his earlier instruction to the jury upon that point, as well as contrary to the decisions of this court.

In the case of Maher v. People, 10 Mich. 212 (81 Am. Dec. 781), a case as to the facts much resembling the case at bar, this court declared the law on the subject under consideration as follows:

"It will not do to hold that reason should be entirely dethroned, or overpowered by passion, so as to destroy intelligent volition. (Citing cases.) Such a degree of mental disturbance would be equivalent to utter insanity, and, if the result of adequate provocation, would render the perpetrator morally innocent. . . . The principle involved in the question, and which we think clearly deducible from the majority of well-considered cases, would seem to suggest, as the true general rule, that reason should, at the time of the act, be disturbed or obscured by passion to an extent which might render ordinary men, of fair average disposition, liable to act rashly or without due deliberation or reflection, and from passion, rather than judgment."

So far as we have been able to learn, this rule has never been departed from in this State.

The record shows that, when arraigned, respondent admitted the homicide, and asked the court to determine what crime had been committed. The testimony of respondent was thereupon taken, and the court then directed that a jury be called to determine what crime had been committed, if any. Upon the trial respondent was again sworn in his own behalf, and in the course of his direct examination he detailed the conversation held with his wife, immediately preceding the homicide. On cross-examination the prosecutor was permitted, over objection, to go into his testimony upon the same subject given before the court at the earlier hearing. Respondent assigns error upon this ruling of the court. We do not think the objection well taken. Having testified (at the trial before the jury) as to what was said by himself and deceased immediately before the homicide, it was competent for the prosecutor to show that he had given a different version of the conversation under oath upon his first examination.

The other assignments of error have been considered, but need no discussion.

Because of the errors pointed out, the judgment is reversed, and a new trial ordered.

BLAIR, C. J., and OSTRANDER, HOOKER, and MOORE, JJ., concurred.

LESINSKI, C. J.   A formal complaint and warrant were
issued against defendant, Carl Clark, on April 12, 1965,
charging him with the second degree murder of his wife,
Dorothy Clark, in violation of CL 1948, Sec. 750.317 (Stat
Ann 1954 Rev Sec. 28.549).   After a formal examination in
open court establishing probable cause, defendant was remanded for trial as charged in the complaint.   Upon the conclusion of proofs, the trial court reduced the charge to manslaughter and submitted the case to the jury on the lesser
offense.   Defendant appeals the manslaughter conviction.
      After leaving work on the morning of April 9, 1965, de-
fendant, along with several of his coworkers, members of a
car pool with whom he traveled to and from work, purchased
some liquor and went to defendant's apartment to play poker.
The poker game lasted until about 5 or 6 p.m. and the players
left.   Mrs. Clark, the deceased, was present in the home,
but did not take part in the game, nor was she seen drinking.
      Clifford Bennett, one of the men who took part in the
poker game, met with other members of the car pool in front
of defendant's apartment building about 11 p.m. on the night
in question.   Bennett, although he knew defendant was not
scheduled to work the night of April 9, 1965, went to defendant's apartment to get some ice for a soda pop.   Bennett
testified defendant answered the door wearing only a T-shirt.
In response to Bennett's request for ice, defendant merely
waved his finger back and forth.   While the door was open,
this witness looked inside the apartment and saw the lower
part of a nude female body lying across the bed.   After the
defendant closed the apartment door, the witness Bennett,
"stood there for a few minutes and . . . heard a couple of
slapping sounds . . . like someone was hitting on something
naked, a naked body."   Bennett placed this incident as having taken place about 11:05 p.m. on the night of April 9,
1965.   Other witnesses testified that they heard "moaning"
or "crying sounds" coming from defendant's apartment between
8:15 and 11 p.m. on the night in question.
      Defendant called the police about 12:02 a.m. on April 10,
1965.   The police arrived at defendant's apartment and found
Mrs. Clark unconscious on the bed.   She was conveyed to Receiving hospital and was pronounced dead at 12:30 or 12:35
a.m. by an attending physician.   An autopsy was performed
which determined the cause of death to be hemorrhage and
shock due to a blunt trauma to the abdomen.   The outer skin
of the abdomen was not broken.   Medical testimony indicated
that the injury was not caused by a sharp instrument.   Defendant, in his statement to the police, gave conflicting
stories.   One story is that he and his wife had been alone
all evening but he left for about 15 minutes to get some cig-
arettes.   Upon his return to the apartment, he found his wife

756

unconscious and called the police. Another story is that
he and the victim had been out to several bars and had returned about 11 p.m. He claimed that he immediately fell
asleep and upon awakening he found himself completely un-
dressed except for his T-shirt, and his wife lying on the
floor beside the bed.

It is urged by defendant that the evidence will not support a verdict of manslaughter because the essential element of provocation was not offered in evidence. We do not
agree.

Manslaughter is not defined by statute. CL 1948, Sec.
750.321 (Stat Ann 1954 Rev Sec. 28.553). Therefore, we
must look to common law for a definition. In People v.
Droste (1910), 160 Mich 66, 79, manslaughter was defined as
"the unlawful killing of another without malice, express or
implied." "Manslaughter is distinguished from murder in
that the element of malice, express or implied, which is
the very essence of murder is absent." 2 Gillespie, Michigan Criminal Law and Procedure (1st ed), Sec. 1381, cited
with approval in People v. Grillo (1948), 319 Mich 586, 590.

Wellar v. People (1874), 30 Mich 16, is instructive in
showing what constitutes manslaughter. The Court stated at
pp 19,20:

"Manslaughter is a very serious felony, and may be punished severely. The discretionary punishment for murder
in the second degree comes considerably short of the maximum punishment for manslaughter. But the distinction is a
vital one, resting chiefly on the greater disregard of human life shown in the higher crime. And in determining
whether a person who has killed another without meaning to
kill him is guilty of murder or manslaughter, the nature
and extent of the injury or wrong which was actually intended, must usually be of controlling importance.

"It is not necessary in all cases that one held for murder must have intended to take the life of the person he
slays by his wrongful act. It is not always necessary that
he must have intended a personal injury to such person. But
it is necessary that the intent with which he acted shall
be equivalent in legal character to a criminal purpose aimed
against life. Generally the intent must have been to commit
either a specific felony, or at least an act involving all
the wickedness of a felony. And if the intent be directly
to produce a bodily injury, it must be such an injury as may
be expected to involve serious consequences, either periling
life or leading to great bodily harm. There is no rule recognized as authority which will allow a conviction of murder where a fatal result was not intended, unless the injury
intended was one of a very serious character which might
naturally and commonly involve loss of life or grievous mischief. Every assault involves bodily harm. But any doctrine
which would hold every assailant as a murderer where death
follows his act, would be barbarous and unreasonable. . . .

757

"In general, it has been held that where the assault is not committed with a deadly weapon, the intent must be clearly felonious, or the death will subject only to the charge of manslaughter. The presumption arising from the character of the instrument of violence, is not conclusive in either way, but where such weapons are used as do not usually kill, the deadly intent ought to be left in no doubt. There are cases on record where death by beating and kicking has been held to warrant a verdict of murder, the murderous intent being found. But where there was no such intent the ruling has been otherwise."

Justice CAMPBELL, in Wellar, supra, also pointed out that provocation is only important in a situation where the slaying was intentional, either express or implied, from the nature of the weapon used. Provocation is important here because it effectively mitigates the intentional slaying and reduces the maximum criminal responsibility to manslaughter.

Under certain circumstances, as here, the trier of fact may find that an assault which caused a death was committed without malice or a desire and intent to take human life. Thus, every manslaughter verdict does not warrant a showing of provocation to sustain a conviction thereon.

Upon a review of the record before us, we find ample evidence to support a conviction of manslaughter. It was, therefore, proper for the court to instruct the jury that defendant could be found guilty of the lesser offense, manslaughter. People v. Milhem (1957), 350 Mich 497; see, also, CL 1948, Sec. 768.32 (Stat Ann 1954 Rev. Sec. 28.1055). . . .

The judgment is affirmed.

J. H. GILLIS and HOLBROOK, JJ., concurred.

(b)   Involuntary Manslaughter

People v. Townsend
214 Mich. 267

(For the opinion of the court in this case, see page 188, supra.)

People v. Barnes
182 Mich. 179

(For the opinion of the court in this case see page 198, supra.)

People v. Wardell
291 Mich. 276

SHARPE, J. Defendant, Harvey Wardell, on April 14, 1938, was convicted of the offense of involuntary manslaughter by the operation of an automobile. The information charged the defendant with having caused the death of Leona Proctor while operating an automobile at an excessive rate of speed and while under the influence of intoxicating liquor, and while Leona Proctor was standing in a safety zone.

Defendant appeals and complains of the following instructions given to the jury:

"Before the defendant may be found guilty of wilfulness or wantonness and recklessness, three necessary elements must be found:

"1. Knowledge of a situation requiring the exercise of ordinary care and diligence to avert injury to another.

"2. Ability to avoid a resulting harm by ordinary care and diligence in the use of the means at hand.

"3. The omission to use such care and diligence to avert the threatened danger when, to the ordinary mind, it must be apparent that the result is likely to prove disastrous.

"To warrant a conviction in this case under the charge of involuntary manslaughter, the negligence of the accused, if there was negligence on his part, must have been the proximate cause of the death of the deceased, and must have been characterized by such a degree of culpable negligence as to amount to gross negligence, and this is the question for you to decide. . . .

"For the purpose of clearly fixing in your mind what the crime of involuntary manslaughter consists of, I will define it again for you; it is the unintentional killing of a person in the commission of an unlawful act, less than a felony, without any intention to do so, in an unlawful manner of an unlawful act, which probably would produce such circumstances, coupled with gross negligence. For example, driving a car while under the influence of intoxicating liquors, where death results, is sufficient, I believe, and goes to make up the offense known as involuntary manslaughter; driving through a stop street where properly and duly designated signs have been placed, where death results."

And of the failure of the trial court to give the following instructions as requested by defendant:

"I charge you ladies and gentlemen, that the offense of manslaughter is not shown if the people show that on the day in question the acts of the defendant were merely slightly different from those of a person of ordinary prudence under the same or similar circumstances, or if the acts of the defendant are the result of inadvertence, thoughtlessness, or inattention. The offense of manslaughter is not made out short of showing on the part of the defendant wilfulness and wantonness, and a knowing disregard for the consequence of his acts. If the people have failed to prove to you beyond a reasonable doubt that the defendant's acts were wilful and wanton, then you may not find him guilty of manslaughter. . . .

759

"I charge you, ladies and gentlemen of the jury, that you may not infer that the defendant's acts were wilful and wanton because the results of his acts may have been dire and shocking."

In People v. Ryczek, 224 Mich. 106, we defined "involuntary manslaughter" as follows:

"Involuntary manslaughter is the killing of another without malice and unintentionally, but in doing some unlawful act not amounting to a felony nor naturally tending to cause death or great bodily harm, or in negligently doing some act lawful in itself, or by the negligent omission to perform a legal duty."

See, also, People v. Townsend, 214 Mich. 267 (16 A.L.R. 902).

In the case at bar the instructions given to the jury were upon the theory of manslaughter committed by doing an unlawful act as distinguished from the doing of a lawful act in a grossly negligent manner.

In People v. Townsend, supra, we said:

"The distinction between involuntary manslaughter committed while perpetrating an unlawful act not amounting to a felony and the offense arising out of some negligence or fault in doing a lawful act in a grossly negligent manner and from which death results must be kept in mind upon the question of pleading."

See, also, People v. Maki, 245 Mich. 455.

The trial court also gave the following instruction:

"In order to find the defendant guilty of involuntary manslaughter in this case, you must, from the testimony, determine whether or not the defendant was guilty of gross and culpable negligence in the operation of his motor car, and that such gross negligence in the operation of his motor car was the proximate cause of the (death of the) deceased, Leona Proctor. . . .

"Gross negligence means something more than ordinary negligence, and something more than heedlessness, thoughtlessness, and inattention. It means wantonness or disregard of the consequences which may result or ensue, and an indifference or disregard of the rights of others, that is equivalent to a criminal intent."

Defendant contends that the charge given by the trial court is not tenable in that involuntary manslaughter is defined in terms of negligence and not in terms of wilfulness; that the decisions under the so-called guest passenger act (1 Comp. Laws 1929, Sec. 4648 (Stat. Ann Sec. 9.1446)) define the nature of the misconduct; that manslaughter in effect requires the finding of conduct on the defendant's part equivalent to an assault; and that if the defendant's conduct is characterized by negligence, however culpable, then a verdict of involuntary manslaughter would not be justified.

We are not in accord with the theory of defendant. The term "gross negligence" as defined in the so-called guest passenger act has no application in a case of manslaughter arising when an unlawful act is committed.

In Riley v. Walters, 277 Mich. 620, 631, we said:

"The term 'gross negligence' as used in a majority of the cases where the term has been defined in this State has no application to the term as ordinarily used under the guest statute where it is used as synonymous with wilful and wanton misconduct."

See, also, Olszewski v. Dibrizio, 281 Mich. 423 (2 N.C.C.A. (N.S.) 456).

And for cases defining civil and criminal negligence see: People v. Barnes, 182 Mich. 179; People v. Schwartz, 215 Mich. 197; People v. McMurchy, 249 Mich. 147.

Defendant claims error on the failure of the trial court to give certain requests to charge as are hereinbefore mentioned. We have examined the requests to charge as offered by defendant and, considering them in connection with the entire charge given, are led to the conclusion that it was not error to fail to give the requested instructions. In effect the jury was told that in order for them to find the defendant guilty of involuntary manslaughter it was necessary for them to find that he was guilty of committing an unlawful act as well as being guilty of gross negligence and that said act or gross negligence was the proximate cause of the death of Leona Proctor.

Such instructions gave defendant ample protection and the conviction is affirmed.

WIEST, BUSHNELL, POTTER, CHANDLER, NORTH, and McALLISTER, JJ., concurred with SHARPE, J. BUTZEL, C. J., concurred in the result.

People v. Orr
243 Mich. 300

SHARPE, J. (dissenting). In denying defendant's motion for a new trial, the trial court stated the facts here presented as follows:

"On a hillside, near the top of the hill, on a cement road between Negaunee and Marquette, known as M-35, a Chevrolet car ran out of gasoline and stopped.

"The Chevrolet was traveling from Negaunee towards Marquette. A Hudson car, traveling in the same direction, drew up behind the Chevrolet and stopped. A Buick car, also traveling in the same direction, came to a stop behind the Hudson car. The three cars were standing on the right-hand side of the center of the traveled part of the highway. The Hudson and Buick cars were waiting for the traffic against them to clear so they might safely proceed around and to the left of the stalled Chevrolet.

"The deceased, Helen Rohrborn, was a passenger in the Buick. It was owned and driven at the time by one Charles Brandt.

"The defendant was driving a high-powered Marmon roadster, from Negaunee, with Marquette as his destination. While the Buick was standing, as related, he ran into its rear. Both cars were badly wrecked, and Helen Rohrborn, who was sitting in the Buick at the time of the collision, was so grievously injured that she shortly died. The collision occurred between daylight and darkness on the evening of September 12, 1926.

"As the defendant was approaching the Buick car he could not see the road ahead beyond the top of the hill. His intention was to pass to the left and around the Buick and the other standing cars unmindful that a car traveling towards Negaunee might block his way. Before he reached the Buick car another car traveling against him came over the hill. There was not sufficient room to pass between the approaching car and the Buick. He could not stop in time to avoid hitting either the approaching car or the Buick. He made an effort to pull out to the right of the Buick, but failed. He claims he was unable to stop because both the service and emergency brakes of the Marmon car were out of order.

"On the theory the defendant drove his car at a rate of speed that was unreasonable and improper having regard to the traffic then on the highway and the safety of the public; and so as to endanger the life of the deceased, and that he did so wilfully, wantonly, negligently and recklessly, he was brought to trial on an information charging him with the offense of manslaughter. Whether, under the evidence, he was guilty of manslaughter or of negligent homicide, was submitted to the jury. He was convicted of manslaughter, and this is a motion to vacate the verdict and for a new trial."

1. Error is assigned on the denial of the motion of defendant's counsel for a directed verdict, made at the conclusion of the people's proofs and again when the proofs were closed. It was based largely upon the claim of the defendant that the proofs would not justify a finding that he was driving at a rate of speed exceeding 35 miles an hour, the maximum then permitted by law. But that is not the sole test to be applied. It leaves out of consideration the question of due care. The rule to be applied was properly stated by the trial judge in his charge, as follows:

"It was the duty of the defendant to drive and operate the car he was driving at a rate of speed that was reasonable and proper in view of the traffic and use of the road and all the circumstances and conditions which existed at the time and place of the accident."

It will serve no useful purpose to review the testimony. We have read it with care, and are satisfied that it justified the verdict rendered. See People v. Barnes, 182 Mich. 179; People v. Schwartz, 215 Mich. 197; People v. Ryczek, 224 Mich. 106; People v. Campbell, 237 Mich. 424. . . .

. . . Error is assigned upon the following from the charge:

"Involuntary manslaughter is where a person, in the commission of an unlawful act, or in the commission of a lawful act in an unlawful manner, unintentionally kills another. The defendant is charged with involuntary manslaughter."

It is urged that our statutes make no distinction between voluntary and involuntary manslaughter; that under this definition the jury may have been led to believe that –

"the law was that if this defendant had committed any unlawful act at the time of this accident, that is, if he had failed to observe any part of the vehicle law of this State, and had unintentionally caused the death of Miss Rohrborn, he was guilty of involuntary manslaughter."

The definition given of manslaughter is in line with what was said in People v. Townsend, 214 Mich. 267 (16 A.L.R. 902). Taken as a whole, the charge very fully instructed the jury as to the nature of the offense and the proofs necessary to sustain it.

6. The verdict as announced was "guilty of involuntary manslaughter." As entered in the journal of the court it reads, "guilty of manslaughter." The statute makes no distinction in providing for the punishment on conviction thereof. There was no error in recording it as stated.

7. The jury were instructed that they might find the defendant guilty of involuntary manslaughter or negligent homicide. As the defendant was convicted of the former, this assignment need not be further considered.

The other errors complained of have received careful consideration. They do not merit discussion. The defendant had a fair and impartial trial. He was ably defended.

The exceptions should be overruled. The trial court should proceed to sentence.

WIEST, J., concurred with SHARPE, J.

CLARK, J. Although defendant requested it, no instruction was given the jury relative to burden of proof. This is reversible error. The situation was not met by giving an excellent instruction on presumption of innocence. Defendant is entitled to a new trial, and that being so, another matter should be considered. In the trial, counsel for defendant did not contend that his client had not been guilty of wilfulness, wantonness, and recklessness, so-called gross negligence, as distinguished from negligence, in effect, that there was no evidence to support the charge of manslaughter, but he makes that contention in this court, and that, doubtless, would be his position in a new trial.

763

The evidence made a case of negligent homicide for the jury, which case is based on negligence, ordinary negligence so-called, as provided by Act No. 98, Pub Acts 1921 (Comp. Laws Supp. 1922, Sec. 15226 (2)). Whether the defendant suffer conviction of manslaughter or of negligent homicide makes some difference to him. In the former the maximum penalty is 15 years, and in the latter 5 years.

The charge of manslaughter is here without evidential support. 26 Mich. Law Rev. 820. Before defendant may be found guilty of wilfulness, or of wantonness and recklessness, which in effect are wilfulness, three necessary elements must be found according to note 69 L.R.A. 516; and text 20 R.C.L. p. 145, heretofore approved by this court:

(1) Knowledge of a situation requiring the exercise of ordinary care and diligence to avert injury to another.

(2) Ability to avoid the resulting harm by ordinary care and diligence in the use of the means at hand.

(3) The omission to use such care and diligence to avert the threatened danger when to the ordinary mind it must be apparent that the result is likely to prove disastrous to another.

The third element at least is wholly lacking. There is no evidence to indicate that when defendant attempted to pass the standing cars it must have been apparent to him, having an ordinary mind, that his attempt was likely to prove disastrous to another. The consequence of disaster was as likely to fall on defendant as upon any other. Just before the coming of defendant's car, August Mellin, husband of the woman at the wheel of the parked Hudson car, had driven a car around and past the stalled Chevrolet. He had done successfully (as had a number of other drivers) practically the same act that defendant attempted. Defendant was mistaken in thinking he had time and opportunity to pass the parked cars. But his act, like that of Mr. Mellin and the other drivers, was not wilful or wanton. At most, a jury might find that defendant did not use due care - was negligent.

It is common error to think that because the result of a negligent act is dire the act itself is wanton. Negligence is negligence be it much or little. The difference between negligence and wilfulness or wantonness is not in degree but in kind. Negligence is characterized chiefly by inadvertence, thoughtlessness, inattention, and the like, while wantonness or recklessness, in effect wilfulness, is characterized, as the words imply, by wilfulness.

We need not pursue the question, as authorities on it are abundant and accessible. Defendant should answer the charge of negligent homicide, not manslaughter.

Conviction set aside. New trial ordered.

NORTH, FELLOWS, and McDONALD, JJ., concurred with CLARK, J.

The late Chief Justice FLANNIGAN did not sit.

The late Justice BIRD took no part in this decision.

People v. Thompson
122 Mich. 411

MOORE, J. The respondent was tried and convicted of manslaughter, in the recorder's court of Detroit, on an indictment found in the circuit court for the county of Wayne. The
case comes here on exceptions before judgment.

The respondent was, in November, 1895, an engineer having
charge of two boilers and other machinery in a building on
Larned street, in Detroit. On the morning of the 6th of November one of the boilers exploded with terrific force, destroying the building in which it was located. As a result of the
explosion, a number of lives were lost. . . .

It is said the court erred in his instructions to the
jury as to the degree of care respondent should exercise in
his care of the boilers; The court was requested to charge
the jury as follows:

"The fact of the explosion, and even the possibility of
guarding against it, do not necessarily make out a case of
culpable negligence. Very few acts in life are done with
such care to prevent accidents as would have been possible.
The law only requires of any one that degree of care and
prudence which persons who are reasonably careful ordinarily
observe. To require more would put everybody under restraints
in the management of his business, and in his dealings with
others, which would be more hurtful in the embarrassments
they would cause than beneficial in the protection they could
give against injuries."

"Whether the absence of the respondent from his boiler
at the time of the explosion was negligent depends upon
circumstances. If you find that the respondent, from his
past experience, from his knowledge of the boiler, and the
flow of oil, and of the burner, had reason to believe, and
in fact did believe, that it was consistent with safety to
be absent from the boiler, as he was, at the time of the explosion, then he was not, in law, guilty of criminal negligence by reason of such absence."

The judge did not give these requests, but gave a general charge as to what would be culpable negligence, which,
in the main, was a correct statement of the law, but it
did not instruct the jury upon the particular questions
raised in these requests. The requests should have been
given. It cannot be that an act done in good faith, based
upon what experience has shown to be safe, is criminally
negligent. Schroeder v. Car Co., 56 Mich. 132; Cheboygan
Lumber Co. v. Delta Transportation Co., 100 Mich. 16; Whalen v. Railroad Co., 114 Mich. 512.

We do not deem it necessary to refer to the other assignments of error. They are either not well taken, or are necessarily decided by what we have already said, or, if error,
are of such a character they will not be likely to be repeated.

765

The conviction is set aside, and a new trial ordered.
The other Justices concurred.

   3. Provocation Formula

                    Maher v. People
                    10 Mich. 212

CHRISTIANCY J.:

   The prisoner was charged with an assault with intent to
kill and murder one Patrick Hunt. The evidence on the part
of the prosecution was, that the prisoner entered the saloon
of one Michael Foley, in the village of Houghton, where said
Hunt was standing with several other persons; that prisoner
entered through a back door and by a back way leading to it,
in his shirt sleeves, in a state of great perspiration, and
appearing to be excited; and on being asked if he had been
at work, said he had been across the lake; that, on entering the saloon, he immediately passed nearly through it to
where said Hunt was standing, and, on his way towards Hunt,
said something, but it did not appear what, or to whom; that
as soon as the prisoner came up to where Hunt was standing,
he fired a pistol at Hunt, the charge of which took effect
upon the head of Hunt, in and through the left ear, causing
a severe wound thereon; by reason of which Hunt in a few
moments fell to the floor, was partially deprived of his
sense of hearing in that ear, and received a severe shock
to his system which caused him to be confined to his bed
for about a week, under the care of a physician; that immediately after the firing of the pistol prisoner left the
saloon, nothing being said by Hunt or the prisoner. It did
not appear how, or with what, the pistol was loaded. The
prisoner offered evidence tending to show an adulterous
intercourse between his wife and Hunt on the morning of the
assault, and within less than half an hour previous; that
the prisoner saw them going into the woods together about
half an hour before the assault; that on their coming *out
of the woods the prisoner followed them immediately (evidence having already been given that the prisoner had followed them to the woods); that, on their coming out of the
woods, the prisoner followed them and went after said Hunt
into the saloon, where, on his arrival, the assault was
committed; that the prisoner on his way to the saloon, a
few minutes before entering it, was met by a friend who informed him that Hunt and the prisoner's wife had had sexual
intercourse the day before in the woods. This evidence was
rejected by the court, and the prisoner excepted. Was the
evidence properly rejected? This is the main question in
the case, and its decision must depend upon the question
whether the proposed evidence would have tended to reduce

                        766

the killing - had death ensued - from murder to manslaughter, or rather, to have given it the character of manslaughter instead of murder? If the homicide - in case death had ensued - would have been but manslaughter, then defendant could not be guilty of the assault with intent to murder, but only of a simple assault and battery. The question therefore involves essentially the same principles as where evidence is offered for a similar purpose in a prosecution for murder; except that, in some cases of murder, an actual intention to kill need not exist; but in a prosecution for an assault with intent to murder, the actual intention to kill must be found, and that under circumstances which would make the killing murder.

Homicide, or the mere killing of one person by another, does not, of itself, constitute murder; it may be murder, or manslaughter, or excusable, or justifiable homicide, and therefore entirely innocent, according to the circumstances or the disposition or state of mind or purpose, which induced the act. It is not, therefore, the act which constitutes the offense, or determines its character; but the quo animo, the disposition, or state of mind, with which it is done. Actus non facit reum nisi mens sit rea;" People v. Pond, 8 Mich. 150.

*To give the homicide the legal character of murder, all the authorities agree that it must have been perpetrated with malice prepense or aforethought. This malice is just as essential an ingredient of the offense as the act which causes the death; without the concurrence of both, the crime can not exist; and, as every man is presumed innocent of the offense with which he is charged till he is proved to be guilty, this presumption must apply equally to both ingredients of the offense - to the malice as well as to the killing. Hence, though the principle seems to have been sometimes overlooked, the burden of proof, as to each, rests equally upon the prosecution, though the one may admit and require more direct proof than the other; malice, in most cases, not being susceptible of direct proof, but to be established by inferences more or less strong, to be drawn from the facts and circumstances connected with the killing, and which indicate the disposition or state of mind with which it was done. It is for the court to define the legal import of the term, malice aforethought, or, in other words, that state or disposition of mind which constitutes it; but the question whether it existed or not, in the particular instance, would, upon principle, seem to be as clearly a question of fact for the jury, as any other fact in the cause, and that they must give such weight to the various facts and circumstances accompanying the act, or in any way bearing upon the question, as in their judgment, they deserve; and that the court have no right to withdraw the question from the jury by assuming to draw the proper inferences from the whole, or any part of, the facts proved, as presumption of law. If courts could do this, juries might be required to find the fact of malice where they were satisfied from the whole evidence it did not exist. I do not here speak of those cases in which the death is caused in the attempt to commit some other offense, or in illegal resistance to public officers, or other classes of cases which may rest upon peculiar grounds of *public policy, and which may or may not form an exception; but of ordinary cases, such as this would have been had death ensued. It is not necessary here to enumerate all the elements which enter into the legal definition of malice aforethought. It is sufficient to say that, within the principle of all the recognized definitions, the homicide must, in all ordinary cases, have been committed with some degree of coolness and deliberation, or, at least, under circumstances in which ordinary men, or the average of men recognized as peaceable citizens, would not be liable to have their reason clouded or obscured by passion; and the act must be prompted by, or the circumstances indicate that it spring from, a wicked, depraved or malignant mind - a mind which, even in its habitual condition, and when excited by no provocation which would be liable to give undue control to passion in ordinary men, is cruel, wanton or malignant, reckless of human life, or regardless of social duty.

But if the act of killing, though intentional, be committed under the influence of passion or in heat of blood, produced by an adequate or reasonable provocation, and before a reasonable time has elapsed for the blood to cool and reason to resume its habitual control, and is the result of the temporary excitement, by which the control of reason was disturbed, rather than of any wickedness of heart or cruelty or recklessness of disposition; then the law, out of indulgence to the frailty of human nature, or rather, in recognition of the laws upon which human nature is constituted, very properly regards the offense as of a less heinous character than murder, and gives it the designation of manslaughter.

To what extent the passions must be aroused and the dominion of reason disturbed to reduce the offense from murder to manslaughter, the cases are by no means agreed; and any rule which should embrace all the cases that have been decided in reference to this point, would come *very near obliterating, if it did not entirely obliterate, all distinction between murder and manslaughter in such cases. We must, therefore, endeavor to discover the principle upon which the question is to be determined. It will not do to hold that reason should be entirely dethroned, or overpowered by passion so as to destroy intelligent volition: State v. Hill, 1 Dev. & Bat., 491; Haile v. State, 1 Swan, 248; Young v. State, 11 Humph., 200. Such a degree of mental disturbance would be equivalent to utter insanity, and, if the result of adequate provocation, would render the perpetrator morally innocent. But the law regards manslaughter as a high grade of offense; as a felony. On principle, therefore, the extent

768

to which the passions are required to be aroused and reason obscured must be considerably short of this, and never beyond that degree within which ordinary men have the power, and are, therefore, morally as well as legally bound to restrain their passions. It is only on the idea of a violation of this clear duty, that the act can be held criminal. There are many cases to be found in the books in which this consideration, plain as it would seem to be in princple, appears to have been, in a great measure, overlooked, and a course of reasoning adopted which could only be justified on the supposition that the question was between murder and excusable homicide.

The principle involved in the question, and which I think clearly deducible from the majority of well considered cases, would seem to suggest as the true general rule, that reason should, at the time of the act, be disturbed or obscured by passion to an extent which <u>might render</u> ordinary men, of fair average disposition, <u>liable</u> to act rashly or without due deliberation or reflection, and from passion, rather than judgment.

To the question, what shall be considered in law a reasonable or adequate provocation for such state of mind, so as to give to a homicide, committed under its *influence, the character of manslaughter? on principle, the answer, as a general rule, must be, anything the natural tendency of which would be to produce such a state of mind in ordinary men, and which the jury are satisfied did produce it in the case before them - not such a provocation as must, by the laws of the human mind, produce such an effect with the <u>certainty that physical effects follow from physical causes</u>; for then the individual could hardly be held morally accountable. Nor, on the other hand, must the provocation, in every case, be held sufficient or reasonable, because such a state of excitement has followed from it; for then, by habitual and long continued indulgence of evil passions, a bad man might acquire a claim to mitigation which would not be available to better men, and on account of that very wickedness of heart which, in itself, constitutes an aggravation both in morals and in law.

In determining whether the provocation is sufficient or reasonable, <u>ordinary human nature</u>, or the average of men recognized as men of fair average mind and disposition, should be taken as the standard - unless, indeed, the person whose guilt is in question be shown to have some peculiar weakness of mind or infirmity of temper, not arising from wickedness of heart or cruelty of disposition.

It is, doubtless, in one sense, the province of the court to define what, in law, will constitute a reasonable or adequate provocation, but not, I think, in ordinary cases, to determine whether the provocation proved in the particular case is sufficient or reasonable. This is essentially a question of fact, and to be decided with reference to the peculiar facts of each particular case. As a general rule, the court, after informing the jury to what extent the passions must be aroused and reason obscured to render the

769

homicide manslaughter, should inform them that the provocation must be one, the tendency of which would be to produce
such a degree of excitement and disturbance *in the minds of
ordinary men; and if they should find such provocation from
the facts proved, and should further find that it did produce
that effect in the particular instance, and that the homicide
was the result of such provocation, it would give it the character of manslaughter. Besides the consideration that the
question is essentially one of fact, jurors, from the mode
of their selection, coming from the various classes and oc-
cupations of society, and conversant with the practical affairs of life, are, in my opinion, much better qualified to
judge of the sufficiency and tendency of a given provocation,
and much more likely to fix, with some degree of accuracy,
the standard of what constitutes the average of ordinary human
nature, than the judge whose habits and course of life give
him much less experience of the workings of passion in the
actual conflicts of life.

The judge, it is true, must, to some extent, assume to decide upon the sufficiency of the alleged provocation, when
the question arises upon the admission of testimony; and when
it is so clear as to admit of no reasonable doubt upon any
theory, that the alleged provocation could not have had any
tendency to produce such state of mind, in ordinary men, he
may properly exclude the evidence; but, if the alleged provocation be such as to admit of any reasonable doubt, whether
it might not have had such tendency, it is much safer, I think,
and more in accordance with principle, to let the evidence go
to the jury under the proper instructions. As already intimated, the question of the reasonableness or adequacy of the
provocation must depend upon the facts of each particular
case. That can, with no propriety, be called a rule (or a
question) of law which must vary with, and depend upon the
almost infinite variety of facts presented by the various
cases as they arise. See Stark. on Ev. Amer. Ed., 1860,
pp. 676 to 680. The law can not with justice assume, by the
light of past decisions, to catalogue all the various facts
and *combinations of facts which shall be held to constitute
reasonable or adequate provocation. Scarcely two past cases
can be found which are identical in all their circumstances;
and there is no reason to hope for greater uniformity in future. Provocations will be given without reference to any
previous model, and the passions they excite will not consult
the precedents.

The same principles which govern, as to the extent to
which the passions must be excited and reason disturbed, apply
with equal force to the time during which its continuance may
be recognized as a ground for mitigating the homicide to the
degree of manslaughter, or, in other words, to the question
of cooling time. This, like the provocation itself, must depend upon the nature of man and the laws of the human mind,
as well as upon the nature and circumstances of the provocation, the extent to which the passions have been aroused, and

770

the fact, whether the injury inflicted by the provocation is
more or less permanent or irreparable. The passion excited
by a blow received in a sudden quarrel, though perhaps equally
violent for the moment, would be likely much sooner to subside than if aroused by a rape committed upon a sister or a
daughter, or the discovery of an adulterous intercourse with
a wife; and no two cases of the latter kind would be likely
to be identical in all their circumstances of provocation.
No precise time, therefore, in hours or minutes, can be laid
down by the court, as a rule of law, within which the passions
must be held to have subsided and reason to have resumed its
control, without setting at defiance the laws of man's nature,
and ignoring the very principle on which provocation and passion are allowed to be shown, at all, in mitigation of the offense. The question is one of reasonable time, depending upon all the circumstances of the particular case; and where
the law has not defined, and can not without gross injustice
define the precise time which shall be deemed reasonable, as
it has with respect to notice of the dishonor of *commercial
paper. In such case, where the law has defined what shall
be reasonable time, the question of such reasonable time,
the facts being found by the jury, is one of law for the court;
but in all other cases it is a question of fact for the jury;
and the court can not take it from the jury by assuming to
decide it as a question of law, without confounding the respective provinces of the court and jury: Stark. Ev., Ed.
of 1860, pp. 768, 769, 774, 775. In Rex v. Howard, 6 C. & P.,
157, and Rex v. Lynch, 5 C. & P., 324, this question of reasonable cooling time was expressly held to be a question of
fact for the jury. And see Whart. Cr. L., 4th ed., Sec. 990,
and cases cited. I am aware there are many cases in which
it has been held a question of law; but I can see no principle on which such a rule can rest. The court should, I
think, define to the jury the principles upon which the question is to be decided, and leave them to determine whether
the time was reasonable under all the circumstances of the
particular case. I do not mean to say that the time may not
be so great as to enable the court to determine that it is
sufficient for the passion to have cooled, or so to instruct
the jury, without error; but the case should be very clear.
And in cases of applications for a new trial, depending upon
the discretion of the court, the question may very properly
be considered by the court.

It remains only to apply these principles to the present
case. The proposed evidence, in connection with what had already been given, would have tended strongly to show the commission of adultery by Hunt with the prisoner's wife, within
half an hour before the assault; that the prisoner saw them
going to the woods together, under circumstances calculated
strongly to impress upon his mind the belief of the adulterous purpose; that he followed after them to the woods; that
Hunt and the prisoner's wife were, not long after, seen coming
from the woods, and that the prisoner followed them, and went
in hot pursuit after Hunt *to the saloon, and was informed by

771

a friend on the way that they had committed adultery the day before in the woods. I can not resist the conviction that this would have been sufficient evidence of provocation to go to the jury, and from which, when taken in connection with the excitement and "great perspiration" exhibited on entering the saloon, the hasty manner in which he approached and fired the pistol at Hunt, it would have been competent for the jury to find that the act was committed in consequence of the passion excited by the provocation, and in a state of mind which, within the principle already explained, would have given to the homicide, had death ensued, the character of manslaughter only. In holding otherwise the court below was doubtless guided by those cases in which courts have arbitrarily assumed to take the question from the jury, and to decide upon the facts or some particular fact of the case, whether a sufficient provocation had been shown, and what was a reasonable time for cooling.

But there is still a further reason why the evidence should have been admitted. No other cause being shown for the assault, the proposed evidence, if given, could have left no reasonable doubt that it was, in fact, committed in consequence of the alleged provocation, whether sufficient or not; and all the facts constituting the provocation, or which led to the assault, being thus closely connected, and following each other in quick succession, and the assault itself in which they resulted, constituted together but one entire transaction. The circumstances which, in fact, led to the assault were a part of the res gestae, which the jury were entitled to have before them, to show what was the real nature of the act, the quo animo, state of mind and intention, with which it was done. The object of the trial should be to show the real nature of the whole transaction, whether its tendency may be to establish guilt or innocence; but, until the whole is shown which might have any bearing one way or the *other, its tendency to establish the one or the other can not be known. Any inference drawn from a detached part of one entire transaction may be entirely false. And, for myself, I am inclined to the opinion, that all the facts constituting the res gestae, so far as the prosecuting counsel is informed of, and has the means of proving them, should, on principle and in fairness to the prisoner, be laid before the jury by the prosecution. They naturally constitute the prosecutor's case. And whenever it may appear evident to the court, that but a part of the facts, or a single fact, has been designedly selected by the prosecution from the series constituting the res gestae, or entire transaction, and that the evidence of the others is within the power of the prosecutor, it would, I think, be the duty of the court to require the prosecutor to show the transaction as a whole. See by analogy, Holden's case, 8 C. & P., 606; Stoner's case, 1 C. & K., 650; Chapman's case, 8 C. & P., 559; Orchard's case, Ibid., note; Roscoe Cr. Ev., 164. Until this should be done it is difficult to see how any legitimate inference of guilt, or of the degree of the

772

offense, can be drawn; as every reasonable hypothesis of innocence, or a lower degree of guilt, is not, it seems to me excluded. Criminal prosecutions do not stand on the same ground, in this respect, as civil cases. In the latter no such presumption is to be overcome; nor is it necessary to exclude every other hypothesis than the one sought to be established: 3 Greenl. Ev., Sec. 29. But however this may be, it was clearly competent for the defendant to show the rest of the transaction, whether known to the prosecution or not. I think, therefore, for the several reasons stated, the evidence offered was erroneously rejected.

After the evidence was closed, the prisoner was called by his counsel to make a statement under the statute. This statement went strongly to corroborate the facts offered to be shown by the evidence rejected. The prisoner's counsel requested the court to charge, that the prisoner's *statement was for the consideration of the jury; that they should receive it as evidence in the cause, and give it such credit as, under the circumstances, they believed it entitled to; which the court refused, and the prisoner's counsel excepted. But the court in this connection did charge, that the statement could not be received in relation to matters of defense excluded by the court, the conduct of Hunt and the prisoner's wife; but that where there were facts and circumstances in relation to the commission of the offense, the jury might consider the prisoner's statement in considering the evidence, and give it such weight as they thought proper.

The only substantial error of the court in relation to this "statement," is that which grew out of the exclusion of the evidence, and was the natural consequence of that error. All he intended to say was, that the statement might be considered by the jury so far only as it had any bearing upon the case; but that, so far as it related to the conduct of Hunt and the prisoner's wife, it had no such bearing. It was, thus far, erroneous; but in other respects substantially correct. It is of little consequence whether the statement be called evidence, or by some other name. It is not evidence within the ordinary acceptation of that term; because not given under the sanction of an oath, nor is the prisoner liable for perjury or to any other penalty, if it be false; not can a full cross-examination be enforced. Yet it is clear the jury have a right to give it such credit, in whole or in part, as under all the circumstances they may think it entitled to.

The judgment should be reversed and a new trial granted.

MARTIN, CH. J. and CAMPBELL, J. concurred.

MANNING J.

I differ from my brethren in this case. I think the evidence was properly excluded. To make that manslaughter *which would otherwise be murder, the provocation - I am not speaking of its sufficiency, but of the provocation itself - must be given in the presence of the person committing the homicide.

773

The cause of the provocation must occur in his presence. PARK J., in Regina v. Fisher, 8 C. & P., 182, in speaking of the cause of provocation, says, "In all cases the party must see the act done." Any other rule in an offense so grave as taking the life of a fellow-being, in the heat of passion, I fear would be more humane to the perpetrator than wise in its effects on society. More especially since the abolition of the death penalty for murder, and the division of the crime into murder in the first and second degree. There is not now the same reason, namely, the severity of the punishment, for relaxing the rules of law in favor of a party committing homicide as before. It would, it seems to me, be extremely mischievous to let passion engendered by suspicion, or by something one has heard, enter into and determine the nature of a crime committed while under its influence. The innocent as well as the guilty, or those who had not as well as those who had given provocation, might be the suffers. If it be said that in such cases the giving of the provocation must be proved or it would go for nothing; the answer is, that the law will not, and should not permit the lives of the innocent to be exposed with the guilty in this way, as it would do did it (sic) not require the cause of the provocation to occur in the presence of the person committing the homicide. See Regina v. Fisher, 8 C. & P., 182; Regina v. Kelly, 2 C. & K., 814; and State v. John, 8 Ired., 330.

I think the judgment should be affirmed.

Judgment reversed, and new trial ordered.

People v. Younger
380 Mich. 678

SOURIS, J. Defendant was convicted by a jury of first-degree murder[1] for killing his wife.[2] The homicide occurred at about 3 o'clock one morning when defendant returned home unexpectedly and found his wife, a female neighbor and his wife's male employer in defendant's home having a drink. It was defendant's claim at trial, and it is his claim on appeal, that the presence of the male in his home at that hour was the culminating act of provocation, preceded by many prior acts of infidelity by his wife and broken promises of reformation, that precipitated his killing his wife in an act of passion, thereby reducing the homicide from one of murder to manslaughter.

Defendant's principal claims on appeal are that (1) he should have been accorded greater freedom than was allowed him in introducing evidence of his wife's past misconduct in support of his claim that he was subjected to such provocation than an ordinary man would kill in the heat of passion and (2) that the jury should have been instructed

774

to consider such evidence of his wife's past misconduct in determining the sufficiency of the asserted provocation to constitute the homicide manslaughter rather than murder. This is not a case in which temporary insanity was pleaded as a defense. See People v. Garbutt (1868), 17 Mich 9 (97 Am Dec 162). Accordingly, we need not express an opinion whether the circuit judge's challenged evidentiary rulings and jury instructions would have been adequate had such defense been in issue.

Murder and manslaughter have been distinguished frequently in our reports. Murder in the first degree requires proof of premeditation, deliberation and malice. Manslaughter, on the other hand, is a homicide which is not the result of premeditation, deliberation and malice but, rather, which is the result of such provocation that an ordinary man would kill in the heat of passion before a reasonable time had elapsed for the passions to subside and reason to resume its control. See People v. Scott (1859), 6 Mich 287; Maher v. People (1862), 10 Mich 212 (81 Am Dec 781); People v. Lilley (1880), 43 Mich 521; People v. Holmes (1896), 111 Mich 364; People v. Poole (1909), 159 Mich 350 (134 Am St Rep 722); and People v. Ryczek (1923), 224 Mich 106.

At the threshold of every manslaughter case, the killing, to be manslaughter and not murder, must have been the product of an act of passion; it must have been committed in a moment of frenzy or of temporary excitement. Manslaughter is homicide devoid of actions which require unimpassioned calculation for their accomplishment. If there be actions manifesting deliberation, it cannot be said, legally, that the homicide was the product of provocation which unseated reason and allowed passion free rein. Thus, the nature and quality of the act of homicide first must be examined to determine whether it is that of an ordinary man responding to the heat of passion or that of an ordinary man functioning with deliberation. Only if the defendant's actions can be found to be acts of passion is it appropriate to inquire into the legal sufficiency of the asserted provocation. In this case of Younger, we conclude that defendant's own conduct on the fatal night precludes a finding that he had been bereft of reason by passions run rampant. A description of his actions, much of which is conceded by defendant and the balance of which is uncontradicted on this record, establishes the point we make.

Defendant, who worked in Detroit and normally returned to his home in Flint only on weekends, arrived at his Flint home unexpectedly at about 3 o'clock one morning and found his wife and two others, one of whom was male, having a drink. He greeted his wife's guests and, as he preceeded through the living room to an adjoining bedroom, his wife told him that one of his dogs had died. Without response, he entered the bedroom, kissed his sleeping child and began to cry. An unspecified time later he left the bedroom and went into the basement where he dug "furiously" into a carrying bag in which he had placed some of his hunting equipment

and, after some difficulty, he found some shells for his
.22-caliber rifle. He then removed the rifle from its
cover, loaded the rifle and returned upstairs. As he did
so, his wife's male guest was departing, having finished
his drink; but the female guest remained.

Defendant's testimony of what transpired next was:

"And as I approached I says, 'Nita -' I advised her, I
says, 'Anita, get on your knees and pray.'

"She said, 'Honey, what's wrong? What's wrong?'

"I says, 'You promised me one thing, you invariably do
just the opposite. They (defendant's children) do not have
to live like this.'

"And from that point on she started saying a lot of things:
'Please give me another chance. I will do better. Don't
do this. What's wrong, Honey? I will do anything that you
say do. You just say it.'

"I said, 'I know what you are going to do, what you have
repeatedly done.'

"Pearl (the female guest) turned around and she made
some remark. I do not know verbatim or exactly what Pearl
said, but my wife remarked to her to do as I had said do.
And at this particular point is when I cursed at her and
she says, 'Dave, I will change. Just give me another chance.
I will change. I will promise I will change.' And at this
precise moment is when I pulled the trigger."

Pearlie Shook, the female guest, testified that defendant
kept his wife on her knees for about 4, 5, or 6 minutes. Her
description of the homicide was:

"A. And he was standing behind the davenport. And he
said to Mrs. Younger something like this: 'Anita, thought
I told you that I would never give you another penny of my
money.'

"And she said, 'What money?' And she say, 'I haven't asked
you for any money. I don't want any money.'

"He say, 'Well, I have the papers here in my pocket to
prove.' You know, I guess the divorce or something, I don't
know. But then he says, 'You are such of a great believer,
get on your knees and pray to your Maker.'

"And she went, like 'Oh, Dave, honey,' you know, 'what's
wrong?' you know.

"Q. Pardon me, Now I'm sorry, I missed that last part.

"A. 'Oh, Dave, honey, what's wrong?'

"So he said, 'Get on your knees and I mean get on them
now,' or something like this. And when she got on her knees
at the davenport like this and start praying and pleading
with him. So he say -

"Q. Do you know what she said exactly? Could you recall?

"A. She was saying, 'Oh, honey, don't do this,' you know.

"He say, 'You know I am going to do this, don't you?' No,
he said - Yes, he said, 'You know I am going to do this,
don't you?'

"She say, 'Honey, I know you will do it.'

"He say, 'No, you know, I am going to do this.'
"So after this she begged, you know, and pleaded, 'Let
me live for Ramata and - '
"Q. For who?
"A. Ramata. That the baby. And I said something like,
'Dave, don't do this. Think about the children,' or something. And he asked me not to move and she told me don't
move because he would shoot me. So I stood there. And by
it being so much noise, her praying and begging him not to
do this, they woke up Renee; that's her daughter. I think
she is six years old. And when Ramata - I mean, Renee, runs
out of the bedroom - But before this, she had begged and begged and Ramata run out of the bedroom.
"Q. You mean Renee?
"A. Renee, yes. The oldest girl. And when she went
out the bedroom she run straight to her mother. So Mrs.
Younger was still pleading and begging, you know, and so I
grabbed the child. And Mr. Younger said something like,
'Look at this bitch squirm,' or something like that; something like that. And he shot her the first time then he
just kept shooting."

It appears, from the closing arguments of both counsel,
that defendant shot his wife 16 times. From the foregoing,
it is apparent to us that defendant did not kill his wife
in a momentary impulse of passion but, rather, that he proceeded methodically to execute her in cold blood. On such
facts, defendant was not entitled to any instruction on manslaughter and, thus, the circuit judge's evidentiary rulings
and his refusal to instruct on the issue of provocation, as
to which defendant complains on appeal, were not reversible
errors. . . .
Affirmed.

DETHMERS, C. J., and KELLY, BLACK, T. M. KAVANAGH, O'HARA,
ADAMS, and BRENNAN, JJ., concurred.

4. Unlawful Act Doctrine - Misdemeanor Manslaughter
Rule

People v. Stubenvoll
62 Mich. 329

CHAMPLIN, J. An information was filed against the respondent for the murder of William Pickel, and upon a trial
the jury returned a verdict of manslaughter.
The death was caused by a pistol ball discharged by respondent, as he claims, for the purpose of frightening the
deceased; and that he intended to shoot over Pickel's head,
but, by accident, the ball took effect in Pickel's body, and
he soon expired.

The Legislature, in 1869, passed an act entitled "An act to prevent the careless use of fire-arms."

The first and second sections of this act make it a misdemeanor for any person, intentionally and without malice, to point, aim, or discharge any fire-arm, without injury, at another person. The third section enacts:

"Any person who shall maim or injure any other person by the discharge of any fire-arm, pointed or aimed, intentionally but without malice, at any such person, shall be guilty of a misdemeanor, and shall be punished by a fine of not less than fifty dollars, or imprisonment in the county jail for a period of not more than one year; and if death ensue from such wounding or maiming, such person so offending shall be deemed guilty of the crime of manslaughter."

The counsel for respondent requested the court to charge the jury:

"If you find that the death of William Pickel resulted from the accidental use, or careless use, of the revolver in the hands of the defendant, without malice, you must acquit him of any offense, under the information in this case, and your verdict will be 'not guilty.'"

And again:

"If you find, as a fact, that the defendant did not intend to do any bodily harm to the deceased, but, through careless use of a revolver, death resulted, he is not guilty of murder in any degree, not of manslaughter, under the information against him in this case, and it will be your duty to acquit."

These requests the court refused to give. They were rightly refused. The public prosecutor was not compelled to frame his information under the third section of the statute cited. The testimony of the prosecution tended to prove murder. It was competent for the prosecutor to file his information simply for murder, and leave the matter to be dealt with as the proof should disclose the character and grade of the crime committed, which might range all the way from murder in the first degree down to a simple assault and battery. The statute has nowhere attempted to define the crime of manslaughter, but has left the offense as known at the common law, and this court properly defined.

He also told the jury that, under the evidence, there could be no conviction for murder in the first degree, and, after defining the different degrees of murder and of manslaughter, he instructed the jury as follows:

"If you find, at the time of the homicide, that the defendant intentionally discharged a pistol at the person of Willie Pickel, while Pickel was running in the highway, with malice in his heart at the time, and that such malice was the moving cause of the act, and as a result of the shot Willie Pickel received a wound from the effects of which he died, the defendant is guilty of murder in the second degree.

"If you find that the defendant was chasing Willie Pickel in the highway, with the intention to compel him to seek a place of shelter from the defendant, and for the purpose of frightening him he discharged a pistol, not intending to inflict any personal injury upon Willie Pickel, but only to frighten him, the defendant was engaged in an unlawful act; and if you find the shot did inflict an injury from which Willie Pickel died, the defendant is guilty of manslaughter.

"If you find that the defendant was chasing Willie Pickel in the highway, intending to overtake him and inflict some personal chastisement on him, and while so chasing him designedly discharged a pistol, not intending to inflict any injury on Pickel by such discharge, but only to frighten him, and as a result of the shot a wound was inflicted on the person of Willie Pickel from the effect of which he died, the defendant is guilty of manslaughter."

These instructions presented the law of the case correctly to the jury. . . .

By his own statement he was armed with a deadly weapon, and, being so armed, he gave chase to the deceased, and if he had caught him he might have slapped him in the face and told him what was right. He was not very angry, but he did not want to be called names. He was trying to scare the boys, and stop their throwing dirt or stones. He took his revolver out to shoot in the air to scare the boys, and when he took it out to do this, while he was pursuing and the deceased fleeing from him, about one hundred feet distant, he says he does not know how it happened, but it went off, and hit and killed the boy Willie Pickel. He also shows that there was an altercation there between him and the boys, they calling names and throwing dirt or stones, one of which hit him on the leg.

It thus appears from his testimony that he meant to do two things, both of which were unlawful:

1. He chased the deceased with intent to slap him in the face, or, in other words, to do him bodily harm.

2. He meant to shoot his pistol - a deadly weapon, loaded with powder and ball - in the air for the purpose of scaring the boys.

Under such circumstances, if death of a person ensues from the act, the crime is, at least, manslaughter, whether he intended to kill the person or not. It seems to me that it would be monstrous to hold that the respondent is not legally responsible for such criminal carelessness as his own story shows he was guilty of. Can it be that human life has come to be so cheap that it can be sacrificed without provocation, and the slayer go unpunished because he did not intend to take life by his rash or careless act? And yet such was the effect of the respondent's requests to charge the jury above quoted.

Mr. Bishop, in his work on Criminal Law, says:

"It is reasonable to hold that, where one uses a deadly weapon without justification, he evinces a disregard for human life and safety amounting to 'malice.'"

Was there any justification for the use of the deadly weapon in this case? Assuredly not. Its use was uncalled for and wanton. The boy chased and killed was but fifteen years old. He had committed no crime, and respondent had no right to lay violent hands upon him, - much less to shoot him.

In the case of State v. Smith, 2 Strob. (S.C.) 77, the prisoner fired a pistol at a person on horseback merely to frighten his horse and cause it to throw its rider, and the ball caused the death of another person. The offense was held to be murder. Mr. Justice Evans, in deciding the case, said:

"If the prisoner's object had been nothing more than to make Carter's horse throw him, and he had used such means only as were appropriate to that end, then there would be some reason for applying to this case the distinction that, where the intent was to commit only a trespass or a misdemeanor, the accidental killing would be only manslaughter."

The above case, in many of its features, is quite similar to this. The occurrence happened after dark. A crowd had assembled in the street, among which was the prisoner. Two children had been sent upon an errand, and, meeting the crowd, had climbed upon the fence, and sat there. Carter rode by upon horseback. The prisoner discharged his pistol, and accidentally hit and killed one of the children. The prisoner said that he did not know that the child was there, and would not have hurt him for the world if he had known it. Again, being asked, when he said he did not mean to kill the negro, "Well, who did you mean to kill?" he hesitated and said: "Really, I did not intend to kill anybody. I shot at that d--d mulatto, but did not intend to kill him." Again, he said: "I shot with this intention: to make Carter's horse cut or caper, and throw him down; and I thought I had elevated the pistol high enough to be out of danger." And again: "I designed a frolic, to scare Carter or his horse, and thought I had raised the pistol so as not to hit anybody."

In this case, if the object of respondent was simply to frighten the boy, the means used were entirely inappropriate for the purpose. If that had been his only object, his giving chase seems effectually to have accomplished it, for they were fleeing from him; and for what reason other than affright? The people's testimony showed that the respondent made threats, and had deliberately taken his pistol from his pocket while behind the tree, and that he pursued, and deliberately took aim, and fired the fatal shot. I think there was testimony in the case that would have justified the court in submitting it to the jury whether the respondent was not guilty of murder in the first degree.

780

Adverting again to decided cases: It has been held that where a parent corrects his child, if the correction exceeds the bounds of due moderation, either in the measure of it, or in the instrument made use of for that purpose, it will be either murder or manslaughter, according to the circumstances. Rex v. Cheeseman, 7 Car. & P. 455; Anonymous, 1 East, P.C. 261; 1 Hale, P.C. 455; Foster, 262.

In Wigg's Case, 1 Leach, 378, a boy having the care of some sheep suffered some of them to escape through the hurdles of the pen, and the master, seeing the sheep escaping, ran towards the boy, threw a stake at the boy, which hit and killed him. The jury, under the direction of the court, found the master guilty of manslaughter.

In the case of Rex v. Sullivan, 7 Car. & P. 641, a lad, in frolic, without meaning harm to any one, took the trapstick out of the forepart of a cart, in consequence of which it was upset, and the carman, who was in it putting in a sack of potatoes, was thrown backward on some stones, and killed. The lad was held to be guilty of manslaughter.

So it was held that where one whips a horse on which another is riding so that it springs out, and runs over and kills a child, he is guilty of manslaughter: 2 Bish. Crim. Law, Sec. 693. It is also manslaughter if, on a sudden quarrel between two persons, a blow intended for one of them accidentally falls upon a third, whom it kills: Rex v. Brown, 1 Leach, 135; 1 East, P.C. 231, 245, 274.

Mr. Bishop says (2 Crim. Law, Sec. 704):

"It appears to be a doctrine of the courts that, if parties become excited by words, and one of them attempts to chastise the other with a weapon not deadly, he will be held for manslaughter, though death is unintentionally inflicted."

And when a man discharges a gun at another's fowls, in mere wanton sport, he commits, if he accidentally kills a human being, the offense of manslaughter, while his intended act is only a civil trespass: 2 Bish. Crim. Law, Sec. 692.

In State v. Roane, 2 Dev. (N.C.) 58, it was held the firing of a gun simply for the purpose of frightening another, by which shooting death is produced, is manslaughter. In this case the prisoner's counsel requested the court to charge the jury "that if the defendant did not intend to kill, but only to frighten the deceased, they should find him not guilty of any offense," which was refused; and the judge charged that if the defendant discharged his gun in a careless, negligent, and heedless manner, and thereby caused the death of the deceased, he was guilty of manslaughter, although he did not intend to kill. Held no error.

And in People v. Fuller, 2 Parker, C.C. 16, it was held that where one carelessly discharged a gun into the street in the night-time, and shot deceased unintentionally, not knowing he was there, it was manslaughter.

Mr. Bishop formulates the doctrine to be drawn from the adjudicated cases as follows (2 Crim Law, Sec. 689):

781

"If an act is unlawful, or is such as duty does not demand, and of a tendency directly dangerous to life, however unintended, it will be murder. But if the act, though dangerous, is not directly so, yet sufficiently dangerous to come under condemnation of the law, and death unintended results from it, the offense is manslaughter; or if it is one of a nature to be lawful properly performed, and it is performed improperly, and death comes from it unexpectedly, the offense still is manslaughter."

Applying the principle to be deduced from the cases referred to, and the doctrine above laid down, to the case under consideration, and viewing the transaction in the light of the most favorable circumstances shown by the testimony, the act of respondent in killing the lad was manslaughter. Indeed, there was no evidence upon which the requests of defendant's counsel could properly be based; for it is impossible to separate the accidental shooting claimed from the other facts which give character to the act as negligent, heedless, and careless, in discharging a loaded pistol at such a time, in such a place, upon such an occasion. From his own testimony there could be no reasonable doubt in the minds of the jury that he was guilty of the crime of manslaughter; and when the case shows that there could be but one conclusion, and that in accordance with the verdict rendered, it will not be disturbed for a misdirection as to the meaning of the phrase "reasonable doubt": People v. Marble, 38 Mich. 125.

When the jury reported their verdict to the court they reported that they found the respondent guilty of voluntary manslaughter, which was reduced to form, and recorded by the clerk, who then said:

"Gentlemen of the jury, you say you find the respondent, Jacob Stubenvoll, guilty of manslaughter in manner and form as the people have in their information charged, - so say you, Mr. Foreman, so say you all?"

The jury answered:

"We do."

This was not error. We discover no error in the record, and the judgment is affirmed.

SHERWOOD, J., concurred.

CAMPBELL, C. J. (dissenting). The verdict in this case is a peculiar one, and can hardly have resulted from anything but gross misapprehension. There was no testimony in the record which could sustain a verdict of voluntary manslaughter, which involves intentional killing upon great provocation. If the killing here was intentional, I agree with my Brother CHAMPLIN that it would have been murder, but I do not think it could be made murder in the first degree. All this, however, is now unimportant, because, by the verdict rendered, respondent has been acquitted of murder.

782

I think there was testimony from which the jury could properly have found the respondent guilty of manslaughter. But the prisoner was himself a witness, and swore to what was an accidental discharge of his pistol, under circumstances which, if believed, made the result one of homicide by misfortune, and not punishable, unless civilly as an actionable injury from negligence.

The criminal law never was aimed at punishing as a crime that which involves no wrong purpose. Involuntary manslaughter, arising from wrong purpose not homicidal, does not exist unless death is caused in an attempt to carry out some unlawful purpose which is _malum in se_, but not felonious. If respondent purposely fired his pistol in the direction of the boy who was killed, the act was dangerous in itself, and might authorize a conviction. But merely firing a pistol is not an unlawful act, and firing in the air is not usually, and would not have been here, a dangerous act. It is laid down by Lord Hale that if a person (although not having the proper legal qualification, and therefore in violation of the statute) kills another accidentally while shooting at a bird, it is no crime, because his intent was no worse than if he had been lawfully qualified, and the act was a misadventure. 1 Hale, 475. Forster, in his concise treatise, takes the same view. Foster, 259. So far as I know, there is no respectable authority which upholds a conviction where the result is one of pure accident, with no serious mischief intended. Any other rule would be cruel and unreasonable.

If the prisoner was believed, the act was not one of his volition at all, but a merely accidental discharge. What he intended to do was an act legally innocent, had his intention been carried out. I think he had a right to go to the jury on this theory, and that the court erred in refusing his request to that effect. If he told the truth, he meant to fire in the air, with the foolish, but not wicked, design of frightening the boys. That is the utmost evil to which the accidental discharge of the pistol could be attached, if it could be to that. The jury might not believe his version, but he had a right to ask, as he did, a charge on the theory that it was true.

I think there should be a new trial.

MORSE, J., concurred.

People v. Rogulski
181 Mich. 481

STEERE, J. Respondent was convicted of the crime of manslaughter in the circuit court of Wayne county, on February 18, 1913, under an information for murder which, in simple form under section 11912, 3 Comp. Laws (5 How. Stat. (2d Ed.) Sec. 15083), charged in one count that:

Respondent "on the 29th day of December, in A.D. 1912, at said township of Dearborn in said county, feloniously, wilfully, and of his malice aforethought, did kill and murder one Walter Dahlman, contrary to the form of the statute in such case made and provided and against the peace and dignity of the people of the State of Michigan.". . .

It is undisputed that Dahlman was killed, at the time and place alleged, by a shot fired from a gun held in respondent's hands. It was claimed on the part of the defense that the shooting was unintentional, in which view the prosecution and court apparently acquiesced, and the court instructed the jury that respondent could not be convicted of either murder or voluntary manslaughter under the testimony, but might be convicted of involuntary manslaughter, or "assault and battery, or even an assault." The record shows respondent was found "guilty of manslaughter" - whether voluntary or involuntary is not stated. He was sentenced to serve not less than two years and not more than five years at Jackson State prison. . . .

On the morning of this tragedy, Dahlman and his two companions went out from Detroit to Dearborn together, taking with them a single-barreled shotgun belonging to Dahlman. . . . They purposed to and did call upon a family named Jubs, living near Dearborn, where Leitz was acquainted. They asked for George Jubs, apparently a younger member of that family, who was not at home. The three then left their coats in the Jubs barn, walked together across a field towards the River Rouge carrying Dahlman's gun, and on the way they fired it two or three times at a mark. In their rambling they crossed the river when one of them saw a field mouse run under a brush, and they all then devoted themselves to trying to find and get it. While they were so engaged, respondent came up and greeted them, asking what they were looking for. Having been informed, he in apparent good nature joined in the hunt for a few minutes, and finally inquired the kind and name of the gun they had, which at that time Leitz was carrying. Leitz, in response, said he did not know, but would tell as soon as he looked, and just as he was giving the information respondent took the gun from his hands. Of what then occurred Leitz testifies:

"Just as I said that he pulled the gun out of my hands. Then he says to the three of us, 'Now you will have to come along with me.' I says to him, 'What is the matter?' He says, 'Never mind, you will have to come along with me.' Just as he says that, Walter stepped, made a kind of step, and says, 'Please, Mister, give me my gun.' Just when he said that he fired and killed him. . . . After Walter was shot, he says, 'I am shot,' and he fell. Rogulski then walked away without looking at the boy who was shot. . . . "

Counsel for the defense state in their brief:

"Respondent was caretaker of the Ford farm at Dearborn,

in Wayne county. Many trespassers had been accustomed to invade the farm and shoot there regardless of notices posted thereon forbidding such conduct. . . .

In submitting the question of involuntary manslaughter to the jury, the court instructed them that if respondent was at the time engaged in an unlawful act, not amounting to a felony, which resulted in the killing, even though death was not intended, he would be guilty of manslaughter, saying among other things:

"Now, I charge you that this man had no business, he had no legal right, to take this gun from these boys. It was a matter that it was not for him to correct, if they were there even as trespassers upon that farm; that even Mr. Ford himself, who was the owner of the place, and had he forbidden persons to go upon that farm and do shooting, would have no right to go down there and take this boy's property from him, and if he did that by force he would be engaged in an unlawful act. And so, in this case, if this man went there for the purpose of taking this gun away from these boys, and he was in the act of taking the gun from them, against their will, taking it way from them, and in the taking it away from them and in the keeping of it and in the carrying of it he even accidentally shot this boy, he is guilty of involuntry manslaughter." (sic)

It is claimed by respondent that this portion of the charge is erroneous on two grounds: First, that under the single, short count of the information filed in this case charging murder a conviction for involuntary manslaughter cannot be had; second, because the court erroneously said to the jury that respondent had no business to take the gun from the boys, and he would be guilty of involuntary manslaughter if he accidentally shot the boy while keeping and carrying away the gun. Such excerpts from the charge must be considered in connection with the evidence in the case and the charge taken as a whole. So considered, we cannot regard them as misleading. The evidence was plain and conclusive that the shooting immediately followed respondent's taking the gun from Leitz, he had not separated from them, but had just stepped back three or four feet, and, facing the three boys, ordered them to come along with him. The entire transaction covered but a very short space of time.

If the evidence showed that respondent obtained possession of this gun from Leitz either by a ruse or by violence, with a wrongful intention to permanently deprive the owner of it and convert it to his own use, by delivering it to Bryant for a reward, or otherwise, his acts would amount in effect to larceny, if not to robbery. If he intentionally but without malice aimed or pointed the gun at Dahlman designing no mischief, but by its discharge death resulted, he was guilty of a careless use of firearms in violation of the statute upon that subject, and the offense was manslaughter.

785

Section 11511, 3 Comp. Laws 5 How. Stat. (2nd Ed.)   Sec. 14560.
Aside from this, it is a general principle of the common law
that any one in possession of and using a dangerous agency,
particularly firearms, must observe all reasonable caution,
and, if by his failure to do so and negligent use of the same,
death results, he may be convicted of manslaughter. Taken as
a whole, we think the charge of the court was very moderate
and extremely favorable to the accused. . . .
    We think the information was sufficient to sustain the
verdict and find no reversible error in the case.
    The conviction and judgment of sentence are affirmed.

    McALVAY, C. J., and BROOKE, KUHN, STONE, OSTRANDER, BIRD,
and MOORE, JJ., concurred.

                        People v. Abbott
                        116 Mich. 263

    HOOKER, J. The defendant was convicted of manslaughter,
as an accessory before the fact, in causing the death of
Viola Stevens through the use of an instrument in an attempt
to cause a miscarriage.
    To understand the points raised, reference should be had
to the statutes relating to the subject. 2 How. Stat. Sec.
9106, provides that the willful killing of an unborn quick
child, by any injury to the mother which would be murder if
it resulted in the mother's death, shall be manslaughter.
Section 9107 makes an attempt to destroy an unborn quick
child through medicine administered to, or instruments used
upon, the mother, manslaughter when followed by the death of
the child or mother, unless necessary to preserve the life
of the mother, or so advised by two physicians. Section 9108
punishes as a misdemeanor the willful employment of drugs,
etc., or instruments upon a pregnant woman, with intent to
procure a miscarriage, subject to the exceptions mentioned in
the preceding section. See 2 How Stat. Sec. 8438; People v.
Olmstead, 30 Mich. 431. The information contained separate
counts for murder and manslaughter, and also a count upon
the last-mentioned section, viz., 9108. In his charge to
the jury the learned circuit judge said that the defendant
could not be convicted of murder, and that he could not be
convicted of statutory manslaughter under section 9107, because Viola Stevens was not shown to have been pregnant with
a quick child, in the sense that such term is used in the
law. He instructed them that the defendant might be convicted of a misdemeanor, under section 9108, or that he might
be found guilty of manslaughter, upon the theory that death
to the mother resulted from the act, which was made unlawful
and punishable by section 9108, under the well-established
rule that "if a person, whilst doing or attempting to do another act, undesignedly kill a man, if the act intended or
attempted were a felony, the killing is murder; if unlawful, -
malum in se, - but not amounting to a felony, the killing is

                            786

manslaughter; if lawful, - that is, not being _malum in se_, - homicide by misadventure merely." See People v. Scott, 6 Mich. 293.

The defendant's counsel take the position that under these statutes there can be no conviction of the offense of murder where death is caused by any of the acts therein made punishable; that there can be no conviction of manslaughter in such cases except when the woman was, at the time of the commission of the act, pregnant with a quick child, as provided in sections 9106, 9107; and that it necessarily follows - the judge having determined and instructed the jury that Viola Stevens was not shown to have been pregnant with a quick child - that the defendant could be convicted, if at all, only of the misdemeanor created by section 9108. This contention rests upon the proposition that such act was not unlawful at the common law, it being no offense to attempt to produce an abortion upon a woman pregnant, but not with a quick child, with her consent, and upon the theory that the legislature has, by section 9107, shown an intention to reduce the offense from murder to manslaughter in cases where a woman pregnant with quick child comes to her death in this way, and upon the fact of its failure to provide in section 9108 additional punishment where the woman upon whom a miscarriage is sought to be produced dies in consequence thereof, from which it is said that it must be inferred that the intention was to make the penalty prescribed by that section the limit in all cases.

We think this theory should not prevail. If we could say that the law recognizes the lawfulness of attempts to produce miscarriages, there would be more force in the contention that a fatal result to the mother would be excusable homicide, though we do not mean to intimate such an opinion; but the legislature have been to the trouble to make the mere attempt to cause a miscarriage punishable by a year's imprisonment, and we cannot believe that they intended that the death of the mother should be treated as a misadventure. It is more reasonable to believe that they left that subject to be governed by existing rules of law. Upon this theory it was reasonable for the circuit judge to say that the defendant could not be convicted of murder, because that would have been the extent of the offense had the child been quick; and it is not to be supposed that the law would be more severe in a case where the child had not quickened than where it had, even if, under existing rules, the passing section 9108 would otherwise have made such offense murder. See Com. v. Railing, 113 Pa. St. 37. Without deciding this question, however, - it being unnecessary, - we must determine whether the conviction of manslaughter can be upheld. It may be, unless it can be said (1) that at common law a conviction could not be based on accidental killing through an unlawful act less than a felony, or (2) that it cannot be based on an act made unlawful by statute.

787

Mr. Bishop asserts that "if the act be both wrongful and in its nature dangerous to life, even if it be a misdemeanor, yet, if the element of danger concurs with the element of the unlawfulness of the act, the accidental causing of death thereby is murder." 2 Bish. Cr. Law, Sec. 691. See Tiff. Cr. Law, 815. Counsel contend that this is not a dangerous act, basing the contention upon the evidence of physicians, which is said to show that not more than 1 per cent of cases are fatal to the woman, where the child has not quickened. We doubt if the effect of this statute is to depend, upon the opinions of witnesses upon the question of the degree of danger. But, however that may be, the act was a misdemeanor, and accompanied by some danger to life, and we shall find much authority for holding that an indictment for manslaughter will lie in such a case.

"If a man happen to kill another in the execution of a malicious and deliberate purpose to do him a personal hurt by wounding or beating him, or in the willful commission of any unlawful act which necessarily tends to raise tumults and quarrels, and consequently cannot but be attended with the danger of personal hurt to some one or other, - as by committing a riot, robbing a park, etc., - he shall be adjudged guilty of murder." 1 Hawk. P.C. (Curw. Ed.) p. 86 Sec. 10.

Again, Bishop says:

"And if the act were not directly dangerous, yet done with the motive of committing a misdemeanor, the offense would be manslaughter; but if, still not being dangerous, the motive were merely the commission of a civil trespasss, the unintended death would not be indictable under all circumstances, though under some it would be manslaughter. To lay down, as to this, an exact rule, sustained by authorities, seems impossible. But, to illustrate, when a man discharges a gun at another's fowls, in mere wanton sport, he commits, if he accidentally kills a human being, the offense of manslaughter, while his intended act is only a civil trespass; and the same is the result when the firing of the gun which produces death is with intent simply to frighten another, or when one carelessly discharges the contents of firearms into the street. And where a lad in a frolic, without meaning harm to any one, took the trap-stick out of the forepart of a cart, in consequence of which it was upset, and the carman, who was in it, putting in a sack of potatoes, was thrown backward on some stones and killed, the lad was held to be guilty of manslaughter. Where one covers another with straw, and sets fire to it, if the intent is to do a serious bodily harm, and death follows, the offense is murder; if merely to frighten, it is manslaughter. (Errington's Case, 2 Lewin, Crown Cas. 217.) . . . Giving one physic in sport, if it kills him, is manslaughter." 2 Bish. Cr. Law, Sec. 692, note 4; Id. Sec. 693.

See People v. Scott, 6 Mich. 292.

Thus it appears that the unlawful act need not always be criminal, and where the act done is not of dangerous tendency, the offense, when death accidentally follows, may be manslaughter. 2 Bish. Cr. Law, Sec. 670, 694. Again Mr. Bishop says:

"Though the intent of the wrong-doer is not to take human life, and the thing which he does is not of the dangerous sort contemplated in the last few paragraphs, still, by accident, it may result in death. And if it does, and if the thing intended was malum in se and indictable, whether as felony or misdemeanor, a discussion in our first volume shows that a felonious homicide is committed." Id. Sec. 694.

See, also, 1 Bish. Cr. Law, Sec. 323-336.

In Com. v. Parker, 9 Metc. (Mass.) 265, it was said:

"The use of violence upon a woman, with an intent to procure her miscarriage without her consent, is an assault highly aggravated by such wicked purpose, and would be indictable at common law. So where, upon a similar attempt by drugs or instruments, the death of the mother ensues, the party making such an attempt, with or without the consent of the woman, is guilty of the murder of the mother, on the ground that it is an act done without lawful purpose, dangerous to life, and that the consent of the woman cannot take away the imputation of malice, any more than in case of a duel, where, in like manner, there is the consent of the parties."

In this case it was held necessary to aver and prove that the woman was quick with child, and the indictment was held bad. The following language is significant:

"There being no averment, in the first count in this indictment, that the woman was quick with child, or any equivalent averment, and the judge who tried the case having instructed the jury that it was not necessary to prove such averment in the third count, the court are all of the opinion that, although the acts set forth are, in a high degree, offensive to good morals and injurious to society, yet they are not punishable at common law, and that this indictment cannot be sustained." Id. 268.

From this and the foregoing authorities we may infer that, had the act been a misdemeanor at the common law, it would have supported an indictment for manslaughter. We are not advised of any authority which limits the application of this rule to acts which were misdemeanors at common law, nor do we see any good reason for so limiting it. In Yundt v. People, 65 Ill. 374, it was held that manslaughter would lie in a case closely analogous to the one before us.

A further contention is that, granting that the act was indictable, the information would not support a conviction under the proof, in that it alleged that the act was committed with force and violence, while the evidence showed that it was done with the consent of Viola Stevens. It is urged that this was a fatal variance. We are cited to the case of People v. Olmstead, 30 Mich. 438, in support of this claim. In that case the information is very brief, and consists of the single statement that respondent, on a day and years and at a place named, "one Mary A. Bowers feloniously, willfully, and wickedly did kill and slay, contrary to the statute in such case made and provided, and against the peace and dignity of the State of Michigan." There was nothing there to indicate the fact of consent, or even the nature of the act. As the court said: "He might, perhaps, be fairly assumed bound to prepare himself to meet a charge of manslaughter under section 9107, 2 How. Stat. The information in this case was more specific. It clearly apprised the defendant of the nature of the offense, unless it was necessary to allege Viola Stevens' consent, and to imit the allegation that the act was committed "with force and arms in and upon one Viola Stevens, in the peace of the people of the State of Michigan then and there being," etc. In our opinion, this was not a fatal variance, especially as it was not necessary to allege or prove the assent of Viola Stevens to the act, and as the offense was the same whether she assented or not. . . .

(The judgment was reversed on other grounds and a new trial ordered.)

The other justices concurred.

People v. Pavlic
227 Mich. 562

(For the opinion of the court in this case see page 194, supra.)

People v. Harris
214 Mich. 145

STEERE, C. J. Defendant was convicted in the circuit court of Monroe county of the crime of manslaughter, committed on April 29, 1919, by running over with an automobile, and killing, a girl 17 years of age named Gertrude Cousino as he was driving north through the village of Erie on his way from Toledo to Detroit along the thoroughfare known as the Dixie highway. Erie is a small unincorporated village about 10 miles south of the city of Monroe, having a few places of business and a number of residences centered around a four corners where an east and west road crosses the Dixie highway. On the cross-road just east of the Dixie highway is located a Catholic school. Miss Cousino was killed not long before 9 o'clock in the morning close to school. Quite a number of them saw the accident and also several older persons who were at or near the crossing. Testimony of the prosecution showed than an automobile (used as a "bread wagon") which carried some pupils to school from

790

north of Erie had just stopped at the northwest corner to
discharge them when Miss Cousino was seen to come out from
the direction of her home onto the east side of the Dixie
highway several hundred feet south of the corner and turn
north, walking along the highway on its right, or east, side
towards the corners, wearing a red hat as certain witnesses
seem to have particularly noticed. An automobile was also
noticed at quite a distance beyond her, coming from the
south at a high rate of speed. The driver of the auto which
brought the pupils from the north and stood at the northwest
corner of the crossing testified that the rapidly approaching
automobile was at least a quarter of a mile further south
when Miss Cousino came out upon the highway, and both were
thereafter in plain sight with nothing between them to obstruct the driver's view until it struck her just before she
reached the crossing. The on-coming car did not sound its
horn nor slacken speed, estimated by various witnesses at
from 20 to 35 miles an hour, and as it struck the girl swept
or carried her along for nearly 30 feet before she fell to
the ground and it ran over her, killing her almost instantly.
The automobile was a Studebaker with two men in it. Defendant was driving and did not stop when he struck her, but stepped on his accelerator and hastened away. A young man just
then in front of the post office north of the four corners,
who heard the accident and saw part of it, caught the number
of the car as it went by increasing its speed. The car
cleared the village at an estimated speed of 40 miles an hour
and further north the men were seen throwing bottles from
their automobile, some of which containing whisky were picked
up by children who saw them thrown. After driving about four
miles north of Erie along the Dixie highway defendant drove
down a cross-road for about a half mile and stopped within
sight of a farm house where he and his companion tore the
license numbers from the automobile and threw them in a ditch.
The farmer and his son near whose place they stopped saw
them do this and then leave the car, walking back east towards the Dixie highway. Notice of the accident and the number of the car were telephoned the sheriff at Monroe and a
deputy from there on his way toward Erie met the two men
walking north on the Dixie highway, stopped and talked with
them, told of his mission and asked if they had seen anything of such an automobile as he described. They denied
having seen any car and the sheriff went on. Later he learned where the automobile was left and other particulars which
led him to return north after these men, whom he overtook and
apprehended before they had reached Monroe. When examined
where they left it their automobile was without license
plates. Mutilated plates found in a ditch near by were issued by the State of Ohio. A broken whisky bottle was in
the car and on shelves concealed under the running board
were found 72 bottles of whisky.

Defendant admitted he was driving the car which struck
the girl to Detroit from Toledo, where he had been employed

in the liquor business, but denied ever having any whisky
in the car. He testified that he did not see the girl until
just as the machine hit her and did not stop for fear he
would be mobbed; that the accident occurred as he was passing a horse and buggy standing in front of a store, or shop,
and a moving hay wagon, when the girl suddenly came out in
front of his machine as the hay wagon passed. The other
occupant of this automobile supported defendant's account
of how the accident occurred. The testimony of witnesses
for the prosecution was positive that no such vehicles were
in the street at the place of the accident or to the south
of it, but that the way was clear and the girl in plain
sight of the approaching car from the time she came out upon
the road until it overtook and struck her. This issue of
fact was submitted to the jury under proper instructions. . . .

It was the claim of the prosecution that the accidental
death of Miss Cousino was caused by defendant while he was
intentionally and recklessly engaged in unlawful acts in
violation of statutory provisions, and such criminal intent
attached to the accidental killing under the law of homicide,
making the offense either murder or manslaughter. As covering the unlawful acts which there was testimony tending to
show defendant was intentionally committing and for the perpetration of which he was using the very instrumentality
which killed Miss Cousino the following statutory provisions
are referred to. As directly relating to the instrumentality
used, section 4817, 1 Comp. Laws 1915, prohibits operating a
motor vehicle upon a public highway in this State at a
greater speed than is reasonable, or so as to endanger the
life or limbs of any person, not in any event to exceed 25
miles an hour, and requiring that on approaching an intersecting highway the operator shall have the vehicle under
control, operated at such speed as is reasonable and proper
with regard to the traffic then on the highway and safety of
the public. Section 4818 provides:

"Upon approaching a person walking in the roadway . . .
a person operating a motor vehicle shall slow down to a
speed not exceeding ten miles an hour and give reasonable
warning of its approach and use every precaution to insure
the safety of such person."

By section 4824 violation of these provisions is punishable as a misdemeanor. . . .

The trial court explained to the jury the different degrees of unlawful killing covered by the information and
distinctly charged that defendant could only be convicted,
if convicted at all, of involuntary manslaughter, which is
quite generally defined by the authorities as the unintentional killing of a person in the commission of an unlawful
act, or -

"the killing of a human being, without any intention to do
so, but in the commission in an unlawful manner, of an un-

lawful act, or of a lawful act, which probably would pro-
duce such consequences." <u>Wharton on Homicide</u> (<u>3d Ed.</u>) p. <u>8</u>.

The fact that the act which caused death was not a misdemeanor at common law does not relieve the killing from
constituting manslaughter if the act is made a misdemeanor
by statute. <u>People v. Abbott</u>, <u>116</u> <u>Mich</u>. <u>263</u>.
Under the facts in this case as submitted to the jury we
can safely rest this inquiry on the following designation of
manslaughter by Justice STONE in <u>People v. Barnes</u>, <u>182</u> <u>Mich</u>.
<u>179</u>:

"There seems to be no conflict in the decisions where
the respondent is violating some statute, <u>and</u> where his
manner is negligent and careless; the courts in such cases
uniformly hold that he is guilty of manslaughter, if the
death of some other person is the result."

The conviction and judgment of sentence will stand
affirmed.

MOORE, WIEST, FELLOWS, STONE, CLARK, BIRD, and SHARPE, JJ.,
concurred.

People v. Carabell
11 Mich. App. 519

A. C. MILLER, J. A circuit court jury found defendant
Alvin J. Carabell guilty of manslaughter, <u>CL 1948</u>, <u>Sec</u>.
<u>750.321</u> (<u>Stat Ann 1954</u> <u>Rev</u>. <u>Sec</u>. <u>28.553)</u>. A motion for new
trial was denied and this appeal followed.

On August 10, 1965, at about 9:30 p.m., in the city of
Flint, Michigan, defendant and two friends went by auto to
a beer store. Defendant remained in the front seat, one
friend remained in the back seat, while the driver entered
the beer store. The deceased approached the vehicle from
the sidewalk, requested a drink and attempted to enter the
car. He was intoxicated. A scuffle ensued between deceased and the defendant. The friend in the back seat was
unable to separate them and went into the beer store. Upon
entry into the car deceased started to sit himself on defendant's lap and grabbed defendant by the throat. When
the friend reappeared, the two were grappling. Deceased
fell to the sidewalk. The witnesses differed as to whether
defendant struck and kicked the deceased, who suffered a
fatal brain hemorrhage. . . .

Defendant . . . contends that it is the duty of the trial

court to give a charge on lesser included offenses for the protection of the constitutional right of the defendant, although such requests were not made by the defense counsel.

In its opinion the trial court stated:

"This court concludes therefore that there seems to be two categories of charges or instructions by the court: First, those which are so essential to a fair trial that the court must charge them irrespective of a request therefor and, second, those charges which are not so essential to a fair trial that a request therefor is required before error can be predicated upon their not being given. This court believes that lesser included offenses belong in the former category and must be given by the court irrespective of a request therefor. But that is not decisive of the present issue. There has been cited absolutely no law by defendant's counsel that assault or assault and battery were in fact lesser included offenses within the range of evidence in this case. There is no question but that the testimony in this case all establishes that the respondent himself was initially assaulted by the deceased. It appears to the court as if the manslaughter conviction was of necessity predicated upon a finding, properly founded in the evidence, that the defendant's response to the deceased's initial attack was excessive and continued after the deceased's attack had been repelled and deceased was rendered helpless. Under normal circumstances assault and battery would be a lesser included offense; however, assault and battery is a misdemeanor and a death resulting from the commission of a misdemeanor is manslaughter regardless of whether defendant had an intent to kill. If this in fact is true, then there would be no lesser included offense of assault and battery." . . .

"(Whereupon a discussion was had, off the record, between defense counsel and the defendant.)

"Mr. Salim: Mr. Carabell states that he agrees with my position, that involuntary manslaughter is not, and we do not desire it to be a factor in this case.

"The Court: All right. The court will find that the evidence in this case indicates either - based upon the issues that are presented, either an action on behalf of the defendant's justification by virtue of self-defense or excessive force used in self-defense; and therefore, it will either be voluntary manslaughter or not guilty, and that will be the ruling of the court."

There was no objection to this ruling. . . .

Voluntary manslaughter was properly defined to the jury as follows:

"Manslaughter has been defined as the unlawful killing of another without malice, express or implied. The offense is one that is committed without malice or premeditation, as a result of temporary excitement by which the control of reason is disturbed, rather than from any wickedness of the heart or cruelty or recklessness of disposition. The general rule is

794

that reason should, at the time of the act, be disturbed or obscured by passion, or, an excitement of any cause to an extent that might render ordinary men of fair average disposition, liable to act rashly or without due deliberation or reflection, and from passion and lack of reason rather than from judgment.

"In short, voluntary manslaughter is the killing of another intentionally, but in a sudden heat of passion due to adequate provocation and without malice."

There was no prejudice. . . .
Affirmed.

McGREGOR, P. J., and J. H. GILLIS, J., concurred.

People v. Marshall
362 Mich. 170

SMITH, J. At approximately 3 a.m. on the morning of February 4, 1958, a car driven by Neal McClary, traveling in the wrong direction on the Edsel Ford Expressway, crashed head on into another vehicle driven by James Coldiron. The drivers of both cars were killed. Defendant William Marshall has been found guilty of involuntary manslaughter of Coldiron. At the time that the fatal accident took place, he, the defendant William Marshall, was in bed at his place of residence. His connection with it was that he owned the car driven by McClary, and as the evidence tended to prove, he voluntarily gave his keys to the car to McClary, with knowledge that McClary was drunk.

The principal issue in the case is whether upon these facts, the defendant may be found guilty of involuntary manslaughter. It is axiomatic that "criminal guilt under our law is personal fault."[1] As Sayre[2] puts the doctrine "it is of the very essence of our deep-rooted notions of criminal liability that guilt be personal and individual." This was not always true in our law, nor is it universally true in all countries even today, but for us it is settled doctrine.

The State relies on a case, Story v. United States,[3] in which the owner, driving with a drunk, permitted him to take the wheel, and was held liable for aiding and abetting him "in his criminal negligence." The owner, said the court, sat by his side and permitted him "without protest so (sic) recklessly and negligently to operate the car as to cause the death of another."[4] If defendant Marshall had been by McClary's side an entirely different case would be presented, but on the facts before us Marshall, as we noted, was at home in bed. The State also points out that although it is only a misdemeanor to drive while drunk,[5] yet convictions for manslaughter arising out of drunk driving have often been sustained. It argues from these cases that although it was only a misdemeanor for an owner to turn his keys over to a drunk

795

driver,[6] nevertheless a conviction for manslaughter may be sustained if such driver kills another. This does not follow from such cases as Story, supra. In the case before us death resulted from the misconduct of driver. The accountability of the owner must rest as a matter of general principle, upon his complicity in such misconduct. In turning his keys over, he was guilty of a specific offense, for which he incurred a specific penalty. Upon these facts he cannot be held a principal with respect to the fatal accident: the killing of Coldiron was not counseled by him, accomplished by another acting jointly with him, nor did it occur in the attempted achievement of some common enterprise.

This is not to say that defendant is guilty of nothing. He was properly found guilty of violation of paragraph (b) of section 625 of the Michigan vehicle code[7] which makes it punishable[8] for the owner of an automobile knowingly to permit it to be driven by a person "who is under the influence of intoxicating liquor." The State urges that this is not enough, that its manslaughter theory, above outlined, "was born of necessity," and that the urgency of the drunk-driver problem "has made it incumbent upon responsible and concerned law-enforcement officials to seek new approaches to a new problem within the limits of our law." What the State actually seeks[9] from us is an interpretation that the manslaughter statute imposes an open-end criminal liability. That is to say, whether the owner may ultimately go to prison for manslaughter or some lesser offense will depend upon whatever unlawful act the driver commits while in the car. Such a theory may be defensible as a matter of civil liability but Gellhorn's[10] language in another criminal context is equally applicable here: "It is a basic proposition in a constitutional society that crimes should be defined in advance, and not after action has been taken."[11] We are not unaware of the magnitude of the problem presented, but the new approaches demanded for its solution rest with the legislature, not the courts.

The view we have taken of the case renders it unnecessary to pass upon other allegations of error. The verdict and sentence on that count of the information dealing with involuntary manslaughter are set aside and the case remanded to the circuit court for sentencing on the verdict of the jury respecting the violation, as charged, of section 625, subd (b) of the Michigan vehicle code, discussed hereinabove.

DETHMERS, C. J., and CARR, KELLY, BLACK, EDWARDS, KAVANAGH, and SOURIS, JJ., concurred.

Footnotes

1. People v. Sobczak, 344 Mich. 465, 470.

2. Sayre, Criminal Responsibility for the Acts of Another, 43 Harv. L Rev. 689, 717.

3. 57 App. DC 3 (16 F2d 342, 53 ALR 246).

4. 57 App. DC 4.

5. CLS 1956, Sec. 257.625, subd (a) (Stat Ann 1960 Rev Sec. 9.2325, subd (a)).

6. CLS 1956, Sec. 257.625, subd (b) (Stat Ann 1957 Cum Supp Sec. 9.2325, subd (b). By PA 1958, No 113, a third and subsequent offense under this section becomes a felony (Stat Ann 1960 Rev Sec. 9.2325 subd (e)).

7. CLS 1956, Sec. 257.625, subd (b) (Stat Ann 1960 Rev Sec. 9.2325, subd (b)).

8. "(c) Any person who is convicted of a violation of paragraph (a) or (b) of this section shall be punished by imprisonment in the county jail or Detroit House of correction for not more than 90 days or by a fine of not less than $50 nor more than $100 or both such fine and imprisonment in the discretion of the court, together with costs of the prosecution.
"On a second or subsequent conviction under this section or a local ordinance substantially corresponding thereto, he shall be guilty of a misdemeanor and punished by imprisonment for not more than 1 year, and, in the discretion of the court, a fine of not more than $1,000."

9. "Any person who shall commit the crime of manslaughter shall be guilty of a felony punishable by imprisonment in the State prison, not more than 15 years or by fine of not more than 7,500 dollars, or both, at the discretion of the court." (CL 1948, Sec. 750.321 (Stat Ann 1954 Rev Sec. 28.553)).

10. Gellhorn, American Rights, 85,86.

11. See US Const., art 1, Sec. 9, 10; Mich Const 1908, art 2, sec. 9. - Reporter

Note

Criminal Law-Manslaughter-Automobile
Owner's Vicarious Responsibility
7 Wayne L. Rev. 483

Defendant, in violation of a Michigan statute,[1] voluntarily surrendered his automobile keys to one he knew was intoxicated. Shortly thereafter, the drunk driver, proceeding in the wrong direction on an expressway, became involved in a two-car head-on collision in which both drivers were killed. When the fatal accident occurred defendant was at his place of residence. The jury found defendant guilty of involuntary manslaughter. On appeal, held, conviction set aside. Although guilty of a misdemeanor in permitting a drunk to drive his car, the owner was not a principal with respect to the accident and therefore was not guilty of involuntary manslaughter. People v. Marshall, 362 Mich. 170,

797

106 _N.W.2d_ 842 (1961).

The law of vicarious responsibility for criminal acts has developed at a significantly slower pace than its tort-law counterpart, the doctrine of respondeat superior.[2] None-theless, today, a person other than the driver of an auto-mobile may be liable for crimes committed by one he permits or procures to drive.[3] Further, where death is caused by a driver known to be intoxicated,[4] inexperienced,[5] or reckless,[6] the owner,[7] or passenger,[8] who sits by the side of the driver and permits him to take control of the wheel may be convicted of manslaughter,[9] or even murder.[10] Criminal responsibility in these cases is seemingly predicted on two grounds. First, that it is criminal negligence to place a dangerous instru-mentality such as an automobile in the hands of a careless or reckless driver; and second, that by the presence of the per-son providing the instrumentality, he is in a position to con-trol its operation and as such he is a party to any subsequent misconduct of the driver.[11]

The court pointed out that the distinguishing fact in the principal case was the defendant-owner's absence from the scene of the crime.[12] It would seem that their decision is based on defendant's lack of ability to control the subse-quent conduct of the driver. Although the court was willing to accept this feature as grounds for its decision, a con-trary result is supportable. Responsibility for the driver's crime should not be imposed on the defendant because he is the owner, nor because he was or was not in a position to control the driver, but rather, because he was a party to the crime. The controlling fact is that defendant author-ized the operation of his car by one he knew was intoxicated and as a direct consequence thereof, two persons were killed. Accordingly, defendant was a party to an unlawful act and under traditional common law definitions, an accessory be-fore the fact[13] to the resulting homicide.[14] Under the theory of misdemeanor-manslaughter a party to a lessor crime is likewise responsible for the resulting homicide, hence the owner should be as guilty as the driver.[15]

Relying on the proposition that one other than a common-law principal may be a party to the crime of manslaughter, several courts have sustained convictions of persons pro-viding the dangerous instrumentality causing death, notwith-standing defendant's absence from the scene of the crime. Thus, a defendant-owner who surrendered possession of his truck to an employee he knew was intoxicated has been found guilty of manslaughter for the homicide caused by the reck-lessness of the drunk driver.[16] The instant case can also be paralleled to that in which a defendant ship-owner per-mitted the operation of a steamer knowing it to have a de-fective boiler, and following a fatal explosion, he along with the captain and engineer were convicted of manslaughter;[17] or to a case where defendant voluntarily provided a gun, to a woman known by him to be drunk, which subsequently was used by the woman as an instrument causing death.[18]

The court in the principal case also speaks of criminal guilt as being based on personal fault. While this sweeping generality is basically true, it requires qualification. Most felonies require proof of a specific intent, but involuntary manslaughter by definition is the unintentional killing of another while engaged in an unlawful or criminally negligent act.[19] Since the act of killing requires no specific intent, it follows that personal fault may attach to anyone who is a participant in the unlawful or criminally negligent act in whic homicide results.[20]

In discussing the extent of vicarious liability for manslaughter it becomes necessary to consider its limitations. People v. Marshall[21] presents a case in which the owner admits knowledge of the driver's drunken condition.[22] Without this knowledge the driver should not be criminally responsible,[23] so the difficulty of proving actual knowledge in these cases will serve to defeat many prosecutions. A second limiting fact would be that of proof of causation. That is, there should be adequate proof that the homicide was a direct consequence of the owner's unlawful act, and proof of an intervening cause should be a successful defense to criminal liability.[24] And finally, the nature of the offense itself would be considered. If it is one which naturally tends to jeopardize the safety of others, responsibility should attach to all parties involved in its commission.[25]

Although the principal case appears to be one of first impression, its problems are as old as the crime of manslaughter. The uncertainty that clouds cases similar to the one here discussed seems to be the result of intermingling traditional tort and criminal law concepts. Distinctions between the two are essential, but it is believed that People v. Marshall fails, as do many of its predecessors, to succinctly define the basic differences. It would appear that the court might better have considered the case by referring to the relationship of the parties involved, defendant's causation of the resulting death, and the nature of the violation involved. With this in mind and from an analysis of the foregoing authority, it would not be too speculative to anticipate other jurisdictions arriving at contrary results if presented with the same situation.

Francis A. Jones, III

Footnotes

1. Mich. Comp. Laws Sec. 257.625 (b) (1948), Mich. Stat. Ann. Sec. 9.2325 (b) (1960). "It shall also be unlawful and punishable as provided in paragraph (c) of this section, for the owner of any motor vehicle or any person having such in charge or in control thereof to authorize or knowingly permit the same to be driven or operated upon any highway or any other place open to the general public, including any area designated for the parking of motor vehicles, within this

state by any person who is a habitual user of narcotic drugs, barbital or any derivative of barbital or any person who is under the influence of intoxicating liquor or narcotic drugs, barbital or any derivative of barbital."

2. Sayre, Criminal Responsibility for the Acts of Another, 43 Harv. L. Rev. 689, 694 (1930).

3. People v. Odom, 19 Cal. App. 2d 641, 66 P.2d (1937) (owner guilty for failure to stop at an accident even though he was not driving); State v. Stonns, 233 Iowa 655, 10 N.W.2d 53 (1943) (an owner held to be an aider-and-abettor to a drunk driving charge); State v. Cook, 149 Kan. 481, 87 P.2d 648 (1939) (all passengers in a car are principals under drunk driving statute); State v. Sarver, 134 Kan. 98 4 P.2d 440 (1931) (both driver and passenger guilty of drunk driving); Commonwealth v. Sherman, 191 Mass. 439, 78 N.E. 98 (1906) (owner as guilty as chauffeur for latter's speeding); State v. Derosia, 94 N.H. 228, 50 A.2d 231 (1946) (owner an aider-and-abettor in hit-and-run accident); State v. Gibbs, 227 N.C. 667, 44 S.E.2d 201 (1947) (both driver and owner guilty of drunk driving); James v. Commonwealthm 178 Va. 28, 16 S.E.2d 296 (1941) (owner an aider-and-abettor in hit-and-run accident).

4. Story v. United States, 16 F.2d 342 (D.C. Cir. 1926), cert. denied, 274 U.S. 739 (1927); Lewis v. State, 220 Ark. 914, 251 S.W. 2d 490 (1952); Ex parte Liotard, 47 Nev. 169, 217 Pac. 960 (1923); State v. Hopkins, 147 Wash. 198, 265 Pac. 481 (1928), cert. denied, 278 US 617 (1928), 27 Mich. L. Rev. 101 (1928), 38 Yale L.J. 392 (1928); see Annots, 59 A.L.R. 695 (1929), 53 A.L.R. 254 (1928), 30 A.L.R. 66 (1923).

5. People v. Ingersoll, 245 Mich. 530, 222 N.W. 765 (1929) (negligent homicide); Pucket v. State, 144 Neb 876, 15 N.W. 2d 63 (1944); Armstrong v. State, 48 Okla. Crim. 146, 289 Pac. 1115 (1930); see Annot., Civil and Criminal Liability of one in Charge of an Automobile Who Permits an Unlicensed Person to Operate it, 137 A.L.R. 475 (1942).

6. Moreland v. State, 164 Ga. 467, 139 S.E. 77 (1927), 41 Harv. L. Rev. 398 (1928), 23 Ill. L. Rev. 393 (1928); Miller v. State, 49 Ga. App. 683, 176 S.E. 688 (1934).

7. Supra notes 4-6; see Annot, 99 A.L.R. 756, 771 (1935).

8. Eager v. State, 325 S.W. 2d 815 (Tenn. 1959), 27 Tenn. L. Rev. 417 (1960).

9. Supra notes 4-8.

10. Berness v. State, 38 Ala. App. 1, 83 So. 2d 607 (1953); State v. Trott, 190 N.C. 674, 130 S.E. 627 (1925); Brewer v. State, 140 Tex. Crim. 9, 143 S.W. 2d 599 (1940).

11. Supra notes 4-8. For application of a conspiracy theory in homicide, applied to all parties participating in highway races, see Jones v. Commonwealth, 247 S.W. 2d 517 (Ky. 1952); State v. Fair, 209 S.C. 439, 40 S.E. 2d 634

(1946). Contra, People v. Lemieux, 176 Misc. 305, 27 N.Y. S.2d 235 (1941).

12. People v. Marshall, 362 Mich. 170, 172, 106 N.W. 2d 842, 843.

13. An accessory before the fact was one who, being absent at the time the crime was committed, assisted, procured, counseled, incited, induced or encouraged another to commit it. People v. Owen, 241 Mich. 111, 216 N.W. 434 (1927). Under older law an accessory before the fact could not be charged or tried as such until the principal was convicted. 1 Wharton, Criminal Law Sec. 269, 276 (12th ed. 1932). It would seem to follow that the defendant in the principal case could never have been tried as an accessory before the fact. But see Regina v. Gaylor, 7 Cox. Crim. Cas. 253 (1857).

14. Early decisions frequently stated the proposition that one could not be an accessory before the fact to manslaughter. Bibithes Case, 4 Coke 43b (K.B. 1597); Adams v. State, 65 Ind. 565 (1879); State v. Robinson, 12 Wash. 349, 41 Pac. 51 (1895). A number of subsequent cases, however, held the reason for precluding the possibility of an accessory before the fact did not apply to involuntary manslaughter. State v. McVay, 47 R.I. 292, 132 Atl. 436 (1926), 40 Harv. L. Rev. 321 (1927), 25 Mich. L. Rev. 72 (1926), Annot., 44 A.L.R. 576 (1926). Today a number of states have enacted statutes abolishing the distinctions between accessories and principals; nonetheless it often becomes necessary in applying these statutes to refer to common law rules to determine liability. See, e.g., People v. Owen, supra note 13.

15. 1 Wharton, Criminal Law and Procedure, Sec. 254 (12th ed. 1957); Sayre, supra note 2, at 703, 704.

16. Stacy v. State, 228 Ark. 260, 306 S.W.2d 852 (1957). This case is not precisely in point, however, because the court also found elements of control in that the defendant-owner was following the truck in his car. The phrase "sits by the driver" used as a reference to the owner's presence in Story v. United States, supra note 4, was construed by the Arkansas court to include one who was in the near vicinity of the accident. It is felt, however, that if the court was willing to go this far, they might well find that one who gives his keys to a drunk driver and remains home "sits by the driver" within the same construction of the Story case. See Note, 12 Ark. L. Rev. 402 (1958). But see People v. Rauch, 252 App. Div. 795, 299 N.Y. Supp. 155 (1937) in which a manslaughter conviction of an automobile owner who permitted an employee to use his car knowing it had defective brakes was reversed. For a Note approving the trial court's conviction see 46 Yale L.J. 1411 (1937).

17. State v. McVay, supra note 14.

18. McCoy v. State, 50 Ga. App. 54, 176 S.E. 912 (1934).

19. 1 Wharton, Criminal Law and Procedure, Sec. 289 (12th

ed. 1957).

20. Note, 23 Ill. L. Rev. 393 (1928).

21. 362 Mich. 170, 106 N.W. 2d 842 (1961).

22. Although defendant's counsel raised a question as to
the admissibility of statements made by the defendant to the
police in this matter, the evidence was admitted at the trial
and was not discussed in the court's question.

23. Lash v. State, 97 Ga. App. 622, 103 S.E. 2d 653 (1958);
State v. Spruill, 214 N.C. 123, 198 S.E. 611 (1938); State
v. Creech, 210 N.C. 700, 188 S.W. 316 (1936).

24. In People v. Pavlic, 227 Mich. 562, 199 N.W. 373 (1924),
defendant illegally sold liquor to one who subsequently died,
but the court found that he was not guilty of involuntary
manslaughter because it appeared that it was the drinking of
the liquor followed by several days of severe exposure that
caused the death. Thus, while defendant's unlawful act might
have contributed to the death it was not the direct cause.
See also Sayre, supra note 2, at 705-708; see Annots., 35
A.L.R. 741 (1924), 15 A.L.R. 244 (1921).

25. Some courts hold that there is no criminal responsibility
for the homicide unless defendant's act was malum in se and
not merely malum prohibitum. 1 Wharton, Criminal Law and
Procedure, Sec. 254 (12th ed. 1957). It is believed, however,
that distinctions between acts malum in se and malum prohibitum are unnecessary. Responsibility for homicide might
better be applied where death results from the violation of
a statute intended and designed to prevent injury to the person. People v. Mitchell, 27 Cal. 2d 278, 166 P.2d 10 (1946);
Commonwealth v. Samson, 130 Pa. Super. 65, 196 Atl. 564 (1938).

5. Final Draft - Michigan Revised Criminal Code

(Manslaughter)

Sec. 2010. (1) A person commits the crime of manslaughter if:

    (a) He recklessly causes the death of, another person; or
    (b) He commits a criminal abortion, as defined in sec-
tion 7015, on a female and thereby causes her death; or
    (c) He intentionally causes or aids another person to
commit suicide; or
    (d) He causes the death of another person under the in-
fluence of extreme mental or emotional disturbance as defined in section 2005 (2).

    (2) Manslaughter is a Class B felony.

Committee Commentary

Section 2010 is a modified version of New York Revised

Penal Law, Sec. 125.15. Its relationship to existing law
is discussed in the Commentary to Sec. 2006 to 2015.

PROBLEM

Defendants had an argument in their home and in an attempt
to keep the defendant husband from leaving the house defendant
wife threatened to place their infant daughter behind the car
on the driveway. The defendant wife had done this on prior
occasions and had thereby induced her husband to remain at home.
As defendant husband left the house his wife followed him with
the baby in her arms and after he entered the automobile she
either placed or threw the baby behind the wheels of the car.
The defendant husband opened the car door and observed the baby
as he was backing out. He continued out the driveway after running over the infant's head and drove a short distance away
before returning to the house. Defendant husband took the baby
to a doctor and upon examination disclosed a skull fracture
and an absence of brain matter.

The defendant husband made a statement to the police which in
part was as follows: "She went to the back of the car with the
baby in her arms. I didn't think she was going to do it. The
motor was running and the car was in motion. I saw her when
she tossed the baby. I felt the bump when I hit. It was too
late to stop then so I kept on going."

The defendant wife signed a statement admitting the basic
facts set forth herein.

As the investigating police officer, what crime will you
seek to prove against the defendant wife? What crime will you
seek to prove against the defendant husband? Should they both
be convicted of the same offense. See People v. Jackson, 1
Mich. App. 207.

C. Negligent Homicide

1. Michigan Compiled Laws (1948)

750.324 Negligent homicide; penalty

Sec. 324. Any person who, by the operation of any
vehicle upon any highway or upon any other property, public
or private, at an immoderate rate of speed or in a careless,
reckless or negligent manner, but not wilfully or wantonly,
shall cause the death of another, shall be guilty of a misdemeanor, punishable by imprisonment in the state prison not
more than 2 years or by a fine of not more than $2,000.00,
or by both such fine and imprisonment. As amended P.A. 1965,
No. 38, Sec. 1, Eff. March 31, 1966.

750.325 Same; manslaughter where due to operation of motor
           vehicle

Sec. 325. The crime of negligent homicide shall be deemed

to be included within every crime of manslaughter charged to have been committed in the operation of any vehicle, and in any case where a defendant is charged with manslaughter committed in the operation of any vehicle, if the jury shall find the defendant not guilty of the crime of manslaughter, it may render a verdict of guilty of negligent homicide. As amended P.A. 1965, No. 38, Sec. 1, Eff. March 31, 1966.

750.326 Immoderate speed not dependent on legal speed

Sec. 326. IMMODERATE SPEED NOT DEPENDENT ON LEGAL RATE OF SPEED - In any prosecution under the 2 next preceding sections, whether the defendant was driving at an immoderate rate of speed shall not depend upon the rate of speed fixed by law for operating such vehicle.

281.677 Negligent homicide; penalty

Sec. 27. Any person who, by the operation of any vessel at an immoderate rate of speed or in a careless, reckless or negligent manner, but not wilfully or wantonly, shall cause the death of another, shall be guilty of a misdemeanor, punishable by imprisonment in the state prison for not more than 2 years or by a fine of not more than $2,000.00 or by both such fine and imprisonment.

281.678 Same; included in charge of manslaughter

Sec. 28. The crime of negligent homicide shall be deemed to be included within every crime of manslaughter charged to have been committed in the operation of any vessel, and in any case where a defendant is charged with manslaughter committed in the operation of any vessel, if the jury finds the defendant not guilty of the crime of manslaughter, the jury may render a verdict of negligent homicide.

2. Definition and General Elements of the Offense

People v. Campbell
237 Mich. 424

MCDONALD J. The defendant was convicted of negligent homicide by the operation of an automobile at an immoderate rate of speed and in a careless, reckless and negligent manner, contrary to the provisions of Act No. 98, Pub. Acts 1921 (Comp. Laws Supp. 1922, Sec. 15226 (2-4)).
After dark, in the early evening of January 31, 1926, he was driving an automobile from the city of Grand Haven in Ottawa county to the village of Spring Lake. Crossing the bridge over Grand river, his way led around a curve on to trunk line M 16. While making this curve, he ran down and

804

instantly killed Sidney Braak and his wife, Rosalin Braak, who were walking in the highway. The defendant was alone in his car and was the only eyewitness to the accident. The night was dark and misty. He testiled (sic) that he was driving about 20 miles an hour and that, though he was watching the road, he did not see them until he came upon them, and it was then too late to turn or stop his car and avoid hitting them.

The people claim that he was driving at an immoderate rate of speed under the circumstances; that he was not keeping a proper look out for pedestrians; and that he did not have his car under such control that he could stop it within the range of his lights.

The first assignment of error which we will discuss raises the question as to the degree of negligence necessary to constitute the offense named in the statute under which the defendant was prosecuted. On the trial, counsel for the defense claimed that to establish the crime the people must prove something more than ordinary negligence, and requested the court to so charge the jury. The request was denied and the jury were instructed, in substance, that the defendant was guilty if he did not use ordinary care.

In their brief, counsel's argument leads to the conclusion that,

"To prove the statutory offense of negligent homicide by the operation of a vehicle, it is necessary to show gross negligence in the sense of very great negligence, or gross failure to exercise proper care; a failure to exercise even slight care."

In this State, under the common law, one is not criminally responsible for death from negligence unless the negligence is so great that the law can impute a criminal intent. If death ensues from negligence which shows a culpable indifference to the safety of others, the negligence is said to be gross or wanton or wilful, and is equivalent to criminal intent, a necessary element of every common-law crime. One whose acts cause death under such circumstances is guilty of involuntary manslaughter or common-law negligent homicide. See People v. Barnes, 182 Mich. 179.

By the enactment of this statute the legislature of 1921 obviously intended to create a lesser offense than involuntary manslaughter or common-law negligent homicide, where the negligent killing was caused by the operation of a vehicle. To do this it eliminated, as necessary elements of the lesser offense, negligence classed as wanton or wilful. Included in these terms is gross negligence. So that in the enactment of the statute there was expressly eliminated, as elements of the crime, all negligence of such character as to evidence a criminal intent; and as we have before pointed out, wanton or wilful or gross negligence was of that character. Therefore, this statute was intended to apply only to cases where the negligence is of a lesser degree than gross negligence.

According to the classification of degrees of negligence by courts and text-book writers, all negligence below that called gross is slight negligence and ordinary negligence. Slight negligence is never actionable either in the civil or criminal law and is not so under this statute. Ordinary negligence is based on the fact that one ought to have known the results of his acts; while gross negligence rests on the assumption that he did know but was recklessly or wantonly indifferent to the results. The common law makes one guilty of the latter degree of negligence criminally responsible; and probably in view of the numerous fatalities caused by the operation of automobiles on our streets and highways, the legislature was led to enact a statute making one criminally responsible for a lower degree of negligence, for any negligence between slight and gross. Terms and classification of negligence are confusing. But, regardless of that, the basic idea of this statute is that every one who places himself in a situation where his acts may affect the safety of others must use every reasonable precaution to guard against injuring them. If he does not do so, and death ensues, he is guilty of negligent homicide under this statute. It is a harsh statute, but finds justification in the serious results that are liable to follow the negligent operation of automobiles on extensively traveled streets and highways. The court did not err in refusing defendant's request to charge and in instructing the jury that death resulting from ordinary negligence constituted an offense under this statute.

Further, it is urged by defendant's counsel that the doctrine of contributory negligence applies to relieve one of criminal responsibility under this statute. The court refused to instruct the jury in accordance with counsel's view, and in that they say he erred. There is some conflict in the authorities on this question, but we think that the great weight of authority sustains the action of the trial court in holding that contributory negligence of the deceased is not a defense in such cases. Such was the holding of this court in People v. Barnes, supra, wherein the rule announced in State v. Campbell, 82 Conn. 671 (74 Atl. 927, 18 Ann. St. Rep. 283), was quoted with approval, as follows:

"The rule of law concerning contributory negligence by the injured person, as a defense in civil actions for damages for personal injuries, had no application to this case. The State was required to prove the alleged unlawful act of the accused and its consequences, but not that the deceased exercised due care to avoid the consequences of that unlawful act. The court did not, either by its refusal to charge as thus requested, or by the language used, give the jury to understand, as the defendant claims it did, that the conduct of the deceased was eliminated from the case. The court properly said to the jury that the State must

806

clearly show that deceased's death was the direct result of the defendant's negligence, but that the injured man's conduct became material only as it bore upon the question of such negligence of the accused, and that if the culpable negligence of the accused was the cause of Mr. Morgan's death, the accused was responsible under the criminal law, whether Mr. Morgan's failure to use due care contributed to his injury or not."

In the Barnes Case the defendant was prosecuted for the negligent killing of one Mary Robb by the operation of an automobile. In speaking of how the contributory negligence of the deceased might be considered by the jury, this court said:

"So we say here that, while the claimed contributory negligence of Mary Robb is no defense in this case, yet it does not follow that her conduct should be eliminated from the case; it should be considered as bearing upon the claimed culpable negligence of the respondent, and the question should all the time be: Was respondent responsible under the law, whether Mary Robb's failure to use due care contributed to her injury or not?"

In the instant case the court eliminated the question from the case by instructing the jury, as a matter of law, that the deceased were not guilty of contributory negligence. In this we think he erred.

The defendant was driving six feet from the curb. The night was dark and misty. He testified that he was keeping a lookout, but that he assumed that no person would be walking out in that part of the highway where he was driving. The deceased were not crossing the highway. They were walking six feet from the curb with their backs to approaching cars. We think it was for the jury to say whether, under all of the circumstances, they were using ordinary care for their own safety in walking six feet out from the curb in a dark and misty atmosphere on an extensively traveled highway with their backs to approaching automobiles. Considering the darkness, the misty atmosphere, the slippery condition of the pavement, their position in the highway, the fact that there was a safer place to walk, and their knowledge of the fact that automobiles would be constantly overtaking them from the rear, were the deceased, at the time of the accident, using ordinary care for their own safety? If they were not, that fact would not be a defense, but it would be an important factor in the case which the defendant would be entitled to have the jury consider. Pedestrians have equal rights with automobiles in the use of the public highways. Their duties are reciprocal. The driver of an automobile has a right to assume that a pedestrian will use ordinary care for his own safety, and any assumption that he has a right to indulge in may be considered by the jury with the other facts in determining his negligence. Pedestrians

in a public highway have a right to assume that the driver
of an automobile will use ordinary care for their protection,
but they may not rest content on that assumption and take no
care for their own safety. Some of my Brethren are of the
opinion that the decedents cannot be said to have been guilty
of contributory negligence, because they had a legal right
to walk any place in the highway, because they had a right
to walk where they were walking at the time of the accident.
It is rather a question of prudence than of legal right. One
may have a right to amble all over a highway, but a man of
ordinary prudence would hardly do so when it is filled with
moving automobiles. It is a matter of common knowledge that
at the present time a highway extensively traveled is a
place of greater danger than a railroad track. With this
knowledge, a pedestrian must be held to exercise a reasonable degree of care for his protection. Were the decedents
exercising such care for their safety under the conditions
existing at the time of the accident? The particular circumstances of the occasion made the question one for the
jury.

Complaint is made that in his charge to the jury the
court called attention to numerous provisions of the motor-
vehicle law, none of which was applicable to any facts in
the case. He instructed the jury as to the care an operator of an automobile should use, and the proper speed at
which the car should be driven in approaching an intersecting highway, bridge, dam, sharp curve or steep descent,
and in traversing an intersecting highway, bridge, dam,
sharp curve or steep descent. There is no evidence that
the defendant violated these provisions of the law, but,
though it was in no way applicable to the facts in the
case, we are not convinced that the jury was confused or
misled by the instruction. But the situation was different in regard to the effect of the instruction as to the
legal rate of speed in cities. Mr. Jorgensen, a witness for
the people, had been permitted to testify as to the rate of
speed the defendant had driven his car in the business section of the city of Grand Haven just before the accident.
So when the court instructed the jury that the driver of
an automobile should not operate it at a greater rate of
speed than 15 miles an hour in the business portion of a
city, he emphasized the fact that the defendant had violated the law shortly before the accident, and at a point
remote from it. The testimony of the witness as to the
rate of speed the defendant was driving in the business
section of the city of Grand Haven was neither material
nor competent. It should have been excluded. Standing
alone it might not have seriously prejudiced the defendant's case. Standing alone, the judge's charge in respect
to the permissible speed in cities might not have misled
the jury; but coupled with the incompetent testimony we
think it constitutes reversible error.

For the reasons indicated the judgment of conviction

is reversed and a new trial granted.

BIRD, SNOW, FELLOWS, and CLARK, JJ., concurred with McDONALD, J.

WIEST, J. (dissenting). The opinion prepared by Mr. Justice McDONALD does not meet with my approval.

Act No. 98, Pub. Acts 1921 (Comp. Laws Supp. 1922, Sec. 15226 (2-4)), defines a crime of lesser degree than manslaughter and denominates it negligent homicide. That act provides:

"Every person who, by the operation of any vehicle at an immoderate rate of speed or in a careless, reckless or negligent manner, but not wilfully or wantonly, shall cause the death of another, shall be guilty of the crime of negligent homicide. . . .

"In any prosecution under this act, whether the defendant was driving at an immoderate rate of speed shall be a question of fact for the jury and shall not depend upon the rate of speed fixed by law for operating such vehicle."

This statute is plain, and application of its provisions to defendant's testimony of how the accident happened established his guilt. The statute rests guilt upon ordinary negligence, involves no intent and excludes need of establishing gross, wilful or wanton negligence or acts malum in se. It leaves questions of whether the rate of speed was immoderate or operation of the vehicle careless, reckless or negligent to depend upon the particular circumstances of each case. It is an innovation in the law of homicide, departs from the doctrines of common-law manslaughter and carries its own yardstick for measuring culpability. In some States a similar culpability is fixed and accountability exacted under statutes defining manslaughter in the fourth degree. Decisions relative to such degree of manslaughter are helpful, but decisions relative to voluntary or involuntary manslaughter, as at common law, afford no help, for they involve considerations not at all applicable under the provisions of this statute. In manslaughter the negligence of the operator of an automobile must be something more than ordinary negligence. As stated, this statute provides for an offense of lesser degree than manslaughter, for it admits, in case of acquittal of manslaughter, of a conviction of negligent homicide. The wilful, wanton and culpable negligence involved in manslaughter are all eliminated in a prosecution under this statute, for it plants negligent homicide upon ordinary negligence causing the death of a human being. In manslaughter it has been held that the negligence must be something more in degree than is sufficient to afford a right of action for damages. In negligent homicide the negligence need be no more than that ordinarily involved in an action for damages.

The law seeks to reach a consequence altogether too frequent under careless driving and to fill a gap through which those guilty of killing a human being too often avoided accountability. With the policy of the law we have no concern, but with its due administration we are much concerned.

Defendant drove his automobile upon and killed two persons walking in the highway. Under his own testimony he was guilty of negligent homicide. The accident happened about 7 o'clock in the evening of January 31, 1926. Defendant testified:

"The pavement was damp and wet that night and it was misty and dark, . . . Just before I started to turn this curve my lights were shining directly in front of me. . . . The curve to the right in the road, or anything on there was not visible to me or within the range of my lights until I had turned my car in that direction. Just as I did turn and started around this curve I hit the people pretty near as soon as I saw them. . . . I was driving about five or six feet from the curb. I could not say how quickly I saw them after I started to make the turn beyond the Three Point Garage. It was just when I saw them I hit them, that was all. I do not know whether they had been walking in the road before or only just come onto the road at that point. I haven't any idea of the facts. As I swung around the curve they were suddenly there in front of me and I struck them almost instantly. I did not have any time either to turn or stop, after seeing them. . . . I cannot explain the accident, how it happened, except the lights to the left of me, at the Three Point Garage, and not seeing to the right of me on account of there not being very much spread of the lights, and I turned to the right and they were there. It was dark on the right side while the bright lights of the garage were over on the left side of the road. I was not driving fast. I judge 20 miles an hour. . . .

"As I went by the garage I could see ahead about 15 feet. I probably could stop my car in 15 feet at the rate at which I was going. When these people were within 15 feet of me I did not see them, I don't believe I did. My lights would show up these people that far, if they were trained on them. They were not trained on them directly, I believe. They were trained straight ahead. I was going to make a curve. It was just previous to making the curve. My lights were shining ahead of me before I made the curve, my lights were not trained on them as I hit them. I could see 15 feet ahead of the car. These people were ahead of my car after I turned. When I made the curve then I saw them. I couldn't say how far ahead of me they were when I saw them. I saw them just as I hit them. . . . At some moment, or second before, I struck these people, I remember I did see them. I couldn't say if they were walking or standing still. I don't know; they were walking towards Spring Lake. I don't believe they saw me at all before I struck them. Before I hit them I don't believe they knew I was there. I did not blow my horn. I was driving with my eyesight blurred. I could see where I was going straight ahead of me but turning to the right I couldn't see where my car was going very well, I did not sound my horn so that I could warn any one that was ahead of me where I couldn't see. Those people were struck by my car without any warning at all. I do not know at what point I was when I struck them. Whether it was in front of the Three Point Garage or not, I do not know. . . . Neither one turned their face towards me when I hit them. . . . I was turning to the right when I hit them, making the curve. As I made the curve that night I did not blow my horn and gave no warning of my approach at all. I could not see very well. It was misty. . . . The spot light was not burning. I don't believe it was in good condition. . . . My judgment is I was going about 20 miles an hour. I think that is the same as I had been driving all the time since I left home. I slowed down a little bit on account of the glare of the lights. I don't remember whether the brakes held or not."

Under defendant's testimony there was no issue of contributory negligence on the part of the pedestrians, and it would have been a mockery of the rights of the people and the due course of justice to have injected such an issue. The only asserted negligence on the part of the persons killed was their walking in the highway with the traffic. Negligence on the part of the persons killed, if any, was no defense. Contributory negligence has no place in the law of crimes. State v. Gray, 180 N.C. 697 (104 S.E. 647); State v. Miller (Or.), 243 Pac. 72; State v. Hanahan, 111 S.C. 58 (96 S.E. 667); Bowen v. State, 100 Ark. 232, (140 S.W. 28); Lauterbach v. State, 132 Tenn. 603 (179 S.W. 130); State v. Weisengoff, 85 W. Va. 271 (101 S.E. 450); State v. Elliott, 94 N.J. Law, 76 (110 Atl. 135); Thornton v. State (Ala.App.), 108 South. 80.
The rule is well settled that contributory negligence on the part of the person killed is no defense. However, defendant's conduct complained of must be viewed in the light of all its attendant circumstances in order to determine whether his act was the cause of the killing, but for no other purpose. Of course, there must be a causal connection established between the negligence of defendant and the killing, but when this is made to appear the issue admits of no consideration of concurrent negligence beyond the purpose we have stated.
In Schultz v. State, 89 Neb. 34 (130 N.W. 972, 33 L.R.A. (N.S.) 403), a manslaughter case, it was said of contributory negligence:

"The State was required to prove the alleged unlawful act of the accused and its consequences, but not that the deceased exercised due care to avoid the consequences of the unlawful act. The authorities are not in conflict as to this question. Uniformly the courts have said a man will not be excused for killing another, even though his victim was negligent. While contributory negligence is a complete defense to an action for private injury resulting from homicide, it is no defense to a prosecution for a public wrong.

21 Am. & Eng. Enc. Law (2d Ed.), 195. We think the refusal of this instruction (contributory negligence) was clearly right for the further reason that the evidence disclosed no theory upon which such an instruction could be predicated."

In Maxon v. State, 177 Wis. 379 (187 N.W. 753, 21 A.L.R. 1484), the charge was manslaughter. In the opinion it was said:

"It is further urged on defendant's behalf that the evidence in this case warrants or requires a determination to the effect that the deceased was himself guilty of negligence in his management of the motorcycle to such an extent that he should be held to have proximately contributed to the collision, and that such contributing negligence by him may be successfully interposed as a bar to this prosecution, as much so as it might or could be in a civil action against him for the resultant damages.

"In a criminal prosecution such as this by the State, in which a defendant is charged with the taking of a human life, the fact that deceased may have in a measure, by his own carelessness, contributed to the unfortunate result cannot be recognized as a defense. The reason is plain, owing to the substantial difference between a criminal action prosecuted on behalf of the State and a civil action instituted to recover the damages resulting from the same accident. While no doubt the entire circumstances surrounding the killing are proper for the consideration of the jury in determining whether or not the defendant was negligent, yet his criminal negligence, if it exists, cannot be wiped out by the fact that the deceased was also negligent."

Negligent homicide, within the meaning of this statute, involves no element of gross or wilful negligence, and the killing could not in any event be adjudged a mere misadventure, if occasioned by the careless, reckless, or negligent operation of the automobile by the accused.

The statute (1 Comp. Laws 1915, Sec. 4818) provides:

"Upon approaching a person walking in the roadway of a public highway, . . . a person operating a motor vehicle shall slow down to a speed not exceeding ten miles an hour and give reasonable warning of his approach and use every reasonable precaution to insure the safety of such person.". . .

This statute fully recognizes the right of persons to walk in the roadway of a public highway, and its mandate of care to be exercised by operators of motor vehicles is to safeguard pedestrians. Defendant did not slow down and gave no warning of his approach because he did not discover the pedestrians in time to do so. He did not see the pedestrians until just as he struck them because he had no view of the roadway. This will be discussed later.

The statute (Comp. Laws Supp. 1922 Sec. 4817) provides:

"No person shall operate a motor vehicle upon a public

812

highway at a rate of speed greater than is reasonable and proper, having regard to the traffic and use of the highway, or so as to endanger the life or limb of any person." . . .

This statute speaks no uncertain language. State v. Schaeffer, 96 Ohio St. 215 (117 N.E. 220, L.R.A. 1918B, 945, Ann. Cas. 1918E, 1137). In that case it was said:

"'Safety first' must not be sacrificed for 'speed first.'. . .
"The day has long been here when the authorities should exercise every power under every law of the State to protect the safety of the public, its life, its limb; and in order to meet every possible situation of danger, some such general, comprehensive and elastic statute as section 12603 is absolutely necessary.
"The careful, conservative driver need have no fear of it, and the reckless, wanton speed-maniac needs to be kept in fear of it."

The Ohio statute mentioned is like ours. Civil accountability is but a slight deterrent; it may be met by insurance. As yet criminal accountability may not be so met. Under the circumstances detailed by defendant the speed of his car was unreasonable and reckless, for he could not see the roadway.
As said in Lauterbach v. State, supra:

"One who disobeys the statutory rule as to speed is acting in defiance of law, and must be held to have anticipated the possibility of any injury caused by his recklessness."

No person may operate a vehicle on a public highway and omit reasonable care on the assumption that there are no pedestrians also using the highway. At night the operator of an automobile must have a light showing the path he is to travel and sufficient to disclose the presence of pedestrians using the same roadway. It is manifest that the lights on defendant's car did not show the roadway because of the curve in the road. He, therefore, came upon the pedestrians with his eyes, as it were, blindfolded. He was aware of the curve in the road, and must be held to have known that, in making the curve, his lights would not show him the roadway. Ordinary prudence required him to slow down to a speed where he could stop if need presented itself, no matter how sudden. Defendant's claim that he was blinded by lights but intensifies his carelessness. Blinded, as he claims, he took the chance of finding the way clear and ran into the pedestrians. He was reckless in so doing. Hammond v. Morrison, 90 N.J. Law, 15 (100 Atl. 154); Osbun v. DeYoung, 99 N.J. Law, 284 (122 Atl. 809). Whether the curve in the road prevented his lamps from lighting the way or the lights of the garage obscured his vision makes no difference. If he could not see where he was going it was imperative that he either stop or slow down to a point where he could stop if need to do so presented itself.
In Hammond v. Morrison, supra, defendant

813

"attempted to excuse himself upon the ground that just before the collision the street lights which he had passed
were reflected into his eyes by the windshield of his car,
so that he was unable to see in front of him."

The court said:

"His own story demonstrates his lack of care. No man
is entitled to operate an automobile through a public
street blindfolded. When his vision is temporarily destroyed in the way which the defendant indicated, it is his duty
to stop his car, and so adjust his windshield as to prevent
its interfering with his ability to see in front of him. The
defendant, instead of doing this, took the chance of finding the way clear, and ran blindly into the trolley car behind which the decedent was standing. Having seen fit to
do this, he cannot escape responsibility if his reckless conduct results in injury to a fellow being."

It was defendant's duty to anticipate the use of the roadway by pedestrians and to keep a lookout for them, and not
to proceed if he had no view of the roadway. If his view,
was prevented by glare of lights, or because his lamps, by
reason of the curve in the road, did not light the way he
proceeded at his peril. An operator of an automobile a-
long a public highway at night is bound to anticipate the
presence of pedestrians upon it.
Hatzakorzian v. Rucker-Fuller Desk Co., 197 Cal. 82 (239
Pac. 709, 41 A.L.R. 1027), was a case for damages, but
many of the questions here presented were there decided and
we, therefore, quote from the syllabus as given in A.L.R.:

"Under a statute requiring a person driving an automobile
on a public highway to drive it in a careful and prudent
manner and at a rate of speed not greater than is reasonable
and proper, having regard to the traffic and use of the highway, a driver is negligent if, on a dark night, with a dark
roadbed, he continues to travel at 20 or 25 miles an hour
after his vision is obscured by the glare of the lights on
an approaching car, so that he could not see any object in
front of him."

(See, also to the same effect Budnick v. Peterson, 215
Mich. 678; Gleason v. Lowe, 232 Mich. 300; Holsaple v.
Supt's of Poor of Menominee Co., 232 Mich. 603.)

"Pedestrians have a right to travel anywhere upon a
public highway, and it is not negligence for them to do so."

(See, also Gibbard v. Cursan, 225 Mich. 311.)

"A pedestrian on a highway is under no legal duty to
look back or watch behind to see whether or not he is in
danger of being struck or run down by any vehicle approaching him from the rear."

(See, also, Nordman v. Mechem, 227 Mich. 86.)

"In the absence of evidence to the contrary, a pedestrian killed while walking on a public highway is presumed to have exercised at all times the requisite degree and amount of care for his own safety and preservation."

(See, also, Petersen v. Lundin, 236 Mich. 590.)

"One driving an automobile along a public highway at night is bound to anticipate the presence of pedestrians upon it."

(See, also, Southall v. Smith, 151 La. 967 (92 South 402, 27 A.L.R. 1194); 2 R.C.L. p. 1184.)

The common-law rule is that pedestrians have a right to walk anywhere upon a public highway. An exercise of this right is in no sense evidence of negligence. There is no rule of law requiring pedestrians on a public highway to walk with or against vehicular regulations. The law of the road is not strictly applicable as between vehicles and pedestrians, the latter having a right to walk on any part of the road. 29 C. J. p. 650.

In Darus v. West, 179 Wis. 279 (191 N.W. 506), the court stated:

"The argument of defendants' counsel is that pedestrians on a country highway must look to the rear at stated intervals of time or space to see if vehicles are coming and to keep out of their way. We are aware of no such rule of law."

In Marton v. Pickrell, 112 Wash. 117 (191 Pac. 1101, 17 A.L.R. 68), an operator of an automobile claimed a pedestrian was guilty of negligence in walking on the side of the highway facing traffic. The court, however, pointed out that the rule of the road had reference to vehicles only. Pedestrians have an undoubted right to travel in any part of a public highway in the country. Prudence may suggest the advisability of walking on the side facing traffic but no law counts it negligence to walk with the traffic. If a pedestrian walks with the traffic he is in the very position where the operator of an automobile is bound to anticipate his presence.

In Belliveau v. Bozoian, 46 R.I. 83 (125 Atl. 82), it was stated:

"It is well established that pedestrians have in general, and under reasonable restrictions as to exercise of care by them, a right to travel anywhere upon a public highway, and it is negligence for a driver of a vehicle upon a public highway to recklessly run upon a pedestrian who is standing or walking with his back toward him."

In Schock v. Cooling, 175 Mich. 313, it was said:

"It is well settled by abundant authority that it is negligence for the driver of the conveyance, having ample space to pass a pedestrian on a highway, to so guide his vehicle as to strike the latter in passing."

In the case at bar defendant had ample space to pass the
pedestrians. Why did he strike them? Because he did not
see them in time to avoid doing so. Why did he not see them?
His vision was obscured by lights along the way and his lamps
did not light the roadway because of a curve in the road. The
emergency with which defendant was confronted, when his lights
did disclose the pedestrians, arose out of his recklessness
in driving at a speed of 20 miles an hour at a point where
he had no view of the roadway.

The distinction between manslaughter and negligent homicide made by this legislation is important. The motor vehicle law establishes a rule of care to be observed and does
not confine its mandate to acts wrong in and of themselves;
it is regulatory of conduct calculated to save human life
and the negligent homicide act exacts accountability for
death occasioned by non-observance of such precautionary
provisions. Festina lente, or hasten slowly, a favorite saying of Augustus Caesar, would be a good thing for some operators of automobiles to recall when about to make a turn
where lamps do not show the way, or lights on the street
blind the vision. Ordinary care and consideration for the
rights of others requires that inconsiderate haste be not
indulged and that vigilance and care be exercised. Lamps
to light the way are not only intended to safeguard the
operator in preserving his life and limb but as well to prevent his driving over persons walking in the highway. Pedestrians are not required to surrender the whole road to
vehicles. Operators of vehicles are required to recognize
the right of pedestrians in the highway and may not drive
them into the ditch or brush them aside. Of course, pedestrians are under obligation to bring their use of the highway in reasonable accord with vehicular use.

It is stated in Elliott on Roads and Streets (4th Ed.),
Sec. 1086:

"All persons have a right to walk in a public highway
as well as to ride or drive upon it; their rights are equal,
and both footmen and drivers are required to exercise such
reasonable care and prudence as the circumstances demand."

The foremost traveler, whether on foot or in a vehicle,
is not bound to give way beyond allowing reasonable room to
pass.

If defendant had struck a vehicle at the same spot instead of pedestrians no one would question his culpability.
The pedestrians were the foremost travelers and defendant
was as reckless in running them down as he would have been
had they been in a vehicle.

We have mentioned and quoted from cases involving manslaughter and also actions in tort to show the degree of
care required by the law, under the circumstances shown by
the testimony of defendant. His testimony and the law established his guilt. The pedestrians killed were, at the
time, in the exercise of their rights and were guilty of
no negligence. To apply the rules relative to common-law

manslaughter would efface the statute. This may not be done. The statute is a valid exercise of the legislative power, and we have nothing to do with the question of whether it is wise legislation or otherwise. Under defendant's testimony there was no error committed by the court sufficient to justify a reversal.

The conviction should be affirmed.

SHARPE, C. J., and STEERE, J., concurred with WIEST, J.

People v. McMurchy
249 Mich. 147

BUTZEL, J. <u>Act No. 98, Pub. Acts 1921</u> (Comp. Laws Supp. <u>1922, Sec. 15226 (2-4)</u>), reads as follows:

"An act to define the crime of negligent homicide, when committed by the operation of a vehicle, and to prescribe penalties for said crime.

"<u>The People of the State of Michigan enact:</u>

"SECTION 1. Every person who, by the operation of any vehicle at an immoderate rate of speed or in a careless, reckless or negligent manner, but not wilfully or wantonly, shall cause the death of another, shall be guilty of the crime of negligent homicide and upon conviction shall be sentenced to pay a fine not exceeding one thousand dollars, or to undergo imprisonment in the State prison for a period not exceeding five years, or by both such fine and imprisonment in the discretion of the court.

"SEC. 2. The crime of negligent homicide shall be deemed to be included within every crime of manslaughter charged to have been committed in the operation of any vehicle, and in any case where a defendant is charged with manslaughter committed in the operation of any vehicle, if the jury shall find the defendant not guilty of the crime of manslaughter such jury may in its discretion render a verdict of guilty of negligent homicide.

"SEC. 3. In any prosecution under this act, whether the defendant was driving at an immoderate rate of speed shall be a question of fact for the jury and shall not depend upon the rate of speed fixed by law for operating such vehicle.

"Approved April 28, 1921."

The provisions of this act were considered by this court in the case of <u>People v. Campbell</u>, <u>237</u> Mich. <u>424</u>. It was held that the offense that this statute defines is homicide caused by more than slight and less than gross negligence.

This act was again under consideration by this court in the case of <u>People v. Maki</u>, <u>245</u> Mich. <u>455</u>. The court held that the information under this law should set out all facts in regard to the offense with such particularity so as to inform the accused of exactly what constituted the negligence. In the <u>Maki Case</u> the validity of the act was also questioned.

817

The decision of the lower court upholding the constitutionality of the act was affirmed, but only by an evenly divided court. The constitutionality of the act is again assailed in the present case, which comes up from the recorder's court of the city of Detroit on a writ of error.

An information was filed against respondent charging that on July 23, 1928, by operation of his automobile in a careless, reckless, and negligent manner, but not wilfully and wantonly, he caused the death of Caroline Plunkett, etc. The details of the alleged homicide are set forth with full particularity. The information states that respondent was driving at a rate of 35 miles an hour; that he did not have his automobile under control so as to be able to slow down, stop, or turn aside said automobile upon approaching pedestrians and others lawfully upon the highway and the intersecting streets; that he did not give any signal of his approach; that he did not slow down his automobile upon approaching the intersection at which Caroline Plunkett was lawfully driving her automobile and as a result thereof, in a careless, reckless, and negligent manner drove his automobile with such force and violence against the automobile driven by said Caroline Plunkett that he inflicted upon her divers injuries from which she died. The information is complete in every detail. Although it does not charge that respondent was driving at an immoderate rate of speed, considering traffic conditions at the time and place of the offense, it does show that he was negligent within the purview of the statute. . . .

The trial court stated that because of the Maki Case, doubt had arisen as to the constitutionality of the act, and for this reason a very large number of negligent homicide cases were being held for trial pending a further expression of this court. He, therefore, rendered an immediate opinion so that an appeal could be taken to this court. In a written opinion, he sustained the motion to quash, and held that the act was unconstitutional. He based his ruling on the grounds that, under this act, drivers of cars never would know whether they are guilty or not until the jury should pass upon their guilt after a fatal accident occurred; that the magistrate to whom the request for a warrant should be presented would not know whether the rate of speed employed by the vehicle that caused the fatal accident was a moderate one or not, and would be obliged to issue the warrant; that it would be mandatory for the trial judge to submit the case to the jury for the reason that the jury alone would have the right to determine whether the rate of speed was moderate or immoderate; that the accused would not know how to plead; that he would not understand the nature of the offense for which he was charged; that it gives legislative powers to the jury; that it gives the jury the power to suspend the laws governing the speed at which vehicles may be operated under the laws of the State of Michigan; that the act covers more than one subject, and that the purpose of the act is not fully set forth in the title thereof. . . .

The inclusion of the provision in regard to immoderate
speed is proper. It in no way affects the speed-limit laws,
the violation of which is punishable under the statutes regulating them. While it is permissible to drive within certain
limits of speed, the law provides that such speed must always
be at a prudent and reasonable rate and not greater than will
permit the driver to stop his car within the assured clear
distance ahead. The speed-limit law provides for the punishment for the violation of its provisions. It does not provide for the additional criminal or civil liability of one
who violates the law and in so doing commits homicide. One
may be guilty of murder and also of another crime that he
commits while in the act of murder. If a person drives at
a rate of speed forbidden by the speed-limit laws, he would
be punishable under such laws. If he commits homicide, he
may be punishable under the act defining negligent homicide.

The commonly-accepted definition of "immoderate" is: "Not
within reasonable limits." If one drives at a rate of speed
that is not reasonable, he is driving at an immoderate rate
of speed and not within reasonable limits. If under those
circumstances he kills a person, he is guilty of negligence.
The term "immoderate speed" constitutes a form of negligence,
and may result in damage to person or property. If it causes
death, it is negligent homicide. For this reason, the entire discussion in this opinion in regard to negligence is
also applicable to negligent homicide by one driving at an
immoderate rate of speed. . . .

The crime of negligent homicide, like that of involuntary
manslaughter and the many forms of crime set forth in the
Maki Case in the opinion upholding the constitutionality of
the law, is determined by the facts in each case, and the
rule to be applied to it is not a matter of conjecture but
a positive one.

We are not concerned with whether the term "negligent
homicide" was adopted as a euphemism for the more harsh
term of "involuntary manslaughter of a lesser degree." Similar standards of measurement are used to determine the respective crimes. Evidently the fear of being convicted of
the crime of involuntary manslaughter did not act as a deterrent to the large number of drivers who through negligence
less than gross have caused death. There is no doubt but
that the legislature was prompted to pass a law to curb reckless, careless, and negligent driving which caused death, in
cases where the negligence was less than gross. The reason
for the law has unfortunately been too well demonstrated
both before and since its enactment. Public records of the
Detroit police department show that the annual death rate
from automobile accidents in that city has more than doubled
during the past ten years. From January 1, 1922, to October
31, 1929, there have been 2,205 such deaths reported to the
police department. In 1926 there were 327 such deaths; in
1927 there were 325; in 1928 there were 322; and for the
first ten months of 1929, there were 294. A very large number of these deaths were caused by the negligence of automobile

drivers. This does not include the very large number of non-fatal injuries which resulted from a similar cause. The records show that the same driver has killed two persons at different times in or near Detroit. Can it be said that the State is powerless in the premises, because no code of laws or rules can be drafted that will fit a multitude of variant circumstances surrounding each case?

Justice COOLEY in People v. Roby, 52 Mich. 577, 579 (50 Am. Rep. 270), in referring to criminal manslaughter, said:

"I agree that as a rule there can be no crime without a criminal intent; but this is not by any means a universal rule. One may be guilty of the high crime of manslaughter when his only fault is gross negligence; and there are many other cases where mere neglect may be highly criminal. Many statutes which are in the nature of police regulations, as this is, impose criminal penalties irrespective of any intent to violate them; the purpose being to require a degree of diligence for the protection of the public which shall render violation impossible."

. . . One may be civilly and criminally responsible for the negligence which causes death, though there may be some factors that would discharge one from liability for civil negligence. The method of determining negligence in both instances is the same. There is no code of rules that fits each and every case of civil negligence.

Dean Green in his article on The Negligence Issue, in 37 Yale Law Journal, 1029, says:

"It would be futile for the law to attempt to deal in detail by way of precise anticipatory rule with each of the infinite number of cases which can be classified as 'negligence' cases. The number of such situations in which the quality of conduct can be measured by standards stated in terms of conduct is relatively small. The torrents of pertinent factors incident to any wholesale attempt along this line are beyond classification and statement. The qualities of personality are themselves numerous; their shadings are countless; the conduct of individuals is incalculable at present in its variety; the possible combinations of these are literally infinite, as infinite as space and time. The number of instances of conduct which could be labelled either as negligent or nonnegligent is beyond the limits of any catalog the law can make. So it is not surprising that in the face of infinity the law does exactly what other sciences do in like situations. It adopts a formula; a formula in terms which will permit its problems to be reduced to a graspable size. This formula, like many other formulas, tends quickly to become ritual and it would seem that it is only this ritual which holds the law's interest. This much it insists upon rigorously, but this is as far as the law's science goes in this direction. It seems to have no interest in the 'physical, mental and moral' qualities and characteristics of personality as such, nor

820

in the qualities and characteristics of the 'ordinary prudent
person.' And while it is intellectually stimulating to inquire into the intelligence, experience, powers of memory,
observation, co-ordination, the reaction time, self-control,
courage, skill, ad infinitum, which the law might require of
defendants, such inquiry is rendered utterly without profit
for the purposes of determining the negligent conduct of any
particular defendant in any particular case. The law does
not make any attempt to require any of them in any one or
more combinations. A formula in these terms has not been
written which can be relied on to fit a single defendant in
a single case."

As stated in this article, no precise anticipatory rules
can be laid down that will govern with particularity each
and every case of criminal or civil negligence. Negligence
can only be defined by general rules. It consists of a want
of reasonable care or in the failure of duty which a person
of ordinary prudence should exercise under all the existing
circumstances in view of the probably injury. . . .
The very same evidentiary facts required to prove civil
liability for negligence may be used to prove criminal liability. It is true that there may be certain defenses as
contributory negligence, etc., which would discharge one
from civil liability but not from criminal liability. . . .
The definition of negligence and of its various grades
has come down to us through a multitude of decisions, and
is neither vague, uncertain, or indefinite. The one opinion
in the Maki Case adverse to the constitutionality of the law
contains excerpts from decisions in numerous cases. A reading of these decisions dispels the doubts as to the constitutionality of the statute here under consideration. . . .

(In a lengthy discussion the court rejected the argument
that the statute was unconstitutional.)

In this discussion of the law of negligence, we have considered the constitutional objections raised. The negligent homicide law does not suspend or repeal existing statutes governing the operation of automobiles; it does not
deprive one of life, liberty, or property without due process of law; it is not an ex post facto law, and the law of
any particular cause can be declared or known before the
offense described in the act has been committed; it does
not delegate legislative powers to the jury, or give a judicial department of the government any legislative powers.
With the words "shall be a question of fact for the jury"
eliminated, the act is valid and constitutional.
The order of the lower court quashing the indictment and
discharging the prisoner is set aside. The lower court is
directed to proceed to try the respondent under the indictment.

WIEST, C. J., and CLARK, SHARPE, and NORTH, JJ., concurred with BUTZEL, J.

821

McDONALD and POTTER, JJ., concurred in the result.
(Concurring opinion of Justice FEAD omitted.)

People v. Robinson
253 Mich. 507

McDONALD, J. The defendant was convicted on a charge of
negligent homicide arising out of the operation of an automobile upon a public highway in such a manner as to cause
the death of one John Hanold.

The people's testimony tends to show that on the evening
of May 17, 1929, the defendant, in company with John Hanold
and another young man, attended a dance near Benton Harbor,
Michigan, where they remained until two o'clock in the morning. While there they drank some beer. The defendant says
he had about three glasses. When the dance was over they
drove to Muskegon. There they loitered about visiting
friends until four o'clock in the afternoon, when they started for home. They drank beer before leaving. On the way
home defendant was driving. He got on the wrong side of the
road and collided with a car approaching from the opposite
direction. In the collision John Hanold was killed.

The theory of the defense is expressed in the following
request to charge:

"You are instructed that if the respondent, Maurice
Robinson, was tired, worn out, and lost consciousness by
falling suddenly to sleep and the impact or collision occurred in consequence thereof, then your verdict should be
not guilty in this case. You are instructed in view of the
previous language that the negligent homicide statute (3
Comp. Laws 1929, Sec. 16743-16745) is predicated on negligence; or, in other words, a failure to use care and caution
that the ordinary prudent man would use and that where the
cause was brought about by the respondent's falling to sleep
on account of being worn out and weariness and in consequence thereof suddenly falls asleep, then there can be no
negligence within the meaning of the negligent homicide
statute, and your verdict should be not guilty. In other
words, if the sole proximate cause of the collision in this
case was caused by the respondent being worn out, fatigued
and losing consciousness by falling asleep, then there is
no criminal negligence."

This request is not a correct statement of the law in
regard to the negligence of one falling asleep while driving an automobile. He may not always be chargeable with
negligence for what he does while asleep, but the rule is
different where he voluntarily puts himself in such a physical condition that he cannot stay awake. The danger of
driving an automobile on the highways by one who is not in
possession of his faculties is a matter of common knowledge.

822

This defendant knew that he had been going without sleep, that he had been drinking that which would disturb his faculties, and that he was not in a fit condition to drive a car. An ordinarily prudent man would have known it. An ordinarily prudent man would have known that this or some other accident would probably happen while driving in that condition. So, under the circumstances as shown by his own evidence, the defendant was negligent in falling asleep. He was negligent in trying to drive a car when a man of ordinary prudence would have known it was not safe for him to do so. It was negligent for him to drive when he was weary and sleepy. It was his duty to stop driving until he had overcome his weariness and regained control of his faculties. The court did not err in refusing to submit the defendant's theory on the question of negligence. The evidence sustains the jury's finding. . . .

The judgment of conviction is affirmed, and the case remanded with directions to enter proper judgment.

BUTZEL, C. J., and CLARK, SHARPE, NORTH, and FEAD, JJ., concurred with McDONALD, J.

(Concurring opinion of Justice WIEST omitted.)

People v. Good
287 Mich. 110

BUSHNELL, J. Defendant Good was convicted of a violation of the homicide statute, the same being section 324 of the Michigan penal code, Act No. 328, Pub. Acts 1931 (Stat. Ann. Sec. 28.556). This statute reads:

"Any person who, by the operation of any vehicle at an immoderate rate of speed or in a careless, reckless or negligent manner, but not wilfully or wantonly, shall cause the death of another, shall be guilty of a felony, punishable by imprisonment in the State prison not more than five years or by a fine of not more than two thousand five hundred dollars."

Appellant's statement of facts is accepted by the people. At about 11:30 p.m., Good, who was employed as a night watchman, on his way to work, was driving north on Mt. Elliot avenue in the city of Detroit. He drove up behind a street car, which was waiting for a stop light, two blocks south of Farnsworth. When the signal changed, Good drove alongside the car as it started up and passed it. About half a block south of Farnsworth avenue, Good observed an automobile parked at the curb; he turned to the left to avoid it and drove through an unprotected safety zone, which was merely outlined on the pavement, striking Mrs. MacKenzie, who was standing therein with her 17-year-old daughter. Mrs. MacKenzie's body was thrown ahead of Good's car and she died about an hour later

823

in the Receiving Hospital. Good's lights and brakes, according to his testimony, were working well, and his windshield was clean. He was 52 years old, had been continuously employed at the same place of business for the last 13 years, except when it was shut down, and was a man of good character. After Good's conviction by the jury, the court ordered that he be placed upon probation for a term of five years under the following conditions:

"1. That said defendant shall not operate a motor vehicle.
"2. That said defendant shall make restitution in the sum of $385 payable as determined by the probation department, and any further sum later imposed by the court.
"3. That said defendant shall be committed to the Detroit house of correction and therein confined for a term of three months. It is hereby ordered by the court, that said term be suspended until the terms of probation are violated."

Two questions are raised in this appeal:
1. Appellant Good complains of the following instruction:

"If you find from the evidence in this case that this deceased person was standing in the highway and that the defendant drove his automobile against her, and that the reason he did drive his automobile against her was that he didn't see her, then I charge you that he is guilty of the negligence which it is necessary for the people to prove in this case."

The night on which the accident occurred was quite dark, the safety zone in which Mrs. MacKenzie and her daughter were standing was poorly lighted and Mrs. MacKenzie's clothing was dark and blended in with the surroundings. Appellant claims that, because of these circumstances, the jury should have been free to determine whether or not his failure to see Mrs. MacKenzie constituted negligence and that the court erred, therefore, in charging in effect that such failure was negligence as a matter of law.

We do not find any error in this charge. An automobile driver, whose view is not obstructed, is bound to see pedestrians who come within the range of his lights. See Lett v. Summerfield & Hecht, 239 Mich. 699; Haney v. Troost, 242 Mich. 693, and Russell v. Szczawinski, 268 Mich. 112. These cases, it is true, involved collisions with large objects, such as trucks and other automobiles, but the same principle is applicable to the present situation where a pedestrian is involved. We are not unaware of the cases in which this court has held that failure to see unusual objects whose presence may not be anticipated, despite the exercise of due care, is not negligence as a matter of law. Martin v. J. A. Mercier Co., 255 Mich. 587 (78 A.L.R. 520) (hole in road); Marek v. City of Alpena, 258 Mich. 637 (bump in road); Garrison v. City of Detroit, 270 Mich. 237 (unlighted abandoned traffic signal), and Bard v. Baker, 283 Mich. 337 (unlawful overhanging load on truck). However, autoists are bound to anticipate that pedestrians may be present on the street.

While the court's charge left very little for the jury to

determine with respect to defendant's negligence, the language of the charge, taken as a whole, is within the law of this State. People v. Dougherty, 232 Mich. 46. . . .
(Second question omitted.)
(Affirmed.)

BUTZEL, SHARPE, POTTER, CHANDLER, NORTH, and MxALLISTER, JJ., concurred with BUSHNELL, J.
(Concurring opinion of Justice WIEST omitted.)

People v. Paulen
327 Mich. 94

NORTH, J. On trial by jury, defendant, Lesley John Paulen, was convicted of negligent homicide under CL 1948, Sec. 750.324, (Stat Ann 1949 Cum Supp Sec. 28.556). Sentence was imposed and he has appealed.

Shortly after 2 a.m. on March 9, 1948, defendant was driving an automobile in a westerly direction on Davison avenue, in Detroit. There are double lines of streetcar tracks on this thoroughfare which is 66 feet wide between curbs. As defendant approached the intersection of Davison avenue with McDougall street Stanley Korzeniecki, apparently petting a dog, was standing a little east of the intersection, facing in a southwesterly direction, just north of the most northerly streetcar track, in what is referred to in the record as a "safety zone" or a "streetcar stop." Defendant was following an automobile driven by David Christopherson who was proceeding "just to the right of the (north) car track." They were traveling at not more than 25 miles per hour. By swerving suddenly to his right Christopherson narrowly missed striking Korzeniecki. Defendant testified he did not see Korzeniecki until after the Christopherson automobile veered to the right and too late to avoid striking Korzeniecki, which resulted in fatal injuries to him. Defendant also testified he was driving "40 or 45 feet" behind the Christopherson car; but that distance was considerably greater according to Christopherson's testimony, who was the only other eye-witness. . . .

Error is also assigned in respect to the charge of the court. First it is asserted that there was prejudicial error in that the trial court charged the jury:

"So, in this case, it was the duty of the defendant to keep a sharp lookout ahead and to see what was ahead of him and not, by reason of his failure to keep a sharp lookout ahead and to see what was ahead of him, to strike this deceased, if he was in lawful occupancy of the highway."

Without holding that, in view of the charge as a whole, the quoted statement would necessitate reversal, we think it should be noted that the use of the word "sharp" in the context was not an accurate statement of the law and might

825

well have misled the jury to require a more strict degree
of care of defendant in driving his automobile than is required by law, which is that degree of care which an ordinarily careful and prudent person would have exercised under
the same or similar circumstances. Hazen v. Rockefeller, 303
Mich. 536.

Another phrase of the charge of the court of which appellant
complains is, we think, much more serious. Early in his charge
the trial judge correctly stated to the jury:

"Those elements (of negligent homicide) are these: First,
that the defendant drove a vehicle on a public highway in
the city limits of the city of Detroit. Second, that he was
negligent in the operation of his vehicle. Third, that his
negligence caused an accident. Fourth, that as a result of
that accident someone received injuries which caused his death.
In this case, members of the jury, there is no controversy
about some of the elements. In other words, the defendant
concedes that he was driving the car. He concedes there was
an accident and that as a result of this accident a man was
killed. He denies that he was negligent, and he also denies
that, even though it should appear that he was negligent, he
denies that it was his negligence which caused the accident.
In other words, those two elements of the offense are the elements which require your decision."

But later and well toward the close of his charge the trial
judge instructed the jury:

"So those are the things you have to give your attention
to, members of the jury, whether this defendant was guilty
of the negligent act charged and whether that negligent act
was proximate cause of the accident. The other elements, as
I said, are conceded, although I will repeat them: The driving of the car, the negligent act, and the negligent act being the proximate cause of the accident, which caused the
death of the pedestrian."

Relative to the portion of the charge which we have itali-
cized, the people's brief states:

"Without a doubt a part of the last quoted sentence as
reported is erroneous but an erroneous part of one sentence
of the entire charge does not constitute reversible error."

Admittedly, under circumstances justifying such course,
we have held that an erroneous statement in the court's
charge when considered with the charge as a whole did not
constitute reversible error. But when, as in the instant
case, the erroneous statement is decisive of the controverted or controlling issue or issues of the case, it cannot be
passed lightly and still say that the defendant has not been
deprived of his constitutional right to a fair trial. When
in the instant case the court, although probably inadvertently, said to the jury that "the negligent act, and the negligent act being the proximate cause of the accident which
caused the death of the pedestrian" are conceded, the court

in practical effect directed a verdict against defendant. In so doing error was committed which commands reversal.

The verdict and judgment are vacated and a new trial granted.

BOYLES, C. J., and REID, DETHMERS, BUTZEL, CARR, BUSHNELL, and SHARPE, JJ., concurred.

3. Final Draft - Michigan Revised Criminal Code

(Criminally Negligent Homicide)

Sec. 2015. (1) A person commits the crime of criminally negligent homicide if:

(a) With criminal negligence he causes the death of another person; or

(b) He intentionally or recklessly causes the death of a person other than himself in the good faith but unreasonable belief that one or more grounds for justification exist under chapter 6.

(2) The jury may consider statutes regulating the actor's conduct in determining whether he is culpably negligent under subparagraph (1)(a).

(3) Criminally negligent homicide is a Class C felony.

Committee Commentary

The title and first sentence are taken from New York Revised Penal Law, Sec. 125.10; the remainder is new. Its relationship to existing law is discussed in the Commentary to Sec. 2006 to 2015.

Committee Commentary to Sec. 2006 to 2015

Relationship to Existing Law

Manslaughter at common law includes several categories. In only one of them, "involuntary manslaughter", is there the intent to kill or inflict serious bodily injury. In this instance the reasonableness of the defendant's reaction is sufficient to reduce the penalties from murder to manslaughter, but not to excuse the killing altogether.

For the remainder, intent to kill or do great bodily injury is not present. If the defendant commits an assault on another, without intent to kill or inflict serious bodily injury, but death results, the crime is manslaughter (People v. Slack, 90 Mich. 448, 51 N.W. 523 (1892); People v. Stubenvoll, 62 Mich. 329, 28 N.W. 883 (1886)). Most of the cases, however, turn on the presence or absence of criminal negligence which causes death. Basically this is determined by looking after the fact to see whether the defendant used the standard of care that was called for under the circumstances, considering the conduct in which the defendant was engaged (cf. People v. Thompson, 122 Mich. 411, 81 N.W. 344 (1899); defendant was a stationary engineer who was absent elsewhere in the building when the boilers blew up; an instruction should have been given that if he had reason to believe and did believe from his past experience that it was consistent with safety for him to be absent from the boilers at the time, he would not be guilty). If the charge is based on a negligent omission to act, the existence of a duty to act must first be proven (People v. Beardsley, 150 Mich. 206, 113 N.W. 1128 (1907)).

The chief difficulties have arisen in relating violations of particular misdemeanor statutes to the issue of negligence, and in attempting to develop a verbal formula describing what criminal negligence is. There is some authority for the existence of a "misdemeanor-manslaughter rule" analogous to the felony-murder rule (in general, see Moreland, The Law of Homicide, ch. 11, 18 (1952)). Whether that rule as such now prevails depends on one's interpretation of People v. Marshall, (362 Mich. 170, 106 N.W. 2d 842 (1961)) in which the prosecuting attorney asserted that the defendant, who was at home in bed at the time, was guilty of manslaughter because he had permitted a person whom he knew to be intoxicated to operate his vehicle; the driver had caused a collision which killed both the driver and the driver of another car. The Supreme Court held that the only offense committed by the defendant was a violation of the Motor Vehicle Code section. This suggests that the misdemeanor-manslaughter rule as such does not pertain in Michigan.

However, the violation of a statute may have some bearing on negligence, particularly if it is causally related to the death. In a case decided some years ago the Court said:

"To make the information for involuntary manslaughter good it must allege that the accused was in the commission of some unlawful act or negligently doing some act lawful in itself, or by the negligent omission to perform a legal duty, and that death resulted therefrom. The distinction between involuntary manslaughter committed while perpetrating an unlawful act not amounting to a felony and the offense arising out of some negligence or fault in doing a lawful act in a grossly negligent manner and from which death results must be kept in mind upon the question of pleading. In the former case it is sufficient to allege the unlawful act with sufficient particularity to identify it and then to charge that as a consequence the defendant caused the death of the deceased, and there is no need to aver in detail the specific acts of the accused; but in case of manslaughter committed through gross or culpable negligence while doing a lawful act the duty which was neglected or improperly performed must be charged as well as the acts of the accused constituting failure to perform or improper performance. . . ." (People v. Townsend, 214 Mich. 267, 273-4, 183 N.W. 177 (1921)).

In another case the court also held that violation of the
speed law bore on the question of mens rea, so that the jury
could consider whether the criminal act "so affected his
mind as to stimulate or induce wanton negligence in recklessly driving his car as claimed, thereby showing its causal
connection with the killing" (People v. Harris, 214 Mich. 145,
151-2, 182 N.W. 678 (1921)). It appears, therefore, that the
violation of the statute certainly bears on both the pleading
question and the question of negligence.

However, the Court has also created verbal distinctions
between "negligence" on the one hand and "wilfulness and
wantonness" on the other, and appears to say that there is
no such thing as a "negligent" manslaughter. In the leading
case, which arose from an automobile collision when the defendant improperly passed a line of stopped cars at the top
of a hill, the court held that before the defendant could be
guilty of manslaughter, the jury must be able to find the defendant "guilty of wilfulness, or of wantonness and recklessness, which in effect are wilfulness" (People v. Orr, 243
Mich. 300, 22 N.W. 777 (1928)). The court went on to say:

"It is common error to think that because the result of a
negligent act is dire the act itself is wanton. Negligence
is negligence be it much or little. The difference between
negligence and wilfulness or wantonness is not in degree but
in kind. Negligence is characterized chiefly by inadvertence,
thoughtlessness, inattention, and the like, while wantonness
or recklessness, in effect wilfulness, is characterized, as
the words imply, by wilfulness." (243 Mich. at 308).

Whether this distinction is the reason for the enactment of
the negligent homicide statute (C.L. 1948, Sec. 750.324) or
the result of it is not clear, but it is more likely the
former. If the verbal hairsplitting in the Orr case means
anything, it must be that manslaughter requires a disregard
of known consequences. In that event one would decide
whether the case is second-degree murder or manslaughter according to how great the probabilities were that someone
would be killed or seriously injured if the defendant per-
sisted in his projected course of activity.

To some extent these matters are affected by statute.
The basic manslaughter statute (C.L. 1948, Sec. 750.321)
does not define manslaughter, but merely provides for its
punishment. It therefore incorporates common-law definitions, to the extent Michigan courts wish to apply and adapt
them. As indicated above, the explanation in the Orr decision
and other similar decisions of the mens rea requirements for
manslaughter underlies the existence of the special statute
(C.L. 1948, Sec. 750.324) governing negligent homicide "by
the operation of a vehicle at an immoderate rate of speed
or in a careless, reckless or negligent manner, but not wilfully or wantonly". Recent amendments make it immaterial
whether the incident occurs on public or private property
(repudiating the holding in People v. Wigle, 350 Mich. 692,

829

86 N.W. 2d 813 (1957)). Negligent homicide is made a lesser included offense to a charge of manslaughter (C.L. 1948, Sec. 750.325). The reference to "immoderate speed" required further statutory explanation that this does not depend on the rate fixed by law for operating the vehicle (C.L. 1948, Sec. 750.326). Because the negligent homicide statute refers to "vehicles", it does not include watercraft. Therefore, the Legislature has passed a special statute covering that situation (C.L. 1948, Sec. 281.677), which is also a lesser-included offense to a charge of manslaughter (C.L. 1948, Sec. 281.678).

Special statutes defining manslaughter include: setting a spring gun or explosive trap which causes death (C.L. 1948, Sec. 750.236); wilfully killing an unborn quick child (C.L. 1948, Sec. 750.323); and causing death by an intentionally pointed or aimed firearm, but without malice (C.L. 1948, Sec. 750.329). A person commits a misdemeanor punishable by not more than 2 years imprisonment or a fine of not more than $2,000 if "because of carelessness, recklessness or negligence, but not wilfully or wantonly, (he) shall cause or allow any firearms under his immediate control, to be discharged so as to kill or injure another person" (C.L. 1948, Sec. 752.861); a similar statute applies to like misuse of a bow or arrow (C. L. 1948, Sec. 752.881).

*   *   *

The Draft preserves some of these features and eliminates others. Section 2006(1)(a) includes as one form of second-degree murder the causing of death by an act done with intent to cause serious physical injury to someone other than the actor. This conceivably could include homicides that are viewed as second-degree murder under the existing statutes, depending on the interpretation placed on the term "serious" in comparison with "grave bodily injury". It does mean that unless the purpose is to inflict this "serious" injury, the resulting death is not murder in the second-degree; whether a homicide resulting from an other intentionaly-committed assault is manslaughter or criminally negligent homicide depends on whether the defendant's acts are "reckless" or "criminally negligent".

Section 2006(1)(b) includes reckless conduct causing death, if it manifests extreme indifference to human life. What amounts to that extreme indifference depends on the circumstances of the particular case, but some special heinousness must be manifested. Recklessly causing death, without more, is manslaughter (Sec. 2010(1)(a)). "Reckless" is defined in Sec. 305(a) and in this application approximates the test set out in the Orr case.

Section 2010(1)(b) is in the same general vein as existing Michigan statutes governing death of a pregnant woman. The subsection applies only to a "criminal" abortion, which does not include any therapeutic abortion as defined in Sec. 7020. If the woman dies as a result of a therapeutic abortion, the doctor is not criminally responsible unless independently he is shown to have acted "recklessly" under Sec. 2010(1)(a) or "criminally negligently" under Sec. 2015(1)(a). Under the Draft, termination of fetal life itself is not manslaughter; a termination before the fetus is born and is alive, under Sec. 2001(2), is abortion under Sec. 7020. The term "alive", incidentally, is intended to point to "life" in the medical sense after birth, and does not incorporate any special legal test.

Section 2010(1)(c) makes intentionally causing or aiding a suicide manslaughter. This embodies two purposes. One is to indicate a duty not to facilitate suicide. The second, and perhaps more important, purpose is to make clear that this activity is not to be viewed as murder under Sec. 2005 unless the defendant uses duress or deception in bringing about the suicidal act.

Section 2010(1)(d) is the new equivalent to the common-law concept of voluntary manslaughter; a homicide under the influence of extreme mental or emotional disturbance for which there is a reasonable explanation or excuse is not either first-degree or second-degree murder under Sec. 2005(2). Section 2010 (1)(d) confirms the fact that the proper category for homicides committed under these circumstances is manslaughter.

Section 2015(1)(a) covers deaths caused through criminal negligence, a concept defined in the general part of the Draft (Sec. 305). Both the Model Penal Code and the New York Revised Penal Law content themselves with this statement alone. There is some merit, however, in indicating specifically the use that may be made of statutes bearing on the actor's criminal conduct. The choice in Sec. 2015(2) is to permit the jury to consider these statutes in deciding whether the defendant departed from the standard of conduct appropriate for him under the circumstances. This formulation should also make it clear that the misdemeanor-manslaughter rule as such is not within the coverage of the Draft.

Section 2015(1)(b) is included to make clear where instances of so-called "imperfect defenses" are to fall. The logic of common-law statements suggests that defenses like self-defense are "confession and avoidance" devices in which, for example, the defendant acknowledges that he intended to kill, but asserts special circumstances which justify or excuse the killing. If he loses on the issue of self-defense, that leaves an "intentional unprivileged" killing which is murder. However, self-defense and the other defenses are usually couched in terms of the "reasonableness" of the defendant's perception of the circumstances or the force required to extricate himself from his predicament. An elimination of self-defense usually rests, therefore, on a determination that the defendant acted rashly, hastily or without good judgment. This in turn is a state of mind much closer to "negligence" than it is to "malice". In fact,

831

most cases of imperfect self-defense, etc., are placed by the jury in the manslaughter category (see E.G., People v. Stallworth, 364 Mich. 528, 111 N.W.2d 742 (1961); People v. Van Camp, 356 Mich. 593, 97 N.W.2d 726 (1959)). Therefore, the matter is spelled out rather than left for later judicial interpretation.

Second-degree murder is a Class A felony with a maximum of 20 years. Manslaughter is a Class B felony with a maximum term of ten years, and culpably negligent homicide a Class C felony with a maximum term of five years.

D. Homicide Under the Michigan Revised Criminal Code
14 Wayne L. Rev. 904

I.
Introduction

The law of homicide in Michigan, as in many states, is replete with obscure common law doctrines such as "malice aforethought," "premeditation and deliberation," "adequate provocation," "heat of passion" and "cooling time." These concepts are confusing and often misleading. The Michigan Revised Criminal Code (Proposed Code) abolishes them, offering instead clear and concise statutory language. This comment attempts to summarize existing Michigan law, demonstrate the effect the Proposed Code will have upon it and point out certain difficulties in the language of the revision.

II.
Murder in the First Degree

A. Existing Michigan Law

Presently, statutory first degree murder includes all murder "perpetrated by means of poison, or lying in wait, or any other kind of wilful, deliberate and premeditated killing, or which shall be committed in the perpetration, or attempt to perpetrate any arson, rape, robbery or burglary . . ."[1] The latter clause sets out the felony-murder rule and will be discussed in section III.

It should be noted that the statute classifies types of murder which will be first degree murder, without defining murder itself. For a definition it is necessary to resort to the common law. An early case, People v. Potter,[2] held that the common law definition of murder was retained under the Michigan statute, stating: "Murder is where a person of sound memory and discretion unlawfully kills any reasonable creature in being, in the peace of the state, with malice prepense or aforethought, either express or implied."[3] This general definition is still accepted.[4] Thus it has been

832

held that the murder statute has no application until the homicide in question is found to be murder.[5]

An understanding of the concept "malice aforethought" is necessary, for it is the integral part of the common law definition. People v. Borgetto[6] defines malice as including every unlawful, unjustifiable, wicked or corrupt motive; not confining it to ill will, anger, hatred or revenge. It denotes a disregard of social duty and may be implied from cruel or deliberate acts against others. The length of time prior to the act during which the actor formed his unlawful purpose is immaterial since "malice aforethought" denotes purpose and design rather than deliberation.[7] This definition is in accord with the general common law rule.[8] Malice may be either express or implied. Express malice requires an intent to cause either the harm that actually results, or harm of the same general nature,[9] while implied malice may arise from the deliberate and unjustified use of a deadly weapon.[10]

The statute makes all murder perpetrated by means of poison or lying in wait murder in the first degree, along with any other wilful, deliberate and premeditated killing. Since the division of murder into two degrees was chiefly for the purpose of apportioning the severity of the punishment,[11] it is easy to see why murder perpetrated by poison or lying in wait is classified as first degree. Murder by these means indicates deliberation and preparation - a previously-planned act. The law considers such an act evidence of the most wicked and depraved type of character and singles out its possessor for the most severe punishment.[12]

Similarly, the first statute dividing murder into degrees,[13] after which the Michigan statute was patterned, used "premeditated" to reintroduce the element of predesign into the concept of murder. Originally "malice aforethought" was synonymous with preconception, but years of judicial interpretation had deprived "aforethought" of all its natural meaning. The insertion of "premeditation" was a resurrection of the original meaning of "aforethought," that is, something preconceived.[14] However, once again judicial interpretation seems to have eroded this concept. Michigan cases have held that the use of a deadly weapon, coupled with evidence of the surrounding circumstances, may give rise to an inference of wilfulness, deliberation and premeditation.[15] Thus, the same element of the actus reus, use of a lethal weapon, may give rise both to implied malice, making a homicide murder, and when coupled with evidence of the circumstances in which it was used, to an inference of premeditation and deliberation, making the crime murder in the first degree.

Furthermore, People v. Vinunzo[16] held that ejusdem generis[17] does not apply to limit "wilful, deliberate and premeditated killing" to murders of the same nature as those perpetrated "by means of poison, or lying in wait," that is, those in which there is a preconceived plan to kill. Such over-broad interpretation has done much to vitiate the distinction be-

833

tween first and second degree murder by holding, in effect, that premeditation will be sufficient if it occurs at any time precedent to the fatal act.[18]

In order for a homicide to constitute murder there must be a criminal intent against life.[19] The early case of _Wellar v. People_[20] held that an intent to kill, or even an intent to inflict personal injury, was not necessary. However, it _was_ necessary that defendant possess an intent legally equivalent to a criminal purpose dangerous to life, that is, a felonious intent. This view is modified by the recent case of _People v. Hansen_,[21] which states that first degree murder requires a deliberate intent to kill. If there was no deliberation or if the intent was to inflict a lesser injury there cannot be a conviction for murder in the first degree, but rather, a lesser degree of homicide. _Hansen_, therefore, appears to make first degree murder in Michigan a specific intent crime.

Michigan also recognizes the doctrine of transferred intent, whereby if the actor intends to shoot and kill A, but misses A and hits B, the murderous intent which he bore toward A is "transferred" to B.[22] Finally, it should be noted that the present Michigan statute requires a mandatory sentence of "solitary confinement at hard labor in the state prison for life."[23]

B. Proposed Changes in the Law

Section 2005(1)(a) of the Proposed Code states that "A person commits the crime of murder in the first degree if: (a) With intent to cause the death of a person other than himself, he causes the death of that person or of another person. . . ."[24] This section, of course, must be read in conjunction with the provisions on justification.[25] Otherwise it would render any intentional killing, even in self-defense, first degree murder.

Section 2005 purports to preserve the core of the existing law of murder.[26] The question of whether it succeeds in this purpose must be examined. The common law concept of "malice aforethought" has been replaced by the proposed mens rea requirement of "intent". As previously discussed, malice could be implied from any cruel or deliberate act against a person;[27] a similar implication could be employed to give meaning to "intent." In fact, this is necessary, for the defendant will usually not have articulated an intention to kill. Rather, we must look to his acts, and from the fact of the killing and its surrounding circumstances, we draw the conclusion that an intent to kill (or malice) must necessarily have been present.

The cases already seem to have equated malice with intent. _People v. Statkiewicz_[28] held that the use of a deadly weapon implied malice. The court said, speaking of a determination (intention) to kill, that death or great bodily

834

harm "might reasonably have been expected, from the nature of the weapon and the manner of its use. . . ."[29] Therefore, substitution of "intent" for "malice aforethought" would appear to work no great change in the substantive law of first degree murder. However, it does have the value of avoiding the use of a term which has been a source of confusion for innumerable juries, principally because of the tortured interpretation given it by the courts.

One of the most striking aspects of this section is its elimination of the terms "wilful, deliberate and premeditated" from the definition of murder in the first degree. This is in accord with the treatment given the offense by a number of revised codes.[30] It is, therefore, necessary to ask whether the elimination of "premeditation" changes the substantive law of Michigan.

As noted earlier, decisions such as People v. Vinunzo[31] have emasculated the doctrine of premeditation, resulting in a requirement of deliberation and premeditation that is satisfied if at any time before the fatal act, the actor deliberately formed the purpose to kill. If the actor habitually carried a lethal weapon, he could be found to have deliberated and premeditated in the time required to draw it out and inflict the fatal injury. The effect of such a rule is to eradicate the entire concept of deliberation and premeditation, and thus its elimination will not greatly change the law of first degree murder as declared by the cases. Again, the proposal has the value of eliminating verbiage rendered excess by judicial interpretation.

Section 2005(1)(a) requires "intent" to cause death as the culpable mental state for first degree murder. The Proposed Code states that, "A person acts intentionally with respect to a result. . . when his conscious objective is to cause that result. . ."[32] adopting the rule of People v. Hansen,[33] where it was held that first degree murder requires an intent to kill. Such a notion is contrary to the general common law concept of murder. Professor Warren states:

By the common law, an unlawful killing with malice aforethought, even though the manifest intent or purpose was to do simply a bodily harm, but not to take life, constituted murder. Therefore purpose or intent to kill does not constitute an essential ingredient in the crime of murder by the common law.[34]

Existing Michigan law on this point is less than clear. The older cases held that an intent to inflict serious bodily harm would be sufficient to sustain a charge of murder in the first degree,[35] while the more recent decisions seem to require a specific intent to kill.[36] The Proposed Code adopts the view of the recent cases for first degree murder and that of the earlier cases as its rule for second degree murder. In this respect Michigan law as to first degree murder remains unchanged.[37]

The Proposed Code also makes explicit the underlying

assumption of the doctrine of transferred intent, whereby
if the actor intends to cause the death of one person and
causes the death of another, he will be guilty of murder
in the first degree.[38] This result is in accord with the
present law[39] and is clearly correct. Otherwise guilt or
innocence would depend upon purely fortuitous circumstances,
such as the actor's marksmanship. Yet the actor would be
equally as culpable and dangerous, and the harm to society
would be equally as great as if he had accomplished his intention. The Proposed Code reaches this result in a straightforward manner by incorporating the rule into the definition
of first degree murder[40] rather than relying on the fiction
of transferred intent.

Section 2005(2) provides that a person will not be guilty
of either first or second degree murder "if he acts under
the influence of extreme mental or emotional disturbance for
which there is a reasonable explanation or excuse."[41] Homicide under such conditions will constitute manslaughter.[42]
The test proposed, while similar to the existing common law
test - acting in the heat of passion, produced by adequate
provocation, and before the blood has had time to cool[43] -
appears to be broader in scope. The Proposed Code places
greater emphasis on the individual circumstances of the actor
by basing the test on the viewpoint of someone in his situation. This new test will be discussed more fully in section V.

By requiring[44] the death caused to be that of someone other
than the actor, section 2005 codifies the notion that sui-[45]
cide or attempted suicide is not a crime under Michigan law.
Furthermore, subsection (3) states that a person does not
commit first degree murder if, without using duress or deception, he causes or aids another person to commit suicide.[46]
The purpose of this section[47] is to reverse People v. Roberts,[48]
which held that a husband who mixed poison at his wife's request and put it within her reach to end her suffering from
a terminal illness was guilty of first degree murder. The result reached by the Proposed Code is preferable to the rule
of Roberts. Causing or aiding another to commit suicide under
such circumstances does not involve the culpability characteristic of first degree murder. Even the common conception of
malice, as wickedness, cruelty, or depravity, is absent in
such a case. In Roberts the defendant bore no ill will toward
his wife, his act was motivated by love and mercy. He is
clearly not in a class with an intentional killer whose homicidal act is motivated by hate.

There is also the limitation that the act must not consist
of using duress or deception. This is consistent with a number of decisions from other jurisdictions.[49] These cases
should be excepted from the mitigatory effect of subsection (3),
for in contrast to cases like Roberts, they do evidence malice
and an intent to kill. It is difficult to distinguish the
case where one pushes another from a cliff, from the case
where he causes him to jump at gunpoint. In both situations

there is an intent to kill which causes a death, fulfilling
the basic requirements for first degree murder under the Proposed Code.

It is necessary to read section 2005(3) in conjunction with
section 2010(c), wherein intentionally causing or aiding a person to commit suicide is deemed manslaughter.[50] Such a reading insures that a defendant not chargeable under the first
degree murder section will not be exculpated. However, it is
not entirely clear how these two sections were meant to interact. The broadly worded manslaughter section seems to cover
all intentionally caused or aided suicides. Yet the murder
section, by including the phrase "without the use of duress
or deception," appears to imply that if duress or deception
were employed, the actor's conduct would be cognizable as
murder in the first degree. This ambiguity should be eliminated, possibly by narrowing the manslaughter section to exclude cases involving deception or duress.

It must be noted that cases of voluntary euthanasia[51] will
be first degree murder under the proposed Code, as the actor
intentionally causes the death of another.[52] Consent will
not be a defense because the "harm" caused is serious.[53] Nor
will the defense of "choice of evils" be available.[54] Clearly,
the case of a mercy-killing is not similar to the "usual" case
of first degree murder, other than in the commission of a
homicidal act. It is much less culpable in that usually it
is committed either upon request or with the consent of the
"victim." By designating such an act murder in the first
degree no weight is given to the attitude of the patient,
as opposed to the usual, unwilling murder victim. The act
is very similar to causing or aiding the commission of suicide without duress or deception. The Proposed Code specifically omits suicide from first degree murder, designating
it as manslaughter.[55] The mental attitude of the actor in
both cases is identical - to relieve another person from suffering. Can it be said that there is such a difference between preparing a hypodermic and handing it to the sufferer
for self-injection, and actual injection by the actor himself
that it will justify the difference in treatment under the
Proposed Code? These parallel acts should receive parallel
treatment. In the words of a careful student of the subject:

> There is no evidence that the majority of the American
> people approve of euthanasia, but it is reasonable to assume
> that most people consider a killing motivated by mercy less
> reprehensible than killing for a base motive. Thus, a speci-
> fic statutory reduction of penalty for mercy killing would
> seem to be the most appropriate solution.[56]

While the broadened concept of "extreme mental or emotional
disturbance" might apply to mitigate the act to manslaughter
in some cases, it is submitted that many mercy-killings,
particularly those committed by physicians, will remain unaffected by this provision. Therefore, specific provisions,

similar to those relating to suicide, should be added to the Proposed Code which exclude cases of euthanasia from the category of first degree murder, and include it in that of manslaughter.

The burden of "injecting the issue" of suicide or extreme mental or emotional disturbance is on the defendant.[57] This means that in addition to merely stating his claim he must produce some evidence to corroborate the claim, which is in accord with present practice.[58] The amount which would carry the burden would be properly a matter for the trial judge's discretion. Certainly it would be less than that necessary to sustain the burden of persuasion. Placing the production burden on the defendant is necessary to discourage unmeritorious claims which would result in placing upon the prosecution the heavy burden of disproving such claims beyond a reasonable doubt. This would be a useless expenditure of time and effort if the claim had no basis in fact. Of course, the Proposed Code's position that the burden of persuasion as to the entire case remains upon the prosecution is correct if the presumption of innocence is to stand.

Finally, it should be noted that the proposed penalty for murder in the first degree is "imprisonment not less than ten years to life."[59] Under present law there is a mandatory life sentence.[60] The provision of the Proposed Code is preferable. Rather than tying the hands of the trial judge, it allows him discretion to impose a sentence commensurate with the individual circumstances of the case.[61]

III.

Felony-Murder

A. Existing Michigan Law

The present felony-murder rule is incorporated into the first degree murder statute, which states: "All murder. . . which shall be committed in the perpetration or attempt to perpetrate any arson, rape, robbery or burglary, shall be murder of the first (1st) degree. . . ."[62] Its purpose is to establish the mens rea for murder in cases where a homicide is perpetrated in the commission of one of the enumerated felonies. It is a fiction in that it imputes to a felon an intent to kill when he may have had none. As stated by Professor Morris:

Its original and present effect is the imputation of a certain state of mind, the _mens rea_ regarded as essential to liability for murder, to one who may or may not in fact have had that intention. The classic _mens rea_ of murder is an intention to kill; that is extended to include an intention to do an act intrinsically likely to kill, possibly formulated sufficiently by an intention to inflict grievous bodily harm. An intention to inflict physical

838

hurt is involved in all versions.[63]

This statement enunciates the reason for the rule; certain acts are inherently dangerous to human life, and their intentional perpetration evidences either an intent to inflict serious bodily harm, or a wanton disregard of the consequences. If a death results the felony-murder rule imputes malice rendering the homicide murder in the first degree.

Before there can be a conviction under this doctrine, there must have been at least an intent to commit the underlying felony.[64] The intent is necessary because the felony-murder rule does not create the mens rea requisite for murder, rather it imputes it from a preexisting criminal intent. An attempt to commit the felony will suffice,[65] and the homicide will be first degree murder even if it was unintentional or accidental.[66]

The rules of complicity also interact with the felony-murder rule. In People v. Peranio[67] a co-felon who had lent his gun to the other co-felons for the purpose of robbery, and who was waiting a short distance away, was convicted of first degree murder when the victim was shot and killed. Although he claimed he would not have joined in the robbery if he had known anyone would be killed, the result appears to be correct. The defendant knew, or should have known, that there is a great likelihood of violence during the commission of an armed robbery. Since the crime is one involving conduct dangerous to human life, he is equally as culpable as the individual who actually fired the shot.

The concept of felony-murder is almost unlimited in its potential breadth of application. For instance, People v. Mihalko[68] held that a person would be guilty of murder even if death came as a result of an independent force if the attempt to perpetrate the felony gave rise to that force. The Michigan rule reached its ultimate extension in People v. Podolski[69] where it was held that when one police officer accidentally shot another in a gun battle ensuing after a robbery, the robbers were guilty of first degree murder.[70] The rationale was that the robbers knew, or should have known, that they were setting in motion a chain of events which would probably result in the use of deadly retaliating force and that they were responsible for the results flowing therefrom. Moreover Podolski broadly interpreted the "commission" of a felony to include the immediate escape therefrom.[71]

People v. Austin[72] refused to extend the rule of Podolski to a case where one of the co-felons was shot and killed by his intended victim. In acquitting the surviving co-felons, the court quoted extensively from Commonwealth v. Redline[73] which held that the killing of a felon by one attempting to thwart the felony was justifiable homicide, and since the killing was lawful, it could not support a charge of murder. The Austin court also quoted People v. Wood,[74] where it was held that the fatal act must have been either actually or

constructively that of the felons. The act could not be
that of the felons unless committed by them or one acting
in concert with them. In failing to make explicit its own
rationale, and in refusing to directly overrule Podolski, the
Austin court left open the possibility that Podolski is still
good law.[75] If principal reliance is placed upon Redline,
Podolski may still be applicable to similar fact situations,
i.e., where the homicide is not justifiable. If Wood is the
main basis for the decision, however, the felony-murder rule
would apply only in cases where the act is imputable to the
felon on agency principles, thus impliedly overruling Podolski.

While the statute designates as first degree murder a homicide committed in the course of one of the four enumerated
felonies, this does not preclude the finding of a lesser degree of homicide if warranted by the evidence.[76] However,
if the evidence admits of no inference other than murder in
the first degree, it is proper to instruct the jury that they[77]
must either convict the defendant of that offense, or acquit.
If death results during the commission of a felony other than
arson, rape, robbery or burglary, the offense will be second
degree murder.[78]

B. Proposed Changes in the Law

As under the existing law, the Proposed Code incorporates
the felony-murder rule into the provision governing first
degree murder.[79] The apparent intent of this section is to
limit application of the felony-murder rule to prevent results such as that reached in Podolski. The proposal limits
application of the rule to cases where one of the felons
causes the death of someone other than one of their number.
This would appear to preclude a finding of guilt in cases
where: a third party kills another third party,[80] the victim[81]
or another third party kills one of the felons, or one of
the felons kills himself.[82] Such a limitation is supported
by the purpose of the rule - to impute the mens rea necessary
for murder to a felon who has killed during the commission
or attempt to commit one of the enumerated felonies. To convict in a case where a third party or the victim kills would[83]
be to impute not only the mens rea but the actus reus. Such
a construction would be contrary to the basic principles of
our criminal law system according to which guilt is personal.[84]

Nor is an extension of the rule to the above situations
justified on the basis of the catchall rationale of deterrence.
In these cases it is clear that the felon did not intent, or
even desire, that the homicide occur. The purpose of deterrence is not served by the imposition of first degree murder
sanctions for an act which, as to the felon, was totally unintentional. One commentator suggests that for a greater
deterrent effect, the sanctions for the underlying felonies
which create the risk of death should be increased, rather[85]
than imposing punishment for the resulting death.

It is necessary to inquire whether the Proposed Code

840

accomplishes its intended purpose of limiting the felony-
murder rule. It states that a person commits first degree
murder if, in committing or attempting to commit one of the
enumerated felonies, "he, or another participant if there
be any, causes the death of a person other than one of the
participants."[86] The key word is "causes." Does it mean
that one of the participants must actually commit the homicide? If not, what does it mean? The proposed rules of
causation are stated as:

Conduct is the cause of a result when:
(a) It is an antecedent but for which the result in question would not have occurred; and
(b) The relationship between the conduct and result satisfies any additional causal requirements imposed by the Criminal Code or by the statute defining the offense.[87]

If subsection (a) is read by itself it defines the classic
"but for," or cause-in-fact test. The draftsmen could not
have equated "cause" as used in the felony-murder rule to
the "but for" test. Otherwise, criminal liability would lie
in every case because, "but for" the felony, the death would
not have occurred. Liability under such a rule could extend
far beyond fact situations such as those posed above. Conviction in such cases were generally based upon a proximate
cause theory – death being the reasonably foreseeable result of engaging in a dangerous felony.[88] The "but for"
rule would include all consequences resulting from an act,
reasonably foreseeable or not.

Subsection (b) is of little assistance, as section 2005
imposes no additional causal requirements. The remainder
of section 320 offers further limitations on the "but for"
rule of causation set out in subsection (1)(a). These limitations, however, are keyed to the mens rea requirement for
causing a particular result. Unfortunately, the Proposed
Code articulates no such requirement in its version of felony-
murder. Clearly, an intent to kill is not necessary since
it would negate the function of the felony-murder rule.
Therefore, section 320(2) would not apply, as it relates
to "intentionally or knowingly causing a particular result."[89]

The Model Penal Code formulation of the felony-murder rule
requires a mental element of recklessness "under circumstances
manifesting extreme indifference to the value of human life."[90]
The commentary to this section describes a reckless homicide
which the draftsmen felt was substantially equivalent to intentional or knowing homicides. Recklessness, they say, pre-
supposes an awareness of a substantial risk of homicide,
and that when this risk reaches the point of extreme indifference to the value of human life, it is the same sort of
indifference possessed by those who perpetrate a homicide intentionally or knowingly.[91]

Perhaps the same sort of mens rea requirement was intended
to be implicit in the Michigan provision. If so, section

841

320(3) must be examined for a possible limitation of "but for" causation in cases where the act of homicide is perpetrated not by one of the co-felons but by a third party. It states:

(3) When recklessly or negligently causing a _particular_ result is an element of an offense, the element is not established if the _actual_ result is not within the risk of which the actor is aware. . . unless:

(a) The actual result differs from the probable result _only_ in the respect that a different person or different property is injured or affected or that the probable injury or harm would have been more serious or more extensive than that caused; or

(b) The actual result involves the same kind of injury or harm as the probable result and is not too remote or accidental in its occurrence to have a bearing on the actor's liability or on the gravity of his offense.[92]

Let us assume that the "particular result" referred to would be an act of homicide committed by one of the felons, while the "actual result" is the death of a third party at the hands of another third party. The general rule of subsection (3) is that if the actual result is not within the risk of which the actor is aware, causation is not established. Is the risk of one third party killing another within the risk of which the felons are aware? Cases such as _Podolski_ would answer affirmatively. The rationale of that decision was that felons know, or should know, that their acts involve a high risk of deadly retaliation by their victims.[93] If this rationale is followed, causation will be established, and the felons will be guilty of the first degree murder. This would not seem to be the result intended by the draftsmen.

If we say that the actual result was not within the risk of which the felon was aware, which is hopefully the result at which the courts will arrive, will causation nevertheless be established under subsection (a) or (b)? Subsection (a) offers two tests. First, the actual result must differ from the probable one _only_ in that a different person is injured. If "only" may be taken at face value, this test will not be met because not only is a different person injured, but a different person inflicted the injury. The second test, that the probable injury would have been more serious than the actual injury, is not applicable.

Subsection (b) also offers two tests, but unlike (a) they are not in the alternative. First, the actual result must involve the same kind of injury or harm as the probable result. This requirement will be satisfied, as both the probable and actual result are death. Further, the actual result must not be too remote or accidental to have a bearing on the actor's liability or the gravity of his offense. This is basically a problem of proximate cause. While it may be

argued that under this rule a court could find the death of
one third party at the hands of another third party not too
remote or accidental a consequence, the recent case of People v. Austin[94] indicates that current judicial feeling is
against such an interpretation. As there is a general feeling throughout the country of limiting, if not abolishing,
the felony-murder rule,[95] there would not appear to be too
great a danger of courts interpreting this test to include
killings committed by third parties. Also, the causal
limitation imposed by section 320 (3)(b) would allow conviction in cases where the felon has taken a hostage who,
when used as a shield, is accidentally killed by third parties.[96] Here the felon has taken a more active part in bringing about the death, his culpability is therefore greater and
the result is not too remote or accidental. Substitution of
"kills," or a similar word for "causes the death of" in section 2005 (1)(b), while eliminating the possibility of a result like that of Podolski, would preclude conviction in so-
called "shield" cases where the act of the felon, in terms
of blameworthiness, is not essentially different from cases
where he actually committed the physical homicidal act.

There remain to be considered two types of cases in which
the felony-murder rule has been applied in other states to
reach an "unfair" result. In Commonwealth v. Bolish[97] the
defendant hired another to set fire to certain property. In
so doing, there was an explosion and the accomplice was killed. In holding that defendant was guilty of murder under
the felony-murder rule, the court based its decision on the
ground that the death was the natural or reasonably foreseeable result of the felony. Conviction in such a case is no
more illogical than conviction in the case of a homicide perpetrated by a third party. Although the death was neither
intended nor desired by the felons, nor was it in furtherance of their felonious design, it occurred during the commission of the felony and was not clearly unforeseeable. However, all the arguments against conviction in the third party
cases are applicable here, there being no great social purpose served by a finding of murder. The Proposed Code, by
requiring that the death caused be of a person other than
one of the felons, rightly prevents such a result.[98]

People v. Cabaltero[99] involved a robbery conspiracy,
during which one of the conspirators shot and killed another
because he thought that the latter, a lookout, had revealed
their criminal purpose. All of the other conspirators were
convicted of first degree murder under the felony-murder
rule. The court held that the murder was committed "in the
perpetration" of the robbery, and consequently, all of the
participants were equally guilty. The court refused to accept the argument that the act was independent of the underlying felony, deciding that if it was committed during the
course of the felony the statutory requirement for felony-
murder was met.

Such a result would not be possible under the Proposed Code since the proposal requires that the homicide be "in furtherance of the crime that (the felon) is committing or attempting to commit. . . ."[106] This rule is preferable to that of Cabaltero.[101] Otherwise, as Professor Morris states, if during the commission of a felony one of the felons chances to see a lifelong enemy and kills him in an act wholly independent of the underlying felony, the others, nevertheless, would be guilty of first degree murder. Such an imposition of liability would be even broader than the doctrine of proximate cause, for such an occurrence would not be reasonably foreseeable. For this very reason a conviction could not be sustained on any theory of deterrence. It would be contrary to the basic precepts of criminal justice to impose liability where there is no causal relationship between the defendant's acts and the criminal result. Generally, causation has two requisites when the act is committed by another: (1) authorization or incitation to commit the act, or (2) knowledge and acquiescence in the act. The only time liability might be imposed in the absence of the above two conditions is when the act is the proximate result of an authorized act.[102] It is clear that in the case under discussion, none of these apply. Since the act is independent of the underlying felony, and therefore not causally related, imposition of criminal liability would be theoretically untenable as well as "unfair."

Closely related is the case where one of the participants enters upon commission of the felony not intending to kill and not anticipating such action by any of the others. The Proposed Code provides a carefully defined and closely drawn affirmative defense in such cases.[103] There must have been more than one participant in the crime and the defendant must not have committed or in any way encouraged the homicide. He must also show that he was not armed with a deadly weapon, that he had no reasonable ground to believe that any of the other participants were so armed or that they intended to engage in homicidal conduct.[104] An identical provision in the revised New York Penal Law[105] has been criticized for being too tightly drawn. Clearly the close drafting could work a hardship. For example, a safecracker, little expecting a death to result but with knowledge that his companions were carrying explosives, could be convicted of first degree murder. However, in spite of the scattered harsh results which might obtain in some individual cases, the strict requirements of the defense are necessary to prevent specious claims of ignorance. Some objective criteria are necessary because of the impossibility of fathoming the subjective mental processes of the defendant.

Under the present statutory provision there are four felonies listed which form the basis for the rule: arson, rape, robbery and burglary.[106] To these the Proposed Code adds escape, kidnapping and sodomy.[107] The four felonies presently comprising the rule were undoubtedly chosen because they were thought to be particularly dangerous to human life, as they involve a high risk of violence. Assum-

844

ing that dangerousness is the criterion for including a
particular crime in the felony-murder category, those added
by the Proposed Code must be considered equally as dangerous
as those presently enumerated. Escape involves forcefully
breaking away from a penal institution, and kidnapping generally involves violence. Sodomy, at first glance, would not
appear to fulfill the criterion of dangerousness. However,
under the Proposed Code, it differs from rape only in that
it involves deviate sexual intercourse, so that all the violence accompanying a forcible rape would also be present in
first degree sodomy.[108]

Finally, the proposal codifies the rule enunciated in
Podolski[109] that the commission of a felony includes the
immediate flight therefrom.[110] This rule is in accord with
common sense, as the felonious act cannot be viewed in a
vacuum, isolated in time. There is just as much reason to
impose liability for first degree murder upon a bank robber
who kills while making his escape as upon one who kills
during the commission of the robbery.

IV.

Murder in the Second Degree

A. Existing Michigan Law

The present statutory provision encompasses all kinds
of murder other than that designated as first degree.[111]
Since that which, theoretically, distinguishes murder in
the first degree is the presence of premeditation and deliberation, second degree murder may be defined as an unlawful killing with malice aforethought but absent any premeditation or deliberation.[112] Such malice will be sufficient even if formed but an instant before the act.[113] An
intent to kill is not necessary; an intent to inflict great
bodily harm is sufficient.[114] While voluntary intoxication
is not a defense, it can mitigate what would have been first
degree murder to second degree if the defendant is found to
have been so inebriated as to be unable to formulate the requisite deliberation and premeditation.[115] Finally, as a
corollary to the felony-murder rule, killing in the perpetration of a felony other than those enumerated under felony-
murder is murder in the second degree.

B. Proposed Changes in the Law

The Proposed Code formulates two types of fact situations
which will constitute second degree murder. The first occurs when the actor, intending to cause serious physical injury to another, causes the death of that person or another
person.[116] In this case there must be a specific purpose
to inflict such an injury or the homicide will not constitute second degree murder.[117]

845

Similar to the section on first degree murder, this provision has the virtue of eliminating the confusing and misleading phrase "malice aforethought," replacing it with a specific intent. Since the intent to cause serious physical injury is substantially equivalent to the usual common law formulation,[118] cases presently viewed as second degree murder because of an intent to do great bodily harm are retained under the Proposed Code. Thus, if a deadly weapon is used upon a vital part of the body, an intent to inflict serious physical injury may be implied.[119]

The second circumstance in which a person commits second degree murder is if:

Under circumstances manifesting extreme indifference to the value of human life, he recklessly engages in conduct which creates a grave risk of death to a person other than himself, and thereby causes the death of another person.[120]

Recklessness, without more, will not give rise to liability under this section but will be manslaughter under section 2010(1)(a).[121] What then is recklessness manifesting extreme indifference to the value of human life and creating a grave risk of death?

This provision is similar to the Model Penal Code's presumption of recklessness under the felony-murder rule.[122] However, such conduct is within felony-murder under the Proposed Code and would not be covered by this section. Apparently this section was meant to include such things as shooting into a crowd of people, derailing a train or bombing an airplane. In such cases, since there may not be a specific intent to cause death or serious physical injury, the mental state must be recklessness. The near certainty of the occurrence of death evidences a mental state much more culpable than mere recklessness - it is tantamount to knowledge or intent and should constitute murder.

The problem inherent in this section is that, outside of these paradigm cases, there will be considerable difficulty in drawing the line between recklessness which constitutes manslaughter and reckless murder. However, it would be impossible to formulate a precise test which would clearly differentiate between the subtle shadings of criminal mens rea capable of being produced by the human mind. Of necessity, the question of whether the recklessness is such as will constitute second degree murder or manslaughter must be left for the jury's determination on the basis of the heinousness evidenced in the particular case. Although one commentator suggests deletion of the word "recklessly,"[123] it is submitted that this would not greatly alleviate the problem, as the key words on the basis of which the jury must decide are "extreme indifference to the value of human life," and "grave risk of death." Furthermore, substitution of "intentionally" or "knowingly" would not accurately reflect the actor's state of mind.

Manslaughter

A. Existing Michigan Law

The present statutory provision for manslaughter does not define the offense but merely provides punishment[124] while retaining the common law definition. At common law manslaughter is divided into two categories, voluntary and involuntary. Generally, voluntary manslaughter involves an intent to kill, but malice is negated by adequate provocation so that the homicide is committed "in the heat of blood." Passion, while not sufficient to constitute an absolute defense, will, if produced by adequate provocation, mitigate to manslaughter an act that otherwise would have been murder.[125] Manslaughter involves less culpability than murder because of the greater disregard for human life characteristic of murder.[126] Whether a particular set of circumstances will constitute provocation depends on the facts of each case.[127] Although many of the cases involve an assault upon the defendant,[128] this is not necessary. Such provoking acts as a threatened assault upon a loved one[129] or the adultery of a spouse[130] have been held sufficient.[131] In determining what will constitute adequate provocation, ordinary or average human nature is taken as the standard.[132] The provocation must be such as "might render ordinary men, of fair average disposition, liable to act rashly or without due deliberation or reflection, and from passion, rather than judgment."[133] This test is purely objective and takes no account of the actor's individual characteristics.

The defendant must also have acted while still under the influence of his passion before his "blood has had time to cool." This, too, is a question of fact for the jury and depends upon the circumstances of the case. Account must be taken of such things as "the nature and circumstances of the provocation, the extent to which the passions have been aroused, and the fact, whether the injury inflicted by the provocation is more or less permanent or irreparable."[134]

Involuntary manslaughter consists of an unintentional killing in the perpetration of some unlawful act less than a felony, the performance of a lawful act in a grossly negligent manner or in the omission of a legal duty.[135] The unlawful act need not be dangerous to life,[136] nor is an intent to kill or inflict serious bodily injury necessary.[137] A number of statutes have been enacted specifically constituting the commission of certain acts which result in death as manslaughter.[138]

If an act, lawful in itself but committed with gross negligence - amounting to wilfulness or recklessness and wantonness - causes death, liability for manslaughter will ensue. Ordinary negligence will not suffice.[139] In order to constitute wilfulness or recklessness and wantonness the actor's conduct must fulfill three requirements: (1) he must have knowledge of a situation which requires ordinary

847

care to avert injury to another person; (2) he must possess
the ability, with the means at hand, to avoid the injury
through the use of ordinary care; and (3) he must omit using
such care to avert the injury when, to an ordinary person,
it would be apparent that the result would probably be disastrous to another.[140]   Many of these cases involve the reckless use of automobiles.[141]   In such a case, if the actor's
conduct does not amount to wilfulness or recklessness and
wantonness he may nevertheless be subject to statutory liability for negligent operation of a vehicle causing death.[142]

An omission to perform a duty which causes death may also
constitute involuntary manslaughter.[143]   However, the duty
must be one arising by law or contract. For example, if a
guardian knew that his ward was in danger and that he could
rescue him without jeopardizing hiw own life, wilful or negligent failure to do so would be manslaughter.[144]   The omission
to perform a mere moral duty, such as saving a drowning stranger, will not result in the imposition of liability.[145]

B. Proposed Changes in the Law

Although not explicitly, the Proposed Code retains the
distinction between voluntary and involuntary manslaughter.
Section 2010 lists four situations in which manslaughter may
occur. The first three, recklessly causing death, committing
a criminal abortion and intentionally causing or aiding suicide, would be classed as involuntary manslaughter. The last,
intentionally causing death under the influence of extreme
mental or emotional disturbance, would be voluntary manslaughter in that it involves an intent to kill.[146]

First, recklessly causing the death of another person constitutes manslaughter.[147]   The definition of recklessness approximates the three criteria requisite for wilful or reckless
and wanton conduct under current Michigan law.[148]   Not only
must the actor have been aware of a substantial and unjustifiable risk that death would result and have consciously disregarded it, but his disregard must be a gross deviation from
the standard of conduct which would be observed by reasonable
people in the same situation.[149]   The requirement of cognizance and conscious disregard of the risk definitively rules
out the possibility of negligence constituting manslaughter
and thus, in substance, codifies the judicially developed
rule previously discussed. Criminally negligent homicide
is treated under a separate section.[150]

The simple concept of recklessness abolishes the distinction between commission of an unlawful act causing death
and commission of a lawful act in an unlawful manner with
the same result.[151]   Cases involving the omission of a legal
or contractual duty also will be cognizable under this section if the actor was aware of and consciously disregarded
the risk of death to the person to whom the duty was owed.
Nonfeasance many (sic) constitute recklessness under the Proposed Code as there is no requirement that the actor must

have created the risk.[152] Similarly, if the defendant was negligently unaware of the risk the crime will be negligent homicide.[153]

While the existence of a misdemeanor-manslaughter rule in Michigan is doubtful,[154] the Proposed Code eliminates all possibility of its existence. The misdemeanor-manslaughter rule encompasses deaths resulting from the commission of _any_ unlawful act less than a felony.[155] The rule has been criticized because of the illogical and harsh results which obtain when it is applied to relatively minor offenses which are malum prohibitum rather than malum in se.[156] It focuses upon the occurrence of such an infraction rather than on the culpability of the actor, that is, his recklessness or negligence. Such a result is not possible under the Proposed Code, which focuses solely upon the criterion of recklessness. If the actor recklessly causes death, whether or not he has incidently committed a misdemeanor, the offense will be manslaughter. If he has not acted recklessly, even though he may be a misdemeanant, there will be no manslaughter.[157]

Second, a person commits manslaughter, if, as a result of a criminal abortion, he causes the death of the female.[158] The abortion must be criminal as defined in section 3015. If it is performed by a physician and is therapeutic,[159] the act will not constitute manslaughter unless it is performed recklessly.[160]

Under the present statutory provisions, an abortion resulting in the death of either the mother or an unborn quick child[161] will be manslaughter.[162] In the Proposed Code generally, homicide must be committed upon a "person," defined as a human being born and alive at the time of the homicidal act.[163] Specifically, under the manslaughter provision, the death caused by a criminal abortion must be that of the mother.[164] This rule is in accord with the common sense conception of homicide and is necessary in order to avoid vitiation of the abortion statute. Otherwise, every criminal abortion would be manslaughter, with the defendant incurring a penalty double that provided for abortion.[165]

Third, intentionally causing or aiding another person to commit suicide will be manslaughter.[166] The first inquiry must be into the meaning of causation as used in this context. Intentionally causing another to commit suicide by means of duress or deception is provided for in first degree murder. Is it possible to cause another to commit suicide without the use of duress or deception? Certainly perpetrating the fatal act could not be meant, as suicide is defined as deliberately terminating one's own existence.[167] One causes a result when his conduct is an antecedent but for which the result would not have occurred.[168] When intentionally causing a result is an element of an offense, causation is not established unless the result is within the purpose or contemplation of the actor.[169] Perhaps, "causes" was intended to mean the suggestion of suicide. This however, raises substantial conceptual problems if one

849

takes into account the free will of the suicide. It would be difficult to apply the concept of causation in such a case, even in the basic "but for" sense. Who can say that the actor's suggestion was the cause-in-fact of the suicide? Perhaps the deceased had already considered the subject and had decided to take his own life, rendering the suggestion superfluous. Similar problems arise with inciting or encouraging suicide, which also might be considered as aiding rather than causing. Possibly the concept of causing suicide should be eliminated altogether. If not, it must be distinguished from aiding suicide. The former would involve a greater degree of culpability because the actor might actually implant the idea of self-destruction in the suicide's mind. In the latter case the actor merely would be assisting in carrying out a preconceived plan. If the suicide is a responsible adult, aiding in his self-destruction must, of necessity, be less culpable if any value is to be placed upon his free will as a human being.

In distinguishing between different cases of aiding suicide, Swiss law looks to the motive of the actor. If it was self-serving, sanctions will be imposed, whereas if it was altruistic there will be no punishment.[170] While the concept of motive as an element of a crime is foreign to American law, nevertheless, it does bear upon the reprehensibility of the actor's conduct.

Although suicide should not be encouraged by the removal of all sanctions in these cases,[171] it appears that there is a real distinction between causing and aiding the commission of suicide, the latter, in cases similar to those of voluntary euthanasia, evidencing a lesser degree of culpability. While the Proposed Code reduces these cases from first degree murder[172] to manslaughter, this might not be sufficient. Perhaps when aiding a person to commit suicide is motivated by mercy, the offense should be mitigated from a Class B to a Class C felony.[173]

Fourth, a person commits manslaughter if he causes the death of another person while "under the influence of extreme mental or emotional disturbance for which there is a reasonable explanation or excuse."[174] Reasonableness is determined "from the viewpoint of a person in the actor's situation under the circumstances as he believes them to be."[175] This test broadens the common law concept of adequate provocation and more effectively parallels the rational processes of the defendant.

Under the proposed rule the provoking disturbance need not be the result of a physical injury, affront or circumstances of a similar nature. It nullifies the common law rule that words alone will never constitute adequate provocation.[176] The provoking circumstances need not emanate from the victim but may be the result of totally external forces. This innovation is significant in that it focuses attention upon the true mitigating factor. The rationale is not that the defendant has a limited right to repay "an eye for an eye";

rather, the law should look to the provoking or disturbing circumstances because of the effect which they might have on the defendant's mental state. Under the proposed test his conduct will be scrutinized solely as to whether his act was the result of extreme emotional or mental disturbance arising from any reasonable source. The fact that the words "explanation or excuse" are used is significant in that defendant's act need not be caused by provoking conduct. Rather, the explanation or excuse may be of wholly non-human origin. For instance, the Model Penal Code cites the example of one who acts under the influence of a traumatic injury.[177]

The Proposed Code also introduces an element of subjectivity into the concept of reasonableness. Whether there is a reasonable explanation or excuse for the defendant's conduct will be judged from the viewpoint of his situation under the circumstances as he believed them to be. This formulation eliminates the rigid objective test of the reasonable man. However, "situation" is an ambiguous term. Though retention of the requirement that the excuse or explanation be reasonable indicates an intention to strike a balance between objectivity and subjectivity, it has been argued that "situation" engulfs and renders the concept of reasonableness meaningless.[178] This need not be the result. That it is possible to reach a balancing point between a purely subjective and purely objective test is made clear from the law of torts. In determining whether a person has been negligent, if he has some physical infirmity his conduct will be judged by the standard of a reasonably prudent man with a like defect.[179] Similar judicial interpretation of this section seems to have been intended and would constitute a workable approach.

Furthermore, the circumstances must be viewed as the actor believed them to be, not necessarily as they existed in fact. Again, this is a significant innovation. Since we are interested in his mental state we must view the circumstances surrounding his crime as he did if we are to accurately determine the culpability of his conduct. Circumstances as they actually existed may have little or no bearing upon such an inquiry.

VI.

Criminally Negligent Homicide

A. Existing Michigan Law

Presently, most cases of criminally negligent homicide are classed as involuntary manslaughter.[180] In order for criminal liability to result the actor's conduct must amount to gross negligence, amounting to wantonness, disregard of probable consequences and indifference to the rights of others - a standard of conduct equally as culpable as criminal intent.[182]

851

Good faith performance of a duty in a manner which has been[183] safe in the past will negative the element of negligence. As in tort law, the defendant's act must be the proximate[184] cause of the victim's death.

In order to curb the serious results of negligent operation of vehicles[185] the legislature has passed a statute making such operation resulting in death a misdemeanor.[186] Either the defendant must have been driving at an immoderate rate of speed, or operating his vehicle in a careless, reckless,[187] or negligent manner, short of wilfulness or wantonness. The charge of negligent homicide committed with a vehicle is deemed to be included in every charge of manslaughter similarly committed, so that if the defendant is acquitted[188] of the latter he may still be convicted of the former. By statute, that which will constitute an immoderate rate of speed is not dependent upon the legal rate.[189] Rather, it is that which is not within reasonable limits under the circumstances.[190] Thus, it is apparent that the same type of evidence necessary to impose civil liability for negligence is necessary to impose criminal liability under this statute.[191] Finally, while the contributory negligence of the victim is not a defense to manslaughter or statutory negligent homicide, it is relevant to the culpable negligence[192] of the defendant.

B. Proposed Changes in the Law

The Proposed Code poses two situations in which a person commits criminally negligent homicide. The first occurs when, with criminal negligence, he causes the death of another person.[193] "Criminal negligence" is defined as the failure to perceive a substantial and unjustifiable risk that a result will occur or that a circumstance exists. The risk must be such that failure to perceive it is a gross deviation from the standard of care that would be observed by a reasonable person in the situation.[194] This section is the counterpart of reckless manslaughter, the only difference being that in recklessness the actor perceives the risk and consciously disregards it.[195] Such conduct evidences a greater indifference to the value of human life and is deserving of the more stringent sanctions which obtain upon a conviction of manslaughter.

Inclusion of the concept of "gross deviation" from a reasonable standard of conduct appears to impose a higher standard than ordinary negligence, but a lesser one than recklessness. Nevertheless, the fact cannot be escaped that in punishing negligence, one is punishing inadvertent rather than conscious conduct. For this reason criminally negligent homicide statutes have been attacked on the ethical-conceptual basis that voluntary causing of harm is the essence of moral fault.[196] In imposing sanctions upon negligent conduct, the statute seems to run counter to the ethical bases of Anglo-

American criminal law, unless it can be said that unaware-
ness itself is a voluntary action.

Ethical questions aside, it is necessary to inquire whether
punishing negligence serves any utilitarian purpose. The
first question is one of deterrence. Professor Hall states
that there is no utility in punishing negligence because, by
hypothesis, the actor is unaware of his action and therefore
not conscious of risk creation or of sanctions. If he does
give thought to the matter his conduct is reckless rather
than negligent.[197] The contrary view is that by imposing
sanctions we can make men utilize their faculties to discover
that they are creating a substantial and unjustifiable risk.
That is, sanctions are imposed to stimulate care that otherwise might not be taken.[198]

The second general reason for the imposition of criminal
sanctions is rehabilitation. It would appear that this is
not relevant in cases of negligent homicide, as few would
contend that imprisonment is the proper pedagogical device
to correct negligence. Though it might be said that it would
impress upon the actor the gravity of his act and teach him
not to repeat it, it seems that the mere thought of having
killed another human being would probably accomplish the
same result.

Third, note must be taken of the concept of retribution,
still a very real factor in criminal law. The draftsmen of
the Model Penal Code state that failure to use one's faculties
may, in cases of gross deviation from reasonable standards
of conduct, be deserving of societal condemnation.[199]

This last formulation returns us to the question of moral
fault. It would appear that the actor is morally blame-
worthy if gross inadvertence to conduct creating a substantial and unjustifiable risk of death to others actually results in death. It is further submitted that Wechsler and
Michael are correct in their belief that by providing sanctions for negligent conduct of this type people can be encouraged to take positive steps to remain cognizant of their
conduct in relation to their surroundings.[200] For these
reasons this provision should remain in the Proposed Code.

Intentionally or recklessly causing the death of another
in the honest but unreasonable belief that the act was justified also will constitute criminally negligent homicide.[201]
This section applies to cases of imperfect defenses, which
are basically pleas of confession and avoidance. For example, if the defendant fails to establish self-defense, his
confession leaves only an intentional, unprivileged killing,
which under both the common law and Proposed Code will be
murder. Since these defenses are usually based on the actor's
reasonable belief of impending harm and the amount of force
necessary to overcome it,[202] it seems logically and conceptually correct to constitute the resulting, unprivileged act
as negligent homicide. Certainly one who acted in the good
faith belief that his conduct was justified is not morally
or culpably in the same class as one who intentionally kills

853

without such belief.

In practice, juries usually have deemed the act manslaughter.[203] The effect of this provision will be definitively to place cases of imperfect defense in a category logically suited to them. No longer will the defendant's fate be left to chance. Furthermore, the penalty will be reduced from that for manslaughter[204] to that for negligent homicide. Such a reduction is desirable in light of the relatively little culpability inherent in the act.

Finally, under the Proposed Code, the jury may consider statutes regulating the actor's conduct in determining whether or not he is culpably negligent.[205] The most obvious example of such reference would be to speed laws in a case where the defendant negligently killed while operating a motor vehicle. This approach is in accord with common sense, because while such statutes may not be definitive of the issue they obviously have a bearing on the reasonableness of the actor's conduct. The same result is reached under the present law.[206] The only suggestion that may be made is that perhaps reference should be made to ordinances as well as statutes because, if the draftsmen did have speed laws in mind, they are largely a matter of local ordinance rather than state statute.

VII

Conclusion

While the Michigan Revised Criminal Code provisions on homicide present a commendably straightforward approach to criminal law, certain alterations are suggested. First degree murder should specifically include causing suicide by means of duress or deception, and the manslaughter provision should specifically exclude these cases. Perhaps "causing" suicide should be omitted from the manslaughter section altogether, leaving only "aiding." Specific provisions mitigating cases of voluntary euthanasia from first degree murder to manslaughter should also be included, making treatment of these cases commensurate with the treatment of aiding suicide. The latter, when motivated by mercy, might be further mitigated from a Class B to a Class C felony. Finally, as to criminally negligent homicide, it is suggested that reference be made to ordinances as well as statutes regulating the actor's conduct in determining his negligence.

Though the Proposed Code contains certain problems and ambiguities, this result is almost inherent in the task of comprehensively revising an entire penal system. Generally, it eradicates many of the difficulties presently existing in the law of homicide and for this reason, is a vast improvement over the present law.

Edwin W. Hecker, Jr.

Footnotes

1. Mich. Comp. Laws Sec. 750.316 (1948), Mich. Stat. Ann. Sec. 28.548 (1954).

2. 5 Mich. 1 (1858).

3. Id. at 5. See 1 F. Wharton & J. Ruppenthal, Wharton's Criminal Law, Sec. 419 (1932).

4. People v. Andrus, 331 Mich. 535, 50 N.W.2d 310 (1951).

5. People v. Austin, 221 Mich. 635, 192 N.W. 590 (1923).

6. 99 Mich. 336, 58 N.W. 328 (1894).

7. Id. at 339, 58 N.W. at 329; Nye v. People, 35 Mich. 15 (1876).

8. 1 O. Warren & B. Bilas, Warren on Homicide, Sec. 66, at 264-69, 273-75 (perm. ed. 1938).

9. People v. Hansen, 368 Mich. 344, 118 N.W.2d 422 (1962).

10. People v. Statkiewicz, 247 Mich. 260, 225 N.W. 540 (1929).

11. People v. Potter, 5 Mich. 1 (1858); R. Moreland, The Law of Homicide 199 (1952).

12. Nye v. People, 35 Mich. 15 (1876).

13. Act of April 22, 1794, 3 Sm. L. 186 (Pa.).

14. R. Moreland, supra note 11, at 200.

15. Lundberg v. Buckhoe, 338 F.2d 62 (6th Cir. 1964); People v. Statkiewicz, 247 Mich. 260, 225 N.W. 540 (1929); People v. Vinunzo, 212 Mich. 472, 180 N.W. 502 (1920).

16. 212 Mich. 472, 180 N.W. 502 (1920).

17. Ejusdem generis is defined as being of the same kind, class, or nature. Thus, where general words follow an enumeration of specific things ejusdem generis applies to limit the scope of the general words to things of the same nature as those enumerated. Black's Law Dictionary 608 (4th Ed. 1951).

18. See People v. Palmer, 105 Mich. 568, 63 N.W. 656 (1895), wherein it was held that if at any time after reentering the bar where his victim was drinking, the defendant deliberately, intentionally and with malice aforethought shot him, he would be guilty of murder. Professor Moreland views the erosion of the concept of premeditation as the natural, and unfortunate, result of the judicial process. He states:
   If history is an acceptable teacher (the legislators) might have anticipated that as in the case of aforethought,: the element of pre-design would eventually be read out of "premeditated" by the judges. Wilful and deliberate being words which fundamentally mean no more than intentional, the first degree murder would then require no more in fact than an unlawful, intentional homicide. . . .if the jury were desirous of going that far.
R. Moreland, supra note 11, at 200. Other states have adopted

similar rules. See 12 Mont. L. Rev. 72 (1951); 21 Md. L. Rev. 349 (1961). That such a view was not always controlling is evidenced by Nye v. People, 35 Mich. 15 (1876), where it is stated: "But it is a perversion of terms to apply the term deliberate to any act which is done on a sudden impulse." Id. at 18.

19. People v. Marshall, 366 Mich. 498, 115 N.W.2d 309 (1962).

20. 30 Mich. 16 (1874).

21. 368 Mich. 344, 118 N.W. 2d 422 (1962).

22. People v. Hodges, 196 Mich. 546, 162 N.W. 966 (1917) (dictum).

23. Mich. Comp. Laws Sec. 750.316 (1948), Mich. Stat. Ann. Sec. 28.548 (1954).

24. Mich. Rev. Crim. Code Sec. 2005(1)(a) (Final Draft L967).

25. Id. Sec. 601-45.

26. Id. Sec. 2005, Comment A.

27. 99 Mich. at 339, 58 N.W. at 329.

28. 247 Mich. 260, 225 N.W. 540 (1929).

29. Id. at 264, 225 N.W. at 541 (emphasis omitted).

30. The model Penal Code recognizes only a single degree of murder, defining it:

> (1) (C)riminal homicide constitutes murder when:
> (a) it is committed purposely or knowingly; or
> (b) it is committed recklessly under circumstances
manifesting extreme indifference to the value of human life.

Model Penal Code Sec. 210.2(1) (Official Draft 1962). Illinois similarly omits any mention of premeditation in defining murder:

> (a) A person who kills an individual without lawful justi-
fication commits murder if, in performing the acts which cause the death:
> (1) He either intends to kill or do great bodily
harm to that individual or another; or knows that such acts will cause death to that individual or another; or
> (2) He knows that such acts create a strong pro-
bability of death or great bodily harm to that individual or another. . . .

Ill. Ann. Stat. ch. 38, Sec. 9-1(a) (Smith-Hurd 1964). Like the Model Penal Code and Illinois, New York defines its single degree of murder without reference to premeditation or de-liberation:

> A person is guilty of murder when:
> 1. With intent to cause the death of another person,
he causes the death of such person or of a third person. . . . or
> 2. Under circumstances evincing a depraved indifference

to human life, he recklessly engages in conduct which creates
a grave risk of death to another person, and thereby causes
the death of another person. . . .

N.Y. Pen. Law Sec. 125.25 (1) -.25 (2).

31. 212 Mich. 472, 180 N.W. 502 (1920).

32. Mich. Rev. Crim. Code Sec. 305(a) (Final Draft 1967).

33. 368 Mich. 344, 118 N.W.2d 422 (1962).

34. 1 O. Warren & Bilas, supra note 8, sec. 65, at 253.

35. People v. Statkiewicz, 247 Mich. 260, 225 N.W. 540 (1929);
Wellar v. People, 30 Mich. 16 (1874).

36. People v. Hansen, 368 Mich. 344, 118 N.W.2d 422 (1962);
see People v. Marshall, 366 Mich. 498, 115 N.S.2d 309 (1962).

37. The Proposed Code's definition of "intentionally" is
essentially equivalent to the Model Penal Code's definition
of "purposely." The Model Penal Code states:

(a) A person acts purposely with respect to a material
element of an offense when:
(i) if the element involves the nature of his conduct or a result thereof, it is his conscious object to engage in conduct of that nature or to cause such a result. . . .

Model Penal Code Sec. 2.02 (2) (a) (i) (Official Draft 1962).
Yet, in addition to categorizing criminal homicide committed
"purposely" as murder, the Model Code similarly classes that
which is committed "knowingly." Id. Sec. 210.2 (1) (a). Its
definition of "knowingly" is similar to that of the Proposed
Code as regards a material element of an offense involving
conduct or circumstances. Mich. Rev. Crim. Code Sec. 305(b)
(Final Draft 1967):

"Knowingly." A person acts knowingly with respect to
conduct or to a circumstance described by a statute defining
an offense when he is aware that his conduct is of that nature
or that the circumstance exists.

Model Penal Code Sec. 2.02 (2) (b) (i) (Official Draft 1962):

A person acts knowingly with respect to a material element of an offense when:

(i) if the element involves the nature of his conduct
or the attendant circumstances, he is aware that his conduct
is of that nature or that such circumstances exist. . . .

However, unlike the Model Code, the Proposed Code does not
provide for the mens rea element of "knowingly" with respect
to a result. Mich. Rev. Crim. Code Sec. 305 (b) (Final
Draft 1967): The Model Penal Code, Sec. 2.02 (2) (b) (ii)
(Official Draft 1962) states:

A person acts knowingly with respect to a material element of an offense when: . . .

857

(ii) if the element involves a result of his conduct, he is aware that it is practically certain that his conduct will cause such a result.

Thus, there is no provision for a murder committed "knowingly" in the proposed section, as there is in the Model Penal Code Sec. 210.2(1)(a) (Official Draft 1962). The latter's formulation of "knowingly" in relation to a result is an awareness that it is practically certain that the conduct will cause the result. Id. Sec. 2.02(2)(b)(ii). However, upon closer examination the apparent deficiency of the Proposed Code proves to be more imagined than real. First, if the actor knows, to the point of certainty, that a result will follow from his act, he will probably be held to have intended the result. See N.Y. Pen. Law Sec. 15.05, Comment. Also, the Model Penal Code, and the Illinois Code which is similar, provide for only a single degree of murder. Ill. Stat. Ann. ch. 38, Sec. 9-1 (Smith-Hurd 1964); Model Penal Code Sec. 210.2 (Official Draft 1962). In Michigan, if the actor is found not to have had the conscious objective of causing death, he may still be guilty of second degree murder if he intended to inflict serious physical injury or if he recklessly engaged in conduct creating a grave risk of death under circumstances manifesting extreme indifference to the value of human life. Mich. Rev. Crim. Code Sec. 2006 (Final Draft 1967). It is submitted that most cases of "knowing" murder under the Model Code would fall into one of these two categories. For example, if carbolic acid were given to the victim for the purpose of drugging him, and death resulted, it would not be first degree murder because it was not the conscious objective of the actor to cause death. Id. Sec. 2005(1)(a). However, since there was an intent to cause serious physical injury, the crime would be murder in the second degree. Id. Sec. 2006(1)(a). Similarly, if the actor tied his victim to a railroad track with the intent of frightening her into transferring the deed to her property, with knowledge that a train was due to pass, the act, if death resulted, would be second degree murder. While there might not have been an intent to cause death, or even serious physical injury, the conduct manifested extreme indifference to the value of life and created a grave risk of death. Id. Sec. 2006(1)(b).

38. Mich. Rev. Crim. Code Sec. 2005(1)(a) (Final Draft).

39. People v. Hodges, 196 Mich. 546, 162 N.W. 966 (1917) (dictum).

40. For an interesting critique of the doctrine of transferred intent and a novel solution to the problems posed by it see Ritz, Felony Murder, Transferred Intent, and the Palsgraf Doctrine in the Criminal Law, 16 Wash. & Lee L. Rev. 169 (1959).

41. Mich. Rev. Crim. Code Sec. 2005(2) (Final Draft 1967).

42. Id. Sec. 2010(1)(d).

43. People v. Milhem, 350 Mich. 497, 87 N.W.2d 151 (1957).

44. Mich. Rev. Crim. Code, Sec. 2005(1)(a) (Final Draft 1967).

45. (1943-1944) Mich. Att'y Gen. Biennial Rep. 342, reasons that although Michigan adopts, by reference, offenses indictable at common law, part of the definition of a crime is its punishment. As there is not authorized punishment applicable to an individual after he has committed suicide, it cannot be a crime. Since the punishment for an attempt is one-half of that authorized for the completed crime, neither can attempted suicide be criminal.

46. Mich. Rev. Crim. Code Sec. 2005(3) (Final Draft 1967).

47. Id. Sec. 2005, Comment C.

48. 211 Mich. 187, 178 N.W. 690 (1920).

49. See e.g., cases collected in Annot., 25 A.L.R.2d 1186 (1951).

50. Mich. Rev. Crim. Code Sec. 2010(c) (Final Draft 1967).

51. Voluntary euthanasia means killing for the benefit of the patient at his request or with his consent. This is to be distinguished from involuntary euthanasia, where the patient is killed for the benefit of another person or persons. An example of the latter would be the killing of a hopeless mental defective because he has absolutely no value to society. The moral and ethical differences between these two types of cases are apparent, and only the former will be considered in this discussion. It would be repugnant to the principles of Anglo-American law to allow any person, no matter how useless, to be exterminated because he constituted a burden upon society. Such cases, it is submitted, should remain within the provision for first degree murder.

52. Mich. Rev. Crim. Code Sec. 2005(1)(a) (Final Draft 1967).

53. Id. Sec. 330(2)(a).

54. Id. Sec. 605(2). The Comment to this section specifically excludes euthanasia.

55. Id. Sec. 2005(3), 2010(1)(c).

56. Silving, Euthanasia: A Study in Comparative Criminal Law, 103 U. Pa. L. Rev. 350 (1954).

57. Mich. Rev. Crim. Code Sec. 2005(2) - (3).

58. Id. Sec. 135 (n). See, e.g., Maher v. People, 10 Mich. 212 (1862); People v. Potter, 5 Mich. 1 (1858).

59. Mich. Rev. Crim. Code Sec. 2005(5) (Final Draft 1967).

60. Mich. Comp. Laws Sec. 750.316 (1948), Mich. Stat. Ann. Sec. 28.548 (1954).

61. See Comment, Sentencing Reform and the Michigan Revised Criminal Code, 14 Wayne L. Rev. p. 891 supra.

62. Mich. Comp. Laws Sec. 750.316 (1948), Mich. Stat. Ann. Sec. 28.548 (1954).

63. Morris, The Felon's Responsibility for the Lethal Acts of Others, 105 U. Pa. L. Rev. 50, 59 (1956).

64. People v. Hearn, 354 Mich. 468, 93 N.W.2d 302 (1958); People v. Wright, 315 Mich. 81, 23 N.W.2d 213 (1946). The Wright court stated: "Admittedly the homicide in the instant case would not constitute murder in the first degree unless defendant was at the scene of the alleged crime either with intent to rob or in the actual act of robbing." Id. at 87, 23 N.W.2d at 216.

65. Mich. Comp. Laws, Sec. 750.316 (1948), Mich. Stat. Ann. Sec. 28.548 (1954); People v. Best, 218 Mich. 141, 187 N.W. 393 (1922).

66. People v. Crandell, 270 Mich. 124, 258 N.W. 224 (1935).

67. 225 Mich. 125, 195 N.W. 670 (1923).

68. 306 Mich. 356, 10 N.W.2d 914 (1943) (beating during attempted robbery resulted in pneumonia from which victim died).

69. 332 Mich. 508, 52 N.W.2d 201 (1952).

70. The facts are analogous to the controversial case of Commonwealth v. Almeida, 362 Pa. 596, 68 A.2d 595 (1949), and the result is identical. Basing its decision on the theory of proximate cause borrowed from the law of torts, the Almeida court reasoned that it was immaterial whether the fatal bullet was fired by the felons or by one of the victim's fellow officers. The felons set in motion a chain of events the proximate result of which was the death of a police officer. Therefore, they were culpable whether or not one of their number actually fired the fatal shot.

71. 332 Mich. at 518, 52 N.W.2d at 205.

72. 370 Mich. 12, 120 N.W.2d 766 (1963).

73. 391 Pa. 486, 137 A.2d 472 (1958), noted in 71 Harv. L. Rev. 1565 (1958), and 56 Mich. L. Rev. 1197 (1958). Redline disapproved but refused to overrule Almeida, distinguishing it on the basis that it involved the death of a police officer rather than a felon.

74. 8 N.Y.2d 48, 167 N.E.2d 736, 201 N.Y.S.2d 328 (1960).

75. Almeida and Redline gave rise to a similar result in Pennsylvania. Torcia, Clarification of the Felony-Murder Statute?, 63 Dick. L. Rev. 119 (1959).

76. People v. Andrus, 331 Mich. 535, 50 N.W.2d 310 (1951); People v. Treichel, 229 Mich. 303, 200 N.W. 950 (1924).

77. People v. Utter, 217 Mich. 74, 185 N.W. 830 (1921).

78. See, e.g., People v. Arnett, 239 Mich. 123, 214 N.W.

231 (1927) (while resisting arrest, defendant killed a sheriff).

79. Mich. Rev. Crim. Code Sec. 2005(1)(b) (Final Draft 1967):
(1) A person commits the crime of murder in the first degree if:
. . .

(b) Acting either alone or with one or more persons, he commits or attempts to commit arson in the first degree, burglary in the first or second degree, escape in the first degree, kidnapping in the first degree, rape in the first degree, robbery in any degree, or sodomy in the first degree, and in the course of and in furtherance of the crime that he is committing or attempting to commit, or of immediate flight therefrom, he, or another participant if there be any, causes the death of a person other than one of the participants.

80. See People v. Podolski, 332 Mich. 508, 52 N.W.2d 201 (1952); Commonwealth v. Almeida, 362 Pa. 596, 68 A.2d 595 (1949).

81. See Commonwealth v. Thomas, 382 Pa. 639, 117 A.2d 204 (1955).

82. See Commonwealth v. Bolish, 391 Pa. 550, 138 A.2d 447 (1958). For an extensive analysis of all the possible interrelationships between felon, victim and third party, see Ludwig, Foreseeable Death in Felony Murder, 18 U. Pitt. L. Rev. 51 (1956).

83. Morris, supra note 63, at 59.

84. See Sayre, Criminal Responsibility for the Acts of Another, 43 Harv. L. Rev. 689 (1930).

85. Morris, supra note 63, at 67-68.

86. Mich. Rev. Crim. Code Sec. 2005(1)(b) (Final Draft 1967) (emphasis added).

87. Id. Sec. 320(1).

88. See, e.g., People v. Podolski, 332 Mich. 508, 52 N.W. 2d 201 (1952); Commonwealth v. Almeida, 362 Pa. 596, 68 A.2d 595 (1949).

89. Mich. Rev. Crim. Code Sec. 320(2) (Final Draft 1967).

90. Model Penal Code Sec. 210.21(1)(b) (Official Draft 1962). The inclusion of reckless murder has been criticized in Danforth, The Model Penal Code and Degrees of Criminal Homicide, 11 Am. U.L. Rev. 147, 158-65 (1962).

91. Model Penal Code, Sec. 201.2, Comment (2) (Tent. Draft No. 9, 1959).

92. Mich. Rev. Crim. Code Sec. 320(3) (Final Draft 1967). (Emphasis added).

93. 332 Mich. 508, 52 N.W. 2d 201. See cases cited notes 80-82 supra.

94. 370 Mich. 12, 120 N.W.2d 766 (1963).

95. Id.; Commonwealth v. Redline, 391 Pa. 486, 137 A.2d 472 (1958); Byrn, Homicide Under the Proposed New York Penal Law, 33 Fordham L. Rev. 173 (1964); Ludwig, supra note 82; Morris, supra note 63; Packer, The Case of Revision of the Penal Code, 13 Stan. L. Rev. 252 (1961); 71 Harv. L. Rev. 1565 (1958); 18 Stan. L. Rev. 690 (1966).

96. E.G., Wilson v. State, 188 Ark. 846, 68 S.W. 2d 100 (1934).

97. 381 Pa. 500, 113 A.2d 464 (1955).

98. Mich. Rev. Crim. Code Sec. 2005(1)(b) (Final Draft 1967).

99. 31 Cal. App. 2d 52, 87 P.2d 364 (1939).

100. Mich. Rev. Crim. Code Sec. 2005(1)(b) (Final Draft 1967).

101. Morris, supra note 63, at 73.

102. Sayre, supra note 84, at 802-04.

103. Mich. Rev. Crim. Code Sec. 2005(4) (Final Draft 1967).

104. N.Y. Pen. Law Sec. 125.25(3).

105. Note, The Proposed Penal Law of New York, 64 Colum. L. Rev. 1469 (1964).

106. Mich. Comp. Laws Sec. 750.316 (1948), Mich. Stat. Ann. Sec. 28.548 (1954).

107. Mich. Rev. Crim. Code Sec. 2005(1)(b) (Final Draft 1967).

108. Arson in the first degree involves setting fire to or exploding a building when the actor knows, or reasonably should know, that a person is inside. Id. Sec. 2805. The risk that the person will be trapped inside and killed is very great under these circumstances.
Burglary in the first degree involves entering or remaining unlawfully in a building while armed with a deadly weapon with the intent to commit a crime therein. Id. Sec. 2610. Here, the deadly weapon coupled with the likelihood of resistance from an occupant of the dwelling clearly involves sufficient dangerousness to be included in felony-murder. Second degree burglary involves similar entry into a building either armed with a deadly weapon, or unarmed if the building is a dwelling. Id. Sec. 2611. Again, the likelihood of an occupant resisting the entry involves danger to life.
A person commits the crime of escape in the first degree if, with the aid of at least two other persons there present, he employs force or a deadly weapon or instrumentality in escaping from a penal facility. Id. Sec. 4605. In so escaping the chances of violence, for instance a running gun battle, are so great that inclusion under felony-murder would seem almost mandatory.
First degree kidnapping involves the intentional abduction of another for any one of a number of purposes, including holding him for ransom, using him as a shield, inflicting physical injury, etc. Id. Sec. 2210(1). Again, there is a

high risk of violence, particularly when the propensity of kidnappers for killing their victim to avoid identification is taken into account.

First degree rape consists of three distinct situations. The first occurs if a male engages in sexual intercourse with a female by forcible compulsion. Id. Sec. 2310(1)(a). Forcible compulsion means either physical force or a threat placing a person in fear of immediate death or serious physical injury or kidnapping. Id. Sec. 2301(h). This situation is clearly dangerous. The female will naturally resist, and a progressive escalation of violence may follow, with the threat to life increasing at each step. Second, a male commits rape. if he engages in intercourse with a female incapable of consent because physically helpless. Id. Sec. 2310(1)(b). Here the presence of danger to life is more questionable. If the actor forcibly rendered her physically helpless, the case falls within the first category. However, if she is helpless for another reason, inclusion under felony-murder is dubious. For example, the actor may have plied his victim with drink to facilitate the accomplishment of his criminal design, with death resulting from too great an intake of alcohol. It is submitted that his act was not inherently dangerous to life, and perhaps his culpability does not warrant imposition of the sanctions concomitant with first degree murder. However, the dangerousness present in the preceding and subsequent situations, coupled with the impracticability of including certain instances of rape and excluding others, necessitate the inclusion in toto of first degree rape in felony=murder. Third, a male is guilty of first degree rape if he engages in intercourse with a female under the age of eleven years. Id. Sec. 2310(1)(c). Here the danger is obvious. See generally Comment, Sex Offenses and Penal Code Revision in Michigan, 14 Wayne L. Rev. p. 934 infra.

Robbery in the first degree is theft using force or threats to overcome resistance while armed with a deadly weapon. Mich. Rev. Crim. Code Sec. 3305 (Final Draft 1967). Second degree robbery is the use of similar force or threats with an accomplice actually present. Id. Sec. 3306. Third degree robbery is simply theft with the use of force or threats. Id. Sec. 3307. In all three degrees it is the use or threat of force which distinguishes robbery, and this distinguishing characteristic classes robbery as a dangerous crime. Whenever physical violence is threatened or employed in a criminal undertaking, the threat to life becomes increasingly great.

First degree sodomy is basically the same as first degree rape except that the act consists of deviate sexual intercourse. Id. Sec. 2315. The same considerations as discussed under rape are applicable.

Similar additions to the felony-murder rule have been adopted in N.Y. Pen. Law Sec. 125.25(3), and Model Penal Code Sec. 210.2(1)(b) (Official Draft 1962).

109. 332 Mich. 508, 52 N.W.2d 201 (1952).

110. Mich. Rev. Crim. Code Sec. 2005(1)(b) (Final Draft 1967). Similar provisions have been adopted in N.Y. Pen. Law Sec. 125.25(3), and Model Penal Code Sec. 2102(1)(b) (Official Draft 1962).

111. Mich. Comp. Laws Sec. 750.317 (1948), Mich. Stat. Ann. Sec. 28.549 (1954).

112. 1 O. Warren & B. Bilas, Warren on Homicide, Sec. 79, at 389 (Perm. ed. 1938).

113. People v. Palmer, 105 Mich. 568, 63 N.W. 656 (1895).

114. People v. Collins, 303 Mich. 34, 5 N.W.2d 556 (1942); Wellar v. People, 30 Mich. 16 (1874(. See People v. Hanse, 368 Mich. 344, 118 N.W.2d 422 (1962).

115. People v. Collins, 303 Mich. 34, 5 N.W.2d 556 (1942).

116. Mich. Rev. Crim. Code Sec. 2006(1)(a)(Final Draft 1967).

117. Id. Sec. 2006. Comment.

118. See id. Sec. 135(h); cases cited note 114 supra; 1 O. Warren & B. Bilas, supra note 112, Sec. 79, at 394.

119. See People v. Statkiewicz, 247 Mich. 260, 225 N.W. 540 (1929).

120. Mich. Rev. Crim. Code Sec. 2006(1)(b) (Final Draft 1967).

121. See id. Sec. 2006, Comment. "Recklessly" is defined as conscious disregard of a substantial and unjustifiable risk that a result will occur. Id. Sec. 305(c).

122. Model Penal Code Sec. 210.2(1)(b) (Official Draft 1962).

123. Danforth, supra note 90.

124. Mich. Comp. Laws Sec. 750.321 (1948), Mich. Stat. Ann. Sec. 28.553 (1954).

125. People v. Milhem, 350 Mich. 497, 87 N.W.2d 151 (1957); People v. Ryczek, 224 Mich. 106, 194 N.W. 609 (1923); People v. Droste, 160 Mich. 66, 125 N.W. 87 (1910).

126. Wellar v. People, 30 Mich. 16 (1874).

127. Maher v. People, 10 Mich. 212 (1862).

128. E.G., People v. Stallworth, 364 Mich. 528, 111 N.W. 2d 742 (1961); People v. Van Camp, 356 Mich. 593, 97 N.W. 2d 726 (1959).

129. People v. Burkard, 374 Mich. 430, 132 N.W.2d 106 (1965).

130. Maher v. People, 10 Mich. 212 (1862).

131. Although it is commonly said that mere words will not constitute adequate provocation, 1 F. Wharton & J. Ruppenthal, Whatron's Criminal Law Sec. 584 (1932), no Michigan case so holding has been found.

132. Maher v. People, 10 Mich. 212 (1862).

133. Id. at 220.

134. Id. at 222.

135. Metropolitan Life Ins. Co. v. McDavid, 39 F. Supp. 228 (E.D. Mich. 1941); People v. Ryczek, 224 Mich. 106, 194 N.W. 609 (1923).

136. People v. Pavlic, 227 Mich. 562, 199 N.W. 373 (1924).

137. People v. Slack, 90 Mich. 448, 51 N.W. 533 (1892).

138. Mich. Comp. Laws Sec. 750.14 (1948), Mich. Stat. Ann. Sec. 28.204 (1962) (using drugs or instruments with intent to procure miscarriage causing death of mother); Mich. Comp. Laws Sec. 750.236 (1948) Mich. Stat. Ann. Sec. 28.433 (1962) (setting spring gun or other explosive device which causes death of another); Mich. Comp. Laws, Sec. 750.322 (1948), Mich. Stat. Ann. Sec. 28.554 (1954) (wilful killing of un-born quick child by injury to mother which would have been murder had mother died); Mich. Comp. Laws Sec. 750.323 (1948), Mich. Stat. Ann Sec. 28.555 (1954) (attempt to destroy un-born quick child resulting in death of child or mother); Mich. Comp. Laws. Sec. 750.329 (1948), Mich. Stat. Ann. Sec. 28.561 (1954) (intentionally aiming firearm, without malice, which causes death).

139. People v. Orr, 243 Mich. 300, 22 N.W. 777 (1928).

140. Id. at 307, 220 N.W. at 779.

141. See, e.g., People v. Wardell, 291 Mich. 276, 289 N.W. 328 (1939).

142. Mich. Comp. Laws Sec. 750.324 (1948), as amended Mich. Stat. Ann. Sec. 28.556 (Supp. 1968).

143. People v. Beardsley, 150 Mich. 206, 113 N.W. 1128 (1907).

144. See 1 R. Anderson, Wharton's Criminal Law and Procedure, Sec. 296 (1957).

145. See People v. Beardsley, 150 Mich. 206, 112 N.W. 1128 (1907).

146. Mich. Rev. Crim. Code Sec. 2010 (Final Draft 1967).

147. Id. Sec. 2010(1)(a). See Model Penal Code Sec. 210.3 (1)(a) (Official Draft 1962).

148. See p. 925 supra.

149. Mich. Rev. Crim. Code Sec. 305(c) (Final Draft 1967).

150. Id. Sec. 2015.

151. People v. Townsend, 214 Mich. 267, 183 N.W. 177 (1921). If death was caused by an unlawful act, it is sufficient to allege that the defendant committed the act and that death occurred as a result of it. However, if death was caused by the performance of a lawful act in a grossly negligent manner, the duty improperly performed must be alleged as well as the

acts which constituted the defendant's improper performance or failure to perform.

152. Mich. Rev. Crim. Code Sec. 305(c) (Final Draft 1967).

153. Id. Sec. 305(d), 2015(1)(a).

154. See People v. Marshall, 362 Mich. 170, 106 N.W.2d 842 (1961), noted in 60 Mich. L. Rev. 102 (1961).

155. R. Moreland, The Law of Homicide 183 (1952).

156. Id.

157. The virtues of replacing the misdemeanor-manslaughter rule with a single standard of recklessness are discussed in Walker, Mens Rea in Manslaughter, 117 New L. J. 950 (1967).

158. Mich. Rev. Crim. Code Sec. 2010(1)(b) (Final Draft 1967).

159. Id. Sec. 7015(3). See Comment, Abortion Reform in Michigan - An Analysis of the Proposed Code's Provisions, 14 Wayne L. Rev. p. 1006 infra.

160. A "quick child" if one that has developed so that it moves within the mother's womb. Black's Law Dictionary 1415 (4th ed. 1951).

161. Mich. Rev. Crim. Code Sec. (1)(a) (Final Draft 1967). A therapeutic abortion performed negligently, which results in the death of the female, may be criminally negligent homicide. Id. Sec. 2015(1)(a).

162. Mich. Comp. Laws Sec. 750.14 (1948), Mich. Stat. Ann. Sec. 28.204 (1962); Mich. Comp. Laws. Sec. 750.323 (1948), Mich. Stat. Ann. Sec. 28.555 (1954).

163. Mich. Rev. Crim. Code Sec. 2001 (Final Draft 1967).

164. Id. Sec. 2010(1)(b).

165. Id. Sec. 1401(2)(b) - (c), 2010(2), 7015(5).

166. Id. Sec. 2010(1)(c).

167. Black's Law Dictionary 1602 (4th ed. 1951); John Hancock Mut. Ins. Co. v. Moore, 34 Mich. 41 (1876).

168. Mich. Rev. Crim. Code Sec. 320(1)(a) (Final Draft 1967).

169. Id. Sec. 320(2).

170. Silving, Euthanasia: A Study in Comparative Criminal Law, 103 U. Pa. L. Rev. 350, 376-77 (1954).

171. In Texas there is authority to the effect that knowingly furnishing another with the means to commit suicide is not criminal if the actor stops short of perpetrating the fatal act. Sanders v. State, 54 Tex. Crim. 101, 112 S.W. 68 (1908).

172. People v. Roberts, 211 Mich. 187, 178 N.W. 690 (1920).

173. The maximum penalty for a Class B felony is imprisonment for ten years, for a Class C felony it is five years.

Mich. Rev. Crim. Code Sec. 1401(2)(b) - (c) (Final Draft 1967).

174. Id. Sec. 2005(2), 2010(1)(d).

175. Id. Sec. 2005(2). Similar provisions are found in N.Y. Pen. Law Sec. 125.20(2), 125.25(1)(a); Model Penal Code Sec. 2103(1)(b) (Official Draft 1962).

176. See R. Perkins, Criminal Law 49-51 (1957).

177. Model Penal Code Sec. 201.3, Comment(5) (Tent. Draft No. 9, 1959).

178. Byrn, Homicide Under the Proposed New York Penal Law, 33 Fordham L. Rev. 173, 179 (1964).

179. W. Prosser, The Law of Torts, Sec. 32, at 155 (3d ed. 1964).

180. See, e.g., People v. Rogulski, 181 Mich. 481, 148 N.W. 189 (1914); People v. Stubenvoll, 62 Mich. 329, 28 N.W. 883 (1886).

181. People v. Campbell, 237 Mich. 424, 212 N.W. 97 (1927).

182. People v. Barnes, 182 Mich. 179, 148 N.W. 400 (1914).

183. People v. Thompson, 122 Mich. 411, 81 N.W. 344 (1899).

184. People v. Barnes, 182 Mich. 179, 148 N.W. 400 (1914).

185. People v. McMurchy, 249 Mich. 147, 228 N.W. 723 (1930).

186. Mich. Comp. Laws Sec. 750.324 (1948), as amended, Mich. Stat. Ann. Sec. 28.556 (Supp. 1968).

187. Id.

188. Mich. Comp. Laws Sec. 750.325 (1948), as amended, Mich. Stat. Ann. Sec. 28.557 (Supp. 1968).

189. Mich. Comp. Laws, Sec. 750.326 (1948), Mich. Stat. Ann. Sec. 28.558 (1954).

190. People v. McMurchy, 249 Mich. 147, 228 N.W. 723 (1930).

191. People v. Robinson, 253 Mich. 507, 235 N.W. 236 (1931); People v. McMurchy, 249 Mich. 147, 228 N.W. 723 (1930).

192. People v. Campbell, 237 Mich. 424, 212 N.W. 97 (1927); People v. Barnes, 182 Mich. 179, 148 N.W. 400 (1914).

193. Mich. Rev. Crim. Code Sec. 2015(1)(a) (Final Draft 1967). Similar provisions have been adopted in N.Y. Pen. Law Sec. 125.10; Model Penal Code Sec. 210.4 (official Draft 1962).

194. Mich. Rev. Crim. Code Sec. 305(d) (Final Draft 1967).

195. Id. Sec. 305(c).

196. Hall, Negligent Behavior Should Be Excluded From Penal Liability, 63 Colum. L. Rev. 632 (1963).

197. Id. at 641.

198. Wechsler & Michael, A Rationale of the Law of Homicide,

37 Colum. L. Rev. 701, 750-51 (1937); Model Penal Code Sec. 201.4, Comment (2) (Tent. Draft No. 9, 1959).

199. Model Penal Code, Sec. 201.4, Comment (2) (Tent. Draft No. 9, 1959).

200. Wechsler & Michael, supra note 198.

201. Mich. Rev. Crim. Code Sec. 2015(1)(b) (Final Draft 1967). This section is unique. Neither the New York Revised Penal Law nor the Model Penal Code contain similar provisions.

202. See, e.g., R. Perkins, supra note 176, at 884-85.

203. E.d., People v. Stallworth, 364 Mich. 528, 111 N.W. 2d 742 (1961); People v. Van Camp, 356 Mich. 593, 97 N.W.2d 726 (1959).

204. Mich. Comp. Laws Sec. 750.321 (1948), Mich. Stat. Ann. 28.553 (1954) (Penalty for manslaughter - maximum of fifteen years imprisonment or fine of $7,500, or both); Mich. Rev. Crim. Code Sec. 1401 (2) (c), 2015 (3) (Final Draft 1967) (Penalty for criminally negligent homicide - maximum of five years imprisonment).

205. Mich. Rev. Crim. Code Sec. 2015(2) (Final Draft 1967).

206. See People v. McMurchy, 249 Mich. 147, 228 N.W. 723 (1930); Mich. Comp. Laws, Sec. 750.326 (1948), Mich. Stat. Ann. Sec. 28.558 (1954).

INTERROGATORIES

1. What constitutes first degree murder under the Michigan statutes?
2. What constitutes second degree murder under the Michigan statutes?
3. What provisions is made in the Michigan law with respect to dueling?
4. What provision is made in the Michigan statutes with respect to deaths resulting from the use of explosives?
5. What were the facts, issue and holding of the Court in People v. Austin, 221 Mich. 635?
6. How is murder in the first degree defined in People v. Austin
7. How is manslaughter and voluntary manslaughter defined in People v. Austin?
8. What were the facts, issue and holding of the Court in People v. Potter? What was the purpose of the first degree murder statute according to the Potter opinion? What is the basic distinction between first and second degree murder according to this case? How does the Court define 1st degree murder?
9. What were the facts, issue and holding of the Court in People v. Scott? What is the basic distinction between first and second degree murder according to opinions in this case?
10. What were the facts, issue and holding of the Court in People v. Case?

11. What were the facts, issue and holding of the Court in
    Wellar v. People? What construction is placed on this case
    by Hecker in 14 Wayne L. Rev. 904?
12. What were the facts, issue and holding of the Court in
    People v. Palmer? What is the basic distinction between
    murder and manslaughter according to this case? What
    interpretation of this case is provided by the Committee
    Commentary to Sec. 2005, Final Draft, Mich. Rev. Crim. Code?
13. What were the facts, issue and holding of the Court in
    People v. Collins? Is voluntary intoxication a defense
    to a manslaughter charge?
14. What were the facts, issue and holding of the Court in
    People v. Carl?
15. What were the facts, issue and holding of the Court in
    People v. Hodges? What is the basic policy underlying the
    doctrine of transferred intent?
16. Trace the history of the felony-murder doctrine.
17. What are the four essential elements of the felony-murder
    doctrine? What condition must be satisfied if the homicide
    is to come within the doctrine? How is legal malice defined?
18. What was the holding of the Court in Commonwealth v. Almeida?
    State the simple syllogism upon which the decision was
    predicated.
19. Does Michigan follow the rule of the Almeida case?
20. In what way was the common law felony-murder rule expanded
    by the Almeida decision? According to Hecker, what is the
    reason for the felony-murder rule? How is the mens rea
    requirement satisfied by the application of the rule?
21. How is the proximate cause rule relevant to the felony-
    murder rule?
22. What grounds have been set forth by some states as a basis
    for rejecting the Almeida case?
23. How many states follow the felony-murder rule?
24. What were the facts, issue and holding of the Court in
    People v. Gordon?
25. What were the facts, issue and holding of the Court in
    People v. Koharski?
26. What were the facts, issue and holding of the Court in
    People v. Peranio? On what basis is the decision defended
    by Hecker?
27. What were the facts, issue and holding of the Court in
    People v. Arnett?
28. What were the facts, issue and holding of the Court in
    People v. Crandell?
29. What were the facts, issue and holding of the Court in
    People v. Wright?
30. What were the facts, issue and holding of the Court in
    People v. Podolski? According to Hecker, how did this
    decision broaden the felony-murder rule? Would the Final
    Draft, Mich. Rev. Crim. Code, Sec. 2005 (1) (b) change the
    Podolski decision? What import would this provision have
    on the so-called "shield" cases?

31. What were the facts, issue and holding of the Court in People v. Austin? Does the Court overrule the Podolski decision? What is the basis of Justice Dethmers dissent? Has the Court rejected the incorporation of the proximate cause rule in the application of the felony-murder doctrine? What construction is placed on this case by the Committee Commentary to Sec. 2005, Final Draft, Mich. Rev. Crim. Code?

32. What were the facts, issue and holding of the Court in People v. Hearn? What constructiin is placed on this case by the Committee Commentary to Sec. 2005, Final Draft, Mich. Rev. Crim. Code?

33. What were the facts, issue and holding of the Court in People v. Bowen?

34. What were the facts, issue and holding of the Court in People v. Hansen? In what way did this decision modify the holding in the Weller case?

35. What were the facts, issue and holding of the Court in People v. Ney? How is malice defined by the Court? What is the distinction between first and second degree murder?

36. What were the facts, issue and holding of the Court in People v. Vinunzo? According to the "Homicide Under the Michigan Revised Criminal Code, 14 Wayne Law Review, what has been the result of the holding of the court?

37. How is homicide defined in Section 2001, Final Draft, Mich. Rev. Crim. Code?

38. Outline the provisions of Section 2005, Final Draft, Mich. Rev. Crim. Code.

39. According to the Committee Commentary to Section 2005, what were the common law clissifications of murder?

40. According to the Committee Commentary to Section 2005, what was the original purpose of the Michigan first degree murder provision? How was this purpose frustrated by judicial interpretation?

41. What was the holding of the Court in People v. Roberts? How would this decision be altered by Section 2005 (3), Final Draft, Mich. Rev. Crim. Code?

42. What was the holding of the Court in People v. Marshall and People v. Andrus? What construction is placed on the Andrus Case by the Committee Commentary to the Final Draft, Mich. Rev. Crim. Code?

43. What was the holding of the Court in People v. Pavlic?

44. What was the holding of the Court in People v. Bucski?

45. What was the holding of the Court in People v. Milhem?

46. What are some of the special circumstances in which the killings are either denominated murder or punished at a level corresponding to murder?

47. What changes would the adoption of Section 2005 make in the existing law?

48. Outline the provisions of Section 2006 of the Final Draft, Mich. Rev. Crim. Code.

49. Outline the provisions of the Michigan Compiled laws relevant to manslaughter.

50. What were the facts, issue and holding of the Court in People v. Lilley? How is voluntary manslaughter defined? What are the basic elements of the offense?

51. What were the facts, issue and holding of the Court in People v. Poole?

52. What were the facts, issue and holding of the Court in People v. Clark?

53. What were the facts, issue and holding of the Court in People v. Townsend? What construction is placed on this case by the Committee Commentary to Sections 2006-2015, Final Draft, Mich. Rev. Crim. Code?

54. What were the facts, issue and holding of the Court in People v. Barnes?

55. What were the facts, issue and holding of the Court in People v. Wardell? How is involuntary manslaughter defined in this case?

56. What were the facts, issue and holding of the Court in People v. Orr? What are the elements of involuntary manslaughter? What construction is placed on the Orr case by the Committee Commentary to Sections 2006-2015, Final Draft, Mich. Rev. Crim. Code?

57. What were the facts, issue and holding of the Court in People v. Thompson? What construction is placed on this case by the Committee Commentary to Sections 2006-2015, Final Draft, Mich. Rev. Crim. Code?

58. What were the facts, issue and holding of the Court in Maher v. People? What is the function of the provocation formula? What constitutes an adequate provocation?

59. What were the facts, issue and holding of the Court in People v. Younger?

60. What were the facts, issue and holding of the Court in People v. Stubenvoll? How is the rule of the case formulated by Bishop? What is the point of the dissenting opinion? What construction is placed on this case by the Committee Commentary to Sections 2006-2015, Final Draft, Mich. Rev. Crim. Code?

61. What were the facts, issue and holding of the Court in People v. Rogulski?

62. What were the facts, issue and holding of the Court in People v. Harris? How is involuntary manslaughter defined in this case? What construction is placed on this case by the Committee Commentary to Sections 2006-2015, Final Draft, Mich. Rev. Crim. Code?

63. What were the facts, issue and holding of the Court in People v. Paulic?

64. What were the facts, issue and holding of the Court in People v. Abbott? Does it make any difference if the victim consented to the unlawful act?

65. What were the facts, issue and holding of the Court in People v. Carabell? How is the misdemeanor-manslaughter rule formulated in this case? How is voluntary man-slaughter defined?

66. What were the facts, issue and holding of the Court in People v. Marshall? Does this case raise any doubts about the application of the misdemeanor-manslaughter rule? What is the rationale of the Court? On what basis is the rule criticized by Hecker?
67. Under what circumstances is vicarious responsibility imposed in automobile negligence cases?
68. What criticism of People v. Marshall is offered in the law review note, "Criminal Law - Manslaughter - Automobile Owner's Vicarious Responsibility", 7 Wayne L. Rev. 483?
69. Under what circumstances is the owner of a motor vehicle criminally responsible for the action of the driver. Give examples.
70. In what respect was the decision of the Court in People v. Marshall inconsistent with the traditional common law with respect to accessory liability?
71. What criticism is offered of the Court's position in People v. Marshall that criminal guilt must be based upon personal fault.
72. Outline the provisions of Section 2010, Final Draft, Mich. Rev. Crim. Code.
73. Answer the questions given in the problem statement on page 803.
74. What provision has been made by statute in Michigan with respect to negligent homicide?
75. What were the facts, issue and holding of the Court in People v. Campbell? What is the difference between gross negligence and ordinary negligence? What degree of negligence is required for conviction of negligent homicide? What are the principal points of the dissenting opinion?
76. What were the facts, issue and holding of the Court in People v. McMurchy?
77. What were the facts, issue and holding of the Court in People v. Robinson?
78. What were the facts, issue and holding of the Court in People v. Good?
79. What were the facts, issue and holding of the Court in People v. Paulen?
80. Outline the provisions of Section 2015, Final Draft, Mich. Rev. Crim. Code.
81. Is intent ever an element in manslaughter?
82. What was probably the reason for the adoption of the negligent homicide statute?
83. What legislation has been adopted in response to People v. Wigle?
84. Is negligent homicide a lesser included offense to a charge of manslaughter?
85. How is malice defined in People v. Borgetto?
86. What is the difference between express and implied malice?
87. What was the purpose for dividing murder into degrees?
88. What was the holding of the Court in People v. Statkiewicz?
89. On what basis does abortion constitute manslaughter? Whose death is required?

90. Does intentionally aiding or causing suicide constitute manslaughter? What problem of proximate cause arises in this area?
91. What criteria must be satisfied if criminally negligent homicide is to be manslaughter?
92. What is the criteria for conviction of negligent homicide under the Michigan statute? In what way is contributory negligence by the victim relevant?
93. What criticism is offered by Hecker of the negligent homicide statute? What public purposes allegedly justify this type of legislation?

CHAPTER VI

ASSAULTS, EXTORTION AND RELATED OFFENSES

A. Assaults

    1. Michigan Compiled Laws (1948)

750.81 Assault and assault and battery

    Sec. 81. ASSAULT AND ASSAULT AND BATTERY - Any person who shall be convicted of an assault or an assault and battery where no other punishment is prescribed shall be guilty of a misdemeanor.

750.81a Assault and infliction of serious injury.

    Sec. 81a. Any person who shall assault another without any weapon and inflict serious or aggravated injury upon the person of another without intending to commit the crime of murder, and without intending to inflict great bodily harm less than the crime of murder, shall be guilty of a misdemeanor, punishable by imprisonment in the county jail or the state prison for a period of not more than 1 year or fine of $500.00, or both.

750.82 Felonious assault

    Sec. 82 FELONIOUS ASSAULT - Any person who shall assault another with a gun, revolver, pistol, knife, iron bar, club, brass knuckles or other dangerous weapon, but without intending to commit the crime of murder, and without intending to inflict great bodily harm less than the crime of murder, shall be guilty of a felony.

750.83 Assault with intent to commit murder

    Sec. 83. ASSAULT WITH INTENT TO COMMIT MURDER - Any person who shall assault another with intent to commit the crime of murder, shall be guilty of a felony, punishable by imprisonment in the state prison for life or any number of years.

750.84 Assault with intent to do great bodily harm less than murder

    Sec. 84. ASSAULT WITH INTENT TO DO GREAT BODILY HARM LESS THAN MURDER - Any person who shall assault another with intent to do great bodily harm, less than the crime of murder, shall be guilty of a felony punishable by imprisonment in the state prison not more than 10 years, or by fine of not more than 5,000 dollars.

750.85 Assault with intent to commit rape, sodomy or gross
        indecency; sexual delinquent

Sec. 85.   Any person who shall assault any female with
intent to commit the crime of rape, and any person who shall
assault another person with intent to commit the crime of
sodomy or gross indecency, shall be guilty of a felony, punishable by imprisonment in the state prison for not more than 10
years, or by fine of not more than $5,000.00, or if such per-
son was at the time of the said offense a sexually delinquent
person, may be punishable by imprisonment in the state prison
for an indeterminate term, the minimum of which shall be 1
day and the maximum of which shall be life.   As amended P.A.
1952, No. 73, Sec. 1, Eff. Sept. 18.

750.86 Assault with intent to maim

Sec. 86.   ASSAULT WITH INTENT TO MAIM - Any person who
shall assault another with intent to maim or disfigure his
person by cutting out or maiming the tongue, putting out
or destroying an eye, cutting or tearing off an ear, cutting
or slitting or mutilating the nose or lips or cutting off or
disabling a limb, organ or member, shall be guilty of a felony,
punishable by imprisonment in the state prison not more than
10 years or by fine of not more than 5,000 dollars.

750.87 Assault with intent to commit felony not otherwise
        punished

Sec. 87.   ASSAULT WITH INTENT TO COMMIT FELONY, NOT OTHER-
WISE PUNISHED - Any person who shall assault another, with
intent to commit any burglary, or any other felony, the punishment of which assault is not otherwise in this act prescribed, shall be guilty of a felony, punishable by imprisonment in the state prison not more than 10 years, or by fine
of not more than 5,000 dollars.

750.88 Assault with intent to rob and steal being unarmed

Sec. 88.   ASSAULT WITH INTENT TO ROB AND STEAL BEING UN-
ARMED - Any person, not being armed with a dangerous weapon,
who shall assault another with force and violence, and with
intent to rob and steal, shall be guilty of a felony, punishable by imprisonment in the state prison not more than 15
years.

750.89 Assault with intent to rob and steal being armed

Sec. 89.   ASSAULT WITH INTENT TO ROB AND STEAL BEING ARMED -
Any person, being armed with a dangerous weapon, or any article
used or fashioned in a manner to lead a person so assaulted
reasonably to believe it to be a dangerous weapon, who shall
assault another with intent to rob and steal shall be guilty
of a felony, punishable by imprisonment in the state prison
for life, or for any term of years.

750.90 Sexual intercourse under pretext of medical treatment

Sec. 90. SEXUAL INTERCOURSE UNDER PRETEXT OF MEDICAL TREATMENT - Any person who shall undertake to medically treat any female person, and while so treating her, shall represent to such female that it is, or will be, necessary or beneficial to her health that she have sexual intercourse with a man, and shall thereby induce her to have carnal sexual intercourse with any man, and any man, not being the husband of such female, who shall have sexual intercourse with her by reason of such representation, shall be guilty of a felony punishable by imprisonment in the state prison not more than 10 years.

750.205 Placing explosives; intent to destroy but without resulting damage

Sec. 205. PLACING EXPLOSIVES WITH INTENT TO DESTROY BUT WITHOUT RESULTING DAMAGE - Any person who places in, upon, under, against or near to any building, car, vessel or structure, gunpowder or any other explosive substance, with intent to destroy, throw down or injure the whole or any part thereof, under such circumstances, that, if the intent were accomplished, human life or safety would be endangered thereby, although no damage is done, is guilty of a felony, punishable by imprisonment in the state prison not more than 15 years.

750.206 Same; with intent to destroy and causing damage to property

Sec. 206. PLACING EXPLOSIVES WITH INTENT TO DESTROY AND CAUSING DAMAGE TO PROPERTY - Any person who places in, upon, under, against or near to any building, car, vessel or structure, gunpowder or any other explosive substance, with intent to destroy, throw down or injure the whole or any part thereof, which explosive substance shall cause the destruction or injury of the property of another, shall be guilty of a felony, punishable by imprisonment in the state prison not more than 25 years.

750.207 Same; with intent to destroy and causing injury to any person

Sec. 207. PLACING EXPLOSIVES WITH INTENT TO DESTROY AND CAUSING INJURY TO ANY PERSON - Any person who places in, upon, under, against or near to any building, car, vessel or structure, gunpowder or any other explosive substance, with intent to destroy, throw down, or injure the whole or any part thereof, which substance upon explosion shall cause injury to any person, shall be guilty of a felony, punishable by imprisonment in the state prison for life. Such convicted person shall not be eligible to parole.

750.235 Same; injuring, intentionally aimed, without malice

Sec. 235. INJURING BY DISCHARGE OF FIRE-ARM INTENTIONALLY BUT WITHOUT MALICE POINTED AT ANOTHER - Any person who shall maim or injure any other person by the discharge of any fire-arm pointed or aimed intentionally, without malice, at any such person shall be guilty of a misdemeanor, punishable by imprisonment in the county jail not more than 1 year or by a fine of not more than 500 dollars.

2. Definitions and General Elements

People v. Sheffield
105 Mich. 117

Respondent was convicted of assault and battery, and sentenced to pay a fine of $100, and to be confined in the county jail for 30 days. Judgment reversed, and respondent discharged. The facts are stated in the opinion.

McGRATH, C. J. This is a prosecution under 3 How. Stat. Sec. 9314b, which provides that -

"If any male person or persons over the age of 14 years shall assault a female child under the age of 14 years, and shall take indecent and improper liberties with the person of such child, without committing or intending to commit the crime of rape upon such child, he shall be deemed a felonious assaulter," etc.

The court instructed the jury that it would be legally competent for them to convict respondent of an assault and battery, it being a lesser offense, and included in the one with which respondent is charged; and the jury found the respondent guilty of assault and battery.

The charge of the court was erroneous, and the verdict cannot stand. The girl's testimony tended clearly to show that respondent was not guilty of any improper liberties. She testified that all respondent did or attempted to do was to put his arm around her waist, and that no offer or threat to take or request to be allowed to take any other liberties with her person was made by respondent. Two young men testified that they saw the pair sitting on the ground; that respondent's arm was around the girl, and that his other hand was under her clothes; that, at all events, they did not see the other hand. There was no middle ground here. The respondent was either guilty as charged, or the jury have been allowed to find that an act not unlawful in itself constituted an assault. Such mere familiarity, participated in and consented to by the child, in the absence of indecent and improper liberties, between a man over 50 years of age and a girl under 14, who have been intimate and frequently in each other's company, does not constitute an assault. An assault involves "every attempt or offer, with force and violence, to do a corporal hurt to another." Drew v. Comstock, 57 Mich. 176. Rape upon a female 14 years of age and upwards involves an assault with intent, an assault and battery, and an assault. The assault must be shown to have been committed. It is included in the major offense, and is a necessary ingredient thereof. Each element going to make up the greater offense is in itself a statutory offense. In that class of cases it has frequently been held that the jury may convict of the lesser offense.

Carnal knowledge and abuse of a girl under 14 years of age is a statutory offense, although she consents. People v. Courier, 79 Mich. 366, People v. Miller, 96 Id. 119, and People v. Abbott, 97 Id. 484, were prosecutions under 3 How. Stat. Sec. 9094. In the first case it was insisted that the offense had not been completed, but the Court held that perfect penetration was not necessary; that force, against the will of the child, was not a necessary element of the crime; that sexual intercourse was sufficient; and that, if an assault was made with that design, the assaulter was guilty of an assault with intent to commit the crime. In the Miller case respondent was convicted of an assault with intent to commit the act, although the people's evidence was to the effect that the offense charged had been committed, and respondent denied even an attempt. In the Abbott case actual sexual intercourse was shown and found. Each of these cases involved, as a lesser crime, the offense charged in the present case, and the testimony embraced that offense. In the Courier case it is said: "If indecent liberties are taken with the child, with no intent to have sexual intercourse, it is punishable as an assault."

The statute in the present case aims at indecent and improper liberties with the person of the child. It is in and of itself the lesser offense in the category of offenses committed with consent. When applied to a case where an assault is not associated, it involves no other statutory offense. Indeed, it is the statute which gives to the act constituting the offense the character of an assault. In People v. Hicks, 98 Mich. 86, the act was done against the protest of the child; hence involved an assault independent of this statute.

The judgment is reversed, and the respondent discharged.

LONG, MONTGOMERY, and HOOKER, JJ., concurred. GRANT, J., did not sit.

People v. Carlson
160 Mich. 426

McALVAY, J. Respondent was convicted before the circuit court for Houghton county of an assault with intent to commit the crime of rape upon a female child of the age of 10 years.

The case is here upon exceptions before sentence. The crime was charged to have been committed on Monday, July 5, 1909, which was celebrated as the Fourth. Respondent, of the age of 17 years, had been celebrating in Red Jacket that day with other young men, and had been drinking more or less. Between 3 and 4 o'clock in the afternoon, he, with one of his companions, went to the Copper Range depot, and sat down by it. After sitting there a short time, his companion says he went away, leaving Carlson sitting there. The girl in question, and her brother, eight years old, had also been to Red Jacket, and were on their way home to Centennial Heights, where they lived. They first saw Carlson and a companion near the depot. He stopped the children, and talked to them and gave them 10 cents, telling them to go back and spend it on ice cream and candy. They went back and spent the money, returning within a short time. They claim that both young men were still at the depot. Carlson, leaving the other, started after them, and, catching up, began to talk with them, and walked on with them until they came to the railroad track, when he said that his brother was coming with six ice cream cones, and told them to take the pathway down by the dam and go in by the road, and he would follow the track and meet them there. They went to the place as directed, and met him there below the dam. He offered the girl $4 if she would lie down on the grass. He said it would be all over quick. The girl refused to lie down, and he coaxed and begged her to do so, raising his offer to $8, $10, and $12. He mentioned other girls who had done so, for him for $4. She continued to refuse and he then began to ask her the kind of stockings, drawers, and garters she wore. He rolled up his trousers and showed her his green stockings. The little girl said she must be going. Respondent said, "No," that his brother would soon come, and they could have all the ice cream. He then asked them to go to another place where his brother would be, and they went with him through the bullrushes and swamp farther away into the bushes. Here he begged and coaxed her to lie down, and she again refused. He then threatened to shoot her if she did not do so, which greatly frightened her. He asked the little boy to feel the revolver in his pocket. The boy felt on the place indicated, but could not tell what he felt. Respondent grabbed the boy and dragged him into the bullrushes, saying that he would shoot him if he screamed. The girl then ran away up to the top of the hill, where she heard her brother call to her. She called back and waited for him until he came up. Respondent, after letting the boy go, ran through the bushes towards his home. The children started towards home. They were crying hard when they met a man and his wife, and told what had happened. These people said they would bring them home. On the way the little girl saw respondent, and pointed him out. The man with her started after him, calling to him. He ran away towards Red Jacket. They met the father of the children near his home, and he was told what had occurred. The girl told her mother as soon as she

879

could sufficiently compose herself.

The testimony of the children is corroborated, except as to what occurred when they were alone with respondent. As to that they are not contradicted by any witness. Respondent did not lay hands upon the girl. He did not show her money, and he did not draw a revolver. The defense offered testimony tending to show that he was under the influence of liquor, and also as to his good character. The question of his condition as to intoxication was a disputed question of fact submitted to the jury. The case as presented here in behalf of respondent in effect accepts the facts established on the part of the people as to what was done by respondent, which is claimed to have constituted the offense charged.

The contentions made are:

(1) That no assault was proven, and consequently a verdict of not guilty should have been instructed by the court.

It is urged that the case made by the people showed nothing more than solicitations or threats made by respondent. There are numerous definitions of what constitutes an assault given by courts and text-writers. We cite two, which, taken together, may be said to include all necessary elements:

"An assault is any attempt or offer, with force or violence, to do a corporal hurt to another, whether from malice or wantonness, with such circumstances as denote, at the time, an intention to do it, coupled with a present ability to carry such intention into effect." 3 Cyc. p. 1020.

"An assault is any unlawful physical force, partly or fully put in motion, creating a reasonable apprehension of immediate injury to a human being." 2 Bishop on Criminal Law (7th Ed.), Sec. 23.

That an assault may be committed without actually touching the person of the one assaulted, is not disputed, and no authorities are required in support of the proposition. Where, as in this case, an assault is threatened, coupled with an unlawful condition, the question to be decided is whether the acts done are sufficient to be submitted to a jury to find an assault as a question of fact, or to be determined by the court as one of law. A careful examination of the undisputed facts in this case, taking into consideration the tender years of these children, the enticing by respondent, the place of the occurrence, his purpose as expressed by his talk with the girl, his threat to shoot (indicating and claiming to be armed with a revolver) unless she submitted to his demand, his violent seizure of the little boy and dragging him into the bullrushes with the threat to shoot him if he screamed, all taken together, satisfies us that the question of an assault was one to be submitted to the jury under proper instructions.

It is insisted that this court has held to the contrary in People v. Dowell, 136 Mich. 306, 310 (99 N.W. 23, 24). It is evident that such contention is founded upon the follow-

880

ing words there used:

"Actual violence or actual assault is essential to the commission of this crime."

We deny that the fair inference from this language is as claimed by respondent. The statement must be taken in connection with the context, and the case there considered. It can be construed to mean no more than that an assault was a material element of the offense charged, and must be proved.

In another case relied upon by respondent, and cited in support of his proposition that threats alone do not amount to an assault, this court, in discussing what would, and what would not, amount to an assault, said:

"The act done must not only be criminal, but it must have proceeded far enough towards a consummation thereof, and this must necessarily be a question for the jury under proper instructions." People v. Lilley, 43 Mich. 525 (5 N.W. 985).

The foregoing language is approved by us as applicable to the instant case, and we think the case is authority for our conclusion herein. This would seem to be the rule laid down in New York in an early case where a like offense was charged, and we do not find that the court has departed from that decision. Hays v. People, 1 Hill (N.Y.), 351. The question was, in our opinion, properly submitted to the jury.

(2) Error is assigned upon the refusal of the court to give a certain charge which combined the necessity of being satisfied beyond a reasonable doubt (a) that defendant had committed an assault upon the little girl; and (b) that at the time of such assault his intention was to ravish and carnally know her; and also to charge as requested with reference to the effect of intoxication upon the question of ability to form an intent. We have examined the charge of the court, and find that upon all the questions raised under these assignments of error the court properly instructed the jury upon the law, and we find no error in the charge.

The verdict of the jury in the case is affirmed, and the cause is remanded for judgment.

OSTRANDER, BROOKE, BLAIR, and STONE, JJ., concurred.

People v. Doud
223 Mich. 120

(For the facts of this case see page 409, supra.)

. . .The charge was laid under section 15228, 3 Comp. Laws 1915, which provides:

"Whoever shall assault another with a gun, revolver, pistol, knife, iron bar, club, brass knuckles or other dangerous weapon, but without intending to commit the

881

crime of murder, and without intending to inflict great
bodily harm less than the crime of murder, shall be deemed
guilty of a felonious assault." . . .

Defendant contends that this statute involves an intent
on the part of the accused to do a bodily hurt to another.
This statute expressly negatives certain felonious intents,
the purpose being to save the declared crime from falling
within other defined felonies.

It is said the offense charged is one intermediate between simple assault and battery and assault with intent to
inflict great bodily harm less than the crime of murder.
(People v. Warner, 201 Mich. 547-557), and it is urged that:

"In every simple assault, there is a criminal intent,
otherwise there is no assault. 'Malice or wantonness' is
the basic essential and a man's intention must meet with
his act in constituting a simple assault;" citing People v.
Carlson, 160 Mich. 426; Tiffany's Criminal Law (How. 4th
Ed.),p. 683.

In finding the defendant guilty the jury must have accepted
the claim of the prosecution that defendant pointed the revolver at Mr. Davenport and made the threat claimed. A secret
intent not to inflict an injury, wholly incompatible with a
declared purpose to injure, accompanied by acts manifesting
a corporal hurt to one immediately menaced thereby, may, of
course, be told to the jury by the accused, and such was permitted in this case, but the trial judge held that defendant's
acts governed and not his secret intention. An assault, under
practically all definitions, must carry on the face of its
attendant circumstances an offer or attempt with force or
violence to do a corporal hurt to another. This involves an
intent or purpose to inflict a corporal hurt to another. It
is not necessary that the prosecution go outside of the disclosed evidence of such intent and establish, by extrinsic
proof, the intent entertained by the accused. The intent to
do an injury may be found and usually is found from the acts
of the accused, and, in the absence of a declaration of intention, or of evidence by the accused, must, if at all, be
so found. The defendant, however, is at liberty to tell his
purpose, even though contradicted by his every act, and have
the same go to the jury. Such is the law of simple assault.

Does the statute under which defendant was convicted change
such rule and constitute it a crime to point a revolver at
another, accompanying the act with a threat of employment of
its lethal power in case a demand made is not complied with,
regardless of the intent of the aggressor? The statute speaks
of an assault with a revolver or other dangerous weapon, and
as the offense covered thereby was formerly punished as a
simple assault, we must infer that, in the use of the term
"assault" the legislature intended the same to carry its ordinary meaning in connection with crimes of offered violence.
Evidently feeling that the penalty for simple assault did not

meet occasions where a dangerous weapon was employed the legislature fixed a greater penalty for such aggravated assaults but did not eliminate the question of intent or purpose, involved in every case of assault of a criminal nature. Whether the statute in question raises the grade of the offense from former simple assaults or seeks to cover offenses not included within assaults with specific intents, we find it midway between offenses involving a purpose to exercise violence and assaults involving a felonious intent.

At the trial defendant was permitted to testify fully as to his intent and claimed he entertained no purpose to inflict injury. Even though such claim was refuted by his acts, demeanor and words, defendant had a right to go to the jury with what he claimed to have been his purpose. The trial judge gave the jury no instruction upon the issue of defendant's intent, although requested to do so, but charged:

"The people say that he pointed the gun at Davenport; and the people say that he pointed the gun under such circumstances as imported an intent to fire his gun off. The people do not say that he did intend to (it is not necessary that they should say it or prove it), but if he pointed a gun under such circumstances that Davenport had reasonable grounds to believe that he intended to fire it off, and it was pointed at Davenport at the time, then he is guilty of the offense charged."

While the fear of one assaulted, arising from reasonable apprehension of bodily hurt, threatened by another having means and ability to inflict the same, is mentioned in some of the books as proper evidence to go to the jury, we do not understand that such fear governs upon the question of the intent or purpose of an accused under this statute. We think defendant was entitled to have the following portion of his sixth request to charge given:

"As to what his intention actually was you must determine that, if you are able to, from the evidence in the case, considering what he did, what he said, and what he testifies to as his intent."

It is claimed that defendant intended no harm to the workmen and had the revolver for its moral effect, to scare them off his land; that the revolver was a borrowed one and he did not know whether it was loaded or not, and in the brief it is said:

"In the case at bar, the attention of the court is invited to the fact that there is no proof whatever that the revolver held by Doud was loaded. The only testimony on the point is that given by Mr. Doud himself, who testified that he did not know whether the gun was loaded or not.
"It has been held that there is no presumption that a revolver so used was loaded and that the burden of proof is on the State;" citing State v. Napper, 6 Nev. 113; Price v.

United States, 85 C.C.A. 247, 156 Fed. 950 (15 L.R.A. (N.S.) 1272): Fastbinder v. State, 42 Ohio St. 341.

The authorities are not in harmony upon the subject of whether, in a prosecution for assault with a dangerous weapon, such as a revolver, the prosecution must establish that it was loaded at the time of its employment. Without considering, except as herein stated, underlying statutes, if any, or specific intents involved in charges of assaults with firearms, we will take a view of the leading cases upon the subject.

In State v. Godfrey, 17 Or. 300 (20 Pac. 625, 11 Am. St. Rep. 830), the charge was, being armed with a Winchester rifle and making an assault and threatening to kill therewith if the person so threatened did not turn back. There was no direct evidence that the gun was loaded. It was held:

"To point an unloaded gun at another, at a distance of from thirty to seventy yards, whereby such other is put in fear, and flees, is not an assault with a dangerous weapon."

In People v. Sylva, 143 Cal. 62 (76 Pac. 814), it was held:

"The pointing of an unloaded gun at the prosecuting witness, accompanied by a threat to shoot him, without any attempt to use it otherwise, is not an assault with a deadly weapon, and cannot sustain a conviction for an assault for want of a present ability to commit violent injury upon the person threatened in the manner attempted."

In State v. Napper, supra, the court held that a conviction of an assault with a deadly weapon with intent to inflict a bodily injury could not be sustained because there was no allegation or proof that the gun which the defendant pointed at witness, and threatening to shoot, was loaded.

An examination of these cases discloses statutes requiring a showing of present ability on the part of an accused to do violence to the person of another.

In Price v. United States, supra, the accused, while engaged in an angry altercation with the complaining witness, without justification, and within shooting distance, drew a revolver and pointed it toward the witness in a threatening manner, putting him in such fear that he got under a table for safety. The court held in substance that an assault with a dangerous weapon cannot be committed by pointing at another an unloaded pistol, although the person toward whom it is pointed does not know that the weapon is not loaded, and is put in fear by such act, but held that a simple assault might be so committed.

In Fastbinder v. State, supra, the defendant was charged with shooting at another with intent to kill. It was held:

"In order to convict of shooting with intent to kill, it must be averred and proved that the gun was loaded with powder and a bullet or some other destructive substance, which, when discharged from the gun, is calculated to produce death."

884

In *Commonwealth v. White*, 110 Mass. 407, it was held:

"If A. menacingly points at B. a gun which B. has reasonable cause to believe loaded, and B. is put in fear of immediate bodily injury therefrom, and the circumstances would ordinarily induce such fear in a reasonable man, A. is guilty of assault, although he knows that the gun is not loaded."

In *Beach v. Hancock*, 27 N. H. 223 (59 Am. Dec. 373):

"The defendant, being engaged in an angry altercation with the plaintiff, aimed a gun at him in an excited and threatening manner, and snapped it twice. It was not, in fact, loaded, but the plaintiff did not know whether it was loaded or not. *Held*, that the defendant had committed an assault."

In *State v. Shepard*, 10 Iowa, 126, defendant was indicted for an assault with a gun with intent to commit murder, and convicted of an assault. It was held:

"The pointing of a gun which is not loaded, in a threatening manner at another, constitutes an assault, when the party at whom it is pointed does not know that it is not loaded, or has no reason to believe that it is not."

In *State v. Smith*, 2 Humph. (Tenn.) 457, it was held that:

"If a person present a pistol at another purporting to be loaded, so near as to have been dangerous to life, if the pistol being loaded, had gone off, it is an assault in law, though the pistol were not in fact loaded."

In *State v. Herron*, 12 Mont. 230 (30 Pac. 140, 33 Am. St. Rep. 576), the charge was an attempt to commit an assault with a deadly weapon. It was said by the court:

"It is not questioned but a loaded rifle is a deadly weapon. In this case a rifle was used. It was used with threats. The defendant said that he would blow Nelson's head off. He thus threatened to do that which he could do only if the gun were loaded. Under these circumstances, on an information for an attempt, must the State prove that the gun was loaded, or if it a matter of defense to show the fact (if it be a fact) that there was no load in the gun? . . .

"Although there is a division of views in the decided cases, we think that the better opinion is that, if a firearm is the alleged deadly weapon - a weapon the only ordinary use of which is by its being loaded - if it be pointed at the complainant in a threatening manner, if defendant make threats to shoot, if the circumstances are such as would exist if one were using a loaded gun - in short, that if all the elements of the evidence be made out, as required by the criminal laws and procedure, except the direct, we may say visual, proof that the weapon is loaded - under these circumstances a direction to the jury to acquit is error; and the fact that the gun was unloaded (if such be the fact) is a matter of defense. Such view seems to be held by the weight of authority, and such is the only practical view in the enforcement of the statute in reference to assaults with a deadly weapon of this character."

In State v. Archer, 8 Kan. App. 737 (54 Pac. 927), it was held:

"The pointing of a revolver which is not loaded in a threatening manner at another is an assault when the party at whom it is pointed does not know that it is not loaded, or has no reason to believe that it is not, and is by the act of the menacing party put in fear of bodily harm."

See, also, McNamara v. People, 24 Colo. 61 (48 Pac. 541); State v. Cherry, 11 Ired. (N.C.) 475.
Several of the cases last cited involved the rule with reference to simple assault and it is claimed on the part of the defendant that the rule applied in cases of simple assault has no application to assaults with a dangerous weapon. Having in mind the language of our statute, that it specifically forbids an assault with a revolver, and the evident reason underlying its enactment, and that it involves no intent or purpose beyond such as relates to simple assaults and raises the grade only when assaults are committed with designated forbidden weapons, we think the cases cited with reference to the rule in simple assaults are applicable. But beyond this we adopt the rule so well stated in the opinion of the Montana court. We, therefore, hold that it was not necessary for the prosecution to show that the revolver was, in fact, loaded. . . .
For the errors pointed out the conviction is reversed and a new trial granted.

FELLOWS, McDONALD, CLARK, BIRD, SHARPE, MOORE, and STEERE, JJ., concurred.

People v. Shaffran
243 Mich. 527

WIEST, J. In an altercation over the existence and location of a way or easement, along the section line between the farms of defendant and Mert Gallivan, defendant struck Gallivan in the back with a stone, fracturing two ribs. Defendant was convicted of an assault with intent to do great bodily harm, less than the crime of murder, and seeks reversal.
The right of way constituted a dispute of long standing. The morning of the assault Gallivan and two of his boys went to the disputed strip to plow. One of the boys took a shotgun along. Defendant and his brother were plowing in a nearby field, and, noticing the Gallivans plowing on the disputed strip, went over and started to turn the furrow back. At this, active hostilities broke out. In the conflict defendant claims he was struck on the head with a club by one of

886

the Gallivan boys and his pantaloons perforated by shot from the gun in the hands of the other Gallivan boy.

At the trial the court would not permit an issue to be tried out on the subject of the right of way and its location. We are asked to hold that defendant had a right to show that the way was an easement appurtenant to his property, and, in the protection of his right therein and preservation of the way, he was justified in employing sufficient force to prevent destruction thereof by the Gallivans. The court was not in error.

In People v. Doud, 223 Mich. 120 (32 A.L.R. 1535), we had occasion to consider the subject and there stated the applicable rule of law, and, as the opinion is readily accessible, we need but repeat that the authorities are uniform in holding:

"In the application of the rule that a man may use such force as is necessary for the protection of his property, it must be noted that the principle is subject to this most important quilification, that he shall not, except in extreme cases, inflict great bodily harm or endanger human life." 2 R.C.L. pp. 555, 556.

The court was not in error in giving the following instruction:

"There has been some testimony here about a road. Now, I charge you that the location of that road, or the rights of these people in that road, is not a question for you to determine at all, and it is not proper to be decided in this case. The only reason the testimony about the road was permissible was to show the relations of the parties, and to show their dealings, and what really brought about the present transaction, but even if this man, the defendant, had a right there - even if he had a right to travel that road, he did not have any right to inflict violence upon Mr. Gallivan, simply to avenge his right to that road, because if he had a right to that road, there is a legal way for him to get that right, and a peaceable way, and he cannot take the law in his own hands to get it."

The missile employed by defendant was capable of inflicting serious bodily injury, and, if such was defendant's purpose, he was guilty even though Gallivan was a trespasser.

The claimed assaults by the younger Gallivans upon defendant were before the jury, and we must accept the verdict as establishing the stone hurling as first in the order of events. We find no reversible error.

The conviction is affirmed.

FEAD, C. J., and NORTH, FELLOWS, CLARK, McDONALD, and SHARPE, JJ., concurred. POTTER, J., did not sit.

People v. Goolsby
284 Mich. 375

WIEST, C. J. The Michigan penal code, Act No. 328, chap. 11, Sec. 82, Pub. Acts 1931 (Comp. Laws Supp. 1935, Sec. 17115-82, Stat. Ann. Sec. 28.277), defines felonious assault as follows:

"Any person who shall assault another with a gun, revolver, pistol knife, iron bar, club, brass knuckles, or other dangerous weapon, but without intending to commit the crime of murder, and without intending to inflict great bodily harm less than the crime of murder, shall be guilty of a felony."

An information under this statute charged defendant with a felonious assault upon Ferdinand Banta "with a dangerous weapon, to-wit: an automobile," and he was tried, convicted and sentenced.

Defendant prosecutes review, and contends that an automobile is not a dangerous weapon within the meaning of the statute.

We state the agreed facts. Ferdinand Banta was a police officer on traffic duty in the city of Flint. Defendant, when asked by the officer to stop, got out of his automobile, used some profanity to the officer, got back into his automobile and, against the wishes of the officer, he deliberately stepped on the gas and told the officer to get out of the way. Without noticing whether the officer did or did not get out of the way, he started across the intersection of the streets, against the signal and against the orders of the officer. The automobile struck the officer, knocked him down and the left rear wheel of the automobile ran over his right foot at the instep, but without breaking any bones.

The statute defines and penalizes an aggravated assault. Some weapons carry their dangerous character because so designed and are, when employed, per se, deadly, while other instrumentalities are not dangerous weapons unless turned to such purpose. The test as to the latter is whether the instrumentality was used as a weapon and, when so employed in an assault, dangerous. The character of a dangerous weapon attaches by adoption when the instrumentality is applied to use against another in furtherance of an assault. When the purpose is evidenced by act, and the instrumentality is adapted to accomplishment of the assault and capable of inflicting serious injury, then it is, when so employed, a dangerous weapon.

It has been held an assault and battery to ride over another with a horse. State v. Sims, 3 Strob. (S.C.) 137. See, also, Mortin v. Shoppee, 3 Carr. & P. 373 (172 Eng. Rep. 462); also driving a cart against a wagon and thereby causing injury, People v. Lee, 1 Wheel. Crim. Cas (N.Y.) 364. In Williamson v. State, 92 Fla 980 (111 South. 124, 53 A.L.R. 250), it was held that an automobile may be so used as to constitute a deadly weapon within the meaning of an aggravated assault. To like effect, see People v. Clink, 216 Ill. App. 357; People v. Anderson, 229 Ill. App. 315; People v. Benson, 237 Ill. App. 467.

Counsel for defendant concede: "that there are any number

of instrumentalities which may technically be considered as
dangerous weapons, depending on the mode in which they are
used and that further, an automobile may be such an instrumentality;" but contend that the statute in this case re-
stricts dangerous weapons to the same type and kind as enumerated in the statute, and an automobile does not come within
that classification.

This involves the doctrine of ejusdum generis. Construction
or interpretation of a penal statute requires consideration of
the evil sought to be penalized. The evil, under legislative
consideration, was that of assaults, aggravated by use of dangerous weapons and, expressive of such purpose, certain instrumentalities were mentioned, not to the exclusion of other
potentially dangerous weapons, but inclusion thereof by the
omnibus term "or other dangerous weapon." The language, so
employed, cannot, considering the purview of the enactment,
be read as though written "or other dangerous weapons of like
character, class or kind."

In People v. Gogak, 205 Mich. 260, defendant was convicted
of carrying a concealed weapon, not specifically mentioned in
the statute. The statute there involved (3 Comp. Laws 1915,
Sec. 15236) specifically mentioned certain weapons, and added
"or other offensive and dangerous weapons or instruments concealed upon his person."

In sustaining the conviction and refusing to apply the doctrine of ejusdem generis, this court said:

"We think it clearly appears that the legislature here intended to go further than the specific things that are mentioned in the statute, and meant to embrace all 'other offensive and dangerous weapons or instruments falling within
the scope and spirit of this statute other than those specifically mentioned."

See, also, People v. Gould, 237 Mich. 156.
The legislative intent is fairly ascertainable from the
declared purpose and the language of the enactment controls,
and the court, in an endeavor to ascertain such intent and
purpose from terms employed, should be circumspect.
The doctrine invoked in exculpation is untenable. . . .
The record discloses no error. Conviction affirmed.

BUTZEL, BUSHNELL, SHARPE, POTTER, CHANDLER, NORTH, and
McALLISTER, JJ., concurred.

People v. Lipski
328 Mich. 194

BUSHNELL, J. Defendant Richard Lipski, a married man,
drove his truck off the highway and stopped an automobile
being driven by a married woman. Lipski got out of his
truck, opened the left door by the driver's seat of the

other car and slid in beside the woman. He held her arms, displayed his affections upon her and asked her to have sexual relations with him. She refused. He made no attempt to force her against her will, but admitted that he would have had such relations had she allowed him to do so. The record is silent as to any previous acquaintance between the parties.

An information charging assault with intent to have sexual relations with a married woman, but not with intent to rape her, was filed against Lipski. The court reduced the charge to assault and battery and quashed the remainder. Thereafter the prosecuting attorney nolle prossed that case. Another complaint was signed by the married woman's husband. The second information charged Lipski with assault on the person named therein, "a married woman, with intent to commit a felony, to-wit: Adultery, he being a married man, but not being then and there married to her."

Defendant moved to quash this information. The trial judge, after considering the briefs and oral arguments, filed a written opinion. He held that, except as to the charge of assault, no such offense existed as that charged in the information. The State was granted leave to appeal from the court's order.

The statute under which the information was drawn, CL 1948, Sec. 750.87 (Stat. Ann. Sec. 28.282) reads as follows:

"Any person who shall assault another, with intent to commit any burglary, or any other felony, the punishment of which assault is not otherwise in this act prescribed, shall be guilty of a felony, punishable by imprisonment in the State prison not more than 10 years, or by fine of not more than 5,000 dollars."

The scope of this statute is broad and the assault is not limited to felonies of a type similar to burglary. Neither does the language include all other felonies because "a specific intent" is requisite. People v. Lilley, 43 Mich. 521, 529.

Adultery, unlike manslaughter which by definition precludes such an intent, is a felony in which intent is a necessary element. 1 Am. Jur, p 685.

Defendant argues that adultery, like incest, requires the consent of both parties, and that such consent, being inconsistent with the nature of an assault, negatives the assault and is therefore not a crime under the statute. See, in this connection, DeGroat v. People, 39 Mich 124, and People v. Burwell, 106 Mich 27.

Adultery is defined by statute as "the sexual intercourse of 2 persons, either of whom is married to a third person." CL 1948, Sec. 750.29 (Stat Ann Sec. 28.218). This statute guards the sanctity of marriage. Where both parties are married it protects each nonparticipating spouse. The spouse of the assaulter should be shielded just as much where the intercourse is with force as where it is with consent. In

890

like manner, the woman who is assaulted and who would be guilty of adultery if she condoned the assaulter's advances, should have her status fully protected when she refuses and resists.

The controlling factor is the marriage relation, and that exists whether intercourse occurs with or without consent. Consent is not expressed nor implied by the language of the statute, and will not be judicially inserted therein.

A charge of assault with intent to commit adultery is within the scope of the statute under which this information was laid. The facts disclosed in this record place defendant sufficiently within the purview of the statute as to require his trial.

The order quashing the information is vacated and the cause is remanded.

BOYLES, C. J., and NORTH, CARR, and SHARPE, JJ., concurred with BUSHNELL, J.

BUTZEL, J. (dissenting). I am unable to concur in the opinion for reversal. The trial court correctly ruled that the well-pleaded allegations of the information amounted only to the crime of assault and battery. Under the common law, the Michigan statutes and decisions, the crime of "assault with intent to commit adultery" does not exist.

Simple incontinence or fornication was not punishable under the common law at the time of the founding of the American colonies. Jurisdiction of this offense had long before been relinquished to the ecclesiastical courts and thus no such offense was included in the body of common law adopted in this country. Anderson v. Commonwealth, 5 Rand (Va) 627 (16 Am Dec 776). Our penal code does not provide that simple fornication - concurrent sexual intercourse without sanction of marriage - is a crime in the absence of a further element in violation of law.

Adultery is the sexual intercourse of 2 persons, either of whom is married to a third person, and its perpetration is a felony. CL 1948, Sec. 750.29, 750.30 (Stat Ann Sec. 28.218, 28.219). Transgression of the martial vows in violation of statute is the element rendering such intercourse a crime.

. Incest is sexual intercourse between 2 persons who are within the degree of relationship, either by consanguinity or affinity, wherein marriage to each other is prohibited, and the commission of incest is likewise a felony. CL 1948, Sec. 750.333 (Stat Ann 1949 Cum Supp Sec. 28.565). Violation of the statutory prohibition against such intimacy between near relatives is the element rendering such intercourse a crime.

The analogous offenses of adultery and incest are thus based upon intercourse in disregard of either marital ties or ties of blood or affinity. In the early case of People v. Jenness, 5 Mich 305, Justice CHRISTIANCY laid down the rule that the act of intercourse must be voluntarily engaged in by the parties in order to constitute the crime of incest. The following portion of the Jenness opinion was quoted by Justice COOLEY in DeGroat v. People, 39 Mich 124, where it was the controlling concept:

"This offense (of incest) can only be committed by the concurrent act of 2 persons of opposite sexes; and the assent or concurrence of the one is as essential to the commission of the offense as that of the other."

In adherence to this established rule, rape and incest have been held mutually exclusive crimes, as the lack of consent essential to rape is repugnant to the concurrence necessary for incest. DeGroat v. People, supra, People v. Burwell, 106 Mich 27.

There is no reason to follow an opposite rule in adultery cases, as the 2 offenses differ only in the status from which the criminal aspect of the act arises. Adultery, like incest, requires the concurrence of both participants. If such mutual assent is lacking, the crime committed would be rape, as it is under the well-settled incest rule of this jurisdiction. To follow the contrary reasoning of the opinion for reversal would in effect overrule the Jenness, DeGroat and Burwell Cases, supra, or would make a distinction where no real difference exists.

Our statute (CL 1948, Sec. 750.333 (Stat Ann 1949 Cum Supp Sec. 28.565)) defines as incest not only fornication between near relatives, but also adultery between them. If, as is stated in the opinion for reversal, there can be the commission of adultery with the consent of only one of such parties, that "adultery" would not constitute incest under the Jenness, DeGroat and Burwell decisions, supra, despite the fact that it would fulfill the statutory definition of incest. This inconsistency is based upon the false premise that mutual assent is unnecessary for the crime of adultery and is avoided by adhering to the rule of concurrence in both the analogous crimes.

The drafters of our penal code (PA 1931, No 328), who presumptively were mindful of our decisions (Lenawee County Gas & Electric Co. v. City of Adrian, 209 Mich 52 (10 ALR 1328)), did not define adultery as requiring the consent of only one of the participants and, until such time as the legislature . directs otherwise, that concept should not be engrafted upon our law.

The record is clear that there was no intent to have illicit relations unless the woman involved concurred, and it is equally clear that she resisted all advances. In the absence of the vital element of concurrence, the offense charged in the information cannot exist.

Stemming from Sir Matthew Hale's language in 1 Pleas of the Crown (1st Am ed) 634, there has been considerable judicial comment regarding the ease with which a sexual charge may be made and the difficulty of disproving it. See the annotations in 60 ALR 1124 and 130 ALR 1489. It would be difficult to

conceive of a charge more susceptible to the foregoing
criticism than the one set forth in the instant case. Some
trivial intentional touching, slight and innocuous, might
lead to a similar felonious charge in future cases.

Without lengthy citation of the numerous authorities recognizing the facility with which threats to prefer sexual
charges, or complaints made in execution of such threats,
lend themselves to extortion schemes, suffice it to say that
the conclusion reached in the foregoing opinion for reversal
might frequently result in blackmailing innocent victims. In
a situation such as the one at bar, simple assault and battery
is the sole offense unless the legislature directs to the contrary. This it has not done.

Affirmed.

REID and DETHMERS, JJ., concurred with BUTZEL, J.

3. Final Draft - Michigan Revised Criminal Code

(Assault in the First Degree)

Sec. 2101 (1) A person commits the crime of assault in
the first degree if:

(a) With intent to cause serious physical injury to
another person, he causes serious physical injury to any
person by means of a deadly weapon or a dangerous instrument;
or

(b) With intent to disfigure another person seriously
and permanently, or to destroy, amputate or disable permanently a member or organ of his body, he causes such an injury to
any person; or

(c) Under circumstances manifesting extreme indifference
to the value of human life, he recklessly engages in conduct
which creates a grave risk of death to another person, and
thereby causes serious physical injury to any person; or

(d) In the course of and in furtherance of the commission or attempted commission of arson in the first degree,
burglary in the first or second degree, escape in the first
degree, kidnapping in the first degree, rape in the first degree, robbery in any degree, or sodomy in the first degree,
or of immediate flight therefrom, he intentionally or recklessly causes serious physical injury to another person who
is not a participant in the commission of the crime.

(2) Assault in the first degree is a Class B felony.

Committee Commentary

Section 2101 is based on New York Revised Penal Law
Sec. 120.10. Its relationship to existing law is discussed
in the Commentary to Sec. 2101 to 2103.

(Assault in the Second Degree)

Sec. 2102. (1) A person commits the crime of assault in the second degree if:

(a) With intent to cause serious physical injury to another person, he causes serious physical injury to any person; or

(b) With intent to cause physical injury to another person, he causes physical injury to any person by means of a deadly weapon or a dangerous instrument; or

(c) With intent to prevent a peace officer from performing a lawful duty, he causes physical injury to any person; or

(d) He recklessly causes serious physical injury to another person by means of a deadly weapon or a dangerous instrument; or

(e) For a purpose other than lawful medical or therapeutic treatment, he intentionally causes stupor, unconsciousness, or other physical or mental impairment or injury to another person by administering to him, without his consent, a drug, substance or preparation capable of producing the intended harm.

(2) Assault in the second degree is a Class C felony.

Committee Commentary

Section 2102, except subsection (1) (d), is adapted from New York Revised Penal Law Sec. 120.05. Subsection (1) (d) is taken from Illinois Criminal Code Sec. 12-2(a) (3) and 12-4 (b) (3). The relationship of the section to present law is discussed in the Commentary to Sec. 2101 to 2103 below.

(Assault in the Third Degree)

Sec. 2103 (1) A person commits the crime of assault in the third degree if:

(a) With intent to cause physical injury to another person, he causes physical injury to any person; or

(b) He recklessly causes physical injury to another person; or

(c) With criminal negligence he causes physical injury to another person by means of a deadly weapon or a dangerous instrument.

(2) Assault in the third degree is a Class A misdemeanor.

Committee Commentary

Section 2103 is adapted from New York Revised Penal Law Sec. 120.00. Its relationship to existing law is discussed in the Commentary to Sec. 2101 to 2103 below.

Committee Commentary to Sec. 2101 to 2103

894

Relationship to Existing Law

The basic concept of assault and battery in Michigan is still that of the common law. The basic statute (C.L. 1948, Sec. 750.81) states only that where no other punishment is prescribed for an assault or an assault and battery, it shall be considered a misdemeanor. Statements in Michigan decisions appear to continue the common-law doctrine that an assault is an attempted battery, so that unless the defendant has the purpose to injure, he does not commit assault (see, e.g., People v. Doud, 223 Mich. 120, 193 N.W. 884 (1923); People v. Sheffield, 105 Mich. 117, 63 N.W. 65 (1895)). Though there are statements in the context of "assault with intent" statutes (see, e.g., People v. Carlson, 160 Mich. 426, 125 N.W. 361 (1910)) which might be interpreted somewhat more broadly, it seems likely that the tort law-derived concept of "intentional creation of the apprehension of receiving a battery" does not prevail in Michigan criminal law.

Common law knew no forms of aggravated battery. Michigan legislation, however, includes a number of statutes aggravating simple assault. The aggravating factors tend to fall into three categories:

(1) Serious physical injury actually inflicted. Assault and infliction of serious or aggravating injury constitute a circuit court misdemeanor (C.L. 1948, Sec. 750.81a); the intent must not be to commit murder or to inflict great bodily harm less than the crime of murder. Torturing a child is a felony punishable by up to 10 years imprisonment (C.L. 1948, Sec. 750.136a). The traditional crime of mayhem is restated to cover injuries to tongue, eyes, ears, nose, lips, and any limb, organ or member of the body (C.L. 1948, Sec. 750.397).

The new statute making it a misdemeanor, punishable by up to two years' imprisonment, to assault a police officer making a lawful arrest is intended chiefly to protect the officer against physical harm, since it operates only when there is injury requiring medical care or attention (C.L. 1948, Sec. 750.479a).

(2) Dangerous means, whether or not resulting in injury. The chief coverage is the felonious assault statute (C.L. 1948, Sec. 750.82), which makes it a felony to assault someone with a gun, revolver, pistol, knife, iron bar, club, brass knuckles or other dangerous weapon, but without the intent either to commit murder or to inflict great bodily harm less than the crime of murder. The term "other dangerous weapon" is not viewed as an ejusdem generis clause, and includes a vehicle (People v. Goolsby, 284 Mich. 375, 279 N.W. 867 (1938)). One may also include the statute prohibiting sending explosives with intent to injure or maim (C.L. 1948, Sec. 750.204), and the section penalizing placing explosives with intent to destroy a building or car under circumstances that if the intent had been carried through human life or safety would be endangered (C.L. 1948, Sec. 750.205), though the latter belongs more in the context of arson than assault.

895

(3) <u>Motivation for the assault</u>. Assault in Michigan
is usually agravated according to the actor's purpose or
motivation in committing the assault. The motives specified
are: intent to commit murder (C.L. 1948, Sec. 750.83); intent to do great bodily harm less than murder (C.L. 1948, Sec.
750.84); intent to commit rape, sodomy or gross indecency (C.L.
1948, Sec. 750.85); intent to maim (C.L. 1948, Sec. 750.86);
intent to commit burglary or a felony not otherwise covered
in an assault with intent statute (C.L. 1948, Sec. 750.87; this
was held to include adultery, People v. Lipski, 328 Mich. 194,
43 N.W.2d 325 (1950)); intent to rob and steal being armed (C.
L. 1948, Sec. 750.89). Though some of these statutes may properly be viewed as singling out aggravating factors, most of
them were apparently intended to codify specific attempt situations. In all of these statutes the specific intent must be
proven beyond a reasonable doubt, (People v. Guillet, 342 Mich.
1, 69 N.W.2d 140 (1955); People v. Shaffran, 243 Mich. 527, 220
N.W. 716 (1928)).
     To complete the description of Michigan statutes, mention
should be made of the several statutes prohibiting dueling
(C.L. 1948, Sec. 750.171-750.173), now totally obsolete, the
prohibition against sending or placing explosives (C.L. 1948,
Sec. 750.204, 750.205), more properly considered in the contexts of arson and malicious destruction of property, and the
sections penalizing unlicensed prize-fighting (C.L. 1948, Sec.
750.442-750.447), a matter now dealt with indirectly through
Sec. 4230-4235 of the Draft.

                *   *   *   *   *

     The Draft embodies a fairly drastic reorientation of
Michigan law. In the first place, it limits assault as a
concept to the infliction of physical injury, defined in
Sec. 135(h) to mean impairment of physical condition or substantial pain. A mere physical touching will not constitute
assault, but harassment; harassment is defined in Sec. 5530
thus:

     "A person is guilty of harassment when, with intent to
harass, annoy or alarm another person:

     1. He strikes, shoves, kicks or otherwise touches a per-
son or subjects him to physical contact; or
     2. In a public place, he uses abusive or obscene language,
or makes an obscene gesture, or

. . .

     5. He engages in a course of conduct or repeatedly com-
mits acts which alarm or seriously annoy such other person
and which serve no legitimate purpose."

     This type of conduct is more appropriate in the context
of loitering and disorderly conduct than in the context of
assault.
     In the second place, the Draft eliminates all "assault

896

with intent" sections. The fact of physical contact is of little more than formal legal significance in the Michigan cases; the critical factor is the purpose or motivation. Unsuccessful or inadequate activity plus intent, however, are the critical elements under the concept of attempt. Therefore, instead of charging assault with intent to commit murder, or assault with intent to commit rape, it is more in order to charge attempted murder or attempted rape. Because the Draft embodies an elaborate codification of doctrines of attempt, it is preferable to eliminate most matters of motivation from the assault context.

Because assault now requires as a minimum the infliction of physical injury, there is no reason why the Draft provisions on attempt cannot be utilized where there is an effort to inflict physical injury or serious physical injury which fails. Though common-law oriented writers criticize the idea of "attempted assault" (see Perkins, An Analysis of Assault and Attempts to Assault, 47 Minn.L.Rev. 71 (1962)), it is directly proper under the Draft. The Draft endorses the statement of the authors of the New York Draft Penal Law:

"The proposed assault formulation, requiring actual physical injury, places the crime of assault in the main category of offenses (robbery, larceny, perjury, etc.) which are committed only when the offender succeeds in his criminal objective. And as with other offenses of this nature, an unsuccessful endeavor (a common law assault not resulting in a battery) constitutes an attempt. "Attempted assault," therefore, becomes a logical and meaningful offense under the proposed Article, having considerable utility in connection with certain specific intent assault crimes . . ." (citing the equivalents to Sec. 2101 (1) (a), 2102 (1) (a), (b) and (f), and 2103 (1) (a) and (b)). (Commission Staff Notes pp 330-31)

Section 2101 comprehends the most serious forms of life-endangering conduct. Subsection (1) (a) covers the intentional infliction of serious physical injury, defined in Sec. 135 (i), by means of a deadly weapon or a dangerous instrument.

Subsection (1) (b) is a modern restatement of the concept of mayhem, and does not differ substantially from the present statutory coverage in Michigan (C.L. 1948, Sec. 750.397).

Subsection (1) (c) should be compared with Sec. 2006 (1) (b) (murder in the second degree). If death results from the defendant's extraordinary recklessness and callousness the crime falls within Sec. 2006 (1) (b); if serious physical injury results the offense falls within Sec. 2101 (1) (c). Mere physical injury under these circumstances comes within Sec. 2103 (1) (b).

Subsection (1) (d) is a "felony-assault" doctrine which should be considered together with Sec. 2005 (1) (b). If serious physical injury results it is assault in the first degree.

Section 2102 (1) (a) provides for increased penalties, though less than under Sec. 2101, for one who intentionally inflicts on someone serious physical injury, as defined in

Sec. 135(i). This corresponds fairly closely to the present aggravated assault statute (C.L. 1948, Sec. 750.81a).

Subsection (1) (b) penalizes the intentional infliction of physical injury, as defined in Sec. 135 (h), by means of a deadly weapon, defined in Sec. 135 (k), or a dangerous instrument, defined in Sec. 135 (1). It resembles fairly closely the present felonious assault statute (C.L. 1948, Sec. 750.82).

Subsection (1) (c) covers physical injury, as defined in Sec. 135 (h), inflicted on a peace officer with intent to prevent him from performing a lawful duty, or "transferred intent" injuries to others who are present. A statute to this effect was passed in 1966 (C.L. 1948, Sec. 750.479a). It should be noted that the state must prove beyond a reasonable doubt that the assaulter must believe the officer is acting lawfully. If there is a good faith but mistaken belief to the contrary, there is no assault under this subsection. There is minimal overlap between this subsection and Sec. 4710 (1), prohibiting obstruction, impairment or hindrance of criminal law enforcement or the preservation of peace by a peace officer by the use or threatened use of violence, force or physical interference or obstacle. Section 4710 makes no distinction in treatment based on the amount of injury inflicted, and places primary emphasis on the motivation. Section 2102 (1) (c), on the other hand, stresses the infliction of physical injury under circumstances calling for increased punishment. The overlap, therefore, is probably minimal, and will be compensated for by Draft provisions on double jeopardy.

Subsection (1) (d) governs the reckless causing of a serious physical injury to another by means of a deadly weapon or a dangerous instrument. The subsection is closely related to Sec. 2103 (1) (c), but calls for increased penalties because serious physical injury, not mere physical injury, is caused by reckless, not merely negligent, conduct.

Subsection (1) (e) places in an aggravated assault category any non-consensual administering of a drug, etc. which is intended to produce and does produce stupor, unconsciousness or other physical or mental impairment or injury. This conduct constituted battery at common law (Clark & Marshall Law of Crimes 655 (6th ed. 1958); Perkins, Criminal Law 81 (1957)). It is placed in the second-degree assault category here because of the hazard to life inherent in substances so introduced into the body. Lawful medical or therapeutic treatment is of course excepted.

Section 2103 sets out the basic coverage of assault. Under subsection (1) (a), the intent is to cause physical injury, as defined in Sec. 135 (h), and the act is the causing of that injury to anyone. There is no specification of the means by which the injury is to be caused.

Subsection (1) (b) probably goes further than existing Michigan law, in that it covers physical injury, as defined

898

in Sec. 135 (8), inflicted as the result of recklessness. Under Sec. 305 (c), this means that the actor must disregard a known substantial and unjustifiable risk that a result will occur. In effect this subsection is the counterpart to manslaughter in the second degree, particularly Sec. 2010 (1) (a); if death results from the recklessness it is second-degree manslaughter, but if physical injury only results, it is third-degree assault (but cf. Sec. 2102 (1) (e) if persious physical injury is recklessly caused by a deadly weapon or dangerous instrument).

Subsection (1) (c) penalizes one who through criminal negligence, as defined in Sec. 305 (d), causes physical injury to someone by means of a deadly weapon, as defined in Sec. 135 (k), or by a dangerous instrument, as defined in Sec. 135 (1)-(m). This embodies a basic concept of criminality now contained in the section which makes it a misdemeanor to maim or injure a person by the discharge of a firearm pointed at another (C.L. 1948, Sec. 750.235), that which makes it a heavily-punished misdemeanor to cause or allow a bow and arrow under one's control carelessly, recklessly or negligently, but not wilfully or wantonly, to kill or injure another (C.L. 1948, Sec. 752.881) and the case which includes using a vehicle to run over a police officer's foot as a form of felonious assault (People v. Goolsby, 284 Mich. 375, 279 N.W. 867 (1938)). It goes further, however, in that it covers any deadly weapon or dangerous instrument, which latter in turn includes any type of vehicle, any vessel and aircraft. Thus negligence in the operation of a motorboat, or using an airplane to "buzz" a populated district, would fall within this subsection if physical injury results.

In a number of the subsection (e.g., Sec. 2101 (1) (a), (b), (c); 2102 (1) (a),(b),(c),(d); 2103 (1) (a)), though the intent is stated in terms of purpose to injure "another person," the objective act is physical injury or serious physical injury to "any person." This is intended to preserve the common-law concept of transferred intent, embodied in Michigan case law (People v. Hodge, 196 Mich. 546, 162 N.W. 966 (1917)).

Note on assaults on school employees. The Committee considered a subsection similar in wording to that covering assaults on peace officers, which would have protected school employees and other persons on school grounds. A majority of the Committee concluded that there was no reason to include special provisions, the more general provisions being adequate in this regard to provide ample protection for teachers and administrators against assaults by pupils or loiterers in school buildings.

(Menacing)

Sec. 2110. (1) A person commits the crime of menacing if, by physical action, he intentionally places or attempts to place another person in fear of imminent serious physical injury.

    (2) Menacing is a Class B misdemeanor.

Committee Commentary

    Section 2110 is adapted from New York Revised Penal Law Sec. 120.15.

    It is not clear under Michigan case law whether the several "assault with intent" statutes cover infliction of the fear of being the victim of a criminal act. In one case (People v. Carlson, 160 Mich. 426, 125 N.W. 361 (1910)), the Supreme Court rejected defendant's contention that a threat to use physical violence not in fact accompanied by physical contact could not constitute an assault with intent to commit rape, and held that such an assault might be committed without an actual touching. Since, however, the Court felt the jury could in fact find an intent to rape, the case is not necessarily authority for the proposition that creating the apprehension of receiving serious physical injury constitutes an assault; the logic of statements in other cases suggests that an attempt or purpose to batter is probably required.

    Section 2110 embodies the idea that one who uses physical menaces to create apprehension in his victim that serious physical injury is imminent should be punished. Menacing based on threat of non-serious physical injury falls within the definition of coercion (Sec. 2125). Less serious abuse constitutes harassment.

(Reckless Endangerment)

    Sec. 2115. (1) A person commits the crime of reckless endangerment if he recklessly engages in conduct which creates a substantial risk of serious physical injury to another person.

    (2) Reckless endangerment is a Class A misdemeanor.

Committee Commentary

    The section is adapted from New York Revised Penal Law Sec. 120.20.

    Absent Sec. 2115, reckless conduct becomes criminal only if it causes death under Sec. 2010 (manslaughter) or injury under Sec. 2103 (1) (b) (assault in the third degree); recklessness which does not in fact produce either result is not otherwise punishable. Section 2115 permits the imposition of penalites on one who clearly manifests his recklessness, as defined in Sec. 305 (c). Functionally it corresponds to utilizing a broadened attempt concept, except that there must be intent or knowledge before there can be attempt. Only one existing statute appears to embody this idea (C.L. 1948, Sec. 750.205), which covers placing explosives with intent to destroy but without resulting damage, "under such circumstances, that, if the intent were accomplished, human life or safety would be endangered thereby." Section 2115 embodies a more general statement of the same idea.

(Promoting a Suicide Attempt)

Sec. 2120. (1) A person commits the crime of promoting a suicide attempt if he intentionally causes or aids another person to attempt suicide.

(2) A person who engages in conduct constituting the offense of promoting a suicide attempt may not be convicted of attempt to commit murder unless he causes or aids the suicide attempt by the use of duress or deception.

(3) Promoting a suicide attempt is a Class C felony.

Committee Commentary

Section 2120 is based on New York Revised Penal Law Sec. 120.30 and 120.35.

Under Sec. 2005 (2) a person does not commit murder if his conduct consists of causing or aiding, without the use of duress or deception, another person to commit suicide; the converse is that use of duress or deception amounts to murder. Intentionally to cause or aid another person to commit suicide, without the use of duress or deception, falls within Sec. 2010 (1) (c) (manslaughter). Section 2120 supplements these provisions where the would-be suicide is unsuccessful in his assisted efforts to kill himself.

Under subsection (1), a person who intentionally causes or aids another to attempt suicide commits the crime of promoting a suicide attempt. This conduct should be spelled out and not left for inclusion by interpretation in Sec. 2101-2103.

Subsection (2) is the counterpart to the provisions of Sec. 2005 (2), and is intended to indicate that there cannot be prosecution both for promoting a suicide attempt and attempted murder unless the state proves the use of duress or deception.

B. Extortion

1. Michigan Compiled Laws (1948)

750.213 Malicious threats to extort money

Sec. 213. MALICIOUS THREATS TO EXTORT MONEY - Any person who shall, either orally or by a writter or printed communication, maliciously threaten to accuse another of any crime or offense, or shall orally or by any written or printed communication maliciously threaten any injury to the person or property or mother, father, husband, wife or child of another with intent thereby to extort money or any pecuniary advantage whatever, or with intent to compel the person so threatened to do or refrain from doing any act against his will, shall be guilty of a felony, punishable by imprisonment in the state prison not more than 20 years or by a fine of not more than 10,000 dollars.

750.214 Extortion by public officers

Sec. 214. EXTORTION BY PUBLIC OFFICERS - Any person who shall wilfully and corruptly demand and receive from another for performing any service, or any official duty, for which the fee or compensation is established by law, any greater fee or compensation than is allowed or provided for the same, and any public officer, for whom a salary is provided by law in full compensation for all services required to be performed by him, or by his clerks or deputies, who shall wilfully and corruptly demand and receive from any person any sum of money as a fee or compensation for any services required by law to be performed by him in his said office, or by his clerks or deputies, shall be guilty of a misdemeanor; but no prosecution for such offense shall be sustained unless it shall be commenced within 1 year next after the offense was committed.

2. Definitions and General Elements of the Offense

People v. Jones
62 Mich. 304

CAMPBELL, C. J. Respondent was convicted under Section 19 c. 153, Rev. Stat. (being Sec. 9093, How. Stat.), which provides that if any person shall verbally, or by written or printed communication, "maliciously threaten to accuse another of any crime or offense," or "maliciously threaten any injury to the person or property of another, with intent thereby to extort money, or any pecuniary advantage whatever, or with intent to compel the person so threatened to do any act against his will," he shall be punished, etc.

The information contains but one count, which avers that respondent, on January 19, 1886, -

"Did verbally and maliciously threaten to accuse one Ellen Roosa of an offense, to wit, of the violation of the internal revenue laws of the United States of America, relating to the sale of spirituous and intoxicating liquors; and he, the said B. F. Jones, did then and there verbally and maliciously threaten injury to the person and property of the said Ellen Roosa, and that the said B. F. Jones did then and there verbally and maliciously threaten her, the said Ellen Roosa, to accuse her of such crime and offense

902

as would cause her, the said Ellen Roosa, to be imprisoned
in the State's prison at Jackson, in the State of Michigan, -
all with the intent to extort money from her, the said Ellen
Roosa, also certain pecuniary advantage, and with further intent of him, the said B. F. Jones, to compel her, the said
Ellen Roosa, to do an act against her will, to wit, to make
a sale and transfer of all her right, title and interest in
and to certain personal property, goods, and chattels then
owned and possessed by her, the said Ellen Roosa, in the city
of Owosso, in the county and State aforesaid, to wit, a one-
half interest in and to the business, furniture, fixtures,
and articles used in carrying on the business of running a
saloon located on Washington street," etc. "of the value of
$700."

It will be observed that in this single count are included
all of the possible violations of the section, with all of
the possible intents, and all are connected together in a
single charge.

It will also appear that no offense is specified, no threatened injury to person or property is specified, no averment
is made of actual injury, or its nature, and the only distinct
evil purposed, as described, is compelling Mrs. Roosa to sell
out her interest in the saloon.

On the trial, objections of various kinds pointed out the
defects, and the court refused to require the people to elect
what grievance to prosecute. Several exceptions were taken,
and we are also asked to set aside the whole proceedings for
these defects.

These statutory provisions have been in force, in form or
substance, for a long time. The object is to put threats of
criminal accusation on a similar footing with threats of personal violence when made for extortion or similar objects.
In cases of actual success in obtaining property, there were
some instances where pressure of threats to accuse of infamous crimes was held to create the same mischief as force,
and to make out robbery. These cases were few and peculiar,
and open to some doubt.

The nature of the mischief requires that the character of
the threat should be set out, so that it may be seen whether
or not a substantial threat was really made, and what it was, -
whether any particular injury or any particular crime. It
is undoubtedly true that vague threats are sometimes made;
but, unless they indicate to the person threatened some charge
which is intelligible, it has not been considered that a
criminal offense is made out under the statute, while, if
mischief actually follows, there are usually other legal
methods which will bring the offender to justice.

It is not the policy of the law to punish those unsuccessful threats which it is not presumed would terrify ordinary
persons excessively; and there is so much opportunity for
magnifying or misunderstanding undefined menaces that probably as much mischief would be caused by letting them be

prosecuted as by refraining from it.

The only case referred to where it has been supposed a threat need not be laid definitely is Rex V. Tucker, 1 Moody, 134; but in that case it was laid specifically in the indictment as having a definite meaning, and was shown by the testimony to have been rightfully interpreted. It is expressly noted by Mr. Harrison (1 Dig. 2005) that the right to have its meaning shown by proof is all the case decided, and it is so described in Car. Crim. Law, 288. The subject is treated at some length by Mr. Russell (2 Russ. Cr. 706 et seq.), and Archbold (Crim. Pl. 605 et seq.). There seems to be no authority for leaving out the particular offense or mischief covered by the threat, or deducible from it, and the intent must be stated specifically, and proved as laid: Id., 2 East, P.C. 1118.

The statutes do not materially change the common law when the threat succeeds, except as they aggravate the character of the crime. It is questioned whether they have introduced anything further as to the nature of the mischief, 2 Russ. 706. In Rex v. Southerton, 6 East, 126, it was pointed out that at common law the offense on which the threat was made must be indictable; and that prosecutions under the revenue laws did not come within the principle.

We do not feel called on to consider whether the crimes and offenses, a threat to accuse of which is punishable, include any but such as are punishable by our own courts. This point was argued, and there are some considerations which favor the idea, as the United States laws punish some similar cases of extortion. But, on the present information, no offense under the revenue laws is specified, and most of them are not indictable, and none coming within any possible meaning of the threat charged here is felonious.

Under this general and indefinite pleading, the jury found a general verdict, and, as no election was required, it is questionable whether the charge could have corrected the mischief had the counts been separate. But in this count there are no definite allegations of the meaning of the threats, either of accusation or of personal injury.

We think the conviction cannot be sustained, and it must be quashed and the prisoner discharged.

The other Justices concurred.

People v. Whittemore
102 Mich. 519

MONTGOMERY, J. Respondent was convicted of maliciously threatening to accuse one Paul Lucas of the crime of perjury, in violation of How. Stat. Sec. 9093.

The facts are that the respondent is an attorney, residing at St. Paul, Minn., and was the attorney of one Joseph Stehr, who had a suit pending in the Minnesota courts against

Paul Lucas and others, involving the title to certain lands
in St. Paul. Respondent came to Alpena in December, 1893,
for the purpose of taking the depositions of witnesses in
the case referred to, and, as subsequent events would indicate, with the further purpose of procuring a deed from Lucas
to his client. On the 13th, 14th, 15th, and 16th of December,
respondent examined Paul Lucas as a witness in the case, before a circuit court commissioner. After the testimony was
concluded, respondent invited Lucas to his room at the hotel,
and, while there, Lucas swears, in substance, respondent
threatened to prosecute him for perjury unless he would deed
the land to his (respondent's) client, for a named consideration. These threats did not prove effectual, and on the 25th
day of January, 1894, respondent made a complaint against
Lucas for perjury, and caused his arrest. An examination was
not had at once, but Lucas was taken to the office of the prosecuting attorney, who permitted him to go at large, with instructions to report to him (the prosecutor); and, apparently,
the prosecutor interested himself in the effort to procure
the deed from Lucas and his wife. On the 27th day of January
the prosecuting attorney and the respondent in this case and
Lucas started to drive from Alpena into the country, where
Lucas resided, to procure the execution of the deed. Mr. J.
H. Cobb, the attorney who now represents the people in this
case, one Charles Golling, Judge Kelley, who presided at the
trial, and the sheriff of Alpena county, followed the party
for the purpose of preventing a consummation of the transaction. The deed was not procured, but Lucas returned to
Alpena, a justice was called in, and the respondent was complained against for the offense here in controversy. . . .
    . . . The circuit judge charged the jury, in effect, that
if the threats were made with the wrongful intent charged,
and were made maliciously, the offense was complete, whether
Lucas was or was not guilty of the offense of perjury. The
respondent complains of this holding, and contends that if
the respondent, having an interest in the matter, believed
that Lucas was guilty of perjury, he had the right to threaten
to prosecute Lucas, unless he should place the title where
it belonged. But we think the law is settled otherwise. 2
Whart. Cr. Law, Sec. 1664; Rose Cr. Ev. *979; Rex v. Gardner,
1 Car. & P. 479; Reg. v. Cracknell, 10 Cox, Cr. Cas. 408;
Com. v. Buckley, 148 Mass. 27; Com. v. Coolidge, 128 Id. 55;
State v. Goodwin, 37 La. Ann. 713. The respondent in the
present case denied having made the threats imputed to him,
or having made any demand upon the prosecuting witness. His
statement of the conversation was, in effect, that he offered
to compromise the litigation with the complaining witness.
    Respondent further contends that the testimony tending to
show that Lucas was in fact guilty of perjury was proper for
two purposes:

"It would tend to show that he was not a truthful witness,
and that the threats were not made maliciously."

It has been held in some cases that, when the question involved is whether the demand for money is a demand for what respondent is in no way entitled to, evidence that the prosecuting witness has been guilty of an offense for which the accused is entitled to demand compensation is admissible, as bearing upon the question of the intent; that is, to determine whether the accused is seeking to recover his own, or to extort money which does not belong to him. Com. v. Jones, 121 Mass. 57; Mann v. State, 47 Ohio St. 556. The reasoning of the latter case is against the clear weight of authority, as is apparent from an examination of the cases hereinbefore cited. In the case of Com. v. Jones, the fact that a demand was made upon the complaining witness was admitted by the accused, and evidence that the complaining witness had been guilty of a wrong against him, for which he was entitled to demand compensation, was held admissible, as having a bearing upon the question of the respondent's intent, he having denied a threat of prosecution. But in the case of Com. v. Buckley, decided by the same court, it was held that evidence that the complaining witness had in fact committed the offense was not competent for the purpose of impeaching him; and it was also said of the other contention made by the respondent here, that it was competent on the question of malice:

"The malice required by the statute is not a feeling of ill will toward the person threatened, but the willful doing of the act with the illegal intent. If the threat was willfully made with the intent to extort money, it was a malicious act, and the fact that the charge was true would be immaterial."

We think there was no error in the ruling in this regard. . .
A careful examination of the record convinces us that there was no legal error committed on the trial.
The conviction will be affirmed, and the case remanded for further proceedings.

McGRATH, C. J., LONG and HOOKER, JJ., concurred. GRANT, J., did not sit.

People v. Watson
307 Mich. 378

BUTZEL, J. Defendant was charged with having orally and by written communication of the 20th day of May, and between said date and the 29th day of August, 1941, maliciously threatened and accused Ray E. Chappel of the crime of adultery and conspiracy to obtain an abortion and with the intent then and there to extort money from him. The crime is set forth in Act No. 328, Sec. 213, Pub. Acts 1931 (Comp. Laws Supp. 1940, Sec. 17115-213, Stat. Ann. Sec. 28.410), under the catchline "Malicious threats to extort money." Defendant appeals from the judgment of conviction.

906

It is necessary to review briefly the sordid facts as testified to by Ray E. Chappel. He conducted a jewelry business on the ground floor of a building at Niles, Michigan. There was a workshop and also a small dark room in which to fit glasses in the rear of the store. Chappel was 64 years of age; his wife was living at the time. Sometime previously he had been involved in an affair similar to the one complained of with another woman. Defendant patronized his store a few times and on March 21, 1941, brought him a small cabinet containing a negligible quantity of old gold. He took it to a room in the rear of his store. She accompanied him. He responded to advances made by her and an illicit relationship ensued. She visited the store from time to time and similar acts took place. About the 17th of May, 1941, or thereabouts, she came to the store, told him she was pregnant, and that he was responsible. She said she had been to Chicago for an examination and that she could have an abortion performed there for $400, but that she could have one at South Bend, Indiana, for $450, and she preferred to go to South Bend which is but a short distance from Niles, Michigan. He gave her $5 for an examination and the illicit relationship continued at the time. A few days later, defendant informed Chappel that she had an examination and that she was strong enough to undergo a criminal operation. It was agreed upon. He paid her $450 a few days later. The following day and for almost three months thereafter she sent him in rapid succession notes describing her necessitous, desperate and at times dangerous physical condition as a result of the operation. The notes as a rule were delivered by messenger to whom Chappel gave money, one time giving $72, then at short intervals, $150, $50, $300, $147.52, $225, $74, $264.50, $200, $371, $328, $504, $275, $375, although he thought he sent more than the enumerated amounts.

On August 29, 1941, Chappel received two notes in one day by messenger. In the first defendant told him about a very serious condition that had developed and asked him not to be angry but that she could not get "anything from him – because he wants to know the cause and reason, et cetera, and full particulars." (Evidently "him" referred to defendant's husband.) "As far as I am concerned I would tell him." If Chappel would send her funds she would repay him from the sale of real estate and he should send reply by bearer. In the same hour, Chappel received another note from defendant as follows:

"Do you want me to go to County House for this treatment? I am ready to air the whole thing – as I am doing the suffering – not you. If you don't – what other course have I – as if it wasn't for you I could tell him all – as I don't care for myself. If you do not reply to this I will send for him to come here and bring an attorney with him as I can't go on like this. You must know this is terrible. I can't help the condition – as you made me get rid of same – paid for it – and left me in this condition.

"Now - think this over Ray dear - I am sorry - but I am sick and just can't help it. Please reply."

In reply to the first note, he wrote that he could not do anything at that time, and in answer to the second note, that the matter was a serious one and he wanted time to think it over and would give her the answer toward the end of the week.

Chappel thereupon consulted a lawyer. On the 4th day of September, 1941, a lady messenger came to the store and asked for a package for defendant. Chappel in the meantime had called in a deputy sheriff who hid in the store when the messenger arrived. The messenger asked for the package for Mrs. Watson and Chappel gave her a sealed enevelope, whereupon the deputy sheriff arrested the messenger. She told him that defendant had sent her after the package and that defendant was around the corner in a big black sedan. Defendant was arrested then and there. She was bound over to the circuit court for trial and duly convicted.

No testimony was introduced in behalf of defendant. There is more than ample testimony to prove beyond a reasonable doubt that defendant threatened to accuse Chappel of a crime in order to extort large sums of money from him. The testimony clearly indicates that defendant visited no hospitals in Niles, South Bend or Chicago, and that the entire threats in order to extort money were founded on false statements by defendant. It is evident that Chappel was a dupe in paying over money to messenger boys from hotels and other places as the notes were presented.

Defendant on appeal contends that the people did not present a prima facie case of extortion as alleged in the information and that the court should have granted a motion to dismiss and directed a verdict of not guilty. Both sides rely largely on the case of People v. Braman, 30 Mich. 460, in which Mr. Justice COOLEY wrote an opinion, concurred in by Mr. Justice CHRISTIANCY, upholding a conviction under the statute, and Chief Justice GRAVES in an opinion concurred in by Mr. Justice CAMPBELL, dissented. As the opinions are available to the profession, for the sake of brevity, we shall not quote from them. We are in accord with the opinion of Mr. Justice COOLEY. We believe the statute is sufficiently broad so as to cover a threat merely to publicly accuse another of a crime and that it does not require a threat to file formal complaint and instigate a criminal prosecution. In People v. Frey, 112 Mich. 251, defendant contended that while evidence of a threat to accuse judicially was necessary to establish the offense of extortion, the proof fell short of showing more than a threat to accuse publicly. The court held that even under defendant's interpretation of the statute, which it did not decide, there was testimony to show a threat to prosecute sufficient to allow the case to go to the jury. In the instant case, the last letter written by defendant satisfies either construction of the statute. It embodied a threat of both public accusation and legal proceedings. It stated that defendant would tell "him" (evidently her husband), that if Chappel did not reply to this she would send for "him to come" and "bring an attorney with him," and that Chappel was responsible for the criminal operation which left her in a dangerous condition. Defendant threatened Chappel with not only telling her husband but also with bringing an attorney along. A fair inference would be that the attorney was to be brought in order to take legal action.

It became a question for the jury to determine whether from the letters and actions of defendant she did maliciously threaten to accuse Chappel of a crime with the intent to extort money from him. The testimony supports the jury's findings and judgment of conviction is affirmed.

BOYLES, C. J., and CHANDLER, NORTH, STARR, WIEST, BUSHNELL, and SHARPE, JJ., concurred.

People v. Percin
330 Mich. 94

BUTZEL, J. This is an appeal from a conviction on the charge of extortion. The 2 counts of the information are as follows:

First, "That Albin Percin and Raymond Claeys . . . on the 16th day of August, A.D. 1947 and on divers other days and dates between said date and the 20th day of August A.D. 1947 . . . did . . . orally and maliciously threaten to accuse others, to-wit: Bernard Kosmol and Henry Pokroppa, of a certain crime and offense, to-wit: giving and furnishing alcoholic beverages to one Clarence Ryan, being . . . a minor[1] . . . with the intent to extort money from and compel the said Bernard Kosmol and Henry Pokroppa to give to them . . . the sum of . . . $200; contrary to the form of the statute, et cetera"; and

Second, "By . . . orally and maliciously threatening to report to the liquor control commission of the State of Michigan the sale of alcoholic liquors . . . to one Clarence Ryan . . . which said report would result in the penalty of . . . $300 and a . . . 30-day suspension of the license of said Bernard Kosmol and Henry Pokroppa, . . . with the intent thereby to extort . . . the sum of . . . $200; contrary to the form of the statute."

The statute reads:

"Any person who shall . . . maliciously threaten to accuse another of any crime or offense, or shall . . . maliciously threaten any injury to the person or property . . . of another with intent thereby to extort money or any pecuniary advantage whatever, . . . shall be guilty of a felony,

909

punishable by imprisonment." <u>CL 1948</u>, <u>Sec.</u> <u>750.213</u> (<u>Stat</u> <u>Ann</u> <u>Sec.</u> <u>28.410</u>).

Percin and Claeys, defendants, were police officers of the Detroit police department. On Saturday, August 16, 1947, they approached Bernard Kosmol, owner with Henry Pokroppa of the Rhein Bar in Detroit, and told him that they knew he had been serving liquor to a minor, one Ryan, then 19 years of age. Percin said that they had not turned the matter over to the inspector. Claeys stated that if it were reported to the liquor control commission, Kosmol could be fined $300 and have his license suspended for 30 days. They asked how much their silence was worth to him. Kosmol told the defendants that he would have to speak to his partner and asked the defendants to come back on Monday. Defendants returned on Monday and spoke to Pokroppa, Kosmol not being present. It was agreed that $200 would be paid. When they returned on Tuesday, Kosmol put them off until the following day. Percin could not come on Wednesday and Claeys was to come alone. Kosmol reported what had occurred to the police department, and when Claeys came in on Wednesday there were 2 inspectors hidden and waiting for him. Kosmol gave Claeys an envelope with marked bills in it, and after Claeys took the envelope he was arrested, the inspectors having witnessed the transaction. Percin was arrested later.

Kosmol, although in this country for some 27 years, could not speak English with ease or fluency, and at the trial some of his answers were confusing. The defendants, by introducing the records of the examination, demonstrated that he was confused as to which of the officers had made the statements at the original meeting, some of which he credited to Percin at the trial, although at the examination he stated Claeys had made them. However, the substance of his testimony remained unshaken during the cross-examination. Imperfect as it was, Kosmol's testimony when combined with the testimony of the other witnesses provided ample evidence which, if believed by the jury, established the guilt of each defendant beyond a reasonable doubt.

In <u>People</u> v. <u>Jones</u>, <u>62</u> <u>Mich.</u> <u>304</u>, we said:

"Vague threats are sometimes made; but, unless they indicate to the person threatened some charge which is intelligible, it has not been considered that a criminal offense is made out under the statute."

Kosmol testified that he did not know that selling liquor to minors was a crime; he thought it was merely an infraction of the rules of the liquor commission. The defendants contend that the threats were so unintelligible that Kosmol did not know he was being threatened with accusation of a crime and for that reason there was no crime committed. This contention is without merit.

There are 2 elements to the crime of extortion, the threat to accuse of a crime or offense, and the intent to extort

910

money. In examining the information in People v. Jones, supra, the Court found that no specific threat was included. The Court stated that general allegations of a threat were insufficient, for there must be a specific threat before a crime has been committed. In the instant case, the specific threat to charge the complainants with selling liquor to a minor was alleged in the information and shown at the trial. As to whether the necessary intent was shown was a question to be decided by the jury from the facts before them. In People v. Braman, 30 Mich. 460, Justice COOLEY said:

"If the meaning of the communication were doubtful, the intent would be a question for the jury."

There was no error in the conviction under the first count.

We find it unnecessary to consider the effect of these threats upon the complainants in reaching our conclusion. As the court said in Commonwealth v. Corcoran, 252 Mass 465, 483 (148 NE 123):

"The gist of the offense described in the statute is the attempt to extort money. Commonwealth v. Goodwin, 122 Mass 19, 33. If the threat be of the kind referred to in the statute, and is made with the intent thereby to extort money, or with the intent to accomplish any of the other objects mentioned therein, the crime has been committed. The language is explicit and is not subject to any exceptions or qualifications. The legislature did not make the commission of the offense dependent upon the state of mind of the person threatened, and there is no occasion for reading into the statute qualifications not there found. If it had been intended that to constitute the offense the person threatened was intimidated or must have understood and appreciated the fact that he was so threatened with the intent to extort money from him, or to accomplish any other purpose set forth in the statute, it is the rational inference that it would have been so declared. People v. Thompson, 97 NY 313, 318."

See, also O'Neil v. State, 237 Wis 391 (296 NW 96, 135 ALR 719).

The above quoted passage applies with equal force to the Michigan statute.

Defendants contend that they were tried under the wrong statute, and that they should have been tried under CL 1948, Sec. 750.123 (Stat Ann Sec. 28.318), which says in part:

"Any . . . officer authorized to serve process or arrest or apprehend offenders against criminal law who shall receive from a defendant or from any other person any money . . . as a consideration, reward or inducement, for omitting or delaying to arrest any defendant, or to carry him before a magistrate . . . or for omitting or delaying to perform any duty pertaining to his office, shall be guilty of a misdemeanor, punishable by imprisonment in the county jail not more than 6 months or by fine of not more than . . . 250

911

dollars."

Defendants claim that this misdemeanor statute applies to police officers and that the extortion statute applies to everyone, and, therefore, it was clearly the legislative intent to punish police officers under the misdemeanor statute only. We need only consider the most obvious of several answers to this claim. The extortion statute punishes for the malicious threat with the intent to extort. These 2 offenses are of a completely different nature, and it is frivolous to suggest that the legislature intended that police officers be treated more leniently than ordinary citizens merely because, by their extortion, they incidentally committed the crime of accepting a reward for the failure to perform their duty.

It is also contended that there was no violation of the second count in the information. This count accused the defendants of the threat to injure the property of the complainant and defendants claim that the injury threatened was not visible tangible property. Though distinct in point of law, "the two counts did not charge inconsistent offenses. Both arose out of the same transaction, both were provable by the same testimony, only one time, place and subject being involved." People v. Lowenstein, 309 Mich 94, 99. There was no need for an election of counts. People v. Mathews, 207 Mich 526, 535; People v. McKinney, 10 Mich 54.

"Where 1 of 2 counts is bad and the other good, a general verdict of guilty will be sustained as to the good count." 1 Gillespie, Michigan Criminal Law and Procedure, Sec. 568.

We find it unnecessary to discuss the second count, since the first count is sufficient to sustain the verdict. People v. McKinney, supra; Shannon v. People, 5 Mich 71.

Defendant Percin, who was not present when the money was paid, alleged 2 additional grounds for reversal. First, that the evidence was insufficient to convict him, and second, that the court erred in its instructions to the jury. These contentions are predicated on the theory that the crime was not completed until the money was handed over, and that Percin, not being then present, was not a principal to the crime. It is clear that the crime was complete before the payment, and that both defendants participated in its commission. As we said before there was sufficient evidence to support the finding of the jury. We have examined the charge most carefully and find that the court was eminently fair, and that there were no errors in the instructions.

Finally, it is contended that the jury was never told of what crime the defendants had threatened to accuse the complainants. The court, in its charge to the jury read the information which included the specific threat and averred that it was a crime. There was no error.

The judgment is affirmed.

REID, C. J., and BOYLES, NORTH, DETHMERS, CARR, BUSHNELL,

and SHARPE, JJ., concurred.

3. Final Draft - Michigan Revised Criminal Code

(Coercion)

Sec. 2125. (1) A person commits the crime of coercion
if he compels or induces a person to engage in conduct that
the latter has a legal right to abstain from engaging in, or
to abstain from engaging in conduct in which he has a legal
right to engage, by instilling in him through use of a threat
a fear that, if the demand is not complied with, the actor
or another will bring about the harm threatened.
(2) "Threat" as used in this section includes:

(a) threatening the imminent use of force against any
person who is present at the time; and
(b) threats as defined in section 3201 (1).

(3) The actor does not commit coercion by instilling in
a person a fear that he or another person will be charged
with a crime, if the actor honestly believes the threatened
charge to be true and his sole purpose is to compel or induce the person to take reasonable action to correct the
wrong which is the subject of the threatened charge. The
burden of injecting the issue is on the defendant, but this
does not shift the burden of proof.
(4) Coercion is a Class A misdemeanor.

Committee Commentary

The section is derived in part from New York Revised
Penal Law, Sec. 135.60, 135.75.
The Michigan statute on malicious threat (C.L. 1948,
Sec. 750.213) combines elements of attempted extortion
(see Commentary to Sec. 3245-3247) and coercion. The
threats specified are to accuse another of any crime or offense or to threaten injury to the victim's person or property, or to his mother, father, husband, wife or child. The
motivation is "to extort money or any pecuniary advantage
whatever, or . . . to compel the person so threatened to do
or refrain from doing any act against his will." Though the
information must allege the specific charge which the defendant threatened to bring (People v. Jones, 62 Mich. 304,
28 N.W. 839 (1886)), it does not appear to matter particularly what the charge is. All that is required is a threat to
accuse another publicly of a crime; a threat to file a formal complaint and instigate a criminal prosecution is not required. (People v. Watson, 307 Mich. 378, 11 N.W.2d 926 (1943)).
Nor is payment of money required to be the objective. A
purpose to force the sale of a business (People v. Jones, 62
Mich. 304, 28 N.W. 839 (1886)) or to force a signature on a
deed (People v. Whittemore, 102 Mich. 519, 61 N.W. 13 (1894)

913

is sufficient. It does not matter whether the complainant is in fact victimized; it is the defendant's motivation that is important (People v. Percin, 330 Mich. 94, 47 N.W. 2d 29 (1951)).

The Draft makes some changes in the present law, changes which correspond to those embodied in the extortion provisions (Sec. 3245-3247). Before coercion can be committed, the victim must actually act or refrain from acting. However, unsuccessful threats can be disposed of as attempted coercion. The threat may be anything listed in Sec. 3201 (1), or a threat of imminent use of force against any person present at the time (Sec. 2125 (2) (a)). The latter must be included specifically because the threat of harm in Sec. 3201 (1) (i) is limited to harm "in the future." The limitation in that definition was to avoid overlap between extortion and robbery. To eliminate any distinction at this point based on the nature of the threat, the section incorporates both the definition of threat used in extortion and the threat specified for robbery (Sec. 3305-3307).

Subsection (3) is the counterpart to the exemption in coverage in extortion where there is an honest claim to the property obtained as restitution or indemmification for harm done. It would be incongruous to hold the actor not guilty of extortion if property passes, but to hold him guilty of coercion if some other act is involved. The subsection also preserves freedom to negotiate out-of-court settlements.

Note on degrees. The New York Revised Penal Law divides coercion into degrees, and the Model Penal Code (Sec. 212.5) calls for aggravation of penalty if the actor's purpose is felonious. The Committee is not persuaded that the utility in subjecting some persons who commit coercion to extended prison terms outweighs the difficulties inherent in classifying the particular threats made.

INTERROGATORIES

1. Outline the provisions of the Michigan statutes relative to assaults and allied offenses.
2. What were the facts, issue and holding of the Court in People v. Sheffield? What interpretation of this case is provided by the Committee Commentary to Section 2101-2103, Final Draft, Mich. Rev. Crim. Code?
3. What were the facts, issue and holding of the Court in People v. Carlson? How is an assault defined in this case? Do threats alone constitute an assault? What interpretation of this case is provided by the Committee Commentary to Sections 2101-2103 and Section 2110, Final Draft, Mich. Rev. Crim.Code?
4. What were the facts, issue and holding of the Court in People v. Doud? How is the holding of the Court characterized

by the Committee Commentary to Sections 2101-2103, Final Draft, Mich. Rev. Crim. Code?

5. What were the facts, issue and holding of the Court in People v. Shaffran? What interpretation of this case is provided by the Committee Commentary to Sections 2101-2103, Final Draft, Mich. Rev. Crim. Code?

6. What were the facts, issue and holding of the Court in People v. Goolsby? What interpretation of the case is provided by the Committee Commentary to Sections 2101-2103, Final Draft, Mich. Rev. Crim. Code?

7. What were the facts, issue and holding of the Court in People v. Lipski? What is the point of the dissenting opinion? What interpretation of this case is provided by the Committee Commentary to Sections 2101-2103, Final Draft, Mich. Rev. Crim. Code?

8. Outline the provisions of Sections 2101-2103, Final Draft, Mich. Rev. Crim. Code. What changes would the aforesaid proposals make in the present law?

9. What is the basic concept of assault and battery in Michigan? What is the source of the concept?

10. What is meant by an aggravated battery? The aggravating factors tend to fall into what categories? Give examples of each category.

11. Outline the provisions of Section 2110, Final Draft, Mich. Rev. Crim. Code. How would this section clarify the present law?

12. Outline the provisions of Section 2115, Final Draft, Mich. Rev. Crim. Code? What is the basic purpose of this provision?

13. Outline the provisions of Section 2120, Final Draft, Mich. Rev. Crim. Code. What is the basic purpose of this provision?

14. Outline the provisions of the Michigan statutes relative to extortion.

15. What were the facts, issue and holding of the Court in People v. Jones? What interpretation of this case is provided by the Committee Commentary to Section 2125, Final Draft, Mich. Rev. Crim. Code?

16. What were the facts, issue and holding of the Court in People v. Whittemore? What interpretation of this case is provided by the Committee Commentary to Section 2125, Final Draft, Mich. Rev. Crim. Code?

17. What were the facts, issue and holding of the Court in People v. Watson? What interpretation of this case is provided by the Committee Commentary to Section 2125, Final Draft, Mich. Rev. Crim. Code?

18. What were the facts, issue and holdings of the Court in People v. Percin? What are the elements of extortion according to this case? What interpretation of this case is provided by the Committee Commentary, Final Draft, Mich. Rev. Crim. Code?

CHAPTER VII

SEXUAL OFFENSES

A. Rape

    1. Michigan Compiled Laws (1948)

750.520 Carnal knowledge

    Sec. 520. Any person who shall ravish and carnally know any female of the age of 16 years, or more, by force and against her will, or who shall unlawfully and carnally know and abuse any female under the full age of 16 years, shall be guilty of a felony, punishable by imprisonment in the state prison for life or for any term of years, or if such person was at the time of the said offense a sexually delinquent person, may be punishable by imprisonment in the state prison for an indeterminate term, the minimum of which shall be 1 day and the maximum of which shall be life. Such carnal knowledge shall be deemed complete upon proof of any sexual penetration however slight. As amended P.A. 1952, No. 73, Sec. 1, Eff. Sept. 18.

    2. Definitions and General Elements of the Offense

People v. McDonald
9 Mich. 150

    There was proof that defendant was twice on a bed with the child Margaret Brown, in indecent positions, the child not objecting.
    The defendant asked the court to instruct the jury, among other things, that when actual consent is given, there can be no assault, and that as carnal knowledge implies assent, this waives the assault. This instruction was refused. Also, that if the jury should believe the defendant twice did what he intended to do, unmolested, and that the child was unharmed, they must find the defendant did not intend to commit the crime, and must discharge him. This instruction was given, but with the qualification, that though acquitted of the main charge, he might be convicted of assault and battery. The defendant also insisted that the information charged no offense known to the law.
    The jury found the defendant "guilty of an assault and battery, but not with an intent to carnally know and abuse."
MARTIN Ch. J.:

As this case comes to us upon exceptions, and not by writ of error, we can only look into those matters which do not "appear of record." The sufficiency of the information is, therefore, not before us.

Whether there is such an offense known to the common law, as an assault with intent carnally to know and abuse, or not, were it questionable, is immaterial; for it is very obvious that there is such an offense known to our statute. Section 5730 of Comp. Laws enacts that, "if any person shall ravish and carnally know any female of the age of ten years or more, by force and against her will, or shall unlawfully and carnally know and abuse any female child under the age of ten years, he shall be punished," etc. Both these offenses are rape, as they come within the common law definition of that offense. The distinction between them relates solely to the character and amount of proof required to convict of the offense. Force and want of consent must be satisfactorily shown in the case of carnal knowledge of a female of the age of ten years or more, but they are conclusively presumed in the case of such knowledge of a female child under that age, and no proof will be received to repel such presumption. . . .

As actual consent of a female child under the age of ten years can not be shown upon a trial for the crime of rape, because the law will not suffer the presumption of incapacity to consent to be repelled, or even attacked, neither, in case of a charge of assault with intent to commit such crime, can consent be shown to negative such intent, for the law will neither suffer nor consider such evidence. There can be no presumption or evidence of consent in cases in which the law declares there exists an absolute inability to consent. As there can be no such implication or evidence, so no proof of consent can be given which shall "waive the assault," and the rule laid down in the cases cited by the prisoner's counsel can only apply when consent is possible.

The jury in this case found a verdict of assault and battery, and negatived the intent charged. This they had a right to do. It is a general rule of criminal law, that a jury may acquit of the principal charge, and find the prisoner guilty of an offense of lesser grade, if contained within it. Thus, upon an indictment for murder, the jury may find a verdict of manslaughter only. So upon an indictment for an assault with intent to kill, the accused may be found guilty of an assault, or assault and battery only. Upon a charge for a felonious assault, the lesser offense of an assault, or an assault and battery, is, under our statutes, included. See Comp. L., Chap. 192.

There was no error in the ruling or charge of the recorder, and judgment should be rendered upon the verdict.

The other justices concurred.

People v. Courier
79 Mich. 366

917

MORSE, J. The respondent was convicted in the recorder's court of Detroit of carnally knowing and abusing a female child under the age of 14 years, and sentenced to the State prison at Jackson for the term of 15 years. The assignments of error all relate to the charge of the court.

The court was asked by respondent's counsel to direct a verdict of not guilty. This request was based upon the testimony of a physician, sworn on behalf of the people, who gave the result of his examination of the little girl, made soon after the alleged assault upon her. It was claimed that his testimony showed that there could not have been a perfect penetration of the child by the defendant without a rupture of the parts, and which, with the blood letting therefrom, would cause great pain, and also outcries from the child, of which pain and outcries there was no evidence, but to the contrary; that the testimony of the physician also showed that there was no rupture or forcing or penetration of the parts, or breaking of the hymen, and therefore the corpus delicti or crime charged in the information had not been proved by the people, and the verdict should have been not guilty. The physician, however, testified that the parts were swollen and inflamed, and evidently caused by contact with the male organ; that the hymen was absent, but its loss had not been recent.

Perfect penetration is not now considered necessary in order to constitute the crime of rape, or carnal knowledge and abuse of a child under the age of 14 years. As was said by the trial court in his charge to the jury, the English and American courts hold that nothing more than res in re is necessary without reference to the extent of the penetration. There was in this case positive evidence of persons, who caught the respondent in the act, that there was penetration to some extent, and sufficient, if the testimony was believed, to constitute the crime charged. The court very properly left the question of penetration to the jury, instructing them that they must find a penetration of the child's body by the male organ. . . .

CHAMPLIN, C. J., CAMPBELL and GRANT, JJ., concurred.

People v. Gengels
211 Mich. 632

STEERE, J. Defendant was tried and convicted in the circuit court of Kent county of the crime of statutory rape under an information containing one count which charged him in proper form with having, on May 24, 1921, assaulted Mildred Sayles, a female child under 16 years of age and "then and there feloniously did unlawfully and carnally know and abuse, contrary to the form of the statute in such case made and provided," etc. It was shown by her own and her father's testimony that at the time of the offense as charged Mildred

918

Sayles was under 16 years of age and attending public school.
She was a large girl, weighing about 135 pounds, who had been
employed at different times as an usher at the Empress and
other theaters in the city of Grand Rapids, where she had
given her age as 16 years for the purpose of securing employment.

Defendant was a Lithuanian 24 years of age and employed
as a cabinet maker in Grand Rapids. He had bought a second-
hand automobile with which he admitted taking the girl riding
at various times, having formed her acquaintance on the street,
denied having sexual intercourse with her on the occasion charged or at any other time, and claimed that he cared for her a
great deal, treated her as his sweetheart, and "acted like a
gentleman."

There were no other witnesses to what occurred between them
on the night in question. She testified positively to his having sexual intercourse with her. He positively denied it.
Much of the record is composed of his lengthy cross-examination
and many of defendant's 26 assignments of error are directed
to that portion of the trial, particularly to claimed prejudicial conduct and comment of the prosecuting attorney in
that connection, and attempts to collaterally impeach defendant's answers on cross-examination as to his commission of
other offenses of like nature.

Defendant's cross-examination disclosed that he had on
various occasions when out with a boon companion driving in
his automobile around the streets of Grand Rapids picked up
and taken riding with them girls willing to accept their in-
vitations and companionship. He admitted acquaintance formed
in that way with several girls they had first met upon the
street and taken riding. Pressed as to his conduct with them
he admitted congenial associations but positively denied sexual intercourse or any improper conduct with them. During
the course of his protracted cross-examination the prosecuting attorney pointed out several young women or girls he had
brought into court, one with a baby in her arms, and interrogated defendant in regard to them. Defendant admitted
knowing them and to having taken them riding in his car, but
insisted in denial of accusing questions that his conduct
when with them had always been honorable and he had acted
like a gentleman. Taking as his text defendant's claim that
he "acted like a gentleman," the prosecuting attorney theatri-
cally featured his cross-examanimation against objection of
defendant's counsel by calling up and pointing out the girls
he had arrayed in court and catechizing defendant as to his
relations with them. . . .

. . . It is also a well established general rule that
upon a trial for felony the prosecution may not introduce
evidence tending to prove that accused has been guilty of
other distinct and independent crimes for the purpose of proving he committed the offense charged. An exception to the
rule recognized in this and many other jurisdictions is in
that class of crimes where guilt depends upon the intent,
guilty knowledge and purpose with which the act charged is

919

done, as some overt act with intent to commit some felony not actually accomplished, or where a series of connected frauds, forgeries, passing counterfeit money, etc., is held competent as tending to establish guilty knowledge and criminal intent. But in the crime charged here proof of the intent goes with proof of the act of sexual intercourse with a girl under the age of consent. It is not necessary for the prosecution to prove want of consent. Proof of consent is no defense, for a female child under the statutory age is legally incapable of consenting. Neither is it any defense that the accused believed from the statement of his victim or others that she had reached the age of consent. 33 Cyc. p. 1438, and cases cited.

In cases involving statutory rape, a qualified exception to the general rule only permits proof of intercourse between the prosecutrix and accused for the purpose of showing opportunity, disposition of the parties and intimate relations tending to break down self-respect and modesty. . . . In the instant case the prosecuting attorney asserted and spectacularly attempted to directly prove, "On the very subject-matter, of course, this trial is about," another rape committed upon another girl at a different time, having no connection with the crime charged, speciously insisting before the jury and attempting indirectly to prove by further suggestive questions the very subject-matter which the court had excluded, claiming that it was admissible by way of impeachment. The course pursued was prejudicial error.

The judgment is reversed and a new trial granted.

FELLOWS, C. J., and WIEST, McDONALD, CLARK, BIRD, SHARPE, and MOORE, JJ., concurred.

People v. Pizzura
211 Mich. 71

MOORE, C. J. From a conviction of the defendant of the offense of statutory rape the case is brought here upon exceptions before sentence. There is very little dispute as to the facts: The defendant and Anna Pizza became acquainted in the city of Detroit some time during the month of June, 1918. Within a short time thereafter she and the defendant, Francisco Pizzura, eloped and began to live together. Shortly thereafter the parents of the girl went to the home of the defendant and induced them to return to the house of the parents of the girl in the city of Detroit, where the young people continued to live together with the knowledge and consent of the parents, from that time until the defendant was inducted into the military service. On November 28, 1918, while the defendant was in the army at Camp Custer, he returned to Detroit on a furlough and went to the Pizza home, remaining there with Anna Piazza all night with the knowledge and consent of her parents, and had intercourse with her at that time. The charge laid in the information is that the intercourse complained of was committed on the 28th day of November, 1918. The testimony shows that Anna Pizza and the defendant represented themselves as husband and wife among their neighbors and acquaintances.

The statute under which the complaint is made is section 15211, 3 Comp. Laws 1915.

The trial judge charged the jury in part as follows:

"Inasmuch as the age of consent to marriage, and the age of the complainant being less or under the full age of sixteen, I charge you, gentlemen of the jury that this complaining witness in this case was unable to enter into the contract of marriage, either a common-law marriage or a ceremonial marriage under the proper authorities of the State."

Section 15211, 3 Comp. Laws 1915, read:

"If any person shall ravish and carnally know any female of the age of sixteen years, or more, by force and against her will, or shall unlawfully and carnally know and abuse any female under the full age of sixteen years, he shall be punished by imprisonment in the State prison for life, or for any such period as the court in its discretion shall direct, and such carnal knowledge shall be deemed complete upon proof of penetration only."

The question naturally arises, Did the defendant "unlawfully and carnally know and abuse" Miss Pizza?

In 22 R. C. L. at page 1175, it is said:

"A man cannot himself be guilty of an actual rape upon his wife. One of the main reasons for this is the matrimonial consent which she gives when she assumes the marriage relation, and which the law will not permit her to retract in order to charge her husband with the offense." Citing many cases which support the text. . . . .

At this time it may be well to ask a few questions. Suppose without any decree of divorce and with Miss Pizza still desiring to hold the defendant as her husband, he should go through the form of a ceremonial marriage with a female person of the age of consent, could he not be convicted of the offense of bigamy? The case of People v. Slack, supra, answers the question in the affirmative. Suppose Miss Pizza, instead of being under the age of 15 years, had been only two days under the age of consent when she began her relations with defendant and they continued to regard each other as husband and wife, could the husband have been convicted of statutory rape for the act of intercourse which occurred two days before his wife was 16 years old; or could he in the last supposed case though she desired to continue as his wife repudiate the role of husband and say to her: "You are no wife of mine." To answer these two supposed cases in the affirmative shocks one's sense of justice and right. When the defendant began and continued his relations with Miss Pizza he was of consenting marriageable age and as to him the marriage was valid. Their relations were voidable only at the option of Miss Pizza. She has not desired to repudiate the marriage contract, but, on the contrary, she desires, so far as the record shows, to hold the defendant to it.

We think the court erred in his charge to the jury and that the conviction should be reversed. As there is no dispute as to the facts, we think the defendant should be discharged.

STEERE, BROOKE, FELLOWS, STONE, CLARK, BIRD, and SHARPE, JJ., concurred.

People v. Crosswell
13 Mich. 427

COOLEY J.:

The defendant was informed against in the circuit court for the county of Kalamazoo for rape, alleged to have been committed upon one Mrs. Crittenden. The information was, in all respects, in the usual form.

On the trial, evidence was adduced that four persons, walking in the road together through or past a piece of woods, saw Mrs. Crittenden and the defendant in the road together a few rods off; Mrs. Crittenden, at the time, lying upon her back with her clothes up to her waist, and the defendant on his knees before her; that he did not have hold of her, or seem to be exercising any control, nor she to be making any resistance; that sexual intercourse took place between them, after which, on some slight noise being made, the defendant got up and ran off, while Mrs. Crittenden came out towards the witnesses smiling, and followed them to a house in the neighborhood where they were going to visit.

The prosecution then offered evidence to show that Mrs. Crittenden at the time was insane. The defendant objected to this as irrelevant, and also because, if insanity was a material fact, it should have been alleged in the information. The court overruled the objection, and the defendant excepted. The evidence given to establish insanity showed that Mrs. Crittenden was forty-eight or forty-nine years of age, in apparent good physical health, of good size and seeming strength; that she had been in the insane asylum at Kalamazoo the preceding year, but was, at this time, residing at home with her husband; that she worked some at home, but appeared to be uneasy, and said she ought to be doing something, but did not know what to do. The most pointed testimony was that of E. H. Van Dazen, the physician, who was in charge of the insane asylum while Mrs. Crittenden was there, who testified that she was in a state of _dementia_ - not idiotic, but approaching towards it; that she had vague appre-

922

hensions of injury, and a predisposition to be with men - a morbid, rather than an active desire, to have sexual intercourse; that that was one way in which her insanity manifested itself; that she was dismissed from the asylum not much improved, but under better control, and with more method in her conduct; that her general health was pretty good, and she was of good size, and apparently a strong woman. The witness did not think she had intelligent understanding at the time the crime was said to have been committed.

The court below, at the conclusion of the case, charged the jury that if the woman was so suffering from mental disease at the time, as to have no intelligent will to oppose the act of the prisoner, and he knew of this her condition, then her failure to oppose him, or her seeming acquiescence, could not be urged against a conviction; and that if he made the attempt upon her person with the intent to have carnal intercourse, and she did not resist because she had no intelligent will to oppose, he was guilty of the offense charged. Under these instructions the jury returned a verdict of guilty.

The exceptions present to us questions which we do not find distinctly passed upon in any adjudged case. The main question, and the only one we deem it necessary to discuss, is, whether the carnal knowledge of a woman non compos mentis, under the circumstances disclosed in the testimony above stated, can be punished as rape under the statutes of this state.

Rape is defined to be "the carnal knowledge of a woman by force and against her will:" 1 East. P.C. 434; 4 Bl. Com., 210. The statute providing for its punishment in this state - Sec. 5730 of Compiled Laws - is in the following words: "If any person shall ravish and carnally know any female of the age of ten years or more, by force and against her will, or shall unlawfully and carnally know and abuse any female child under the age of ten years, he shall be punished," etc. This statute does not change the nature of the offense as it stood at the common law, nor does it describe two distinct offenses, but the carnal knowledge of the female child under the age of ten years is held to be rape, on the ground that, from immaturity and want of understanding, the child must be deemed incapable of assenting, and the act presumed to be the result of force: People v. McDonald, 9 Mich. 150; Commonwealth v. Sugland, 4 Gray, 7. And it is insisted in this case than an insane woman, or one not mentally competent to exercise an intelligent will, is in the same position, as respects this crime, as a child under ten years of age, and that carnal knowledge of her person would constitute the offense notwithstanding her acquiescence.

If the case before us can be regarded as rape, it is apparent that it must fall within the first clause of the section quoted, since the other is confined, by its express terms, to carnal knowledge of female children under the age of ten years, and can not be extended by analogy, to embrace other cases. But to warrant a conviction under the first

clause of the section, the carnal knowledge must have been
by force and against the will of the woman; and as there were
facts before the jury, in this case, from which they might
fairly infer that the woman, and not the man, was the soliciting party, and the charge of the judge must be construed in
the light of the testimony, the real question to be determined
is, whether that is by force and against the will, where the
woman assented to and desired its commission, but without
possessing, at the time, the mental capacity which would render her responsible for her own conduct?

The general rule requires, not only that there should be
force, but that the utmost reluctance and resistance on the
part of the woman, should appear: People v. Morrison, 1 Park.
C.R., 625; Woodin v. People, Ibid., 464. The essence of the
crime is said to be, not the fact of intercourse, but the injury and outrage to the modesty and feelings of the woman, by
means of the carnal knowledge effected by force: Pennsylvania v. Sullivan, Addis, 143; 2 Bish. Cr. L., Sec. 944; 3
Greenl. Ev., Sec. 210. As these circumstances are wanting in
the present case, it becomes important to ascertain whether
any other circumstances can be regarded as legal equivalents.

There are undoubtedly some cases where the law not only
does not require actual force to be proved, but where force
is presumed, and not suffered to be disproved. The case of
carnal intercourse, with a female child, under ten years of
age, has already been alluded to, but the rule in that case
is not an arbitrary one, but is based upon a well understood
fact in nature, that the child, at that tender age, is without desire for such intercourse, and the presumption that it
is against her will is therefore in accordance with the general fact. Nature, indeed, does not definitely fix the period
at which the child might become capable of understanding the
character of the act, and assenting to it; and the statute
has therefore named the age of ten years as the period when
the conclusive presumption of opposing will shall cease. The
rule in this case, we apprehend, depends less upon mental
capacity than upon physical considerations, and the age named
is not the age of consent, either at the common law or by
the statute. It was, indeed, at one time supposed that if
the female was over ten years of age, but under twelve, intercourse with her must necessarily be rape, because the capacity to consent was wanting; but the courts did not so hold,
and statutes were passed making the act a misdemeanor where
the female was between the age of ten and the age of consent,
but where, not being against her will, it did not fall within
the definition of rape: 1 Hale P.C., 631; 4 Bl. Com., 212;
1 Russ. Cr., 693.

In the case of Regina v. Camplin, 1 Den. C.C., 89; Same
Case, 1 C. & K., 746, it appeared that the prisoner gave the wom
liquor for the purpose of exciting her, but which had the
effect to make her quite drunk; and while she was in a state
of insensibility, he took advantage of it and violated her.
The court held the act to be rape. The prosecutrix showed

924

by her words and conduct, up to the latest moment at which
she had sense or power to express her will, that it was
against her will that intercourse should take place. It was
no answer to the charge, therefore, that she had no opposing
will at the moment when intercourse actually took place,
since the prisoner had actually mastered it by means of the
stupefying drug, which was the same, as was well remarked by
one of the judges, as if it had been overcome by a blow.

In Rex v. Charter, 13 Shar's J.P., 746, cited in 1 Bish.
Cr. L., Sec. 343, note, and 2 Arch. Cr. Pl. & Pr., 167 (306),
the prisoner had carnal knowledge of the person of a woman
laboring under delirium, and who was insensible to the act.
The act was held to be rape; but the decision can hardly be
regarded as establishing an exception to the general doctrine
as to this crime. If the woman was insensible, some degree
of physical force must actually have been employed by the
prisoner; and no more resistance is required by the law, in
any case, than the condition of the woman will permit her to
make.

The facts, in the case last cited, made it open to the
objection which appears to have been taken in The State v.
Crow, 10 West. Law J., 501; Note to Whart. & St. Med. Juris.,
Sec. 463, where the defendant was charged with the crime of
rape committed upon an insane woman. That case is sometimes
referred to as holding that all carnal intercourse with an
insane woman is rape; but the point involved was a very different one, and the decision sanctions no such doctrine. It
is not a little remarkable that, while it is insisted by the
prosecution in this case that all intercourse with a woman
in this condition must be rape, because she has no capacity
to consent, it was there urged by the defense, that no intercourse with her, even by force, could be rape, because she
had no will to oppose. Rape, it is said, must be against the
will of a person who has no will? This argument made it necessary for the court to determine what is meant by the word will,
as used by the law in this connection, and we quote from the
decision so much as has a bearing upon this question: "Is
it true," said the court, "that an idiot or insane person has
no will? What is the definition of these two words? Do they
imply a loss of will or a mere unsoundness of mind? These
words are thus defined by Webster: 'Idiot - a natural fool;
a fool from birth; a human being in form, but destitute of
reason, or the ordinary intellectual power of man. Insane -
unsound in mind or intellect; mad; deranged in mind, and one
of the words used to define insanely, is foolishly.' 'Fool'
is defined to be 'one who is destitute of reason or the common power of understanding; an idiot.' In Chitty's Med. Juris.
an idiot is defined to be 'a person who has been defective in
intellectual powers from the instant of his birth, or at least
before the mind had received the impression of any idea.'
Again, Chitty says that 'idiocy consists in a defect or steril-
ity of the intellectual power, while lunacy or madness consists in a perversion of the intellect.' All these definitions

imply either a <u>weakness</u> or <u>perversion</u> of the mind or its
powers, not their <u>destruction</u>. Hence, an idiot cannot be
said to have <u>no will</u>, but a <u>will weakened or impaired</u>; a
will acting, <u>but not</u> in conformity to those rules and motives and views which control the action of persons of sound
mind. Indeed, in an insane person the will is too often
fearfully active, and entirely uncontrollable by reason or
perversion of it. Nor is this the most conclusive answer to
the argument. If there is no will, how are voluntary actions
continued? Actions, like respiration, are instinctive, and
independent of the will; but eating, and numerous other acts
which necessarily imply the exercise of the will, are performed by idiots and insane persons, and their exercise demonstrates the existence of a will - of a will that can assent
to or dissent from what are clearly voluntary acts. I have,
therefore, no hesitation in holding that both idiots and insane persons are possessed of a will, so that it may be legally and metaphysically said, that a carnal knowledge may be
had of their persons <u>forcibly</u> and against their will."
  From the brief note of the scotch case of <u>McNamara</u>, <u>Arkley</u>,
<u>521</u>, <u>524</u>, in <u>2 Bish. Cr. L.</u>, Sec. <u>939</u>, <u>note</u>, a similar de-
fense would seem to have been made there. The woman, in that
case, was an idiot; and the court told the jury that if they
believed the defendant "had actually penetrated the girl,
<u>and that she had shown any physical resistance, to however</u>
<u>small an extent</u>, the offense would be complete, <u>in consequence</u>
<u>of her inability to give a mental consent</u>."
  Both these cases, while not perhaps distinct authorities
to that effect, clearly imply that the same circumstances
must exist to constitute rape in the case of an idiot or insane woman, as where the woman is of sound mind. The word,
<u>will</u>, as employed in defining the crime of rape, is not con-
strued as implying the faculty of mind by which an intelligent
choice is made between objects, but rather as synonymous with
<u>inclination</u> or <u>desire</u>; and in that sense it is used with pro-
priety in reference to persons of unsound mind.
  We are aware of no adjudged case that will justify us in
construing the words "against her will," as equivalent in
meaning, with "without her intelligent assent," nor do we
think sound reason will sanction it. But, though the definition of the offense implies the existence of a will in the
woman, which has opposed the carnal knowledge, no violence
is done to the law by holding, in any case where the woman,
from absence of mental action, does not willingly acquiesce,
that the physical force necessary to effectuate the purpose,
however slight, is against her will. As was said by Alder-
son B., in <u>Camplin's Case</u>, above cited, a woman may be supposed to have a general will not to be ravished; and the man
is not to be excused because she was prevented, or was unable, to exercise it in the particular case. If, therefore,
a man knowing a woman to be insane, should take advantage of
that fact, to have knowledge of her person, when her mental
powers were so impaired that she was unconscious of the nature

of the act, or was not a willing participator, we should
have no difficulty in holding the act to be rape, notwithstanding distinct proof of opposition might be wanting. All
such cases stand upon reasons which clearly distinguish them
from the case now before us, where the will was active, though
perverted, and all idea of force or want of willingness is
distinctly disproved.

There are cases in which it has been held that.if the
woman's consent is obtained by fraud, she at the time supposing the man to be her husband, the crime of rape is not
committed: Rex v. Jackson, Russ. & R., 487; Regina v. Saunders, 8 C. & P., 265; Regina v. Williams, Ibid., 286; Regina
v. Clarke, 29 E. L. & E., 542; State v. Murphy, 6 Ala., 765;
Wyatt v. State, 2 Swan, 394. But there are some cases in
this country to the contrary, and they seem to us to stand
upon much the better reasons, and to be more in accordance
with the general rules of criminal law: People v. Metcalf,
1 Whart. C. C. 378, and Note 381; State v. Shepard, 7 Conn.,
54. And in England, where a medical practitioner had knowledge of the person of a weak-minded patient, on pretense of
medical treatment, the offense was held to be rape: Regina
v. Stanton, 1 C. & K., 415; Same Case, 1 Den. C. C., - The
outrage upon the woman, and the injury to society, is just
as great in these cases as if actual force had been employed;
and we have been unable to satisfy ourselves that the act
can be said to be any less against the will of the woman
when her consent is obtained by fraud, than when it is extorted by threats or force.

Undoubtedly, fraud would be much more readily inferred
in a case of mental derangement than where the woman's powers
of mind were unimpaired; but in the present case, no circumstance of either fraud or force was required by the charge
of the court to the completion of the offense, nor is it
suggested that any such circumstance existed. The naked
fact of intercourse, with knowledge of the mental condition,
was held sufficient. As one who has knowledge of the facts
which prove insanity must be supposed to know that insanity
exists, it would follow that, in any case of doubt, a man's
guilt or innocence would depend upon the preponderance of
testimony on the question of the woman's competency. As
marriage with an insane person is void, it might become a
serious question whether the ceremony could protect the too
partial bridegroom from prosecution for rape, where he had
relied upon manifestations which, to him, appeared the evidences of genius, but which experts should convince a jury
were only the vagaries of a disordered imagination.

The conclusion at which we have arrived is, that rape,
at the common law or under our statute, is not committed
upon the person of a woman over ten years of age, where no
circumstance of either force or fraud accompanies the carnal
knowledge. The circuit court must be advised that, in the
opinion of this court, the conviction was erroneous, and that
the verdict should be set aside and a new trial granted.

CAMPBELL and CHRISTIANCY JJ. concurred, and MARTIN CH. J. concurred in the result.

Moran v. People
25 Mich. 356

CHRISTIANCY, CH. J.

Plaintiff in error was tried in the Recorder's Court of the City of Detroit, upon an information charging him with having committed a rape upon Frances Jackson, a female of the age of ten years and more, to wit: of the age of sixteen years. The information was in the usual form, that he did ravish and carnally know the said Frances by force, and against her will.

The bill of exceptions is as follows:

"And on said trial, the People, to maintain the issue on their part, introduced evidence which tended to prove, that the father of the complaining witness, shortly before she was sixteen years of age, brought her to the house of the defendant, in Detroit, to be treated for consumption, the defendant claiming to be skilled in the treatment of diseases of that kind; that her father left her at defendant's house; that the defendant made an examination of her, and, after such examination, told her that the 'whites' had collected in her stomach; that she was ulcerated; that her uterus was inverted; that to save her life it would be necessary to enlarge her 'parts,' so that the 'whites' might pass off, to break the ulcers, and to turn the uterus; that he could do this with instruments, but the operation would probably kill her; that the only way would be for him to have carnal connection with her; that when she objected, he told her that it was what he did to all women who came to be treated by him; that he had told her father that it would be necessary, and he understood all about it, and had authorized the defendant to have connection with his daughter; that she relying upon these representations, and believing them to be true, permitted the defendant to have connection with her; that if it had not been for such representations she would not have yielded; and that said representations were false, and known by the defendant to be so.

"The defendant, to maintain the issue on his part, introduced evidence tending to rebut that given by the prosecution.

"The court charged the jury as follows:

"'If you find that the defendant represented to the complaining witness that, as a part of his medical treatment, it was necessary for her to have carnal connection with him; that such representations were false and fraudulent; that she believed it, and, relying upon it, consented to the solicitations of the defendant, and had connection with him; and that such representations were made for the purpose of inducing

928

her to give such consent, and that without it she would not have yielded, the defendant is guilty of the crime charged against him.

"'If the complaining witness did not believe the representations; was not deceived by them; or had sense and intelligence enough to know better than to believe them; or by the reasonable exercise of such faculties as she has, might have known better, and that the act was wrong, the defendant is not guilty.'

"To said charge, and each and every part thereof, the defendant then and there excepted."

It will be noticed that this charge leaves out, and wholly ignores, all idea of force as a necessary element of the crime charged; and the jury were, in effect, told that the defendant might be found guilty of the rape, though he neither used, nor threatened to use, any force whatever in case of her refusal, and though she might have assented without any constraint produced by the fear or apprehension of force, or any dangerous, or serious, consequences to herself, if she refused or resisted.

This feature of the charge is assigned as error, and presents the only question raised in the case by the plaintiff in error.

The definition of rape, as generally given in the English books, is, that "Rape is the unlawful carnal knowledge, by a man of a woman, forcibly (or by force), and against her will:" 3 Coke's Inst. (Thomas' Ed. 549; 1 Hale P.C., 628; Hawkin's P. C. (Cur. Ed.), 122; 4 Bl. Com., 210; 1 Russ. on Cr. (Greenl. Ed.), 675. This definition depended, perhaps, partly upon the common law, but mainly upon two early, and rather loosely worded English statutes, one of which (Stat. Westm. 2, Ch., 34) expressly made force an element in the crime, if the party were attainted at the king's suit (though not when the proceeding was by appeal), and the other (Stat. Westm. 1, Ch., 13), which did not require force as an element, except as it might be inferred from the word, "ravished:" See 2 Bish. Cr. L., Sec. 1067 to 1069, where the substance of these statutes is given. And, as remarked by Mr. Bishop (2 Bish. Cr. L., Sec. 1073), the more correct definition to be gathered from these statutes would have been "Rape is the unlawful carnal knowledge, by a man of a woman by force, when she does not consent." The difference between the two definitions, however, would seem to be important, only in cases where the female with whom the connection is had, may be said to have no will, as in the case of an idiot, or insane person, or one in a state of unconsciousness, in which cases, if anywhere, the force necessary to accomplish the act itself without resistance, could possibly be held to constitute the force contemplated by the definition of the offense: See Rex v. Ryan, 2 Cox C. C., 115; Reg. v. Fletcher, Bell C. C., 63; Reg. v. Camplin, 1 Den. C. C., 89. But this particular class of cases has no special bearing upon the case now before us (and we do not discuss it); nor are we embarrassed by any uncertainty in the definition of the offense.

Our statute have adopted substantially the definition first above given from the English authorities. Section 5730, Compiled Laws (of 1857), declares, "If any person shall ravish and carnally know any female of the age of ten years or more, by force and against her will . . . he shall be punished," etc.

In the interpretation of this statute it is clear that the terms "by force," must not be wholly rejected or ignored, but that some effect must be given to them; and the language of the provision certainly requires something more to be shown than if these words had been omitted; and it is equally clear that if that particular kind and amount of force only is required which is always essential to the act of sexual connection itself, when performed with the assent of the woman, then no effect whatever is given to the term "by force," but the interpretation and the effect of the statute will be precisely the same as if these words were not contained in it. This interpretation, therefore, is not permissible. Some effect must be given to the words; and such has been the almost, if not entirely, uniform course of decision, both in England and in this country, where the definition of the offense is substantially the same as that given by our statute, when the charge has been for the actual commission of a rape upon a female of the age of proper discretion, of sound mind, and in full possession of her faculties, however fraudulent the means, or false the pretenses, by which her consent was procured. I have not been able to find a single well-authenticated case, where the question was directly raised, in which it has been directly decided the other way. The anonymous case cited in the note to 1 Wheeler's Cr. Cases, 381, and referred to by Mr. Wharton (Cr. Laws, Sec. 1144), and by Mr. Bishop (2 Cr. Law, Sec. 1080), to the effect, that force is not necessary in the commission of rape, but that stratagem may supply its place, is stated as a mere rumor of a decision made at Albany by Chief Justice Thompson, and, as very properly remarked by the court in Walter v. The People, 50 Barb., 144, "loose statements of this kind are entitled to no consideration whatever." In State v. Shepard, 7 Conn., 55, the woman was asleep, and did not discover the fact until defendant had violated her person; and her first impression was that it was her husband; as soon as she awoke and became sensible of the situation, he sprang from the bed. The charge was for an assault with intent to commit a rape. The prisoner's counsel contended that, if there was any carnal knowledge obtained, it was a rape, and the prisoner could not be convicted of the mere assault with intent, etc., as the less offense was merged in the greater. The only question discussed was, whether proof of a rape would sustain an indictment for an attempt to commit it; and, as very properly remarked by the counsel for plaintiff in error in the case before us, the counsel for the prisoner in that case overlooked a good

defense in the attempt to maintain a frivolous one. The case
of Regina v. Stanton, 1 C. & R., 415, has been sometimes cited
as sustaining nearly the same doctrine as that cited from the
note to Wheeler's Cr. Cases. But it was the case of an indictment for an assault with intent to commit a rape, where the
prisoner, a physician, had obtained access to the person of
the woman under pretense of administering an injection, and
commenced to have carnal connection with her, when she, discovering it, got up and ran out of the room. This was clearly
an assault, and the only question was, whether the intent existed as charged. As it did not appear that the prisoner had
intended to use force, in case of resistance, it was, of course,
but an assault only, and was so held by the court; but when
the court say, (sic)that, if that intent had appeared, it
would have constituted the completed offense of rape, they
express an opinion upon a question not in the case. This is
not the only case in which it seems to have been obscurely
shadowed forth, that, when the defendant has succeeded in obtaining the connection without force, actual or threatened,
and without resistance, by falsely personating the husband,
the mere intent to use force, had it become necessary to accomplish his purpose, would satisfy the requirement of force
involved in the definition of rape (See Rex v. Jackson, Russ
& Ry. C. C., 487);and a similiar idea seems to have been obscurely intimated in some American cases. But, with all deference, I must be allowed to suggest, whether it has not resulted from confounding two distinct offenses - the completed
offense of rape, and the attempt, or an assault with the intent to commit it. And I am compelled to say, I am wholly
unable to discover how the intent to resort to force in such
cases, when it is not in fact either resorted to, or in any
manner threatened, can be at all material upon the question,
whether a rape has been committed, or how such intent, never
brought to the notice of the woman by word or act, can satisfy
the requirement of force in the legal definition of the offense; and such, I think, is the prevailing view of the English courts (See, among other cases, Reg. v. Saunders, 8 C.
& P., 265; Reg. v. Williams, Id., 286; Reg. v. Clarke, Dears.,
397; Reg. v. Fletcher, Law Reports, 1 Cr. Cases Reserved, 39;
14 Law T. (N. S.), 573; 12 Jur. (N. S.), 505), as well as of
the American courts; though such intent would, of course, constitute a necessary and controlling element in a charge for
an assault with intent to commit a rape, though in no way
communicated to the intended victim.
     But if we admit that the intent to resort to force, if re-
quired to accomplish the criminal purpose, in a case like the
present would, though never used or threatened, constitute the
transaction a rape, this would not sustain the charge in the
present case, which did not even require the existence of
such intent.
     The true rule as to force in cases of rape generally, was
recognized by this court in People v. Valentine Cornwell (not
Crosswell v. The People, as printed in the report), 13 Mich.

931

433, where it was said, that "the essence of the crime is not the fact of intercourse, but the injury and outrage to the feelings of the woman by means of the carnal knowledge effected by force." And there being no force used or threatened in that case, but strong grounds for believing that the woman was the soliciting party, the connection was properly held not to constitute rape, though the woman was not of sound mind, and had no intelligent understanding at the time the act was committed, but was in good physical health. In cases where the woman is entirely insensible from idiocy, or from the effect of drugs administered (though the point is not here involved), it may be entirely right to hold a very slight degree of force sufficient; and that amount of force which, in such cases, would always be necessary, beyond what would be required with a consenting party, might, perhaps, properly be held, as it sometimes has been held, sufficient to make the transaction a rape, as suggested by my brother Cooley in People v. Cornwell, ubi (sic) supra.

And when drugs are administered, or procured to be administered, by the criminal, for the purpose of taking away or lessening the power of resistance, and having that effect, there may be no ground for distinction between the force thus exerted by him through the agency of the drugs, and that directly exerted by his hand and for the same purpose.

The only question really involved in People v. Cornwell, above cited, was whether, under the circumstances of that case, the defendant could be held guilty without proof of force in any form, actual or threatened, and it was, I think, properly held by us that he could not. But after disposing of this, the only question in the case, an intimation was thrown out - for which I admit, and claim, a full share of the responsibility - that when a woman's consent is obtained by fraud, she at the time supposing the man to be her husband, the connection thus obtained may constitute rape. No such question was involved or argued; and we suppose it to be well understood by judges and the profession, that intimations and suggestions of this kind, in no way necessary to the decision of the case, are not always, or generally, as carefully considered and examined as the questions upon which the case itself turns; and hence the familiar rule, that judicial opinions are to be considered as authority, and construed, only secundum subjectam materiam.

If the statute, or the definition of rape, did not contain the words "by force," or "forcibly," doubtless a consent procured by such fraud as that referred to, might be treated as no consent; but the idea of force can not thus be left out and ignored, nor can such fraud be allowed to supply its place, though it would doubtless supply, and satisfy all the other terms of the definition; and, so far as the intimation in question is to be understood as going further and dispensing with all idea of force, it must be understood as an intimation of the court of what, in their opinion, the law ought to be, rather than what it is. And, upon abstract principles of right and wrong, a sexual connection obtained by falsely and fraudulently personating the husband of a woman, or by a physician fraudulently inducing a female patient to believe such connection essential to a course of medical treatment, must be considered nearly, if not quite, as criminal and prejudicial to society as when obtained by force or any apprehension of violence, and it might, and in my opinion would, be judicious for the legislature to make some provision for punishment in cases of this kind. But it is not for the judiciary to legislate, by straining the existing criminal law to bring such cases within it.

For the reasons given, I think the judgment of the recorder's court should be reversed, and a new trial awarded.

And with reference to a new trial, it is proper for the guidance of the recorder's court, to consider the nature of the evidence set forth in the record, and which will probably appear upon the new trial, and to determine what charge the state of facts would warrant, or whether there was anything in the evidence which would authorize the jury to find that the carnal connection was obtained "by force, and against the will" of the party injured.

We think it is well and properly settled that the terms "by force," do not necessarily imply the positive exertion of actual physical force in the act of compelling submission of the female to the sexual connection, but that force or violence threatened as the result of non-compliance, and for the purpose of preventing resistance, or extorting consent, if it be such as to create a real apprehension of dangerous consequences, or great bodily harm, or such as in any manner to overpower the mind of the victim so that she dare not resist, is, and upon all sound principles must be, regarded, for this purpose, as in all respects equivalent to force actually exerted for the same purpose. See Reg. v. Hallett, 9 C. & P., 748; Reg. v. Day, Id., 722; Wright v. The State, 4 Humph, 194; Pleasant v. The State, 8 Eng., 360; and see Strang v. The People, 24 Mich., 1. Nor, as appears by the case last cited, need the threats be of force to be used in accomplishing the act, as in that case the principal threat was, that if she refused he would take her away where she could never get back. In fact, we think the terms of the statute in reference to force, are satisfied by any sexual intercourse to which the woman may have been induced to yield, only through the constraint produced by the fear of great bodily harm, or danger to life or limb, which the prisoner has, for the purpose of overcoming her will, caused her to apprehend as the consequence of her refusal, and without which she would not have yielded.

It remains only to apply these principles to the present case.

Considering the way, and the purpose for which, the girl had been placed by her father under the care and treatment of the defendant as her physician, the evidence had a tendency to show, and the jury might properly have found, that the girl was induced by the defendant to submit to the sexual

933

intercourse with him, from the fear and under the apprehension, falsely and fraudulently inspired by the defendant for the purpose of overcoming her opposition, that, if she did not yield to such intercourse, he intended to, and would, use instruments "for the purpose of enlarging her parts," and that such operation with instruments would be likely to kill her. And if the jury should so find - with or without the other facts submitted to them by the charge given - and that she would not otherwise have yielded, it would be their duty to find the defendant guilty of the crime charged.

The judgment must be reversed, and a new trial awarded.

CAMPBELL, J., concurred.

COOLEY, J.

As my brethren are agreed in this case, I concur in the result while not fully assenting to all that is expressed in the opinion.

GRAVES, J., did not sit in this case.

Note

This case resulted in 1883 in the adoption of a statute making it a felony to procure sexual intercourse with a female under the pretext of medical treatment. See C. L. 1948, Sec. 750.90, at page 876, supra. - - Ed.

People v. Marrs
125 Mich. 376

GRANT, J. . . .

. . . Counsel alleges as error that the court refused to direct a verdict for the respondent. The evidence on the part of the people tended to show that the prosecutrix was 18 years old, and mentally and physically weak; that she had never before kept company with young men; that respondent had met her but once before; that he came that night under a promise to take her to her father's home; that she had a bundle done up to take home with her; that respondent told her that he could not take her home that night, but would take her out riding that evening, around the town, but instead drove a long way out of the city, into the country, and assaulted her in the buggy; that she made such resistance as she could, but finally became exhausted, when he accomplished his object. He testified that he took her our riding a week before, and took improper liberties with her than, and sought to have intercourse with her, but she refused. These statements are denied by her. He then testified that the act of intercourse was entirely voluntary upon her part. It is unnecessary to state further the disgusting details. It

934

is not at all surprising that a jury would place but little confidence in the testimony of the respondent, whose own testimony showed him to have no regard for the honor or virtue of woman. We think the case was one for the jury.
. . . It was competent for the prosecution to show the mental and physical condition of the prosecutrix, as bearing upon the extent of the resistance the law required her to make. . . .
. . . The most important and difficult question arises upon the following instruction:

"The respondent may be convicted of an assault with intent to commit the crime of rape, although the jury may find that the complainant did not resist to the extent necessary to render the offense rape, provided they find that he assaulted the complainant with intent to have intercourse with her against her will, by using whatever force might be necessary to overcome whatever resistance she made; and the fact that the respondent had intercourse with complainant, if you find that he did have, would not be in the way of a verdict of assault with intent to commit rape."

The question presented is this: May a respondent be convicted of an assault with intent to commit rape, where the act of sexual intercourse was afterwards committed by consent, or failure to make the resistance which the law requires? Consent, or failure to use the proper resistance, at any time before the act of intercourse has actually occurred, precludes conviction for rape. Condonation never excuses or forgives the criminal act, and affords no defense to the criminal. Com. v. Slattery, 147 Mass. 423 (18 N.E. 399). Where the prosecutrix first objected and afterwards consented, the prisoner was convicted of assault. Reg. v. Hallett, 9 Car. & P. 748. Where the resistance was not such as to constitute the crime of rape, it was held that the respondent might be convicted of assault with intent to commit the crime. State v. Bagan, 41 Minn. 285 (43 N. W. 5). It was also held that a subsequent yielding and consent to sexual intercourse do not relate back and cover the assault with intent to commit the crime. State v. Hartigan, 32 Vt. 607 (78 Am. Dec. 609). Under a charge of the crime of rape, though the court might have inclined to the opinion that the testimony was not sufficient to convict of that crime, the court say: (sic)

"We easily arrive at a different conclusion when the jury have only found the assault with intent, etc. Of course, if there was consent on the part of the prosecutrix, there could be no such violence, in legal contemplation, as to render the prisoner guilty; for, if the liberties were taken with her consent, there could be no rape, nor yet an assault with that intent. But where the assault is made by the prisoner with the intent to commit the offense, and this is clearly shown, the jury might convict, though not satisfied that at the time he consummated his purpose there was such want of consent as

935

to constitute the higher crime. It is true that the jury must be satisfied, before they could convict for the assault, that the prisoner intended to gratify his passions on the person of the prosecutrix at all events, and notwithstanding any resistance on her part; and yet this might be done, though they were not satisfied that the resistance on her part was so continued and persistent as to prove guilt of the higher crime, when he succeeds in having a carnal knowledge." State v. Cross, 12 Iowa, 66, 68, 69 (79 Am. Dec. 519).

That case is cited with approval, under a similar state of facts, in State v. Atherton, 50 Iowa, 189 (32 Am. Rep. 134).

Bishop says:

"If, after the assault, and before penetration, the woman yields her consent, the offense of assault with intent to ravish is committed; for the consent does not undo what was done before." 1 Bish. New Cr. Law, Sec. 766.

The theory of these cases appears to be that the assaulter of female virtue cannot defend himself from an actual assault with intent to accomplish his object by force, by showing that he subsequently obtained the assent of his victim, or that she did not continue that resistance which is essential to a conviction. We think this is a salutary doctrine, and well supported by the authorities.

Conviction reversed, and new trial ordered.

The other Justices concurred.

People v. Myers
306 Mich. 100

SHARPE, J. Defendant Roger Myers, a single man of the age of 17 years, was convicted by a trial judge sitting without a jury of the crime of rape, as defined in the penal code, Act No. 328, Sec. 520, Pub. Acts 1931 (Comp. Laws Supp. 1940, Sec. 17115-520, Stat. Ann. Sec. 28.788).

The people charge that the crime was committed August 8, 1941. The complaining witness, a single woman, whose name is omitted from this opinion for obvious reasons, testified that on the evening in question she had gone to the Rouge Park pool for a swim; that she came out of the pool about 9:45 p.m. and went to a point on Plymouth road to wait for a bus to return to Plymouth; that while waiting for a bus, a car drove by with three young men in it; that the car returned and the young men invited her to go for a ride; and that upon her refusal, she was ordered, at the point of a gun, to get into the car. She said: "I got in that car because I was frightened. I thought if I didn't they might either hit me over the head with the gun or shoot me." She

936

further testified that as they drove, she learned that the young men had been planning a holdup; that they drove out into the country and parked the car on a side road, where all three of the young men had intercourse with her; and that later the parties returned and let the complaining witness out at the city limits of Plymouth. On the same evening, she reported the matter to the police; and at a later date, she went to Detroit to a "showup" where she identified Roger Myers and Richard Dubey from a number of men.

On October 29, 1941, the trial court found defendant Myers guilty and remanded him to the custody of the sheriff to await the report of the probation department. On November 21, 1941, Myers was placed on probation for a term of five years. On March 23, 1942, the order of probation was revoked and Myers was sentenced for a term of not less than 10 years nor more than 20 years with no recommendation. Subsequently, a motion for a new trial was made and on June 12, 1942, was denied.

Defendant Myers appeals and contends that the finding of the court as to his guilt was contrary to the great weight of the evidence.

There is evidence in the record that all three of the young men including Myers had intercourse with the girl. It is admitted that at some period during the trip the sum of $29 was extracted from the girl's pocketbook and later divided among the three young men. It is also an admitted fact that the guns used were imitation and one of them had been recently purchased from a five-and-ten cent store.

It is claimed that the prosecutrix did not resist to the utmost. The prosecutrix testified as follows:

"I know what the meaning of the word 'sexual intercourse' is. Richard Dubey had sexual intercourse with me at that time. His private parts entered my private parts. I struggled with him. I tried to push him away, but he was, didn't do any good because he was laying on top of me. Dubey eventually got off of me. Roger Myers come over to the car. Well, when he got in the car I had, I was sitting up there and he says, 'Don't be bashful.' I said well, I didn't want to have intercourse with him either, and then he pulled the gun out, that was a smaller gun than the one was had before. That is Rogers Myers. He says, 'I don't want to use this gun,' but he says, 'I may have to.' Well, then I was forced to have intercourse with him. He pushed me down. He had intercourse with me. His private parts entered my private parts."

In People v. Geddes, 301 Mich. 258, we said: "The degree of resistance required to be shown in rape cases is generally said to be 'resistance to the utmost.'" But, it is well settled that failure to resist is excused if the will of the prosecutrix was overcome by fear of the defendant. Strang v. People, 24 Mich. 1, and Moran v. People, 25 Mich. 356 (12 Am. Rep. 283). In our opinion, there was competent evidence, if believed by the trial judge, to find defendant guilty beyond

a reasonable doubt of the offense named. The conviction
of defendant is affirmed. . . .

CHANDLER, STARR, WIEST, and BUSHNELL, J. J., concurred
with SHARP, J.

(Concurring and dissenting opinions relative to probation
revocation procedures omitted).

Hirdes v. Ottawa Circuit Judge
180 Mich. 321

Mandamus by Mike Hirdes against Orien S. Cross, circuit
judge of Ottawa county, to compel respondent to vacate an
order denying relator's motion to dismiss a writ of capias
in an action brought against him by Leonard Vis. Submitted
March 28, 1914. (Calender No. 25.913.) Writ denied April
7, 1914.

STONE, J. Relator was arrested by the sheriff of Ottawa
county on a writ of capias ad respondendum, issued out of the
circuit court for said county at the suit of Leonard Vis.
Relator was held to bail in the sum of $2,000 on an order
made by the respondent, which bail relator gave. Attached
to the writ were three affidavits; one of Leonard Vis, the
plaintiff, one of Maggie Vis, his wife, and one of Harry Vis,
his brother. . . .
In the affidavit of Leonard Vis, he swears that the said
Mike Hirdes, contriving and wrongfully and unjustly intending to injure him and deprive him of the comfort, fellowship,
society, aid, and assistance of his said wife, and alienate
and destroy her affection for him, on the 20th day of March,
1913, at the city of Zeeland, wrongfully, wickedly, and unjustly debauched and carnally knew deponent's wife, and did
then and there have sexual intercourse with her, as deponent
is informed and believes. In another part of the affidavit
the plaintiff states that the defendant caused the said wife
to become intoxicated in order that he might carry out his
wicked purpose of seducing her, as he was informed and believed. The affidavit further states that affiant makes the
affidavit for the purpose of procuring a writ of capias ad
respondendum, and claims that he has a just cause of action
against the said Mike Hirdes, and is damaged in the sum of
$10,000. The affiant then refers to the accompanying affi-
davits of his wife and brother.
It is necessary that we should critically examine the affidavit of the wife, Maggie Vis. She therein states that
she was 20 years of age, the wife of Leonard Vis, and resided
with him in the city of Zeeland; that on the 20th day of March,
1913, in the absence of her husband, Mike Hirdes came to deponent's home and furnished her with a quart of whisky, part
of which she drank, and became intoxicated; that the said
Hirdes then and there took advantage of deponent's condition

and had sexual intercourse with her; that she did not have will power enough, being in an intoxicated condition, to resist the actions of said Mike Hirdes, which purpose he could not have accomplished had she not been intoxicated. We quote from the affidavit:

"Deponent further says that she gave the said Mike Hirdes no occasion whatever to think or believe that she would be open and subject to his embraces, and that in order to have sexual intercourse with her he first procured the liquor, gave it to her, and caused her to be intoxicated. . . . Deponent further says that she refused to have sexual intercourse with him, whereupon he procured this liquor, and, while in the state of intoxication, and not being able to resist, he took advantage of her and had sexual intercourse.". . .

Upon the trial of the case under a proper declaration, would it be competent for the wife, Maggie Vis, to testify that the said Mike Hirdes furnished her with whisky, and caused her to become so intoxicated that she was not in a condition to resist the action of said Hirdes, and that, while in such condition produced by him, he had sexual intercourse with her, she not being able, by reason of such intoxication, to resist his acts and conduct? We are of opinion that it would be competent for her to so testify, and, should those facts be shown to the satisfaction of a jury, that they would be warranted in finding that the conduct of the said Hirdes, under such circumstances, amounted to rape.

In the case of <u>People v. Croswell</u>, <u>13</u> <u>Mich.</u> <u>427</u> (<u>87</u> <u>Am.</u> <u>Dec.</u> <u>774</u>), Justice COOLEY, after defining the crime of rape,

"In the case of <u>Regina v. Camplin</u>, <u>1</u> <u>Den. C. C.</u> <u>89</u>; same case <u>1 C. & K.</u> <u>746</u>, it appeared that the prisoner gave the woman liquor for the purpose of exciting her, but which had the effect to make her quite drunk; and, while she was in a state of insensibility, he took advantage of it and violated her. The court held the act to be rape. The prosecutrix showed by her words and conduct, up to the latest moment at which she had sense or power to express her will, that it was against her will that intercourse should take place. It was no answer to the charge, therefore, that she had no opposing will at the moment when intercourse actually took place, since the prisoner had actually mastered it by means of the stupefying drug, which was the same, as was well remarked by one of the judges, as if it had been overcome by a blow. . . . If the woman was insensible, some degree of physical force must actually have been employed by the prisoner; and no more resistance is required by the law, in any case, than the condition of the woman will permit her to make. . . . The outrage upon the woman, and the injury to society, is just as great in these cases as if actual force had been employed; and we have been unable to satisfy ourselves that the act can be said to be any less against the will of the woman when her consent is obtained by fraud than when it is extorted by threats or force."

In _33 Cyc._, at pages 1426 and 1427, it is said:

"So, if ability to resist is taken away by administering drugs, even though the woman may be conscious, sexual intercourse with her is rape. . . . And if the woman is intoxicated to the extent of being unable to resist, the act is without her consent and is rape" - citing many cases.

Especially should this be the rule if the state of intoxication is produced by the defendant. . . .

In our opinion, the circuit judge did not err in so holding, and the writ of mandamus must therefore be denied, with costs against relator.

McALVAY, C. J., and BROOKE, KUHN, OSTRANDER, BIRD, MOORE, and STEERE, JJ., concurred.

3.   Final Draft - Michigan Revised Criminal Code

(Definitions)

Sec. 2301. The following definitions apply in this chapter:

(a) "Sexual intercourse" has its ordinary meaning and occurs upon any penetration, however slight; emission is not required.

(b) "Deviate sexual intercourse" means any act of sexual gratification between persons not married to each other, involving the sex organs of one person and the mouth or anus of another.

(c) "Sexual contact" means any touching of the sexual or other intimate parts of a person not married to the actor, done for the purpose of gratifying sexual desire of either party.

(d) "Female" means any female person who is not married to the actor. Persons living together as man and wife are married for purposes of this chapter, regardless of the legal status of their relationship otherwise. Spouses living apart under a decree of judicial separation are not married to one another for purposes of this chapter.

(e) "Mentally defective" means that a person suffers from a mental disease or defect which renders him incapable of appraising the nature of his conduct.

(f) "Mentally incapacitated" means that a person is rendered temporarily incapable of appraising or controlling his conduct owing to the influence of a narcotic or intoxicating substance administered to him without his consent, or to any other act committed upon him without his consent.

(g) "Physically helpless" means that a person is unconscious or for any other reason is physically unable to communicate unwillingness to an act.

(h) "Forcible compulsion" means physical force that overcomes earnest resistance; or a threat, express or implied, that places a person in fear of immediate death or serious physical injury to himself or another person, or in fear that he or another person will be immediately kidnaped.

Committee Commentary

The bulk of the section is derived from New York Revised Penal Law, Sec. 130.00. Subparagraph (b) incorporates elements from Illinois Criminal Code Sec. 11-2, and the special definitions of marriage in subsection (d) are taken from Model Penal Code Sec. 213.6 (2). The several definitions will be discussed in the context of the sections which follow.

(Sexual Misconduct)

Sec. 2305. (1) A person commits the crime of sexual misconduct if:

(a) Being a male, he engages in sexual intercourse with a female without her consent; or

(b) Being a female, she engages in sexual intercourse with a male without his consent; or

(c) He engages in deviate sexual intercourse with another person without the latter's consent.

(2) Sexual misconduct is a Class B misdemeanor.

Committee Commentary

The section is derived from New York Revised Penal Law Sec. 130.20. It sets the basic dividing line between criminal conduct of both a heterosexual and a homosexual character.

Non-consensual heterosexual intercourse. The "carnal knowledge" or rape statute (C. L. 1948, Sec. 750.520) covers any intercourse with a woman 16 or older "by force and against her will". Force is required sufficient to overcome "utmost resistance" (People v. Myers, 306 Mich. 100, 10 N.W.2d 323 (1943)), but the victim's weak physical and mental powers may be taken into account in deciding how much resistance is expected of her (People v. Marrs, 125 Mich. 376, 84 N.W. 285 (1900)). Once resistance is overcome, only slight penetration of the penis into the vulva is required; there need not be complete penetration or emission (People v. Courier, 79 Mich. 366, 44 N.W. 571 (1890)). If the victim yields before penetration, the defendant cannot be convicted of rape, but can be found guilty of assault with intent to rape because of his activity prior to consent (People v. Marrs, 125 Mich. 376, 84 N.W. 284 (1900)).

941

Michigan case law is inconsistent on the question of whether intercourse with a mentally defective woman or a drugged or intoxicated woman is rape, or whether rape can be committed by procuring intercourse by fraud. In an early case the Supreme Court held that intercourse with an insane woman, not procured through force or fraud, did not constitute rape at common law (People v. Crosswell, 13 Mich. 427 (1865)), and that intercourse under the pretext of medical treatment could not be rape unless the dire descriptions of what would happen if surgical treatment rather than intercourse were used so put the girl in fear that she became incapable of resistance (Moran v. People, 25 Mich. 356 (1872). The latter case was compensated for by an 1883 statute (C.L. 1948, Sec. 750.90) which makes it a felony to procure intercourse with a female under pretext of medical treatment. In a civil action the Supreme Court indicated that intercourse with a woman unable to resist because of intoxication is rape, particularly if the defendant intentionally produced her state of intoxication (Hirdes v. Ottawa Circuit Judge, 180 Mich. 321, 146 N.W. 646 (1914)). . . .

(Rape in the First Degree)

Sec. 2310. (1) A male is guilty of rape in the first degree if:

(a) He engages in sexual intercourse with a female by forcible compulsion; or
(b) He engages in sexual intercourse with a female who is incapable of consent by reason of being physically helpless; or
(c) He engages in sexual intercourse with a female who is less than 11 years old.

(2) Rape in the first degree is a Class A felony.

Committee Commentary

The section is derived from New York Revised Penal Law Sec. 130.35. Its relationship to existing law is discussed in the Commentary to Sec. 2310 to 2312 below.

(Rape in the Second Degree)

Sec. 2311. (1) A male commits the crime of rape in the second degree if, being 18 years old or more, he engages in sexual intercourse with a female less than 14 years old.

(2) Rape in the second degree is a Class C. Felony.

Committee Commentary

The section is derived from New York Revised Penal Law Sec. 130.30. Its relationship to existing law is discussed in the Commentary to Sec. 2310 to 2312 below.

(Rape in the Third Degree)

Sec. 2312. (1) A male commits the crime of rape in the third degree if:

(a) He engages in sexual intercourse with a female who is incapable of consent by reason of some factor other than being less than 16 years old; or

(b) Being 21 years old or more, he engages in sexual intercourse with a female less than 16 years old.

(2) Rape in the third degree is a Class A misdemeanor.

Committee Commentary

The section is adapted from New York Revised Penal Law Sec. 130.25. Its relationship to existing law is discussed in the Commentary to Sec. 2310 to 2312 below.

Committee Commentary to Sec. 2310 to 2312

Relationship to Existing Law

As indicated in the Commentary to Sec. 2305 Michigan law defines as rape forcible intercourse with a woman not married to the defendant, and any intercourse with a girl under 16. The first clause of the statute (C.L. 1948, Sec. 750.520) continues the common-law concept of forcible rape; since only intercourse with a girl under 10 was common-law rape (People v. McDonald, 9 Mich. 150 (1861)), the remainder of the statute amplifies the common-law coverage.

Section 2305 sets the basic norm for criminal heterosexual intercourse, particularly in Sec. 2305 (1) (a) and (b). Sections 2310-2312 therefore, may be viewed as aggravated forms of the sexual intercourse penalized in Sec. 2305.

Section 2312 creates two possibilities for third-degree rape. One is intercourse with a woman incapable of consent for any reason other than the fact she is under 16. The definition of consent in Sec. 2330 means that Sec. 2312 (1) (a) applies when the woman is mentally defective, as defined in Sec. 2301 (e), so that she is incapable of appraising the nature of her conduct, or mentally incapacitated, as defined in Sec. 2301 (f), so that she is temporarily incapable of appraising or controlling her conduct because a narcotic or intoxicating substance has been given her without her consent, or by reason of any other act done to her without her consent. Sexual intercourse with a physically helpless person, though non-consensual under Sec. 2330, comes within first-degree rape and not third-degree.

The second possibility under Sec. 2312 is intercourse with a girl less than 16 years old, when the actor is twenty-one or older. The difference in age is substantial enough that intercourse of this nature is escalated into the rape category from sexual misconduct.

Section 2311 is concerned with another variation on statutory rape. If the girl is less than 14 and the actor 18 or older, the intercourse becomes second-degree rape, punished slightly more heavily than third-degree rape. If the boy is 16 or 17, the intercourse constitutes sexual misconduct only (Sec. 2305).

Section 2310 restates the gist of rape both at common law and under present Michigan law. First-degree rape may be committed in one of three ways. The first is through forcible compulsion, defined in Sec. 2301 (h) as physical force which overcomes earnest resistance, or as an express or implied threat which places the victim in fear of immediate death or serious physical injury to herself or someone else or of an immediate kidnapping of herself or someone else. This does not change existing law in any material way.

The second is through sexual intercourse with a woman incapable of consent because she is physically helpless, defined in Sec. 2301 (g) as unconsciousness or any other state which renders a person physically unable to communicate assent. This, too, is consistent with common-law rape cases (Perkins, Criminal Law 122-23 (1957)).

The third is intercourse with a child younger than 11. Conduct of this character is so dangerous to the child that it deserves severe penalties. In this respect also, common-law coverage is substantially retained, except that the critical age is 11 rather than 10.

The definition of sexual intercourse in Sec. 2301 (a) preserves the existing law that only a slight penetration is necessary and that emission is not required.

B. Debauchery, Seduction and Fornication

1. Michigan Compiled Laws (1948)

750.339 Males under 15, debauching by females

Sec. 339. FEMALES DEBAUCHING MORALS OF MALES UNDER 15 YEARS OF AGE - Any female person over the age of 15 years, who shall knowingly and wilfully debauch the person and deprave the morals of any boy under the age of 15 years, either by lewdly inducing or enticing any such boy to carnally know any such female person, or by indecent bodily contact with the person of any such boy communicating to him any venereal or other loathsome disease, shall be guilty of a felony, punishable by imprisonment in the state prison not more than 5 years.

750.340 Same; debauching by males

Sec. 340. MALES DEBAUCHING MORALS OF MALES UNDER 15 YEARS

OF AGE - Any male person over the age of 15 years who shall debauch and deprave the morals of any boy under 15 years of age, by enticing or soliciting such boy to commit the abominable and detestable crime against nature, either with any man or beast, shall be guilty of a felony, punishable by imprisonment in the state prison not more than 5 years.

750.341 Female patient in institution for insane, ravish, abuse

Sec. 341. RAVISHING, ETC., FEMALE PATIENT IN ANY STATE OR COUNTY INSTITUTION FOR THE CARE OF THE INSANE - Any person who shall ravish or carnally know and abuse any female who is a patient in any state or county institution for the care of the insane, feeble-minded, epileptic or mentally incompetent shall be guilty of a felony, punishable by imprisonment in the state prison not more than 15 years nor less than 5 years; and such carnal knowledge shall be deemed complete upon proof of penetration only.

The term "patient" as used herein shall be construed to mean any female committed to any state or county institution aforesaid and who has not been discharged according to law.

In all prosecutions under the provisions of this section the validity of the commitment shall not be questioned.

750.342 Female ward, carnal knowledge

Sec. 342. CARNAL KNOWLEDGE OF FEMALE WARD BY GUARDIAN, ETC. - Any guardian of any female under the age of 18 years, or any other person to whose care or protection any such female shall have been confided, who shall defile her by carnally knowing her while she remains in his care, custody or employment, shall in any case not otherwise provided for be guilty of a felony, punishable by imprisonment in the state prison for not more than 10 years or by a fine of not more than 5,000 dollars.

750.532 Punishment

Sec. 532 PUNISHMENT - Any man who shall seduce and debauch any unmarried woman shall be guilty of a felony, punishable by imprisonment in the state prison not more than 5 years or by fine of not more than 2,500 dollars; but no prosecution shall be commenced under this section after 1 year from the time of committing the offense.

2. Definitions and General Elements

People v. Bailey
341 Mich. 592

(For the opinion in this case see page 113, supra.)

MARSTON, J:

The defendant was convicted for the seduction of Alice
J. Morey. There were three counts in the information: the
<u>first</u> charged him with committing the offense on the 28th
of July, 1873, in the county of Calhoun; the <u>second</u>, with
the commission of a like offense on the same day in the
township of Penfield, in said county; and the <u>third</u>, with
a like offense, under and by means of a promise of marriage,
on the same day, in the county of Calhoun. . . .

Illicit intercourse alone would not constitute the offense charged. In addition to this the complainant, relying upon some sufficient promise or inducement, and without
which she would not have yielded, must have been drawn a-
side from the path of virtue she was honestly pursuing at
the time the offense charged was committed. Now, from her
own testimony it would seem that the parties had illicit
intercourse as opportunity offered. "Such is the force
and ungovernable nature of this passion, and so likely is
its indulgence to be continued between the same parties,
when once yielded to, that the constitution of the human
mind must be entirely changed before any man's judgment
can resist the conclusion" that where parties thus indulge
their criminal desires it shows a willingness upon her part
that a person of chaste character would not be guilty of,
and that although a promise of marriage may have been made
at each time as an inducement, it would be but a mere matter
of form, and could not alone safely be relied upon to establish the fact that she would not have yielded had such a
promise not been made.

We do not wish to be understood as saying that, even as
between the same parties, there could not be a second or even
third act of seduction; but where the subsequent alleged acts
follow the first so closely, they destroy the presumption of
chastity which would otherwise prevail, and there should be
clear and satisfactory proof that the complainant had in truth
and fact reformed, otherwise there could be no seduction. The
object of this statute was not to punish illicit cohabitation.
Its object was to punish the seducer, who, by his arts and
persuasions, prevails over the chastity of an unmarried woman,
and who thus draws her aside from the path of duty and rectitude she was pursuing. If, however, she had already fallen,
and was not at the time pursuing this path, but willingly submitted to his embraces as opportunity offered, the mere fact
of a promise made at the time would not make the act seduction.

Nor will illicit intercourse which takes place in consequence of and in reliance upon a promise made, make the act
seduction. If this were so, then the common prostitute, who
is willing to sell her person to any man, might afterward make

the act seduction by proving that she yielded relying upon
the promise of compensation made her by the man, and without which she would not have submitted to his embraces. Illicit intercourse, in reliance upon a promise made, is not
sufficient therefore, to make the act seduction. The nature
of the promise, and the previous character of the woman as
to chastity, must be considered. And although the female may
have previously left the path of virtue on account of the
seductive arts and persuasions of the accused or some other
person, yet if she has repented of that act and reformed,
she may again be seduced. We do not say that there may not
have been a reformation in this case; indeed there may have
been many, but they were unfortunately fleeting. Had a reasonable time elapsed between the different acts, a presumption in favor of a reformation might arise, but we think no
such presumption could arise in this case, and that the burden of proving such would be upon the prosecution.

In this connection we may discuss another question raised.
Upon cross-examination of the complaining witness she was
asked whether previous to this time she had ever had connection with any other man. This was objected to as irrelevant, and the objection was sustained. It does not clearly
appear from the record what particular time the question referred to, whether to a time previous to the first alleged
act of intercourse with the defendant, or previous to the
trial. If the latter, the ruling was clearly correct. -
People v. Brewer, 27 Mich. 134. If the former, then we think
the question, under the objection made, was proper. In the
examination of this question, and also of the one last discussed, we have derived but little benefit from an examination
of the authorities. Seduction was not punishable by indictment at common law, and the cases which discuss these questions are all under statutes which differ in some respect
from ours.

In most of the states their statute makes the seduction
of a woman of "previous chaste character" an indictable offense, while there are no such words, nor any of like import
in ours, - and the courts have held that the words "previous
chaste character" mean that she shall possess actual personal
virtue, in distinction to a good reputation, and that a single
act of illicit connection may therefore be shown on behalf
of the defendant. If, however, we are correct in what we
have already said upon the question as to what is necessary
to make an act of illicit intercourse seduction, then the
chastity of the female at the time of the alleged act is in
all cases involved, and the presumption of law being in favor
of chastity, the defense have a right to show the contrary.
This, upon principle, we consider the correct doctrine, and
that it necessarily follows from what we have said upon the
other question. . . .

Questions were also raised as to the charge of the court
relative to the effect of good moral character, and some

others which are not likely to arise again, under previous decisions of this court which seem to have been overlooked, and we do not consider it necessary therefore to discuss them.

The conviction should be set aside and a new trial granted, and directions given to the court below accordingly.

The other Justices concurred.

People v. Defore
64 Mich. 693

CHAMPLIN, J. Respondent was convicted of the crime of seduction. But one act was charged or claimed to have been committed, and that the prosecutrix swore was under a promise of marriage. No attempt was made to show that she was not a woman of previous chaste character. On her direct and cross-examination she testified to the use of considerable force by respondent before he accomplished his purpose, and said she would not have consented if she could have prevented it. Her testimony given on cross-examination before the justice, signed by her, was produced and identified by her, and was introduced and read to the jury, as follows:

"I did not consent to his doing that to me, and would not, only he held me so tight I could not help it. I would not have said anything about this matter, or made Peter any trouble, only I found I was in a family way. If it had not been for that, I would have let him gone where he liked."

The counsel for defendant requested the circuit judge in writing, to charge and instruct the jury as follows:

"1. If the jury find from the evidence that there was any other inducement or motive which induced or led the prosecutrix to submit herself to the defendant, except the promise of marriage, then the jury cannot convict the defendant of seduction.

"2. To convict the defendant of seduction, the jury must find two facts, viz.: (1) That the prosecutrix consented to the act of copulation with the defendant freely and willingly; (2) that she was induced to thus consent by reason of a promise of marriage made by defendant prior to the act of connection.

"3. If you find from the evidence that she submitted to the act of connection unwillingly, or through force or fear of defendant, the jury cannot convict the defendant of seduction.

"4. If the jury find from the evidence, that the prosecutrix submitted herself to the defendant partly because of a promise of marriage, and partly through force or fear of defendant, then the jury cannot convict the defendant of seduction.

"5. The jury must find from the evidence, before they can convict the defendant of seduction, that there was a promise of marriage between the defendant and prosecutrix, made prior to the act of connection, and that said promise was understood and relied upon by her, and that she yielded to the act with defendant because of said promise, and did so freely and with full consent.

"6. If the jury find from the evidence that the prosecutrix would not have submitted herself to have connection with defendant on the sixteenth day of November, 1884, without the force used by defendant, as testified to by her, then the jury cannot convict the defendant of seduction.

"7. If the jury find from the evidence that the act was done against the will and wishes of the prosecutrix, then the jury cannot convict.

"8. In order to convict the defendant of seduction, the jury must find from the evidence a promise of marriage made by the defendant to the prosecutrix, and in consideration of such promise she freely and willingly consented to have connection.

"9. If the prosecutrix was compelled by force or fear of defendant, in whole or in part, to submit to the act of connection, then the act would not be seduction, and the jury cannot convict."

The circuit judge declined to so instruct the jury, and on his own motion charged and instructed them as follows:

"Gentlemen of the Jury: This action is brought by the people against the defendant under the provisions of the statute which provides for the punishment of any man who shall seduce or debauch an unmarried woman. In this case the defendant is charged with having seduced and debauched the complaining witness, Nettie Josephack, on the sixteenth day of November, 1884, in the township of Jordan, in this county. The testimony on which the people rest is the testimony of the complaining witness. Her testimony stands before you uncontradicted by any other witness in the case. You therefore have no conflict of testimony to reconcile, except it be conflicting statements of the complaining witness. The fact that the complaining witness and the defendant had sexual intercourse on that day, in that township, is not disputed; and you may take that fact as established in examining this case. The question for you to determine, then, is, what were the inducements that led to this sexual intercourse? They may be, or they may have been, occasioned in three ways:

"1. It may have been from the mutual desire of the parties, without undue influence of either, to gratify their passions. In that case, if you should find such was the case, then your verdict will be ,'Not guilty.'

"2. It may have been by the seductive influence of the defendant. But the complaining witness has testified to no acts in that line except the promise of marriage. Therefore, in order to convict this defendant of the offense here charged, under the testimony before you, you will have to find that the inducement which led to her submitting her person to the carnal intercourse of the defendant was the fact that he, for that reason, promised to marry her. If you find that that was the reason of her submitting to his embrace, then your verdict will be, 'Guilty.'

"3. If you should find from the testimony in the case that she gave no consent whatever; that the intercourse was obtained by force and compulsion, - such an obtaining of carnal intercourse with a woman is rape, and it is a higher crime than the one you are brought here to consider. It would be against public policy to allow a prosecuting officer to bring a charge of seduction where the crime was rape, because if the law allowed him to do so, he might allow parties to escape with a light punishment where State's prison for a long term of years was the punishment that should be meted out for that offense.

"The crime of rape consists of, or is defined by Bouvier to be: 'A carnal knowledge of a woman by a man, forcibly and unlawfully, against her will.' Therefore, to find that this man committed a rape on this woman, you will have to find that he committed that 'forcibly and unlawfully, and against her will.' If she consented to the connection, it was not rape.

"Therefore, gentlemen, I think that you will, in this case, have but two matters to consider. I think you may dispense with any theory that this defendant committed the higher crime of rape under the testimony in the case, and you will be left simply to determine whether it was by the mutual consent of the parties, resulting from long acquaintance, and the very intimate relation that existed between them, upon a contract of marriage before entered into, or whether it was upon a promise at that time of a future marriage on condition that she would submit to his embraces. If you find the former, he is not guilty; if you find the latter, your verdict will be, 'Guilty.'"

The errors assigned upon this record are the following:

"1. The court erred in refusing to grant the requests submitted by defendant's counsel, and in refusing to instruct the jury as stated in said several requests; that the refusal of each and every one of said defendant's requests was error.

"2. The charge of the court, on his own motion, as as (sic) whole, was error.

"3. The court erred in that part and portion of this charge where he charges the jury in relation to the crime of rape, because the same is contrary to law, and in this case misleading to the jury, and contrary to the evidence.

"4. The court erred in taking from the jury in his charge the consideration of the question of rape.

"5. The court erred in his charge wherein he instructs the jury as follows: 'I think you may dispense with any theory that this defendant committed the higher crime of rape.

"6. The court erred in submitting the case to the consideration of the jury under the testimony in the case as the evidence is not sufficient to support the verdict."

It is claimed that the assignment of error based upon the refusal to give the nine requests to charge is too general to be considered, and particularly as some of such requests were given and others were improper. The object of assignments or error is to point out specifically what is relied upon as error. This is accomplished by the first assignment, which in terms assigns error upon the refusal to give each and every one of defendant's requests. This applies to each request separately, and no good reason is perceived for repeating each request in the assignments, which would only tend to prolong the record without lending any perspicuity to the errors assigned. The second assignment of error is too general, and cannot be considered.

The first request to charge was properly refused in the form in which it was asked. The testimony showed no other inducement or motive than a promise of marriage, except it might be the mutual desire of the parties; and this the court called the jury's attention to, and told them, if they found that the act was done by the mutual consent of the parties to gratify their passions, the respondent was not guilty. The second request was covered substantially by the charge as given, as was also the eighth.

The third and sixth requests were properly refused. The respondent was on trial for the offense created by the statute of seducing and debauching an unmarried female. Under this statute, the offense is committed if the man has carnal intercourse to which the woman assented, if such assent was obtained by a promise of marriage made by the man at the time, and to which, without such promise, she would not have yielded. People v. Millspaugh, 11 Mich. 278, 282, 283. The offense consists in enticing the woman from the path of virtue, and obtaining her consent to the illicit intercourse by promises made at the time. The evidence should be such as to satisfy the jury beyond a reasonable doubt upon these points. The promise and yielding her virtue in consequence thereof is the gist of the offense. If she resists, but finally assents or yields, induced thereto or in reliance upon the promise made, the offense is committed. Boyce v. People, 55 N.Y. 644.

An act of intercourse induced simply by mutual desire of the parties to gratify a lustful passion would not constitute the crime charged in the information. The charge of seduction and debauchery implies that a pure woman will resist, and that the natural sentiment of virtue and of purity will be over-

come by promise of marriage and other means, and submission
to his desires finally obtained through such inducements.
And it has been held that, when the female submitted through
a promise of marriage conditioned upon the act resulting in
pregnancy, the crime was committed. People v. Hustis, 23 Hun.
58; Kenyon v. People, 26 N.Y. 203. The requests last referred
to leave out of consideration the concurrent influence of the
promise of marriage as a producing cause of yielding assent,
or, to use the language of the request, in submitting to the
act.

The fourth and ninth requests were properly refused. The
crime of rape is not embraced in that of seduction; and it
would be improper for the judge, upon a trial for seduction,
to instruct the jury upon the law relative to the crime of
rape. Reynolds v. People, 41 How. Pr. 179.

The judge, however, should charge that, if the jury
should find that she did not assent to the act of intercourse, the offense was not committed. The respondent was
entitled to have his seventh request given. This request
is not covered by the charge of the court, which was finally
reduced to two propositions; namely, whether the act was done
by the mutual consent of the parties, or whether it was upon
a promise at that time of a future marriage on condition that
she would submit to his embraces. He withdrew from the jury
whether she gave no consent whatever, and the intercourse was
obtained by force and compulsion. For this error assigned,
the conviction must be set aside, and a new trial ordered.

It may be well, as there must be a retrial, to point out
one or two errors in the charge not specifically assigned
as error.

The attention of the jury was called to the fact that the
people rested their testimony upon the testimony of the complaining witness, and that her testimony stood before them
uncontradicted by any other witness in the case. He also
told the jury that the fact that the complaining witness and
the defendant had sexual intercourse on that day, in that
township, was not disputed; and the jury might take that
fact as established in examining the case. This was erroneous. The weight of the evidence, and the credit to be
given to the testimony of the complaining witness, was a
question exclusively for the jury, and it was error for the
court to charge the jury that they should consider any facts
testified to by her as established simply because she had
testified to them, and had not been contradicted. These
facts which he directed the jury to regard as established
were a part of the res gestae. The law presumed the respondent innocent of the crime charged until such presumption was
rebutted and overcome by evidence; and the jury must weigh
this presumption against her testimony, and ascertain what
the facts are. Her testimony may have been of such a character or so contradictory as not to obtain any credit with
the jury. Indeed, the judge told the jury that they had no
conflict of testimony to reconcile except it was the con-

952

flicting statements of the complaining witness.

Another error in the charge appears. It is the duty of the trial judge, in a criminal case, to instruct the jury in reference to the presumptions of law applicable to the case before them, distinguishing those which are conclusive from those which are disputable. The presumption of innocence is present in every criminal case; and he should instruct the jury to that effect, and that it stands good until overcome by evidence which convinces the jury beyond a reasonable doubt that the respondent is guilty. The charge of the court entirely overlooks this presumption, and nothing was said upon the subject.

Let an order be entered reversing the judgment, and granting respondent a new trial.

The other Justices concurred.

People v. Smith
132 Mich. 58

CARPENTER, J. Defendant was convicted of the crime of seduction. The information charged that the offense was committed on the 30th of April, 1901, in the township of Homestead, in the county of Benzie. The complaining witness testified that she was 20 years old in August, 1901; that she had sexual intercourse with the defendant on or about the date named in the information, and also in February and early in April, 1901; that on each of these occasions defendant promised that, if she got in the family way, he would marry her; that she became pregnant, and was delivered of a child on the 19th of January, 1902.

At the conclusion of the people's case, counsel for the defendant requested the court to instruct the jury -

"To render a verdict of not guilty, as the evidence in the case discloses . . . that respondent had illicit intercourse with the complaining witness in February and in April prior to the time charged. It follows that she is not a person who could be seduced at the time alleged in the complaint, warrant, and information. And there has been no sufficient promise to marry proven. She could not be said to be a chaste person at the time alleged."

This request was denied, to which defendant excepted. In his charge to the jury, the court said:

"The girl, Miss Brown, has gone on the stand, and testified that the respondent had, on every occasion when they had intercourse promised to marry her. I charge you, as a matter of law, that, if this respondent did have sexual intercourse with this girl at the time alleged in the information, and, in order to persuade her to allow him to have such sexual intercourse, did make this promise, no matter whether he intended to carry this promise out or not, if this girl relied on his promises and inducements at that time, and allowed him to have sexual intercourse with her, and if she was a chaste character, then I charge you that the defendant is guilty of this crime as charged in the information."

To this part of the charge defendant assigns error.

In the case of People v. Clark, 33 Mich. 112, the lower court permitted the jury to find the defendant guilty of seduction because of illicit intercourse in August, 1873, though the complaining witness testified that she had such intercourse with the defendant not only in August, but on the preceding 28th of July. In deciding this case the court said:

"We do not wish to be understood as saying that, even as between the same parties, there could not be a second, or even third, act of seduction; but, where the subsequent alleged acts follow the first so closely, they destroy the presumption of chastity which would otherwise prevail, and there should be clear and satisfactory proof that the complainant had in truth and fact reformed; otherwise there could be no seduction. . . . And, although the female may have previously left the path of virtue on account of the seductive arts and persuasions of the accused or some other person, yet, if she has repented of that act, and reformed, she may again be seduced. We do not say that there may not have been a reformation in this case. Indeed, there may have been many, but they were unfortunately fleeting. Had a reasonable time elapsed between the different acts, a presumption in favor of a reformation might arise; but we think no such presumption could arise in this case, and that the burden of proving such reformation would be upon the prosecution."

This decision is decisive of the case at bar. As the people introduced no evidence whatever tending to show a reformation on the part of the complaining witness after the illicit intercourse of the preceding February and early in April, it was the duty of the court to direct the acquittal of defendant, as requested.

There is, in our judgment, however, a more serious error in the case. All that the defendant did, according to the testimony of the complaining witness, to induce her to have illicit intercourse with him, was to promise to marry her if she became pregnant. Does sexual intercourse, induced by such a promise, constitute seduction? In the case of People v. De Fore, 64 Mich., at page 699 (31 N.W. 585, 8 Am. St. Rep. 863), Justice CHAMPLIN says:

"And it has been held that, when the female submitted through a promise of marriage conditioned upon the act resulting in pregnancy, the crime was committed. People v. Hustis, 32 Hun, 58; Kenyon v. People, 26 N.Y. 203 (84 Am. Dec. 177)."

People v. Hustis sustains the proposition for which it is cited. This decision, however, was made in a lower court, consisting of three judges, one of whom filed a vigorous dissenting opinion. The only argument advanced in the majority opinion was the claim that the case was ruled by Kenyon v. People, above cited in the quotation from Justice CHAMPLIN'S opinion. The case of Kenyon v. People holds this, and only this: That it is a sufficient promise of marriage, under the New York statute creating the crime of seduction (in which illicit connection under promise of marriage is the gist of the offense), "that the defendant promised to marry the prosecutrix if she would have carnal connection with him." The case of Kenyon v. People is, therefore, no authority upon the question under discussion, and furnished no justification whatever for the decision of People v. Hustis.

The best definition of seduction contained in our Reports was framed by Mr. Justice MONTGOMERY, when, as circuit judge he tried the case of People v. Gibbs, and will be found in the report of that case in 70 Mich., at page 430 (38 N.W. 257):

"Seduction may be defined to be the act of persuading or inducing a woman of previous chaste character to depart from the path of virtue by the use of any species of arts, persuasions, or wiles which are calculated to have, and do have, that effect, and resulting in her ultimately submitting her person to the sexual embraces of the person accused."

This is in harmony with the case of People v. Clark, 33 Mich., at page 116, where it was said:

"Illicit intercourse alone would not constitute the offense charged. In addition to this, the complainant, relying upon some sufficient promise or inducement, and without which she would not have yielded, must have been drawn aside from the path of virtue which she was honestly pursuing at the time the offense charged was committed."

As well as the case of People v. De Fore, 64 Mich., at page 699 (31 N. W. 585, 8 Am. St. Rep. 863), where it was said:

"An act of intercourse, induced simply by mutual desire of the parties to gratify a lustful passion, would not constitute the crime charged in the information. The charge of seduction and debauchery implies that a pure woman will resist, and that the natural sentiment of virtue and of purity will be overcome by a promise of marriage and other means, and submission to his desires finally obtained through such inducements."

Where the woman is a young, inexperienced girl, the courts very properly hold that promises and means are sufficient

which would not move a woman of mature years. People v.
Gibbs, 70 Mich., at page 427 (38 N.W. 257). The complaining witness in this case, however, was not a young and inexperienced girl. She was nearly 20 years of age, and, it
is apparent knew quite well the consequences of her act.
She cannot complain, therefore, if she is judged by the
rules applicable to ordinary pure women.

Is a promise to marry, conditioned upon the illicit intercourse resulting in pregnancy, calculated to induce a pure
women to yield her chastity? In our judgment, this question admits of but one answer. Such a promise has no tendency to overcome the natural sentiment of virtue and purity.
The woman who yields upon such a promise is in no better
position than as though no promise whatever had been made.
No wrong is done her if she is put in the class with those
who commit the act to gratify their desire. She was willing to lose her virtue if some provision was made to conceal its loss. If pregnancy does not result from the illicit
intercourse, her conduct is, in every respect, as culpable
as that of her companion. If pregnancy does result, his
conduct becomes more culpable than hers when, and not until,
he refuses to marry her. The commission of the offense
cannot depend upon the happening of a subsequent event,
though it is to be noted in this case that the complaint
is made, not of the intercourse in February, 1901, when the
complaining witness lost her virtue, but of the intercourse
in the following April, which apparently resulted in her
becoming pregnant.

The verdict must be set aside, and a new trial ordered.

The other Justices concurred.

3. Final Draft - Michigan Revised Criminal Code

Committee Commentary to Sec. 2305

... Consensual heterosexual intercourse. Fornication is not
a crime at common law (Perkins, Criminal Law 328, 330 (1957)).
No Michigan statute punishes fornication as such; only when
accompanying circumstances make it adultery or seduction is
there criminal law coverage (People v. DeFore, 64 Mich. 693,
31 N.W. 585 (1887); People v. Rouse, 2 Mich. N.P. 209 (Allegan Circuit 1871). Debauching a female ward is a felony.
(C.L. 1948, Sec. 750.342).

What is consented to in fact may not in legal contemplation be viewed as consensual. At common law, intercourse
with a girl under 10 was considered to be rape, whether consented to in fact or not (People v. McDonald, 9 Mich. 150
(1861)). By statute any intercourse with a girl less than
16 years old is rape (C.L. 1948, Sec. 750.520); the girl
is legally incapable of giving consent, and it does not
matter that the defendant reasonably believed she was above
the statutory age (People v. Gengels, 218 Mich. 632, 188 N.W.

398 (1922)). If, however, the couple entered into what
would amount to a binding common-law marriage relationship
if they were of age, there can be no charge of statutory
rape; the relationship created, under the law in force at
that time, a voidable and not a void marriage (People v.
Pizzura, 211 Mich. 71, 178 N.W. 235 (1921)).

Another statute makes it a felony for a woman to "debauch"
a male under 15 through intercourse (C. L. 1948, Sec. 750.339).
Under that statute as interpreted, the woman must know that
the boy is less than 15 years old, but her knowledge or belief can be inferred circumstantially (People v. Bailey, 341
Mich. 592, 67 N.W. 2d 785 (1954)).

Note on seduction. It is a felony for a man to seduce
and debauch an unmarried woman (C. L. 1948, Sec. 750.532).
The section does not cover intercourse as such; it requires
some sufficient promise or inducement which causes the woman to yield (People v. Clark, 33 Mich. 112 (1876)). The
usual inducement is a promise to marry (People v. Defore, 64
Mich. 693, 31 N.W. 585 (1887)). The woman must consent;
rape cannot be charged alternately as seduction (People v.
DeFore, 64 Mich. 693, 31 N.W. 585 (1887)). The defendant's
promise must be unconditional; a promise to marry the girl
if she becomes pregnant is not enough (People v. Smith, 132
Mich. 58, 92 N.W. 776 (1902)).

The statute has not been before the Michigan Supreme Court
since 1916 (People v. Turton, 192 Mich. 331, 158 N.W. 870
(1916)), and in that and most of the earlier cases convictions
were reversed. On the civil side, the Legislature in 1935
severely limited the availability of actions for seduction
by requiring pleading and proof that the woman seduced was
not 18 years of age or over at the time of the seduction,
(C. L. 1948, Sec. 600.2910). Roughly equivalent protection
is provided through the definition of sexual misconduct in
Sec. 2305, the definitions of rape (Sec. 2310-2312) and the
definitions of sexual abuse (Sec. 2320-2322), so that there
is no need for a separate criminal seduction statute. Therefore, its repeal is recommended.

Note on carnal knowledge of female ward. It is a felony
for a guardian to have intercourse with a female ward 17 or
younger (C.L. 1948, Sec. 750.342). The statute has never
been before the Supreme Court. Its repeal without equivalent coverage is recommended because sexual misconduct (Sec.
2305) and second- and third-degree rape (Sec. 2311-2312)
provide sufficient coverage if the problem should arise.

C. Homosexual Intercourse

    1. Michigan Compiled Laws (1948)

750.158 Penalty

957

Sec. 158. Any person who shall commit the abominable and detestable crime against nature either with mankind or with any animal shall be guilty of a felony, punishable by imprisonment in the state prison not more than 15 years, or if such person was at the time of the said offense a sexually delinquent person, may be punishable by imprisonment in the state prison for an indeterminate term, the minimum of which shall be 1 day and the maximum of which shall be life. As amended P.A. 1952, No. 73, Sec. 1, Eff. Sept. 18.

750.159 Emission need not be proved

Sec. 159. In any prosecution for sodomy, it shall not be necessary to prove emission, and any sexual penetration, however slight, shall be deemed sufficient to complete the crime specified in the next preceding section. As amended P.A. 1952, No. 73, Sec. 1, Eff. Sept. 18.

750.338 Gross indecency; between male persons

Sec. 338. Any male person who, in public or in private, commits or is a party to the commission of or procures or attempts to procure the commission by any male person of any act of gross indecency with another male person shall be guilty of a felony, punishable by imprisonment in the state prison for not more than 5 years, or by a fine of not more than $2,500.00, or if such person was at the time of the said offense a sexually delinquent person, may be punishable by imprisonment in the state prison for an indeterminate term, the minimum of which shall be 1 day and the maximum of which shall be life. As amended P.A. 1952, No. 73, Sec. 1, Eff. Sept. 18.

750.338a Same; female persons

Sec. 338a. Any female person who, in public or in private, commits or is a party to the commission of, or any person who procures or attempts to procure the commission by any female person of any act of gross indecency with another female person shall be guilty of a felony, punishable by imprisonment in the state prison for not more than 5 years, or by a fine of not more than $2,500.00, or if such person was at the time of the said offense a sexually delinquent person, may be punishable by imprisonment in the state prison for an indeterminate term, the minimum of which shall be 1 day and the maximum of which shall be life. As amended P.A. 1952, No. 73, Sec. 1, Eff. Sept. 18.

750.338b Same; between male and female persons

Sec. 338b. Any male person who, in public or in private, commits or is a party to the commission of any act of gross indecency with a female person shall be guilty of a felony, punishable as provided in this section. Any female person who, in public or in private, commits or is a party to the commission of any act of gross indecency with a male person shall be guilty of a felony punishable as provided in this section. Any person who procures or attempts to procure the commission of any act of gross indecency by and between any male person and any female person shall be guilty of a felony punishable as provided in this section. Any person convicted of a felony as provided in this section shall be punished by imprisonment in the state prison for not more than 5 years, or by a fine of not more than $2,500.00, or if such person was at the time of the said offense a sexually delinquent person, may be punishable by imprisonment in the state prison for an indeterminate term, the minimum of which shall be 1 day and the maximum of which shall be life. As amended P.A. 1952, No. 73, Sec. 1, Eff. Sept. 18.

2. Definitions and General Elements

People v. Schmitt
275 Mich. 575

TOY, J. Defendant was charged in the information with having committed "the abominable and detestable crime against nature with one Kella Anderson."

He waived jury trial, and, after trial by the court, was convicted and sentenced to be confined in the Michigan State Prison of Southern Michigan for a term of 2 to 15 years.

On appeal defendant claims that Act No. 328, Sec. 158, 159, Pub. Acts 1931, apply to the crime of sodomy as defined by common law, and do not apply to the act here proven by the people to have been committed by defendant.

The penetration proved by the prosecution was per os.

The trial court held that the statute applied to such an act, and was not limited to the common-law definition of sodomy.

We think the trial court was in error.

In construing a statute wherein a public offense has been declared in the general terms of the common law, without more particular definition, the courts generally refer to the common law for the particular acts constituting the offense. 8 R. C. L. p. 334.

This rule is followed in Michigan. People v. Hodgkin, 94 Mich. 27 (34 Am. St. Rep. 321); Peck v. Molhoek, 249 Mich. 360; Garwols v. Bankers Trust Co., 251 Mich. 420.

At common law, penetration per os did not constitute sodomy, or the "crime against nature." Rex v. Jacobs, R.

& R. 331 (168 Eng. Rep. 830); Munoz v. State, 103 Tex. Cr. App. 439 (281 S. W. 857); State v. Johnson, 44 Utah, 18 (137 Pac. 632); Koontz v. People, 82 Col. 589 (263 Pac. 19); State v. Murry, 136 La. 253 (66 South. 963); People v. Boyle, 116 Cal. 658 (48 Pac. 800); Kinnan v. State, 86 Neb. 234 (125 N. W. 594, 27 L. R. A. (N. S.) 478, 21 Ann. Cas. 335).

The history of legislation in this State relative to this offense will be found in People v. Hodgkin, supra. There we recognized the common-law definition as applicable to the statute. Since then there has been no change in the act, except in relation to the degree of proof required, and to the penalty. The legislature has shown no disposition to depart from the common-law definition, therefore it remains. Garwols v. Bankers Trust Co., supra. This is evidenced further from the fact that the offense of fellatio is now prohibited and made felonious by Act No. 328, Sec. 338, Pub. Acts 1931, which reenacted Act No. 198, Pub. Acts 1903. See People v. Swift, 172 Mich. 473.

The act committed by defendant does not come within the provisions of Act No. 328, Sec. 158, 159, Pub. Acts 1931, therefore the proof being at variance with the information the conviction is set aside and the defendant discharged.

NORTH, C. J., and FEAD, WEST, BUTZEL, BUSHNELL, and EDWARD M. SHARPE, JJ., concurred. POTTER, J., took no part in this decision.

People v. Dexter
6 Mich. App. 247

FITZGERALD, J. On August 9, 1965, a complaint and warrant were issued against Harvey James Dexter, charging him with the following offenses:

Count 1: Being a male person, did then and there in a private place, to-wit, North American Van Lines, 3110 North Turner street, city of Lansing, county of Ingham, State of Michigan, attempt to procure the commission by a male person, to-wit, Edwin Lee Woodard, of an act of gross indecency, in violation of CLS 1961, Sec. 750.338 (Stat Ann 1954 Rev Sec. 28.570).

Count 2: Did then and there assault one Edwin Lee Woodard with intent to commit the crime of gross indecency, a felony contrary to the provisions of CLS 1961, Sec. 750.85 (Stat Ann 1962 Rev Sec. 28.280).

Count 3: Did then and there feloniously attempt to commit the abominable and detestable crime against nature, to-wit: sodomy, with Edwin Lee Woodward, by having unnatural carnal copulation with said Edwin Lee Woodard, contrary to CLS 1961, Sec. 750.158 (Stat Ann 1962 Rev Sec. 28.355).

Count 4: Did then and there assault one Edwin Lee Woodard with intent to commit the crime of sodomy, a felony, contrary to the provisions of CLS 1961, Sec. 750.85 (Stat Ann 1962 Rev Sec. 28.280).

The jury returned a verdict of guilty on all four counts. Dexter was sentenced to 3 months to 5 years on counts 1 and 3 and 9 months to 10 years on counts 2 and 4, all to run concurrently.

Appellant raises the question of whether the counts charging gross indecency merged into the sodomy counts. Michigan follows the common-law definition of sodomy. People v. Hodgkin (1892), 94 Mich 27. At common law, sodomy covered only copulation per anum. "Penetration per os did not constitute sodomy, or the 'crime against nature'," People v. Schmitt (1936), 275 Mich 575, 577, and cases therein cited. The legislature has shown no inclination to depart from the common-law definition of sodomy. Penetration per os, fellatio, is prohibited by the gross indecency statute. People v. Schmitt, supra. The elements of gross indecency and sodomy differ.

In the case at bar, there was testimony from the complaining witness that the defendant did attempt penetration per anum. He further testified that the defendant sought to have an act of fellation performed on him. Thus, both sodomy and gross indecency were properly in issue and there was no merger of counts. . . .

The contention that the gross indecency statute is unconstitutionally vague is not tenable. In People v. Hicks (1893), 98 Mich 86, the Supreme Court commented on the statute which makes taking indecent and improper liberties a crime. The Court said:

"In this case, as in State v. Millard, 18 Vt 574 (46 Am Dec 170), it may be said that 'no particular definition is given by the statute of what constitutes the crime. The indelicacy of the subject forbids it and does not require of the court to state what particular conduct will constitute the offense. The common sense of the community, as well as the sense of decency, propriety, and morality which most people entertain, is sufficient to apply the statute to each particular case, and point out what particular conduct is rendered criminal by it'."

This general principle was later applied to acts of gross indecency in People v. Carey (1922), 217 Mich 601. The Court stated at 603:

"The information in the language of the statute informed defendant of the crime for which he was to be tried. It should not state the evidence by which it is to be proved, nor should it describe the particular act charged."

Statutes of the indecent liberties or gross indecency type penalize "conduct that is of such character that the common sense of society regards it as indecent and improper'. People v. Szymanski, (1948), 321 Mich 248, 252. The gross indecency statute is not vague or bereft of guidelines.

Defendant did not object to the instructions given the

jury on gross indecency even though he was given an express
opportunity to do so. This failure of timely objection
waives any right the defendant might have had to object now
to the instructions. People v. Mallory (1966), 2 Mich App
359; GCR 1963, 516.2.

The other questions raised by appellant have been considered and deemed without merit.

Affirmed.

QUINN, P. J., and T. G. KAVANAGH, J., concurred.

People v. Askar
8 Mich. App 95

T. G. KAVANAGH, P. J. Defendant was convicted of sodomy.
He appeals.

The appeal makes five assertions of error - the first
questioning the sufficiency of the evidence, the second
challenging the construction of the statute as forbidding
anal intercourse between male and female, and the remaining
three asserting that the trial court's rulings and the conduct of the prosecutor prevented the defendant from having
a fair trial.

Concerning the sufficiency of the evidence we find no
error. There was indeed evidence of the commission of the
offense charged and since the weight of the evidence and
credibility of the witnesses is for the jury's consideration we will not disturb their findings in this regard.
See People v. Petrosky (1938), 286 Mich 397; People v. Sch-
ram (1965), 1 Mich. App. 279.

Similarly we are not persuaded of error in the construction of the statute. The defendant maintains that the term
"mankind" as used in the statute does not include women.

"It is a cardinal rule of statutory construction that the
legislative intent must be gathered from the language used,
if possible, and that such language shall be given its ordinary meaning unless a different interpretation is indicated." Goethal v. Kent County Supervisors (1960), 361 Mich.
104, 111. "Mankind" is a generic term embracing all of humanity. Black, Law Dictionary (4th ed 1951), p 1115. There
is nothing in the statute to indicate that the legislature
used the term in a more restrictive sense.

The statute does not define the crime of sodomy. The
Michigan Supreme Court has held that in construing the
statute we must refer to the common law for the particular
acts constituting the offense. People v. Schmitt (1936),
275 Mich 575. At common law, sodomy is a carnal copulation
between human beings in an unnatural manner. 2 Wharton,
Criminal Law and Procedure, Sec. 751; 2 Bouvier, Law Dictionary (8th ed 1914), p 3088. The act which defendant is
alleged to have performed clearly falls within the terms of

962

this definition. We hold that such conduct constitutes
the crime of sodomy under our statute. . . .
(Reversed on other grounds.)

QUINN and McGREGOR, J. J., concurred.

People v. Livermore
9 Mich. App. 47

HOLBROOK, P. J. Defendant Julie Livermore, was charged
with, and convicted by jury trial of, committing an act of
gross indecency with another female person contrary to CLS
1961, Sec. 750.338a (Stat Ann 1954 Rev Sec. 28.570(1)). Defendant was sentenced to a term of 1-½ to 5 years in the
Detroit house of correction.

The pertinent facts are as follows: On the evening of
July 6, 1965, defendant visited Mrs. Carolyn French at the
public camping grounds at Sunrise lake in Osceola county,
Michigan. Mrs. French had been tent-camping with her 4
children at Sunrise lake for several days.

About 9 p.m. that same evening, defendant and Mrs. French
were observed, by complainant Jerry Branch and others, to
be in close bodily contact with each other, which continued
for approximately 1 hour. The defendant and Mrs. French then
entered the latter's tent.

Later, on receiving a complaint, Troopers Robert Bratschi
and LeRoy Fladseth of the Michigan State police, proceeded
to the Sunrise lake camping grounds. They arrived there
about midnight, talked to the complainant and others and
then stood within 15 feet of the French tent. Obscene language and conversation indicative of sexual conduct occurring between 2 female persons was overheard by the troopers
for about 10 minutes. From the information received from
complainant, the obscene language and conversation, and
noises overheard, the troopers took action under the belief
that a felony had been committed or was being committed at
that time. They approached the tent, identified themselves
as State police officers, and requested admittance; there
was no reply; the troopers unzipped the outer flap, and aided by a flashlight observed a cot located directly in front
of the doorway on which defendant and Mrs. French were lying, partially covered by a blanket; the 2 females were advised that they were under arrest and after taking several
flash pictures, the troopers permitted them to dress in
private. . . .

The applicable statute, CLS 1961, Sec. 750.338a (Stat
Ann 1954 Rev Sec. 28.570 (1)), reads in part as follows:

"Any female person who, in public or in private, commits
or is a party to the commission of, or any person who procures or attempts to procure the commission by any female
person of any act of gross indecency with another female

person shall be guilty of a felony."

Defendant claims on appeal that since the information charges a "public place", evidence of events occurring inside the tent were inadmissible. It is her contention that the tent was being used as a residence and therefore was a "private place"even though pitched in a public camping area.

In ruling on defendant's motion to suppress, the written opinion of the trial judge stated:

"Defendants in the individual cases above have moved to suppress films and photographs taken by and the testimony of two State police officers at a tent belonging to defendant French in the public park at Sunrise lake,Osceola county, on the night of July 6, 1965. It is the contention of defendants that the photographs taken and observations made by the police officers were without their consent and the result of an unauthorized entry by the police officers into said tent which had the status of a private residence.

"The motion was made before Honorable Rupert Stephens, now deceased, and was submitted upon the basis of a transcript of testimony taken upon the preliminary examination of the defendants.

"For the purposes of argument, the court will consider the tent as the equivalent of a private residence notwithstanding its location in a public park. The question thereupon is, did the officers make a lawful entry therein upon reasonable grounds for believing that a felony had been committed within.

"It is the opinion of the writer who has succeeded to the case upon the death of Judge Stephens, that the testimony of the officers at the preliminary examination indicated an observation by them of conversations, over a period of 10 minutes during which period the officers were standing approximately 15 feet from the tent, of abnormal and unlawful conduct within the tent by 2 females. The conversations need not be described in length; sufficeth to say that they were indicative of sexual conduct occurring between 2 female persons, conduct of such nature as to constitute gross indecency, a felony under the laws of the State of Michigan, and of such nature as to indicate to the average person with reasonable certainty that the female persons so speaking were engaged in such conduct. Upon hearing such conversations and upon concluding, as they did conclude and as they were justified in reasonably concluding, that the statute had been violated, they were entitled to make an entry for the purpose of making an arrest and this they did. The evidence obtained and their observations made following their lawful entry may properly be received in evidence and the motions to suppress are denied."

Defendant's motion to suppress went only to the proofs - i.e., defendant did not at any time prior to trial file a motion to dismiss the information as being defective in

substance. Had this been done, the prosecution could have
moved for an amending of the information. In any event,
the exact place of the crime whether public or private is
not a material element of the offense of gross indecency. . . .

Review of the record and disposition of the previous
questions raised by appellant constrain us to conclude
that the trial court properly denied defendant's motion to
dismiss. We find that the evidence presented by the prosecution was sufficient to sustain defendant's conviction.

Affirmed.

BURNS and McGREGOR, JJ., concurred.

3. Final Draft – Michigan Revised Criminal Code

(Sexual Misconduct)

Sec. 2305. (1) A person commits the crime of sexual
misconduct if: . . .

(c) He engages in deviate sexual intercourse with another person without the latter's consent.

(2) Sexual misconduct is a Class B misdemeanor.

Homosexual intercourse. All homosexual activity, whether
consented to or not, and whether indulged in by minors or
adults, is heavily punished by Michigan statutes. Assault
with intent to commit sodomy or gross indecency is a felony
punishable by up to ten years imprisonment (C. L. 1948,
Sec. 750.85). The "abominable and detestable crime against
nature" is a felony punishable by up to 15 years imprisonment (C. L. 1948, Sec. 750.158). Emission need not be proven
and any sexual penetration, however slight, is legally sufficient (C. L. 1948, Sec. 750.159). Gross indecency between
males, whether in public or private, is a felony punishable
by up to 5 years imprisonment (C. L. 1948, Sec. 750.338),
and equivalent punishment is provided for like activity between females (C. L. 1948, Sec. 750.338a). In all of these
sections a "sexually delinquent person" receives an indeterminate sentence with a maximum of life.

Other deviate sexual activity. The statutory definition
of sodomy includes intercourse with an animal (C. L. 1948,
Sec. 750.158). Intercourse with a dead body is not covered
by statute.

*   *   *   *   *

Section 2305 provides three types of criminal activity.
The first is sexual intercourse by a male with a female
without her consent. The chief impact of Sec. 2305 (1) (a)
is to continue the concept of statutory rape. The definition of consent in Sec. 2330 is such that a girl under sixteen

is legally incapable of consenting to intercourse. However, only males less than 21 years old fall into this category, because sexual intercourse by a male 21 or older with a girl 15 or younger is third-degree rape under Sec. 2312. if the girl is under 14 and the male 18 or older, sexual intercourse becomes second-degree rape under Sec. 2311. The purpose of Sec. 2305 (1) (a) is to penalize intercourse between minors who do not differ more than 7 years in age span, provided the girl is 14 or 15 years old.

The second subsection continues the basic coverage of the present Michigan statute penalizing a female over 15 years old who has intercourse with a boy under 15 years (apparently 15-year-old girls are sexless, or non-predatory) (C. L. 1948, Sec. 750.339). However, the age of the victimized male partner is set at the same point provided in Sec. 2305 (1) (a). Subsection (1) (b) provides the outside limit of criminality for a woman who has voluntary intercourse with a minor male; rape is limited to acts initiated by a male, and sodomy does not include heterosexual vaginal intercourse.

The third subsection covers deviate sexual intercourse without consent. This means that only homosexual conduct with a person less than 16 years old constitutes sexual misconduct, provided the defendant partner is less than 21. HOMOSEXUAL CONDUCT IN PRIVATE BETWEEN CONSENTING ADULTS IS NOT CRIMINAL UNDER CHAPTER 23 AS PRESENTED IN THIS DRAFT. Deviate sexual intercourse is defined in Sec. 2301 (b) as any act of intercourse involving the sex organs of one person and the mouth or anus of another. Therefore, Sec. 2305 (1) (c) also includes male-female contacts of this nature, if there is no consent.

It should be noted that the definition of "sexual intercourse" is (sic) Sec. 2301 (a) continues the traditional rule that slight penetration only is required and emission not required. Private activity between spouses is totally outside the Draft, because "deviate sexual intercourse" as defined in Sec. 2301 (b) excludes activity between husband and wife, and the definition of "female" in Sec. 2301 (d), a term of art in the rape sections (Sec. 2310-2315), is limited to a woman not married to the actor. For purposes of chapter 23, however, a special definition of marriage is provided. If a couple is living as man and wife, they are married for purposes of this Chapter even though as a matter of domestic relations law they might be viewed as unmarried, and indeed as legally incapable of contracting a lawful marriage. Conversely, if there is a judicial decree of separation, the couple is deemed not married even though no decree of divorce has been entered. This is intended to provide the same protection to the person of the wife against unwanted sexual advances from her husband (taking the most usual situation) that Sec. 3240 (2) provides for property which the wife has following separation. It is, however, slightly more limited than Sec. 3240 (2) in that a judicial decree of separation is required under Sec. 2301 (d), and not simply a de facto separation.

Note on bestiality and necrophilia. The present statutes penalize bestiality (C. L. 1948, Sec. 750.158) but not necrophilia (intercourse with a dead body). Conduct of this nature is rare and is of course pathological. No special coverage of either practice is provided in this chapter. If any prosecutions are brought for this sort of activity and no defense of mental defect or disorder is or may be made under Sec. 705 the information can be laid under Sec. 5560 (abuse of corpse) in the instance of necrophilia and Sec. 5565 (cruelty to animals) in a case of bestiality.

(Sodomy in the First Degree)

Sec. 2315. (1) A person commits the crime of sodomy in the first degree if:

(a) He engages in deviate sexual intercourse with another person by forcible compulsion; or
(b) He engages in deviate sexual intercourse with a person who is incapable of consent by reason of being physically helpless; or
(c) He engages in deviate sexual intercourse with a person who is less than 11 years old.

(2) Sodomy in the first degree is a Class A felony.

Committee Commentary

The section is derived from New York Revised Penal Law Sec. 130.50. Its coverage is discussed in the Commentary to Sec. 2315 to 2317 below.

(Sodomy in the Second Degree)

Sec. 2316. (1) A person commits the crime of sodomy in the second degree if, being 18 years old or more, he engages in deviate sexual intercourse with another person less than 14 years old.

(2) Sodomy in the second degree is a Class C felony.

Committee Commentary

The section is derived from New York Revised Penal Law Sec. 130.45. Its coverage is discussed in the Commentary to Sec. 2315-2317.

(Sodomy in the Third Degree)

Sec. 2317. (1) A person commits the crime of sodomy in the third degree if:

(a) He engages in deviate sexual intercourse with a
person who is incapable of consent by reason of some factor
other than being less than 16 years old; or
(b) Being 21 years old or more, he engages in deviate
sexual intercourse with a person less than 16 years old.

(2) Sodomy in the third degree is a Class A misdemeanor.

Committee Commentary

The section is derived from New York Revised Penal Law
Sec. 130.40. Its coverage is discussed in the Commentary
to Sec. 2315 to 2317 below.

Committee Commentary to Sec. 2315 to 2317

Relationship to Existing Law

An (sic) indicated in the Commentary to Sec. 2305, present Michigan law covers all homosexual acts and all heterosexual intercourse other than vaginal. Very heavy felony
penalties attach to these prohibited activities. Heterosexual vaginal intercourse is not a crime in Michigan, however, unless it constitutes seduction, incest or adultery.
The Draft rests on the premise that there is no more reason to penalize private consensual homosexual acts between
adults than there is to penalize non-marital heterosexual
intercourse. To some both are equally immoral, to others
both are equally distasteful, to still others distinctions
may be drawn. However, the experience in Michigan and elsewhere has been that efforts to control changing sexual mores
by law, and particularly by criminal law, are doomed to failure. Seduction (see Commentary to Sec. 2305) is still a
prohibited act, but it has fallen into total disuse in the
past fifty years. Adultery, too, remains a crime in form
only. Private activity cannot effectively be regulated;
when prosecutions for private activity are sought, they are
sought by intermeddlers or by a disgruntled relative.
Furthermore, efforts to cope with homosexuality by criminal prosecutions are inconsistent both with medical experience and with the general doctrine of responsibility
in the Draft. Medical writings approach consensus that homosexuality is symptomatic of psychological disorder, stemming from a failure to achieve mature psychic development,
and that it cannot be cured unless the underlying psychological deviation is cured (see the medical authorities summarized in George, Legal, Medical and Psychiatric Considerations in the Control of Prostitution, 60 Mich. L. Rev. 717,
753-57 (1962); Sexual Behavior and the Law 434-77 (Slovenko
ed. 1964)). Criminal penalties are no more able to cure
homosexuality than they are mental disease or defect, and
Sec. 705 exempts persons in the latter category from criminal responsibility. There may also be an incipient problem
of cruel and unusual punishment, based on the analogy to the

decisions holding that an addict cannot be punished for
his addiction (Robinson v. California, 82 S. Ct. 1417, 370
U.S. 660, 8 L. Ed.2d 758 (1962)) or a chronic alcoholic for
being intoxicated (Driver v. Hinant, 356 F.2d 761 (4th Cir.
1966)).

Moreover, most arrests are made through police vice squad
decoys (see The Consenting Adult Homosexual and the Law: An
Empirical Study of Enforcement and Administration in Los
Angeles County, 13 U.C.L.A. L. Rev. 643-686-742, 795-97 (1966));
enforcement is often discriminatory.

However, homosexual activities based on compulsion, or
perpetrated on a young person or on anyone incapable of resisting the deviate sexual advance, are completely imper-
missible. A violent homosexual assault is as dangerous to
the victim as a heterosexual attack. Fear, anger or resentment is as much a by-product of a homosexual attack on an intoxicated or physically helpless person as it is of a heterosexual assault. If there is concern for the welfare of a
mental incompetent when there is a heterosexual contact,
there is as much concern when the contact is homosexual or
otherwise aberrant. Homosexual activity with a child going
through the transition from pre-pubertal sexuality to mature
sexual adjustment exposes him to much greater danger of last-
ing phychological damage than does a heterosexual contact,
except perhaps for an incestuous relationship. All of these
acts are made criminal by the Draft. Public sexual acts are
included in the concept of disorderly conduct. In general,
what would be criminal heterosexual activity under the heading of rape is sodomy in a corresponding degree if it involves deviate sexual intercourse.

Therefore, Sec. 2317 elevates what would otherwise be
sexual misconduct under Sec. 2305 to the felony range if
the victim is unable to consent because of mental defect or
mental incapacity, or if the victim is less than 16 and the
actor 21 or older.

Sodomy in the second degree corresponds to rape in the
second degree; Sec. 2316 applies if the victim is less than
14 and the actor 18 or older.

Sodomy in the first degree corresponds to rape in the
first degree. Section 2315 is violated if deviate sexual
intercourse is effected through forcible compulsion as defined in Sec. 2301 (h) if the victim is physically helpless as defined in Sec. 2301 (g) or if the victim is less
than eleven years old.

Though the primary concern is with homosexual contacts,
the definition of "deviate sexual intercourse" in Sec. 2301
(b) includes non-vaginal heterosexual intercourse, other
than between spouses.

D. Indecent Liberties, etc.

    1. Michigan Compiled Laws (1948)

750.336 Child under 16, indecent liberties; penalty

Sec. 336. Any person or persons over the age of 16 years, who shall assault a child under the age of 16 years, and shall take or attempt to take indecent and improper liberties with the person of such child, without committing or intending to commit the crime of rape or the crime of sodomy or gross indecency upon such child, shall be guilty of a felony, punishable by imprisonment in the state prison for not more than 10 years, or by fine of not more than $5,000.00, or if such person was at the time of the said offense a sexually delinquent person, may be punishable by imprisonment in the state prison for an indeterminate term, the minimum of which shall be 1 day and the maximum of which shall be life. As amended P.A. 1952, No. 73, Sec. 1, Eff. Sept. 18; P.A. 1954, No. 51, Sec. 1, Eff. Aug. 13.

750.145 Same; contributing to neglect or delinquency of

Sec. 145. CONTRIBUTING TO NEGLECT OR DELINQUENCY OF CHILDREN - Any person who shall by any act, or by any word, encourage, contribute toward, cause or tend to cause any minor child under the age of 17 years to become neglected or delinquent so as to come or tend to come under the jurisdiction of the juvenile division of the probate court, as defined in section 2 of chapter 12a of Act No. 288 of the Public Acts of 1939, as added by Act No. 54 of the Public Acts of the First Extra Session of 1944, and any amendments thereto, whether or not such child shall in fact be adjudicated a ward of the probate court, shall be guilty of a misdemeanor.

750.145a Accosting, enticing or soliciting child for immoral purposes

Sec. 145a. Accosting, enticing or soliciting child. Any person who shall accost, entice, or solicit a child under the age of 16 years with intent to induce or force said child to commit an immoral act, or to submit to an act of sexual intercourse, or an act of gross indecency, or any other act of depravity or delinquency, or shall suggest to such child any of the aforementioned acts, shall on conviction thereof be deemed guilty of a misdemeanor, punishable by imprisonment in the county jail for not more than 1 year.

750.145b Same; second offense, penalty

Sec. 145b. Any person who shall be adjudged guilty a second or any subsequent time of a violation of the preceding section of this act, the offense being charged as a second or subsequent offense, shall be guilty of a felony.

2. Definitions and General Elements

People v. Hicks
98 Mich. 86

LONG, J. Respondent was convicted on an information charging him with having made an assault on one Elsie Hoertz, a female child of the age of eight years, and taking indecent and improper liberties with her person.

The prosecution was brought under section 9314b, 3 How. Stat., which provides:

"If any male person or persons over the age of 14 years shall assault a female child under the age of 14 years, and shall take indecent and improper liberties with the person of such child, without committing or intending to commit the crime of rape upon such child, he shall be deemed a felonious assaulter, and on conviction thereof shall be punished by imprisonment in the State prison not more than 10 years, or by fine not exceeding $1,000, or both such fine and imprisonment, in the discretion of the court."

The respondent was a man 62 years of age. On the day in question, he went to the rear of the house of the child's father, ostensibly to see him, but was told by the mother that her husband was not at home but would return in about 20 minutes. Back of the house was a shed, in which was the child cracking some nuts. The respondent entered the shed, and what took place there is in dispute between the respondent and the child. It becomes necessary to state the claims of the parties, in view of the charge of the court.

The child says that when he entered the shed he said: "What pretty legs you have got." She said: "Can't you see my legs there?" He then put his hand under her clothes, - as she expresses it, "under my pants," illustrating where he put his hand by putting her hand to her side. She told him she would tell her mother, and at once went into the house. The mother of the girl was called as a witness. She stated that her daughter came in, and told her that the man picked up her dress, and reached way up under her clothing, to her private parts. The witness was permitted, under objection, to detail the whole conversation with her daughter.

The respondent testified in his own behalf that he found the girl cracking nuts; that she was sitting on a block; that he bent down on one knee in front of her, and took the hammer and cracked some; that he got to fooling with her about them, taking some from her; that she commenced to crack one, and he was going to get it, or reached to get it, when she, sitting straddle of the block, put up her knee to hold him off, and that he took hold of her leg, and moved it away, to get the nut; that he put his hands upon her in no other way. She said she would tell her ma, and went into the house. He left immediately after that, and did not wait to see her father. . . .

It is contended by respondent's counsel that, to constitute the offense under this statute, the respondent must be shown to have taken liberties with the private parts of the child. We do not think the act susceptible of that construction. The Legislature evidently did not intend so to limit its meaning. The offense is in taking indecent and improper liberties with the person of such child. Surely, the Legislature did not intend that the offense should not be regarded as committed unless the indecent liberties were taken with the private parts of the child. It certainly would be indecent for a man to place his hands upon certain other parts of the body of a female child, with intent to take liberties with her. "Indecent and improper liberties with the person of such child" means such liberties as the common sense of society would regard as indecent and improper. In this case, as in State v. Millard, 18 Vt. 577, it may be said that "no particular definition is given by the statute of what constitutes this crime. The indelicacy of the subject forbids it, and does not require of the court to state what particular conduct will constitute the offense. The common sense of the community, as well as the sense of decency, propriety, and morality which most people entertain, is sufficient to apply the statute to each particular case, and point out what particular conduct is rendered criminal by it." The prosecution in that case was for indecent exposure of the person.

We think there was manifest error in the charge. The court stated what took place between the parties in the shed up to the time when the respondent said he attempted to take the nut from the child, and added, "So far they both agree." The parties did not agree up to the point. On the contrary, the respondent positively denied that he put his hands upon the girl, or that he had any intent to commit any indecency. If his story be true, he was without fault, and could not have been convicted of an assault even; while, if the story of the girl be true, he was addressing indecent language to her from the outset, and had committed an offense against her. The way the case was left to the jury under this charge could not but have prejudiced his case.

The theory of the defense was not stated to the jury in the general charge. The jury should have been told that, if they believed the respondent's testimony, it was their duty to acquit. We think the charge unfair in this respect.

The verdict and judgment must be set aside, and a new trial ordered.

McGRATH, GRANT, and MONTGOMERY, JJ., concurred with LONG, J. HOOKER, C. J., concurred in the result.

People v. Sanford
149 Mich. 266

GRANT, J. The indictment in this case contains two counts. The first charges a felonious assault upon one Mary I. Batson, a female 12 years of age, with intent to

972

commit the crime of rape. The second charges the respondent with taking indecent and improper liberties with the person of Mary I. Batson, without committing, or intending to commit, the crime of rape. The respondent was convicted of assault and battery. The evidence on the part of the people is that the respondent pursued the girl, who ran from him, caught her, threw her upon the floor, and put his hand upon her person under her clothes above her knee, and tore her underskirt. The respondent testified that he had a scuffle with her on the porch, but that it was a friendly scuffle; that she grabbed a pocket piece from his hand; and that he got hold of her and took it away from her.

The evidence was sufficient to sustain a verdict of assault and battery, if the jury believed the story of the girl. They found the assault and battery, but evidently without the intent to commit the crime of rape, or without having taken any indecent liberties with her person. The judge instructed the jury as follows:

"If you are not able to say beyond a reasonable doubt that the respondent is guilty of one of these two offenses, to wit, of assault with intent to commit the crime of rape, or taking indecent or improper liberties with her person, if you should find beyond a reasonable doubt that he took hold of her in an insulting and lustful manner, threw her down on the floor, or placed his arms around her waist in an insulting and improper manner, you would be justified in finding him guilty of assault and battery."

The main point raised is that the crime of assault and battery is not included in either of the offenses charged in the information and the court erred in instructing the jury that he might be convicted of that crime. We need not determine the question whether the respondent could have been convicted of assault and battery under the first count, where no battery is specifically alleged. A battery is not necessarily, though usually, involved in an assault with intent to commit rape. The better practice is for the prosecutor to allege a battery if he intends to rely upon it. An assault and battery is necessarily involved in the crime of taking indecent and improper liberties with a female child under the age of 14 years, as provided in 3 Comp. Laws, Sec. 11719.

"Any indecent liberties taken with the person of a female against her will is an assault and battery." Tiffany on Criminal Law (4th Ed.) p. 685.

It follows that the respondent was properly convicted under this count. No requests were preferred upon this point. Other errors are assigned, but they are not of sufficient importance to discuss.

We find no error, and the conviction is affirmed.

McALVAY, C. J., and CARPENTER, HOOKER, and MOORE, JJ., concurred.

WIEST, J. Defendant was convicted of an assault upon
a girl, 13 years of age, and taking indecent and improper
liberties with her person, and prosecutes review by appeal.

Under the conviction the lesser offense of assault was
merged in the major crime. The court instructed the jury:

"I imagine that I can believe that a man would put his
arm around a child, a girl of the age of Florence Cotton,
with intent to take indecent liberties. He is guilty the
minute he touches her, of the offense. It rests with his
intent. What does he intend to do? These crimes are effected by beginning rather subtly and approaching the worst
degree of the crime later on. In my estimation, a man who
has the wrong intent may start with even the placing of his
hand on the shoulder of a female child, not necessarily
around her. If he has the intent to follow these actions
up, there is no particular place where it begins, if he has
the intent to accomplish something that is vilely wrong as
against this particular female, there is no particular place
where the touching of her or the assault itself becomes indecent liberties, becomes the crime of indecent liberties,
if it is just a sequence of what he begins in the first
place and intends to follow up. It might even be the laying of a finger on her, if the intent is to follow it up.
It is necessary to touch the body in order to bring this
kind of a crime within the statute. I was going to say to
this jury, and I don't have to say it, that any man 44 years
of age, the father of seven children, three of whom are
married, who would go to bed as this man admits he did,
with this girl, that that might take care of the question
of assault in itself, but I don't have to go that far. If
this man laid his hands on this little girl, laid a hand on
her shoulder, or a finger on her cheek, or an arm around her
waist, with the intent to follow his act up, he is guilty
of taking indecent liberties with this female child."

The instruction was erroneous and highly prejudicial
in that it permitted a verdict of guilty of taking indecent and improper liberties upon a finding of assault with
intent to commit that crime.

An assault or an assault and battery is necessarily involved in the crime of taking indecent and improper liberties with a female child under the age of 14 years. People v. Sanford, 149 Mich. 266; People v. Dupree, 175 Mich.
632; People v. Place, 226 Mich. 212.

The major crime of taking indecent and improper liberties
is not committed by an intent, short of consummation. The
liberties, penalized by the statute, are such "as the common sense of society would regard as indecent and improper."
People v. Hicks, 98 Mich. 86; People v. Healy, 265 Mich. 317.

The trial judge seems to have had the idea that intent was

involved. Ordinarily this would have placed an undue burden upon the prosecution but in this case, as given in the instruction to the jury, it was a weapon against the accused and held him guilty if his intent was bad in even touching the shoulder of the girl.

The prosecuting attorney claims that the error mentioned was cured by the following instruction:

"Before you can find the defendant guilty, you will have to find that the defendant actually took some indecent and improper liberties with the person of Florence Cotton, as charged in the information. As I said before, it will have to be some physical act. . . . That is, he cannot be convicted unless you find that there was some physical connection between him and this girl, made with intent to commit indecent liberties, or to follow up his act and gain the confidence of this girl, until he might accomplish whatever purpose he set out to accomplish, and you find that to be indecent. Before you will be justified in finding him guilty, you must be satisfied that he committed some physical act which, in the light of all the facts, was indecent and improper, or a chain in the entire act, which, if you find it to be more than what the court suggested, the laying of his hand on her shoulder, or his arm around her waist, was a part of the whole act which he had the intention to commit, which , in the light of all the facts, was indecent and improper in its nature, and contrary to the sense of decency, and by which he actually assaulted her person."

This still carried the question of intent and was so connected with the mentioned previous instruction as to be but further confusion of the real issues.

The prosecuting attorney asks for affirmance on the ground that there has been no miscarriage of justice.

Defendant has a right to have a jury pass upon the evidence under proper instructions. This right he has not had. The record has been examined and the error found of such a character and so prejudicial to defendant's rights as to command reversal and a new trial.

The conviction is reversed with a new trial and defendant remanded to await such trial.

NORTH, C. J., and FEAD, BUTZEL, BUSHNELL, EDWARD M. SHARPE, and POTTER, JJ., concurred. TOY, J., did not sit.

People v. Healy
265 Mich. 317

SHARPE, J. The information in this case charged the defendant with taking indecent and improper liberties with the person of a female child 10 years of age. Upon the trial she testified that defendant, standing in front of

975

his house, said he had a job for her and would pay her a nickel; that she went into the front room with him, and that he said they would better go into the kitchen as some-body might see them; that in the kitchen he told her to sit down; that she "was wearing bloomers with rubber bands in the bottom, he pulled up both legs of the bloomers about half way between the knees and the thigh," and told her he was going to draw a picture; that he had a paper and sat down in a chair and began drawing her legs with a pencil; that some of the other children called to her and she want-ed to go and he gave her a nickel and told her not to tell anybody and she said "yes."

The defendant testified that he worked in an automobile plant and that painting was a "side line" with him; he had taken drawing lessons in school and had painted about 10 pictures; that he had drawn faces, but not a picture of a living person; that this child was the first model he ever had. He described what occurred as she did, and said he asked her not to tell because "she started whimpering, I thought she would go home crying, and something would be thought wrong." He was at that time 41 years of age. Dr. Byers testified that he had purchased a picture from the defendant and "knew he was an artist."

The case was tried before the judge without a jury. He stated:

"In this case it does not appear that the respondent was guided by any immoral motive or any immoral intent; it does not appear that he was guided by passion or lust, or that he intended to place his hands in any manner upon the pri-vate parts of this little girl. Had he so intended there was ample opportunity to do that."

He, however, found that defendant's conduct was "impro-per" and convicted him "of taking improper liberties."

The purpose of the statute (Act No. 328, Pub. Acts 1931, Sec. 336) is to punish male persons who take indecent and improper liberties with the persons of female children. The liberties referred to are such "as the common sense of society would regard as indecent and improper." People v. Hicks, 98 Mich. 86, 90. Had the father or mother been pre-sent, it is doubtful if they would have objected to what was done by the defendant. The record discloses no inde-cent and improper liberties taken with the person of the little girl.

The conviction is set aside and the defendant discharged.

McDONALD, C. J., and WEADOCK, POTTER, NORTH, FEAD, WIEST, and BUTZEL, JJ., concurred.

People v. Szymanski
321 Mich. 248

CARR, J. Defendant was convicted in the recorder's

court for the city of Detroit of the crime of taking indecent liberties with the person of a 9-year-old girl,
without committing or intending to commit the crime of rape,
in violation of Act No. 328, Sec. 336, Pub. Acts 1931 (Comp.
Laws Supp. 1940, Sec. 17115-336, Stat. Ann. Sec. 28.568).
The information filed in the case alleged that the offense
was committed on the 26th day of May, 1945, in the city of
Detroit. It was the claim of the prosecution on the trial
that the conduct charged against defendant occurred in a
certain theater on the afternoon of the date alleged. Defendant's testimony discloses that he was 26 years of age
at that time. Trial by jury was waived and the case was
heard before the court. Defendant has appealed from the
verdict and sentence.

It is claimed on behalf of defendant that the evidence
in the case was insufficient to establish with the requisite degree of certainty that the offense charged was actually committed. The statute cited provides:

"Any male person or persons over the age of sixteen years,
who shall assault a female child under the age of sixteen
years, and shall take indecent and improper liberties with
the person of such child, without committing or intending
to commit the crime of rape upon such child, shall be guilty
of a felony."

The child against whom the offense is claimed to have been
committed, herein referred to as the complaining witness,
testified that she entered the theater in company with a
younger sister and another girl 10 years of age. The children sat together and the youngest fell asleep. A man,
claimed by the people to have been defendant, sat down beside the complaining witness. In describing the alleged offensive conduct, she further testified:

"As soon as he moved in and sat down, he put his hand up
my dress. I think I told Adrien to move over, so she did;
then I moved over a seat and he moved over a seat, too. He
put his hand on the bare skin of my leg, but he didn't move
his hand very high, though, up my dress or whatever it was
I was wearing. I didn't tell Adrien why I wanted her to
move over until after I got out of the show because I was
scared. I was so scared I didn't know what to do. He did
it until the show was over, I guess, and then I went out
with Adrien in a hurry and I told her; then I went home and
told my mother, and my mother came back with Adrien."

It is argued by defendant's counsel that the conduct
described in the testimony quoted was not sufficient to constitute the offense defined by the statute. Reliance is
placed on language found in the opinion of this Court in
People v. Hicks, 98 Mich. 86. There the defendant was charged with the crime of taking indecent liberties with the person of a female child, and the child against whom the offense was claimed to have been committed gave testimony

similar in character to that of the complaining witness in the instant case. However, in the Hicks Case, the child's mother was permitted to detail a conversation in which the child made statements indicating that defendant had taken more objectionable liberties with her person than her testimony on the trial suggested. In holding that such testimony by the mother was incompetent and prejudicial, the Court expressed doubt if, without such testimony, the jury would have convicted of any greater offense than assault and battery. If is significant to note that the Court did not state that a verdict of guilty of the more serious offense charged could not have been sustained on the basis of the testimony of the occurrence as given by the girl. It is significant to note also that in the case cited defendant was apparently well acquainted with the girl and with her parents. The case was reversed, not because of the insufficiency of competent evidence to establish the offense, but because of error in the admission of the testimony in question and also error in the charge of the court.

In the case at bar, the circumstances surrounding the offense charged against the defendant were materially different from those involved in People v. Hicks, supra. Here the parties concerned were not acquainted, and there is nothing in the record to indicate that the complaining witness had ever previously seen the man who sat beside her in the theater. The testimony is undisputed that he placed his hand on her bare leg under her dress, and that he kept it there for some time. The circumstances under which the act was done indicate the motivating purpose and intent. Clearly, the occurrence was not accidental. The fright of the complaining witness at the time and her subsequent complaints to her companion and to her mother are significant. The statute penalizes conduct that is of such character that the common sense of society regards it as indecent and improper. People v. Healy, 265 Mich. 317; People v. Visel, 275 Mich. 77. The offense against the person of the complaining witness, as detailed in her testimony, was of such character as fully to justify the conclusion of the trial judge that the offense charged in the information had been committed. The claim that the corpus delicti was not sufficiently established is without merit. People v. Lakin, 286 Mich. 282. . . . . . . The verdict and sentence are affirmed.

BUSHNELL, C. J., and SHARPE, BOYLES, REID, NORTH, DETHMERS, and BUTZEL, JJ., concurred.

People v. Noyes
328 Mich. 207

SHARPE, J. On April 14, 1949, an information was filed in the circuit court of Kalamazoo county charging defendant with the crime of statutory rape and also charging defendant

978

with taking indecent liberties with the person of a female child under the age of 16 years. Upon trial by jury, defendant was convicted of taking indecent liberties with such child.

The information charged that the offense occurred on January 10, 1947. The record shows that defendant was married and living with his wife and 2 children. On the day in question, defendant's wife was in a hospital following the birth of a third child. The complaining witness lived with her parents next door to where defendant and family lived. At the time the alleged crime was committed, she was 11 years of age and unusually well developed for a girl of that age. She had, by the consent of her mother, been given some information on sexual matters by defendant.

The girl testified that her mother had been taking care of defendant's children on the day in question; that between the hours of 4:30 and 6 p.m., defendant returned to his home; and that the following occurred:

"I was straightening up the bedroom when he came home, and he came in the bedroom. He talked a little bit, and then put his hands -. He said 'Hi'; then he put his hands on my breasts and played with my breasts. This was through my dress. Then he reached his hands under the dress and played with my privates. That was on my bare flesh. This took place in the bedroom at his home. I was right on the bed, but not all the time. When he was feeling of my privates, I think I was sitting on the bed.

"Q. Tell us what happened from there on?
"A. He then - he had intercourse with me.
"Q. What do you mean by intercourse?
"A. He put his privates in mine.
"Q. You are sure that happened?
"A. Yes.
"Q. How long did that take place, do you know? How long did he keep his privates in yours?
"A. I don't remember.
"Q. What did he do then?
"A. Well, what do you mean?
"Q. You say he put his privates in yours; then what?
"A. Well, then he took it out and I went out of the room."

She also testified that on prior occasions she had intercourse with defendant. Defendant denied that he had committed any crime with or upon the girl and claimed that on the day in question he arrived home between 5:30 and 6 p.m., but that he did not see her there on that day. He also claimed that the charge was brought against him because there had been trouble between his family and that of the complaining witness.

The cause was submitted to a jury who returned a verdict of not guilty of rape, but guilty of taking indecent liberties with a female child under the age of 16 years.

Upon leave granted, defendant appeals and urges that there was a total lack of evidence to sustain a conviction under the indecent liberties statute. CL 1948, Sec. 750.336 (Stat Ann Sec. 28.568). It should be noted that the crime of taking indecent liberties is not a lesser offense to the crime of rape. See People v. McGovern, 306 Mich 427. One may be prosecuted under an information in which both offenses are charged. See CL 1948, Sec. 767.82 (Stat Ann Sec. 28.1022)

There was testimony from which a jury could have convicted defendant of the crime of rape and in our opinion there is evidence from which a jury could convict defendant of the crime of taking indecent liberties. In the case at bar, the jury evidently did not believe that a rape had been committed. There is evidence that defendant put his hands on the girl's breasts and played with her privates on the bare flesh. There can be no question that such actions are indecent. We reject defendant's claim that there was no testimony to support the charge of taking indecent liberties.

It is also urged that the trial court was in error in failing to instruct the jury on the elements constituting the crime of taking indecent liberties. It appears that the trial court gave the following charge to the jury:

"The burden of proof, members of the jury, in a criminal case rests with the people, and the people must prove by legal testimony and beyond a reasonable doubt a state of facts which will justify conviction. The burden is upon the people during the entire trial to satisfy you and each of you as to the guilt of the defendant, and they must so satisfy you beyond a reasonable doubt of the defendant's guilt of the crime charged. . . .

"The second count in the information charges an offense known as taking indecent and improper liberties with a female child under the age of 16 years. The statute defining this offense, so far as the same is material, provides as follows, and I quote the statute:

"'Any male person or persons over the age of 16 years who shall assault a female child under the age of 16 years, and shall take indecent and improper liberties with the person of such child, without committing or intending to commit the crime of rape upon such child, shall be guilty of a felony.'

"Before this defendant can be convicted of this charge, the second charge of indecent liberties, in other words, it must appear that he made an assault upon the complaining witness, that is, that he laid hands upon her in such a manner as to constitute an assault, and took indecent and improper liberties with her person.

"Indecent and improper liberties with the person of such child means such liberties as the common sense of society would regard as indecent and improper. No particular definition is given by the statute of what constitutes this crime. The common sense of the community as well as the sense of

decency and propriety and morality which most people entertain is sufficient to apply the statute to each particular
case and point out what particular conduct is rendered criminal by it, that is, by the statute."

The principal objection to this charge is that in instructing the jury, the court failed to use the term "without committing or intending to commit the crime of rape."
We note that the trial court in instructing the jury read
the statute relating to the crime of taking "indecent and
improper liberties" and in doing so included the following
words: "without committing or intending to commit the crime
of rape." In our opinion the reading of the statute relating to the crime is an instruction to the jury and is to be
considered by them as any other given instruction. The
failure of the trial court to repeat this element of the
crime is not error. . . .

No prejudicial error being found sufficient to grant a
new trial, the judgment of conviction is affirmed.

BOYLES, C. J., and REID, NORTH, DETHMERS, BUTZEL, CARR,
and BUSHNELL, JJ., concurred.

3. Final Draft - Michigan Revised Criminal Code

(Sexual Abuse in the First Degree)

Sec. 2320. (1) A person commits the crime of sexual
abuse in the first degree if:

(a) He subjects another person to sexual contact by
forcible compulsion; or
(b) He subjects another person to sexual contact who
is incapable of consent by reason of being physically helpless; or
(c) He subjects another person to sexual contact who
is less than 11 years old.

(2) Sexual abuse in the first degree is a Class C felony.

Committee Commentary

The section is adapted from New York Revised Penal Law
Sec. 130.65. Its relationship to existing law is discussed
in the Commentary to Sec. 2320 to 2322 below.

(Sexual Abuse in the Second Degree)

Sec. 2321. (1) A person commits the crime of sexual
abuse in the second degree if:

(a) He subjects another person to sexual contact who
is incapable of consent by reason of some factor other than
being less than 16 years old; or

981

(b) He subjects another person to sexual contact who is less than 14 years old.

(2) Sexual abuse in the second degree is a Class A misdemeanor.

Committee Commentary

The section is adapted from New York Revised Penal Law Sec. 130.60. Its relationship to existing law is discussed in the Commentary to Sec. 2320 to 2322 below.

(Sexual Abuse in the Third Degree)

Sec. 2322. (1) A person commits the crime of sexual abuse in the third degree if he subjects another person to sexual contact without the latter's consent.

(2) A person does not commit a crime under this section if:

(a) The other person's lack of consent was due solely to incapacity to consent by reason of being less than 16 years old; and

(b) The other person was more than 14 years old; and

(c) The actor was less than 6 years older than the other person.

(3) Sexual abuse in the third degree is a Class B misdemeanor.

Committee Commentary

The section is adapted from New York Revised Penal Law Sec. 130.55. Its relationship to existing law is discussed in the Commentary to Sec. 2320 to 2322 below.

*   *   *   *   *

Committee Commentary to Sec. 2320 to 2322

Relationship to Existing Law

Activities preliminary to illicit or criminal sexual acts are penalized under present law. Assaults with intent to commit rape, sodomy or gross indecency constitute a felony (C.L. 1948, Sec. 750.85). Accosting, enticing or soliciting a child under 16 for immoral purposes is a misdemeanor (C.L. 1948, Sec. 750.145a); upon a second or subsequent conviction the act becomes a felony (C.L. 1948, Sec. 750.145b). Taking indecent liberties with a child under 16, not involving the commission of or intent to commit rape, sodomy or gross indecency on the child, is a felony (C.L. 1948, Sec. 750.336). The touching does not have to be of the child's genitalia; "(t)he common sense of the community, as well as the sense of decency, propriety, and morality

which most people entertain is sufficient to apply the
statute to each particular case, and point out what particular conduct is rendered criminal by it." (People v. Hicks,
98 Mich. 86, 56 N.W. 1102 (1893)). One conviction was based
on the fact that the defendant placed his hand on a little
girl's leg while she sat in a darkened theatre (People v.
Szymanski, 321 Mich. 248, 32 N.W.2d 451 (1948)). The typical
case, however, involves more obviously sexually-motivated
touchings (People v. Noyes, 328 Mich. 207, 43 N.W.2d 331
(1950) (breasts and genitalia)). The crime requires "immoral intent"; an amateur painter did not violate the statute when he hiked a young girl's skirt and sketched her
leg (People v. Healy, 265 Mich. 317, 251 N.W. 393 (1933)).
It is a felony for a woman more than 15 to lewdly induce
or entice" a boy under 15 to have intercourse (C.L. 1948,
Sec. 750.339), and a felony for a male over 15 to entice or
solicit a boy under 15 to commit sodomy (C.L. 1948, Sec.
750.340).

Sections 2320-2322 provide systematic coverage of "sexual
contacts", defined in sec. 2301 (c) as any touching of the
sexual or other intimate parts of a person not married to
the actor, done for the purpose of gratifying the sexual
desire of either party. The sections therefore constitute
a special codified sexual assault.

Section 2322 provides the basic definition of sexual
abuse, which is non-consensual sexual contact. However,
so that heavy petting between contemporaries is not brought
within the coverage of criminal law, there is no criminality
if lack of consent under Sec. 2312 is based solely on the
"victim's"age, the "victim" is either 14 or 15 years old,
and the actor is less than six years older than the "victim".
As the language is drafted, the contact may be either heterosexual or homosexual.

Section 2321 corresponds in general with second-degree
and third-degree rape (Sec. 2311-2312) and second-degree
and third-degree sodomy (Sec. 2316, 2320). If inability
to consent is based on mental defect or mental incapacity,
or if the partner is less than 14, the penalties increase
somewhat, though they are still indicated within the misdemeanor range.

Section 2320 provides felony-level penalties if the sexual contact is through forcible compulsion as defined in
Sec. 2301 (h), or if it is perpetrated on one who is physically helpless or less than 11 years old. It thus corresponds to first-degree rape (Sec. 2310) and first-degree
sodomy (Sec. 2315).

E.   Indecent Exposure

    1.   Michigan Compiled Laws (1948)

750.335A   Indecent exposure

Sec. 335a. Any person who shall knowingly make any open
or indecent exposure of his or her person or of the person
of another shall be guilty of a misdemeanor, punishable by
imprisonment in the county jail for not more than 1 year,
or by a fine of not more than $500.00, or if such person was
at the time of the said offense a sexually delinquent person, may be punishable by imprisonment in the state prison
for an indeterminate term, the minimum of which shall be 1
day and the maximum of which shall be life: Provided, That
any other provision of any other statute notwithstanding,
said offense shall be triable only in a court of record.
P.A. 1931, No. 328, Sec. 335a, added by P.A. 1952, No. 73,
Sec. 1, Eff. Sept. 18, 1952.

2. Definition and General Elements

People v. Kratz
230 Mich. 334

STEERE, J. Defendant was convicted in the circuit
court of Muskegon county on September 17, 1923, of violating the provisions of section 15467, 3 Comp. Laws 1915, in
the particular that he did (as charged in the information),
"then and there designedly make an open, indecent and obscene exposure of his person in the presence of Margaret
Leversay, Lucile Leversay and Alice Jones, contrary to the
form of the statute in such cases made and provided," etc.
The material provisions of the section under which defendant was prosecuted are as follows:

"If any man or woman, married or unmarried, . . . shall
designedly make any open, indecent or obscene exposure of
his or her person, . . . every such person shall be punished
by imprisonment in the county jail." . . .

When arraigned defendant stood mute, waiving nothing,
and when the case was brought to trial his counsel interposed an objection to any testimony on the ground that the
information under which defendant was arraigned did not set
out any offense known to the law of this State. The court
held the information sufficient in that it followed the
language of the statute.
As a general rule it is held sufficient to charge the
offense in the language of the statute although in a certain class of cases it has been held not sufficient. This
belongs to that class of cases of which it was said in State
v. Millard, 18 Vt. 577 (46 Am. Dec. 170), a prosecution involving indecent exposure of the person:

"No particular definition is given, by the statute, of
what constitutes this crime. The indelicacy of the subject

forbids it, and does not require of the court to state what
particular conduct will constitute the offense. The common
sense of the community, as well as the sense of decency,
propriety and morality, which most people entertain, is sufficient to apply the statute to each particular case, and
point out what particular conduct is rendered criminal by it."

See, also, People v. Giradin, 1 Mich. 90; People v. Carey,
217 Mich. 601; State v. Bauguess, 106 Iowa, 107 (76 N.W. 508).
In the latter case the wording of the statute in stating
the offense is "any open and indecent exposure of his or her
person," as in the instant case. The statutory description
of the offense, which the information follows, contains no
words of obscure or technical meaning. The well settled and
generally known significance of the phrase "indecent and obscene exposure of the person" is the exhibition of those private parts of the person which instinctive modesty, human
decency or natural self-respect requires shall be customarily
kept covered in the presence of others.

Kratz was an elderly man who, though married, at the time
of the alleged offense apparently lived alone, on Howden
street in Muskegon Heights not far from railroad tracks and
a gas plant across the tracks on the same side of the street,
with a vacant lot between grown over with small trees and
bushes which was called by witnesses "the woods."

Margaret and Lucile Leversay and Alice Jones were school
girls respectively 12, 10 and 9 years old who passed Kratz'
place as they went to and from school. He had talked with
them as they went by, gave or offered them money at times
and a street acquaintance existed between them. Briefly
stated, the story of defendant's misconduct on September 17,
1923, is that when the two Leversay girls passed Kratz' place
at about 1 o'clock on their way to the afternoon session of
school he went out to the sidewalk and dropping a dime on it
told Margaret to pick it up, which she did not do, but the
girls then crossed over the street and went on. Kratz picked
up the dime and walked up the street past them and into the
edge of the woods, appearing to the children as they came by
and motioning them towards him and made, as they told it, an
indecent and obscene exposure of his person to them. When
they went home that evening after school he came out of his
place and walked by them saying something as he passed, and
going into the woods he circled around to the front of them.
He then asked Margaret if he did not give her a quarter the
other day to go to a show, which she admitted, and he then
said to her "I have got another one just like it, come into
the woods with me." When she asked what he wanted her to go
into the woods for he replied he would tell her when they
got there. She told him to go to the other side of the
woods and wait there, and she would come over soon. He then
started through the woods in the direction indicated. The
three children hurried to the police station and told an officer, who, after hearing their complaint, went to the place

indicated and finding Kratz waiting there took him into custody.

The Jones girl, who was going home from school with the Leversay girls that evening, saw no indecent exposure. She stated that she knew Kratz but "wouldn't take the money he gave me," and briefly related what occurred in her presence as follows:

"We had been to school that day. After school that night, he (Kratz) wouldn't let us go home. He kept making motions at us - Margaret and Lucile they told him to go on the other side and wait. And then we went and told Mr. Smith about him. We was coming right on straight and he wouldn't let us go any further from school, and kept making motions and motions at us."

A witness named Thompson who was working on the sidewalk near there testified to seeing Kratz pick money up from the sidewalk which the Leversay girl had thrown down, and also of his motioning for her.

Kratz testified that he knew the girls, had given Margaret a quarter at her request a week or more before September 17th, thought he saw them go to and come from school that day, but denied the offense charged or any other improper conduct towards these girls. Asked "Did you ever hand her (Margaret) any money and have her refuse to take it and you have to go and get it?" he replied, "I did not. I laid ten cents on the sidewalk one time and picked it up again. I didn't give it to her - just to show her I had it."

Error is urged against the charge of the court in not making plain that the exposure must be public, and it is contended that "under the charge as given a person might be convicted if the exposure was in a private place." "Public" and "private" as applied to places are not absolute in meaning but relative as used in contradistinction of each other. The statute makes no reference to place, either public or private. The gist of the offense is an intentional or designedly made "open, indecent or obscene exposure of the person," necessarily in the presence of others. The court amply, and fairly for defendant, instructed the jury on that requisite as follows:

"The term 'openly' as used in this information and in the law under which the prosecution is had, means public in the sense that it was not concealed, that it was not private, that it was made in such a place and such a manner as to be a public exposure, that it was not within a concealed place or enclosure, but that it was made publicly to the people who were there in view, and by that, gentlemen, is not meant necessarily that it was a public ground or in a public place in the sense of its being upon public property. It may have been upon private property, but it must have been openly and publicly with relation to the people that were there situate."

The court's charge fully instructed the jury in plain and impartial terms as to the nature of the offense charged, presumption of innocence, burden of proof beyond any reasonable doubt, cautioned against prejudice and, in all respects, covered the various rights of an accused in a criminal case.

Complaint is made of leading questions asked the children by the prosecutor. The eldest of the two girls who testified to the offense was a child of 12 years. When called as witnesses the situation and subject-matter upon which they were interrogated naturally tended to embarrass and, at times, confuse them. Counsel on the respective sides were impartially favored during their examination by the polite replies "Yes, ma'am" and "no ma'am." All attending circumstances presented a situation in the examination of these children bringing it within that class of cases in which it has been frequently held the trial court may without error permit a considerable degree of latitude to the prosecutor when examining immature and diffident children necessarily called as witnesses. It is noticeable that when the direct-examination of the two witnesses to the exposure reached the point in their narratives and they were asked to tell what then happened or what defendant did, each in a few simple and graphic words without leading questions or suggestion told of a vulgar demonstration to them by him constituting a designedly open, grossly indecent and obscene exposure of his person. His absolute denial raised a plain issue of fact which was left to the jury under proper instructions.

We find no reason to disturb the result. The conviction will stand affirmed.

McDONALD, C. J., and CLARK, BIRD, SHARPE, MOORE, FELLOWS, and WIEST, JJ., concurred.

People v. Ring
267 Mich. 657

BUSHNELL, J. Defendant, the proprietor and operator of a nudist colony, described as the Sun Sports League camp, was convicted of a violation of section 335, of the penal code, Act No. 328, Pub. Acts 1931.

The section reads:

"Any man or woman, not being married to each other, who shall lewdly and lasciviously associate and cohabit together, and any man or woman, married or unmarried, who shall be guilty of open and gross lewdness and lascivious behavior, or who shall designedly make any open or indecent or obscene exposure of his or her person, or of the person of another, shall be guilty of a misdemeanor, punishable by imprisonment in the county jail not more than one year, or by fine of not more than five hundred dollars. No prosecution shall be commenced under this section after one year from the time of committing the offense."

The camp, operated near State highway M-89 in Allegan county in a more or less secluded location in the country, consisted of tents, a building made of paper and another building about 8 X 10 feet in size, partially boarded up, all surrounded by a second growth of scrub oak in a clearing of about three acres. It lay about a mile and a half from the highway and was reached by a road claimed by appellant to be private.

After viewing the camp and the inhabitants thereof from an overhanging bluff on adjoining property, the officers visited the camp without a search warrant, and found about 15 or 20 naked men and women and children, best described by a neighboring property owner as "cavorting around," some on the bank of a creek and others engaged in harmless amusements such as volley ball. The group consisted of the defendant, his wife and two children, six other couples who were married, three unattached men and two other children.

At the trial, defendant's request for the exclusion of the witnesses from the courtroom was denied. This was entirely within the discretion of the court, and no abuse is shown of that discretion. People v. Burns, 67 Mich. 537.

The sheriff was permitted to testify, over objection, to what appeared to him to have been improper conduct on the part of a man and woman. This, however, did not occur in the presence of the accused. The court did not give appellant's request to charge, which was as follows:

"There was some testimony in this case from the sheriff as to the conduct of two persons upon the rollway. These persons were not under respondent's observation at the time and he is in no manner responsible for their conduct, if there was such conduct."

The failure to give the charge was not error. A jury's conception of what constitutes indecent exposure may very properly be influenced by both the purpose and result of the exposure, so that testimony as to conduct on the premises was admissible. . . .

The appellant in his brief submits the clear question:

"Is one who, on his own property, privately goes without clothing, in the presence of persons whose sense of decency, propriety and morality is not offended, guilty of a violation of Act No. 328, Sec. 335, Pub. Acts 1931?"

The answer, in the light of the facts presented in the record, is "Yes." It is clearly shown that the appellant designedly made an open exposure of his person and that of others in a manner that is offensive to the people of the State of Michigan. Such exposure is both open and indecent.

It is not necessary that the crime itself be particularly well defined. The average jury, composed of members of the community, has an instinctive realization of what constitutes a violation of the act. Instinctive modesty, human

988

decency and natural self-respect require that the private
parts of persons be customarily kept covered in the presence of others. People v. Kratz, 230 Mich. 334.

The case was fairly tried, the determination of the jury
will not be disturbed, and the conviction is affirmed.

NELSON SHARPE, C. J., and POTTER, NORTH, FEAD, WIEST,
BUTZEL, and EDWARD M. SHARPE, JJ., concurred.

People v. Hildabridle
353 Mich. 562

In separate actions, consolidated for trial and appeal,
Earl Hildabridle, Marvin Weissenborn, Harold R. Carter and
Ruth Carter were convicted of indecent exposure. Reversed.

DETHMERS, C. J. (dissenting). Defendants were convicted
by jury in circuit court of the crime of knowingly making
open and indecent exposure of their persons in violation of
CLS 1956, Sec. 750.335a (Stat Ann 1954 Rev Sec. 28.567 (1)).
The court placed them on probation for 2 years, making it
a condition thereof that each serve 30 days in the county
jail and pay a $250 fine and $100 costs. They appeal.

Two State police officers had gone on business to "Sunshine Gardens," a nudist camp operated on private property
in a secluded area. While there they had seen certain nude
persons, secured their names and obtained warrants for their
arrest. Thereafter, 1 of those 2 officers, in company with
another officer, went to the camp with the warrants to arrest the persons therein named. While there, they saw other
naked men, women, boys, and girls, out of doors, some standing, some sitting, some walking around, several in the vicinity of a pool, all exposed to the view of each other. Included were the defendants, adults, and also 4 girls, then
8, 10, 11 and 12 years of age, respectively, and a 17-year-
old boy, before whom the 4 defendants stood nude with private parts exposed. The officers then and there arrested
defendants. Their prosecutions ensued.

We decline to take the exsursion into the field of the
definitions, desirability, and delights of nudism, psychiatic
considerations or purportedly applicable quotations from the
Scriptures suggested in the briefs, or the flights of fantasy to which the subject may beckon. Consideration will
be limited to questions of law raised by appellants, of
which most are scarcely novel and none deserving of extended
discussion.

It is urged that there was illegal search and arrest on
private property; that the statute is vague, indefinite, fails
to define "open" and "indecent" exposure, is not sufficiently
explicit to inform persons as to what conduct will render
them liable to its penalties, and that it is, for these reasons, repugnant to the due process clause of the 14th Amend-

ment and void; that it does not, by its terms, apply to
the organized practice of nudism; that it is not violated
by nakedness on private property; that nudity, per se, is
not obscene and every exposure of the person not indecent,
particularly when the exposure does not offend the morals
or sense of decency of those present and there are no other
avert acts of indecency or obscenity aside from the bare
fact of nudity. These points have been considered and answered in People v. Ring, 267 Mich 657 (93 ALR 993), and the cases
therein discussed. The distinguishing feature in that case
that there was testimony that one couple was engaged in what
appeared to be improper conduct was not treated as of such
controlling importance or so vital to the reasoning and
holdings in this Court's opinion in Ring as to render them
inapplicable here. Nor are they any less so because the
statute then in effect prohibited designedly making an open
or indecent or obscene exposure, while, by reason of subsequent amendment, it now is directed to knowingly making
an open or indecent exposure. The comments on the Ring Case,
commencing at 33 Michigan L Rev 936, do not persuade us that
it ought now to be overruled. They do clearly indicate that
Ring governs and applies to the factual situation presented
here.

Though the term "exposure," qualified by such adjectives
as "open," "indecent," "obscene," "immodest," or others of
like import, be difficult of definition, the practice need
not for that reason be permitted to run rife in Michigan.
As indicated in Ring and cases therein considered, the average jury, composed of members of the community, can be expected to represent and embrace a cross section of the community thinking and moral standards which are first reflected in the legislative enactment by the people's chosen representatives and, once again, in the statute's application
to the facts of the case by the jury in arriving at its finding and verdict that certain conduct is violative thereof.
That a jury found it to have been violated by defendants' exposure of their persons to the young children in this case
and the exposure of the children themselves should be surprising to neither the pure in heart nor the lewd.

In Roth v. United States, 354 US 476 (77 S Ct 1304, 1 L
ed2d 1498), the court considered statutes couched in the same
general terms as those of the statute before us, the words
obscene and "indecent" having been employed there, as here,
without further definition. The court held that the statutes,
applied according to the proper standard for judging obscenity,
do not violate constitutional requirements of due process by
failing to provide reasonably ascertainable standards of guilt.
The court further held that obscenity is not, as defendants
here claim for nudism, within the area of constitutionally
protected freedom of speech and, finally, that the proper standard for judging obscenity, adequate to withstand the charge of
constitutional infirmity, is whether, to the average person,
applying contemporary community standards, the conduct in ques-

tion has a tendency to excite lustful thoughts. The Michigan statute depends, for its force in proscribing indecent exposure, upon employing that precise standard which inheres, as we have seen above, in jury application of the statute to the facts at bar under court instructions entirely consistent therewith, as they were in this case. The logic of Roth with respect to inapplicability of the guarantee of freedom of speech is as persuasive in a consideration of the applicability of the right to peaceably assemble, which defendants contend is violated by their convictions in this case. Nakedness has not, until now, been held an essential element of that right, and obscenity should prove as severe a limitation on that right as it was held, in Roth, to be on the right of free speech.

The claim of prejudicial remarks by the prosecuting attorney, entitling defendants to a new trial, is without merit, it neither appearing that the jury comprehended them nor that they were prejudicial in character.

The convictions should be affirmed.

CARR and KELLY, JJ., concurred with DETHMERS, C. J.

VOELKER, J. I dissent.

I dissent and vote to reverse and discharge these defendants for 2 reasons: first, because there was a total lack of proof (let alone proof beyond a reasonable doubt) of their guilt; second, because their conviction was the result of the use of evidence obtained by an illegal search.

The pertinent portion of the statute under which these defendants were prosecuted and convicted provides as follows: "Any person who shall knowingly make any open or indecent exposure of his or her person or of the person of another shall be guilty of a misdemeanor." (CLS 1956, Sec. 750.335a (Stat Ann 1954 Rev Sec. 28.567 (1)).)

First we need more facts.

The people's proofs affirmatively show that when the police arrived the defendants were sitting or standing in various leisurely attitudes alone or in family and other groups at or near a depressed pool or pond; that there was not the slightest evidence by word or gesture of any act or sign of obscenity, lewdness, indecency or immorality. Except for the fact, that they were entirely unclothed they might have been any group of people enjoying a rural week-end outing. As one of the officers testified at the trial, "Well, some were standing, others walking around, some were sitting, children were playing on playground equipment."

It also seems pertinent to further identify these defendants to see what kind of people they are. The proofs show that they are all working-class people nearing or past middle age. At the time of the trial one defendant was 62, unmarried, and had worked 42 years continuously for one employer in an automobile factory; the childless married woman defendant worked in an Ohio supermarket; her 43-year-old husband had

991

worked 16 years as a machinist for the same employer; the
father of the 3 children and remaining defendant (whose wife
has since died) had worked as an inspector in an automobile
factory for 26 years. All had previously visited the camp
and were nudists by conviction. With the exception of one
defendant who had shortly after his discharge from military
service been convicted on his plea of guilty to the larceny
of chickens in Ohio back in the depression years, it appears
that none had ever been arrested and convicted of any crime,
sexual or otherwise, except occasional minor traffic offenses.

A portion of the unrebutted testimony of the proprietress
of the nudist camp follows: This 140-acre nudist camp was
the home of herself and her husband; they had lived there
approximately 12 years and owned it for 14; they maintained
printed regulations, including a rule against drinking or
the bringing of intoxicants on the premises; violators of
this rule were requested to leave and if they failed to do
so the police were called, usually the State police. Police
response to such calls had occasionally occurred while there
were nude people in the area, none of whom were ever disturbed or arrested by the police, the last call being several
summers before; that otherwise there had been no complaints
about the conduct of people in the camp in its 14 years of
existence; that in all that time the proprietress had never
seen or heard reported any improper actions by anybody on
the premises, and that all of the present defendants had been
there before.

While this nudist camp had operated for some 14 years it
also appears that none of the various testifying officers
who participated in the arrests had ever received or heard
of any complaint against the place. The closest to a complaint was the testimony of a State trooper who said a few
disgruntled motorists whom he had ticketed in the area had
occasionally twitted him about the place. So the presumably
outraged community boils itself down to a knot of determined
police officers who for some undisclosed reason after 14
years finally made up their minds and set a trap to tip over
the place. And tip it they did.

I now turn to the legality of the search.

In his opinion my Brother states that prior to the day in
question 2 State police officers had "gone on business" to
the nudist camp and there saw certain nude persons and later
obtained warrants for their arrest and that one of these officers had still later gone to the camp with a third officer
to serve these warrants on the day that these present defendants were observed, photographed and arrested.

In view of what follows I must point out that my Brother
is somewhat in error: on the earlier "business" visit to
which he alludes only 1 of the 2 police officers was a State
policeman; the other was a detective on the Battle Creek
city police force then physically out of the city of his employment. There is another small error: both officers had
not earlier "gone on business" to the nudist camp; this claim

992

was advanced on behalf of but 1 of them: to the visit of the
city police officer who was out of his bailiwick; the State
police officer candidly testified that he accompanied the
other city police officer there for the avowed purpose of
getting evidence against any nudists he might then happen
to see.

In view of the serious question in this case on the issue
of illegal search and arrest we shall look a little further
into the precise nature of this claimed "business." The State
policeman on his cross-examination at the preliminary examination of these present defendants testified that he had gone
there on June 15, 1956, with a detective of the Battle Creek
police "on a matter that he (the latter) was concerned with."
The instant arrests were made on June 30th. This exchange
followed.

"Q. Were you there (on June 15th) for the purpose of obtaining evidence?
"A. I was with Lt. Schoder (the Battle Creek detective)
on a matter that he was concerned with and I had my camera
with me and it was my every intention to gather evidence if
there was any showing of indecent exposures."

At the trial this same officer testified that he went with
officer Schoder "more or less as company for him."
The fact is that the record in this case is barren of any
testimony that these 2 officers went to the camp on June 15th
for any other purpose than as an initial step in a plan to
conduct a later mass raid on the place. Lt. Schoder (the
Battle Creek officer who had ostensibly "gone on business"
to the camp on June 15th) testified at both the preliminary
examination and the trial of these defendants. Nowhere does
he state or remotely imply that his so-called "business" trip
to Sunshine Gardens was ever anything but solely to get the
goods on the nudist and help arrest them. Thus on cross-examination at the preliminary examination:

"Q. You accompanied Detective Whalen on the 15th of June?
"A. Yes.
"Q. And you accompanied the police officers in the raid
on the 30th of June?
"A. I accompanied them out there to serve these warrants.
"Q. I didn't ask you your reason. But you accompanied
them?
"A. You said on the raid. The reason I went was to serve
the warrants. I was going out to see if I could identify
(naming the 3 June 15th nudists).
"Q. You weren't interested in any raid?
"A. I was interested in locating those people because we
had the warrant.
"Q. And you just pitched in and helped when you got there?
"A. That's right."

So it develps that the only real or claimed "business" that
this Battle Creek police officer had out at this remote and

993

secluded nudist camp located entirely out of his bailiwick was in turn to "accompany" the man who was "accompanying" him, that is, the State police detective whose main avowed purpose or "business" in going there was somehow to find some way to get evidence on any nudists.

We should add that even if Lt. Schoder had had some legitimate business at the nudist camp on June 15th in our opinion that would still not legalize the search then made or the evidence obtained by Detective Whalen on that date (upon which he later "swore out" the warrants he ostensibly sought to serve on June 30th), else by the same reasoning police officers need henceforth merely arrange to accompany plumbers or inspectors or utility meter men, say, upon suspected private premises and thereafter legalize their then or subsequent illegal searches and arrests under the guise that they had originally accompanied someone there on "business." This cannot be sound law.

In designating the affair of June 30th as a raid we are merely adopting the frank terminology of officer Whalen during the preliminary examination and also at the trial. That he had himself a nice problem in successfully penetrating this nudist camp he conceded with admirable candor. He further testified at the examination that the camp was "a dense wild area;" that there was "some question about the gathering of evidence out there;" and that he and his fellow officers had discussed ways and means of solving the "problem in gathering evidence" and of obtaining pictures because of "the fact that it was secluded and it was difficult to get on the property without trespassing."

Further indication that the ostensible warrant-serving party of June 30th was in reality a planned raid for new and bigger game - with the warrants for other persons serving as the legal foot-in-the-door - is the fact that the 3 carloads of cruising police officers joined the first carload of 2 warrant-serving officers within less than 2 minutes of a radio call. Our experience with raids upon nudists' camps is mercifully limited, but we very much doubt that it would take 4 carloads of police officers to gather in the 3 nude defendants therein named. It seems most unlikely that the arrest of 3 naked nudists (one of them a woman) could have presented any such grave problems either of subjugation or of potential danger to the police.

To say that the admitted raid and mass arrests on June 30th was legalized under the guise of serving warrants on other people obtained by an illegal visitation on June 15th is a new wrinkle in Operation Bootstrap. The whole business of serving the warrants on June 30th appears on this record to have been a clumsy and transparent attempt to get around the vexing police problem of illegal search. Moreover (and further demonstrating the apparent police strategy), even assuming arguendo that the June 15th "business" visit of the 2 officers was legal - as the people claim - they (or at least the State policeman present) could plainly have then arrested the 3 nudists they then saw on the premises for a misdemeanor committed in their presence (CL 1948, Sec. 764.15 (Stat Ann 1954 Rev Sec. 28.874)), always assuming, as they and the people do and as we do not, that the deportment of the defendants then constituted a violation of the "indecent exposure" statute.

That one or both of these officers may have been disappointed over the results of their earlier alleged "business" visit and have wanted to wait for a bigger week-end bag, including children (June 15th was a week day; June 30th fell on a Saturday), is of course sheer speculation, but the fact is that the ultimate lack of warrants for the arrests of these defendants did not appear measurably to deter these very same officers in making their mass arrests without warrants on June 30th. (Mrs. Weissenborn took sick and died after her arrest and before this appeal; the cases of certain other nudists were continued; and it appears that still others were released after questioning.)

Despite all this my associate devotes but part of 1 sentence in his opinion to the question of the legality of the search and arrest - merely to note that the defendants had raised the issue. Yet to say that the search and arrests here were illegal is an understatement. It was indecent - indeed the one big indecency we find in this whole case: descending upon these unsuspecting souls like storm troopers; herding them before clicking cameras like plucked chickens; hauling them away in police cars and questioning them for upwards of 5½ hours; and taking still more pictures; and then, final irony, swearing out warrants that one of their own number was the aggrieved victim of an indecent exposure - of which more presently. If this search was legal then any deputized window-peeper with a ladder can spy upon any married couple in the land and forthwith photograph and arrest them for exposing themselves indecently to him.

In People v. Marxhausen, 204 Mich. 559 (3 ALR 1505), the warrantless police raided the defendant's island home in the Detroit river during his absence and found and removed contraband liquor from his home, from an improvised cellar, and also from "other points on the premises." In an eloquent and resounding opinion Mr. Justice FELLOWS struck down the search (pp 562, 563) and among other things had this to say (after quoting our State constitutional provisions against unreasonable searches and seizures and the "due process" provision):

"Like provisions are found in the Fifth Amendment to the Federal Constitution. Similar provisions are found in the constitutions of the various States of the Union. By these provisions the rights of the individual are secured; the provisions of the Federal government and its officers, and the provisions of the State constitutions securing the citizen from arbitrary, unlawful conduct on the part of the State and its officers. These provisions not only secure the individual in his person, his home, and his property from invasion through unbridled and unrestrained executive or administrative will. It ought not to be necessary to recall the fact that it is of the essence of a free government that the individual shall be secure in his person, his home and his property from unlawful invasion, from unlawful search, from unlawful seizure. The writing of these provisions into the Federal Constitution, into every constitution of every State in the Union was not an idle ceremony. With a clearness of vision our forefathers provided for a lawful search and seizure, one supported by oath or affirmation, describing the place to be searched and the person or things to be seized; and in the same section safeguarded the rights of the individual by inhibiting unreasonable and unlawful search. They provided an orderly manner for search and seizure and prohibited all others."

He then (p 565) quoted from the terse Chatham:

"'Every man's house is called his castle. Why? Because it is surrounded by a moat, or defended by a wall? No. It may be a straw-built hut; the wind may whistle around it, the rain may enter it, but the kind cannot.'"

He concludes thus (pp 566, 567):

"These events which we have but given in outline occurred within the memory of the men who formulated and adopted the Fourth Amendment. In clear and unmistakable language these men wrote into the fundamental law of the nation to be afterwards incorporated into the fundamental law of the various States of the Union the safeguard against unlawful and unreasonable search and seizure of the person and property of the citizen, irrespective of whether such unlawful and unreasonable search and seizure had the sanction of legislative approval or rested in the arbitrary will of the executive and administrative arm of the State. Does the search of defendant's premises and the seizure of his property in the instant case offend the rights secured to him by this provision of the fundamental law of the State? These officers had no search warrant issued upon oath or affirmation, no search warrant of any kind. They entered the home of defendant by command of no court, they searched his premises by virtue of no process. They justify, if at all, under administrative will and mandate not recognized by the Constitution, and unauthorized in a government of laws. That 'the end justifies the means' is a doctrine which has not found lodgment in the archives of this Court. The search and seizure detailed in this record was an unauthorized trespass and an invasion of the constitutional rights of this defendant. (emphasis added.)

"These rights of the individual in his person and property should be held sacred, and any attempt to fritter them away under the guise of enforcing drastic sumptuary legislation (no matter how beneficial to the people it may be claimed to be), must meet with the clear and earnest disapproval of the courts."

This is the case our Court pays scant lip service to in the Ring Case (p 660) and then proceeds to ignore. We now find that an island home and premises was immune from warrantless search in Marxhausen (where no question existed about the illegality of what was found) but not a nudist camp as in the Ring Case and in this case - where grave questions exist as to guilt. We believe this is to invoke the doctrine of "the end justifies the means" so eloquently warned against in Marxhausen. We further believe that this, as in Marxhausen, is to fritter away the rights of the individual in his person and property under the lofty guise of benefiting the people. It seems that we are now prepared to burn down the house of constitutional safeguards in order to roast a few nudists. I will have none of it.

If these convictions can stand, based upon this search, then police officers may henceforth raid at will the locker rooms of clubs, art classes, and exhibitions, sunbathers at homes and at picnics and beaches and virtually any private or secluded place where the officers may hope to dredge up some "dirt" and whenever they may decide by barracks-room debate that a suspected practice is immoral or indecent. It would be to say any nudity anywhere becomes both open and indecent regardless of the circumstances and simply because some irritated or overzealous police officers may think so. It would be to impose not the moral standards of the community but the moral standards of the patrolman on some of the most intimate and private concerns of human life.

If the opinion of my Brother prevails we will have found a new way to get around irksome constitutional inhibitions against unreasonable searches and seizures: 2 police officers will make a visit to such private premises as they may in their wisdom conclude they want to get the goods on; they will pretend that 1 or both of them have some "business" there; if pressed they will admit that their real business was to accompany each other; and, finally, this explanation will so completely disarm and satisfy this Court that, without any discussion, we will categorically hold that the search and subsequent use of evidence obtained thereby is entirely legal. To such a proposition I will not be a party.

I say and hold that the search and arrests in this case were unreasonable and unlawful. I shall presently attempt to show that even if the officers were there legally that what the search disclosed did not in these circumstances constitute a violation of this statute. Before doing so I shall discuss another ground for reversal.

The charging part of the various original complaints and warrants against these defendants (their cases were consolidated for preliminary examination and trial) named one or the other of individual raiding officers as the victim of the indecent exposure. These defendants were examined under such complaints and warrants and were thereafter bound over to circuit court for trial upon a testimonial record addressed to those complaints and warrants. In circuit court (and for the first time) informations were filed against them as follows: that each did "in the presence and within the view of divers good people of this State, unlawfully and designedly did make an open, indecent and obscene exposure of his person, by then and there standing,naked and uncovered to the view of said persons for a long space of time, to-wit: several minutes, to the great scandal of said people, and to the manifest corruption of their morals."

Entirely aside from the fact that there is not a shred of testimony in this long record that anyone was ever scandalized or corrupted by what took place, I consider this circumstance reversible error. So far as this record discloses the informations appear to have been changed by the prosecuting attorney without any prior leave of court; consequently these defendants were never examined or given an opportunity to be examined on the offense charged in the filed informations. This was not a routine change to correct an obvious mistake or typographical error in the complaints and warrants; this was to our mind a basic change and shift from the whole tenor of the earlier documents.

It is no answer to say that the defendants did not specifically raise the question below or here. Under our law they were entitled to a preliminary examination on the sworn complaints and warrants upon which they were arrested. They got it. If for reasons of doubt or expediency the prosecuting attorney later had serious second thoughts about the utility or wisdom of naming only one or the other of the raiding officers as the morally offended one, we think he should at least have called the change to the attention of court and counsel so that either a formal amendment could have been moved for and argued or so that counsel could timely have moved either for a continuance or, more likely, for a remand for new examination under the changed informations. We do not raise or pass on the question of the sufficiency of the informations; the point is that they differed materially from the complaints and warrants.

These people were entitled to an examination as to the identity and knowledge possessed by these anonymous new aggrieved citizens who for the first time were alluded to in the changed informations. They did not get it. They were never given a chance to be confronted by or to examine their new and nameless accusers or to prepare for trial on the basis of their possible testimony. Criminal prosecutions in this State are initiated by sworn complaint (followed by warrant) made by persons possessing knowledge of the facts; they are not initiated by informations filed by prosecutors based upon hearsay. Put another way, these defendants were tried

upon informations upon which there existed no corresponding
complaints and warrants. We think this circumstance en-
titles them at least to a new trial.
   I now pass to the basic question in this case: of whether -
all question of search aside - any violation of this statute
occurred.

   Lest I henceforth be heralded as the patron saint of
nudism (which I probably will be anyway), I hasten to pre-
face what follows by stating that I am not a disciple of
the cult of nudism. Its presumed enchantments totally elude
me. The prospect of displaying my unveiled person before
others, in beholding others thus displayed, revolts and hor-
rifies me. I think these people have carried an arguably
valid basic idea (the deliberate de-emphasis of the prevailing Western body taboo, with the anticipated lessening and
ultimate disappearance of the undoubted eroticism frequently
attendant upon such taboo - that is, the very opposite of indecency) to excessive lengths.
   Having said all that, I have at once veered to the heart
of this case. It is this: whatever I or my associates (or
the circuit judge or the prosecutor or the police, for that
matter) may personally think of the practice of nudism has
nothing to do with the case. More controlling is the fact
that there are a number of earnest people in this world (including these defendants) who do subscribe to organized
nudism and who think that it is morally, mentally and physically healthful. But we need not speculate on or defend or
attack the philosophy of nudism. The question before us is
much simpler. Were these defendants guilty of making an indecent exposure? I say no.
   It is said that there are hardy bands of sincere and
earnest folk amond us who likewise insist that all mental,
moral and physical health depends absolutely upon the regular consumption of vast quantities of bran. Others possess
a similar passion for goats' milk. Few molest them or even
bother their heads about them unless they try too strenuously
to impose or inflict their queer beliefs upon those who happen
to loathe these items. Thus, on the facts before us, do I
equate the criminality of private social nudism - at least
so far as a violation of this statute is concerned. Private
fanaticism or even bad taste is not yet a ground for police
interference. If eccentricity were a crime, then all of us
were felons.
   My Brother plants his case largely upon the Michigan <u>Ring
Case</u> and the United States Supreme court <u>Roth Case</u> in affirming these convictions, writing as follows:

   "Though the term 'exposure', qualified by such adjectives
as 'open', 'indecent', 'obscene', 'immodest', or others of
like import, be difficult of definition, the practice need

999

not for that reason be permitted to run rife in Michigan."

Is he speaking of indecent exposure or of nudism? He does not say. Whether of one or the other, there is no evidence in this record or elsewhere that either has been or is running "rife" (that is: prevalent, existing generally) in Michigan. If he means to equate one with the other (as he seems clearly to mean) then he has begged 1 of the 2 large issues in this case, entirely ignoring the other: the question of search, and I cannot agree. This is to indulge in a presumption of guilt, not of innocence; to pass a moral judgment; to assume that a statute means what one may privately want it to mean or thinks it should mean - regardless of the facts. This is further to say that all nakedness, whether public or private, whatever the circumstances, is always indecedent and criminal. I cannot agree.

From the undoubtedly valid premise that some degree of nudity must always be involved in order for an exposure to be indecent, the Ring Case and the opinion of my Brother in this case have leapt to the erroneous conclusion that nudity is synonymous with indecency; the opinions imply that the more nudity present the more indecent the exposure. Both cases proceed upon the basic assumption that nudity in itself is obscene or indecent. As I shall presently undertake to show, this is a demonstrable fallacy. If this assumption were valid few artists could continue to work from live models, or, veering somewhat to a related field, the curators of our art galleries and museums would have to turn to the cultivation of fig leaves; and that stalwart badge of middle-class respectability, the National Geographic magazine, would be banished from the hearth to the censor's shears.

My Brother further writes as follows:

"That a jury found it (the statute) to have been violated by defendants' exposure of their persons to the young children in this case and the exposure of the children themselves should be surprising to neither the pure in heart nor the lewd."

For all its emotional and rhetorical appeal, this passage states less a fact than a resounding moral judgment. Moreover it carries implications that are simply not so: it implies that these defendants were charged with exposing themselves to children and, also, with exposing the children whereas we have seen that the complaint and warrant charges only indecent exposure by these defendants before a named police officer and that the subsequent informations named nobody; it implies that the jury answered a special question or brought in some sort of special verdict, whereas the verdict was simply a general one of guilty; and it implies that the children testified at the trial, whereas they did not and moreover there is no testimony from any witness that they or anybody was scandalized or corrupted by what he saw. If the passage

discloses anything it is why my Brother thinks these defendants should stay convicted - because children were present.
Now concern for little children is always touching and understandable; and my colleague possesses no exclusive franchise
on it; but if these convictions must be affirmed simply because my associate thinks the prosecutions and the jury verdict may have been inspired by a concern for children, we suggest that there might have been other statutes and apter procedures available to such an end. Moreover, and whether other
courses were available or not, the presence of children constituted no valid ground for making an illegal search or for
arresting these defendants for an exposure which neither the
proofs show, nor obviously none of the participants regarded,
as indecent.

To my mind the presence of the children, far from accentu-
ating any indecency, was itself additional proof and insurance
that no indecency or immorality was contemplated or intended
by these defendants. It is particularly monstrous to think
that their parents would intentionally have exposed their
children to that which they thought was indecent, and if they
nevertheless had, which the people seem to claim, then the
prosecution should be censured for not taking far more drastic
action to punish all concerned and to save the children from
any repetition. So much for the presence of children in this
case.

If one concedes (which I do not) that the private practice
of social nudism constitutes a violation of the "indecent exposure" statute, the legality of the search phase of the Ring
Case cited by my Brother can at least arguably be rationalized
(something which the Court there did not attempt to do) and
distinguished from this case as follows: both the record and
report in the Ring Case show that the officers there - and
while entirely off the premises - were able to observe a
naked man and woman, the former feeling the latter's privates.
If the officers could behold such a spectacle without trespassing, presumably so could others, and since few would be
hardy enough to argue that such a public display did not constitute an act of indecent exposure, then the officers per-
force were seeing an actual misdemeanor being committed in
their presence for which they could make a lawful arrest without a warrant. And if while thus upon the premises bent upon
making that arrest (but not some 2 weeks later, as here) they
saw thereon still another person committing a misdemeanor (the
naked nudist camp proprietor in the Ring Case) it would at
least be arguable that under such circumstances the arresting-
bent police may have had a right also to arrest this brand
new misdemeanant. The search and arrest as to him would at
least have had some veneer of legality - something entirely
lacking in this present case, where all stages of the search
were conceived and born in illegality.

If instead the Ring Case means (and unfortunately the
Court's murky opinion there is susceptible of such interpretation) that police officers may without any color of authority

conduct a raid upon private property upon mere suspicion
that a misdemeanor theretofore entirely out of their presence may be taking place (which is our case), then the case
is utterly bad law, never followed in Michigan before or
since, and the Ring Case must be overruled.

One trouble (among others) in the Ring Case was that it
neglected adequately to distinguish between the question of
illegal search and arrest and the further question of whether
private nudism was or was not a violation of the then version of this statute. We were then evidently so determined
to smite nudism that we virtually overlooked the real issue
on the search and flatly assumed guilt. This short cut to
guilt is accentuated in the present opinion from which I
dissent - where the grave question of the legality of the
search is barely alluded to and the defendants' guilt is
also flatly assumed.

The Roth Case cited by my Brother had to do with the mail-
ing and public dissemination of allegedly obscene printed
matter. My Brother neglects to point out that in the Roth
Case there was a blazing dissent by Justice Douglas, joined
in by Justice Black, or that Chief Justice Warren, while
concurring in the result, filed a separate opinion expressing sharp concern over the wisdom of the broad language employed in the majority opinion. But most of all my Brother
overlooks the important fact that the Roth Case was concerned with the public dissemination of allegedly obscene writings, a situation which might have had the persuasiveness
of some analogy here if we were concerned with a public display of their nudity by the defendants in this case (as
though they had boldly walked down the main street of Battle
Creek), but certainly not to a private practice of their belief in nudism in a place so remote and secluded that the
prosecuting officials had to resort to the tactics displayed
in this case in their efforts to try to get any evidence on
them.

My Brother would swallow whole the "test" of the Ring
Case - that the average jury, composed of members of the
community, has an instinctive realization of what constitutes a violation of the act - attempting to tie it up with
some broad dicta in the majority opinion in the Roth Case
about "contemporary community standards" and similar language
impliedly questioned by the Chief Justice and flatly rejected
by 2 of the ablest justices. We have already pointed out
why we think this language in the Roth Case (and the same
would apply to the Ring Case) could not apply to the elabor-
ately private conduct of these defendants in this case. Although I say that such a test is in any event inapplicable
to these defendants, since my Brother nevertheless seeks to
apply it, we will see what Mr. Justice Douglas has to say
about such a similar test in the Roth Case (Roth   v. United
States, 354 US 476, 512 et seq.):

"Any test that turns on what is offensive to the community's

standard is too loose, too capricious, too destructive of
freedom of expression to be squared with the First Amendment. Under that test, juries can censor, suppress, and
punish what they don't like, provided the matter relates
to 'sexual impurity' or has a tendency'to excite lustful
thoughts.' This is community censorship in one of its
worst forms. It creates a regime where in the battle between the literati and the Philistines, the Philistines are
certain to win. If experience in this field teaches anything, it is that 'censorship of obscenity has almost always been both irrational and indiscriminate.' Lockhart &
McClure, Literature, The Law of Obscenity, and the Constitution, 38 Minn L Rev 295, 371. The test adopted here accentu-
ates that trend. . . .

"The legality of a publication in this country should
never be allowed to turn either on the purity of thought
which it instills in the mind of the reader or on the degree
to which it offends the community conscience. By either
test the role of the censor is exalted, and society's values
in literary freedom are sacrificed."

We join with Justice Douglas in questioning the wisdom
of such a rule even in those "public" situations where it
might otherwise be said properly to apply, but we utterly
reject any such test or rule that would make a juryman the
omniscient community litmus of that to which, by hypothesis,
neither he nor the community at large has ever been exposed.
If trained judges on this Court can disagree on the applicability of this statute to these facts, we can see no merit
and much danger in a rule that would ignore and reject our
differences in favor of the presumably infallible intuitions
of the average lay juryman; and especially is this so in
situations where, as here, the moving facts are undisputed
and the big question resolves itself largely into one of
statutory interpretation.

If private nudism is to be banished in this State as
contrary to the public morality we think the attempt must
be made by the legislature and not by the police or by this
Court, and certainly not by stretching out of shape the law
of search and seizure and the proper meaning of this statute.
That segments of the legislature itself entertained doubts
that the previous version of this statute ever applied to
the practice of nudism is shown by the fact that long after
the Ring Case and only about a year before the arrests in
this case it drafted a new statute aimed expressly at banish-
ing nudism. The house committee to which the bill was assigned appears to have refused to report it out on the ground
that existing laws were sufficient. The attorney general (now
Mr. Justice KAVANAGH) agreed, basing his decision squarely on
the then "indecent exposure" statute and the Ring Case. (1955
OAG, p234) Needless to say this Court is not bound by the
attorney general's interpretation of statutes or of our decided cases, nor is that officer at liberty - in areas where

we have written - to interpret the law contrary to his best
guess as to the meaning of our utterances, however wrong
those utterances and regardless of how that officer might
or might not otherwise feel. The most this tends to show
is that the prosecutions here were probably brought in apparent good faith - beyond showing, as noted, the doubt that
existed in the legislature itself.

Our decision in the Ring Case has been roundly criticized
in 33 Michigan L Rev 936, the writer pointing out that the
"disconcerting" result there reached was not only hard to
reconcile with the then recent Burke Case (another "nudist"
case where on substantially similar moving facts under a
similar statute the New York court reversed conviction),
but that the Ring Case stands virtually alone in its con-
trariness to the clear weight of authority throughout the
country. "The Michigan court is seemingly without precedent," the comment concludes (p 941), "in holding that an
indecent exposure occurs and the community sense of decency
is offended regardless of the accompanying circumstances.
All cases have tacitly implied that what makes the act offensive is the relationship which it bears to the public in
general or to the people there present, and some cases have
expressly pointed this out (Citing cases.)"

When student editors start sniping at our decisions with
such deadly accuracy, perhaps the time has come for all of
us to take a second long look at the Ring Case. Instead of
sniping I prefer using in this instance a blunt instrument.
The plain fact is that the Ring Case is less a legal opinion
than an exercise in moral indignation. An aroused judge has
instead used this Court as a platform from which to tell the
world what he thinks about such queer new-fangled shenanigans
as nudism. Now moral indignation is all very well, and many
of us might do with more of it, but to indulge in it at the
expense of basic constitutional rights and individual liberties can be an expensive and dangerous luxury. Moral indignation is a poor substitute for due process. The embarras-
sing Ring Case is hereby nominated for oblivion.

Finally neither the Ring Case nor my Brother's opinion in
this case makes any effort to dredge below the surface and
grapple with the probable meaning of this statute. The effort is long overdue and I shall now proceed with the grappling and dredging. I shall pose some hypothetical situations in an attempt to show what this statute means - and
also what it does not mean. No effort will be made to cover
all possible situations nor shall we seek exactly to define
or limit indecent exposure (which would probably neither be
possible nor desirable); and while we concede that there are
doubtless certain twilight areas difficult of pragmatic definition, we equally insist that such areas are relatively
narrow and that there exist and it is possible to delineate
broad zones of behavior lying clearly within or without the
proper purview of this statute.

1: Richard Rowe is the drum major of his college; it is the half time of the big homecoming football game; the band is swinging into the traditional college march. The goose-stepping drum major is strutting with peacock magnificence; all eyes are upon him. Suddenly his skin-tight trousers rip and let go unmistakably exposing his nude person to 50,000 cheering fans. Would this be an indecent exposure under our statute? Clearly not. And why not? Because the exposure was obviously accidental, poor Richard did not mean it, indecently or otherwise - and the crowds of hysterically mirth-stricken beholders would not possibly take it that way. Any such prosecution would be laughed out of court.

Comment: We note that the unmistakable exposure here was as public and open as one could readily imagine, but the hapless Richard is guiltless of indecent exposure for at least 2 reasons: he did not mean it that way and it was not taken that way.

2: Richard Rowe is a chronic sleepwalker. One night at midnight he goes for a somnambulistic stroll and walks naked down to the corner mailbox to mail an imaginary letter. A strange woman beholds him and screams for the police. They arrive and take poor Richard to the station. Upon police confirmation of his affliction would he be prosecuted for indecent exposure? Probably not, and if he were any court or jury in the land would doubtless let him go. Why? Because he didn't mean it, there was no intention of indecency, he didn't even know what he was doing.

Comment: Here the woman "exposee" was no less shocked and horrified than if Richard were a lusting pathological exhibitionist who carefully planned it that way - but still there is no valid case because her sense of shock did not combine with his conscious intent to indecently expose his person to her. We are now ready for a tentative definition: The statute envisages a combination of 2 things: a reasonably inferable indecent intention by the exposer as well as a reasonably-to-be expected reaction of shock and shame on the part of the probable exposee.

3: Richard Rowe does the same thing as in example 2 except that this time he carefully planned it that way. The same woman beholds him. Is he guilty of indecent exposure? Most certainly yes.

Comment: Where the exposure is openly, knowingly and deliberately made before others who may reasonably be expected to be shocked by the performance, the exposure is clearly indecent.

4: Richard Rowe intentionally does the same as in example 3, but the woman is stone blind and being led by a seeing-eye dog and no one else sees him as Richard scampers home. Was there an indecent exposure? Probably not, because there was no exposee present who was conscious or aware of what would otherwise have clearly been an indecent exposure.

5: The police find sleepwalker Richard Rowe of example

2 wandering aimlessly about the public streets.

6: The police find naked Richard Rowe the non-sleepwalker flitting from behind tree to tree along a residential street but with no one else present.

7: The patrolling police behold Richard Rowe standing in silhouette with his privates exposed in the bedroom window of his lighted home.

Comments on 5, 6 and 7: No indecent exposure in 5 (as in 2) because no intention. An open and indecent exposure in 6 and 7 because of the deliberate intention to indecently expose the person and the reasonable chance that he would be seen by a passer-by who would be shocked and outraged by the sight.

8: Richard Rowe embraces nudism and, along with the defendants in this case, parades in a nude missionary expedition down the main street of Battle Creek and all are gathered in by the police.

Comment: Clearly guilty of indecent exposure because the exposure is openly and knowingly made before persons who may reasonably be expected to be shocked and outraged by the performance and there is no question of illegal search or arrest involved. The claimed pureness of heart or sincere beliefs of the exposers here will not save them because they will be deemed to know that the probable beholders (unlike those at a private nudist retreat) would not share their beliefs and would instead be shocked by the sight.

9: The police place a ladder against Richard Rowe's home and climb it and look through the curtained window into the bathroom where he and his wife and 3 small children are naked and having sun lamp treatments or taking baths.

Comment: No crime of indecent exposure because though there is a common naked exposure of mixed sexes knowingly and openly made, none of the participants meant or took it indecently and, further, any other persons who might reasonably be expected to see them and be shocked thereby could only do so by trespassing or making an illegal search.

10. Our present case.

Comment: No crime of indecent exposure for precisely the same reasons as in example 9 above.

We have now seen that the statute envisages a combination of 2 things: an actual or reasonably inferable indecent intention by the exposer joined with a reasonably-to-be-expected reaction of shock and outrage by the probable or potential exposees. We have seen that the absence of one or the other element can be fatal to guilt. Where, as here, both elements are missing and neither the exposers intend their exposure indecently nor do the exposees remotely take it that way (of which there is not a contrary shred of proof in this record) then it follows all the more that there can be no crime of indecent exposure under our statute.

The crime of indecent exposure naturally suggests the presence of an "exposee" as well as an exposer. Who were the exposees in this case? The raiding and warrantless police? The complaints and warrants say yes, but, as noted, the information either says otherwise or leaves the issue in doubt. We recoil from the idea that police can invade private premises and (after stoically taking photographs) claim they were shocked by what they beheld. Was it the proprietress, Mrs. Adams, who helped run the place for so many years? The question answers itself. Was it the defendants and other adult nudists? We are not told, but again we find it hard to swallow the idea that dedicated and convinced participants in the practice of private social nudism - themselves nude - may become suddenly scandalized or corrupted by the sight of their companions and turn around and prosecute each other for indecent exposure.

Perhaps (along with my Brother) the people meant the now motherless Weissenborn children. They were mercifully spared participation in the trial of this case, but to surmise without a shred of evidence that they were corrupted by seeing their mother and father without any clothes (along with some other mostly middle-aged people some distance away) is to gratuitously invest childhood with evil and erotic tendencies before mere nakedness and to reject the observations and researches of virtually every anthropologist and sociologist who has contributed to the literature of human mores. See Sumner, Folkways, under index entry "Nakedness." Also, see 33 Michigan L Rev 936 for similar references.

Guilt or innocence of indecent exposure is not a matter of measuring the amount of human flesh exposed; one does not caliper the revealed epidermis and certify guilt as increasing by the square inch; the indecency of an exposure is always a matter of intent to be gathered from all of the circumstances. The plain fact is that often the less the exposure the more plainly indecent it becomes, by that very circumstance alone; the plain fact is that usually there is involved an aggressive and unmistakably erotic attempt to focus the attention of others solely on the sexual organs of the exposer, and, as any weary patrolman knows (if some judges may have forgotten), most usually on a certain engorged portion of the male anatomy. To link these poor defendants, however deluded, with such gross and panting immorality is a kind of back-handed indecency in itself.

Most simply put, then, where the exposure is neither meant nor taken as indecent there cannot be a violation of this statute. Unless this over-long opinion were written entirely in vain, I should by now have demonstrated at the very least that a reasonable doubt exists that this statute applies to the conduct of these people. It is elementary under our Anglo-American legal system that where such a doubt exists the vote must be for innocence.

In a world locked in a death struggle between the David of democracy and the Goliath of giant totalitarianism, it serves David illy for the court of last resort of one of democracy's greatest industrial bastions - the State of Michigan - to put its stamp of approval on such a dubious departure from our traditional procedures and historic safeguards against invasion of our individual rights - the right to be secure from unreasonable search and seizure and the right in all criminal proceedings to receive the benefit of any reasonable doubt.

That these defendants here may have been raided, arrested and prosecuted from the loftiest of motives is no answer; it is no excuse that the bold invasion of individual rights and liberties unfolded here was motivated by pureness of heart. These defendants can take little comfort that they were prosecuted with love and their conviction possibly accompanied by a warm glow of community virtue. The busiest snoopers and moral vigilantes among us are doubtless convinced of 3 things: of their own unfaltering rectitude; that what they do is always for our own best good; and that any among us who dare question the legality of their activities are soaked in sin.

For all practical purposes this is probably the court of last resort for these defendants; we are their last hope. Whatever we may privately think about the practice of nudism should not cloud our decision in this case. Our reversal of these convictions is no more an indorsement by us of nudism than our occasional necessary reversal of a murder conviction constitutes a judicial indorsement of murder. If nudism must go in Michigan it must go by right not might. The bald inescapable fact is that the prosecuting officials in this case badly over-reached themselves. The time has now come for us to say so.

The convictions here are reversed and the defendants discharged. All film and prints of the defendants in the possession of the prosecution and police shall be returned forthwith to their counsel.

SMITH and BLACK, JJ., concurred with VOELKER, J.

EDWARDS, J. (concurring). I concur with Mr. Justice VOELKER'S result in this case, but only upon the first of the grounds which he discusses pertaining to illegal search and seizure. The officers who made these arrests did so after entering upon property privately owned and posted as "private." Their justification for their entrance was a claimed attempt to serve warrants for arrest previously procured upon sworn information. The record discloses 2 warrants based upon a complaint made on June 15, 1956, pertaining to a claimed indecent exposure of the persons named on that same date.

The record discloses no attempt to serve these warrants or to arrest these people on that date or subsequently until June 30th when the entry complained of by appellants was made by the officers. It should be noted that none of the defendants-appellants in this proceeding are identified as those for whom warrants were issued. Under these circumstances, I agree with Justice VOELKER that the warrants were obtained as a subterfuge for gaining entrance and without any purpose of making the specific arrests for which they called. See Gouled v. United States, 255 US 298, 305 (41 S Ct 261, 65 L ed 647):

"The prohibition of the Fourth Amendment is against all unreasonable searches and seizures and if for a government officer to obtain entrance to a man's house or office by force or by an illegal threat or show of force, amounting to coercion, and then to search for and seize his private papers would be an unreasonable and therefore a prohibited search and seizure, as it certainly would be, it is impossible to successfully contend that a like search and seizure would be a reasonable one if only admission were obtained by stealth instead of by force or coercion."

It may, however, be argued that the invasion of these private premises by the officers was justified under the "open field" rule. Hester v. United States, 265 US 57 (44 S Ct 445, 68 L ed 898). See annotation, 74 ALR 1416, 1454.

My Brother's opinion has provided sufficient facts to indicate that the officers in question, absent lawful warrant, did illegally invade the curtilage of the dwellings here concerned.

In People v. Taylor, 2 Mich. 250, 252, this Court, adopting a quotation from Chitty, has thus defined "curtilage":

"In its most comprehensive and proper legal signification it includes all that space of ground and buildings thereon, which is usually enclosed within the general fence, immediately surrounding a principal messuage, out-buildings and yard, closely adjoining to a swelling-house, but it may be large enough for cattle to be levant and couchant therein."

If a man's house be his castle, the most casual view of the premises involved here, as portrayed in photographic exhibits, indicates the scene of this arrest was the courtyard.

This record convinces the writer that the arrests were made in violation of article 2, Sec. 10, of the Michigan Constitution (1908).

KAVANAGH, J., did not sit.

3.   Final Draft - Michigan Revised Criminal Code

(Indecent Exposure)

Sec. 2325. (1) A person commits the crime of indecent exposure if, with intent to arouse or gratify sexual desire of himself or of any person other than his spouse, he exposes his genitals under circumstances in which he knows his conduct is likely to cause affront or alarm.

    (2) Indecent exposure is a Class C misdemeanor.

Committee Commentary

The section is a modified form of Model Penal Code, Sec.
213.5.

Under the present statute, knowingly to make any open or
indecent exposure of the "person" of the actor or another is
a misdemeanor, or in the case of a "sexually delinquent person," a felony punishable by an indeterminate sentence up to
life (C.L. 1948, Sec. 750.335a). The term "openly" means
"public in the sense that it was not concealed, not private,
but that it was made publicly to the people who were there
in view, and it is not meant necessarily that it was in a
public place or upon public property" (People v. Kratz, 230
Mich. 334, 203 N.W. 114 (1925) (syll. 5)). The more controversial application of the statute has been to nudist colonies.
In one case (People v. Ring, 267 Mich. 657, 255 N.W. 373 (1934)),
the exposure by nudists to one another was considered offensive
to the "people of the state" even if not to the participants;
"(i)nstinctive modesty, human decency and natural self-respect
require that the private parts of persons be customarily kept
covered in the presence of other" (267 Mich. at 662). A
somewhat different attitude, however, is indicated in a more
recent case (People v. Hildabridle, 353 Mich. 562, 92 N.W. 2d
6 (1958)), though reversal of the nudists' conviction in the
case was based on the illegality of the search by which evidence of nudism was obtained:

"Yet to say that the search and arrests here were illegal
is an understatement. It was indecent - indeed the one big
indecency we find in this whole case; descending upon these
unsuspecting souls like storm troopers; herding them before
clicking cameras like plucked chickens; hauling them away in
police cars and questioning them for upwards of 5½ hours and
taking still more pictures; and then, final irony, swearing
our warrants that one of their own number was the aggrieved
victim of an indecent exposure . . . . If this search was
legal then any deputized window-peeper with a ladder can spy
upon any married couple in the land and forthwith photograph
and arrest them for exposing themselves indecently to him."
(353 Mich. at 572-73 (Voelker, J.))

It would appear, therefore, that invocation of the statute
against nudism is difficult if not impossible, though on
evidentiary grounds.

Section 2325 retains the basic coverage of the present
statute by penalizing any exposure of the genitalia done with
intent to arouse or gratify the actor's sexual desire or that
of another to whom he is not married, under circumstances in
which he knows his act will probably cause affront or alarm.
Under Sec. 2325, it is not the place, but the purpose of the

exposure and the likelihood of psychological alarm to others, that determine the actor's criminality.

F. Lack of Consent and Mistake as to Consent Under the Michigan Revised Criminal Code

(Lack of Consent)

Sec. 2330. (1) Whether or not specifically stated, it is an element of every offense defined in this chapter that the sexual act was committed without consent of the victim.

(2) Lack of consent results from:

    (a) Forcible compulsion.
    (b) Incapacity to consent.
    (c) If the offense charged is sexual abuse, any circumstances, in addition to forcible compulsion or incapacity to consent, in which the victim does not expressly or impliedly acquiesce in the actor's conduct.

(3) A person is deemed incapable of consent if he is:

    (a) Less than 16 years old.
    (b) Mentally defective.
    (c) Mentally incapacitated.
    (d) Physically helpless.

Committee Commentary

The section is taken from New York Revised Penal Law Sec. 130.05.

The general provision on the legal effect of consent by the person affected by the actor's conduct (Sec. 330) is adequate as a general guide. Sexual offenses, however, are a special enough case that consent provisions applicable to this chapter only are needed. A concentration of the definition of consent in one section also simplifies the language of the various sections which define crimes, because it is possible by the phrase "without consent" to incorporate the terms of Sec. 2330 by reference.

Subsection (1) lays down the general rule that consent by the victim takes the situation out of the criminal law. This produces no change in the forcible rape case, but changes the present law in most other kinds of sex offense.

Subsection (2) states that consent is wanting whenever there is forcible compulsion, as defined in Sec. 2301 (h) whenever there is incapacity to consent, further defined in subsection (3), and in the case of sexual abuse (Sec. 2320-2322), whenever there is not express or implied acquiescence to the actor's conduct.

Subsection (3) defines the limits of legal incapacity to consent. Anyone under the age of 16 is legally unable to

consent to homosexual or heterosexual activity. The age
limit used is that now embodied in the rape statute and indicated as preferred in the Model Penal Code (cf. Sec. 213.3,
213.4). The other three forms of legal incapacity are mental
incapacity, as defined in Sec. 2301 (f), and physical helplessness, as defined in Sec. 2301 (g). Usually these three
terms are used expressly in sections aggravating rape, sodomy
or sexual abuse, but their inclusion in Sec. 2330 eliminates
any possible effort to make the term "without consent" control
the more specific designation of "physically helpless" or
"mentally incapacitated".

(Mistake as to Consent)

Sec. 2331. (1) An actor does not commit a crime under
any of the sections of this chapter if the other person did
not in fact consent, but if the actor at the time he engaged
in the conduct constituting the offense did not know of the
facts or conditions responsible for the incapacity to consent,
including the age of the other person.
(2) The burden of injecting the issue of mistake under
this section is on the defendant, but this does not shift
the burden of proof.

Committee Commentary

Subsection (1) is an expanded version of New York Revised
Penal Law Sec. 130.10; subsection (2) incorporates the state-
ment of burden of injecting the issue used elsewhere in the
Draft.
The general provisions of the Draft on mistake of fact
(Sec. 325 (a)) might suffice to cover special problems of
error inherent in sexual offenses under this chapter. However, because of the lack of a satisfactory pattern of coverage of problems of mistake in case law under the present
Michigan statutes, a special statement is included in Sec. 2331.
Under the present law, mistake as to age is no defense in
the case of statutory rape, but is relevant when a female older than 15 is charged with debauching a male under 15 (People
v. Bailey, 341 Mich. 592, 67 N.W. 2d 785 (1954)). A recent
California decision (People v. Hernandez, 39 Cal. Rptr. 361,
393 P.2d 673 (1964)) applies the reasonable mistake of fact
doctrine to statutory rape, but it cannot be said at the present time that there is a general trend in this direction in
modern state cases. Other elements in sexual offenses are
also usually treated as objective acts, so that in effect the
actor is penalized for the act of intercourse on a strict liability basis. Since the initiator of sexual activity always
intends intercourse, no special indication of mens rea or culpability is required either under existing statutes or under the
Draft.
Section 2331 confirms that a mistake about the factors that
make a person legally or factually unable to consent, whether

because of age, mental defect, mental incapacity or physical helplessness, is always relevant to bar conviction. There is no requirement that the mistake be "reasonable." Since under subsection (2) the burden of injecting the issue of mistake is on the defendant, and since usually there is no other source of information about his mistake than the defendant himself, this means that in most cases he will need to take the stand on his own behalf in order to discharge his burden of injecting the issue. At this point the jury should be competent to judge his credibility, so that no "substantive" limitation of reasonableness is required.

Note on lack of chastity of sexual partner. Lack of chastity on the part of the sexual partner is not a direct legal defense under Michigan law. Evidence about prior relations between the defendant and the complainant is factually relevant, however, on the question of consent in rape (cf. People v. Gengels, 218 Mich. 632, 188 N.W. 398 (1922)) other than statutory rape, or of whether a woman who has charged seduction consented to intercourse only on a promise of marriage (People v. Clark, 33 Mich. 112 (1876)). The Model Penal Code (Sec. 213.6 (4)) makes it an affirmative defense in certain cases of corruption of minors and sexual assault that the alleged victim had promiscuous sexual relations with others. The Draft, however, contains no such provisions, on the basis that the present doctrines which utilize the test of relevancy to issues in the case, now set out in Michigan case law, are preferable, particularly in light of the amplified doctrine of mistake in Sec. 2331, and the unwarranted slanders on the complainant's sexual life that the defendant's "oath-helpers" are likely to perpetrate, particularly in third-degree rape and sexual misconduct cases.

Note on "sexually delinquent persons". In 1952 the Legislature created the category of "sexually delinquent persons", against whom indeterminate sentences of up to life imprisonment may be imposed. The statutory definition is:

"any person whose sexual behavior is characterized by repetitive or compulsive acts which indicate a disregard of consequences of the recognized rights of others, or by the use of force upon another person in attempting sex relations of either a heterosexual or homosexual nature, or by the commission of sexual aggressions against children under the age of 16." (C.L. 1948, Sec. 750.10a)

The information must allege that the defendant is a sexually delinquent person (C.L. 1948, Sec. 767.61a), and trial of the case includes evidence about the defendant's condition. Special limitations are placed on freedom of prisoners outside the walls if they were convicted for a sexual act of murder involving a sexual act (C.L. 1948, Sec. 769.2a).

These provisions, it is submitted, cannot be preserved without serious danger to fairness of trial and without impairing substantially the overall objectives of the Draft.

Permitting proof of "sexual delinquency" means that the prosecutor can spread before the jury the defendant's complete history of asocial activity, which almost guarantees his conviction.
If he engages in the activity mentioned in the definition of
"sexually delinquent person," he does so either because he is
a recidivist or because he suffers from a mental defect or disease that renders him without capacity to conform his conduct
to the requirements of law (Sec. 705), in which case he should
be hospitaliized and not condemned to a life sentence. Therefore, the term "sexually delinquent person" does not appear in
the Draft, and the existing provisions are recommended for repeal on the basis of adequate coverage elsewhere in the Draft.

G. Sex Offenses and Penal Code Revision in Michigan
          13 Wayne Law Rev. 734
                    I.
               Introduction

    The scope of this comment is limited to chapter twenty-
three of the Michigan Revised Criminal Code (Proposed Code)
entitled Sexual Offenses. Certain offenses that are collo-
quially referred to as sex offenses do not fall within the
ambit of chapter twenty-three. Among those offenses therefore excluded from consideration in this presentation are prostitution, obscenity, bigamy, incest, and adultery. While these
offenses are no less important than those included in this discussion, an in depth analysis will render a more significant
contribution than would coverage on a broader basis necessarily
relegated to superficial treatment. Offenses included in the
discussion are rape, sodomy, sexual abuse, and indecent exposure.

                         II

             Unlawful Heterosexual Conduct

A. Existing Michigan Law
    Principal among unlawful heterosexual acts is the offense
of rape. Forcible intercourse with a woman and intercourse
with a child under the age of ten were rape at common law.[1]
A series of codifications leading up to the current Michigan
rape statute[2] adopt the common law concept of forcible rape
and raise the age of consent to sixteen. The statute prohibits two separate though related offenses - forcible rape
and statutory rape.
    The first element of forcible rape is "carnal knowledge,"[3]
an archaic designation for the act of sexual intercourse.
This element of the crime is satisfied by any "penetration
however slight."[4] Since the essence of the crime is the non-
consensual imposition on the woman, the prosecution need only
show some penetration,[5] the existence of which is a question
of fact for the jury.[6] The gratification of the assailant is

irrelevant, and it is universally held that emission is not essential to the completion of the crime.[7]

Although it is not patently clear from the statute, a man does not commit rape by having sexual intercourse with his wife, regardless of her age, even though he uses force against her will.[8] Implicit in the definition of the crime is "unlawful carnal knowledge," an essential component of the common law crime. Unlawful in this context means not authorized by law, and since sexual relations between husband and wife are sanctioned by law a man who takes his wife by force is not guilty of rape.[9]

The act must be "by force and against her will."[10] As is frequently the case with antiquated statutory language, the denotative sense of this phrase is not clear. The import of this constituent of the crime is whether the woman was willing or unwilling. Clearly the element is satisfied where the victim's resistance is overcome by physical violence.[11] However, something more than the physical force necessary to the consummation of the sexual act is required.[12] A corollary of this proposition is the law's requirement that the victim resist to the "utmost."[13] While the law requires "utmost" resistance from the victim, and if she consents or yields prior to penetration there is no rape,[14] the law does not require foolhardy resistance. So if the victim's will is overcome by fear induced through threats of "great bodily harm, or danger to life or limb" the requirement of force is fulfilled.[15] The prosecution may introduce evidence reflecting on the victim's mental or physical infirmities in order that they be considered in assessing the amount of resistance required of the victim.[16]

The state of the victim's mind with respect to "unwillingness" has led to some interesting consent problems. In a Massachusetts case the defendant argued that his victim was "so drunk as to be utterly senseless," and therefore his act was not "against her will" as required by the statute since her will was inactive.[17] The court dismissed the defendant's argument stating that the essence of the statutory language was "without her consent," and since she was insensible she was not capable of consent.[18] The statutory requirement had been satisfied. While no Michigan case has specifically decided the point,[19] the preceding opinion reflects the general American rule with respect to temporary incapacity.[20]

Lack of capacity of a more permanent character such as idiocy or insanity presents yet a different problem. The weight of authority in this country is that sexual intercourse with a woman incapable of consent by reason of mental infirmity is rape.[21] An early Michigan case, apparently still good law, held that sexual intercourse with a mental incompetent was not rape unless the defendant knew that the woman was mentally deficient.[22] As a result of this requirement Michigan rape coverage is narrower than most American jurisdictions. Intercourse with a female patient of a mental institution is punishable by statute in Michigan.[23] The statute

1015

has been interpreted by the Michigan Attorney General to cover any female subsequent to the issuance of a commitment order, regardless of whether she is ever physically confined.[24] There is an obvious disharmony of reason between the case law rule and the statutory rule as interpreted. If a man is not guilty of rape by virtue of intercourse with a mental deficient unless he knows that she is mentally deficient, why should his act magically become criminal where the woman has been adjudged insane but not confined? This inconsistency should be resolved.[25]

Fraudulent procurement of consent leading to prosecution for rape appears in two general classes of cases: pretended medical treatment and pretended husbands. There formerly existed a distinction in Michigan, in the medical treatment context, between consent to the act in fact, under the guise that intercourse would somehow be beneficial to the patient's health, and consent to some treatment that turned out to be intercourse unbeknown to the patient. The latter kind of consent was tantamount to no consent at all, and therefore the act was rape. However, the former kind of consent, consent to intercourse in fact, was held to negate a charge of rape.[26] The rule of that case has since been overturned by statute, making it a felony to induce intercourse under pretext of medical treatment.[27]

The somewhat bizzare cases of fraudulently obtained consent involve the mistaken husband. Somehow the identity of the actor is mistaken for that of the victim's husband, as in a darkened room. The sham marriage is a variation of the mistaken husband situation. In these cases the defendant typically induces the victim's consent by staging a mock ceremony. The common law resolution of the mistaken husband cases has been exculpation of the defendant on the ground that the essential element of force is lacking.[28] Such instances of fraudulently obtained consent should not be placed beyond the ambit of the criminal law. Both the identity of the actor and her relationship to the actor are of determinative importance to the woman, and consent resting on such mistake of fact is equivalent to no consent at all. While the point has never been specifically decided in Michigan, there is good reason to believe that such conduct will not fall within the statute.[29]

Since the statute does not require that the victim be chaste, a prostitute may be the victim of rape. Evidence of bad reputation for chastity is admissible, however, but only for the narrow purpose of reflecting on whether the "victim" actually consented to the act.[30] Such a rule of evidence is heralded by one authority for its wisdom because "the jury usually supplies the common sense which the law itself seems to have overlooked at this point."[31]

Statutory rape is an offense designed to protect an interest quite different from that guarded by the offense of forcible rape.[32] Forcible rape is designated as a criminal act for the obvious purpose of protecting the person and

1016

feelings of females from unwilling violation. Criminality
is attached to statutory rape[33] for the purpose of protecting
females of tender years from acts of indiscretion, the
physical and sociological ramifications of which, due to
their presumed immaturity of judgment,[34] they do not fully appreciate. Like forcible rape, statutory rape requires some
penetration, and a man cannot be charged with rape of his
wife, even though she is below the statutory age, except where
he aids or abets another in the commission of the act.[35] A
woman may, of course, be the victim of forcible rape even
though she is below the age of sixteen, statutory rape being
merely a strict liability modification of common law rape.

Statutory rape significantly departs from forcible rape
with respect to the element of "force and against her will."
The cases recite in various forms this distinction by noting
that for statutory rape force is either not a necessary element,[36] irrelevant[37] or conclusively presumed.[38] These recita-
tions are distinctions without a difference, the practical
effect of which is that the act need not be accomplished by
force nor must it be against the victim's will. A fortiori
it is no excuse that the victim was willing or consented even
where she was the perpetrating party or where she lied about
her age.[39]

Since the offense of statutory rape is in the form of
strict liability, evidence reflecting on the "victim's" chastity, or more properly the lack thereof, is not admissible[40]
for the purpose of establishing consent. It has even been
held that evidence showing that the victim was a prostitute
is inadmissible.[41] Michigan courts have carved out two narrow
exceptions to this rule: lack of chastity may be shown for
the purpose of indicating that someone other than the defendant committed the crime,[42] and evidence showing the prosecutrix
to be a nymphomaniac or sexual psychopath is admissible, but
only for the purpose of reflecting on her credibility.[43]

Protection of interest parallel to those protected by the
statutory rape provision is provided by two other Michigan
statutes: carnal knowledge of a female ward[44] and debauching a male under the age of fifteen years.[45] Carnal knowledge of a female ward, under the age of eighteen, by her
guardian is designated as a felony under the statute. In
spite of the fact that this statute was enacted more than
fifty years ago, it has never been construed in any reported
case. It should be noted that, except for increasing the
age limit by two years, this statute is a duplication of the
protection afforded by the statutory rape provision.

The statute prohibiting female persons, over the age of
fifteen, from inducing or enticing a boy under fifteen to
engage in sexual intercourse designates the offense as a
felony. It is interesting to note that the statute has been
construed by only one reported case in the more than seventy
years since its enactment.[46] This statute is substantially
different from the statutory rape statute in that it requires[47]
actual knowledge that the victim is under the statutory age.

In Michigan, the seduction of an unmarried woman, despite
her age, is a felony by statute.[48] Seduction is defined as
sexual intercourse the assent to which was obtained by an
inducing promise, usually of marriage.[49] The essence of the
criminal act is the inducement of the female to deviate from
her virtuous avenue by means of promise.[50] Accordingly, some
inducing promise must be shown by the prosecution. However,
a promise of monetary compensation is not enough to sustain
a conviction.[51] Similarly, a promise to marry the woman "if"
she becomes pregnant will not support a prosecution for seduction.[52] The woman also must have been chaste at the time
of the seduction to constitute a punishable offense,[53] but
the prosecutrix is presumed to be chaste until the contrary
is shown.[54] Should the defendant in fact marry the victim
there can be no prosecution.[55]

B.   Revised Criminal Code Proposals

The Proposed Code covers unlawful intercourse in four
separate sections: rape in the first degree,[56] rape in the
second degree,[57] rape in the third degree[58] and sexual misconduct.[59]

The Proposed Code retains the prohibition against forcible
rape, without significant deviation from existing law in
language that is conducive to uniform interpretation.[60] The
archaic designation of "carnal knowledge" is abandoned in
favor of the term "sexual intercourse" which is defined as
having "its ordinary meaning and occurs upon any penetration,
however slight; emission is not required."[61]

The issue of the husband's liability for ravishing his
wife is resolved by defining a "female" as "any female person who is not married to the actor."[62] In addition, the
definition of "female" adopts the Model Penal Code approach
to situations that are closely akin to the normal marital
relationship although slightly removed in fact or in law.[63]
For the purposes of rape prosecutions, persons living together as a man and wife are considered married and spouses
living apart under judicial decree are considered not married.[64]
Where the parties have been living together as man and wife
there appears to be no good reason to impose criminal sanctions based on the artificial distinction between a de facto
marriage and a solemnized marriage,[65] especially in view of
the Proposed Code's removal of the criminal sanction from
adultery.[66] The reasons for eliminating the possibility of
a rape accusation where spouses are living apart without the
benefit of judicial decree include the substantial possibility
of resumption of sexual relations and reconciliation, coupled
with the danger of fabricated spiteful charges.[67] Existing
law is retained under the Proposed Code by rendering a husband liable, as a principal to the offense, where he solicits,
aids or abets another in the commission of rape upon his wife.[68]

The Proposed Code's substitution of "forcible compulsion"
for the present requirement of "by force and against her will"

is questionable. The draftsmen are to be applauded for
their effort to define "forcible compulsion."[69] Under the
existing statute there is no statutory definition for "by
force and against her will." The case law has forged the
descriptive term "utmost resistance," but this requirement
is sufficiently ambiguous to permit a construction that the
victim must have been physically incapable of additional
struggle against the assailant.[70] The uncertainty inherent
in the narration of such a standard to the jury is obvious.
It is doubtful that the Proposed Code's description of "forcible compulsion" as "physical force that overcomes earnest
resistance" is any improvement over "utmost resistance." In
fact the very purpose of the definition, a clearer proscription is probably jeopardized since the trial judge will not
have the benefit of case law interpretations within which to
structure his charge to the jury.

A second ambiguity with respect to the definition of
"forcible compulsion" is whether the test is to be objective,
a reasonably prudent woman under the circumstances, or subjective, the actual apprehension of the victim under the circumstances. Since the proffered definition is identical to
that contained in the New York Penal Law it seems reasonable
to assume that the draftsmen intend the same interpretation
as that set out in the New York Penal Law comments - a subjective test.[71] A choice between these criteria requires a
balancing of the policy favoring an assurance that the resistance is not feigned, half-hearted or ambivalent, against
the policy favoring protection of women from serious bodily
injury through the facilitation of prosecutions. The choice
is admittedly a value judgment, but it is submitted that it
is better to protect the interests of timid females at the
possible expense of the aggressive male.[72]

The following definition would be both more meaningful to
a jury and clearly adopt the subjective test:

Forcible compulsion means physical force that overcomes
resistance at least as great as the maximum resistance the
victim could offer under the circumstances to prevent penetration while avoiding serious risk of death or serious
physical injury to the victim or another person, including
the serious risk that the victim or another person will be
immediately kidnapped.[73]

The risk of death, injury or kidnapping of another person is
taken into account, as it is under the Proposed Code's definition, for the purpose of clarifying whether a woman who submits to intercourse as a result of risk imposed upon another
is the subject of a rape.[74] There is apparently no good reason to distinguish between the aggressor who compels submission by threats directed against the victim personally
and the aggressor who compels submission by the imposition
of risk of serious harm on another.

The "state of the victim's mind" issue is approached by
the Proposed Code in a most comprehensive fashion and with
a most interesting distinction. Sexual intercourse with a

1019

woman incapable of consent by reason of being physically
helpless[75] is classified as rape in the first degree, while
intercourse with a woman incapable of consent by reason of
mental defect[76] or mental incapacity[77] is classified as rape
in the third degree. The apparent distinction, upon which
the disparity in punishment assigned these offenses is based,
is the difference between volitional, although unreasoned,
activity and non-volitional activity. Where the intercourse
is non-volitional, i.e., physical helplessness, there is no
conscious acquiescence and no consent by definition; the aggravated character of the act merits rape in the first degree.
Where the intercourse is volitional although unreasoned due
to a permanent or temporary mental infirmity, i.e., mental
defect or mental incapacity, there is a conscious acquiescence
amounting to consent in fact but for policy reasons not consent in law; the less aggravated character of the act deserves a lesser penalty. The assessment of penalties commensurate with the grievousness of the act makes good sense.
Where the victim is "helpless" the actor is acting with the
same disregard for personal safety as a forcible rapist. However, the magnitude of the disparity in penalties is a value
judgment. Suffice it to note that first degree rape is punishable by an indeterminate term with a maximum of twenty
years,[78] and third degree rape carries a penalty of a definite
term with a maximum of one year.[79] There is, however, a not-
able ambiguity in the Proposed Code's treatment of this area.
Since the definition of mental incapacity excludes those individuals who administer intoxicating substances to themselves,
except where the act is accomplished by force or the victim
is unconscious, no conviction may be had for intercourse with
an individual so incapacitated. Whether an indictment for
sexual misconduct would be appropriate is open to speculation[80]
as that section prohibits intercourse "without her consent."[81]
Lack of consent is defined as "incapacity to consent," a circular definition for this purpose. As pointed out previously,
the "self-intoxicated" case has never been specifically decided in Michigan.[82] Presented with an opportunity, the legislature should declare the position of the law with specificity.
Where the intoxicated victim offers appropriate resistance
and the assailant sucessfully (sic) overcomes that resistance,
an indictment for first degree rape is proper. Similarly,
where the victim's cognition has been reduced to a state of
dormancy, an indictment for first degree rape should lie as
the victim is physically helpless (unconscious). The circumstances applicable to consideration here are those in which
the woman does not offer active resistance although she remains conscious. Where the mature woman has voluntarily reduced her inhibiting mechanisms to a state of ambivalence,
especially where she engages in joint indulgence in drugs
or liquor, it is ludicrous for her to claim later she has
been raped. "Conditions affecting only the woman's capacity
to 'control' herself sexually (should) not involve criminal
liability."[83]

The Proposed Code's position with respect to the cases of

fraudulently obtained consent is not clear from the comments.
It is assumed that the draftsmen advocate a general repeal
of existing criminal statutes including the statute covering
pretended medical treatment. Where the victim consents to
some medical treatment that in fact turns out to be intercourse, unbeknown to the patient, the act would fall under
the sexual misconduct section since the act of intercourse
was "without her consent."[84] However, where the victim does
consent to intercourse in fact, although she is mistaken as
to some collateral fact, it is not possible to unequivocally
declare the state of the law under this formulation. In
this category of cases are those where the woman engages in
intercourse under the guise that it will be beneficial to her
health, or with a man whose identity she mistakes for that of
her husband, or with a man she mistakenly believes to be her
husband as a result of a sham marriage. Under existing case
law these fact situations would not support a conviction for
rape due to the lack of force.[85] Presumably, the absence of
the element of force from the sexual misconduct section would
liberate these cases from the restrictive position of existing law. Since these collateral facts are essential to the
victim's grant of consent, the actor who obtains consent by
virtue of fraudulent misrepresentation of such collateral
matters should not be free from criminal liability. The uncertainty here present should be resolved by supplementing
section 2305 (1) with the following provision.

(1) A person commits the crime of sexual misconduct if:
. . .
    (d) Being a male or a female, the actor knows that the
other person is unaware that a sexual act is being committed
upon that person or that the other person submits because
that person falsely supposes that the actor is that person's
spouse.[86]

This provision requires knowledge on the part of the actor,
excluding cases of mutual mistake.
    The Proposed Code offers a number of significant and long
overdue alterations in the area of statutory rape. Initial
among the proposed changes is a subclassification of offenses
on the basis of age disparity between the male and female,
assigning penal sanctions accordingly. An individual less
than fifteen years of age is not subject to criminal responsibility, but rather his conduct falls under the Juvenile
Code and the jurisdiction of the probate court.[87] The scheme
is tabulated below for convenient reference in conjunction
with the ensuing discussion.[88]

Victim's Age	Actor's Age	Maximum Penalty
Less then 11	15 and over	20 Years (felony)
11 to 14	18 and over	5 years (felony)
11 to 14	15 to 18	90 days (misdemeanor)
14 to 16	21 and over	1 year (misdemeanor)
14 to 16	15 to 21	90 days (misdemeanor)

The Proposed Code retains coverage equivalent to the
common law by specifying that intercourse with a child less
than eleven years old is rape in the first degree.[89] A
sexual experience of this nature with a child who almost
certainly has not reached puberty,[90] is a risk in the order
of the highest magnitude[91] that reflects a "most deserving
of severe penal sanction. The remaining provisions constitute a more complex system for covering conventional statutory rape. The obvious import of this graduated scheme is
that the greater age disparity merits a more severe sanction.

Recent penal law revisions in other jurisdictions have
adopted graduated schemes of statutory rape offenses.[92] The
Michigan proposal places primary emphasis on three arbitrary
age classes of the female, considering the male's age in an
incidental fashion. The Model Penal Code approach,[93] liability
predicated on age differential as a function of the male's age
with respect to the female's age, seems simpler, more rational
and more equitable. Where the female is between the ages of
eleven and sixteen and the male is more than four years older
than the female the offense would be a felony, but where the
age disparity is four years or less the offense would be a
misdemeanor.

The rape offenses scheme provides coverage equivalent to
existing statutes on carnal knowledge of a female ward and
debauching a male under fifteen. The two significant changes
in this area are the age alterations and sharply reduced penalties for both offenses. Debauching a male under fifteen is
currently a felony punishable by imprisonment for a maximum
of five years.[94] Such conduct would fall under the proscription for sexual misconduct which makes it a misdemeanor for
a female to engage in intercourse with a male under the age
of sixteen[95] (ninety day maximum). Carnal knowledge of a
female ward under eighteen by her guardian is a felony punishable by imprisonment for a maximum of ten years.[96] Under
the Proposed Code this conduct falls squarely within the statutory rape scheme set out in the table above, the nature of the
offense being dependent upon age disparity. However, there
is a noteworthy exception in that consensual intercourse with
females over sixteen does not subjject the actor to criminal
liability. There appears to be no good reason to extend the
age limit of statutory rape to eighteen simply because the
female is a ward of the actor. The age of consent should be
dependent upon sexual and psychological maturity rather than
the form of legal relationship.

The draftsmen recommend repeal of the seduction statute
indicating that "(r)oughly equivalent protection is provided"
in the chapter on sexual offenses.[97] This statement is unfounded since inducing intercourse by promise is not punishable under the Proposed Code's provisions. However, repeal
should be urged on the basis of the policy that provoked the
legislature to expunge all civil actions for breach of promise
to marry and seduction of persons eighteen and over,[98] i.e.,
the danger of fraudulent claims without a corresponding good
reason for retaining the statute.

1022

One of the most important of the bids to alter existing law is the section providing for the defense of mistake of fact with respect to the capacity to consent.[99] The general American rule that mistake of fact is no defense to statutory rape, in spite of the prosecutrix' misrepresentations[100] or defendant's efforts to ascertain the true facts,[101] has for years been severely criticized in legal texts and journals.[102] American adherence to this "no defense" position is in sharp contrast with European law and even our own general principles of criminal law.[103] However, the rule has in recent years suffered encroachment by statute in Illinois, New York and New Mexico,[104] and by judicial edict in California in People v. Hernandez.[105]

It is widely recognized that there are instances of statutory rape where it is the male who is the "victim" of a sexually sophisticated female[106] whose physical appearance is woefully misleading; that recidivism among statutory rapists is nonexistent; and that the statutory rapist is generally not an abnormal youth who represents a threat to public security as does the classic rapist.[107] Relations with females who appear to be chronologically mature violates only social and religious conventions that are widely disregarded, and does not violate our traditional principles of criminal culpability, particularly the principle of mens rea.[108]

However, the Proposed Code advocates a subjective test in line with the Hernandez case. The reason for allowing the defense of mistake of fact is the avoidance of injustice where the "victim" holds herself out objectively as a mature female. Where a male engages in sexual relations with a female who appears to be over the age of consent, the law confers a harsh realization on the innocent mind of the defendant by later convicting him of rape. On the other hand, the policy of the statute is to protect immature females from their own immaturity. This policy is enhanced by facilitating prosecutions. The existence of either a subjective or an objective defense of mistake of fact dilutes the policy of the statute to some extent, but an objective standard at least requires that the defendant's belief be reasonable. Since the defendant's belief is to be based on the objective appearance of the female, it is not too much to ask that the defendant's interpretation of that appearance be objective. The best reconciliation of these competing interests is an objective standard. To demand of the defendant that his belief be reasonable at least approaches traditional principles of culpability without abrogating the basic policy of the statute. It should be noted that the defendant's burden of establishing the defense will become increasingly more difficult as the age of the victim decreases. For this reason it is urged that section 2331 be altered to encompass only reasonable mistake of fact.[109]

The mistake section applies also to incapacity by reason of mental defect, mental incapacity and physical helplessness. These modes of incapacity are not significantly different from incapacity by reason of age in that they are based on parallel policies. Therefore, the preceding discussion applies equally as well to these forms of incapacity.

C. Analysis

The Proposed Code's coverage of forcible rape generally retains current coverage while attempting a resolution of existing ambiguities through comprehensive definitions. The proposal is successful in promulgating a rational scheme enhanced by precise definitions, with three exceptions: the definition of "forcible compulsion" should be more comprehensive and establish clearly whether it is a subjective or objective test; the definition of incapacity to consent with respect to self-induced intoxication should be specific; and the existence of doubt regarding the cases of fraudulently obtained consent should be resolved by adding a specific provision.

The statutory rape proposal is a well reasoned and long overdue modification of existing law. The introduction of the graduated offense scheme, while it could be simpler and more equitable, is certainly an improvement. The defense of mistake of fact brings the offense of statutory rape within the general principles of criminal law, but a reasonable mistake test would be more appropriate than the proposed subjective test.

There are, however, other considerations relevant to heterosexual offenses not noticed in the Proposed Code: defense of prostitution in statutory rape actions, corroboration of charges and a restrictive statute of limitations. The statute of limitations and corroboration are reserved for later discussion.

Since the offense of statutory rape is predicated upon the necessity of protecting the virtue of immature females, inquiry into the virtue or chastity of the victim would be anomalous. However, it is incongruous to hold that the statute exists for the protection of prostitutes.[110] A good example of the potential injustice is provided by a New York case[111] wherein the defendant was convicted of statutory rape of a female who operated out of a hotel room as a prostitute. The woman had in fact previously been convicted of prostitution, testifying at her trial that she was twenty-three years old. Illinois provides a defense of prostitution against a charge of statutory rape.[112] Where the young girl has so far departed from sexual norms that she enters into relationships on a commercial basis, the purpose of the statute has failed with respect to that individual. Having failed in its purpose, the statute should not be operative in favor of prostitutes who subsequently decide that they have been raped. Accordingly, the lead of Illinois should be followed in establishing prostitution as a defense to statutory rape of females between eleven and sixteen. Prostitution in this context should be defined as sexual intercourse in exchange of compensation rather than mere promiscuity.[113] The reason for defining prostitution in this manner is to minimize the possibility of "oath helpers," individuals that swear to prior acts of intercourse simply to assist a comrade.

III

Unlawful Deviate Sexual Conduct

A. Existing Michigan Law

Principal among the prohibitions against deviate sexual conduct is the offense of sodomy. The crime derives its name from the ancient city of Sodom, reputedly destroyed for notorious unnatural sex practices in violation of the biblical edict "thou shall not lie with mankind, as with womankind."[114] Michigan's statutory proscription of sodomy, due to its vague statutory definition, has been held to adopt the common law crime of sodomy.[115] As a result, the sodomy statute covers penetrations of animals and humans per anum but not per os,[116] and the rule of an early Michigan case that emission must be shown, has been overturned by a subsequent statute.[117] Other statutory enactments, carrying identical penalties, prohibit acts of "gross indecency" between persons, regardless of sex, in public or private.[118] Regrettably, the judiciary has not been disposed to relate the meaning of the legislative cipher "gross indecency" with any specificity. The supreme court has held that an indictment in the form of the statute is sufficient to appraise the defendant of the charge against him since "(t)he common sense of the community, as well as the sense of decency, propriety, and morality which most people entertain is sufficient to apply the statute to each particular case. . . ."[119] The gross indecency statutes are not unconstitutional for vagueness,[120] and as such probably cover every conceivable form of sexual activity that any substantial group of individuals considers indecent.

The most that can be said of the current status of Michigan law with respect to deviate sexual conduct is that it probably prohibits any and all sexual activity, in public or private, heterosexual or homosexual, other than conventional petting or coitus. Consent is, of course, no defense.

B. Revised Criminal Code Proposals

The Proposed Code's coverage of deviate sexual conduct would work sweeping change in the law. Criminality would attach only to nonconsensual conduct, assessing penalties in accordance with the degree of aggravation or age disparity in a manner identical with the aforementioned rape provisions.

The unwieldy and unnecessarily vague phrases "abominable and detestible crime against nature"[121] and "gross indecency"[122] are abandoned in favor of the phrase "deviate sexual intercourse," which is defined as "any act of sexual gratification

between persons not married to each other, involving the
sex organs of one person and the mouth or anus of another."[123]
This retreat from the use of language, borrowed from another
era,[124] that is repugnant to modern theory of constitutionality,[125] is to be commended.

The most severe penalty (twenty year maximum) under the
graduated scheme is assigned to deviate sexual intercourse
by forcible compulsion, or with a person physically helpless,
or with an infant under eleven years of age.[126] The definitions of physically helpless and forcible compulsion are the
same in this context as for rape.[127] As in the case of rape,
sexual impositions by force, or upon physically incapacitated
persons, or upon children of extreme immaturity are extraordinarily dangerous to the individual victim and a serious
threat to public security, deserving of severe sanction. The
remaining sections covering deviate sexual intercourse correspond to the system of statutory rape provisions.[128]

Victim's Age	Actor's Age	Maximum Penalty
Less than 11	15 and over	20 years (felony)
11 to 14	18 and over	5 years (felony)
11 to 14	15 to 18	90 days (misdemeanor)
14 to 16	21 and over	1 year (misdemeanor)
14 to 16	15 to 21	90 days (misdemeanor)

This graduated scheme, based on age disparity, follows
that adopted by New York in its recent penal law revision.[129]
The systematic concept was formalized in the early drafts
of the Model Penal Code based on the theory that it is advisable to deter seduction of the young by older perverts,
with relatively harsh penalties, while avoiding attaching
serious criminality to occasional experimentation between
adolescent contemporaries.[130] Empirical evidence, such as
there is, tends to justify this distinction. The famous
Kinsey study indicates that nearly sixty per cent of the male
population in America has had some sort of homosexual experience, usually in their youth.[131] While the magnitude of
Kinsey's figures has been questioned,[132] there can be little
doubt that his estimates bear a significant relationship to
actuality. Surely no one would contend that such passing
sexual experimentation by something approaching sixty per
cent of the population is deserving of penalties equivalent
to the most heinous of crimes.

Deviate sexual intercourse with persons incapable of consent by reason of mental incapacity is classified, as in the
rape context, as a Class A misdemeanor[133] (one year maximum).
The discussion in the rape section parallels the considerations relevant here.[134] It should also be noted that the
defense of mistake of fact is available in deviate sexual
intercourse prosecutions as well as rape prosecutions and

and consequently open to the same criticisms.[135]

The most important alteration of law under the proposal is the elimination of criminality from deviate sexual activity between consenting adults in private. The premise underlying this position is that it is not a proper function of the criminal law to regulate private morality,[136] a premise to be examined in detail in the following section. Accordingly, the Proposed Code would punish homosexual activities accomplished by compulsion, perpetrated on the young, or displayed in public[137] even though consensual, while relegating the control of private morality to religious and sociological institutions. This view reflects a philosophy that has been extremely popular in legal texts and journals but apparently not among the legislatures. Illinois is presently the only jurisdiction that exempts homosexual conduct, between consenting adults in private, from criminal liability.[138] The recent penal code revision in New York retained the prohibition against consensual sodomy,[139] but the penalty for violation (ninety day maximum)[140] is in sharp contrast to the existing Michigan penalty (fifteen year maximum).[141]

C. Analysis

The proposed scheme for unlawful deviate sexual intercourse is comprehensive, well-integrated and complete with definitions. The graduated penalty provisions based on a varying degree of aggravation are sound. The definitions are a marked improvement over existing law, although open to specific objection as previously discussed.[142] It is important to note that this portion of the Proposed Code is characterized by a distinct alteration in penalties, some reduced and some increased. However, space limitation does not permit a discussion of penal theory in this presentation.[143] The most striking change is the elimination of punishment for deviate sexual activity between consenting adults in private, an issue requiring detailed analysis.

The regulation of deviate sexual conduct between consenting adults in private requires discussion at three levels, though not clearly distinct and somewhat overlapping: the ethical level - the relationship between morality and legal sanction; the legal level - the relationship between existing jurisprudential doctrines and legal sanction; and the practical level - the relationship between enforcement and legal sanction.

To set the problem in its ethical context the following premise is taken as self-evident. Every legal sanction must be justifiable, for the deprivation of life, liberty or property is itself a crime without the impetus of law based on reason. It is the justification about which the controversy centers. The publication of the British study[144] in 1957, commonly referred to as the Wolfenden Report, precipitated the latest bout over the legal regulation of morality.[145] The report advised that homosexual practices between consenting adults in private be excluded from criminal liability on the following ground:

Unless a deliberate attempt is to be made by society, acting through the agency of the law, to equate the sphere of crime with that of sin, there remains a realm of private morality and immorality which is, in brief and crude terms, not the law's business.[146]

The ensuing controversy has been championed by two eminent legal scholars. Lord Devlin takes exception to the Wolfenden Report's conception of what is properly "the law's business," equating immoral conduct to treason.[147] His thesis is that a set of common moral values is essential to the existence of a society and therefore private conduct that threatens a moral principle, while not a menace to others, is a threat to the existence of society. The conclusion is that the law is justified in controlling private homosexual activity to prevent a chink in the moral cement of society just as it is justified in the "supression of subversive activities."[148]

H. L. A. Hart aligns himself with John Stuart Mill on the issue of the enforcement of morality, taking the position that the only justification for the regulation of private conduct is the prevention of harm to other individual members of society.[149] Hart diverges from the strict principles of Mill in distinguishing between what he terms "legal moralism" and the enforcement of a "moral principle and nothing else" or "paternalism." The distinguishing example cited by Hart is a statute punishing cruelty to animals. The justification for such a statute is not the immorality of the act, "paternalism," but rather the prohibition of inflicting suffering albeit only of an animal, "legal moralism."[150] A law cannot be justified without showing an imposition on some sentient being. While mere knowledge that someone may be doing something wrong might distress some member of society, punishment on this basis is tantamount to punishment simply because someone objects to what is being done. The only liberty that could exist in such an atmosphere is the liberty to do those things to which no one seriously objects - an illusory liberty at best.[151] As Hart points out, the principle of legality is seriously undercut by a law prohibiting that which some group feels is immoral, without justification, and is reminiscent of the Nazi period in Germany during which a statute was enacted punishing activity deserving of punishment according "to the fundamental conceptions of a penal law and sound popular feeling."[152]

Devlin's fear, that society would collapse as an eventual result from the weakening of society's moral bonds through relaxation of the regulation of private sexual donduct, is not supported by history.[153] On the entire Eurpoean Continent only Austria and Germany punish private homosexual conduct between consenting adults.[154] Indeed, if Dr. Kinsey's statistics are accurate, our society was on the verge of collapse in 1948.[155] Devlin's tolerance limit, that limit where legal regulation should be imposed, is that which arouses feelings of "intolerance, indignation, and disgust."[156]

1028

The problem is that there is no demonstrable correlation between such elusive tags and their destructive influence on society, and there are serious difficulties associated even with determining the real feelings of the community.[157]

Assuming _arguendo_ that most men regard homosexuality as a "vice so abominable that its mere presence is an offence,"[158] that tenet itself demands examination.[159] If a man contend that the law should condemn homosexuality, it is advisable to inquire of his reasons. The response may be based on: prejudice - homosexual creatures are morally inferior because they are effeminate; emotion - they make me sick; rationalization - everyone knows homosexuality is sinful; fantasy - homosexuality causes earthquakes (as the Emperor Justinian believed):[160] or personal aversion - blind hate attributable to unacknowledged self suspicion. None of these justify the restriction of another man's freedom. Accordingly, "(a) conscientious legislator who is told a moral consensus exists must test the credentials of that consensus."[161] If none of the aforementioned reasons are acceptable justification, the legislator must uncover some other reason to support the law. Does such a reason exist?

Careful reflection on the justification of law should lead to a conclusion in accordance with that of Hart. The enforcement of morality _qua_ "intolerance, indignation and disgust" without demonstrable individual harm, at the expense of liberty, is simply not worth the price. The regulation of private homosexual conduct between consenting adults is, on this basis, itself immoral.

An examination of morality legislation at the legal level indicates that the regulation of consensual homosexuality between adults in private is curiously out of step with constitutional doctrines. The contention presented here is not that such regulation is unconstitutional; it clearly is not as of this date, although the trend is not favorable to the continuing validity of such regulation. Rather the ensuing discussion is intended to point up the discriminatory application of legal doctrines between homosexual offenses and the remainder of the criminal law. In this respect it is hoped that the legislature will examine the disparity and articulate a justification.[162]

A line of cases leading to the Supreme Court's latest pronouncement, in Griswold v. Connecticut,[163] have established a constitutionally protected right of privacy. The majority opinion draws upon several provisions of the Bill of Rights stating that the protections afforded by these amendments are incumbent upon the states through the fourteenth amendment. _Griswold_ struck down a Connecticut statute that forbade the use of contraceptive devices by married couples, on the ground that the statute abridged a right of privacy that lay within the penumbra of fundamental constitutional guarantees.[164] It is but a short extension of the "zone of privacy" enshrouding marital sexual relations to include homosexual acts between consenting adults in private, particularly

1029

if the state can demonstrate no convincing justification for such regulation.[165]

Punitive measures directed at homosexuality also may encounter difficulty with the cruel and unusual punishment prohibition of the eighth amendment.[166] While psychiatric opinion is not unanimous on the causes or nature of homosexuality, there is a substantial school believing that homosexuality in certain cases has a compulsive element. That is to say, that certain homosexuals do not have the voluntary capacity to conform their conduct to the requirements of law.[167] Robinson v. California[168] held invalid a state statute making it a crime to be a narcotics addict, on the ground of cruel and unusual punishment. An attempt was made two years later to apply the Robinson rule to a sodomy case in Perkins v. State.[169] Robinson was distinguished on the basis that punishment based on the status of narcotics addiction is different from punishment based on an overt homosexual act.[170] Evidently Judge Craven felt a twinge of injustice, even though he felt constrained to uphold the conviction on constitutional grounds, for he drew into question the wisdom of penal theory with respect to homosexuals when he commented at the end of his opinion that "(p)utting Perkins into the North Carolina Prison system is a little like throwing Brer Robbit into the Briar-patch."[171]

The Perkins decision has definitely not foreclosed the issue.[172] Two recent circuit court decisions, Driver v. Hinnant[172] and Easter v. District of Columbia,[173] have held that since a chronic alcoholic lacks the voluntary capacity to conform his conduct to law, no conviction can be had for that particular conduct for "(t)o do so would affront the Eighth Amendment, as cruel and unusual punishment. . . ."[174] Accepting current medical opinion that homosexuality contains elements of compulsiveness, punishment of homosexual offenders may well come under this rule.[175]

An examination of the issue at the practical level is divorced from any judgments respecting the morality of homosexuality. This aspect of the issue focuses on the enforcement of existing law and its ancillary effects.[176] Basic to the discussion is a recognition that homosexuals have a moral code of their own and, even if they are capable of controlling their conduct, they are not likely to be deterred by threat from conduct that they consider moral.[177] If estimates of homosexuality are at all realistic, there is a significant proportion of the public regularly flouting the law.[178] In face of such apparently widespread violation of law, enforcement is far from uniform or regular.[179] One striking aspect of discriminatory enforcement is reflected by the nearly total failure to prosecute lesbian activity.[180] Since most homosexual activity is conducted in private, the possibility of enforcement, assuming an impetus for enforcement,[181] is exceedingly dim due to search and seizure limitations. The practical result of sporadic and discriminatory enforcement is the breeding of a general disrespect for the law on the part of the unfortunate few

1030

who are punished for indulging in acts that are practiced on a relatively broad basis.

Another undesirable practical effect of existing law is the victimization of homosexuals by blackmailers.[182] The luckless homosexual encountered by a blackmailer is deterred from resorting to the law and exposing the blackmailer by the threat of criminal punishment. Since the homosexual may not be aware of the physician-patient privilege, he may be reluctant to seek psychiatric help or other assistance for his emotional problems.[183] Removing the criminal sanctions from homosexuality will not remove the social stigma attached to homosexual conduct and therefore will not eliminate the blackmail problem. However, the removal of such a weapon from the blackmailer's arsenal should at least diminish the threat of extortion.

An evaluation of the considerations relevant to the prohibition of deviate sexual conduct between consenting adults in private does not weigh in favor of the retention of existing law. On ethical ground there appears to be no justification for such prohibition. Current law seems to be out of phase with existing legal doctrines although there is a discernible trend toward judicial rectification of that anomaly. As a practical matter, the disadvantageous effects of the law are not balanced by corresponding benefits. Objective perusal of these considerations compels a redefinition of the law.

IV

Illicit Sexual Contacts Without Penetration

A. Existing Michigan Law

This section of the discussion deals with conduct antecedent to criminal sexual penetration and sexually motivated touchings that do not require sexual penetration. Three types of offenses fall into this category; assault, indecent liberties and enticings.

Assault with intent to commit rape, sodomy or gross indecency is a felony punishable by imprisonment up to ten years.[184] Criminal assault in general is an attempt to commit a nonconsensual immediate touching of the victim by a show of force or violence, coupled with the apparent present ability to complete the act.[185] Assault with intent to commit rape, sodomy or gross indecency is, however, a specific intent crime. The burden is on the prosecution to show that the defendant intended specifically to commit rape, sodomy or gross indecency.[186] That the assailant voluntarily desisted before completion of the act does not necessarily negate the intention at the time he commenced the attack, to commit rape, sodomy or gross indecency.[187] If the victim is below the statutory age of consent, it is necessary only that the defendant intend the act; it is of no consequence that he did not intend to overcome resistance.[188] If, how-

ever, the requisite intent is not proved in such a case,
and the act is not completed, an indictment will still lie
for indecent liberties.[189]   It is also important to note
that the specific intent mens rea may not exist where the
defendant's mental faculties are numbed, as by alcohol.[190]

The specific intent must be accompanied by active steps
toward accomplishment of the intended act.[191]   An actual
touching is not a necessary element of the offense,[192] although it usually is present. The steps necessary are those
that would constitute an ordinary assault if it were not
for the specific intent.[193] Should the victim consent before the intended act is consummated, but after initial resistance, the assailant is still chargeable with the assault because the offense is complete before the victim acquiesced.[194]   In accordance with the familiar phrase "mere
words do not constitute an assault," illicit solicitations
unaccompanied by actual or attempted physical contact do not
give rise to a charge of assault.[195]

The attempt or act of taking indecent liberties with a
child under sixteen years of age is a felony carrying the
same penalty as assault.[196]   Indecent liberties in this context means "such liberties as the common sense of society
would regard as indecent and improper."[197]   Some touching
is essential to the commission of the crime,[198] but it need
not be of the child's "private parts."[199]

It is clear that the offense is not a lesser degree of
statutory rape.[200]   This offense and the offense of assault
with intent to commit rape, sodomy or gross indecency are
mutually exclusive,[201] and it is error to omit the statutory
phrase, "without committing or intending to commit the crime
of rape, sodomy or gross indecency," from the charge to the
jury.[202]

Conduct directed toward inducing youths to commit immoral
acts is currently prohibited by three different Michigan
statutes. It is a misdemeanor to "accost, entice, or solicit"
a person under sixteen years of age with the intent to induce the commission of or submission to an immoral act.[203]
The offense requires active steps toward the consumation(sic)
of the intended act coupled with the requisite intent, and
it has been held that merely inviting a thirteen year old
boy to enter an automobile is not enough to sustain a conviction.[204]   The statutes covering the debauching of a boy
under fifteen by a female[205] and by a male,[206] discussed
previously,[207] include punishment for soliciting or enticing the same.

B. Revised Criminal Code Proposals

The Proposed Code categorizes indecent touchings under
the sexual abuse scheme. The prohibition is against "sexual contact" which is defined as "any touching of the sexual
or other intimate parts of a person not married to the actor,
done for the purpose of gratifying sexual desire of either
party."[208]   The comments to the identical New York provision
state that it is not necessary that there be a direct contact

with the victim's body to constitute a "sexual contact";[209]
a touching through clothing will be sufficient. The
Proposed Code's definition in this respect could be clearer
by providing specifically for direct or indirect contacts.
It should be noted that the phrase "for the purpose of gratifying sexual desire" will place a burden on the prosecution
that may prove difficult to satisfy. The protection of children from illicit manipulations could be diluted by placing
such an onus on the prosecution.[210] A decision concerning
whether to include such a provision requires a balancing of
society's interest in protecting the young, against the interest of protecting innocent defendants from fraudulent or
imagined charges. However, corroborating evidence is not required to sustain a conviction.[211] In this respect the prosecution's burden will be light, at the expense of defendants.
With this factor operating to the disadvantage of defendants,
it is desireable (sic) to include the gratification phrase as
a mitigating factor. A compromise in this fashion would glean
the most laudable benefits from each provision without serious
sacrifice of either interest.

Sexual abuse in the first degree corresponds to first degree rape and first degree sodomy but with a five year maximum sentence. Covered by this section are sexual contacts
by forcible compulsion, or with a physically helpless person, or with a child under eleven years of age.[212] The previous discussion with respect to forcible compulsion is applicable here.[213] The lower penalty in this context, while
still a felony, is justified by the correspondingly less
severe threat of physical and psychological injury to the
victim.

Sexual abuse in the second degree encompasses "sexual contacts" with individuals who are incapable of consent by reason of mental defect, mental incapacity or being less than
fourteen years old.[214] The gist of the offense is the victim's lack of appreciation for the nature of the conduct.
While the aggressor's conduct is deserving of criminal punishment, it lacks the danger element sufficient to elevate
the offense to a felony status. Accordingly, the offense is
a Class A misdemeanor (one year maximum).

Sexual abuse in the third degree covers all other nonconsensual "sexual contacts." For purposes of this section,
lack of consent carries an expanded definition; "the victim
does not expressly or impliedly acquiesce in the actor's
conduct."[215] This expanded definition of "without consent"
was thought necessary for coverage of sexual advances not
characterized by force or violence although still objectionable. Taking indecent liberties with persons in crowds supposedly falls into this category.[216]

Third degree sexual abuse also covers "sexual contacts"
with persons incapable of consent by reason of being less
sixteen years of age. However, if the victim is over fourteen
but less than sixteen and the actor is less than six years
older than the victim, no criminality is attached to the act.[217]
The reason for exculpation, "so that heavy petting between

contemporaries is not brought within the coverage of criminal law. . . .,"[218] seems sound. However, the age disparity specified is debatable. An examination of the extremes reveals that heavy petting resulting in sexual touchings between an actor just under twenty and an individual just over fourteen will be exculpated. From the defendant's point of view, it may be contended that fourteen year old girls commonly disguise their age with cosmetics, high heel shoes, and other manifestations, making it very difficult to ascertain age from appearances. However, the defense of mistake of fact is available to the defendant.[219] Another significant point is that "sexual contact" may be either heterosexual or homosexual. It is submitted that the policy of protecting the young from sexual experience would be better served, without serious injustice to youthful offenders, by reducing the age differential from six years to four years.

C. Analysis

The gradation and definitional aspects of the Proposed Code's provisions are here again the striking features and deserve commendation. Under the provisions for assault, a physical injury is essential to the offense.[220] The sexual abuse sections therefore provide coverage for sexual impositions that would not be covered elsewhere. Assault with intent to commit rape, sodomy or gross indecency under existing law receives equivalent coverage under the sexual abuse scheme. The current prohibition against indecent liberties is covered by sexual abuse, but the existing statute also covers attempts. Provision for attempts is made elsewhere in the Proposed Code and not susceptible to discussion under sex offenses.[221]

Since the proposed sexual abuse provisions require an actual touching, the existing Michigan statutes prohibiting the enticement to commit or submit to an immoral act do not come within the sexual abuse coverage. Such enticements or solicitations will fall under the chapter on attempts.[222]

V

Indecent Exposure

A. Existing Michigan Law

Indecent exposure is a misdemeanor by statute in Michigan.[223] The offense requires an intentional exposure, so an inadvertent or accidental exposure is not criminal.[224] However, where the defendant is reckless in his behavior by exposing himself where he is likely to be observed by others, his intent will be presumed.[225] It is essential that the offense be committed in public view, and it has been held that this element is statisfied (sic) where the act took place on the private property of the defendant but open to the public view.[226] It is of course necessary that some other person observe the act.[227] The consent of the observers has led to an interesting question particularly with regard to nudist camps.

In an early Michigan case, People v. Ring,[228] members of a nudist camp were convicted of indecent exposure. The authorities viewed the camp from an overhanging bluff on adjoining property prior to entering the camp and making the arrests. The camp was apparently not well secluded as a neighboring property owner described their activity as "cavorting around."[229] The case has been interpreted by the Michigan Attorney General as authority for labeling cult nudism illegal.[230]

A more recent decision casts serious doubt on the continuing viability of the Ring case. In People v. Hildabridle[231] the supreme court reversed a conviction for indecent exposure arising out of the practice of nudism. However, the reversal rested on two grounds: illegal search and seizure and nonviolation of the statute. The doubt surrounding the decision is a result of a divided court. Three justices voted for reversal on the dual grounds of illegal search and seizure and that private cult nudism did not violate the statute.[232] The three remaining justices voted for affirmance of the conviction.[234] It could be argued that the Ring case is not inconsistant with Hildabridle on the basis that the defendants in Ring were exposed to public view while the defendants in Hildabridle were not.[235] However, it remains possible that cult nudism could be brought within the statute should the issue be presented to the court absent the complicating search and seizure problem.[236]

B. Revised Criminal C ode Proposal

The Proposed Code prohibits exposure of the actor's genitals, with the specific intent to gratify a sexual desire, under circumstances that he knows would cause affront or alarm.[237] The express requirement of exposure of genitals is a sensible improvement over current statutory language prohibiting exposure of "his or her person." Under the existing language it is conceivable that an attempt might be made by some zealous group to use the statute for regulation of wearing apparel. This possibility is foreclosed under the proposal. The regulation of "swim fashions," "short shorts" and other items of wearing apparel is better left to local control.[238]

The specific intent element contained in the proposed section, "with intent to arouse or gratify sexual desire of himself or of any person other than his spouse," raises some serious problems. The prosecution must prove the subjective intention of the defendant in a specific intent crime, and the familiar rule that a man is presumed to intend the "natural and probable consequences of his act" will not satisfy a specific intent requirement.[239] Two hypothetical examples will serve to illustrate the problem.

CaseI: A man exposes himself to his spouse under circumstances where he is likely to be observed by others (e.g., in a car at a drive-in theater) intending only to arouse his spouse, hoping that no one else will observe the act.

1035

Case II: A man exposes himself on a public street for the purpose of urinating, intending only to relieve himself, while harboring the somewhat spurious hope that no one will happen along and observe him.

Note that in neither case does the actor maintain the specific intent to "arouse or gratify sexual desire of himself or of any person other than his spouse." In Case I the actor's specific intent is to arouse his spouse, an intent expressly excluded from the statute. In Case II the actor's intent is merely to relieve himself, intending no sexual consequences whatsoever. In both cases the actor's conduct may be characterized as negligent, or possibly reckless, and in both cases his conduct falls without the statute.

The statutory purpose of prohibiting indecent exposure is to prevent displays that would be shocking or disturbing to public sensibilities. It should make no difference that the actor was merely indifferent to the mental integrity of others and not an exhibitionist. The purpose of prohibiting indecent exposures would be better served by the following suggested statutory form.

A person commits the crime of indecent exposure if he exposes his genitals under circumstances in which he knows or should have known that his conduct is likely to cause affront or alarm.

Under this form negligent or reckless, as well as intentional, exposures may be prosecuted. The criminality of the act would depend upon the reasonableness of the exposure. For example, where the defendant's only purpose was to relieve himself, an exposure on a busy street obviously would be a violation, but an exposure in a secluded woodlot would be a violation only if the offender had actual or constructive knowledge that he would be observed by others who would be disturbed.

As the comments to the Proposed Code point out, it is the purpose of the exposure and the likelihood of psychological alarm rather than the place that is determinative of the criminality of the act.[240] This statement is founded on two different elements of the proscription: "intent to arouse or gratify" and "knows his conduct is likely to cause affront or alarm." To sustain a conviction under this section it would have to be shown that the defendant knew that his act would shock others and that it was his intent to gratify some sexual desire. This aspect of the statute probably would eliminate the possibility of a prosecution for private cult nudism. The suggested statutory form set out above would not diminish this result. The retention of "likely to cause affront or alarm" in the suggested form would exclude private nudism since nudists supposedly are not disturbed by the naked view of their fraternal membership. The facts presented in the Ring case (nudism open to public view) would, however, be subject to prosecution under this form.

C. Analysis

The Proposed Code's provision is drawn in clear and concise terms not characteristic of the existing statute. The specific intent provision does not appear to serve any salutary purpose, however, and should be stricken in view of the severe restriction it places on the section.

With respect to the application of the criminal law to private cult nudism, it should be questioned whether such prohibition is justifiable assuming even that it is desirable. Although less emotional, the issue here is not different from the prohibition of private homosexual practices, i.e., the justification of law is the prevention of harm to other individuals.[241] The prohibition of private cult nudism requires an articulation of the harm threatened to others.[242]

Ethical questions aside, it now appears doubtful that a state can prohibit the practice of nudism on constitutional grounds. A Tennessee statute[243] was recently struck down as a violation of the due process clause of the fourteenth amendment in <u>Roberts v. Clement</u>.[244] The majority opinion rested its decision on the denial of due process because the statute was unduly vague and indefinite. In a concurring opinion Judge Darr indicated that the Tennessee statute should not fall for violation of "procedural" due process but rather for violation of "substantive" due process. The statute infringed on more than the defendant's ability to present a proper defense - procedural due process; it also infringed upon the constitutionally protected substantive rights of privacy[245] and freedom of association.[246] If a state seeks to prohibit such conduct in more precise terms than did Tennessee in order to avoid the void for vagueness doctrine, it may be hard pressed to show sufficient state interest to overcome Judge Darr's arguments.[247] In any event, constitutional protection from illegal search and seizure renders the possibility of prosecution for nudism that is truly private extremely remote.[248]

VI

Conclusion

Before summarizing the preceding discussion it should be pointed out that there are two additional considerations not noticed in the proposal that deserve reflection in conjunction with comprehensive revision.

In order that the possibility of fraudulent charges be minimized, a requirement of prompt complaint should be added to the sex offense chapter.[249] Since juries tend to be sympathetic to alleged victims, there is a substantial danger that a defendant will be convicted on stale evidence. For example, a willing participant to intercourse may later become a vindictive complainant upon discovering that she is pregnant. A victim that truly has been subjected to an act of sexual outrage should not delay in bringing the offense to the attention of authorities. The additional dangers of

1037

blackmail and psychopathic complaint would be reduced by a prompt complaint requirement.

Current Michigan law requires that an indictment be brought within six years after the alleged commission of the offense.[250] Seduction prosecutions are an exception, the indictment for which must be brought with one year.[251] Evidence of delay in making complaint is admissible, but only for the purpose of reflecting on the credibility of the complainant.[252] It is suggested that the Model Penal Code be followed by requiring that the action be instituted within three months of occurrence except where the complainant is less than sixteen years of age or otherwise incompetent to make complaint, in which case the action must be instituted within three months after the parent or guardian learns of the offense.[253] Since complainants in this latter category lack the capacity to become willing participants, consistency of reason demands that their personal failure to bring complaint cannot operate in favor of the defendant. Likewise, the fear of parental anger or confusion as to the significance of the act may delay the complaint, factors that should not prevent prosecution.

The Proposed Code makes no provision with respect to corroboration of the complainant's allegations. Sex offenses are easily charged and difficult to disprove. The fear that innocent defendants might be convicted on the bare accusations of complainants is as old as the law itself.[254] Accordingly, some jurisdictions have a general requirement of corroboration to support convictions for sex offenses.[255] Professor Mueller supports his assertion that corroboration is "indispensable in order to avoid easily trumped-up charges," with the following example from West Virginia.[256] The prosecutrix explained how a doctor had raped her, while she was under anesthetic, by describing how he knelt down to perpetrate the act. The defense promptly showed that the physician had artificial legs and could not possibly kneel down.

But Dean Wigmore takes a contrary position. His contention is not that the fear of fraudulent or imaginary charges is unrealistic, for he carefully documents the existence of such a danger.[257] Rather his position is that the partial protection afforded defendants by the common sense of the jurymen and the power of the trial judge to set aside a verdict based upon insufficient evidence,[258] should be supplemented by an alteration of the rules of evidence to permit inquiry into the complainant's moral character and mental disposition.[259] The partial protection that Wigmore suggests exist are open to question. Sex offense accusations are fraught with reason-impairing emotion that may prevent common sense of the jury from meeting our noble expectations. Indeed, the jury's sympathy may well lie with the complainant rather than the defendant. Where a judge sets aside a verdict rendered solely on the testimony of the complainant he runs the risk of invading the function of the jury, credibility generally being exclusively for the jury's deter-

mination.[260] In any event, Wigmore's suggested alterations
of the rules of evidence, to permit inspection of the victim's chastity and mental disposition, are in part inconsistent with the policy of the substantive law. To the extent that the victim has been subjected to a nonconsensual
imposition, moral or mental disposition is irrelevant. If
prior conduct or psychiatric opinion is admitted into evidence the impact on the jury is obvious. The jury is not
likely, assuming they have the capacity, to distinguish between evidence admitted for the purpose of reflecting on
credibility and evidence admitted for any other purpose. The
practical effect may be the acquittal of a guilty defendant.
Another adverse effect could be the failure to bring any
charges in order to avoid placing the victim's moral virtue
on trial.

The danger of convicting innocent defendants is substantial.
The legislative concern with this risk is reflected by the
corroboration requirement commonly found in seduction statutes
and occasionally encountered in rape, sodomy and indecent exposure statutes.[261] On the other hand, sex crimes are among
the most repulsive offenses to be found in any penal code. A
general requirement of corroboration will place an extremely
onerous burden on the prosecution in certain cases that may
well prevent the conviction of some offenders. These competing considerations present a most perplexing dilemma.
Three factors permit a resolution that is at least palat-
able. The first is the prompt complaint requirement proposed above. To a certain extent, prompt complaint reduces
the risk of fraudulent allegations without unduly burdening
the prosecution. Secondly, Michigan jurisprudence contains
a built-in safeguard mitigating the harshness of an absolute
rule - the trial judge's discretionary power to comment on
the evidence, testimony and character of witnesses.[262] While
the judge's comments are not binding on the jury, the impact
of his tested judgment on the ultimate triers of fact is
found to be substantial. In this respect the jury will be
reminded of the solemn nature of their undertaking whenever
the trial judge foresees the risk of convicting an innocent
defendant on the bare accusation of the complainant. Finally, the Anglo-American adversary system provides protection
of the defendant's interests by assuring him of counsel who
is duty bound to remind judge and jury of the impending risk.
In view of these factors, a statutory corroboration requirement is not desirable.

The chapter of the Proposed Code covering sexual offenses
is a nearly total adoption of the sex offense provisions of
the New York Penal Law. In general the Proposed Code is a
marked improvement over current Michigan law. Certain aspects of this chapter, however, require more meticulous consideration. Those aspects are discussed in detail within
this presentation and are merely summarized at this point.
The "forcible compulsion" definition should be more comprehensive and encompass a subjective test in line with the

definition suggested. The uncertainty with respect to the
capacity to consent where the victim is under the influence
of a self-induced intoxicant should be resolved by specifically excluding the possibility of prosecution under such
circumstances. The cases of fraudulently obtained consent
should be anticipated by supplementing section 2305 (1) with
the subsection suggested. The highly desirable mistake of
fact section should be based on an objective rather than a
subjective test. The Proposed Code should also provide for
a defense of prostitution against a charge of statutory rape.
The specific intent formulation of the proposed indecent exposure section is extremely restrictive and should be replaced by the aforementioned suggested form. Finally, the
entire chapter should be subject to a prompt complaint requirement. In deference to the draftsmen of the Proposed
Code it must be pointed out that the foregoing list of criticisms is not to be interpreted as a general indictment of
the proposal. In spite of the fact that this commentator
finds fault with specific provisions, the Proposed Code in
its present form is a much needed improvement over existing
Michigan law.

J. Terry Moran

Footnotes

1. People v. McDonald, 9 Mich. 149 (1861). See generally
R. Perkins, Criminal Law 110-11 (1957).

2. Mich. Pub. Acts 1952, No. 73, Sec. 750.520, Mich. Stat.
Ann. Sec. 28.788 (1954). Any person who shall ravish and
carnally know any female of the age of 16 years, or more, by
force and against her will, or who shall unlawfully and carnally know and abuse any female under the full age of 16
years, shall be guilty of a felony, punishable by imprisonment in the state prison for life or for any term of years.
. . . Such carnal knowledge shall be deemed complete upon
proof of any sexual penetration however slight.

3. Id.

4. Id.

5. People v. Rivers, 147 Mich. 643, 111 N.W. 201 (1907);
People v. Scouten, 130 Mich. 620, 90 N.W. 332 (1902).

6. People v. Courier, 79 Mich. 366, 44 N.W. 571 (1890).

7. See, e.g., Comstock v. State, 14 Neb. 205, 15 N.W. 355
(1883); cf. People v. Courier, 79 Mich. 366, 44 N.W. 571 (1890).

8. People v. Pizzura, 211 Mich. 71, 178 N.W. 235 (1920) (a
common law marriage will suffice). However, a man may be convicted of rape upon his wife as principal to the crime if he
aids, abets or procures another to commit the physical act.
People v. Chapman, 62 Mich. 280, 28 N.W. 896 (1886); cf. People v. Flynn, 96 Mich. 276, 55 N.W. 834 (1893).

9. See R. Perkins, supra note 1, at 115.

10. Mich. Pub. Acts 1952, No. 73, Sec. 750.502, Mich. Stat. Ann. Sec. 28.788 (1954).

11. Moran v. People, 25 Mich. 355 (1872).

12. Id.

13. People v. Geddes, 301 Mich. 258, 3 N.W.2d 266 (1942); People v. Crosswell, 13 Mich. 427 (1865).

14. Brown v. People, 36 Mich. 203 (1877).

15. Moran v. People, 25 Mich. 355, 365 (1872); accord, People v. Myers, 306 Mich. 100, 10 N.W.2d 323 (1943); People v. Flynn, 96 Mich. 276, 55 N.W. 834 (1893).

16. People v. Marrs, 125 Mich. 376, 84 N.W. 284 (1900).

17. Commonwealth v. Burke, 105 Mass. 376, 377 (1870).

18. Id. at 380-81.

19. But cf. Hirdes v. Ottawa Circuit Judge, 180 Mich. 321, 146 N.W. 646 (1914) (civil case).

20. Even though there is no consent in fact and no resistance, the offense of rape may be committed. This is true where the victim is non compos mentis, asleep, or where drugs or intoxicating drinks are used. 44 Am. Jur. Rape, Sec. 6, (1942) (footnotes omitted).

21. See 44 Am. Jur. Rape, Sec. 10-11 (1942); R. Perkins, supra note 1, at 123.

22. People v. Crosswell, 13 Mich. 427 (1865).

23. Mich. Comp. Laws Sec. 750.341 (1948), Mich. Stat. Ann. Sec. 28.573 (1954).

24. There is no difference in the criminality of the act between the commission of this offense upon an insane, feeble-minded or epileptic person who has been ordered confined in an institution but not yet physically confined, and the com-mission of the same offense upon such a person who is already actually confined.
(1928-1930) Mich. Att'y Gen. Biennial Rep. pt. 1, at 135, 139.

25. The mental deficiency issue under the Proposed Code is discussed at pp. 942-43 infra.

26. Moran v. People, 25 Mich. 355 (1872) (dire descriptions of the consequences of failure to submit to intercourse so as to put the patient in great fear, however, would negate consent resulting in rape).

27. Mich. Comp. Laws Sec. 750.90 (1948), Mich. Stat. Ann. Sec. 28.285 (1962).

28. Bloodworth v. State, 65 Tenn. 492 (1872). See generally Annot., 91 A.L.R.2d 591 (1963). The common law result has

1041

been altered by statute in some jurisdictions. Id. at 601-12.

29. In Moran v. People, 25 Mich. 355 (1872), the court indicated that the mistaken husband case would not be different from the facts before the court (pretended medical treatment) holding that force is necessary to a conviction for rape. Dictum suggesting a contrary result in People v. Crosswell, 13 Mich. 427 (1865), was repudiated in Moran as erroneous.

30. People v. Ryno, 148 Mich. 137, 111 N.W. 740 (1907).

31. R. Perkins, supra note 1, at 117.

32. Forcible rape and statutory rape are found within the same statute. Mich. Pub. Acts 1952, No. 73, Sec. 750.520 Mich. Stat. Ann. Sec. 28.788 (1954).

33. Less than the full age of sixteen years in Michigan. See text of statute set out at note 2 supra. Age is a question to be determined by the trier of fact. People v. Commack, 317 Mich. 410, 26 N.W. 2d 924 (1947).

34. See pp. 934-37 supra.

35. See p. 935 supra.

36. People v. Courier, 79 Mich. 366, 368, 44 N.W. 571, 572 (1890).

37. People v. Bennett, 205 Mich. 95, 100-01, 171 N.W. 363, 365 (1919).

38. People v. McDonald, 9 Mich. 632, 188 N.W. 398 (1922).

39. People v. Gengels, 218 Mich. 632, 188 N.W. 398 (1922).

40. People v. Goulette, 82 Mich. 36, 45 N.W. 1124 (1890); People v. Glover, 71 Mich. 303, 38 N.W. 874 (1888).

41. State v. Rash, 27 S.D. 185, 130 N.W. 91 (1911), citing People v. Abbott, 97 Mich. 484, 56 N.W. 862 (1893).

42. People v. Russell, 241 Mich. 125, 216 N.W. 441 (1927).

43. People v. Bastian, 330 Mich. 457, 47 N.W. 2d 692 (1951).

44. Mich. Comp. Laws Sec. 750.342 (1948), Mich. Stat. Ann. Sec. 28.574 (1954).

45. Mich. Comp. Laws Sec. 750.339 (1948), Mich. Stat. Ann. Sec. 28.571 (1954).

46. People v. Bailey, 341 Mich. 592, 67 N.W. 2d 785 (1954).

47. The words "knowingly and willfully," as used in the statute, disclose a legislative intent that . . . knowledge that the boy is under 15 years of age shall be essential to the commission of the crime. Id. at 594, 67 N.W. 2d at 786.

48. Mich. Comp. Laws, Sec. 750.532 (1948), Mich. Stat. Ann. Sec. 28.800 (1954).

49. People v. DeFore, 64 Mich. 693, 31 N.W. 585 (1887); People v. Millspaugh, 11 Mich. 277 (1863).

50. People v. Clark, 33 Mich. 112, 116 (1876).

51. Id. at 116-17. But cf. People v. Gibbs, 70 Mich. 425, 38 N.W. 257 (1888) wherein promise of a gift by a 50 year old man to a 15 year old girl was held sufficient.

52. People v. Smith, 132 Mich. 58, 62-63, 92 N.W. 776, 777 (1902).

53. People v. Turton, 192 Mich. 331, 334, 158 N.W. 870, 871, (1916).

54. People v. Brewer, 27 Mich. 133, 137 (1873). But this is not to say that the victim must be a virgin, for a return to a chaste life prior to the seduction will reinstate the presumption of chastity and support a conviction. See People v. Squires, 49 Mich. 487, 13 N.W. 828 (1882); People v. Clark, 33 Mich. 112 (1876).

55. People v. Gould, 70 Mich. 240, 38 N.W. 232 (1888). But if the defendant thereafter deserts his spouse after marrying her to avoid prosecution he shall be guilty of a felony under Mich. Comp. Laws Sec. 750.164 (1948), Mich. Stat. Ann. Sec. 28.361 (1962).

56. Mich. Rev. Crim. Code Sec. 2310 (Final Draft 1967).

57. Id. Sec. 2311.

58. Id. Sec. 2312.

59. Id. Sec. 2305.

60. (1) A male is guilty of rape in the first degree if:
        (a) He engages in sexual intercourse with a female by forcible compulsion; or
        (b) He engages in sexual intercourse with a female who is incapable of consent by reason of being physically helpless; or
        (c) He engages in sexual intercourse with a female who is less than 11 years old. Id. Sec. 2310.

61. Id. Sec. 2301 (a).

62. Id. Sec. 2301 (d).

63. Model Penal Code Sec. 213.6 (2) (Official Draft 1962). See also N.Y. Pen. Law Sec. 130.00, Comment at 271 (however a judicial separation decree is irrelevant so long as a valid marital status exists).

64. Mich. Rev. Crim. Code Sec. 2301 (d) (Final Draft 1967).

65. See People v. Pizzura, 211 Mich. 71, 178 N.W. 235 (1920); State v. Ward, 204 S.C. 210, 28 S.E. 2d 785 (1944); Model Penal Code Sec. 207.4, Comment (4) at 245 (Tent. Draft No. 4, 1955).

66. The adultery and cohabitation statutes are for practical purposes dead letters. . . . The threat of uninvoked penalties is an empty one, and full enforcement would not be tolerated. . . . (I)t is preferable to eliminate the fiction of criminal law controls on the marriage morals of Michigan. Mich. Rev. Crim. Code Sec. 7010, Comment at 493 (Final Draft 1967

67. Model Penal Code Sec. 207.4, Comment (4) at 245 (Tent. Draft No. 4, 1955). See also Frazier v. State, 48 Tex. Crim. 142, 86 S.W. 754 (1905).

68. Mich. Rev. Crim. Code Sec. 415 (Final Draft 1967).

69. "Forcible compulsion" means physical force that overcomes earnest resistance; or a threat, express or implied, that places a person in fear of immediate death or serious physical injury to himself or another person, or in fear that he or another person will be immediately kidnapped. Id. Sec. 2301 (b).

70. Model Penal Code Sec. 207.4, Comment (6) at 246-7 (Tent. Draft No. 4, 1955). See generally Note, The Resistance Standard in Rape Legislation, 18 Stan. L. Rev. 680 (1966).

71. The definition "does not require the victim to have 'reasonable cause to believe' that the actor will carry out his threat." N.Y. Pen. Law Sec. 130.00 Comment at 273.

72. Model Penal Code Sec. 207.4, Comment (6) at 247 (Tent. Draft No. 4, 1955). But see Note, supra note 70 at 685.

73. Ct. Note, supra note 70, at 684-85, 688. The kidnaping provision is derived from the Model Penal Code. Its inclusion is desirable because the threat of abduction is no less fear inducing than the threat of physical injury.

(F)ormerly we relied on the formulation with regard to first degree felonies to embrace kidnapping threats. Since, when we came to draft our kidnapping provisions, we did not make all kidnapping felonies of the first degree, it became necessary to provide expressly for kidnapping.

Model Penal Code, Sec. 213.1, Comment at 143 (Official Draft 1962).

74. E.G., mother submits to save her child. Model Penal Code Sec. 207.4, Comment (6) at 247 (Tent. Draft No. 4, 1955). Girl submits to save the life of her escort. State v. Olsen, 138 Ore. 666, 7 P.2d 792 (1932).

75. "'Physically helpless' means that a person is unconscious or for any other reason is physically unable to communicate unwillingness to an act." Mich. Rev. Crim. Code Sec. 2301 (g) (Final Draft 1967).

76. Mental defect is defined as "a mental disease or defect which renders him incapable of appraising the nature of his conduct." Id. Sec. 2301 (e).

77. Mental incapacity is defined as "temporarily incapable of appraising or controlling his conduct owing to the influence of a narcotic or intoxicating substance administered to him without his consent, or to any other act committed upon him without his consent." Id. Sec. 2301 (f).

78. Id. Sec. 1401.

79. Id. Sec. 1415.

80. Id. Sec. 2305 (1) (2).

81. Id. Sec. 2330 (2) (b). Note that the definition of mental incapacity includes only intoxication procurred without the victim's consent. Id. Sec. 2301 (f).

82. See P. 936 & note 19 supra.

83. Model Penal Code Sec. 213.2, Comment at 144 (Official Draft 1962). See also Model Penal Code Sec. 207.4, Comment (7) at 248 (Tent. Draft No. 4, 1955).

84. Mich. Rev. Crim. Code Sec. 2305 (1) (a) (Final Draft 1967); see p. 937 supra.

85. See p. 937 & notes 28 & 29, supra.

86. See Model Penal Code Sec. 213.1 (2) (c) (Official Draft 1962). It should be noted that the penalty under the sexual misconduct section (maximum ninety days) is considerably less severe than the penalty under existing law for intercourse under pretense of medical treatment. Mich. Comp. Laws Sec. 750.90 (1948), Mich. Stat. Ann. Sec. 28.285 (1962) (maximum ten years).

87. Mich. Rev. Crim. Code Sec. 701 (Final Draft 1967).

88. See generally Mich. Rev. Crim. Code Sec. 2305, 2310-12 (Final Draft 1967).

89. Id. Sec. 2310 (1) (c).

90. See Chaneles, Child Victims of Sexual Offenses, 31 Fed. Prob. 52 (June, 1967).

91. Model Penal Code Sec. 207.4, Comment (1) at 242 (Tent. Draft No. 4, 1955).

92. See Minn. Stat. Ann. Sec. 617.02 (1964); 6 N.M. Stat. Ann. Sec. 40A-9-3, 40A-9-4 (1953); N.Y. Pen Law Sec. 130.20-35.

93. Model Penal Code Sec. 213.3 (Official Draft 1962).

94. Mich. Comp. Laws Sec. 750.339 (1948), Mich. Stat. Ann. Sec. 28.571 (1954). See p. 939 supra.

95. Mich. Rev. Crim. Code Sec. 2305 (1) (b) (Final Draft 1967). Section 2330 (3) (a) deems a person incapable of consent if under the age of sixteen.

96. Mich. Comp. Laws Sec. 750.342 (1948), Mich. Stat. Ann. Sec. 28.574 (1954). See p. 939 supra.

97. Mich. Rev. Crim. Code Sec. 2305, Comment at 182 (Final Draft 1967).

98. Mich. Comp. Laws Sec. 551.301 (1948), Mich. Stat. Ann. Sec. 25.191 (1957).

99. Mich. Rev. Crim. Code Sec. 2331 (Final Draft 1967).

100. People v. Lewellyn, 314 Ill. 106, 145 N.E. 289 (1924); Farrell v. State, 152 Tex. Crim. 488, 215 S.W. 2d 625 (1948).

101. Manning v. State, 43 Tex. Crim. 302, 65 S.W. 920 (1901).

102. See, e.g., Myers, Reasonable Mistake of Age: A Needed Defense to Statutory Rape, 64 Mich. L. Rev. 105 (1965); Comment, Forcible and Statutory Rape: An Exploration of the Operation and Objectives of the Consent Standard, 62 Yale L.J. 55 (1952).

103. The primordial concept of mens rea, the guilty mind, expresses the principle that it is not conduct alone but conduct accompanied by certain specific mental states which concerns, or should concern the law.

104. Ill. Ann. Stat. Ch. 38, Sec. 11-4 (b) (1) (Smith-Hurd 1964) (reasonable belief); 6 N.M. Stat. Ann. Sec. 40A-9-3 (1953); N.Y. Pen. Law Sec. 130.10.

105. 61 Cal. 2d 529, 393 P.2d 673, 39 Cal. Rptr. 361 (1964) (subjective belief).

106. See McGeorge, Sexual Assaults on Children, 4 Med. Sci. & L. 245 (1964).

107. See Myers, supra note 102, at 122-25 and authorites cited therein.

108. See note 103 supra. Cf. Model Penal Code Sec. 207.1, Comment at 206-07 (Tent. Draft No. 4, 1955).

109. But see Israel, The Process of Penal Law Reform - A Look at the Proposed Michigan Revised Criminal Code, 14 Wayne L. Rev. p. 772 Supra, at 826.

110. See Ploscowe, Sex Offenses: The American Legal Context, 25 Law & Contemp. Prob. 217, 222 (1960); Model Penal Code Sec. 207.4, Comment (13) at 254 (Tent. Draft No. 4, 1955).

111. People v. Marks, 146 App. Div. 11, 130 N.Y.S. 524 (1911).

112. Ill. Ann. Stat. ch. 38, Sec. 11-4 (b) (2) (Smith-Hurd 1964).

113. But see Model Penal Code Sec. 213.6 (4) (Official Draft 1962).

114. Leviticus 18:22. See generaly 48 Am. Jur. Sodomy Sec. 1-7 (1943).

115. "(T)he abominable and detestable crime against nature either with mankind or with any animal. . . . ." Mich. Pub. Acts 1952, No. 73, Sec. 750.158, Mich. Stat. Ann. Sec. 28.355

(1962). Offenses declared in general statutory language adopt the common law for particularization of the elements of the crime. People v. Schmitt, 275 Mich. 575, 267 N.W. 741 (1936).

116. People v. Dexter, 6 Mich. App. 247, 148 N.W. 2d 915 (1967).

117. "(I)t shall not be necessary to prove emission, any sexual penetration, however slight shall be deemed sufficient. . . ." Mich. Pub. Acts 1952, No. 73 Sec. 750.159, Mich. Stat. Ann. Sec. 28.356 (1962), overturning People v. Hodgkin, 94 Mich. 27, 53 N.W. 794 (1892).

118. Mich. Pub. Acts 1952, No. 73, Sec. 750.338, Mich. Stat. Ann. Sec. 28.570 (1954) (acts between male persons). Mich. Pub. Acts 1952, No. 73, Sec. 750.338a, Mich. Stat. Ann. Sec. 28.570 (1) (1954) (acts between female persons). Mich. Pub. Acts 1952, No. 73 Sec. 750.338 (b), Mich. Stat. Ann. Sec. 28.570 (2) (1954) (acts between males and females).

119. People v. Carey, 217 Mich. 601, 602-03, 187 N.W. 261, 262 (1922). The court quoted with approval from an earlier case that "(c)ourts will never allow its (sic) records to be polluted by bawdy and obscene matters." Id. at 603, 187 N.W. at 262.

120. People v. Dexter, 6 Mich. App. 247, 148 N.W. 2d 915 (1967).

121. Mich. Pub. Acts 1952, No. 73, Sec. 750.158, Mich. Stat. Ann. Sec. 28.355 (1962).

122. Mich. Pub. Acts 1952, No. 73, Sec. 750.338, Mich. Stat. Ann. Sec. 28.570 (1954); Mich. Pub. Acts 1952, No. 73, Sec. 750.338a, Mich. Stat. Ann. Sec. 28.570 (1) (1954); Mich. Pub. Acts 1952, No. 73, Sec. 750.338b, Mich. Stat. Ann. Sec. 28.570 (2) (1954).

123. Mich. Rev. Crim. Code Sec. 2301 (b) (Final Draft 1967).

124. "(T)he infamous crime against nature, committed either with man or beast. . . ." 4 Blackstone, Commentaries Sec. 215.

125. If the statute were a new one, it would be obviously unconstitutional for vagueness. The former concern for the feelings of those reading the statute has yielded to the necessity that an indicted person know of what he is charged. Euphemisms have no place in criminal statutes. Perkins v. State, 234 F. Supp. 333, 336 (W.D.N.C. 1964).

126. Mich. Rev. Crim. Code, Sec. 2315 (Final Draft 1967).

127. The definition of forcible compulsion is open to the same criticism here as it was in connection with rape, it being of no consequence that the victim of deviate sexual intercourse may be male as well as female. See pp. 941-42 supra.

128. See Mich. Rev. Crim. Code Sec. 2305 (1) (c), 2315-17 (Final Draft 1967). It is of no consequence to the comparison that the victim of deviate sexual intercourse may be male as well as female. See pp. 944-45 supra.

129. N.Y. Pen. Law Sec. 130.20, 13040-50.

130. Model Penal Code Sec. 207.5, Comments (3)-(4) at 280 (Tent. Draft No. 4, 1955).

131. A. Kinsey, W. Pomeroy & C. Martin, Sexual Behavior in the Human Male 371 (1948).

132. See N. St. John-Stevas, Law and Morals 29-30 (1964); Wheeler, Sex Offenses: A Sociological Critique, 25 Law & Contemp. Prob. 258, 264 (1960).

133. Mich. Rev. Crim. Code Sec. 2317 (1) (a) (Final Draft 1967).

134. See pp. 942-43 supra.

135. See pp. 946-47 supra.

136. Mich. Rev. Crim. Code Sec. 2317, Comment at 186 (Final Draft 1967).

137. Public homosexual displays are covered by the Proposed Code's provisions for loitering. Id. Sec. 5540 (1) (c), notwithstanding the statement that such conduct is "included in the concept of disorderly conduct." Id. Sec. 5525, Comment at 187.

138. Ill. Ann. Stat. ch. 38, Sec. 11-1 to 11-20 (Smith-Hurd 1964). The Model Penal Code reporters originally adopted this position but the proposal was defeated by the council.

Some members believe that the Reporters' position is the rational one but that it would be totally unacceptable to American legislatures and would prejudice acceptance of the Code generally. Other members oppose the position. . . . on the ground that sodomy is a cause or symptom of moral decay in a society and should be repressed by law.

Model Penal Code Sec. 207.5, Comment (1) at 276 (Tent. Draft No. 4, 1955). See Schwartz, Morals Offenses and the Model Penal Code, 63 Colum. L. Rev. 669 (1963).

139. N.Y. Pen. Law Sec. 130.38. See Ploscowe, Sex Offenses in the New Penal Law, 32 Brooklyn L. Rev. 274, 286 (1966) (critical: "It is obvious once again that change is not necessarily progress.") The New York proposed code would have removed criminality from private consensual conduct. See Note, The Proposed Penal Law of New York, 64 Colum. L. Rev. 1469, 1545 (1964).

140. N.Y. Pen. Law Sec. 70.15 (2).

141. Mich. Pub. Acts 1952, No. 73, Sec. 750.158, Mich. Stat. Ann. Sec. 28.355 (1962) (life maximum for a sexually delinquent

person).

142. See p. 947 supra.

143. See generally Comment, Sentencing Reform and the Michigan Revised Criminal Code, 14 Wayne L. Rev. p. 891 supra.

144. Report of the Committee on Homosexual Offenses and Prostitution, CMD. No. 247 (1957) (hereinafter cited as Wolfenden Report).

145. See, e.g., P. Devlin, The Enforcement of Morals (1965) (hereinafter cited as Devlin); H. Hart, Law, Liberty and Morality (1966) (hereinafter cited as Hart); N. St. John-Stevas, Law and Morals (1964); Dworkin, Lord Devlin and the Enforcement of Morals, 75 Yale L. J. 986 (1966); Ison, The Enforcement of Morals, 3 U. Brit. Colum. L. Rev. 263 (1967).

146. Wolfenden Report at 24.

147. Devlin at 13-14.

148. Id.

149. Hart at 4-5. See also Fletcher, Sex Offenses: An Ethical View, 25 Law & Contemp. Prob. 244 (1960). A hybrid position is attributable to Norman St. John-Stevas that only "those moral offenses which affect the common good are fit subjects for legislation." N. St. John-Stevas, supra note 145, at 27. However, the assessment of the public good via empirical study interjects serious difficulty. Id. at 27-31.

150. Hart at 46-48.

152. Id. at 12.

153. See Hart at 50-52; Ison, supra note 145, at 266-69.

154. N. St. John-Stevas, supra note 145, at 120. Such predominantly Catholic countries as France, Italy, Mexico and Uruguay do not attempt regulation of private sexual relationships between consenting adults. Model Penal Code, Sec. 207.5, Comment (1) at 278 (Tent. Draft No. 4, 1955).

155. See N. St. John-Stevas, supra note 145, at 118-19.

156. Devlin at 17.

157. Ison, supra note 145, at 267-69.

158. Devlin at 17.

159. See generally Dworkin, supra note 145, at 994-1002.

160. Hart at 50.

161. Dworking, supra note 145, at 1001.

162. See generally Comment, Deviate Sexual Behavior: The Desirability of Legislative Proscription, 30 Albany L. Rev. 291 (1966); Note, The Crimes Against Nature, 16 J. Pub. L. 159, 177-83 (1967); Comment, supra note 150, at 599-603.

163. 381 U.S. 479 (1965). See 64 Mich. L. Rev. 197-288 (1965) for a series of articles by renowned professors discussing the Griswold case.

164. 381 U.S. at 485. The search and seizure provision of the fourth amendment is not entirely distinct from a right of privacy entitled to constitutional protection. In Smayda v. United States, 352 F.2d 251 (9th Cir. 1965), homosexuals were apprehended and convicted on evidence obtained by clandestine surveillance of a public toilet by means of a concealed hole drilled in the ceiling. In spite of the fact that a large number of innocent users were necessarily observed during the surveillance, the court held that there was no unreasonable search and seizure of a constitutionally protected area. See 17 Hastings L.J. 835 (1966) (critical). However, the recent Supreme Court decision in Katz v. United States, 389 U.S. 347 (1967) apparently strips Smayda of its basic underpinnings by declaring constitutional protection for persons in public phone booths where the surveillance is without benefit of judicial decree issued upon probable cause.

165. One state court that has considered the question rejected the constitutional privacy argument on the rather unconvincing ground that "(i)t is sufficient to say that sodomy has been a crime over the centuries." State v. White, -- Mr. --, --, 217, A.2d 212, 215 (1966). But cf. Bielicki v. Superior Court, 57 Cal. 2d 602, 371 P. 2d 288, 21 Cal. Rptr. 552 (1962). "(L)icense to make such an inspection of a toilet stall is not the equivalent of authority to invade the personal right of privacy of the person occupying the stall." Id. at 609, 371 P. 2d at 292, 21 Cal. Rptr. at 556.

166. "Excessive bail shall not be required, nor excessive fines imposed, nor cruel and unusual punishments inflicted." U.S. Const. amend. VIII.

167. See George, Legal, Medical and Psychiatric Considerations in the Control of Prostitution, 60 Mich. L. Rev. 717, 753-57 (1962); Glueck, An Evaluation of the Homosexual Offender, 41 Minn. L. Rev. 187, 194-205 (1957), and the authorities collected therein.

168. 370 U.S. 660 (1962).

169. 234 F. Supp. 333 (W.D.N.C. 1964).

170. Id. at 337.

171. Id. at 339.

172. 356 F.2d 761 (4th Cir. 1966).

173. 361 F.2d 50 (D.C. Cir. 1966).

174. 356 F.2d at 764. It should be noted, however, that voluntary intoxication is not within the rule. Nor are other criminal acts of the chronic alcoholic, not characteristic of his affliction, exempt from punishment. Id.

175. Subsequent to the preparation of this comment the Supreme Court handed down its decision in Powell v. Texas, 88 S. Ct. 2145 (1968), wherein the Court refused to apply the Robinson rule to an alcoholic. The Justices concurring in the majority opinion were not convinced of the compulsiveness of alcoholism, but the indication is that this factor would not be controlling since an overt public act was involved. However, Mr. Justice White's special concurrence, the deciding vote in a five-four decision, suggests that the result would be different could compulsiveness be definitively established. In any event the issue with respect to homosexuals remains open.

176. For an exceedingly fine empirical study of the enforcement of homosexual laws, see Comment, The Consenting Adult Homosexual and the Law: An Empirical Study of Enforcement and Administration in Los Angeles County, 13 U.C.L.A.L. Rev. 647 (1966).

177. See Comment, Deviate Sexual Behavior: The Desirability of Legislative Proscription, 30 Albany L. Rev. 291, 300-1 (1966).

178. See A. Kinsey, W. Pomeroy & W. Pomeroy & C. Martin, Sexual Behavior in the Human Male (1948). "(Eight) per cent of the males are exclusively homosexual . . . for at least three years between the ages of 16 and 55. This is one male in every 13. (Four) per cent of the white males are exclusively homosexual throughout their lives. . . ." Id. at 651. See also G. Mueller, Legal Regulation of Sexual Conduct 16-19 (1961); Note, supra note 162, at 171-75.

179. Ploscowe, Sex Offenses: The American Legal Context, 25 Law & Contemp. Prob. 217, 221 (1960). See Comment, supra note 177, at 297-99; Note, supra note 162, at 171-75.

180. A survey covering a ten year period in New York City found only three cases of sodomy prosecution of females while "tens of thousands" of males were prosecuted. Bowman & Engle, A Psychiatric Evaluation of Laws of Homosexuality, 29 Temp. L.Q. 273, 281 (1956). A survey conducted by Kinsey covering 1696 to 1952 revealed not a single conviction of a female for homosexual activity. A. Kinsey, W. Pomeroy, C. Martin & P. Gebhard, Sexual Behavior in the Human Female 484-486 (1953). But see People v. Livermore, 9 Mich. App. 47, 155 N.W. 2d 711 (1967) (conviction for "gross indecency" between females).

181. "Only an intellectually numb person can still maintain that the criminal law, with the traditional means at its command, can enforce the sexual standard which it endoreses. It cannot, and we must face the fact." G. Mueller, supra note 178 at 17.

182. The experience of the English attorney general's office has been that 95 per cent of all blackmail cases reported to

that office concerned homosexuals. E. Schur, Crimes Without Victims: Deviate Behavior and Public Policy 83 (1965). A recent New York indictment for extortion involved seventeen defendants, part of a nationwide ring, who specialized in victimizing prominent homosexuals. N.Y. Times, March 3, 1966, at 1, col. 3. See generally Comment, supra note 177, at 302-04; Note, supra note 162, at 175-177.

183. Model Penal Code Sec. 207.5, Comment (1) at 278 (Tent. Draft No. 4, 1955).

184. Mich. Pub. Acts 1952, No. 73, Sec. 750.85, Mich. Stat. Ann. Sec. 28.280 (1962). If the defendant is a "sexually delinquent person" a maximum life sentence may be imposed. Id. A sexually delinquent person is defined as "any person whose sexual behavior is characterized by repetitive or compulsive acts. . . ." Mich. Pub. Acts 1952, No. 73, Sec. 750.10a, Mich. Stat. Ann. Sec. 28.200 (1) (1962).

185. People v. Carlson, 160 Mich. 426, 125 N.W. 361 (1910). See generally R. Perkins, Criminal Law 86-96 (1957).

186. People v. Guillett, 342 Mich. 1, 69 N.W. 2d 140 (1955).

187. People v. Richardson, 224 Mich. 66, 194 N.W. 612 (1923).

188. People v. Goulette, 82 Mich. 36, 45 N.W. 1124 (1890).

189. People v. Dowell, 136 Mich. 306, 99 N.W. 23 (1904).

190. The trier of fact must consider all factors reflecting on the state of the defendant's mind in determining if he had the capacity, and did in fact, entertain the specific intent. People v. Guillett, 342 Mich. 1, 69 N.W. 2d 140 (1955).

191. People v. Courier, 79 Mich. 366, 44 N.W. 571 (1890).

192. People v. Sanford, 149 Mich. 266, 112 N.W. 910 (1907).

193. People v. Courier, 79 Mich. 366, 44 N.W. 571 (1890).

194. People v. Marrs, 125 Mich. 376, 84 N.W. 284 (1900).

195. See, e.g., State v. White, 52 Mo. App. 285 (1893). However, it has been held that an action for assault will be sustained where the defendant's conduct leads to injury as a result of mental distress intentionally inflicted by the defendant. State v. Williams, 186 N.C. 627, 120 S.E. 224 (1923). See generally Annot., 12 A.L.R. 2d 971 (1950).

196. Mich. Pub. Acts 1952, No. 73, Sec. 750.336, Mich. Stat. Ann. Sec. 28.568 (1954). Any person or persons over the age of 16 years, who shall assault a child under the age of 16 years, and shall take or attempt to take indecent and improper liberties with the person of such a child, without committing or intending to commit the crime of rape or the crime of sodomy or gross indecency upon such child, shall be guilty of a felony.

197. People v. Hicks, 98 Mich. 86, 90, 56 N.W. 1102, 1104

(1893); accord, People v. Szymanski, 321 Mich. 248, 32 N.W. 2d 451 (1948).

198. People v. Noyes, 328 Mich. 207, 43 N.W. 2d 331 (1950); People v. Visel, 275 Mich. 77, 265 N.W. 781 (1936).

199. People v. Hicks, 98 Mich. 86, 90, 56 N.W. 1102, 1104 (1893). See People v. Szymanski, 321 Mich. 248, 32 N.W. 2d 451 (1948) (man placing his hand on girl's leg in a theater). For cases decided in favor of the defendant, see People v. Healy, 265 Mich. 317, 251 N.W. 393 (1933) (artist raising child's bloomers to sketch her legs); People v. Sheffield, 105 Mich. 117, 63 N.W. 65 (1895) (defendant placed his arms around the waist of a young girl with whom he was acquainted).

200. People v. Eddy, 252 Mich. 340, 233 N.W. 336 (1930).

201. People v. Oberstaedt, 372 Mich. 521, 127 N.W. 2d 354 (1964).

202. People v. Parmalee, 206 Mich. 4, 172 N.W. 399 (1919).

203. Mich. Comp. Laws Sec. 750.145a (1948), Mich. Stat. Ann. Sec. 28.341 (1962).

204. People v. Pippin, 316 Mich. 191, 25 N.W. 2d 164 (1946).

205. Mich. Comp. Laws Sec. 750.339 (1948),Mich. Stat. Ann. Sec. 28.571 (1954).

206. Mich. Comp. Laws Sec. 750.340 (1948), Mich. Stat. Ann. Sec. 28.572 (1954).

207. See p. 939 supra.

208. Mich. Rev. Crim. Code Sec. 2301 (c) (Final Draft 1967).

209. N.Y. Pen. Law Sec. 130.55, Comment at 307.

210. See Ploscowe, Sex Offenses in the New Penal Law, 32 Brooklyn L. Rev. 274, 281-82 (1966).

211. Unlike the New York code from which the Proposed Code's proposals are largely drawn, the Michigan proposal contains no corroboration requirement. The relative merits of such a proposal are discussed at pp. 966-68 infra. See N.Y. Pen. Law Sec. 130.15.

212. Mich. Rev. Crim. Code Sec. 2320 (Final Draft 1967).

213. See pp. 941-42 supra.

214. Mich. Rev. Crim. Code Sec. 2321 (Final Draft 1967). For a detailed discussion of mental incapacity and mental defect see pp. 942-43 supra.

215. Mich. Rev. Crim. Code Sec. 2330 (2) (c) (Final Draft 1967).

216. See N.Y. Pen. Law Sec. 130.05, Comment at 275. The example cited is an illicit touching in a crowded subway.

217. Mich. Rev. Crim. Code, Sec. 2322 (2) (Final Draft 1967).

218. Id., Comment at 189; N.Y. Pen. Law Sec. 130.55, Comment at 308.

219. Mich. Rev. Crim. Code Sec. 2331 (Final Draft 1967).

220. Id. Sec. 2101-03.

221. Id. Sec. 1001-20.

222. Id.

223. Mich. Pub. Acts 1952, No. 73, Sec. 750.335a, Mich. Stat. Ann. Sec. 28.567 (1) (1954). If the offender is classified as a "sexually delinquent person" a maximum penalty of life imprisonment may be imposed. See note 184 supra.

224. People v. Kratz, 230 Mich. 334, 203 N.W. 114 (1925).

225. Peyton v. District of Columbia, 100 A. 2d 36 (D. C. Ct. App. 1953); cf. People v. DeVine, 271 Mich. 635, 261 N.W. 101 (1935).

226. People v. DeVine, 271 Mich. 635, 261 N.W. 101 (1935); cf. Prople v. Ring, 267 Mich. 657, 255 N.W. 373 (1934).

227. People v. Kratz, 230 Mich. 334, 203 N.W. 114 (1925). It is sometimes said that at least one other person in addition to the observer must have been able to see the act if he had looked. Green v. State, 106 Ga. App. 485, 127 S. E. 2d 383 (1962).

228. 267 Mich. 657, 255 N.W. 373 (1934), noted in 33 Mich. L. Rev. 936 (1935).

229. 267 Mich. at 659, 255 N.W. at 373.

230. In response to the introduction of legislation that would have prohibited nudism, the attorney general opined that present law, as interpreted by the Ring Case, was adequate prohibition of the practice of nudism. (1955-1956) Mich. Att'y Gen. Biennial Rep. pt. 1, at 234.

231. 353 Mich. 562, 92 N.W. 2d 6 (1958), noted in 5 Wayne L. Rev. 256 (1959).

232. I say and hold that the search and arrests in this case were unreasonable and unlawful. . . . (E)ven if the officers were there legally . . . what the search disclosed did not in these circumstances constitute a violation of this statute.
353 Mich. at 576, 92 N.W. 2d at 12 (Voelker, J., with Smith & Black, JJ., concurring).

233. Dethmers, Carr and Kelly, JJ. Judge Kavanagh, former Michigan Attorney General who wrote the opinion on the Ring case, note 230 supra, did not participate in the decision.

234. Id. at 594, 92 N.W. 2d at 20 (Edwards, J., now federal circuit judge for the Sixth Circuit).

235. See People v. Hildabridle, 353 Mich. 562, 582-83, 92 N.W. 2d 6, 14-15 (1958).

236. But see Roberts v. Clement, 252 F. Supp. 835 (E.D. Tenn. 1966), discussed p. 965 infra.

237. Mich. Rev. Crim. Code Sec. 2325 (Final Draft 1967).

238. Cf. Ill. Ann. Stat. ch. 38, Sec. 11-9, Comment at 639-40 (Smith-hurd 1961).

239. See R. Perkins, Criminal Law 671-74 (1957).

240. Mich. Rev. Crim. Code Sec. 2325, Comment at 190 (Final Draft 1967).

241. See pp. 952-54 supra.

242. It seems in fact something of a mystery why those who engage in (nudism's) strange practices are willing to suffer both the stings of outraged public opinion and voracious, ravenous insects in order to pursue its illusory rewards. . . . But . . . in our triune form of government it is the particular duty of the judiciary to protect individuals and minorities in their constitutional rights even though their beliefs and activities may be heretical or unpopular.
Roberts v. Clement, 252 F. Supp. 835, 850 (E.D. Tenn. 1966) (Concurring opinion of Darr, J.) According to some psychologists nudity may have a very beneficial effect on certain persons. See Time, Feb. 23, 1968, at 68.

243. Tenn. Code Ann. Sec. 39-3009 (Supp. 1967).
It shall be unlawful for any person, firm or corporation to operate or carry on, or engage in the operation of a nudist colony in this state. It shall also be unlawful for any person to engage in nudist practices in this state.

244. 252 F. Supp. 835 (E. D. Tenn. 1966).

245. Id. at 848. See also Griswold v. Connecticut, 381 U.S. 479 (1965), discussed pp. 954-55 supra.

246. 252 F. Supp. at 850. See U. S. Const. amends. I, XIV.

247. Cf. Griswold V. Connecticut, 381 U. S. 479 (1965).

248. See, e.g., People v. Holdabridle, 353 Mich. 562, 92 N. W. 2d 6 (1958).

249. See Model Penal Code Sec. 207.4, Comment (23) at 264-65 (Tent. Draft No. 4., 1955).

250. Mich. Comp. Laws Sec. 767.24 (1948), Mich. Stat. Ann. Sec. 28.964 (1954).

251. Mich. Comp. Laws Sec. 750.532 (1948), Mich. Stat. Ann. Sec. 28.800 (1954).

252. Turner v. People, 33 Mich. 363 (1876); People v. Gage, 62 Mich. 271, 28 N. W. 835 (1886).

253. Model Penal Code Sec. 213.6 (5) (Official Draft 1962).

254. Speaking of sodomy Blackstone remarks that "it is an offence of so dark a nature, so easily charged, and the negative so difficult to be proved, that the accusation should be clearly made out; for if false it deserves a punishment inferior only to that of the crime itself." Blackstone, Commentaries *215.

255. E. G., Iowa Code Ann. Sec. 782.4 (1950); N.Y. Penal Law Sec. 130.15. See also Model Penal Code Sec. 207.4, Comment (22) at 253-64 (Tent. Draft No. 4, 1955); Ploscowe, Sex Offenses: The American Legal Context, 25 Law & Contemp. Prob. 217, 223 (1960).

256. G. Mueller, Legal Regulation of Sexual Conduct 38-39 (1961).

257. 3 J. Wigmore, Evidence Sec. 924a (3d ed. 1940). "Judging merely from the reports of cases in the appellate courts, one must infer that many innocent men have gone to prison because of tales whose falsity could not be exposed." Id. at 459.

258. 7 J. Wigmore, Evidence Sec. 2061 (3d Ed. 1940).

259. 3 J. Wigmore, Evidence Sec. 924b (3d Ed. 1940).

260. That credibility is for the determination of the jury is as old as the jury system itself. "For one excellence of the trial by jury is, that the jury are triers of the credit of the witness, as well as of the truth of the fact." Blackstone, Commentaries *214. See People v. Koukol, 262 Mich. 529, 247 N.W. 738 (1933). See generally 58 Am. Jur. Witnesses Sec. 862 (1948).

261. See statutes and cases collected in 7 J. Wigmore, Evidence Sec. 2061 n 2. (3d ed 1940 & Supp. 1964).

262. Mich. Gen. Ct. Rule 516.1 (1963). Relevant constructional considerations are found in People v. Padgett, 306 Mich. 545, 11 N. W. 2d 235 (1943), cited with approval in People v. Oates, 369 Mich. 214, 217, 119 N.W. 2d 530, 532 (1963).

H. Prostitution and Pandering

   1. Michigan Compiled Laws (1948)

750.448 Soliciting and accosting

   Sec. 448. SOLICITING AND ACCOSTING — Any person who shall accost, solicit or invite another in any public place, or in or from any building or vehicle, by word, gesture or any other means, to commit prostitution or to do any other lewd or immoral act, shall be guilty of a misdemeanor.

750.449 Admitting to place for purpose of prostitution

Sec. 449. ADMITTING TO PLACE FOR PURPOSE OF PROSTITUTION -
Any person who shall receive or admit or offer to receive or
admit any person into any place, structure, house, building
or vehicle for the purpose of prostitution, lewdness or assignation, or who shall knowingly permit any person to remain
in any such place for any such purpose, shall be guilty of a
misdemeanor.

750.450 Aiders and abettors

Sec. 450. AIDERS AND ABETTORS - Any person who shall aid,
assist or abet another to commit, or offer to commit, any
act prohibited by the 2 next preceding sections of this chapter shall be guilty of a misdemeanor.

750.451 Second and subsequent convictions

Sec. 451. SECOND AND SUBSEQUENT CONVICTIONS - Any person
who shall be adjudged guilty a second time of a violation of
any of the preceding sections of this chapter, the offense
being charged as a second offense, shall be guilty of a misdemeanor, punishable by imprisonment in the county jail not
more than 1 year or by a fine of not more than 500 dollars;
and any person adjudged guilty a third or any subsequent
time of a violation of any of said sections, the offense
being charged as a third or subsequent offense, shall be
guilty of a felony, punishable by imprisonment in the state
prison for not more than 2 years.

750.452 House of ill-fame, keeping, maintaining or operating

Sec. 452. KEEPING, ETC. A HOUSE OF ILL-FAME - Any person
who shall keep, maintain or operate, or aid and abet in keeping, maintaining or operating a house of ill-fame, bawdy
house or any house or place resorted to for the purpose of
prostitution or lewdness shall be guilty of a felony punishable by imprisonment in the state prison for not more than
5 years or by a fine of not more than 2,500 dollars.

750.453 Incriminating testimony and immunity of witnesses

Sec. 453. INCRIMINATING TESTIMONY AND IMMUNITY OF WITNESS
EXCEPT FOR PERJURY - No person shall be excused from attending and testifying, or producing any books, papers or other
documents before any court or magistrate, upon any investigation, proceeding or trial, for a violation of any of the
provisions of this chapter, upon the ground or for the reason that the testimony or evidence, documentary or otherwise,
required of him may tend to degrade or incriminate him; but
no person shall be prosecuted or subjected to any penalty or
forfeiture for or on account of any transaction, matter or
thing concerning which he may so testify or produce evidence,

documentary or otherwise, and no testimony so given or produced shall be received against him upon any criminal investigation, proceeding or trial: Provided, That no person so testifying shall be exempt from prosecution and punishment for perjury committed in so testifying.

750.454 Leasing house for purposes of prostitution

Sec. 454. LEASING HOUSE KNOWING IT IS TO BE USED FOR PURPOSES OF PROSTITUTION, ETC. - Any person who shall let any dwelling house, knowing that the lessee intends to use it as a house of ill-fame or place of resort for the purpose of prostitution and lewdness, or for the purpose of gambling for money or other property, or who shall knowingly permit such lessee to use the same for such purpose, or who shall receive any rent for any dwelling, house, room or apartment which is used as a house of ill-fame or place of resort for prostitutes, or for the purpose of prostitution and lewdness, or for the purpose of gambling for money or other property, having reasonable cause to believe such house, room or apartment is used for any such purpose, shall be guilty of a misdemeanor, punishable by imprisonment in the county jail not more than 6 months or by fine of not more than 250 dollars: Provided, That no person shall be liable for receiving rent as aforesaid for any period prior to the time when he shall have reasonable cause to believe that such house, room or apartment is used for any such purpose.

750.455 Pandering

Sec. 455. PANDERING - Any person who shall procure a female inmate for a house of prostitution; or who shall induce, persuade, encourage, inveigle or entice a female person to become a prostitute; or who by promises, threats, violence or by any device or scheme, shall cause, induce, persuade, encourage, take, place, harbor, inveigle or entice a female person to become an inmate of a house of prostitution or assignation place, or any place where prostitution is practiced, encouraged or allowed; or any person who shall, by promises, threats, violence or by any device or scheme, cause, induce, persuade, encourage, inveigle or entice an inmate of a house of prostitution or place of assignation to remain therein as such inmate; or any person who by promises, threats, violence, by any device or scheme, by fraud or artifice, or by duress of person or goods, or by abuse of any position of confidence or authority, or having legal charge, shall take, place, harbor, inveigle, entice, persuade, encourage or procure any female person to enter any place within this state in which prostitution is practiced, encouraged or allowed, for the purpose of prostitution; or who shall inveigle, entice, persuade, encourage, or procure any female person to come into this state or to leave this state for the purpose of prostitution; or who upon the pretense of marriage takes or detains a female person for the purpose of sexual intercourse; or who shall receive or give or agree to receive or give any money or thing of value for procuring or attempting to procure any female person to become a prostitute or to come into this state or leave this state for the purpose of prostitution, shall be guilty of a felony, punishable by imprisonment in the state prison for not more than 20 years.

750.456 Placing wife in a house of prostitution

Sec. 456. PLACING WIFE BY FRAUD, ETC., IN HOUSE OF PROSTITUTION - Any person who by force, fraud, intimidation or threat places or leaves, or procures any other person to place or leave his wife in a house of prostitution or to lead a life of prostitution, shall be guilty of a felony, punishable by imprisonment in the state prison for not more than 20 years.

750.457 Earnings of prostitute, acceptin

Sec. 457. ACCEPTING MONEY, ETC., FROM EARNINGS OF PROSTITUTE - Any person who shall knowingly accept, receive, levy or appropriate any money or valuable thing without consideration from the proceeds of the earnings of any woman engaged in prostitution, or any person, knowing a female to be a prostitute, shall live or derive support or maintenance, in whole or in part, from the earnings or proceeds of the prostitution of said prostitute, or from moneys loaned or advanced to or charged against her by any keeper or manager or inmate of a house or other place where prostitution is practiced or allowed, shall be guilty of a felony, punishable by imprisonment in the state prison not more than 20 years. And such acceptance, receipt, levy or appropriation of such money or valuable thing, shall, upon any proceeding or trial for violation of this section, be presumptive evidence of lack of consideration.

750.458 Detaining female in house of prostitution for debt

Sec. 458. DETAINING FEMALE IN HOUSE OF PROSTITUTION FOR DEBT CONTRACTED WHILE THERE - Any person who attempts to detain any female person in a disorderly house or house of prostitution because of any debt or debts she has contracted, or is said to have contracted while living in said house, shall be guilty of a felony, punishable by imprisonment in the state prison for not less than 2 nor more than 20 years.

750.459 Transporting female for prostitution

Sec. 459. TRANSPORTING FEMALE FOR PROSTITUTION - Any person who shall knowingly transport or cause to be transported, or aid or assist in obtaining transportation for, by any means of conveyance, into, through or across this state, any female person for the purpose of prostitution or with the intent and purpose to induce, entice or compel such female person to become a prostitute shall be guilty of a felony, punishable by imprisonment in the state prison for not more than 20 years; any person who may commit the crime in this section mentioned may be prosecuted, indicted, tried and convicted in any county or city in or through which he shall so transport or attempt to transport any female persons as aforesaid.

750.460 Acts committed outside state

Sec. 460. ACTS COMMITTED OUTSIDE STATE - It shall not be a defense to a prosecution for any of the acts prohibited in the next 5 preceding sections of this chapter that any part of such act or acts shall have been committed outside this state, and the offense shall in such case be deemed and alleged to have been committed and the offender tried and punished in any county in which the prostitution was intended to be practiced or in which the offense was consummated, or any overt act in furtherance of the offense shall have been committed.

750.461 Competency of female as witness though wife of accused

Sec. 461. COMPETENCY OF FEMALE AS WITNESS THOUGH WIFE OF ACCUSED - Any such female person referred to in the 6 preceding sections shall be a competent witness in any prosecution under this chapter to testify for or against the accused as to any transaction or as to any conversation with the accused or by him with another person or persons in her presence, notwithstanding her having married the accused before or after the violation of any of the provisions of this chapter, whether called as a witness during the existence of the marriage or after its dissolution. No complaint shall be entertained or warrant issued against any female giving testimony in any proceeding under this chapter by reason of or arising from any testimony so given by such female witness, nor shall any such testimony or any part thereof be used in any way in connection with or as a basis for a criminal prosecution against said witness. No such female witness shall be permitted to refuse to answer any question involving a violation of the provisions of this chapter on the ground that such answer might tend to incriminate or degrade said witness: Provided, That no person so testifying shall be exempt from prosecution and punishment for perjury committed in so testifying.

750.462 Female under 17, in house of prostitution

Sec. 462. FEMALE UNDER 1& YEARS OF AGE NOT TO BE EMPLOYED OR REMAIN, ETC., IN HOUSE OF PROSTITUTION - Any person who, for any purpose whatever, other than prostitution, shall take or convey to, or employ, receive, detain or suffer to remain in any house of prostitution, house of ill-fame, bawdyhouse, house of assignation or in any house or place for the resort of prostitutes or other disorderly persons, any female of the age of 17 years or under, shall be guilty of a misdemeanor.

750.167 Definition, subsequent offenses - Disorderly Persons

Sec. 167. Any person of sufficient ability, who shall refuse or neglect to support his family; any common prostitute; any window peeper; any person who engages in an illegal occupation or business; any person who shall be drunk or intoxicated or engaged in any indecent or obscene conduct in any public place; any vagrant; any person found begging in a public place; any person found loitering in a house of ill-fame or prostitution or place where prostitution or lewdness is practiced, encouraged or allowed; any person who shall knowingly loiter in or about any place where an illegal occupation or business is being conducted; any person who shall loiter in or about any police station, police headquarters building, county jail, hospital, court building or any other public building or place for the purpose of soliciting employment of legal services or the services of sureties upon criminal recognizances; any person who shall be found jostling or roughly crowding people unnecessarily in a public place; any person who telephones any other person or causes any other person to be telephoned and uses any vulgar, indecent, obscene, threatening or offensive language, or suggesting any lewd or lascivious act over any telephone, shall be deemed a disorderly person. When any person, who has been convicted of refusing or neglecting to support his family under the provisions of this section, is then charged with subsequent violations within a period of 2 years, such person shall be prosecuted as a second offender or third and subsequent offender as provided in section 168 of this act, if the family of such person is then receiving any form of public relief or support. As amended P.A. 1956, No. 110, Sec. 1, Eff. Aug. 11; P.A. 1964, No. 144, Sec. 1. Eff. Aug. 28.

802.104 Prostitutes; complaint, imprisonment, term, release

Sec. 4. Every person more than 15 years of age, who is a common prostitute shall, upon conviction thereof, be punished by imprisonment in the Detroit house of correction a term of 3 years. Complaints under this section may, in cities having a police justice, be made to said police justice, who shall hear, try and determine the same. In the townships, villages, and cities which have no police justice, said complaints shall be made to a justice of the peace, who shall hear, try and determine the same; but said justice of the peace shall, within 30 days after he has determined the said complaint, if the said person is found guilty, file in the office of the county clerk of his county, copies of all the proceedings under the same, and of the testimony which copies shall, by the said clerk, be forthwith submitted to the circuit judge of said county, who shall in writing approve or disapprove of the finding of said justice of the peace, which approval or disapproval shall be filed by said judge in the office of said clerk, and shall be final. If said judge disapproves of said finding, the clerk shall certify the same under the seal of the circuit court to the superintendent of said house of correction, and said superintendent shall, upon the receipt of the certificate, release the person in whose case it is made. It is hereby made the duty of any sheriff, constable, or superintendent of police in this state, to serve said certificate upon the requisition of the said clerk, on the superintendent of said house.

802.105 Same; parole, rules and regulations

Sec. 5. The inspectors of the Detroit house of correction may establish rules and regulations under which women confined in the said house, by virtue of the preceding section, may upon reformation or marked good behavior, be absolutely discharged from imprisonment therein, or be released conditionally from residence in said house before their term of imprisonment has expired, which rules and regulations shall be approved by the circuit judge of the county of Wayne and the recorder of the city of Detroit: Provided, That the persons released conditionally may at any time before the expiration of their term of imprisonment be returned to a residence in said house under and by the written order of the said inspectors, which order shall be authority for any officer of said house, sheriff or policeman, to arrest and return said persons.

408.619 Applicants not to be sent to certain places

Sec. 19. Prostitution, Licentious Show. An employment agency shall not knowingly procure, entice, send or aid or abet in procuring, enticing or sending a woman or girl to practice prostitution, or to enter as an inmate or a servant a house of ill fame, or other place resorted to for prostitution, or for the purpose of taking part or performing in unclean, nude, licentious, lewd or vicious shows. . . .

408.621 Penalties

Sec. 21. PENALTIES. Any person found guilty of the violation of any section of this act shall be guilty of a felony and shall be subject to a fine of not less than 300 dollars or more than 1,000 dollars, or by imprisonment not to exceed 4 years or both, at the discretion of the court.

2. Definitions and Elements of the Offenses

Neither the statutes nor the cases in Michigan specifically define "prostitution." This is probably because the
word has a commonly understood meaning though prostitution
was not an offense at the common law.[1] Prostitution has
been variously defined in those jurisdictions taking the
trouble to do so as "the common lewdness of a woman for gain"
or as '"the practice of a female in offering her body to an
indiscriminate intercourse with men for money or its equivalent."'[2]

A house to which persons resorted for purposes of prostitution was known as a bawdy house, a house of prostitution,
or a house of ill-fame. The keeping of such a house was a
nuisance at common law, and the owner of the house was guilty
of a misdemeanor at common law if he rented the house with
knowledge that it was to be used for the purpose of prostitution.[3] -- Ed.

Footnotes

1. R. Perkins, Criminal Law 335 (1957)

2. Ibid.

3. Ibid.

People v. Johnson
260 Mich. 117

CLARK, C. J. Defendant, charged with procuring a female
inmate for a house of prostitution (3 Comp. Laws 1929, Sec.
16862), was convicted and sentenced, and has appealed.

The evidence is that the female came to defendant's house
and was taken in by defendant and there remained.

The word procure, as used in the statute, means to acquire or to get. The female here was procured or acquired
or gotten within the meaning of the statute. To show the
procuring the female as an "inmate for a house of prostitution," evidence was properly received of arrest and conviction of a prostitute from the house (50 C. J. p. 813), and
that a female inmate committed an act of prostitution in
the house. . . .

We find no reversible error. Affirmed.

McDONALD, POTTER, SHARPE, NORTH, FEAD, WIEST, and BUTZEL,
JJ., concurred.

People v. Jackson
280 Mich. 6

WIEST, J. Defendant reviews his conviction of the crime of pandering, under an information charging that, on or about the 1st of May, 1932, at the city of Flint, in Genesee county, and between that date and the 10th day of January, 1936, he "did knowingly accept, receive, levy and appropriate large sums of money of the United States of America without consideration from the proceeds of the earnings of Georgia Coleman, a woman engaged in prostitution, and he, the said Nathaniel Jackson knowing said Georgia Coleman, a female, to be a prostitute did live and desire (derive?) support and maintenance from the earnings and proceeds of the prostitution of said Georgia Coleman."

The statute, <u>Act No. 328</u>, <u>Sec. 457</u>, <u>Pub. Acts 1931</u> commonly known as the penal code, provides:

"Any person who shall knowingly accept, receive, levy or appropriate any money or valuable thing without consideration from the proceeds of the earnings of any woman engaged in prostitution, or any person, knowing a female to be a prostitute, shall live or derive support or maintenance, in whole or in part, from the earnings or proceeds of the prostitution of said prostitute, . . . shall be guilty of a felony. . . . And such acceptance, receipt, levy or appropriation of such money or valuable thing, shall, upon any proceeding or trial for violation of this section, be presumptive evidence of lack of consideration.". . .

It is . . . contended that the statute (<u>Act No. 328</u>, <u>Sec. 457</u>, <u>Pub. Acts 1931</u>) in making "acceptance, receipt, levy or appropriation of such money or valuable thing . . . presumptive evidence of lack of consideration," is unconstitutional in casting upon defendant the burden of going forward with the evidence and negativing the presumption. The identical point was considered in <u>State v. Pippi</u>, <u>supra</u>, and found to have no merit.

Defendant gave no testimony and, therefore, we do not have the question of weighing the evidence against the statutory presumption. Employment of the statutory presumption did not deprive defendant of any right.

"Every accused person, of course, enters upon his trial clothed with the presumption of innocence. But that presumption may be overcome, not only by direct proof, but, in many cases, when the facts standing alone are not enough, by the additional weight of a countervailing legislative presumption. If the effect of the legislative act is to give to the facts from which the presumption is drawn an artificial value to some extent, it is no more than happens in respect of a great variety of presumptions not resting upon statute. . . .

"The point that the practical effect of the statute creating the presumption is to compel the accused person to be a witness against himself may be put aside with slight discussion. The statute compels nothing." <u>Yee Hem v. United States</u>,

268 U.S. 178 (45 Sup. Ct. 470).

In that case the court quoted the following from Mobile, J. & K. C. R. Co. v. Turnipseed, 219 U.S. 35 (31 Sup. Ct. 136, 32 L. R. A. (N. S.) 226, Ann. Cas. 1912A, 463):

"'That a legislative presumption of one fact from evidence of another may not constitute a denial of due process of law or a denial of the equal protection of the law it is only essential that there shall be some rational connection between the fact proved and the ultimate fact presumed, and that the inference of one fact from proof of another shall not be so unreasonable as to be a purely arbitrary mandate. So, also, it must not, under guise of regulating the presentation of evidence, operate to preclude the party from the right to present his defense to the main fact thus presumed.'"

We find no reversible error and the conviction is affirmed.

FEAD, C. J., and NORTH, BUTZEL, BUSHNELL, SHARPE, POTTER, and CHANDLER, JJ., concurred.

People v. Saunders
29 Mich. 269

CAMPBELL, J.

Respondent was convicted under section 7702 of the Compiled Laws, of letting a dwelling house, "knowing that the lessee intended to use it as a place of resort for the purpose of prostitution and lewdness." The same section contains a prohibition and penalty against knowingly permitting a lessee to use a dwelling-house for such purposes, but the information was confined to the offense of letting with guilty knowledge. . . .

. . . It was necessary in this case not only to prove the intended and actual use of the dwelling for the unlawful purpose, but to show that respondent knew it was so intended when he first leased it. It is not likely that persons who come to an understanding on such a purpose will express it in writing, or even express it at all. Criminal agreements are often, if not usually, made tacitly. They can only be proved by circumstances. If a person leases a house to a woman of ill-repute, and knows of that repute, and the house is thenceforth used for unlawful purposes, and such use is known to him, these facts must be regarded as having a tendency to create belief in his guilty knowledge, or, at all events, as bearing upon that fact. . . .

The attention of the court was called to the question, and the judge was asked to charge that there was no evidence that defendant knew the house was resorted to, or that it was resorted to in fact, for the purposes named, but this was refused.

1065

The testimony tended to show nothing more than the evil repute of the lessee, and of other women who had been seen in the house. There was no evidence of any acts of lewdness committed there, and no evidence that men resorted there at all. If there had been proof that the house was resorted to by men as well as women of ill-fame, the jury could draw any reasonable inference from such facts. But the law does not punish the mere letting of houses to bad characters. It is the use of the house, and not merely the repute of its inmates, which the particular statute under consideration was intended to reach.

Whatever may be the probability that the house will be improperly used when in such hands, yet there must be clear proof of intent to satisfy the law, and the fact of such use, from which in this case the intent was sought to be derived, is not to be assumed without proof, direct or circumstantial. If the inmates commit offenses elsewhere, the landlord is not made responsible for what is not done on his premises. And the court erred in allowing the case to be disposed of without testimony tending to establish the misuse of the house.

We do not wish to be understood as holding that if there is clear proof of a letting with the distinct understanding that the house is to be used for unlawful purposes, any proof of actual use would be necessary. The crime may be complete at the time of the letting, and such is the meaning of the statute. But in the case before us there was no proof of such design that could have sufficed without the evidence of the actual use, and therefore the evidence became essential....

For the errors before noted, the conviction should be set aside and a new trial granted, and directions given to the court below accordingly.

COOLEY, and CHRISTIANCY, JJ., concurred.

GRAVES, Ch. J., did not sit in this case.

People v. Gastro
75 Mich. 127

CHAMPLIN, J. The respondent was charged with unlawfully keeping and maintaining a house of ill fame, resorted to for the purpose of prostitution and lewdness, contrary to the statute, at the village of Bessemer, Gogebic county. She was convicted, and sentenced to be imprisoned in the Detroit house of correction for 18 months at hard labor.

The prosecution called witnesses, and was permitted, against the objections of the attorneys for respondent, to prove the character of the house occupied by her, from what they had heard, for a long space of time. The respondent's attorneys insisted that the proofs should be confined to the day named in the information, but -

"The court ruled the testimony must show the offense charged was committed on the day laid; but, as bearing upon that question, evidence was admissible, and would be received, as to the time within one week of that alleged."

There was no error in permitting the testimony as to the ill fame of the house to extend back one week or even longer if the respondent was the keeper of the house during that time. The court rightly held that the proof must show that the offense was committed on the day alleged in the information, the elements of the offense being -

1. That it was a house of ill fame.
2. That the respondent kept it.
3. That it was resorted to for the purpose of prostitution and lewdness.

The testimony to establish the fact that the house was resorted to for the purpose of prostitution and lewdness consisted of that given by David F. Foley, George Hogle, and Floyd C. McIntryre, who each testified to the bad reputation of the house, and that they went to her house together in the night-time a few days before her arrest, and found respondent there, and a man by the name of Martin; that they were not in bed; that Martin made his home at said respondent's house; that they also found one other woman at respondent's house; who was in bed with a man whom they had known for some length of time as a single man, although they would not swear that he had not married the woman before such night, but they did not think he had done so; that the woman and man got up, and she used some indecent language.

Hogle testified that respondent called said Martin "a pimp," or "her pimp," and also called him and others "pimps."

The witness Foley was sheriff, and testified to certain admissions made by the respondent after the arrest, and while she was imprisoned in jail. These were objected to as not having been made voluntarily. In reply to a question from the court, the witness stated that such statement was made without question or suggestion, and was entirely of her own offer. He thereupon testified that respondent stated to him that she kept a whore-house.

The bill of exceptions contains the statement that -

"The above were all the witnesses sworn on the trial of the cause, and the foregoing is the substance of all the evidence on the part of the prosecution."

There was no error in admitting the testimony of the sheriff as to respondent's admissions.

The circuit judge in charging the jury said:

"We have some testimony with reference to the language which was used in the house, as to what the characters of the inmates were, - whether they were prostitutes or not. We have the testimony of one witness who says that this respondent made the remark that this man, whatever his name is, was 'her pimp.' We all know what that is when we are outdoors, and we should know what it means when we are here, just as well as when we are outdoors. We know, as a matter of fact, that it is a man who has intercourse with a loose woman, and usually she is taking care of him, - supporting him. When she says such a man is 'her pimp,' that is what she means. Well, there is a case of unwarranted sexual intercourse if you believe that to be true.

"Now, under the testimony we have the girl there; and there is testimony of one or more witnesses tending to show that respondent, on a certain occasion just after this woman was caught in bed with a man not her husband, made the remark to her that she was a whore. There is some evidence of that kind. Now, language of that kind, made use of by the respondent herself to this woman, would be pretty strong evidence against her that that other woman was a whore, and that she had such a kind of a house there. It is her own statement as to what the character of the woman was; and being her own house, if she had that kind of a woman around there habitually, and they frequented it (they certainly, according to the evidence, frequented it at one time), you have a right to consider that as pretty strong evidence as bearing upon the character of the people who come to that house.

"There is evidence by Mr. Foley, by which he swears that she said she kept a whore-house. Now it is for you to say whether she told him that or not. If you believe that she did tell Mr. Foley that she kept a whore-house, that is very strong evidence in favor of the guilt of this woman. People do not usually admit themselves guilty of crime when they are not guilty. It is more usual to deny it, and they most always do deny it. If a man, charged with crime, admits that he is guilty of it, it is pretty conclusive evidence, and evidence sufficient for you to act upon in finding him guilty. It is evidence, at least, that I should not fail to act upon if I was on the jury."

The court committed several errors in giving the above instructions. The testimony of Hogle was that the respondent called the man Martin "a pimp," or "her pimp," and also called Hogle and others "pimps." The court was not warranted in determining the language used by her, and applying it to Martin as "her pimp." It was for the jury to say whether she called Martin "a pimp," or called him "her pimp."

The circuit judge assumed that she called him "her pimp," and then proceeded to define the word "pimp," which definition differs essentially from the common acceptance of the term as defined by lexicographers. Worcester defines it as -

"One who provides gratifications for the lust of others; a procurer; a panderer."

Webster's definition is the same. The circuit judge says

a pimp –

"Is a man who has intercourse with a loose woman, and usually she is taking care of him, – supporting him."

Words sometimes acquire a peculiar signification, in a particular locality, different from their ordinary meaning, but, when such is the case, it is a fact requiring proof, and not a fact which the court can take judicial notice of; the rule being that courts will take judicial notice of the ordinary meaning of English words, but not of uncommon or extraordinary meanings applied in isolated cases or in particular localities. The word "pimp" is not so far as we are informed, a technical word, nor has it acquired any peculiar or appropriate meaning in the law. It is therefore to be construed and understood according to the common and approved usage of the language. How. Stat. Sec. 2. . . .

The counsel for defendant requested the court to charge the jury that "a single act of illicit intercourse is not sufficient to convict." In O'Brien v. People, 28 Mich. 213, it was held that the language of this statute refers to persons of bad character, and the word "resorted" implies that the house was visited frequently by that class of persons; and hence it is argued that, as the testimony in this case shows only a single instance of a person being found in the house, in the absence of testimony that men were seen resorting there, the offense was not made out. It has been held that a single act of prostitution, or habitual acts by one person, do not constitute the house bawdy. Com. v. Lambert, 12 Allen, 177; State v. Evans, 5 Ired. 603; State v. Garing, 75 Me. 591.

In Com. v. Lambert the court said that the permission, by the keeper of a house, of a single act of illicit intercourse within it does not of itself constitute the offense described in the statute.

"To hold that it did, would be to leave wholly out of view the meaning of the phrase 'resorted to,' as used in those sections of the statute."

The statute is designed to prohibit the keeping and maintaining of a house which persons are permitted to frequent for the purpose of unlawful sexual intercourse, and to prevent the existence of such places of resort. A single act of lewdness or prostitution would not constitute the offense which the statute prohibits and punishes; but, if the house is shown to be a house of ill fame, and it is also shown that persons resort there for the purpose of prostitution or lewdness, proof of a single act of prostitution would be sufficient upon this branch of the case.

I do not decide that it is necessary to show an actual illicit intercourse. If it be shown that the inmates are prostitutes, or the house is the resort of prostitutes, and males are seen frequenting the house at night, evidence of these

and kindred facts might be sufficient to satisfy a jury
that the house was resorted to for the purpose of prostitution. Under the testimony appearing in this case the request
should have been given.

The judgment must be reversed, and a new trial is granted.

MORSE, CAMPBELL, and LONG, JJ., concurred. SHERWOOD, C. J.,
did not sit.

People v. Cox
107 Mich. 435

HOOKER, J. Section 1997a, 3 How. Stat., declares that
"all keepers of bawdy houses, or houses for the resort of
prostitutes, . . . shall be deemed disorderly persons;" and
by the succeeding section the first offense is made punishable by a fine of $50 and costs of prosecution, or by im-
prisonment in the county jail or Detroit house of correction
not exceeding 30 days, or the person convicted may be required
to give sureties for good behavior for the period of three
months.

Section 9286, 3 How. Stat., provides that -

"Every person who shall keep a house of ill fame, resorted to for the purpose of prostitution or lewdness, and
every person who shall solicit, or in any manner induce,
a female to enter such house for the purpose of becoming
a prostitute, or shall by force, fraud, deceit, or in any
like manner procure a female to enter such house for the
purpose of prostitution or of becoming a prostitute, shall
be deemed guilty of a felony, and upon conviction thereof
shall be punished by imprisonment in the State prison not
more than five years, or in the county jail not more than
one year, or by fine not exceeding one thousand dollars,
or by both such fine and imprisonment, in the discretion of
the court."

The defendant appeals from a conviction under the latter
section, upon an information which charges that -

"Heretofore, to wit, on the 1st day of December, A.D.
1894, and on divers other days and times between that day
and the 1st day of January, A. D. 1895, . . . he unlawfully
and feloniously did keep and maintain a certain house of ill
fame, resorted to for the purpose of prostitution and lewdness."

To this information a plea of former conviction was interposed, setting forth the warrant upon which said conviction
was had, and stating that in that proceeding he was prosecuted for keeping the same house, and that it was a continuation of the same offense for which he is now prosecuted. The
warrant mentioned shows that he was proceeded against as a

1070

disorderly person, under the section first mentioned, the charge being -

"That heretofore, to wit, on the 23d day of March, A. D. 1895, and for ten days preceding that day, at the township of Duncan, in said county, Ira Cox, of said township of Duncan, has been and is a disorderly person, within the meaning of section 1 of Act No. 264 of the Public Acts of Michigan of 1889, being section 1997a of Howell's Annotated Statutes of the State of Michigan, for that the said Ira Cox, at the township of Duncan, in said county, during and at times aforesaid, was the keeper of a house for the resort of prostitutes."

It will be noticed that the present prosecution is for an alleged offense anterior to that upon which he was first convicted.

Two questions are presented for our consideration:

1. Whether a continuous keeping of a house of ill fame, resorted to for the purpose of prostitution, etc., is a continuing offense, so that a conviction bars another prosecution for such keeping previous to the time of the indictment upon which a conviction has been had.

2. If so, whether a conviction, under the disorderly act, of keeping a house for the resort of prostitutes, bars a prosecution for keeping a house of ill fame, resorted to for the purposes of prostitution, at a time previous to the first indictment.

To establish guilt under the disorderly act, it is necessary to show that the house is kept for the resort of prostitutes. Under the other act, the house must be resorted to for purposes of prostitution and lewdness by men or women, or both, and it must be a house of ill fame. The first falls short of the second, as it may or may not be a house of ill fame, and acts of prostitution may or may not be committed there. The act implies that it shall be a rendezvous for prostitutes, - a place which they visit or haunt (see Webst. Dict. "Resort"); and it may be open to question whether the the disorderly act would apply to a person who kept a house where prostitutes merely made it their permanent residence. But such a person might be punishable under the other statute, if the house was a house of ill fame, and was resorted to (i. e., visited) for the purpose of prostitution and lewdness. These acts are made criminal under separate statutes, but they are of the same nature. The act of keeping a disorderly house is the gravamen of the offense in each. A given state of facts may permit an election by the prosecutor as to which of two offenses he will charge; but in this case, as keeping a disorderly house is a vital incident under both statutes, he should not be permitted to bring successive charges under both acts for one and the same transgression. The lesser offense is necessarily included in the greater, and "as the government cannot begin with the highest, and then go down step by step, bringing the man into jeopardy for every derelic-

1071

tion included therein, neither can it begin with the lowest and ascend to the highest, with precisely the same result." We think, therefore, that one should not be prosecuted under both statutes for one and the same unlawful act.

It remains to inquire whether this doctrine can be applied in this case, in view of the fact that the charge in this case covers time anterior to the charge in the former. Can the continuous keeping of a house under either of these statutes be treated as more than one offense? Technically speaking, when one engages in a business, he cannot be said to engage a second time in the same venture. He may engage in a similar business elsewhere, or upon another occasion, after bringing the first venture to a close. The same may be said about keeping a saloon or brothel. So long as it is uninterrupted, it is really but one act of keeping. To hold otherwise at once raises the question of duration of the offense. Shall the same be measured by years, months, weeks, days, hours, or by still shorter intervals? On the other hand, is there no difference between the offender of a day, and one whose business has run a year? And, further, after one has incurred and suffered one conviction, may he continue the unlawful act _ad libitum_, safe from further prosecution, by reason of the former conviction?

The injustice of dividing a continuous act into as many offenses as there are days in the period of its continuation was early seen and asserted. The principle was applied in a case where four charges were made of infractions of the law upon one and the same day, in the case of Crepps v. Durden, Cowp. 640. That case arose under a statute prohibiting labor upon the Lord's day, and it was held that a conviction upon proof that a baker sold a hot loaf upon that day was a bar to prosecution for selling other loaves upon the same day, the court saying that: "There is no idea conveyed by the act itself that, if a tailor sews on the Lord's day, every stitch he takes is a separate offense. . . . There can be but one entire offense on one and the same day." In re Snow, 120 U.S. 281, involved the question before us; and it was held that the offense of illegal cohabitation as husband and wife was a "continuous offense, having duration, and not an offense consisting of an isolated act." The court refused to permit more than one conviction for such act, and called attention to the great injustice of cumulative penalties, which would be possible under the practice insisted upon by the prosecutor, and said, "It is to prevent such an application of penal laws that the rule has obtained that a continuing offense of the character of the one in this case can be committed but once, for the purposes of indictment or prosecution, prior to the time the prosecution is instituted." Again it is said, alluding to such cumulative sentences, "No case is cited where what has been done in the present case has been held to be lawful, but the uniform current of authority is to the contrary, both in England and in the United States;" citing the case of Crepps v. Durden, supra. A number of the American cases are cited in the opinion, which it is unnecessary to repeat here. See, also, Com. v. Robinson, 126 Mass. 259, which is thought to be in harmony with the rule laid down in the case of Snow. In re Nielsen, 131 U.S. 176, is another case in point, and is decisive of both questions in the case. The case of People v. Gault, 104 Mich. 575, is distinguishable from this case, as it arose under a statute which provided that the transactions of each day should be a separate offense. It is, in our opinion, well settled that a prosecution upon a charge laid at a date anterior to a former indictment is, in such a case as this, barred by a conviction upon such former indictment, where the offense charged is a continuing one.

The defendant, therefore, had the right to go to the jury upon the question of fact raised by the plea in bar, and the conviction must therefore be set aside, and the respondent discharged. See People v. Jones, 48 Mich. 554. Order accordingly.

The other Justices concurred.

People v. Lee
307 Mich. 743

BUSHNELL, J. Defendant Hattie Lee was arrested, arraigned and examined on a warrant which charged that "between July 17, 1942 and July 18, 1942," she "feloniously did keep, maintain or operate a house of ill fame," which was "resorted to for the purpose of prostitution and lewdness." . . . Defendant has appealed from the sentence imposed by the court after the jury found her guilty. . . .

. . . The essential elements of the statutory offense (Michigan penal code, Act No. 328, Sec. 452, Pub. Acts 1931 (Comp. Laws Supp. 1940, Sec. 17115-452, Stat. Ann. Sec. 28.707)), of keeping a house of ill fame are: (1) That the place in question was a house of ill fame; (2) That the defendant kept or aided in the keeping of the house, and, (3) That it was resorted to for the purpose of prostitution and lewdness. People v. Gastro, 75 Mich. 127; People v. Russell, 110 Mich. 46; People v. Wheeler, 142 Mich. 212; and 2 Gillespie's Michigan Criminal Law & Procedure, Sec. 1725.

The second element of the offense is satisfied by defendant's concession that she was renting the place. That the place was a house of ill fame may be proved by showing its reputation; that it was resorted to for the purposes named may be shown by the testimony of persons having knowledge of this fact. O'Brien v. People, 28 Mich. 213.

James Gilmour, a member of the police force of the city of Muskegon, testified that he had patrolled the neighborhood on and off for about 15½ years, and that the place had the reputation of being a house of ill fame. Peter Rechlitz,

1073

a detective sergeant, also testified to the same effect. This was sufficient to satisfy the requirement regarding the reputation of the house in question.

"In order to sustain a conviction it is not necessary to show actual illicit intercourse. If it is shown that the inmates are prostitutes, and that men frequented and resorted to the place at night, evidence of these and kindred facts may be sufficient to satisfy a jury that the house was resorted to for the purpose of prostitution." 2 Gillespie's Michigan Criminal Law & Procedure, Sec. 1725.

See, also, People v. Martin, 176 Mich. 381.

At the preliminary examination two officers of the Michigan State police testified that they visited the premises on July 17 and 18, 1942. Their testimony as to what they observed while in the house was sufficient to establish that the place was resorted to for the purpose of prostitution, and there was ample evidence produced before the examining magistrate to require that the defendant be held for trial. See People v. Dellabonda, 265 Mich. 486. . . .

Defendant complains that the court erred in allowing the prosecutor to subpoena certain women and then attempt to prove by police officers that these women were prostitutes. All of these women were in the house at the time of the raid and, as stated in People v. Russell, supra, 48:

"It was competent to show that one of the inmates of the house was a female who had borne the reputation of being a common prostitute."

This matter was considered in People v. Tomczak, 250 Mich. 679, where one of the defendant's witnesses was impeached and such impeachment testimony was objected to. The court said in that case:

"The point is well taken if limited to impeachment, but without merit when considered upon the subject of the character of the house in which she lived."

1 Wigmore on Evidence (3d Ed.), p. 509, Sec. 78, reads:

"A house of ill fame, or disorderly or bawdy house, signifies a house commonly resorted to or lived in by prostitutes for purposes of prostitution; thus, one element in the offense of keeping it may be the kind of persons resorting to or living in it. Now it is usually understood by courts that this element of the crime involves, not merely the actual but also the reputed character of these persons as prostitutes; in which case their reputed character becomes a fact in issue; and this is the general result of the precedents." . . .

It is also contended that it was improper to inquire into the reputation of the defendant, although she lived in the house in question. Evidence as to the character of a keeper of a house of ill fame is admissible as tending to show the character of the house. . . .

As stated in <u>Batesville v. Smythe</u>, <u>138</u> <u>Ark.</u> <u>276</u> (<u>211</u> <u>S.W.</u> <u>140</u>):

"There is a conflict in the authorities as to the admissibility of proof of the reputation of the accused person, the same as other inmates of a house of prostitution; but we think the weight of authority sustains the view that such proof is competent. The universally conceded rule is that guilt of a person accused of crime cannot be established by proof of general reputation; but an exception to that rule, or rather an instance of nonapplication of the rule, is that the character of a house may be established by the reputation of its inmates and frequenters, and this applies to the proof of reputation of the accused person as an inmate of the house. . . . The judgment is affirmed.

BOYLES, C. J., and CHANDLER, NORTH, STARR, WIEST, BUTZEL, and SHARPE, JJ., concurred.

3. Final Draft - Michigan Revised Criminal Code

CHAPTER 62. PROSTITUTION OFFENSES

Section
6201. Prostitution.
6205. Patronizing a Prostitute
6210. Prostitution and Patronizing a Prostitute: No Defense
6215. Sexual Conduct: Definition.
6220. Promoting Prostitution: Definition of Terms.
6221. Promoting Prostitution in the First Degree.
6222. Promoting Prostitution in the Second Degree.
6223. Promoting Prostitution in the Third Degree.
6225. Permitting Prostitution.

(Prostitution)

Sec. 6201. (1) A person commits the crime of prostitution if he engages in or agrees or offers to engage in sexual conduct with another person in return for a fee.
(2) Prostitution is a Class B Misdemeanor.

Committee Commentary

The section is adapted from New York Revised Penal Law Sec. 230.00. Its relationship to existing law is explained in the Commentary to Sec. 6201 to 6215 below.

(Patronizing a Prostitute)

Sec. 6205. (1) A person commits the crime of patronizing a prostitute if:

1075

(a) Pursuant to a prior understanding, he pays a fee to another person as compensation for that person or a third person having engaged in sexual conduct with him; or

(b) He pays or agrees to pay a fee to another person on an understanding that in return that person or a third person will engage in sexual conduct with him; or

(c) He solicits or requests another person to engage in sexual conduct with him in return for a fee.

(2) Patronizing a prostitute is a Class B misdemeanor.

Committee Commentary

The section is adapted from New York Revised Penal Law Sec. 230.05. Its relationship to existing law is explained in the Commentary to Sec. 6201 to 6215 below.

(Prostitution and Patronizing a Prostitute: No Defense

Sec. 6210. In any prosecution for prostitution or patronizing a prostitute, the sex of the two parties or prospective parties to the sexual conduct engaged in, contemplated, or solicited is immaterial, and it is no defense that (a) both persons were of the same sex, or (b) the person who received, agreed to receive or solicited a fee was a male and the person who paid or agreed or offered to pay the fee was a female.

Committee Commentary

The section is identical with New York Revised Penal Law Sec. 230.10. Its relationship to existing law is explained in the Commentary to Sec. 6201 to 6215 below.

(Sexual Conduct: Definition)

Sec. 6215. "Sexual conduct" as used in the preceding sections includes "sexual intercourse" and "deviate sexual intercourse" as defined in section 2301.

Committee Commentary to Sec. 6201 to 6215

Relationship to Existing Law

The common law did not punish prostitution as such (3 Burdick, Crimes, Sec. 973 (1946)). The primary coverage of prostitution is under the disorderly conduct statute (C. L. 1948, Sec. 750.167), which includes among disorderly persons "any common prostitute." In addition, a special statute applicable to Wayne county provides for the commitment of a "common prostitute" to the Detroit House of Correction for a three-year term (C. L. 1948, Sec. 802.104), though she may be paroled earlier (C. L. 1948, Sec. 802.105).

The public activity of a prostitute in soliciting or accosting another to commit prostitution is also declared a misdemeanor (C. L. 1948, Sec. 750.448).

The traditional term "prostitute" includes only a female (George, Legal, Medical and Psychiatric Considerations in the Control of Prostitution, 60 Mich. L. Rev. 717, 722-23 (1962) (hereinafter cited as Control of Prostitution")); homosexual "fags" would be punished under the basic sodomy provision (C. L. 1948, Sec. 750.158) or the gross indecency provision (C. L. 1948, Sec. 750.338). The soliciting and accosting statute, however, could cover homosexual acts, since it includes solicitation to do "any other lewd or immoral act."

Whether the customer can be viewed as a criminal turns on the language of the accosting statute, disorderly conduct, statute and doctrines of accomplice liability (see Control of Prostitution at 729-30). The disorderly conduct statute (C. L. 1948, Sec. 750.167) includes "any person found loitering in a house of ill-fame or prostitution or place where prostitution or lewdness is practiced, encouraged or allowed"; this could include the male customer. The soliciting section (C. L. 1948, Sec. 750.448) covers "any person" who accosts, solicits or invites another "in any public place, or in or from any building or vehicle" to commit prostitution; taken literally, this could include the male customer who initiates the contact. As a third possibility, a special aiding and abetting section (C. L. 1948, Sec. 750.450) might include the male as an accomplice. However, there are no reported decisions on the question in Michigan.

The Draft covers all kinds of commercial sexual activity, whether heterosexual or homosexual and whether by a male or female prostitute. Section 6201 defines as prostitution the engaging in, or agreement or offer to engage in sexual conduct with someone else in return for a fee. Sexual conduct according to Sec. 6215 includes sexual intercourse as defined in Sec. 2301 (a) and deviate sexual intercourse as defined in Sec. 2301 (b). Because Sec. 6201 uses the term "any person" it includes either a male or a female who engages in either heterosexual or homosexual activity for a fee. This is made explicit by Sec. 6210, which states that it is no defense that both of the persons engaging or to engage in the sexual conduct were of the same sex or that the customer is a female and the defendant a male.

Prostitution is punished as a Class B misdemeanor in the Draft. Prostitution is probably in most instances symptomatic of mental abnormality (see Control of Prostitution at 745-53); routine punishment will not alter the basic pattern of conduct. The penalty indicated, therefore, is almost exclusively to facilitate enforcement by keeping prostitutes out of sight. Whether there is a Robinson v. California issue remains to be seen; for the time being it probably does not prevent continuation of anti-prostitution legislation because of the want of empirical data on the degree to which the prostitute can control his or her activity.

The Draft expressly makes it a crime to patronize a prostitute, defined as either (1) paying a fee for an act of prostitution already performed, (2) paying a fee for such an act to be performed, or (3) soliciting or requesting someone else to engage in sexual conduct for a fee. The habitual resorting to prostitutes may itself suggest psychopathology (see Control of Prostitution at 758-60); punishment will achieve no more in this instance that it will in the case of the prostitution itself. However, there may be some indirect gain in working with the prostitute if she seeks rehabilitation, because she feels no discrimination in the law between her and her partner, and to have a criminal charge available against the customer may in fact be a means of facilitating his cooperation with prosecuting authorities. Punishment is indicated at the Class B misdemeanor level, the same punishment assessed against the prostitute.

(Promoting Prostitution: Definition of Terms)

Sec. 6220. The following definitions are applicable in the following three sections:

(a) A person "advances prostitution" if, acting other than as a prostitute or a patron of a prostitute, he knowingly causes or aids a person to commit or engage in prostitution, procures or solicits patrons for prostitution, provides persons or premises for prostitution purposes, operates or assists in the operation of a house of prostitution or a prostitution enterprise, or engages in any other conduct designed to institute, aid, or facilitate an act or enterprise of prostitution.

(b) A person "profits from prostitution" if, acting other than as a prostitute receiving compensation for personally-rendered prostitution services, he accepts or receives money or other property pursuant to an agreement or understanding with any person whereby he participates or is to participate in the proceeds of prostitution activity.

Committee Commentary

The section embodies the substance of New York Revised Penal Law, Sec. 230.15. Its significance is discussed in the Commentary to Sec. 6220 to 6225 below.

(Promoting Prostitution in the First Degree)

Sec. 6221. (1) A person commits the crime of promoting prostitution in the first degree if he knowingly:

(a) Advances prostitution by compelling a person by force or intimidation to engage in prostitution, or profits from such coercive conduct by another; or
(b) Advances or profits from prostitution of a person less than 17 years old.

1078

(2) Promoting prostitution in the first degree is a Class B felony.

Committee Commentary

The section is adapted from New York Revised Penal Law Sec. 230.30. Its significance is discussed in the Commentary to Sec. 6220 to 6225 below.

(Promoting Prostitution in the Second Degree)

Sec. 6222. (1) A person commits the crime of promoting prostitution in the second degree if he knowingly:

(a) Advances or profits from prostitution by managing, supervising, controlling or owning, either alone or in association with others, a house of prostitution or a prostitution business or enterprise involving prostitution activity by 2 or more prostitutes; or
(b) Advances or profits from prostitution of a person less than 20 years old.

(2) Promoting prostitution in the second degree is a Class C felony.

Committee Commentary

The section is adapted from New York Revised Penal Law Sec. 230.25. Its significance is discussed in the Commentary to Sec. 6220 to 6225 below.

(Promoting Prostitution in the Third Degree)

Sec. 6223. (1) A person commits the crime of promoting prostitution in the third degree if he knowingly advances or profits from prostitution.
(2) Promoting prostitution in the third degree is a Class A misdemeanor.

Committee Commentary

The section is adapted from New York Revised Penal Law Sec. 230.20. Its significance is discussed in the Commentary to Sec. 6220 to 6225 below.

(Permitting Prostitution)

Sec. 6225. (1) A person commits the crime of permitting prostitution if, having possession or control of premises that he knows are being used for prostitution purposes, he fails to make reasonable efforts to halt or abate that use.
(2) Permitting prostitution is a Class B misdemeanor.

Committee Commentary

The section is adapted from New York Revised Penal Law Sec. 230.40. Its significance is discussed in the Commentary to Sec. 6220 to 6225 below.

Committee Commentary to Sec. 6220 to 6225

Relationship to Existing Law

The bulk of legislation affecting prostitution is directed toward the pander, pimp and those directly profiting from prostitution activities (see Control of Prostitution at 724-29). Michigan has several statutes in this category.

The pandering statute (C. L. 1948, Sec. 750.455) makes it a felony punishable by a maximum of twenty years to procure a female inmate for a house of prostitution, to induce or entice a female to become a prostitute, to use promises, threats, violence or any scheme to cause a woman to enter or remain in a house of prostitution or assignation, to use similar devices to cause her to enter a place in which prostitution is practiced or allowed, to procure anyone to enter or leave the state to practice prostitution, to take a person or detain her for purposes of intercourse in the pretext of marriage, or to receive or give or agree to receive or give any money or thing of value for procuring or attempting to procure a woman to become a prostitute or enter or leave the state for purposes of prostitution. Procuring means to acquire or get, and it is enough to support a conviction that the evidence shows that a woman came to the defendant's house to practice prostitution, was taken in by the defendant and remained there (People v. Johnson, 260 Mich. 117, 244, N.W. 251 (1932)).

It is also a felony punishable by up to five years' imprisonment to keep a house of ill-fame (C. L. 1948, Sec. 750.452). The elements of the offense are (1) that the place in question is a house of ill fame, (2) that the defendant kept or aided in keeping it, and (3) that it was resorted to for purposes of prostitution or lewdness (People v. Lee, 307 Mich. 743, 12 N.W. 2d 418 (1943); People v. Wheeler, 142 Mich. 212, 105 N.W. 607 (1905); People v. Cox, 107 Mich. 435, 65 N.W. 283 (1895)). A single act of illicit intercourse does not make a place a disorderly house, it must be frequently visited by a number of persons, though specific acts of intercourse need not be proved. (People v. Gastro, 75 Mich. 127, 42 N.W. 937 (1889)). A special section permits a grant of immunity to witnesses (C. L. 1948, Sec. 750.453).

Related provisions forbid one to place his wife in a house of prostitution or leave her there (C. L. 1948, Sec. 750.456); to detain a female in a house of prostitution for debt contracted while she was there (C. L. 1948, Sec. 750.458); to permit a female under 17 to remain in a house of prostitution for any purpose whatever other than prostitution (C.L. 1948, Sec. 750.462) or to admit anyone into any building or

1080

place for purposes of prostitution, lewdness or assignation (C.L. 1948, Sec. 750.449). It is also a felony punishable by up to twenty years' imprisonment to transport a woman into, through or across the state for purposes of prostitution (C.L. 1948, Sec. 750.459).

Accepting money from the earnings of a prostitute, without any consideration, is a felony punishable by up to twenty years' imprisonment (C.L. 1948, Sec. 750.457). The section carries a presumption that the receipt of money or property is without consideration; the presumption was sustained as constitutional (People v. Jackson, 280 Mich. 6, 273 N.W. 327 (1937)).

It is a misdemeanor to lease a dwelling house knowing that the lessee intends to use it for prostitution or to continue to receive rent if there is reasonable ground to believe that the premises is being used for prostitution or gambling (C.L. 1948, Sec. 750.454). If the charge is based on the fact of renting, the defendant must be shown to have had the knowledge at the time the lease was exeucted (People v. Saunders, 29 Mich. 269 (1874)); the alternative of receiving rent, however, can be based on negligence, since the term is "reasonable cause to believe."

It is also a felony for a private employment agency to send a woman or girl to a place of prostitution (C.L. 1948, Sec. 408.619, 408.621).

The Draft brings these various activities together in three degrees of promoting prostitution and the crime of permitting prostitution. Promoting prostitution may consist either of "advancing prostitution" as defined in Sec. 6220(a) or "profiting from prostitution" as defined in Sec. 6220(b).

A person advances prostitution if he knowingly (a) causes or aids a person to engage in prostitution, or (b) procures or solicits patrons for prostitution, or (c) provides persons or premises for prostitution, or (d) operates or assists in operating a house of prostitution or other prostitution enterprise like a call-girl operation, or (e) does anything else designed to facilitate prostitution. It thus includes elements of procuring, transportation for purposes of prostitution, keeping a house of prostitution, and pandering.

A person profits from prostitution by receiving or accepting money or property which is viewed as proceeds from prostitution. This of course is defined to exclude the prostitute, in order not to permit overlap with Sec. 6201. This is the equivalent of the "living on the earnings" provisions in the present statute.

Any one of the alternatives in advancing or profiting, if proven, constitutes third-degree promoting under Sec. 6223. This is a Class A misdemeanor. However, if the promoting involves a prostitution operation by two or more prostitutes, or if the person victimized is less than 20 years old, the crime becomes second-degree promoting under Sec. 6222, and moves into the Class C felony range. Even heavier penalties are imposed if the promoting is done by force or intimidation or if the prostitute is under 17 years old; first-class promoting under Sec. 6221 is a Class B felony.

A problem of interpretation might arise under Sec. 6220 and 6223 in the case of the lessor or provider of premises. To clarify the matter, and to recognize that this form of facilitation is in a sense at third remove from the actual practice of prostitution, (sic) Sec. 6225 defines the crime of permitting prostitution as the failure to make reasonable efforts to halt or abate the use of one's premises for prostitution purposes. The crime can in effect be committed through negligence. Punishment is set at the Class B misdemeanor level.

INTERROGATORIES

1. Outline the provisions of the Michigan rape statute. What are the two offenses prohibited by this statute?
2. What were the facts, issue and holding of the court in People v. McDonald? What construction is placed on this case by the Committee Commentary, Final Draft, Mich. Rev. Crim. Code?
3. What were the facts, issue and holding of the court in People v. Courier? What construction is placed on this case by the Committee Commentary, Final Draft, Mich. Rev. Crim. Code?
4. What were the facts, issue and holding of the court in People v. Gengels? In what respect is lack of chastity relevant to a rape prosecution?
5. What were the facts, issue and holding of the court in People v. Pizzura?
6. According to Moran, 13 Wayne L. Rev. 734, what are the basic purposes of the statutory rape law?
7. What were the facts, issue and holding of the court in People v. Crosswell? What construction is placed on this case by the Committee Commentary, Final Draft, Mich. Rev. Crim. Code?
8. What were the facts, issue and holding of the court in Moran v. People? What construction is placed on this case by the Committee Commentary, Final Draft, Mich. Rev. Crim. Code? What legislation was adopted in response to the decision?
9. Is the decision in the Moran case still the law of Michigan?
10. What were the facts, issue and holding of the court in People v. Marrs? What construction is placed on this case by the Committee Commentary, Final Draft, Mich. Rev. Crim. Code?
11. What were the facts, issue and holding of the court in People v. Myers? What construction is placed on this case by the Committee Commentary, Final Draft, Mich. Rev. Crim. Code?
12. What is meant by the requirement that the victim resist to the "utmost?"

13. What were the facts, issue and holding of the court in Hirdes v. Ottawa Circuit Judge? What construction is placed on this case by the Committee Commentary, Final Draft, Mich. Rev. Crim. Code?

14. According to Moran, 13 Wayne Law Rev. 734, what are the elements of rape? Is the gratification of the assailant relevant to the completed offense? Under what circumstances is consent in fact not consent in law? Can a prostitute be the victim of statutory rape? Is lack of chastity ever relevant in a statutory rape prosecution?

15. Outline the provisions of Sections 2301, 2305, 2310, 2311, and 2312 of the Final Draft, Mich. Rev. Crim. Code. Would these provisions make any substantial change in existing law?

16. Outline the provisions of the Michigan statutes relevant to debauchery and seduction.

17. What were the facts, issue and holding of the court in People v. Bailey? What interpretation of this case is offered by the Committee Commentary, Section 2331, Final Draft, Mich. Rev. Crim. Code?

18. What were the facts, issues and holdings of the court in People v. Clark? What interpretation of this case is offered by the Committee Commentary Sec. 2331, Final Draft, Mich. Rev. Crim. Code?

19. What were the facts, issue and holding of the court in People v. Defore? What interpretation of this case is offered by the Committee Commentary, Sec. 2305, Final Draft, Mich. Rev. Crim. Code?

20. What were the facts, issue and holding of the court in People v. Smith? What interpretation of this case is provided by the Committee Commentary, Sec. 2305, Final Draft, Mich. Rev. Crim. Code?

21. According to Moran, 13 Wayne Law Rev. 734, what are the basic defenses to a prosecution for seduction? How is seduction defined? What is the essence of the offense?

22. Is fornication a crime in Michigan?

23. Outline the provisions of the Michigan statutes relevant to homosexual and other deviate sexual intercourse.

24. According to Moran, 13 Wayne L. Rev. 734, what is the source of the term "sodomy?" Are there any significant gaps in the Mich. statutes dealing with deviate sexual behavior? Does sodomy include sexual intercourse per os? On what basis is it argued that the Michigan Gross Indecency Statute is unconstitutional?

25. As discussed by Moran, 13 Wayne L. Rev. 734, what are the basic arguments pro and con relative to the imposition of criminal sanctions in the area of private adult consensual homosexuality? In what way is the case of Griswold v. Connecticut and the Eighth Amendment germane to the controversy?

26. What were the facts, issue and holding of the court in People v. Schmitt?

27. What were the facts, issues and holdings of the court in People v. Dexter?

28. What was the issue and holding of the court in People v. Askar? Is sodomy defined by statute? What is the common law definition of the offense?

29. What were the facts, issue and holding of the court in People v. Livermore?

30. How is deviate sexual intercourse defined in Sec. 2301, Final Draft, Mich. Rev. Crim. Code? How does Sec. 2305 (1) (c) differ from the present law applicable to homosexual intercourse? What rationale is offered in support of the change in policy?

31. What constitutes bestiality? What punishment is provided under Michigan law?

32. What constitutes necrophilia? Is it punished under Michigan law? Would it be punished under the Revised Criminal Code? What rationale is offered in support of the policy?

33. What constitutes sodomy under the Revised Criminal Code?

34. Outline the provisions of the Michigan law relevant to taking indecent liberties, contributing to the delinquency of minors and enticing or soliciting immoral acts on the part of minors.

35. What were the facts, issue and holding of the court in People v. Hicks? How are "improper liberties" defined? Must there be a touching of the child's genitalia?

36. What were the facts, issue and holding of the court in People v. Sanford?

37. What were the facts, issue and holding of the court in People v. Visel?

38. What were the facts, issue and holding of the court in People v. Healy? Is immoral intent a required element?

39. What were the facts, issue and holding of the court in People v. Szymanski? What constituted the actus reus of the crime? How is the case distinguished from the Hicks case?

40. What were the facts, issues and holdings of the court in People v. Noyes? What evidence was offered of sexual motivation in the case?

41. Outline the provisions of the Final Draft, Mich. Rev. Crim. Code dealing with sexual abuse.

42. Outline the provisions of Michigan's indecent exposure statute. Does the statute define indecent exposure?

43. What were the facts, issue and holding of the court in People v. Kratz? What is the meaning of the term "openly" relative to the definition of the indecent exposure offense?

44. What were the facts, issue and holding of the court in People v. Ring?

45. What were the facts, issue and holding of the court in People v. Hildabridle? On what basis does Justice Edwards concur? What are the main points of the dissenting opinion? How does the attitude of the court's majority differ from the attitude of the court in People v. Ring?

46. How does Sec. 2325 (1), Final Draft, Mich. Rev. Crim. Code define indecent exposure?

47. Outline the provisions of Sec. 2330, Final Draft, Mich. Rev. Crim. Code.
48. Outline the provisions of Sec. 2331, Final Draft, Mich. Rev. Crim. Code.
49. How is the term "sexually delinquent persons" defined in the present law? In what important respect would Sec. 2331 change the present law?
50. Outline the provisions of the Michigan statutes relative to prostitution and pandering. What statute is most relevant to prostitution?
51. Do any of the Michigan statutes define prostitution?
52. How is prostitution generally defined?
53. Was operating a house of prostitution an offense at the common law?
54. What were the facts, issue and holding of the court in People v. Johnson? What evidence was found to be sufficient to support the conviction?
55. What were the facts, issue and holding of the court in People v. Jackson? What legal presumption was sustained?
56. What were the facts, issue and holding of the court in People v. Saunders? What mens rea requirement must be satisfied?
57. What were the facts, issue and holding of the court in People v. Gastro? Is a single act of illicit intercourse sufficient to make a place a disorderly house? Must specific acts of intercourse be proven?
58. What were the facts, issues and holding of the court in People v. Cox?
59. What were the facts, issue and holding of the court in People v. Lee? What are the elements of the offense of keeping a house of ill fame according to the Cox and Lee cases?
60. How is prostitution defined in Sec. 6201, Final Draft, Mich. Rev. Crim. Code?
61. Outline the provisions of Sec. 6205, 6210, and 6215, Final Draft, Mich. Rev. Crim. Code.
62. Does the term "prostitute" include a homosexual fag? What provisions of the present law are applicable?
63. What provisions of the present law are applicable to the male customer of a prostitute?
64. Outline the provisions of Sec. 6220, 6221, 6222, 6223, and 6225 of the Final Draft, Mich. Rev. Crim. Code.

CHAPTER VIII

ABDUCTION, FALSE IMPRISONMENT, AND KIDNAPPING

A. Abduction and False Imprisonment

    1. Michigan Compiled Laws (1948)

750.11 Taking a woman and compelling her to marry

    Sec. 11. TAKING A WOMAN AND COMPELLING HER TO MARRY -
Any person who shall take any woman unlawfully <u>and</u> against
her will, and by force, menace, or duress, compel her to
marry him or any other person, or to be defiled, shall be
guilty of a felony, punishable by imprisonment in the state
prison for life or any term of years.

750.12 Taking woman with intent to compel to marry

    Sec. 12. TAKING A WOMAN WITH INTENT TO COMPEL HER TO
MARRY - Any person who shall take any woman unlawfully
and against her will with intent to compel her by force,
menace or duress, to marry him or any other person, or to
be defiled, shall be guilty of a felony, punishable by imprisonment in the state prison not more than 10 years.

750.13 Enticing away female under 16

    Sec. 13. ENTICING AWAY FEMALE UNDER 16 YEARS FOR PURPOSE
OF MARRIAGE, ETC. - Any person who shall take <u>or</u> entice away
any female under the age of 16 years, from her father, mother,
guardian, or other person having the legal charge of her person, <u>without their consent</u>, either for the purpose of prostitution, concubinage, sexual intercourse or marriage, shall be
guilty of a felony, punishable by imprisonment in the state
prison not more than 10 years.

    2. Definitions and Element of Offenses

People v. Bristol
23 Mich. 118

    The defendant was charged with the abduction of Mary
L. Cottrell, a female under sixteen years of age, for the
purpose: 1. Of marriage; 2. of concubinage; 3. of
prostitution; each purpose being alleged in a separate
count. The plea was not guilty, and the verdict was guilty
as charged in the second count.

1086

The counsel for the People, to maintain said issue, on their part, introduced witnesses and gave testimony tending to show that respondent, on the 11th day of June, A.D. 1870, at the township of Cottrelville, in the county of St. Clair, made an agreement with Mary L. Cottrell, a female under the age of sixteen years, to wit: of the age of thirteen years, to elope with him and go to Chicago to get married; that afterwards, on the same day, the said Mary L. Cottrell was at a neighbor's house, by permission of her father, William A. Cottrell, at a sewing or quilting bee; that the respondent came there with a horse and buggy and requested said Mary to take a ride with him; that she went with him and they rode together to Detroit, where respondent registered at a hotel, an assumed name and place of residence, as follows: "H. Clark and wife, Mt. Clemens," that he called for a room at a hotel, and that they occupied the same room and same bed during the night, and that said respondent then and there the same night had sexual intercourse with her; that respondent told her at Detroit that they were just the same as married, but that they ought not to sleep together until married; that the next day they rode together to Disco, in the county of Macomb, and there spent the night, occupying the same bed, and where respondent again had sexual intercourse with her; that the next day they rode together to the city of St. Clair, in said county of St. Clair, and the respondent took her to the house of a relative of his, and soon after their arrival in said city they were found by her father, and the respondent was arrested; that the father of said Mary did not consent to her going away from the custody of her father, who had the legal charge of her person, without his consent, and against his will; that respondent is a relative of the mother of said Mary, by marriage, and had been living and making his home at the house of said William A. Cottrell, father of the girl, for about two years prior to the time he took her away; that he had been a teacher of the district school which Mary attended; that respondent and Mary had talked with each other about marrying, about two years prior to their going away; that Mary asked him one day, going to the school-house, which of the girls he liked the best, and he answered, I like you the best, and said she must wait six years for him; that he expected to get part of his father's property, and to have a home in Chicago, and that she should have a piano, silk dresses and gold rings; that they were engaged to be married some time before they went away together; that Mary wanted to marry respondent, and on the way to Detroit, at New Baltimore, she expressed a desire to get married, and was put off by respondent, and told to wait until they got to Detroit; that respondent was informed by her that her father did not wish her to go with him, and that her father had threatened to punish her if she was ever seen with him or went with him at all; that after they had started for Detroit, he asked her if they hadn't

Facts

1087

better turn around and go home and get her father's consent; that she said no, that she was afraid to go home then, on account of the punishment her father had threatened; that after they had got to St. Clair, and before the arrest of respondent, he talked of getting a carriage, and going to Vicksburg, a town north of St. Clair, and talked of going to Chicago; that respondent had sexual intercourse with her before he took her away from Cottrelville to Detroit.

The defendant made a statement, denying having ever had any improper sexual intercourse with said Mary L. Cottrell. The following requests to charge, preferred by the defendant, were refused, to wit:

Issue

1. That under our statute the crime charged consists in the purpose for which the female is taken or enticed away - the mere taking or enticing not being criminal, unless done with one of the purposes mentioned in the statute.
2. If the jury believe that the defendant's purpose was seduction, and that he did "seduce and debauch Mary L. Cottrell, an unmarried woman," then he is guilty under the law punishing seduction, but cannot be convicted under the information in this case.
3. If the jury believe that the defendant had carnal intercourse with Mary L. Cottrell, to which her assent was obtained by a promise of marriage, and to which, without such promise, she would not have yielded, then his offense is seduction, and not punishable under this information.
4. That the proof that the defendant had connection with Miss Cottrell several different times will not support the charge of concubinage, or justify the jury to convict the defendant of an intent or purpose to make her a concubine.

And the said circuit judge charged the jury as follows: The crime consists in the taking and enticing away any female under the age of sixteen years, from her father, mother, guardian or other person having the legal charge of her person, without their consent, either for the purpose of prostitution, concubinage or marriage. One or all of three purposes are necessary, and unless some one of the purposes is satisfactorily proved, the defendant cannot be convicted.

The law supposes a child of the tender age of less than sixteen to be incapable of an understanding consent, and no act of hers can do away with the necessity of the parent's or guardian's consent. Her willingness or unwillingness to go with the accused is of no importance, except so far as it might enable you to determine whether she was taken or enticed away. (The very term enticing away implies her consent)

Any one who designedly, by means of gaining the affections of a female child under sixteen years, gains such an influence over her as to make her desirous of going with him and yielding to his wishes, may be presumed to have enticed her away

1088

if she yield to such influence and goes away with him. In
such case she could hardly be said to have a will of her
own. Her will and wishes would be subordinate to, and controlled by, his will or wishes, however expressed. Words
of enticement or persuasion are not necessary if by the acts
and conduct proved there is satisfactory evidence that he
had got such a control over her that his will and desires
controlled or guided her actions, and that she went with
him, yielding to his will.

If a defendant should use his position as a teacher, as
a relative or member of the family, his superiority in age
or position, and give such a young girl to understand that
she was the object of his affections, permit her to express
a premature love without chiding, and listen to her suggestions to elope with him, and afterwards furnish the means
and take her away, it would be a question of fact with you
whether he was not the enticer, and responsible party in
such proceeding. You may ask yourselves, is it reasonable
to suppose that so young a girl could or would be the seducer
and enticer of a person of the age and position of the defendant, or is it most reasonable to conclude that he was
the actor and she the one, whose youth and inexperience
yielded to his persuasions.

The law assumes the man to be the stronger, and everywhere
seeks to protect the weak from the passions and power of the
stronger. It is necessary, and our laws undertake to provide for that necessity, for the preservation of society,
that the young and weak shall be protected from the old and
strong; and, universally, females are treated as the weak,
and the law makes them its peculiar wards. It acts upon the
theory that men are the active agents or movers, and women
are the passive dependents upon man's gallantry and recipients of his protecting love.

Hence, there are no laws punishing women for seduction,
abduction or other offenses against modesty requiring superior power or strength. They are supposed to be incapable
of committing such offenses. They look to us for protection,
whilst we must take care of ourselves, no matter what may be
their blandishments to lead us astray. After arriving at
the age of maturity they are capable of assent; they cease
in that respect from a certain kind of minority, but before
that the law protects them and their parent's rights over
them, and they cannot do anything to take themselves away
from that protection, or doing away with the necessity of
parent's assent. Enticing or taking away a child within the
age of sixteen from a neighbor's house, where she is permitted to be for a visit or other temporary purpose, would
be a taking from the father's custody as much as if from his
house.

It is not claimed that the purpose of prostitution is
proved. The prosecution claims that one of the purposes
charged, that of concubinage, has some proof in its support.
The legal definition of concubinage, as attended by the

statute, and as applicable to this case, is "The carnal
connection between a man and a woman unmarried, or the cohabitation of a man with a woman to whom he is not united
by marriage." If you find that the purpose of defendant
in taking or enticing the girl, was that of carnal connection with her, or to cohabit with her, then, if the other
necessary facts are found to be proved, he may be found
guilty under the second count, charging purpose of concubinage. The length of time he intended to cohabit or continue
the improper connection with her, is immaterial. Proof of
actual cohabitation or intercourse, if satisfactorily proved, would tend to prove with what purpose the taking or enticing was done. If you should find that he started away
with Mary with the then-intended purpose of marriage or concubinage, the crime would be complete, though before consummation of his purpose he was arrested or prevented from
its consummation; or even if, after taking her away for such
purpose, he repented, and did not carry out his purpose,
that fact would be an appeal to mercy, but not to justice
or the rules of law; the crime was complete whenever he took
her away (if you so find), for either of the purposes expressed in the statute, no matter how far he may have gone,
or how soon he may have returned.
   In weighing the testimony of the girl claiming to have
been abducted, you will consider her age and situation, you
will ask yourselves what you would expect of your own children of that age, and by your experience as men you will
judge of the probability of her statements - whether she
would be likely to remember all that had occurred: Did she
intend to state things truly or falsely? Did she intend to
cover up any thing, or state any thing not said or done, or
differently from the way it was said or done, intentionally,
with a design to injure defendant, or indifferently as to
his rights? If either, her testimony should be carefully
scrutinized, if not entirely rejected. In considering it,
judge by her appearance, and all the other surroundings of
the case. Has she been in any way substantially corroborated?
Is there any other proof to sustain her - if so, what, and
by whom? Did defendant take her in his buggy away with him?
Did they ride together to Detroit? Did defendant call for
a room there for both, as husband and wife? Did he register
an assumed name? Did he spend the night in the same room or
in the same bed? Did they, not being married, cohabit together, and have you other, or any, proof of other acts tending to show his purpose? Then, if the proof convinces you
beyond reasonable doubt that the girl was under sixteen, that
she was taken or enticed away by defendant for either of the
purposes of prostitution, concubinage, or marriage, without
her father's consent, you have a simple duty - to announce
by your verdict your convictions. But there must be no reasonable doubt as to proof of any element of the crime. A
reasonable doubt is such as would hinder or prevent you from
entering any important undertaking. It is not a mere doubt,

1090

but must be founded upon such a lack of proof as to compel you to say that you are not by the proof convinced of his guilt.

You are the sole judges of what facts have been proved, and if, in giving illustrations of the applications of the general rules of law, I have alluded to facts, you are to have no impression of what I may think of the facts, or of what facts I may think have been proved. If I have given you any such impression, it has been by inadvertence, and you must divest yourselves of it. With the court's opinion of what the facts are you have nothing to do. Judge of the facts for yourselves; find what facts have been proved tending to prove the crime charged; apply the law as I have announced it to you to the facts you find proved, and then render your verdict according to your conscientious convictions, without regard to sympathy or consequences. If you are satisfied beyond a reasonable doubt by the proofs and law that the defendant is guilty, then say so, and leave the result to the court. If not so satisfied, say not guilty, with equal disregard of consequences. Do your duty honestly, according to your oaths and consciences; and the law, the prisoner and the People must be satisfied.

The defendant excepted in due form to the refusals to give the charges requested, and to each and every part of the charge given specifically.

Dwight May, Attorney-General, for the people.

John Atkinson, for the defendant.

Per Curiam:

The exceptions chiefly insisted upon relate to the nature of the crime intended to be covered by the statute, and to the charge of the court as trenching upon the province of the jury.

The statute (2 Comp. L., Sec. 5734), under which the prosecution was had, punishes any one who takes or entices any female under sixteen years of age, from her father, mother or guardian, etc., without their consent, either for the purpose of prostitution, concubinage or marriage.

Two points are raised on the statute, viz: First, that inasmuch as the evidence tended to show that whatever unlawful design existed was carried out, the offense should *Issue* have been charged as seduction; and second, that there could be no offense in any enticing with a design of having illicit intercourse, unless it was to be continuous, and that concubinage would not exist without some relation of more or less permanence. We do not think it material whether the *Reason* offense when complete would amount to seduction or not, as they are both felonies, and there is no room for the doctrine of are merger. (sic) If the offense committed comes within the terms of the statute, the prosecution was properly laid.

We think the statute intended, in enumerating marriage,

1091

prostitution and concubinage, to cover every purpose of
unlawful enticement to sexual intercourse. The word "concubinage" had no settled common-law meaning, and if we look
at the derivation and the usage of etymologists, we shall
find it to be a comprehensive term, covering any illicit
intercourse. We have no doubt the legislation was intended
to cover all such cases, and if the question had been more
doubtful, we should not be disposed to explain away the
meaning of a wholesome statute in order to create an exception clearly within the mischief, and leave entirely unpunished attempts to destroy the virtue of young females,
merely because there was no design after ruining them, or
taking any further notice of them. Such a claim does not
appeal very strongly to equitable consideration.

The exception to the charge is too general. But we do
not think the court can be properly charged with having
gone beyond propriety in the fulness of the instructions
given to the jury. There was nothing said which, so far
as appears, could have possibly misled them, and no comments
were made which exceeded a proper judicial discretion.
The conviction was right, and judgment should be rendered
upon it.

People v. Congdon
77 Mich. 351

MORSE, J. This is a very singular case, and the result
of the trial in the court below is astonishing, and almost
incomprehensible. Gordon Congdon is the grandfather and
Desire Rosenbach the mother of Lizzie Austin, a girl about
14 years of age at the time of the trial. Charles Rosenbach is the husband of Desire Rosenbach. The defendants
were informed against in the circuit court for the county
of Berrien, under the statute, for the abduction of the
said Lizzie Austin.

Section 9099, How. Stat., reads as follows:

"Every person who willfully, and without lawful authority, shall forcibly or secretly confine or imprison any
other person within this State against his will, or shall
forcibly carry or send such person out of this State, or
shall forcibly seize or confine, or shall inveigle or kidnap, any other person, with intent either to cause such
person to be secretly confined or imprisoned in this State
against his will, or in any way held to service against his
will, shall be punished by imprisonment in the State prison
not more than ten years, or by fine not exceeding one thousand
dollars."

The information was filed October 9, 1888, and consisted
of three counts.

The first count charged a conspiracy to commit the criminal

1092

acts mentioned in the statute.

The second count charges that the respondents, on July 22, 1888, at Benton township, -

"Willfully, and without lawful authority therefor, did forcibly and secretly inveigle and kidnap one Lizzie Austin, with intent to cause the said Lizzie Austin to be secretly confined in the State of Michigan, to wit, at Benton Township, in said county, against her will, and to be held to service against her will."

The third count charges that the respondents, on July 22, 1888, at the town of Benton, -

"With force and arms, in and upon one Lizzie Austin, did make an assault, and the said Lizzie Austin then and there, willfully and without lawful authority therefor, and without the consent and against the will of the said Lizzie Austin, did forcibly seize and secretly confine for a long space of time, to wit, the space of one day, at the township of Benton, in said county, with intent then and there to cause the said Lizzie Austin to be sent out of the State of Michigan, and did then and there, afterwards, to wit, on the twenty-third day of July, 1888, forcibly send the said Lizzie Austin out of the State of Michigan."

The trial commenced January 22, and closed January 23, 1889. All three of the respondents were found guilty.

Lizzie Austin was the daughter of John and Desire Lawrence. When she was eight years old she was adopted by Stephen M. and Kate M. Austin, husband and wife. The proceedings for this adoption were in the probate court, under Act No. 26, Laws of 1861 (How. Stat. Sec. 6379), and the articles of adoption were signed by the Austins and Lawrences, and acknowledged by them. Lizzie made her mark under the name of Mary E. Lawrence, and it is certified by the notary that she also acknowledged the instrument. July 9, 1883, the probate court entered its decree, changing the name of the child from Mary E. Lawrence to Mary E. Austin, and declaring her to be the heir at law of said Stephen M. and Kate M. Austin. From that date until about July 22, 1888, she lived with the Austins as their child. Her mother procured a divorce from her father in the meantime, and remarried and moved to Chicago. The mother had some correspondence with Mrs. Austin wanted $250, which Mrs. Rosenbach though to be too high.

On Sunday, July 22, 1888, Mr. & Mrs. Rosenbach were staying at the house of one Fleming, in Benton Harbor, at which place the Austins resided. Congdon, the grandfather, also lived at Benton Harbor. Saturday night, Lizzie stayed overnight at the residence of a brother of Mrs. Austin. On her way to the Austins on Sunday she met her grandfather, who told her her mother was at Fleming's and asked her if she did not wish to see her. Lizzie answered, "Yes," and went with her grandfather to visit her mother. At Fleming's she

also met Mr. Rosenbach. Her mother asked her if she would
go to Chicago, and live with them. Lizzie willingly consented. Rosenbach went to get a team; but, being unable to
procure one, he and lizzie traveled on foot into the country
towards Three Oaks, a station on the Michigan Central Railroad. They stopped at several farm-houses, seeking a conveyance, and finally found one. A farmer drove them to Three
Oaks, where they took a train for Chicago. Lizzie remained
at Chicago about a week, when Austin, with a deputy-sheriff
of Berrien county, took her forcibly from the custody and
care of her mother, and brought her, against her will, to
Mrs. Austin's, where she has ever since remained.

Upon the trial, Lizzie, then about 14 years old, was sworn
by the prosecution, after they were forced to do so by the
demand of the defense and the reluctant ruling of the court
that they must obey the law in this respect, and she testified that no force, threats, promises, or other inducements
were used by her mother, or any of the respondents, to compel,
or even to coax, her to go to Chicago; that she had long wished to leave the Austins, and go to her mother; that she gladly
and willingly went; and that if she had her own way she would
at the time she was testifying go home with her mother.

No evidence was adduced to show any force used, or any undue means of any kind resorted to, to take this girl away
from the Austins "against her will," which is the gist of
the offense under the statute, nor was she confined or deprived of her liberty for a moment. It is true, one witness
swore that while she was going with her grandfather to Fleming's, to see her mother, Congdon had hold of her arm; but
the witness did not notice that the girl was manifesting any
unwillingness to go with him. All the other testimony in
the case is overwhelmingly to the effect that the child went
gladly with her grandfather to see her mother, as would have
been natural; and that she went willingly, on foot, with her
stepfather, until a team was procured to take them to a station.

The case seems to have been tried from the beginning by
the prosecution and the court on a wrong theory. The question submitted to the jury, in effect, was who had the best
right to the custody of the child. The court told the jury,
in substance, that Mr. and Mrs. Austin were to be considered
the real parents of the child, and that, while the own mother
had a right to see the child, yet she had no right to seek to
estrange the child from its foster-parents -

"And she must, however hard it may be, have a due regard
for the feelings and rights of the foster-parents, and, if
there should be reason or cause for the child's being taken
away from the care, custody, or control of the foster-parents,
there is another remedy to be pursued. . . . While we have no
law so harsh that it will forbid the mother to look upon or
see her child, and talk with her, . . . yet she must, when
she so converses with this little girl, have a due regard for

the feelings of the Austins; and she must not have sought to estrange the love or feelings of that little girl in any way or particular."

The court also said:

"As to the influence exercised by the defendants, gentlemen, if any, with Lizzie Austin, to create a desire in her mind to go to Chicago, to live with her mother, I instructed you this morning, and I now repeat it: In case you find that there was a consent on the part of this little girl to go to Chicago, - if she was willing, if she went of her own free will and accord, - then it becomes your duty to find a verdict of not guilty. But if you find that that consent, even if there was a consent, was brought about by reason of force, or promises, or anything of that sort; for instance, if these defendants, or any one of them, having in mind a common object, and each of them seeking to carry out that object, had purposely gone to this little girl at the time and place charged or testified to, and, knowing her age, and knowing that what they might say to her might tend to influence one of that age, and have an undue influence upon her, - then, in case they held out any inducement in the way they would clothe her; if they instituted comparisons between the house she then lived in and the home they would give her; if they did this, intending to destroy her love for her foster-parents, or cause her to form an intent or desire to go; if they did anything of that kind, - then they would be guilty.

"If, as I said before, you find that she consented, and that, even though they made inducements, those inducements had nothing to do with her going away, then your duty is to find a verdict of not guilty. You look at the testimony in the case, and it is for you to say whether or not there was undue influence of that kind, with the intent to cause her to leave her foster-parents."

There was no evidence in the case that anything was said to her about how she would be clothed, or what kind of a home her mother would give her, and nothing in the case to warrant this reference in the charge. This was after the jury had been out, and returned for further instructions. A juryman asked:

"Would any influence, under the circumstances, brought to bear upon this little girl by any of the defendants be regarded as undue influence?

"Court. No, gentlemen. There might be such a thing as a good influence, as an effort upon their part to influence her for the better or for good; and a bad influence is one such as I have instructed you upon."

Under this charge the jury were justified, if they followed the instructions, in finding the mother guilty of the crime charged, if they found simply that she asked Lizzie to go home with her, and such asking induced her to go. There was no evidence in the case tending to show that any fraud or duress was used, nor any flattery, allurements, or promises, even, employed, to get this girl away from the Austins, beyond the mere asking if she wanted to go. The record shows that she went gladly and freely, out of her natural love for her mother, and for no other reason. She wants to live with her mother now; and there appears no good reason why she should not do so, except the articles of adoption, and the action of the probate court thereon.

The jury should have been directed, on the facts, to find a verdict of not guilty as to all of the defendants. The statute was not intended to reach a case like this. There is a statute designed to meet cases of this kind, where the child is under 12 years of age (How. Stat. Sec. 9104, as amended by Pub. Acts of 1885, p. 275), and referring especially to adopted children. It punishes the father or mother, as well as any other person, for violation of the statute. But it wisely limits the age of the child to 12 years, recognizing the fact that above that age the wishes of the child have some standing in the courts, as well as its welfare. . . .

The conviction of the respondents must be set aside, and each of them discharged from further custody or prosecution under the information filed in the court below.

The other Justices concurred.

People v. Fleming
267 Mich. 584

BUTZEL, J. William Fleming, defendant, was convicted of attempting to entice away a female child 14 years of age from her parents, without their consent, for the purpose of concubinage. Upon a supplementary information being filed charging him with two prior convictions for felonies, he was sentenced as a third offender to Jackson State prison for a term of not less than five nor more than ten years. The trial court stated that he was impressed with the importance of the questions raised by the defense, and believed them to be of sufficient merit to warrant an appeal. He therefore directed that, in the event of such an appeal, the expense be borne by the county.

The testimony of numerous witnesses called at the trial on behalf of the people established the following facts: On March 30, 1933, defendant called at the home of a 14-year old child, and had several conversations, first with her mother, and later with both parents. He represented that he was a physician with an invalid wife, and desired the services of the child to look after his wife while he was out on professional calls. He offered to give the child board, and permit her to attend a school near his home, and also to pay her a small wage. On his first visit, defendant

1096

asked that he be permitted to take the little girl away for
a few minutes to see his wife. When the child conditioned
her acceptance upon her younger sister also being taken a-
long, defendant replied that the car would be too crowded,
as he had to meet three old ladies up town, and there would
not be room for all. Defendant made many inconsistent statements, which caused the child's parents to become suspicious
and send for the sheriff. The latter came to the house with
his deputy, interviewed defendant, and finally ordered him
to drive to the sheriff's office for further investigation.
After the sheriff had alighted from his car and gone to unlock the office, defendant escaped by starting his own car
just as the deputy was stepping out of it. He was apprehended some time later. There is no question but that the
statements made by defendant to the child's parents were false
in every respect. He assumed a false name, was not a physician, and had no home, and there was no showing that he had
a wife. He admitted to the sheriff that his statements were
untrue.

At the conclusion of the testimony by the witnesses called
on behalf of the people, defendant did not take the stand,
nor were any witnesses called on his behalf. His attorney
requested the court to instruct the jury to render a verdict
of "not guilty," on the ground that no evidence had been
presented by the people to show what intent defendant had.
The motion for a directed verdict was denied, and the defense rested its case. The jury then returned a verdict
of guilty as charged.

Concubinage has been defined as any form of illicit intercourse. People v. Bristol, 23 Mich. 118; People v. Cummons,
56 Mich. 544. However, the difficulty with this case is
that defendant's purpose in attempting to entice the child
away from her home is unknown. It is necessary for the people not only to charge, but to prove the intent on the part
of respondent when the corrupt intent is made a necessary ingredient of the crime charged. People v. Bilitzke, 174 Mich.
329. The rule was stated by Mr. Justice CHRISTIANCY in Roberts
v. People, 19 Mich. 400, 414, as follows:

"We think the general rule is well settled, to which there
are few, if any, exceptions, that when a statute makes an offense to consist of an act combined with a particular intent,
that intent is just as necessary to be proved as the act itself, and must be found by the jury, as a matter of fact, before a conviction can be had. But especially, when the offense created by the statute, consisting of the act and the
intent, constitutes . . . substantially an attempt to commit
some higher offense than that which the defendant has succeeded in accomplishing by it; we are aware of no well-founded
exceptions to the rule above stated."

The prosecuting attorney contends that the circumstances,
as well as the defendant's character, were such as to permit
of no other inference than that he wanted to secure the child

for the purpose of concubinage. He claims the proofs indicate that the child's parents were poor and had a large family, and that it therefore could not reasonably be inferred that defendant attempted to secure the possession of the child for the purpose of exacting money. He also calls attention to the following statement by Mr. Justice COOLEY in People v. Carrier, 46 Mich. 442, 446:

"It was also insisted that there was no evidence to go to the jury tending to show that the defendant enticed the woman from Barry's custody, or that, if he did, his purpose was either prostitution, concubinage, or marriage. The facts were that defendant induced a brother of the girl to persuade her to meet him at a place away from Barry's house, and that after the interview which there took place the girl went off at once to Canada. How far, if at all, this was induced by the persuasions of the defendant was left to the jury on the facts."

However, Justice COOLEY went on to state that the prosecution had thrown light upon the intent by a showing of previous illicit relations and of the subsequent conduct of the parties.

Were the previous record of defendant in the instant case examined, it would be found that both of his former convictions were for making "an indecent and obscene exposure of the person of another," that the exposure was of a female in both cases, and that it was of a female child in at least one of the cases. It is quite possible that defendant may be a pervert, with a strong psychopathic disposition toward the commission of the offense of indecent exposure of the person of another, and that such was his intent in the instant case. There are strong indications that defendant requires the attention of a psychiatrist and possibly institutionalizing, but that does not establish his guilt of the charge in the instant case. There is no evidence that defendant attempted to entice the child away for the particular purpose of concubinage, and for this reason the conviction must be set aside and a new trial ordered. Under the circumstances, it will be unnecessary to discuss whether defendant may be sentenced as a third-term offender, or whether his two previous offenses were felonies or misdemeanors.

The conviction is set aside and defendant is remanded to the custody of the sheriff for a new trial.

NELSON SHARPE, C. J., and POTTER, NORTH, FEAD, WIEST, BUSNHELL, and EDWARD M. SHARPE, JJ., concurred.

3. Final Draft - Michigan Revised Criminal Code

(Definition of Terms)

Sec. 2201. The following definitions apply in this chapter:

1098

(a) "Restrain" means to restrict a person's movements unlawfully and without consent, so as to interfere substantially with his liberty by moving him from one place to another, or by confining him either in the place where the restriction commences or in a place to which he has been moved. Restraint is "without consent" if it is accomplished by (i) physical force, intimidation or deception, or (ii) any means, including acquiescence of the victim, if he is a child less than 16 years old or an incompetent person and the parent, guardian, or other person or institution having lawful control or custody of him has not acquiesced in the movement or confinement.

(b) "Abduct" means to restrain a person with intent to prevent his liberation by either (i) secreting or holding him in a place where he is not likely to be found, or (ii) using or threatening to use deadly physical force.

(c) "Relative" means a parent or stepparent, ancestor, sibling, uncle or aunt, including an adoptive relative of the same degree through marriage or adoption.

Committee Commentary

The section is adapted from New York Penal Law, Sec. 135.00. The significance of the definitions is discussed in the commentaries to the sections which follow.

(Unlawful Imprisonment in the First Degree)

Sec. 2205. (1) A person commits the crime of unlawful imprisonment in the first degree if he knowingly restrains another person under circumstances which expose the latter to risk of serious physical injury.

(2) Unlawful imprisonment in the first degree is a Class A misdemeanor.

Committee Commentary

The section is adapted from New York Revised Penal Law Sec. 135.10. Its relationship to existing law is set out in the Commentary to Sec. 2205 to 2206 below.

(Unlawful Imprisonment in the Second Degree)

Sec. 2206. (1) A person commits the crime of unlawful imprisonment in the second degree if he knowingly restrains another person.

(2) A Person does not commit a crime under this section if (a) the person restrained is a child less than 16 years old, (b) the actor is a relative of the child, and (c) his sole purpose is to assume control of the child. The burden of injecting the issue is on the defendant, but this does not shift the burden of proof.

(3) Unlawful imprisonment in the second degree is a Class B misdemeanor.

1099

Committee Commentary

The section is adapted from New York Revised Penal Law Sec. 135.05, 135.15. Its relationship to existing law is explained in the Commentary to Sec. 2205 to 2206 below.

Committee Commentary to Sec. 2205 to 2206

Relationship to Existing Law

False imprisonment, defined as the unlawful confinement of a person, is a common-law misdemeanor (Perkins, Criminal Law 129-34 (1957)). Though there is no case law so indicating, conceivably false imprisonment could be charged in Michigan. A few statutes embody certain aspects of false imprisonment: taking a woman and compelling her to marry (C.L. 1948, Sec. 750.11); taking a woman with intent to compel her to marry (C.L. 1948, Sec. 750.12); enticing away a female under sixteen for an immoral purpose (C.L. 1948, Sec. 750.13); and detaining a woman in a house of prostitution for debt (C.L. 1948, Sec. 750.458). The first three statutes are lumped together as abduction. The taking must be without consent (People v. Congdon, 77 Mich. 351, 43 N.W. 986 (1889)), and in the case of a child under sixteen, the defendant's purpose must be to have illicit sexual relations (People v. Fleming, 267 Mich. 584, 255 N.W. 305 (1934); People v. Bristol, 23 Mich. 118 (1871)). Abduction, therefore, can be viewed as a specialized form of false imprisonment.

The Draft redonominates the offense as unlawful imprisonment. The act by which the crime is committed is "restraint", defined in Sec. 2201 (a) to be substantial interference with the victim's liberty by either moving him from one place to another or confining him. The culpability requirement is "knowingly", which means under Sec. 305 (b) that knowledge of the circumstances is sufficient. The restraint must be unlawful, which means that the question of legality of interference may be contested in the criminal courts. Whether, for example, an improper arrest of a citizen by a police officer amounts to unlawful imprisonment turns on (a) whether the arrest was in fact unlawful under the circumstances, (b) whether the officer knew that his interference with the citizen's liberty was unlawful but intended to act anyway, (c) whether the person arrested consented to the interference with his liberty, and (d) whether the circumstances of the unlawful arrest manifest a "substantial" interference with the citizen's liberty. Only when the arrest is unlawful, known to be unlawful, is not consented to, and is viewed as a substantial interference with the citizen's liberty is there unlawful imprisonment.

The sole basis for aggravating unlawful imprisonment from the second to the first degree is exposure of the person restrained to the risk of serious physical injury, a term

1100

defined in Sec. 135 (i). Compare the basis for aggravating assaults in Sec. 2101-2103 and the crime of reckless endangerment (Sec. 2115).

At times the criminal law is invoked to continue a parental battle over custody of children (cf. People v. Nelson, 322 Mich. 262, 33 N.W. 2d 786 (1948); People v. Congdon, 77 Mich. 351, 43 N.W. 986 (1889)). This is minimized in Sec. 2206 by subsection (2). The crime of unlawful imprisonment in the second degree is not committed if the victim is less than sixteen years old, the defendant is a relative as defined in Sec. 2201 (c) and the sole motivation for the restraint is to take control of the child. This exception does not apply to Sec. 2205, however, because no child should be exposed to serious physical injury in a custody dispute. It should be noted that under the definition of "restraint without consent" under Sec. 2201 (a), agreement to the taking of a child under sixteen is legally irrelevant, but is relevant above that age if no physical force, intimidation or deception is used. Note also that under Sec. 2205 (2) the only acceptable motive for the restraint is to gain custody; any other purpose is unprivileged.

Because the circumstances underlying the restraint by a relative are peculiarly within the knowledge of the actor and his relatives, and perhaps not readily accessibly to the prosecutor, the burden of injecting the issue is placed on the defendant in Sec. 2206 (2), but this does not shift the burden of proof on the state to prove criminality beyond a reasonable doubt.

B. Kidnapping

    1. Michigan Compiled Laws (1948)

750.349 Kidnaping

Sec. 349. CONFINING PERSON AGAINST WILL, ETC. - Any person who wilfully, maliciously and without lawful authority shall forcibly or secretly confine or imprison any other person within this state against his will, or shall forcibly carry or send such person out of this state, or shall forcibly seize or confine, or shall inveigle or kidnap any other person with intent to extort money or other valuable thing thereby or with intent either to cause such person to be secretly confined or imprisoned in this state against his will, or in any way held to service against his will, shall be guilty of a felony, punishable by imprisonment in the state prison for life or for any term of years.

Every offense mentioned in this section may be tried either in the county in which the same may have been committed or in any county in or through which the person so seized, taken, inveigled, kidnaped or whose services shall be sold or transferred, shall have been taken, confined,

1101

held, carried or brought; and upon the trial of any such offense, the consent thereto of the person, so taken, inveigled, kidnaped or confined, shall not be a defense, unless it shall be made satisfactorily to appear to the jury that such consent was not obtained by fraud nor extorted by duress or by threats.

750.350 Same; child under 14

Sec. 350. ENTICING AWAY, ETC., CHILD UNDER 14 YEARS OF AGE - Any person who shall maliciously, forcibly or fraudulently lead, take or carry away, or decoy or entice away, any child under the age of 14 years, with intent to detain or conceal such child from its parent or guardian, or from the person or persons who have lawfully adopted said child or from any other person having the lawful charge of said child, shall be guilty of a felony, punishable by imprisonment in the state prison for life or any term of years. In case such child shall have been adopted by a person or persons other than its parents, in accordance with the statute providing for such adoption, then this section shall apply as well to such taking, carrying, decoying or enticing away of such child, by its father or mother, as by any other person.

2. Definition and Elements of the Offense

People v. Nelson
322 Mich. 262

REID, J. Defendant was convicted by a jury of kidnapping a young child, his nephew, under section 350 of the Michigan penal code (Act No. 328, Pub. Acts 1931, Comp. Laws Supp. 1940, Sec. 17115-350, Stat. Ann. Sec. 28.582). From the judgment imposing sentence, defendant appeals.

Carl Nelson and Constance Nelson, the parents of the child in question, were married in November, 1940, at Ironwood, Michigan, and continuously lived together in New York city from Christmas eve, 1940, until the latter part of May, 1946, during part of which time Carl Nelson was in the armed service of the United States. Carl Nelson was an actor and Constance, a social service worker. Their son, Carl David Nelson, was born August 26, 1942.

Differences arose between the parents. Constance Nelson for protection for herself and her child applied to domestic relations court in New York, family division, May 27, 1946. We are not fully informed as to the nature of the disposition of the matter made by the family division of the domestic relations court, but some disposition of the matter in differences was made so that Constance Nelson had physical charge of the child. She did not apply for a divorce in

1102

New York State and she testified that the supreme court
of New York State has not granted her custody of the child.
There seems to have been accorded to Carl Nelson the right
to have his son at least for stated periods for visitation.
During one such visit about June 1, 1946, Carl Nelson, the
father, took his son from New York State to the residence of
his parents in Escanaba, Michigan, without the mother's permission. The mother, Constance, returned to Michigan and
on June 29, 1946, accompanied by her two brothers, who she
says are "good husky chaps," she went to the Nelson residence
in Escanaba. They stopped in front of the house; she saw
the little boy on the lawn, got out of the car, ran across
to the child, and picked him up. Defendant, who was there,
tried to stop her by putting his hand in front of her. She
took the boy to the home of her parents, the Victor home, in
Ramsay, Michigan.

On the morning of July 3, 1946, Carl Nelson, the father,
and Herbert Nelson, the defendant, accompanied by William
Van Laanen and John Bergquist, drove to Ramsay in defendant's
car, which they parked on a hill a short distance east of
the Victor home. Carl Nelson and defendant got out of the
car. Van Laanen and Bergquist remained in the car.

Defendant claims he did not take the child Carl David
but the jury by their verdict indicate that they believed
the testimony of witness Edward Olson, who testified that
defendant picked up the child on the yard back of the house,
and ran toward the road. Van Laanen testified that he saw
Carl (the father) coming out of the yard with the child in
his arms. Bergquist testified to the same effect, and that
at no time did he see defendant Herbert have the child.
There is no testimony to dispute the defendant's claim that
from the instant the child was taken to the automobile, he
has been in the exclusive custody of his father.

The four men, Carl Nelson (the father), Herbert Nelson
(the defendant), Van Laanen and Bergquist, drove to Pembine,
Wisconsin, let Carl with the boy, Carl David, our of the car,
and left them there. Defendant knew that Carl intended to
go to Owosso, Michigan, with the child. Defendant returned
to Escanaba, where he was later arrested.

There is no testimony to show that defendant in the transaction of taking the boy had any motive other than to assist
his brother, the father of the boy, in getting the boy back
into his (the father's) physical custody. All the facts, including the fact that the defendant let his brother with the
boy out of the car at Pembine, Wisconsin, strongly indicate
that defendant's motive was to assist his brother and not to
serve any other purpose on defendant's part as to the custody
of the boy. The acts on which the prosecution relies to show
that the defendant may have had some motive of his own to
serve are simply the acts of defendant in assisting the father
in getting the son back into the father's custody.

The statute under which the prosecution is brought (Act

No. 328, Sec. 350, Pub. Acts 1931 (Comp. Laws Supp. 1940, Sec. 17115-350, Stat. Ann. Sec. 28.582)), enacted under the title of "kidnaping," is as follows:

"Any person who shall maliciously, forcibly or fraudulently lead, take or carry away, or decoy or entice away, any child under the age of 14 years, with intent to detain or conceal such child from its parent or guardian, or from the person or persons who have lawfully adopted said child or from any other person having the lawful charge of said child, shall be guilty of a felony, punishable by imprisonment in the State prison for life or any term of years. In case such child shall have been adopted by a person or persons other than its parents, in accordance with the statute providing for such adoption, then this section shall apply as well to such taking, carrying, decoying or enticing away of such child, by its father or mother, as by any other person."

The leading case relied on for the prosecution's theory is State v. Brandenberg, 232 Mo. 531 (134 S.W. 529, 32 L.R.A. (N.S.) 845). The reasoning in that case to support a conviction of the mother's agent is as follows (pp. 537, 538):

"The parental affection flowing from both father and mother to a child of tender years would be a protection to such child as long as it remained in the actual and immediate custody of either of them, and the filial love of the child would in most cases enable either parent to properly control its conduct; but these safeguards to the child would not exist between it and a mere agent, like the defendant in this case, who was not bound to it by any tie of consanguinity.

"It is apparent that one of the objects of the statute under consideration was to protect parents against the mental anguish which necessarily follows the decoying away and retaining of their children, and if a child be taken or decoyed away from one parent by another parent, the mental anxiety of the parent who thus loses the child would not be nearly so great as in the case at bar, where the child passed into the hands of one who was under no obligation, and perhaps no inclination, to properly care for it."

In the Brandenberg Case, the defendant took the child from its father's custody to St. Louis, Missouri, and took it to San Francisco, California, where defendant claims the mother of the child agreed to meet him later, the parents then being as yet undivorced. The reasoning in that case, as quoted above, has applicability to the facts of that case where the mother did not immediately obtain the custody for herself.

The reasoning in the Brandenberg Case entirely fails of applicability to the case at bar, where the defendant turned the child immediately into the father's arms, and the father left the scene with the child in his custody with no possibility of the unfavorable results of the agent (as distinguished from

1104

the parent) continuing in the custody, as cited in the Brandenberg Case.

The trial court in the case at bar properly ruled that no order of the domestic relations court of New York city had been shown awarding the custody to either parent. We are not concerned with the question as to which parent should be awarded the custody, temporary or permanent, of the child Carl David Nelson. The question here is whether defendant acting for the father and in the immediate presence of the father of the child (no court order forbidding), is to be considered as a felon under Act No. 328, Sec. 350, Pub. Acts 1931 (Comp. Laws Supp. 1940, Sec. 17115-350, Stat. Ann. Sec. 28.582) for aiding the father to immediately and in person obtain the physical custody of his own child.

If no suit for divorce or separation has been filed between husband and wife and there is no order of court awarding the custody of a child to the mother, persons who act merely as agents of and for account of the father in taking the child from the custody of the mother are not guilty of kidnapping. See State v. Elliott, 171 La. 306 (131 South. 28, 77 A.L.R. 314), in which case the court annulled a conviction and sentence of appellant, one of three persons who obtained the physical custody of a child four years of age from its mother against her protest at the request and authorization of the child's father, who was not present. In that case the court ruled that the trial judge should have granted the requested charge that if the jury found that no suit for divorce or separation had been filed and there was no order awarding the custody to the mother and that the defendants in taking the child were acting merely as the agents of and for account of the father, they were not guilty of kidnapping under the statute.

We consider the statute in question (Act No. 328, Sec. 350, Pub. Acts 1931 (Comp. Laws Supp. 1940, Sec. 17115-350, Stat. Ann. Sec. 28.582)) does not in all cases make a good-faith agent of the parent liable as a felon, unless there can be said to be an independent custody on such agent's part or an unreasonable delay in transferring the child to the parent, the principal.

The welfare of the child is paramount. The prosecution in this case in effect requests us to rule that the intervening parent, regardless of what the child's welfare may require or what the circumstances of the intervening parent are, may not authorize an agent to act in his behalf to retrieve the custody of a child. We decline so to rule.

"Where one parent is entitled to the possession of a minor child as against all the world except the other parent, and where the father and mother are equally entitled to its possession, one of them does not commit the crime of kidnapping by taking exclusive possession of the child; and a person who assists a parent under such circumstances is not guilty of the crime. But it has been ruled that where the

1105

agent of one of the parents, acting alone and not in company with his principal, takes a child from the other parent without his consent, he is guilty of kidnapping although both parents are equally entitled to the possession of the child." 8 R. C. L. p. 297.

For the latter statement, State v. Brandenberg, supra, is cited.

Defendant in this case was not shown to have violated the statute (Act No. 328, Sec. 350, Pub. Acts 1931 (Comp. Laws Supp. 1940, Sec. 17115-350, Stat. Ann. Sec. 28.582)) because the criminal intent required by the statute is not shown. On the contrary, in this case a lawful intent is clearly shown, namely, that the father should immediately obtain direct physical custody of his own child.

The judgment is reversed. The cause (sic) is remanded to the circuit court with direction to set aside the sentence (without a new trial), discharge the defendant and cancel his bond.

BUSHNELL, C. J., and SHARPE, BOYLES, NORTH, DETHMERS, BUTZEL, and CARR, JJ., concurred.

3. Final Draft - Michigan Revised Criminal Code

(Kidnaping in the First Degree)

Sec. 2210. (1) A person commits the crime of kidnaping in the first degree if he intentionally abducts another person with intent to:

(a) Hold him for ransom or reward; or
(b) Use him as a shield or hostage; or
(c) Facilitate the commission of any felony or flight thereafter; or
(d) Inflict physical injury upon him, or to violate or abuse him sexually; or
(e) Terrorize him or a third person; or
(f) Interfere with the performance of any governmental or political function.

(2) A person does not commit a crime under subsection (1) if he voluntarily releases the victim, alive and not suffering from serious physical injury, in a safe place prior to trial. The burden of injecting the issue of voluntary safe release is on the defendant, but this does not shift the burden of proof. This subsection does not apply to a prosecution for or preclude a conviction of kidnaping in the second degree or any other crime.

(3) Kidnaping in the first degree is a Class A felony.

Committee Commentary

The section is adapted from Model Penal Code Sec. 212.1 and from "Middle Atlantic Code"* Sec. 562. Its relationship to existing law is discussed in the Commentary to Sec. 2210 to 2211, below.

* The drafters of this code have asked that the state's identity be kept confidential until the measure has been formally presented to the legislature for action.

(Kidnaping in the Second Degree)

Sec. 2211. (1) A person commits the crime of kidnaping in the second degree if he intentionally abducts another person.

(2) A person does not commit a crime under this section if (a) the abduction is not coupled with intent to use or to threaten to use deadly physical force, (b) the actor is a relative of the person abducted, and (c) his sole purpose is to assume control of that person. The burden of injecting the issue is on the defendant, but this does not shift the burden of proof.

(3) Kidnaping in the second degree is a Class B felony.

Committee Commentary

The section is adapted from New York Revised Penal Law Sec. 135.20. Its relationship to existing law is explained in the Commentary to Sec. 2210 to 2211 below.

Committee Commentary to Sec. 2210 to 2211

Relationship to Existing Law

Kidnaping is an aggravated form of false imprisonment which originally involved transportation out of the realm, and thus beyond the power of the sovereign's authority to protect the victim by law (Perkins, Criminal Law 134-137 (1957); Note, A Rationale of the Law of Kidnaping, 53 Colum. L. Rev. 540, 541 (1953)). Michigan, like most states, has a special kidnaping statute (C. L. 1948, Sec. 750.349), which covers unlawful confinement for the purpose of carrying or sending the victim out of the state, or of extorting money or other valuables, or of holding in secret confinement or imprisonment within the state, or of holding to service against the victim's will. Punishment is for any term of imprisonment up to life. The statute remains for practical purposes without actual construction by the Supreme Court (cf. People v. Nelson, 322 Mich. 262, 33 N.W.2d 786 (1948)).

The Draft retains the basic thrust of the present statute, except that the involuntary servitude aspects in most cases will now constitute unlawful imprisonment in the second degree (Sec. 2206). The basic act for kidnaping in Sec. 2211 is "abduction" defined in Sec. 2201 (b) to mean restraint, defined in Sec. 2201 (a), with intent to prevent the victim's liberation by either secreting or holding him in a place where he is unlikely to be found, or using or threatening to use deadly physical force, defined in Sec. 135 (j). It is thus the factor of either secrecy of restraint or the actual or threatened use of life-endangering physical force that sets kidnaping apart from unlawful imprisonment. In effect, then, kidnaping is an aggravated form of unlawful imprisonment, as it was at common law.

Section 2210 aggravates the penalties for kidnaping if the actor has a further purpose than that embodied in the definition of abduction itself. The first is the intent to hold the victim for ransom or reward. This is almost always the clearest possible indication of professional criminality, and poses substantial risk to the victim's life (see 53 Colum. L. Rev. 540, 548-49 (1953)). The second is the purpose to use the victim as a shield or hostage, again a potentially highly dangerous motivation. The third is to facilitate the commission of a felony or a subsequent escape; this bears a close relationship to the second, though it is of course broader. The fourth is the purpose to inflict bodily injury on the victim or to misuse him sexually. The definition of bodily injury in Sec. 135 (h) is restricted enough that there is considerable potential harm to the victim of this type of kidnaping. A fifth motivation is to terrorize the victim or another person. Several cases recently reported in Michigan fit this pattern; compare also the fact situation in People v. Hansen,368 Mich. 344, 118 N.W.2d 422 (1962), in which the victim killed the would-be terrorizer. The final motivation listed is to interfere with the performance of any governmental or political function. This would include, for example, kidnaping a police officer to prevent an alarm from being given, or kidnaping an official so that he would be unable to participate in legislative debates, sign official papers, or whatever. (In general, see Model Penal Code Tent. Draft No. 11, pp. 17-18 (1960).)

None of the purposes listed in Sec. 2210 must actually be carried out in order for the crime to be committed; the crime is complete when there is restraint coupled with intent to secrete or use or threaten use of deadly physical force. Most of these purposes if carried through either pose substantial danger to the life of the victim or create strong incentive to the criminals to kill the victim to eliminate the chief medium for their identification and apprehension. Ransom kidnaping statutes in a number of states like New York, Illinois and California have been construed to require imposition of the death penalty if the victim sustains the slightest bodily injury (see Model Penal Code Tent. Draft No. 11, pp. 19-20 (1960); Note, 53 Colum. L. Rev. 540, 549-50 (1963)). What was originally intended as a protection to the victim, through deterring infliction of serious harm to the ransom kidnap victim, was converted

1108

through judicial construction into an invitation to the
criminal to kill the victim once the latter suffered even
a slight injury; since the defendant thereby became eligible
for the death penalty he was in no worse case legally if he
killed the victim and thus removed the best prosecution witness against him. The Draft provides that there is no kidnaping in the first degree if the defendant voluntarily releases the victim alive and not suffering from serious physical injury, in a safe place before trial. This modified
the Model Penal Code provision by leaving first-degree penalties intact if there is serious physical injury to the
victim. The criminal thereby obtains a limited means of
effectuating second thoughts about the propriety of his acts.
Because the burden of injecting this issue is on the defendant, he must in effect inform the public where, when and in
what condition the victim was released. But in theory this
eliminates any legal encouragement to the criminal to kill
his victim if other than serious physical injury has been
inflicted and indeed encourages him to release the victim.
If voluntary release takes place, only kidnaping in the
first degree is eliminated as a legal possibility; kidnaping in the second degree, unlawful imprisonment in either
degree or assault in any of its degrees are unaffected by
release.

Death of the victim as such does not aggravate kidnaping.
This is because any death which the criminal causes is already murder under Sec. 2005 (1) (b), and the causation test
is the "but for" test of Sec. 302. Death of the victim
through accident, e.g. in an automobile collision caused by
tire failure, would be at most culpably negligent homicide,
with the fact of a law violation pertinent in determining
negligence (cf. People v. Harris, 214 Mich. 145, 151-52,
182 N.W. 678 (1921)).

The New York and "Middle Atlantic" codes permit a relative
to avoid kidnaping responsibility if his motivation is to
gain control of the victim. This is too broad an exception.
Therefore the Draft limits it to those abductions in which
there is no use or threat to use deadly physical force, and
to those cases in which the only motivation is to obtain
custody or control. Any purpose listed in Sec. 2210 auto-
matically takes the case out of the exemption in Sec. 2211 (2).

INTERROGATORIES

1. Outline the provisions of the Michigan statutes relevant
    to abduction and false imprisonment.
2. How is the crime of false imprisonment defined by Perkins?
3. What Michigan statutes embody aspects of false imprisonment?
4. What statutes are lumped together as abduction?
5. What were the facts, issue and holding of the court in
    People v. Bristol?

6. What were the facts, issue and holding of the court in People v. Congdon? What is the mens rea requirement for the offense?
7. What were the facts, issue and holding of the court in People v. Fleming? What must be the defendant's purpose?
8. Outline the provisions of Sec. 2201, 2205, and 2206, Final Draft, Mich. Rev. Crim. Code.
9. Outline the provisions of Mich. Comp. Laws, Sec. 750.349 and 750.350.
10. According to Perkins, how was the offense of kidnaping originally defined?
11. What were the facts, issue and holding of the court in People v. Nelson?
12. Outline the provisions of Sec. 2210 and 2211, Final Draft, Mich. Rev. Crim. Code. Would these provisions alter the present law?

CHAPTER IX

OFFENSES INVOLVING THEFT

A. Larceny

  1. Michigan Compiled Laws (1948)

750.356 Larceny

  Sec. 356. Any person who shall commit the offense of
larceny, by stealing, of the property of another, any money,
goods or chattels, or any bank note, bank bill, bond, promissory note, due bill, bill of exchange or other bill, draft,
order or certificate, or any book of accounts for or concerning money or goods due or to become due, or to be delivered, or any deed or writing containing a conveyance of
land, or any other valuable contract in force, or any receipt,
release or defeasance, or any writ, process or public record,
if the property stolen exceed the value of $100.00, shall be
guilty of a felony, punishable by imprisonment in the state
prison not more than 5 years or by fine of not more than
$2,500.00. If the property stolen shall be of the value of
$100.00 or less, such person shall be guilty of a misdemeanor.
As amended P.A. 1957, No. 69, Sec. 1, Eff. Sept. 27.

750.356a Same; from motor vehicles or trailers; attached
          accessories; breaking or entering, damaging

  Sec. 356a. Any person who shall commit the offense of
larceny by stealing or unlawfully removing or taking any
wheel, tire, radio, heater or clock in or on any motor vehicle, house trailer, trailer or semi-trailer, shall be
guilty of a felony, punishable by a fine not to exceed
$1,000.00, or by imprisonment in the state prison not more
than 5 years.
  Any person who shall enter or break into any motor vehicle, house trailer, trailer or semi-trailer, for the purpose of stealing or unlawfully removing therefrom any goods,
chattels or property of the value of not less than $5.00, or
who shall break or enter into any motor vehicle, house trailer, trailer or semi-trailer, for the purpose of stealing or
unlawfully removing therefrom any goods, chattels, or property regardless of the value thereof if in so doing such person breaks, tears, cuts or otherwise damages any part of
such motor vehicle, house trailer, trailer or semi-trailer,
shall be guilty of a felony, punishable by a fine not to exceed $1,000.00, or by imprisonment in the state prison not
more than 5 years.

750.356b Breaking and entering coin operated telephone,
          penalty

Sec. 356b. Any person who breaks or enters into any coin operated telephone or a coin device attached to or an integral part thereof for the purpose of stealing or unlawfully removing therefrom any money, regardless of the value thereof, if in so doing such person breaks, tears, cuts or otherwise damages any part of the telephone or any coin device attached to or an integral part thereof, is guilty of a misdemeanor, punishable by a fine not to exceed $200.00 or by imprisonment for not more than 1 year, or both. P.A. 1931, No. 328, Sec. 356b, added by P.A.1961, No. 81, Sec. 1, Eff. Sept. 8, 1961.

750.357 Larceny from the person

Sec. 357. LARCENY FROM THE PERSON - Any person who shall commit the offense of larceny by stealing from the person of another shall be guilty of a felony, punishable by imprisonment in the state prison not more than 10 years.

750.357a Larceny of livestock

Sec. 357a. LARCENY OF LIVESTOCK - Any person who shall commit the offense of larceny by stealing the livestock of another shall be guilty of a felony.
The term "lovestock" shall apply to horses, stallions, colts, geldings, mares, sheep, rams, lambs, bulls, bullocks, steers, heifers, cows, calves, mules, jacks, jennets, burros, goats, kids and swine.

750.358 Larceny at a fire

Sec. 358. LARCENY AT A FIRE - Any person who shall commit the offense of larceny by stealing in any building that is on fire, or by stealing any property removed in consequence of alarm caused by fire, shall be guilty of a felony, punishable by imprisonment in the state prison not more than 5 years or by a fine of not more than 2,500 dollars.

750.359 Larceny from vacant dwelling

Sec. 359. LARCENY, ETC., FROM VACANT BUILDING - Any person or persons who shall steal or unlawfully remove or in any manner damage any fixture, attachment or other property belonging to, connected with or used in the construction of any vacant structure or building, whether built or in the process of construction or who shall break into any vacant structure or building with the intention of unlawfully removing, taking therefrom or in any manner damaging any fixture, attachment or other property belonging to, connected with or used in the construction of such vacant structure or building whether built or in the process of construction, shall be guilty of a misdemeanor, punishable by imprisonment in the county jail of not more than 1 year or by a fine of not more than 500 dollars.

750.360 Larceny; places of abode, work, storage, conveyance, worship and other places

1112

Sec. 360. Any person who shall commit the crime of larceny by stealing in any dwelling house, house trailer, office, store, gasoline service station, shop, warehouse, mill, factory, hotel, school, barn, granary, ship, boat, vessel, church, house of worship, locker room or any building used by the public shall be guilty of a felony.

750.361 Same; or maliciously removing journal bearings or brasses

Sec. 361. LARCENY OR MALICIOUSLY REMOVING JOURNAL BEARINGS OR BRASSES - Any person who shall steal or maliciously remove, take, change, add to, take from or in any manner interfere with any journal bearings or brasses or any parts or attachments of any locomotive, tender or car, or any fixture or attachment belonging to, connecting with or used by any railway, railroad or transportation company in this state shall be guilty of a misdemeanor, punishable by imprisonment in the state prison for not less than 1 year nor more than 2 years: Provided, That if the stealing or removal of such journal bearings or brasses, or any parts or attachments of any locomotive, tender or car, or any fixture or attachment belonging to, connected with, or used on any locomotive, tender or car as aforesaid shall be the cause of wrecking any train, locomotive or other car in this state, whereby the life of any person or persons shall be lost as a result of the felonious or malicious stealing, nothing in this section shall be construed as preventing prosecution for such crime.

Possession of any journal bearings or brasses or any parts or attachments of any locomotive, tender or car, or any fixture or attachment belonging to, connected with, or used by any railroad, railway or transportation company in this state, without the authority of the railroad company owning or leasing the same, shall be prima facie evidence that the same has been stolen or maliciously taken or removed by the person in whose possession the same is found or proved to have been.

750.362 Same; by conversion, etc.

Sec. 362. LARCENY BY CONVERSION, ETC. - Any person to whom any money, goods or other property, which may be the subject of larceny, shall have been delivered, who shall embezzle or fraudulently convert to his own use, or shall secrete with the intent to embezzle, or fraudulently use such goods, money or other property, or any part thereof, shall be deemed by so doing to have committed the crime of larceny and shall be punished as provided in the first section of this chapter.

750.362a Same; rented motor vehicle, trailer or other tangible property; penalty

1113

Sec. 362a. Any person to whom a motor vehicle, trailer or other tangible property is delivered on a rental or lease basis under any agreement in writing providing for its return to a particular place at a particular time who refuses or wilfully neglects to return such vehicle, trailer or other tangible property, after the expiration of the time stated in a notice in writing proved to have been duly mailed by registered or certified mail addressed to the last known address of the person who rented or leased the motor vehicle, trailer or other tangible property, and with intent to defraud the lessor, is guilty of larceny. If the vehicle, trailer or other tangible property exceeds the value of $100.00 he shall be guilty of a felony punishable by imprisonment for not more than 2 years or by a fine of not more than $1,000.00, or both. If the vehicle, trailer or other tangible property is of the value of $100.00 or less, he shall be guilty of a misdemeanor. P.A.1931, No. 328, Sec. 362a, added by P.A.1964, No. 241, Sec. 1, Eff. Aug. 28, 1964, as amended P.A.1966, No. 297, Sec. 1, Eff. March 10, 1967.

750.363 Same; by false personation

Sec. 363. LARCENY BY FALSE PERSONATION - Any person who shall falsely personate or represent another, and in such assumed character shall receive any money, or other property whatever, intended to be delivered to the party so personated, with intent to convert the same to his own use, shall be deemed by so doing, to have committed the crime of larceny, and shall be punished as provided in the first section of this chapter.

750.364 Same; from libraries

Sec. 364. LARCENY FROM LIBRARIES - Any person who shall procure, or take in any way from any public library or the library of any literary, scientific, historical or library society or association, whether incorporated or unincorporated, any book, pamphlet, map, chart, painting, picture, photograph, periodical, newspaper, magazine, manuscript or exhibit or any part thereof, with intent to convert the same to his own use, or with intent to defraud the owner thereof, or who having procured or taken any such book, pamphlet, map, chart, painting, picture, photograph, periodical, newspaper, magazine, manuscript or exhibit or any part thereof, shall thereafter convert the same to his own use or fraudulently deprive the owner thereof, shall be guilty of a misdemeanor.

750.365 Same; from car or persons detained or injured by accident

Sec. 365. LARCENY FROM CAR OR PERSONS DETAINED OR INJURED BY ACCIDENT - Any person who shall steal from any car, while detained by accident or injury to any railroad, locomotive, tender or car, or who shall steal the property of,

1114

or rob any person detained, injured or killed by reason of any accident or injury to any such railroad, locomotive, tender or car, shall be guilty of a felony, punishable by imprisonment in the state prison for not more than 20 years or by a fine of not more than 10,000 dollars.

At the trial of any case arising under this section, it shall be sufficient prima facie proof of the existence of any railroad company named in the indictment to show that such company was doing business as a railroad company at the time named in the indictment.

750.366 Same; railroad passenger tickets

Sec. 366. LARCENY OF RAILROAD PASSENGER TICKETS - Any person who shall feloniously or fraudulently take and carry away any railroad passenger ticket or tickets belonging to any railroad company or companies, shall be guilty of a felony.

The words "railroad passenger ticket or tickets" as used in this section shall be construed to embrace any ticket, card, pass, certificate or paper providing, or intended to profice, for the carriage or transportation of any person or persons upon any railroad, and shall include, not only tickets of any railroad company fully prepared for use, but those not fully prepared for use, and all others which have been once used. At the trial of any case arising under this section, it shall be sufficient prima facie proof of the existence of any railroad company named in the indictment to show that such company was doing business as a railroad company at the time named in the indictment.

750.367 Taking or injuring trees, shrubs, vines, plants

Sec. 367. TAKING OR INJURING FRUIT, SHADE, ORNAMENTAL TREES, SHRUBS, VINES, ETC. - Any person who shall wrongfully take and carry away from any place any fruit tree, ornamental tree, shade tree, ornamental shrub, or any plant, vine, bush, or vegetable there growing, standing or being, with intent to deprive the owner thereof, or who shall without right and with wrongful intent, detach from the ground or injure any fruit tree, ornamental tree, shade tree, ornamental shrub, or any plant, vine, bush, vegetable or produce shall be deemed by so doing to have committed the crime of larceny and shall be punished as provided in the first section of this chapter.

750.367a Larceny of rationed goods, wares and merchandise

Sec. 367a. LARCENY OF RATIONED GOODS, WARES OR MERCHANDISE - Any person who shall steal any goods, wares or merchandise, the manufacture, distribution, sale or use of which is restricted or rationed by the federal government, or any of its agencies or instrumentalities, during a state of war between the United States and any other country or nation, shall be guilty of the applicable crime or crimes set forth in Act No.

328 of the Public Acts of 1931, as amended,[1] and upon conviction thereof shall be punished by not to exceed double the fines and imprisonment therein provided. Any prosecution hereunder shall be in circuit court or in a court having similar criminal jurisdiction. The term "steal" as used in this section shall be construed to include the obtaining of any such property or the possession thereof in any manner or by any means defined, or the penalty for which is prescribed, by any section of chapters 31, 36, 52 or 61, or section 280 of chapter 43 of Act No. 328 of the Public Acts of 1931 as amended.[2]

Footnotes

1. Sections 750.1 et seq.

2. Sections 750.174 et seq., 750.218 et seq., 750.356 et seq., 750.280.

750.367b Taking possession of and use of airplane

Sec. 367b. TAKING POSSESSION OF AND USE OF AN AIRPLANE - Any person who shall, wilfully and without authority, take possession of or use an airplane, and any person who shall assist in or be a party to such taking possession of or use of an airplane, belonging to another, shall be guilty of a felony, punishable by imprisonment in the state prison for not more than 5 years.

750.406 Military stores, larceny, embezzlement or destruction

Sec. 406. LARCENY, EMBEZZLEMENT OR DESTRUCTION OF MILITARY STORES - Any person who, during any war, rebellion or insurrection against the United States, or against this state, shall wilfully and maliciously embezzle, steal, injure, destroy or secrete any arms or ammunition, or military stores or equipments of the United States, or of this state, or of any officer, soldier or soldiers in the service of the United States, or of this state, or shall wilfully and maliciously destroy, remove or injure any buildings, machinery or material used or intended to be used in the making, repairing or storing of any arms, ammunition, military stores or equipment for the service of the United States, or of this state, whether such buildings, machinery or materials be public or private property, shall be guilty of a felony, punishable by imprisonment in the state prison for not more than 5 years or by a fine of not more than 2,500 dollars.

426.155 Reception into booms or manufacture of logs without consent of owner; misdemeanor

Sec. 5. If any person having the possession or control of any boom, in any of the waters of this state shall, knowingly, run, turn, admit or receive into such boom, or cause to be run, turned, admitted or received into such boom, any log, spar, boomstick, shinglebolt, railroad tie or fence post not his own, without the consent of the owner thereof; or if any person being in the possession or having the control of any saw-mill, shingle-mill, or any structure made for the purpose of manufacturing lumber, shingles or timber, shall knowingly manufacture into lumber, shingles, timber, pickets or posts, any log, spar, or shinglebolt not his own, without the consent of the owner thereof, shall be deemed guilty of a misdemeanor, and punished as provided in section 4 of this act.[1]

Footnote

1. Section 426.154

287.308 Stealing or holding in possession dog; penalty

Sec. 8. Any person who shall steal or take without the consent of the owner and without lawful authority, any dog registered under the provisions of this act, or any person excepting dog wardens who shall harbor or hold in his possession any stray dog of which he is not the owner and does not report such possession to the sheriff of the county or the police department of the city in which he is holding such dog within 48 hours after such person came in possession of said dog, where the value of such dog shall not be in excess of $100.00, shall be guilty of a misdemeanor, and where the value of such dog shall be in excess of $100.00 shall be guilty of a misdemeanor and upon conviction thereof shall be fined not less than $50.00 nor more than $500.00, or imprisoned in the county jail for not more than 1 year, or both such fine and imprisonment in the discretion of the court.

2. Definitions and Elements of the Offense

In re Rogers
308 Mich. 392

WIEST, J. . . . Petitioner is confined in the State prison at Jackson and seeks release by habeas corpus on the alleged ground that he was convicted of the crime of larceny, in the circuit court for the county of Huron, in November, 1930, and sentenced to the State prison at Jackson for a period of not exceeding 30 years and not less than 15 years; that the penalty for such offense could not exceed 5 years and he has been in prison under such sentence 12½ years. . . .

Upon arraignment, petitioner pleaded guilty to the charges and former convictions but in the journal of the court he was recorded as guilty of "grand larceny" and so sentenced. In common parlance the term "grand larceny" may have a meaning

1117

but in point of law it is unknown by such term. Had this error in nomenclature been seasonably brought to the attention of the circuit court the proper correction should and could have been made but, inasmuch as petitioner now presents the matter as a ground for his release, it is not too late to permit the record to be made to speak the truth. The writ of certiorari has brought before us the proceedings in the circuit court and under our constitutional power, it being apparent that the errors in the court journal and the commitment of sentence are ministerial, the record is remanded to the circuit court with direction to make the same, nunc pro tunc, speak the judicial determination relative to the conviction and the grounds for the sentence imposed and a supplemental commitment issued and forwarded to the warden of the State prison at Jackson. . . .

The mentioned charge in the information of two previous felonies and imprisonment of petitioner, upon his plea of guilty, authorized the court, in imposing sentence, to consider petitioner a third offender and subject to the imprisonment imposed. Act No. 175, Chap. 9, Sec. 11, Pub. Acts 1927, as amended by Act No. 24, Pub. Acts 1929 (3 Comp. Laws 1929, Sec. 17339 (Stat. Ann. Sec. 28.1083)). Petitioner's application for release is denied.

NORTH, C. J., and STARR, BUTZEL, BUSHNELL, SHARPE, BOYLES, and REID, JJ., concurred.

People v. Taugher
102 Mich. 598

GRANT, J. The respondent was convicted, under a common-law information, of the larceny of a buggy. The entire evidence upon which he was convicted is stated in the record as follows:

"That on the 19th day of July, 1893, Mrs. Taugher, wife of the defendant, came to the city of Muskegon with a horse and buggy, and while in said city her buggy was smashed by an electric car, and that Fred W. Thompson, superintendent of the electric railway, procured of Peter Damm, complaining witness in this cause, a buggy for the use of Mrs. Taugher, to enable her to return to her home, - the buggy to be returned by her on the following day; that Mrs. Taugher did not return the buggy; that afterwards, and on the 25th day of July, 1893, Mrs. Taugher and defendant, James Taugher, came together to said city of Muskegon with said buggy, and were met on one of the streets of said city by said Thompson and said Peter Damm; that Thompson said to Damm: 'Here is your buggy; now, take it, and I will pay for one day, and they must pay for the rest;' that at this time defendant was in the buggy, and his wife on the sidewalk, close to the buggy; that Peter Damm then laid his hand on one of the

1118

thills of the buggy, and said, 'This is my buggy, and I
want it right here, now;' that then Mrs. Taugher said to
Thompson, 'When are you going to fix my buggy?' that Thompson replied; 'I have nothing to do with it; you must see
Mr. Nims, the president of the company, about it; that defendant did not leave the buggy, and that Damm made no further effort to obtain the buggy; that defendant said, 'Let
me have the buggy to take my wife to Nims' office, and I
will return it on my way back,' to which Peter Damm consented, and released his hand from the thill of the buggy; that
this conversation occurred about 11 o'clock in the forenoon;
that Taugher and wife went to Nims' office, Taugher remaining in the buggy while his wife went to Nims' office, and
were seen there and in the street in front of the office by
Peter Damm, and that defendant remarked to Damm, 'We are
waiting for Mr. Nims;' that the buggy was not returned to
Damm, but was driven by Taugher and wife out to their farm
being the home of defendant, and the place where Mrs. Taugher wanted to go on the day of the accident to her buggy.
The next day, Damm drove out to the farm, saw Taugher, and
told him he had come for the buggy. Taugher told him that
his wife was out picking berries, and had the buggy with
her. Taugher also said he had two horses, - a colt and an
older one. Taugher then had one horse hitched to a culti-
vator, and a colt was seen by Damm running in a pasture on
the farm. Taugher also told Damm that his wife would not
give up the buggy until her own was fixed, and told Damm
that he should go to the street-car company for his buggy,
to which Damm replied, 'You want me to have a lawsuit to
accommodate you?' and Taugher said, 'I guess you will have
to.' That Damm then searched Taugher's premises, but did
not find the buggy; that Damm then returned to the city,
and caused the arrest of Taugher for the larceny of a buggy;
. . .that, at the time of Taugher's arrest at the farm, Taugher told the officer that he (Taugher) never stole a buggy;
that his wife went to town, and met with an accident, and
that she got the buggy from Thompson, and still had it in
her possession; that he (Taugher) had nothing to do with it
whatever, and that the buggy was then in the barn; that at
the time of defendant's arrest the officer did not search
the barn or premises of Taugher, but brought defendant to
the city of Muskegon, and the next day went again to Taugher's
premises with Damm, and searched the farm, but did not find
the buggy; that on the same day, and after his return to the
city of Muskegon, the officer went to the jail where defendant was confined, and asked him where the buggy was; that
defendant said in response that the buggy was up in the barn;
that the officer then said to defendant: 'You know better;
it was not there yesterday, and it is not there today;' that
Taugher inquired if the officer had been up to the farm, and
was told 'Yes;' that the officer then told defendant that he
had made inquiries of Mrs. Taugher, and that she told him
that the buggy was not there to-day, and was not there yester-

1119

day; that defendant thereupon told the officer that it was no use to pick him, as he would get nothing out of him; that defendant also told the officer that may be some friends of mine in town may have the buggy;' that the officer asked for their names, and was told by Taugher that he would not give their names, - that he would not put anybody in trouble."

The respondent introduced no evidence.

Issue It is contended by the attorney for the people that the respondent intended to steal the buggy from the outset, and that he requested and obtained the consent of Mr. Damm to use the buggy temporarily with felonious intent. We do not think that a felonious taking is established by the proof. He was in the lawful possession of the buggy when Damm approached him upon the street and demanded possession. Damm, by placing his hand upon the thill, did not recover possession.

The people rely upon the case of People v. Camp, 56 Mich. 548. In that case the respondent obtained possession of a horse from a boy, the son of the owner, who evidently had no authority to act for his father, and afterwards secreted him.

Reason A felonious taking is essential to establish the crime of larceny at the common law. Respondent's possession was lawful until the demand. He would be liable in a civil action of replevin or trover, but no criminal intent is shown.

Held It follows that the conviction must be set aside, and the respondent discharged.

The other Justices concurred.

People v. Bradovich
305 Mich. 330

WIEST, J. An information in the recorder's court for the city of Detroit charged defendants with the crime of larceny in a store of three men's suits of the total value of $113. The offense charged was laid under the criminal code, Act No. 328, chap. 52, Sec. 360, Pub. Acts 1931 (Comp. Laws Supp 1940, Sec. 17115-360, Stat. Ann. Sec. 28.592). Defendants waived trial by jury and upon trial before the court were found guilty of an attempt to commit the crime mentioned. On appeal defendants claim error because the information did not charge an attempt to commit, but only larceny consummated.

Issue
facts The evidence disclosed that defendants were in the store of the Bond Clothing Company, located at 1000 Woodward avenue in the city of Detroit, and were observed, by a salesman, taking clothing from a rack and concealing it beneath their own clothing. The salesman notified the manager who posted men at the exits from the room on the second floor where defendants took the clothing, stopped the elevator, and notified the police, who arrived within five or six minutes; and then the manager and the police went to the

1120

second floor in the elevator and there saw defendants walking toward a table in the front part of the room where defendants removed the stolen property from beneath their clothing and laid the same on the table. Under the evidence defendants were clearly guilty of larceny, and the question is whether they could be convicted of the lesser offense of attempt to commit that crime without a count to such effect in the information. There is no merit in the point.

We held in People v. Rose, 268 Mich. 529 (syllabus), that: *Rule*

"Conviction may be had of lesser offense not charged in information where it is necessarily included within greater offense that is charged."

In People v. Baxter, 245 Mich. 229, 232, we said:

"Defendant invokes the rule, operative in some jurisdictions by judicial holdings, and in others by statute, that there can be no conviction of an attempt to commit a felony if the evidence establishes consummation of the felony. This is the rule in Illinois. People v. Lardner, 300 Ill. 264 (133 N.E. 375, 19 A.L.R. 721). But the rule is not general, and does not prevail in this jurisdiction. If an information admits a conviction of an attempt to commit a felony, an accused may be found guilty of the attempt, though the evidence shows a completed offense. People v. Miller, 96 Mich. 119; People v. Blanchard, 136 Mich. 146. Such a verdict may be illogical, but the people cannot complain, and the defendant must accept it, even though less in measure than his just deserts; at least he cannot be heard to say that he has suffered injury. . . .

The trial judge was evidently of the opinion that, inasmuch as the defendants had shed their plunder without leaving the store, they had thus purged the taking thereof and gave defendants the benefit of a doubt created thereby. If so, in point of law the judge was mistaken. The crime of larceny was completed when defendants removed the clothing from the rack and concealed it beneath the clothing they were wearing.

Defendants claim there was no asportation from the store of the clothing so concealed. Removal of the clothing from the rack and concealing it under their own clothing constituted asportation. See note 19 A. L. R. 724.

As said before, defendants were guilty of larceny and were not injured in any respect by the adjudication of the court that they were guilty of an attempt to commit the crime of larceny. Defendants did not testify.

It is urged that they discarded the plunder of their own free will. What they did indicated knowledge of inability to escape and, therefore, they unloaded what they had stolen, evidently having the childish opinion that they could thus free themselves from the crime they had committed.

The convictions are affirmed. *Held*

BOYLES, C. J., and CHANDLER, NORTH, STARR, BUTZEL, BUSHNELL, and SHARPE, JJ., concurred.

MOORE, J. The respondent was convicted in the superior
court of Grand Rapids of the offense of larceny of property
belonging to Gertrude Anderson. There are many assignments
of error, but the important question in the case is whether
the facts shown by the testimony constitute the offense of
larceny. The respondent offered no testimony. The jury, in
order to convict, must have believed the testimony offered
by the people, which was to the following effect: In the
early part of 1897 the respondent came to Grand Rapids as
a solicitor for a life-insurance company of which S. F. Angus
was the Detroit manager. She made the acquaintance of Miss
Earle, one of the examining physicians of the life-insurance
company, and through her made the acquaintance of Miss Anderson, who was keeping house, with one servant, in Grand Rapids.
She solicited Miss Anderson to become insured, but Miss Anderson did not consent. About the middle of February an arrangement was made that Miss Martin was to board with Miss
Anderson, and she did so from then until the 15th of April,
when Miss Martin left Grand Rapids.

Miss Anderson had a bicycle. About the 1st of March there
was talk between them about purchasing a bicycle, and Miss
Martin said she was going to have a new wheel, and should
buy it very cheap, through a friend of hers and, if Miss Anderson wanted one, she could get one for her, and she thought
she could sell the old wheel to a lady she knew in Detroit.
Miss Anderson at this time was employed in the office of the
United States engineer, where there were a number of persons
employed. A little later Miss Martin suggested to Miss Anderson that she thought she could get wheels for her associates in the office, considering them also as friends, at the
same price. Miss Anderson decided to take a wheel, and then
told her associates what Miss Martin proposed. Miss Martin
came to the office March 13th, and arranged to take the orders for wheels for Miss Anderson and several of her associates. Miss Martin sat down at Miss Anderson's desk, and
wrote what she said was a letter to the friend through whom
she was to get the wheels, E. J. Moran. Miss Anderson was
to have a high-grade Cleveland wheel at a cost of $38, which
amount she paid in cash to Miss Martin. Mr. Schauroth gave
her an indorsed government check for $100 and $14 in money.
Capt. Townsend gave her a check for $38. Mr. Wallace gave
her $18, and Miss Martin offered to loan him $20 to make up
his $38.

Miss Martin folded up what had been delivered to her, and
folded up the letter, and put them all in an envelope, and
asked Miss Anderson to go with her to the express office to
buy the money order, which Miss Martin said she wanted to
get off that night. This was between half past 4 and 5
o'clock. On the way to the express office Miss Martin said

she must first go to the office of Dr. King to get the $20 she was to let Mr. Wallace have. The two went to the office, and Miss Martin went in, and, after being gone for awhile, returned, and reported that Dr. King was not in, and she would have to see him later. She then said she must go to the U. B. A. Home on business, and Miss Anderson walked up there with her. They then came down town. It was nearly 6 o'clock, and, fearing the money-order department of the express office would be closed later, they went to the express office, and arranged that the checks which had been given Miss Martin should be received and cashed by the express company, and a money order be issued to Miss Martin later, when she had collected the $20 of Dr. King. It was then so late that Miss Anderson went home, and left Miss Martin to finish the business. Miss Martin returned to the express office, and bought an order for $50, and one for $43, in favor of S. F. Angus, Detroit, and one for $28 in favor of Mrs. F. B. Martin, Detroit, and no other orders on that day or on the 14th, 15th, or 16th of March were issued to Isma Martin, and none were issued in favor of E. J. Moran. About 7 o'clock or after, Miss Martin returned to the residence of Miss Anderson, and held up a piece of paper some distance from her, and said, "Here is the receipt for that money." After this the women talked about the wheels, which did not come. About a week before Easter, Miss Martin showed Miss Anderson a letter, which she said was from her friend through whom she was getting the wheels, saying if they would wait until Easter Monday the wheels would have the late improvements. The next Thursday after Miss Martin showed this letter, she left the house, saying she was going to Detroit, and would return the following Monday. She did not return, and Miss Anderson did not see her again until she saw her in court after her arrest. Miss Anderson never received any wheel. She testified that she never consented that Miss Martin should use the money she gave her for any other purpose than to purchase for her a bicycle.

It is the position of the people that from the foregoing facts, and the necessary and reasonable inferences to be drawn from them, the jury were warranted in finding the respondent guilty of larceny. The position of respondent is stated in a request to charge reading as follows:

"If you find from the evidence in the case that the money was delivered by Gertrude Anderson to respondent, intending at the time of the delivery to pass the title to the same, no matter how fraudulent the transaction on the part of the respondent turned out to be, you must acquit the respondent of the offense charged."

In support of this proposition counsel cite 2 Archb. Cr. Pl. 372; 1 Whart. Cr. Law, Sec. 964, 965; 2 East P. C. 668; Ross v. People, 5 Hill, 294; 2 Bish. Cr. Law, Sec. 808; Hildebrand v. People, 56 N.Y. 396 (15 Am. Rep. 435); People v. McDonald, 43 N. Y. 61; Zink v. People, 77 N. Y. 126 (33

Am. Rep. 589).

While it is conceded by the people that Miss Anderson consented to part with the possession of her money, they contend that her consent was fraudulently obtained, and that she did not intend to part with the title of her property to Miss Martin, but that it was delivered to her for a special purpose, and for that reason the offense is larceny; citing People v. Shaw, 57 Mich. 403 (58 Am. Rep. 372); Stinson v. People, 43 Ill. 397; Welsh v. People, 17 Ill. 339; Murphy v. People, 104 Ill. 533; Com. v. Barry, 124 Mass. 325; People v. Abbott, 53 Cal. 284 (31 Am. Rep. 59).

It is sometimes difficult to determine in a given case whether the offense is larceny or whether it is a case of false pretenses. We think the rule to be gathered from the authorities may be stated to be: In larceny, the owner of the thing stolen has no intention to part with his property therein; in false pretenses, the owner does intend to part with his property in the thing, but this intention is the result of fraudulent contrivances. If the owner did not part with his property in the thing, but simply delivered the possession, the ownership remaining unchanged, for the purpose of having the person to whom the property was delivered use it for a certain special and particular purpose, for the owner, the title would not pass, and its felonious conversion would be larceny. A distinction is made between a bare charge for special use of the thing, and a general bailment; and it is not larceny if the owner intends to part with the property and deliver the possession absolutely, although he has been induced to part with the goods by fraudulent means. If, by trick or artifice, the owner of property is induced to part with the possession to one who receives the property with felonious intent, the owner still meaning to retain the right of property, the taking will be larceny; but if the owner part (sic) with not only the possession, but the right of property also, the offense of the party obtaining the thing will not be larceny, but that of obtaining the goods by false pretenses. As was said in Loomis v. People, 67 N. Y. 329 (23 Am. Rep. 123):

"There is, to be sure, a narrow margin between a case of larceny and one where the property has been obtained by false pretenses. The distinction is a very nice one, but still very important. The character of the crime depends upon the intention of the parties, and that intention determines the nature of the offense. In the former case, where, by fraud, conspiracy, or artifice, the possession is obtained with a felonious design, and the title still remains in the owner, larceny is established; while in the latter, where title, as well as possession, is absolutely parted with, the crime is false pretenses. It will be observed that the intention of the owner to part with his property is the gist and essence of the offense of larceny, and the vital point upon which the crime hinges and is to be determined."

1124

In this case the respondent made the acquaintance of the prosecutor, and pretended he had a check he wanted cashed. The prosecutor went with him to a saloon, where they met a confederate of respondent, and dice were thrown. The respondent asked the prosecutor to lend him $90, saying he was sure to win, and that, if he did not, he had the check, which he would get cashed and pay him back. The money was loaned, the dice were thrown, respondent lost, and the prosecutor insisted upon having his money back. The check was then put up and lost, and the confederates went away carrying the money with them. The court said the respondent was properly convicted.

In Stinson v. People, 43 Ill. 397, it is said: "If the owner parts with the possession voluntarily, but does not part with the title, expecting and intending the same thing shall be returned to him, or that it shall be disposed of on his account, or in a particular way, as directed or agreed upon, for his benefit, then the goods may be feloniously converted by the bailee, so as to relate back, and make the taking and conversion a larceny, if the goods were obtained with that intent;" and the conviction of larceny was held to be proper. This was a case where the prosecutor had been induced to wager his money with one of the respondents, and had delivered it to a third person, who was selected as a stake-holder, the other confederate depositing what was represented as a package containing a like amount of money, but which was in fact waste paper.

The case of People v. Shaw, 57 Mich. 403, is an instructive one. Shaw and Jones were confederates. Shaw claimed to be an agent for a tea house, and explained the method of selling tea by means of cards. While he was doing this, Jones came up, and pretended to be a stranger, and took part in the transaction, which resulted in Brown letting Shaw have $80, which Shaw bet with Jones. The card was drawn, and Shaw lost, and he at once delivered the money to Jones. Justice CAMPBELL, in writing the opinion, made use of the following language: "There is some rather attenuated discrimination to be found in the books between such cheats as induce a person to give temporary custody of his property to another, who keeps or disposes of it, and those whereby he is induced to part with it out and out. We do not think it profitable to draw overnice metaphysical distinctions to save thieves from punishment. If rogues conspire to get away a man's money by such tricks as those which were played here, it is not going beyond the settled rules of law to hold that the fraud will supply the place of trespass in the taking, and so make the conversion felonious;" and sustained the conviction of respondents for larceny.

Applying these rules of law to this case, what is the result? It must be borne in mind that Miss Anderson was not buying of Miss Martin a bicycle for $38, but was intrusting to her, as her friend and agent, $38 to be used for a special purpose. She did not intend, when she gave

1125

Miss Martin the possession of the property, to also give
her the title to it, so that it might be said the money belonged to Miss Martin. She parted with the possession so
the money might be devoted to a specific purpose for the
benefit of Miss Anderson. If, at the time she obtained
the property, the respondent obtained it by false representations, intending at the time to convert it to her own use,
and with the intent to deprive Miss Anderson of her property,
she was guilty of larceny. . . .

Conviction is affirmed, and case remanded for further
proceedings therein.

The other Justices concurred.

People v. McHugh
286 Mich. 336

POTTER, J. Defendant was arrested upon a complaint made
November 23, 1935, charging him with a violation of section
362 of the Michigan penal code of 1931 (Act No. 328, Pub.
Acts 1931 (Comp. Laws Supp. 1935, Sec. 17115-362, Stat Ann.
Sec. 28.594)). The information charged:

"That James P. McHugh, late of the said city of Detroit,
in said county, heretofore, to-wit, on the 9th day of January,
A. D. 1934, at the said city of Detroit, in the county aforesaid, $1,300 in lawful money of the United States of America,
and of the value of $1,300, of the personal property, goods
and chattels of Otto Kraft, was delivered to and came into
the possession of James P. McHugh, and afterwards and while
the said goods and chattels then in his possession as aforesaid, he, the said James P. McHugh, to-wit, on the 9th day
of January, A. D. 1934, at the city of Detroit aforesaid,
the said property of the value aforesaid, feloniously and
fraudulently did embezzle and convert to his own use.

"Therefore, the said James P. McHugh the property of the
said Otto Kraft aforementioned in manner and form aforementioned in manner and form aforesaid, feloniously did steal,
take and carry away; contrary to the form of the statute,"
et cetera. . . .

. . . Section 362, of Act No. 328, Pub. Acts 1931, provides:

"Any person to whom any money, goods or other property,
which may be the subject of larceny, shall have been delivered, who shall embezzle or fraudulently convert to his own
use, or shall secrete with the intent to embezzle, or fraudulently use such goods, money or other property, or any part
thereof, shall be deemed by so doing to have committed the
crime of larceny and shall be punished as provided in the
first section of this chapter."

The information charged in apt language an offense under
this section of the penal code and the testimony was sufficient

1126

to sustain the conviction of the respondent. There is nothing in People v. Doe, alias Meyer, 264 Mich. 475, which militates against this contention. . . .

. . . It is contended the offense charged against defendant is one unknown to the law. On the contrary, it is charged in accordance with the provisions of Act No. 328, Sec. 362, Pub. Acts 1931.

Issue

"Under our Constitution the power to enact laws is vested in the legislature. . . . To declare what shall constitute a crime, and how it shall be punished, is an exercise of the sovereign power of a State, and is inherent in the legislative department of the government." People v. Hanrahan, 75 Mich. 611 (4 L. R. A. 751).

The legislature, in the exercise of the sovereign power delegated to it by the Constitution, passed the section of the statute under which the defendant was tried and convicted. The information charged in apt language a violation of this provision of the statutes and it cannot be said the information did not charge an offense known to the law. It may be, as pointed out in People v. Doe, alias Meyer, supra, that the offense is neither common-law larceny nor embezzlement, but is one of the crimes provided by statute law to occupy the noman's land surrounding the offenses against property at common law. . . . There was testimony tending to show the statute was directly applicable to the offense with which defendant was charged. We find no error in defendant's conviction which is affirmed. *Held*

Reason

Legislative Powers

WIEST, C. J., and BUSHNELL, SHARPE, CHANDLER, NORTH, and McALLISTER, JJ., concurred. BUTZEL, J., took no part in this decision.

People v. Long
50 Mich. 249

(For the opinion in this case see page 123, supra)

People v. Shaunding
268 Mich. 218

Brenton Shaunding was convicted of entering a horse shed, without breaking, with intent to commit larceny therein. Reversed, and new trial granted. . . . *Held*

facts

necessity of Intent

BUSHNELL, J. The trial court was in error in excluding testimony offered by the respondent as to his belief that he had the right to take the property in question from the place from which it was taken.

"The felonious intent is an essential and inseparable *Issue*

1127

ingredient in every larceny, and if a person takes property
under a claim of right, however unfounded, he has not committed larceny." People v. Hillhouse, 80 Mich. 580,586.

The judgment is reversed, and a new trial is granted.

NELSON SHARPE, C. J., and POTTER, NORTH, FEAD, WIEST,
BUTZEL, and EDWARD M. SHARPE, JJ., concurred.

People v. Henry
202 Mich. 450

STONE, J.   The defendant was convicted of the crime of
larceny of $26 lawful money of the United States, from the
person of one Samuel Harris, under an information charging
robbery, being armed with a dangerous weapon, in violation
of section 15206, 3 Comp. Laws 1915. Upon the trial the evidence was very conflicting. On the part of the people it
was testified that about 12 o'clock midnight of July 29, 1917,
the defendant entered the saloon of Harris in the city of
Detroit being armed with a revolver which he discharged into
the ceiling in the presence of Harris, who testified:

"The defendant came up to me right away with his gun saying: 'Give me the money or I will kill you.' I was standing
by the cash register behind the bar and he stuck the gun at
me. He says 'Give me money.' I told him, 'Wait, I will give
it right away.' He said, 'Come on, give me your money or I
will kill you right away.' He pointed the revolver at me,
shaking it that way. I was scared to turn around, thinking
he might shoot me in the back, so I said, 'Come on behind,
I will give it to you.' I opened the register, grabbed whatever I could give and put it on the bar," and that defendant
took the money and went away.

On the part of the defendant it was testified that defendant went into the saloon of Harris earlier in the night and
had been there induced by Harris to enter a gambling game
called a "crap" game, then in progress in the saloon, in which
he lost $27; that he asked Harris to restore the money, which
he refused to do; whereupon he went to his home, a short distance from the saloon, but soon returned to the saloon with
a revolver. The defendant testified:

"The first thing as I stepped up to the door I made a
shot into the ceiling. I was careful not to shoot any one.
Right after that I stuck the revolver in my coat pocket.
When I entered the saloon, I had no gun in my hand. There
were some people scattered around the back side of the saloon.
I said 'Give me my money,' to the saloon and to the fellows
that robbed me. I said nothing to Harris. After the shot
I saw him come from the back end, from around the barrels.
Harris said to me, 'Hey, there, what is the matter?' I said,
These fellows got my money and I would like to have some one

1128

restore it back.' He said, 'I don't want any of that thing around here; I will pay you, how much is it?' I said. '$27.00.' And he went over to where the gamekeeper was sitting and brought me back $26.00. He said he didn't want that disturbance at that time of night. I told him, 'Thank you,' and walked out. . . . I went back there to get the money they robbed me of, and went home to get my gun."

The court was requested by defendant's counsel, among other things, to charge the jury as follows:

"5. I further charge you, gentlemen of the jury, that in considering all of the evidence in this case touching the matters involved, you will take into consideration all of the evidence in the case, and if you find, gentlemen of the jury, that the defendant only used that necessary force to repossess himself of his own property, which had been taken from him by crap game shooting in said saloon, then you cannot hold the defendant guilty of robbery as charged in the information.

"6. The Revised Statutes, chapter 156, of 1897 (2 Comp. Laws 1915, Sec. 7795 et seq.), provides that any person obtaining money by card playing or shooting craps or shooting dice or any gambling device whatever, if the sum obtained by said playing is less than $25 the person obtaining said money is subject to a fine of $100 or to be confined in jail for three months, or both such fine and imprisonment; if the person playing such crap game receives more money from such gambling than said sum of $25, then, if convicted, he shall be subject to a fine of $500, or twelve months in the county jail, or both such fine and imprisonment, in the discretion of the court. I further charge you, gentlemen of the jury, that this same statute which I have mentioned gives the loser of his money - which would be this defendant, if he lost his money in said saloon and by that method of crap shooting and gaming - a right to recover the same in cases of assumpsit for money had and received, or in an action of trespass on the case, or by replevin for and on behalf of the plaintiff. Therefore, I charge you that if this money was obtained by gambling, as aforesaid, from the defendant, that the prosecuting witness or any one who was present shooting crap games in said saloon, could not acquire any title to said property, because it is in contravention of the law to play such games, and they never come into the legal possession of said money; if you find these facts to be true from the evidence, gentlemen of the jury, you must acquit the defendant, as he is not guilty of the charge as set up in the information."

Neither of said requests was given. The trial court charged the jury in part as follows:

"I will charge you, if this defendant voluntarily went into what is known as a crap game and lost his money in that

1129

way and he came back and endeavored through violence and at the point of a revolver to secure his money back from Mr. Harris, I charge you, gentlemen of the jury, that under those circumstances that he would be guilty of robbery.

"It may be true, that if a man in your presence is attempting to steal your property and attempting to carry it away, you have a right to defend yourself, and you have a right to overcome him, and you have a right to retake your property; there is no question about that, but after voluntarily surrendering your money or surrendering your property, and then the property is out of your possession, out of your sight, then, gentlemen of the jury, it is not your province or any man's province, rather, to undertake to take the law into his own hands, and by force and violence to make a reparation of the wrong done to him. That is for the courts, that is for the legal channels in the peaceful, orderly administration of the law, rather than by any man taking it by violence into his own hands. . . .

"But if this defendant went in there, as under the theory of the people, and did what they said he did, that is the people's witnesses, then, gentlemen of the jury, you should convict him, and if he went back there and did what the complainant, Harris, has said he did, that he came into the place and shot off the gun and pointed it at Harris, and secured the money which he had lost in a crap game, and attempted to take from Mr. Harris what he had previously lost in a crap game, then, gentlemen of the jury, he is guilty of the charge in the information. . . .

"But if he (the defendant) did lose the money at that crap game and then he went away and afterwards came back and held Mr. Harris up, as he described, laboring under the theory that he had lost his money in the previous crap game, and resented it, and attempted to get it back, I say to you, gentlemen of the jury, under those circumstances, the defendant would be guilty of the charge in this information. . . .

"Now, this information contains the charge of robbery - being armed with a dangerous weapon with intent to kill if resisted. It also contains the charge of larceny from the person. If you do not believe the defendant guilty of robbery, being armed with a dangerous weapon and if resisted with intent to kill, you may convict this defendant of larceny from the person, if you believe him guilty of that beyond a reasonable doubt. . . .

"This information contains also the charge of larceny. If you do not find the defendant guilty of the two offenses which I have just enumerated that are included in this information, beyond a reasonable doubt, then you may convict this defendant of larceny, if you believe him guilty of that beyond a reasonable doubt, gentlemen. If you find him guilty of that beyond a reasonable doubt, gentlemen of the jury, then fix the value of the property taken in your verdict."

After conviction the defendant was sentenced to imprisonment in the Detroit house of correction for a term of not less than 6 months, nor more than 5 years. He has brought the case here on writ of error. Error is assigned upon the refusal to charge as requested above, and to that part of the charge above set forth.

As defendant was not convicted of robbery and was only convicted of larceny, it is suggested that if there was error in that part of the charge relating to robbery it was harmless error. But it should be borne in mind that, without defining the crime of larceny, the jury were instructed that they might convict of larceny if they believed the defendant guilty of that crime, beyond a reasonable doubt. Yet the element of felonious intent is present in larceny, the same as in robbery. We are of the opinion that the foregoing request to charge should have been given. Our statute gives a right to the loser to recover the money or property lost in a gambling game - and among other actions gives that of replevin - thus recognizing the money or property as belonging to him. Hess v. Culver, 77 Mich. 598, 601; Lassen V. Karrer, 117 Mich. 512.

We are also of the opinion that there was prejudicial error in the charge. If the defendant in good faith believed that the money which he demanded was his money, and that he was entitled to its possession, he could not be guilty of either robbery or larceny in taking it, because there would be no felonious intent, "and if the defendant, for any reason whatever, indulged no such intent, the crime cannot have been committed." People v. Walker, 38 Mich. 156; State v. Koerner, 8 N.W. 292 (78 N.W. 981).

A case very much in point is that of Thompson v. Commonwealth in the court of appeals of Kentucky, 18 S.W. 1022. The opinion being brief, we quote it:

"The appellant was convicted of the crime of robbing J. R. Barnes. The money that the appellant is accused of robbing said Barnes of, was won by Barnes from appellant that evening at an unlawful game; and the appellant thereafter presented his pistol on Barnes, and compelled him to return him the money thus won. Under our statute the title to the money won by Barnes did not pass to him, or from the appellant, nor did the right to its possession pass to Barnes, as against the appellant. It is a uniform rule that a person is not guilty of stealing that which belongs to him, and to which he has a right. Robbing is larceny, accompanied by violence, and putting the person from whom the property is taken in fear. Here the fact that the appellant was entitled to the money, and Barnes' possession of it was not rightful, as against the appellant, stripped the appellant's act of feloniously taking the property of another with the fraudulent intention of permanently depriving the owner of it."

The judgment was reversed. To the same effect are the following cases: State v. Hollyway, 41 Iowa, 200; People v. Hall, 6 Parker's Cr. R. (N.Y.) 642; Rex v. Hall, 3 Car. & Payne, 409.

The last cited case was an indictment for robbing John Green, a gamekeeper of Lord Ducie, of three hare wires and a pheasant. It appeared that the prisoner had set three wires in a field belonging to Lord Ducie, in one of which this pheasant was caught; and that Green, the gamekeeper, seeing this, took up the wires and pheasant, and put them into his pocket; and it further appeared that the prisoner, soon after this came up and said: "Have you got my wires?" The gamekeeper replied that he had, and a pheasant that was caught in one of them. The prisoner then asked the gamekeeper to give the pheasant and wires up to him, which the gamekeeper refused; whereupon the prisoner lifted up a large stick, and threatened to beat the gamekeeper's brains out if he did not give them up. The gamekeeper fearing violence did so. Baron Vaughan said:

"I shall leave it to the jury to say whether the prisoner acted on an impression that the wires and pheasant were his property; for, however he might be liable to penalties for having them in his possession, yet, if the jury think that he took them under a _bona fide_ impression that he was only getting back the possession of his own property, there is no _animus furandi_, and I am of opinion that the prosecution must fail."

There was a verdict of not guilty.

In our opinion the question of felonious intent in the instant case should have been submitted to the jury, under appropriate instructions as to both robbery and larceny, along the lines above indicated.

We find no other reversible error in the record. For the errors pointed out the judgment is reversed and a new trial granted.

OSTRANDER, C. J., and BIRD, MOORE, STEERE, BROOKE, FELLOWS, and KUHN, JJ., concurred.

People v. Williams
368 Mich. 494

DETHMERS, J. Defendants were convicted of larceny in a building. The parties agree that the applicable statute is CL 1948, Sec. 750.360 (Stat Ann 1954 Rev. Sec. 28.592), which reads:

"Any person who shall commit the crime of larceny by stealing in any dwelling house, house trailer, office, store, gasoline service station, shop, warehouse, mill, factory, hotel, school, barn, granary, ship, boat, vessel, church, house of woship, locker room or any building used by the public shall be guilty of a felony."

The structure in which the people allege the larceny

1132

occurred is described as being 7 feet, 7 inches high, 15
feet, 1 inch long, and 33 inches wide. According to the
owner's testimony it is constructed of metal, attached to
the land, bolted down to cement, entirely enclosed, a covered shed, it has overlapping doors with a steel bar coming
down through the outside door and a padlock attached through
the steel rod. In it tires were stored and displayed in 2
tiers, with a capacity for 100 tires. It had been constructed on the premises and located about 38 feet from the main
gasoline service station building located on the same premises.
On the night in question the doors had been closed and locked,
but afterwards the mentioned rod on the door had been sawed   *Facts*
apart, the lock removed, the door opened, and 5 tires taken.

Is the structure in which the larceny was committed a   *Issue*
building within the meaning of the quoted statute? Defendants say it is merely a tire rack. They suggest that it
comes within the meaning of CL 1948, Sec. 750.114 (Stat Ann
Sec. 28.309), making it a misdemeanor to break and enter,
with intent to commit the crime of larceny, "any outside
show case or other outside enclosed counter used for the display of goods." We think the structure here involved is
considerably more than a show case or counter in the ordinarily accepted sense of the terms.

Defendants cite Rouse v. Catskill & N. Y. Steamboat Co.,
59 Hun (66 SC NY) 80 (13 NYS 126), in which it was held that
a vessel is not a building within the meaning of an ordinance prohibiting the sale of liquor in a building; Town of
Union v. Ziller, 151 Miss 467 (118 So 293, 60 ALR 1155), in
which a metal billboard was held not to be a building under
an ordinance prohibiting metal buildings; Truesdell v. Gay,
79 Mass 311, in which a wall around 3 sides of the stack of
an iron furnace to protect the stack from earth sliding down
a hill behind it is not a building within the lien law, to
permit a lien to attach to it; Whiteley v. Mayor and City
Council of Baltimore, 113 Md 541 (77 A 882), in which it was
held that, in a street opening proceeding in which it was
required that a map be filed showing lots and buildings to
be taken, it was not necessary to show a portable school-
house thereon because it was intended to be there only temporarily and was not a building to be taken or destroyed for
the street opening; Bailey v. Ohio, 26 Ohio Cir Ct 375, in
which a chicken coop 37-3/4 inches by 38 inches by 2 feet
high, which was moved from place to place and not attached
to the ground, was not a building within the meaning of a
statute defining burglary as breaking and entering any
building, because lacking any permanency of location as
a structure. These are of scant assistance to defendants
here with respect to the structure of the size, permanent
character and type of construction and attachment to the
realty here involved.

In Truesdell the follwoing was said:

"The word 'building' cannot be held to include every species

1133

of erection on land, such as fences, gates or other like structures. Taken in its broadest sense, it can mean only an erection intended for use and occupation as a habitation or for some purpose of trade, manufacture, ornament or use, constituting a fabric or edifice, such as a house, a store, a church, a shed."

This structure comes well within this definition of a building.

In Sanchez v. People, 142 Colo 58 (349 P2d 561, 78 ALR 2d 775), we find in the syllabi (p2d) the following:

"1. All stationary structures within State, no matter of what substance they may be constructed, are within term 'building' as used in burglary statute, so long as they are designed for use in position in which they are fixed."

"2. Although a telephone booth may be only a closet by dictionary definition when within another structure, it is a 'building' within purview of burglary statute when set apart."

"4. Under statute defining burglary as entry with felonious intent into any building, defendant who was prying cover off coin box in outside telephone booth was guilty of 'burglary.'"

By the same token, whatever term might be applicable to the structure here involved if it were inside another building, set apart and outside, as it was, it was a building within the meaning of the applicable statute. . . .

Affirmed.

CARR, C. J., and KELLY, SOURIS, and OTIS M. SMITH, JJ., concurred with DETHMERS, J.

BLACK and KAVANAGH, JJ., concurred in result.

ADAMS, J., did not sit.

Note

In the case of People v. Parsons, 105 Mich. 177, 184-185, the following instruction, summarizing the elements of larceny, was approved by the Michigan Supreme Court:

"Larceny has been defined to be the felonious taking and carrying away by any person of the goods and personal property of another, with the felonious intent of converting it to his own use and making it his own property, without the consent of the owner, - the word 'felonious' meaning that he has no color of right or excuse for the act. The intent must be, not to deprive the owner temporarily, but permanently, of his property. . . . According to all definitions, there must be a taking and carrying away; it must be with felonious intent; it must be the personal goods of another; and it must

1134

be without the consent, and against the will, of the owner."...

3. Final Draft - Michigan Revised Criminal Code

(Theft: Definition)

Sec. 3205. (1) "Theft" means:

(a) Knowingly to obtain or exert unauthorized control over the property of the owner; or

(b) Knowingly to obtain by deception control over property of the owner; and under subparagraph (a) or (b);

(c) To intend to deprive the owner permanently of the property.

(2) If the prosecution is based on theft by deception, and the deception is that defined in section 3201 (a) (v) failure to perform standing alone is not evidence that the defendant did not intend to perform.

Committee Commentary

The significance of the elements of the definition of theft is discussed in the Commentary to Sec. 3205 to 3208 below.

(Theft in the First Degree)

Sec. 3206. (1) A person commits the crime of theft in the first degree if he commits theft of:

(a) Property which exceeds 1000 dollars in value; or

(b) Property of any value taken from the person of another.

(2) Theft in the first degree is a Class B felony.

Committee Commentary

The significance of the section is discussed in the Commentary to Sec. 3205 to 3208 below.

(Theft in the Second Degree)

Sec. 3207. (1) A person commits the crime of theft in the second degree if he commits theft of:

(a) Property of any value and the property is taken in a building or from a vehicle; or

(b) Property which exceeds 250 dollars in value but does not exceed 1,000 dollars in value, and which is not taken from the person of another.

(2) Theft in the second degree is a Class C felony.

(3) If theft in the second degree is committed as defined

1135

in subsection (1) (a), the court in its discretion may after conviction reduce the crime to any class of misdemeanor or a violation.

Committee Commentary

The significance of the limitations and the reduction possibility is discussed in the Commentary to Sec. 3205 to 3208 below.

(Theft in the Third Degree)

Sec. 3208. (1) A person commits the crime of theft in the third degree if he commits theft of property which does not exceed 250 dollars in value and which is not taken from the person of another or in a building or from a vehicle.

(2) Theft in the third degree is a Class B misdemeanor.

Committee Commentary

The significance of the limitations is discussed in the Commentary to Sec. 3205 to 3208 below.

Committee Commentary to Sec. 3205 to 3208

Relationship to Existing Law

A. Summary

The chief aims in drafting this section and those which follow have been (1) to eliminate the confusing distinctions between larceny, larceny by trick, larceny by conversion, embezzlement of several different kinds, and obtaining property by false pretenses, perpetuated in the present Michigan statute and case law, (2) to define with greater clarity and in light of modern economic circumstances the line between criminal and non-criminal acquisitive conduct, and (3) to lay the ground work for a more rational classification of offenders in the property crimes area to reduce unwarranted disparity in punishments.

The structure of the crime of theft is greatly simplified:

(1) The defendant's acts must constitute either obtaining or exerting unauthorized control, as defined in Sec. 3201 (e) and (f), or obtaining by deception as defined in Sec. 3201 (e) and (a).

(2) These acts must be done "knowingly". The element of knowledge extends to every element referred to in Sec. 3205 (1) or (2), including the act of obtaining, the exertion of unauthorized control, the deception practiced (and see the language in Sec. 3201 (a)), the nature of the property and the fact of ownership in another. This precludes any concept of strict liability or any use of recklessness or negligence in imposing criminal responsibility.

(3) Even if the state establishes the elements described

above, it must also prove beyond a reasonable doubt that the defendant intended to deprive the owner permanently of his property, the term "deprive. . . permanently" being defined as in Sec. 3201 (b).

It is clear that the Draft does not expand the present Michigan Law except in one limited respect. The term "deception in Sec. 3201 (a) includes representations as to future as well as present or past fact, law as contrasted with fact, and opinion as contrasted with fact, and thus is arguably broader than the concept of false pretenses under traditional Michigan law. Otherwise, and in the language of Indiana Annotated Statutes Sec. 10-3029 (Burns 1964), the provision is intended "to unify several traditionally distinct offenses against person and property in order to eliminate pointless procedural obstacles to the conviction of thieves and swindlers." It also eliminates the welter of conflicting punishment provisions embodied in existing statute law.

B. Derivation

The basic definition resembles in many respect Illinois Criminal Code Sec. 16-1 (a) - (b), though it is not identical with it. Its basic approach is also similar to that of Indiana Annotated Statutes Sec. 10-3030 (Burns 1964), Minn. Criminal Code Sec. 609.52, New York Revised Penal Law Sec. 155.05 and Wisconsin Statutes Sec. 943.20 (1963). It differs from these provisions, and follows the lead of Model Penal Code Sec. 223.2, by keeping separate the crimes of extortion and receiving stolen property.

C. Relationship to Existing Law

1. Larceny.

Basically the law of Michigan on larceny is the common law, since the primary statute (C.L. 1948, Sec. 750.356), uses the term larceny without redefining it. One may, therefore, safely utilize the traditional concept of larceny as the taking and carrying away of personal property from the possession of another with intent to deprive the owner permanently of his property. No formal distinction exists between grand and petit larceny. (In re Rogers, 308 Mich. 392, 13 N.W.2d 862 (1944)), though a treatment distinction prevails under C.L. 1948, Sec. 750.356, based on the value of the property taken.

Considering the individual elements in isolation, a physical taking of possession is required for larceny (People v. Taugher, 102 Mich. 598, 61 N.W. 66 (1894)), but any removal of the goods from the place where they are found is sufficient (People v. Bradovich, 305 Mich. 329, 9 N.W.2d 560 (1943) (dictum)). If the property is delivered over, however, other than in circumstances in which fraud is used to obtain a possessory interest and not title, there is no

1137

larceny because of the lack of asportation (People v. Martin, 116 Mich. 446, 74 N.W. 653 (1898); cf. People v. Shaw, 57 Mich. 403, 24 N.W. 121 (1885)). Under certain circumstances embezzlement statutes might apply (see subdivision 2 below), and if title passed because of representations legally classified as fraudulent, the crime of obtaining property by false pretenses might lie (see subdivision 3 below). Many traces of these distinctions appear in the Michigan cases. But the Michigan statutes also include a somewhat anomalous provision denominated larceny by conversion (C. L. 1948, Sec. 750.362) which blurs the line between larceny and embezzlement by making one who "embezzles or fraudulently converts to his own use" property which has been delivered to him guilty of larceny. The Michigan Supreme Court has held this to emphasize not the circumstances of delivery but the fact of conversion (People v. McHugh, 286 Mich. 336, 282 N.W. 168 (1938); People v. Doe alias Meyer, 264 Mich. 475, 280 N.W. 270 (1933)). This has meant that some problems traditional to larceny law as it exists in most states have been minimized, but that other problems of overlapping coverage have arisen in relation to the several embezzlement statutes.

Common-law larceny came to embody many refined distinctions concerning what could be the subject matter of property (see Hall, Theft, Law and Society 80-97 (2d ed. 1952)), but these problems are largely eliminated by the lengthy definition of property in C. L. 1948, Sec. 750.356:

"of the property of another, any money, goods or chattels, or any bank note, bank bill, bond, promissory note, due bill, bill of exchange or other bill, draft, order or certificate, or any book of accounts for or concerning money or goods due or to become due, or to be delivered, or any deed or writing containing a conveyance of land, or any other valuable contract in force, or any receipt, release or defeasance, or any writ, process or public record."

While some possibility exists of disputes as to the coverage of this language, Michigan cases do not reveal the litigation about what can be the subject matter of larceny that one encounters in many jurisdictions.

The intent stated is the intent to deprive the owner permanently of his interest. The word "owner", however, is not controlling in the usual sense, for larceny can be committed by the holder of title who surreptitiously takes back a liened chattel (People v. Long, 50 Mich. 249, 15 N.W. 105 (1883)) or the maker of a note who takes the instrument from the payee (People v. Gregg, 170 Mich. 168, 135 N.W. 970 (1912) (dictum)). Though there is little or no Michigan authority in point, one may assume that as in other jurisdictions "intent to deprive permanently" means in application "lack of purpose to return the property with reasonable promptitude and in substantially unimpaired condition". But if the defendant believes that the property is his or his to deal with in the particular way, this is factually inconsistent with an intent permanently to deprive or its equivalent; evidence is therefore admissible showing a claim of right, and the jury cannot disregard the issue (see, e.g., People v. Shaunding, 268 Mich. 218, 225 N. W. 770 (1934); People v. Alburn, 132 Mich. 24, 92 N.W. 494 (1902)). This is true even though the defendant is mistaken as to his legal rights (People v. Henry, 202 Mich. 450, 168 N.W. 534 (1918)).

Other legislation in Michigan affects the larceny area. Larceny from the person is punished more heavily than ordinary larceny (C. L. 1948, Sec. 750.357) but must be charged as a separate offense. Larceny by false personation is a special and separate offense (C. L. 1948, Sec. 750.363), though in the absence of this special statute the offense would be either larceny or obtaining property by false pretenses, according to whether title had passed or not (People v. Martin, 116 Mich. 446, 74 N.W. 653 (1898)). Certain types of property receive specific protection, though with punishment provisions inconsistent with the basic larceny statute: livestock (C. L. 1948, Sec. 750.357a); parts of railway rolling stock (C. L. 1948, Sec. 750.361); library materials (C. L. 1948, Sec. 750.364); railroad passenger tickets (C. L. 1948, Sec. 750.366); trees, shrubs, plants, etc. (C. L. 1948, Sec. 750.367); rationed goods in wartime (C. L. 1948, Sec. 750.367a); military stores during war or insurrection (C. L. 1948, Sec. 750.406); logs and other wood products (C. L. 1948, Sec. 426.155) and dogs (C. L. 1948, Sec. 287.308). Other statutes take account of the place or circumstances of the larcenous act: at a fire (C. L. 1948, Sec. 750.358); from a vacant dwelling (C. L. 1948, Sec. 750.359); from buildings or transportation facilities (C. L. 1948, Sec. 750.360; see People v. Williams, 368 Mich. 494, 118 N. W.2d 391 (1962)); from libraries (C. L. 1948, Sec. 750.364); from railroad cars after an accident (C. L. 1948, Sec. 750.365); and from motor vehicles (C. L. 1948, Sec. 750.356a; see People v. Hadesman, 304 Mich. 481, 8 N.W.2d 145 (1943)).

Because of the vast possibilities for variances between pleading and proof under these many statutes, a special statute (C. L. 1948, Sec. 767.60) endeavors to minimize the difficulties somewhat by permitting conviction of any of the offenses if one is pleaded. Another section liberalizes the requirements for specifying the property taken in some pleadings (C. L. 1948, Sec. 767.61).

The Draft alters this picture in a number of important respects. The chief advance is that by the simple definition of theft in Sec. 3205, incorporating as it does the definitions of "deprive" (Sec. 3201 (b), "obtain" (Sec. 3201 (e)) and "obtain or exert (unauthorized) control" (Sec. 3201 (f)), the artificial distinctions between the several kinds of larceny, embezzlement, and obtaining property by false pretenses are swept away. The gravamen of the offense will be the obtaining of control over property in which another has an interest and the deliberate diversion of it for the offender's own purposes. A unitary definition will enable the courts to examine predatory conduct against property much more realistically than has the multitude of overlapping and inconsistent statutes which now exists in Michigan. At the same time, however, the traditional defense of claim of right is preserved in Sec. 3240 (1), and domestic squabbles over property are minimized through Sec. 3240 (2).

The use of a single definition of theft also will work a procedural advantage both to the state and to the defendant. The state will be protected to a substantial degree against a finding of a variance when a conviction is appealed. The defendant, however, will no longer be in the position of having to defend against an array of statutory crimes when any one of them is alleged against him, the situation he now faces under C. L. 1948, Sec. 767.60.

The simplified definition of theft will be effective only if the existing special coverage legislation is repealed.

The punishment provisions retain the traditional use of value of the property affected as a basis for increased penalties. A standard based on value has the advantage of simplicity of application, particularly when the alternative is a long list of factors which can or must aggravate the penalty for theft. In general, the greater the value of the property, the greater the harm to the complaining witness and indirectly, to the community. Professional criminals also usually seek the greater value rather than the lesser. None of the new legislation, including the Model Penal Code, wholly dispenses with value as one of several standards for determining penalty. Thus it seems preferable to continue the familiar traditions.

The Draft also takes special account of theft from the person. These thefts have an added element of danger to the person of the victim which may result from the bodily contact. Moreover, most pickpocket and purse-snatching activity indicates professionalism, which in turn warrants increased punishment.

A somewhat greater problem lies in the continued recognition of theft in a building or from a vehicle as a felony. This is the coverage of the present Michigan statutes (C.L. 1948, Sec. 750.360; C.L. 1948, Sec. 750.356a). From a corrections standpoint it is difficult to justify the imposition of felony-grade punishment on people who steal small amounts in buildings or from motor vehicles. However, given the fact that the present Michigan arrest statutes (C. L. 1948, Sec. 764.15, 764.16) permit officers to arrest only for misdemeanors committed in their presence and private citizens to arrest for misdemeanors not at all, shoplifting and theft from automobiles will be virtually non-preventable if the offenses are misdemeanors. Hopefully it may be possible in the future to modernize the law of arrest by permitting officers to arrest on reasonable grounds to believe a misdemeanor has been committed and citizens to arrest for misdemeanors actually committed in

their presence; if so, the special references to the place
of theft should be eliminated from Sec. 3207. Until that
time, however, enforcibility requires the continuation of
the special coverage now embodied in Michigan statutes and
the Draft. However, to minimize some of the hardships which
this may entail, the Draft empowers the court in its discretion to reduce the offense to a misdemeanor or a violation
after conviction.

B. Embezzlement

1. Michigan Compiled Laws (1948)

750.174 Embezzlement

Sec. 174. Agent, servant, employee, trustee, bailee,
custodian. Any person who as the agent, servant or employee of another, or as the trustee, bailee, or custodian
of the property of another, or of any partnership, voluntary association, public or private corporation, or of this
state, or of any county, city, village, township, or school
district within this state, shall fraudulently dispose of or
convert to his own use without the consent of his principal,
any money or other personal property of his principal which
shall have come to his possession or shall be under his
charge or control by virtue of his being such agent, servant, employee, trustee, bailee or custodian, as aforesaid,
shall be guilty of the crime of embezzlement, and upon conviction thereof, if the money or personal property so embezzled shall be of the value of $100.00 or under, shall be
guilty of a misdemeanor; if the money or personal property
so embezzled be of the value of more than $100.00, such per-
son shall be guilty of a felony, punishable by imprisonment
in the state prison not more than 10 years or by a fine not
exceeding $5,000.00.

Prima facie proof of intent. In any prosecution under this
section, the failure, neglect or refusal of such agent, servant, employee, trustee, bailee or custodian to pay, deliver,
or refund to his principal such money or property entrusted
to his care upon demand shall be prima facie proof of intent
to embezzle. As amended P.A. 1957, No. 69, Sec. 1, Eff.
Sept. 27

750.175 Same; public officer, agent or servant

Sec. 175. EMBEZZLEMENT BY PUBLIC OFFICER, HIS AGENT, ETC. -
Any person holding any public office in this state, or the
agent or servant of any such person, who knowingly and unlawfully appropriates to his own use, or to the use of any other
person, the money or property received by him in his official
capacity or employment, of the value of 50 dollars or upwards,
shall be guilty of a felony, punishable by imprisonment in
the state prison not more than 10 years or by fine of not more

1141

than 5,000 dollars.

In any prosecution under this section the failure, neglect or refusal of any public officer to pay over and deliver to his successor all moneys and property which should be in his hands as such officer, shall be prima facie evidence of an offense against the provisions of this section.

750.176 Same; administrator, executor or guardian

Sec. 176. EMBEZZLEMENT BY ADMINISTRATOR, EXECUTOR OR GUARDIAN - Any general or special administrator of any executor or guardian, who has been appointed by a judge of probate and who has collected any goods, chattels, money or effects of the deceased or ward, and who has wilfully appropriated the same to his own use and who has been ordered by the judge of probate forthwith to deliver to his successor in trust, ward or any person lawfully entitled thereto, all the goods, chattels, money or effects of the deceased or ward in his hands, and who shall wilfully omit, neglect or refuse for 60 days to obey said orders, shall be deemed to have committed the crime of embezzlement, and shall be guilty of a felony, punishable by imprisonment in the state prison for not more than 10 years, or by fine not more than 5,000 dollars: Provided, That in case such order shall be appealed from, said period of 60 days shall be reckoned from the affirmance of the order in the circuit or supreme court.

750.177 Same; chattel mortgagor, vendee or lessee

Sec. 177. Any person who shall embezzle, fraudulently remove, conceal or dispose of any personal property held by him subject to any chattel mortgage or written instrument intended to operate as a chattel mortgage, or any lease or written instrument intended to operate as a lease, or any contract to purchase not yet fulfilled with intent to injure or defraud the mortgagee, lessor or vendor under such contract or any assignee thereof, shall, if the property so embezzled, removed, concealed or disposed of, is of the value of more than $100.00, be guilty of a felony, punishable by imprisonment in the state prison not more than 2 years, or by a fine of not more than $1,000.00. If the property so removed, concealed or disposed of is of the value of $100.00 or less, the person so offending shall be guilty of a misdemeanor. As amended P.A. 1959, No. 119, Sec. 1, Eff. March 19, 1960.

750.178 Same; chattel mortgage, lease or contract property, by others

Sec. 178. Any person who shall fraudulently embezzle, remove, conceal or dispose of any personal property which has been mortgaged, leased or purchased under a contract to purchase not yet fulfilled by another knowing such personal prop- to have been so martgaged, leased or purchased, with intent to injure or defraud the mortgagee, lessor or vendor under

1142

such contract, or any assignee thereof, shall, if the property so embezzled, removed, concealed or disposed of, is of the value of more than $100.00, be guilty of a felony, punishable by imprisonment in the state prison not more than 2 years or by a fine of not more than $1,000.00. If the property so removed, concealed or disposed of is of the value of $100.00 or less, the person so offending shall be guilty of a misdemeanor. As amended P.A. 1959, No. 119, Sec. 1. Eff. March 19, 1960.

750.179 Same; railroad passenger tickets

Sec. 179. EMBEZZLEMENT OF RAILROAD PASSENGER TICKETS – Any officer, agent, clerk or employe of any incorporated railroad company who shall fraudulently embezzle, dispose of or convert to his own use any railroad passenger ticket or tickets, whether such tickets are fully prepared for use, or not so fully prepared, or use tickets which have been once used, and which have come to his hands or charge by virtue of his office or employment, shall be guilty of a felony.

In any prosecution under this section, it shall be lawful to include in a charge, as 1 offense, all acts constituting such offense committed between certain days set forth, and it shall be sufficient to set forth by general description the tickets alleged to have been unlawfully taken; and it shall be sufficient to maintain the charge if it shall be proved on trial that any such ticket or tickets were, within the period set forth, embezzled, disposed of, or converted by the defendant charged in said prosecution as alleged.

At the trial of any case arising under this section, it shall be sufficient prima facie proof of the existence of any railroad company named in the indictment to show that such company was doing business as a railroad company at the time named in the indictment.

The words "railroad passenger ticket or tickets" as used in this section shall be construed to embrace any ticket, card, pass, certificate or paper providing, or intended to provide, for the carriage or transportation of any person or persons upon any railroad, and shall include, not only tickets of any railroad company fully prepared for use, but those not fully prepared for use, and all others which have been once used.

750.180 Same; bank, deposit, trust company, or credit union

Sec. 180. Any president, director, secretary, cashier, treasurer or other officer, teller, clerk, agent, receiver or conservator, or agent or employee of such receiver or conservator of any bank, trust company, credit union or safe or safety and collateral deposit company, who embezzles, abstracts or wilfully misapplies any of the moneys, funds, credits or property of the bank, trust company, credit

union or safe or safety and collateral deposit company,
whether owned by it or held in trust, or who, without
authority of the directors or proper officers, issues, or
puts forth any certificate of deposit, draws any order or
bill of exchange, makes any acceptance, assigns any note,
bond, draft, bill of exchange, mortgage, judgment or decree,
or who makes any false entry in any book, report or statement of the bank, trust company, credit union or safe or
safety and collateral deposit company with intent in either
case to injure or defraud the bank, trust company, credit
union or safe or safety and collateral deposit company or
any company, corporation or person or to deceive any officer of the bank, trust company, credit union or safe or
safety and collateral deposit company, or any agent, receiver or conservator, or agent or employee of such receiver or conservator appointed to examine the affairs of
such bank, trust company, credit union or safe or safety
and collateral deposit company; and any person who with
like intent aids or abets any officer, clerk, agent, receiver or conservator, or agent or employee issue or cause
to be issued or put in circulation, any bill, note or other
evidence of debt to circulate as money, shall be guilty of
a felony, punishable by imprisonment in the state prison
not more than 20 years. As amended P.A. 1960, No. 31, Sec.
1, Eff. Aug. 17.

750.181 Same; property belonging to himself and another

Sec. 181. Any agent, servant, employee, trustee, bailee,
custodian, attorney-at-law, collector or other person, who,
in any manner receives or collects money or any other personal property which is partly the property of another and
partly the property of such agent, servant, employee, trustee,
bailee, custodian, attorney-at-law, collector or other person, and who shall embezzle or fraudulently dispose of or
convert to his own use, or take or secrete with intent to
embezzle or convert to his own use, such money or personal
property, without the consent of the part owner of such
money or personal property, shall, if the money or personal
property so embezzled is of the value of $100.00 or under,
be guilty of a misdemeanor; if the money or personal property so embezzled is of the value of more than $100.00, he
shall be guilty of a felony, punishable by imprisonment in
the state prison not more than 10 years or by a fine of not
more than $5,000.00.

In any prosecution for such crime it shall be no defense
that such agent, servant, employee, trustee, bailee, custodian, attorney-at-law, collector or other person was entitled to a compensation out of such money or personal property as compensation for collecting or receiving the same
for and on behalf of the owner thereof, but it shall be no
embezzlement on the part of such agent, servant, employee,
trustee, bailee, custodian, attorney-at-law, collector or
other person to retain his reasonable collection fee on the

1144

collection or any other valid interest he may have in such money or personal property.

In any prosecution under this section, the failure, neglect or refusal of such agent, servant, employee, trustee, bailee, custodian, attorney-at-law, collector or other person to pay, deliver or refund to the proper person such money or personal property entrusted to his care, upon demand, shall be prima facie proof of intent to embezzle. As amended P.A. 1959, No. 119, Sec. 1, Eff. March 19, 1960.

750.182 Same; warehouseman or forwarder of property receipted
          for

Sec. 182. EMBEZZLEMENT OR CONVERSION BY WAREHOUSEMAN OR FORWARDER OF PROPERTY RECEIPTED FOR - Any warehouseman or forwarder, or other person who shall have issued a receipt or certificate for flour, wheat, pot or pearl ashes, or any grain, produce or thing of value, or shall receive property on deposit or for sale on a specific contract or understanding, and shall, after issuing said receipt or certificate or receiving such property, embezzle, dispose of or convert to his own use, such property or the moneys received on the sale of such property, contrary to such receipt or certificate, or to the previous contract or understanding, shall be guilty of a felony.

750.182a Falsification of school records, penalty; suspension
          of teacher's certificate

Sec. 182a. Any officer or employee of a school district who shall wilfully falsify any record required to be kept under the provisions of Act No. 26 of the Public Acts of the First Extra Session of 1948, as amended, being sections 388.1 to 388.41, inclusive, of the Compiled Laws of 1948, or any other school law of this state, having a bearing on school aid, shall be guilty of a misdemeanor, punishable by a fine of not more than $2,500.00 or imprisonment in state prison for not more than 2 years, or both, in the discretion of the court. The teacher's certificate of any person who shall be convicted of wilfully falsifying any such record shall be suspended for a period of 5 years and for such additional period as the superintendent of public instruction may determine. P.A. 1931, No. 328, Sec. 182a, added by P.A. 1953, No. 90, Sec. 1, Imd. Eff. May 19, 1953.

750.488 Retention of fees by state officers and employees
          on salary

Sec. 488. RETENTION OF FEES BY STATE OFFICERS AND EMPLOYEES ON SALARY - Any officer or employe of the state government, having a salary fixed by law who shall retain any fees received for performance of his official duties, or who shall not promptly turn over to the state treasurer or credit to the proper funds such fees when collected, shall

be guilty of a misdemeanor, punishable by imprisonment in
the state prison not more than 2 years or by a fine of not
more than 1,000 dollars. Any one convicted under the provisions of this section shall be promptly removed from office.

500.1456 Agent, solicitor or broker as fiduciary, intent
          to embezzle

Sec. 1456. Any money, substitute for money or thing of
value whatsoever, received by any agent, solicitor or broker
as premium or return premium, on or under any policy of insurance or application therefor, shall be deemed to have
been received by such agent, solicitor or broker in his
fiduciary capacity, and any agent, solicitor or broker who
embezzles, or fraudulently converts or appropriates to his
own use, or, with intent to embezzle, takes, secretes or
otherwise disposes of, or fraudulently witholds, appropriates, lends, invests or otherwise uses or applies any money,
substitute for money or thing of value received by him as
premium or return premium on or under any policy of insurance
or application therefor, contrary to the instructions or
without the consent of the insurer, for or on account of
which the same was received by him, shall be deemed guilty
of larceny by embezzlement, and shall be punished as provided in the criminal statutes of this state, irrespective of
whether or not such agent, solicitor or broker has, or claims
to have, any commission or other interest in such money, substitute for money or thing of value. P.A. 1956, No. 218,
Sec. 1456, Eff. Jan 1, 1957.

2. Definitions and Elements of the Offense

People v. Bergman
246 Mich. 68

SHARPE, J. Defendant was convicted, under section 15310,
3 Comp. Laws 1915, of embezzling certain moneys which came
into his hands as clerk, agent, and servant of Armour &
Company, his employer, and seeks review by writ of error.
Defendant had been in the employ of the company at Grand
Rapids for more than 13 years. His duties required him to
secure orders from retail dealers in that city and mail them
to the company at Chicago. Shipments were made direct to
the customers. Invoices were sent to defendant by mail. It
was his duty to make collections thereof. When doing so,
customers would sometimes make claim for a credit for shortages or damaged goods. It was defendant's duty to take a
statement of such claim and send it to the company for adjustment. He did not always do so. He would credit it on
the bill, and accept a check in payment for the balance.
Several of the dealers so testified, as well as the defendant

1146

himself. He did not report such credits to the company,
but assumed to remit to them the full amount of the bill.
This necessarily resulted in a shortage in his account with
the company and a corresponding shortage in the customer's
accounts with it. The checks accepted by him were made payable to the company. It was arranged that he should take
these checks to a bank in Grand Rapids, indorse them with a
stamp provided by the company for that purpose, and secure
a draft for the amount, payable to the company, and mail it
to the Chicago office. He had a few customers whose checks
were drawn on other banks, and were not accepted by the bank
which issued the drafts. He would, as he claims, get these
cashed at the bank on which they were drawn, and deposit the
proceeds to make up the amount of the draft. His shortage
became so great that he felt compelled to report that the
draft was in part in payment of accounts other than those
for which the checks were given. The record discloses that
he deposited all of the checks, and, as he claims, all of
the money, received from customers in the bank of deposit
and forwarded drafts therefor. He testified that his shortage was due entirely to the allowances he had made to customers when they paid their accounts.
    The trial court, in his instructions to the jury, after
stating the manner in which the defendant conducted business,
as testified to by him, said to them that these allowances
were made by him -

"without any authority, and that is embezzlement. There
isn't any doubt about it, because he admits it all himself,
so there is nothing for the jury to pass on. He has converted to his own use, for the purpose of making unauthorized allowances on these accounts, money that belonged to his
employer, Armour & Company."

    Error is alleged upon this instruction.
    Embezzlement is not an offense at common law. It is a
creature of statute. There is entire harmony in the definitions defining it. In Tiffany's Criminal Law, p. 789,
it is said:

"The offense of embezzlement consists in the application
to the party's own use of property which came to his hands,
under trust, by reason of his employment in a particular
capacity; and the misapplication of it from the purpose for
which he received it."

    See, also, 20 C.J. p. 407, and 9 R.C.L. p. 1264.
    Under the statute, the fraudulent disposal of and con-
version to his own use applies only to "any money or other
property of another which shall have come to his possession,
or shall be under his charge by virtue of" his office or employment. The crime consists in the intentional unlawful appropriation of the money or the property of the employer by
the employee. People v. Butts, 128 Mich. 208, 214. The dis-

tinction between it and larceny is that, while in the latter there must be a felonious taking, in the former there must be an unlawful appropriation of that which comes into possession rightfully. Taylor v. Kneeland, 1 Doug. 67, 72. In People v. McKinney, 10 Mich. 54, Mr. Justice CAMPBELL said, page 109:

"The term embezzlement . . . when used in statutes . . . has almost, if not quite, universally been confined to the misappropriation of property, by those to whose care it has been confided as officers or agents."

When the defendant made the allowances to customers, he received a check for the amount of the account less the shortage. The money represented by the shortage did not at any time come into his hands, nor was it ever under his control. It was his duty to collect it, but he did not do so, although he credited the shortage and receipted and accepted checks for the balance. But, unless it was actually received by him, he was not guilty of embezzling it. It cannot be said that he fraudulently misappropriated or converted to his own use that which never came into his possession.

Counsel for the prosecution rely on the following from 9 R.C.L. p. 1275:

"To appropriate 'to one's own use' does not necessarily mean to one's personal advantage. Every attempt by one person to dispose of the goods of another, without right, as if they were his own, is a conversion to his own use."

The defendant made no attempt to dispose of the goods shipped to customers. They were never in his possession.

The judgment is reversed, and a new trial ordered.

FEAD, FELLOWS, WIEST, CLARK, and McDONALD, JJ., concurred. NORTH, C. J., and POTTER, J., did not sit.

Note

In the application of the aforesaid statutes it is first necessary to find that the person held the property allegedly embezzled in a capacity covered by the statute under which prosecution is being brought. There are several Michigan cases illustrative of this requirement.

In People v. Burns, 242 Mich. 345, the defendant was charged with embezzlement under the statute applicable to public officers. He claimed that he was not an officer within the meaning of the statute as he was not required to handle money in the capacity of a probation officer. He had appropriated a check from the county treasurer which was given to him for delivery to a pensioner. His conviction was sustained on the ground that he was a public officer within the meaning of the statute and that it was no defense that he had no legal right to the possession of the check. It was enough that the money came into his hands by virtue of his office.

1148

In People v. Andrews, 249 Mich. 616, the defendant was charged with the embezzlement of some bonds delivered to him for the purpose of investing in a real estate development in which the owner of the bonds was interested. The court held that the defendant could not be convicted under the statute which punished "embezzlement by any agent, servant, or employee, . . ." because the defendant did not fit any of those classifications, but his conviction was sustained under a statute which punished embezzlement by ". . . any person to whom any money, goods, or other property. . ." was delivered.

Also relevant to this problem is the case of People v. Belz which follows this note. -- Ed.

People v. Belz
257 Mich. 302

McDONALD, J. The defendant has appealed from a judgment of conviction on a charge of embezzlement. At the time the offense is alleged to have been committed, he was president and general manager of the Marx Brewing Company, a Michigan corporation. As such he received a stipulated salary. By resolution of the board of directors, he was authorized to withdraw funds from the bank for corporate purposes upon checks signed by himself as president. In this manner, on February 21, 1928, he drew a check for $1,695 payable to the order of Oschs, Crowley & Horger, automobile dealers, of Dearborn, Michigan. This check was paid out of the company's funds. It was not for corporate purposes, but was used in payment of an automobile which defendant purchased in his own name and for his own use. On February 23, 1928, he caused the amount represented by this check to be entered in the books of the corporation as a charge against himself. It was never paid. The facts are not in dispute.

The information was drawn under Act No. 48, Pub. Acts 1927 (3 Comp. Laws 1929, Sec. 16980), which defines embezzlement by agents, servants, and employees. It is charged in the information that the money alleged to have been embezzled by the defendant came into his possession as agent, servant, and employee of the Marx Brewing Company, and, in that capacity, he fraudulently disposed of it and converted it to his own use. The defendant contends that he was not the agent, servant, or employee of the company; that the property embezzled did not come into his possession as such; that it came into his possession as president of the company; that the president of a corporation is not an agent, servant, or employee within the meaning of the statute, and that therefore he is not guilty of the crime charged.

With this contention we are unable to agree. The question is not whether the president of a corporation comes within

1149

the scope of the statute. We need not consider the general
status of officers and directors of incorporated companies;
for, in this case, the defendant's authority to withdraw
corporate funds upon his check did not arise from his position as president. It was expressly conferred on him by
resolution of the board of directors. He was made the agent
of the company to handle its funds. As president he had no
control over the money in the bank. He was employed by the
directors of the company to manage its business, subject to
their supervision, and was empowered to draw checks for corporate purposes. For these services he was paid a stipulated
salary. Nothing further was necessary to create the relation
of master and servant. The fact that he was also president
did not alter this relation. He was given powers and duties
that did not belong to the president. He was employed and
paid for certain services, and in respect to them his relation was the same as though he had no official connection
with the corporation. He was an agent, servant, and employee
of the corporation within the meaning of the statute. The
court did not err in holding that he was properly informed
against under an applicable statute.

Equally untenable is the defendant's contention that
felonious disposition was not established because he caused
the transaction to be entered and openly carried as a charge
against himself in the books of the corporation.

It is true the books show that $1,695 was charged against
the defendant in February, 1928, and was carried as a debit
entry until March, 1930. An audit in March revealed this
charge and others totaling $10,000. These charges and the
transactions which gave rise to them were without the knowledge and consent of the board of directors or any other of
the officials. They were not known except to the defendant
until they were uncovered by the audit. If there had been
an honest intent on the part of defendant in using the corporation money for his own purposes, it would seem that he
would have obtained permission from the directors to have
it charged against him on the books. The defendant was not
a witness on the trial, and, in the absence of any explanation by him, it may be said that the entry indicates an intention to repay the money when it was discovered; but that
would not remove the criminality from the act in taking it
without the consent of the corporation and converting it to
his own use. People v. Butts, 128 Mich. 208.

We find no error. The judgment of conviction is affirmed.

CLARK, C. J., and POTTER, SHARPE, NORTH, FEA , WIEST, and
BUTZEL, JJ., concurred.

People v. Wadsworth
63 Mich. 500

MORSE, J. The respondent was convicted of embezzlement

1150

upon a trial in Delta county, a change of venue having been
taken to that county from Marquette, where the information
was filed and the alleged offense committed.

The information consisted of two counts, - one attempting
to charge the defendant with the embezzlement of the money
of John Dillon, and the other charging him with such embezzlement as the de facto treasurer of the city of Ishpeming.
The trial proceeded upon the theory of the first count. . . .

The undisputed facts will be found to disprove any embezzlement under the law.

John Dillon was elected city treasurer of Ishpeming for
the year 1883. He had held the office two terms immediately
previous thereto. It seems that a peculiar method of elect-
ing this officer prevails in Ishpeming.

The candidate is nominated and elected upon his running
qualities, - his capacity to get votes, - but the money to
secure such nomination and election is put up by some bank,
which also furnishes the bonds. After the election, the
candidate elected qualifies, and there his duties begin and
end. The taxes are paid into the bank, and collected and
disbursed by it. The treasurer has no further concern about
the matter, and is, of course, entirely ignorant of the duties
of his office. The bank pays to him the fees allowed by law,
and the profits made by the use of the money thus necessarily
deposited in the bank seem to be a sufficient remuneration
to the bank for its trouble and expense in the matter.

The respondent during these years was the managing member
of the banking house of D. F. Wadsworth & Co., private bankers. During the first two terms of Dillon's office the
funds received by respondent's bank were deposited in the
bank the same as other moneys deposited by its customers,
and mingled with them. The tax moneys were not kept or deposited as a separate fund, not to be used by the bank save
for legitimate tax purposes, but became at once a part of the
common cash funds of the bank, to be used and paid or loaned out the same as other moneys. Indeed, the bank could
have no possible object in entering into such an arrangement as was made, unless it could use the tax money in any
way it chose until it was wanted for the purposes for which
it was levied. Dillon and the whole business community well
understood the use that was being made of this money, and
that it was not kept separate from the other funds of the
bank, or intact.

When Dillon was elected the third time, he testifies he
made the same arrangement. The money was to be kept and
used as before. It was so kept and used.

Unfortunately, however, for the city, the bank of D. F.
Wadsworth & Co. did a losing and unprofitable business in
the year 1883. In the afternoon of December 29, 1883, between the hours of 3 and 5 P.M., the Cleveland Iron Mining
Company paid its taxes into the bank, to wit, $11,942. This
money was nearly if not all paid out to other depositors on
Monday, the thirty-first. On the second of January, 1884,

1151

the bank made a general assignment for the benefit of its creditors. At the time of the failure the bank was owing the city about $30,000. . . .

It appears without question that the moneys collected or paid in from taxes were deposited on an account called "City Taxes," and, after the taxes were all in, the books were balanced up in the business, and everything credited to this account, and the balance due the treasurer was credited to an account called "City Treasurer's Account." The moneys were deposited the same as any other deposits, as soon as collected, and mingled with other funds. The bank held itself liable to the city treasurer for that amount. This had been the practice for years, and with other treasurers before Dillon. . . .

For this, and all the other evidence, it clearly appears that Wadsworth received and kept and used this tax money in the business of his bank, the same exactly as he did all the other moneys deposited with him in the usual course of his business; that he supposed, and had reason to suppose, that he had a right to use this money as he did the other moneys; that he believed, and had reason to believe, when he received this particular sum of nearly $12,000, that the whole obligation of his bank to the city treasurer, including this sum with the rest, was to be assumed and paid by the Marquette County Bank, a solvent institution; that he had not the least idea of his own failure, or that he would be forced to make an assignment; that he only made the assignment because of the failure of the arrangement of transfer, and the insistence of the mayor of the city, who assumed to represent that municipality as a creditor of the bank, that he should do so, and that at once. He endeavored to pay and secure the city, as far as he could. In other words, the intent to defraud the city, or any one else, is absolutely wanting. His character up to the date of his failure, in the language of the mayor, had "always been excellent," for a series of years. "I never knew of his doing a mean or dishonest act."

There can be no embezzlement under our statutes where there is no intent to defraud. There are cases where one uses the money of another as he has no right to use it, and thereby converts and appropriates it to his own use, in which the statute will infer a fraudulent intent, and punish the act as an embezzlement.

But such is not this case. When the money was deposited or taken into the bank under the practice of years, and by the arrangement with Dillon, the money ceased to be the property of Dillon, and became the money of the bank. The respondent became obligated to refund to the city or to Dillon, when called for, any balance that might be due, not in the same identical money deposited, but in the funds of the bank. The relation of debtor and creditor was established. The money deposited was loaned to the bank, to be repaid when called for. Wadsworth, in paying out the funds deposited to pay taxes, in the usual course of his business, only did what he was in effect authorized to do by Dillon. That the city

1152

has lost its tax levy is as much the fault of Dillon as of Wadsworth.

There is no evidence tending to show that Wadsworth used a dollar of this money for his own private gain or advantage....

If the respondent in this case is guilty of embezzlement, then any debtor who borrows money on the faith and belief that he can repay it, and by misfortune in business is unable to do so, is guilty of the like offense. . . .

The case is one of a failing debtor borrowing money off one to pay a loan to another, with the reasonable hope of being speedily able to meet all his obligations. This is not the case where one, in violation of the law, or of his duty to his employer, uses money not his own, and which he knows he has no right to use, in speculation for his own profit, or in pandering to his appetites, or love of luxury, with the hope of being able to replace it before its use is discovered, and concealing the taking of it by false entries, or otherwise.

It is a case where a banker, known to be doing business, in part at least, upon the profits arising from the use of the deposits in his bank, is unable to meet his obligations, and fails. The depositor in such a case is a creditor of the bank, and there is nothing about his relation with the bank that can make its failure an embezzlement of the funds he has voluntarily placed there in the usual course of business, without any special agreement that his money shall be kept separate from the other funds, and not used as are all general deposits. Deposited without such agreement, he parts with his title, and loans his money to the bank. The bank, therefore, cannot embezzle his money, because he has none in its hands. The bank owes him a certain amount, to be paid when called for. A mere failure to pay a loan can never be an embezzlement.

The respondent should have been acquitted, upon the evidence, by the direction of the court below. The judgment against him is reversed, and he will be discharged from any further custody, under the information filed against him in this case.

The other Justices concurred.

People v. Bauman
105 Mich. 543

HOOKER, J. The defendant appeals from a verdict and sentence upon a charge of embezzlement. He sold cigars for the complainant, and was authorized to make collections. Incidental expenses, such as money used in saloons, were adjusted from time to time, but he was expected to make reports of collections and expenses at short intervals, if not daily. The testimony introduced on behalf of the prosecution

1153

tended to show that the defendant had collected moneys from customers which he had failed to report and had denied receiving and that he was short upwards of $100. The testimony for the defendant does not dispute a possible shortage, but tends to establish the facts that there was no intentional concealment; that it was usual for him to appropriate some of the money collected, and apply it upon his salary; that he was sometimes overpaid, or had drawn or used, to the extent of $75 or $100 in advance of his earnings; but that it was never with the fraudulent or felonious design of cheating or defrauding his employer.

In his charge to the jury the court said:

"He is charged with not having done that; that is to say, with not having turned in the moneys which he collected. Now, if you find from the evidence in this case that he retained these moneys, it is not necessary that he appropriate them to his own use. If he retained the moneys, if he made these collections, and kept them, if you are satisfied beyond a reasonable doubt that that is the case, then, of course, it will be your duty to convict, and your verdict will be guilty. . . . If you are satisfied from the evidence in this case, beyond a reasonable doubt, that the defendant did make these collections, and that he did not turn the moneys in, - all the money which he collected, - barring, of course, the amount which he was authorized to spend, if you believe that he was authorized by C. P. Collins & Co. to spend a portion of what he collected for the purpose of advertising their business, but if you believe that he kept more than that, then, of course, it will be your duty to convict. . . . If you believe that he had authority to spend a certain amount, then, of course, you must find that he had no authority to spend any more than that. If he spent any more than that, he was doing it upon his own authority, and without authority from the firm, and that was spending money which he had no right to spend; and if he spent any more money than he was authorized by the firm, and failed to account to the firm for the moneys which he collected, barring the amount which he was authorized to spend, then he made such an appropriation of this money as he was not entitled to make; and, if you believe that he did that, - failed to account to this firm for these moneys which he collected, - then it will be your duty to convict."

Under this charge, the mere retention of money, or its expenditure for the purposes of the firm in excess of the amount agreed upon for expenses, if accompanied by a bare failure to report or account for accurately, was sufficient to authorize a conviction. If leaves out the important question of criminal intent, - the design to wrong, cheat, or defraud the owner, - which is a necessary element of embezzlement. It may be that the facts found by the jury were sufficient to prove the existence of this intent had that question been submitted to them but we cannot assume that they

1154

found it.

The judgment must be reversed, and a new trial granted. ***Held***

The other Justices concurred.

People v. Hurst
62 Mich. 276

CAMPBELL, C. J.   Respondent was convicted of embezzling $275, alleged to have been put in his hands by one Lena J. Smith as her agent. Respondent was a lawyer, and also engaged more or less in renting houses. Mrs. Smith formed his acquaintance while seeking to rent a house. She got ***Facts*** him to lend $400 for her, which he did on mortgage. She further said she had $1,100 more to lend. He said he had a place for $700, which he actually lent on first mortgage. He also showed her a letter from a man who had a parcel of 40 acres of land to sell, and he wanted her to give him the money to buy it, as he knew of a purchaser who would buy at an advance. She handed him $400 to buy the land, and said he might have the profit. He told her where the land was, but she could not remember, and did not testify upon that point. This was on March 31, 1882. The embezzlement is charged as of that day.

About the middle of April she saw him at his house, intoxicated. She asked him for her papers, and if he had invested the money, and he shook his head, and said he had been "on a drunk." She asked for her money, and he gave her $100, and a chattel mortgage which he owned for $25. She asked him if that was all he had, and he said it was, and promised to pay the balance in a month or two, and asked her to wait on him. She called on him frequently, and in the fall he conveyed to her 40 acres of land in Cheboygan county as security until he could pay her. He said he was selling some land for a lady in Springwells; and, if he succeeded, his commissions would exceed his debt to her, and he would pay her, and she could return the deed, which she need not record, but he would pay for recording. She agreed to wait on him, and hold the deed as security a little longer, until he could sell the 25 acres referred to. She subsequently dunned him frequently, and, finding he had an interest in a patent right, asked him to assign that to her as security, which he did.

There was some other testimony which was material, in favor of defendant, on which his counsel made some points, which we do not now think it necessary to decide.

In our opinion, the testimony did not make out a case of embezzlement. Before that offense can be made out, it must ***Issue*** distinctly appear that the respondent has acted with a felonious intent, and made an intentionally wrong disposal, indicating a design to cheat and deceive the owner. A mere failure to pay over is not enough if that intent is not plainly apparent. . . .

1155

In this case there was nothing indicating concealment or a felonious disposition. A candid admission was made at once on inquiry, and partial payment was made and security given at different times, when asked. The debt was admitted and recognized as a debt on both sides. Whatever wrong may have been done, there was no embezzlement proven.

The conviction must be quashed, and the court below advised to discharge the prisoner.

The other Justices concurred.

People v. Douglass
293 Mich. 388

WIEST, J. Defendant was convicted of the crime of embezzlement and sentenced. Upon appeal he alleges 20 errors, one of which and its counterparts, has merit.

The information charged that defendant, as agent and employee of the St. Joe Machines, Inc., fraudulently converted to his own use $4,000 in money belonging to that company. It appears that defendant had a patent license covering a pipe-cutting machine and entered into contract with the machines company to build the machine under his supervision and advance him money for expenses of traveling and selling the same. During the first year one machine was sold and, after the company received some of the proceeds, defendant was found indebted to the company to the amount of $2,500, and was without means to make payment. Thereupon defendant, by another contract, gave the company the right to manufacture and sell the machines until the profits would liquidate any indebtedness due the company. Subsequently defendant obtained an order from the York Ice Machinery Company at a price of $5,500. This was the second machine sold. The president of the St. Joe company demanded that defendant assign to that company all the money to be paid by the York company and stated the machine would not be shipped otherwise. Defendant, after demur, made the assignment and was given an agency appointment in order to collect payment from the York company. At that time defendant owed the St. Joe company $6,579.82. The machine was shipped to York, Pennnsylvania, and installed by defendant and the York company paid $5,500 to defendant. Defendant tendered his check for $2,500 to the St. Joe company, which was refused, and demand made for $4,000. Upon defendant's refusal to pay the $4,000 and his assertion that the assignment was under duress and void, he was charged with embezzlement of $4,000.

On appeal defendant contends that his motion for a directed verdict, on the ground that the proofs did not show any violation of law, should have been granted, inasmuch as the money was retained by defendant under claim of right of virtue of contract relations antedating the mentioned assignment.

1156

There is no merit in this claim.

Error is assigned upon the following instruction:

"As I have said, this offense that is charged is that of embezzlement and a simple definition of embezzlement is the illegal and wrongful appropriation of the money intrusted to one's care, and to appropriate means to take to one's self, or to use, in one's own personal way," the claim being that this definition leaves out the essential element of felonious intent.

The charge against defendant involved felonious intent on his part, and the jury should have been so instructed. It was not sufficient merely to read to the jury the statutory provision relative to embezzlement. Act. No. 328, Sec. 174, Pub. Acts 1931 (Comp. Laws Supp. 1940, Sec. 17115-174, Stat. Ann. Sec. 28.371).

Defendant claimed that the assignment of his right to the money was under duress and, therefore, void and he offered the company the amount due it and kept only what he was entitled to retain under the previous contract.

This claim of right, if bona fide, though unfounded in point of law, had bearing upon the question of his felonious intent.

In American Life Insurance Co. v. United States Fidelity & Guaranty Co., 261 Mich. 221, we said:

"An essential of the crime (embezzlement) is a felonious or fraudulent intent. . . .

"The mere failure to pay over moneys belonging to another, without a felonious intent, is not embezzlement. People v. Hurst, 62 Mich. 276; Fleener v. State, 58 Ark. 98 (23 S.W.1)."

We there quoted with approval the following from 20 C.J. p. 436:

"If property is converted without concealment, and under a bona fide claim of right, the conversion is not embezzlement, however, unfounded the claim may be. The mere absence of concealment and secrecy, however, is no defense, if there is a fraudulent intent, and no claim of right."

To like effect see 18 Am. Jur. p. 586, Sec. 27.

The question is not whether the assignment was under duress, rendering it void, but whether defendant, in good faith, even though mistaken in point of law, retained the money under assertion of bona fide claim of right to do so.

The trial judge not only failed so to instruct the jury but gave the following erroneous and prejudicial charge:

"So the question for you to decide is, have the people satisfied you beyond a reasonable doubt and to a moral certainty that their claims made against Mr. Douglass have been sustained. That is, did he assign his interest in the proceeds from this machine to the St. Joe Company. Did they, in turn, make him their agent to collect it and did he collect the proceeds, $5,500, and did he fail to pay $4,000 of it at least over to the St. Joe Company. If the people

1157

have satisfied these four elements beyond a reasonable doubt and to a moral certainty you will find the respondent guilty as charged. If they have failed so to satisfy you, your verdict would be not guilty."

[margin handwritten: Reason]

This instruction eliminated the essential issue of felonious intent and barred the defense involving intent offered by defendant.

[margin handwritten: Held]

The conviction is reversed and a new trial granted.

BUSHNELL, C. J., and SHARPE, POTTER, CHANDLER, NORTH, McALLISTER, and BUTZEL, JJ., concurred.

People v. Butts
128 Mich. 208

MOORE, J. . . .

This testimony discloses, as plainly as words can express, that, while respondent was secretary of the company, funds belonging to the company came into his possession, which he appropriated to his own use; not inadvertently and unintentionally, but designedly and intentionally, knowing the funds belonged to the company, and not to himself. Taking his own version of the transaction, there is not a single element of the offense described by the statute lacking. Act No. 114, Pub. Acts 1897 (3 Comp. Laws Sec. 11591); People v. Warren, 122 Mich. 504 (81 N.W. 360, 80 Am. St. Rep. 582). It is true, the respondent says he intended to return the money, but that does not do away with the offense. It is doubtless true that nearly every employe who misappropriates funds intends to return them to his employer, and to do this before the misappropriation is discovered. But this intention does not prevent the act from becoming a crime. The crime consists in the intentional appropriation of the money by the employe of the employer. It is true, too, that respondent claims that one or more of the directors of the company knew what he was doing, and did not object to it. This is denied by the other officers of the company, but, whether true or false, it does not excuse the respondent. Two or more of the directors of the company could not appropriate the funds of the company to their own personal use, and be justified in doing so. The judge did not charge the jury that the testimony of the respondent made out a case against him, but left the question of intent to the jury. This was quite as favorable to the respondent as he had a right to ask. People v. Hawkins, 106 Mich. 479 (64 N.W. 736); People v. Schottey, 116 Mich. 1 (74 N.W. 209). . . .

[margin handwritten: Facts / Issue]

[margin handwritten: Held]

The verdict is affirmed, and the case will be remanded to the court below, with instructions to proceed to judgment.

MONTGOMERY, C. J., Hooker and Grant, JJ., concurred.
LONG, J., did not sit

[handwritten bottom: Offense completed when intention formulated to convert to his own use.]

NORTH, C. J. Appellant was convicted by a jury of embezzling and converting to his own use $10,000 of the funds
of Rands, Inc., a Michigan corporation, located in Detroit.
This corporation was practically owned and wholly under the
control of William C. Rands. The defense urged was that the
accused took and used the $10,000 under the express authority
of his employer and that later defendant decided to keep the
amount so taken in the belief that he was justly entitled
thereto as part payment for money due him from his employer
under a specific agreement, the details of which are unimportant for decision herein.

Appellant asserts as error that the trial judge failed to
fully cover in his charge to the jury the defendant's theory
of defense, notwithstanding an appropriate request to so charge
was preferred. It was a part of defendant's claim and theory
of defense that prior to the time he countersigned and cashed
the check for $10,000 and used the proceeds for his own stock
transactions Mr. Rands gave him permission to do so. Mr.
Rands, the complaining witness, denied there was any such
arrangement or permission. Clearly if defendant had Rands'
permission to use the funds alleged to have been embezzled,
no crime was committed. A controlling issue of fact was thus
presented. On this phase of the case defendant testified:

"He (Mr. Rands) said,'You better go in and buy yourself
some Hiram Walker stock if you need anything more help yourself out for your own account. Go ahead and use it.' . . .
He said to me, 'If you need anything, go ahead and use it,'
and I said, 'I have used a few hundred shares of stock,'
and he said, 'All right, go ahead but don't carry the place
away.' . . . I proceeded to take the property of Rands, Inc.,
without telling anybody about it. I did it with Mr. Rands'
advice."

In the court's opinion, filed at the time he denied defendant's motion for a new trial, the following statement
is made:

"Rands took the witness stand first and testified very
largely as to formal matters. He testified in general terms
that he did not authorize use by defendant of the $10,000
which the defendant was charged with embezzling at any time
or for any purpose. Afterwards Hoefle, the defendant, took
the stand and with great detail narrated the time, place
and substance of the agreement he claimed to have had with
Rands, which authorized him to use the money as he did."

The following request to charge was presented by defendant:

"The testimony of Mr. Hoefle shows that at the time he
drew and cashed this $10,000 check he did so under authority

1159

of William C. Rands, that he had no intention at that time to keep and not return the money, but did intend to return it; and if you find that to be the fact then you must find that the defendant is not guilty of the charge of embezzling and converting this money to his own use feloniously and fraudulently as charged."

A careful reading of the court's charge discloses that this request was not given nor was it covered by any portion of the charge to the jury. Instead the charge, in so far as it outlined the theory of defense, was wholly confined to another issue of fact presented by the testimony, to-wit, that defendant subsequent to taking and using the money, believing he had a right to do so, decided to retain it and apply it in payment on an indebtedness which he claimed was due him from Mr. Rands. This we think deprived defendant of a fair trial. It is the duty of a trial court, if proper request is made, to cover in the charge to the jury the theory upon which the defense is founded, if it is supported by competent testimony.

"A party is entitled to have specific charges upon the law applicable to each of the various hypotheses or combinations of facts which the jury, from the evidence, might legitimately find, and which have not been covered by other instructions." People v. Parsons (syllabus), 105 Mich. 177.

See, also, People v. Cummins, 47 Mich. 334.
Surely it was of greatest importance to the defendant that the jury should be charged that the burden was on the people to show beyond a reasonable doubt that the $10,000 was taken and used by defendant without the consent or approval of Mr. Rands or Rands, Inc. Failure to outline and submit to the jury this theory of the defense was prejudicial error.
While it has not been urged in the people's brief, it may be noted in passing that the above quoted request to charge, as presented by defendant, was not in technically correct language. It would have been unfair and prejudicial to the people's case for the court to have said to the jury:

"The testimony of Mr. Hoefle shows that at the time he drew and cashed this $10,000 check he did so under authority of William C. Rands."

Such statement by the court would in all probability have led the jury to understand the charge as meaning that by Mr. Hoefle's testimony the fact was established that the money was used under the authority of Mr. Rand. Notwithstanding the imperfection in the request as presented, this theory of the defense was specifically called to the attention of the court and it thereupon became the duty of the court in the trial of a criminal case to fairly cover this theory of the defense in the charge to the jury. . . .
For the reason hereinbefore indicated the defendant's conviction must be set aside and a new trial ordered.

1160

FEAD, WIEST, BUTZEL, BUSHNELL, EDWARD M. SHARPE, and
TOY, JJ., concurred. POTTER, J., took no part in the decision.

People v. Dixon
259 Mich. 229

FEAD, J. Defendant was convicted of embezzlement of an
order for payment of $178, drawn by the auditor general of
the State upon the State treasurer, and described in the information both as money and as a check.

In 1927 and 1928, defendant was superintendent of maintenance, in Saginaw county, for the State highway department.   *FACTS*
As part of his duties, he kept a time book of the labor of
men employed under him. From the time book, his wife made
daily report sheets which defendant filed in the Saginaw office of the department, where pay roll vouchers were compiled from them. Upon the vouchers, individual pay checks
were issued by the auditor general and sent to defendant,
who distributed them to the employees.

The check in question was issued to W. M. Brown and bears
indorsement in his name. It was further indorsed by defendant and applied by him in payment of his personal debt to a
merchant. He said he had paid Brown the money, in pursuance
of a somewhat general practice of advancing money to his men
or cashing their checks for them.

In general, the people presented testimony that there
was no W. M. Brown on the State highway work under defendant's charge; that Brown's name appeared on daily reports
some 122 times in 1927 and 1928; that several employees
listed on defendant's reports as working on the same section
with Brown at different times and others having general duties
in the county did not know him, but would have known him if
he had been employed as shown by the reports; that in 16 instances Brown's name appeared at the bottom of the daily reports as though added after the reports were made, the name
being in handwriting different from Mrs. Dixon's and similar
to defendant's; that defendant cashed all of Brown's checks,
usually at the same time and place as he cashed his own; that
defendant listed a fictitious F. H. Brown as an employee, and
when delivery of his check was attempted by another representative of the department accompanying defendant, defendant claimed to have paid Brown in advance so he could go
away; that defendant had received and cashed four other checks,
three of the payees in which denied receipt of the check or
money or right thereto, and, the other being dead, similar
testimony as to his check was given by his wife and son. A
handwriting expert gave his opinion that the indorsement of

1161

W. M. Brown's name on the various checks and of F. H. Brown's name and the additions of the names to the daily reports were in defendant's handwriting.

Defendant claimed W. M. Brown was a genuine employee and checks to him represented actual labor. Several witnesses testified they knew Brown, that he worked for defendant, and that F. H. Brown was also an employee. Defendant explained that the four other checks disclaimed by the payees represented purchase of materials, and, to avoid delay, were handled as labor bills in a manner which, while irregular, contained no actual wrong to the State. He said Brown's indorsements were genuine and the daily reports were wholly in his wife's handwriting.

In addition, the witnesses testified to many details, and, of course, displayed the common lapses of memory, contradictions, indications of bias and favoritism which are ordinary incidents of a long trial. The credibility of witnesses was an important consideration, and the testimony on both sides was strong enough to present a clear issue for the jury and prevent a ruling that the verdict was against the great weight of the evidence.

Testimony of the disposition of other checks by defendant was offered and received upon the question of his intent and was strictly so confined in the charge. It was competent. 3 Comp. Laws 1929 Sec. 17320.

In the opening statement, the people charged that W. M. Brown, as an employee of the department, was a fictitious person. Upon this statement, defendant argues that the check, therefore, had no payee, was not valid, and could not be the subject of embezzlement. He cites no authority for the position. A check or order for the payment of money is valuable only if and because money can be obtained on it. Embezzlement of a check or order intrusted to an agent does not depend upon the technical validity or effect of the instrument, but occurs when it is misappropriated by the agent to the injury of the principal. People v. Hanaw, 107 Mich. 337. . . .

We discover no reversible error in the record, and judgment is affirmed, with costs.

CLARK, C. J., and McDONALD, POTTER, SHARPE, NORTH, WIEST, and BUTZEL, JJ., concurred.

People v. Hawkins
106 Mich. 479

HOOKER, J. The Standard Oil Company of Ohio, a foreign corporation, has for several years done business in Michigan, having a general office in Detroit, through which its business for a portion of the State was done. This business consisted principally in selling petroleum to customers in this State. The oil was, as a rule, shipped to Detroit in

1162

tank and other cars, and there stored until sold, being then reshipped. In some instances, however, the oil was shipped direct from Ohio to the purchaser. All money received for sales of oil in that portion of the State that was within the jurisdiction of the Detroit office was sent to that office, and came to the hands of the defendant, who was bookkeeper and assistant cashier. He was convicted of embezzling $2,600 of the company's money, and the case comes here upon exceptions before sentence.

The errors complained of are said to be:

(1) The failure of the court to direct a verdict for defendant, upon the ground that he was not the servant or agent of the Standard Oil Company, within the embezzlement statute, and that he embezzled none of its money. . . .

1. The first question hinges upon the statute. 3 How. Stat. Sec. 4161d6. This statute was added to the general act providing for the incorporation of domestic manufacturing companies, and was enacted in the year 1889. It provides that foreign corporations "organized . . . either wholly or in part for any of the purposes" contemplated by the act referred to, "upon recording copies of their charter or articles of incorporation, . . . as provided in section nine" of said act, "and upon filing . . . a resolution" authorizing any agent duly appointed to acknowledge service of process for the company, etc., "and appointing an agent for service of process," may carry on business in this State, and "shall enjoy all the rights and privileges, and be subject to all the restrictions and liabilities, of corporations existing under this act." This corporation did not avail itself of the opportunity afforded by this statute, by filing its articles as therein provided. The theory upon which the first assignment of error rests is that the statute (section 4161d6) prohibits the non-complying foreign corporation from doing business in this State, and that, therefore, all contracts made by it are void, and all business done by it or upon its behalf is illegal; that it could neither acquire nor hold any property in this State, nor could it make a lawful contract of agency. The underlying question is, manifestly, the construction to be placed upon the statute; for, if it does not involve a prohibition of business by the corporation, the whole argument of defendant's counsel upon this branch of the case must fall. . . .

But, if it should be held that the act under consideration was prohibitive, and that the company could not make or enforce contracts, it would not follow that this defendant could not be guilty of embezzlement. In fact, he was the agent of the company, whether it was a lawful enterprise or engagement, or not. By virtue of his relation, he became possessed of property which was not his, and which belonged to the company if to anybody. He acted for, and permitted himself to be held out as the agent of, the company, and received money from various persons who were willing to pay. He was a de facto servant, and it is unnecessary that his

1163

relation should have grown out of a lawful contract of agency. It was enough if he acted, and was permitted to act, as such. . . .

We find no error, and think that the conviction should be affirmed, and the recorder's court directed to proceed to judgment. Ordered accordingly.

GRANT and MONTGOMERY, JJ., concurred with HOOKER, J. LONG, J., did not sit.

(Dissenting opinion of Justice McGRATH omitted.)

People v. Hanaw
107 Mich. 337

HOOKER, J. The defendant is charged with embezzlement, and the evidence indicates that complainant indorsed and gave to him for collection, for his use and benefit, a check held by complainant upon a firm in New York. The defendant sent the check to New York, and received a draft payable to his order for a part of the sum, and deposited this draft with his banker, at Jackson, receiving credit for the amount. The complaint and warrant charged the embezzlement against him as "agent, clerk, servant, and collector," and as an embezzlement of a large amount of money, to wit, $398.50, of the value of $398.50, of the goods and chattels then and there belonging to the complainant, and that said goods and chattels then and there came to the possession of the defendant by virtue of his employment, etc. . . .

Again, it is urged that the draft came lawfully into the possession of the defendant; that he had a right to cash it, inasmuch as a portion of the proceeds was his own; and that, inasmuch as this is true, embezzlement cannot be predicated upon the deposit of the draft. It is true that the defendant had a right to convert the draft into money, and take his commission, and pay the remainder to his principal, but this is not what he did. He converted into money or its equivalent, and did not pay his principal. He had no right to sell the draft with this unlawful design to misappropriate, and the law will not separate the act of sale from the intent to convert, but will say that with such an intent he had no right to sell the draft. The parties had a joint interest in this draft, and the statute is expressly aimed at the misappropriation of the principal's share in such cases. In the case of <u>Com. v. Smith</u>, <u>129</u> <u>Mass.</u> <u>110</u>, it is said:

"The fact that the defendant received for the goods of his employers a check payable to his own order did not vest in him the title to the check or its avails. The relation of debtor and creditor did not exist, and the specific proceeds of the sales, whether in cash or in checks payable to their agent's order, belonged to his employers, and were held in trust for them. . . . The transaction is the same whether

1164

the defendant received the price of the goods sold in bank
bills from the hand of the purchaser, or in a check, upon
which he received the money or a credit at the bank." . . .
    The conviction is affirmed. *held*
    The other Justices concurred.

                    People v. Glazier
                     159 Mich. 528

                                                    750.175

    BLAIR, J. Respondent was indicted upon presentment by
a grand jury, charging him in 31 counts with violations of
section 11612 of the Compiled Laws. All of the counts of
the indictment are in the same form, except that some of
them charge respondent, as State treasurer, with knowingly
and unlawfully appropriating, at different times, to his
own use, different sums belonging to the State, and in his
custody as State treasurer. Certain counts charge the ap-
propriations to be to the use of the Chelsea Savings Bank,
while other counts allege an appropriation to the use of
himself and the Chelsea Savings Bank jointly.
    At the close of the testimony the prosecution elected to
go to the jury upon the 10 counts, alleging, with proper
variations of time and amount, as in the ninth count:

    "That on, to wit, the day and year aforesaid, at, to wit,
the city of Lansing, in the county of Ingham aforesaid, the
said Frank P. Glazier, so holding the office of State treasurer as aforesaid, did knowingly, unlawfully, and feloniously appropriate to the use of the Chelsea Savings Bank, a
body corporate under the laws of the State of Michigan, a
large sum of money, to wit, the sum of $12,213.15, of the
value of $50 and upwards, to wit, of the value of $12,213.15,
the property of and belonging to the said State of Michigan,
which had been received and was then held by him in his official capacity aforesaid as State treasurer of the State
of Michigan, contrary to the form of the statute in such
case made' and provided, and against the peace and dignity
of the people of the State of Michigan". . . .
    . . . If we have correctly interpreted the law, it was
unlawful for respondent to deposit any of the State's money
in the Chelsea Savings Bank, and his deposits therein may
properly be considered as a continuing series of unlawful
acts all flowing from the one preconceived design to use
the State's money for the benefit of himself, his institutions, and his bank. This construction receives support
from the language of section 3 of the act (3 Comp. Laws,
Sec. 11614), viz:

    "A failure or refusal of any public officer to pay over
and deliver to his successor all moneys and property which
should be in his hands as such officer shall be prima facie
evidence of an offense against the provisions of section 1
of this act." . . .

                        1165

(1) The receipt of public moneys by a public official entitled to receive them.

(2) The appropriation of the moneys, knowing them to be public moneys, to a use which, as a matter of law, is unauthorized.

(3) The failure or refusal to pay over the money, which he ought to have on hand.

The provisions of section 11614, 3 Comp. Laws, plainly imply that a felonious intent is not an element of the crime. In our opinion it was the intention of the legislature to provide that any public officer, who devoted the public funds in his custody and control to any other purposes than those to which the law authorized their appropriation, must account for them to his successor, or be guilty of a felony, no matter how good his intentions may have been. People v. Warren, 122 Mich. 504 (81 N. W. 360, 80 Am. St. Rep. 582). Under this statute the public officer uses the public funds for an unauthorized purpose at his peril. If he is able to account for them at the proper time, he incurs no criminal responsibility under this statute, however bad his motives, but can only be prosecuted for the offense described in section 1201, or under the general embezzlement statute. If he is unable to account, he is criminally responsible, however good his motives.

The exceptions are overruled, and the record remanded for further proceedings in accordance with the law.

OSTRANDER, HOOKER, McALVAY, and BROOKE, JJ., concurred.

People v. Gregg
170 Mich. 168

STEERE, J. The respondent, Perry Gregg, was convicted in the circuit court of Eaton county in June, 1911, of embezzling, or fraudulently converting to his own use, a certain promissory note, of the alleged value of $35.84, belonging to another and previously delivered to him for a particular purpose. The information filed against him contained two counts. The first was framed under section 11570, 3 Comp. Laws, which is as follows:

"If any person to whom any money, goods, or other property which may be the subject of larceny, shall have been delivered, shall embezzle or fraudulently convert to his own use, or shall secrete with the intent to embezzle, or fraudulently use such goods, money or other property, or any part thereof, he shall be deemed by so doing to have committed the crime of larceny."

To this was added a second count, charging simple larceny. The jury found respondent guilty "as charged in the first count of the information, the same being the count

1166

charging the defendant with embezzlement of the note under paragraph 11570, of the <u>Compiled Laws of 1897</u>."

To this was added a second count, charging simple larceny. The jury found respondent guilty "as charged in the first count of the information, the same being the count charging the defendant with embezzlement of the note under paragraph 11570, of the <u>Compiled Laws of 1897</u>."

The note had been previously given by respondent, who was the maker, to William H. Van Auken, the complaining witness herein, who was the payee. It fell due October 15, 1909. The prosecution claimed it was never paid, but that respondent, having received it from the owner for a certain specified purpose, embezzled and fraudulently converted it to his own use, thereby committing the crime of larceny.

The evidence introduced by the respective parties as to the manner in which respondent acquired possession of the note was irreconcilable. Testimony offered by the prosecution tended to show that about October 1, 1910, the note being then about a year past due and unpaid, Van Auken visited respondent, who was a farmer, and negotiated a purchase from him of some lambs which were to be delivered about the 1st of November following; that the agreed price was 6 cents per pound and $5 extra, and any additional rise which might occur in the market before the time of delivery; that he told respondent the collection of his note was a reason why he wished to make the purchase; that he then gave him the note to be applied in part payment of the purchase price, and said to him, "If you take the note, you will know your lambs are sold and I will know they are bought;" that the lambs were never delivered as agreed, and some time subsequent to the date set for their delivery he interviewed respondent on the subject, who then stated in profane and violent language that he owed Van Auken nothing, did not have any note which belonged to him, had sold the lambs and spent the money, and would do nothing about the note, refusing to return the same when demanded. It was the claim and testimony of respondent that he had never sold the lambs, which belonged to his wife, to Van Auken; that there was some talk on the subject about the time claimed, in which Van Auken tried to buy them, but no agreement was reached or note then given to him; that he owed Van Auken nothing at that time, having previously taken up the note in question, paying the same in full, in cash, to Van Auken, amounting in principal and interest, to $40. It is manifest that the witnesses thus testifying could not be honestly mistaken. One side or the other must have deliberately falsified. These issues of fact were decided by the jury in favor of the prosecution.

The case is before us on exceptions to refusal of the court below to rule that the evidence was insufficient to support the information, and to instructions given the jury; the errors relied on being thus stated:

1167

CHARGE TO JURY

"(1) The refusal of the trial judge to direct a verdict of not guilty.
"(2) The failure of the trial judge to give the jury
such a charge as defendant was entitled to under the law.
"(3) The refusal of the court to grant a new trial."

The first question, therefore, to consider, is whether
the testimony of the prosecution, taken as a whole, contained facts sufficient to constitute the offense charged. If
so, it was for the jury to decide, under proper instructions.
It is the theory and claim of respondent that the testimony
of the prosecution shows at most but a contract of purchase
and sale and a breach of such contract - a part payment of
the agreed purchase price by delivery and acceptance of the
note and an agreement by respondent to deliver the lambs,
for which he could only be held liable in a civil suit for
resulting damages; that, when Van Auken delivered the note
in part payment on the purchase, he parted with both possession and title to it and passed the same to respondent, who
cannot be found guilty of embezzling or stealing his own
property.

This case does not involve the much discussed "shadow
line" between false pretenses and larceny, or between larceny and embezzlement. The provisions of the statute under
which the information is laid dispose of the latter, and the
evidence fails to show any misrepresentations by respondent
as to existing facts by which complaining witness was misled. False promises or false assurances as to future transactions are not false pretenses in law. Though, like bonds,
certificates of stock, or paper money, the intrinsic value
of a promissory note is insignificant, it has real value in
the right of property which it represents, and is itself
property which may be the subject of larceny. The fact that
respondent had originally given this note to Van Auken, who
had a civil right of action against him, independent of the
note, would not defeat a criminal prosecution. The maker of
a note may be guilty of its larcency or embezzlement from the
payee to whom he has given it, though his indebtedness is unaffected by the act. Commonwealth v. Eichelberger, 119 Pa.
254 (13 Atl. 422, 4 Am. St. Rep. 642).

Must we conclude from the people's testimony that the note
became respondent's property? Van Auken voluntarily delivered it and parted with the possession, but did he transfer and
part with the title also? Its delivery was for a specified
purpose, as part payment on the purchase price of the lambs,
a payment on account. There is no proof it was applied to
such purpose; defendant denies that it was, and all the testimony is to the effect that it was not. It is not inferable
from the people's testimony that Van Auken intended to for-
give the debt and surrender the note, and pass title therein
to respondent, whether the lambs were delivered or not. It
is fairly deducible from the transaction that the note was
delivered conditionally; that the ownership and title to the

1168

note remained in Van Auken, only to pass when the deal was consummated, and he had received the consideration therefor by delivery of the lambs. Respondent kept the note and sold the lambs to others, putting it beyond his power to do that which would fulfill the condition under which he received the note, and which would invest him with the title. The jury could fairly infer from the testimony as a whole that he did not apply it in part payment on the property purchased and never intended to do so. He himself testifies that he did not. We cannot agree that the payee of the note is shown to have parted with the title. The principle involved in this question has been held to be the actual intent of the owner as disclosed by what he said and did at the time he delivered possession of the property. In the case of Queen v. Russett, 2 Q. B. Div. 312, there was a purchase and sale of a horse, with part payment and promised future delivery, which was never made. The seller was prosecuted for larceny of the part payment. It was claimed that the sale was fraudulent; the seller removing the animal elsewhere under circumstances indicating he never intended to deliver it. Under the proof in that case a material question was the distinction between false pretenses and larceny, but whether or not the payor of a part payment parted with the title to the money paid was involved. The respondent contended that the purchaser, who testified, "I never expected to see the L8 back, but to have the horse," parted absolutely with both the possession and property in the money paid, and therefore respondent's taking it was not larceny, but, if any crime, obtaining money by false pretenses. In confirming a conviction, the court said, amongst other things:

"In my judgment the money was merely handed to the prisoner by way of deposit, to remain in his hands until completion of the transaction by delivery of the horse. He never intended, or could have intended, that the prisoner should take the money and hold it, whether he delivered the horse or not. . . . I need only to refer to the contract, which provides for payment of the balance on delivery of the horse, to show how impossible it is to read into it an agreement to pay L8 to the prisoner whether he gave delivery of the horse or not. It was clearly only a deposit by way of part payment of the price of the horse, and there was ample evidence that the prosecutor never intended to part with the property in (sic) the money when he gave it into the prisoner's possession."

An examination of the charge of the court, with reference to the numerous allegations of error launched against it, leads to the conclusion that most of the claimed errors are founded on the contentions of respondent already discussed and decided, and to review them in detail would be but repetition. The charge is very full and detailed, covering, with unusual emphasis and prominence, the various rules of law relative to burden of proof, reasonable doubt, and presumption of innocence designed to safeguard the rights

1169

of the accused. The portions of the charge touching
simple larceny, under the second count in the information,
require no consideration, as the respondent was not convicted under that count. The court fairly submitted defendant's claim, based on the opposing testimony, to the
jury to determine, as an issue of fact, with proper explanation of their province and duties in passing upon the credibility of witnesses. As to what constituted the statutory
offense of which respondent was convicted, the court instructed the jury, in part, as follows:

"But if, on the other hand, you find that he received
the note under the circumstances as claimed by the people,
and afterwards at any time conceived the idea of converting the note to his own use, and did fraudulently so convert said note, then he would be guilty of embezzlement,
and you should so designate in your verdict. . . . Now, by
the term 'convert' - that is, converting the note to his
own use - or 'embezzle' is meant simply the wrongful or
fraudulent appropriation to one's own use of money or goods
left in his possession by another. From what I have said
to you, gentlemen, you will understand that to convict in
this case you should be satisfied beyond a reasonable doubt
that Mr. Gregg had an intent either when he took the note
or later on to deprive Mr. Van Auken of its value. . . .
The intent is the essence of the offense, and, unless the
intent to wrong is present at the time of the commission
of the offense, then no crime has been committed."

Objection is made to the use of the word "fraudulently,"
instead of "feloniously," in instructing the jury as to
what constituted the offense, and that the jury were not
instructed that to constitute the crime the act must have
been done with a felonious intent. The court followed the
language of the statute in that respect. If the respondent fraudulently converted or used the property as specified
in the act he did it, under the provisions of the act, with
a felonious intent. We cannot see how any assistance would
have been given the jury by using, or even defining, "feloniously." It is not imperative that the jury shall be given
technical definitions, but it is sufficient if the purport
of the words as applied to their duties in deciding the
facts be explained to them. It is true that, in order to
convict, they must have found a felonious intent. "Feloniously" is a technical word of the legal vocabulary, originally essential in indictments charging any offense involving forfeiture of goods and lands to the crown, or, in this
country, any crime involving death or imprisonment in the
penitentiary. It imports that the act charged was done with
a mind bent on that which is criminal, with an unlawful and
wicked intent. When applied to a violation of a criminal
statute, if the facts proven show the statute was intentionally violated and establish a felony, then the crime
was committed feloniously. State v. Snell, 78 Mo. 240.

1170

The language of the charge more than once clearly covered this proposition.

We find no prejudicial error in the case, and the conviction is affirmed.

MOORE, C. J., and McALVAY, BROOKE, BLAIR, STONE, and OSTRANDER, JJ., concurred. BIRD, J., did not sit.

Note

Gillespie summarizes the elements of embezzlement in Michigan as follows:

"1. That the defendant occupied, or, acted in, a fiduciary relation covered by the statute;

2. That by virtue of such relationship the property or money claimed to have been embezzled came into his possession or under his control, and;

3. That he wrongfully converted or appropriated the same to his own use, with intent to defraud, without the consent of his principal."[1]

1. Gillespie, Michigan Criminal Law and Procedure, Sec. 1318, (2nd ed. 1953).

3. Final Draft - Michigan Revised Criminal Code

Committee Commentary

2. Embezzlement

Embezzlement is a statutory offense created because of the holdings of common-law courts that one who receives property as a bailee, agent, employee, fiduciary, etc., and who later decides to convert the property to his own use does not commit larceny because he has not "taken and carried away property in the legal possession of another." Legislatures in every state have hastened to legislate to reach common kinds of wilful misappropriation, but usually in an "after the fact" fashion in which, if the courts hold an existing statute inapplicable to a particular type of possession, a new statute is enacted covering the specific relationship. This has produced statutory chaos in which some relationships are not covered at all, others covered by two or more statutes bearing different punishments and still others covered by two or more statutes carrying the same penalties, but with the possibility every present of a variance requiring reversal.

The Michigan statutes are according to pattern. In addition to a general embezzlement statute (C. L. 1948, Sec. 750.174), there are statutes covering public officers (C. L. 1948, Sec. 750.175); insurance agents and brokers (C. L. 1948, Sec. 514.10); persons employed by building and loan associations,

1171

(C.L. 1948, Sec. 489.27); administrators, executors and
guardians (C. L. 1948, Sec. 750.176); chattel mortgagees
(C.L. 1948, Sec. 750.177); anyone who embezzles encumbered
personal property (C.L. 1948, Sec. 750.178); railroad employees who embezzle tickets (C.L. 1948, Sec. 750.179, and
see People v. Beebehyser, 157 Mich. 239, 121 N.W. 751 (1909)
which held this not to include an employee of a street railway company); bank and credit union employees (C.L. 1948, Sec.
750.180), warehousemen and forwarders (C.L. 1948, Sec. 750.182);
state officers retaining fees (C.L. 1948, Sec. 750.488) and
arresting officers who do not forward recognizance monies in
traffic cases (C.L. 1948, Sec. 257.728) or deposit interim
bonds (C.L. 1948, Sec. 750.584).

In application, it is necessary first to find that property
is involved which the person holds in a capacity recognized
in the statute under which the prosecution is brought (People
v. Andrews, 249 Mich. 616, 229 N.W. 401 (1930); People v.
Burns, 242 Mich. 345, 218 N.W. 704 (1928); People v. Belz,
257 Mich. 302, 241 N.W. 219 (1932)). The creation of a debtor-
creditor relationship (People v. Wadsworth, 63 Mich. 500, 30
N.W. 99 (1886)) or the giving of unauthorized credit for damaged goods (People v. Bergman, 246 Mich. 68, 224 N.W. 375
(1929)) does not amount to embezzlement because there is no
property involved. Nor does embezzlement lie if property
is utilized or expended for purposes of the employer or principal, even though this is not specifically authorized or
does not in fact result in gain for the employer or principal
(People v. Bauman, 105 Mich. 543, 63 N.W. 516 (1895)). It
does not matter, however, that the property taken is not enforcible in a civil action (People v. Dixon, 259 Mich. 229,
242 N.W. 896 (1932)), that the corporate principal is not
licensed to do business in the state (People v. Hawkins, 106
Mich. 479, 64 N.W. 736 (1895)) or that the offender has a
claim to some but not all the property converted (People v.
Hanaw, 107 Mich. 337, 64 N.W. 231 (1895)). No particular
form of activity is specified under most of the statutes; the
diversion may take any shape possible considering the kind
of property involved (cf. People v. Andrews, 249 Mich. 616,
229 N.W. 401 (1930) (bonds); People v. Burns, 242 Mich. 345,
218 N.W. 704 (1928) (pension checks); People v. Dixon, 259
Mich. 229, 242 N.W. 896 (1932) (cashing fictitious paychecks);
People v. Belz, 257 Mich. 302, 241 N.W. 219 (1932) (company
check to purchase personal car); People v. Lay, 193 Mich. 476,
160 N.W. 467 (1916) (salary checks in excess of amount authorized)). Public officers may be held on the basis of a failure
to turn over monies when required by law (People v. Glazier,
159 Mich. 528, 124 N.W. 582 (1910). Mere non-payment or non-
production in other cases, however, is not sufficient (People
v. Hurst, 62 Mich. 276, 28 N.W. 838 (1886)); it is necessary
to establish that the defendant intentionally departed from
the terms or conditions under which he held the property with
the awareness he had no lawful claim to do so. A defendant,
therefore, can submit evidence that he thought he was author-

ized to act as he did, and the court must give appropriate instructions to the jury on the point (People v. Douglas, 292 Mich. 388, 292 N.W. 341 (1940); People v. Hoefle, 276 Mich. 428, 267 N.W. 644 (1936); American Life Ins. Co. v. U.S.F. & G. Co., 261 Mich. 221, 246 N.W. 71 (1933)). If the intent is present, however, a purpose to make restitution in the future does not take away criminality (People v. Butts, 128 Mich. 208, 87 N.W. 224 (1901)).

The Draft supplants all the statutes now existing, because it covers anyone who "exerts unauthorized control over the property of the owner" (Sec. 3205 (1) (a)). This eliminates the many pleading problems and the wide disparity in penalties which arise from existing law and dispenses with distinctions which have only historical significance. It does not, however, expand present law unless there is still some relationship uncovered by the many existing statutes; the stress on "unauthorized control" over property of the "owner" removes from consideration any issue of the specific character of the relationship.

C. False Pretenses

1. Michigan Compiled Laws (1948)

750.217a Solicitation of information anent employment, residence, assets, or earnings by false personation

Sec. 217a. Any individual who on his own behalf, or as officer, agent, partner, employee, or representative of any entity, solicits or aids or abets another in soliciting information from any person as to his or any other person's place of employment, residence, assets or earnings, by any means whatever with the intent of misleading the person into believing that the information is being sought by or on behalf of, or for the purposes of, any governmental agency or commission is guilty of a misdemeanor. P.A. 1931, No. 328, Sec. 217a, added by P.A. 1961, No. 62, Sec. 1, Eff. Sept. 8, 1961.

750.218 False pretenses with intent to defraud

Sec. 218. Any person who with intent to defraud or cheat, shall designedly, by color of any false token or writing or by any false or bogus check or other written, printed or

1173

engraved instrument, by spurious coin or metal in the
similitude of coin, or by any other false pretense, cause
any person to grant, convey, assign, demise, lease or
mortgage any land or interest in land, or obtain the signature of any person to any written instrument, the making
whereof would be punishable as forgery, or obtain from any
person any money or personal property or the use of any instrument, facility or article or other valuable thing or
service, or by means of any false weights or measures obtain a larger amount or quantity of property than was bargained for, or by means of any false weights or measures
sell or dispose of a less amount or quantity of property
than was bargained for, if such land or interest in land,
money, personal property, use of such instrument, facility
or article, valuable thing, service, larger amount obtained or less amount disposed of, shall be of the value of
$100.00 or less, shall be guilty of a misdemeanor; and if
such land, interest in land, money, personal property, use
of such instrument, facility or article, valuable thing,
service, larger amount obtained or less amount disposed
of shall be of the value of more than $100.00, such person
shall be guilty of a felony, punishable by imprisonment in
the state prison not more than 10 years or by a fine of not
more than $5,000.00. As amended P.A. 1957, No. 69, Sec. 1
Eff. Sept. 27.

750.219 Financial condition, false statements

Sec. 219. WRITTEN FALSE STATEMENTS ABOUT FINANCIAL CON-
DITION TO OBTAIN CREDIT, ETC. - Any person shall be guilty
of a misdemeanor, punishable by imprisonment in the county
jail for not more than 1 year, or by a fine of not more
than 500 dollars, who, either individually or in a representative capacity:

First, shall knowingly make a false statement in writing
to any person, firm or corporation engaged in banking or
other business respecting his own financial condition or
the financial condition of any firm or corporation with
which he is connected as a member, director, officer, employe or agent, for the purpose of procuring a loan or credit in any form or an extension of credit from the person,
firm or corporation to whom such false statement is made,
either for his own use or for the use of the firm or corporation with which he is connected as aforesaid; or

Second, having previously made, or having knowledge that
another has previously made a statement in writing to any
person, firm or corporation engaged in banking or other
business respecting his own financial condition or the financial condition of any firm or corporation with which he is
connected as aforesaid, shall afterwards procure on faith
of such statement from the person, firm or corporation to
whom such previous statement has been made, either for his
own use or for the use of the firm or corporation with which

1174

he is so connected, a loan or credit in any form, or an extension of credit, knowing at the time of such procuring that such previously made statement is in any material particular false with respect to the present financial condition of himself or of the firm or corporation with which he is so connected; or

Third, shall deliver to any note broker or other agent for the sale or negotiation of commercial paper, any statement in writing, knowing the same to be false, respecting his own financial condition or the financial condition of any firm or corporation with which he is connected as aforesaid, for the purpose of having such statement used in furtherance of the sale, pledge or negotiation of any note, bill or other instrument for the payment of money made or endorsed or accepted or owned in whole or in part by him individually or by the firm or corporation with which he is so connected; or

Fourth, having previously delivered or having knowledge that another has previously delivered to any note broker or other agent for the sale or negotiation of commercial paper a statement in writing respecting his own financial condition or the financial condition of any firm or corporation with which he is connected as aforesaid, shall afterwards deliver to such note broker or other agent for the purpose of sale, pledge or negotiation on faith of such statement, any note, bill or other instrument for the payment of money made or endorsed or accepted or owned in whole or in part by himself individually or by the firm or corporation with which he is so connected, knowing at the time that such previously delivered statement is in any material particular false as to the present financial condition of himself or of such firm or corporation.

750.219a Telephone service, use of false credit or telephone number or use of number without authority

Sec. 219a. Any person who knowingly obtains or attempts to obtain telephone service or the transmission of a telephone message by the use of any false or fictitious telephone credit number or telephone number, or by the use of any telephone credit number or telephone number of another without the authority of the person to whom such credit number or telephone number was issued, is guilty of a misdemeanor. If the total value of telephone service obtained in a manner prohibited by this section exceeds $100.00, the offense shall be prosecuted as a felony. P. A. 1931, No. 328, Sec. 219a, added by P. A. 1961, No. 93, Sec. 1, Eff. Sept. 8, 1961, as amended P. A. 1967, No. 255, Sec. 1, Eff. Nov. 2.

750.219c Telecommunication, use with intent to avoid payment

Sec. 219c. Any person who knowingly obtains or attempts to obtain, by the use of any fraudulent scheme, device, means or method telegraph or telephone service or the transmission of a message, signal or other communication by telephone or telegraph, or over telephone, telegraph or other communication facilities with intent to avoid payment of charges therefor is guilty of a misdemeanor. P. A. 1931, No. 328, Sec. 219c, added by P. A. 1961, No. 93, Sec. 1, Eff. Sept. 8, 1961.

750.220 Property valuation or indebtedness, false statements

Sec. 220. WRITTEN FALSE STATEMENT OF PROPERTY VALUATION, ETC., TO OBTAIN CREDIT - Any person who wilfully and knowingly makes any false statement in writing of his or her property valuation, real or personal, or both, or of his or her indebtedness, for the purpose of obtaining credit from any person, company, co-partnership, association or corporation, shall be guilty of a misdemeanor, punishable by imprisonment in the county jail for not more than 1 year or by fine of not more than 500 dollars.

750.221 Blind or defective, false statements

Sec. 221. FALSELY REPRESENTING SELF AS BLIND, ETC. - Any person who shall falsely represent himself or herself as blind, deaf, dumb, crippled or physically defective for the purpose of obtaining money or any other thing of value, and any person thus falsely representing himself or herself as blind, deaf, dumb, crippled or otherwise physically defective, and securing aid or assistance on account of such representation, shall be guilty of a misdemeanor.

400.60 False statement to obtain relief; penal and civil liability; removal of officer or employee; information furnished by recipient; failure to report change of status

Sec. 60. Any person who by means of wilful false statement or representation or by impersonation or other fraudulent device obtains or attempts to obtain, or aids or abets any person to obtain (a) assistance or relief to which he is not entitled; or (b) a larger amount of assistance or relief than that to which he is justly entitled; or any officer or employee of a county, city, or district department of social welfare who authorizes or recommends relief to persons known to him to be ineligible or to have fraudulently created their eligibility; or any person who knowingly buys or aids or abets in buying or in disposal of the property of a person receiving assistance or relief without the consent of the director or supervisor of the state department, shall, if the amount involved shall be of the value of $500.00 or less, be deemed guilty of a misdemeanor, and shall, if the amount involved shall be of the value of more than $500.00, be deemed guilty of a felony, and upon conviction shall be punished as provided by the laws of this state: Provided, That if anyone receives assistance or relief through means enumerated in this section, in which prosecution is deemed unnecessary, the state department or county departments may take

1176

the necessary steps to recover from the recipient the total amount paid as assistance or relief, plus interest at 5 per cent per annum. On conviction of the violation of the provisions of this section of any officer or employee of any county, city, or district department of social welfare, such officer or employee shall be removed or dismissed from office. There is hereby imposed upon every person receiving relief under this act either upon his own application or by his inclusion, to his knowledge, in the application of another the continuing obligation to supply to the department issuing the relief: (a) the complete circumstances in regard to his income from employment or from any other source or the existence of income, if known to him, of other persons receiving relief through the same application; (b) information regarding each and every offer of employment for himself or, if known to him, of the other persons receiving relief through the same application; (c) information concerning changes in his circumstances or those of other persons receiving relief through the same application which would decrease the need for relief; and (d) the circumstances or whereabouts, known to him, of relatives legally responsible for his support or for the support of other persons receiving relief through the same application if changes in such circumstances or whereabouts could affect the amount of assistance available from such relatives or affect their legal liability to furnish support. Any person who shall neglect or refuse to submit to the department issuing relief the information required by this section shall, if the amount of relief granted as a result of such neglect or refusal be less than $500.00, be guilty of a misdemeanor, and if the amount of relief granted as a result of such neglect or refusal be $500.00 or more, shall be deemed guilty of a felony, and upon conviction shall be punished as provided by the laws of this state. As amended P. A. 1950, Ex. Sess., No. 18, Sec. 1, Eff. March 31, 1951.

2. Definition and Elements of the Offense

People v. McAllister
49 Mich. 12

CAMPBELL, J. Respondent was convicted of obtaining of the firm of Prindle & Larned of Kalamazoo, by false pretenses, a bill of hardware amounting to seven dollars and one cent, and sentenced to three years' imprisonment. The false pretence charged was that he owned a house and lot on Portage street, near the gas works in Kalamazoo, and was building an addition to the house, and wished to buy the articles for use in such building.

The information does not show, and the testimony throws no more light, how this pretence operated as a fraud, or

1177

that good the truth of the statement said to have been made, would have done the complaining witnesses. It was entirely compatible with the averment that respondent may have owned other property, or that the house might be a homestead, and in no way subject to legal process, or encumbered to its value. It does not appear that respondent was given to understand that the question asked him about his building was put for the purpose of ascertaining whether it was safe to trust him. He made no representations at all when he asked for credit for this small bill until an inquiry was made, and the only question asked him was the single one whether he was building. This contained no intimation that he was expected to give information concerning the ownership or value of property, or that his credit would depend upon his answer. There can be no offence under the statute unless the party knows or has reason to believe that his representations are relied on as the grounds of credit. And there is nothing in the testimony indicating this; neither does the information point out how any fraud could result from such statements standing alone and unexplained.

On the trial the claim was that the seller of the goods expected to have a mechanic's lien. But he asked and he obtained no information whatever that had any tendency to show that such a lien would arise, or would be of any value. While we need not refer to it to make out error, it appears very distinctly that respondent had just such property as he claimed to have, and there is nothing to indicate that the trifling difference in location made or could have made any difference in the honesty of the transaction. The court erred in admitting any testimony under the information and in allowing any conviction. There was nothing which had any legal force to prove the crime alleged.

The judgment must be reversed and the prisoner discharged from prison

The other Justices concurred.

People v. Brown
71 Mich. 296

CAMPBELL, J. Respondent was convicted of obtaining two promissory notes - one of $200, and one of $80 - on false pretenses. From the testimony the case seems to have been one of the Bohemian oat cases; but it is claimed that no offense was charged in the information. The purport of this was as follows: It charges that Alva Ellie and respondent, with fraudulent design, etc., represented to one Harmon Hartwell that respondent was agent for an incorporated company, designated as the "Bohemian Oat & Cereal Company," having its chief office at Ypsilanti; that it was a good, responsible, and reliable company, that fulfilled all its contracts, and

1178

had a paid-up capital of $100,000, and was so wealthy and financially responsible that it would be impossible for it to avoid payment of all its liabilities; that it intended in good faith to carry out all contracts, and any contract made with it through its said agent would be fairly and honestly fulfilled, and it had thus far fulfilled all its obligations, and was not a fraudulent or swindling company, but honest, fair, and trustworthy, and any deal with it would be fairly and in good faith carried out.

That Hartwell, relying on these representations, was induced to sign and deliver the two notes to Ellis and respondent, who obtained them by the false and fraudulent representations, and with the fraudulent design mentioned. The information then negatives the allegations imputed to respondent specifically.

The information does not point out for what consideration these notes were given, or to whom they were payable, or whether negotiable or not. It does not show that the corporation, directly or by agent, made any agreement or had any dealings with Hartwell. In other words, it does not show in what way it concerned Hartwell whether the Bohemian Oat & Cereal Company was an honest and responsible or dishonest and swindling concern. There is nothing to connect the notes with any fraud practiced on Hartwell. A falsehood not acted on can be no fraud; and, so far as this information goes, the statements concerning the corporation had no more to do with the notes than any other irrelevant lies would have had. Unless Hartwell dealt with it, the condition or character of the company could not concern him.

The information charged no offense. The conviction under it cannot be sustained, and must be reversed and set aside, and respondent discharged.

The other Justices concurred.

People v. Wakely
62 Mich. 297

CHAMPLIN, J.   The defendant was informed against and convicted of obtaining personal property by false pretenses. Objections are taken to the sufficiency of the information.

We are of opinion that the information is sufficient, under our statutes relative to pleadings in such cases. How. Stat. Sec. 9226, 9539.

It was incumbent upon the prosecution to prove, not only the representations and pretenses made, but their falsity, substantially as alleged in the information. These were as follows:

"That Hudson J. Wakely, . . on the fourth day of August, 1884, at the city of Ionia, in the county of Ionia, with intent to cheat and defraud one Margaret J. Schild, and fraudu-

lently obtain one single top-buggy with improved Brewster
spring, of the value of one hundred and fifty dollars, of
the goods and chattels and property of her, the said Margaret J. Schild, did designedly falsely represent and pretend to one John Schild, who was the agent of the said
Margaret Schild, and had the authority from her to see and
dispose of said buggy, that he, the said Hudson J. Wakely,
owned in fee simple, clear and free from all liens or incumbrance, one hundred and twenty acres of good farming
land in Montcalm county, Michigan, worth six thousand dollars;
and said Hudson J. Wakely well knew at the time he made said
representations that said John Schild was the agent for said
Margaret J. Schild, as herein stated.

"And also that said Hudson J. Wakely, at the same time
and place, with intent to cheat and defraud said Margaret
J. Schild, and fraudulently obtain said top-buggy from her,
did further designedly falsely represent and pretend to the
said John Schild, as agent for said Margaret J. Schild, and
with intent to obtain said buggy as aforesaid, that his
brother, that is to say, the brother of said Hudson J. Wakely, to wit, one John Q. Wakely, owned one hundred and sixty
acres of good farming land near Carson City, Michigan, and
that his brother was worth at least twenty-five thousand
dollars, free and clear of all liens and incumbrances.

"And the said John Schild, believing the said false pretenses and representations so made as aforesaid, was then
and there deceived thereby, and was induced, by means of the
false pretenses and representations so made as aforesaid, to
deliver, and did then and there, heretofore, to wit, on the
fourth day of August, 1884, deliver, to said Hudson J. Wakely,
one single top-buggy with improved Brewster spring, of the
value of one hundred and fifty dollars, and the property of
said Margaret J. Schild, and take the promissory note for
one hundred and fifty dollars of said Hudson J. Wakely and
John Q. Wakely in payment for said buggy; but in express reliance of the said false and fraudulent representations made
by said Hudson J. Wakely as to the pecuniary responsibility
of himself and said John Q. Wakely, said note being for the
sum of one hundred and fifty dollars, and to become due in
six months from August 4, 1884; whereas, in truth, the said
Hudson J. Wakely did not own said land in Montcalm county,
Michigan, and was not responsible for said note, and was not
worth the sum of six thousand dollars over and above his exemption, but, on the contrary, was not worth any property
liable to execution.

"And, further, that the said John Q. Wakely was not at
said time the owner of one hundred and sixty acres of land
near Carson City, Michigan, and was not worth at least twenty-
five thousand dollars as herein stated, and was not good and
responsible for the amount of said note; and said note is entirely worthless and of no value, and would not have been accepted nor taken except for the fraudulent representations
made by the said Hudson J. Wakely, as herein stated; and

1180

neither said Hudson J. Wakely nor John Q. Wakely are good for, nor responsible for, the amount of said note nor said buggy obtained, as herein stated, upon said false and fraudulent representations."

As the case developed upon the trial, the people failed to prove that the representations made by the respondent that he owned a farm near Greenville that was worth six thousand dollars, free and clear from all incumbrance, were false; and the circuit judge charged the jury that those representations, if made, must be taken as true; and he left it to the jury to determine whether the further representations with reference to John Q. Wakely were made, and whether or not they were false.

The testimony introduced to show what John Q. Wakely was worth fell far short of establishing the falsity of the representations. Much of it was hearsay, and much other was incompetent. The court should have taken the case from the jury. The people failed to make a case.

The object of the statute is to punish cheats, and it must be made to appear, not only that some person has been defrauded, but that the person making the representations intended to defraud the person by the representations made.

The complaint is that the accused falsely represented his financial condition, and that of his brother, to induce Margaret J. Schild to take a note signed by the accused and his brother for $150, in paymnent for a buggy.

As to his own condition, he represented that he was the owner of a farm near Greenville worth $6,000, free and clear, and it turns out that this representation was true, so far as this case was concerned, as stated by the learned judge. This being conceded, how does it appear that he intended to defraud Margaret J. Schild out of her buggy? Can it be said that a person worth $6,000, in a farm free and clear of all incumbrance, either intends to or does perpetrate a fraud in giving his note to the amount of $150 for property purchased? Whether it be true or false that his brother whose name was upon the note was worth $25,000 made no difference, unless the vendor of the buggy was actually defrauded in the transaction. No steps have been taken to enforce collection of the note, and no evidence was introduced to show that at the time he made the representations he was not worth $6,000.

It is true that there need be but one false pretense, and though several are set out in the information, yet if any of them are proved which amounts in law to a false pretense, the information is sustained. But it does not amount in law to a false pretense unless made with a fraudulent intent, and the person parting with the property is actually defrauded.

In all cases of this kind three things, at least, must concur: the intent to defraud, the false pretense made with the intent, and the fraud accomplished. If the respondent was worth $6,000 at the time he purchased the buggy, no change in his circumstances since relate back so as to fasten upon him an intent at that time to defraud.

When it is necessary to show a particular intent in order to establish the offense charged, proof of previous acts of the same kind is admissible for the purpose of proving guilty knowledge or intent. People v. Hennssler, 48 Mich. 52. . . . The errors assigned based upon the receipt of such testimony are overruled.

It was competent to allege in the information that the false representations were made to an agent, and if he has authority to sell the article obtained by such false pretense, it will be sufficient, although the principal did not act upon the representations made otherwise than through the agent.

The judgment must be reversed, and a new trial ordered.

The other Justices concurred.

Higler v. People
44 Mich. 299

COOLEY, J. The plaintiff in error has been convicted in the Recorder's Court of Detroit upon an information charging him with obtaining twenty-five dollars of one Burley by false pretenses. The pretense alleged was "that he, the said John Higler, was then and there engaged in store-keeping in Cadillac Wexford County, Michigan." No further representations are set up as accompanying this false pretense, whereby it was made effective. The question now is whether the information will sustain the conviction.

The statute under which the information was filed is as follows:

"Every person who, with intent to defraud or cheat another, shall designedly, by color of any false token or writing, or by any other false pretense, cause any person to grant, convey, assign, demise, lease or mortgage any land . . or obtain from any person any money, personal property or valuable thing, or by means of any false weights or measures, obtain a larger amount or quantity of property than was bargained for, . . . shall be punished by imprisonment," etc. Public Acts, 1879, p. 197.

It is said that this statute enumerates certain kinds of false pretenses, and that according to a familiar rule of construction the "other" pretenses which the statute intends can be those only which are of a kindred nature to those which are mentioned. State v. Simpson, 3 Hawks 620; State v. Sumner 10 Vt. 589. But the rule has no application, because this statute does not attempt an enumeration of the pretenses that shall be held criminal. False tokens are mentioned, but the term is general, not particular, and the same may be said of false writings. The idea suggested to the mind by these is something cognizable to the sight or touch. "Any

1182

other false pretense" is a specification equally general, and will embrace other classes.

It is said further that the pretense, to be within the statute, must be one calculated to deceive a man of ordinary prudence, and that if it be a false representation of facts, these facts must be such as were calculated to influence a person of common caution to part with that which was obtained. Is the false representation that one is a "store-keeper" a pretense of this sort? It may be true and yet the man be utterly without responsibility and without character; and in that case the fact of the business would offer no security that a loan made in reliance upon it would be repaid. The term is indefinite: it may mean a wholesale merchant, or a petty dealer in toys or candies; it may imply a principal, or an agent or a servant; it may be applied to one notoriously without capital and who lives by his wits rather than by legitimate trades; in short, disconnected from all else, it can never indicate that the person who bears the designation is one who can safely be trusted with a loan.

All this is true; and if the reliance in accommodating another person with a loan were pecuniary means of responsibility, it might be very conclusive. But, notoriously, the fact is otherwise. Men are trusted in large amounts every day who have no pecuniary responsibility, and are known to have none. Sometimes the reliance for repayment will be a supposed business ability; sometimes on a business that would be injured by the existence of overdue debts; but most often, perhaps, a reputation for integrity. And if in any case the existence of any particular fact would be likely to beget confidence, there is no reason why a false assertion of its existence should not be a criminal pretense, as much as would a false assertion of pecuniary responsibility, provided it is equally relied upon, and equally effectual to accomplish the fraud designed.

Pecuniary responsibility is no more a necessary attendant upon a commission in the army than upon the keeping of a store; but the false assertion that one holds such a commission has been held a false pretense. Regina v. Hamilton 1 Cox C. C. 244; s.c. on appeal 9 Q.B. 271; Thomas v. People 34 N.Y. 351. So the pretense that one is buying horses as a gentleman's servant may be a criminal false pretense, though the fact of service by itself would not be likely to inspire confidence except in connection with the further fact, expressed or understood, that the master was to pay the purchase price. Rex v. Dale, 7 C. & P. 352.

Now it is unquestionable that the fact that one is a store-keeper is one which would be likely to give a degree of confidence and credit. There is an implication, if not of solvency, at least of the possession of considerable means, in the very idea that one is keeping a store; with no knowledge of his responsibility one would sooner trust him for small sums than if he had no business, or if his business were unknown. A store-keeper is not expected to refuse payment of small debts, whether payment can or cannot be enforced; it is inconsistent with business prosperity that he should do so, and <u>prima facie</u> he will have in his hands the means whereby such debts may be paid. And if such a person, when away from home, had occasion to borrow a few dollars for expenses, a lender would trust, not to his responsibility, but to his honor, for re payment, and would probably ask no questions further, after learning what was his business.

But the question of the materiality of the pretense is one rather of fact than of law. If it was false, and had a tendency to deceive, and did actually deceive and accomplish the intended fraud, the case is within the statute. <u>Regina v. Hamilton</u>, supra.

"The materiality and the influence of the pretenses in question is for the jury to determine on evidence by verdict; unless some inducing circumstances upon the face of the indictment show that the pretenses are clearly immaterial and could not influence credit. The averment of the pretenses by the indictment is only to give the defendant notice of what may be proved against him; the mode of obtaining need not be pleaded; and if any pretense is capable of defrauding, that is sufficient." <u>Thomas v. People</u>, supra. The pretenses in that case were that the prisoner was a chaplain in the army, just returned from the army and wanted money to get home with; and it was said of them: "A court cannot say, as a matter of law, that these were not material representations, and were not calculated to deceive; and to induce credit; and were not within the statute, which speaks of obtaining by any false pretense."

In this case the jury has found that the pretense was both false and effectual. There are no exceptions in the case, but the question of sufficiency is raised upon the face of the information itself. It is a question, therefore, whether the pretense is one which can, under any circumstances, be within the statute, and not whether it was so in the particular case under the facts disclosed by the evidence. As was said in <u>Thomas' Case</u>, we cannot say as a matter of law that the pretense was not within the statute.

The judgment must be affirmed.

GRAVES and MARSTON, JJ., concurred.

CAMPBELL, J., dissenting. I think our previous decisions and the general course of authority lead to the result that the statute only intends to reach such pretenses as are reasonably calculated to defraud. A merchant or any other business man would never trust another merely because he is a storekeeper, because a person may undertake such a business whenever he pleases, without either capital or credit, and may never have property enough to be subject to execution. Without some statement as to capital or business, it cannot be supposed reasonably safe to give credit. The cases which have held a false statement of office or position sufficient are mainly, and so far as original authority goes are, I think, entirely cases where the character assumed involves such elements as to make it safe to trust the party from that alone. They are (sic) such instances as officers of the army and navy, government officers, and English university commoners. An officer of the army or navy is liable to punishment for any sort of dishonest conduct, and officers appointed to honorable positions are presumably reputable. Moreover, all of these have a pecuniary income which is known to every one, and the assumption of their character is a representation of their means and station. The conditions of residence in an English university make it entirely safe for a local tradesman to trust a commoner to any reasonable extent.

When the position involves in itself no trustworthiness, it seems to me the assumption of it falsely cannot be a sufficient ground by itself to convict under the statute.

People v. Summers
115 Mich. 537

Jacob L. Summers was convicted of obtaining a promissory note under false pretenses. Affirmed. . . .

MOORE, J. . . .
Complaint is made of that portion of the charge reading as follows:

"It is not every representation that is false that will amount to a false pretense within the statute, and sustain a charge of obtaining a signature to an instrument by false pretenses. It must be one calculated to deceive and induce action on the part of the one to whom it is made. A representation as to an existing fact or thing so evidently and plainly false that no one would be deceived, that no one should believe or can be induced to act upon it, cannot sustain a charge of false pretense. Formerly it was held that, to sustain a charge of false pretense with intent to deceive and cheat or defraud, the pretense must be one that is calculated to deceive and induce action on the part of a person of ordinary prudence, capacity, and intelligence; but, as I understand, that is not now the rule, and whether the representation is calculated to deceive and induce certain action may depend upon the capacity, intelligence, and learning of the person or persons to whom the statement or representation is made. And in this case you may, in judging of this question, take in consideration the education, business ability, experience, and learning of the Fischers, as shown by the evidence; and if you find that the representation charged in this count, if made, was, in view of their capacity and ability, calculated to deceive them as to the character of the paper, and did induce them to sign it, even though you should be of the opinion that a

1185

person of ordinary prudence, capacity, and intelligence ought not to be deceived by it, you may still find that the representation was calculated to and did induce them to sign the paper. It is for you to determine whether it was calculated to and did induce their signing from all the circumstances shown."

The authorities are not uniform as to just what the rule is in relation to the character of the pretense used. The trial court, in disposing of the motion for a new trial, stated the rule, as we think it now prevails, so clearly that I quote it here:

"While there are many cases supporting the contention of the respondent that, when the pretenses used are of a character such that a person of ordinary intelligence and prudence could not be deceived by it, they do not constitute false pretenses within the statute, I think the best-considered cases hold to a different doctrine. The design of the statute was to protect the weak and shield the credulous against the arts and wiles of the shrewd and designing; and the real question on this point ought to be, and under the statute and in reason is, Was the pretense designedly false, and made to induce the action claimed, and was it successful? Its success may depend upon the weakness or strength of the party played upon. Men of much good judgment and discretion are often deceived by false pretenses used by skilled and crafty confidence men, that possibly to the ordinary jury would seem ought not to deceive anybody, while much less plausibility of pretense will rapidly capture and deceive the unwary, unlearned, and inexperienced. It ought not to be the law that one may escape the penalty of a crime in deceiving the weak to their injury by false pretenses by establishing that, if the party was not so weak, he would not have succeeded in deceiving him."

We have examined the other assignments of error, but do not think it necessary to refer to them further than to say we deem them without merit. The verdict is affirmed, and cause remanded for further proceedings.

The other Justices concurred.

People v. Bird
126 Mich. 631

The respondents were arrested under a complaint and warrant charging them with a fraudulent conspiracy to obtain from one Thomas J. Curtis, by divers false pretenses, subtle means and devices, $300, and that by said false pretenses, etc., the respondents obtained from said Curtis $300. The complaint is a general one, and does not set forth the specific means by which the conspiracy was carried

out. The first count in the information is general, like
the complaint. The second count is one for false pretenses,
and sets forth the specific methods resorted to by the respondents to accomplish their object. The methods, in substance, were that the respondents represented to said Curtis
that they were the apostles of Christ; that said Curtis and
they were to be the judges of the people in that part of the
country; that the son of Curtis was to be Christ in his
second coming; that they (respondents) were sent by the Lord
to tell Curtis these things; and that the Lord required of
him to pay to them $300, to make a home for them. The re-
spondents were convicted.

GRANT, J. . . .
It is urged that the pretenses were so absurd and irrational that they do not come within the statute. This
question has been adjudicated against the contention of
the respondents in People v. Summers, 115 Mich. 537 (73 N.
W. 818), where many authorities upon the point are cited.
Mr. Curtis, from whom the respondents obtained the money,
was evidently an ignorant and weak man. It appears from
his own testimony and from other evidence that his mind
is unbalanced upon the subject of religion. The statute
is designed for the protection of such, and for the punishment of those who will take advantage of their weaknesses
to perpetrate fraud.
. . . It is next urged that, though the respondents held
peculiar views, yet that they were honest in their belief.
We agree with counsel that their views were peculiar. Whether they were honest in them was a question for the jury.
The court, in very clear language, instructed the jury that,
if they were honest in their religious belief, no matter
how misguided they might be, they could not be convicted.
The evidence is that Bird and Williams were very active in
preaching their doctrines to Mr. Curtis, that it was his
duty to give them money, and that the Lord had so directed.
We think, also, that there was evidence from which the jury
might reasonably infer that respondents Lawrence and Ray
were parties to the fraud, although they did not make direct
representations to obtain the money.
We find no error in the record, and the conviction is
affirmed.

The other Justices concurred.

People v. Henssler
48 Mich. 49

MARSTON, J. The respondent was charged with obtaining
the endorsement of Martin Kline to a promissory note by
false pretenses, and upon trial had was convicted. The
case comes here upon exceptions before judgment. . . .

1187

. . . . That if Kline endorsed the note for an unlawful
and immoral purpose, he was not within the protection of
the statute, and the respondent should be acquitted. This
objection as we understand it, under the facts in this case,
means that if the money to be obtained from a negotiation
of the note after its endorsement, was to be used by the
respondent for an unlawful or immoral purpose, and such fact
was known to the person before endorsing, there could be no
conviction. This position is based upon the theory that
the statute upon which this prosecution was founded, was
in some way intended to protect the party deceived and defrauded but not to punish the party guilty thereof. When
a crime has been committed the law seeks to punish the party
guilty thereof. The injured individual has been wronged,
and his object, motive or complicity therein may affect any
remedy that he might have against the perpetrator thereof.
In every crime there is in addition to this wrong done the
individual, also a public wrong. This the State punishes,
and except in certain trivial cases, the person injured has
no control over and cannot prevent or interfere with the
public prosecution by the State authorities. The penalty
attached to the commission of the offense charged in the
information is imposed upon public grounds, and the fact
that the party deceived or defrauded may have supposed or
known the money obtained on his endorsement would be used
for immoral or unlawful purposes would not purge the guilt
of the accused. His offense was not lessened by the fact
that he intended to put the money, when obtained, to a bad
use. . . .

As we discover no error in the record, the Recorder must
be instructed to proceed to judgment.

The other Justices concurred.

People v. Lintz
251 Mich. 367

FEAD, J. Defendants were convicted of obtaining money
from Arthur L. Loveland under false pretenses. They negotiated a trade of Loveland's house for a farm owned by
Walter Franklin. The testimony of the people was that defendants represented to Loveland that the farm was incum-
bered by a mortgage of $565, which he would have to pay to
make the trade; they said Whitesell would pay it and Loveland could reimburse him; Loveland gave them the money to
repay Whitesell; there was no mortgage on the premises, and
defendants appropriated the money to their own use. . . .

Defendants' principal point, urged to obtain a discharge
as well as reversal, is that, assuming the false representations proved, the offense was not made out because Loveland
was not defrauded. The argument is that, as he was willing
and had agreed to pay the additional $565 on the trade and

1188

Issue

he received all he had agreed to take, without being called upon to pay any greater sum, he lost nothing, even though defendants appropriated the money to themselves. It seems no less than a truism that one may be as well defrauded by being tricked into paying money to a person to whom or purpose to which he has not agreed as by being led to pay more money then he has agreed. The criminal character of the act is determined by the means used in obtaining the money. *People v. Lennox*, 106 Mich. 625.

The other errors assigned need not be discussed as they are unlikely to arise on a new trial.

Judgment is reversed, and new trial ordered.

WIEST, C. J., and BUTZEL, CLARK, McDONALD, SHARPE, and NORTH, JJ., concurred. POTTER, J., did not sit.

People v. Lennox
106 Mich. 625

GRANT, J. The gist of the crime charged in the information is that the respondent "did designedly falsely represent and pretend to said Robert B. Shank that he, the said Cornelius Lennox, had received from one Walter A. Newton a subscription of $10, with payment in full thereon by said Walter A. Newton," whereas the said Walter A. Newton had not subscribed nor paid him the $10, and had subscribed and paid to him only $1. The allegations in regard to the subscription book or paper, and that said Newton had written his name and amount therein, are merely descriptive of the means used, and of evidence to sustain the charge. The information would be perfectly good if it contained nothing about the subscription book or paper. "The defendant's knowledge of the falsity of the pretenses is material, and hence must be averred, unless the pretenses stated are of such a nature as to exclude the possible hypothesis of the defendant's ignorance of their falsity." *People v. Fitzgerald*, 92 Mich. 331, and the authorities there cited. That case was reversed because the information did not allege that the respondent knew he was not authorized by the association to collect the money for the benefit of the person named in the subscription paper. It was held that the respondent might have been ignorant of the fact that the paper he presented was a false and fraudulent statement. The present case comes clearly within the exception to the general rule stated in the above authority. The allegation of the information in this case negatives any possible hypothesis of ignorance. In *People v. Behee*, 90 Mich. 356, the information was held bad because it did not allege that Barbour was the agent of the Detroit Stove Works, from whom it was charged that the money was fraudulently obtained, and because it did not allege that the respondent knew the

1189

representations to be false. These representations were that he was authorized to collect money for a poor woman whose son was killed on the railway, and who was her only support. He might honestly have believed that he was authorized. Consequently the scienter was important and material. Had Behee been charged with falsely representing to B. that A. had subscribed and paid him $10, and obtained $5 from B. on this representation, that case would be in point. The information must be held good.

The proofs fully sustain the charge, and conclusively show that the respondent represented to Shank that Newton had subscribed and paid $10, whereas in fact he had subscribed and paid but $1. It is, however, insisted that no criminal intent necessary to the offense is shown, because the respondent used the money obtained for the purpose of establishing the school, and had purchased articles necessary to start it. What he did with the money is immaterial. The law does not sanction the obtaining of money under false pretenses, though the object to which it is devoted be meritorious. The criminal character of the act is not determined by the subsequent use of the money, but by the means used in obtaining it.

We find no error in the record, and the verdict is affirmed, and the court below directed to proceed to sentence.

The other Justices concurred.

People v. Etzler
292 Mich. 489

BUTZEL, J. Defendant was convicted of the crime of obtaining money under false pretenses. In substance, the information charged that he represented that he would sell a Dodge automobile to one Hamilton, and that defendant falsely represented that said automobile was free and clear of all incumbrances except a mortgage in the amount of $330.84 to the Farmington State Bank, in Farmington, Michigan, but in fact there was the further incumbrance of a chattel mortgage for $570.20 to the General Finance Corporation, and that by these false and fraudulent representations the complaining witness, Hamilton, was induced to part with a Ford car and the sum of $164.83 in cash.

The record shows that defendant incorporated an automobile sales business under the name of Redford Motors Sales, Inc., and became its president. It borrowed money to conduct its business and gave as security what purported to be "floor plan" mortgages on automobiles identified by motor and serial numbers to the General Finance Corporation. The automobile involved in the instant case appeared to be covered by such a chattel mortgage which was duly recorded. By its terms, the mortgagor agreed not to in-

cumber, sell, or remove the property from its place of
business without first obtaining a discharge of the mortgage. Without disclosing the existence of such document,
defendant, on behalf of his company, sold the car in question to Mr. Hamilton and, in payment therefor, the latter
turned over a used car on which he was allowed $497.17,
paid an additional sum in cash, and was to pay the additional sum of $330.84 to the Farmington State Bank. The dealer
only turned over to the finance company the $100 check given
by Hamilton, and made no further payments which would entitle it to a release of the alleged chattel mortgage. The
finance company replevied the automobile from Hamilton who
finally made a settlement by agreeing to pay the mortgagee
the sum of $361.50.

Defendant asks us to hold that mere failure to disclose
the existence of an incumbrance without an affirmative
statement in so many words that there was no incumbrance
is insufficient proof of intent to obtain money by means
of false pretenses. We cannot so rule. The false pretense
can be the failure to speak when it was necessary to do so.
If defendant sold the new automobile without revealing the
fact that it was mortgaged, he was deliberately acting a
falsehood, and such conduct is as objectionable as a spoken
falsehood. People v. Clark, 10 Mich. 310. One may make
false pretense by act as well as by word. People v. Schultz,
210 Mich. 297.

BUSHNELL, C. J., and SHARPE, POTTER, CHANDLER, NORTH,
McALLISTER, and WIEST, JJ., concurred.

Held: Conviction affirmed

People v. Widmayer
265 Mich. 547

SHARPE, J. In a written complaint, made by Frank Dendel
on the 21st day of November, 1932, to a justice of the peace,
it was alleged that the defendants on the 31st day of March,
1932, "did, with intent to cheat and defraud one Frank Dendel, designedly, by color of a false receipt, and by means
of false pretenses, to-wit: that certain lots in Grand Oakland Memorial Park purchased by said Frank Dendel would be
resold by them for him in August, 1932, for the sum of $1,200;
that they were representatives of Grand Oakland Memorial Park
and were fully informed of the values of said property and
the operations upon said property; that the Lutheran Cemetery was to be moved upon said Memorial Park in block T,
raising the value of said lot to $1,200 which they would
obtain for him in August, 1932, and many other false pretenses, and said A. F. Widmayer and E. T. Going did obtain
from said Frank Dendel money to the value of more than $50,
to-wit: of the value of $290."

The defendants were apprehended and brought before the
justice, and an examination had on December 23, 1932, after

1191

which they were bound over to the circuit court of Allegan county for trial. When arraigned on an information in which the charge was stated as in the complaint, they moved to quash it and for their discharge, upon the ground that the proofs submitted on the examination disclosed no criminal offense. The motion was denied, and by leave of this court the question is before us for adjudication.

Dendel was the only witness who was sworn on the examination. He testified that the defendants came to see him about March 1, 1932, and urged him to purchase some lots in the Grand Oakland cemetery; that he at that time owned 11 lots therein, for some of which he had paid $420; that defendants said the cemetery "had opened up the resale department;" that he did not want to sell his lots; that they stated to him "the advantages of purchasing more lots at that time. They said that the cemetery was to be moved on block T. They said the resale department would get for this lot later $1,200. They said they would get the $1,200 the 1st of August this year, 1932. . . . On March 1, 1932, I purchased another lot of them. I would not have bought the lot except for what they told me then. I would not have bought. I didn't want to buy it. That lot is not worth anything to me now. I can't sell it."

He further testified that he was 68 years of age, and had done some business during that time selling farm products; that he had made a similar complaint against one Armstrong for swindling him in the sale of cemetery lots, but settled it and withdrew the complaint; that if the defendants paid him $1,200 "it would be all right with me. That is why I started this prosecution. I was beat."

The only statements in any way tending to support the charge of obtaining the money of the complaining witness by false pretenses are:

1. That the cemetery would be moved upon block T.
2. That the lot purchased by him would be resold by August 1, 1932, and he would be paid $1,200 for it.

The first of these was clearly a representation as to a future event, and the second a promise or undertaking to do something in the future. The rule of law is well established that, to sustain a conviction, "The false pretenses must refer to some existing fact, and statements concerning what would occur in the future are not a sufficient basis for the charge." People v. Segal (syllabus), 180 Mich. 316.

See, also Biddle v. United States, 84 C.C.A. 415 (156 Fed. 759); 25 C.J. p. 589, and 11 R.C.L. p. 831.

It is apparent that the purpose of the complaining witness was not to secure a conviction under the criminal law, but to compel the defendants to pay to him the money to which he claimed to be entitled.

"It is right that men should pay their debts, and not culpable for creditors to collect by legitimate means and

1192

methods; but making merchandise of the criminal law is not a lawful method." Koons v. Vauconsant, 129 Mich. 260, 263 (95 Am. St. Rep. 438).

The testimony taken on the examination disclosed no violation of the statute, and the motion to quash the information and discharge the defendants should have been granted. An order will be here entered remanding the case, with instructions to do so.

McDONALD, C. J., and WEADOCK, POTTER, NORTH, FEAD, WIEST, and BUTZEL, JJ., concurred.

People v. Reynolds
71 Mich. 343

LONG, J. The respondent in this cause was tried and convicted in the circuit court for the county of Tuscola for obtaining a stock of drugs and groceries of one Florence L. Coy by false pretenses, and brings the case into this Court upon exceptions. . . .

The only allegations in the information showing the falsity of the pretenses are:

"Whereas, in truth and fact, the said DeElbert A. Reynolds well knew that said real-estate mortgage was not a gilt-edged mortgage," etc.

These are not allegations that the pretenses were false in fact. A false pretense was defined in a Massachusetts case to be "a representation of some fact or circumstance, calculated to mislead, which is not true." Com. v. Drew, 19 Pick. 184. This statute, like all criminal statutes, must be construed strictly, and nothing not within its words be held to be within its meaning. The most obvious proposition is that the pretense must be false (People v. Tompkins, 1 Park. Crim. R. 224); and the doctrine undoubtedly is that if it is not false, though believed to be so by the person employing it, it is insufficient. It being, therefore, necessary to prove the falsity of the pretense, it is necessary to aver it in the information. State v. De Lay, 93 Mo. 98 (5 S.W. Rep. 607). In this respect the information is fatally defective, and no conviction could be sustained under it.

The verdict and judgment of the court below must be set aside, and the respondent discharged.

The other Justices concurred.

People v. Fitzgerald
92 Mich. 328

1193

MORSE, C. J. The respondent was convicted upon the following information, and sentenced to the State prison at Jackson for the term of five years:

"STATE OF MICHIGAN,
   County of Wayne,   as:
      City of Detroit,

"The recorder's court of the city of Detroit:

"In the name of the people of the State of Michigan, Samuel W. Burroughs, prosecuting attorney in and for the said county of Wayne, who prosecutes for and on behalf of the people of said State in said court, comes now here in said court, in the November term thereof, A. D. 1891, and gives the said court here to understand and be informed that Maurice Fitzgerald, late of said city of Detroit, heretofore, to wit, on the 9th day of July, A. D. 1891, at the said city of Detroit, in the county aforesaid, with intent to cheat and defraud Joseph H. Berry and Thomas Berry, co-partners doing business under the firm name of Berry Bros., and fraudulently to obtain two dollars in money, and of the value of two dollars, did designedly and falsely represent and pretend to Joseph H. Berry, one of the members of the firm of Berry Bros., that he, the said Maurice Fitzgerald, was authorized by the Consolidated Brotherhood of Railroad Trainmen, Switchmen, and Firemen to collect money for the benefit of Mrs. Algoe, by handing said Joseph H. Berry, member of the firm of Berry Bros., as aforesaid, the following subscription list, to wit:

"'Consolidated Brotherhood of R. R. Trainmen, Switchmen, and Firemen.
"'To whom it may concern:
"'We, the B. of R. R. T., Switchmen, and Firemen, ask any sum of shippers and business men they may wish to give for the benefit of Mrs. Algoe, dependent mother of one of our switchmen, killed June 6, 1891. Mr. Frank Algoe leaves a dependent mother, and it will be appreciated by the above.
"'(Seal) BROTHERHOOD OF RAILWAY BRAKEMEN, B.O.R.R.B.'

"And believing the said false pretenses and representations so made as aforesaid by the said Maurice Fitzgerald, he, the said Joseph H. Berry, of the firm of Berry Bros., as aforesaid, was deceived thereby, and was then and there induced by means of the said false pretenses and representations, so made as aforesaid, to deliver, and did then and there deliver, two dollars in money, and of the value of two dollars, of the property of the said Berry Bros., to him, the said Maurice Fitzgerald, and the said Maurice Fitzgerald did then and there designedly, by means of the said false pretenses and representations, so made as aforesaid, unlawfully and fraudulently obtain from the said Berry Bros. two dollars in money, and of the value of two dollars, of the goods and property of the said Berry Bros., with intent then and there the said firm of Berry Bros. to cheat and

1194

defraud of the same; whereas, in truth and in fact, the said Maurice Fitzgerald was not at that time, nor at any other time, authorized by the Consolidated Brotherhood of R. R. Trainmen, Switchmen, and Firemen to collect any money for the benefit of Mrs. Algoe, or any other person, - to the great damage and deception of the said Berry Bros., and to the evil example of all others in like cases offending, contrary to the form of the statute in such case made and provided, and against the peace and dignity of the people of the State of Michigan.

"Samuel W. Burroughs
"Prosecuting Attorney."

It is contended that this information is defective under the ruling of this Court in People v. Behee, 90 Mich. 356, for the reasons stated in the brief of respondent, as follows:

"1. The information fails to allege that said Joseph H. Berry had any connection with Berry Bros., as agent or otherwise, or that he was authorized by said Berry Bros. to give money in charity or for any other purpose.
"2. It fails to allege a scienter. FRAUDULENT
"3. It fails to allege that the pretenses were false in fact." INTENT

1. The allegation that Joseph H. Berry, the person to whom the false representations were made, was a member of the copartnership of which the money was fraudulently obtained, is sufficient to meet the first objection.

2. The information is defective because of its failure to allege that respondent knew that he was not authorized by the brotherhood named to collect money for the benefit of Mrs. Algoe. The defendant stood mute, and is therefore entitled to raise the question here.

"The defendant's knowledge of the falsity of the pretenses is material, and hence must be averred, unless the pretenses stated are of such a nature as to exclude the possible hypothesis of the defendant's ignorance of their falsity." 2 Whart. Crim. Law (9 ed.), Sec. 1225; Whart. Crim. Pl. & Pr. (9th ed.), Sec. 164; State v. Smith, 8 Blackf. 489; State v. Bradley, 68 Mo. 140; People v. Behee, 90 Mich. 356; People v. Reynolds, 71 Id. 343

This case does not come within the exception to the general rule laid down by Wharton. Under our statute, where the intent is the gist of the offense, the ignorance of the defendant of the falsity of his representations would take away the fraudulent intent. It is possible, under the case stated in the information, that the defendant was ignorant of the fact that the paper he presented to Berry was a false and fraudulent statement. He might have supposed the paper genuine, and that he was authorized to collect money by virtue of it. If the proof in the case had stopped where the information does, the defendant could not have been convicted. It was necessary in order to convict him to go further, and prove that he knew that he was not authorized to collect this money.

3. The false pretense in this case was his representation that he was so authorized by the presentment of this subscription paper, which implied such authority. This pretense is alleged to be false in fact in the following language, which is sufficient:

"Whereas, in truth and in fact, the said Maurice Fitzgerald was not at that time, nor at any other time, authorized by the Consolidated Brotherhood of R. R. Trainmen, Switchmen, and Firemen to collect any money for the benefit of Mrs. Algoe, or any other person."

The judgment must be reversed, and the defendant discharged.

LONG, GRANT, and MONTGOMERY, JJ., concurred. McGRATH, J., did not sit.

People v. Bagwell
295 Mich. 412

SHARPE, J. Defendant was found guilty by a jury in the circuit court for the county of Bay upon an information charging that Cline Bagwell "On the 8th day of April in the year 1936 at the city of Bay City in said county, did with intent to defraud, obtain from Cora Brown $900 in checks and currency and 42 shares of preferred stock in the Consumers Power Company, of the value of $4,200 by falsely and fraudulently representing to Cora Brown that a net income of $1 per month was being and had been earned by each 1/7500th interest in . . . oil lease interests owned by Michigan Producers & Refiners, Inc., to-wit, et cetera.". . .

The information in this case was filed under Act No. 328, Sec. 218, Pub. Acts 1931 (Comp. Laws Supp. 1940, Sec. 17115-218, Stat. Ann. Sec. 28.415). Under this statute, the elements of the offense consist of a false representation as to a past or existing fact made with intent to defraud and resulting in the accomplished fraud. . . .

The record shows that there was evidence of the falsity of the claims made as to the earnings of the oil wells; evidence that the complaining witness made the investments because of such representation; and evidence that by reason of the investment she was defrauded. The weight of the evidence was purely a matter for the consideration of a jury.

The questions involved were properly submitted to the jury and the conviction is affirmed.

BUSHNELL, C. J., and BOYLES, CHANDLER, NORTH, McALLISTER, WIEST, and BUTZEL, JJ., concurred.

1196

McGRATH, C. J. Respondent was convicted of obtaining
money upon false pretenses. The complaint set forth that
respondent, with intent to cheat and defraud one Seig, and
fraudulently obtain from him $350, applied to Seig for a
loan of said amount, and did represent that he was the owner
of a one-half interest in two lots of land, and to induce
Seig to loan him the said $350, and to take a mortgage as
security on said lots, and with intent to cheat and defraud
said Seig, he represented that "the said lots were of the
value of $1,200, and that there was then and there and at
that time a house of the value of $1,200 on said lots, . . .
whereas, in truth and in fact, at the time the said Charles
Oscar, Jr., made the said false and fraudulent representations aforesaid, said lots were not worth the sum of $1,200,
and were not worth to exceed $100. There was not then and
there any house whatever on said lots." The warrant and
return of the justice set forth the offense in the same
language. An examination was had, and the respondent bound
over. The justice made return that –

"It appearing to me upon the examination of said Charles
Oscar, Jr., that the offense so charged in the complaint
and warrant, as aforesaid, has been committed, and that said
offense is not cognizable by a justice of the peace, and
that there is probable cause to believe the said Charles
Oscar, Jr., to be guilty of the commission thereof, I," etc.

The information charged, in addition to what is set forth
in the complaint, warrant, and return, that respondent represented –

"That the said lots were of the value of $1,200, and that
there was then and there and at that time a new house of the
value of $1,200 on said lots, and that said house was new,
and that it cost more than $1,200 to build the same."

Upon the arraignment of the respondent, his attorneys
moved to quash the information, for the reason –

1. That respondent had never had any preliminary examination of and concerning said charges in the said information,
and had never waived the same.
2. Because the original complaint charged no offense
known to the law.

The motion was overruled.
The court was right in denying the motion. The complaint
alleged, in substance, that respondent represented that there
was a house of the value of $1,200 upon the lots, whereas
there was in fact no house thereon. The complaint did set
forth an offense of which the statements alleged to have been
made by respondent respecting values, which might be regarded

as mere opinions, were not essential elements. The additional matters set up in the information, as brought out upon the examination, related to that offense, and was a part of the same transaction. People v. Annis, 13 Mich. 510. The testimony clearly tended to show that there was no house, in the sense that the word is generally used, upon the premises; that the dwelling upon the lots had been destroyed by fire some time before; that the premises were situate in a distant county, and that there was upon the lots an old building, the estimated cost of the construction of which was $30. The court instructed the jury that the representations as to value were not material allegations for the purpose of obtaining a conviction upon, and that "as to whether he made a statement of its value (referring to the value of the lots), and as to what its true value may be, is only a circumstance to be considered by you in determining the intent with which he made the other statements, - as to there being a new house upon the land, and what it cost to build it."

Complaint is made that the court instructed the jury:

"Something has been said, gentlemen, about this man having other property, and about Seig not commencing any private action to recover his money. It matters not whether respondent had any other property or not, in this case. If he made the false pretenses as claimed by the people, in the manner claimed by the people, he is guilty, if they have established it beyond a reasonable doubt. The crime charged was the false pretenses in regard to this particular property, not in regard to something else. Mr. Seig was entitled as a man and a citizen, in the reception of that mortgage, to the truth in regard to the security that was being offered. A man cannot come in at a later day, if he is guilty, and excuse his guilt or wipe it away by saying, 'I had other property; if you had chosen you could have sued me and recovered. Mr. Seig was not obliged to do that. I speak of that, gentlemen, in connection with the fact that something has been said by counsel in regard to it."

This instruction states the correct rule. Seig declined to part with his money unless its payment was secured. The offer of security, which was represented to be ample was the means employed to induce him to part with his money. As is said in Com. v. Coe, 115 Mass. 481, 502:

"The offense consists in obtaining property from another by false pretenses. The intent to defraud is the intent, by the use of such false means, to induce another to part with his possession and confide it to defendant when he would not otherwise have done so. Neither the promise to repay nor the intention to do so will deprive the false and fraudulent act in obtaining it of its criminality. The offense is complete when the property or money has been obtained by such means, and would not be purged by subsequent restoration or repayment. Evidence of ability to make the repayment is

1198

therefore immaterial and inadmissible. The possession of
the means of payment is entirely consistent with the fraud
charged. The evidence offered on this point did not touch
the question of falsity and fraud of the means by which the
loan was obtained, and was properly rejected."
The conviction is affirmed.

The other Justices concurred.

3. Final Draft - Michigan Revised Criminal Code

Committee Commentary

3. Obtaining Property by False Pretenses

The crime of obtaining property by false pretenses is also
a statutory offense made necessary because of technicalities
of common-law larceny. For larceny it was necessary that
possession be obtained; if, no matter how much fraud may have
appeared in the inducements offered, the complainant willingly parted with title, then possession went with it and the
defendant did not convert "property in the legal possession
of another." The Michigan false pretenses statute (C.L. 1948,
Sec. 750.218) is in the tradition of the statutes enacted
everywhere to compensate for the limited coverage of common-
law larceny. The chief incongruity is in the statute penalizing the obtaining of relief payments on the basis of false
representation (C.L. 1948, Sec. 400.60), which carries a different penalty than the basic statute.
Because the statutory language is comprehensive as to what
can be obtained and what is a sufficient transfer, the chief
questions for litigation have been what can be a false pretense and what the actor's intent must be. A pretense must
be material, in that it is a significant factor in the transaction (People v. McAllister, 49 Mich. 12, 12 N.W. 891 (1882))
and relates to the transaction in question (People v. Brown,
71 Mich. 296, 38 N.W. 916 (1888)). It must also be false and
must be instrumental in causing the complainant to part with
his property (People v. Wakely, 62 Mich. 297, 28 N.W. 871
(1886); Higler v. People, 44 Mich. 299, 6 N.W. 664 (1880)).
It makes no difference that the victim is unduly credulous
(People v. Bird, 126 Mich. 631, 86 N.W. 127 (1901); People
v. Summers, 115 Mich. 537, 73 N.W. 818 (1989)) or that the
property was obtained for an immoral purpose (People v. Henssler, 48 Mich. 49, 11 N.W. 804 (1882)). The gravamen of the
offense is loss of the opportunity to bargain (People v.
Lintz, 251 Mich. 367, 232 N.W. 404 (1930)), so that it does
not matter that the complainant in fact received value in
return (People v. Lennox, 106 Mich. 625, 63 N.W. 971 (1895)).
The failure to speak when it is incumbent to do so can be a
false pretense (People v. Etzler, 292 Mich. 489, 290 N.W. 879
(1940)). However, not everything can be a false pretense as

1199

a matter of law. The statement must relate to a past or existing fact, so that a statement of "law" or a statement referring to a future event cannot qualify (People v. Widmayer, 265 Mich. 547, 251 N.W. 540 (1933); People v. Reynolds, 71 Mich. 343, 38 N.W. 923 (1888)). The defendant must believe his representations to be false (People v. Fitz-Gerald, 92 Mich. 328, 52 N.W. 726 (1892)), but if contrary to his belief they are true he does not commit the crime (People v. Reynolds, 71 Mich. 343, 38 N.W. 923 (1888); cf. People v. Etzler, 292 Mich. 489, 290 N.W. 879 (1940)). Intent is of course a jury question (People v. Bagwell, 295 Mich. 412, 295 N.W. 207 (1940)). A purpose to make restitution in the future is no defense (People v. Oscar, 105 Mich. 704, 63 N.W. 971 (1895)).

The Draft changes the present law in several respects. First, it removes the technical distinctions between larceny and obtaining by bringing what is now the crime of obtaining within the ambit of Sec. 3205(2), "obtains by deception control over property of the owner." This phrase is defined in Sec. 3201(f) so as to eliminate disputes based on whether or not "title" as opposed to "possession" passed. Second, the definition of "deception" in Sec. 3201(a)(ii) turns on the impression which the offender's total activity has on the victim, and thus eliminates non-functional distinctions based on "fact" as against "law", "fact" as contrasted with "opinion", or "present of past fact" as opposed to "future events." A promise which there is no intent to perform is specifically a form of deception, though mere non-performance alone will not establish this, a position no different from that taken by courts today in both civil cases and federal mail fraud prosecutions. However, some scope is given to the jury to decide what kinds of "exaggeration" are to be tolerated in the community, since "puffing by statements unlikely to deceive ordinary persons in the group addressed" does not amount to deception (Sec. 3205(1)). Third, disparity in punishment is reduced by having the major forms of acquisitive conduct brought within a single definition and accordingly covered by a single punishment provision.

D. Appropriation of Lost Property

1. Michigan Compiled Laws (1948)

LOST GOODS AND STRAY BEASTS

434.1 Lost money or goods; notice of finding

Sec. 1. When any person shall find any lost money, or lost goods if the owner thereof be known, he shall immediately give notice thereof to such owner; if the owner thereof be unknown, and such money or goods be of the value of 3

1200

dollars or more, the finder shall, within 2 days, cause
notice thereof to be posted in 2 public places within the
township where the same were found; and shall also, within
7 days give notice thereof in writing to the township clerk
of such township and pay him 25 cents for making an entry
thereof in a book to be kept for that purpose

434.2 Same; notice by publication

Sec. 2. If the money or goods so found be of the value
of 10 dollars or more, and the owner thereof be unknown,
the finder thereof shall also, within 1 month after such
finding, cause notice thereof to be advertised in some newspaper in the same county, if one be published there, and if
not, then in some newspaper published in an adjoining county,
and continued therein for 6 successive weeks.

434.3 Taking up of animal running at large

Sec. 3. It shall be lawful for any resident freeholder
of any township in this state to take up any stray horses,
mules, or asses, by him found going at large in such township, beyond the range where such horses, mules, or asses
usually run at large; and also to take up between the first
day of November and the thirty-first day of March, any stray
neat cattle, sheep or swine, by him found going at large
therein, beyond the range where such animals usually run
at large.

434.4 Same; notice to owner, to township clerk, to county
          clerk, entry, fees

Sec. 4. Such finder shall immediately give notice thereof
to the owner of any such animal, if known to him; but if the
owner thereof be unknown, such finder shall, within 10 days,
cause notice thereof to be entered with the township clerk,
in such book as aforesaid, containing a description of the
color, age, and natural and artificial marks of such animals,
as near as may be, together with the name and residence of
such finder, and shall pay to said township clerk the sum of
50 cents for entering the same, and sending notice as hereinafter required; and the township clerk shall, immediately upon receipt of such notice make and send to the county clerk
a copy of the same, who shall, immediately upon receipt thereof, enter the same in a book to be kept by him for that purpose, and the finder shall pay to the township clerk the further sum of 25 cents, which sum shall be sent with the notice
as aforesaid to the county clerk, and the same shall be the
amount of fees said county clerk shall be entitled to receive
for his services.

434.5 Same; publication of notice

Sec. 5. If the owner of any such animal or animals shall
not, within 1 month, appear and reclaim them, and such animal

or animals taken up at the same time shall be of the value
of 10 dollars or more, the finder shall cause such notice
to be published in a newspaper in the same county, if one
be published there, and if not, then in a newspaper published in an adjoining county, and continued therein for 6 successive weeks.

434.6 Appraisal of lost goods or stray animals; filing, fees

Sec. 6. Every finder of lost goods or stray animals, of
the value of 10 dollars or more, shall, within 3 months, and
before any use shall be made thereof, procure an appraisal
of the same to be made and certified by a justice of the
peace of his township, which appraisal he shall within said
3 months, cause to be filed with the township clerk; and he
shall pay to such justice 50 cents for such appraisal and
certificate, and 6 cents for each mile necessarily traveled
by him in such service, and to the clerk 6 cents for filing
the certificate.

434.7 Lost money or goods; restitution to owner

Sec. 7. If the owner or person entitled to the possession
of any such money or goods, other than stray animals, shall
appear at any time within 1 year after such entry with the
township clerk, and make out his rights thereto, he shall
have restitution of the same, or of the value thereof, upon
his paying all the costs and charges aforesaid, together with
a reasonable compensation to the finder for keeping and taking care of the same, and for his necessary travel and expenses in the case; which charges shall, in case of disagree-
ment between the owner and finder, be determined by some
justice of the peace of the township, who shall certify the
same.

434.8 Same; remaining in finder; township entitled to one-
       half of value

Sec. 8. If no owner or person entitled to the possession
of the same shall appear in 1 year, then such lost money or
goods shall remain to the finder, he paying ½ of the value
thereof to the treasurer of the township, according to said
appraisement, after deducting from such value all the fees
and charges aforesaid, to be determined and certified by a
justice of the peace as aforesaid; and upon the neglect or
refusal to pay the said ½ of the value, the same shall be
recovered by the township treasurer, in an action of debt,
or on the case.

434.9 Stray beasts; restitution to owner

Sec. 9. If the owner or person entitled to the possession
of any such stray beast, shall appear within 6 months after
such entry with the township clerk, and shall make out his
right thereto, he shall have restitution of the same, upon

1202

paying all lawful charges as before provided in the case
of lost goods.

434.10 Same; sale; notice, finder as bidder, proceeds

Sec. 10. If such owner or person entitled to the possession of the same, shall not appear and make out his title to
the animal or animals within the said 6 months, such animal
or animals shall be sold at the request of the finder, by
any constable of the township, at public auction, upon first
giving notice thereof in writing, by posting up the same in
3 of the most public places in such township, at least 10
days before such sale, and the finder may bid therefor at
such sale, and the money arising therefrom, after deducting
all the lawful charges aforesaid, and the fees of the constable, which shall be the same as upon a sale on execution,
shall be deposited in the treasury of the township and notice
thereof shall be given by the constable making such sale, to
the township clerk, whose duty it shall be to charge the same
to the treasurer of the township.

434.11 Same; proceeds of sale, receipt by owner or township

Sec. 11. If the owner or person entitled to the possession
of any such animal, shall appear within 1 year after the entry
with the township clerk as aforesaid, and establish by his
own affidavit, or otherwise, to the satisfaction of the township treasurer, his title thereto, he shall be entitled to
receive the money so deposited in the township treasury, from
the proceeds of the sale; and if no owner or person entitled
to the possession of the same shall appear within the said
year, such money shall belong to the township.

434.12 Finder; preclusion from certain benefits; wilful
        neglect to comply, penalty

Sec. 12. If the finder of any lost money, goods, or stray
beasts, shall neglect to cause the same to be entered, advertised, or notice thereof to be posted, as directed in
this chapter, he shall be precluded from all the benefits
of this chapter, and from all claim for keeping such goods
or animals, or on account of any charges in relation thereto; and if any party shall willfully, and with fraudulent
intent to convert the same to his own use, neglect to make
such entry, or to cause the same to be advertised, as hereinbefore provided, for 30 days, he shall be deemed guilty
of a misdemeanor, and on conviction thereof shall be fined
not less than 10, nor more than 50 dollars, and in the de-
fault of the payment thereof, be imprisoned in the county
jail for a period not exceeding 90 days.

434.13 Unlawful taking of animal taken up as stray, liability

Sec. 13 If any person shall unlawfully take away any
animal, taken up as a stray pursuant to the provisions of

this chapter, without paying all the lawful charges incurred in relation to the same, he shall be liable to the finder thereof to the value of such animal, which may be recovered in an action of trespass, or on the case.

434.14 Moderate working of horses, etc., taken up; value of labor deducted from charges

Sec. 14. If any horses, mules or oxen, of sufficient age and strength, and used to work, shall be taken up under the provisions of this chapter as strays, and shall not be reclaimed by the owner within 1 month after the entry thereof with the township clerk, the person taking up the same may moderately and carefully work such horses, mules or oxen, within the township where they were so taken up; and the value of such labor shall be deducted from the charges aforesaid.

2. Definitions and Elements of the Offense

People v. Coulon
151 Mich. 200

McALVAY, J. From a conviction for the crime of larceny respondent upon a writ of error has brought his case to this court for review. He was charged with stealing $30 of the money of Allen Bryans, lost with other money, amounting to $80, at Banfield in Barry county, and which respondent had found. Respondent admitted he had found $50. This amount was returned to Bryans. The complaint was made for the larceny of the balance.

The errors assigned are all upon the charge of the court, refusals to charge, and to instructions given to the jury which returned into court after being out for a time. We will discuss the assignments of error in the order presented in respondent's brief. He asked the court, among other requests, to charge as follows:

"I instruct you, gentlemen of the jury, that if the prosecution has failed to prove to a moral certainty that the defendant in this case found eight-five (85) dollars that then regardless of any suspicions or feelings or belief that you may have, it is your duty to bring in a verdict of 'not guilty.' I further instruct you that if the prosecution has failed to prove to a moral certainty that on Christmas last the defendant conceived the fraudulent intent at the time he found the money to convert it to his own use, that it is then your duty to bring in a verdict of 'not guilty.' I instruct you further, gentlemen of the jury, that if the prosecution has failed to establish to a moral certainty that defendant conceived the fraudulent intent on Christmas, at the time of the finding of the money, to convert it to his own use, that whatever intent the defendant may have had afterwards is entirely immaterial in this case and that your verdict should be 'not guilty.'"

The court refused to give this request and we think properly. The first paragraph of the request relative to the amount of money found is admitted to have been covered by the court. Three requests are in fact combined and each of them requires the court to charge that the elements of the offense must be proved to a moral certainty. This court has never established a rule that the judge must so charge. It is only necessary that the jury should be satisfied beyond a reasonable doubt of the guilt of a person charged with a crime, and it is not necessary for the court in his charge upon that proposition to go any further.

In the general charge the court six times instructed the jury that they must be satisfied beyond a reasonable doubt as to every element of the offense charged, and, using the words of respondent's request, said:

"But in a criminal cause the burden of proof is with the people to satisfy a jury to a moral certainty and beyond a reasonable doubt before a conviction is authorized."

The material portions of the second and third paragraphs of this request, relied upon by respondent, relate to the question of criminal intent and when the same was formed. The general charge of the court also properly covered this proposition. After charging that, unless the jury were satisfied beyond a reasonable doubt that respondent found $80 as claimed, he must be acquitted; that if $50 was all that he found he was not guilty; the court continued as follows:

"Should you find from the proof and beyond a reasonable doubt that respondent found $80, or thereabouts, then you should consider whether when he picked it up, and discovered what it was, he conceived a fraudulent purpose of converting it or any part of it to his own use; that is, at that time did he form and have the intent to convert it to his own use and defraud the owner of it whoever he might be. If he did he is guilty of larceny under the statute and your verdict would be 'guilty.' If he did not, he should be acquitted by a verdict of 'not guilty.'"

The fourth and sixteenth assignments of error relate to the refusal of the court to charge as follows:

"If, having no fraudulent intent at the time he found and took possession of the money, he afterwards converted the property to his own use in derogation of the owner's right, he is not guilty of larceny because there is no wrongful taking."

In the charge already quoted the court has fixed the time explicitly when respondent must form and have the criminal intent in order to be convicted of the larceny of the money, and the language repeated in a slightly different form could

1205

not have been misunderstood by the jury. They were specifically charged that he must have conceived that intent at the time he picked up this money. "If he did he was guilty of larceny. . . . If he did not he should be acquitted." If that is the law on the subject, as is admitted by counsel on both sides, the charge is absolutely unambiguous. The giving of this request under discussion was unnecessary and its omission was without prejudice. The trial judge directed the attention of the jury to the question of intent, in view of the evidence, as to what respondent said and did at the time of the finding and afterwards. This evidence, it is claimed in respondent's brief, tends to exonerate the accused. The court evidently in his charge so treated it, but in such a way that the jury would consider all of it, and draw their conclusion from such consideration. Respondent's seventh request, which relates to the proposition that the evidence in the case must exclude every other reasonable hypothesis but guilty and that beyond a reasonable doubt, was given in substance by the court in the main charge. The eighth request was argumentative and properly refused. . . .

No prejudicial error appearing in the case, the conviction is affirmed.

GRANT, C. J., and BLAIR, MOORE, and CARPENTER, JJ., concurred.

People v. Harmon
217 Mich. 11

STONE, J. In March and April, 1920, James Harmon was engine foreman and yard conductor, and Bert F. Coe was assistant conductor in the employ of the Grand Trunk Railroad Company at Lansing, Michigan. An information was filed charging them with the larceny of 16 Fisk automobile tires of the value of $250. Mr. Harmon was tried and convicted. His case is here on exceptions before sentence.

It is the claim of the people that on February 25, 1920, Robert Scarf, shipping clerk for the Detroit branch of the Fisk Tire & Rubber Company, prepared a shipment of 32 Fisk tires, of various sizes, for the Giles Tire service of Lansing, Michigan; that these tires were arranged in 9 bales; that Mr. Scarf called up the cartage company and consigned the tires in the usual course of business to the consignee for whom they were prepared; that they were shipped over the Grand Trunk railroad. It is the further claim that the shipment was received at the Grand Trunk station in Detroit and loaded in Lansing car No. 47, and that the car arrived at Lansing, and the tires were checked out as received at Lansing in the usual manner. This date was March 7th. It is also claimed that about two days later the Giles Service Company called for these tires and it then developed that they were short 7 bales, a shortage of 25 tires. It is also

1206

claimed that on April 9, 1920, 14 new tires corresponding to
the tires shipped as above were found in the cellar of Earl
Finkbinder's home in Lansing, where they had been placed by
Mr. Harmon and later two more tires were taken off the car
of one Coe, which were with the 14 found when they first came
into the hands of the defendant James Harmon. It is claimed
these 16 tires corresponded with 16 of the tires missing in
the Giles shipment, and that no shipment of a similar lot of
16 tires, or containing 16 similar tires, was ever shipped
from the Detroit Fisk branch, and that the Detroit branch
furnishes all tires shipped in Michigan. It is admitted that
these tires were brought to Mr. Finkbinder's home by the defendant about three weeks before April 8, 1920. The claim
of the people is that Mr. Harmon and Mr. Coe stole these tires.
   The claim of the defendant is stated by his counsel as
follows:

"The evidence on behalf of respondent tends to show that
the Grand Trunk railroad owned a piece of land bordering its
tracks, some 30 or 40 rods from its freight shed. In the
southeast corner of this piece of land were some stockyards.
The balance of the land was not used by the Grand Trunk for
railroad purposes and had for the last three years been leased by the Grand Trunk to the respondent and used by the respondent as a garden spot. . . . The respondent introduced evidence
showing that one morning in the latter part of January or the
first of February, in passing from his home to his work, he
crossed his garden patch and saw some automobile tires lying
there in a hole; that these tires were partially covered with
snow so that only one or two of them showed; that he left
them there a week or ten days; that during this time nobody
removed the tires and that therefore he removed the tires from
the garden spot and put them in his garage. At the time he
put the tires in his garage his automobile was in the repair
shop. About the middle of February he returned his car to
the garage and not having room for the tires and the car, he
spoke to Finkbinder, from whom he rented the garage, about
them and Finkbinder permitted him to store them in his (Finkbinder's) cellar. The tires were in Finkbinder's cellar about
three weeks when respondent was called to the police station
where he met Detective O'Brien and was asked in reference to
the tires. He then told O'Brien about finding the tires as
herein set forth. Respondent also told Finkbinder the same
detailed statement in reference to the tires at the time they
were placed in Finkbinder's cellar. Respondent has never
claimed the tires as his own. In fact, whenever he referred
to the tires both before his arrest, at the time of his arrest, and since his arrest, he has always detailed the same
history as to the method in which the tires came into his
possession. It is true that he never advertised the tires
in the lost and found column of the papers, nor did he ever
ask the Grand Trunk if any tires had been lost by that road."

   It is the claim of defendant that there should have been a

directed verdict in his favor because there is no evidence
that any crime has been committed. This contention seems
to be principally based upon the theory that there is no
evidence that the tires were actually delivered to the Grand
Trunk Railroad Company in Detroit, and the further claim that
there is no evidence that they were actually received by the
railroad company in Lansing.

Mr. Scarf testified to the putting up of the order and that -

"When these tires were ready I called up the cartage company and the last I saw of them was when I rolled them on his
wagon at the door of the shipping department. That was February 25th. The cartage man brought back the bill of lading,
signed by the railroad company, dated the 26th or 27th. I
turned it over to the billing clerk. The shipment left our
store room the 25th and it was delivered to the railroad the
next morning, the 26th. That has the Grand Trunk railroad
stamp on it. In the nine bales that went from our company
to the cartage company there were 32 tires and these tires
cover a portion of that shipment and the bales are described
in the shipment. I have investigated all the records and
find no other loss or claim or shipment of a similar character. These 16 tires and the 7 at the Grand Trunk do not
make up the complete invoice; there are 9 tires to be recovered yet. The Detroit branch furnishes all tires used
in Michigan and they are shipped from Detroit."

Mr. Reedy testified in part:

"February 26, 1920, I received two shipments of 9 bales
of tires from the Fisk Rubber Company consigned to Giles
Tire Service, Lansing. I got my signature here where I
loaded 9 bales of tires in a special Lansing car, No. 47. . . .

"Q. You don't know anything about it except what your
records show, you don't remember anything about it do you?

"A. No, except what the records show.

"Q. And the usual thing would have been for you as checker to have turned it over to the loader and for the loader
to have put it on the truck car, wouldn't it?

"A. Yes, sir.

"Q. And that is probably what happened in this case,
isn't it?

"A. I presume. I have no personal knowledge as to whether these tires ever went on a car or not. We have a system
of tickets but I cannot tell whether I got the ticket back
or not.

"Q. So you don't know?

"A. No."

Redirect-examination by Mr. Boice:

"Our records indicate it was loaded. The handing to the
loader and loading it to the car was almost simultaneous,
all at one time. I was right there. I loaded this myself
and checked up the bills."

Later on he testified:

"I loaded this particular shipment into 47 car myself."

Homer Phillips, a checker at the station at Lansing, testified in part:

"I remember having some tires pass through my hands March 7th. I had a checking list and as the loader counted them I checked them out. The circle around the item 'Giles Tire Service, 9 Bales rubber tires' indicates that I checked 9 bales out of the car.

"Q. Does that mean that you checked out the entire 9?

"A. It indicates there was supposed to be nine in the shipment and the loader who loaded the 9 on, called 9 bales of tires and I checked it right there with the circle."

On cross-examination:

"Q. But you would stand there with this list in your hand?

"A. Certainly.

"Q. And the loader - you would have your pencil in your hand?

"A. Certainly.

"Q. And the loader would say 15 drums, you would put a ring around there, that is if he called that off, 15 drums you would check that off?

"A. Yes.

"Q. That is all you know about it, absolutely, is what he said?

"A. Certainly, that is all."

Recross-examination by Mr. Person:

"Q. You don't know how many bales there were do you?

"A. No exactly, only from what they called of course."

After this testimony was given we do not think it was a far-fetched inference that these tires were not only shipped from Detroit over the Grand Trunk, but that they were received at its warehouse in Lansing. Especially is this so as there is no question about part of this shipment finding its way to the warehouse.

Error is assigned upon the receipt of the shipping bill, the bill of lading and the checking list, but we think each of these papers was sufficiently identified to make to competent evidence. Counsel say: (sic)

"It is the claim of the respondent that the charge of the court was unfair to the respondent, argumentative as to several paragraphs and sentences; that said charge in effect amounted to a directed verdict of guilty; that the court nowhere and at no time in said charge submitted to the jury the theory of respondent's defense or the questions of fact involved therein; that in no part of the charge is the theory of the law in reference to lost articles and the rights of the finder in reference thereto explained and submitted to the jury."

Counsel preferred 11 written requests to charge. These were not given except as covered by the general charge. Many of these requests related to the rights and duties of the finder of lost property. We quote two of them:

"9. If you find that these tires were located on land on which the respondent had a lease and a right of possession and a right of use, then I charge you that the respondent had the right to remove the tires from such lands of his and that he had no duty to inquire or search for the owner in any way, and that in so removing said tires it was proper for him to store and preserve them either on his own property or by an arrangement with others, and that such storing and preserving of such property is no evidence of a larceny but is the carrying out of the honest duty of the respondent.

"10. I charge you that if the respondent found these tires on lands which he had the right to occupy, then in moving the tires from said land and preserving them at some other place, he was but acting within his rights and he had no duty to make inquiry of the Grand Trunk or anybody else as to the ownership of the tires."

Whatever may be the decisions in other commonwealths these requests to charge were not correct statements of the law in this State. See chapter 141, 2 Comp. Laws 1915, and especially sections 7446 and 7450.

The charge was a very long one. Among other statements the jury was told:

"Now, such intent, if he found them as he claims, you would have to find was formed by him at the time he first removed them, not afterwards. If his purpose in removing them from the pit, when he first found them, was to remove them from the pit and convert to his own use and deprive the owner of them permanently then he had a felonious intent. But if he removed them from the pit for the purpose of preserving them, so the owner might have them later, and later on formed the purpose of stealing them, he would not be guilty of the crime of larceny.

"Now, that may sound very fine drawn to some of your people, but that is the law, because under our statute, if the finder of property takes no steps as pointed out in the statute to give notice to the owner or to find the owner, and after finding and having the property in his possession forms the intent to convert it to his own use, he is guilty of another offense but not of larceny. . . .

"Now the mere fact that he did not report it to the police or that he did not advertise it does not make him guilty of the crime here charged, but what he did and what a person of average intelligence and right thinking would have done under the same circumstances, may be considered by you upon the

1210

question of his intent. He says he took the automobile tires and stored them, and he tells you where they were placed. What was his purpose? A man under the circumstances, here disclosed by the testimony and the respondent might take the automobile tires and store them, holding them for the owner. When he removed them from where he says he found them, what was his purpose? Was it to hold them for the owner or to deprive the owner of them and take them himself? If his purpose was to hold them for the owner and he had nothing to do with placing them in the pit where he found them, then he would not be guilty of any larceny, but if at the time he found them or at the time he removed them from the place where he found them, his purpose was to convert them to his own use and deprive the owner thereof permanently, whoever the owner might be, then he would be guilty of larceny provided you find that these tires were part of the shipment from Detroit. . . .

"He claims that the tires in court, 16 tires here were found by him on his ground in that pit, along the last of January or the first of February, 1920. Now, if he so found them, those tires are no part of the shipment made from Detroit on the 26th day of February, 1920. I am calling your attention to these matters because of the issue of fact to be decided by you from the evidence. . . . If you find that the tires here in court were in the possession of the respondent previous to their shipment from Detroit, or the time they could have reached the city of Lansing, then your verdict must be not guilty."

The case was carefully and ably tried. So far as the requests of counsel were proper to be given to the jury, they were fully covered by the general charge. The jury simply did not believe the story of the defendant.
The conviction is affirmed, and the case is remanded for further proceedings.

STEERE, C. J., and CLARK, BIRD, and SHARPE, JJ., concurred.
MOORE, WIEST, and FELLOWS, JJ., did not sit.

3. Final Draft - Michigan Revised Criminal Code

(Appropriation of Lost Property)

Sec. 3215 (1) A person commits the crime of appropriation of lost property if he obtains or exerts control over property of another which he knows to have been lost or mislaid, or to have been delivered under a mistake as to the identity of the recipient or as to the nature or amount of the property, without in either instance taking reasonable measures to discover and notify the owner.
(2) "Reasonable measures" includes but is not necessarily limited to notifying the identified owner or any peace officer.

1211

(3) Appropriation of lost property is a Class B misdemeanor.

Committee Commentary

A. Summary

   The definition of theft in Sec. 3205 eliminates any question about whether one who appropriates lost, mislaid or misdelivered property, other than under a claim of right, commits
a crime. However, though few appear to believe that this conduct should be exempt from criminal penalties, neither do many
maintain that it should be treated as ordinary theft. This
section, therefore, creates a special crime of appropriation
of lost property which is punished less heavily than theft
under Sec. 3208 and so ensures that this conduct will not fall
within Sec. 3208 by judicial construction. The burden placed
on the finder is to take reasonable measures to discover and
notify the owner, a duty already imposed by the law of property in Michigan.

B. Derivation

   The first paragraph is a modified version of Model Penal
Code Sec. 223.5. The definition of "reasonable measure" is
taken from Indiana Annotated Statutes Sec. 10-3032 (Burns 1964).

C. Relationship to Existing Law

   The criminality, if any, at common law of one who misappropriated lost or mislaid property turned again on the
technical doctrine of possession. If a man saw and picked
up property which he believed to be the identifiable but mislaid property of someone else with the intent to convert it
permanently to his own use, this was larceny, because the "possession" remained in the loser (cf. People v. Coulon, 151 Mich.
200, 114 N.W. 1013 (1908)). However, if he picked it up with
the intent to hold it for the loser, but later determined to
convert the property to his own use, it would not be larceny
because there was no "trespassory taking" (see instruction in
People v. Harmon, 217 Mich. 11, 185 N.W. 679 (1921)); the conduct might constitute a form of embezzlement depending on the
breadth of the language in the particular embezzlement statute
invoked. Michigan law, what little of it there is, appears to
have preserved these distinctions, with the additional compli-
cation that C.L. 1948, Sec. 434.1-434.12, requires finders of
goods of over a certain value to register their finding with
the township clerk (which may raise a question of the application of the statute to incorporated areas). It has been held
that compliance with the statute is a condition to "possession"
in the "finder" (People v. Harmon, 217 Mich. 11, 185 N.W. 679
(1921)).

   Though there is no Michigan authority on the matter, cases
have arisen in other jurisdictions as to whether one who

1212

receives an unintended overpayment or property concealed
unknowingly in property intended to be delivered commits larceny if he thereafter discovers the error and appropriates
the money or property to his own use. Criminality usually
is determined on the basis of whether "title", "possession"
or "mere custody" had passed, though this has been an artificial legal determination unrelated in fact to the actual
state of mind of the parties, since neither was aware of the
overpayment or presence of the concealed item at the time
the transfer of control was made. (See, e.g., Sapp v. State,
157 Fla. 605, 26 So.2d 646 (1946); Cooper v. Commonwealth,
110 Ky. 123, 60 S.W. 938 (1901); Bailey v. State, 58 Ala.
414 (1877); Commonwealth v. Hays, 14 Gray (Mass.) 62 (1859);
Rex v. Hudson (1943) K.B. 458.)

   The Draft utilizes the Model Penal Code provision covering
lost, mislaid and misdelivered property because (a) it recognizes the similarity in circumstances involved in all three
instances, a similarity that too often was obscured by the
common-law doctrines of possession in larceny, and (b) it
acknowledges in its lesser punishment provisions the difference in attitude and degree of dangerousness between the individual who decides to take advantage of unexpected opportunity to capitalize on another's error or misfortune (well
embodied in the "finders keepers, losers weepers" folk saying) and the one who deliberately preys on another's property. In the instance of misdelivered goods, the Draft will
forestall any question in cases arising in the future of whether ordinary theft or a special variety is involved. At
the same time, however, it must be recognized that People v.
Harmon, 217 Mich. 11, 185 N.W. 679 (1921), creates a special
problem because of its concern with compliance with the provisions of C.L. 1948, Sec. 434.1-434.12 covering lost of mislaid property. The Draft speaks of "reasonable measures to
discover and notify the owner," and not of "compliance with
statutes governing lost and unclaimed property." The basis
for this is that if compliance with the special Michigan
statutes is the only way in which criminality can be avoided,
the result will be strict liability in a great many instances,
for most laymen (and lawyers) are totally unaware of these
provisions. A person might take steps which would appear to
him and to a jury at a later time as imminently reasonable
but which would not amount to the registration and publication required by statute, and would therefore be criminally
responsible. Accordingly, non-compliance should not necessarily be equated with criminality; the test of reasonableness should be applied to each case as it arises. To give
the citizen a measure of guidance, however, notice to the
identified owner or to police precludes criminality. At the
same time the Revision Committee recommends, as do the drafters of the Model Penal Code (Tent. Draft No. 2, p. 86 (1954)),
that the statute on lost and unclaimed property be revised to
take account of the special coverage of the matter in the
Criminal Code itself. Since the statements in the Harmon

case verge on dictum, this legislative solution is in no way precluded.

THE MICHIGAN REVISED CRIMINAL CODE AND OFFENSES INVOLVING THEFT
14 Wayne L. Rev. 969

I
Introduction

One of the most significant changes made by the Michigan Revised Criminal Code (Proposed Code) involves the law relating to crimes against property. The proposed coverage of offenses involving theft contains comprehensive provisions prohibiting fraudulent appropriation of property.[1] The Proposed Code attempts to eliminate the inadequacies of present Michigan law while retaining its basic principles as to misappropriation. To achieve this, the proposal consolidates in one offense, theft, several traditionally distinct property crimes,[2] and incorporates new provisions to meet the failure of current statutes to reach certain misappropriations.

II
Consolidation of Larceny, Embezzlement and Obtaining Property by False Pretenses

A. Historical development

Historically, misappropriation of property has been covered by three different offenses: larceny, embezzlement and obtaining property by false pretenses. The earliest development, common law larceny, punished the taking and carrying away of personal property of another with the intent to deprive permanently.[4] Situations where the accused fraudulently appropriated property that he had possessed rightfully as a fiduciary were not within the prohibition since the wrongful act did not include a "taking."[5] Pressured by the growth of fiduciary relationships, legislatures created the crime of embezzlement to punish agents, bailees and public officers who appropriated property that had been entrusted to them.[6] Similarly, legislatures originated the crime of obtaining property by false pretenses when courts refused to find a "taking" if the misappropriated property was obtained by false representations.[7] In essence, the three offenses involve the same elements - the knowing appropriation of property by the accused, without the consent of the rightful owner and with an intent to deprive him thereof.[8]

B. Present Michigan Law

Michigan law retains the traditional distinctions between

1214

larceny, embezzlement and obtaining property by false pretenses. The rationale for these distinctions is purely historical and serves no useful purpose today.[10] Community standards do not differentiate between swindlers and other thieves since the wrongful acts committed involve similar types of conduct, involving the same kind of harm to society.[11] Professor Perkins has pointed out that such "distinctions. . . are useless handicaps from the standpoint of the administration of criminal justice."[12] These technical and antiquated distinctions have resulted in inequities both as to procedure and punishment.[13]

The conviction of thieves and swindlers is hindered by procedural technicalities evolving from these statutory distinctions, despite Michigan's limited attempts to treat crimes of misappropriation as one. By statute, an indictment for larceny may contain counts for embezzlement, larceny by conversion, larceny or obtaining property by false pretenses. The jury may convict for any of the offenses charged[14] as the prosecutor is not required to elect between them.[15] One court even held that in a trial for embezzlement it is not error for the prosecutor to refer to the defendant as a young thief, since embezzlement is the "equivalent" of larceny.[16]

Nevertheless, these attempts at synthesis have not alleviated the unfair consequences of recognizing the offenses as separate. In many instances the prosecutor may charge both larceny and embezzlement when the facts are not clear as to whether the accused had rightful possession of the property in the first instance. The jury must make this factual determination. Since a general verdict of guilty does not specify which crime has been committed,[17] the conviction may be reversed because of the purely technical distinctions between larceny, embezzlement and obtaining property by false pretenses.

Approximately thirty-five separate Michigan statutory provisions pertain to property crimes. These sections were enacted as new property interests requiring protection developed. As a result of this piecemeal evolution, a multitude of misappropriation offenses covers the same or similar behavior with substantially different penalties.[18] The general larceny statute is reinforced by provisions protecting specific property: trees, shrubs and plants; airplanes; live stock; library material; and parts of railway rolling stock.[19] Other provisions provide punishment for larceny from particular places and under certain circumstances.[20] The crime of embezzlement has multiplied to protect new methods of entrusting property. Separate provisions punish embezzlement by public officers; administrators, executors and guardians; mortgagors, vendees, and lessees; agents and servants; and warehousemen.[21] As a result, the larceny and embezzlement statutes contain a wide variety of penalties for substantially similar conduct.[22]

C. The Proposed Code

The Proposed Code attempts to eliminate the conglomeration of statutory coverage and the unwarranted distinctions of present misappropriation offenses.[25] Section 3205 is not intended to change the existing law of fraudulent appropriation; the primary purpose of this provision is to set forth a simple description of theft.[25]

Section 3205 (1) (a). The Michigan Legislature attempted to remove the distinction between larceny and embezzlement by enacting a statute establishing embezzlement as a form of larceny.[26] This statute merely blurred the line between the two offenses since judicial decisions applied it merely as a "filler" for the "no-man's land surrounding the offenses."[27] The Proposed Code would clarify this area by unifying larceny and embezzlement within a single description of theft. Section 3205 (1) (a) prohibits knowingly obtaining or exerting unauthorized control over the property of the owner thus effectively consolidating both offenses.[28] The present notion of larcenous conduct as a "taking and carrying away"[29] is reduced to a simple test of obtaining or exerting unauthorized control, while behavior consisting of exerting unauthorized control encompasses existing embezzlement prohibitions. Retention of Michigan's broad scope of proscribed acquisitional conduct is assured by the definition of "obtains or exerts unauthorized control,"[30] and the exclusion of any form of strict liability is enforced by requiring all misappropriations to be done "knowingly."[31] The Proposed Code would not require that the accused exert control over property pursuant to a specified relationship as does present embezzlement law.[32] This section simply requires the exertion of unauthorized control in any capacity, removing the problem of discovering the appropriate relationship for the relevant embezzlement statute.[33]

Section 3205 (1) (b). The existing elements of obtaining property by false pretenses are a false representation of past or existing facts[34] and a knowing intent to defraud.[35] Statements concerning what will occur in the future[36] or mere expressions of opinion[37] cannot be used as a basis for conviction. The accused must believe his representations to be false, and they must actually be so.[38] Obtaining property by false pretenses is distinct from larceny because "in larceny, the owner of the thing stolen has no intention to part with his property therein; in false pretenses, the owner does intend to part with his property . . ."[39] This distinction presents the usual punishment disparity problems.[40] Another statute covering falsely obtaining relief payments adds confusion since it prescribes a different penalty for essentially the same fraudulent behavior.[41]

Section 3205 (1) (b) is the Proposed Code's alteration of present obtaining property by false pretense offenses into the consolidated form of theft. The crime is complete when one obtains "by deception control over property of the owner."[42] A comprehensive definition of deception removes the distinctions between misrepresentations of fact, law and opinion, and eliminates the technical distinction between larceny and obtaining property by false pretenses.[43]

The Proposed Code appears to broaden existing concepts of false pretenses. By making the creation or reinforcement of a false impression the determinative aspect of deception, this section permits[44] a conviction where the deception consists of true statements. This is a desirable extension since the criminal prohibition is to deter the use of false impression, and not to regulate the technical mechanisms employed to create the impression. Deception also includes an actor's promises to perform that which he does not intend to perform or knows will not be performed.[45] As a result, breach of contract may result in theft liability. Most authorities are reluctant to subject persons engaging in such conduct to criminal sanctions for the reason that many businessmen might be convicted on little more evidence than their non-performance of a contract.[46] This fear should be alleviated by subsection (2), stating that "failure to perform standing alone is not evidence that the defendant did not intend to perform."[47]

The definition of "deception" includes conduct which establishes a false impression; no reference is made to the victim's gullibility. The Proposed Code's test is whether the victim was actually duped by the actor's conduct, not whether this conduct would deceive a man of ordinary intelligence. This is desirable since people are entitled to the protection of the criminal law even though they are not of ordinary intelligence.[48]

Presently, the mere stating of an opinion will not subject one to liability for obtaining property by false pretenses.[49] The Proposed Code has excluded from its definition of deception[50] reasonable commercial "puffing by statements unlikely to deceive ordinary persons in the group addressed"[51] and falsification with no pecuniary significance.[52] The draftsmen have recognized the possibility of injustice if courts are permitted to impose criminal liability on the basis of the assertions and implications found in today's mass advertising[53] - since, in the usual instance, mass advertising cannot be varied according to the intellectual capacity of the recipients.

Under the existing false pretense statute the crime is not committed unless "the person sought to be deceived relied thereon to his detriment."[54] Under the Proposed Code, theft evidently would retain the necessity of reliance[55] since the accused must <u>obtain control</u> over the property <u>by deceiving</u> the rightful owner.[56] This requirement is in keeping with the traditional notion that the causal connection between the harm done and the conduct of the defendant is a prime consideration in imposing criminal liability.[57]

<u>Section 3205 (1) (c)</u>. This section specifies the criminal state of mind that must accompany the conduct described in subsections (a) and (b) as an intent "to deprive the owner permanently of the property."[58] The Proposed Code requires that the fraudulent appropriation be permanent in order to

accommodate the present concept that stealing and swindling do not include conduct of a temporary nature.[59] The phrase "deprive permanently," defined in section 3201, attempts to encompass all existing misappropriation offenses.[60]

The requirement of an intent to deprive permanently is derived from larcenous crimes where it is easy to infer from the "taking."[61] Because embezzlement involves the unauthorized use of property such an intent would not be evident at the time of taking, but could, in most cases, be inferred at the time of the unauthorized use. The intent required for a conviction under existing law must be "felonious or fraudulent,"[62] with the purpose of depriving the owner of his property. Since withholding property for an extended period of time or under circumstances such that the major portion of its value, use or benefit is lost to the owner falls within the definition of "deprive . . . permanently,"[63] it would appear that the proposed intent requirement does not greatly differ from a "felonious or fraudulent" intent to deprive. The definition also covers cases where a thief obtains property and subsequently uses, conceals or abandons it knowing that the owner will probably be permanently deprived of it.[64]

One troublesome aspect of the intent requirement is that the Proposed Code does not specify whether the mental element of the crime must consist of the intent to permanently deprive the rightful owner of his property at the moment of acquisition. Presently, the imposition of the larceny sanction merely requires that the accused intend a permanent deprivation, not specifying at what point in time this intent must be proven.[65] A thief may not possess the necessary intent at the time he acquires control of the property, but may later use or deal with it intending to permanently deprive the owner of the property. The formulation of this intent at some time subsequent to the taking should be sufficient to invoke criminal sanctions, since the social harm is identical to that which occurs when the requisite intent is possessed upon acquisition. The statutory language appears to solve the problem, as section 3205 prohibits obtaining or exerting unauthorized control when accompanied by an intent to permanently deprive. The exertion of unauthorized control is a continuous activity; it can occur after the actor has obtained the property. Under this analysis, theft may consist of prohibited exertion of control subsequent to the initial acquisition if it is accompanied by an intent to deprive permanently.

III
APPROPRIATION OF LOST PROPERTY

A. Present Michigan Law

Most states, in their concern for property rights, require finders to notify a known owner or post an advertisement for an unknown owner.[66] Michigan has followed the common law requirement, that a finder is bound to hold the goods for the

1218

true owner,[67] with a property statute requiring an actor to give proper notice of the finding.[68] Failure to comply with the statute precludes a claim to the goods after the specified waiting period and may result in conviction for a misdemeanor.[69] The imposition of criminal liability for misappropriation of lost or mislaid property is usually founded on the concept of possession.[70] If the property is lost there is no possession of which the owner may be deprived.[71] When property is "mislaid" the owner is held to have constructive possession, and the finder may be convicted of larceny.[72] However, one may only be charged with larceny[73] if he intended to convert the mislaid property at the time of finding.[74] The concept of possession and the intent requirement have made difficult the imposition of criminal liability for the appropriation of lost property. Presently, there is no criminal sanction for appropriating property or money after discovering either the receipt of an unintentional overpayment or a mistaken delivery.[75]

B. The Proposed Code

The draftsmen have recognized the social desirability of protecting ownership rights in lost, mislaid or misdelivered property and in deterring those who deliberately capitalize on the misfortunes of the owner. Section 3215 creates the new crime of appropriation of lost property which is distinct from the general theft provision and imposes a separate penalty.[76] This section is aimed at punishing only those who deliberately prey upon another's property. The Proposed Code imposes a duty on a finder to take reasonable measures to discover and notify the owner when he "obtains or exerts control over property of another which he knows to have been lost or mislaid, or to have been delivered under a mistake . . ."[77] The section provides: "'(r)easonable measures' includes but is not necessarily limited to notifying the identified owner or any peace officer."[78]

As this provision imposes sanctions for a failure to take reasonable measures after the actor has found the property, his intent at the initial acquisition is no longer the primary consideration.[79] The finder will not be guilty merely because he used the property temporarily. By making the failure to act the prime factor in imposing liability, the issue of constructive possession is rendered obsolete since the Proposed Code takes no account of the manner in which the defendant obtained the property. This view is desirable since the social harm is not the original taking but the failure of the actor to restore the property to the owner.

The provision specifying the measures a finder may perform to avoid liability should never be construed as the minimum with which he must comply to satisfy the statute. The concern in People v. Harmon[80] for compliance with the lost property statute indicates that the Michigan courts may construe the language of "reasonable measures" as the statutory prescription for relieving a finder of liability. In Harmon, the defense counsel requested to have the jury charged "that he (the finder) had no duty to . . . search for the owner in any way . . . "[81] According to the court, this request was not a correct statement of the law in view of a statute requiring the defendant to advertise the lost property.[82] In light of this case, the draftsmen recommend "that the statute on lost and unclaimed property be revised to take account of the special coverage of the matter in the Criminal Code itself."[83] A minimum notification requirement would place an unreasonable burden on those who find an article of little or no value or those who take other apparently reasonable measures.[84] This section merely establishes two specific courses of action which a finder may take.[85] Other measures could be taken which, even though possibly not as effective as notifying a peace officer, would negate criminality in view of the surrounding circumstances.[86] The language of the proposed section, "includes but is not necessarily limited to notifying,"[87] is intended as a safeguard against the adoption of a blanket notification requirement.

An early draft of the Model Penal Code (Model Code) provided a positive guide for reasonableness by stating that account shall be taken of "the nature and value of the property, the expense and inconvenience borne by him . . ."[88] The Model Code further suggested "delivery of the property to the occupant of the premises or operator of the vehicle where the property was found" as a reasonable measure appropriate to many finding situations.[89] It is suggested, in view of the Proposed Code's intent to apply a flexible standard without establishing any specific measures as a minimum requirement, that this provision be added to the proposal.

Section 3215 appears adequately equipped to prevent wrongdoers from capitalizing on the errors and mistakes of others. However, there seems to be a significant difference between one who fraudulently obtains property and one who acts upon the common notion of "finders keepers, losers weepers."[90] The affirmative invasion of another's property interest seems more culpable than the retention of "fortunes" presented by chance.[91] The Proposed Code recognizes this distinction by segregating misappropriation of lost property from the consolidated forms of theft. . . .

Footnotes

1. Crimes against property involve three types of criminal conduct: damage to property, trespass and misappropriation. For offenses involving Criminal Damage to Property see Mich. Rev. Crim. Code Sec. 2701-30 (Final Draft 1967). See id. Sec. 2605=-7 for Criminal Trespass to Property.

2. Larceny, embezzlement of several different kinds, and obtaining property by false pretenses are consolidated into a single offense, theft. Id. Sec. 3205.

3. Appropriation of Lost Property, Theft of Services and

Theft by Failure to Make the Required Disposition of Funds Received or Held represent new provisions. See id. Sec. 3215, 3220, 3225.

4. See Kenny's Outlines of Criminal Law Sec. 220 (19th ed. J. Turner 1966), describing larceny as the most ancient of offenses involving dishonesty, in which the main purpose of the conduct is the enrichment of the perpetrators.

5. See 2 W. Russell, Crime 1062 (12th ed. J. Turner 1964) (embezzlement activities from common law larceny).

6. For statutory enactments see id. at 1063-64.

7. The law of larceny would not apply when the defendant's fraud induced the victim to part with title as well as possession of the property. 2 R. Anderson, Wharton's Criminal Law and Procedure Sec. 580-620 (1957).

8. Taking property from a person creates a greater danger to the person than embezzlement. Thus the distinction was made between offenses involving physical harm and those involving material harm to their victims, i.e., burglary, robbery and extortion, and misappropriation offenses. Kenny's Outlines of Criminal Law Sec. 220 (19th ed. J. Turner (1966)). See Mich. Rev. Crim. Code Sec. 3245 (Final Draft 1967) (extortion); id. Sec. 3307 (robbery).

9. See People v. Bergman, 246 Mich. 68, 224 N.W. 375 (1929) (differentiating embezzlement from larceny). Embezzlement requires the unlawful appropriation of property rightfully in the accused's possession. See United States v. Chrysler Brougham Sedan, 74 F. Supp. 970 (E.D. Mich. 1947) (differentiating larceny and obtaining property by false pretenses).

10. J. Hall, Theft, Law and Society 98 (2d ed. 1953):
For if we examine the criminal statutes of almost any state, we find that the ancient hands of the Anglo-Saxons and Normans stretch across the centuries and dominate large sections of our criminal law today. These statutes contain long lists of specifically described property, harking back to the ferae naturae concept, things affixed to the freehold, and choses in action. Thus the modern American statutes, with rare exception, are of a piece with the legislation that started as far back as the thirteenth century. They are not based upon an analysis of the entire problem but represent cumulative narrow amendments to the common law where gaps existed or developed. The present substantive criminal law is the result of historical accidents which gave rise to specific formulas, a particularistic method of legislation, and the spinning of tenuous, complicated technicalities from the plethora of case material which arose in the last two centuries.

11. Model Penal Code, App. A at 105-06 (Tent. Draft No. 1, 1953).

12. R. Perkins, Criminal Law 272 (1957).

13. The draftsmen intend to eliminate pointless procedures

and the welter of conflicting punishments by unifying the traditionally distinct offenses. Mich. Rev. Crim. Code Sec. 3205, Comment (Final Draft 1967).

14. Mich. Comp. Laws Sec. 767.69 (1948), Mich. Stat. Ann Sec. 28.1009 (1954).

15. Id.

16. People v. Sanders, 139 Mich. 442, 102 N.W. 959 (1905).

17. In People v. Stuart, 274 Mich. 246, 264 N.W. 359 (1936), the defendant was charged with having committed the crimes of embezzlement and larceny. A general verdict of guilty was held to be insufficient and the conviction was reversed.

18. To avoid the possibility of variance between pleadings, a special statute was enacted to permit conviction of any of the offenses if one is pleaded. Mich. Comp. Laws Sec. 767.60 (1948), Mich. Stat. Ann. Sec. 28.1000 (1954).

19. Mich. Comp. Laws Sec. 750.367 (1948), Mich. Stat. Ann. Sec. 28.599 (1954) (trees and plants - punished as provided in 1st larceny section); Mich. Comp. Laws Sec. 750.364 (1948), Mich. Stat. Ann. Sec. 28.596 (1954) (libraries - guilty of a misdemeanor); Mich. Comp. Laws Sec. 750.361 (1948), Mich. Stat. Ann. Sec.28.593 (1954) (railroad property - imprisment for one to two years); Mich. Comp. Laws Sec. 750.357a (1948), Mich. Stat. Ann. Sec. 28.589(1) (1954) (live stock - guilty of a felony); Mich. Comp. Laws Sec. 750.367b (1948), Mich. Stat. Ann. Sec. 28.599(2) (1954) (airplane - imprisment for not more than five years).

20. Mich. Comp. Laws Sec. 750.357 (1948), Mich. Stat. Ann. Sec. 28.589 (1954) (larceny from the person - imprisonment for not more than ten years); Mich. Comp. Laws Sec. 750.358 (1948), Mich. Stat. Ann. Sec. 28.590 (1954) (larceny from burning building - imprisonment for not more than five years or a fine of not more than $2500); Mich. Comp. Laws Sec. 750.359 (1948), Mich. Stat. Ann. Sec. 28.591 (1954) (larceny or pillaging vacant buildings or those under construction - imprisonment in the county jail for not more than one year or a fine of not more than $500); Mich. Comp. Laws Sec. 750. 365 (1948), Mich. Stat. Ann. Sec. 28.597 (1954) (larceny from wrecked railroad cars or their passengers - imprisonment in the state prison for not more than twenty years or a fine of not more than $10,000).

21. Mich. Comp. Laws Sec. 750.175 (1948), Mich. Stat. Ann. Sec. 28.372 (1962) (embezzlement by public officer - imprisonment for not more than ten years or a fine of not more than $5,000); Mich. Comp. Laws Sec. 750.177 (1948), Mich. Stat. Ann. Sec. 28.374 (1962) (embezzlement by mortgagor, vendee or lessee - imprisonment not more than two years or a fine of not more than $1,000); Mich. Comp. Laws Sec. 750.181 (1948), Mich. Stat. Ann. Sec. 28.378 (1962) (embezzlement by agent or servant - imprisonment not more than ten years or a fine of

not more then $5,000); Mich. Comp. Laws Sec. 750.182 (1948), Mich. Stat. Ann. Sec. 28.379 (1962) (embezzlement by warehouseman - guilty of a felony).

22.   Each of the sections has its own sanctions, and as a result conduct consisting of misappropriation is subject to maximum penalties ranging from two to twenty years imprisonment and $100 to $10,000 in fines.

23.   The punishment for committing theft under the Proposed Code is determined by the value of the property appropriated . Since taking from the person creates a greater danger to society, it warrants a higher penalty. If the stolen property exceeds $1,000 in value, or was taken from the person of another, the offense will be theft in the first degree. Mich. Rev. Crim. Code Sec. 3206 (Final Draft 1967). If the value of the property exceeds $250 but not $1,000, or if it was taken from a building or vehicle, the offense is theft in the second degree. Id. Sec. 3207. Property less than $250 in value and not taken from the person of another, a building or a vehicle is thieft in the third degree. Id. Sec. 3208.

24.   Id. Sec. 3205, Comment.

25.   A special section containing definitions of terms used in the substantive provisions makes possible the concise description of the crime in Sec. 3205. See id. Sec. 3201.

26.   See Mich. Comp. Laws Sec. 750.362 (1948), Mich. Stat. Ann. Sec. 28.594 (1954) (larceny by conversion or embezzlement).

27.   People v. Doe, 264 Mich. 475, 481, 250 N.W. 270 (1933).

28.   Mich. Rev. Crim. Code Sec. 3205 (1) (a) (Final Draft 1967).

29.   People v. Parsons, 105 Mich. 177, 63 N.W. 69 (1895). See also People v. Johnson, 81 Mich. 573, 45 N.W. 1119 (1890).

30.   Mich. Rev. Crim. Code Sec. 3201(f) (Final Draft 1967).

31.   Id. Sec. 305(b). "Knowingly" . A person acts knowingly with respect to conduct or to a circumstance described by a statute defining an offense when he is aware that his conduct is of that nature or that the circumstance exists."

32.   People v. Andrews, 249 Mich. 616, 229 N.W. 401 (1930); People v. Burns, 242 Mich. 345, 218 N.W. 704 (1928).

33.   The lack of property involved still excludes unauthorized credit and debtor-creditor relationships from being embezzlement. People v. Bergman, 246 Mich. 68, 224 N.W. 375 (1929) (unauthorized credit); People v. Wadsworth, 63 Mich. 500, 30 N.W. 99 (1886) (debtor-creditor relationships).

34.   People v. Bagwell, 295 Mich. 412, 295 N.W. 207 (1940).

35.   People v. Lee, 259 Mich. 355, 243 N.W. 227 (1932).

36.   People v. Widmayer, 265 Mich. 547, 251 N.W. 540 (1933).

37.   People v. Jacobs, 35 Mich. 36 (1876).

1223

38. People v. Reynolds, 71 Mich. 343, 38 N.W. 923 (1888). But cf. People v. Etzler, 292 Mich. 489, 290 N.W. 879 (1940).

39. Zink v. People, 77 N.Y. 114, 121 (1879), cited with approval in People v. Martin, 116 Mich. 446, 74 N.W. 653 (1898).

40. The maximum penalty for obtaining property by false pretenses is imprisonment for not more than ten years or a fine of not more than $5,000. Mich. Comp. Laws Sec. 750.218 (1948), Mich. Stat. Ann. Sec. 28.415 (1962). See note 20 supra for punishment of larceny.

41. Mich. Comp. Laws Sec. 400.60 (1948), Mich. Stat. Ann. Sec. 16.460 (1960) (false statement to obtain relief - if amount granted is more than $500 such person shall be guilty of a felony).

42. Mich. Rev. Crim. Code Sec. 3205(1)(b) (Final Draft 1967). Fraudulent use of credit cards is prohibited in a separate section of the Proposed Code. Id. Sec. 4045.

43. Id. Sec. 3201 (a)

44. It would be possible for one to use a combination of true statements without qualifying them which could result in the creation of a false impression.

45. Mich. Rev. Crim. Code Sec. 3205(2) (Final Draft 1967).

46. For a discussion of the reluctance to classify promises made without intention to perform as false pretenses see Chaplin v. United States, 157 F.2d 697 (D.C. Cir. 1946).

47. Mich. Rev. Crim. Code Sec. 3205(2) (Final Draft 1967).

48. See People v. Summers, 115 Mich. 537, 73 N.W. 818 (1898), which held that although a man of ordinary intelligence would not have been deceived, it may still be found from all the circumstances that the representations did induce the person to act.

49. See People v. Jacobs, 35 Mich. 36 (1876) (expression of opinion made with fraudulent intent cannot sustain a conviction).

50. Mich. Rev. Crim. Code Sec. 3201(a) (Final Draft 1967).

51. Id.

52. E.G., fraudulent assertions as to his social affiliations by a salesman to encourage a sale would be excluded under the Proposed Code. See id. Sec. 3201(a).

53. See Model Penal Code Sec. 206.2, Comment (8) at 70 (Tent. Draft No. 2, 1954), for a discussion of allowing commercial "puffing" as a reasonable compromise between no exception and an unrestricted exemption for opinions.

54. People v. Larco, 331 Mich. 420, 429, 49 N.W.2d 358, 366 (1951).

55. Mich. Rev. Crim. Code Sec. 3201(a) (Final Draft 1967).

People v. McAllister, 49 Mich. 12, 12 N.W. 891 (1882) held there could be no conviction unless the defendant knows that his representations are relied upon by the party defrauded.

56. To obtain property by deception means to use methods to induce one to part with his possession and thus, if the victim is induced he must have done so in reliance.

57. See Kenny's Outlines of Criminal Law Sec. 13 (19th ed. J. Turner 1966) (discussion of causation in the criminal law).

58. Mich. Rev. Crim. Code Sec. 3205 (1) (c) (Final Draft 1967).

59. Unauthorized use of property will not subject the user to theft liability in Michigan. See id. Sec. 3235, Comment; id. Sec. 3230 (unauthorized use of a propelled vehicle.)

60. Id. Sec. 3201 (b) states:
To "deprive . . . permanently" means:
(i) To withhold property or cause it to be withheld from a person permanently or for so extended a period or under such circumstances that the major portion of its economic value, or of use and the benefit thereof, is lost to him; or
(ii) To dispose of the property so as to make it unlikely that the owner will recover it. . . .

61. See id. Sec. 3205, Comment (the draft does not expand existing Michigan law).

62. American Life Ins. Co. v. United States Fidelity & Guar. Co., 261 Mich. 221, 246 N.W. 71 (1933).

63. Mich. Rev. Crim. Code Sec. 3201 (b) (i) (Final Draft 1967).

64. Id. Sec. 3201 (b) (i)-(ii).

65. People v. Johnson, 81 Mich. 573, 45 N.W. 1119 (1890). But cf. People v. Harmon, 217 Mich. 11, 185 N.W. 679 (1921) (defendant must intend to convert at the time of obtaining the lost property).

66. See Riesman, Possession and the Law of Finders, 52 Harv. L. Rev. 1105, 1124 (1939) (discussion of American finder statutes and case law holding finder responsible for lost property).

67. Wood v. Pierson, 45 Mich. 313, 7 N.W. 888 (1881).

68. Mich. Comp. Laws Sec. 434.12 (1948), Mich. Stat. Ann. Sec. 18.701-702 (1957) (lost money or goods, notice of findings, notice by publication).

69. Mich. Comp. Laws Sec. 434.12 (1948), Mich. Stat. Ann. Sec. 18.712 (1957).

70. See Riesman, supra note 66, at 1121. The mislayer retains constructive possession (whereas a loser does not) which implies that the mislayer has at least a subconscious knowledge of where he left the article.

71. Id.

72. The common law in America does impose criminal liability on a finder when the circumstances involve constructive possession. Id. But cf. People v. Coulon, 151 Mich. 200, 114 N.W. 1013 (1908) (no reference as to whether the property was lost or mislaid).

73. Compliance with the lost property statute establishes possession in the finder. Cf. People v. Harmon, 217 Mich. 11, 185 N.W. 679 (1921).

74. In People v. Coulon, 151 Mich. 200, 114 N.W. 1013 (1908), the court correctly instructed the jury that the finder is guilty of larceny if
    when he picked it up . . . he conceived a fraudulent purpose of converting it or any part of it to his own use; that is, at that time did he form and have the intent to convert it to his own use and defraud the owner of it whoever he might be.
Id. at 202, 114 N.W. at 1014 (emphasis added).

75. There are no Michigan cases on this type of lost property situation. However, see Sapp v. State, 157 Fla. 605, 26 So. 2d 646 (1946) (defendant accepted a mistaken overpayment intending to deprive the owner thereof); Cooper v. Commonwealth, 110 Ky. 123, 60 S.W. 938 (1901) (charging larceny of receipt of mistaken overpayment with a subsequent intent to appropriate).

76. See Mich. Rev. Crim. Code Sec. 3215, Comment (Final Draft 1967), stating that the definition of theft in Sec. 3205 eliminates any question of lost property being included within theft.

77. Id. Sec. 3215 (1).

78. Id. Sec. 3215 (2).

79. See Model Penal Code Sec. 206.5, Comment (2) (Tent Draft No. 2, 1954) (stating that the usual search for an initial fraudulent intent is largely "make believe"). However, it is arguable that his intent at the time of the finding could be considered on the issue of reasonable measures.

80. 217 Mich. 11, 185 N.W. 679 (1921) (charge that the defendant had no duty to inquire or search was refused in view of the lost property statute).

81. Id. at 17, 185 N.W. at 681.

82. Id. The court is referring to Mich. Comp. Laws Sec. 434.1-2 (1948), Mich. Stat. Ann. Sec. 18.701-702 (1957) (lost money or goods, notice of finders, notice by publication).

83. Mich. Rev. Crim. Code Sec. 3215, Comment at 233 (Final Draft 1967).

84. A minimum notification provision would be contrary to the intention of the draftsmen. See id. (stating that strict enforcement of statutes could result in strict liability since most people are unaware of these provision).

85. See id. Sec. 3215 (2).

86. See Mich. Rev. Crim. Code Sec. 3215, Comment at 233 (Final Draft 1967).

87. Id. Sec. 3215 (2)

88. Model Penal Code Sec. 206.5 (Tent. Draft No. 2, 1954). But see Model Penal Code Sec. 223.5 (Official Draft 1962).

89. Model Penal Code Sec. 206.5 (Tent. Draft No. 2, 1954). But see Model Penal Code Sec. 223.5 (Official Draft 1962).

90. Conduct under Sec. 3215 is excluded from Sec. 3205 covering the consolidated theft offenses and a lesser punishment is provided. See Mich. Rev. Crim. Code Sec. 3215 (3) (Final Draft 1967) (appropriation of lost property is a Class B misdemeanor).

91. See Frankel, Criminal Omissions: A Legal Microcosm, 11 Wayne L. Rev. 367 (1965) (discussing omissive larceny and lost or mislaid property protection).

INTERROGATORIES

1. Outline the provisions of the Michigan statutes relevant to larceny.
2. Do the Michigan statutes redefine common law larceny? What is the traditional concept of larceny?
3. What is the distinction between grand and petit larceny?
4. What were the facts, issue and holding of the court in In re Rogers? What is the meaning of the term nunc pro tunc?
5. What were the facts, issue and holding of the court in People v. Taugher? Is an actual physical taking required for larceny?
6. What were the facts, issue and holding of the court in People v. Bradovich? Does removal of goods from the place where they are found satisfy the element of taking?
7. What were the facts, issue and holding of the court in People v. Martin? What light does this case shed on the asportation requirement?
8. How does taking property by false pretenses differ from larceny?
9. What were the facts, issue and holding of the court in People v. McHugh?
10. What were the facts, issue and holding of the court in People v. Long? How is the term "owner" expanded by this decision?
11. What was the holding of the court in People v. Shaunding? What is the meaning of the term "intent to deprive permanently?"

12. What were the facts, issue and holding of the court in People v. Henry? Is this a case of mistake vitiating the required mens rea?
13. What were the facts, issue and holding of the court in People v. Williams?
14. What are the elements of larceny according to People v. Parsons?
15. Outline the provisions of Sec. 3205, 3206, 3207 and 3208, Final Draft, Mich. Rev. Crim. Code. What changes would these provisions make in the existing law of larceny?
16. Outline the provisions of the Michigan statutes relevant to embezzlement.
17. Why was it necessary to create the statutory offense of embezzlement?
18. What were the facts, issue and holding of the court in People v. Bergman? What element of embezzlement was lacking in this case?
19. What were the facts and holding of the court in People v. Burns?
20. What were the facts and holding of the court in People v. Andrews?
21. What were the facts, issue and holding of the court in People v. Belz?
22. What were the facts, issue and holding of the court in People v. Wadsworth?
23. What were the facts, issue and holding of the court in People v. Bauman? What factor defeated the charge?
24. What were the facts, issue and holding of the court in People v. Douglas? How did the defendant defeat the mens rea requirement?
25. What were the facts, issue and holding of the court in People v. Butts?
26. What were the facts, issue and holding of the court in People v. Hoefle? What prevented satisfaction of the mens rea requirement?
27. What were the facts, issue and holding of the court in People v. Dixon? Does it matter that the property was not enforcible in a civil action?
28. What were the facts, issue and holding of the court in People v. Hawkins? What was the nature of the defense?
29. What were the facts, issue and holding of the court in People v. Hanaw? Is it a defense that the defendant has a legal claim to some of the property?
30. What were the facts, issue and holding of the court in People v. Glazier? Is felonious intent an element under the applicable statute?
31. What were the facts, issue and holding of the court in People v. Gregg?
32. According to Gillespie, what are the basic elements of embezzlement?
33. Outline the provisions of the Michigan statutes relevant to the crime of false pretenses.

34. What were the facts, issue and holding of the court in People v. McAllister? Must the pretense be material?
35. What were the facts, issue and holding of the court in People v. Brown?
36. What were the facts, issue and holding of the court in People v. Wakely? Must the pretense be false in fact? Must it be instrumental in causing the complainant to part with his property?
37. What were the facts, issue and holding of the court in People v. Higler? What conditions must be met if the false pretenses are to satisfy the culpability requirement? What was the basis of the dissenting opinion?
38. What was the holding of the court in People v. Summers? Does it make any difference that the victim is unduly credulous?
39. What were the facts, issue and holding of the court in People v. Bird?
40. What were the facts, issue and holding of the court in People v. Henssler?
41. What were the facts, issue and holding of the court in People v. Lintz? What is the gravamen of the offense?
42. What were the facts, issue and holding of the court in People v. Lennox? Is it a defense that the complainant in fact received value?
43. What were the facts, issue and holding of the court in People v. Etzler? Under what conditions may silence constitute a false pretense?
44. What were the facts, issue and holding of the court in People v. Widmayer?
45. What were the facts, issue and holding of the court in People v. Reynolds?
46. What were the facts, issue and holding of the court in People v. Fitzgerald? Must the defendant believe his representations to be false?
47. What were the facts, issue and holding of the court in People v. Bagwell?
48. What were the facts, issue and holding of the court in People v. Oscar? Is intent to make restitution in the future a defense to false pretenses?
49. Outline the provisions of the Michigan statutes relevant to appropriation of lost property.
50. What were the facts, issue and holding of the court in People v. Coulon? Why is appropriation of lost property at the time of finding larceny?
51. What were the facts, issue and holding of the court in People v. Harmon? Why is an appropriation of lost property subsequent to the time of finding not considered larceny? Would such conduct constitute embezzlement? Of what significance is the registration requirement relative to the element of possession.

CHAPTER X

BURGLARY AND POSSESSION OF BURGLAR'S TOOLS

A. Burglary

   1. Michigan Compiled Laws (1948)

   Chapter XVI. BREAKING AND ENTERING

750.110 Breaking and entering

   Sec. 110. Any person who shall break and enter with intent to commit any felony, or any larceny therein, any tent, hotel, office, store, shop, warehouse, barn, granary, factory or other building, structure, boat or ship, railroad car or any private apartment in any of such buildings or any unoccupied dwelling house, shall be guilty of a felony punishable by imprisonment in the state prison not more than 10 years. Any person who breaks and enters any occupied dwelling house, with intent to commit any felony or larceny therein, shall be guilty of a felony punishable by imprisonment in the state prison for not more than 15 years. For the purpose of this section "any occupied dwelling house" includes one that does not require the physical presence of an occupant at the time of the breaking and entering but one which is habitually used as a place of abode.

As amended P.A. 1968, No. 324, Sec. 1, Eff. Nov. 15.
1968 Amendment. Added the last sentence.

750.111 Entering without breaking

   Sec. 111. Any person who, without breaking, shall enter any dwelling,house, tent, hotel, office, store, shop, warehouse, barn, granary, factory or other building, boat, ship, railroad car or structure used or kept for public or private use, or any private apartment therein, with intent to commit a felony or any larceny therein, shall be guilty of a felony punishable by imprisonment in the state prison not more than 5 years, or fined not more than $2,500.00. As amended P.A. 1964, No. 133, Sec. 1, Eff. Aug. 28.

750.112 Burglary with explosives

   Sec. 112. BURGLARY WITH EXPLOSIVES - Any person who enters any building, and for the purpose of committing any crime therein, uses or attempts to use nitro-glycerine, dynamite, gunpowder or any other high explosive, shall be guilty of a felony, punishable by imprisonment in the state prison not less than 15 years nor more than 30 years.

750.113 Coin or depository box; opening or attempting to
         open

Sec. 113. OPENING OR ATTEMPTING TO OPEN COIN BOX, ETC. -
Any person who maliciously and wilfully, by and with the aid
and use of any key, instrument, device or explosive, blows
or attempts to blow, or forces or attempts to force an entrance into any coin box, depository box or other receptacle
established and maintained for the convenience of the public,
or of any person or persons, in making payment for any article
of merchandise or service, wherein is contained any money or
thing of value, or extracts or obtains, or attempts to extract
or obtain, therefrom any such money or thing of value so deposited or contained therein, shall be guilty of a misdemeanor,
punishable by imprisonment in the county jail not more than 6
months or by a fine of not more than 250 dollars.

750.114 Breaking and entering; outside show case or counter

Sec. 114. BREAKING AND ENTERING OUTSIDE SHOW CASE, ETC. -
Any person who shall break and enter, or enter without breaking, at any time, any outside show case or other outside enclosed counter used for the display of goods, wares or merchandise, with intent to commit the crime of larceny, shall
be guilty of a misdemeanor, punishable by imprisonment in the
county jail not more than 6 months or by a fine of not more
than 250 dollars.

750.115 Same; or entering without breaking; building, tents,
         boats, railroad cars; entering public buildings
         when expressly denied

Sec. 115. Any person who shall break and enter, or shall
enter without breaking, any dwelling, house, tent, hotel,
office, store, shop, warehouse, barn, granary, factory or
other building, boat, ship, railroad car or structure used
or kept for public or private use, or any private apartment
therein, or any cottage, clubhouse, boat house, hunting or
fishing lodge, garage or the out-buildings belonging thereto, or any other structure, whether occupied or unoccupied,
without first obtaining permission to enter from the owner
or occupant, agent, or person having immediate control thereof, shall be guilty of a misdemeanor: Provided, That this
section shall not apply to entering without breaking any place
which at the time of such entry was open to the public, unless such entry has been expressly denied.
This section shall not apply in cases where the breaking
and entering or entering without breaking were committed by
a peace officer or some one under his direction in the lawful performance of his duties as such peace officer.

    2. Definitions and Elements of the Offense

                          1231

GRAVES, J. The plaintiffs were prosecuted by the same information for a joint attempt at burglary, and were convicted. The burglary was set forth as at common law, but the pleader saw fit to add that Harris was armed and Williams not armed. As we understand the record, it is now contended that, by this means, the information assumed to implead the two as having jointly attempted to commit what, if the attempt had been carried out, must have been a separate and distinct crime by each, and would not have been a single joint offense on the part of both; and the argument is drawn from the regulations in the statute which limit the penalty in case a burglar is armed, etc., to twenty years' imprisonment, and in other cases to fifteen years.

The two provisions, it is said, make two different crimes, and the information, in setting up that one party was armed and the other not, imputed an attempt by each to perpetrate a crime different from that alleged to have been attempted by the other. The point suggests several considerations into which we need not enter. It may be a question whether, where two make an attempt in concert, and one is actually armed, it will not apply to both. For the purpose of apportioning the punishment, the statute distinguishes between simple burglary and burglary when attended by certain facts which are naturally regarded as increasing its enormity. In case the perpetrator is armed with a dangerous weapon, and there is some one lawfully in the dwelling house, the penalty may be twenty years' imprisonment; but if the circumstances of aggravation are not present the imprisonment cannot exceed fifteen years. Burglary is a common law offense, and not a crime ordained by legislation; and it is a single or identical offense, as it was originally. The statute does not carve it into two. It exposes it to different grades of punishment, according as it may or may not be accompanied by the incidents specified in the statute. It may be laid according to the common law, and without referring to the facts on which the imposition of the higher penalty depends; but in such case the punishment cannot exceed the lesser penalty. The accusation will support nothing more. Where the facts are supposed to warrant it, and the higher penalty is contemplated, the crime must be described with the attending facts which justify that penalty.

The various breakings resembling burglary which have been declared criminal by the legislature, are distinguishable from the ancient offense of the common law. They owe their definition to the statute, and the statute must be consulted to ascertain their ingredients. When they are charged they must be set forth in substance, as in the statute, with all descriptive incidents, whether negative or otherwise. Koster v. People 8 Mich. 431; Byrnes v. People, 37 Mich. 515. Re-

curring to the objection in the record, and its failure on
its own theory is evident. It construes <u>Comp</u>. <u>L</u>. <u>Sec</u>. <u>7561</u>
as constituting a distinct crime composed of the facts speci-
fied therein, and denoted by being described as in the statute; and, proceeding on this foundation, the claim is put
forth that when the information said that Harris was armed,
it charged him with an attempt to commit the offense in that
section, whilst Williams was accused of an attempt to commit
the offense in the section following. The premises do not
warrant the conclusion. Pursuing the theory contended for,
the statement that Harris was armed was not enough to meet
the requirements of section 7561. The further fact that
there was some person lawfully in the house, was indispensable.

The statement that one was armed and the other not, standing alone and without the other facts belonging with it to
constitute the aggravated case described by the statute, is
wholly destitute of force. It adds nothing to the essential
charge and detracts nothing from it. It is mere surplusage,
and the legal effect of the information is to charge the parties with a joint attempt to commit a burglary punishable by
not to exceed fifteen years' imprisonment.

It is next objected that the information is bad for want
of due certainty in showing that something was done as com-
mencement of a burglary. The averment is that they "feloniously and burglariously to break and enter the said dwelling house, did insert between the upper and under sash of
an outside window of said dwelling house a certain instrument, to wit: a knife." We think this is a sufficient allegation to sustain the judgment. It embodies a charge of the
beginning of a breaking burglariously with intent to effect
a burglarious entry. The specific intent is set up, and a-
long with it and in pursuance of it the direct application
of a kind of force which common knowledge recognizes as em-
ployable for such ends.

Nothing further is necessary. The judgment is affirmed.

The other Justices concurred.

People v. Shaver
107 Mich. 562

MONTGOMERY, J. The respondent was convicted of burglary,
and brings the case here on exceptions. It is contended that
the information fails to charge any offense known to the law.
The charge, after fixing the time and place, is that the respondent, at about the hour of 1 o'clock in the night-time,
with force and arms, the dwelling house of Benjamin F. Rowson,
there situate, feloniously did break and enter, with intent
the goods and chattels of said Benjamin F. Rowson, in said
dwelling house then and there being, feloniously to steal,

1233

take, and carry away, no person then and there being, being put in fear, etc.

2 How. Stat. Sec. 9132, reads as follows:

"Every person who shall break and enter any dwelling house in the night-time, with intent to commit the crime of murder, rape, robbery, or any other felony, or larceny, or, after having entered with such intent, shall break any such dwelling house in the night-time, any person being lawfully therein, and the offender being armed with a dangerous weapon at the time of such breaking or entry, or so arming himself in such house, or making an actual assault on any person being lawfully therein, shall be punished by imprisonment in the state prison not more than twenty years."

Section 9133 as follows:

"Every person who shall break and enter any dwelling house in the night-time, with such intent as is mentioned in the preceding section, or who, having entered with such intent, shall break such dwelling house in the night-time, the offender not being armed nor arming himself in such house with a dangerous weapon, nor making any assault upon any person then being lawfully therein, shall be punished by imprisonment in the state prison not more than fifteen years."

The contention is that an information for burglary should so describe the offense as to bring it within one or the other of these sections, and that, if an attempt is made to bring it under the latter section, it is the duty of the prosecutor to aver that the accused was not armed, etc., The counsel for the people contends, on the other hand, that the statute creates no new offense, but provides for different degrees of punishment for burglary, the punishment being augmented if the offender is armed, etc., but if not armed, or if the offense is not so charged, the lesser penalty is to be inflicted, and that the offense may still be charged as at the common law. Both parties rely upon Harris v. People, 44 Mich. 305. That case was one of an attempt to commit burglary, and the question involved was whether it was necessary to describe the attempted burglary as coming within one or the other of the above-quoted sections. This was held unnecessary, and while we recognize that, as the charge was a charge of an attempt, the case is not necessarily controlling, the reasoning of the court, if followed, rules this case. Mr. Justice GRAVES, speaking for the court, said:

"Burglary is a common-law offense, and not a crime ordained by legislation; and it is a single or identical offense, as it was originally. The statute does not carve it into two. It exposes it to different grades of punishment, according as it may or may not be accompanied by the incidents specified in the statute. It may be laid according to the common law, and without referring to the facts on which the imposition of the higher penalty depends, but in such case the punishment cannot exceed the lesser penalty. The accusation will support nothing more. Where the facts are supposed to warrant it, and the higher penalty is contemplated, the crime must be described with the attending facts which justify that penalty."

It is true, this language is followed by the statement:

"The various breakings resembling burglary which have been declared criminal by the legislature are distinguishable from the ancient offense of the common law. They owe their definition to the statute, and the statute must be consulted to ascertain their ingredients. When they are charged, they must be set forth in substance as in the statute, with all descriptive incidents, whether negative or otherwise."

But the learned justice is here plainly referring to those breakings which are for the first time constituted offenses by statute, and which are not such at the common law. We think the reasoning of this case is sound, and it follows that a common-law information for burglary is still good.

It is suggested that the information is not good as a common-law information, for the reason that at the common law burglary consisted of the breaking and entering of a dwelling house in the night-time with intent to commit a felony, and that this information charges the intent to commit a larceny, which, it is said, may or may not be a felony. This objection is without force. Larceny is a common-law felony. See <u>Drennan v. People</u>, 10 <u>Mich</u>. 169. . . .

(Conviction reversed on other grounds.)

The other Justices concurred.

People v. White
153 Mich. 617

McALVAY, J. Respondent was convicted in the circuit court for Clinton county of breaking and entering in the night-time a store building not adjoining to or occupied with a dwelling house, with intent to commit the crime of larceny, being charged under section 11547, 3 <u>Comp. Laws</u>. The case is before us on exceptions before judgment. The following taken from the record will indicate what occurred upon the trial material to the question now before the court:

"To the foregoing information the respondent pleaded not guilty, and by his attorney in open court at the beginning of the trial said respondent admitted that he was guilty of the larceny of the goods in question, but denied that he was guilty of the burglary contained in the information.

"Said cause was tried in open court before a jury chosen and sworn on the 10th day of December, A.D. 1907, and upon said trial said respondent took the stand in his own behalf

1235

and testified that on or about the night in question, he, while intoxicated, walked along the street which passed in front of the store in question, and that he left said street and passed along the side of the said store building to a point about sixty feet from the said street and there saw a window of said store raised about a couple of inches so he could put his hands under the window, which window was held down by its own weight only, and that he did put his hands under the window and pushed it up far enough so that the opening would admit his body, and that he crawled through said window into the store. He also testified that he was drunk at the time, and did not before he went into the store through the window, or at the time he was going into the store through the window, have any intention of stealing anything in the store, but he admitted that after he went into the store he did steal, take and carry away a horse blanket and a fur overcoat. The respondent further testified that he and another workman had been working in and about the said store building in repairing the same on two different days a few days previous to the night in question, and that in doing their work they had occasion to and did raise this window, and the testimony in the case on behalf of the people tended to show that the window had stops or plugs for the purpose of holding the same in place, and that as far as the proprietors of the store had knowledge the window had not for a long time been opened or raised previous to the time respondent worked at repairing the building; and they had no knowledge that it was raised on that occasion, and that the proprietors of the store building in question had no knowledge that said window was opened to any extent on the night in question, and that as far as they had knowledge the window was closed completely in the usual manner prior to and at the time respondent gained entrance into the building as testified to by him. The testimony of the people showed, however, that an employe, who was deceased at the time of the trial, had charge of the room and window in question on the day preceding the entering into the building by respondent, and no person on the part of the people testified positively that the window was not open on the night in question as testified to by respondent.

"The testimony of the people was to the effect that said horse blanket and said fur overcoat were worth less than $25."

Upon the theory that such an entering as was testified to and admitted by respondent did not in law amount to a burglarious breaking and entering, his attorney presented four requests to charge the jury to the effect that respondent could not be found guilty of burglary, and that under the evidence he could be convicted of no graver offense than larceny. The court refused to charge the jury as requested, and upon the point at issue charged as follows:

"Now you will notice that the charge here in this information says that the respondent feloniously did break, and enter this building with intent to commit the crime of larceny therein. Under the evidence which is undisputed as to the material points in that regard, the court has assumed the burden and now instructs you that as to the breaking and entering the court charges you that under the evidence there was such a breaking and such an entering as satisfies the law so far as committing this offense was concerned in this case.

"In other words, the manner in which the respondent himself says that he went through the window and entered the building, the court thinks as a matter of law, and now instructs you, is a sufficient breaking and entering to constitute the crime of burglary, providing the other elements that are necessary to make up the crime are found to exist, so that you need not take up any time in the jury room in passing upon the question of breaking and entering."

The errors alleged are that the court erred in refusing to give the requests, and in charging as above quoted. The only matter for the court to determine is whether the admitted facts in the case constitute a burglarious breaking and entering.

It is insisted upon the part of the respondent that the lifting of a window which is partly open, in order to make an aperture large enough to admit the intruder, is not a breaking. Several eminent text-writers and decisions of courts of other States are cited in support of this contention. The tendency of the courts of late has been to hold that but the slightest force is necessary to constitute a breaking. For example: pushing open a closed door; opening a screen door which is held by its springs, the door of the house being open; removing a screen; entering through an unfastened transom which hung in place by its own weight; entering a mill through a hole cut for the purpose of allowing a belt to run, by pushing aside the belt; entering a mill house through a small hole under the sill; taking goods from a building by thrusting the arm through an opening either made or enlarged for the purpose; entering a house by coming down through the chimney; lifting a cellar door; raising the sash of a window, shut down close, but not fastened; pulling down an upper sash; all have been held to be a sufficient burglarious breaking.

In this State the same tendency appears. It was held that the removal of an iron cellar-window grating was a breaking within the statute (People v. Nolan, 22 Mich. 229); also pushing open a closed but unfastened transom swinging horizontally on its hinges (Dennis v. People, 27 Mich. 151). It was held that the fact that a respondent slightly raised a window in the daytime, so that the bolts which fastened it down would not be effectual, would not divest his subsequent breaking and entering through the window in the nighttime of the character of burglary. People v. Dupree, 98 Mich. 26.

Respondent urges that because this window was raised two

inches there was no "breaking," but admits in his brief
that had the window been closed and he had raised it, although it was not fastened and it was necessary to overcome but its weight, it would have constituted a "breaking." As stated above, such reasoning is supported by
respectable authority. This, however, does not appeal to
our judgment as sound reasoning. We think the rule adopted
in the instances above quoted is a reasonable one. It is,
in effect, that if any force at all is necessary to effect
an entrance into a building, through any place of ingress,
usual or unusual, whether open, partly open or closed, such
entrance is a breaking sufficient in law to constitute burglary, if the other elements of the offense are present. We
think such holding is in harmony with Dennis v. People, and
People v. Dupree, supra.

A recent Tennessee case is exactly in point. The respondent entered a house in the night-time through a window
found partially raised from the bottom, which he opened
sufficiently to admit his person. In this case the court
considers many of the instances referred to in this opinion,
and cites the cases. The opinion concludes:

"It seems to us a useless refinement to hold that the
various instances above cited are sufficient evidence of
breaking, and that the further raising of a window partly
open is not sufficient evidence, when the opening in the
window is enlarged by the person entering so as to make the
aperture sufficient to admit his body. Here is a material
change of the status, and the change is accomplished by the
application of force." Claiborne v. State, 113 Tenn. 261
(68 L.R.A. 859), and cases cited.

The circuit was not in error in holding the acts of respondent a sufficient breaking and entering. The conviction is affirmed. The cause will be remanded to the court
below for the entry of a judgment in accordance with the
verdict, and respondent will be brought before that court
for sentence.

OSTRANDER, HOOKER, MOORE, and CARPENTER, JJ., concurred.

People v. Griffith
133 Mich. 607

MOORE, J. Respondent was convicted of the offense of
burglary. He was sentenced for four years to prison. His
counsel, in their brief, say:

"But one question is presented by this record, and that
is this: Since the taking effect of Act No. 34, Pub. Acts
1899, can one who is guilty of breaking and entering the
barn of another in the night-time, intending to steal therein, be informed against and convicted, over objection, of

burglary of that other's dwelling house?"

It is their claim "that the act of 1899 has restricted the common-law offense of burglary to the breaking and entering in the night-time of the actual dwelling house of another, with felonious intent," etc., and that the trial, conviction, and sentence of the respondent cannot be sustained.

The respondent was convicted under an information which charged him with having in the night-time of October 25, 1902, feloniously and burglariously broken and entered the dwelling house of one Warren, with intent to commit the crime of larceny therein. The testimony showed respondent broke into a barn at the time alleged in the information, and stole therefrom several bags of beans. This barn was within an inclosure which surrounded the dwelling house of Mr. Warren as well as his barn. The enactment of the law of 1899 did not do away with the common-law offense of burglary. The principles involved are fully discussed in Harris v. People, 44 Mich. 305 (6 N.W. 677), and People v. Shaver, 107 Mich. 562 (65 N.W. 538), and it is sufficient to refer to them.

The judgment is affirmed.

The other Justices concurred.

People v. Evans
150 Mich. 443

BLAIR, J. Respondent was charged with and convicted of the offense of burglary. The alleged crime was committed on the night of December 31, 1906, by breaking and entering a corncrib and chicken house upon the farm of one Morris Scofield, who was the complaining witness. The door of the corncrib was fastened with a strap hasp and staple. The door on the chicken coop was fastened by a stick braced against it on the outside. In accordance with his custom, Mr. Scofield was not living in his dwelling house on the farm at the time in question, but was living in the city of Benton Harbor, where he resided during the winter months. He went to the farm nearly every day to feed the stock and take care of it, but hired one Groves to feed and take care of the stock on Christmas Day, 1906, and New Years Day, 1907. Groves and his wife lived in a tenant house upon this same farm, some 20 or 25 rods from Scofield's dwelling house, and had worked for Scofield by the day during the fall of 1906, but quit working for him regularly when he moved into town, about November 25th.

"After that he helped me a day or two or three hauling in corn fodder. After he quit working he did not work for me at all except occasionally he did my chores, I think, once or twice. On New Years Day and Christmas I did not go

1239

to the farm and Groves did my chores on those two days. I hired him to do it. . . . I authorized Groves to feed the chickens and horses and cows on the farm on New Years and also Christmas but I never told him to feed them any other time, only on these two days. Groves paid no rent for the tenement house and I paid Groves money for doing the chores on Christmas and New Years. I went out to the farm every day except New Years and Christmas."

Groves pleaded guilty to the offense of burglary and testified in behalf of the people. Among other things he testified:

"I was in Scofield's employ at the time. After the fall work was done he wanted me to do chores for him and I did so. I would take care of his stock. . . . I was authorized by Mr. Scofield to supervise things in general when he was not there. I looked after the stock, horses and chickens. At that time I was his hired man and lived in the tenant house."

On the night of December 31st, respondent went to the house of Groves with a team and wagon, and he, Groves, and two other men went to the corncrib; some one of the four unfastened and opened the door, and a quantity of corn was taken and afterwards carried to Benton Harbor and disposed of. The next day respondent returned to the place and certain chickens were taken from the chicken coop.

Respondent was sworn and testified in his own behalf that he had nothing to do with the actual taking of the corn and chickens other than transporting them in his wagon and that what he did was at the request of Groves, believing in good faith that Groves had a lawful right to take and dispose of the property; that the corn was sold by Groves, who took the money and gave respondent $2 for the use of his team and services; that the chickens were sold by respondent for $4.88, which money he gave to Groves. He also testified that Groves told him that he had charge of the premises and was Scofield's hired man. . . .

The assignments of error argued in the brief of respondent's counsel are:

1. That the court erred in charging that "under the evidence in this case, there was a breaking, that is, by some one, some of the four parties who are named."

It is contended that –

"Since breaking is the essential element of the offense, it must be left with the jury to say from the evidence whether the people have proven this essential element beyond all reasonable doubt and to a moral certainty. It is a question of fact for the jury; not a question of law for the court."

The entire paragraph, in which the expression complained of is, is (sic) as follows:

1240

"The word 'breaking,' too, has a technical meaning in the law. It does not necessarily mean to break a lock. Unfastening anything which has been fastened will constitute a breaking under the law. Where anything is shown to be shut up, no matter how, or fastened, if it is opened by another person or unfastened, that constitutes a breaking within the meaning of the law, and so, under the evidence in this case, there was a breaking, that is, by some one, some of the four parties who are named."

While it is true that the breaking which constitutes an essential element of the offense of burglary must have been with a felonious intent, we think the jury must be presumed to have understood from this paragraph of the charge, taken in connection with the remainder of the charge, that all that the court meant to have them understand as having been proved in the case was that the opening of the doors, which was undisputed, was sufficient to constitute an actual breaking, and, so understood, the charge is not subject to criticism.

The contentions of the respondent were fairly submitted to the jury, and they were instructed that if Mr. Groves had the oversight and charge of the premises, and had a right to enter the corncrib and chicken coop, there was no burglary committed in the case, and, further, if they should find that respondent had good reason to believe that Groves had charge of the property, and could dispose of it as he pleased, in that event respondent would not be guilty of burglary nor larceny either. . . .

The judgment is affirmed.

McALVAY, C. J., and CARPENTER, Grant, and MOORE, JJ., concurred.

People v. Huffman
315 Mich. 134

STARR, J. On jury trial defendant was convicted under an information containing two counts, the first of which charged him with feloniously breaking and entering a store building in the nighttime with intent to commit larceny in violation of section 110 of the penal code, and the second count of which charged him with larceny from the store building in violation of section 360 of the penal code. The jury returned a general verdict of "guilty as charged" but did not specify under which count or of which offense he was convicted. The trial judge sentenced him to prison for a minimum of 5 and a maximum of 15 years but did not specify on which count or for which offense the sentence was imposed. Having obtained leave, he appealed. Subsequent to filing his claim of appeal, defendant moved for leave to file a delayed motion for a new trial on the ground that the general

1241

verdict of "guilty as charged" was invalid and that his sentence under this verdict was void. This motion was denied by the trial court.

No question is raised as to the weight of the evidence, and it was stipulated that the testimony be omitted from the record. It was also stipulated that the evidence submitted to the jury was sufficient to justify defendant's conviction under either or both of the counts; that the two offenses charged related to, and arose out of, the same transaction; and that no motion was made to compel the prosecution to elect between counts. No question is raised regarding misjoinder or duplicity of counts.

The principal question presented is whether or not the trial judge erred in receiving a general verdict of "guilty as charged." The statutory penalty for the offense charged in the first count is imprisonment for not more than 15 years (penal code, Sec. 110), and the penalty for the offense charged in the second count is imprisonment for not more than four years or a fine of not more than $2,000 or both (penal code, Sec. 503). It should be noted that the minimum sentence of five years imposed by the trial court exceeded the maximum sentence of four years provided by statute for the offense charged in the second count.

Defendant contends that each count of the information charged a separate and distinct felony; that the penalty for each offense was different; and that the trial court erred in accepting a general verdict of "guilty as charged." In 1 Gillespie's Michigan Criminal Law & Procedure, p. 676, Sec. 568, it is stated:

"Where an information contains more than one count charging different offenses, the verdict must point out the offense of which the defendant is found guilty, and a general verdict of guilty is void and requires a new trial."

In the case of People v. Stuart, 274 Mich. 246, the information charged defendant in separate counts with having committed the statutory offenses of embezzlement and larceny. Upon trial without a jury the circuit judge entered a verdict of "guilty as charged." On appeal defendant contended that he was charged with two separate and distinct offenses and that the record did not disclose of which offense he was convicted. The offense of embezzlement was punishable by a maximum sentence of 10 years, while the offense of larceny was punishable by a maximum of five years. In vacating the judgment and sentence and granting a new trial, we said (p. 248):

"The essential elements of these two statutory offenses are different. It is a matter of right that defendant should have knowledge and have a proper record made of the exact offense of which he was convicted. . . . The general determination of the trial court that defendant was 'guilty as charged' was no more than a general verdict.

"'A general verdict of guilty, without specifying the

count or offense on which it is founded, is invalid where there are several counts, each of which charges a separate and distinct offense, of a nature and character radically different from that in the other counts, and having no necessary connection.' 16 C. J. p. 1105." . . .

In the present case it is clear that the offense of breaking and entering a store building in the night-time with intent to commit larceny, as charged in the first count of the information, is a separate and distinct offense from that of larceny from a store building, as charged in the second count. As said in People v. Stuart, supra, "The essential elements of these two statutory offenses are different." Furthermore, the evidence required to establish the offense charged in the first count is substantially different from that required to establish the offense charged in the second count. The two counts were not framed and used as different methods of charging separate, distinct, and inconsistent offenses, and it should be borne in mind that the statutory penalties for these offenses are substantially different.

Although it was stipulated that the evidence justified defendant's conviction under either or both of the counts in the information, we, nevertheless, hold to our established rule that it was error to receive a general verdict of guilty when the two offenses charged were separate, distinct, and different in character, required substantially different evidence to establish them, and were punishable by different statutory penalties.

The jury's general verdict did not indicate under which count defendant was convicted or of what offense he was found guilty. The trial court imposed only one sentence and did not indicate for which offense it was imposed. If the sentence imposed related to the offense of larceny charged in the second count, it was void because it exceeded the maximum statutory penalty for that offense. Defendant was entitled to know of what offense he was found guilty and for what offense he was sentenced. People v. Stuart, supra. The jury's general verdict of "guilty as charged" and the court's sentence did not furnish him with this information. . . .

We conclude that the jury verdict in the present case was void. This does not entitle defendant to a discharge, but necessitates a new trial. People v. Little, 305 Mich. 482; 1 Gillespie's Michigan Criminal Law & Procedure, p. 676, Sec. 568.

The judgment of conviction is reversed, the sentence is vacated and a new trial granted.

BUTZEL, C. J., and CARR, SHARPE, BOYLES, REID, and NORTH, JJ., concurred. BUSHNELL, J., took no part in the decision of this case.

People v. Williams
368 Mich. 494

(For the opinion in this case see page 1132, supra.)

(Definition of Terms)

Sec. 2601. The following definitions are applicable to this chapter:

(a) "Building", in addition to its ordinary meaning, includes any structure, vehicle, railway car, aircraft, or watercraft used for lodging of persons therein or for carrying on business; each unit of a building consisting of two or more units separately secured or occupied is a separate building.

(b) "Dwelling" means a building which is used or usually used by a person for lodging.

(c) "Enter or remain unlawfully". A person "enters or remains unlawfully" in or upon premises when he is not licensed, invited, or otherwise privileged to do so. A person who, regardless of his intent, enters or remains in or upon premises which are at the time open to the public does so with license and privilege unless he defies a lawful order not to enter or remain, personally communicated to him by the owner of the premises or some other authorized person. A license or privilege to enter or remain in a building which is only partly open to the public is not a license or privilege to enter or remain in that part of the building which is not open to the public. A person who enters or remains upon unimproved and apparently unused land, which is neither fenced nor otherwise enclosed in a manner designed to exclude intruders, does so with license and privilege unless notice against trespass is personally communicated to him by the owner of the land or some other authorized person, or unless notice is given by posting in a conspicuous manner.

(d) "Premises" includes any building, as defined in subparagraph (a) and any real property.

Committee Commentary

The section is adapted from New York Revised Penal Law Sec. 140.00. The significance of the several definitions is discussed in the context of the sections which follow in Chapter 26.

(Burglary in the First Degree)

Sec. 2610. (1) A person commits the crime of burglary in the first degree if he knowingly enters or remains unlawfully in a dwelling with intent to commit therein a crime against a person or property, and if, in effecting entry or while in the dwelling or in immediate flight therefrom, he or another participant in the crime is armed with explosives or a deadly weapon.

(2) Burglary in the first degree is a Class A felony.

Committee Commentary

The section is based on New York Revised Penal Law Sec. 140.30. Its relationship to existing law is discussed in the Commentary to Sec. 2610 to 2612 below.

(Burglary in the Second Degree)

Sec. 2611. (1) A person commits the crime of burglary in the second degree if he knowingly enters or remains unlawfully in a building with intent to commit therein a crime against a person or property, and if either:

(a) In effecting entry or while in the building or in immediate flight therefrom, he or another participant in the crime is armed with explosives or a deadly weapon; or

(b) The building is a dwelling and he enters or remains unlawfully therein.

(2) Burglary in the second degree is a Class B felony.

Committee Commentary

The section is adapted from New York Revised Penal Law Sec. 140.25. Its relationship to existing law is discussed in the Commentary to Sec. 2610 to 2612 below.

(Burglary in the Third Degree)

Sec. 2612. (1) A person commits the crime of burglary in the third degree if he knowingly enters or remains unlawfully in a building with intent to commit therein a crime against a person or property.

(2) Burglary in the third degree is a Class C felony.

Committee Commentary

The section is based on New York Revised Penal Law Sec. 140.20. Its relationship to existing law is discussed in the Commentary to Sec. 2610 to 2612 below.

Committee Commentary to Sec. 2610 to 2612

Relationship to Existing Law

Common-law burglary is defined as the breaking and entering of a dwelling house in the nighttime with intent to commit a felony within (People v. Shaver, 107 Mich. 562, 65 N.W. 538 (1895)). A "breaking" was any act or use of force necessary to effect an entrance into a building (People v. White, 153 Mich. 617, 117 N.W. 161 (1908)). A dwelling house comprehended any building within the curtilage, which included adjacent outbuildings (People v. Griffith, 133 Mich. 706, 95 N.W. 719 (1903)). Both the breaking and the entry had to be without consent or a claim of right (People v. Evans, 150 Mich.

443, 114 N.W. 223 (1907)). The burglary constituted a completely separate offense from any crime actually committed after entry was gained to the building (People v. Huffman, 315 Mich. 134, 23 N.W.2d 236 (1946)).

Michigan has long had statutory coverage under the heading of "breaking and entering". This legislation has been considered not to abrogate common-law burglary, which still in form exists (People v. Griffith, 133 Mich. 706, 95 N.W. 719 (1903); People v. Harris, 44 Mich. 305, 6 N.W. 677 (1880)), but modern prosecutions appear to be laid exclusively under the statutes.

The two primary statutes are breaking and entering with intent to commit a felony or larceny (C.L. 1948, Sec. 750.110), and entering without breaking for a like purpose (C.L. 1948, Sec. 750.111). The two sections eliminate certain restrictions inherent in common-law burglary. Under 1964 amendments, the time of the criminal act is not legally significant. Nor is the crime any longer limited to dwelling houses; C.L. 1948, Sec. 750.110 applies to "any tent, hotel, office, store, shop, warehouse, barn, granary, factory or other building, structure, boat or ship, railroad car of any private apartment in such buildings or any unoccupied dwelling house". If the dwelling house is occupied, the maximum penalty increases from 10 to 15 years. In C.L. 1948, Sec. 750.111, the coverage is "any dwelling, house, tent, hotel, office, store, shop, warehouse, barn, granary, factory or other building, boat, ship, railroad car or structure used or kept for public or private use, or any private apartment therein". The apparent legislative purpose is to eliminate all distinctions based on the nature of the structure (cf. the interpretation of the term "building" in the larceny from the building statute, in People v. Williams, 368 Mich. 494, 118 N.W.2d 391 (1962)). The element of breaking, however, continues to have significance, because breaking and entering brings a maximum of 10 or 15 years, while entry alone carries a maximum of 5 years only.

There are certain other related statutes. The section entitled "burglary with explosives" (C.L. 1948, Sec. 750.112), punishes with a 15 to 30 year term entry followed by use of explosives to commit a crime inside the premises. Opening or attempting to open a coin box or other receptacle is a misdemeanor (C.L. 1948, Sec. 750.113). So is breaking and entering an outside showcase (C.L. 1948, Sec. 750.114; cf. People v. Williams, 368 Mich. 494, 118 N.W. 2d 391 (1962)). Finally, breaking and entering, or entering without breaking, various structures without first obtaining permission is a misdemeanor (C.L. 1948, Sec. 750.115).

Sections 2610-2612 retain some features of the present statutes and reject others. The basic activity is the same as that in the sections on criminal trespass (Sec. 2605-2607), a knowing entry into or remaining on premises under circumstances in which this is unlawful. Two factors set burglary apart from criminal trespass, however. One is the

1246

fact that the entry or failure to leave is motivated by the intent to commit a crime on the property against a person or property. This limitation is intended to prevent the commission of a minor regulatory statute escalating what is otherwise criminal trespass to the felony level. The second is the limitation that entry must be in a building, as defined in Sec. 2601 (a). This is all that is embodied in Sec. 2612 (burglary in the third degree).

Section 2611, burglary in the second degree, incorporates the basic definition of burglary in Sec. 2612, but aggravates it if a criminal participant is armed with explosives or with a deadly weapon, as defined in Sec. 135(k). This accomplishes in part the purpose of the present statute defining burglary with explosives (C.L. 1948, Sec. 750.112), and in part recognizes the special danger to occupants of the building when the defendant or an accomplice is armed. A second alternative aggravating factor is that the building is a dwelling as defined in Sec. 2601 (b).

Section 2610 builds further on the aggravating elements in Sec. 2611 (1) (b); increased penalties flow from the fact that in a dwelling the defendant or an accomplice is armed with explosives or a deadly weapon. It thus combines both the elements that are stated in the alternative in Sec. 2611.

The Draft does not follow the New York pattern of aggravating burglary when physical injury is inflicted on a person within the building. Intentionally or recklessly inflicting serious physical injury constitutes assault in the first degree under Sec. 2101 (1) (d). There seems to be no reason to take account of the same circumstances to aggravate burglary also. It is even more incongruous to punish accidental or negligent infliction of serious physical injury, or any infliction of any physical injury, more severely than intentionally or recklessly inflicting serious physical injury; this is the result under the New York Revised Penal Law because first-degree burglary is more severely punished than first-degree assault.

It is evident that the primary function of burglary as a criminal law concept is to serve as a crystallized doctrine of attempt. The attempt provisions of the Draft cure many of the difficulties traditionally encountered in utilizing common-law attempt; burglary, therefore, might be eliminated completely. However, burglary, or in Michigan terminology, breaking and entering, is so firmly a part of our law that it is probably unrealistic to eliminate it. The drafters of the Model Penal Code sum up the problem thus:

"If we were writing on a clean slate, the best solution might be to eliminate burglary as a distinct offense . . . But we are not writing on a clean slate. Centuries of history and a deeply embedded Anglo-American conception like burglary cannot easily be discarded. The needed reform must therefore take the direction of narrowing the offense to something like the distinctive situation for which it

was originally devised: invasion of premises under circumstances specially likely to terrorize occupants." (Tent.
Draft No. 11, p. 57 (1960))

Burglary is therefore continued in the present Draft.

B. Possession of Burglar's Tools

   1. Michigan Compiled Laws (1948)

750.116 Burglar's tools, possession

   Sec. 116. POSSESSION OF BURGLAR'S TOOLS - Any person
who shall knowingly have in his possession any nitroglycerine, or other explosive, thermite, engine, machine,
tool or implement, device, chemical or substance, adapted
and designed for cutting or burning through, forcing or
breaking open any building, room, vault, safe or other depository, in order to steal therefrom any money or other
property, knowing the same to be adapted and designed for
the purpose aforesaid, with intent to use or employ the
same for the purpose aforesaid, shall be guilty of a felony,
punishable by imprisonment in the state prison not more
than 10 years.

   2. Definition and Elements of the Offense

People v. Jefferson
161 Mich. 621

   George Jefferson was convicted of having skeleton keys
in his possession, and sentenced to imprisonment for not
less than five nor more than ten years in the State prison
at Jackson. Affirmed.

   HOOKER, J. The defendant has appealed from a conviction,
based on section 11589, 3 Comp. Laws, which provides that:

   "Every person who shall knowingly have in his possession,
any engine, machine, tool or implement, adapted and designed for cutting through, forcing or breaking open any building, room, vault, safe or other depository, in order to steal
therefrom any money or other property, knowing the same to
be adapted and designed for the purpose aforesaid, with intent to use or employ the same, for the purpose aforesaid,
shall be, on conviction thereof, punished by imprisonment
in the State prison not more than ten years, or by imprisonment in the county jail not more than one year, or a fine
not exceeding one thousand dollars, or both such fine and
imprisonment, at the discretion of the court."

Numerous errors were assigned, most of which will be disregarded, for two reasons, viz:

(1) Noncompliance with Sup. Ct. Rule 40, which requires that the brief of appellant "shall contain a clear and concise statement of the . . . errors upon which he relies."

(2) Failure to discuss questions raised by the various assignments.

In view of the fact that the case is a criminal one, we overlook the omission of these requirements so far as to examine the case upon the more important question, which seems to be whether there was evidence tending to prove the guilty knowledge and intent required by the terms of the statute, viz:

(1) Knowledge of possession of implements.
(2) Knowledge of their adaptation to and design for the criminal purpose.
(3) Intent to use them for such purpose.

The implements in question were produced and shown to have been found on the defendant's person when he was arrested. They were skeleton keys, and we append a drawing of them.

A witness testified that defendant told him that he was taking them to Battle Creek. This indicated the first essential; i.e., knowledge of possession.

There was testimony that tended to show that such instruments are used by burglars, and that they are used for picking locks and opening doors; that the defendant was a burglar and sneak thief by occupation, and had been for years; that he called at the jail on an inmate; that he claimed to be in haste to leave town, and gave different places as his destination. If the jury believed defendant to be engaged in the occupation of burglary and thieving, it was a natural inference that he knew that the implements were adapted to and designed for use in burglaries, and that his intention was to thus use them. This testimony was competent, and the questions discussed were all questions which were for the jury. People v. Howard, 73 Mich. 10 (40 N.W. 789); People v. Edwards, 93 Mich. 636 (53 N.W. 778); People v. Jones, 124 Mich. 179 (82 N.W. 806).

The judgment is affirmed.

OSTRANDER, MOORE, BLAIR, and STONE, JJ., concurred.

People v. Dorrington
221 Mich. 571

WIEST, C. J. Defendant was convicted of feloniously

1249

having in his possession "five skeleton keys, a time bomb outfit and two steel rods," adapted and designed for cutting through, forcing and breaking open buildings, rooms, vaults, safes and other depositories, in order to steal therefrom, well knowing the implements to be adapted and designed for such purpose and with intent to use and employ the same for breaking and entering. We have stated but the substance of the charge. Defendant was convicted and sentenced to prison for an indeterminate term of 5 to 10 years. Defendant assigns error upon rulings of the trial court, remarks of the prosecuting attorney, and insists the verdict is against the great weight of the evidence and the trial court was in error in not granting a new trial.

The evidence at the trial disclosed that the "five skeleton keys," were common house keys, the "time bomb outfit," was a cheap alarm clock with a battery rigged up to ring the bell, and the "two steel rods" were knitting needles. The prosecution claimed the house keys were adapted to unlocking common locks; the alarm clock and battery could be arranged to set off an explosive and the knitting needles could be used to push a key out of a lock or turn it in the lock.

The statute under which defendant was prosecuted provides:

"Every person who shall knowingly have in his possession, any engine, machine, tool or implement, adapted and designed for cutting through, forcing or breaking open any building, . . . knowing the same to be adapted and designed for the purpose aforesaid, with intent to use or employ the same for the purpose aforesaid." . . . 3 Comp. Laws 1915, Sec. 15334.

Three essential elements are involved in this crime: First. The tool or implement must be adapted and designed for breaking and entering. Second. It must be in the possession of one who has knowledge that it is adapted and designed for the purpose of breaking and entering. Third. It must be possessed with intent to use or employ the same in breaking and entering.

Are common house keys, an alarm clock with a battery to ring its bell, and knitting needles, in and of themselves, burglar's tools? To ask the question is to answer it. Such things are not designed for breaking and entering but for an entirely different purpose. It is not enough, to constitute their possession criminal, to say that they may be employed in breaking and entering. This statute has some provisions against strained use thereof which seem to have been overlooked in this prosecution. The term "adapted and designed" means something more than mere common household articles capable of use in breaking and entering. To come within the statute, the tools must not only be adapted, that is, capable of being used in breaking and entering but as well designed, that is contrived or taken to be employed for such purpose.

Keys and tools may be so contrived as to clearly indicate the criminal purpose of possessing them. But house keys, and an alarm clock with a battery to ring its bell, and knitting needles, in a home, serve a legitimate purpose, and bear a harmless character, for they have been contrived for a useful purpose, and they afford no basis for an inference of possession for a criminal purpose. They remain house keys and clocks and needles, unless intended to be used for the purpose of breaking and entering. It is not enough that they may be used in breaking and entering, but the intent to so employ them must appear in order to constitute the crime here charged.

Keys, of course, are designed to open locks, and one may have as many house keys in his home as he may desire, and if he has more keys than locks, that fact justifies no inference that they are burglar's tools. It is not a crime to have house keys, an alarm clock and knitting needles in a home. It is a crime to have keys, bombs and rods for the purpose of breaking and entering. There is no evidence in this record, and no circumstance disclosed, warranting any inference that defendant possessed the keys, clock and knitting needles for the purpose of breaking and entering.

The trial judge instructed the jury that, in order to find the defendant guilty, they would have to find "that he had the intent to use and employ them (the keys, clock and needles) for the purpose of committing a larceny upon a building, vault, safe or other depository that he was to break into." There are cases where the tools and implements are so clearly contrived and adapted for breaking and entering as to warrant a finding that their possession could not possibly be for any other purpose, but house keys, an alarm clock and knitting needles bear no such villainous character. The police explained how this alarm clock and battery could be arranged to set off a bomb. We apprehend from such explanation that any alarm clock can be so arranged. That an alarm clock may be made to serve a nefarious purpose does not make it unlawful to have such a time piece and a battery to ring its bell. Knitting needles are not burglar's tools. The motion to discharge the defendant should have been granted. . . .

The conviction is reversed and a new trial granted.

FELLOWS, McDONALD, CLARK, BIRD, SHARPE, MOORE, and STEERE, JJ., concurred.

People v. Edwards
93 Mich. 636

DURAND, J. The respondent was convicted of a violation of section 9175, How. Stat., which reads as follows:

"Every person who shall knowingly have in his possession

1251

any engine, machine, tool, or implement adapted and designed for cutting through, forcing, or breaking open any building, room, vault, safe, or other depository, in order to steal therefrom any money or other property, knowing the same to be adapted and designed for the purpose aforesaid, with intent to use or employ the same for the purpose aforesaid, shall be, on conviction thereof, punished by imprisonment in the State prison not more than ten years, or by imprisonment in the county jail not more than one year, or a fine not exceeding $1,000, or both such fine and imprisonment, at the discretion of the court."

The respondent insists that no conviction can be had under this statute unless the information charges, and the evidence shows, the particular building intended to be broken into, and who is the owner of it. This contention cannot be sustained. If it is necessary, before a conviction can be had under this statute, to establish the location and ownership of the particular building intended to be broken into, it would be necessary in most cases to wait until the person having such tools in his possession with the intent to use them feloniously is caught in the very act of burglary, which is another and entirely distinct offense. Such a construction would render this statute practically nugatory, and would entirely defeat its purpose and object. This statute was enacted to make the crime of burglary more infrequent, and, as far as possible, to prevent it. It is aimed at that class of criminals who provide themselves with implements to make the commission of the crime of burglary easy, and who go about the country from place to place with the intent to use them whenever they find an opportunity to do so. The possession of such implements, and a general intent to use them in the felonious manner mentioned in the statute, is all that is necessary; and in this case the showing of such an unlawful possession and felonious intent on the part of the respondent in the county of Ionia was all that was required to be shown. It was not necessary to allege or prove any intent to use them in a particular place, or for a specified purpose, or in any definite manner. In this respect the offense charged is similar to that of having in possession counterfeit bills, with intent to use them as true, and in such a case it is never necessary to aver or prove the time, place, or manner in which the bills were intended to be uttered. Com. v. Tivnon, 8 Gray, 375; Archb. Crim. Pl. 513. The crime is complete when it satisfactorily appears that a person is found to be knowingly equipped with tools and implements adapted and designed for burglarious purposes, he knowing the same to be so, and having the felonious intent to employ them for that purpose when an opportunity satisfactory to him presents itself, or when he finds a building or place sufficiently unguarded to prompt him to take the risk of an attempt.

There is no error in the record, and the judgment is affirmed.

The other Justices concurred.

3. Final Draft - Michigan Revised Criminal Code

(Possession of Burglar's Tools)

Sec. 2615. (1) A person commits the crime of possession of burglar's tools if he:

(a) Possesses any explosive, tool, instrument, or other article adapted, designed, or commonly used for committing or facilitating the commission of an offense involving forcible entry into premises or theft by a physical taking; and

(b) Intends to use the thing possessed, or knows that some person intends ultimately to use the thing possessed in the commission of an offense of the nature described in subparagraph (a).

(2) Possession of burglar's tools is a Class C felony.

Committee Commentary

The section combines elements from C.L. 1948, Sec. 750.116, and New York Revised Penal Law Sec. 140.35.

The present Michigan statute penalizes one who knowingly has in his possession certain specified explosives and instruments "adapted and designed for cutting or burning through, forcing or breaking open any building, room, vault, safe or other depository in order to steal therefrom any money or other property", with knowledge that what is possessed is so adapted, or else their actual use for the purpose. The three intent elements, therefore, are (1) knowledge of the fact of possession, (2) knowledge of their adaptation to and design for the criminal purpose, and (3) intent to use them for that purpose (People v. Jefferson, 161 Mich. 621, 126 N.W. 829 (1910)). Language in one Michigan case (People v. Dorrington, 221 Mich. 571, 191 N.W. 831 (1923)) seems to say that because ordinary household items like regular keys, alarm clocks and knitting needles are not "adapted and designed" for the commission of a crime, they cannot be burglar's tools. Other parts of the same opinion, however, and decisions in other states, make the difference turn on the amount of independent proof necessary to show the requisite knowledge and intent when the instruments are inherently innocuous. Thus, the fact of possession of nitroglycerine, skeleton keys or special taps by one who offers no explanation about their intended use may carry the case to the jury, while fairly specific proof of intent is necessary if the items in the defendant's possession have legitimate uses. It is unnecessary to allege

1253

or prove an intent to burglarize a specific building; all that is required is proof of a general intent to use the instrument in a felonious manner whenever an opportunity presents itself (People v. Edwards, 93 Mich. 636, 53 N.W. 778 (1892)).

Section 2615 continues much of the coverage of the present statute. A general statement of "any explosive, tool, instrument, or other article" replaces the longer listing in the present statute, but the requirement of adaption, design or common use for committing certain crimes is retained as a qualification. Under the Draft, the offenses ultimately covered include any forcible entry into premises, which usually will mean burglary in one of its degrees but might include criminal trespass in the first or second degree, and theft committing by a physical taking. The culpability element may be either an intent to use the thing possessed to commit one of the enumerated offenses, or knowledge that some person intends so to use it. The latter alternative brings the professional or amateur supplier within the coverage of the section, and is similar in operation to the offense of distributing abortifacients (sec. 7045).

INTERROGATORIES

1. Outline the provisions of the Michigan statutes relevant to burglary?
2. What restrictions inherent in the common law have been eliminated by the breaking and entering statutes? Does the element of breaking continue to have significance?
3. What were the facts, issue and holding of the court in People v. Harris? Does common law burglary still exist in Michigan?
4. What were the facts, issue and holding of the court in People v. Shaver? How is burglary defined by the common law?
5. What were the facts, issue and holding of the court in People v. White? How is "breaking" defined by the decision?
6. What were the facts, issue and holding of the court in People v. Griffith? What interpretation is given by the court to the term "dwelling house."
7. What were the fact, issue and holding of the court in People v. Evans? Does both the breaking and entry have to be without consent or claim of right?
8. What was the issue and holding of the court in People v. Huffman? Does burglary constitute a completely separate offense from any crime actually committed after entry?
9. What were the facts, issue and holding of the court in People v. Williams?
10. Outline the provisions of Sec. 2601, 2610, 2611, and 2612, Final Draft, Mich. Rev. Crim. Code.

11. Why did the Committee decide not to treat burglary under the law of attempt?
12. Outline the provisions of the Michigan statute on possession of burglar's tools.
13. What were the facts, issue and holding of the court in People v. Jefferson? What are the three elements of guilty knowledge required by the statute?
14. What were the facts, issue and holding of the court in People v. Dorrington? What are the three elements of the crime of possession of burglar's tools? What is the relationship between the nature of the tool and the independent proof needed to establish guilty knowledge?
15. What were the facts, issue and holding of the court in People v. Edwards? Is it necessary to allege or prove an intent to burglarize a specific building?
16. Outline the provisions of Sec. 2615, Final Draft, Mich. Rev. Crim. Code. Would these provisions work any substantial change in the existing law?

CHAPTER XI

ROBBERY

robbery

1. Michigan Compiled Laws (1948)

Chapter LXXVII. ROBBERY

750.529 Armed robbery; aggravated assault

Sec. 529. Any person who shall assault another, and shall feloniously rob, steal and take from his person, or in his presence, any money or other property, which may be the subject of larceny, such robber being armed with a dangerous weapon, or any article used or fashioned in a manner to lead the person so assaulted to reasonably believe it to be a dangerous weapon, shall be guilty of a felony, punishable by imprisonment in the state prison for life or for any term of years. If an aggravated assault or serious injury is inflicted by any person while committing an armed robbery as defined in this section, the sentence shall be not less than 2 years' imprisonment in the state prison. As amended P.A. 1959, No. 71, Sec. 1, Eff. March 19, 1960.

750.530 Unarmed robbery

Sec. 530. ROBBERY UNARMED - Any person who shall, by force and violence, or by assault or putting in fear, feloniously rob, steal and take from the person of another, or in his presence, any money or other property which may be the subject of larceny, such robber not being armed with a dangerous weapon, shall be guilty of a felony, punishable by imprisonment in the state prison not more than 15 years.

750.531 Bank, safe and vault robbery

Sec. 531. BANK, SAFE AND VAULT ROBBERY - Any person who, with intent to commit the crime of larceny, or any felony, shall confine, maim, injure or wound, or attempt, or threaten to confine, kill, maim, injure or wound, or shall put in fear any person for the purpose of stealing from any building, bank, safe or other depository of money, bonds or other valuables, or shall by intimidation, fear or threats compel, or attempt to compel any person to disclose or surrender the means of opening any building, bank, safe, vault or other depository of money, bonds, or other valuables, or shall attempt to break, burn, blow up or otherwise injure or destroy any safe, vault or other deposi-

tory of money, bonds or other valuables in any building
or place, shall, whether he succeeds or fails in the perpetration of such larceny or felony, be guilty of a felony,
punishable by imprisonment in the state prison for life or
any term of years.

750.514 Seizing locomotive with mail or express car
              attached

Sec. 514. SEIZING LOCOMOTIVE WITH MAIL OR EXPRESS CAR
ATTACHED - Any person who shall unlawfully seize upon any
locomotive, with any express or mail car attached thereto,
and run away with the same upon any railroad, or shall aid,
abet or procure the doing of the same, shall be guilty of
a felony, punishable by imprisonment in the state prison
not more than 10 years, or by fine of not more than 5,000
dollars.

750.516 Forcible detention of railroad train

Sec. 516. FORCIBLE DETENTION OF RAILROAD TRAIN FOR
PURPOSE OF ROBBERY, ETC., - Any person who shall wilfully
and maliciously, with intimidation or threat of life with
firearms, dynamite, or other dangerous devices stop a
railroad train, or cause the officers or employes of said
railroad company to stop or leave the train, or detach the
train 1 part from another, or compel the engineer of fireman to run the train contrary to their general order, or
any part thereof in this state, for the purpose of wrecking or robbing said train, or the passengers or employes
thereon, or the express or mail cars of such train, shall
be guilty of a felony, punishable by imprisonment in the
state prison for life or for any term of years.

750.517 Entering train for robbing by meand of intimidation

Sec. 517. ENTERING RAILROAD TRAIN OR CARS FOR PURPOSE OF
ROBBING BY MEANS OF INTIMIDATION - Any person or persons who
shall enter upon any railroad train, passenger car, mail car
or express car, with intent to rob said railroad train, passenger car, mail car, express car or the passengers or employes on said cars, by means of intimidation or by threat
of life to the passengers or employees upon said cars or in
charge of said cars in this state, shall be guilty of a
felony, punishable by imprisonment in the state prison for
life or for any term of years.

2. Definition and Elements of the Offense

Saks v. St. Paul Mer. Indemnity Co.
308 Mich. 719

BOYLES, J. Plaintiff brought suit against the defendant indemnity company to recover for money taken from plaintiff by robbers, for the loss of which plaintiff claims to have been indemnified by the defendant in a robbery policy. The case was submitted to the circuit court for Wayne county on a stipulation of facts, the circuit judge filed a written opinion finding for plaintiff, and entered judgment against defendant for $765. The only ground urged by defendant for reversal is that the policy of insurance on which suit was based does not cover the loss sustained by plaintiff, under the agreed facts. . . .

In short, defendant claims that it is not liable because the loss did not occur inside the building.

The Saks Cafe, operated by the plaintiff and described in said policy, is a night club so-called. On November 30, 1941, at about 2 a.m., plaintiff had closed his place of business, had counted the day's receipts, segregated the money for business purposes into four different envelopes, and after the money had been thus segregated it was turned over to plaintiff's wife who put it in her purse. The total amount of the cafe money was $1,185.50. Besides this, she had other money belonging to herself in the purse. At the time of closing the place of business and while the money was being counted, the plaintiff, his wife, the head-waiter, and the night watchman were in the cafe. Having completed the counting of the money and turning it over to Mrs. Saks, the parties went out of the cafe to get into their cars which were parked in the driveway on the north side of the building. When Mr. Saks and the other parties left the cafe to go to their cars, they left by the side door. Mrs. Saks and the headwaiter left ahead of Mr. Saks and were in their cars waiting for him. Mr. Saks got into the car after the door of the cafe, by which he had left, had closed and automatically locked. Then three masked men came up, exhibited guns and forced all parties to get out of their cars and re-enter the cafe. They returned to the cafe by the same side door from which they had left.

After re-entering the cafe, one of the robbers took the plaintiff into the cafe kitchen and cross-examined him as to where the money was. Although plaintiff's wife had put all the money from the cafe business into her purse and had left her purse with the money in it in the car, plaintiff thought the robbers had taken her purse at the time they made them get out of the car. While the one robber was questioning the plaintiff in the cafe kitchen, another one had forced the night watchman to lie on the floor in the main part of the cafe and had the headwaiter standing with his face to the wall. The remaining robber was questioning plaintiff's wife.

Plaintiff did not know that the money was still in the car and kept insisting he did not have any more money. The robber watching plaintiff struck him on the side of

1258

the head with his revolver. Plaintiff's wife heard the
blow and told the one with her that the money was in her
purse in the car. Thereupon the robber who was questioning plaintiff's wife went out to the car, got the purse and
the money and brought it back into the cafe. He took the
money out of the purse and kept it. He left the purse on
a table, called the other robbers and they all left the
cafe.

While the robbers were questioning Mr. Saks in the
kitchen, they made continuous threats of bodily harm to
all of the parties if they did not divulge the whereabouts
of the money. They were very loud in their threats and
inflicted a gash in the head of the plaintiff. After the
robbers had removed the money from the purse they threatened all parties with bodily harm if they made any outcry
as the robbers ran from the building. The amount taken
by the robbers was in excess of $1,000. The policy of in-
surance limited recovery to a loss of $700, so that the
maximum amount that could be recovered by plaintiff would
be $700 plus interest.

The stipulation of facts which we find in the record
recites that a copy of the policy is thereto annexed.
There is no copy of the policy in the record. However,
the circuit judge in his opinion found, and the statement
is not controverted, that "robbery" is defined in the policy as "the felonious and forcible taking of insured property." Defendant makes no claim that the offense shown by
the facts does not constitute the crime of robbery. Under
our statutes, an essential element of robbery armed is assaulting another and stealing or taking away money or other
property from his person or in his presence. Act No. 328
Sec. 529, Pub. Acts 1931 (Michigan penal code) (Comp. Laws
Supp. 1940, Sec. 17115-529, Stat. Ann. Sec. 28.797).

This is a case of first impression in this State.
Counsel for defendant relies on Axt v. London & Lancashire
Indemnity Company of America (C.C.A.), 131 Fed. (2d) 370.
Plaintiff relies on Cartier Drug Co. v. Maryland Casualty
Company of Baltimore, Maryland, 181 Wash. 146 (42 Pac. (2d)
37). The facts in the latter case are quite similar to
those in the instant case and the reasoning of the court
is convincing. The court said:

"The sole question in the case, as we see it, is: At
what place was Cartier robbed of the $473.57? In the ad-
ministration of criminal law, two distinct elements are
held to be necessary to the crime of robbery: (1) Putting
the victim in fear of violence to his person or property;
and (2) the taking of money, property, or thing of value
from his person or in his presence.

"Whatever the crime may be, under any state of facts
where one of such elements exists and the other does not,
it is not robbery. The first element being present, the
crime of robbery is consummated only when the victim is

1259

deprived of dominion over his money or property."

The money taken in the instant case by the robbers
was the property of Mr. Saks, not his wife's property.
The offense of robbery armed was perpetrated against Mr.
Saks, in his presence, inside the building, when the robber removed his money from his wife's purse and took it
away. The crime was not consummated until the whereabouts
of the money had been disclosed, it had been taken into the
building, appropriated by the robbers and taken away. If
Mr. Saks had been able to prevent the taking away of the
money, after it had been returned to the building, the
crime of robbery armed would not have been consummated.
It would have been an attempt, only. The crime of robbery
armed was committed inside the building, within the meaning of the policy.

We conclude that plaintiff's loss is within the coverage of the policy. Judgment affirmed.

NORTH, C. J., and STARR, BUTZEL, BUSHNELL, and REID, JJ.,
concurred with BOYLES, J.

(Dissenting opinion of Justice SHARP omitted.)

People v. Kolodzieski
237 Mich. 654

SHARPE, C. J.   Defendant was convicted on a charge of
robbery, "being armed with a dangerous weapon, with intent,
if resisted, to kill or maim." 3 Comp. Laws 1915, Sec.
15206. From the testimony it appears that two men entered
a butcher shop owned by Joseph Samulowicz in the city of
Detroit on the 2d of July, 1925, armed with revolvers, compelled the owner and his helper to lie upon the floor, took
the money, $41.96, in the cash register therefrom, and then
locked the men in the ice box. Both the owner and his helper positively identified the defendant as one of these men.
The defense was an alibi.

1. There was testimony to sustain the verdict. While
several witnesses (relatives of defendant) testified that
he was at another place when the crime was committed, we
cannot say that the verdict was against the great weight
of the evidence.

2. Four persons whose names appeared on the information
as witnesses were not present at the trial or called as
witnesses. The officer in charge of the case testified
that he had been unable to locate two of them. The others
were police officers in the city.

Defendant's counsel made no request that they should be
called, and, in view of the nature of the charge and the
defense offered, it is apparent that no prejudice resulted
from their failure to appear. People v. Higgins, 127 Mich.

1260

291.

3. Error is assigned on the instruction of the court that the jury could not convict of larceny from the person. This is a lesser offense, included in the charge of robbery. People v. Covelesky, 217 Mich. 90. There was no evidence tending to show the commission of the lesser offense. The evidence is undisputed that the men who took the money were armed with a dangerous weapon, and that their threats clearly indicated an intent to kill or maim, if resisted. The defense was an alibi. The only question for the jury to pass upon was whether the defendant was one of the men present and participating in the commission of the crime. Under these circumstances, we think the court was warranted in instructing that the offense of larceny from the person should not be considered. People v. Repke, 103 Mich. 459; People v. Beverly, 108 Mich. 509; People v. Onesto, 203 Mich. 490. The duty to instruct as to lesser offenses in homicide cases is reviewed at length in a note in 21 A.L.R. 603.

The other errors assigned have been considered. We deem them without merit.

The judgment is affirmed.

BIRD, SNOW, STEERE, FELLOWS, WIEST, CLARK, and McDONALD, JJ., concurred.

People v. Allie
216 Mich. 133

BIRD, J. Defendant was charged under section 15208, 3 Comp. Laws 1915, with having committed a robbery in the city of Detroit. A trial resulted in his conviction. Error has been assigned on the charge of the trial court. By way of instruction the trial court said to the jury they could find one of three verdicts. They could find defendant guilty as charged; they could find him guilty of larceny from the person; or they could find him not guilty. Defendant's counsel agrees with this, but insists that it does not go far enough; that there were two other verdicts which could have been found, namely, "an attempt to commit a robbery and assault and battery." He further insists that the failure to so instruct the jury was reversible error and he argues that this view is sustained by the recent statutory rape cases in which we have held that the trial court must, upon his own initiative, instruct the jury as to the lesser offenses included in the offense charged. The cases referred to are People v. Garner, 211 Mich. 44, and People v. Harvey, 212 Mich. 393.

The prosecutor replies, in substance, that if defendant is correct in his position as to the two additional verdicts, he should have called the trial court's attention

1261

to the omission at the time. Not having done so, he cannot be heard to say that the omission was reversible error, and cites the following cases in support thereof: People v. Brott, 163 Mich. 150; People v. Driscoll, 47 Mich. 414; People v. Waller, 70 Mich. 239; People v. Raher, 92 Mich. 167; People v. Warner, 104 Mich. 337; People v. Smith, 106 Mich. 437.

Both counsel appear to be well fortified in their respective contentions. It, therefore, devolves upon the court to point the way to a single and consistent rule in such cases. The statute appears to support defendant's contention as to the number of verdicts which could have been rendered. Section 15616, 3 Comp. Laws 1915, provides that:

"Upon an indictment for any offense consisting of different degrees, as prescribed in this title, the jury may find the accused not guilty of the offense in the degree charged in the indictment, and may find such accused person guilty of any degree of such offense inferior to that charged in the indictment, or of an attempt to commit such offense."

This statute would clearly give a defendant in a criminal case the right to have the jury instructed that he could be convicted of any of the included offenses. This court has held specifically that one charged with robbery may be convicted of assault with intent to rob. People v. Blanchard, 136 Mich. 148. And the rule elsewhere appears to be that he may be convicted of assault and battery. 1 McClain on Criminal Law, p. 463; 23 R.C.L. p. 1162; 22 Cyc. p. 481.

We think it clear under the terms of the statute that the defendant was entitled to have an instruction that he could be found guilty of an attempt to commit the crime of robbery or of assault and battery. The question then arises whether it was reversible error for the trial court to neglect to give this instruction upon his own initiative. . . .

In the present case the court did not advise the jury that they could convict the defendant of an attempt to commit the crime of robbery nor of assault and battery. Its attention was not challenged to it in any way. No request to that effect was proffered, and we are of the opinion that, after counsel has neglected to call it to the attention of the trial court at the time, he should not now be permitted to come before the appellate court and have the case reversed on that ground.

This being the only question that calls for our consideration, the judgment of conviction will be affirmed.

STEERE, C. J., and WIEST, STONE, and SHARPE, JJ., concurred with BIRD, J.

(Dissenting opinion of Justice CLARK omitted.)

People v. Calvin
60 Mich. 113

1262

MORSE, J. The respondent in the circuit court for the county of Bay pleaded not guilty to the following information:

"State of Michigan, County of Bay, ss. - The Circuit
            Court for the County of Bay:

"John E. Simonson, prosecuting attorney for the county of Bay aforesaid, for and in behalf of the People of the State of Michigan, comes into said court, in the June term thereof, A.D. 1885, and gives it here to understand and be informed, that Hulbert Calvin and Skill Doyle, late of the city of Bay City, in the county of Bay, and State of Michigan, heretofore, to-wit: On the seventeenth day of June, in the year 1885, at the city of Bay City, in said Bay county, with force and arms in and upon Louis White in the peace of the People of the State of Michigan, then and there being, feloniously did make an assault; and him, the said Louis White, in bodily fear then and there feloniously did put, and one ten-dollar gold coin of the currency of the United States of America, of the value of ten dollars, and to wit, about two dollars in silver money of the currency of the United States of America, of the value of two dollars, which money complainant is unable to more fully describe, all of the value of twelve dollars, of the goods, chattels, and property of Louis White, then and there from the person, and against the will of him, the said Louis White, feloniously did steal, rob, take, and carry away, contrary to the form of the statute in such case made and provided, and against the peace and dignity of the People of the State of Michigan.

                    "John E. Simonson
          "Prosecuting Attorney for the county of Bay."

Which information was duly verified.

Upon a trial under such information, the court instructed the jury that the respondent could not be convicted of robbery, but might be, under the information, if they found the evidence sufficient, found guilty of larceny from the person. He was convicted of the latter crime, and sentenced to the State's prison at Jackson for three years.

After the evidence was taken, and just previous to this ruling of the court, the counsel for respondent moved to quash the information, but the record is silent as to the reasons stated therefor.

The failure of the court to grant this motion and his instruction to the jury, are assigned as error. It is claimed upon the part of the defendant, that by this action he was charged and tried for one crime, - robbery, - and convicted of another and totally different one; that larceny from the person is not contained within the charge of robbery; and, also, that the information for the latter offense is fatally defective in its failure to state whether the defendant was armed or unarmed: How. Stat. Sec. 9089, 9091. . . .

1263

The question now arises whether the common-law offense of robbery exists in this State, in view of the statutes above noted: How. Stat. Sec. 9089, 9091. The information charges sufficiently the common-law offense: 2 Archb. Crim. Pr. 1295; 2 Bish. Crim. Proc. Sec. 1002.

Our statutes seem to carve the crime of robbery under the common law, into two grades, as above set forth; and these two divisions of the offense embrace together, all of the essential ingredients of the common-law crime. A punishment is affixed to each. It was not the intention of the Legislature to create a new crime, but to define two grades of the offense, and provide a different punishment for each. Com. v. Clifford, 8 Cush. 217.

Having thus covered the crime by statutory definitions and punishment, it would seem as if the offense of robbery in this State must be informed against under one or the other of these statutes. We must consider the common-law crime superseded by the statute, and punished only when prosecuted under one of the provisions of the statute; and the offense must be laid in conformity therewith: Bish. St. Cr. Sec. 520.

There is no other punishment provided for robbery. We are corroborated in this view of the intention of the Legislature by the general statute, which provides in effect that every indictable offense at the common law, for the punishment of which no provision is expressly made by any statute of this State, shall be punished as a misdemeanor: How. Stat. Sec. 9434. It certainly was not the intention of the Legislature to class any kind of robbery, or punish the same, only as a misdemeanor. It follows, then, that a common-law information for robbery is not permissible in this State, but the crime must be laid under the statute.

Under this view of the case it remains to be seen whether or not this information can be treated as a good information for larceny from the person. . . .

(The court found a good information for larceny from the person.)

There being no error in the record, the judgment of the court below is affirmed.

The other Justices concurred.

People v. Powler
142 Mich. 225

Ernie Powler was convicted of robbery and sentenced to imprisonment for not less than ten and not more than fifteen years in the State prison at Jackson. Reversed, and a new trial ordered. . . .

GRANT, J. The respondent in this case was the one impleaded with the respondent in <u>People v. Scofield</u>, ante, 221, in which an opinion is handed down herewith. The proceedings before the court were the same in both cases. As it was decided in <u>People v. Calvin</u>, <u>60 Mich. 119</u>, that the common-law crime of robbery is superseded in this State by the statute, it follows that the finding and commitment do not describe any crime known to the law of Michigan. Had the court found respondent guilty of assault with intent to rob, the conviction could have been sustained under several decisions. <u>People v. Blanchard</u>, <u>136 Mich. 146</u>, and authorities there cited. See, also, <u>People v. Calvin</u>, supra.

Section <u>11486</u>, <u>3 Comp. Laws</u>, defines robbery when not armed with a dangerous weapon. It is not contended that respondent was sentenced under this statute, or pleaded guilty to that crime.

Judgment reversed, and new trial ordered.

BLAIR, MONTGOMERY, OSTRANDER, and HOOKER, JJ., concurred.

People v. Locke
275 Mich. 333

EDWARD M. SHARPE, J. Respondent was convicted on the charge of having on the 12th day of August, 1931, assaulted and robbed one Almond Foster in his grocery store of the sum of $7, and that at the time of committing said assault and robbery he was armed with a dangerous weapon and intended to kill or maim if resisted. The defense was an alibi.

It is the claim of the people that while respondent did not actually commit the robbery himself, yet he was a participant in that he planned the robbery, furnished the guns for the holdup, and waited outside in an automobile while the robbery was committed. When the cause came on for trial the respondent did not take the stand and testify and the people had to rely largely upon the testimony of three convicts, two of whom were confessed perjurers.

The respondent claims error in the admission of the testimony of Frank O'Malley, a detective connected with the Grand Rapids police force, relating to a conversation he had with the respondent after respondent's arrest.

"Q. Will you tell the jury the conversation you had with Mr. Locke.

"A. I told Mr. Locke he was charged with a holdup that happened on the 12th day of August, 1931. I asked him what he knew about it and he said he didn't know anything about it. He turned to me and said, 'O'Malley, you don't think I am a holdup man, do you?' And I said, 'I wasn't there, I don't know.' I said, 'I don't know, you went out with a man by the name of - - - did I say Bill, you went out with a man by the name of Jim Westrate and Dever and picked up

1265

another man by the name of Lapham out in the country some time ago with the intention of hijacking a man,' and I said, 'is that true?' And he said 'yes, I did, but,' he said, 'we didn't go to the man's place.'"

Section 17320, 3 Comp. Laws 1929, provides in part that:

"In any criminal case where defendant's motive, intent, the absence of, mistake or accident on his part, or the defendant's scheme, plan or system in doing an act, is material, any like acts or other acts of the defendant which may tend to show his motive, intent, the absence of, mistake or accident on his part, or the defendant's scheme, plan or system in doing the act, in question, may be proved, whether they are contemporaneous with or prior or subsequent thereto; notwithstanding that such proof may show or tend to show the commission of another or prior or subsequent crime by the defendant." . . .

In the case at bar the information was drawn under the following statute:

"If any person shall assault another, and shall feloniously rob, steal and take from his person any money or other property, or shall feloniously assault another with intent to rob or steal any money or other property, which may be the subject of larceny, such robber being armed with a dangerous weapon, or any article used or fashioned in a manner to lead the person so assaulted to reasonably believe it to be a dangerous weapon, with intent, if resisted, to kill or maim the person robbed or assaulted, . . . he shall be punished by imprisonment in the State prison for life or any number of years." 3 Comp. Laws 1929, Sec. 16722.

The word "feloniously" as used in this statute implies intent to commit the crime of robbery or stealing. People v. Quigley, 217 Mich. 213; State v. Fordham, 13 N.D. 494 (101 N.W. 888); State v. Rechnitz, 20 Mont. 488 (52 Pac. 264). Consequently intent is a necessary element of the crime described in 3 Comp. Laws 1929, Sec. 16722. The acts of respondent referred to in O'Malley's testimony did not result in the commission of any crime and at most tended to show a disposition to commit such an offense. We are unable to see how this purported act would show any motive, intent, or scheme to commit the crime with which defendant was charged.

The admission of this testimony constituted error, the conviction is reversed, and a new trial granted.

NORTH, C. J., and FEAD, WIEST, BUTZEL, BUSHNELL, and POTTER, JJ., concurred. TOY, J., did not sit.

People v. Quigley
275 Mich. 333

WIEST, J. Just before noon, on the 18th day of March, 1921, two men entered the bank of G. A. Blakeslee Company, in the village of Galien, where Theron N. Chilson, cashier, was on duty alone seated at his desk behind a glass partition, and one of them covered the cashier with a revolver and commanded him to hold up his hands, and, remarking that he was not quick enough about it, fired through the glass partition. The bullet did not strike the cashier. The other man then climbed over the partition and opened the door and let his companion in and at the point of the revolver the cashier was forced to unlock the day door to the money vault and open the burglar chest. In the cashier's desk there was about $5,000 in cash and in the burglar chest about $60,000 in industrial, municipal, and liberty bonds, which they took, and after striking the cashier on the back of the head, causing a wound requiring medical attention and two stitches, they went to the street door where an automobile with a driver was awaiting them and drove away. Six days later defendants entered a brokerage office at the union stock yards, Chicago, and Quigley was there introduced under the false name of H. C. Walters, and he handed a package of bonds of the par value of $8,200, and a part of the bonds stolen from the bank, to the broker and requested that they be sold. A purchaser was found, and check drawn by the broker to H. C. Walters, but further identification being required, and both defendants being nervous and endeavoring to unduly hurry matters, the suspicion of the broker became aroused and he notified the police and defendants were arrested and brought to this State and tried, convicted and sentenced for the robbery.

Defendants bring the case here for review on writ of error, claiming the information was insufficient; that the testimony of identity of defendants should not have been submitted to the jury; that defendants should have been found not guilty under the evidence, and that the charge of the court was erroneous in several particulars. No motion was made for a new trial or to quash the information.

Omitting formal parts the information charged:

"That Frank Quigley and Fred Hague, heretofore, to wit: on the 18th day of March, in the year one thousand nine hundred and twenty-one, at the county of Berrien aforesaid; did then and there feloniously, with force and arms in and upon one Theron N. Chilson make an assault, and him, the said Theron N. Chilson, did beat, maim, injure, and wound and feloniously did then and there put him, the said Theron N. Chilson, in bodily fear and danger of his life, and money, bonds, securities, bank notes, other valuables, personal property, goods and chattels, of the value of to wit: Sixty thousand dollars of the goods, chattels and property of G. A. Blakeslee Company, bankers, in the bank, safe and depositories of said bank, then and there being found in said county and State, against the will of the said Theron N.

Chilson, the cashier of said G. A. Blakeslee Company, feloniously did then and there, and by force and violence, steal, take, rob and carry away, contrary to the form of the statute in such case made and provided," etc.

The statute, section 15229, 3 Comp. Laws 1915, so far as applicable to the charge made, provides:

"That whoever, with the intent to commit the crime of larceny, or any felony, shall . . . injure or wound, . . . or shall put in fear any person for the purpose of stealing from any building, bank, safe, or other depository of money, bonds, or other valuables, . . . shall, whether he succeeds or fails in the perpetration of such larceny or felony, be punished," etc.

It is urged that the information is fatally defective as a charge of common-law robbery as it neither charges that property was taken from the person of the party assaulted or that it was taken by force. The statute under which this information was laid does not undertake to denounce the common-law robbery, it does not remit the pleader to the common-law definition of what constitutes robbery. This statute does not make it necessary to charge that the property was taken from the person of the party assaulted, but only from any building, bank, safe, or other depository of money, bonds, or other valuables, and accomplished by confining, maiming, injuring or wounding, or attempting to do so, or putting in fear any person who might interfere with the plan. Such person so put in fear or assaulted might be a patrolman on the street or a customer in the bank or one just entering or leaving the bank, provided the assault was made in the perpetration of the offense. This information can be laid down upon the statute and be found to contain all the essential averments required. But it is said that the intent of the assault is not averred nor the purpose thereof, as required by the statute. The statute requires an intent to commit the crime of larceny, or any felony, or an assault or putting in fear for the purpose of stealing from any building, bank, safe or other depository of money, bonds or other valuables. An intent is, therefore, involved. Is such intent sufficiently charged in the information? To hold that an information charging two men with entering a bank and there feloniously assaulting the cashier and putting him in bodily fear and danger of his life, and then and there, that they did, by force and violence and against the will of the cashier, feloniously rob and carry away $60,000 in money, bonds and securities from the bank, safe and depository, does not charge that the assault was made with intent to commit a larceny or felony or for the purpose of stealing from the bank would offend common sense. There is no presumption of permissible inference that what they did do they did not intend to do; the presumption is the

1268

other way, and upon the trial, from what they did do, the
jury could find the intent.

An intent, of course, is a secret of a man's mind, and
he can disclose it by declarations or by his actions. And
actions sometimes speak louder than words. It would seem
that an intent to commit a larceny, or the purpose of stealing from a bank, sufficiently appears charged when it is
charged that there was a felonious assault and as a part
thereof a felonious stealing and robbery from the bank depository, and such is the law.

The information charges a felonious assault upon the
cashier of the bank and a felonious putting of him in bodily
fear and a felonious stealing and robbery of the money and
bonds and securities from the bank. We do not commend this
information as a model, but hold it sufficient after conviction when it is attacked for the first time in this court.

In State v. Hughes, 31 Nev. 270 (102 Pac. 562), the defendant was convicted of the crime of assault with intent
to commit robbery, and it was urged that the indictment was
not sufficient because it did not allege that the acts done
by defendant were done with the intent to commit the crime
of robbery. In passing upon this question the court said:

"The record does not disclose that the indictment was
demurred to or that a motion in arrest of judgment was interposed. The sufficiency of the indictment appears, therefore,
to be questioned for the first time upon appeal. The indictment, it must be admitted, is far from being a model.
Where, however, the sufficiency of an indictment is questioned for the first time upon appeal, it will not be held insufficient to support the judgment, unless it is so defective
that by no construction, within the reasonable limits of the
language used, can it be said to charge the offense for which
the defendant was convicted. . . .

"The word 'feloniously' used in the body of the indictment, in a legal sense, means, 'done with intent to commit
crime.' Its use in an indictment has uniformly been held
to be a sufficient averment of the intent necessary to constitute the crime. State v. Douglas, 53 Kan. 669 (37 Pac.
172); State v. Halpin, 16 S.D. 170 (91 N.W. 605); People
v. Willett, 102 N.Y. 251 (6 N.E. 301); Phelps v. People, 72
N.Y. 334; People v. Dumar, 42 Hun (N.Y.), 80; State v.
Rechnitz, 20 Mont. 488 (52 Pac. 264); State v. Smith, 31
Wash. 245 (71 Pac. 767); State v. Boyle, 28 Iowa, 522; People v. Butler, 1 Idaho, 231; People v. Lopez, 90 Cal. 569
(27 Pac. 427); Commonwealth v. Adams, 127 Mass. 15; 3 Words
and Phrases Judicially Defined, p. 2731.

"Had the word 'feloniously' been used directly to qualify
the word 'assault' it could be said with a greater degree of
clearness that the intent is sufficiently alleged. However,
in view of the fact that the formal part of the indictment
acquainted the defendant with the specific crime with which
he was intended to be charged, and the body of the indictment contains language which is capable of being construed

1269

into the equivalent of a charge of the essential element of intent, and the indictment not having been questioned in the lower court, we are not disposed to hold it fatally defective. There is nothing whatever to indicate that the defendant was misled by the form of the indictment, or that he at any time failed to fully appreciate that he was indicted for and was being tried for the crime of assault with intent to rob."

In State v. Bannister, 79 Vt. 524 (65 Atl. 586), it was claimed that the use of the word "feloniously" does not supply the requirement that the indictment should allege the intent with which the respondent received the goods. It was held:

"By the use of the word 'feloniously' in the indictment the prosecutor charged the respondent with the commission of a grave crime. Bishop says, 1 New Crim. Law, Sec. 427: 'Felonious, - standing alone, rather designates the grade of the crime - that it is "felony" in distinction from misdemeanor - than any particular form of the felonious intent. Yet, in a sort of general sense, it points to the intent which enters into a felony.'"

In State v. Fordham, 13 N.D. 494 (101 N.W. 888), the defendant was convicted of robbery. It was contended on behalf of defendant that the information did not state the facts constituting a public offense in this, that it did not allege an unlawful intent, and animus furandi; and that felonious intent required the same allegation and proof as in larceny. The court said:

"The defendant also urges that it was error to overrule his demurrer to the information upon the ground that it does not allege, directly or in substance, that the property was taken with intent to steal it. Robbery is defined in the statute as 'a wrongful taking of personal property in the possession of another, from his person or immediate presence, and against his will, accomplished by means of force or fear.' The information in this case charges that the property was wrongfully and feloniously taken. . . . It is true that a taking with intent to steal is essential to constitute the crime of robbery, but the intent to steal is covered by the use of the word 'wrongful.' 'Wrongful,' in this connection, means not a mere taking without authority of law, but the word is to be construed in its most comprehensive meaning, and includes within its meaning a taking with an evil motive or with a criminal mind. In this connection it is synonymous with 'felonious;' and it is well settled that the word 'felonious,' when used in defining the crime of robbery or larceny, implies an intent to steal. People v. Moore, 37 Hun (N.Y.), 84; State v. Bush, 47 Kan. 201 (27 Pac. 834, 13 L.R.A. 607); State v. Hogard, 12 Minn. 293; State v. Rechnitz, 20 Mont. 488 (52 Pac. 264); People v. Ah Sing, 95 Cal. 654 (30 Pac. 796)."

In People v. Butler, 1 Idaho, 231, the point urged against the indictment was that it nowhere showed: "the intent of the defendant to steal or rob." The court held:

"This point is not well taken; we think the intent of the defendant to steal or rob clearly and sufficiently appears in the indictment. It charges first a felonious assault upon the person robbed, by the defendant putting him feloniously in bodily fear, thereby the felonious and violent robbing, taking and carrying away by defendant from his person of the property. The words 'felonious' and 'rob' carry with them the intent, and are sufficient."

In State v. Rechnitz, 20 Mont. 488 (52 Pac. 264), the court said:

"But the mental element of any larceny must, we think, be still marked by using the word 'feloniously,' or by equivalent words. There must be accompanying the taking an evil intention. It has been long settled that in an indictment for a common-law felony it is necessary to aver that the act charged to have been done was done 'feloniously.' . . . The word 'feloniously' is descriptive of the act charged. It means that the act was done with a mind bent on doing that which is wrong, or, 'as it has been sometimes said, with a guilty mind.'"

We have examined the information with care, having in mind the provisions of the statute, and have examined the cases cited by counsel and many other cases, and we are of the opinion that the information fully informed defendants of the true nature of the charge and was sufficient in law. . . .

It is claimed that the court in the charge instructed the jury that if defendants were jointly engaged in disposing of the bonds and were both taking part in the attempt to dispose of them both parties were in possession of the bonds as a matter of law, and it is insisted that whether Hague was in possession of the bonds was a question for the jury. The court charged upon this subject:

"Now, it is also the claim of the people in this case, gentlemen of the jury, that some six days thereafter the 18th day of March, 1921, namely on the 24th day of March, 1921, these two respondents appeared at the banking house or brokerage house of Slaughter & Company, in the city of Chicago, somewhere near the stock yards, and that at that time they had in their possession the bonds which have been introduced in evidence, of the par value of $8,200 and offered to sell these bonds to the banking house. It is the claim of the people that those bonds which were in the possession of the defendants at that time were the same bonds, or part of the same bonds which were stolen from the bank on March 18th. In this connection I charge you, gentlemen of the jury, that the evidence discloses that upon the 24th day of March, 1921, these bonds were actually in the physical

1271

possession of the respondent Quigley, and that the respondent Hague was with him. I charge you as a matter of law that if Mr. Hague and Mr. Quigley were jointly engaged in the undertaking on that occasion of disposing of those bonds, if they were both interested in the disposal of those bonds, and were both taking part in the attempt to dispose of those bonds, then, as a matter of law, both parties were in possession of the bonds on that occasion, and it does not matter that the bonds were actually, physically, in the possession of one of them. In law, if both were engaged in the common undertaking of the disposing of the bonds, then as a matter of law they would be in the possession of both of them."

This instruction left to the jury the question of fact involved and correctly stated the law. 25 Cyc. p. 140. The charge of the court relative to the possession of recently stolen property was without error, having in mind the evidence and the issues thereon left to the jury. People v. Hogan, 123 Mich. 233; People v. Walters, 76 Mich. 195; People v. May, 199 Mich. 574.

An effort was made by defendants to explain the possession of the stolen property but evidently this only led to further fasten the crime upon them. Possession of recently stolen property, accompanied by an active and hurried effort under an assumed name to dispose thereof is evidence to go to the jury upon the issue of whether the accused stole the same. The charge fairly and fully instructed the jury as to all the issues and gave the law applicable thereto.

We find no reversible error, and the convictions are affirmed.

STEERE, C. J., and STONE, CLARK, BIRD, and SHARPE, JJ., concurred. MOORE and FELLOWS, JJ., did not sit.

People v. McKeighan
205 Mich. 367

KUHN, J. It was the claim of the people on the trial of this case that the defendant induced certain other parties, viz., Harry Davis, Walter Davidson, William Cooper and Joseph Feeney, to commit the crime of assault and robbery, not being armed with a dangerous weapon (3 Comp. Laws 1915, Sec. 15208), upon one Fred Spencer. The information charges the defendant as a principal in the commission of this offense. He was tried separately from the other parties involved, they having pleaded guilty to the charge of assault and robbery. The testimony tended to show that on the evening of November 24, 1917, Davis, Cooper, Davidson and Feeney were at the home of Mr. and Mrs. Cooper, which was adjoining to the apartments occupied by the defendant and his family in the same building, both of these apartments being over a garage belonging to the defendant. That during the evening

1272

Spencer came to the Cooper home and there engaged in a game
of dice or playing what is known as "craps." It is further
claimed that after the game had been going on for some time,
the defendant came to the apartment, but took no part in the
playing of the game. That Spencer won some money from the
other men, it is claimed by the use of crooked dice. The testimony further shows, and it is the claim of the prosecution,
that the defendant advised some of these men to go and get
their money back, and that he told Mr. Cooper, who was to
take Spencer in his automobile when he left the apartment,
to stop the automobile so that the others implicated might
get their money back and have a settlement with Spencer.
Witness Davis, who had previously pleaded guilty to an assault and robbery charge, testified with reference to his
conversation with the respondent as follows:

"He said, 'Make him give it to you.' He said, 'If I was
you I would make him give it to me and stick him up, and
make him give it to me.' Then he went over and spoke to
Cooper a minute. Then he told me that Cooper said he would
stop at North and Parkland provided there was no row."

There is testimony to the effect that the respondent
called Spencer into a room before he left, where the sum
of $20 was given by Spencer to the respondent as "kick in"
money after threats of violence were made by respondent.
That afterwards Cooper did stop his automobile for the purpose of lighting the tail light thereon, and that thereafter
Davis, Feeney and Davidson did take from Spencer certain
money. The evidence further tends to show that Spencer had
$100 on his person when he joined in the game, and that at
the time that he was claimed to have been robbed he had $133,
all of which was taken from him, which it is claimed tended
to show that he was robbed of $100 which he did not win at
gambling, but which he had when he joined in the game. The
trial resulted in a conviction of respondent, and the case
is brought here by writ of error after sentence.
It is claimed that the information is insufficient, in
that it charges the respondent as a principal, and that
there is nothing in the information to inform the respondent of what connection it was claimed he had in the commission of the offense other than that he directly committed
it, and that although the statute (3 Comp. Laws 1915, Sec.
15757) provides that an accessory shall be indicted, tried
and punished as a principal, it does not intend to permit an
information to be drawn without giving sufficient facts to
inform the respondent of the exact nature of the charge.
With this contention we do not agree, as the statute has
clearly abolished all distinctions previously existing between principals and accessories, and in express terms applies to indictments (including informations). . . .
The information was clearly sufficient to warrant the
conviction.
Counsel for the respondent claim that the trial court
erred in refusing to give the following request to charge:

1273

"If you find that the money alleged to have been stolen was won in an illegal game of dice, from Davis and the other parties who participated in securing a return of the same, then that money would not be the property of Spencer and your verdict must be not guilty."

- and contend that the present case is ruled by the case of People v. Henry, 202 Mich. 450. In that decision it is stated that -

"Our statute (2 Comp. Laws 1915, Sec. 7795) gives a right to the loser to recover the money or property lost in a gambling game, and, among other actions, gives that of replevin, thus recognizing the money or property as belonging to him."

The statute in question provides:

. . . "and any person that shall lose any sum of money, or any goods or articles of value, by playing or betting on cards, or by any other device in the nature of such playing and betting, and shall pay or deliver the same or any part thereof to the winner, the person so paying or delivering the same may sue for and recover such money in an action for money had and received, to the use of the plaintiff; and such goods or other articles of value in an action of replevin or the value thereof in an action of trover, or in a special action on the case."

The statute points out that where money is lost, the loser may recover from the winner the money illegally obtained in an action for money had and received, and further provides that goods or other articles of value may be recovered by an action of replevin. A careful reading of this statute has satisfied us that it was the intent of the legislature to provide that the action of replevin may be resorted to where the money could be positively identified, but as it is quite apparent that this would be difficult to do in most instances, the further action for money had and received is provided for in cases where the money cannot be identified. In the instant case the testimony conclusively shows that the money was commingled with the money which Spencer had on his person at the time he started the game, and that it would have been hard to identify the exact money which was lost in the game. Moreover, the record shows that it is the claim of the people that more money was taken from Spencer than he actually won in the game. Under the facts in this case, in our opinion, it clearly became a question for the jury to determine whether or not the respondent aided and abetted the commission of the alleged offense, and the subject for inquiry now is whether the various elements constituting the crime were properly submitted to the jury in the charge by the trial court. One of the essential elements of this crime that it is necessary to prove beyond a reasonable doubt is that the respondent had a felonious intent at

1274

the time of counseling, aiding and abetting the commission
of the said offense of robbery. It was therefore necessary
that the learned trial judge should give clear and explicit
instructions as to this important feature of the alleged offense. The learned trial judge charged with reference to
this as follows:

"Now if you find by the evidence in this case, beyond a
reasonable doubt, that the respondent counseled, advised
and knew and had a criminal intent at the time that he advised with the other men, and you find the other men did
proceed to hold up, rob, and take the money away from the
man Spencer, then under our law the respondent is equally
guilty with the other parties who absolutely took the money
away from him."

This, in our opinion, was not a sufficient statement of
the necessary intent. It should have been clearly stated
that it was necessary that the respondent had a criminal intent to rob, steal or take from the person of Fred Spencer
property that could have been the subject of larceny. An
intent to commit a simple assault would not justify a conviction upon the charge alleged in the information. . . .
(Reversed on other grounds.)

BIRD, C. J., and MOORE, STEERE, BROOKE, FELLOWS and
STONE, JJ., concurred. OSTRANDER, J., did not sit.

People v. Henry
202 Mich. 450

(For the opinion in this case see page 1128, supra.)

People v. Kruper
340 Mich. 114

BUSHNELL, J. Defendants Henry Kruper and Ignatius Sadak
were granted leave to appeal from sentences imposed after
they were found guilty of the crime of extortion. Defendants were tried jointly before a jury on an information containing counts of extortion and robbery unarmed. . . .

The complaining witness, Henry J. Druzynski, lives with
his wife and child in the city of Detroit. At the time he
was in the haberdashery business, although the suggestion
was made in his cross-examination that he was also operating a baseball numbers pool. This he denied. He apparently
was acquainted with defendant Sadak, who had visited at his
home on August 14, 1949. About a week later, at 1 o'clock
in the morning, Druzynski and his friend, Stanley Novak,
left a bar on East 7-Mile Road in the city of Detroit to enter

1275

his car. He noticed another automobile parked about 20
feet away facing in the same direction. As Druzynski got
into his car with Novak, Sadak approached and told Cruzyn-
ski he wanted to talk to him. He got out and went with
Sadak to the sidewalk, where Kruper, approaching from the
car in the rear, joined them. In the conversation that ensued the defendants demanded $200. According to Druzynski,
they said: "We aren't fooling and we are going to get it."
He further testified:

"So they gave me a good shaking up. They both shook me
up by the arms. They held me by the arms. I got frightened, scared and afraid of everything, so I said 'I haven't
got that kind of money.' Then Iggy said to me 'You've got
lots of money. We will take you home.' So they both grabbed me and attempted to take me to my house."

When asked how much money he had, Druzynski took $9 out
of his pocket, consisting of a $5 bill and 4 ones, and
stated that that was all he had. Sadak looked at the money,
made some obscene remarks, and gave it back, saying: "Wait
a minute," and then, according to Druzynski, Sadak took $5
out of the money and kept it. Druzynski further testified:

"Then Iggy said to me, 'You got a nice boy and wife,' and
that is when Kruper walked over to the car and said something
to Novak who was still in the car. In the meantime while he
went down there Iggy grabbed me by the arm and he said, 'Look,
if you think we are kidding around or fooling around, we have
got 3 irons laying in the car.' I said I didn't want to go
to the car because he was going to show me he had 3 irons.
I said I'd take his word for it. He did not say what kind
of irons they were. He just said '3 irons.' Novak was still
in the car talking to Kruper and they had a little scuffle
there. I saw the scuffle. It was a little shaking up job.
I actually saw it."

Kruper then ordered Novak to get out and go home and
Sadak got into the car with Druzynski and rode with him to
another bar, where an unsuccessful attempt was made to borrow
$200. Kruper had followed in his car. The conversation was
continued, with Druzynski pleading for more time, and finally an appointment was made for the next morning at a designated place. After Kruper and Sadak left, Druzynski went
to the Davison avenue police station and reported the facts
and the police arranged to be present at the proposed meeting.

An important question in the case is that of election of
counts.

The elements of the crime of extortion as stated in the
statute (CL 1948, Sec. 750.213 (Stat. Ann Sec. 28.410)) are
as follows:

"Any person who shall, either orally or by a written or
printed communication, maliciously threaten to accuse another of any crime or offense, or shall orally or by any

written or printed communication maliciously threaten any injury to the person or property or mother, father, husband, wife or child of another with intent thereby to extort money or any pecuniary advantage whatever, or with intent to compel the person so threatened to do or refrain from doing any act against his will, shall be guilty of a felony, punishable by imprisonment in the State prison not more than 20 years or by a fine of not more than $10,000."

The statute pertaining to the crime of robbery unarmed (CL 1948, Sec. 750.530 (Stat Ann Sec. 28.798)) reads:

"Any person who shall, by force and violence, or by assault or putting in fear, feloniously rob, steal and take from the person of another, or in his presence, any money or other property which may be the subject of larceny, such robber not being armed with a dangerous weapon, shall be guilty of a felony, punishable by imprisonment in the State prison not more than 15 years."

The primary distinction between the offense of robbery and extortion is that in robbery the taking must be without the consent of the party robbed, while in extortion the taking is with consent. However, in both crimes may exist the elements of the use of force, violence, fear, et cetera. See 2 Gillespie, Michigan Criminal Law and Procedure (1st ed), Sec. 1169-1173, pp 1467-1470, and Sec. 1844, pp 2044-2045.

These crimes are not completely inconsistent in the eyes of the law. The threat to do "injury to the person or property," or to the class enumerated in the extortion statute, when accompanied by force, actual or constructive, and property or money is given up in consequence of that force, these elements can constitute robbery. Whenever the elements of force or putting in fear enter into the taking, and that is the cause which induces the party to part with his property, such taking is robbery. This is true regardless of how slight the act of force or the cause creating fear may be, provided, in the light of the circumstances, the party robbed has a reasonable belief that he may suffer injury unless he complies with the demand. In the light of this relationship between the 2 crimes, the people were not required to elect under which count they should proceed.

The verdict and the sentences are affirmed.

BUTZEL, C. J., and CARR, SHARPE, BOYLES, REID, DETHMERS, and KELLY, JJ., concurred.

3. Final Draft - Michigan Revised Criminal Code

CHAPTER 33. ROBBERY

Section
3301. Definition of Terms.

(Definition of Terms)

Sec. 3301.   (1)   The definitions contained in section 3201 are applicable in this chapter unless the context otherwise requires.

(2)   "In the course of committing a theft" embraces acts which occur in an attempt to commit or the commission of theft, or in flight after the attempt or commission.

(Robbery in the First Degree)

Sec. 3305.   (1)   A person commits the crime of robbery in the first degree if he violates section 3307 and is armed with a deadly weapon or dangerous instrument.

(2)   Possession then and there of an article used or fashioned in a manner to lead any person who is present reasonably to believe it to be a deadly weapon or dangerous instrument, or any verbal or other representation by the defendant that he is then and there so armed, is prima facie evidence under subparagraph (1) that he was so armed.

(3)   Robbery in the first degree is a Class A felony.

(Robbery in the Second Degree)

Sec. 3306.   (1)   A person commits the crime of robbery in the second degree if he violates section 3307 and is aided by another person actually present.

(2)   Robbery in the second degree is a Class B felony.

(Robbery in the Third Degree)

Sec. 3307.   (1)   A person commits the crime of robbery in the third degree if in the course of committing a theft he:

(a)   Uses force against the person of the owner or any person present with intent to overcome his physical resistance or physical power of resistance; or

(b)   Threatens the imminent use of force against the person of anyone who is present with intent to compel acquiescence to the taking of or escaping with the property.

(2)   Robbery in the third degree is a Class C felony.

(Claim of Right Not a Defense)

Sec. 3310.   No person may submit in defense against a prosecution for robbery in any of its degrees that there was no theft because the taking was under a claim of right, claim of right is not a defense under this chapter.

*   *   *   *   *

Committee Commentary to Chapter 33

A. Summary

The Draft retains the basic coverage of the present statutes. However, it draws the line clearly between robbery and extortion in the basic definition of Sec. 3307, and provides for increased penalties in degree format by reason of increased danger to the victim because there are two or more criminal participants (Sec. 3306) or the criminal is armed or creates the impression that he is armed (Sec. 3305).

B. Derivation

Section 3305 restates the present Michigan Law (C.L. 1948, Sec. 750.529). Section 3306 is adapted from New York Revised Penal Law Sec. 160.10. Section 3307 embodies elements from Wisconsin Statutes Sec. 943.32 (1965) and Model Penal Code Sec. 222.1

C. Relationship to Existing Law

"Common law robbery was theft of property from the person or in the presence of the victim by force or by putting him in fear either of immediate bodily injury or of certain other grievous harms, including arson of the dwelling and even accusation of sodomy" (Model Penal Code, Tent. Draft No. 11, p. 68 (1960)). The Michigan Supreme Court has called it "assaulting another and stealing or taking away money or other property from his person or in his presence (Saks v. St. Paul Mercury Indemnity Co., 308 Mich. 719, 14 N.W. 2d 547 (1944). The nature of the crime is further indicated by the fact that larceny from the person, assault with intent to rob and assault with intent to rob and assault and battery are lesser included offenses on a charge of robbery (People v. Kolodzieski, 267 Mich. 654; 212 N.W. 958 (1927); People v. Allie, 216 Mich. 133, 184 N.W. 423 (1921); People v. Blanchard, 136 Mich. 146, 98 N.W. 983 (1904)). The intent element appears to be a blending of the intent necessary for larceny with that for assault (People v. Locke, 275 Mich. 333, 266 N.W. 370 (1936); People v. Quigley, 217 Mich. 213, 185 N.W. 787 (1921)). Michigan robbery legislation is viewed as superseding the common law but in fact dividing it into two grades (People v. Powler, 142 Mich. 225, 105 N.W. 611 (1905); People v. Calvin, 60 Mich. 113, 26 N.W. 851 (1886); cf. People v. Quigley, 217 Mich. 213, 185 N.W. 787 (1921)).

The two basic statutes are robbery unarmed (C.L. 1948, Sec. 750.530) and robbery armed (C.L. 1948, Sec. 750.529). There is a counterpart assault with intent statute which can be invoked when no property is in fact obtained (C.L. 1948, Sec. 750.88). There is a lesser included offense to a charge of robbery unarmed. Two special kinds of robbery are forcible detention of a railroad train (C. L. 1948, Sec. 750.516) and bank, safe and vault robbery (C. L. 1948, Sec. 750.531).

Though the statutes contain no specific reference to defenses against a charge of robbery in any of its statutory

1279

forms, the traditional inclusion of larceny in the elements
of the offense has led to decisions that a belief the actor
has a right to take or recover the property is a defense
both to larceny and to robbery (People v. McKeighan, 205
Mich. 367, 171 N.W. 500 (1919); People v. Henry, 202 Mich.
450, 168 N.W. 534 (1918)). Whether there is also a defense
against the assault elements requires consideration of the
general justification of use of force to protect one's property; relatively few robbery situations are appropriate to
invoke these doctrines. (See Sec. 620 and 625 and the Commentaries to them).

In many jurisdictions the problem of avoiding overlap between robbery and extortion has been a difficult one. The
problem is less acute in Michigan because our extortion statute is not a true extortion statute; in other states our
statutory definition would be found under the headings of
coercion and attempted extortion (see commentary to Sec. 3245-
3247). The only Michigan decision which attempts to distinguish them does so on the basis of "consent" (People v. Kruper, 340 Mich. 114, 64 N.W. 2d 629 (1954); see commentary
to Sec. 3205-3208), but this appears to be a legal abstrac-
tion bearing no evident relationship to actual circumstances.
The basic problem may be viewed as unsettled in present Michigan law.

Though for purposes of arrangement, first-degree robbery
is placed first, it is more convenient in explaining the
thrust of Chapter 33 to consider the several sections in the
inverse order to that in which they actually appear.

Section 3307 makes several important changes in Michigan
law. One is in the scope of the basic concept of robbery
itself. The present approach is that unless property is
actually taken from the person or presence of the victim,
there is no robbery. If the actor tries to rob and is prevented or is unsuccessful, the matter must be disposed of as
attempted robbery or assault with intent to rob. This em-
phasizes the property aspects of the crime and treats it as
an aggravated form of theft. If, however, one is primarily
concerned about the physical danger or appearances of physical danger to the citizen, and his inability to protect
himself against sudden onslaughts against his person or property, then the actual taking of property diminishes in importance. Chapter 33 embodies the judgment that repression
of violence is the principal reason for being guilty of robbery. For this reason it utilizes in Sec. 3301 the Model
Penal Code language of "in the course of committing a theft"
which extends from the attempt state through the phase of
flight. This also eliminates the question of what is a
lesser-included offense to a charge of robbery.

The next portion of Sec. 3307 concerns itself with the
means used to acquire or attempt to acquire the property.
Subsection (1) (a) turns on the actual use of force against
the owner, and works no change in existing law. Subsection
(1) (b), however, involves threat of immediate force against

the person of the owner or someone present as a means to
part the owner from his property. It is at this point that
the Draft endeavors to distinguish as clearly as possible
between robbery and extortion. The definition of "threat"
in extortion (Sec. 3201 (1), 3247) covers a menace "to cause
physical harm in the future to the person threatened or to
any other person (Sec. 3201 (1) (i)), which contrasts with
"imminent use of force" in Sec. 3307 (1) (b). "Physical confinement or restraint" (Sec. 3201 (1) (iii)) might or might
not involve in particular instances "imminent use of force
against the person" (Sec. 3307 (1) (b)), but the chances of
overlap are minimal enough (cf. the facts in People v. Kruper, 340 Mich. 114, 64 N.W. 2d 629 (1954)) that further qualification of the language of Sec. 3307 (1) (b) is probably unnecessary.

Section 3307 (1) (b) does not specify any relationship between the person actually threatened and the owner. The important considerations should be whether the actor intends
to coerce the owner into parting with his property by the
threats he uses and whether under the circumstances the
threat is or might be effective. There is no purpose served
by calling it robbery if threats are directed against the
wife or child of the owner, but something else if the same
threats are directed toward the owner's fiancee or a child
of a complete stranger who happens to be present.

The punishment for robbery in the third degree is indicated at the lowest felony level, and is the same as that
for the least serious form of extortion, extortion in the
second degree (Sec. 3246).

Section 3306 authorizes increased punishment for one who
commits robbery while aided by another. The reason is the
increased likelihood of an assault on the victim. Michigan
law, as indicated earlier in the Commentary, does not now
contain any mention of assistance by accomplices. The Draft,
however, includes this as the factor which sets robbery in
the second degree apart from robbery in the third degree,
because where two or more persons commit the crime it indicates greater planning and therefore a greater likelihood
that the criminals are professionals. There is also more
likelihood that violence will erupt, since each criminal
reinforces the others. Inclusion of the factor of actual
aid does not affect the doctrine of vicarious responsibility
of accomplices for the criminal acts of the principal. This
matter is dealt with in the general provisions of the Draft
covering complicity.

The punishment category for robbery in the second degree,
a Class B felony, equals that for the more serious form of
extortion, extortion in the first degree (Sec. 3247).

Section 3305 is the most serious form of robbery. The
aggravating factors are use of a dangerous weapon or death
or injury to a non-criminal who is present "in the course
of committing a theft." Prima facie evidence provisions

covering use of dummy weapons or representations that the
robber is armed make it possible to convict armed robbers
on appearances, but leave it open to them to show that they
were not in fact armed so that the offense should be either
robbery in the second or in the third degree.

The present Michigan robbery armed statute (C. L. 1948,
Sec. 750.529) authorizes an increased maximum and minimum
punishment if the offender is armed with a dangerous weapon
or inflicts serious bodily injury or an aggravated assault
on the victim. The Draft preserves both ideas, but evidences the relationship between this and ordinary robbery
in a more logical arrangement, that of first-degree robbery
in relation to second or third-degree robbery and not robbery armed in relation to robbery unarmed.

The defendant must be armed or create the impression that
he is armed with a deadly weapon or a dangerous instrument.
These terms are defined in Sec. 135 and have been utilized
in Chapter 21 (Assaults). This confirms the close relationship that this chapter bears both to Chapter 21 and Chapter
32.

What to do about the use of dummy weapons is a difficult
matter. The basic robbery statute is designed to protect
the citizen from fear for his person or that of another. This
should be aggravated only when there is either actual serious
physical injury inflicted on the victim or when the robber
actually possesses an instrument which is in fact capable of
inflicting such injuries. (See the definition of "serious
physical injury" in Sec. 135.) Indeed, under the present
Michigan law the robber might as well be armed as not, since
he receives increased punishment for using either a water
pistol or a real pistol. However, it is very difficult to
prove that a robber actually is armed with a dangerous weapon unless he is arrested on the spot. In an effort to balance needs for enforcement with the demands for appropriate
penalties, the Draft makes possession of something reasonably believed to be a deadly weapon or dangerous instrument
as defined in Sec. 135, or a representation by the defendant
that he has one, prima facie evidence that he is armed. If
in fact he refutes this, the proper conviction is of robbery
in the third degree (Sec. 3307).

The Draft does not preserve the special statutes on train
robbery and bank, safe and vault robbery. Train robbery
does not appear to be a current problem, and bank robbery
does not pose any special danger to person or property not
already reached under Sec. 3306 and 3307. The Draft embodies the view taken by the American Law Institute:

"A more difficult question is posed by the fairly common
statutes penalizing with special severity robbery or burglary
of banks or trains. Here are particularly desirable and
well-defended prizes, presumably chosen as targets by the
most desperate and well-organized criminals. On the other
hand, one reads of pathetic attempts of clumsy amateurs to
rob banks; and the criteria which would lead to designating

bank robbery for special treatment take us logically on to building and loan companies, credit unions, express companies, paymasters, post offices, jewelry stores, and truck loads of whiskey, silk, or other valuable commodities. It is difficult, if not impossible, to draft an acceptable legislative definition of this category of unusually tempting victims. This, plus the fact that most states get along without special laws on the subject, supports our judgment against making exceptional provision here." (Model Penal Code, Tent. Draft No. 11, p. 72 (1960)).

Because of the considerable risk to life that first-degree robbery transactions involve, the penalty category indicated is a Class A felony; Sec. 3305 therefore is one of the handful of very serious offenses contained in the Draft.

As indicated earlier in the Commentary, at least two Michigan decisions state that a claim of right to the property taken is a defense against a charge of robbery. This flows logically from the traditional definition of robbery as in effect larceny by assault. A claim of right means that there is no larceny, so that in turn and as a matter of logic there can be no robbery. Only the assault can be punished. Since robbery under Sec. 3307 of the Draft occurs in the course of committing or attempting to commit theft, and since claim of right is a defense to a charge of theft (Sec. 3240 (1)), a claim of right would also be available as a defense under Chapter 33 unless a contrary doctrine is indicated.

However, the chief concern in Chapter 33 is for the protection of the lives and physical or mental well-being of citizens. Therefore, there is little point in retaining the common-law defense, since the danger to the citizen from the use or threat of force is present no matter what the origin of the claim by the defendant to the property may be. There is an added policy in favor of non-retention of the defense, namely that citizens should be encouraged to assert their property rights through orderly processes of law rather than by force. The Draft, therefore, in Sec. 3310, specifically eliminates a claim of right as a defense to robbery in any of its degrees. In taking this position the Draft does not in fact decree punishment of those who under present law would be innocent of crime. It only affects the character of criminality and perhaps the maximum term of imprisonment, in that under existing doctrine the defendant would be convicted of an aggravated form of assault despite his claim of right, while under the Draft he is punished for robbery in one of its degrees as originally charged in the information.

INTERROGATORIES

1. Outline the provisions of the Michigan statutes relevant to the crime of robbery.

2. Is there any difference in Michigan in the authorized penalty for robbery if the defendant uses a dummy weapon instead of a deadly weapon?

3. What were the facts, issue and holding of the court in Saks v. St. Paul Mer. Indemnity Co.? How is robbery defined in this case?

4. What were the facts, issue and holding of the court in People v. Kolodzieski? What are the lesser included offenses on a charge of robbery?

5. What were the facts, issue and holding of the court in People v. Allie?

6. What were the facts, issue and holding of the court in People v. Calvin?

7. What was the issue and holding of the court in People v. Powler?

8. What were the facts, issue and holding of the court in People v. Locke? The intent required for robbery represents a blending of the intent requirements for what other crimes?

9. What were the facts, issue and holding of the court in People v. Quigley? Does the Michigan robbery statute supersede the common law?

10. What were the facts, issue and holding of the court in People v. McKeighan? Is a claim of right to the property in question a defense to the crime of robbery? Is such a claim a defense to the element of assault?

11. What were the facts, issue and holding of the court in People v. Henry?

12. What were the facts, issue and holding of the court in People v. Kruper? What is the basic distinction between extortion and robbery in Michigan?

13. Outline the provisions of Sec. 3301, 3305, 3306, 3307, and 3310, Final Draft, Mich. Rev. Crim. Code? What important changes would these provisions make in the law of robbery?

CHAPTER XII

FORGERY, COUNTERFEITING, AND FRAUD

A. Forgery and Counterfeiting

   1. Michigan Compiled Laws (1948)

      Chapter XLI. FORGERY AND COUNTERFEITING

750.248 Forgery of records and other instruments, venue

   Sec. 248. (1) Any person who shall falsely make, alter, forge or counterfeit any public record, or any certificate, return or attestation of any clerk of a court, public register, notary public, justice of the peace, township clerk, or any other public officer, in relation to any matter wherein such certificate, return or attestation may be received as legal proof, or any charter, deed, will, testament, bond or writing obigatory, letter of attorney, policy of insurance, bill of lading, bill of exchange, promissory note, or any order, acquittance of discharge for money or other property, or any waiver, release, claim or demand, or any acceptance of a bill of exchange, or indorsement, or assignment of a bill of exchange or promissory note for the payment of money, or any accountable receipt for money, goods or other property, with intent to injure or defraud any person shall be guilty of a felony, punishable by imprisonment in the state prison not more than 14 years.

   (2) The venue in a prosecution under this section may be either in the county in which the forgery was performed, or in a county in which any false, forged, altered or counterfeit record, deed, instrument or other writing is uttered, and published with intent to injure or defraud. As amended P.A. 1964, No. 101, Sec. 1 Eff. Aug. 28; P.A. 1967, No. 64, Sec. 1, Eff. Nov. 2.

750.249 Same; uttering and publishing

   Sec. 249. UTTERING AND PUBLISHING FORGED INSTRUMENTS - Any person who shall utter and publish as true, any false, forged, altered or counterfeit record, deed, instrument or other writing mentioned in the preceding section, knowing the same to be false, altered, forged or counterfeit, with intent to injure or defraud as aforesaid, shall be guilty of a felony, punishable by imprisonment in the state prison not more than 14 years.

750.250 Forgery of notes, etc., issued for debt of state, political subdivisions

   Sec. 250. FORGERY OF NOTES, ETC., ISSUED FOR DEBT OF

STATE - Any person who shall falsely make, alter, forge or counterfeit any note, certificate, bond, warrant or other instrument, issued by the treasurer or other officer authorized to issue the same, of this state, or any of its political subdivisions or municipalities, with intent to injure or defraud as aforesaid, shall be guilty of a felony, punishable by imprisonment in the state prison not more than 7 years.

750.251 Forgery of bank bills and promissory notes

Sec. 251. FORGERY OF BANK BILLS AND NOTES - Any person who shall falsely make, alter, forge, or counterfeit any bank bill or promissory note payable to the bearer thereof, or to the order of any person, issued by this state, or any of its political subdivisions or municipalities or by any incorporated banking company in this state, or in any of the British provinces of North America, or in any other state or country, or payable therein, at the office of any banking company incorporated by any law of the United States or of any other state, with intent to injure or defraud any person, shall be guilty of a felony, punishable by imprisonment in the state prison not more than 7 years.

750.252 Possession of counterfeit notes, etc., with intent to utter same

Sec. 252. POSSESSION OF COUNTERFEIT NOTES, ETC., WITH INTENT TO UTTER SAME - Any person who shall have in his possession at the same time, 10 or more similar false, altered, forged or counterfeit notes, bills of credit, bank bills or notes of this state, or any of its political subdivisions or municipalities, payable to the bearer thereof, or to the order of any person, such as are mentioned in the preceding sections of this chapter, knowing the same to be false, altered, forged or counterfeit, with intent to utter the same as true, and thereby to injure and defraud as aforesaid, shall be guilty of a felony, punishable by imprisonment in the state prison not more than 7 years.

750.253 Uttering counterfeit notes, etc.

Sec. 253. UTTERING COUNTERFEIT NOTES, ETC. - Any person who shall utter or pass, or tender in payment as true, any such false, altered, forged or counterfeit note, certificate or bill of credit for any debt of this state, or any of its political subdivisions or municipalities, any bank bill or promissory note, payable to the bearer thereof, or to the order of any person, issued as aforesaid, knowing the same to be false, altered, forged or counterfeit, with intent to injure or defraud as aforesaid, shall be guilty of a felony, punishable by imprisonment of not more than 5 years or by fine of not more than 2,500 dollars.

750.254 Possession of counterfeit bank, state or municipal bills or notes

Sec. 254. POSSESSION OF COUNTERFEIT BANK BILLS, ETC. -
Any person who shall bring into this state, or shall have
in his possession, any false, altered, forged or counterfeit
bill or note in the similitude of the bills or notes payable
to the bearer thereof, or to the order of any person issued
by or for this state, or any of its political subdivisions
or municipalities, or any bank or banking company, established in this state, or in any of the British provinces in North
America, or in any other state or country, with intent to utter or pass the same, or to render the same current as true,
knowing the same to be false, forged or counterfeit, shall
be guilty of a felony, punishable by imprisonment in the state
prison not more than 5 years, or by fine of not more than
2,500 dollars.

750.255 Tools and implements for counterfeiting bills or
        notes

Sec. 255. TOOLS AND IMPLEMENTS FOR COUNTERFEITING NOTES -
Any person who shall engrave, make or mend, or begin to engrave, make or mend, any plate, block, press or other tool,
instrument or implement, or shall make or provide any paper
or other material, adapted or designed for the forging and
making any false or counterfeit note, certificate or other
bill of credit in the similitude of the notes, certificates,
bills of credit issued by lawful authority for any debt or
any false or counterfeit note or bill in the similitude of
the notes or bills issued by any bank or banking company established in this state, or within the United States, or in
any of the British provinces in North American, or in any
foreign state or country; and any person who shall have in
his possession any such plate or block, engraved in whole
or in part, or any press or other tool, instrument or implement, or any paper or other material, adapted and designed as aforesaid, with intent to use the same, or to cause or
permit the same to be used in forging or making any such
false or counterfeit certificates, bills or notes, shall be
guilty of a felony, punishable by imprisonment in the state
prison not more than 10 years or by fine of not more than
5,000 dollars.

750.256 Testimony of president and cashier of bank

Sec. 256. TESTIMONY OF PRESIDENT AND CASHIER OF BANK -
In all prosecutions for forging or counterfeiting any notes
or bills of the bank before mentioned, or for altering, publishing or tendering in payment as true, any forged or counterfeit bank bills or notes, or for being possessed thereof, with
intent to alter and pass the same as true, the testimony of
the president and cashier of such bank may be dispensed with,
if their place of residence shall be out of this state, or
more than 40 miles from the place of trial; and the testimony
of any person acquainted with the signature of the president
or cashier of such banks, or who has knowledge of the differ-

1287

ence in appearance of the true and counterfeit bills or
notes thereof, may be admitted to prove that any such bills
or notes are counterfeit; and the lawful existence of any
bank out of this state shall be presumed upon evidence that
such bank is actually engaged in the business of a bank.

750.257 Sworn certificate, evidence

Sec. 257. SWORN CERTIFICATE MADE EVIDENCE - In all prosecutions for forging or counterfeiting any note, certificate,
bills of credit or other security issued in behalf of the
United States, or in behalf of any state or territory, or
for uttering, publishing or tendering in payment as true,
any such forged or counterfeit note, certificate, bill of
credit, or security, or for being possessed thereof with intent to utter or pass the same as true, the certificate under
oath of the secretary of the treasury, or of the treasurer
of the United States, or of the secretary or treasurer of
any state or territory on whose behalf such note, certificate, bill of credit or security, purports to have been
issued, shall be admitted as evidence for the purpose of
proving the same to be forged or counterfeit.

750.258 Connecting parts of instruments

Sec. 258. CONNECTING PARTS OF INSTRUMENTS - If any person shall connect together different parts of several bank
notes or other genuine instruments in such a manner as to
produce an additional note or instrument, with intent to
pass all of them as genuine, the same shall be deemed a
forgery, in like manner as if each of them had been falsely
made or forged.

750.259 Affixing fictitious signature

Sec. 259. AFFIXING FICTITIOUS SIGNATURE - If any fictitious or pretended signature, purporting to be the signature
of an officer or agent of any corporation, shall be fraudulently affixed to any instrument or writing, purporting to
be a note, draft or other evidence of debt, issued by said
corporation, with intent to pass the same as true, it shall
be deemed a forgery, though no such person may ever have
been an officer or agent of such corporation, nor ever have
existed.

750.260 Counterfeiting and possession of coins

Sec. 260. COUNTERFEITING AND POSSESSION OF COINS - Any
person who shall counterfeit any gold or silver coin, current by law or usage within this state, and every person
who shall have in his possession at the same time, 5 more
pieces of false money or coin, counterfeited in the similitude of any gold or silver coin current as aforesaid, knowing the same to be false and counterfeit, and with intent to

utter or pass the same as true, shall be guilty of a felony, punishable by imprisonment in the state prison for life, or for any term of years.

750.261 Same; possession of less than 5 counterfeit coins

Sec. 261. POSSESSION OF LESS THAN 5 PIECES OF COUNTERFEIT COIN - Any person who shall have in his possession any number of pieces less than 5, of the counterfeit coin mentioned in the next preceding section, knowing the same to be counterfeit, with intent, to utter and pass the same as true, and any person who shall utter, pass or tender in payment as true, any such counterfeit coin, knowing the same to be false and counterfeit, shall be guilty of a felony, punishable by imprisonment in the state prison not more than 10 years, or by a fine of not more than 5,000 dollars.

750.262 Same; tools

Sec. 262. TOOLS, ETC., FOR COUNTERFEITING COINS - Any person who shall cast, stamp, engrave, make or mend, or shall knowingly have in his possession, any mould, pattern, die, puncheon, engine, press or other tool or instrument, adapted and designed for coining or making any counterfeit coin, in the similitude of any gold or silver coin, current by law or usage in this state, with intent to use or employ the same, or to cause or permit the same to be used or employed in coining or making any such false and counterfeit coin as aforesaid, shall be guilty of a felony, punishable by imprisonment in the state prison not more than 10 years, or by a fine of not more than 5,000 dollars.

750.263 Forging and counterfeiting trade marks, etc.

Sec. 263. FORGING AND COUNTERFEITING TRADE MARKS, LABELS, STAMPS, ETC. - Any person who shall knowingly and wilfully forge or counterfeit, or cause or procure to be forged or counterfeited, any representation, likeness, similitude, copy or imitation of the private stamp, brand, wrapper or label, usually affixed by any mechanic, druggist, apothecary, or manufacturer to, and used by such mechanic, druggist, apothecary or manufacturer on, or in the sale of any goods, wares or merchandise and with intent to deceive or defraud the purchaser or manufacturer of any goods, wares or merchandise whatsoever, upon conviction thereof, shall be guilty of a misdemeanor, punishable by imprisonment in the count jail for a term of not more than 1 year, or by a fine of not more than 500 dollars.

750.264 Possession of dies, plates, etc., used in sale of
         goods

Sec. 264. POSSESSION OF DIES, PLATES, LABELS, ETC., USED BY MANUFACTURER, ETC., IN SALE OF GOODS - Any person who shall have in his possession any die, plate, engraving, or printed label, brand, stamp, wrapper, or any representation, likeness, similitude, copy or imitation of the private stamp, wrapper or label, usually affixed by any mechanic or manufacturer, druggist or apothecary to, and used by such mechanic, druggist, apothecary or manufacturer on, or in the sale of any goods, wares or merchandise, with intent to use or sell the said die, plate, engraving or printed stamp, label or wrapper, for the purpose of aiding or assisting in any way whatever, in vending any goods, wares or merchandise, in imitation of, or intended to resemble and be sold for the goods, wares and merchandise of such mechanic, druggist, apothecary or manufacturer, contrary to the provisions of the next preceding section shall, upon conviction thereof, be guilty of a misdemeanor, punishable by imprisonment in the county jail of not more than 1 year, or by fine of not more than 500 dollars.

750.265 Selling goods bearing forged labels, etc., intent to defraud

Sec. 265. SELLING GOODS BEARING FORGED LABELS, BRANDS, ETC., WITH INTENT TO DEFRAUD – Any person who shall vend any goods, wares or merchandise, having thereon any forged or counterfeit stamps, labels or brands, imitating, resembling or purporting to be the stamps, or labels of any mechanic, manufacturer, druggist or apothecary, knowing the same to be forged or counterfeited, and resembling or purporting to be imitations of the stamps, labels or marks of such manufacturer or mechanic, with intent to defraud, shall be guilty of a misdemeanor, punishable by imprisonment in the county jail of not more than 1 year, or by fine of not more than 500 dollars.

750.265a Union label; counterfeiting, imitation, unauthorized use

Sec. 265a. Any person who counterfeits or imitates any union label, or who uses any union label without authority of the particular labor organization or association of working-men whose union label is being so used, shall be guilty of a misdemeanor. A union label for the purposes of this section is defined as a trademark, term, design, symbol or device of a labor organization or association of working-men adopted by them to distinguish their craft, trade or work or membership in or indicating work done by such labor organization or association of working-men. P.A. 1931, No. 328, Sec. 265a, added by P.A. 1957, No. 62, Sec. 1, Eff. Sept. 27, 1957.

750.266 Forged railroad passenger tickets

Sec. 266. FORGERY AND SELLING, ETC., OF FORGED RAILROAD PASSENGER TICKETS – Any person who shall falsely make, forge, or counterfeit any railroad passenger ticket, purporting to be made or issued by any railroad company or companies doing business within or without the state, with intent to injure or defraud, whether made by writing, printing, stamping, punching, obliteration, or otherwise, shall be deemed an alteration within the meaning of this section.

Any person who shall sell, or offer to sell or who shall have in his possession with intent to sell, any such false, forged, altered or counterfeit railroad passenger ticket knowing the same to be false, forged, altered or counterfeit, shall be guilty of a felony.

The words "railroad passenger ticket or tickets", as used in this section, shall be construed to embrace any ticket, card, pass, certificate or paper providing, or intended to provide for the carriage or transportation of any person or persons upon any railroad, and shall include not only tickets of any railroad company fully prepared for use, but those not fully prepared for use, and all others which have been once used. At the trial of any case arising under this section, it shall be sufficient prima facie proof of the existence of any railroad company named in the information or indictment to show that such company was doing business as a railroad company at the time named in the information or indictment.

MICHIGAN ELECTION LAW OF 1954

168.544c Nominating petitions; size, form, contents

Sec. 544c. . . .
It shall be unlawful for any person to sign more nominating petitions for the same offices than there are persons to be elected to the office.

Any person who shall sign a petition with a name other than his own shall be guilty of a misdemeanor.

Any person knowingly making a false statement in a certificate on any petition or any person not a circulator who signs as such or any person who signs a name as circulator other than his own shall be guilty of a misdemeanor.

Any person who shall aid or abet another in any of the above listed acts shall be deemed to have committed the act.

The provisions of this section except as otherwise expressly provided shall apply to all petitions circulated under authority of the election law. P.A. 1954, No. 116, Sec. 544c, added by P.A. 1965, No. 312, Sec. 1, Eff. Jan. 1, 1966.

168.937 Forgery, penalty

Sec. 937. Any person found guilty of forgery under the provisions of this act shall, unless herein otherwise provided, be punished by a fine not exceeding $1,000.00, or by imprisonment in the state prison for a term not exceeding 5 years, or by both such fine and imprisonment in the discretion of the court. P.A. 1954, No. 116, Sec. 937, Eff. June 1, 1955.

MICHIGAN VEHICLE CODE

257.257 Alteration or forging of documents, penalty

Sec. 257. It shall be deemed to be a felony for any person to commit any of the following acts:

1. To alter with fraudulent intent any certificate of title, registration certificate or registration plate, issued by the department;
2. To forge or counterfeit any such document or plate purporting to have been issued by the department;
3. To alter or falsify with fraudulent intent or forge any assignment upon a certificate of title;
4. To hold or use any such document or plate knowing the same to have been so altered, forged, or falsified. P.A. 1949, No. 300, Sec. 257, Eff. Sept. 23.

257.905 Financial responsibility chapter, penalty for violation

Sec. 905. Any person who shall forge, or without authority, sign any evidence of ability to respond in damages as required by the secretary of state in the administration of chapter 5 and any person who shall violate any provisions of chapter 5 for which no penalty is otherwise provided, shall be guilty of a misdemeanor and upon conviction shall be fined not less than $100.00 nor more than $1,000.00, or imprisoned not more than 90 days or both. Any person whose operator's or chauffeur's license or registration card or other privilege to operate a motor vehicle has been suspended or revoked and restoration thereof or issuance of a new license or registration is contingent upon the furnishing of proof of financial responsibility and who during such suspension or revocation or in the absence of full authorization from the secretary of state drives any motor vehicle upon any highway or knowingly permits any motor vehicle owned by such person to be operated by another person upon any highway except as permitted hereunder shall be punished by a fine of not more than $500.00 and by imprisonment for a period of not less than 2 days nor more than 1 year or by both such fine and imprisonment. P.A. 1949, No. 300, Sec. 905, Eff. Sept. 23, as amended P.A. 1951, No. 270, Sec. 1, Eff. Sept. 28.

Department of Agriculture

285.82 Unlawful acts, penalty

Sec. 22. Any person who shall wilfully alter destroy any warehouse receipt, or record of warehouse receipts required by this act, or issue a warehouse receipt without preserving a record thereof; or issue a warehouse receipt when the commodity or commodities enumerated therein are not in fact in the building or buildings it is certified they are in, or shall, with intent to defraud, issue a second or other receipt for any commodity for which, or for any part of which, a former valid receipt is outstanding and in force; or shall while any valid receipt is outstanding and in force, sell, pledge, mortgage, or encumber, or transfer contrary to the provisions of this act or permit the same to be done without the written consent of the holder of such receipt, or, if any person receives any such property or helps to dispose of the same, he shall, upon conviction, be punished by a fine not exceeding $10,000.00 or by imprisonment in the state prison not exceeding 5 years, or both.

BABCOCK TEST

288.56 Standard Babcock testing glassware, scales and
          weights

Sec. 6. . . .

Standard weights

(e) STANDARD WEIGHTS

The standard cream test weight shall be 9 grams and the allowable tolerance therefor shall not exceed ½ grain (30 milligrams).

Every person, firm, company association, corporation or agent thereof buying and paying for milk or cream on the basis of the amount of butterfat contained therein as determined by the Babcock test shall use standard Babcock test bottles, pipettes, weights and scales as defined in this act, and it shall be unlawful for any such person, firm, company, association, corporation or agent thereof to falsely manipulate, under-read or over-read the Babcock test or any other contrivance used for determining the quality or value of milk or cream where the value of said milk or cream is determined by the percentage of butterfat contained in the same or to make a false determination by the Babcock test or otherwise, or to falsify the record of such test or to read the test at any temperature except the correct temperature which shall be between 135 degrees and 140 degrees Fahrenheit, or to pay on the basis of any test, measurement or weight except the true test, measurement or weight.

OIL, GAS AND MINERALS

319.19 Penal acts; punishment

Sec. 19. Any person who, for the purpose of evading this act, or of evading any rule, regulation or order made hereunder, shall intentionally make, or cause to be made, false entry or statement of fact in any report required by this act o by any rule, regulation or order made hereunder, or who, for such purpose, shall make or cause to be made false entry in any account, record, or memorandum kept by any person in connection with the provisions of this act, or of any rule, regulation or order made thereunder; or who, for such purpose, shall omit to make, or cause to be omitted, full, true, and correct entries in such accounts, records, or memoranda, of all facts and transactions pertaining to the interest or activities in the petroleum industry of such person as may be required by the supervisor under authority given in this act or by any rule, regulation or order made hereunder; or, who, for such purpose, shall remove out of the jurisdiction of the state, or who shall mutilate, alter, or by any other means falsify any book, record, or other paper pertaining to the transactions regulated by this act, or by any rule, regulation or order made hereunder; shall be deemed guilty of a felony and shall be subject, upon conviction in any court of competent jurisdiction, to a fine of not more than $1,000.00 or imprisonment for a term of not more than 3 years, or to both such fine and imprisonment.

CHRISTMAS TREES, BOUGHS AND OTHER TREES

320.418 Violation of act; forgery

Sec. 8. Violation of any of the provisions of this act is a misdemeanor. The forgery of any bill of sale or other evidence of title prescribed by the department of agriculture is a misdemeanor. P.A. 1962, No. 182, Sec. 8, Eff. March 28, 1963.

GAME LAW OF 1929

314.25 Violations; penalty

Sec. 25. Any person carrying or transporting a shotgun with buckshot, ball load, slug load or cut shell or a rifle other than .22 caliber rim fire during any season open to the taking of deer or elk with firewarms or a bow and arrow during any season open to the taking of deer with bow and arrow, who shall refuse to show his license herein provided for, to any sheriff, deputy sheriff, constable or conservation officer on demand, or any person who shall sell, loan, give or in any manner transfer said license, tag or seal to another person, or any person who shall attempt to use the license, tag or seal of another, or attach or allow to be

attached the tag or seal of his license to any deer or elk
or part thereof, except wuch as he may have lawfully killed
himself, or any person who shall alter any deer or elk hunting license in any way, or any person who shall affix to
any deer or elk hunting license a date other than the date
upon which it was issued, or any person who shall purchase
more than 1 deer or elk hunting license for any 1 deer or
elk hunting season, except duplicates, shall be deemed and
held to be guilty of violating the provisions of this section in addition to violating any of the other provisions
under this license, and may be fined upon conviction as provided in section 28 of this chapter. As amended P.A. 1952,
No. 252, Sec. 1, Eff. Sept. 18; P.A. 1957, No. 207, Sec. 1,
Eff. Sept. 27, P.A. 1964, No. 254, Sec. 1, Eff. Aug. 28.

314.32 License to trap; offenses relating to issuance and
         use, exception; nonresidents

Sec. 32. It shall be unlawful for any person:

(a) To make use of any kind of a trap for the purpose
of trapping any of the wild animals in this state without
first having procured a license therefor in accordance with
the provisions of this act;

(b) To obtain a trapping license by fraud or false
statement, or use or attempt to use any such license so
procured, or to loan or permit another to use his license
or to use the trapping license of another or to alter any
trapping license in any way, or to affix to any trapping
license a date other than the date upon which it was issued,
or to purchase more than 1 trapping license for any 1 trapping season, except as otherwise provided for in this act:
Provided, however, That, except for the trapping of beaver
and otter, the owner or lessee or his minor children shall
not be required to obtain a license to trap on enclosed
farm lands on which he is regularly domiciled;

(c) Who is not a resident of this state to procure a
license to trap. As amended P.A. 1949, No. 305, Sec. 1,
Imd. Eff. June 16; P.A. 1957, No. 207, Sec. 1, Eff. Sept. 27.

UNIFORM NARCOTIC DRUG ACT

335.67 Unlawful acts

Sec. 17. (1) Fraud. No person shall obtain or attempt
to obtain a narcotic drug, or procure or attempt to procure
the administration of a narcotic drug, (a) by fraud, deceit,
misrepresentation or subterfuge; or (b) by the forgery or alteration of a prescription or of any written order; or (c)
by the concealment of a material fact; or (d) by the use of
a false name or the giving of a false address.

(2) Information not privileged. Information communicated
to a physician in an effort unlawfully to procure a narcotic

drug, or unlawfully to procure the administration of any such drug, shall not be deemed a privileged communication.

(3) <u>False statements</u>. No person shall wilfully make a false statement in any prescription, order, report or record, required by this act.

(4) <u>False personation</u>. No person shall, for the purpose of obtaining a narcotic drug, falsely assume the title of, or represent himself to be, a manufacturer, wholesaler, apothecary, physician, dentist, veterinarian, or other authorized person.

(5) <u>False or forged prescription or order</u>. No person shall make or utter any false or forged prescription or false or forged written order.

(6) <u>False or forged label</u>. No person shall affix any false or forged label to a package or receptacle containing narcotic drugs.

(7) Deleted. P. A. 1966, No. 117, Sec. 1.

(8) <u>Application of section</u>. The provisions of this section shall apply to all transactions relating to narcotic drugs under the provisions of section 8, in the same way as they apply to transactions under all other sections. As amended P.A. 1959, No. 187, Sec. 1, Eff. March 19, 1960; P.A. 1966, No. 117, Sec. 1, Eff. March 10, 1967.

335.153a Narcotic drugs; fraudulent procurement

Sec. 3a. Any person who shall obtain or attempt to obtain any narcotic drugs, or who procures or attempts to procure the administration of any narcotic drugs, from a person duly licensed under the provisions of Act No. 343 of the Public Acts of 1937, as amended, being sections 335.51 to 335.78 of the Compiled Laws of 1948, by fraud, deceit, misrepresentation or subterfuge, or by the forgery or alteration of a prescription or written order, or by the concealment of a material fact, or by the use of a false name or the giving of a false address, or who shall wilfully and knowingly make a false statement in any prescription, report, record or order, or who shall, for the purpose of obtaining a narcotic drug, falsely assume the title of or represent himself to be a producer, manufacturer, wholesaler, apothecary, physician, dentist, veterinarian or practitioner, or make or utter any false or forged order or prescription, or who shall affix any false or forged label to a package or receptacle containing narcotic drugs, shall be guilty of a felony. P.A. 1952, No. 266, Sec. 3a, added by P.A. 1955, No. 198, Sec. 1, Imd. Eff. June 17, 1955, as amended P.A. 1958, No. 176, Eff. Sept. 13.

BASIC SCIENCES

338.8 Unlawfully procuring certificate of eligibility;
      penalty

1296

Sec. 8. If any person shall unlawfully obtain or procure a certificate of eligibility under the provisions of this act, whether by false and untrue statements contained in his application to the board, or other fraud or misrepresentation, or if any person shall forge, counterfeit or alter any certificate of eligibility issued under the provisions of this act, or if any person shall practice healing without securing the certificate required under this act, he shall be guilty of a felony, and shall be subject to the penalties prescribed therefor by law.

WAREHOUSEMEN AND WAREHOUSE RECEIPTS

444.107 Violations defined; penalty

Sec. 7. Any person who shall wilfully alter or destroy any register or certificate or receipt provided for in this chapter or issue any receipt or certificate without entering or preserving in such book the registered memorandum; or who shall knowingly issue any certificate or receipt therein provided for when the commodity or commodities therein enumerated are not in fact in the building or buildings it is certified they are in, or shall, with intent to defraud, issue a second or other certificate for any such commodity for which, or for any part of which, a former valid certificate or receipt for any part of the commodities mentioned in this chapter is outstanding and in force, sell, encumber, ship, transfer or remove from the elevator, warehouse or building where the same is stored, any such certified property, or knowingly permit the same to be done, without the written consent of the holder of such certificate or receipt, or if any person knowingly receives any such property or helps to remove the same, he shall, upon conviction, be punished by fine not exceeding 10,000 dollars, or by imprisonment in the state prison not exceeding 5 years.

2. Definition and Elements of Forgery

People v. Larson
225 Mich. 355

BIRD, J. In 1917 defendant was a member of the banking firm of Brewster, Larson & Company, operating private banks at Copemish and Arcadia, in Manistee county, and Mesick, in Wexford county. By reason of losses occasioned by bad and worthless paper, the banks of Copemish and Mesick, in the latter part of the year 1917, were hard pressed for funds. In order to relieve this situation and restore confidence

1297

in the banks, defendant induced four farmers and one merchant living in the vicinity to become partners in the bank of Copemish and Mesick, and induced each of them to advance $1,000 to the banks. This help for a time steadied the situation, but the banks were so badly involved that within two years thereafter they were obliged to go into the hands of a receiver and have their affairs wound up. The investment by the five men resulted disastrously to them and they caused defendant and Charles W. Beatty, who managed the Mesick bank, to be arrested for obtaining money from them and obtaining their signatures to the partnership agreement by false pretenses, in violation of 3 Comp. Laws 1915, Sec. 15320. Defendant Larson demanded a separate trial. This was given him and he was convicted and sentenced to prison.

1. A motion was made to quash the information on the grounds: (a) That no offense is set forth in the complaint. . . .

(a) The statute under which the information is filed provides that:

"Every person who, with intent to defraud or cheat, shall designedly, by color of any false token or writing or by any false or bogus check or other written, printed or engraved instrument, by spurious coin or metal in the similitude of coin, or by any other false pretense, cause any person, natural or corporate, to grant, convey, assign, demise, lease or mortgage any land or interest in land, or obtain the signature of any person, natural or corporate to any written instrument, the making whereof would be punishable as forgery, or obtain from any person, natural or corporate, any money or personal property or the use of any instrument, facility or article or other valuable thing or service, or by means of any false weights or measures obtain a larger amount or quantity of property than was bargained for, or by means of any false weights or measures sell or dispose of a less amount or quantity of property than was bargained for, if such land or interest in land, money, personal property, use of such instrument, facility or article, valuable thing, service, larger amount obtained or less amount disposed of, shall be of the value of twenty-five dollars or less, shall be punished by a fine not exceeding one hundred dollars or imprisonment in the county jail not exceeding three months and if such land, interest in land, money, personal property, use of such instrument, facility or article, valuable thing, service, larger amount obtained or less amount disposed of shall be of the value of more than twenty-five dollars, such person shall be punished by imprisonment in the State prison not more than ten years or by a fine not exceeding five hundred dollars and imprisonment in the county jail not more than one year." 3 Comp. Laws 1915, Sec. 15320.

Counsel make the point that the copartnership agreement

1298

is not such a written instrument "the making whereof would
be punishable as forgery," and they argue that partnership
agreements are not expressly mentioned in the forgery statute
(Sec. 15432), and unless they can be found therein no prosecution could be maintained under section 15320. They also
contend the articles of copartnership could have no legal
efficacy in aiding anyone to defraud a third party.

While the general statute authorizing prosecutions for
forgery does not expressly mention partnership agreements,
we think the forging of names to a partnership agreement, if
it creates a liability, is, in the law, forgery, and under
section 15320 is open to prosecution as such. Commonwealth
v. Hutchison, 114 Mass. 325. In the case cited the same
question is raised on a similar statute. The question involved was as to whether a copartnership agreement could be
the subject of forgery, and the court held that a prosecution for forgery of such an instrument could be maintained.
Forgery includes any act which fraudulently makes an instrument purport to be that which it is not. People v. Marion,
29 Mich. 35. There is no statutory definition of forgery.
At the common law it is defined to be the making of a false
document with intent to defraud. People v. Van Alstine, 57
Mich. 73. The articles of copartnership in the instant case,
when signed by the five men, were recorded in the office of
the county clerk, and filed away in the vault of the bank.
The moment these five men placed their signature to the paper
they became liable for the debts of the copartnership, and
at that moment, if their testimony is to be believed, they
were defrauded. . . .

   WIEST, C. J., and FELLOWS, McDONALD, CLARK, SHARPE, MOORE,
and STEERE, JJ., concurred.

McGinn v. Tobey
62 Mich. 252

   MORSE, J. The bill of complaint in this cause was filed
to set aside a deed purporting to have been executed by complainant to Thomas J. Navin, of certain premises in the county
of Lenawee, being a lot and store building thereon, in the
city of Adrian, and a farm in the township of Hudson; and
also to release a mortgage upon the same premises, executed
by said Navin to Sylvester B. Smith and Thomas J. Tobey
while he held the apparent record title to said premises,
and to have the same decreed and declared to have no force
or validity as a mortgage lien upon the lands.

   Sylvester B. Smith and Thomas J. Tobey were copartners
in the banking business at the time the mortgage was taken,
and Smith was made a defendant to the bill. During the taking of proofs he died, and the suit proceeds against Tobey
as survivor.

1299

At the time of the execution of this deed the defendant Navin was a member of the law firm of Merrit & Navin, in Adrian, and mayor of that city. He had the confidence and respect of all classes, and was very popular. The complainant, a man about 60 years of age, intrusted some of his business to Navin, and had implicit faith in his honesty and professed friendship.

The proofs show that in the spring of 1881 Navin negotiated with complainant for the rent of his store, and a bargain was entered into between them by which Navin was to lease the store for three years at the rate of $450 per year, payable in monthly installments. Navin was to draw the lease in duplicate, each party to hold a copy.

On the thirtieth of April, Navin informed complainent that he had the papers drawn, and McGinn went to his office to execute the lease. The copy which complainant took away was read to him by Navin, and he also read it himself, and, after the suggestion of some little change in the instrument, which was made, he signed it. The apparent duplicate lay upon the table, but was not read to or by McGinn. After he signed his copy he signed the other, supposing it to be an exact counterpart of his own, and left it in Navin's possession.

At the time McGinn was in the office to execute the lease Navin did not say to him that the other paper was a copy; but he laid the two documents together upon the table for McGinn to sign, and complainant supposed it to be a copy from the previous talk that two copies, one for each, were to be made. The paper signed and left was upon a blank of about the same character and size of the lease, and partly printed and written, as was his copy. Navin paid the rent regularly, monthly in advance, up to February 1, 1882.

About six months after the execution of the lease, Navin told complainant that he had lost his copy, and wanted his to make out another one for himself. Complainant let him have it, but he did not return it, and afterwards, when rent was paid, Navin would take the lease from his safe, and Mc-Ginn would make the indorsement upon it, and hand it back to Navin, who would return it to the safe.

Some time in February, 1882, Navin became involved in numerous forgeries and criminal speculations, and fled the country. It was then soon discovered that he had put upon record a deed from McGinn to him of the store, lot, and the farm, dated June 2, 1881, the words "June 2nd" being written over an erasure.

September 29, 1881, Navin executed to Smith & Tobey a mortgage upon the premises described in the deed, which, upon its face, purported to be given as security for the payment of a certain promissory note for $6,000, payable one year from date, with interest at 8 per cent, but in reality executed, as the testimony shows, as collateral security for advances made, and to be made, by the bank of Smith & Tobey to Navin; they holding, at the same time, other col-

1300

lateral security for the same purpose.

All the time from the execution of the lease to the flight of Navin, McGinn was in possession of the farm by a tenant. When Smith & Tobey took the mortgage, they knew of the previous ownership of the farm and store by complainant. They relied upon an abstract of the title from the records of Lenawee county, which showed title in Navin, and had no converse with McGinn about it.

The day Navin left the county he drew $750 from the bank, and about that time his mother deeded to Smith & Tobey a house and lot in Adrian, worth about $8,000, the title being in her, as further security for Navin's indebtedness to them. This lot was purchased by Navin, and he had nearly completed the house upon it, probably with his own means, or that of persons whom he had swindled. About a month thereafter, Smith & Tobey, for some reason, deeded these premises back to Mrs. Navin, the mother of Thomas J.

The counsel for defendant Tobey contend that the bank was innocent of any complicity in the fraud of Navin upon complainant by which the deed was obtained; that it invested its money in good faith upon the security of the mortgage, believing the title to the lands to be in Navin, as it so appeared from the records; and that, under the equitable rule that, when one of two innocent parties must suffer loss, the one must bear the loss who, by his careless or negligent conduct, has made it possible that either should suffer, the mortgage must be considered a valid and subsisting lien upon the premises, and the complainant's bill dismissed.

This was the view of the court below, from which the complainant appeals to this Court.

It is claimed by the counsel for complainant that the deed is a forgery, and can pass no title to the most innocent of purchasers or incumbrancers; that, if not technically a false instrument in such a sense as to come within the literal definition of forgery, it is yet the same as a forged deed in its effect; that it is absolutely void, and not voidable; that the deed was never delivered by McGinn, and that, without delivery, it is void from the beginning; that the complainant never intended to sign any such instrument, – his mind did not go with the act, – and that, therefore, in contemplation of the law, he never did sign it; that it is no more his deed than if he had signed it in his sleep.

It is very evident that the deed of these premises to Navin was not in fact the deed of the complainant. He never meant to execute a deed, and never knew that he had executed one until confronted with his signature to the same, after Navin had gone away to escape arrest. As was well said by Chief Justice Ryan, in _Griffiths v. Kellogg, 39 Wis. 294,_ the deed, "if not a forgery, was akin to forgery." That was a case where a lightning-rod agent induced a woman to sign a promissory note for a greater sum than she owed, by reading the instrument to her as of the less and real sum of her agreed obligation. The court said: "The note in suit was as little hers as if the transaction between her and the lightning-rod man had not taken place and he had forged the note."

The person who relies upon the records for the authenticity and validity of a deed does not stand in as favorable a position as a good-faith holder of negotiable paper.

In this case, if the name of complainant had been forged by Navin, without the presence or knowledge of McGinn, and placed upon the record, the abstract of title upon which defendant Tobey and his copartner relied would not have disclosed the forgery, any more than it did the fraud, of Navin. It seems to us that, in order to make them bona fide holders of this mortgage as against the lands of McGinn, they were bound to go further than the abstract, and to examine the deed. This they did not do.

But we consider this deed clearly a forgery, under the best definitions of that offense. Bishop defines "forgery" to be "the false making or materially altering, with intent to defraud, of any writing, which, if genuine, might apparently be of legal efficacy, or the foundation of a legal liability:" 2 Bish. Crim. Law (7th Ed.), Sec. 523. It is the "fraudulent making and alteration of a writing, to the prejudice of another man's rights:" 4 Bl. Comm. 247. The signature to this instrument is genuine, but the body of the deed is false, and the signing of complainant's name, without knowledge of such falsity, cannot cure it and make it a true and valid instrument in the hands of any one. A genuine signature cannot change the character of an instrument of this kind, unless the intent to do so goes with the signature.

It does not seem to me that the question of the complainant's negligence in signing this supposed copy of the lease without reading it, if this is a forgery, as I think it is, can be considered in this case; for, if the deed is in law a forgery, the question of good faith cannot arise: Camp v. Carpenter, 52 Mich. 375; Austin v. Dean, 40 Id. 386; D'Wolf v. Haydn, 24 Ill. 525; Griffiths v. Kellogg, 39 Wis. 293; Crawford v. Hoeft, 58 Mich. 21.

I do not think, either, that Smith & Tobey could be considered good-faith holders by a simple examination of the abstract of title. The alteration in the date of the deed would have appeared upon examination of the original document, but was not shown by the registry. And the singular circumstance of their deeding the house and lot back to Mrs. Navin, and notifying the attorneys of complainant that they were about to do so, and telling them that they did this so that McGinn might attach Navin's interest in the same, coupled with the fact that they knew of McGinn's occupancy of the farm, and did not ask him about the pretended transfer to Navin, and the further fact that they also knew that the house built upon the lot deeded by Mrs. Navin to them was paid for, in part, by funds of Navin, drawn out of their own

1302

bank, leads me to strongly suspect, to say the least, ~~their entire good faith in the transaction~~. They are not innocent parties without such fault, in my mind, as to take the
value of this mortgage out of this old man, when they could
have easily obtained its amount from Navin's property, which
they have voluntarily returned to his mother.

~~There is no gross negligence shown upon the part of com-
plainant~~. McGinn was not bound to suppose that a man of
the position and character in the community that Navin then
held, and who was his professed friend, was likely to thus
rob him of his hard earnings. He read the lease, and it
was read to him. ~~What must have been this deed was very
similar to the lease~~. It was ~~placed before him as a copy~~,
and in ~~signing it he only did what the ordinary business
man, having any confidence in the honesty and integrity of~~
another, would have done.

To require that he should have dealt with Navin upon the
principle that "every man is a rascal," and none honest, or
lose his property, would be to encourage in law a distrust
and doubt of human nature not commendable or to be desired.

We think, under the circumstances, he had a right to put
a little faith in the integrity of one honored and trusted
by the community where he lived, and was not so negligent
in signing the duplicate without reading it as to lose his
rights in the premises against one holding on the faith of
the record title, without notice of the fraudulent inception
of the deed.

~~The decree of the court below is reversed, with costs of
both courts, and a decree will be entered here granting the
relief prayed in complainant's bill~~.

CAMPBELL, C. J., and CHAMPLIN, J., concurred. SHERWOOD,
J., concurred in the result.

People v. Marion
29 Mich. 31

CAMPBELL, J.

This case, which was before us at the last term (28 Mich.,
255) upon a question relating to the meaning of the information, now comes up after a further trial and second conviction, on exceptions to the rulings of the recorder.

A point was raised at the trial which, if sustained, would
have put an end to the prosecution, and it is therefore necessary to consider it in the outset. It was objected that
the information did not properly allege the forgery of the
certificate of acknowledgment or of the appended clerk's certificate, and that as the forgery of the power of attorney
was not set up in any issuable way, the charge was entirely
defective.

When this case was formerly before us, it was held by the court that the only forgery fairly indicated by the information was that of the acknowledgment and clerk's certificate, and that the express reference to those gave the defendant to understand that this was all he would have to meet. It is now urged that the charge does not even indicate this in any sufficient form. The ground of the objection is that defendant is only charged with uttering a forged power of attorney, and that the certificates form no part of the power, which is complete without them.

It is not claimed that such acts would not be the subject of forgery if purporting to have been made within the State, nor that the information does not clearly show that the forgery relied on was the fabrication of those documents; but the defense is based on the want of any sufficient allegation of the forgery of any thing but the instrument to which they were appended.

It is very well settled that a deed or a power of attorney may be valid as between the parties, and completely bind the grantor without any acknowledgment, unless the contrary is very plainly enacted. The acknowledgment is of a deed already executed. And if a defendant were charged with forging or uttering a forged deed, it would probably be no defense in most cases that the deed was not acknowledged.

But there are many purposes for which an unacknowledged deed is entirely useless. It does not prove itself. It cannot be recorded. It is invalid as against purchasers without notice, and cannot be proved by the registry though actually recorded.

Our statutes contemplate that all deeds shall be acknowledged, and provide for compulsory measures of proof where the grantor fails or refuses to makes (sic) the acknowledgment. - Comp. L. Sec. 4216-4224. An unacknowledged deed is regarded as exceptional and improper. Where a married woman's separate acknowledgment is required the deed is void as to her without it, and it is a necessary step in the conveyance. - Dewey v. Campau, 4 Mich. R., 565; Fisher v. Meister, 24 Mich. 447.

Common usage and the language of many sections of our statutes will not permit us to hold that where a deed has been acknowledged, the statutory certificate may not properly be regarded as forming a part of the complete instrument. An acknowledged deed being the rule, and one not acknowledged the exception, it is the most natural form of expression to call the entire document a deed. Throughout the bill of exceptions the term "power of attorney" is frequently and generally used to embrace the appended certificates, even where objection is made to testimony affecting the latter. When a deed or the record of a deed is offered in evidence on a trial no one would imagine that all certificates belonging to it were not offered with it. An objection to such an offer, that the deed was not admissible alone, would be deemed frivolous. And an inspection

1304

of our recording laws will show that no meaning whatever
can be attached to many provisions without giving such an
interpretation to the various terms "deeds," "mortgages,"
"conveyances," and the like, as will include all their appur-
tenances. A similar remark applies to the tax laws, where
the provision making deeds prima facie evidence occurs earlier in the section than that which requires them to be witnessed, acknowledged, and recorded, as in other cases. -
Comp. L. Sec. 1057.

We can see no reason for applying to an indictment for
forgery any different rule than that which would apply in
other cases, so long as the defendant is clearly informed
of the precise charge against him. The statutes have been
frequently amended so as to prevent failures of justice on
trivial grounds. And where a word susceptible of two meanings is used with such averments as to show which sense is
intended, the charge should be held good.

It may not be useless to refer to two or three precedents
which bear upon this matter. In England it is made a specific felony to forge the attestation of a power of attorney.
Mr. Archbold gives a form of indictment with two counts, one
for the forging and the other for the uttering, and in the
latter uses language almost identical with that used in the
case before us, so far as this particular point is concerned.
The uttering is referred to a certain "forged power of attorney" with the name of the witness forged as an attesting
witness to the execution thereof, the defendant knowing the
witness's name and handwriting to be forged. The attestation is treated throughout as a part of the instrument, and
there is no charge of uttering it separately.

In Queen v. Ritson, L.R., 1 C.C.R., 200, the parties to
a genuine deed were held guilty of forgery for dating it
back when they drew it, so as to appear to have been made
earlier than a bankruptcy assignment. The language of the
judges is very strong. Blackburn, J., defines forgery to
include any act which fraudulently makes an instrument "purport to be that which it is not." And while the date of a
deed is not usually material, yet in that case it became so.
It has been held by this court that whatever may be the
date of a deed, the time of its actual delivery is presumptively fixed by the acknowledgment, as not made previously. -
Blanchard v. Tyler, 12 Mich. R. 339. And this ruling went
upon the ground that the deed was incomplete for the purposes of record until acknowledged, and that such papers are
intended to be recorded.

In Regina v. Keith, 29 Eng. L. & Eq., 558, it was held
that a prisoner who had engraved an ornamental border similar to that used upon certain bank bills was guilty of engraving "part of a note" purporting to be part of the bill
or note of the bank in question, although he had gone no
further. The court say (sic) the statute uses the term
"note" not in its strict sense as the legal promise or obligation, but in its popular sense, which includes every-

thing appearing on the paper, and that the ornamental part of a bank note is as much a part of the note as the words. No one would be deceived by a counterfeit which lacked it.

We think this rule sensible and just. And we think the information in the present case sufficiently described the power of attorney as one purporting to be acknowledged and certified, so as to make all the certificates a part of the description of that complete instrument.

It was also objected that our statutes do not punish the forgery of such certificates and similar official documents as purport to have been made elsewhere than within this State. As the acknowledgment and certifying of deeds of land in Michigan can only be had by virtue of the power given by our own laws for that purpose, they would necessarily be included by the narrowest interpretation. But there is no reason to believe our statutes were not designed to cover any forgeries or utterings of forgeries here which could be used here for fraudulent purposes. . . .

We find no error in the record. It must be certified to the recorder's court that judgment should be rendered on the verdict.

GRAVES, Ch. J., and COOLEY, J., concurred.

CHRISTIANCY, J., did not sit in this case.

People v. Van Alstine
57 Mich. 69

CHAMPLIN, J. The respondent, Charles Van Alstine, was convicted in the circuit court for the county of Hillsdale upon an information charging him, jointly with Charles A. Parker and Edward C. Cleveland, with the forging and uttering of a deed of forty acres of land, lying in the township of Somerset, in Hillsdale county.

The deed purported to be executed by Eleanor Van Alstine, in the presence of Parker and Cleveland, and acknowledged by the grantor before Parker, as a notary public of Lenawee county. It bears date the 9th day of May, 1876. The legal title to the land at the date of the deed was in Eleanor Pelton. It was claimed by the prosecution that she was one and the same person with Eleanor Van Alstine. She had for several years lived with the respondent, Van Alstine, and the evidence showed that he treated her as his wife, and claimed her to be such; that she had united with him in the execution of a deed of land as Eleanor Van Alstine, although she was never married to him by any formal ceremony, and her estate was administered after her death, which occurred in August, 1876, as the estate of Eleanor Pelton. She left as heirs at law two sisters, a Mrs. Giddings and a Mrs. Wescott. She died testate, and her will was admitted to probate in Hillsdale county, an executor appointed, her estate

1306

appraised, and the ordinary steps taken to administer her estate. At the time the executor made his inventory, the title of record to the southwest quarter of the northwest quarter of section twenty-six, township five south, range one west, being in the town of Somerset, county of Hillsdale, appeared to be in Eleanor Pelton, and he included it in his inventory as property belonging to the estate. Afterwards, and in 1876, the respondent, Van Alstine, placed upon record in the office of the register of deeds for Hillsdale county a quitclaim deed of said lands, bearing date May 9, 1876, and purporting to have been executed by Eleanor Van Alstine to him, in the presence of the other two respondents. It is claimed by the prosecution that this deed was forged by the respondent. The case comes here upon exceptions before judgment.

The information contains ten counts. Counsel for respondent insists that the first nine are not sufficient upon which to convict the defendant, for the reason that they contain no allegations that Eleanor Van Alstine had any interest in the land.

Forgery was a misdemeanor at the common law. From the earliest times in the history of the criminal law of England statutes have been passed upon the subject. As early as 1413 a statute (1 Hen. V. ch. 3) was enacted which recited that many persons had been deprived of their property by false deeds, wherefore it was enacted "that the party so grieved shall have his suit in that case, and recover his damages; and the party convict shall make fine and ransom at the king's pleasure." Again, the English statute of 5 Eliz. ch. 14, Sec. 2, prohibited the making or forging of any false deed, etc., "to the intent that the state of freehold or inheritance of any person in lands, etc., shall not be molested, troubled, defeated, recovered, or charged;" and the third section fixes a penalty for any person to forge or make any false charter, deed or writing, to the intent that any person shall have or claim any estate or interest for term of years of, in or to any lands. The forgery of deeds was made felony, without benefit of clergy, by 2 Geo. II. ch. 25. The precedents framed under the English statutes, and especially those under the second section of 5 Eliz. ch. 14, on account of the particular phraseology of the enactments, uniformly set out the title of the party whose estate in the land was intended to be molested. 2 Stark Cr. L. 481; 3 Chit. Cr. L. 1062. The necessity of doing so is apparent from the provisions of the law. It is an essential ingredient of the offense, and must therefore be stated.

But our statute is more broad and general in its terms. It provides that every person who shall falsely make, alter, forge or counterfeit any deed with intent to injure or defraud any person shall be punished, etc. (How Stat. Sec. 9213), and sec. 9226 provides that in any case where an intent to defraud, without naming therein the particular person or body corporate intended to be defrauded, and on the trial of such indictment it shall be deemed sufficient, and shall not be deemed a variance, if there appear to be an intent to defraud the United States, or any state, county, city, or township, or any body corporate, or any public officer in his official capacity, or any copartnership or member thereof, or any particular person. There is no statutory definition of forgery. At the common law it is defined to be the "making of a false document with intent to defraud;" and the offense may be said to be complete when any person falsely makes any of the writings enumerated in the statute "with intent to deceive in such a manner as to expose any person to loss or to the risk of loss."

Forgery

There is such a marked difference between the English and our statute upon the subject, that neither precedents nor decisions based upon the former can be of service or authority under the latter, which, as we have seen, does not limit the operation of the statute to persons having interests in the same or other lands; and to so limit it would seem to be in direct contravention of the statute,—would greatly narrow its operation, and defeat its most important objects. It is apparent, upon the most cursory consideration, that fraud by means of a false or forged deed may be perpetrated, not only upon the owner of the land, but upon strangers to the title who are induced to rely upon the genuineness of the forged deed to advance or loan money upon the faith of the legal validity of such instrument. It was long ago held that a person could be guilty of forgery in signing his own name to a deed of land which he had already conveyed, when he antedated the instrument for the purpose of defrauding. 2 Russ. Cr. 322, 323. In this view of the statute it can neither be necessary nor advisable to set out in the information the title of the person intended to be defrauded, nor in what the forgery consisted. It is not necessary, for the reason that such facts are not essential ingredients of the offense. I do not consider it advisable as a matter of general practice to do so, because, if stated, the proof must correspond with the averment, or the defendant must be acquitted. 2 East's Cr. L. 988.

It was said in People v. Marion 28 Mich. 255, that it is proper to set out, in at least one count of the information, with particularity, in what the forgery consisted; but the public prosecutor is not obliged to do so, and when he does, it is done ex mera gratia to the accused. I do not think it necessary that the information should contain any averment that Eleanor Van Alstine had any interest in the land at the time it is claimed the forgery was committed. The gist of the offense is the intent to defraud. The validity of the objection depends entirely upon the effect and operation of the statute upon which it is founded, and it is usually sufficient if the information is so framed that the offense is described in the words of the statute, or according to its

1308

legal effect and operation. Where the instrument alleged
to have been forged is one enumerated in the statute, and
appears to be complete on its face, to be effectual, all
that is necessary is to aver that the act was done with intent to defraud. But how or in what manner the party was
to be defrauded, is no ingredient of the crime, but is mere
matter of evidence, which all the authorities agree need
not be set out in the information. West v. State 22 N.J.
Law 212, Archb; Cr. Pro. 23, 194; 2 East's Cr. L. 989, Sec.
59; The King v. Powel 2 W. Bl. 787; Taylor's Case 1 Leach
215; Rex v. Goate 1 Ld. Raym 737.
    The land which this deed purported to convey had an
actual potential existence, definitely described and located, and the deed on its face appeared to work some effect
upon the property, and was complete in itself for that purpose. It did not require the aid of averments of extrinsic
facts to render its deception complete. I do not think the
distinction which counsel for respondent seeks to raise between executed and executory contracts exists. The test,
whether the party can be guilty of a forgery, does not consist in determining whether the instrument forged, if genuine, would be of any force or effect. A draft, falsely made,
is no less a forgery because the drawee has no funds, and is
under no obligation to pay if the draft had been genuine.
A deed falsely made by a grantor, after he had conveyed all
interest in the land, is no less a forgery because, if genuine, it would convey no title. Forgery may be committed
when the name forged is fictitious, and I can see no reason why it should be necessary to aver what interest the
alleged grantor, whose name is forged, had in the land
described in the deed. In some cases it would be immaterial, and in others mere matter of evidence, bearing upon
the intent to defraud, as it is in this case. . . .
    The exceptions are overruled, and the court below is
advised to proceed to judgment.

H.

The other Justices concurred.

Leslie v. Kennedy
249 Mich. 553

SHARPE, J. In the spring of 1925 the defendants were
the owners and subdividers of certain real estate near
Detroit, in the county of Wayne. They had in their employ
as a salesman one Russell Carrier. He had formerly been
employed by Joe and Louise Schiappicasse as a chauffeur.
Soon after entering the employ of the defendants, Carrier
induced Mrs. Schiappicasse to purchase a lot in the subdivision. She paid him $20, and instructed him to have
the name of her brother, Jerome Henley, inserted in the

contract as purchaser, as she was buying it for him. On March 30th Carrier prepared a preliminary purchase agreement covering lot 293, and had his wife sign the name "Jerome Henley" thereto, and turned this agreement and the $20 deposit into the office of the defendants, the deposit being credited to Henley on defendants' books. About a week later, Mrs. Schiappicasse told Carrier that she did not want to complete the purchase, and he said "it would be all right." She did not ask for the return of the deposit, nor was it made to her. No entry was made in defendants' books relative thereto.

In the month of May following, Carrier's brother introduced plaintiff to him as a prospective purchaser of a lot in the subdivision. The three of them afterwards visited the property, and Carrier then told plaintiff that a down payment of $20 had been made on lot 293, and that he could give plaintiff the advantage of it by transferring the deal to him. Later, plaintiff decided to make the purchase. Carrier, after consulting with T. G. Harris, the sales manager under whom he worked, prepared a land contract for the sale of lot 293 by defendants to Jerome Henley, dated May 7, 1925, for the sum of $1,000, of which $200 was acknowledged to be paid and the balance in monthly instalments, secured the signature of defendants thereto, and himself signed the name of Jerome Henley as purchaser. He attached an assignment of the contract from Henley to the plaintiff, and signed Henley's name to it. To this was appended the following, signed by plaintiff: "I, Arthur Leslie, accept this transfer and agree to carry out all provisions named in said contract." The contract provided:

"That no sale, transfer, assignment or pledge of this contract shall be in any manner binding upon the seller unless either said Charles J. Kennedy or Charles A. Kandt first consents thereto in writing."

To comply therewith, Carrier procured the signature of Charles J. Kennedy to an indorsement reading: "The transfer of this contract is accepted by the undersigned."

Plaintiff borrowed $180 from Carrier's brother, and paid it to Carrier. This, with the $20 paid by Mrs. Schiappicasse made up the down payment required and the contract with its indorsements was turned over to plaintiff. He made additional payments thereon, amounting to $318.16. On April 20, 1928, he was in default in the sum of $206.79, and defendants caused a notice to be served on him that unless this amount was paid on or before April 30, 1928, forfeiture would be declared. He made no further payments, and on May 31, 1928, a notice of forfeiture was served.

Plaintiff had theretofore complained to defendants that lot 289, cornering on an alley, had been pointed out to him as the lot he had purchased, and on August 11th he notified defendants that for this reason he elected to rescind, tendered an assignment of his contract, and demanded payment of the moneys paid by him on the contract.

On August 15th defendants began proceedings before a circuit court commissioner to obtain possession of the lot, pending the disposition of which plaintiff filed the bill of complaint herein, praying for rescission and a return of the moneys paid. In a cross-bill defendants seek foreclosure of the contract.

The trial court found that plaintiff had failed to establish his claim of misrepresentation in the location of the lot, but held that Carrier had committed forgery in signing Henley's name to the contract and assignment; that the defendants, on discovery of it, could have set it aside, and that "If, upon discovery, one party could repudiate it, why not the other?" and granted plaintiff the relief prayed for in his bill. From the decree entered so adjudging, the defendants have appealed.

It is elementary that an intent to defraud is the gist of the offense of forgery. Prine v. Singer Sewing Machine Co., 176 Mich. 300. The facts, and we have stated them at some length, fail to disclose any such intent on the part of Carrier. He had no authority and no legal right to sign Henley's name to the contract and assignment. But he personally gained nothing by doing so. His only purpose was to secure to plaintiff on his down payment the credit of the $20 paid by Mrs. Schiappicasse. The only person benefited thereby was the plaintiff. The defendants have ratified such act, and by their consent, indorsed upon the assignment, have secured to plaintiff an enforceable contract; one which they have been at all times ready to perform and on which plaintiff is credited with more than $500 of the purchase price. We see no reason why he should be permitted in a court of equity to rescind the contract for this reason.

We are in agreement with the trial court in holding that the claim of misrepresentation as to the lot intended to be purchased by plaintiff is not supported by a preponderance of the evidence. It will serve no useful purpose to set forth the testimony bearing upon it.

The decree is reversed, and one will be entered here dismissing plaintiff's bill and granting the defendants the relief prayed for in their cross-bill. There will be remand to the circuit court for such further proceedings thereunder as may be necessary. The defendants will recover costs.

WIEST, C. J., and BUTZEL, CLARK, POTTER, NORTH, and FEAD, JJ., concurred. McDONALD, J., did not sit.

In re Stout
371 Mich. 438

SMITH, J. Petitioner, an inmate of Ionia State Hospital,

1311

appeared *in propria persona* alleging his detention to be illegal. The record discloses that petitioner was committed to said hospital by order of the recorder's court on September 25, 1931. This order of commitment was issued pursuant to the statute then in force providing such disposition "when a party accused of any felony shall appear to be insane." CL 1929, Sec. 17241, as amended by PA 1931, No. 317. . . . Petitioner alleges that his detention is illegal in that at the time of commitment he was not a person accused of a felony. Based on the averment of said petition a writ of habeas corpus was issued, directed to the medical superintendent of the hospital, with ancillary writ of certiorari to recorder's court. Returns to the writs have been duly filed.

Petitioner was informed against in recorder's court for the city of Detroit on September 2, 1931, on a charge of forgery under the statute, pursuant to CL 1929, Sec. 17048. . . . The information charged that petitioner on July 23, 1931, had in his hands a certain draft for the payment of money in the amount of $43.25, made out to the Properties Holding Company, and further charged as follows: "and the said Clyde C. Stout did then and there, with intent to injure and defraud, falsely, feloniously, fraudulently, indorse, write and forge upon the back of said draft or order for the payment of money the indorsement and signature of the payee thereof, viz: Properties Holding Company, by C. C. Stout, without right and authority so to do, and with intent then and there to injure and defraud."

The record reveals that subsequent to the arraignment, the trial court on September 15, 1931, appointed a sanity commission pursuant to the provisions of the aforementioned statute, CL 1929, Sec. 17241. The sanity commission found petitioner to be an insane person not possessing mental capacity "to undertake his defense." Thereafter, one of the judges of recorder's court found defendant (petitioner herein) to be "insane and irresponsible (sic) not a proper person to be tried at this time" on the charge pending against him, and ordered that he be removed to the State hospital at Ionia until cured or otherwise discharged.

Petitioner sets forth several grounds as a basis for his contention. However, the only allegation meriting review is whether in fact petitioner was, at the time of the commitment, "a person accused of a felony."

Petitioner claims that because he signed his own name to the check, it was not a felony within the meaning of the statute. A reading of the statute provides adequate answer. As applied to this case, it reads substantially as follows: every person who shall falsely make a bill of exchange or indorsement with intent to injure or defraud any person shall be guilty of a felony. CL 1929, Sec. 17048. Forgery includes "any act which fraudulently makes an instrument 'purport to be that which it is not.'" People v. Marion,

1312

29 Mich 31, 35. Petitioner was charged in the information
with falsely and fraudulently indorsing upon the back of
the draft (a bill of exchange) the indorsement of the payee,
without authority and with intent to injure and defraud.
Upon the face of it, the act charged is a felony; therefore
the sanity proceedings were not invalid.

The writ is dismissed.

CARR, C. J., and DETHMERS, KELLY, and O'HARA, JJ., concurred with SMITH, J.

KAVANAGH, J., concurred in result.

(Dissenting opinion of Justice SOURIS and concurring
opinion of Justice BLACK omitted.)

People v. Watkins
106 Mich. 437

LONG, J. Respondent was convicted upon an information
which charged the uttering and publishing of a forged chattel mortgage as true, knowing it to be false, forged and
counterfeit. The only contention is that the uttering and
publishing of this instrument as true, although false, counterfeit, altered, and forged, is not a crime under the statute under which the prosecution was had.

2 How. Stat. Sec. 9213, provides:

"Every person who shall falsely make, alter, forge, or
counterfeit . . . any charter, deed, will, testament, bond
or writing obligatory, letter of attorney, policy of insurance, bill of lading, bill of exchange, promissory note,
or any order, acquittance, or discharge for money or other
property, or any acceptance of a bill of exchange, or indorsement or assignment of a bill of exchange or promissory
note for the payment of money, or any accountable receipt
for money, goods, or other property, with intent to injure
or defraud any person, shall be punished by imprisonment in
the state prison not more than fourteen years, or in the
county jail not more than one year."

Section 9214 provides:

"Every person who shall utter and publish as true any
false, forged, altered, or counterfeit record, deed, instrument, or other writing mentioned in the preceding section,
knowing the same to be false, altered, forged, or counterfeit, with intent to injure or defraud as aforesaid, shall
be punished by imprisonment in the state prison not more
than fourteen years, or in the county jail not more than one
year."

This chattel mortgage purported to have been given by
Samuel W. Nichols and others to respondent, as trustee, to
secure the payment of $229.28, and to secure which payment

1313

the parties did grant, bargain, sell, and mortgage to respondent the goods and chattels mentioned in the mortgage. The mortgage contained this provision:

"The consideration of these presents is such that if the said first parties shall pay or cause to be paid to the second party, his representatives or assigns, the debt aforesaid, with interest at eight per cent per annum until paid, according to one promissory note bearing even date herewith, and to which this mortgage is collateral security, executed by said first parties, and the charges hereinafter mentioned, then this instrument and said note shall be void and of no effect; and the said first parties hereby agree to pay the same accordingly."

The term "chattel mortgage" is not mentioned in the statute, and it is therefore contended that the statute is not broad enough to cover the case of uttering and publishing such instrument.

In the case of People v. Caton, 25 Mich. 388, the respondent was convicted of uttering as true a forged mortgage upon real property. The court there held that the statute could not bear so restricted a meaning as was contended for, and that the term "deed," used in the statute, covered this mortgage. It was there said:

"The statute employs a general term, which covers instruments given for a great variety of purposes, and it gives no indication of an intent to confine its operation to deeds of lands. . . . There is abundant reason to believe, on the other hand, that the word is used in the broad legal sense in which it is understood at the common law; for the purpose of the legislature has evidently been to give, by the use of general words, such an enumeration of the instruments likely to be the subject of forgery as to embrace all the valuable writings by the false making or altering of which innocent persons might be in danger of being defrauded."

The word "deed," as used in the statute, must have the common-law definition. A deed is construed at the common law to be "a written instrument under seal, containing a contract or agreement, which has been delivered by the party to be bound and accepted by the abligee or covenantee." 1 Bouv. Law Dict. (15th Ed.) p. 493; 2 Bl. Comm. 295; Shep. Touch. 50. The definition given by Mr. Washburn is: "A writing containing a contract sealed and delivered by the party thereto." 3 Washb. Real. Prop. 553. As was said in People v. Caton, supra, the statute cannot bear so restricted a meaning as contended for.

The conviction must be affirmed.

The other Justices concurred.

People v. Swetland
77 Mich. 53

1314

MORSE, J. On July 25, 1885, the defendant bought of George W. Parker a piece of land in Kalamazoo county. On the same day she executed a mortgage for $700 to him upon the said land. The theory of the prosecution in this case, as developed on the trial, was that the respondent or some one else forged a discharge of this mortgage, and that she put it on record, or caused it to be recorded, and afterwards used the abstract showing said mortgage to be discharged to effect two other loans, - one from D. T. Allen, and the other from Mrs. Amy E. Day.

The respondent was tried and convicted in the Kalamazoo circuit court for uttering this forged discharge. The case is brought here on exceptions before sentence. The respondent was charged with uttering and publishing -

"As a true, a certain false, forged, and counterfeited acquittance and discharge for money of a certain real-estate mortgage," -

And the alleged forged discharge is set out in full in the information.

It is contended that there was no evidence of uttering, as charged in the information. The evidence showed that either the respondent or her sister took the false discharge to the office of the register of deeds, and had it recorded, and took it away again. It is claimed that the mere taking of it to be recorded was not an uttering; that it certainly was not the uttering of it as an "acquittance and discharge for money." It is said the mortgage was collateral to the notes which represented the debt, and that these notes were still held by Parker, and the only effect of putting the discharge on record was to show the real estate apparently clear of the lien. There may be some ingenuity in this argument, but there is no merit in it. If this false discharge had been genuine, as it purported to be, it would have been an acquittance and discharge, not only of the lien upon the real estate, but of the notes as well, and would therefore have been an acquittance and discharge for money. It would have been the voucher or receipt for the payment of $700, the amount secured by the mortgage. . . .

The discharge was dated August 10, 1886. August 8, 1887, the respondent executed a mortgage for $350 to Allen upon part of the lands embraced in the Parker mortgage. Allen testified that the respondent when she negotiated the loan furnished him with an abstract of the title of the land. This abstract he identified, and it was introduced in evidence, showing the Parker mortgage as discharged. It is claimed by respondent's counsel that, while this might have a tendency to show her guilty of obtaining money of Allen under false pretenses, it had no bearing upon her guilt or innocence of the offense for which she was being tried, and it was therefore prejudicial as well as incompetent evidence in this case. We think it had a direct bearing upon the issue in this case. It not only presented a motive upon respondent's part for the commission of the crime charged against her, but it had a tendency to prove that she uttered this alleged false discharge knowing it was forged. She must have known what the abstract contained, and she uses it knowing it to be false, if it were forged, for one of the purposes which may have been, and probably was, the object of uttering this forged discharge by placing it upon record. Such placing upon record must have been either for the purpose of selling the land apparently free from any lien, or obtaining a loan upon it under the same appearance of the title, or for the purpose of defrauding the mortgagee. The fact that she deliberately uses this discharge, by means of this abstract, to obtain a loan, knowing that the mortgage is undischarged, is a most weighty circumstance, tending to show that she recorded this discharge, or directed its record, knowing it to be forged. Indeed, the presenting of this abstract, when she knew it to be false, was an uttering of this discharge with intent to defraud. . . .

It is claimed that, until the corpus delicti was proven, the statements of the respondent to Knappen were not admissible. There are some cases where the corpus delicti - generally in homicide - is clearly separated and distinct from the question as to who committed the offense, if any is found to have been committed. In such cases the evidence to establish the corpus delicti must first be given, before acts or admissions of the accused can be put in evidence. But the present case is one where the body of the offense - the uttering of a forged instrument, knowing it to be false - is so intimately connected with the question whether or not the respondent is guilty of the crime that there can be no such separation. The corpus delicti in this case depends entirely for its existence upon the acts and intent of the respondent, so that her acts and admissions, if admissible at all, were admissible at any stage of the proceedings upon the trial.

The conviction of the respondent must be set aside, and a new trial granted.

SHERWOOD, C. J., CHAMPLIN and LONG, JJ., concurred. CAMPBELL, J., did not sit.

People v. Kemp
76 Mich. 410

CHAMPLIN, J. In 1884, M. J. Murphy & Co. was a corporation, organized and existing under the laws of the State of Michigan, having its principal office for the transaction of its business in the city of Detroit. In that year this corporation entered into a contract with the proper authorities for the employment of convicts, in the manufacture of chairs, at the State House of Correction and Reformatory at

Ionia.

In carrying on this branch of its business the corporation purchased considerable quantities of lumber from different parties, which was delivered at the prison. The respondent, Kemp, was a stockholder in the corporation, and from November, 1884, until July, 1887, had entire charge of its business at Ionia as its superintendent and general manager. The manner in which the business was conducted in the purchase of lumber was for Kemp to make the purchases, and forward to the home office in Detroit the bills or invoices of purchase from time to time, showing the date, from whom purchased, and the quantity and price; and the corporation would forward by mail from the home office a check upon the People's Savings Bank in Detroit for the amount, payable to the order of the person furnishing the lumber.

After the business had been conducted in this manner for some time, Kemp requested that the checks should be sent directly to him for delivery to the parties, giving as a reason that the parties delivering lumber disliked to be obliged to be running to the post-office for their checks, and preferred to get them where they delivered their lumber. After this request the checks were mailed directly to Kemp, that he might deliver them to the payees named therein. During the time and between September 29, 1885, and December 15, 1886, Kempt sent to the home office by mail several invoices of lumber, purporting to have been purchased of James Faber; the total amount being 145,713 feet, at a cost of $1,602.68.

Among the checks sent to Kempt to pay James Faber for lumber was one for $137.94, dated May 14, 1886.

It is claimed on the part of the people that these invoices were false and fraudulent; that the person named in the invoices was a myth; and that Kemp, when he received the checks payable to the order of James Faber, either forged the name "James Faber" upon the back of the checks or caused it to be done; and that he uttered the checks so forged as true, with the knowledge that the name "James Faber" was forged, with intent to defraud. These checks came back to M. J. Murphy & Co., in the regular course of business, through its banker, the People's Savings Bank of Detroit, and when so received from the bank, they were indorsed with the names "James Faber," and below it "J. B. Kemp." The checks so indorsed were first presented to and paid by the banking-house of W. C. Page & Co., at Ionia, Michigan, and by them remitted to the People's Savings Bank of Detroit for credit.

An information was filed against Kemp charging him with forgery, and with uttering an order for money, knowing it to be forged, with intent to defraud; upon which he was tried and convicted of the offense of knowingly uttering a false, forged, and counterfeited indorsement upon the back of an order for the payment of money, as true, with intent to cheat and defraud as charged.

These are five counts in the information.

1317

The fourth reads as follows:

"That said Joseph B. Kemp, heretofore, to wit, on the fourteenth day of May, A. D. 1886, at the city of Ionia aforesaid, having in his possession a certain other order for money, whose tenor is as follows, to wit:

"'$137.94.   M.J. MURPHY & CO.   No. 8,819
                    "DETROIT, MICH, May 14, 1886.

"'Pay to the order of James Faber one hundred thirty-seven and 94-100 dollars.

                         "M. J. MURPHY & CO.
              "'Geo. E. Wasey, Sec'y-Treasurer

"'TO PEOPLE'S SAVINGS BANK
              "'Detroit, Mich.'

"Upon which said order for money there was then and there a certain false, forged, and counterfeited indorsement in the words following, that is to say, 'James Faber,' - feloniously did utter and publish as true said false, forged, and counterfeited indorsement of said order, with intent then and there to injure and defraud, he (the said Joseph B. Kemp), at the time he so uttered and published said false, forged, and counterfeited indorsement of said order, then and there well knowing the said indorsement to be false, forged, and counterfeited."

The statute under which the respondent was charged reads as follows:

"Every person who shall falsely make, alter, forge, or counterfeit any . . . bill of exchange, promissory note, or any order . . . for money or other property, or any acceptance of a bill of exchange, or indorsement or assignment of a bill of exchange or promissory note for the payment of money, . . . with intent to injure or defraud any person, shall be punished," etc. How. Stat. Sec. 9213.

"Every person who shall utter, and publish as true any false, forged, altered, or counterfeited . . . instrument or other writing mentioned in the preceding section, knowing the same to be false, altered, forged, or counterfeit, with intent to injure or defraud as aforesaid, shall be punished," etc. Id. Sec. 9214.

Upon the trial of the cause counsel for Kemp objected to the introduction of any testimony under the fourth count above quoted, for the reason that there is no such offense known to the statute, and this objection is insisted upon here, and the position is taken that this statute cannot, by its terms or the language therein used, be construed to cover the forging or the uttering of an indorsement upon an order for the payment of money; that the statute does not

1318

make it a crime to forge an indorsement upon an order for the payment of money; that the statute applies only to the forging of indorsements upon two classes of instruments, namely, bills of exchange and promissory notes.

It is true that the information denominates the instrument "an order for money," but it sets out the instrument in full, and the indorsements thereon, and states that the forgery consisted of forging the name "James Faber," indorsed thereon, so that it makes no difference by what name the pleader calls the instrument, if it is set forth in full and is embraced in the terms of the statute. All bills of exchange are orders for money, and an information for forging a bill of exchange, setting forth the instrument in full, and stating what particular part was forged, and calling it an order for money, would not be bad on that account.

The instrument set forth in the information is a check, and a check is a bill of exchange, drawn by a customer upon his banker, payable on demand. . . .

All checks come within the meaning and definition of a bill of exchange, but all bills of exchange are not checks. The main distinctions between them are pointed out in Bank v. Bank, 10 Wall. 604, 647, and other cases cited above. They are commercial paper, and are governed by the same rules as to presentment and notice of non-payment as inland bills of exchange, payable on demand. . . .

The forging of the indorsement upon a check is punishable under the statute which makes it a crime to forge an indorsement upon a bill of exchange, and the information in this case sufficiently charges the offense.

It is alleged that the court erred in receiving in evidence the orders, papers, and the testimony concerning them, before there was any attempt to offer proof of the corpus delicti.

We do not think that any error was committed in this respect. The proof introduced respecting the invoices, the drawing and forwarding of the checks, the payment thereof by W. C. Page & Co., and the condition they were in when presented to and paid by that company, was all relevant testimony to establish the forgery and uttering of the paper. The point is fully covered by the opinion in People v. Marion, 29 Mich. 31.

The court permitted the prosecutor to introduce testimony which tended to prove that the respondent had forged and uttered other checks at or prior to the time of the forgery alleged in the information, for the purpose of showing the fraudulent character of the act of the respondent in passing the paper alleged to have been forged. The court said:

"I understand the rule to be that the prior utterances of forged papers, knowing them to be forged, prior to the commission of the offense alleged, certainly have a tendency to show that there was a scheme on the part of the accused to get money in that way, and would be admissible in evidence,

1319

and upon that theory I receive them."

This ruling of the court is supported by the case of People v. Marion, above cited, where it is said (on page 37) that —

"The principal criminal element in forgery consists in the fraudulent purpose, and the proofs of fraud must be substantially the same in criminal and civil cases. It can only be made clear by a full understanding of the entire surroundings of the transaction."

The other papers introduced, and which the prosecutor claimed had been forged and uttered by Kemp, were of a similar kind to those in question, and were a part of the transaction relating to the business carried on at Ionia, and consisted of what was claimed to be false invoices of lumber purchased, for which checks were sent to Kemp by M. J. Murphy & Co. to be delivered to the person named in the invoices. The testimony tended to show the scheme of respondent, and his intent to defraud M. J. Murphy & Co. and was admissible for that purpose as part of the res gestae. . . .

After the testimony was all introduced on the part of the people, the counsel for respondent requested the court to take the case from the jury, or direct them to render a verdict of not guilty. This the court rightly refused to do. There was testimony in the case which, if believed, tended to show that Kemp forged the name "James Faber," and also that he uttered the check with the forged indorsement of the name of the payee, knowing it to be forged. The prosecutor introduced testimony which tended to prove (and it was for the jury to say that it did prove) that there was no such person as James Faber who sold lumber to M. J. Murphy & Co.; that Kemp forwarded to the home office in Detroit invoices of lumber purchased by him of James Faber; that M. J. Murphy & Co. sent by mail to Kemp checks to be delivered by him to James Faber in payment for this lumber, which came back to it through the bank upon which they were drawn with the name of J. B. Kemp thereon as second indorser, in the genuine handwriting of respondent. These facts raised a strong inference that Kemp himself either forged the name "James Faber" upon the check, or caused it to be done, and there was opinion testimony to the effect that the name "James Faber" was written by respondent. The weight of this testimony, and its convincing effect, was for the jury.

The errors assigned are overruled, and the judgment is affirmed.

SHERWOOD, C. J., MORSE, and CAMPBELL, JJ., concurred. LONG, J., did not sit.

People v. Parker
114 Mich. 442

LONG, C. J. On April 26, 1897, an information was filed in the Muskegon circuit, charging that –

"On the 27th day of February, 1897, at the city of Muskegon, . . . the respondent feloniously did utter and publish as true a certain false, forged, and counterfeited paper writing, promissory note, order for the payment of money, or order for other property, which said false, forged, and counterfeited paper writing, promissory note, order for the payment of money, or order for other property was in the words and figures following: 'Canvass of 1896. 428. Name, Stewart-Hartshorn Co. hereby agree to pay, on publication, $65.00 (sixty-five dollars), for the insertion of 1 page and 1 display heading. Stewart-Hartshorn Co., – Name of firm. Street address, 520 W. Ave. Business, Shade-rollers,' – with intent then and there to injure and defraud, he, the said Harry J. Parker, at the time he so uttered and published the said false, forged, and counterfeited paper writing, promissory note, order for the payment of money, or order for other property, as aforesaid, then and there well knowing the same to be false, forged, and counterfeited, contrary to the statute in such case made and provided," etc.

To this information the respondent pleaded guilty, and his plea was duly entered of record. Thereafter the respondent, by his attorney, moved the court for an order staying sentence and judgment, for the reasons: (1) That there was no offense alleged or set out in the information; (2) that the written instrument described and set forth in the information, as appears upon the face of said information, is not the subject of forgery, whereby the uttering and publishing of the same as true, knowing the same to be forged, etc., is not a crime. This motion was overruled.

It is contended by counsel for respondent:

(1) That the instrument set forth in the information is not one enumerated in the statutes of this State which may be made the subject of forgery.

(2) That, if it were such an instrument as would be the subject of forgery at the common law, the allegations in the information are insufficient to constitute the uttering and publishing of a forged instrument like the one in question a crime, within the meaning of the common-law rule, as the paper upon its face is no more than nudum pactum, which at common law was never the subject of forgery, without the averment of extrinsic facts showing why and in what manner the paper could be made available as a legal document.

1. Section 9214, 2 How. Stat., provides that:

"Every person who shall utter and publish as true any false, forged, altered, or counterfeit record, deed, instrument, or other writing mentioned in the preceding section, knowing the same to be false, altered, forged, or counterfeit, with intent to injure or defraud as aforesaid, shall

1321

be punished by imprisonment," etc.

The preceding section provides:

"Every person who shall falsely make, alter, forge, or counterfeit any public record, or any certificate, return, or attestation of any clerk of a court, public register, notary public, justice of the peace, township clerk, or any other public officer, in relation to any matter wherein such certificate, return, or attestation may be received as legal proof, or any charter, deed, will, testament, bond or writing obligatory, letter of attorney, policy of insurance, bill of lading, bill of exchange, promissory note, or any order, acquittance, or discharge for money or other property, or any acceptance of a bill of exchange, or indorsement or assignment of a bill of exchange or promissory note for the payment of money, or any accountable receipt for money, goods, or other property, with intent to injure or defraud any person, shall be punished," etc.

We are satisfied that this instrument, whatever it may be called, is not one of the instruments mentioned in the statute which is the subject of forgery. It is not a promissory note; it is not an order for the payment of money. As was said in People v. Smith, 112 Mich. 192:

"An order for money has a well-understood meaning, and it would hardly include the case of one who requests or directs another to solicit and receive subscriptions. Usually such an order contains a request or direction to a third party, who is indebted to the maker of the order, to pay such money to the person named."

All the present instrument purports is that Stewart-Hartshorn Company agrees to pay, on publication, $65 for the insertion of one page and one display heading. What is to be inserted is not mentioned in the instrument. What is to be published cannot be known from the instrument itself. What Stewart-Hartshorn Company was to pay for is not stated, and we think counsel correct in pronouncing it nudum pactum. It is not apparent how this instrument could injure any one.

2. We think it is well settled that, to constitute forgery at the common law, the forged instrument must be one which, if genuine, would bind another, and that it must appear from the indictment that such is its legal character, either from the recitals or description of the instrument itself, or, if that does not show it to be so, then by averment of matter aliunde which will show it to be of that character. In People v. Shall, 9 Cow. 778, the respondent was indicted for the forgery of "a certain promissory note, which said note has been and is lost, and the tenor and substance of which said false, forged, and counterfeited note is as follows: 'Three months after date, I promise to pay to Sebastian I. Shall, or bearer, the sum of three dollars in shoe-

making at cash price, the work to be done at his dwelling house near Simon Vrooman, in Minden. David W. Houghtaling,' - with intent to defraud the said David W. Houghtaling." (sic) There was also a count in the indictment for uttering and publishing this instrument as true, knowing it to be forged, etc. The indictment contained no averment of any extrinsic matter giving the instrument forged, allowing it to have been genuine, any force or effect beyond what it bore on its face. There was a conviction and motion in arrest of judgment, which was overruled. Mr. Justice Cowen, in delivering the opinion of the court, said:

"It is scarcely necessary to observe that the instrument set out in this indictment is not a promissory note, within the statute of Anne, and it is agreed that the writing does not come within any of the statutes of forgery, it being payable neither in money nor goods, but labor. The indictment is therefore based upon the common law. Another defect renders it utterly void, of itself, as a common-law contract. It expresses no value received, nor any consideration whatever, and no action could be maintained upon it, if genuine, as a special agreement to perform labor, without averring and proving a consideration dehors the instrument. The indictment avers no extrinsic fact by which it might be operative, nor is it conceivable how matter for such an averment could exist. . . . It does not come within any of the cases sustaining indictments, but to me it appears to be directly within the cases cited holding that instruments purporting to be void on their face, and not shown to be operative by averment, if genuine, are not the subject of forgery. How is it possible, in the nature of things, that it should be otherwise? Void things are as no things. Was it ever heard of that the forgery of a nudum pactum - a thing which could not be declared on or enforced in any way - is yet indictable? It is the forgery of a shadow."

The same rule was laid down in People v. Tomlinson, 35 Cal. 503, in which are cited as sustaining the same doctrine. . . .

We are satisfied that respondent was improperly convicted under this information, and that he should have been discharged upon the motion in arrest of judgment. The information will therefore be quashed, and the respondent discharged.

The other Justices concurred.

People v. Parmelee
309 Mich. 431

BUSHNELL, J. Defendant George Parmelee, 62 years of age, lives on a farm near the Saginaw-Genesee county line, and has operated an oil and gasoline station for the last 8 or 10 years. He was convicted by a jury on a charge of forging and uttering an "accountable receipt," contrary to the provisions of sections 248 and 249 of the penal code, Act No. 328, Pub. Acts 1931 (Comp. Laws Supp. 1940, Sec. 17115-248, 17115-249, Stat. Ann. Sec. 28.445 and 28.446). Upon a motion for new trial the trial judge set aside the conviction of forgery, but permitted the conviction on the charge of uttering a forged "accountable receipt" to stand. Parmelee appeals from a sentence placing him on probation for three years and the imposition of a fine of $150 and costs in the amount of $100.

John Turnwald, the complaining witness, who has been a farmer all his life, owns a farm located partly in Maple Grove, Saginaw county, and partly in Shiawassee county. He has had business dealings with Parmelee over a period of 15 years. On July 1, 1937, he sold 900 lbs of beans at $6 per hundred to Parmelee, for which he received Parmelee's check for $54. On November 15th of that year Parmelee wrote Turnwald a letter in which he claimed that Turnwald was indebted to him in the sum of $34.65. On December 2d he wrote him another letter in which he asserted that this money was due because of the agreement that was made at the time the beans were purchased and the drop in their market price between July 1st and October 1st. In March of 1938 Parmelee brought suit against Turnwald in justice court on the claimed agreement. While the justice court suit was pending, he again wrote Turnwald on May 14, 1938, in an attempt to force a settlement. In this letter Parmelee mentioned for the first time a receipt for $54 which he claimed Turnwald had given him. Parmelee neither obtained a settlement nor a verdict and appealed the case to the circuit court, where Turnwald again prevailed. Later, Parmelee was arrested and charged with forging and uttering an "accountable receipt."

In the criminal trial the check was offered in evidence over Parmelee's objection that:

"There is no dispute over this paper and it has no bearing on the case. It is not a proper exhibit, as it has no connection with any dispute in this case."

The court overruled the objection on the ground that the check was part of the original transaction. The receipt which was received in evidence without objection reads:

"Date, July 1, 1937. Mr. John Turnwald received of George Parmelee $54 to apply on beans. Price to be what I get for bal. of my beans between now and November 1. It is strictly understood there is to be no other agreements. 4# beans.
                    X John Turnwald
                      and Geo. Parmelee."

Turnwald testified that the first time he saw the receipt was in the justice court; that he did not know where it came from; and that he never signed it. He identified the check

and said he indorsed it when he cashed it. Leroy Smith, a
member of the Michigan State police force, who has pursued
the investigation of handwriting since about 1930, testified,
from comparisons made at the State police laboratory in 1938
of Turnwald's indorsement on the check and the signature on
the receipt, that, in his opinion, Turnwald's signature on
the receipt was a tracing of his signature on the back of the
check. He amplified his testimony with the statement that
the signatures were identical and "a perfect match" which
could happen only once in "1,000,910,000,000 times." . . .

The information sufficiently charges a violation of the
statutes which make it a felony to falsely make, alter,
forge, et cetera, and utter any "accountable receipt." Sections 248 and 249 of the penal code, Act No. 328, Pub. Acts
1931 (Comp. Laws Supp. 1940, Sec. 17115-248, 17115-249, Stat.
Ann. Sec. 28.445 and 28.446).

Parmelee claims that the paper in question is not an "accountable receipt." It does not lie in his mouth to make
this claim because he brought an action in the justice court
upon the instrument, and cannot now deny its "accountable"
nature.

The variance asserted in the recital of the receipt in the
information and the language of the exhibit itself are not
sufficient to make the receipt inadmissible in the criminal
action.

The cited statutes require proof of fraudulent intent and
appellant claims that no evidence of such intent was produced.
If the receipt is a forged one, the intent to defraud by uttering it was sufficiently shown by the action which Parmelee
brought on it against Turnwald in the justice court. . . .

The sentence imposed is affirmed.

NORTH, C. J., and STARR, WIEST, BUTZEL, SHARPE, BOYLES,
and REID, JJ., concurred.

People v. Brown
178 Mich. 155

OSTRANDER, J. Respondent who is charged in the information
as "L. Brown, whose first name is unknown, but whose person is
well known," was convicted by a jury of the offense of having
uttered and published as true a certain false, forged, and
counterfeit order for the payment of money, with intent to injure and defraud. The order, set out in the information is
as follows:

"$10.00.   Detroit, Mich., Feb. 2, 1913.
"German-American Bank: Pay to the order of L. Brown, ten
and 00/100 dollars, value received, and charge the same to
"No. 2.
                                   L. BROWN."

1325

It is indorsed, "L. Brown." The testimony for the people tended to prove that on the 2d day of February, 1913, which was Sunday, the respondent called at the store of one Hilson, told him he had some money in the bank that he could not get until Monday, and asked him to give him $10 for his check, which Hilson did; Hilson indorsed the check, presented it at the bank on the following morning, and was told that respondent had no account there; that respondent had not since repaid him the money or taken the check. It also appeared that Hilson had known the respondent from childhood - 25 or 28 years - that respondent drew the check in his (Hilson's) place of business. Hilson testified:

"Q. This check, therefore, you understood to be his check?
"A. Yes, sir.
"Q. On the back, that you understood to be his signature?
"A. Yes; he wrote it out right in my store.
"Q. So all that you complain of is that he had no account at the bank, and you could not get the money?
"A. Yes, sir.
"Q. But the check is in his handwriting?
"A. Yes; he wrote it.
"Q. Made by him as maker and indorsed by him?
"A. Yes, sir.
"Q. You do not claim that it is anybody else's check but his?
"A. His check."

The testimony tended further to prove that the respondent had no account and no money in the bank upon which the check was drawn, and that he had stated to the detective of the police department who arrested him that he got hard up for money, made out the check, and cashed it with a friend of his, and calculated to make it good; that he had no money in the bank. Upon this testimony the people rested. Thereupon the attorney for the respondent moved the court to discharge the respondent and to quash the information, because it appeared that the instrument was not forged. After a considerable colloquy the people recalled the witness Hilson, who stated that he had known the respondent since boyhood; that his name is Leon Novakowski; that he had heard of his using the name of L. Brown; that they were from the same town, which respondent left many years ago; that he knew him there as Leon Novakowski, but had afterwards heard that he went by the name of L. Brown; that it was about ten years since he had first heard him called Leo Brown; that he understood the respondent was signing his own name to the check; that he did not understand that he was signing the name of any other person to the check or any assumed name, but knew that he was going by the name of L. Brown. No testimony was offered on the part of respondent; his counsel simply stated to the jury that, if he was guilty of any offense, it was misrepresenting that he had an account at the bank.

1326

3 Comp. Laws, Sec. 11659 (5 How. Stat. (2d Ed.) Sec. 14695), referred to in the information, prescribes the punishment for persons who shall falsely make, alter, forge, or counterfeit any order for money or other property, with intent to defraud or injure any person, and section 11660 provides that every person who shall utter and publish as true any false, forged, altered, or counterfeit instrument mentioned in the preceding section, knowing the same to be false, altered, forged or counterfeit, with intent to injure or defraud, shall be punished by imprisonment in the State prison not more than 14 years or in the county jail not more than 1 years.

The recorder submitted the question of respondent's guilt to the jury, and, upon the verdict being returned, sentenced him to be confined in the State's prison at Marquette for a term of not less than 5 years. A motion to set aside the verdict and judgment and grant a new trial was refused. The cause is here on exceptions, of which we need to consider but one, which is that the court erred in refusing to discharge the respondent at the close of the people's case. It is obvious that the motion should have been granted; there being no testimony tending to prove that the check was a false, altered, forged, or counterfeit instrument. Upon the hearing, the attorney general confessed error.

The verdict must be set aside, and the respondent discharged.

STEERE, C. J., and MOORE, McALVAY, BROOKE, KUHN, STONE, and BIRD, JJ., concurred.

Houseman-Spitzley Corp. v. Bank
205 Mich. 268

STONE, J. This case grew out of certain fraudulent transactions of one Stephen I. Kux as hereinafter stated. Kux was, in June, 1917, in the employ of the plaintiff as its west side salesman. About the 19th of that month he came to B. C. Spitzley, president of the plaintiff corporation, with a proposition that he join the plaintiff in the purchase of certain property located on the west side of the city of Detroit. He represented that a considerable profit could be made by taking an option upon the property and reselling it at an advance price, before the option should expire. He stated that because of his connection with the plaintiff, he felt that he ought to give it a chance to share in the proposition. He represented that the land was owned by one Fred Maples, who lived in Dearborn, and that Maples was willing to sell at $600 per lot, and would give a 90-day option at that price, upon the payment of $500; and he proposed that plaintiff should pay one-half of that sum, and that he

1327

should pay the other half.

Because Kux was a trusted employee of the plaintiff, and because Mr. Spitzley did not have time to make a personal investigation, other than to ascertain the location of the property upon the map, he assented to the proposition, stipulating that the option should be taken in the name of the plaintiff, and that Kux should immediately undertake the sale of the lots.

A check payable to the order of Maples for $250 was, on June 20, 1917, drawn on the defendant, the American State Bank, signed by the plaintiff, and handed to Kux to take to Maples, as plaintiff's half of the option money. The following day Kux brought to Mr. Spitzley what purported to be the option signed by Maples, which recited the consideration of $500, the description of the lots to be conveyed, and the purchase price. The option was dated July 19th instead of June 19th, and Mr. Spitzley inquired why it was dated ahead. Kux replied that he had made a mistake in dating it, but that it was satisfactory to Maples, and that it was to their advantage, as it gave them an extra 30 days.

Kux's story was a complete fabrication. He knew of no one by the name of Maples, had no transaction with the owner of the property, and had written the names of Maples and the witnesses to the option agreement, himself. He also wrote the name Fred Maples upon the back of the check, and deposited it in his own account in the Federal State Bank. That bank obtained credit for the check through the clearing house, and the check was charged against plaintiff's account in the American State Bank. . . .

At the trial at the circuit, verdict and judgment were directed against the plaintiff, because the trial court was of the opinion that certain transactions between plaintiff and Kux, after the discovery of the forgery, and before notice to defendants, released the latter from liability. It appeared that upon August 2, 1917, Kux, while in jail, was persuaded to make a complete confession of his crime before an assistant prosecuting attorney, and plaintiff's attorney, and that at the time of the confession, Kux voluntarily transferred to plaintiff all the property which he owned, being an automobile which he was purchasing from a dealer upon a title retaining contract. . . .

(Kux also assigned to the plaintiff a land contract. However, the value of the assignments by Kux was inadequate to cover plaintiff's losses from various frauds by Kux.)

That the indorsement of a fictitious payee's name by one not authorized to do so is to be treated as a forgery, as held in Harmon v. National Bank, 153 Mich. 73, 79 (17 L.R.S. (N.S.) 514, 126 Am. St. Rep. 467), does not seem to be questioned by either party, and by the record it appears that the ground upon which the court directed the verdict was that plaintiff by its delay in giving notice, coupled with the acceptance of the forger's property, had estopped itself to claim that the payment of the check was unauthorized. . . .

1328

We are of the opinion that the great weight of authority is as claimed by counsel for plaintiff; that the defendants have not sustained the burden of showing prejudice or injury; and that it does not appear that defendants would have been in any better condition had they received notice of the forgery on the day of Kux's confession. He had not been allowed to escape, but was in custody upon complaint of plaintiff at the time of notice. Upon this record we think the plaintiff was entitled to a directed verdict in its favor.

The judgment below is reversed and a new trial granted, with costs to appellant.

BIRD, C. J., and OSTRANDER, MOORE, STEERE, BROOKE, and FELLOWS, JJ., concurred. KUHN, J., did not sit.

Watrous v. Allen
57 Mich. 362

COOLEY, C. J. The purpose of the bill in this case is to obtain a perpetual injunction against the carrying on of the business of dealing in intoxicating drinks on certain premises in the village of Meredith, in the county of Clare.

The allegations of the bill are as follows:

On February 28, 1884, Thomas J. McClenna was owner of the premises in question, and sold the same to the defendants James D. Allen and William F. Holtz, and made and delivered to them a deed thereof. This deed contained the following proviso:

"Provided always, and this contract and the estate in said premises hereby created is subject to the express condition, that if the parties of the second part, their heirs and assigns, shall at any time sell or keep for sale upon said above-granted premises, or knowingly permit any person under them so to sell or keep for sale, any spirituous or intoxicating liquors, whether distilled or fermented, the entire title and estate in and to said premises hereby sold and created shall cease, and the title to said premises shall thereupon at once revert to and vest in the parties of the first part, their heirs and assigns forever, and shall be lawful for the said parties of the first part, their heirs and assigns to re-enter upon said premises, and said parties of the second part, their heirs and assigns, and every person claiming under him or them, wholly to remove, expel, or put out. . . ."

On or about the first day of August, 1884, William O'Brien took possession of the lot so conveyed to Allen and Holtz, and has commenced the sale of intoxicating liquors thereon as a regular business. O'Brien was aware when he did so of the condition in the McClennan deed, which the bill avers was stricken out by Allen wrongfully the act of striking it out

1329

being an act of forgery. O'Brien was warned not to enter upon such business before he did so, but refused to heed the warning. The bill avers special injury to complainant Watrous as owner of the lands conveyed to him by McClennan, and prays that the estate so conveyed to Allen and Holtz be decreed to be forfeited for breach of condition; that the defendants, and all persons holding from or under them, be enjoined and restrained from giving, delivering, selling or keeping for sale any spirituous or intoxicating liquors, whether distilled or fermented on said premises, and for other and further relief. . . .

That a condition like that in this case is valid in law was decided in Smith v. Barrie, 56 Mich. 314, at the last term of this Court, and is not now in question. A perpetual injunction should be decreed, and complainant should recover his costs.

SHERWOOD and CHAMPLIN, JJ., concurred.

CAMPBELL, J. I think the case is not one for equity.

Note

Gillespie summarizes the principal elements of forgery as follows:

"(1) The making of any false document enumerated in the statute, with

(2) Intent to injure or defraud another, and

(3) The exposure of some person to loss or risk of loss through such act."[1]

1. Gillespie, Michigan Criminal Law and Procedure, Sec. 1485 (2nd ed. 1953).

3. Final Draft – Michigan Revised Criminal Code

(Definition of Terms)

Sec. 4001. The following definitions are applicable in this chapter unless the context otherwise requires:

(a) "Written instrument" means (i) any paper, document or other instrument containing written or printed matter or its equivalent; and (ii) any token, stamp, seal, badge, trademark or other evidence or symbol of value, right, privilege or identification, which is capable of being used to the advantage or disadvantage of some person.

(b) "Complete written instrument" means one which purports to be a genuine written instrument fully drawn with respect to every essential feature thereof.

(c) "Incomplete written instrument" means one which contains some matter by way of content or authentication but which requires additional matter in order to render it a complete written instrument.

(d) To "falsely make" a written instrument means to make or draw a complete written instrument in its entirety, or an incomplete written instrument, which purports to be an authentic creation of its ostensible maker, but which is not either because the ostensible maker is fictitious or because, if real, he did not authorize the making or drawing thereof.

(e) To "falsely complete" a written instrument means to transform, by adding, inserting or changing matter, an incomplete written instrument into a complete one, without the authority of anyone entitled to grant it, so that the complete written instrument falsely appears or purports to be in all respects an authentic creation of its ostensible maker or authorized by him.

(f) To "falsely alter" a written instrument means to change, without authorization by anyone entitled to grant it, a written instrument, whether complete or incomplete, by means of erasure, obliteration, deletion, insertion of new matter, transposition of matter, or in any other manner, so that the instrument so altered falsely appears or purports to be in all respects an authentic creation of its ostensible maker or authorized by him.

(g) "Forged instrument" means a written instrument which has been falsely made, completed or altered.

(h) "Intent to defraud means

(a) A purpose to use deception as defined in section 3201 (a) or to injure someone's interest which has value as defined in section 3201 (m); or

(b) Knowledge that the defendant is facilitating a fraud or injury to be perpetrated or inflicted by someone else.

(i) "Property is defined as in section 3201 (i).
(j) "Services" is defined as in section 3220.
(k) "Government" is defined as in section 3201 (d).

Committee Commentary

This section defines terms only, not criminal activity itself. It is adapted from New York Revised Penal Code, Sec. 170.00. Subparagraph (h) is based on a phrase in Model Penal Code, Sec. 224.1. For a general discussion of the relationship of Draft provisions to existing law, see the Commentary to Sec. 4001-4007 below.

(Forgery in the First Degree)

Sec. 4005. (1) A person commits the crime of forgery in the first degree if, with intent to defraud, he falsely makes, completes or alters a written instrument which is or purports to be, or which is calculated to become or to represent if completed:

   (a) A deed, will, codicil, contract, assignment, commercial instrument, or other instrument which does or may evidence, create, transfer, terminate or otherwise affect a legal right, interest, obligation or status; or
   (b) A public record, or an instrument filed or required by law to be filed or legally fileable in a public office or with a public employee; or
   (c) A written instrument officially issued or created by a public office, public employee or government agency.

   (2) Forgery in the second degree is a Class C felony.

Committee Commentary

   This section aggravates the penalty for what is otherwise forgery in the third degree because the forged instrument directly affects deed, will, contract or commercial instrument transactions, or purports to be fileable with or issued from a public office. It is adapted from New York Revised Penal Code, Sec. 170.10. Its relationship to present Michigan law is discussed in the Commentary to Sec. 4001-4007 below.

(Forgery in the Third Degree)

   Sec. 4007. (1) A person commits the crime of forgery in the third degree if, with intent to defraud, he falsely makes, completes or alters a written instrument.
   (2) Forgery in the third degree is a Class A misdemeanor.

Committee Commentary

   This section, which incorporates the terms specially defined in Sec. 4001, creates the basic line of separation between criminal and non-criminal conduct in this area. It is adapted from New York Revised Penal Code Sec. 170.05. The relationship of the Draft to existing Michigan law is explained in the Commentary to Sec. 4001-4007 below.

Committee Commentary to Sec. 4001 to 4007

Relationship to Existing Law

   Forgery is defined at the common law to be "the making of a false document with intent to defraud" (People v. Larson, 255 Mich. 355, 196 N.W. 412 (1923)) or "the false making or materially altering, with intent to defraud, of any writing, which, if genuine, might apparently be of legal efficacy, or the foundation of a legal liability' . . .(,) the 'fraudulent' making and alteration of a writing, to the prejudice of another man's right" (McGinn v. Tobey, 62 Mich.

1332

252, 259-260, 28 N.W. 818 (1886)). The stated intent is
the intent "to defraud" (Leslie v. Kennedy, 249 Mich. 553,
229 N.W. 469 (1930)), though that is not further defined in
the case law. The act of forgery is anything "which fraudulently makes an instrument 'purport to be that which it is
not'" (In re Stout, 371 Mich. 438, 440-41, 124 N.W. 2d 277
(1963)), and includes the execution of a totally false document (e.g.,People v. Larson, 225 Mich. 355, 196 N.W. 412 (1923)
(co-partnership agreement); People v. Watkins, 106 Mich. 437,
64 N.W. 324 (1895) (chattel mortgage); People v. Swetland, 77
Mich. 53, 43 N.W. 779 (1889) (discharge of mortgage); People
v. Marion, 29 Mich. 31 (1874) (deed)), adding a signature to
an otherwise proper document (Houseman-Spitzley Corp, v.
American State Bank, 205 Mich. 258, 171 N.W. 543 (1919)
(forged endorsement of payee); Harmon v. Old Detroit National
Bank, 153 Mich. 73, 116 N.W. 617 (1908) (fictitious payee);
People v. Kemp, 76 Mich. 410, 43 N.W. 439 (1889) (endorsement of fictitious payee); People v. Van Alstine, 57 Mich.
69, 23 N.W. 594 (1889) (deceased owner's name on deed)), or
an unauthorized striking out of part of a valid instrument
after it has been executed (Watrous v. Allen, 57 Mich. 362,
24 N.W. 104 (1885)). Any kind of a deed or contract instrument can be the subject of forgery. However, it must be an
enforcible instrument in form (People v. Parker, 114 Mich.
442, 72 N.W. 250 (1897) (a subscription form which the court
assumes to be totally without legal effect)). But the requirement is only that the basic character of the instrument
be enforcible; one defendant was successfully prosecuted
even though he lost an action to enforce an accountable receipt on the merits before the forger was discovered (People v. Parmelee, 309 Mich. 431, 15 N.W. 2d 696 (1944)). And
care should be taken to distinguish instances in which the
factual allegations in the writing are false in fact but
the instrument is exactly what it purports to be. An example is a deed to land which the vendor does not own or a
promissory note secured by property which the promisor does
not own. This is not forgery (People v. Brown, 178 Mich. 155,
144 N.W. 477 (1913)).

Present statutes, many of them duplicative, restate the
common-law tradition. The primary criminal code sections
cover forgery of records and other instruments (C.L. 1948,
Sec. 750.248), of notes issued by the state or a political
subdivision (C.L. 1948, Sec. 750.250), and of bank bills and
promissory notes (C.L. 1948, Sec. 750.251). It is also a
crime to issue or circulate spurious bank notes (C.L. 1948,
Sec. 750.95). Affixing a false signature of a corporate officer to a note, etc., is a form of forgery (C.L. 1948, Sec.
750.259). Connecting several parts of genuine instruments
to create an instrument which is not what it appears to be
is considered forgery (C.L. 1948, Sec. 750.259). There are
also four special coverage statutes in the Penal Code itself
on forging and counterfeiting trademarks, labels, stamps,
etc. (C.L. 1948, Sec. 750.263), counterfeiting and imitating

a union label (C.L. 1948, Sec. 750.265a), forging railroad
tickets (C.L. 1948, Sec. 750.266; People v. Smith, 125 Mich.
566, 84 N.W. 1068 (1901)), and making or counterfeiting slugs
(C.L. 1948, Sec. 752.802).

In addition there are a number of forgery sections scattered throughout the Compiled Laws, with penalties inconsistent
with the counterpart Penal Code provisions. They penalize
forgery of names on initiative or referendum petitions (C.L.
1948, Sec. 168.484), forgery in the context of elections
(C.L. 1948, Sec. 168.937), forgery or alteration of certificates and plates issued under the Motor Vehicle Code (C.L.
1948, Sec. 257.257), forgery of a certificate of financial
responsibility under the Motor Vehicle Code (C.L. 1948, Sec.
257.905), alteration of a warehouse receipt (C.L. 1948, Sec.
285.82), falsification of a cream test report (C.L. 1948,
Sec. 288.56), alteration or falsification of records relating to transactions affecting oil and gas production (C.L.
1948, Sec. 319.19), endorsement of a document by a forester
whose registration has expired (C.L. 1948, Sec. 338.735),
forgery of documents under the statute regulating cutting
and sale of Christmas trees (C.L. 1948, Sec. 320.418), alteration of a deer-hunting license (C.L. 1948, Sec. 314.25),
alteration of a trapping license (C.L. 1948, Sec. 314.32),
forgery, counterfeiting or alteration of certificate of
eligibility to practice healing arts (C.L. 1948, Sec. 338.8)
alteration of a certificate or license of a master, pilot,
engineer or operator under the Vessel Regulation Act (C.L.
1948, Sec. 408.278), alteration of a private detective
agency license (C.L. 1948, Sec. 338.805), forgery, alteration or counterfeiting of any stamp or label of the Liquor
Control Commission (C.L. 1948, Sec. 436.46a), forgery or
alteration of a prescription to obtain a narcotic drug (C.L.
1948, Sec. 335.67), similar prohibitions in C.L. 1948, Sec.
335.153a), and alteration of a warehouse receipt (C.L. 1948,
Sec. 444.107).

It is evident both from the case law description of forgery
and the language of these several statutes that the crime of
forgery bears a close relationship to the crime of obtaining
property by false pretenses (or theft by deception under this
Draft, Sec. 3205) and to various offenses protecting the integrity of governmental licensing activities. That relationship is quite clearly expressed in the present false pretense statute (C.L. 1948, Sec. 750.218), which defines a
false pretense, among other things, as "under color of any
false token or writing or by any false or bogus check or
other written, printed or engraved instrument." It might
be asked why theft and attempted theft are not sufficient
coverage of what is now denominated as forgery. The drafters of the Model Penal Code faced the problem in this way:

"In drafting a Model Penal Code, it is necessary to ask
ourselves why this expanded concern for authenticity is not
satisfied by the penal law dealing with false pretense and

fraud. In earlier days the law of false pretense might well have been inadequate because of limitations on its scope. For example, it would have been necessary to prove that property was obtained by the misrepresentation, which would not be the case if a forged deed were given as a gift. In addition, the limitations of traditional attempt law would have prevented punishment of a forger or counterfeiter apprehended after the false documents had been made, but before any attempt to pass them off. It is obviously even more important to convict the forger, often a highly skilled professional criminal, than the individuals to whom he sells or gives the forgeries to be palmed off by them.

"If the shortcomings of other branches of the criminal law are remedied in a modern code that deals effectively with fraud, attempt, complicity, and professional criminality, the need for a separate forgery offense is much diminished. We retain forgery as a distinct offense partly because the concept is so embedded in statute and popular understanding that it would be inconvenient and unlikely that any legislature would completely abandon it, and partly in recognition of the special effectiveness of forgery as a means of undermining public confidence in important symbols of commerce, and of perpetrating large scale frauds. . . ." (Tent. Draft No. 11, pp. 79-80 (1960)).

Following the lead of all recent codification efforts, the Draft retains forgery, though with more explicit definitions than are found in the present Michigan statutes.

Section 4001 is the definitional section for the several offenses set out in the sections which follow. The language of subparagraphs (a) through (g) is taken directly from the New York Revised Penal Code Sec. 170.00, but with the possible exception of the term "badge" in the definition of "written instrument" in Sec. 4001 (a) it clearly restates Michigan law. Subparagraph (h) has been added for two reasons. One is to tie the concept of "intent to defraud" to the coverage of "deception" of Sec. 3205 and 3201 (a) and to the idea of an interest with "value" as delineated in Sec. 3201 (m). A false birth certificate showing mixed blood intended to bring about the "blackballing" of an applicant to a private country club would not be a subject of forgery. The second is to follow the lead of the Model Penal Code in expanding intent to include the alternative of "knowledge that the defendant is facilitating a fraud or injury to be perpetrated or inflicted by someone else", a slightly modified version of what was added to Sec. 224.1 (1) of the Model Penal Code. As the Commentary to that section states,

"This is to make it clear that a forger commits an offense even though he does not defraud the person to whom he sells or passes the forged writings, as where the transferee takes with knowledge of the forgery for the purpose of passing the writings as authentic." (P.O.D. p. 176 (1962).

1335

Section 4005 reserves for the most serious punishment acts of forgery that impair public trust and confidence in governmental or corporate financial issues. A lack of public confidence in the validity of instruments of these kinds can have disastrous impact on governmental processes and the economy. In fact, these are written instruments which were first specifically protected at the common law (see Commentary to Sec. 223.1, Model Penal Code, Tent. Draft No. 11, pp. 78-79 (1960)). It is quite difficult for the average citizen to protect himself against skilled forgeries of documents or certificates like these. Professional criminals are also most likely to concentrate their efforts on reproducing written instruments in these categories. Accordingly, the most serious penalties, those for a Class B felony, are reserved for those who forge the enumerated instruments. It should be noted, however, that the forged item must appear to be "part of an issue." A secured promissory note of a governmental or private corporation would not come within this section, but within Sec. 4006 (1); only bonds, stocks, certificates and the like which are part of a larger issue fall within Sec. 4005. How many "companions" there must be for there to be an "issue" will be a matter of judicial interpretation in the particular case.

Section 4006 also uses the basic definitional terms set out in Sec. 4001, but provides for increased penalties because of what the forged instrument appears to be. Subparagraph (1) includes all deeds, wills and contractual instruments relating to secured transactions. These are the "symbols of commerce" that the Model Penal Code drafters desire to protect. The second and third subparagraphs authorize increased penalties because the forged instrument purports to be a public record, or something that can be filed so as to become a public record, or a document issued or created by a governmental office or agency. Increased penalties for forging these instruments can be justified on at least two grounds. One is the citizen's lack of suspicion about or inclination to question public documents, which makes the successful perpetration of a fraud more likely than if a non-governmental document were forged and uttered. The other is that the circulation of spurious records or recordable instruments tends to weaken public confidence in the authentic records themselves, and thus public confidence in governmental processes as such. The punishment is set at the Class C felony level because the amount of harm to property interests or government functions is much greater than for third-degree forgery, though less than first-degree forgery.

Section 4007 utilizes the several terms defined in Sec. 4001 to delineate criminal from non-criminal conduct in the area of forgery. The false making, completion or alteration of any written instrument which does not come within the subcategories of Sec. 4006 (forgery in the second degree) or Sec. 4005 (forgery in the first degree) will be within the coverage of Sec. 4007; in this sense its coverage is residual. Forgery of trademarks, membership cards, theater tickets, bus transfers, and the like would almost certainly be within this section's ambit. Because the harm done is relatively slight, the crime is indicated at the Class A misdemeanor level.

* * * * *

Note on the counterfeiting of coins and currency. Michigan statutes now penalize the counterfeiting and possession of coins (C.L. 1948, Sec. 750.260), the possession of less than five counterfeit coins (C.L. 1948, Sec. 750.261), the possession of tools for counterfeiting coins (C.L. 1948, Sec. 750.262) and the making or counterfeiting of slugs (C.L. 1948, Sec. 752.802). An early United States Supreme Court case distinguishes between state penalties for counterfeiting itself and for possessing counterfeit or passing it (Fox v. Ohio, 46 U.S. 410 (1847)); the former is stated in dictum as being exclusively a federal concern, while jurisdiction to take cognizance of the latter is concurrent. The Michigan Supreme Court early held that the Michigan statute was valid even before the Fox case was decided (Harlan v. People, 1 Doug. 207 (1843)), and a Connecticut appellate court has recently held the same thing (State v. Scarano, 149 Conn. 34, 175 A.2d 360 (1961)). At the time the several Michigan statutes were first passed (and see also C.L. 1948, Sec. 750.254 (possession of counterfeit bank bills)), state banks in Michigan of course circulated their own notes as currency. The federal tax on state bank notes, in effect since 1867 (now 26 U.S.C.A. Sec. 4881–4885; see Veazie Bank v. Fenno, 75 U.S. 533 (1869)), made this a thing of the past. Therefore, only the counterfeiting of United States coins and currency can fall within the terms of the present Michigan statutes. Though one may assume that the Draft could constitutionally include a section covering at least the possession of counterfeit coins or the possession of counterfeit coins or the possession of tools designed to make them, there is no point to be served in drafting provisions to this effect because of the complete federal coverage of this activity (18 U.S.C.A. Sec. 471–474, 485–487, 489–491). Therefore, the Draft does not include the word "money" in the definition of "written instrument" borrowed from New York Revised Penal Code Sec. 170.00 (1) or in the definition of "valuable instruments" in Sec. 4005 (1). It still may be possible to bring United States coins or currency within the term "symbol of value" "capable of being used to the advantage. . . of some person" in Sec. 4001 (a), and to include it within the coverage of "part of an issue of . . . valuable instruments issued by a government" in Sec. 4005 (1). But elimination of the words "money" and "counterfeit" from the Draft places some practical limitation on the likelihood of this being done. At the same time, the term "stamp" remains in Sec. 4001 (a) and 4005 (1), so that postal and other stamps issued by the federal government will con-

tinue to be included within the coverage of Michigan forgery
law. This is because there are so many official state revenue
stamps in common usage.

B. Fraud

1. Introductory Note

Both the judicial and legislative departments have played
an important role in the development of the law of fraud and
deceit.[1]
In the development of the common law it was held that
where the owner of the goods voluntarily gives up possession
to the accused, there could be no charge of larceny because
the accused has possession and there is no trespassory element. However, where possession was obtained by fraud, trick
or artifice, the fraud vitiates the consent of the owner and
the accused does not obtain lawful possession. Therefore,
the subsequent appropriation by the accused is trespassory.[2]
This is generally classified as "Larceny by Trick." This
is the case in Michigan where the Supreme Court has held
that the trick or fraud will supply the place of trespass.[3]
Where as a result of the fraud or trick the owner intended
to pass both possession and title the crime is false pretenses on the theory that one does not commit a trespass where
he has legal possession, and title.[4] However, if the "chattel
was received with innocent intent and later appropriated as
a result of a change of mind, the wrongful appropriation is
not larceny (but embezzlement) because the misdeed was by one
having lawful possession."[5]
The early common law concerning fraud was influenced by
the doctrine of caveat emptor, and declined to treat as criminal cases those takings made possible by simple deception.
"The classic justification was given by Holt, C. J., in 1703:
'(W)e are not to indict one for making a fool of another.'
R. v. Jones, 91 Eng. Rep. 330. But through the development
of common law cheats the principle was modified as to certain kinds of fraud which were aimed indiscriminately at any
member of the public, rather than at a particular person,
and which were thought to be such that ordinary prudence
was an insufficient protection; . . ."
The common law development was supplemented by a host of
relatively specific legislative acts in Michigan as in other
jurisdictions. These statutes are set forth in the next
section. It should be noted that the common law crime of
gross frauds and cheats has been preserved in Michigan. C.L.
1948, Sec. 750.280. - Ed.

1. Kadish and Paulsen, Criminal Law and Its Processes -
   Cases and Materials, 2nd ed., Little, Brown & Co., 1969.,
   p.625.

1338

2. Perkins, *Criminal Law*, Foundation Press, 1957., pp. 203-204.

3. People v. Shaw, 57 Mich. 403.

4. Perkins, supra note 3.

5. Ibid.

6. Kadish and Paulsen, supra note 1.

2. Michigan Compiled Laws (1948)

Chapter XLIII. FRAUDS AND CHEATS

750.271 Domestic corporations, securities, fraudulent issue and sale

Sec. 271. FRAUDULENT ISSUE AND SALE OF SECURITIES OF DOMESTIC CORPORATIONS - Any person or persons who shall fraudulently issue or cause to be issued, any stock, scrip, or evidence of debt, of any bank, insurance, mining or other incorporated company of this state, or who shall sell or offer for sale, hypothecate, or otherwise dispose of any such stock, scrip or other evidence of debt, knowing the same to be so fraudulently issued, shall be guilty of a felony, punishable by imprisonment in the state prison not more than 10 years.

750.272 Foreign corporations, stock, fraudulently issued, sale

Sec. 272. KNOWINGLY SELLING FRAUDULENTLY ISSUED STOCK OF FOREIGN CORPORATIONS - Any person or persons who shall sell or offer for sale any stock fraudulently issued, and purporting to be the stock, scrip or evidence of debt of any corporation located out of the state of Michigan, knowing the same to be so fraudulently issued, or shall hypothecate, or in any manner dispose of the same for value, shall be guilty of a felony, punishable by imprisonment in the state prison not more than 10 years.

750.273 Signature, fraudulently obtaining

Sec. 273. FRAUDULENTLY OBTAINING SIGNATURE TO NOTE, ETC., - Any person who shall, by representing that he is the agent of any person, company, firm or corporation, or by any other means, fraudulently obtain the signature of any person with the intent to cheat and defraud such person, to any promissory note, bill of exchange, due bill, order, contract or any paper writing whatever, shall be guilty of felony, punishable by imprisonment in the state prison not more than 10 years or by fine of not more than 5,000 dollars.

750.274 Note, fraudulent signature; knowingly purchasing, collection

Sec. 274. PURCHASING AND ATTEMPTING TO COLLECT A NOTE, KNOWING SIGNATURE WAS FRAUDULENTLY OBTAINED - Any person who shall receive into his possession for collection or sale or who shall purchase any promissory note, bill of exchange, due bill, order, contract, or paper writing whatever, obtained in the manner mentioned in the preceding section of this chapter, knowing the same to have been obtained with the intent to cheat and defraud, and any person who shall take any steps to collect any promissory note, bill of exchange, due bill, order, contract, paper or writing whatever, knowing the signature to have been obtained by fraud, with intent to cheat and defraud, shall be guilty of a felony, punishable by imprisonment in the state prison not more than 10 years, or by fine of not more than 5,000 dollars.

750.275 Warranty deed or similar words, use

Sec. 275. USE OF WORDS "WARRANTY DEED" OR SIMILAR WORDS - Any person who shall print, sell or keep for sale any blank forms of deeds containing the words "warranty deed", or "warranty-deed-covenant-own-acts", or any similar words printed or written thereon, unless such deed is in fact an absolute warranty deed, and any person who shall knowingly use any such deed for the purpose of conveying title unless the same is an absolute warranty deed, shall be guilty of a misdemeanor.

750.276 Promise to vendee of grain to sell at fictitious
          price, signature to note

Sec. 276. PROCURING SIGNATURE TO NOTE, ETC., AS CONSIDERATION FOR PROMISE TO VENDEE OF GRAIN TO SELL SAME AT FICTITIOUS PRICE - Any person who, either for his own benefit, or as the agent of any corporation, company, association or person, procures the signature of any person or maker, indorser, guarantor or surety thereon, to any bond, bill, receipt, promissory note, draft, check or any other evidence of indebtedness as the whole or part consideration for any bond, contract, agreement or promise given to the vendee of any grain, seed or other cereals, binding the vendor or any other person, corporation, company or association, or the agent thereof, to sell for such vendee any grain, seed, or cereals at a fictitious price, or at a price equal to or more than twice the market price of such grain, seed or cereals, shall be guilty of a felony.

750.277 Same; sale and transfer

Sec. 277. SALE AND TRANSFER OF NOTE, ETC., SIGNATURE TO WHICH WAS PROCURED AS CONSIDERATION FOR PROMISE TO VENDEE OF GRAIN TO SELL AT FICTITIOUS PRICE - Any person who shall sell, barter or dispose of, either for his own benefit or as the agent of any corporation, company, association or person, any bond, bill, receipt, promissory note, draft, check or other evidence of indebtedness, knowing the same to have been ob-

tained as the whole or part consideration for any bond, contract, agreement, or promise given to the vendee of any grain,
seed or cereals, binding the vendor or any other person, corporation, company or association, or agent thereof, to sell
for such vendee any grain, seed or cereals, at a fictitious
price, or at a price equal to or more than twice the market
price of such grain, seed, or cereals, shall be guilty of a
felony.

750.278 Fraudulent warehouse receipts, executing and deliver-
        ing

Sec. 278. KNOWINGLY EXECUTING AND DELIVERING FRAUDULENT
WAREHOUSE RECEIPTS - Any warehouseman or forwarding merchant
or any other person, or the agent or servant of any warehouseman or forwarding merchant or other person, who shall knowingly execute and deliver to any person a receipt or certificate
purporting to be for flour, wheat, pot or pearl ashes, or any
grain, produce or thing of value, as being at the time of executing and delivering such receipt in possession of such
warehouseman or forwarding merchant, or other person, or in
store for the person or persons, copartnership, or firm named
in any such receipt or certificate, without being at the time
of executing and delivering such receipt in the actual possession of such flour, wheat, pot or pearl ashes, or any
grain, produce or thing of value, as expressed in such certificate or receipt, shall be guilty of a felony, punishable
by imprisonment in the state prison not more than 5 years or
by fine of not more than 2,500 dollars.
The sending or forwarding to a person who shall be duly
entitled or authorized to receive the same, by the public
mails, or through the government postoffice, or by the hands
of any person, of any such receipt or certificate as aforesaid, shall be deemed to be a good and lawful delivery thereof, within the meaning of this section.

750.279 Personal property, fraudulent disposition

Sec. 279 FRAUDULENT DISPOSITION OF PERSONAL PROPERTY -
Whenever money, or any goods, wares or merchandise or other
personal property, shall be delivered, committed or entrusted to, or put in charge of any person as agent with written
instructions, or upon any written agreement signed by the
party so instructed as agent, or such written instructions
shall be delivered or such written agreement shall be made,
at any time after delivery to such agent, of any money or
goods, wares, merchandise, or other personal property, which
instructions or agreements shall express the appropriation,
purpose, or use to which such money shall be applied, or the
terms, mode or manner of the application or employment of
such money, or which shall express or direct the disposition
or use to be made by such agent, of any goods, wares, merchandise or other personal property shall be so delivered,

1341

or entrusted to such agent; if the person to whom any such
money or goods, wares, merchandise or other personal property
in any other way or manner, or for any other purpose, use or
intent, than such as shall be expressed in such written instrument or agreement touching the same, the person or persons so doing, shall be guilty of felony.

750.280 Gross frauds and cheats at common law

Sec. 280. GROSS FRAUDS AND CHEATS AT COMMON LAW - Any
person who shall be convicted of any gross fraud or cheat
at common law, shall be guilty of a felony, punishable by
imprisonment in the state prison not more than 10 years or
by a fine of not more than 5,000 dollars.

750.281 Livery stable keepers, defrauding

Sec. 281. DEFRAUDING LIVERY STABLE KEEPERS - Any person
who, directly or indirectly, hires from the owner or keeper
of any livery stable any horse, mare, stallion, filly, gelding, pony, mule, hack, carriage, buggy, surrey, wagon, sleigh
or sled, with intent to defraud such owner or keeper, shall
be guilty of a misdemeanor.
Proof that such person refused to pay for such horse, mare,
stallion, filly, gelding, pony, mule, hack, carriage, buggy,
surrey, wagon, sleigh or sled, or that he absconded without
paying or offering to pay for the same, shall be prima facie
evidence of such fraudulent intent.
It shall be the duty of the owner or keeper of every livery
stable within this state to keep a copy of this section, printed in large plain English type, posted in a prominent place
in the barn or stable where his business is carried on, and
no conviction shall be had under this section until it be
made to appear to the satisfaction of the court that the provisions of this section have been complied with by the person making complaint.

750.282 Public utility service, injury, interference, use

Sec. 282. FRAUDULENT CONNECTING, USING, ETC., OF WATER,
STEAM, ELECTRIC OR GAS SERVICE AND SUPPLY - Any person who
wilfully or fraudulently injures, or suffers to be injured,
any motor, wire, line, pipe or appliance belonging to any
water, steam, electric or gas company, or prevents any water,
steam, electric or gas meter belonging to such company from
duly registering the quantity of water, steam, electric current or gas measured through the same, or in any way hinders
or interferes with its proper action or just registration,
or attaches any line, wire or pipe to any line, wire, pipe
or main belonging to such water, steam, electric or gas company, or otherwise uses or burns or causes to be burned or
used any water, steam, electric current or gas supplied by
such company, without the written consent of such company, or

1342

its duly authorized agent or officer, unless the same passes through a meter or is measured by a motor set by said company, or fraudulently uses its water, steam, electric current or gas, or wastes the same, shall, for every such offense, if such water, steam, electric current, gas or damage so caused shall be of the value of 50 dollars or less, be guilty of a misdemeanor. If such water, steam, electric current, gas or damage so caused, shall exceed in value the sum of 50 dollars, such person shall be guilty of a felony: Provided, That such criminal prosecution shall not in any way impair the right of such company to a full compensation in damages by civil suit.

The provisions of this section shall extend and apply to all offenses against all water, steam, electric or gas companies and boards or municipalities owning or operating plants for producing, manufacturing, furnishing, transmitting or conducting water, steam, electricity or gas, either natural or artificial.

In all prosecutions under this section it shall be prima facie evidence on the part of the people of the violation of the provisions of this section to show that the defendant other than a lessor had control of or occupied the premises where the offense was committed, or received the benefit of such water, steam, electric current or gas so used or consumed.

750.283 Preventing fraud in sale of fruits and vegetables; closed package

Sec. 283. PREVENTING FRAUD IN SALE OF FRUITS AND VEGETABLES. In this section unless the contents otherwise require, the term "closed package" shall be construed to mean a barrel, box, basket, carrier or crate, of which all the contents cannot readily be seen or inspected when such package is prepared for market. Fresh fruits or vegetables in baskets or boxes, packed in closed or open crates, and packages covered with burlap, tarlatan or slat covers shall come within the meaning of the term "closed package."

Every person who, by himself, his agent or employe, packs or repacks fresh fruits or vegetables in closed packages intended for sale in the open market, shall cause the same to be marked in a plain and indelible manner, as follows:

First, With his full name and address, including the name of the state where such fresh fruits and vegetables are packed, before such fresh fruits or vegetables are removed from the premises of the packer or dealer;

Second, The name and address of such packer or dealer shall be printed or stamped on said closed packages in letters not less than ¼ inch in height.

No person shall sell, offer, expose or have in his possession for sale, in the open market, any fresh fruits or

1343

vegetables packed in any package in which the faced or shown surface gives a false representation of the contents of such package, and it shall be considered a false representation when more than 20 per cent of such fresh fruits or vegetables are substantially smaller in size than or inferior in grade to, or different in variety from, the faced or shown surface of such package, natural deterioration and decay in transit or storage excepted.

Any person who violates any of the provisions of this section shall be guilty of a misdemeanor. The commissioner of agriculture is hereby charged with the enforcement of this section and is given power unto himself and his inspectors to enter into and upon any premises where fruits and vegetables are graded or packed or stored to inspect the same as to grade, pack and condition.

750.284 Genuine article, selling goods other than, when marked

Sec. 284. SELLING OTHER THAN GENUINE GOODS, ETC., UNDER A GENUINE LABEL, STAMP, ETC., - Any person who, from any box, phial, case, package or other form of enclosure, having thereon impressed, or in any manner attached, the printed label, brand, engraving, stamp, mark or other device of any mechanic or manufacturer, druggist or apothecary, shall sell, barter or trade therefrom, or therein, any other goods, wares or merchandise than such as are the genuine production of the manufacturer or mechanic, druggist or apothecary, whose label, mark, stamp or device may be imprinted upon or affixed to such box, or other form of enclosure, with intent to deceive such purchaser, shall be guilty of a misdemeanor.

750.287 Articles marked sterling or sterling silver, fraud in sale

Sec. 287. FRAUD IN SALE OF ARTICLES MARKED "STERLING" OR "STERLING SILVER" - Any person who knowingly makes or sells, or offers to sell or dispose of, or has in his possession with intent to sell or dispose of, any article of merchandise marked, stamped, or branded with the words "sterling" or "sterling silver", or encased or enclosed in any box, package, cover or wrapper, or other thing in or by which the said article is packed, enclosed or otherwise prepared for sale or disposition, having thereon any engraving or printed label, stamp, imprint, mark or trade-mark, indicating or denoting by such marking, stamping, branding, engraving or printing, that such article is silver, sterling silver or solid silver, unless 925/1000 of the component parts of the metal of which the said article is manufactured are pure silver, shall be guilty of a misdemeanor, punishable by imprisonment in the county jail for not more than 1 year or by a fine of not more than 500 dollars.

750.288 Coin or coin silver, fraud in sale of articles
          marked

Sec. 288. FRAUD IN SALE OF ARTICLES MARKED "COIN" OR "COIN SILVER" - Any person who knowingly makes or sells, or offers to sell or dispose of, or has in his possession with intent to sell or dispose of, any article of merchandise marked, stamped or branded with the words "coin", or "coin silver", or encased or enclosed in any box, package, cover or wrapper, or other thing in or by which the said article is packed, inclosed or otherwise prepared for sale or disposition, having thereon any engraving or printed label, stamp, imprint, mark or trade-mark, indicating or denoting by such marking, stamping, branding, engraving or printing, that such article is coin or coin silver, unless 900/100 of the component parts of the metal of which the said article is manufactured are pure silver, shall be guilty of a misdemeanor, punishable by imprisonment in the county jail of not more than 1 year or by a fine of not more than 500 dollars.

750.289 Common carrier, false billing of goods

Sec. 289. FALSE BILLING OF GOODS TO COMMON CARRIER - Any person offering goods, property or effects to any common carrier within this state for the purpose of transportation shall furnish to such carrier a true description of the goods, property or effects so offered, and any person who shall knowingly offer any goods, property or effects to any common carrier for transportation within this state with a false description of the same, or who shall offer any such goods, property or effects under a false billing, false classification or false weight and thereby procure or attempt to procure the transportation of any such goods, property or effects at a less cost than would be due under a true description, true billing, true classification or true weight, shall be guilty of a misdemeanor.

750.290 Imitation leather, boots and shoes

Sec. 290. BOOTS AND SHOES COMPOSED OF IMITATION LEATHER - The term "imitation leather" as used herein shall, for the purposes of this section, be defined to be all leather composed in whole or in part of paper, scraps and portions of hides of animals, used in the manufacture of boots or shoes, which being pressed together with an adhesive substance to keep such component parts intact, is used in place of solid leather in the making of such foot gear.

Every person within this state, who is engaged in the manufacture, sale, exchange, or offers for sale, or has in possession with intent to sell, boots or shoes in the construction of which any imitation leather is used, shall cause to be stamped upon such boots or shoes the words "imitation leather" in a distinct and legible manner: Provided, however, That the letters in the words "imitation leather" shall not be less than 1/8 of an inch in length.

When such imitation leather shall be used either as soles, in-soles, heels or counters of such boots or shoes, the words "imitation leather" shall be stamped upon the outside of the soles near the heel of such boots or shoes; and when such imitation leather shall be used in the making of any other part or parts of such boots or shoes, the words "imitation leather" shall be stamped thereon, in a conspicuous place: Provided, however, Excepting the soles of such boots or shoes the words "imitation leather" need not be stamped upon the outside thereof.

The possession of any boots or shoes which are composed in whole or in part of any imitation leather and which are not stamped as herein required, shall be prima facie evidence of intent to sell the same.

Any person who shall knowingly violate any of the provisions of this section, shall be guilty of a misdemeanor.

750.291 Boarding house keepers, defrauding

Sec. 291. DEFRAUDING BOARDING HOUSE KEEPERS - Any person who shall stop, put up, board or lodge at any boarding house as a guest or boarder by the day, week or month, or shall procure any food, entertainment or accommodation without paying therefor, unless there is a distinct and express agreement made by such person with the owner, proprietor or keeper of such boarding house for credit, with intent to defraud such owner, proprietor or keeper out of the pay for such board, lodging, food, entertainment or accommodation, or any person who, with intent so to defraud, shall obtain credit at any boarding house for such board, lodging, food, entertainment or accommodation, by means of any false show of baggage or effects brought thereto, shall be guilty of a misdemeanor: Provided, That no conviction shall be had under the provisions of this section unless complaint shall be made within 10 days of the time of the violation hereof.

750.292 Hotel, motel, inn, restaurant, cafe; defrauding; limitation

Sec. 292. Any person who shall put up at any hotel, motel, inn, restaurant or cafe as a guest and shall procure any food, entertainment or accommodation without paying therefor, except when credit is given therefor by express agreement, with intent to defraud such keeper thereof out of the pay for the same, or, who, with intent to defraud such keeper out of the pay therefor, shall obtain credit at any hotel, motel, inn, restaurant or cafe for such food, entertainment or accommodation, by means of any false show of baggage or effects brought thereto, is guilty of a misdemeanor. No conviction shall be had under the provisions of this section unless complaint is made within 60 days of the time of the violation hereof. As amended P.A. 1962, No. 19, Sec. 1, Eff. March 28, 1963.

1346

750.293 Same; prima facie evidence

Sec. 293. PRIMA FACIE EVIDENCE – Obtaining such food, lodging or accommodation by false pretense, or by false or fictitious show of baggage or other property, or refusal or neglect to pay therefor on demand, or payment thereof with check, draft or order upon a bank or other depository on which payment was refused, or absconding without paying or offering to pay therefore, or surreptitiously removing or attempting to remove baggage, shall be prima facie evidence of such intent to defraud mentioned in the 2 next preceding sections of this chapter.[1]

1. Sections 750.291, 750.292.

750.294 Animals, fraudulent registration as pure-bred

Sec. 294. FRAUDULENT REGISTRATION OF ANIMALS AS PURE-BRED – Any person who shall by fraud or misrepresentation obtain, or attempt to obtain, the registration of animals as pure-bred upon the herd books of any of the recognized registry associations, when such animals are not entitled to such registration, or who shall by fraud or misrepresentation obtain, or attempt to obtain, any false record of the transfer of ownership of any such registered animals, or who shall designedly make any false statements in reference to the breeding, ownership, color, markings or registration of animals or in reference to any application for the registration or transfer of animals, shall be guilty of a misdemeanor, punishable by imprisonment in the county jail for not more than 1 year or by a fine of not more than 500 dollars.

750.195 Milk and butter fat production, fraudulent practices

Sec. 295. FRAUDULENT PRACTICES IN RECORDING MILK AND BUTTER FAT PRODUCTION OF COWS – Any person who shall connive at, commit or attempt to commit any fraudulent or dishonest practice in connection with the making of official or semi-official records of milk and butter fat production of cows, shall be guilty of a misdemeanor, punishable by imprisonment in the county jail for not more than 1 year or by a fine of not more than 500 dollars.

750.296 Condense milk, marking, sale

Sec. 296. SALE AND MARKING OF CONDENSED MILK – Every container of evaporated, concentrated or condensed whole milk, and every container of evaporated, concentrated or condensed skimmed milk, sold or offered for sale or had in possession or custody with intent to sell by any person within this state, shall have plainly printed thereon in the English language, or attached thereto on some firmly affixed tag or label, a formula for extending the said evaporated, concentrated or condensed milk and said evaporated, concentrated or condensed skimmed milk, respectively, with water.

The formula for the extension of said evaporated, concentrated or condensed whole milk shall be such that the resulting milk product shall not be below the Michigan standard of milk solids or fat for whole milk, and shall be in the following form: By adding .... parts of water to 1 part of the contents of this can a resulting milk product will be obtained which will not be below the legal standard for whole milk. The formula for the extension of said evaporated, concentrated or condensed skimmed milk shall be such that the resulting milk product shall not be below the Michigan standard of milk solids for skimmed milk, and shall be in the following form: By adding ...... parts of water to 1 part of the contents of this can a resulting milk product will be obtained which will not be below the legal standard for skimmed milk.

Any person and the servant or agent of any person, who sells, exchanges or delivers, or has in his custody or possession with intent to sell, exchange or deliver any container of evaporated, concentrated or condensed milk, within this state, not marked or labeled in compliance with the provisions of this section, shall be guilty of a misdemeanor.

750.297e Kosher food products; definition of "kosher"; sale
            and marking of foods; investigation; penalty

Sec. 297e. (1) As used in this section, "kosher" means prepared or processed in accordance with orthodox Hebrew religious requirements sanctioned by a recognized orthodox rabbinical council.

(2) A person who, with intent to defraud, sells or exposes for sale any meat or meat preparations, article of food or food products, and falsely represents the same to be kosher, whether such meat or meat preparations, article of food or food products are raw or prepared for human consumption, either by direct statement orally, or in writing, which might reasonably be calculated to deceive or lead a reasonable man to believe that a representation is being made that such food is kosher or falsely represents any food products or the contents of any package or container to be so constituted and prepared, by having or permitting to be inscribed thereon the word "kosher" in any language; or sells or exposes for sale in the same place of business both kosher and nonkosher meat or meat preparations, or both kosher and nonkosher food or food products, either raw or prepared for human consumption, and who fails to indicate on his window signs and all display advertising, in block letters at least 4 inches in height, "kosher and nonkosher meat sold here" or "kosher and nonkosher food sold here"; or who exposes for sale in any show window or place of business both kosher and nonkosher meat or meat preparations, or kosher and nonkosher food and food products, either raw or prepared for human consumption, and who fails to display over each kind of meat or meat preparation so exposed a sign in block letters at least 4 inches in height

reading "kosher meat" or "nonkosher meat", or "kosher food" or "nonkosher food", or who displays on his window, door, or in his place of business, or in handbills or other printed matter distributed in or outside of his place of business, words or letters in Hebraic characters other than the word "kosher", or any sign, emblem, insignia, 6-pointed star, symbol or mark in simulation of same, without displaying in conjunction therewith in English letters of at least the same size as such characters, signs, emblems, insignia, symbols or marks, the words "we sell kosher meat and food only" or "we sell nonkosher meat and food only", or "we sell both kosher and nonkosher meat and food" is guilty of a misdemeanor. Possession of nonkosher meat and food, in any place of business advertising the sale of kosher meat and food only, is presumptive evidence that the person in possession exposes the same for sale with intent to defraud, in violation of the provisions of this section.

(3) A person who, with intent to defraud, sells or exposes for sale in any hotel, restaurant or other place where food products are sold for consumption on or off the premises, any meat or meat preparations, article of food or food products, and falsely represents the same to be kosher, whether such meat or meat preparations, article of food or food products be raw or prepared for human consumption, either by direct statement orally, or in writing, which might reasonably be calculated to deceive or lead a reasonable man to believe that a representation is being made that such food is kosher or falsely represents any food product or the contents of any package or container to be so constituted and prepared, by having or permitting to be inscribed thereon the word "kosher" in any language; or sells or exposes for sale in the same place of business both kosher and nonkosher meat or meat preparations, or both kosher and nonkosher food or food products, either raw or prepared for human consumption, and who fails to indicate on his window signs and all display advertising, in block letters at least 4 inches in height, "kosher and nonkosher food sold here"; or who exposes for sale in any show window or place of business both kosher and nonkosher food or food products, either raw or prepared for human consumption, and who fails to display over each kind of food or food preparation so exposed a sign in block letters at least 4 inches in height reading "kosher food" or "nonkosher food", or who displays on his window, door or in his place of business, or in handbills or other printed matter distributed in or outside of his place of business, words or letters in Hebraic characters other than the word "kosher", or any sign, emblem, insignia, 6-pointed star, symbol or mark in simulation of same, without displaying in conjunction therewith in English letters of at least the same size as such characters, signs, emblems, insignia, symbols or marks the words "we sell both kosher and nonkosher food", is guilty of a misdemeanor. Possession of nonkosher food, in any place of business advertising the sale

1349

of kosher food only, is presumptive evidence that the person in possession exposes the same for sale with intent to defraud, in violation of the provisions of this section.

(4) No person shall:

(a) Wilfully mark, stamp, tag, brand, label or in any other way or by any other means of identification represent or cause to be marked, stamped, tagged, branded, labeled or represented as kosher food or food products not kosher or not so prepared.

(b) Wilfully remove, deface, obliterate, cover, alter or destroy, or cause to be removed, defaced, obliterated, covered, altered or destroyed the original slaughterhouse plumba or any other mark, stamp, tag, brand, label or any other means of identification affixed to foods or food products to indicate that such foods or food products are kosher.

(c) Knowingly sell, dispose of or have in his possession, for the purpose of resale to any person as kosher, any food or food products not having affixed thereto the original slaughterhouse plumba or any other mark, stamp, tag, brand, label or other means of identification employed to indicate that such food or food products are kosher or any food or food products to which such plumba, mark, stamp, tag, brand, label or other means of identification has or have been fraudulently affixed.

(5) The department of agriculture shall investigate, inspect and supervise the sale of meat and meat preparations and enforce the provisions of this act. The department may promulgate rules and regulations for the enforcement and administration of this act in accordance with the provisions of Act No. 88 of the Public Acts of 1943, as amended, being sections 24.71 to 24.80 of the Compiled Laws of 1948, and subject to Act No. 197 of the Public Acts of 1952, as amended, being sections 24.101 to 24.110 of the Compiled Laws of 1948.

(6) Any person who violates the provisions of this section is guilty of a misdemeanor. P.A. 1931, No. 328, Sec. 297e, added by P.A. 1966, No. 78, Sec. 1, Imd. Eff. June 10, 1966.

750.298 Medicine, practicing under false or assumed name

Sec. 298. PRACTICING MEDICINE UNDER FALSE OR ASSUMED NAME - Any person who shall practice medicine or advertise or practice medicine under a false or assumed name, or under a name other than his own, shall be guilty of a misdemeanor, punishable by imprisonment in the county jail not more than 1 year or by a fine of not more than 500 dollars.

750.298a Representation that service under supervision of physician or that product or appliance approved by medical profession

Sec. 298a. If any person, partnership, corporation or

enterprise shall offer to furnish any service, product or
appliance designed or represented to affect human health,
well-being or appearance, and shall advertise, state or
represent in any offer, inducement or contract that the rendering of such service will be under the guidance or supervision of a physician, or that such product or appliance has
been indorsed or approved by the medical profession, it shall
be unlawful for such person, partnership, corporation or enterprise to render such service or cause or permit the same
to be rendered except by or under the direct, continuing
personal supervision of a physician licensed to practice in
Michigan, or to furnish such product or appliance unless the
same had, in fact, been indorsed or approved in writing by
a bona fide organization of licensed physicians. Any person violating any provisions of this section is guilty of a
misdemeanor punishable by a fine not to exceed $1000.00 or
imprisonment for not more than 1 year, or both. P.A. 1931,
No. 328, Sec. 298a, added by P.A. 1966, No. 302, Sec. 1,
Eff. March 10, 1967.

750.299 Agricultural seeds, false statement

    Sec. 299. FALSE STATEMENTS REGARDING AGRICULTURAL SEEDS -
Any person or his agent or employe, who, in writing or in
a newspaper, circular or other publication published in this
state, makes or disseminates any statement or assertion of
fact concerning the superior qualifications, quality, value
or locality where grown of any agricultural seeds sold or
offered for sale in this state, or the possession of rewards,
prizes or distinctions conferred on account of such seeds,
or the motive or purpose of such sale, intended to give the
appearance of an offer advantageous to the purchaser, or as
an inducement for the planting of such seeds, which is untrue or calculated to mislead and to induce a person to purchase such seeds, is guilty of a misdemeanor.

750.300 Insurance company, killing or injuring animals to
         defraud

    Sec. 300. KILLING OR INJURING ANIMALS WITH INTENT TO
DEFRAUD INSURANCE COMPANY - Any person who shall injure or
kill any horse, mule or other live stock which shall be insured by any insurance company authorized to do business in
this state, when such killing or injury shall be with the
wilful intent on the part of such person to defraud such insurance company, whether such person shall be the owner of
such insured property or not shall be guilty of a felony,
punishable by imprisonment for not more than 2 years or by
a fine of not more than 1,000 dollars.

    3. Definition and Elements of the Offense

        Black's Law Dictionary (4th ed.)

"FRAUD. An intentional perversion of truth for the purpose of inducing another in reliance upon it to part with some valuable thing belonging to him or to surrender a legal right; a false representation of a matter of fact, whether by words or by conduct, by false or misleading allegations, or by concealment of that which should have been disclosed, which deceives and is intended to deceive another so that he shall act upon it to his legal injury. Brainerd Dispatch Newspaper Co. v. Crow Wing County, 196 Minn. 194, 264 N.W. 779, 780. Any kind of artifice employed by one person to deceive another. Goldstein v. Equitable Life Assur. Soc. of U.S. 160 Misc. 364, 289 N.Y.S. 1064, 1067. A generic term, embracing all multifarious means which human ingenuity can devise, and which are resorted to by one individual to get advantage over another by false suggestions or by suppression of truth, and includes all surprise, trick, cunning, dissembling, and any unfair way by which another is cheated. Johnson v. McDonald, 170 Okl. 117, 39 P.2d 150. "Bad faith" and "fraud" are synonymous, and also synonyms of dishonesty, infidelity, faithlessness, perfidy, unfairness, etc. Joiner v. Joiner, Tex. Civ. App. 87 S.W. 2d 903, 914, 915.

It consists of some deceitful practice or willful device, resorted to with intent to deprive another of his right, or in some manner to do him an injury. As distinguished from negligence, it is always positive, intentional. Maher v. Hibernia Ins. Co. 67 N.Y. 292; Alexander v. Church, 53 Conn. 561, 4 A. 103; Studer v. Biestein, 115 N.Y. 316, 22 N.E. 243, 7 L.R.A. 702; McNair v. Southern States Finance Co. 191 N.C. 710, 133 S.E. 85.88. It comprises all acts, omissions, and concealments involving a breach of a legal or equitable duty and resulting in damage to another. Coppo v. Coppo, 163 Misc. 249, 297 N.Y.S. 744, 750. And includes anything calculated to deceive, whether it be a single act or combination of circumstances, whether the suppression of truth or the suggestion of what is false, whether it be by direct falsehood or by innuendo, by speech or by silence, by word of mouth, or by look or gesture. People v. Gilmore, 345 Ill. 28, 177 N.E. 710, 717. Fraud as applied to contracts, is the cause of an error bearing on a material part of the contract, created or continued by artifice, with design to obtain some unjust advantage to the one party, or to cause an inconvenience or loss to the other. Civil Code La. art. 1847. Strauss v. Insurance Co. of North America, 157 La. 661, 102 So. 861, 865; Jesse French Piano & Organ Co. v. Gibbon, Tex. Civ. App. 180 S.W. 1185, 1187.

Fraud, in the sense of a court of equity, properly includes all acts, omissions, and concealments which involve a breach of legal or equitable duty, trust, or confidence justly reposed, and are injurious to another, or by which an undue and unconscientious advantage is taken of another. 1 Story Eq. Jur. Sec. 187; Howard v. West Jersey & S.S.R. Co., 102 N.J. Eq. 517, 141 A. 755. 757.

Fraud is either actual or constructive. Actual fraud

1352

consists in deceit, artifice, trick, design, some direct
and active operation of the mind; it includes cases of the
intentional and successful employment of any cunning, deception, or artifice used to circumvent or cheat another; it is
something said, done, or omitted by a person with the design
of perpetrating what he knows to be a cheat or deception.
Constructive fraud consists in any act of commission or omission contrary to legal or equitable duty, trust, or confidence
justly reposed, which is contrary to good conscience and operates to the injury of another. Or, as otherwise defined, it
is an act, statement or omission which operates as a virtual
fraud on an individual, or which, if generally permitted,
would be prejudicial to the public welfare, and yet may have
been unconnected with any selfish or evil design. Or, according to Story, constructive frauds are such acts or contracts
as, though not originating in any actual evil design or contrivance to perpetrate a positive fraud or injury upon other
persons, are yet, by their tendency to deceive or mislead
other persons, or to violate private or public confidence,
or to impair or injure the public interests, deemed equally
reprehensible with actual fraud. 1 Story, Eq. Jur. Sec. 258.
Code Ga. 1882, Sec. 3173 (Civ. Code 1910, Sec. 4622); People v. Kelly, 35 Barb. N.Y. 457; Jackson v. Jackson, 47 Ga.
99; Massachusetts Ben. L. Ass'n v. Robinson, 104 Ga. 256, 30
S.E. 918, 42 L.R.A. 261; Allen v. United States Fidelity &
Guaranty Co., 269 Ill. 234, 109 N.E. 1035, 1038.
     Fraud is also classified as fraud in fact and fraud in
law. The former is actual, positive, intentional fraud.
Fraud disclosed by matters of fact, as distinguished from
constructive fraud or fraud in law. McKibbin v. Martin, 64
Pa. 356, 3 Am. Rep. 588; Cook v. Burnham, 3 Kan. App. 27,
44 P. 447. Fraud in law is fraud in contemplation of law;
fraud implied or inferred by law; fraud made out by construction of law, as distinguished from fraud found by a
jury from matter of fact; constructive fraud (q.v.). See
2 Kent. Comm. 512-532; Deloney v. Valentine, 154 N.Y. 692,
49 N.E. 65; Lovato v. Catron, 20 N.M. 168, 148 P. 490, 492,
L.R.A. 1915E, 451; Furst & Thomas v. Merritt, 190 N.C. 397,
130 S.E. 40, 43.
     Fraud is also said to be legal or positive. The former is
fraud made out by legal construction or inference, or the
same thing as constructive fraud. Newell v. Wagness, 1 N.D.
62, 44 N.W. 1014. Positive fraud is the same thing as actual
fraud. Douthitt v. Applegate, 33 Kan. 395, 6 P. 575, 52 Am.
Rep. 533; Nocatee Fruit Co. v. Fosgate, C.C.A. Fla., 12 F.
2d 250, 252. . . . "

                    Alderman v. People
                      4 Mich. 414

Error to Wayne circuit.

At the March term of the Wayne circuit court, in 1854, the defendants were indicted, with one Henry H. Bush, for a conspiracy to defraud. They pleaded the general issue to the indictment, and were tried and convicted at the May term, 1855. A motion for new trial, and also in arrest of judgment, was made and overruled, and sentence was passed on the Aldermans in August, 1855.

A bill of exceptions was signed in the case, which was returned with the writ of error, and special errors were assigned upon matters contained in the indictment and bill of exceptions.

The indictment in the first count charged that the defendants, being of Oakland county, with intent to cheat and defraud the persons after named, doing business in Detroit, of their goods, on June 1, 1853, at White Lake, in Oakland county, did conspire with Bush to cheat and defraud said persons of their goods, and the value thereof; that, to consummate said fraud, Bush was to convey a quantity of land owned by him, worth about $1,000, and being all he had, to Major Alderman, under a pretended sale, to be held by him as the apparent owner, till Bush should transfer to him the stock of goods after mentioned; that no real consideration was to be paid for said land; but Alderman was to make advances to establish the credit of Bush in Detroit; that Bush was thereupon to go to Detroit and make as large purchases of goods as he could on credit, and take them to White Lake; that after the goods, to prevent suspicion, had been exposed a while for sale, the whole stock which Bush might have should be transferred to Major Alderman, under a pretended sale, in order to prevent the creditors of Bush from reaching them, or collecting anything from him; that, as a pretended consideration for the goods, Alderman was to reconvey the land to Bush, at a price to be expressed in the deed, a good deal higher than it was worth; and in order still to prevent the creditors from reaching the land in the hands of Bush, he was to execute back to Alderman a mortgage for about what it was really worth, to secure a pretended balance between the value of land and the value of the goods; that, after such transfer, Bush was to refuse to pay his debts, Alderman was to buy them in at a nominal rate, cheating his creditors out of the balance; and that, whatever might be finally made in the operation should be shared, one-third to Alderman and two-thirds to Bush; that, in pursuance of such conspiracy, Bush conveyed the land described to Alderman; that Alderman made advances to Bush to sustain his credit in Detroit; that Bush went to Detroit and made large purchases of goods on credit, of divers persons, naming them; that the goods were taken to White Lake and exposed for sale, when, on December 12, 1853, the whole stock was transferred to Alderman, on a pretended sale, without consideration; that Major Alderman reconveyed the land to Bush, for the expressed consideration of $2,000, being a good deal more than it was worth; that Bush, to keep said land away from his

1354

creditors, gave back to Alderman a mortgage for $1,000, being
all the land was worth; that all the parties, Major and William
Alderman, and Bush, were present at all such transactions,
acting and assisting, concurring in and assenting to the same. . . .
  (By the Court, COPELAND, J.: . . .
  The first count charges that the defendants "did conspire,
combine, confederate and agree, falsely and fraudulently, to
cheat and defraud said persons and mercantile houses, and
others doing business as aforesaid, etc., of diverse large
quantities of goods, and the prices and value thereof." This
charge is more general than that which has, in any case which
has come under our notice, received the sanction of the English courts, more general than that in the King V. Gill, which
has always been regarded as the extreme of laxity, as we have
seen in Queen v. Parker. The only words in the object stated,
indicating an offense, are the words cheat and defraud. But
those words, say the courts in Com. v. Eastmen, Com. v. Shedd
and State v. Hewett, "do not import any known common law offense. If punishable at all as a crime, it is only when the
cheat is effected by false tokens of false pretenses. To
make such an object of conspiracy a criminal act, the combination or agreement must be to cheat and defraud in some of the
modes made criminal by statute, and the indictment must contain allegations which show that the cheat and fraud agreed
upon are embraced in such statute provisions, and that, if
perpetrated, would be punishable as a criminal offense."
  But it is claimed that the object of the conspiracy was
agreed to be accomplished by criminal means. What, then,
are the means by which the alleged object of the conspiracy
was to be accomplished? Bush and his wife were to convey to
Alderman one hundred and thirty acres of land, together with
forty acres then held in Alderman's name. As a consideration
for such conveyance, Alderman was to give up to Bush notes
and securities he then held against him, amounting to $800;
was to sign a note to one Bassey for $180, as security for
Bush, and advance him money to keep up his credit, as alleged,
to the amount of $250, being something more than the land, as
alleged in the indictment, was worth, subject to certain liens.
That Bush should go to Detroit, and on his sole credit and account, purchase goods, take them to White Lake, and there expose them to sale; that subsequently, Bush should sell the
remainder of the goods so purchased, with any others he might
have on hand, to Alderman, who was to convey to Bush the one
hundred and seventy acres of land, and take back a mortgage.
  None of these alleged means are in themselves immoral, even.
There is no allegation whatever, that in obtaining the goods,
any false pretense, false token, or other device, was to be
used - nothing, certainly, tending to support the alleged object of the conspiracy - to cheat and defraud.
  It is said the alleged means are criminal, in that they
come within the provisions of section 17, of chapter 142, Revised Statutes, which makes it a misdemeanor for any person
to secrete, assign, convey or otherwise dispose of any of his

1355

property, with intent to defraud any creditor, or to prevent such property from being made liable for the payment of his debts, or for any person to receive such property with such intent. Admitting that to be so, it affords no support to this indictment, for none of the offenses named in said section are alleged as the object of this conspiracy. There are no allegations in either part of either count which show that the cheat and fraud agreed upon are embraced in any statute provision.

The judgment must be reversed.

Present - COPELAND, DOUGLASS, GREEN, PRATT, MARTIN, JJ.

JOHNSON, J. decided the cause in the court below, and did not participate.

DOUGLASS, J.: I concur in the opinion that the indictment is insufficient, and that the judgment below should be reversed on that ground; but, it being unnecessary for the determination of the case, I decline expressing an opinion upon any of the other questions presented by the bill of exceptions.

People v. Getchell
6 Mich. 496

MARTIN Ch. J.:

We think the recorder erred in excluding the evidence offered by the defendant.

The indictment charges that on the 11th of December, 1858, he, by means of false pretenses, obtained the indorsement of Strong to a note of one hundred and fifty-dollars, made by himself. The statute under which the indictment was found, provides that "every person who, with intent to defraud or cheat another, shall designedly, by color of any false token or writing, or by any other false pretense, obtain the signature of any person to any written instrument, the making whereof would be punishable as forgery, or obtain from any person any money, personal property or valuable thing, shall be punished," etc.: 2 Comp. L. Sec. 5783.

The object of the defense in this case, in offering the rejected evidence, was to show that there was no intent to cheat or defraud - the untruth of the pretense being admitted. A falsehood does not necessarily imply an intent to defraud, for it may be uttered to secure a right, and, however much and severely it may be reprobated in ethics, the law does not assume to punish moral delinquencies as such. To defraud is to deprive another of a right, of property or of money, and this may be accomplished by falsehood, by withholding the right or property, or by force. In the present case, the prosecutor insists that he was defrauded because he was induced to indorse a note by the false representation of the defendant that a prior note for the same amount, indorsed by him, was defective, and had been destroyed; that he was thereby induced to lend his name for double the amount he otherwise would. The simple fact of procuring, by falsehood, the indorsement, was not an offense within the statute; it must have been procured with the intent to defraud, and where an intent is made the gist of an offense, that intent must be shown by such evidence as, uncontradicted, will fairly authorize it to be presumed beyond a reasonable doubt. It is true that a man is presumed to intend the natural consequences of his acts, but, under this statute, it is not the consequence, but the intention, which fixes the crime. There are no natural consequences, strictly speaking, to this act. It is itself an indifferent act, as the consequences will depend upon what he does with the paper, and this will depend upon his will - in other words, his intent. It was, therefore, necessary for the prosecutor to show something more than the application, the falsehood, and the indorsement, before he could ask a conviction; he should have shown those facts which, in the absence of all other proof, would warrant the jury in finding an intent to defraud, unless such intent is fairly to be inferred from the circumstances attending the act itself. If the fact of negotiating both notes would justify such a finding, yet the presumption thus raised might be repelled by the defendant, by exhibiting in evidence such a state of facts as would show that fraud was not designed, or could not have resulted. This he attempted to do by showing the relations of himself and Strong, the obligation of Strong to indorse his paper, his refusal to do so notwithstanding his contract, the necessity for the money for their joint benefit, and the appropriation of the avails of the note in their business, and according to the terms of their agreement. All this was refused, and the evidence offered for that purpose ruled out.

We think this evidence would legitimately tend to disprove the presumption of an intent to defraud, and should have been allowed to go to the jury to enable them to determine _quo animo_ the indorsement was procured.

These considerations render an examination of the other errors assigned unnecessary.

A new trial should be granted.

CHRISTIANCY and CAMPBELL JJ. concurred.

MANNING J.:

When, by false pretenses, the signature of a person is obtained to a written instrument, where the signing of the name by a third person to such instrument would be punishable as forgery, the law implies an intent to cheat or defraud; and nothing more need be shown to warrant a conviction. But the fraudulent intent implied from the act itself is not conclusive on the party. He may show there was in fact no intention to defraud.

The recorder seems to have erred in supposing the implication of law was conclusive, and not prima facie evidence
only, of the criminal intent. In this I think he erred.

New trial ordered.

People v. Umlauf
88 Mich. 274

McGRATH, J. The defendant was convicted upon an information
which charged that he, -

"With intent to cheat and defraud one George Bacon, and
obtain from him, the said George Bacon, the sum of $300 in
money as the price of a certain stallion, then and there
owned by him, said Frank Umlauf, and which he, the said Frank
Umlauf, then and there offered for sale to the said George
Bacon, said stallion being then and there named 'Frank,' did
knowingly give to him, the said George Bacon, a certain false
pedigree of the said bay stallion Frank, then and there owned
as aforesaid by the said Frank Umlauf, which said false pedigree was printed upon a certain card given to the said George
Bacon by the said Frank Umlauf, and was as follows:

"'Frank.

"'Bay stallion, foaled on June 27, 1882, by Bill Weller;
he by Scotia, the sire of Ned Weller, 2:29½; Roachamine, 2:22;
Jackson (stallion), 2:40½; dam Clydesdale, sired by Clydesdale Jock, no record; by Ricks' Royal George, 2:27½; by St.
Lawrence, Jr.; by St. Lawrence.'
"He, the said Frank Umlauf, then and there well knowing
the said pedigree so given by him to the said George Bacon
of the said stallion Frank to be false."

The statute (Act No. 9, Laws of 1887, 3 How. Stat. Sec.
9209d) under which the conviction was had reads as follows:

SECTION 1. The People of the State of Michigan enact,
That every person who knowingly or designedly by means of
any false pretense shall obtain from any club, association,
society, or company for improving the breed of cattle, horses,
sheep, swine, or other domestic animals, a certificate of
registration of any animal in the herd register or other register of any such club, association, society, or company, or
a transfer of any such registration, and every person who
shall knowingly give a false pedigree of any animal, with
intent to defraud, upon conviction thereof, shall be punished by imprisonment in the State prison for a term not exceeding three years, or in a county jail for a term not exceeding one year, or by a fine not exceeding one thousand
dollars, or by both such fine and imprisonment, in the discretion of the court."

The defendant testified that he did not know how the horse

1358

Frank was bred; that one Peltier told him that he (Peltier) knew all about the horse, and had known him since he was a year old.

"I knew nothing about it. I cannot read. I know that there is a picture of a horse on the card; that is all I know. I suppose the pedigree handed me was right. I don't know whether it is right or not. I supposed it was right."

It appeared that one Tripp had at one time owned the horse, and had bought it from one Tebo; that Tripp had handled the horse for defendant, and that it was through Tripp that Umlauf purchased the horse from one Allor.

George Bacon, the complaining witness, testified that at the time of the purchase of the horse witness asked defendant if he had a pedigree of the horse, and he said, "Yes."

"He stepped behind the counter, got it, and gave it to me. I asked if it was a true pedigree, and he said it was."

It further appeared that eight or ten cards of the kind set up in the information were printed at the Monitor office; that the copy from which they were printed was in the handwriting of one Gibbs, and was brought to the office by Gibbs. Gibbs testified that he wrote the copy at Tripp's direction; that Tripp gave him the pedigree of the horse, and he simply did the clerical work; that Tripp referred him to one Peltier, and witness asked Peltier about certain points in the breeding, and witness used the information; that he relied upon Tripp and Peltier, and talked with no one else; that he had no talk with Umlauf about it, except that afterwards he met him, and Umlauf asked him if he saw Tripp about some bills for his horse, and "I said, 'Yes, they are printed;' and he paid me for them. That is all the conversation I ever had with him." Tripp is called, is shown the card, and says:

"Well, part of this is, as near as I can judge, right, and the balance I don't consider I can give you. I traded and got the horse myself, and I got the horse with the pedigree I gave Gibbs. I got it from Charles Tebo. He told me just the same as I told Gibbs. I told him the way he told me. Tebo told me he was from St. Lawrence, and out of a Clydesdale and Hambletonian mare. Umlauf was with me when I done the trading. He held the horse, while I went to look at the stallion and hitch him up. I didn't give Gibbs a copy. I got the facts about the pedigree of the horse from Tebo. I did not get them from Umlauf. Umlauf knew nothing about the pedigree of the horse. I told Gibbs the same as I told you now; and if Umlauf had anything to do with the pedigree, I don't know anything about it."

One Allor testified that —

"The day Umlauf and Tripp came down and traded with me I told them the sire of Frank was the Bill Webb horse. I did not give them any such information as that on the card. Frank

was foaled in the spring of 1880. When Tripp and Umlauf
came down there, Tripp done the talking. Umlauf did not
say a word about the trade. The horse was a good horse,
worth $300 for breeding, when I let him go."

Alva Bacon, son of complaining witness testified that defendant told him that the card was a true pedigree of the
horse. One Cottrell testified that Ned Weller never had a
record of 2:29½, nor had Roachmaine one of 2:22, but both
had quite a local reputation. All this testimony except
that of the defendant was brought out by the prosecution.
It further appeared that Jackson, Scotia, and St. Lawrence
were horses of local reputation, and one witness testified
that there was no special breeding in any of the horses named;
that not a single horse on the list would be considered of
the least value in the world by horsemen, except as a common
all-work horse; that there is not a standard horse's name in
all the lot; that Ned Weller was just a good roadster.

Upon this record it does not appear that there was any
testimony tending to show that defendant knowingly gave a
false pedigree of the horse with intent to defraud. It
appeared that the horse was sired and foaled in the immediate neighborhood, and that several of the horses named in
the card were neighborhood horses of local reputation. The
horse in question was nine years of age, and had passed
through several hands before reaching defendant. There was
no record kept of his lineage. It rested in memory alone.
Tripp claims to have obtained his information from Tebo, and
Allor claims to have informed Tripp. Gibbs obtained his information from Tripp and Peltier, and Tripp and Gibbs do not
agree. Umlauf did not contribute any of the matter put into
the card. He could not read it when printed, and the proofs
do not show that he knew what representations the card contained. In an action to recover back the purchase money it
might be sufficient to show that the information contained
in the card was false, without proof of either knowledge of
its falsity or intent to defraud, but here both knowledge and
intent must be shown; and, while the intent to defraud might
be inferred from actual knowledge, it cannot be presumed in
the entire absence of proof of knowledge. It may be true
that Allor "told them" that the sire of Frank was the Bill
Webb horse, and that he was foaled in the spring of 1880,
although it may well be doubted whether that information
came home to Umlauf; yet it was not shown that he had any
knowledge that the card contained any other representations.

An unregistered account of the strain of an animal especially where that animal, as well as its ancestry, has changed
hands a number of times, must necessarily be based upon hearsay, and the Legislature has wisely made guilt dependent upon
actual knowledge and intent to defraud.

The conviction must be set aside, and a new trial ordered.

The other Justices concurred

1360

People v. Willson
205 Mich. 28

STEERE, J. Respondent brings this case here for review before sentence on his conviction in the circuit court of Oakland county under an information charging him with having as supervisor of the township of Royal Oak falsely and fraudulently reported a wrong valuation of that township to the board of supervisors and its committees of equalization at the June and October, 1916, sessions thereof with intent to defraud and cheat the county of Oakland and its taxpayers. . . .

Various errors are assigned against the charge which is claimed to be argumentative and prejudicial in designated particulars not requiring discussion here, beyond an assignment involving the testimony relative to the township treasurers' shortages. In one portion of the charge the court told the jury that:

"As bearing on the question of respondent's good faith in his action in reporting the valuation of his township to the board of supervisors, at their October session, you may take into consideration whether or not there were any shortages in the account of the township treasurer of Royal Oak in 1915 and 1916, which came to respondent's knowledge."

And later in the charge instructed the jury that —

"The prior and subsequent circumstances were admitted only for the purpose of aiding you in arriving at a correct conclusion as to whether or not the acts of fraud were actually committed as alleged in the information."

The question of whether any or all of the township treasurers were short in their accounts constituted in itself an independent collateral matter which at that time had not been judicially determined. The law is well settled that it would be error for the trial court to instruct the jury they might consider a collateral offense, even by the respondent himself, as evidence of the fact or substantive act of the offense charged. People v. Thacker, 108 Mich. 652; People v. Giddings, 159 Mich. 523 (18 Ann. Cas. 844; People v. MacGregor, 178 Mich. 436). When the court in its last distinct utterance upon the subject told the jury in general that those prior and subsequent matters relative to township affairs could be used by them in arriving at a correct conclusion as to whether or not the acts of fraud were actually committed as charged he, as said in People v. Thacker, supra, "went farther than any of the cases go, and announced a doctrine that would be exceedingly dangerous to follow," particularly under the condition of the record in this case.

As the verdict must be set aside, and a re-trial granted for the errors noted, it seems advisable to briefly refer to two assignments of error which it is tenaciously insisted

1361

entitle respondent to an order of discharge. They are in brief that his counsel's motion to quash the information and later for a directed verdict in his behalf should have been granted because it is not shown or claimed that the county of Oakland "ever suffered a dollar of loss" by reason of the charged fraudulent report; and that because interrogated in the inquisitorial proceedings under Act No. 196, Pub. Acts 1917, as to matters covered by the information against him his statutory and constitutional rights preclude this prosecution.

To constitute the charged criminal perpetration of fraud against the county under the statute it is not essential to prove that the municipal corporation as such sustained direct pecuniary loss. Respondent in reporting the assessed valuation of his township to the board of supervisors was performing an official duty essential to the correct and valid performance of a governmental duty by the county through its official agents in raising public funds for the State and county by taxation. "Fraud" and "bad faith" are often synonymous, and particularly so as applied to the conduct of a public official. "Fraud" in such connection imports acts, concealments or omissions involving a breach of legal or official duty, trust or confidence imposed, injurious to another or to the public, or any portion of the public toward whom that duty is owed, which results in undue or unconscionable advantage to the official, or those in whose behalf it is perpetrated. We have no hesitation in concluding that if it was shown respondent knowingly, designedly and with intent to deceive, falsely reported in his official capacity to the county, or its board of supervisors representing it, a valuation of his township for assessment purposes $2,000,000 less than the true amount, on the faith and as a result of which $12,000 excessive and unlawful State and county taxes were unwittingly imposed upon and collected from that portion of the county outside the township he represented, which as he knew rightfully should have been imposed upon it, defendant would be guilty of the statutory fraud charged. . . .

For the reasons stated the verdict must be set aside and a re-trial granted.

BIRD, C. J., and MOORE, BROOKE, FELLOWS, STONE, and KUHN, JJ., concurred. OSTRANDER, J., did not sit.

Note

Gillespie summarizes the essential elements under the statutes relating to frauds and cheats as follows:

"(1) An intent to defraud;
(2) The commission of a fraudulent act, and,
(3) The fraud accomplished."[1]

1362

It should be noted that Gillespie cites as authority for the above enumerated elements the case of <u>People v. Lee</u>, <u>259 Mich. 355</u>. This case involved a prosecution for false pretenses. It is apparent, however, that the elements for fraud by false pretenses involves the same elements as fraud by other prohibited forms of misrepresentation under Chapter XLIII of the Criminal Code concerning frauds and cheats. - Ed.

1. Gillespie, <u>Michigan Criminal Law and Procedure</u>, Sec. 1529, (2nd ed. 1953)

4. Final Draft - Michigan Revised Criminal Code

The prolix and multifarious provisions of the Mich. Rev. Crim. Code dealing with the general subject of frauds and cheats do not, in the opinion of the Editor, substantially contribute to an understanding of the present law and are therefore omitted.

INTERROGATORIES

1. Outline the provisions of the Michigan statutes relevant to forgery and counterfeiting.
2. Do the Michigan statutes on forgery depart from the common law tradition?
3. What explains the similarity between the law of forgery and the law of false pretenses?
4. What gaps existed in the law of false pretenses that required enactment of forgery laws?
5. Does the forger commit an offense even though he does not defraud the person to whom he sells or passes the forged writings?
6. What aspect of the counterfeiting problem falls exclusively within federal jurisdiction? Why are state counterfeiting laws still needed?
7. What were the facts, issue and holding of the court in People v. Larson? How is forgery defined?
8. What were the facts, issue and holding of the court in McGinn v. Tobey? What was the actus reus of forgery in this case?
9. What were the facts, issue and holding of the court in People v. Marion? What constituted the actus reus of the offense?
10. What were the facts, issue and holding of the court in People v. Van Alstine? What constituted the actus reus of the offense?
11. What were the facts, issue and holding of the court in Leslie v. Kennedy? What is the nature of the intent required?
12. What were the facts, issue and holding of the court in In re Stout? What constituted the actus reus of forgery

in this case? How is the definition of forgery further
explicated?

13. What were the facts, issue and holding of the court in
People v. Watkins? What constituted the actus reus of the
offense?

14. What were the facts, issue and holding of the court in
People v. Swetland? What constituted the actus reus of the
offense?

15. What were the facts, issue and holding of the court in
People v. Kemp? What constituted the actus reus of the
offense?

16. What were the facts, issue and holding of the court in
People v. Parker? What kind of instruments may be the
subject of forgery?

17. What were the facts, issue and holding of the court in
People v. Parmelee? To be the subject of forgery must the
instrument be enforcible in a civil action?

18. What were the facts, issue and holding of the court in
People v. Brown? Is it forgery to give a deed to land
which you do not own?

19. What were the facts, issue and holding of the court in
Houseman-Spitzley Corp. v. Bank? What constituted the
actus reus of the offense?

20. What were the facts, issue and holding of the court in
Watrous v. Allen? What constitutes the actus reus of the
offense?

21. According to Gillespie, what are the principal elements of
forgery?

22. Outline the provisions of Sec. 4001, Final Draft, Mich.
Rev. Crim. law? Do these provisions clearly restate the
Mich. law? In what way is the intent element expanded?

23. Outline the provisions of Sec. 4005, Final Draft, Mich.
Rev. Crim. Code? What conduct is singled out for the
most serious punishment?

24. Have both the judicial and legislative departments of
government played an important role in the development
of the law of fraud?

25. In the early common law what problem was posed in the law
of larceny where the owner of goods voluntarily parted
with possession? What is the function of fraud in establishing the trespassory element required for larceny by
trick?

26. What crime is involved where the victim parted with both
possession and title as a result of the trick or fraud?

27. How does embezzlement differ from larceny by fraud or trick?

28. What role did the doctrine of caveat emptor play in the early
law of fraud and deceit? What has been the legislative response to the problem?

29. Has the common law crime of gross frauds and cheats been
preserved in Michigan?

30. Outline the provisions of the Michigan statutes relevant to
frauds and cheats.

31. How is fraud defined by Black's Law Dictionary?

32. How is actual fraud distinguished from constructive fraud?

33. What is the difference between fraud in fact and fraud in law?
34. How does legal fraud differ from positive fraud?
35. What were the facts, issue and holding of the court in Alderman v. People? Why was the conviction reversed?
36. What were the facts, issue and holding of the court in People v. Getchell? What is the gist of the offense to cheat and defraud? What is the nature of the proof required to satisfy the mens rea requirement? What is the point of the concurring opinion?
37. What were the facts, issue and holding of the court in People v. Umlauf? Can intent be presumed in the absence of proof of knowledge?
38. What were the facts, issue and holding of the court in People v. Willson? Is proof of pecuniary loss a necessary element in a prosecution for fraud?
39. According to Gillespie, what are the essential elements in a prosecution for fraud under the Michigan statutes? Do these elements differ from those required for fraud by false pretenses?

CHAPTER XIII

OFFENSES AGAINST PUBLIC ORDER AND ADMINISTRATION

A. Treason, Subversion and Criminal Syndicalism

    1. Michigan Constitution of 1963

Article 1, Section 22. Treason; definition, evidence

    Sec. 22. Treason against the state shall consist only in
levying war against it or in adhering to its enemies, giving
them aid and comfort. No person shall be convicted of treason
unless upon the testimony of two witnesses to the same overt
act or on confession in open court.

    2. Michigan Compiled Laws (1948)

CHAPTER LXXXIV. TREASON AND SUBVERSION

750.544 Treason; punishment

    Sec. 544. Any person who shall commit the crime of trea-
son against this state shall be punished by imprisonment in
a state prison for life.

750.545 Misprision of treason

    Sec. 545. MISPRISION OF TREASON - Any person who shall
have knowledge of the commission of the crime of treason
against this state, and shall conceal the same, and shall
not, as soon as may be, disclose and make known such treason to the governor thereof, or to some judge of a court of
record within this state, shall be guilty of a felony, and
shall be punished by imprisonment in the state prison not
more than 5 years, or by a fine of not more than 2,500 dollars.

750.545a Subversion against state; penalty

    Sec. 545a. Every person who shall commit the crime of sub-
version against this state shall be punished by imprisonment
in the state prison for life, or any term of years, in the
discretion of the court. P.A. 1931, No. 328, Sec. 545a, added by P.A. 1951, No. 138, Sec. 1, Eff. Sept. 28, 1951.

750.545b Same; misprision felony

    Sec. 545b. Any person who shall have knowledge of the com-
mission of the crime of subversion against this state and
shall conceal the same, and shall not, as soon as may be, dis-

close and make known such subversion to the judge of a court
of record within this state, shall be guilty of a felony.
P.A. 1931, No. 328, Sec. 545b, added by P.A. 1951, No. 138,
Sec. 1, Eff. Sept. 28, 1951.

750.545c Same; defined

Sec. 545c. Any person who shall knowingly be a member,
organizer or officer of any association, corporation or organized group of persons whose purpose as known to him is to
commit subversion shall be guilty of the crime of subversion.
P.A. 1931, No. 328, Sec. 545c, added by P.A. 1951, No. 138,
Sec. 1, Eff. Sept. 28, 1951.

750.545d Same; aid by corporations, forfeiture of charter

Sec. 545d. Any corporation doing business under the laws
of the state of Michigan which, by corporate action, lends
any aid by gifts of money or by any other payments of money,
or furnishes the services of personnel or lends its name or
credit to any person, association, firm or corporation engaged in acts of subversion, knowing them to be so engaged,
shall forfeit its charter or certificate of authority and
shall be fined not more than the total amount of the assets
of the corporation.

750.46 Definition

Sec. 46. CRIMINAL SYNDICALISM DEFINED - Criminal syndicalism is hereby defined as the doctrine which advocates crime,
sabotage, violence or other unlawful methods of terrorism as
a means of accomplishing industrial or political reform. The
advocacy of such doctrine, whether by word of mouth or writing, is a felony punishable as provided in this chapter

750.47 Advocacy of criminal syndicalism, penalty

Sec. 47. Any person who by word of mouth or writing,
advocates or teaches the duty, necessity or propriety of
crime, sabotage, violence or other unlawful methods of terorism as a means of accomplishing industrial or political reform; or prints, publishes, edits, issues or knowingly circulates, sells, distributes or publicly displays any book,
paper, document, or written matter in any form, containing or
advocating, advising, or teaching the doctrine that industrial
or political reform should be brought about by crime, sabotage,
violence or other unlawful methods of terrorism; or openly,
wilfully and deliberately justifies by word of mouth or writing the commission or the attempt to commit crime, sabotage,
violence or other unlawful methods of terrorism with intent
to exemplify, spread or advocate the propriety of the doctrines
of criminal syndicalism; or organizes or helps to organize, or
becomes a member of or voluntarily assembles with any society,
group or assemblage of persons formed to teach or advocate
the doctrines of criminal syndicalism, or who commits or attempts

to commit crime, sabotage, violence or other unlawful methods of terrorism for the purpose of accomplishing industrial or political reform, shall be guilty of a felony, punishable by imprisonment in the state prison not more than 10 years or by a fine of not more than $5,000.00

750.48 Red flag, display

Sec. 48. DISPLAY OF RED FLAG - Any person who shall display a red flag in any public assembly, parade or demonstration in this state is guilty of a felony.

The use of such a flag at any such assembly, parade or demonstration shall be considered as prima facie evidence of its use as an emblem of anarchy.

3. Statutory Construction

People v. Burman
154 Mich. 150

The following complaint was made against defendants: That on the 28th day of July, A. D. 1907.

"Within the corporate limits of the city of Hancock, county of Houghton, and State of Michigan, in and on a certain street of said city, to wit, on Quincy street, one of the public thoroughfares and streets of the said city of Hancock, did then and there make, aid, abet, countenance, and assist in making a disturbance and improper diversion, to the annoyance and disturbance of citizens and travelers, by then and there aiding, abetting, countenancing, and assisting in making and exciting loud and boisterous and profane language and noises within the hearing and to the disturbance of citizens and travelers on the said street, and within the said city of Hancock; and by then and there, for the purpose of exciting a disturbance of the peace within said city, aiding, abetting, countenancing, and assisting in raising up, exhibiting, and carrying red flags, to wit, 10 red flags, while marching on said street and public thoroughfare, well knowing that said procession and assembling together and marching with said red flags would excite anger and indignation and produce fear and fright of many of the citizens and travelers upon the streets of said city of Hancock and elsewhere, and create breaches of the peace; and by then and there aiding, abetting, countenancing, and assisting in exciting the anger, indignation, and fear of the citizens and travelers on said street; and by then and there aiding, abetting, countenancing, and assisting with divers other persons in forming a procession to carry red flags, for the purpose of defying the law and government of the said city of Hancock; and by then and there aiding, abetting, countenancing, and assisting in defying and insulting the law and govern-

1368

ment of the city of Hancock, by then and there aiding, abetting, countenancing, and assisting, together with divers
other persons, in creating boisterous and disorderly conduct,
and boisterous and loud language, within the hearing of citizens and travelers upon the said street; and by then and there
after being duly warned by the marshal of the said city of
Hancock, and requested not to carry or exhibit red flags which
would cause boisterous noises, threatening or unlawful language,
disturbances of the peace, and riots on the streets of said
city, and well knowing that assembling together and marching
upon the said street with red flags would bring together upon
the said street a large crowd of people who believed that red
flags are carried by anarchists or persons believing in overthrowing the established government, and defying the established law and government, in aiding, abetting, countenancing, and
assisting, together with divers other persons, in marching and
parading upon Quincy street carrying red flags, creating threatening and excited conduct and disturbance of the peace, causing
fear and excitement of the citizens and travelers upon the
said street; and by then and there aiding, abetting, countenancing and assisting in gathering, and causing to gather a large
crowd, to wit, 1,000 people or thereabouts, upon the said Quincy
street, to the interference and prevention of lawful traffic
upon the said street, and to the danger of creating riots and
destruction of life and property; and by then and there aiding,
abetting, countenancing, and assisting together with divers
other persons, in blockading and interfering with the lawful
traffic and use of said street, endangering the lives and property of citizens and travelers upon said street of the city of
Hancock, and to the annoyance and disturbance of the peace,
and of citizens and travelers, and to the evil example of all
others in the like cause offending, contrary to and in violation of Ordinance No. Ten (10) of the ordinances of the said
city of Hancock, entitled 'Police Regulations,' passed and approved on, to wit, the 9th day of March, A. D. 1898."

Ordinance No. 10 referred to in said complaint, reads as
follows:

"That any person who shall make, aid, abet, countenance
or assist in making any riot, noise, false alarm of fire, disturbance or improper diversion or commit any nuisance in any
street or alley, or in or on any public or private property
within the village to the annoyance or disturbance of citizens
or travelers, shall, on conviction, be punished by a fine of
not more than $20.00 or by imprisonment for a period not exceeding twenty days, or by both such fine and imprisonment,
together with the costs of prosecution, in the discretion of
the court."

Defendants were tried before a justice of the peace, and
found guilty. They appealed to the circuit court. There the
case was tried before a jury, and there, too, they were found
guilty. They bring the case to this court for review. There

1369

was testimony introduced in the circuit court tending to prove every material averment in said complaint. Special attention is called to the circumstance that this testimony showed that the day before the parade occurred that defendants were advised by the city marshal not to carry red flags, because it was feared "it would cause a disturbance and riot on our streets if they did so." The testimony also showed that the defendants are socialists, and on the said 28th day of July, 1907, which was Sunday, they participated with others in a socialistic parade in the streets of the city of Houghton. Defendants introduced testimony tending to prove that among socialists the red flag is not an emblem of bloodshed and violence, but is an emblem of their order, and signifies brotherhood. They also introduced testimony tending to prove that another ordinance passed by the council of the city of Hancock forbade the carrying of red flags in processions, that they knew of this ordinance, and decided to disregard it because they had been advised that it was invalid.

CARPENTER, J. (after stating the facts). When the trial commenced, the complaint had two counts. The second count is set forth in this opinion. The first count merely charged that the defendants "did then and there make, aid, abet, countenance, and assist in making a disturbance, to the annoyance and disturbance of citizens and travelers, contrary to, and in violation of, Ordinance No. 10." Defendants' counsel asked that the people be compelled to elect between these two counts. The trial court reserved his decision upon this motion until the conclusion of the case. He then compelled the people to elect, and they elected to proceed under the second count. It is now contended that they were entitled to have this election made at the beginning of the trial. It is sufficient to say of this contention that the defendants were not injured by the action of the trial judge. The trial proceeded precisely as it would had the election been made at an earlier time.

2. The trial judge denied the application of defendants for a separate trial. It is contended that this was error. Section 3100, 1 Comp. Laws, provides that, on appeal to the circuit court from a conviction for the "violation of any ordinance," the "proceedings . . . shall be the same as on appeal in criminal cases cognizable by justices of the peace." In the latter cases it is provided (section 11,956, 3 Comp. Laws) that joint defendants "shall be tried separately or jointly in the discretion of the court." The decision of the trial judge that these defendants should be tried jointly is not, therefore, open to review in this court.

3. The people were permitted to prove –

"That the general public of the city of Hancock, the citizens, and travelers on Quincy street (the street upon which the defendants paraded), regarded the red flag as an emblem of anarchy and a danger signal to the government and all law-abiding citizens."

Witness Dr. J. E. Scallon testified:

1370

"The red flag in the popular mind of the citizens of Hancock represents, practically, anarchy, whether the party calls itself socialists, anarchist-socialists, democrat-communists, or whatnot. In the popular mind they are considered Reds.

"Q. What do you mean by 'Reds?'

"A. Men organized to destroy the present forms of government by violence."

This testimony was objected to as immaterial, incompetent, and irrelevant. The counsel making this objection said "the point we make here is how the people regarded the red flag has nothing to do with it." We are asked now to say that this testimony was erroneously admitted. It is said that the testimony is immaterial. We think this objection untenable. The gist of the offense of defendants is that they infuriated the local public by carrying these flags in the parade. The existence of that sentiment was therefore a very material fact, and that was the fact which this testimony tended to prove. The point is now made that the witnesses who gave this testimony did not show themselves qualified to give it. The objection made by the counsel did not suggest, and would not natually suggest, this point to the trial judge. Nor do we think that it was well taken if it had been clearly made.

4. It is insisted that a verdict should have been directed in defendants' favor. Their counsel urge that they had a right to parade and display the red flag, the emblem of their order, and that the ordinance prohibiting it - which ordinance defendants are not charged with violating - was invalid. That ordinance apparently was general in its nature, and forbade the display of a red flag in any parade whatever. Whether or not there might be occasions when defendants had a lawful right to parade with a red flag - and this would be a question which would arise upon the validity of said ordinance - we are not called upon to determine, and we ought not and will not attempt to determine in this case. The question here is not whether the defendants have in general a right to parade with a red flag. It is this: Had they such right, when they knew that the natural and inevitable consequence was to create riot and disorder? Defendants knew this red flag was hated by those to whom it was displayed, because it was believed to represent sentiments detestable to every lover of our form of government. They knew that it would excite fears and apprehension, and that by displaying it they would provoke violence and disorder. Their right to display a red flag was subordinate to the right of the public. They had no right to display it when the natural and inevitable consequence was to destroy the public peace and tranquility. It is idle to say that the public peace and tranquility was disturbed by the noise and violence, not of defendants, but of those whose sentiments they offended. When defendants deliberately and knowingly offended that sentiment, they were responsible for the consequences which followed, and which they knew would follow. It is also idle to say that these

others were wrongdoers in manifesting in the manner they did their resentment at defendants' conduct. This merely proves that they and defendants were joint wrongdoers; that they, as well as defendants, violated the ordinance in question. The object of this proceeding is not to redress the grievance of these other wrongdoers, but it is to redress the grievance of the public whose rights they and defendants jointly invaded. The guilt of their associate wrongdoers does not lessen defendants' responsibility. It is sufficient to say that defendants by their conduct did "aid, countenance, and assist in making a riot, noise, and disturbance," and therefore violated Ordinance No. 10 of the city of Hancock. This reasoning is sustained by authority. Says Chief Justice CHAMPLIN, speaking for the entire court in People v. Johnson, 86 Mich. 177 (13 L.R.A. 163):

"In general terms the offense (breach of the peace) is a violation of public order, a disturbance of the public tranquility, by any act or conduct inciting to violence, or tending to provoke or excite others to break the peace."

See, also, State v. White, 18 R. I. 473. It does not avail defendants to say that they have a right to propagate their political views. That right is not denied. But we do deny and emphatically deny that in propagating their views they may commit a crime or violate any constitutional law or valid municipal ordinance.

Defendants rely upon the Frazee Case, 63 Mich. 396. There the petitioner, who had taken part in a Salvation Army parade, had violated an ordinance of which the court said:

"It left practically within the unlimited discretion of the mayor . . . the power of determining whether processions shall be allowed."

This ordinance was held void. That the reasoning of that case does not apply to this is clearly shown by the following quotations from that opinion:

"There may be times and occasions when such assemblies may for a while be dangerous in themselves because of inflammable conditions among the population. . . . It is only when political, religious, social, or other demonstrations create public disturbances or operate as nuisances, or create or manifestly threaten some tangible public or private mischief, that the law interferes. And, when it interferes, it does so because of the evil done, or apparently menaced, and not because of the sentiments or purposes of the movement, if not otherwise unlawful; and things absolutely unlawful are not made so by local authority, but by general law. . . . It is lawful to provide for dealing with the mischief, but it is not lawful to go beyond reasonable measures and precautions in anticipating it. . . . These processions might, no doubt, become nuisances, as any others might do so, but it cannot be assumed that they will."

Other complaints are made. They need no special attention. They are all answered either by an application of the principles herein stated, by other elementary principles of law, or by a proper construction of the record.

The judgment is affirmed.

GRANT, C. J., and HOOKER, MOORE, and McALVAY, JJ., concurred.

People v. Immonen
271 Mich. 384

NORTH, J. This is an appeal by Unto Edward Immonen and Eric Fahle Burman who were convicted of and sentenced for violating section 48 of the Michigan penal code (Act No. 328, Sec. 48, Pub. Acts 1931) which reads:

"Display of red flag - Any person who shall display a red flag in any public assembly, parade or demonstration in this State is guilty of a felony.

"The use of such a flag at any such assembly, parade or demonstration shall be considered as prima facie evidence of its use as an emblem of anarchy."

In the summer of 1933 through the activities of representatives of several organizations a children's camp was organized and maintained for a period of two weeks at Eben Junction in Alger county. The Eben Educational Society granted the use of its hall incident to the camp program. By some this hall was referred to as the Community building, by others as the Communist hall. About 50 children between 9 and 16 years of age attended the camp. Some paid a small fee, others attended without charge. Their time was occupied by class work and athletic activites. To some extent discipline among the children was maintained by means of self-imposed government. Defendant Immonen and his wife, Ruth Lake Immonen, were appointed to supervise the sports and physical educational activities. Defendant Burman was the manager of a cooperative store in the immediate vicinity of the camp. He furnished supplies and appeared to take an interest in the camp program; although he denied having such interest.

On August 5 and 6, 1933, a red flag was flown from the camp flagpole in the immediate vicinity of the camp building and close to the township highway. There is testimony that at a meeting of the children they decided to display a red flag at the camp. Neither of defendants were present at this meeting. The flag was made by the girls attending the camp. "It was a red flag with a scythe in it and a hammer; a while scythe and a white hammer on a red cloth." The flag was first observed by defendant Immonen on the morning of August 5th flying from the pole which had been erected by other camp attaches. The flying of this flag at the camp was reported to deputy sheriff Peter Arsenault, at Munising. This officer together with

1373

another deputy sheriff and other men went to the camp and talked with the persons who appeared to be in charge. Immonen being pointed out to Arsenault, the latter approached Immonen and said: "What are you fellows flying this red flag for; don't you know it is against the law?" The officer thereupon told Immonen that they wanted the flag taken down and that they would give him 30 minutes in which to do so. Immonen said: "Suppose it doesn't come down;" and to this the officer replied: "We will see it is taken down." Thereupon Arsenault and the men with him left the camp in their automobile but stopped when a short distance away in the vicinity of Burman's store, evidently to await results. They were then approximately 400 feet from the camp and in sight of the flag. While the officer and his companions were sitting in the car defendant Burman approached them and said: "What the hell business is it of you fellows to interfere with the flag?" Arsenault replied: "It is this much business, if you want to fly a flag you fly an American flag." Thereupon Burman said: "Well, I will show you," or as later testified by the witness, "We will show you what business it is," or "What business we have flying a red flag." Burman then left and went into his store. The last above quoted testimony was given by deputy sheriff Arsenault. Defendant Burman's version of the incident as covered in his testimony is as follows:

"Well, the first question I asked was if they were interested in that flag. Someone replied that they were. Then I asked them what their opinion or idea was about the flag, I meant. I didn't mention the flag but what their idea was about - someone answered from the car that if any flag is flying it has got to be the American flag. Then I asked the question: Haven't any society a right to fly any emblem in their affairs in their private affairs or assemblies, what they wish, and one man from the back seat replied, 'Not in this State.' Then the driver (Mr. Arsenault) jumped out and walked towards me in a threatening manner."

Another witness quotes defendant Burman as saying:

"Well, the other societies they can have their flags up. Why can't we have ours?"

At the time of the above noted conversation members of the State police had arrived at the camp. They chopped or pushed down the flagpole and took possession of the flag. When the police left the camp Immonen walked down to the cooperative store and there engaged in an argument relative to the flag. Other members of the camp immediately re-erected the flagpole and some of the girls sewed four red bandana handkerchiefs together, and this improvised flag was promptly flown from the camp flagstaff. With the exception of one witness the testimony is that Immonen took no part in the actual work of re-erecting the flagpole and again displaying the flag, but he admits he was aware at the time that this activity was going on at the camp; and did not interfere or advise against it.

1374

One witness testified that Immonen directed the children in putting up the pole and again flying the flag.

On the following day the red flag was again flying at the camp. The sheriff of Alger county and State police arrived there a little before noon. On this occasion the pole was taken down and cut into pieces and the improvised flag seized. The officers went into the camp building and made some search. While they were there defendant Burman, having been informed of their presence, came from his living rooms over the cooperative store, entered the camp building and came in contact with the sheriff. The latter testified to the following conversation between them:

"I said to Mr. Burman, 'You were notified yesterday about this red flag flying here, wasn't you?' and he says to me, he says, 'What the hell business have you got in here?' He says, 'What business of yours is it, taking the flag down?'

"'Now,' I says, 'Burman, you were notified yesterday about this flag and my officers had a conflict with you yesterday about this, knowing that it was against the State law to fly this flag it is flying again. I am putting you under arrest.'"

Defendant Burman's version of the conversation is as follows:

"I made a common greeting to him - 'hello,' and he replied the same way. After that the sheriff asked me if I was in charge of this. I told him, 'No, I am not; I don't have anything to do with it.' Then he asked me if I am not the leader around here, and I replied, 'To my knowledge I don't consider myself a leader.'"

Some of the officers went into an office room in the southwest portion of the hall where they came in contact with defendant Immonen. The sheriff testified in substance that he asked Immonen what was the idea of this flag raising here after being notified yesterday not to raise the flag. There was no reply to this question but at this time Immonen admitted he was the instructor at the camp. On this phase of the record we quote the following from the testimony of defendant Immonen:

"The sheriff came in and he asked me if I was one of the instructors and I nodded. I was sitting at the table and the typewriter was at my side. And right behind the sheriff one of the troopers, the sergeant, came in. . . . And the trooper asked me who was in charge and I refused to answer, because I didn't know for sure who really was in charge and at that he hit me in the pit of the stomach, which made me feel rather dizzy and I sat down for a while."

Both Immonen and Burman were arrested and placed in the officer's automobile. One of the men who accompanied the sheriff testified that while in the automobile with Burman: "I told Mr. Burman if he didn't fly the red flag he wouldn't go to jail." "He said, 'I have been a citizen here for 20 years, and I know what I am doing.'" Defendant Burman denied having made the

1375

statement just above quoted. Further statement of the facts disclosed by this record is not essential at this point to a consideration of the main questions presented for review.

Appellants challenge the constitutionality of the statute under which they were prosecuted and convicted. In this connection it is noted that the statutory provision consists of two paragraphs. The first paragraph defines the offense, while the second creates a presumption of evidence. Appellants' contention is that the enactment is in violation of article 2, Sec. 2, 4, 16, 19, of the State Constitution for the following reasons: The statute prohibits or tends to prohibit the right peaceably to assembly and to consult for the common good (Sec. 2); it interferes with, restrains and abridges liberty of speech (Sec. 4); it compels one to be witness against himself and deprives him of life and liberty without due process of law (Sec. 16); and further the statute is so framed that the accused in a criminal prosecution is deprived of the right to be informed of the nature of the accusation made against him (Sec. 19). Appellants further claim the enactment is invalid in that it contravenes the 14th Amendment of the Constitution of the United States wherein it is provided:

"No State shall make or enforce any law which shall abridge the privileges or immunities of citizens of the United States; nor shall any State deprive any person of life, liberty, or property, without due process of law; nor deny to any person within its jurisdiction the equal protection of the laws."

On this phase of the case appellants in their brief urge:

"It will be observed that there appears no limitation whatever in relation to the purpose of the display of the flag and it makes no difference whether the flag is displayed by a debate club, a religious society, a college club or a political unit. Any display of the red flag at any public assembly, parade or demonstration is made an offense. The right to display a flag falls within the constitutional guarantee of free speech, and as such is embraced in the 14th Amendment to the Federal Constitution."

Constitutionality of the statute can only be determined from a proper point of view. The legislative purpose must not be ignored. The thing forbidden by the statute must be considered as a whole; not dissected into a multiplicity of parts and from a finding that no one of such parts constitutes a wrong which may be prohibited, conclude that therefore taken as a whole the course of conduct covered by the statute cannot be made an offense by legislative fiat and that the attempt to do so is violative of constitutional rights. In the statute now under consideration the forbidden display of a red flag is confined to such display "in any public assembly, parade or demonstration." Herein we are concerned only with its display at a "public assembly." Under this record there can be no question but that there was such a display at a public assembly, and a somewhat persistent effort to renew and continue such display.

In this connection it becomes necessary to consider whether there is justification from the standpoint of public peace and safety for legislation prohibiting the display of a red flag. How does it differ, if at all, from a flag of any other color or design? Of what is the red flag emblematic, for what does it stand, what does it teach? We hold it to be a matter of common knowledge that the red flag when displayed in the manner forbidden by the statute is the emblem, the advocate and teacher of anarchy. This is as much a matter of common knowledge and should be and is as much a matter of which every court can take judicial notice as that the stars and stripes are the emblem of freedom, and wholly inimical to the teaching of anarchists. To this point reference is made to our decision in People v. Burman, hereinafter quoted. See, also, Murdock v. Clark (C.C.A.), 53 Fed. (2d) 155.

In general acceptance and properly there is a marked distinction between anarchism and communism, notwithstanding there is authority for saying "anarchism is a variety of communalism." Webster's Dictionary (1925). But it is not of controlling importance in the instant case whether the red flag was displayed as an emblem of anarchism or communism, or of either. Nor is it decisive herein that one may advocate the adoption by peaceable and orderly means of the principles of anarchy or of communism, or of other forms of government notwithstanding the advocated governmental principles may be wholly incompatible with and even abhorrent to our present form of government. See Stromberg v. California, hereinafter cited. Such advocacy is not prohibited by the statute. The sole test here is the right or power of the legislature to prohibit the use of the red flag in the manner specified in the statute. We hold such statutory provision valid because by its use incident to the advocacy of radical changes of government the red flag has become definitely identified with the element in such movements which has advocated and does advocate the use of force in the overthrow of our present form of government. The red flag is not an emblem of peaceful means of accomplishing governmental revolution. Instead, in common acceptance, it is a challenge and a threat of the use of force and the resort to destruction incident to governmental revolution. Because the red flag is the insignia of such doctrines and teachings, its use in the manner forbidden by the statute will cause a breach of public peace and endanger the lives and property of citizens generally. To some degree such was the development in the instant case. Hence the legislature in the exercise of police power may within the limitations of the statute forbid the display of the red flag.

The obvious and well-known result of the display of a red flag incident to a public assembly, parade or demonstration is a matter of record in this court in a decision affirming conviction under an ordinance in consequence of a breach of

1377

the peace caused by displaying red flags in a public parade. We quote it in part:

"The question here is not whether the defendants have in general a right to parade with a red flag. It is this: Had they such right, when they knew that the natural and inevitable consequence was to create riot and disorder? Defendants knew this red flag was hated by those to whom it was displayed, because it was believed to represent sentiments detestable to to every lover of our form of government. They knew that it would excite fears and apprehension, and that by displaying it they would provoke violence and disorder. Their right to display a red flag was subordinate to the right of the public. They had no right to display it when the natural and inevitable consequence was to destroy the public peace and tranquility. . . . It is sufficient to say that defendants by their conduct did 'aid, countenance, and assist in making a riot, noise, and disturbance.'"
People v. Burman, 154 Mich. 150, 156 (25 L.R.A. (N.S.) 251).

It must be concluded that there was and is not only justification but an apparent necessity for the enactment of the statutory provision. When such justification or necessity exists then within reason any so-called rights of individuals must yield to the limitation necessarily imposed thereon; and in this requirement there is no invasion of a constitutional right. The enactment of this statute is clearly within the proper exercise of the police power of a sovereign State.

"That attribute of sovereignty known as 'police power,' though difficult of definition, includes the power of legislation deemed essential for protection of the public peace, good order, morals, safety, and health." Locke v. Ionia Circuit Judge 184 Mich. 535, 539.

This statute does not interfere with the right of citizens to peaceably assembly and consult relative to the common welfare; nor does it impair freedom of speech, assuming (as appellants assert) "the display of a flag is tantamount to the expression of speech, within the meaning of constitutional provisions."

"The right (of free speech) is not an absolute one, and the State in the exercise of its police power may punish the abuse of this freedom. There is no question but that the State may thus provide for the punishment of those who indulge in utterances which incite to violence and crime and threaten the overthrow of organized government by unlawful means. There is no constitutional immunity for such conduct abhorrent to our institutions." Stromberg v. California, 283 U. S. 359, 368 (51 Sup. Ct. 532, 73 A.L.R. 1484).

If the activities of defendants and the organization with which they are identified are within the law, no good reason appears why the symbol of such activities should not be something other than the red flag with its inseparable traditions of advocacy of the use of unlawful means for the accomplish-

1378

ment of an end. Because of the fixed symbolical significance
of the red flag its display in the manner forbidden is an argument in favor of sedition, sabotage and direct action in political matters; and this is true notwithstanding the avowed purpose of an advocate to the contrary or the assertion that the
display of the red flag is not intended to be violative of the
law. Hence prohibition of its display in the limited manner
provided in the statute does not infringe the right of free
speech.

Counsel for appellants review at length and rely upon the
Stromberg Case, supra. Their brief asserts it to be "the leading case in the country;" and that the statute passed upon in
that case was "neither as broad nor as general as the one involved in the case at bar." Reference to the Stromberg decision discloses at once that it in no way sustains the contention
of appellants herein. Yetta Stromberg was convicted in the
State courts of having violated a California statute (section
403-a of the penal code) which undertook to make it a felony
if one displayed a red flag or a flag of any color or design
in any public place or at a public assembly (1) as an emblem
of opposition to organized government; (2) as a stimulus to
anarchistic action; or (3) as an aid to propaganda of a seditious character. In the United States Supreme Court her conviction was set aside and the case remanded for the reason
that conviction in the State court was under the general terms
of the statute rather than specifically under any one of the
three clauses of the statute above noted; and in effect the
first of the three clauses was held unconstitutional. Chief
Justice Hughes, delivering the prevailing opinion, said:

"The basis of the decision, as more fully stated in the
opinion of the two concurring justices (People v. Mintz, 106
Cal. App. 725 (290 Pac. 93), was this: 'The constitutionality
of the phrase of this section of opposition to organized
government, is questionable. This phrase can be eliminated
from the section without materially changing its purposes.
The section is complete without it, and with it eliminated it
can be upheld as a constitutional enactment by the legislature
of the State of California.' Accordingly, disregarding the
first clause of the statute, and upholding the other clauses
the conviction of the appellant was sustained.

"We are unable to agree with this disposition of the case.
The verdict against the appellant was a general one. It did
not specify the ground upon which it rested. As there were
three purposes set forth in the statute, and the jury was instructed that their verdict might be given with respect to any
one of them, independently considered, it is impossible to say
under which clause of the statute the conviction was obtained. . . .

"We have no reason to doubt the validity of the second and
third clauses of the statute as construed by the State court
to relate to such incitements to violence.

"The question is thus narrowed to that of validity of the
first clause, that is, with respect to the display of the flag

1379

'as a sign, symbol or emblem of opposition to organized government.' . . . Thus it was said (in the opinion of the State court) that the clause (1) 'might be construed to include the peaceful and orderly opposition to a government as organized and controlled by one political party by those of another political party equally high-minded and patriotic, which did not agree with the one in power. It might also be construed to include peaceful and orderly opposition to government by a legal means and within constitutional limitations.' . . . The first clause of the statute being invalid upon its face, the conviction of the appellant, which so far as the record discloses may have rested upon that clause exclusively, must be set aside."

Consideration of the decision in the Stromberg Case discloses that it in no way sustains a contention that in the exercise of its police power a State may not forbid conduct which will result in a breach of the peace, imperil human lives or jeopardize the safety of private property. Instead, the holding of Chief Justice Hughes is directly to the contrary.

Incident to appellants' claim that the statute is unconstitutional in that it compels one to be a witness against himself, deprives him of life and liberty without due process of law, and denies him equal protection of the law, it is urged that the statute creates a presumption of the guilty of an accused; and that it is ambiguous, vague, indefinite, and discriminatory. It is asserted in appellants' brief:

"The effect of the presumption of anarchy created by the statute is to deprive the defendants of their presumption of innocence and to place the burden of proof upon them in the first instance. Presumption of guilt in such a case is denial of due process."

In support of the above appellants cite our recent decision in People v. Licavoli, 264 Mich. 643. The distinction in the statutory provision passed upon in the Licavoli Case and the statute now under consideration is obvious. The prevailing opinion in the Licavoli Case is based upon the fact that the legislature in the act then and before the court attempted to make a fact or circumstance which had no logical connection whatever with the offense charged evidence of the guilt of the accused. As stated in that opinion by Mr. Justice WIEST:

"The presumption so declared by the enactment is not a rational deduction or inference from fact to fact, but an arbitrary fiat of the legislature."

This is not true of the statutory provision under which appellants herein were charged and convicted. Here the added clause reads:

"The use of such a flag at any such assembly, parade or demonstration shall be considered as prima facie evidence of its use as an emblem of anarchy."

In so providing, the legislature merely embodied in the statute recital of a matter of common knowledge and common acceptance, as we have hereinbefore stated. In this instance that which the legislature decreed should be prima facie evidence is confessedly inherent in, and an essential element of, the course of conduct of forbidden and made criminal by the statute. It is not "an arbitrary fiat of the legislature." Instead there is a rational connection between the statutory offense and the inference to be drawn therefrom which is made prima facie evidence of anarchy. There can be no doubt of the power of the legislature to enact rules of evidence provided such rules do not contravene constitutional rights; and the portion of the statute last above quoted is an appropriate declaration of legislative intent and purpose.

We are unable to agree with appellants that the statute is in any way ambiguous, vague or indefinite, nor is it discriminatory. Incident to this latter phase of the case it is noted in appellants' brief that certain organizations or societies actually use or may use the red flag as their symbol, and that workmen at times use a red flag as a signal of danger. It may well be questioned whether the use of a red flag under any of the circumstances above noted or similar circumstances would fall within the statute, surely the one last suggested does not. But the obvious answer to any and all such supposed uses of the flag is that if the enactment is a valid exercise of the police power, as we hold it is, any person displaying the red flag in violation of the statute must accept the consequences. In so displaying a red flag one is not exercising any inherent or vested right protected by the constitutional provisions. People v. Burman, supra. It follows from what has already been stated herein that we do not find the act under consideration to be in any way in violation of the provisions of the 14th Amendment to the Federal Constitution above quoted. In short, as against any objection here urged, the statute is constitutional.

We have already referred somewhat to the factual aspect of this case, but have noted only in part the testimony relative to defendants having violated the quoted statute. Consideration of the whole record satisfies us that the people submitted sufficient competent testimony to make the issue of the guilt or innocence of the defendants a question of fact for the jury.

The trial judge construed this statute as creating an offense of which one could not be convicted except it was established "beyond a reasonable doubt that the red flag was used as an emblem of anarchy." Such construction was erroneous. Instead, as asserted in appellants' brief:

"It is clear from reading the law that the prohibition is general and is not limited by the presumption concerning 'anarchy.' . . . We submit . . . the prohibition against the display of the red flag in a public assembly, parade or demonstration is a general prohibition. . . . This would, therefore, indicate that 'anarchy' was not properly an issue in this case charging the display of the red flag."

1381

The erroneous construction of the statute by the circuit judge led him into holding, against repeated objections of defendants' counsel, that testimony as to communism and anarchy was admissible. On direct examination of one of the people's witnesses the following testimony was given:

"Q. Is it a matter of general knowledge with the people at Eben that he (Burman) is leader of the Communist party out there?
"A. Yes, sir."

The following is from the direct testimony of another of the people's witnesses:

"The fellow I saw at Marquette two or three days before talking at a Communist meeting was Mr. Immonen."

Still another of the people's witnesses on direct examination testified:

"Q. Then you know of your own knowledge, that Mr. Burman was a candidate on the Communistic party ticket for judge of probate?
"A. He told me he was the leader of the Communist party, getting up a ticket of his own. . . . .
"Q. Did he say he was a candidate for judge of probate on the Communist ticket?
"A. Yes."

All of the foregoing and other testimony of like character was received over defendants' objections. This same erroneous construction of the statute resulted in the case being submitted to the jury under a prejudicial charge. We quote in part:

"I further charge you that individuals may violate this statute by words either spoken or written, even though they have committed no act of physical injury or violence. It is the power of words that has the potent force to violate the provisions of this statute. It is the dangerous doctrine of anarchy and its supporters that ought to be punished.

"If the evidence in this case convinces you, beyond a reasonable doubt, that the party to which these defendants belong has an avowed hostility to this government and an open antagonism to all political parties which profess to support the same form of government, then they would be guilty of anarchy according to the statute which I have just read."

Clearly the guilt or innocence of each of these defendants turned upon the simple and sole issue of whether he committed the statutory offense; and the statutory offense is the "display (of) a red flag in any public assembly, parade or demonstration in this State." Nothing else. The testimony admitted as a part of the people's direct case just above noted was of such a character as to prejudice the jury against each of the defendants. It and the portion of the charge to the jury above quoted constituted prejudicial error in that the defendants were thereby deprived of a fair and impartial trial. This necessitates reversal.

Numerous other assignments of error are urged in behalf of appellants. Many of them are without merit and the others are of such a character that they are unlikely to occur on a retrial of this case. We think it sufficient to note that on the record made at this trial the court might well have given certain of defendants' requests to charge which were neither given nor covered. Among these are the following:

"Mere remonstrating with an officer concerning the legality or illegality of his acts does not constitute a crime.
"If you find from the evidence that defendant Burman, was merely remonstrating with the officers concerning the legality of their acts that would not make him guilty of the crimes charged.
"Absence of disapproval or opposition by the defendants in connection with the display of the red flag is not itself sufficient to make them guilty."

On this appeal we need not and do not determine the question as to whether failure to give the above requests would alone constitute reversible error; and further, it may be noted that upon a retrial of the case these or similar requests to charge might or might not be proper, depending upon the record made at a subsequent trial.

The conviction of each of these defendants is vacated and a new trial granted.

POTTER, C. J., and NELSON SHARPE, FEAD, WIEST, BUTZEL, BUSHNELL, and EDWARD M. SHARPE, JJ., concurred.

People v. Ruthenberg
229 Mich. 315

WIEST, J. Convicted of criminal syndicalism defendant prosecutes review on exceptions before sentence. The information charged:

"That heretofore, to wit, on the 20th day of August A. D. 1922, in the township of Lake . . . (Berrien county, this State), C. E. Ruthenberg did voluntarily assemble with a certain society, group and assemblage of persons, to wit, the Communist Party of America, formed to teach and advocate the doctrines of criminal syndicalism."

Act No. 255, Pub. Acts 1919 (Comp. Laws Supp. 1922, Sec. 15585 (2, 3)), defines the crime of criminal syndicalism, specifies acts constituting the offense and fixes the penalty:

SECTION 1. Criminal syndicalism is hereby defined as the doctrine which advocates crime, sabotage, violence or other unlawful methods of terrorism as a means of accomplishing industrial or political reform. The advocacy of such doctrine,

1383

whether by word of mouth or writing, is a felony punishable as in this act, otherwise provided.

"SEC. 2. Any person who by word of mouth or writing, advocates or teaches the duty, necessity or propriety of crime, sabotage, violence or other unlawful method of terrorism as a means of accomplishing industrial or political reform; or prints, publishes, edits, issues or knowingly circulates, sells, distributes or publicly displays any book, paper, document, or written matter in any form, containing or advocating, advising or teaching the doctrine that industrial or political reform should be brought about by crime, sabotage, violence or other unlawful methods of terrorism; or openly, willfully and deliberately justifies by word of mouth or writing, the commission or the attempt to commit crime, sabotage, violence or other unlawful methods of terrorism with intent to exemplify, spread or advocate the propriety of the doctrines of criminal syndicalism; or organizes or helps to organize or becomes a member of or voluntarily assembles with any society, group or assemblage of persons formed to teach or advocate the doctrines of criminal syndicalism is guilty of a felony and punishable by imprisonment in the State prison for not more than ten years or by a fine of not more than five thousand dollars, or both, at the discretion of the court."

A national delegate convention of the Communist Part of America was called by the central executive committee of the party to meet at Bridgman, Berrien county, this State, in August, 1922. Delegates to the convention were not informed of the place of meeting, but under direction proceeded from city to city toward Bridgman and were finally steered there. Near Bridgman, an isolated hotel and cottages furnished accommodations for the 75 persons attending the convention and a natural amphitheatre amid the woods afforded a place for sessions. Every person attending had a party or assumed name. No communication with the outside world was permitted. Each participant in the convention was assigned a number and given a large manilla portfolio in which to place all papers and documents at the close of each day, to be taken up by the "grounds committee" for safe keeping. Defendant's party name was "Damon" and his portfolio was number 50. These portfolios were deposited each night, by the committee, in two barrels, sunk in the ground at a distance from the hotel and covered with sand, leaves and sticks. Regulations of the "grounds committee" provided:

No incriminating literature or document shall be kept in baggage or in rooms. All such matter must be turned over to the committee every evening. The grounds committee must arrange for the safe keeping of this matter."

A central wash tub in which to burn incriminating papers was also maintained.

Convention sessions were held. Defendant, as a member of the central executive committee of the Communist Party of

America, by virtue of his office, attended the convention as a fraternal delegate with the right to address, and did address the convention. One duly elected delegate in attendance was a special employee of the United States department of justice, bureau of investigation. A delegate from the Comintern (Communist or Third International), Moscow, Russia, was present, and a delegate from the Hungarian federation and another from the Red Trade International at Moscow were present and participated in the convention. Defendant reached the convention on August 15th and remained there until arrested on August 22d.

Federal officers, investigating activities of Communists traced down the convention place, recognized certain Communists in attendance, and laid the matter before the sheriff of Berrien county. The Communists in attendance recognized the Federal officers and laid plans to disperse, with right to foreigners to go first, and many of the delegates hurriedly left. The sheriff, with a number of deputies and the Federal officers, visited the convention place one morning and arrested defendant and 16 others, without warrants for arrest or search, seized their baggage, and took them to the county jail. The sheriff then learned of the depository of the grounds committee and made search, found the barrels and seized their contents.

The information as filed contained four counts. The court quashed the first, second and third counts, on motion of defendant, leaving the fourth count as the charge. Defendant insists that this statute violates sections 2, 4, 16 and 19, article 2, of the Constitution of this State, and section 1 of the Fourteenth Amendment to the Constitution of the United States. Does this statute contravene the right of the people to peaceably assemble? To so hold would require us to say that it is violative of the Constitution to make it a crime for one, in sympathy with and on his own volition to join in an assemblage of persons formed to teach or advocate crime, sabotage, violence or other unlawful methods of terorism as a means of accomplishing industrial or political reform. We cannot make any such holding.

Does the statute prevent freedom of speech? This statute reaches an abuse of the right to freely speak, write and publish sentiments, and is squarely within the accountability allowed to be exacted, in the very provision invoked. This statute does not restrain or abridge liberty of speech.

As said of a similar statute in People v. Steelik, 187 Cal. 361, 375 (203 Pac. 78):

"The legislature has power to punish propaganda which has for its purpose the destruction of government or the rights of property which the government was formed to preserve."

See, also, State v. Hennessy, 114 Wash. 351 (195 Pac. 211).

In Schaefer v. United States, 251 U.S. 466 (40 Sup. Ct. 259), the accused invoked the constitutional right of free speech, in a prosecution under the espionage act, and received

1385

this merited rebuke:

"But simple as the law is, perilous to the country as disobedience to it was, offenders developed and when it was exerted against them challenged it to decision as a violation of the right of free speech assured by the Constitution of the United States. A curious spectacle was presented: that great ordinance of government and orderly liberty was invoked to justify the activities of anarchy or of the enemies of the United States, and by a strange perversion of its precepts it was adduced against itself. . . . Verdicts and judgments of conviction were the reply to the challenge and when they were brought here our response to it was unhesitating and direct. We did more than reject the contention; we forestalled all shades of repetition of it including that in the case at bar. Schenck v. United States, 249 U. S. 47 (39 Sup. Ct. 247); Frohwerk v. United States, 249 U. S. 204 (39 Sup. Ct. 249) Debs v. United States, 249 U. S. 211 (39 Sup. Ct. 252); Abrams v. United States, 250 U. S. 616 (40 Sup. Ct. 17)."

See, also, Gilbert v. Minnesota, 254 U. S. 325 (41 Sup. Ct. 125); State v. Holm, 139 Minn 267 (166 N. W. 181, L.R.A. 1918C, 304).

In People v. Lloyd, 304 Ill. 23, 37 (136 N.E. 505), a prosecution under a similar criminal syndicalism act, the court stated, in answer to the claim that the act violated the right of free speech:

"It would be a strange Constitution, indeed, that would guarantee to any man the right to advocate the destruction by force of that which that Constitution guarantees to the people living under its protection."

See, also, People v. Most, 171 N.Y. 423 (64 N.E. 175, 58 L.R.A. 509); State v. Boyd, 86 N.J. Law, 75 (91 Atl. 586).

The reasons advanced here against the constitutionality of the act have been urged against similar acts in other jurisdictions and found to have no merit. The act does not violate the Fourteenth Amendment to the Federal Constitution.

Defendant claims the statute is too vague to form the basis of a prosecution for felony and is a nullity because it punishes as a felony the enunciation of a doctrine without regard to the intent, the occasion, the result or the imminent result of the enunciation. The legislature may, to safeguard security of persons and property, denounce as criminal specified acts inimical thereto, and make guilt of an offender rest upon his voluntary act, without any felonious intent. This statute involves no felonious intent. It does involve voluntary action, its denunciation of assembling with a society, group or assembly, formed to teach the doctrines of criminal syndicalism, is dependent upon whether the act of joining is voluntary or not. To act voluntarily involves election to so act, and election to be such requires knowledge that the assembly one makes choice to join, and to participate in the purposes thereof, was formed to teach or

1386

advocate criminal syndicalism. But this does not constitute
felonious intent, to be denounced in the statute or averred
in the information. It was held in State v. Hennessy, supra,
under a similar statute, that felonious intent was not involved.

It is claimed the provisions of the statute do not fix an
ascertainable standard of guilt and are not adequate to inform persons, accused of violation thereof, of the nature and
cause of accusation against them. It is said in support of
this that the term "sabotage" is subject to a variety of innocent meanings, and the term "violence" is not necessarily
limited to physical or criminal violence. The naivete of
this should make a Communist smile. One need read but little
to discover what the terms sabotage and violence mean with
reference to industrial or political agenda advocated by radi-
cals. The term sabotage is so well understood by Communists
as to be employed in the theses (sic) and resolutions adopted
at the third world congress of the Communist International
without any explanation to exclude possible innocent meaning.
Dictionaries have explained the meaning of sabotage for many
years. Sabotage has had a well understood meaning every since
French industrial workers threw their sabots, or wooden shoes,
into machinery. It signifies a wilful act of destruction and
has so been understood by writers for many years. Non-criminal
sabotage, such as loafing on the job, of course, does not fall
within the act. . . .

It is also said there has been no overt act by the Communist party committed within this State, and no showing of
intent to commit any in the immediate future, and it is
claimed it is without the power of the State to make it a
felony to join an assembly formed to teach or advocate criminal syndicalism unless it is shown that activities are carried out within the State. This statute does not make criminality dependent upon the commission of an overt act. It
reaches those who advocate or teach the commission of crime
as a means to accomplish an end, and those who, by choice,
assemble with them. An overt act along the lines of such advocacy or teaching would constitute an entirely different
crime punishable now by other laws of the State.

As said in State v. Laundy, 103 Or. 443 (204 Pac. 958,
206 Pac. 290):

"If it is within the power of the legislature to declare
that a given act, when done, constitutes a crime, then it is
likewise within the power of the legislature to declare that
to advocate the doing of such act is a crime; for, if public
policy requires the punishment of him who does an act, it
likewise may require the punishment of him who incites the
doing of such act, whether the act is actually done or not.
State v. Quinlan, 86 N.J. Law, 120 (91 Atl. 111)."

And this applies with equal force to one who voluntarily
joins an assembly formed to teach or advocate criminal syndicalism.

The power vested in, and the duty resting upon this State, under its republican form of government guaranteed by the Constitution of the United States, is well stated in People v. Lloyd, supra:

"The citizens of this State are citizens of the United States, and the citizens of the United States residing within the borders of this State are citizens of this State. Each citizen owes a duty to these two separate sovereignties. The State is a part of the Nation, and owes a duty to the Nation to support the efforts of the National government to secure the safety and protect the rights of its citizens, and to preserve, maintain, and enforce sovereign rights of the Nation against public menace, and to that end the State may require its citizens to refrain from any act which will interfere with or impede the National government in effectively defending itself against such public enemies. . . .

"There is embodied in the Constitution of the United States and the Constitution of each of the 48 States a bill (or declaration) of rights, guaranteeing to every citizen, among other things, the right of private ownership of property, and the right of each individual to use and enjoy his property. . . . The advocacy within in any one of the several States to overthrow the representative form of government of the United States, or of the several States, is therefore an assault upon the established government of each and every one of the 49 separate sovereignities, and it would be strange indeed if any one of these sovereignties did not have the right to protect itself against destruction. The overthrow of the National government would be a direct blow at the representative form of government now secured to each of the several States, and the overthrow of the government of any one of the several States would be an indirect assault upon the government of each of the other 47 States.

"The State of Illinois is therefore interested in the preservation of our National government and the government of each and every one of her sister States, and she, without doubt, has the right under the police power inherent in every government to enact laws for the preservation and protection of her government. . . .

"Manifestly the legislature has authority to forbid the advocacy of a doctrine designed and intended to overthrow the government, without waiting until there is a present and imminent danger of the success of the plan advocated. If the State were compelled to wait until the apprehended danger became certain, then its right to protect itself would come into being simultaneously with the overthrow of the government, when there would be neither prosecuting officers nor courts for the enforcement of the law. The act under consideration makes the advocacy of the overthrow of the government a felony, and provides for the punishment of the advocate, and so it is not necessary that there be a real or actual effort to carry out the program that he advocates."

See, also, People v. Gitlow, 195 App. Div. 773 (187 N.Y. 132 (136 N.E. 317); Gilbert v. Minnesota, 254 U. S. 326 (41 Sup. Ct. 126).

What we have said covers all questions meriting disscussion, disposes of defendant's requests to charge and shows that defendant has no cause to complain of the instructions given the jury.

We find no reversible error in any of the points presented, and the conviction is affirmed and the circuit court advised to proceed to judgment.

McDONALD, SHARPE, STEERE, and FELLOWS, JJ., concurred with WIEST, J.

BIRD and MOORE, JJ., concurred in the result. CLARK, C. J., did not sit.

PER CURIAM. Writ of error to review judgment on conviction. All questions presented by the writ of error have been determined by our opinion in this case on exceptions before sentence (ante, 315). We adhere to that opinion.

Conviction and judgment affirmed.

4. Final Draft - Michigan Revised Criminal Code

(Treason)

Sec. 5505. (1) A person commits the crime of treason, if he levies war against the state of Michigan or adheres to its enemies, giving them aid and comfort.

(2) No person shall be convicted of treason unless upon the testimony of two witnesses to the same overt act or upon confession in open court.

(3) Treason is a Class A felony.

Committee Commentary

The section is taken from Constitution (1963) Art. I, Sec. 22 and C.L. 1948, Sec. 750.544.

Treason at common law consisted of regicide or attempted regicide, promotion of revolt, counterfeiting the great seal, levying war against the Crown or adhering to enemies of the Crown (Perkins, Criminal Law 368-70 (1957)). Treason is defined in the United States Constitution as "levying war against (the United States), or in adhering to their enemies, giving them aid and comfort" (Const. Art. III, Sec. 3). This is the obvious source of the definition in the Michigan Constitution (Art. I, Sec. 22); the statute only provides the penalty (life imprisonment under C.L. 1948, Sec. 750.544). Both the Constitution and the statute preserve the so-called "two-witness rule" regulating the amount of evidence necessary to convict (see also Perkins, Criminal Law 375 (1957)). There is no recorded treason conviction in the history of the state. Misprision of treason is also a felony punishable by up to five years imprisonment (C.L. 1949, Sec. 750.545); no prosecutions appear to have been brought under this section either.

There are also three obsolete statutes, one making it a felony to incite Indian tribes to violate a treaty (C.L. 1948, Sec. 750.348), a second making it a felony to incite soldiers to desert during any war, rebellion or insurrection against the United States or Michigan (C.L. 1948, Sec. 750.405), and a third, dating from 1863, making it a misdemeanor to resist or incite resistance to a military draft (C.L. 1948, Sec. 750.407). There is no decision law on any of them.

The aftermath to World Wars I and II produced several statutes governing subversive activity of one variety or another. One reached anarchy and criminal syndicalism. Syndicalism is defined as doctrine which "advocates crime, sabotage, violence or other unlawful methods of terrorism as a means of accomplishing industrial or political reform"; this constitutes a felony (C.L. 1948, Sec. 750.46). Advocacy of criminal syndicalism or commission of acts for the purpose is punishable by a maximum term of ten years (C.L. 1948, Sec. 750.147). It is also a felony to display a red flag (C.L. 1948, Sec. 750.48). When these statutes were attacked in the 1920's and 1930's they were upheld as constitutional (People v. Immonen, 271 Mich. 384, 261 N.W. 59 (1935) (red flag statute); People v. Ruthenberg, 229 Mich. 315, 201 N.W. 358 (1924) (criminal syndicalism)).

In 1950-52 several new statutes were enacted. One is the Michigan Communist Control Law (C.L. 1948, Sec. 752.321-752.332). The other principal additions covered subversion (C.L. 1948, Sec. 750.545a), concealment of knowledge of subversion (C.L. 1948, Sec. 750.545b); joining a group formed to commit subversion (C.L. 1948, Sec. 750.545c) and facilitation of subversion by a corporation (C.L. 1948, Sec. 750.545d).

These statutes have not had a friendly reception from the courts, and are apparently totally unenforced and unenforcible. Any portion of these statutes purporting to penalize subversion against the United States is unconstitutional because Congress has occupied the field through the Smith Act and other federal legislation (Pennsylvania v. Nelson, 76 S.Ct. 477, 350 U.S. 497, 100 L.Ed. 640 (1956)). The Michigan Supreme Court followed this precedent and declared the Communist Control Law unconstitutional (Albertson v. Attorney-General, 345 Mich. 519, 77 N.W. 2d 104 (1956)).

The Draft takes the position that the only crime necessary to be preserved in this context is treason as defined in the Constitution. The pervasive federal legislation in fact offers all the protection that is needed against conspiracy to overthrow the national government, and the possibility of a conspiracy to overthrow the government of Michigan alone seems remote. In any event, the classical definition of treason is

broad enough to cover overt acts as they appear, and most if
not all of the activities that one can conceive of as being
directed against the State of Michigan are independently
criminal under other provisions of the Draft. Accordingly,
repeal of the various anti-subversion statutes is recommended.

Punishment is indicated at the Class A felony level, which
is less than the present life imprisonment but at the top level
of punishments under the Draft. In fact this has only emotional and educational importance, since there has never yet been
a case of treason against the State of Michigan

B. Riot

    1. Michigan Compiled Laws (1948)

RIOTING AND RELATED CRIMES

752.541 Riot

    Sec. 1. It is unlawful and constitutes the crime of riot
for 5 or more persons, acting in concert, to wrongfully engage in violent conduct and thereby intentionally or recklessly cause or create a serious risk of causing public
terror or alarm.

752.542 Incitement to riot

    Sec. 2. It is unlawful and constitutes incitement to riot
for a person or persons, intending to cause or to aid or a-
bet the institution or maintenance of a riot, to do an act
or engage in conduct that urges other persons to commit acts
of unlawful force or violence, or the unlawful burning or
destroying of property, or the unlawful interference with a
police officer, peace officer, fireman or a member of the
Michigan national guard or any unit of the armed services
officially assigned to riot duty in the lawful performance
of his duty.

752.543 Unlawful assembly

    Sec. 3. It is unlawful and constitutes an unlawful as-
sembly for a person to assemble or act in concert with 4 or
more persons for the purpose of engaging in conduct constituting the crime of riot, or to be present at an assembly
that either has or develops such a purpose and to remain
thereat with intent to advance such purpose.

752.544 Felony; penalty

    Sec. 4. (1) A violation of sections 1 or 2[1] is a felony,
punishable by not more than 10 years in prison or a fine of
not more than $10,000.00, or both.

    (2) A violation of section 3[2] is a felony, punishable by
not more than 5 years in prison or a fine of not more than

$5,000, or both.

1. Sections 752.541, 752.542

2. Section 752.543

750.523 Same refusal to aid officer

Sec. 523. REFUSAL TO AID OFFICER TO DISPERSE OR ARREST RIOTERS - If any person present, being commanded by any of the magistrates or officers aforesaid, to aid and assist in seizing and securing such rioters, or persons so unlawfully assembled, or in suppressing such riot, or unlawful assembly, shall refuse or neglect to obey such command, or when required by any such magistrate or officer to depart from the place of such riotous or unlawful assembly, shall refuse or neglect so to do, he shall be deemed to be 1 of the rioters or persons unlawfully assembled, and shall be liable to be prosecuted and punished accordingly.

750.524 Same; neglect of officers to suppress

Sec. 524. NEGLECT OF OFFICERS TO SUPPRESS UNLAWFUL ASSEM-BLIES - Any mayor, alderman, supervisor, president, trustee or member of a common council, justice of the peace, sheriff or deputy sheriff, having notice of any such riotous or tu-multuous and unlawful assembly as is mentioned in this chapter, in the township, city or village in which he lives, who shall neglect or refuse immediately to proceed to the place of such assembly, or as near thereto as he can with safety, or shall omit or neglect to exercise the authority with which he is in-vested by this chapter, for suppressing such riotous or un-lawful assembly, and for arresting and securing the offenders, shall be guilty of a misdemeanor, punishable by imprisonment in the county jail not more than 6 months or a fine of not more than 250 dollars.

750.525 Same; use of force to quell

Sec. 525. USE OF FORCE TO QUELL UNLAWFUL ASSEMBLIES - If any persons, who shall be so riotously or unlawfully assembled, and who shall have been commanded to disperse, as before pro-vided, shall refuse or neglect to disperse, without unneces-sary delay, any 2 of the magistrates or officers before men-tioned may require the aid of a sufficient number of persons, in arms or otherwise, as may be necessary, and shall proceed in such manner as in their judgment shall be expedient, forth-with to disperse and suppress such unlawful, riotous or tu-multuous assembly, and seize and secure the persons composing the same, so that they may be proceeded with according to law.

750.526 Same; armed force in dispersing to execute order of certain officials

Sec. 526 CONTROL OF ARMED FORCE - Whenever an armed force shall be called out in the manner provided by law for the purpose of suppressing any tumult or riot, or to disperse any body of men acting together by force, and with intent to commit any felony, or to offer violence to persons or property, or with intent, by force or violence, to resist or oppose the execution of the laws of this state, such armed force, when they shall arrive at the place of such unlawful, riotous or tumultuous assembly, shall obey such orders for suppressing the riot or tumult, and for dispersing and arresting all persons who are committing any of the said offenses, as they may have received from the governor, or from any judge of a court of record, or the sheriff of the county, any chief of police or his duly authorized representative, or any member of the Michigan state police, and also such further orders as they shall there receive from any 2 of the magistrates or officers mentioned in the first section of this chapter.

750.527 Same; death ensuing from efforts to disperse

Sec. 527. DEATH ENSUING FROM EFFORTS TO DISPERSE UNLAWFUL ASSEMBLIES OR RIOTS - If, by reason of any of the efforts made by any 2 or more of the said magistrates or officers, or by their direction, to disperse such unlawful, riotous or tumultuous assembly, or to seize and secure the persons composing the same, who have refused to disperse though the number remaining may be less than 12, any such person, or any other person there present as spectators or otherwise, shall be killed or wounded, the said magistrates and officers and all persons assisting by their order, or under their direction, shall be held guiltless and fully justified in law; and if any of the said magistrates or officers, or any person acting by their order, or under their direction, shall be killed or wounded, all the persons so unlawfully, riotously or tumultuously assembled, and all other persons who, when commanded or required, shall have refused to aid or assist the said magistrates or officers, shall be held answerable therefor.

750.528 Same; destroying dwelling house or other property

Sec. 528. RIOTOUSLY DESTROYING DWELLING HOUSE OR OTHER PROPERTY - Any of the persons so unlawfully assembled, who shall demolish, pull down, destroy or injure, or who shall begin to demolish, pull down, destroy or injure any dwelling house or any other building, or any ship or vessel, shall be guilty of a felony, and shall be answerable to any person injured, to the full amount of the damage, in an action of trespass.

EMERGENCY POWERS OF GOVERNOR

10.31 Governor may proclaim state of emergency; orders, rules

Sec. 1. During times of great public crisis, disaster,

rioting, catastrophe, or similar public emergency within the state, or reasonable apprehension of immediate danger thereof, when public safety is imperiled, either upon application of the mayor of a city, sheriff of a county, the commissioner of the Michigan state police, or upon his own volition, the governor may proclaim a state of emergency and designate the area involved. Following such proclamation or declaration, the governor may promulgate such reasonable orders, rules and regulations as he deems necessary to protect life and property, or to bring the emergency situation within the affected area under control. Without limiting the scope of the same, said orders, rules and regulations may provide for the control of traffic, including public and private transportation, within the area of any section thereof; designation of specific zones within the area in which occupancy and use of buildings and ingress and egress of persons and vehicles may be prohibited or regulated; control of places of amusement and assembly, and of persons on public streets and thoroughfares; establishment of a curfew; control of the sale, transportation and use of alcoholic beverages and liquors; control of the possession, sale, carrying and use of firearms, other dangerous weapons, and ammunition; and control of the storage, use, and transportation of explosives or inflammable materials or liquids deemed to be dangerous to public safety. Such orders, rules and regulations shall be effective from the date and in the manner prescribed in such orders, rules and regulations and shall be made public as provided therein. Such orders, rules and regulations may be amended, modified, or rescinded, in like manner, from time to time by the governor during the pendency of the emergency, but shall cease to be in effect upon declaration by the governor that the emergency no longer exists.

10.32 Construction of act

Sec. 2. It is hereby declared to be the legislative intent to invest the governor with sufficiently broad power of action in the exercise of the police power of the state to provide adequate control over persons and conditions during such periods of impending or actual public crisis or disaster. The provisions of this act shall be broadly construed to effectuate this purpose.

10.33 Misdemeanor

Sec. 3. The violation of any such orders, rules and regulations made in conformity with this act shall be punishable as a misdemeanor, where such order, rule or regulation states that the violation thereof shall constitute a misdemeanor.

2. Statutory Construction

Note

There are no Michigan Supreme Court decisions construing the aforesaid statutes. - Ed.

3. Final Draft - Michigan Revised Criminal Code

Note

C.L. 1948, Sec. 750.521 and 750.522, referred to in the Committee Commentary to the Mich. Rev. Crim. Code provisions hereinafter set forth, were repealed by the Michigan legislature in 1968 and replaced by C.L. 1948, Sec. 752.541, 752.542, 752.543, and 752.544, supra, pages

(Riot)

Sec. 5510. (1) A person commits the crime of riot if, with 5 or more other persons, he wrongfully engages in tumultuous and violent conduct and thereby intentionally or recklessly causes or creates a grave risk of causing public terror or alarm.

Committee Commentary

The section is based on New York Revised Penal Law, Sec. 240.05.

Under the traditional criminal law, a riot "is a tumultuous disturbance of the peace by three or more persons acting together (a) in the commission of a crime by open force, or (b) in the execution of some enterprise, lawful or unlawful, in such a violent, turbulent and unauthorized manner as to create likelihood of public terror and alarm" (Perkins, Criminal Law 346 (1957)).

The Michigan riot statutes, which date back to 1846, incorporate the common law tradition by referring to an "unlawful, riotous or tumultuous" assembly, though on the pattern of the English Riot Act of 1714 they vary the traditional number of a minimum of three rioters to twelve or more persons if they are armed with clubs or other dangerous weapons, or otherwise a minimum of thirty persons (C.L. 1948, Sec. 750. 521). The statutes are primarily of procedural significance. The section mentioned above authorizes municipal authorities and police who are on duty at the time to order the rioters to disperse; this is functionally equivalent to the British procedure of "reading the riot act" (Perkins, Criminal Law 348-49 (1957)). If the rioters do not disperse they may be immediately arrested and proceeded against (C.L. 1948, Sec. 750.522). The officers may require bystanders to assist in dispersing the mob; if they later refuse they are legally to be treated as rioters (C.L. 1948, Sec. 750.523). If the rioters do not disperse, whatever force that in the judgment of the officials is "expedient" may be used to quell the riot (C.L. 1948, Sec. 750. 525); any armed force that appears is to be under the

control of local officials and police (C.L. 1948, Sec. 750.526).
If the officers cause someone's death in quelling the disturbance they are to be "guiltless"; if one of those repressing the riot is killed, all the rioters "shall be held answerable therefore" (C.L. 1948, Sec. 750.527). To destroy a dwelling house or other property in the course of a riot is a felony (C.L. 1948, Sec. 750.528).

There is no modern case law interpreting these provisions. The older decisions all dealt with riot as creating a special situation of self-defense when the defendant had killed a member of a mob (People v. Curtis, 52 Mich. 616, 18 N.W. 385 (1884); Patten v. People, 18 Mich. 314 (1869); Pond v. People, 8 Mich. 150 (1860)).

The Governor also is empowered to proclaim a state of emergency in "times of great public crises, disaster, rioting, catastrophe or similar public emergency within the state . . . when public safety is imperiled" (C.L. 1948, Sec. 10.31); violation of any orders, rules or regulations promulgated by the Governor under those circumstances is a misdemeanor (C.L. 1948, Sec. 10.33).

The Draft restates the common-law test for riot. It does not retain the minimum munber of three persons, but picks as an appropriate number five persons. Punishment for the crime is indicated at the lowest felony level.

(Unlawful Assembly)

Sec. 5515. (1) A person commits the crime of unlawful assembly if he assembles with 5 or more other persons for the purpose of engaging in conduct constituting the crime of riot or if, being present at an assembly that either has or develops such a purpose, he remains there with intent to advance that purpose.
(2) Unlawful assembly is a Class A misdemeanor.

Committee Commentary

The section is adapted from New York Revised Penal Law, Sec. 240.10.

At the common law, persons moving to carry out their design of riot committed a misdemeanor called rout (Perkins, Criminal Law 345-46 (1957)); the unlawful assembly in preparation for rout was also punishable under that designation (Perkins, Criminal Law 344-45 (1957)). The sequence of crimes thus was unlawful assembly, rout and riot; the earlier crimes merged into the later as the transaction progressed.

This tradition is also incorporated by reference into the statutes described in the Commentary to Sec. 5505 through the term "tumultuously assembled" (C.L. 1948, Sec. 750.521); the catchline uses the traditional term "unlawful assemblies." There are no Michigan cases in point.

Section 5515 is intended to reach those who have assembled for the purpose of rioting or who are on their way to the scene of a riot, but who have not yet begun to riot, or who associate with a group of known potential rioters with intent to aid their cause. It thus comprises both unlawful assembly and rout at the common law, and constitutes in effect as expanded concept of attempted riot. Punishment is indicated at the Class A misdemeanor level.

(Failure of Disorderly Persons to Disperse)

Sec. 5520. (1) A person commits the crime of failure as a disorderly person to disperse if he participates with 5 or more persons in a course of disorderly conduct likely to cause substantial harm or serious inconvenience, annoyance or alarm, and intentionally refuses or fails to disperse when ordered to do so by a peace officer or other public servant engaged in executing or enforcing the law.

(2) Failure of disorderly persons to disperse is a Class B misdemeanor.

Committee Commentary

The section is adapted from Model Penal Code Sec. 250.1 (2).

As indicated in the Commentary to Sec. 5510, a special statute (1 Geo. I, Stat. 2, c. 5 (1714)) made it a capital felony if a riotous group of twelve or more persons failed to disperse within an hour after a magistrate read the statute to them (Perkins, Criminal Law 348-49 (1957)). This statute is too recent to be a part of the common law, but it is the obvious pattern for the 1846 Michigan statute (C.L. 1948, Sec. 750.521 et seq.).

Section 5520 endeavors to establish an interim offense between the unlawful assembly and riot concepts and ordinary disorderly conduct under Sec. 5525. There must be a group of at least five persons who are in a state of disorderly conduct likely to cause substantial harm or serious inconvenience, annoyance or alarm. This in itself suggests an aggravated form of disorderly conduct. Moreover, the group members must deliberately refuse or fail to disperse when they are ordered to do so by an official lawfully engaged in law enforcement. Both elements must be proven. Because this conduct is less serious than unlawful assembly but more serious than ordinary disorderly conduct, punishment is indicated at the level of a Class B misdemeanor.

Under the Constitution (Art. I, Sec. 3), the people have the right peaceably to assemble. A disorderly assemblage is obviously not at the same time a "peaceable" assembly, and thus is not within the area of constitutional protection.

C. Disorderly Conduct

1. Michigan Compiled Laws (1948)

1397

CHAPTER XXVIII. DISORDERLY PERSONS

750.167 Definition, subsequent offenses

Sec. 167. Any person of sufficient ability, who shall refuse or neglect to support his family; any common prostitute; any window peeper; any person who engages in an illegal occupation or business; any person who shall be drunk or intoxicated or engaged in any indecent or obscene conduct in any public place; any vagrant; any person found begging in a public place; any person found loitering in a house of ill-fame or prostitution or place where prostitution or lewdness is practiced, encouraged or allowed; any person who shall knowingly loiter in or about any place where an illegal occupation or business is being conducted; any person who shall loiter in or about any police station, police headquarters building, county jail, hospital, court building or any other public building or place for the purpose of soliciting employment of legal services or the services of sureties upon criminal recognizances; any person who shall be found jostling or roughly crowding people unnecessarily in a public place; any person who telephones any other person or causes any other person to be telephoned and uses any vulgar, indecent, obscene, threatening or offensive language, or suggesting any lewd or lascivious act over any telephone, shall be deemed a disorderly person. When any person, who has been convicted of refusing or neglecting to support his family under the provisions of this section, is then charged with subsequent violations within a period of 2 years, such person shall be prosecuted as a second offender or third and subsequent offender as provided in section 168 of this act, if the family of such person is then receiving any form of public relief or support.

750.167a Person hunting with firearms while drunk or intoxicated deemed disorderly person; confiscation of weapon; may not apply for license for period of 3 years

Sec. 167a. Any person who shall be drunk or intoxicated while hunting with a firearm or other weapon under a valid hunting license shall be deemed to be a disorderly person. Upon conviction of such person, the weapon shall be confiscated and shall be delivered to the department of conservation for disposition in the same manner as weapons confiscated for other violations of the game laws. Upon conviction of the offense set forth herein the person so convicted, in addition to any punishment imposed pursuant to section 168, and as a part of any sentence imposed on him, shall be forbidden to apply for or possess a hunting license for a period of 3 years following the date of conviction, and violation of the conditions of such sentence shall be deemed to be a misdemeanor.

750.168 Punishment

Sec. 168. Any person convicted of being a disorderly person shall be guilty of a misdemeanor.

CHAPTER XXIX. DISTURBING MEETINGS

750.169 Disturbance of religious meetings

Sec. 169. DISTURBANCE OF RELIGIOUS MEETINGS - Any person who, on the first day of the week, or at any other time, shall wilfully interrupt or disturb any assembly of people met for the worship of God, within the place of such meeting or out of it, shall be guilty of a misdemeanor.

750.170 Disturbance of lawful meetings

Sec. 170. DISTURBANCE OF LAWFUL MEETINGS - Any person who shall make or excite any disturbance or contention in any tavern, store or grocery, manufacturing establishment or any other business place or in any street, lane, alley, highway, public building, grounds or park, or at any election or other public meeting where citizens are peaceably and lawfully assembled, shall be guilty of a misdemeanor.

750.103 Cursing and swearing

Sec. 103. CURSING AND SWEARING - Any person who has arrived at the age of discretion, who shall profanely curse or damn or swear by the name of God, Jesus Christ or the Holy Ghost, shall be guilty of a misdemeanor. No such prosecution shall be sustained unless it shall be commenced within 5 days after the commission of such offense.

750.337 Women or children, improper language in presence

Sec. 337. INDECENT, ETC., LANGUAGE IN PRESENCE OF WOMEN OR CHILDREN - Any person who shall use any indecent, immoral, obscene, vulgar or insulting language in the presence or hearing of any woman or child shall be guilty of a misdemeanor.

2. Case Law

People v. O'Keefe
218 Mich. 1

SHARPE, J. The defendant was convicted and sentenced under section 15483, 3 Comp. Laws 1915. The complaint charged that he -

"was guilty of disorderly conduct, for that the said defendant then and there was making and assisting in making a noise, disturbance and improper diversion by which the peace and good order of the neighborhood was disturbed."

The only witness sworn was Police Officer Roche. He testified that while near the corner of Griswold street and Michigan avenue in Detroit he noticed the defendant and another man

1399

among a number of people standing in the safety zone waiting
to board a street car; that they "seemed to be moving around;"
that as the car stopped they -

"began to push and jostle unnecessarily, and at that time I
ran from the sidewalk out to where they were;"

that they each had a light overcoat on their arms. Over objection of defendant's counsel, he was permitted to indicate
how they apparently jostled one person, the inference being
that they were getting ready to pick his pocket. He attempted to arrest both of them, but the man other than the defendant broke away and fled and was not afterwards apprehended.

The court charged the jury that there was no evidence of
any noise having been made, that they must confine their deliberations to "disturbance and improper diversion." . . .

We do not think the elements necessary to establish an offense under this statute were proven.

The statute has long been on our books. It reads, in part,
as follows:

"If any person shall make or excite any disturbance or contention in any . . . street, . . . he shall be deemed guilty
of a misdemeanor."

As first enacted, the limit of punishment was 10 days.
This has, by amendment, been increased to 90 days. In the
langugage of the statute, there must be a "disturbance or contention." It does not appear that any person other than the
officer was "disturbed" or that there was any "contention"
until he sought to make the arrest. It seems clear to us
that the offense charged was not proven and that defendant's
motion for a directed verdict of "not guilty" should have
been granted. . . .

The conviction and sentence are set aside and the defendant discharged.

The late Justice STONE took no part in this decision.

People v. Kelly
99 Mich. 82

GRANT, J. 1. It is first contended that Act No. 264,
Laws of 1889, is in conflict with section 20 of article 4
of the Constitution, in that it embraces more than one object.
The act is entitled -

"An act relative to disorderly persons, and to repeal
chapter 53 of the Compiled Laws of 1871, as amended by the
several acts amendatory thereof."

Section 2 of the act provides that -

"Any person complained of as being a disorderly person,
and who shall be convicted or shall plead guilty, shall be

1400

punished by a fine not exceeding $50 and costs of prosecution, or by imprisonment in the county jail or the Detroit House of Correction not exceeding 30 days, or he may be required to enter into a recognizance with sufficient sureties for his good behavior for the term of three months. Any person who shall be convicted a second time of being a disorderly person, the offense being charged as a second offense, shall be punished by a fine not exceeding $100 and costs of prosecution, or by imprisonment in the county jail or the Detroit House of Correction not less than 30 days nor more than three months; and for a third and all subsequent convictions, the offense being charged as a third or subsequent conviction, the punishment shall be a fine not exceeding $100 and costs of prosecution, or imprisonment in the county jail or the Detoit House of Correction or the State House of Correction and Reformatory at Ionia not less than six months nor more than two years."

Section 1 enumerates those who come under the term "disorderly persons." Among these are drunkards and tipplers. The precise contention is that the title gives no information as to what acts constitute a disorderly person, and that the third offense, of which the respondent was found guilty, is not expressed therein. The title to this act is the same as the titles to other acts for the punishment of disorderly persons, which have been, from time to time, enacted by the Legislature, and the sections of those acts defining who are disorderly persons have been substantially the same. The term "disorderly persons" is comprehensive, and properly includes all those who are designated in the body of the act. It is within the purview of the title to include different degrees of punishment for first, second, and subsequent convictions. The crime does not consist in the fact of two or more convictions, but in the fact that the respondent has been convicted as a disorderly person for the second or more times. Upon such subsequent trial, he must be found guilty of being a disorderly person; and, in order to impose the heavier punishment, former convictions must be proven. This objection to the law is not well founded. . . .

Judgment affirmed.

The other Justices concurred.

People v. Bartz
53 Mich. 493

CHAMPLIN, J. Respondent was convicted in the Recorder's court of the city of Detroit of knowingly and willfully assaulting Frank Lewis, a member of the Metropolitan Police department, by discharging at and towards him a revolver loaded with cartridge and ball. It was charged that on the 22d day of December, 1883, respondent broke the public peace in the

city of Detroit by wantonly discharging a revolver in one of
the public streets, in the presence and hearing of Policeman
Lewis, who, deeming it necessary as a means of preserving the
public peace, and as a means of preventing a further breach
thereof on the part of respondent, arrested and took him in
custody, and while on the way to the station the respondent
committed the assault for which he was convicted. The record shows that the jury must have found the fact that the
respondent, about eleven o'clock at night, wantonly discharged his revolver while in the public street, at the corner of
Michigan Grand avenue and Randolph street. The officer who
made the arrest was standing on the opposite side of the avenue, and saw the flash and heard the report and saw the respondent and another man start and run up Randolph street to (Fort
and across to) Brush street. The officer pursued and arrested respondent at this point. He had not been out of sight of
the officer from the time he fired the shot until he overtook
and arrested him. The verdict of the jury is conclusive upon
the facts that respondent wantonly discharged his revolver in
the public street, and that he willfully committed the assault
upon the officer while in his custody and under arrest for the
offense. Two questions only are presented for our determination: First, Was it a breach of the public peace to wantonly
discharge a revolver at the place named in the information
under the circumstances shown by the evidence? Second, Was
the offense committed in the presence of the officer so as to
authorize him to arrest respondent without written warrant
from a magistrate?

It was said in Galvin v. State 6 Cold. (Tenn.) 294, that
"a breach of the peace is 'a violation of public order, the
offense of disturbing the public peace. An act of public in-
decorum is also a breach of the peace.'" The term "breach
of the peace" is generic, and includes riotous and unlawful
assemblies, riots, affrays, forcible entry and detainer, the
wanton discharge of firearms so near the chamber of a sick
person as to cause injury, the sending of challenges and provoking to fight, going armed in public without lawful occasion,
in such manner as to alarm the public, and many other acts of
a similar character. The wanton discharge of firearms in the
public streets of a city is well calculated to alarm the public and cause them to be apprehensive of individual safety;
and I think the Recorder was entirely correct when he instructed the jury that such act constituted a breach of the peace.

Was the offense committed in the presence of the officer?
If it was, he was authorized to make the arrest without a warrant. I think it was committed in his presence. The distance
was the width of the avenue. He was in sight of the person
discharging the pistol, and did not lose sight of him while
pursuing to make the arrest. Had the shooting occurred in the
daytime, no such question would be raised. A person's presence does not depend upon whether he can be distinctly seen
or discerned by another. An assemblage of persons in a room
lighted with gas do not cease to be present when the gas is

1402

turned off and they are left in total darkness. The presence
of the officer in this case was so apparent to respondent that
he deemed it prudent to absent himself as soon as he discharged
the revolver. The court instructed the jury, as matter of law,
that when a pistol is fired off in the way the testimony tended to show this was, so the officer could see the flash of the
pistol and hear the shot, and the person who fired the shot
would have been in sight if it had been light so he could have
seen him, it was sufficiently in his presence in the meaning of
the law. I think the charge was correct. If the person discharging the pistol had committed a homicide, and the officer
had started for a magistrate to obtain a warrant, instead of
immediately arresting him, and the offender had escaped, the
officer would have justly been considered reprehensible for
gross dereliction of duty.

The exceptions are overruled, and the Recorder advised to
proceed to judgment.

COOLEY, C. J. and SHERWOOD, J. concurred.

(Concurring opinion of Justice CAMPBELL is omitted.)

People v. Johnson
86 Mich. 175

CHAMPLIN, C. J. Main street, in the village of Naubinway,
Mackinac county, runs east and west. A street runs north from
Main street, upon which is located the house of one Bruce. Between 9 and 10 o'clock of the 28th day of December, 1890, as
the respondent, John Johnson, and one McAlister were walking
along Main street, Johnson "shouted" or "whooped" in a loud
voice twice. The shout was heard by Frank Murry, who was marshall of the village, and who was at the time standing upon
the door-step of Mr. Bruce's house. He started towards Main
street and proceeded down that street until he came to Johnson
and McAlister, and asked, "Who done that hollering?" and Mc-
Alister replied that it was Johnson, and he then arrested him
for it, and attempted to take him to the jail or lock-up. Johnson resisted, and Murry used his club, and sent for Deputy-Sheriff Lull, whereupon they handcuffed Johnson, and dragged him to
the jail. It is not necessary in this action to describe or
comment upon the conduct of Murry while taking his prisoner to
the jail, and after they arrived there.

The prosecuting attorney filed an information against Johnson for resisting the officer, Frank Murry, -

"While in the lawful execution of the duties of his office
in attempting to arrest him, the said John Johnson, for then
and there being drunk, intoxicated, disorderly, and yelling,
and disturbing the public peace, in the public streets of the
village of Naubinway, in the presence of him, the said Frank
Murry, he, the said Frank Murry, being then and there engaged

1403

in his lawful attempts to maintain, preserve, and keep the peace," etc.

Upon trial Johnson was convicted. There was a conflict of testimony as to what occurred at the time of the arrest, but in the rulings here made we have taken the testimony of the people as that upon which the conviction must stand if it can be supported. By Murry's testimony he was over 150 feet away, and upon another street, when he heard the shout. There is no testimony showing that he was in sight of Johnson and McAlister, nor that he knew who it was who shouted, but he based his arrest upon the statement of McAlister that it was Johnson. There was not any riot, noise, or disturbance when he reached them. No other persons are shown to have been upon Main street when Murry first accosted Johnson and McAlister. He had no warrant for the arrest of either Johnson or McAlister.

Under the facts above stated two questions are raised:

1. Did Johnson, by the act of "shouting" or "whooping" in the public street of the village when on his way home, accompanied by McAlister, at the time of night stated, commit a breach of the peace?

2. If yes, was the offense committed in the presence of the officer, Murry?

1. We have had occasion to define the substance and nature of this offense in the following cases: Quinn v. Heisel, 40 Mich. 576; Way's Case, 41 Id. 299; People v. Bartz, 53 Id. 495; Davis v. Burgess, 54 Id. 514; Robinson v. Miner, 68 Id. 549; Ware v. Circuit Judge, 75 Id. 492. In general terms the offense is a violation of public order, a disturbance of the public tranquillity, by any act or conduct inciting to violence, or tending to provoke or excite others to break the peace. Each case where the offense is charged must depend upon the time, place, and circumstances of the act.

The circuit judge instructed the jury that –

"To be intoxicated and yelling on the public streets of a village, in such a manner as to disturb the good order and tranquillity of that village, would be an act of open violence, and would be a breach of the peace, which, if committed in the presence of an officer, would justify him in making the arrest."

This was a correct statement of the law, and was applicable, under the testimony in this case. Hawley, Arrest, p. 38; Moseley v. State (Tex.), 4 S.W. Rep. 907; State v. Lafferty, 5 Har. (Del.) 491; Bryan v. Bates, 15 Ill. 87; State v. Freeman, 86 N.C. 683; City Council v. Payne, 2 Nott & McC. 475; State v. Bowen, 17 S.C. 58.

2. Was the offense committed in the presence of the officer, Murry, so as to authorize him to make the arrest without a warrant? To restate the facts: Johnson was not in the view of the officer. He did not know who it was that raised the shout. He arrived at the place after the occurrence, and inquired, "Who done that hollering?" and was told by McAlister that it was

Johnson, and he then arrested him. At that time Johnson was
not engaged in making any noise or disturbance. At the time
the officer heard the shout he was over 150 feet away, upon
another street. It was not in his presence, and when he arrived there was perfect tranquillity. To authorize an arrest
without a warrant, the offense must be committed in the presence
of the officer, and the arrest must be made immediately. The
officer did not act upon his own knowledge, but upon information he had gained by inquiries from McAlister. If he could
make the arrest under such circumstances without a warrant,
then there is no reason why he could not have made it the next
day, or a week after, upon inquiry and information that Johnson was the person whom he heard shouting.

People v. Bartz, 53 Mich. 493, is cited as supporting the
proposition that the offense was committed in the presence of
of Murry. The facts in that case were different from the facts
in this. In that case the officer who made the arrest saw the
flash made when the pistol was discharged, heard the report,
and saw the respondent, Bartz, and pursued and arrested him.
Bartz had not been out of sight of the officer from the time
he discharged the pistol until the officer overtook and arrested him.

It is claimed by counsel for the people that Johnson, being
intoxicated in a public street, was liable to be arrested
therefor without warrant, under Act No. 4, Laws of 1887 (3 How.
Stat. But this position is one taken in this Court for the
first time. The case was tried below upon the charge and theory
that Murry made the arrest for a breach of the peace. The officer made the arrest for that offense, as is apparent from his
inquiry of Mr. McAlister. He did not inform Johnson that he
arrested him for being intoxicated, and does not testify that
he was intoxicated. McAlister is the only one who testified
that Johnson was intoxicated, and that he was taking him home.
The judge put the case to the jury upon the theory that the
arrest was made for committing a breach of the peace, and the
people will not be permitted, after trial and conviction of
respondent upon that theory, to change ground, and claim that
he was arrested for being intoxicated under the act cited.

The conviction must be set aside, and the prisoner discharged.

The other Justices concurred.

Davis v. Burgess
54 Mich. 514

SHERWOOD, J. This is an action of trespass for assault and
battery and false imprisonment. The plaintiff was a private
citizen, and the defendant, at the time of the arrest complained
of, was a policeman in the city of Detroit. On the 31st of
August, 1882, the defendant claims he went into a pawnbroker's
shop in Detroit to assist a young man in obtaining a watch he

had left in pawn there; he saw the plaintiff, who was acting
as clerk for the pawnbroker, Mr. Van Baalen, at the time, and
Davis ordered him out of the shop, using profane and indecent
language towards him as he left. The next day, about noon,
Davis found Burgess upon the street, and told him there was a
gentleman at the pawnbroker's shop who wished to see him. Burgess went there in company with another officer, and while
there Davis asked Burgess for his name and his number, which
was given, and thereupon Davis called the defendant almost
everything indecent, saying he would have his buttons off of
him, etc., and would make complaint against him. Davis' language was very indecent and profane. This was while they were
in the shop. Defendant did nothing but walked out of the shop
and across the street, and then started for a street car. Davis
followed him, continuing his profanity and abuse, calling the
defendant a son of a bitch, and other mean names, and by so
doing gathered a crowd around them upon the street, and then
he went into his store. Defendant told him that such language
should not be used upon the public street, and was about to
enter the car when Davis again came upon the street, and standing upon the sidewalk, renewed his vile and profane attack upon defendant, who was then going across the street, hailed him
and again assailed him with vulgar, profane and indecent language in the presence of citizens, among whom were ladies, passing along the street. Burgess went to the plaintiff and asked
him for his name, which he refused to give saying to defendant,
"If you lay your hand upon me I'll shoot you," calling him at
the same time a vile name. Defendant thereupon arrested the
plaintiff, took him to the city attorney's office and made complaint against him under the city ordinance, which provides
that "no person shall be guilty of using indecent or immoral
language, nor be guilty of any indecent or immoral conduct or
behavior on any public street, lane, alley, square, park, or
space in said city," the penalty being fine or imprisonment.
The city attorney took the complaint but for some reason failed
to prosecute it. Davis was discharged. This is the defendant's
statement of the facts, and he claims that if found true by the
jury they constitute a perfect defense to the plaintiff's action.

The defendant was sworn in his own behalf, and upon most of
the material facts stated by him he was contradicted by the
plaintiff, whose version of the matter presents an entirely different case; but with this we have little to do.

The court having charged the jury, in substance, that the
only question for them to consider was that of damages, it is
only needful for us to review the case as presented on the part
of the defendant, and if, from his showing, he was not justified,
the verdict must stand.

There seems to be no question that the official position of
the defendant in the city of Detroit, at the time the arrest was
made, constituted him a conservator of the peace. The arrest
was made without warrant. At the time it was made (mid-day)
the plaintiff was on the sidewalk, where citizens, men and women,

1406

were constantly passing and repassing, and there, in a loud, boisterous manner, he called the defendant a "God damned son of a bitch," and continued to use other indecent language. When defendant asked for his name he refused to give it to the officer, and threatened to kill him if he laid his hands on him. Only a few minutes before, the plaintiff had used the same and other profane language towards the defendant in the presence of a crowd upon the street.

There is no question about the officer's right to arrest for a breach of the peace committed in his presence without process. Did the language and conduct of the plaintiff on that occasion amount to a breach of the peace? The answer to this question must necessarily determine the decision in this case. The offense, whatever its character, was committed in the presence of the officers in the public street in a city, in the presence of citizens. The language used was not only vile and profane, but forbidden under penalties both by the by-laws of the city and the statutes of our State. It was against decency and public morals, of the most aggravating character, well calculated to arouse the passions and induce personal violence which was threatened if the officer laid hands upon the offender.

Now, what is understood by "a breach of the peace?" By "peace," as used in the law in this connection, is meant the tranquillity enjoyed by the citizens of a municipality of community where good order reigns among its members. It is the natural right of all persons in political society, and any intentional violation of that right is "a breach of the peace." It is the offense of disturbing the public peace, or a violation of public order or public decorum. Actual personal violence is not an essential element in the offense. If it were, communities might be kept in a constant state of turmoil, fear and anticipated danger from the wicked language and conduct of a guilty party, not only destructive of the peace of the citizens but of public morals, without the commission of the offense. The good sense and morality of the law forbid such a construction. I think the language and conduct of Davis in this case, as it appears on the record, shows him guilty of a breach of the peace, and in the act of committing it at the time he was arrested. The court should have submitted the defendant's case, as he made it, to the jury under proper instructions, to ascertain the truth of the facts as stated by him and his witnesses. This the court did not do, and the failure was error.

The case of Quinn v. Heisel 40 Mich. 576, cited by counsel for plaintiff, is not in point. In that case the officer who was sued for making the arrest, as the plaintiff's testimony tended to show, made it after the offense had occurred, and the testimony was submitted to the jury under a proper charge, who found for the plaintiff. Neither do I see anything in Sarah Way's Case 41 Mich. 299, necessarily conflicting with the views here expressed.

It can make no difference that the officer was made the

subject of the offender's wrong acts and conduct on the occasion. Officers are entitled to the same protection as other
persons. It was the offense against the public which the people could punish, and the officer only acted for them in making the arrest. He had no personal interest in the matter. If
the people failed to prosecute further, it was not the officer's
fault; and if the plaintiff was guilty of the offense for which
he was arrested, he cannot have suffered from the failure to
prosecute. I think the judgment at the circuit should be
REVERSED, and a new trial granted.

COOLEY, C. J. and CHAMPLIN, J. concurred.

CAMPBELL, J. I am not satisfied that the case was not properly presented to the jury.

Note

In Robinson v. Miner and Haug, 68 Mich. 549, 572., with
respect to breaches of the peace and arrest therefor, Justice
CAMPBELL in the opinion of the court commented as follows:

"I never have understood that actual violence was necessary
to constitute a breach of the peace, but that any means used
causing disquiet, disorder, and threatening danger and disaster
to the community is equally sufficient to constitute the offense; and it may be questioned both upon reason and authority
whether, in criminal cases arising to the grade of breach of
the peace, due process of law ever required that process should
issue before making the arrest of the peace-breacker."

3. Final Draft - Michigan Revised Criminal Code

(Disorderly Conduct)

Sec. 5525. (1) A person commits the crime of disorderly
conduct if, with intent to cause public inconvenience, annoyance or alarm, or recklessly creating a risk thereof, he:

(a) Engages in fighting or in violent, tumultuous
or threatening behavior; or
(b) Makes unreasonable noise; or
(c) In a public place uses abusive or obscene language,
or makes an obscene gesture; or
(d) Without lawful authority, disturbs any lawful assembly or meeting of persons; or
(e) Obstructs vehicular or pedestrian traffic; or
(f) Congregates with other persons in a public place
and refuses to comply with a lawful order of the police to
disperse; or
(g) Creates a hazardous or physically offensive con-

1408

dition by any act that serves no legitimate purpose.

(2) Disorderly conduct is a Class C misdemeanor.

Committee Commentary

The section is taken from New York Revised Penal Law, Sec. 240.20.

At common law, "any wilful deed committed without lawful justification or excuse, which unreasonably disturbed the public peace and tranquility, or tended strongly to cause such a disturbance" constituted the misdemeanor of "breach of the peace" (Perkins, Criminal Law 341 (1957)). This tradition is apparently still part of Michigan criminal law, though it has largely been superseded by specific statutes.

Before something can be a breach of the peace at common law, there must be some sort of violent conduct (Robinson v. Milner, 68 Mich. 549, 37 N.W. 21 (1888)) that disturbs the public (People v. O'Keefe, 218 Mich. 1, 187 N.W. 282 (1922)). Robinson therefore held a liquor law violation not to constitute a breach of the peace (under the arrest statute) because there was no act of violence, and O'Keefe that a pickpocket who jostled under circumstances in which only a police officer observed him did not commit an act producing public disturbance.

However, a number of acts have been held to be breaches of the peace: discharging a firearm on a public street (People v. Bartz, 53 Mich. 493, 19 N.W. 161 (1884)); using grossly indecent, profane and abusive language toward another person on a public street and in the presence of others (Davis v. Burgess, 54 Mich. 514, 20 N.W. 540 (1884)); yelling on a public street (People v. Johnson, 86 Mich. 175, 48 N.W. 870 (1891)) and being drunk in the street (People v. Jones, 2 Mich. N.P. 194 (1871) (interpreting the "breach of the peace" provision in the arrest statute)).

Much of the coverage is now statutory. The basic disorderly conduct statute (C.L. 1948, Sec. 750.167) penalizes (a) one who persistently fails to support his dependents, (b) a common prostitute, (c) a window peeper, (d) a person who engages in an illegal occupation or business, (e) a person who is drunk or intoxicated or engaged in any indecent or obscene conduct in any public place, (f) a vagrant or baggar, (g) a person found loitering in a house of prostitution or other place where "lewdness" is practiced, (h) a person who knowingly loiters about any place where an illegal occupation or business is being conducted, (i) a person who loiters on specified public premises to solicit legal employment or the services of sureties, (j) a person who is found jostling or roughly crowding persons unnecessarily in a public place, and (k) any person who uses vulgar, indecent, obscene, threatening or offensive language, or who suggests any lewd or lascivious act over the telephone. The punishment is at the misdemeanor level, but increases if the defendant is a multiple offender (C.L. 1948, Sec. 750.168).

Other statutes penalize disturbances of meetings, including school meetings (C.L. 1948, Sec. 340.970), religious meetings

(C.L. 1948, Sec. 750.169) and any other kinds of meetings where citizens are peaceably and lawfully assembled (C.L. 1948, Sec. 750.170). The Attorney-General has ruled that a person who makes a disturbance on a residentail street which bothers persons in nearby houses violates the latter section (see (1945-46) Op's Mich. Atty. Gen. 703 (May 16, 1946)). Civil penalties may also be invoked against those who disturb religious meetings or engage in certain kinds of activity within two miles of the meeting or obstruct the highway leading to the place of worship (C.L. 1948, Sec. 752.525-752.530).

It is a misdemeanor to "wilfully blaspheme the holy name of God, by cursing or contumeliously reproaching God" (C.L. 1948, Sec. 750.102), to "profanely curse or damn or swear by the name of God, Jesus Christ or the Holy Ghost," if one "has arrived at the age of discretion" (C.L. 1948, Sec. 750.103), or to use improper language in the presence of women of children (C.L. 1948, Sec. 750.337).

The Draft preserves part of the present statute law under the label of disorderly conduct, but allocates some of the coverage to harassment and loitering. Nonsupport is covered in sec. 7040, and matters relating to prostitution and gambling in other chapters of the Draft. Vagrancy as such is not within the coverage of the Draft.

Before any of the specific conduct constitutes disorderly conduct, the actor must either intend to cause public inconvenience, annoyance or alarm, or recklessly create a risk that that will happen. The statute is not in form a strict liability offense.

Subsection (1)(a) covers the sort of public activity that is traditionally within the common-law concept of breach of the peace. The language is in the common-law form.

Subsection (b) covers the unreasonable noise that has been held to be a form of a breach of the peace and within the statute prohibiting disturbances of peaceable assemblies.

Subsection (c) preserves the prohibition against abusive or obscene language, or the making of obscene gestures, in a public place. This is a generally unfocused use of the prohibited language. Using the language with the intent to harass a particular person, and misuse of the telephone, constitute harassment under sec. 5530 and harassing communications under sec. 5535.

Subsection (d) prevents disturbance of any lawful meeting or assemblage of persons, and thus continues the present statutory coverage.

Subsection (3) covers obstruction of vehicular or pedestrian traffic. In order, however, to prevent any misuse of this provision to interfere with free speech and peaceable assembly, the definition of "obstruct" in Sec. 5501 (a) does not include a gathering of persons to hear a person speak or otherwise communicate.

Subsection (f) is in effect a possible preliminary to the crime of failure of disorderly persons to disperse under Sec.

1410

5520. A crowd about to interfere with a <u>lawful</u> arrest would
violate this subsection if its members refused to move away
at the order of the police to disperse. An order by an officer that a peaceable assembly disperse would not be a <u>law-
ful</u> order (see Const. (1963) Art. I, Sec. 2).

Subsection (g) is an <u>ejusdem generis</u> provision that covers
any action not specifically defined that creates a hazardous
or physically-offensive condition and that is not for a legitimate purpose.

Because none of the conduct in itself works irreparable harm,
penalties are indicated to be at the Class C misdemeanor level.

4. The Michigan Revised Criminal Code and Offenses Against Public Order

I.
INTRODUCTION

The purpose of this comment is to analyze Chapter 55 of
Title F of the Michigan Revised Criminal Code (Proposed Code):
Offenses Against Public Order. Specifically, this will entail the examination of the sections chosen, a discussion of
the impact of these provisions on existing statutes and case
law and the evaluation of the proposed changes. It is not the
purpose of this comment to discuss all of the provisions of
Chapter 55, many of which are self-explanatory or do not involve difficult social or legal issues. The sections that
have been chosen for discussion are section 5525 - Disorderly
Conduct; section 5520 - Failure of Disorderly Persons to Disperse; section 5515 - Unlawful Assembly; and section 5510 -
Riot.

An underlying consideration running throughout is that of
protecting the rights of free speech and assembly guaranteed
by both the Federal and Michigan Constitutions.[1] A close examination discloses the concern of the draftsmen with threats
to the abridgment of these cherished rights and the discussion
of constitutional questions will be made where relevant when
treating particular sections.

II.
DISORDERLY CONDUCT, SECTION 5525; FAILURE OF DISORDERLY PERSONS TO DISPERSE, SECTION 5520

A. The Nature of the Offense

At common law, and as continued in many statutes, breach
of the peace can be defined as any conduct "which disturbs or
tends to disturb the tranquility of the citizenry."[2] The disturbance may be the result of the conduct of the actor or the
reaction of those witnessing such conduct.[3] Thus, activity,

though carried out in a peaceful manner, which provokes or threatens violence by others would render the actor guilty of breach of the peace.

Disorderly conduct is not a common law crime. It covers much of the same territory as breach of the peace; but since it is strictly statutory in origin there is no exact or precise common definition available.[4] What constitutes the nature of the offense of disorderly conduct varies from state to state. In some states the offense is limited to that activity which disturbs or causes the disturbance of good order and tranquility and, thus, is closely analogous to common law breach of the peace. Other statutes include as disorderly conduct certain activities which do not have as their natural and probable effect a breach of the peace and, consequently, are broader in scope. Michigan's existing disorderly conduct provision[6] falls in this latter category. It is a catch-all statute, classifying as disorderly, acts ranging from failing to support one's family to being drunk in public. The case law on this statute is limited,[7] and there has been only one case of record interpreting it in a manner relevant to the Proposed Code.[8] Most of the Michigan litigation in this area has been concerned with common law breach of the peace. If the Proposed Code is adopted, some of the breach of the peace cases may be helpful in interpreting the offense of disorderly conduct, but those that are found to contravene the policies of the provision will not be of controlling importance.[9]

B. Proposed Sections 5525 and 5520

The proposed disorderly conduct provision will limit the existing statutory coverage and the common law concept of breach of the peace in two important ways. First, it eliminates from disorderly conduct those activities which, although the proper subject of criminal sanction, do not disturb or are not likely to disturb public order. Thus, only conduct violent in nature or likely to provoke violence is treated in section 5525. Second, since section 5525 (1) refers to activity undertaken "with intent to cause public inconvenience, annoyance or alarm, or recklessly creating a risk thereof,"[10] it appears to be the purpose of the draftsmen to limit disorderly conduct to situations where the conduct of the actor is disorderly, excluding from consideration the possible reaction of others to the activity. Activity which is peaceful in itself but which provokes violence in others would not appear to render the actor guilty of disorderly conduct.[11] Thus, section 5525 adopts a narrower definition than that existing at common law for breach of the peace, where one could commit the offense by exciting others to an actual or potential violent reaction.[12]

Section 5525 (1) further limits disorderly conduct to activity causing public annoyance or alarm. Apparently, it is the intent of the draftsmen to require the disturbance of more than one person before conduct will be deemed disorderly. This has the effect of eliminating most intra-family disputes from its coverage.[1]

1412

However, it is not clear whether the conduct which disturbs the public must take place on public property. Even with the broad definition of "public place" appearing in section 5501 ("place to which the public or a substantial group of persons has access") there are still some places, such as private apartments, which would not be included. However, since certain subsections of section 5525 make no reference to "public place," those subsections should be read to exclude the public property requirement. Therefore, activity carried on in a private residence which disturbs members of the public at large would come under the purview of the disorderly conduct provision.

Subsection (1) (a) contains the usual prohibition against fighting or other "violent, tumultuous or threatening behavior."[14] This provision is quite straightforward, condemning those acts which are obviously in the category of nuisance.

Subsection (1) (b) prohibits the making of "unreasonable" noise. The term "unreasonable" is well chosen. The application of this provision will depend upon the circumstances under which the challenged activity is performed. Thus, it may not be unreasonable to address an open air meeting with a loudspeaker on the occasion of a celebration of a holiday, while to carry on the same activity in the middle of the night in a residential area would be unreasonable.

Subsection (1) (c),[15] prohibiting the uttering of abusive or obscene language in public, extends the disorderly conduct provision beyond acts which cause physical harm or alarm. Such language is not considered to have enough communicative function to warrant constitutional protection.[16] Consequently, there would be no need for invoking the "clear and present danger" rule before such speech could be punished.[17] Similarly, it need not be shown that abusive or obscene language did, or would, provoke disorder, since to do so would mean that the speaker would go unpunished if an audience was unwilling or too well-behaved to react violently to such language.[18]

Subsection (1) (d)[19] continues Michigan's statutory coverage dealing with the disturbance of public meetings.[20] Such a provision is grounded on the conviction that while there is a basic constitutional right to conduct a meeting, there is no constitutional protection afforded for disturbing meetings.[21] The necessity of this provision becomes more acute when it is noted that if the police do not have the statutory authority to eject and arrest hecklers at a meeting, the only other alternative to prevent a potential breach of the peace may be to terminate the speaker's presentation. Such a result would be repugnant to our traditional notions of free speech as it would grant the power to those opposed to particular views to prevent those views from being presented at a public meeting. To allow the rights of assembly and speech to be limited by private censorship in the form of threatening and tumultuous behavior is clearly unjustifiable.[22]

Subsection (1) (e)[23] makes it unlawful to obstruct pedestrian or vehicular traffic. Lest this provision be used to violate

1413

the constitutional rights of speech and assembly, subsection 5501 (a) defines "obstruct" in such a fashion that a gathering of people to hear a speaker would not lead to the arrest of the speaker for disorderly conduct.[24] Since subsection 5501 (a) exempts _all_ gatherings to hear a speaker from the operation of the disorderly conduct provision the draftsmen have avoided a possible clash between local licensing ordinances, dealing with permits for assemblies and parades, and section 5525. Thus, even if a speaker fails to secure a permit as required by such an ordinance and proceeds to hold an open-air meeting which results in the blocking of traffic, such an activity will not render him liable for disorderly conduct. This result is desirable since it allows both the disorderly conduct provision and the licensing ordinance to stand on their separate merits. If the ordinance is a valid exercise of local police power, then the speaker should be punished for violating it. On the other hand, the state should not create the situation whereby local law enforcement agencies could use a disorderly conduct statute to enforce a licensing ordinance.[25]

Subsection (1) (f)[26] proscribes the failure to disperse upon the giving of a lawful order by the police. Such a provision is of vital importance in dealing with the situation where people assemble - for lawful or unlawful purposes - and the police fear an outbreak of violence or disorder. Since section 5525 focuses on the intent of the actor, the necessity of such a provision as subsection (1) (f) is apparent. This can best be shown by means of an example.

The problem of a potential hostile reaction by members of an audience angered by a speaker's presentation has already been mentioned. In such a situation it would be difficult to show that the speaker intended to cause a violent reaction in his audience, particularly since such reaction would be directed against himself. Does this mean that the police are powerless to prevent the disorder that may be imminent?[27] If after taking into consideration all relevant facts concerning the possibility of violent reaction it is the reasonable belief of the police that a disturbance could best be averted by stopping an inflammatory speaker, then such an order to the speaker would be "lawful". Failure of the speaker to respond to the order would be strong evidence of his intent to provoke disorder and would render such refusal actionable under subsection (1) (f).

However, ordering a speaker to stop his speech because of its controversial nature should be the last step taken by the police in their efforts to preserve order. If it can be shown that a disturbance could have been averted merely by ejecting or restraining a few hecklers or by calling additional officers to the scene, then such an order to disperse directed toward the speaker should not be deemed "lawful" under subsection (1) (f). Such a conclusion best implements the purpose of section 5525, which is to focus primarily on the intent of the actor. To allow greater discretion to police officers

would allow punishment for the utterance of unpopular views -
an obvious contravention of the limitation of common law
breach of the peace which section 5525 was intended to achieve.

It should be noted, however, that this interpretation of the
proposed statute is narrower than current holdings enunciated
by the Supreme Court with respect to regulation of speech by
the police and judiciary. In _Feiner v. New York_[28] the plaintiff was arrested and convicted of disorderly conduct when he
refused to stop speaking after twice being so ordered by a
police officer in attendance. Feiner had mounted a small stand
on a street corner in Syracuse and with the aid of a loudspeaker addressed a gathering crowd on the subject of the civil
rights of Negroes. During his speech Feiner urged that Negroes
"rise up in arms for their rights." As he spoke the crowd grew
larger, finally spilling from the sidewalk into the street. At
no time did the listeners become angered or threatening, and
there was only one incident reported of possible violence; one
man told the police to get that sonofabitch" off the stand or
he would.

The Supreme Court upheld Feiner's conviction.[29] In so doing
they reiterated that any intervention or punishment of the right
of free speech must meet the "clear and present danger" test.
But, the Court held that this requirement was satisfied if the
police in good faith believed a breach of the peace to be imminent. What the Court did not specify was the procedures, if
any, the police must employ to prevent a breach of the peace
before ordering a speaker to stop speaking.[30] It is suggested
that Feiner could not have been convicted under proposed section 5525 absent a sufficient presentation by the police that
ordering the stoppage of the speech was the only reasonable
method available to prevent a breach of the peace.[31]

Subsection (1) (f), refusal to comply with a lawful order
to disperse, should be read in conjunction with section 5520,
failure of disorderly persons to disperse.[32] The latter offense is similar to what is commonly called "reading the riot
act" where an appropriate official goes before a riotous assembly and demands that the crowd disperse.[33] Section 5520
is an aggravated form of subsection (1) (f) but there are
significant differences.

The most obvious, but one that must be stressed, is that
section 5520 applies only when a person is already pursuing
a course of disorderly conduct. In this respect it is more
limited than section 5525 (1) (f) where the actor's conduct
becomes disorderly only through refusal to obey a lawful order
to disperse. Admittedly, this may prove to be an attenuated
distinction at times, but it is one that must be kept in mind,
particularly when dealing with the problem of possible violent
reaction by an audience. If the police find it necessary to
intervene and disperse an assembly because of the threat of
violence and if the speaker refuses to comply with such an
order, then such a refusal would render him liable for criminal
prosecution under section 5525 (1) (f). However, in that section 5520 requires disorderly conduct to be present before the
order to disperse is intentionally disobeyed, such a speaker

1415

would not qualify for the aggravated punishment for failure as a disorderly person to disperse.

The second distinction between section 5525 (1) (f) and section 5520 is the minimum gathering of persons necessary for the application of each. Subsection (1) (f) speaks only of congregating "with other persons" and refusing a lawful order to disperse. Presumably, if a person congregates with two others this would satisfy the requirements of the plural "persons" and bring each of the three under subsection (1) (f).[34] Section 5520, on the other hand, places the minimum number of persons required to be gathered at five, and if they are engaged in disorderly conduct and intentionally fail to disperse, each will be criminally liable for failure as disorderly persons to disperse.

Third, section 5520 speaks of "intentionally" refusing or failing to disperse upon an officer's command. This would call for proving that the disorderly person knew of the order to disperse. With particular reference to large congregations of demonstrators it may often occur that some members of the crowd were not aware of the police order.[35] Also, it would appear that an individual would have a good defense under section 5520 if he could show that he was unable to disperse, because of the people pressing in around him.[36] Thus, he would lack the requisite intent to qualify under section 5520.[37]

Subsection (1) (g)[38] is a dragnet provision to catch activity that is a nuisance but does not fall within any of the other specific categories of conduct. Thus, such activity as strewing tacks on a street, throwing firecrackers and any of the endless variety of such pranks would be prohibited.[39] Since this subsection is limited to activity which serves no "legitimate purpose" it should be noted that this provision is not meant to supplant existing tort law on the subject of nuisance. Thus, it will not have the effect of rendering criminal all activities that may bring public discomfort such as maintenance of dumping grounds, excessive smoke from a power plant and pollution of streams from commercial activity, all of which may bring about civil liability.

C. Evaluation

Proposed section 5525 is a vast improvement over Michigan's existing coverage of disorderly conduct. While the present statute suffers from being clumsy and overly broad, section 5525 is concise and straightforward. It effectively classifies in one provision that conduct likely to be annoying or dangerous to public order. By eliminating from disorderly conduct coverage activities which, although socially or morally worrisome, do not pose a threat of breaching the peace - such as public drunkenness - the courts can concentrate solely on those policies underlying regulation of activities which pose a violent threat to society. In focusing primarily on the intent of the actor - not just on his conduct - the draftsmen have given careful recognition to the protection of fundamental first amendment freedoms and, thus, it is believed that all the provisions contained in section 5525 will meet constitutional standards.

One question left open by section 5525 is that of the applicability of subsection (1) (c), which regulates the use of abusive or obscene language in public, to a verbal encounter between a police officer and a citizen. It is certain that subsection (1) (c) will not be invoked in the situation where only the police officer hears the language. Subsection (1) (c) applies only when the public is affected and, as previously stated, only when a plurality of persons are subject to verbal abuse.[40] This leaves unanswered the question of whether (1) (c) will apply in the situation where an individual enters into a verbal controversy with a police officer and others overhear. Presumably, if such a person used obscene or abusive language he would be punishable as a disorderly person.

The possibility of abusing the proposed disorderly conduct statute by applying subsection (1) (c) in such situations becomes acute in the ghetto areas of our large cities where it is reputedly standard practice for the police on the beat to stop, question and perhaps take into cusotdy for interrogation a large number of persons.[41] Realistically, many of the people so affected will be innocent of any charge. Since the relationship between the police and ghetto residents often verges on open hostility, there is a strong likelihood that verbal resistance or reaction will occur. Because conditions are crowded in such areas and a stopped police car often draws an audience, it is likely that others will overhear the verbal altercation between the officer and the person he has stopped, thus rendering such person criminally liable under subsection (1) (c) if he uses foul or abusive language. Since, as in most offenses of the nature of disorderly conduct, the officer at the scene has great discretion in deciding whether or not to make an arrest, a potentially dangerous situation is created. What is feared as a result of such discretion is that arrests and convictions will be had not because of the threat to the tranquility of the neighborhood, but rather because the officer found the remarks personally offensive. Add to this the strained relations that often exist between the police and residents of ghetto areas and you have the ingredients for an explosive situation - one which section 5525 is supposed to aid in averting. Finally, the theme running throughout this discussion is the problem of discriminatory enforcement of the law. The legislature should be wary of adopting a provision that would lend itself to the worsening of relationships between minority groups and the police - in effect a worsening of relationships between such groups and the rest of society, since too often the blue uniform is the symbol of the outside world.

It is suggested that the legislature may want to add a provision to section 5525 which would exempt arguments with peace officers from the operation of disorderly conduct, as suggested

1417

by the draftsmen of the Model Penal Code.[42] Such a provision
would not be alarming in that section 5525 as it is drafted
seeks protection against conduct that has as its tendency public violence. It is reasonable to suggest that a policeman,
carefully trained in his profession, would be the least likely
person to be provoked by the offensive language of others.[43]
In addition, the job of a policeman is such that he often is
involved with people to whom coarse language is common while
in the eyes of the bulk of society these same words are con-[44]
sidered indecent. It offends one's sense of justice to allow
punishment to be meted out to a person who is arrested (often
on the basis of "reasonable cause" for suspicion), subsequently cleared of the original charge, but held on the strength of
the indignation shown at the time of his arrest.[45]

III.
UNLAWFUL ASSEMBLY, SECTION 5515; RIOT, SECTION 5510

A. The Nature of the Offenses

Like the right of free speech, the right to assemble freely
is not absolute.[46] Unlawful assembly is generally defined as
a gathering together of persons with the common intent to achieve[47]
a purpose, lawful or unlawful, in a riotous or tumultuous manner.
At common law it was necessary that at least three people be[48]
gathered in order to constitute the offense of unlawful assembly,
while the number where the offense is statutory varies from jur-[49]
isdiction to jurisdiction. But, under both the common law and
the statutes, less than the requisite number of persons can be
convicted of the offense,[50] as long as the minimum number participated in the assembly.

To constitute the offense of unlawful assembly, it is necessary that the group act with a common purpose or intent. This
is meant to require a showing that the minimum number of persons
provided for in the statute had a common intent to commit a violent act,[51] even though the assemblage consists of a far greater
number. The common intent may be formed either before[52] assembling or at anytime after the gathering takes place. Thus,
a meeting may start as a peaceful assembly, but if later the
purpose to commit an unlawful violent act develops and those attending concur, then the offense of unlawful assembly has been
established.[53]

It has been asserted that not all assemblies at which violent or boisterous activity is carried on fall within the statu-[54]
tory definition of unlawful assembly. Where the purpose of
the assembly was lawful and subsequently violent or tumultuous
activity takes place, the lawful assembly is transformed into
an unlawful one only where the violence endangers public peace
and order.[55]

At common law the intermediary offense between unlawful assembly and riot was called rout. It is generally defined as
the"moving forward of an unlawful assembly toward the execution

1418

of its unlawful design."[56] Therefore the crime of rout consists of an unlawful assembly plus an unsuccessful attempt to accomplish its purpose.[57] The definition of rout was intended to cover those situations where preparation for riot has taken place but where the gathering is apprehended before it can actually begin to carry out its activity.

At common law the offense of riot was committed when those that are unlawfully assembled began the perpetration of their unlawful design.[58] An unlawful assembly was a necessary prerequisite to the offense of riot,[59] but, as discussed in connection with unlawful assembly, the fact that the group originally gathered for a peaceful purpose is not controlling if riotous activity is the result of such an assemblage.[60] The minimum number of participants necessary to constitute the offense was three.[61]

One of the necessary elements of the crime of riot is that those assembled act with a common purpose or intent. It is not enough to show that those charged all participated in a common disorder. Thus, in one leading case it was held that thirty people exploding firecrackers on the Fourth of July in the same location did not constitute a riot in that the participants were each engaged in their own activity and, hence, demonstrated no common intent or purpose.[62] This is not meant to say that there must be a well-laid plan or conspiracy, rather only that there must be evidence of some concerted action toward the furtherance of a common goal.[63]

B. Unlawful Assembly and Riot in Michigan

The existing statute dealing with unlawful assembly in Michigan[64] merely declares that the proper officials should order those unlawfully assembled to disperse, without defining what constitutes unlawful assembly. There has been little case law interpreting or applying the statute.[65]

The existing Michigan statute[66] on riot closely parallels the English Riot Act of 1714.[67] Consequently, it is provided that certain officials shall proceed to unlawful assemblies and order the dispersal of the gathering.[68] It is further provided that such officials can command bystanders to help in suppressing the rioters.[69] If the group fails to disperse or if others fail to aid in suppressing the riot, they shall be deemed guilty of the offense.[70] Any represser shall be guiltless if he kills one of the rioters, and if one of the rioters kills one of those repressing the riot, all rioters will be held answerable.[71] The minimum number set to constitute a riot is twelve if they are armed and thirty if unarmed.[72]

C. Michigan Revised Criminal Code Sections 5515 and 5510

The unlawful assembly provision section 5515,[73] is a more limited definition than the common law offense. For example, the minimum number of participants is set at five; however, many of the essential elements of the common law definition are retained. Thus, there must be a common intent or purpose

1419

between at least five of those so assembled but, as at common law, the intent need not be formed before the assembling takes place. The most limiting factor in this definition of unlawful assembly is that it applies only to assemblies called for the purpose of rioting, or those, originally peaceful in nature, that develop a violent and tumultuous intent. Thus, the offense of unlawful assembly incorporates the common law crime of rout. The draftsmen have excluded a body of American case law dealing with the illegality of assemblies where an unlawful, though not necessarily violent, act is advocated.[74] It has been held in certain jurisdictions that any assembling to do an unlawful act satisfies the definition of unlawful assembly.[75]

The draftsmen of the proposed Code carefully skirted an area of doubtful constitutionality in drafting the unlawful assembly provision: that is, the situation where a peaceful assembly is convened and there is a hostile or violent reaction by others to the views being expressed. This is the same problem faced with respect to the disorderly conduct provision[76] and, again, the draftsmen avoided an unjustifiable (and probably unconstitutional) result by focusing on the conduct and intent of those participating in the assembly. Therefore, peaceful assemblies (even where called for an unlawful purpose) which cause an outbreak of violence by those hearing the words spoken or who are opposed to the auspices of the meeting will not render the peaceful members of the assemblage guilty of unlawful assembly.[77]

Turning to the riot provision, it is seen that the Proposed Code has adopted the basic common law definition of the offense but has raised the minimum number of participants to five. It is necessary to prove that at least five persons were engaged in a common disturbance of a violent or tumultuous nature but, again keeping in mind the breadth of the constitutional interpretation of freedom of assembly, such violent or tumultuous activity must be "wrongful" before the participants can be deemed guilty of riot.[78] There is some authority for the proposition that statutes which prohibit all violent activity, without regard to its lawfulness are unconstitutional abridgements of the freedoms of speech and assembly.[79]

Although there is no specific provision in the Proposed Code, it would seem that the killing of a rioter by one repressing it or defending himself against a mob would be justified along traditional lines of self-defense or other legal justification. Thus, policemen or other peace officers who kill in the line of duty will be protected as will those private citizens who have no other means of escape than the use of force.[80]

It is significant and wise that the draftsmen left out of proposed section 5510 a provision similar to the existing Michigan statute which provides that if a represser of the riot is killed, all rioters will be answerable for murder. It is believed that the inclusion of such a provision in the

1420

proposed riot section might create a reluctance by the judiciary to apply riot penalties. Or, perhaps, they may just declare that the requirements of the provision have not been fulfilled as a means of avoiding wide-ranging criminal liability. The nature of what is called riot today is vastly different from the concept as it existed when the present Michigan statute was enacted in 1846. Due to the nature of the large urban disorders involving hundreds or even thousands of persons, it would be difficult to find a common intent or purpose to commit an act such as murder. Prohibition of such conduct is best left to the law of conspiracy.[81] Furthermore, to include such a provision in the riot statute would contravene to a degree the felony-murder section which delineates[82] specific crimes warranting the application of such a rule.

D. Evaluation

Proposed section 5515 - prohibiting unlawful assemblies - is not likely to have much effect on the substantive law of Michigan. The Michigan cases which have dealt with this crime are unanimous in declaring that only tumultuous or violent assemblies are to be deemed unlawful.[83] Section 5515 is in accord with this view, declaring as unlawful only those assemblies which have as their "intent" the commission of the crime of riot. The main difference between section 5515 and existing statutory coverage (and the most positive contribution it makes to Michigan Law) is that the Proposed Code's provision on unlawful assembly sets out a definition of the offense. Thus, the judiciary and the public will have a readily available delineation of what the "law" is.

The question left open by section 5515, and one which cannot be answered by reference to existing Michigan law, is just how far the judiciary is likely to extend coverage of unlawful assembly. Looking to other jurisdictions, the New York case of People v. Most[84] presents the furthest extension of the unlawful assembly concept.[85] In that case Most, an avowed anarchist, addressed a meeting in New York City to protest the hanging in Chicago of some fellow anarchists who had participated in the Haymarket Riot. Most was greeted by the 80 to 100 persons gathered to hear him as "our leader, Father Most," and he proceeded to harangue against, among others, the Supreme Court and the governor of Illinois, predicting that they would meet the same fate as those that were hanged. He urged those attending the meeting to arm themselves because the day of the revolution was close at hand. Finally, Most stated that they would kill five hundred for each of the five that were hanged in Chicago. The audience greeted each prediction with applause, and at one point a man in the audience jumped to his feet in response to Most's statement that the revolution was close and shouted: "Why not tonight? We are ready and prepared."

The court of appeals upheld Most's conviction for unlawful assembly which was defined in the statute as any "act tending

1421

towards a breach of the peace, or an injury to person or property, or any unlawful act." The court stated that unlawful assembly required the common intent of three or more persons to engage in such activity and that such concert was shown by the fact that at least two members of the audience concurred in the ideas of the speaker. By their adoption of the language, as exhibited by their conduct, they could be shown to have participated in the unlawful design of Most. Thus, the requisite assemblage was established.

The court also made short shrift of Most's argument that his words were not threats but "prophesies" by stating that the nature of the language used was for the jury to decide. But the court went further to hold that it would be no defense even if the threats only related to acts contemplated in the future. Given the circumstances of the case - an inflammatory speech before "a crowd of ignorant, misguided men" - the fact that the unlawful and riotous acts were suggested to take place in the future would not alleviate the great potential harm to public peace.

Today the facts presented in Most may seem bizzare, but one does not have to look far to find similar situations occurring. The orators may not be anarchists and they may not advocate wholesale murder but some revolutionaries - of whatever political makeup - exhort their followers to activity which can only euphemistically be described as extra-legal in nature. It is therefore relevant in inquire whether a similar type of harangue would render a speaker guilty under proposed section 5515.

It is clear from the Most decision and from subsequent decisions[86] that language which poses a highly potential threat of violent outburst, if adopted by a sufficient number of those listening, will satisfy the assemblage requirement of the crime of unlawful assembly. Since unlawful assembly is a complete crime in itself, it need not be shown that riotous activity actually took place. Thus, under proposed section 5515, if four others concurred in the words used by the speaker, the necessary assemblage would be established.

The next step would be to show a common intent or purpose running between the speaker and his audience as required by the unlawful assembly provision. This probably could be done but it would still leave the more difficult problem of sufficiently isolating the nature of this common intent. In Most the problem was relatively easy. The defendant's "ravings," as they were termed by the court, dealt almost exclusively with bringing violence to bear on the alleged enemies of the anarchist movement. In most instances, inciting speakers present a panoply of legitimate demands and grievances along with their inflammatory tirade. Because of the usual mixture of valid social protest and dangerous incitement, conclusively finding a concerted purpose existing between the speaker and those that he has excited so that such a speaker can be punished may become manifestly difficult.

Also, whether a conviction will lie may turn on the attitude of the audience. If, as in Most, there is almost unanimous agreement by those listening to engage in violent and tumultuous activity, courts may be more disposed to punish such speakers. Large, unruly crowds almost inevitably pose a serious threat to society.

As to the question of the temporal relationship between the speech and the proposed activity probably no definitive answer can be given. If the activity proposed is of a highly dangerous nature (such as physical violence), the societal interest in preventing such occurrences is much greater and the judiciary will probably be unimpressed by the time gap, if one can be shown, between the threatened outburst and its suggested time of occurrence.[87]

Finally, the problem existing sub silentio throughout this discussion is that of the constitutional right of free assembly. The issue was not faced by the court in Most, decided in 1891, since it was not until the 1920's that it was first held that the fourteenth amendment protected against abridgment of first amendment freedoms by the states.[88] Today states cannot punish language merely because of its unpopular or shocking nature.[89] The Supreme Court is zealous in its protection of the right to make one's views known. If the Court can find a protected exercise of the rights of free speech and assembly, it is unlikely to affirm a conviction based on the exercise of these freedoms.[90]

For these reasons it is felt that the proposed unlawful assembly provision will be of only limited efficacy in dealing with the problem of a speaker agitating and inciting[91] a crowd to riotous behavior. The facts would probably have to be nearly as extreme as those in People v. Most[92] before a conviction could be upheld under proposed section 5515.

Many of the evils at which riot legislation was originally aimed simply do not exist today. Before the institution of local police departments, there was the threat that an armed band of thugs could have a community at its mercy.[93] Lacking any form of peace-keeping apparatus, such a community easily could have been powerless to defend itself effectively. Riot legislation served its purpose by declaring riot a felony and giving private citizens the right to use deadly force in preventing its occurrence.[94] Moreover, it empowered certain local officials to order rioters to disperse and to call private citizens to arms. If either these officials or private citizens failed to respond to such duties they were subject to criminal prosecution, and the community could be held civilly liable for any damage that resulted from the negligence of their officials in responding to a riotous situation.[95]

Needless to say, this rationale is not relevant today. Trained police departments have taken over the function of preserving the peace and it is no longer necessary - and, indeed, it would be highly dangerous - to require private citizens to take up arms to suppress outbreaks of violence. Riot control demands a high degree of expertise.[96] Leaving protection to amateurs determined to meet force with force would

1423

create the possibility that the riot would actually be escalated instead of suppressed. Thus, when the unwanted provisions are stripped away from the original riot acts there is left the most minor function of such acts - declaration of riot as a felony. This is all that is left of the common law concept of riot, and it is all that the draftsmen included in proposed section 5510.

However, even acknowledging that many of the conditions that formerly prompted riot legislation do not exist today, it still seems that making riotous and tumultuous conduct a crime has justification: first, to create an offense for situations where, because of the great masses of persons involved, there is a serious threat posed to society;[97] second, to establish an offense similar to conspiracy but which does not necessitate the proof of common intent to commit particular acts;[98] finally, by separating mob behavior (which by its nature is more dangerous) from individual disorderliness the policy considerations underlying the separate provisions are made clear. By reading the proposed riot provision together with the disorderly conduct[99] and failure as disorderly persons to disperse[100] provisions it can be seen that the draftsmen have adopted an orderly graduated scheme of punishment that depends upon the circumstances under which activity is undertaken and the number of persons involved. It is fair to punish those participating in large public disturbances at the felony level,[101] while providing a lesser penalty for those at the scene not actually participating but who fail to disperse upon a police command[102] and reserving an even lower penalty for those involved in acts of individual misconduct.[103]

It is important to point out at this juncture that no statute, or group of statutes, which seeks to punish those involved in upheavals of the sort that have swept our cities of late will ever prevent a riot from occurring - no matter how severe the penalty for participation or acts committed. As long as society deals only with the effects of rioting (and this appears to be the current emphasis) leaving the causes untouched, the best that can be hoped for is that our police and other law enforcement agencies will develop a technical expertise in handling mass outbreaks of violent behavior.

It is often asserted that civil disorders draw most of their participants from the criminal segment of the population, the highly impoverished and the young. This so-called "riffraff" theory[104] of riots did not obtain in Detroit in 1967 where the median income of the rioters was nearly the same as that of the entire Negro population, family stability characteristics were about the same and the educational achievement was higher for those that rioted than for the negro population as a whole.[105] Furthermore, only ten per cent of those arrested were juveniles; the largest group, thirty-one per cent, representing those thirty and older.[106] Finally, of 1,200 non-juvenile male persons arrested eighty-three percent were employed, two-thirds had no previous convictions and an additional twenty per cent had only one previous conviction.[107] Thus, we are involved in more than

1424

a revolt against material deprivation. In fact, the hard-core slum dwellers were conspicuous by their absence in the 1967 outbreak of violence. What we do have is a striving for dignity and self-esteem by a large segment of society. A striving that has, regrettably, spilled over into violence. This situation was probably most succintly summed up by one expert in this area when he stated:

The riots were an outburst of frustration over unmet demands for dignity and for economic and political power. They were a tragic, violent, but understandable declaration of manhood and an insistance that Negroes be able to participate in and to control their own destinies and community affairs.[108]

This is the context in which any legal declaration, not just riot legislation, affecting urban areas must be examined. Proposed section 5510 will only be as "good" as the legislative and social reaction to the situations and conditions that comprise the problem of our metropolises. The passing of strong, effective statutes dealing with civil disorder while failing to pass comparable legislation striking at the causes of disorder can only lead to further deterioration of the conditions existing in our cities today.

IV.

CONCLUSION

Sections 5525 and 5520 - disorderly conduct and failure of disorderly persons to disperse - are carefully drafted provisions that will be welcome additions to Michigan's criminal statutory coverage. It is recommended that, with the addition of the section dealing with arguments with policemen, they be adopted.

Sections 5515 and 5510 - unlawful assembly and riot - are also well-drafted but they will be of lesser use to law enforcement officials. If past judicial response can be used as an indicator, it is suggested that most of those participating in large urban riots will be punished for their individual criminal acts rather than for the crime of riot.[109] Sections 5515 and 5510 are no panacea for dealing with this social phenomenon (no single piece of legislation could be that), but they will be of some use in certain circumstances.[110] Thus, in the situation where a speaker agitates for violence or in a small scale disturbance in which the potential harm is great, but no property or personal damage has yet been done, these provisions will be helpful in forestalling larger disorder.

David D. Jozwiak

Footnotes

1. U.S. Const. Amend. I provides:

Congress shall make no law respecting an establishment of religion, or prohibiting the free exercise thereof; or abridging the freedom of speech, or of the press; or the right of the people peaceably to assemble, and to petition the Government for a redress of grievances.

The comparable provisions of the Michigan Constitution of 1963 concerning the right of assembly and freedom of speech are:

Sec. 3. The people have the right peaceably to assemble, to consult for the common good, to instruct their representatives and to petition the government for redress of grievances.
. . .

Sec. 5. Every person may freely speak, write, express and publish his views on all subjects, being responsible for the abuse of such right; and no law shall be enacted to restrain or abridge the liberty of speech or of the press.

Mich. Const. art. I, Sec. 3, 5.

2. Model Penal Code Sec. 250.1, Comment (Tent Draft No. 13, 1961)

3. 12 Am. Jur. 2d Breach of the Peace Sec. 4 (1964).

4. Id. Sec. 29.

5. See People v. Ohneth, 330 Ill. App. 247, 89 N.E. 2d 433 (1949).

6. Mich. Comp. Laws Sec. 750.167 (1948), Mich. Stat. Ann. Sec. 28.364 (1962).

7. See Mich. Stat. Ann. Sec. 28.364, nn. 11-30 (1962), for a listing of the cases.

8. Donovan v. Guy, 347 Mich. 457, 80 N.W. 2d 190 (1956).

9. See Mich. Rev. Crim. Code Sec. 110 (Final Draft 1967).

10. Id. Sec. 5525 (1).

11. However, he may become a disorderly person if he intentionally fails to respond to a lawful order to disperse. See discussion pp. 993-94 infra.

12. See People v. Burman, 154 Mich. 150, 117 N.W. 589 (1908) (parading with red flag would incite others to violence.)

13. Thus, foul language used within the home of another would not be covered. See Ware v. Loveridge, 75 Mich. 488, 42 N.W. 997 (1889) (interpreting as common law breach of the peace). But activity carried on in a private home which disturbs other members of the public may bring a person within this provision of the act.

14. Mich. Rev. Crim. Code Sec. 5525 (1) (a) (Final Draft 1967) provides:

A person commits the crime of disorderly conduct if, with intent

to cause public inconvenience, annoyance or alarm, or recklessly creating a risk thereof, he:

   (a) Engages in fighting or in violent, tumultuous or threatening behavior. . . .

15. Id. Sec. 5525 (1) (c) provides:

A person commits the crime of disorderly conduct if, with intent to cause public inconvenience, annoyance or alarm, or
recklessly creating a risk thereof, he:
. . .
(c) In a public place uses abusive or obscene language, or
makes an obscene gesture. . . .

16. This is the so-called "fighting words" exception to first
amendment protection that originated in Chaplinsky v. New Hampshire, 315 U.S. 568 (1942). In that case Chaplinsky was convicted under a New Hampshire statute which forbade addressing
others with "offensive, derisive or annoying" words in a public place. He appealed to the Supreme Court on the theory that
the statute unlawfully abridged the freedom of speech guaranteed by the Constitution. In affirming the conviction the Court
noted that the first amendment freedoms are not absolute, that
certain classes of speech do not warrant constitutional protection and that provocative and insulting language is such a
class. It was held that: "the profane, the libelous, and the
insulting or "fighting" words . . . by their very utterance inflict injury or tend to incite an immediate breach of the peace."
Id. at 572. Thus, it has become accepted doctrine that a state
can punish certain types of language which, much like the common law concept of assault are likely to provoke a violent reaction in others. As long as the statute prohibiting such language is narrowly drawn, and the standard constituting provocative and insulting language is that "likely to provoke the
average person to retaliation," the one using such words may
be constitutionally punished. Id. at 573-74. See, E.G.,
Feiner v. New York, 340 U.S. 315 (1951); Kunz v. New York, 340
U.S. 290 (1951). See also Z. Chafee, Free Speech in the United
States 149 (1941).

17. The "clear and present" danger rule that serves as a guide-
line for the judiciary to follow in deciding whether one can be
punished for engaging in activity that has basic first amendment protection was enunciated in Schenck v. United States, 249
U.S. 47 (1919). In this case Schenck was indicted and convicted under the Espionage Act of 1917 for conspiring to obstruct
the recruitment of civilians during the First World War. He
appealed his conviction, in part, on the basis that passing out
literature to inductees in front of conscription stations was
protected by the first amendment's free speech provision. In
writing for a unanimous Court, Justice Holmes noted that the
use of circulars to make political views known would have been
"in ordinary times" protected by the first amendment, but that

(w)hen a nation is at war many things that might be said in

time of peace are such a hindrance to its effort that their utterance will not be endured so long as men fight and that no Court could regard them as protected by any constitutional right.

Id. at 52. It was held that:

The questions in every case is whether the words used are used in such circumstances and are of such a nature as to create a clear and present danger that they will bring about the substantive evils that Congress has a right to prevent.

Id. at 52. Thus, the "clear and present" danger rule demands: (1) the existence of a valid state interest to be protected; (2) the existence of circumstances whereby the exercise of free speech may defeat this interest; and (3) speech which because of its "proximity and degree" has as "its tendency" the intent to defeat a valid state interest.

18. Model Penal Code Sec. 250.1, Comment (Tent. Draft No. 13, 1961).

19. Mich. Rev. Crim. Code Sec. 5525 (1) (d) (Final Draft 1967) provides:

A person commits the crime of disorderly conduct if, with intent to cause public inconvenience, annoyance or alarm, or recklessly creating a risk thereof, he:

. . .

(d) Without lawful authority, disturbs any lawful assembly or meeting of persons . . .

20. Mich. Comp. Laws Sec. 340.970 (1948), Mich. Stat. Ann. Sec. 15.3970 (1968) (disturbance of school meetings); Mich. Comp. Laws Sec. 750.169 (1948), Mich. Stat. Ann. Sec. 28.366 (1962) (religious meetings; Mich. Comp. Laws Sec. 750.170 (1948), Mich. Stat. Ann. Sec. 28.367 (1962) (disturbance of other public meetings).

21. See Fellman, Constitutional Rights of Association, 1961 Sup. Ct. Rev. 74, 98.

22. Id.

23. Mich. Rev. Crim. Code Sec. 5525 (1) (e) (Final Draft 1967) states:

A person commits the crime of disorderly conduct if, with intent to cause public inconvenience, annoyance or alarm, or recklessly creating a risk thereof, he:

. . .

(e) Obstructs vehicular or pedestrian traffic. . . .

24. Id. Sec. 5501 (a) states:

To "obstruct" means to render impassable without unreasonable inconvenience or hazard. A gathering of persons to hear a person speak or otherwise communicate does not constitute an obstruction.

25. Such a licensing ordinance may be deemed defective in that it constitutes a prior restraint on the exercise of free speech. See Near v. Minnesota ex rel. Olson, 283 U.S. 697 (1931). Subsequent decisions have extended the doctrine of prior restraint in declaring licensing ordinances invalid as an unconstitutional restraint on free speech in three situations: (1) when the ordinance is discriminatively administered, Niemotko v. Maryland, 340 U.S. 268 (1951); (2) the statute may give the administrator too much discretion in deciding who shall get a permit, Kunz v. New York, 340 U.S. 290 (1951); (3) when the standard used in deciding whether to grant a permit may be wrong, Hague v. CIO, 307 U.S. 496 (1939) (prohibiting all assemblies where official anticipated disorder deemed void). See Stewart, Public Speech and Public Order in Britain and the United States, 13 Vand. L. Rev. 625, 627-29 (1960).

26. Mich. Rev. Crim. Code Sec. 5525 (1) (f) (Final Draft 1967) provides:

A person commits the crime of disorderly conduct if, with intent to cause public inconvenience, annoyance or alarm, or recklessly creating a risk thereof, he:

. . .

(f) Congregates with other persons in a public place and refuses to comply with a lawful order of the police to disperse. . . .

27. See Feiner v. New York, 340 U.S. 315 (1951).

28. Id.

29. The majority opinion accepted the fact as established by the lower court that Feiner was guilty of inciting to riot. With respect to Sec. 5525 it may be argued that incitement is covered by Sec. 5525 (1) (c) which prohibits the uttering of abusive or obscene language in public. Such a conclusion is untenable and it is believed that incitement to riot is not covered by the disorderly conduct provision.

As stated earlier, it was the intent of the draftsmen in adopting subsection (1) (c) to codify the "fighting words" doctrine pronounced in Chaplinsky v. New Hampshire, 315 U.S. 568 (1942). Since such words are deemed to have so little communicative value they are beyond the scope of first amendment protection. Id. Still, it is possible to view fighting words as incitement to a breach of the peace in that the addressee may be moved to violent reaction toward the speaker. See Stewart, Public Speech and Public Order in Britain and the United States, 13 Vand. L. Rev. 625, 634 (1960). Even so, the threat of a breach of the peace would be highly generalized and, under the ruling in Chaplinsky, the standard of guilt would be what language the court deemed reasonably likely to provoke violence on the part of those hearing the words, regardless of what the speaker subjectively intended or what reaction the addressee had. Id.

Incitement to riot, on the other hand, occurs when a speaker solicits a specific act of violence on the part of his audience.

The degree of guilt necessary is the intent to cause a breach of the peace, coupled with inflammatory language which causes a likelihood that disorder will follow. Id. at 635 n. 83. The standard to be used is the clear and present danger rule, and unlike "fighting words," words are not merely thrust out of first amendment protection.

Even though the "fighting words," prohibition and incitement to riot conceptually overlap at times, it is suggested that they are sufficiently dissimilar so that the latter offense would not be caught by the disorderly conduct provision. Depending upon the context in which the language is used, incitement to riot may be punishable under Mich. Rev. Crim. Code Sec. 1010 (Final Draft 1967). According to that provision the crime of criminal solicitation would occur when the actor has the specific intent to encourage others to engage in a specific criminal act. But as noted in the Comment to Sec. 1010, "(a) general exhortation to 'go out and revolt' does not constitute criminal solicitation. . . ." Id. at 94. Before the language used could be actionable under this provision the actor would have to propose some concrete form of action on the part of his audience.

30. See Stewart, supra note 29, at 632, where the author comments on the Feiner holding by stating:

Assuming that the majority is laying down this rule for police intervention, rather than for punishment afterwards, it appears that a speaker who incites to riot may be stopped by police who apprehend in good faith that disorder is imminent. It is irrelevant that they could have preserved the peace without interrupting the speech. (footnotes omitted).

31. What would constitute reasonable alternatives to interfering with the speaker would ultimately depend upon a court's rather than the policeman's interpretation of the situation. The proper approach would embody a presumption in favor of the speaker's constitutional rights of assembly and speech. Only if the police could show that the speaker was inciting a situation whereby there was a clear and present danger of disorder - that, in effect, there were no reasonable alternatives to use in controlling an unruly audience - would they be justified in intervening and arresting the speaker for disorderly conduct if he failed to desist.

32. Mich. Rev. Crim. Code Sec. 5520 (1) (Final Draft 1967) states:

A person commits the crime of failure as a disorderly person to disperse if he participates with 5 or more persons in a course of disorderly conduct likely to cause substantial harm or serious inconvenience, annoyance or alarm, and intentionally refuses or fails to disperse when ordered to do so by a peace officer or other public servant engaged in executing or enforcing the law.

33. See Mich. Comp. Laws Sec. 750.521 (1948), Mich. Stat. Ann. Sec. 28.789 (1954), for the comparable Michigan provision.

34. See People v. Carcel, 3 N.Y.2d 327, 144 N.E. 2d 81, 165 N.Y. S. 2d 113 (1957 (requiring the coming together of at least 3 persons).

35. See, e.g., In re Bacon, 240 Cal. App. 2d 34, 49 Cal. Rptr. 322 (1966).

36. See, e.g., People v. Garvey, 6 Misc. 2d 266, 79 N.Y.S. 2d 456 (1948).

37. But see In re Bacon, 240 Cal. App. 2d 34, 49 Cal. Rptr. 322 (1966), where it was held a blanket request to all persons illegally remaining in a university building after closing was sufficient. Since the order to leave was given repeatedly over a loudspeaker the defendants' assertion that they were not individually requested to leave was deemed unconvincing.

38. Mich. Rev. Crim. Code Sec. 5525 (1) (g) (Final Draft 1967) provides:

A person commits the crime of disorderly conduct if, with intent to cause public inconvenience, annoyance or alarm, or recklessly creating a risk thereof, he:
. . .
(g) Creates a hazardous or physically offensive condition by any act that serves no legitimate purpose.

39. See Model Penal Code Sec. 250.1, Comment (Tent. Draft No. 13, 1961).

40. See pp. 989-90 supra.

41. Wakefield, supernation at Peace and War, Atlantic Monthly, Mar. 1968, at 39, 65-68.

42. Model Penal Code Sec. 250.1, Comment (Tent Draft. no. 13, 1961).

43. Id.

44. Id.

45. Id.

46. But, although the rights of free speech and assembly are fundamental, they are not in their nature absolute. Their exercise is subject to restriction, if the particular restriction proposed is required in order to protect the state from destruction or from serious injury, political, economic or moral. Whitney v. California, 274 U.S. 357, 373 (1927) (Brandeis, J., concurring). For purposes of this comment the usual limitations placed on the right of assembly are the requirements of public order. Thus, riot and unlawful assembly set limits on the exercise of this first amendment freedom. See Fellman, Constitutional Rights of Association, 1961 Sup. Ct. Rev. 74, 84.

47. State v. Butterworth, 104 N.J.L. 579, 142 A. 57 (1928) 46

Am. Jur. Riots and Unlawful Assembly Sec. 3 (1943).

48.   See statutes collected in Annot., 71 A.L.R. 2d 875, 878 n.9 (1960).

49.   46 Am. Jur., supra note 47, Sec. 4.

50.   Reynolds v. State, 82 Tex. Crim. 505, 199 S.W. 1092 (1918).

51.   Id.

52.   The requisites of the crime of unlawful assembly have been held met when a speaker solicits an unlawful act and two or more persons indicate agreement with him.   People v. Most, 128 N.Y. 108, 27 N.W. 970 (1891).

53.   See State v. Cole, 249 N.C. 733, 107 S.E. 2d 732, cert. denied, 361 U.S. 867 (1959).

54.   People v. Kerrick, 86 Cal. App. 542, 261 P. 756 (1927).

55.   Garcia Dominnicci v. District Court, 71 P.R.R. 122 (1950).

56.   46 Am. Jur., supra note 47, Sec. 7.

57.   Id.

58.   Model Penal Code Sec. 250.1, Comment (Tent Draft No. 13, 1961).

59.   State v. Woolman, 84 Utah 23, 33 P.2d 640 (1934).

60.   See Blakeman v. City of Wichita, 93 Kan. 444, 144 P. 816 (1914).

61.   Spring Garden Ins. Co. v. Imperial Tobacco Co., 132 Ky. 7, 116 S.W. 234 (1909).

62.   Aron v. City of Wausau, 98 Wis. 592, 74 N.W. 354 (1898).

63.   46 Am. Jur., supra note 47, Sec. 11-12.

64.   Mich. Comp. Laws Sec. 750.521-622 (1948), Mich. Stat. Ann. Sec. 28.789-790 (1954).

65.   There have been some cases in which it was held that in order to constitute a breach of the peace there must be some actual or threatened breach of the peace.   Robinson v. Miner, 68 Mich. 549, 37 N.W. 21 (1888).   In People v. Dixon, 188 Mich. 307, 154 N.W. 1 (1915), the Michigan Supreme Court held that an assembly gathered to watch a movie on Sunday in violation of a statute did not pose a threat of breaching the peace.
  The operator of the theater could be convicted of violating the Sunday statute but the peaceful assembly of persons could not be construed as falling within Mich. Comp. Laws, Sec. 750. 521 (1948), Mich. Stat. Ann. Sec. 28.789 (1954).   Thus, a conviction based on Mich. Comp. Laws Sec. 750.522 (1948), Mich. Stat. Ann. Sec. 28.790 (1954) (failure of those unlawfully assembled to disperse) was invalid.   Accord, Yerkes v. Smith, 157 Mich. 557, 122 N.W. 223 (1909) (playing baseball on Sunday); People v. Richards, 150 Mich. 434, 114 N.W. 230 (1907) (absent overt act of violence those gathered to watch a movie on Sunday were not unlawfully assembled).   From these limited

authorities it appears that unlawful assembly has been defined in such a manner as to include only those assemblies which have as their purpose violent or tumultuous conduct, excluding those assemblies having an unlawful but nonviolent, purpose. See (1914) Mich. Att'y Gen. Rep. 128, 207. But see People v. Burman, 154 Mich. 150, 117 N.W. 589 (1908), in which it was held that parading with a red flag posed such a potential threat of a breach of the peace that the defendant could be convicted under an ordinance which prohibited the making of a riot, noise or other disturbance.

66. Mich. Comp. Laws Sec. 750.521 (1948), Mich. Stat. Ann. Sec. 28.789 (1954).

67. The Riot Act of 1714, 1 Geo. 1 c5.

68. Mich. Comp. Laws Sec. 750.521 (1948), Mich. Stat. Ann. Sec. 28.789 (1954).

69. Mich. Comp. Laws Sec. 750.522 (1948), Mich. Stat. Ann. Sec. 28.790 (1954).

70. Mich. Comp. Laws Sec. 750.522-523 (1948), Mich. Stat. Ann. Sec. 28.790-791 (1954).

71. Mich. Comp. Laws Sec. 750.527 (1948), Mich. Stat. Ann. Sec. 28.795 (1954).

72. Mich. Comp. Laws Sec. 750.521 (1948), Mich. Stat. Ann. Sec. 28.789 (1954).

73. Mich. Rev. Crim. Code Sec. 5515 (1) (Final Draft 1967) provides:

A person commits the crime of unlawful assembly if he assembles with 5 or more other persons for the purpose of engaging in conduct constituting the crime of riot or if, being present at an assembly that either has or develops such a purpose he remains there with intent to advance that purpose.

74. Annot., 71 A.L.R. 2d 875, 893-94 (1960).

75. Coverstone v. Davies, 38 Cal. 2d 315, 239 P.2d 876, cert. denied, 344 U.S. 840 (1952).

76. See p. 991 supra.

77. See DeJonge v. Oregon, 299 U.S. 353 (1937), in which the Supreme Court declared that a state statute which punished those that participated in a meeting called under the auspices of the Communist Part to be an unlawful abridgment of the right of assembly. The Court stated that no matter who sponsored the meeting as long as it was conducted in a peaceful and lawful manner those attending were exercising constitutionally protected rights.

78. Mich. Rev. Crim. Code Sec. 5510 (1) (Final Draft 1967) provides:

A person commits the crime of riot if, with 5 or more other persons, he wrongfully engages in tumultuous and violent conduct and thereby intentionally or recklessly causes or creates a grave risk of causing public terror or alarm.

79. See Bridges v. California, 314 U.S. 252-265 (1941) (Black, J.) (dictum); Carmichael v. Allen, 267 F. Aupp. 985 (N.D. Ga. 1967) (dictum).

80. See Mich. Rev. Crim. Code Sec. 630 (2) (c) (Final Draft 1967) (proposed alternative provision):

(2) A peace officer is justified in using deadly physical force upon another person . . . only when he reasonably believes that it is necessary:

. . .

   (c) To lawfully suppress a riot or insurrection.

81. See Mich. Rev. Crim. Code Sec. 1015 (Final Draft 1967). The concept of riot is analogous to that of conspiracy and can be viewed as an extension of the law concerning criminal collusion. There need only be proved that there was a concerted purpose to engage in "violent or tumultuous" conduct, while conspiracy demands there be a common intent to engage in particular unlawful acts. Due to the obvious dangerousness of mob behavior it is abundantly fair to punish such concerted behavior but, at the same time, it would seem unfair to extend the rather tenuous collusion demanded for a conviction of riot to punishing all rioters for the murder committed by one of them.

82. Mich. Rev. Crim. Code Sec. 2005 (1) (b) (Final Draft 1967) provides:

A person commits the crime of murder in the first degree if:

. . .

(b) acting either alone or with one or more persons he commits or attempts to commit arson in the first degree, burglary in the first or second degree, escape in the first degree, kidnapping in the first degree, rape in the first degree, robbery in any degree, or sodomy in the first degree and in the course of and in furtherance of the crime that he is committing or attempting to commit, or immediate flight therefrom, he, or another participant if there by any, causes the death of a person other than one of the participants.

83. See note 65 supra.

84. 128 N.Y. 108, 27 N.E. 970 (1891).

85. See Fellman, Constitutional Rights of Association, 1961 Supt. Ct. Rev. 74, 85-86.

86. See Lair v. State, 316 P.2d 225 (Okla. Crim. 1957); State v. Martinez, 53 N.M. 432, 210 P.2d 620 (1949).

87. Cf. Yates v. United States, 354 U.S. 298 (1957); Dennis v. United States, 341 U.S. 494 (1951) (Communist conspiracy cases).

88. See Fellman, supra note 85, at 87.

89. Terminiello v. City of Chicago, 337 U.S. 1 (1949).

90. Id. See Fellman, supra note 85.

91. See note 29 supra for a discussion of incitement to riot as related to the disorderly conduct statute. Such incitement is not dealt with specifically by the Proposed Code but conviction could be had under the criminal solicitation provision, Mich. Rev. Crim. Code Sec. 1010 (Final Draft 1967).

92. 128 N.Y. 108, 27 N.E. 970 (1891).

93. See Spring Garden Ins. Co. v. Imperial Tobacco Co., 132 Ky. 7, 116 S.W. 234 (1909), where a masked band invaded a town, virtually took it over and in the process caused extensive property damage.

94. Model Penal Code Sec. 250.1, Comment (Tent. Draft No. 13, 1961).

95. Thus, riot legislation acted like a civil defense program for early communities where there existed no organized police force to do the job for them.

96. See Wills, The Second Civil War, Esquire, Mar. 1968, at 76 (interview with Col. Rex Applegate, U.S. Army, ret., a leading authority on riot control in the United States).

97. Model Penal Code Sec. 250.1, Comment (6) at 20 (Tent. Draft No. 13, 1961).

98. Id. See, e.g., People v. Kerrick, 86 Cal. App. 542, 261 P. 756 (1927).

99. Mich. Rev. Crim. Code Sec. 5525 (Final Draft 1967).

100. Id. Sec. 5520.

101. Id. Sec. 5510 (2) (Class C felony).

102. Id. Sec. 5520 (2) (Class B misdemeanor).

103. Id. Sec. 5525 (2) (Class C misdemeanor).

104. See generally Grimshaw, Changing Patterns of Racial Violence in the United States, 40 Notre Dame Law, 534-542-43 (1965).

105. Rubin, Analyzing Detroit's Riot: The Causes and Responses, Reporter, Feb. 22, 1968, at 34.

106. Id. at 35.

107. Id.

108. Id.

D. Obstructing Government Operations

        1. Michigan Compiled Laws (1948)

750.479 Resisting, obstructing officer in discharge of duty

Sec. 479. RESISTING, ETC., OFFICER IN DISCHARGE OF DUTY -
Any person who shall knowingly and wilfully obstruct, resist
or oppose any sheriff, coroner, township treasurer, constable
or other officer or person duly authorized, in serving, or
attempting to serve or execute any process, rule or order made
or issued by lawful authority, or who shall resist any officer
in the execution of any ordinance, by law, or any rule, order
or resolution made, issued, or passed by the common council
of any city board of trustees, or common council or village
council of any incorporated village, or township board of any
township or who shall assault, beat or wound any sheriff,
coroner, township treasurer, constable or other officer duly
authorized, while serving, or attempting to serve or execute
any such process, rule or order, or for having served, or attempted to serve or execute the same, or who shall so obstruct,
resist, oppose, assault, beat or wound any of the above named
officers, or any other person or persons authorized by law to
maintain and preserve the peace, in their lawful acts, attempts
and efforts to maintain, preserve and keep the peace, shall be
guilty of a misdemeanor, punishable by imprisonment in the
state prison not more than 2 years, or by a fine of not more
than 1,000 dollars.

750.217 Disguising with intent to intimidate, etc.

Sec. 217. DISGUISING WITH INTENT TO INTIMIDATE, ETC., -
Any person who shall in any manner disguise himself, with intent to obstruct the due execution of the law, or with intent
to intimidate, hinder or interrupt any officer or any other
person, in the legal performance of his duty, or the exercise
of his rights under the constitution and laws of this state,
whether such intent be effected or not, shall be guilty of a
misdemeanor, punishable by imprisonment in the county jail
not more than 1 year or by fine of not more than 500 dollars.

2.   Case Law

Tryon v. Pingree
112 Mich. 338

MOORE, J. This is an action for malicious prosecution and
false imprisonment. Verdict and judgment were given for defendant, and plaintiff brings the case into this court.
In August, 1894, the plaintiff was secretary of the board
of fire commissioners of the city of Detroit, and had the
custody of its books and papers. The defendant at this time
was mayor of the city of Detroit. The act creating the board
of fire commissioners provided: "The books and accounts kept
by said board shall at all times be subject to the inspection
of the mayor and controller." Mr. Greusel was employed by the

Detroit Tribune, a leading paper of Detroit, to look up and prepare matter for publication pertaining to the fire department. An article was published which the commissioners claimed untruly reflected upon the management of the department, and they directed the secretary not to permit Mr. Greusel to examine any more of the books belonging to the department. Upon the refusal of Mr. Tryon to permit an examination of the books by Mr. Greusel, the managing editor of the Tribune wrote a letter to the mayor, stating the refusal by Mr. Tryon to allow Mr. Greusel to examine the books, and saying that they had information which led them to believe that serious irregularities existed in the management of the fire department, and asked the mayor to request Controller Moore to make an examination of the books in the presence of Mr. Greusel. It was also claimed by the mayor that he had received information of irregularities from other sources.

The mayor and the controller visited the office of the fire department, and found the assistant secretary in charge. He was informed by the mayor that he had come, as mayor, to examine the books. A few books and papers were examined, but those in the safe were not produced for his inspection. The next day the mayor, accompanied by Mr. Greusel, visited the office, and found the plaintiff in charge. The mayor requested that Mr. Greusel be allowed to examine the books as his representative. This was refused. He then demanded to see the books himself, and was told that he could not do so until Mr. Goodfellow, president of the commission, was notified. Later in the day, Mr. Pingree, accompanied by his secretary, two policemen, and Mr. Greusel, again visited the office. Mr. Tryon was not there. The books were not produced for examination, and, after a delay of an hour, the mayor and his secretary left the office. Mr. Greusel remained, with written authority from the mayor to examine the books in his behalf.

After leaving the office, Mr. Pingree met Mr. Tryon and Mr. Goodfellow on their way to the fire department. Some conversation ensued. The mayor stated that he had left Mr. Greusel to examine the books. He was informed by Mr. Goodfellow that the commission was in charge of that office, and that he would go down and throw Greusel out; and the defendant stated he would go along and see him thrown out. A whispered conversation occurred between Mr. Tryon and Mr. Goodfellow, and Mr. Tryon went on ahead of the others. When Mr. Pingree and Mr. Goodfellow reached the offices, they were closed, and the doors locked. A controversy arose. A number of firemen were called by Mr. Goodfellow to eject Mr. Greusel. Mr. Pingree attempted to protect him. Then Mr. Elliott and other seized and held Mr. Pingree and Mr. Greusel was thrown downstairs. Mr. Pingree remained for a time, and demanded to see the books. His demand was refused. About 6 o'clock of the same day, Mr. Pingree, with his secretary, Mr. McLeod, and several policemen, again visited the offices of the fire department, and demanded to see the books. His demand was refused, upon the ground that it was after office hours. On the evening of the same day, Mr.

Pingree summoned to his office Mr. Flowers, a lawyer, Police
Justice Sellers, John G. Hawley, a lawyer, and others. It
is claimed by the defendant that he fully and fairly stated
all of the facts of which he was advised to Mr. Hawley, his
lawyer, and that he was advised by Mr. Hawley that the plaintiff and Mr. Goodfellow, Mr. Elliott, and other persons were
guilty of a conspiracy. Mr. Hawley dictated a complaint charging conspiracy, in the presence of both of the police justices.
The complaint was sworn to by Mr. Pingree. Police Justice Sellers issued a warrant. It is claimed that this ended his connection with the criminal case. On the part of the plaintiff
it is claimed that, at the examination, he was represented by
private counsel, and that he instigated the arrest and the subsequent prosecution of the case. Mr. Tryon was arrested, gave
bail, and at the examination, after the witnesses were sworn,
upon advice of the prosecuting attorney, was discharged. He
then brought this suit, with the result already stated.

A good many questions are raised by the record and briefs.
It is admitted that the mayor had the right to examine the
books in his official capacity; but it is claimed by the plaintiff that, in all he did, he was not acting as mayor, but was
seeking to help Mr. Greusel personally, and was actuated by
improper motives. It is also claimed by the plaintiff that
the mayor could not delegate his right to examine the books
to Mr. Greusel. It is urged that Mr. Pingree did not fully
and fairly state all the facts he knew to Mr. Hawley. It is
contended that to obstruct an executive officer is not a crime,
either at common law or by statute, and that the complaint
which was made did not charge an offense. A large number of
assignments of error were taken. These have all had careful
consideration; but it will not be necessary, in our view of
the case, to discuss all of them.

The charge of the trial judge, so far as it is necessary to
quote it, was as follows:

"I give you defendant's sixth request, as modified: 'That,
the warrant having been issued by a court having jurisdiction
of the preliminary examination of all offenders or offenses
committed in Detroit, the judgment of the court that there is
such a crime as the one charged, and that there was reason to
think the persons charged had committed it, protects all persons concerned in the issue or execution of the warrant, as
far as false imprisonment is concerned.' I charge you that
it is the law of this case that there can be no recovery as
against the defendant on the count in this declaration for
false imprisonment. I understand it to be the law as laid
down in Wheaton v. Beecher, 49 Mich. 348, that, when the offense stated in the warrant is such an offense that the justice has jurisdiction of the subject-matter, the warrant will
protect the officer serving it, and also all parties making
the complaint. I charge you that in this case the justice
did have jurisdiction of the subject-matter for which this
warrant was issued, and that, having jurisdiction of the subject-matter, there can be no recovery in this case upon any

1438

ground of false imprisonment. The question that I shall leave to you is simply one question for you to determine, or two questions, rather, and that is upon the count in this declaration charging the defendant with malicious prosecution. Indeed, in order to sustain an action for malicious prosecution, it is necessary that two things should be proven: <u>First</u>, that there should be malice, - and, in a case of malicious prosecution, I understand malice to be an intentional wrongdoing. This malice may be inferred from want of probable cause; that is, if there was no probable cause for the issuing of the warrant, then a jury may infer from that a malice such as is required by law. But, gentlemen of the jury, want of probable cause is to be inferred or to be proven or established before you in this case on these premises: I charge you that if the defendant in this case, Mr. Pingree, fully, fairly, and honestly stated the facts as they appeared to him, and as he knew them, to John G. Hawley, or to the police magistrate, and that, upon such a statement, this warrant was issued, then there can be no recovery in this case for malicious prosecution, even if the advice of John G. Hawley was wrong, or the warrant was issued without authority of law, or the warrant did not state any offense against the law. The principle which governs in this case is laid down by the Supreme Court of the State, and is as follows: 'Every man of common information is presumed to know that it is not safe in matters of importance to trust to the legal opinion of any but recognized lawyers. When a person resorts to the best means in his power for information, it will be such proof of honesty as would disprove malice, and operate as a defense proportionate to his diligence.' And in <u>Perry v. Sulier</u>, <u>92</u> <u>Mich.</u> <u>75</u>, it is said that 'the person seeking and receiving such advice is, in law and in morals, justified in acting upon it, provided that he fully and fairly states the facts to the attorney.' Now, that is the question for you to decide, and the sole question involved in this case for your determination. And this language also has been used by the Supreme Court, which covers the law in this case which I think it necessary to submit to your consideration, and the rule fully stated, that, if a prosecutor has fairly submitted to his counsel all the facts that he knows, capable of proof, and he has acted <u>bona fide</u> on the advice given, he negatives the want of probable cause, and is not liable in an action of malicious prosecution. . . . If you shall find that the statement made by Mayor Pingree or Mr. Pingree, of the facts as they were shown to him, and as he knew them, and of all the facts, was fairly stated to John G. Hawley, and the warrant obtained after that statement, then the defendant in this case is not liable for any damages; but if you shall find the facts were not fairly stated, that he was actuated by malice, that he did not conduct himself in a <u>bona fide</u> way, or did not come up to any of the principles laid down in the law as I have stated it to you, then the plaintiff would be entitled to recover such damages as you shall see fit to give him under the rule that I have already laid down in giving the requests of the plaintiff

1439

on the subject of damages, which is needless for me here to repeat."

We must assume that the provision of the charter of Detroit (chapter 16, sec. 24), authorizing the mayor to examine the books of the fire commissioners at all times was designed to promote the public interest, by securing honesty and accuracy in the management of the affairs of the department under the control of the fire commissioners. Any obstacle that should be unlawfully interposed to prevent such an examination for a proper purpose would be an obstruction of the functions of government, and indictable as such at the common law. It is said that the offense of obstruction of officers is confined to court officers, bailiffs, etc., and does not extend to officers who have to do with executive duties, as contradistinguished from those having judicial functions, and those who are charged with the enforcement of judicial mandates, conservators of the peace, etc., and that no case can be found where one has been convicted for such an offense. This does not necessarily imply that acts constituting an obstruction of government are not indictable at common law, and we should be reluctant to hold that acts of trespass, not otherwise criminal, would not become criminal if the object and effect were to prevent the governor, or legislators, or other State officers from performing the duties pertaining to their respective departments. We cannot think that the mother country, which punishes seditious libels and slanders, would have tolerated acts which actually interrupted official action; and it is possible that the English law would justify the conclusion that such an act would be punishable as a contempt against the king's prerogative, by fine and imprisonment, at the discretion of the king's court of justice. 4 Bl. Comm. 122. Mr. Bishop, in dealing with the question, has no apparent hesitancy in saying that the obstruction of governmental functions is criminal, where the act is of sufficient magnitude to deserve notice. 1 Bish. New Cr. Law, Sec. 457. He says (section 480) that "of natures akin to treason, yet of inferior rank, are the various obstructions of the governmental machinery. The leading ones have been particularized in this chapter, but all other obstructions of the like sort and magnitude are also common law offenses." It is fair to say that he adds: "Practically, the law of this chapter is greatly circumscribed by the rule that it does not notice small things." Just where the line is which marks the limit of crime, and separates it from the realm of "small things which the law does not punish," is hard to say; but we are impressed with the gravity of an act which prevents executive officers of the nation, State, or cities from performing the duties of their offices.

If it be a fact that it was suspected that irregularities existed in the management and use of the funds of the fire department of Detroit, the public was interested in knowing the truth, and had the right, through its mayor, to ascertain it; and, if interested parties were able to prevent it, with impunity, there would be no means of protecting the government

1440

in its rights except the slow process and uncertain efficiency of civil proceedings. Whether the charge was well or ill founded is another question. The warrant was sufficient to charge a most flagrant case, and being, in our opinion, good upon its face, the plaintiff's remedy then, if he had been wronged, was confined to an action for malicious arrest or prosecution, and the trial court did not err in directing a verdict for the defendant upon the count for false imprisonment.

While we are convinced that obstruction of the performance of an official duty is an offense at common law, we understand that the inquiry may always be made in a court of justice whether the obstruction is of an official or a private act. If the latter, it cannot be said that it is an obstruction of, or interference with, governmental functions. Hence evidence tending to show the defendant's object should not have been excluded. 2 Bish. New Cr. Law, Sec. 1010 and cases cited. . . .

The judgment of the circuit court is reversed, and a new trial ordered.

People v. Smith
131 Mich. 70

GRANT, J. Respondent was convicted of resisting an officer. The treasurer of the village of Benzonia, in July, 1901, by virtue of his tax roll and warrant, levied upon certain personal property as the property of Otis Smith for a tax levied against him. While in the act of removing it, the respondent interfered, and resisted the officer. Two defenses were interposed:

1. That the property seized belonged to respondent, although in the possession of Otis Smith, and he offered to show ownership in himself.
2. The illegality of the organization of the village of Benzonia.

Both defenses were ruled out, and respondent was convicted. Upon the first point counsel for respondent relies upon People v. Clements, 68 Mich. 655 (36 N.W. 792, 13 Am. St. Rep. 373). In that case a sheriff levied upon exempt property, and it was held that the debtor was not compelled to submit to a trespass without reasonable resistance. That case does not apply to property not exempt, and which is seized by virtue of a tax warrant, and the officer has already seized and is in possession of the property. The treasurer in this case loaded the property, and was in the public highway in the act of removing it, when the respondent forcibly interfered. Under Sears v. Cottrell, 5 Mich. 251, the levy was lawful.

The village of Benzonia was organized by an act of the legislature in 1899. Its organization cannot now be collaterally attacked. Carleton v. People, 10 Mich. 250, 255; Coe v. Gregory,

1441

53 Mich. 19 (18 N.W. 541).
Conviction affirmed.

HOOKER, C. J., MOORE and MONTGOMERY, JJ., concurred.
LONG, J., did not sit.

People v. King
230 Mich. 405

McDONALD, J.   The defendants are traveling evangelists.
They were convicted of resisting the execution of an ordinance
and the order of the mayor of Alma, Michigan.   The people's
testimony tends to show that the defendants began holding religious meetings on June 13, 1925, in Wright Park, a city park
in Alma, Michigan.   The park adjoins the Michigan Old People's
Masonic Home and Hospital.   No formal permission was given by
the city, but the meetings continued without objection until
complaints came in of excessive noise and misuse of the park.
The city commission then decided to deny the use of the park
to the defendants after Saturday, June 18, 1925, and left the
matter to the mayor, the city manager, and the chief of police,
who caused the defendants to be notified that the meetings
must be discontinued after Saturday night.   Notwithstanding
this notice, the defendants announced that meetings would be
held as usual.   The defendant King spoke in defiance of the
city authorities, told the people that they were not living
in Rome, that the park belonged to them, and the mayor had no
right to deny to them the use of it.   By order of the mayor,
the park was closed on Sunday, July 19, 1925.   The gates were
roped off and the chief of police, with several regular policemen and special officers, were stationed at the park to prevent its use by the defendants.   Before the time announced for
the meeting, the mayor went to the park and talked to the defendants.   He told them that they could not use the park.   Defendant King insisted that the mayor was wrong, and said that,
notwithstanding his order, they would hold their meetings.   Two
of the defendants sought places of entrance not guarded by the
police, and entered the park.   They were ejected.   They then
addressed the people who had congregated in large numbers on
the outside, and advised them to break down the fence and go
into the park.   The crowd followed this advice, and broke over
into the park in spite of the efforts of the officers to restrain them.   The meeting was held according to schedule.   This
prosecution followed.
   The defendants denied many of the claims of the people
though there is little dispute as to the material facts.   They
were convicted and have brought the case to this court on exceptions before sentence.
   The errors assigned relate to the admission of evidence,
to the refusal to give certain requests, and to the charge as
given.

The prosecution was brought under section 14994, 3 Comp. Laws 1915, which provides:

"If any person shall knowingly and wilfully obstruct, resist, or oppose any sheriff, coroner, township treasurer, constable, or other officer or person duly authorized, in serving, or attempting to serve or execute any process, rule or order made or issued by lawful authority, or shall resist any officer, in the execution of any ordinance, by-law, or any rule, order or resolution made, issued or passed by the common council of any city, board of trustees or common council or village council of any incorporated village or township board of any township, or shall assault, beat or wound any sheriff, coroner, township treasurer, constable, or other officer duly authorized, while serving, or attempting to serve or execute any such process, rule or order, or for having served or attempted to serve or execute the same, or shall so obstruct, resist, oppose, assault, beat, or wound any of the above named officers, or any other person or persons authorized by law to maintain and preserve the peace, in their lawful acts, attempts and efforts to maintain, preserve, and keep the peace, every person so offending shall, on conviction thereof, be punished." . . .

The first question discussed in defendants' brief is presented by ten requests to charge, and in substance is, that the court should have held, as a matter of law, that there was no question for the jury, and should have directed a verdict of not guilty. In other words, it is the defendants' claim that there was no offense committed under the statute; that the order of the mayor was not such an order as is contemplated by the statute; that the officers were not engaged in the execution of an ordinance; and that, considering the testimony most favorable to the people's case, the defendants were guilty of nothing more than a violation of an ordinance.

The ordinance in question is known as ordinance No. 67, and is entitled:

"An ordinance to regulate the use of the public parks of the city of Alma, Michigan."

The applicable part reads as follows:

"No person shall deliver any oration, address, speech, sermon, or lecture therein unless he shall have first received permission from the common council of the city of Alma, or the mayor or other lawful authority so to do; nor shall any public meeting be held therein unless leave is first obtained."

The statute under which this prosecution is brought makes it an offense for any person to "resist any officer in the execution of an ordinance," etc. Counsel for the defendants insist that, at the time when the offense is alleged to have been committed, the officers were not engaged in the execution of an ordinance and an effort to prevent its breach. To execute an ordinance, within the meaning of the statute, is to carry it into effect, to enforce its commands. The purpose

of this ordinance is to regulate the use of public parks. One
of the regulations is that such a park shall not be used for
public meetings without permission. In issuing a permit or
preventing the use of the park when a permit has been refused,
the officers are carrying into effect the purpose of the ordinance. They are executing it. The contention of counsel is
wholly without merit. At the time of the alleged offense the
officers were engaged in the execution of an ordinance.

Equally without merit is the claim that the only order contemplated by the statute is a court order. The statute expressly states an "order made or issued by lawful authority."
The ordinance authorizes the mayor to issue permits for the
use of the park. It was his duty to enforce the ordinance.
He could only do so by direction to the chief of police; and
when he ordered the chief to prevent the defendants from using
the park on the day in question, it was an "order issued by
lawful authority." The court correctly overruled the defendants' contention that if there had been any offense committed,
it was merely a violation of the ordinance and not of the
statute.

The objections to the refusal of the court to submit certain requests to the jury and to the charge as given may be
answered by saying that if there were any errors committed in
respect to those matters, they were without prejudice to the
defendants, because, under the undisputed evidence and the
law applicable thereto, the court might properly have directed
a verdict of guilty.

In determining what constitutes resistance to the execution
of the ordinance, the conduct of the defendants must be viewed in connection with the attending conditions and circumstances.
The officers had to deal not only with the defendants but with
a more or less excited crowd of several hundred people, most of
whom were in sympathy with the defendants, and in respect to
the holding of the meeting were under their absolute control.
It was the crowd incited by the defendants that finally over-
came the efforts of the officers to prevent the meeting. King
and one of the other defendants were ejected from the park by
two of the officers. King claimed that in doing so the officer
tore his coat. He got up on a barrel near the fence and addressed the crowd for 15 or 20 minutes. He showed his torn
coat. He attacked the mayor, and said that the people had a
right to use the park, that it was a public place. He said
that the mayor was not doing his duty, that he had a notion to
appoint himself mayor and let the people into the park, and
that if the mayor did not come and open it he, King, had a
right to do so. The defendant George Garner testified:

"When King announced he would make himself mayor - declare
himself mayor - words to that effect, it was a little loud;
he stated the mayor had over-stepped the mark, and he said,
'I have a notion to appoint myself as mayor and order the people to go in the park, go right in the park and we will hold
the meeting.'"

Other witnesses for the defendants testified as follows:

1444

"I saw King shortly after that standing up on something raised, talking to the people; the first thing I heard Mr. King say, he held up his right arm, and he had his coat sleeve nearly torn off. It was held a little at the top, and he was talking about the injustice of the officers. . . . I have never heard anyone that could stir up a crowd with regard to religion like King; he is the best talker I ever heard. He enthused me with his talk. I believed what he said and that was my spirit of mind when I went to the park on Sunday. I believed when I went to the park that I had a perfect right in the park on Sunday. Mr. King stood on a barrel and talked to the crowd fifteen or twenty minutes, and he told the people that it was a public place and they had a right to enter and they did enter the park. . . . I heard most of the talk King gave for fifteen minutes in front of the park; I might have heard all but I didn't pay attention to all. . . .

"Q. You heard him say it was a public park, and he kept motioning to the crowd to go on in, and the crowd went on in when he motioned to them?

"A. Some of them did. There was a crowd in the park before King got through talking; about half the crowd, two hundred, was on the outside and that crowd went through after he got through talking."

Defendant George Garner also testified that he and the other defendants went to the park with a "fixed determination" to hold the meeting notwithstanding any opposition from the officers. He said:

"When we were evicted from the park we told them that we were going to have that meeting. The officers, including Campbell (the chief), were in uniform and he told us he was a police officer. I have had quite an experience with police officers and at that time I intended to hold that meeting after he told us not to. . . . We held the meeting. We intended to do first what we did, but not with any violence."

It is not necessary to make further reference to testimony given in behalf of the defendants. That which we have referred to shows that, knowing they had been forbidden to use the park, the defendants went there with a fixed determination to hold the meeting. They found the park closed. Two of them gained entrance, but were ejected by the police. They were warned by the police officers to keep out. Instead of yielding to the law they persuaded their followers, who were present in large numbers, to enter and take possession of the park. What they did is undisputed, but their contention seems to be that they are not guilty of resisting the execution of the ordinance, because they did not resort to physical violence. To constitute an offense under this statute, it was not necessary that they should kick and fight and bite their way into the park. Their conduct under the circumstances was just as effective in resisting the officers as though they had used physical force.

If all of the testimony except that given by the defendants and their witnesses had been eliminated from the record, the jury would have been justified in finding them guilty. In view of this fact, we shall not spend any time in discussing technical objections to the proceedings of the trial. In the verdict of guilty there was no miscarriage of justice.

The judgment of conviction is affirmed. The court will proceed to sentence.

BIRD, C. J., and SHARPE, SNOW, STEERE, FELLOWS, WIEST, and CLARK, JJ., concurred.

People v. Boyd
174 Mich. 321

McALVAY, J. Respondent in this case was prosecuted before the circuit court for the county of Hillsdale and by a jury was convicted of the common-law offense of obstructing the administration of justice. The case is before this court on exceptions before judgment.

At the time of the commission of the alleged offense, there was a case pending against the respondent in the circuit court, aforesaid, upon an information filed therein against him, which case was upon the October, 1911, calendar of said court, which court convened October 9, 1911, and when the cause was reached upon the calendar the prosecutor answered that he was ready; that a motion for a continuance was filed by respondent, and the case was put at the foot of the calendar for further showing to be made on October 23d. Upon the said information therein the name of Nuel Craig was indorsed as a witness, and he was subpoenaed to appear and testify October 23d.

In the instant case the respondent is charged in the information (omitting the formal parts) as follows:

"On the 18th day of October, in the year one thousand nine hundred eleven, at the township of Cambria, in the said county of Hillsdale, one William J. Boyd, of said city of Hillsdale, having on the 9th day of October, A.D. 1911, been duly arraigned in the circuit court for the county of Hillsdale, on an information charging him with having kept a place where intoxicating liquors were kept for sale, sold, and furnished, in violation of Act No. 207 of the Public Acts of Michigan for the year 1889, as amended, and his plea thereto of not guilty having been entered by order of said court, and said cause having been set for trial at the October, 1911, term of said court, and one Nuel Craig having been duly summoned as a witness for the people on the trial of said cause to appear in said court on the 23d day of October, 1911, to testify in said cause, yet the said William J. Boyd, well knowing the premises, and with intent to obstruct and hinder the due course of justice, then and there wilfully and unlawfully dissuaded, hindered, bribed, hired, carried, and spirited away the said Nuel Craig, for the purpose of preventing him from appearing to

1446

testify as a witness on the trial of said cause, as aforesaid, to the obstruction and hindrance of public justice."

Upon the trial evidence was introduced tending to show that respondent knew that Craig was the principal witness on the preliminary examination of the case in which he had been subpoenaed in the circuit court to testify; that respondent, having made arrangements and agreed to pay Craig $50 to leave the State and not be present to testify, took him in an automobile, with the driver of the car, on the night of October 18, 1911, from Hillsdale county to Pioneer, Ohio; that after lunch, paid for by respondent, they went to Montpelier, Ohio, where respondent left Craig at the Wabash depot, handing him $50, and then respondent, with the driver, returned to Hillsdale in the car. No evidence was introduced on the part of respondent.

The assignments of error which are relied upon by respondent relate to rulings of the court upon objections, and will be discussed in the order presented.

The respondent objected to receiving any testimony in the case under the information, for the reason that it alleged no offense known to the law. This was overruled and exception taken. At the close of the testimony on the part of the people, a motion was made on his part to strike out all the testimony in the case for the same reason, which was also denied.

The contention of the respondent is that this information contained no allegation showing that the court in the original case against respondent had any jurisdiction, for the reason, among others, that it did not show that the local-option law was in force in Hillsdale county.

The question presented is one of first impression in this court. At the common law, to dissuade or prevent, or to attempt to dissuade or prevent, a witness from attending or testifying upon the trial of a cause is an indictable offense. 29 Cyc. p. 1333, and cases cited. In Canada it is made an offense by the Code. Can. Cr. Code, Sec. 180. By United States statute it is made an offense to impede or obstruct the due administration of justice by certain acts done with reference to a cause pending or contemplated to be brought in some Federal court.

Some of the United States have also enacted statutes of like character. We have no statute in this State upon the subject. The case is therefore prosecuted as a common-law offense, and in case of a conviction is punishable under section 11795, 3 Comp. Laws (5 How. Stat. (2d Ed.) Sec. 14987), which reads as follows:

"Every person who shall commit any indictable offense at the common law, for the punishment of which no provision is expressly made by any statute of this State, shall be punished by imprisonment in the county jail not more than two years, or fine not exceeding two thousand dollars, or both, in the discretion of the court."

It appears to be well settled upon authority that –

"Where dissuasion of or interference with a witness in a criminal proceeding is the basis of the charge, it is not necessary to allege that an indictment was found in the original case, the sufficiency of such indictment, or the guilt or innocence of the person therein charged." 15 Enc. Pl. & Prac. p. 27.

The question in the instant case is not the guilt or innocence of the respondent in the main case, nor the sufficiency of the information or the jurisdiction of the court, but whether the respondent is guilty of obstructing or interfering with the administration of justice. In an examination of the authorities we find none in conflict with the authority above cited. In one of the earliest authorities, where the exact question was before the Supreme Court of the State of Vermont (in 1847), that court said:

"Much of the argument at the bar has been expended upon supposed irregularities in the original proceedings against Goodale & Poor, and insufficiencies in the indictment against them prepared and laid before the grand jury. That indictment is not recited, and need not be in the present; it is not, consequently, before us. In offenses of this kind guilt or innocence does not depend upon the guilt or innocence of the original party, against whom the witness may be subpoenaed, or recognized, to appear; nor upon the sufficiency or insufficiency of the original indictment. To thwart or obstruct the due administration of justice by violence, bribery, threats, or other unlawful means, whether in preventing the attendance of witnesses, jurymen, or other officers of court, is a high-handed offense, which strikes at the vitals of judicial proceedings, and subjects to severe animadversion in every well-ordered community. The attempt to commit such an act, it is well settled, is itself a substantive offense, punishable by the common law.

"In this instance, the attempt was unsuccessful; the witness, Warren, attended court and testified before the grand jury, as he had bound himself by recognizance to do. Moreover, the parties against whom he appeared must be taken to have been innocent of the crime imputed to them; and, in addition to this, the indictment against them, if in the description of the offense it followed the complaint filed before the magistrate, I am inclined to think was fatally defective. Still, all these circumstances are entirely consistent with the respondent's guilt. Since the case of State v. Keyes, 8 Vt. 57 (30 Am. Dec. 450) (1836), it is quite unnecessary to pursue this subject at any length." State v. Carpenter, 20 Vt. 9, 12.

See, also, 3 Bishop's New Criminal Procedure, Sec. 897; 2 Wharton's Criminal Law (11th Ed.), Sec. 1597. See, also, State v. Holt 84 Me. 509 (24 Atl. 951); Commonwealth v. Berry, 141 Ky. 477 (133 S.W. 212, 33 L.R.A. (N.S.) 976, Ann. Cas. 1912C, 516), and notes.

The court was not in error in admitting the testimony under

the information, for the reason that the information sufficiently charged an offense.

It is further contended that the record shows that there was no obstruction to the due course of justice by the acts of respondent, if he committed them; and that, at most, these acts could only be charged as an "attempt." The charge in the information is that respondent, "well knowing the premises," and "with intent to obstruct and hinder the due course of justice, then and there wilfully and unlawfully dissuaded, hindered, hired, carried, and spirited away the said Nuel Craig, for the purpose of preventing him from appearing to testify as a witness on the trial of said cause."

There was evidence in the case tending to show that respondent had carried and spirited away this witness, for the purpose of preventing him from appearing and testifying. This charges a substantive offense; that respondent did this with intent to obstruct and hinder the due course of justice; therefore, when the acts charged were committed, the offense charged was complete. As will be seen from some of the cases already cited supra, only an "attempt" was charged. Respondents in these cases were charged with "endeavoring to dissuade, hinder, and prevent witness from appearing and testifying," and were held guilty, although the witness was not thereby prevailed upon to leave the jurisdiction. This objection was included in the motion to strike out the testimony and direct a verdict for respondent, on the ground that the offense proved was not the offense charged in the information. We determine that the court properly overruled the motion and submitted the facts to the jury. . . .

We find no error in the record of this case. The conviction is affirmed, and the case will be remanded to the circuit court, with directions to proceed to judgment.

STEERE, C. J., and MOORE, BROOKE, STONE, OSTRANDER, and BIRD, JJ., concurred. KUHN, J., did not sit.

Note

In People v. Ormsby, 310 Mich. 291, the court commented as follows with respect to the common law offense of obstructing justice. The term, to obstruct justice, connotes an interference with the orderly administration of law. In 46 C. J. p. 868, it is stated: "The phrase 'obstructing justice' means impeding or obstructing those who seek justice in a court, or those who have duties or powers of administering justice therein." . . .

The more common examples of obstruction of justice are the bribery and influencing of officials and officers intrusted with the enforcement of law, coercion of witnesses, interference with the obtaining of testimony, resisting an officer, and other acts generally calculated to interfere with the orderly process of the administration of law. . . .

1449

TITLE E: OFFENSES AGAINST PUBLIC ADMINISTRATION

CHAPTER 45.   OBSTRUCTION OF PUBLIC ADMINISTRATION . . .

(Definition of Terms)

Sec. 4501.   The following definitions apply in this chapter unless the context otherwise requires:

(a) "Government" includes any branch, subdivision or agency of the government of this state or any locality within it.

(b) "Governmental function" includes any activity which a public servant is legally authorized to undertake on behalf of a government.

(c) "Public servant" means any officer or employee of government, including legislators and judges, and any person participating as an adviser, consultant or otherwise in performing a governmental function; but the term does not include witnesses.

(d) "Peace officer" includes any public servant vested by law with a duty to maintain public order or to make arrests for crime, whether that duty extends to all crimes or is limited to specific crimes.

Committee Commentary

The definitions will be discussed in the context of the individual sections which follow. They are derived primarily from Model Penal Code Sec. 240.0. The definition of "peace officer" follows Wisconsin Criminal Code Sec. 939.22 (22) (1963). The definition of "governmental function" is a logical extension of the definition of "government" and was included primarily to avoid any possible suggestion that the term was limited by the "governmental" vs. "proprietary" function distinction found in certain areas of local government law.

(Obstructing Government Operations)

Sec. 4505.   (1) A person commits the crime of obstructing government operations in the second degree if he intentionally obstructs, impairs or hinders the performance of a governmental function by using or threatening to use violence, force, or physical interference or obstacle.

(2) This section shall not apply to:

(a) The obstruction, impairment or hindrance of unlawful action by a public servant.

(b) The obstruction, impairment or hindrance of the making of an arrest.

(c) The obstruction, impairment or hindrance of any

governmental function in connection with a labor dispute with
the government.

(3) Obstruction of government operations if a Class B
misdemeanor.

Committee Commentary

Summary

This section is designed to deal generally with the intentional obstruction of governmental activities. Interference
with the activities of peace officers is covered by Sec. 4506,
imposing a higher penalty. Section 4505 would still be available in such a situation, however, as an alternative, lesser
included offense. There are two areas of physical interference with government administration that are entirely exempt-
ed from the operation of Sec. 4505. Interference with an arrest raises special problems that are dealt with in Sec. 4625.
Obstructions stemming from governmental labor disputes are also
excluded on the ground that they involve special considerations
not within the competence of the Committee.

The basic aim of Sec. 4505 is three-fold. First, it seeks
to expand the coverage of the present law to encompass protection of all governmental functions. Second, it seeks to
limit the proscribed means of obstruction to physical interferences. Third, it seeks to impose a uniform mens rea requirement for all illegal obstructions: that the individual
act with a purpose to obstruct.

Derivation

Section 4505 is derived from Model Penal Code Sec. 242.1
and New York Revised Penal Law Sec. 195.05, but is more limited in coverage than either. It is also based in part on C.L.
1948, Sec. 750.479.

Summary of Present Law

There are at least 15 statutory provisions which presently
proscribe obstruction of government officials in performance
of their duties. The key provision is Penal Code Sec. 479
(C.L. 1948, Sec. 750.479) which deals with resisting arrest
as well as obstruction. The complicated phraseology of that
section leaves some question as to exactly how far it extends
in prohibiting obstructions of government operations.

It provides that:

Any person who shall knowingly and wilfully obstruct, resist or oppose any sheriff, coroner, township treasurer, constable or other officer or person duly authorized, in serving,
or attempting to serve or execute any process, rule or order
made or issued by lawful authority, or who shall resist any
officer in the execution of any ordinance, by law, or any rule,
order or resolution made, issued, or passed by the common

1451

council of any city board of trustees, or common council or
village council of any incorporated village, or township board
of any township or who shall assault, beat or wound any sheriff, coroner, township treasurer, constable, or other officer
duly authorized, while serving or attempting to serve or execute any such process, rule or order, or for having served,
or attempted to serve or execute the same, or who shall so obstruct, resist, oppose, assault, beat or wound any of the above
named officers, or any other person or persons authorized by
law to maintain and preserve the peace, in their lawful acts,
attempts and efforts to maintain, preserve and keep the peace,
shall be guilty of a misdemeanor, punishable by imprisonment
in the state prison not more than 2 years, or by a fine of not
more than 1,000 dollars.

Closely related to Sec. 479 is C.L. 1948, Sec. 750.217, which
makes it a misdemeanor, punishable by one year in the county
jail, to disguise oneself with the intent to intimidate, hinder
or interrupt any officer in the performance of his duty or the
exercise of his legal rights. There are also various provisions
which proscribe obstructions of particular officers in connection
with particular duties. These include: C.L. 1948, Sec. 286.7
(agriculture commissioner; duties relating to apiaries); C.L.
1948, Sec. 287.15a (agriculture commissioner; duties relating
to testing cattle for TB); C.L. 1948, Sec. 287.149 (agriculture
commissioner; regulation of sale and distribution of livestock
remedies); C.L. 1948, Sec. 288.8 (agriculture department or commissioner of health; duty to insure wholesome milk); C.L. 1948,
Sec. 289.40 (dairy and food commissioner; general duties); C.L.
1948, Sec. 290.629 (superintendent of weights and measures; general duties); C.L. 1948, Sec. 300.25 (director of conservation;
duties regarding wildlife); C.L. 1948, Sec. 408.94 (factory
inspector; Department of Labor); C.L. 1948, Sec. 427.14 (hotel
inspector); C.L. 1948, Sec. 408.340 (Commissioner of Labor; ski
area safety); C.L. 1948, Sec. 750.241 (firemen). These provisions vary considerably in language, although they are all
aimed at basically the same type of obstruction as Sec. 479.
All of these provisions provide for normal misdemeanor punishment, however, while Sec. 479 permits a possible penalty of
two years in the state prison.
In addition to the foregoing statutory provisions, the common-law offense of obstructing justice would obviously cover
various obstructions of government operations. The scope of
the common law offense was best described in People v. Ormsby,
310 Mich. 291, 299-300, 17 N.W. 2d 187 (1945): "'The term to
obstruct justice' connotes an interference with the orderly
administration of law. . . . The more common examples of obstructing justice are the bribery and influencing of officials
and officers entrusted with the enforcement of law, coercion
of witnesses, interference with the obtaining of testimony, resisting an officer, and other acts generally calculated to interfere with the orderly process of the administration of law."

Scope of government activities protected

1452

Section 4505 applies to the obstruction of any government function, _i.e._, any activity which a public servant is legally authorized to undertake on behalf of the government (see Sec. 4501 (2)). This represents an extension of coverage beyond present provisions, though the degree of extension is not entirely clear. All interferences with the administration of law probably are proscribed already by present Sec. 479. That provision bars resistance of "any officer in the execution of any ordinance, by law, or any rule, order or resolution made, issued, or passed (by any local government)." Judicial decisions indicate that the reference to "any officer" emcompasses government officials generally (see People v. King, 236 Mich. 405, 210 N.W. 235 (1926) (mayor); People v. Smith, 131 Mich. 70, 90 N.W. 666 (1902) (treasurer)), and that the reference to "execution" encompasses the general administration of the law as well as the use of criminal or civil enforcement procedures (see King, supra, at 409 (issuance of a permit is "execution" of ordinance)). Thus, Sec. 4505 would not seem to go beyond present law insofar as it bars obstruction of the general application of statutes and regulations.

The additional scope of Sec. 4505 comes in its applicability to other governmental functions, which cannot properly be described as the administration of statutory commands. Examples of such activities are legislative investigations, addresses to public meetings, the training of employees at special schools, etc. The language of present Sec. 479 seemingly would not extend to these activities. The various miscellaneous provisions cited supra, however, often would cover these activities, since they frequently refer to obstruction of a particular officer with respect to any of his duties. Moreover, there is one case which can be viewed as suggesting that the common-law crime of obstructing justice might extend to all forms of governmental activities (see Tyron v. Pingree, 112 Mich. 338 (1897) (involving attempt by a mayor to examine the books of the fire department)).

In any event, the Committee has found no sound reason for limiting the government functions protected by Sec. 4505. Interference with "nonlaw-administration" activities may cause even greater injury to the efficiency of government operations than would an interference with the execution of various laws. Certainly no reason exists to continue to bar interference with such activities when conducted by the various officials listed in the special provisions cited supra, _e.g._, the commissioner of agriculture, without imposing a similar ban with respect to similar activities of more important government officials, _e.g._, the Governor.

Prohibited act: obstruction by physical interference or threat thereof

Section 4505 follows the present pattern of Michigan provisions in proscribing interference with government operations that "obstructs," "impairs" or "hinders" the performance of a governmental function. These terms are presently used in several

1453

provisions (see, e.g., C.L. 1948, Sec. 287.15a ("prevent, hinder or obstruct"); C.L. 1948, Sec. 286.7 (resist, impede or hinder)).

Section 4505 applies only to obstruction through the use or threat to use "violence, force, or physical interference or obstacle." The key here is the reference to "physical interference." Force and violence, of course, are only forms of physical interference; therefore, the references to these terms add nothing in and of themselves to the scope of the statute. They are included primarily as a way of emphasizing that "interference" encompasses more than obstruction by assault. The reference to physical "obstacle" serves a similar function. Creation of a physical obstacle would of course constitute use of physical interference, and the specific reference to obstacles is included only to re-emphasize that Sec. 4505 goes beyond obstruction by force.

The application of Sec. 4505 to non-violent physical activity follows present law. While most cases have involved the use of force, the courts in Michigan and other states have long recognized that any affirmative physical action can constitute an illegal obstruction (see People v. King, 236 Mich. 405, 411-412, 210 N.W. 235 (1926); 3 Wharton, Criminal Law, Sec. 1284 (Anderson Ed., 1957)). Various illustrations of illegal obstructions that do not involve force or violence can be given, e.g., tampering with an officer's car to prevent him from answering a call, frustrating an inspector's test by placing a foreign substance in the material he is testing (cf. Johnson v. State, 99 Fla. 1311, 128 So. 853 (salt placed in orange juice)) and the use of "non-violent" demonstration techniques, e.g., sit-ins, lie-ins, mass blockades, etc., to prevent public officials from carrying out their duties. The justification for punishing these activities is clear when one recalls that the crux of crimes against public administration is the unjustified disruption of government action, not the personal harm to the individual official involved. This point was clearly made in People v. King, supra, in which the defendants led a group of followers to break down a fence which the police had constructed to keep them out of a public park:

"(Defendants) contention seems to be that they are not guilty of resisting the execution of the ordinance, because they did not resort to physical violence. To constitute an offense under this statute, it was not necessary that they should kick and fight and bite their way into the park. Their conduct under the circumstances was just as effective in resisting the officers as though they had used physical force." (236 Mich. 405, 411-12).

Section 4505 also follows present practice in its application to obstructions by threats to use physical interference. Of course, the use of a threat is not proscribed in and of itself, but only when it produces an obstruction, i.e., when the threat dissuades an officer from the performance of his duty. Michigan courts have long recognized that threats which have

that effect are criminal (see People v. Jones, 2 Mich. N.P.
194 (1871)). A variation of this rule adopted in some states
holds that a threat cannot constitute an obstruction unless
the individual involved has the present ability and apparent
intention to execute his threats (see Reed v. State, 103 Ark.
391, 147 S.W. 76; 3 Wharton, supra at Sec. 1284). No reference is made to this factor in Sec. 4505 because it really
relates to the basic issue of causation (i. e., did the officer fail to act because of the threat?) and mens rea (i. e.,
did the individual expect that his threats would have this
impact on the officer?).

The suggestion was made that Sec. 4505 not be limited to
obstructions by physical interference, but, consistent with
the philosophy of King, supra, be extended to all activities
which impede governmental administration. The present Michigan law on this score is unclear. On the one hand, there are
no Michigan obstruction cases in which there was not some overt
physical act (leaving aside People v. Boyle, 174 Mich. 321
(1913), which relates to the special problem of tampering
with witnesses). On the other, Michigan accepts the common-
law offense of obstruction and that offense has been viewed
as including obstruction by entirely passive means (see 3
Wharton supra at Sec. 1284, and cf. cases interpreting 18 U.
S.C. 1503). Also, in Tyron v. Pingree, 112 Mich. 338 (1897),
the court suggests in dictum that the mere refusal of one public official to permit his superior to examine certain records
in and of itself constituted a common-law offense. It should
be noted, however, that the facts also indicated a threat to
throw the superior out of the office. The Committee felt that
although there is some validity in this common-law position,
Sec. 4505 nevertheless should be limited to instances of physical interference. If the section were to include all activities which obstruct government operations, irrespective of the
absence of physical interference, it could unduly restrict
legitimate opposition to government activities. Thus, in the
District of Columbia one court held under such an unlimited
provision that a pedestrian who argued with a police officer,
thereby distracting him from performance of his duty, had obstructed government operations (1958 American Law Institute
Proceedings 391). Another illustration might be an individual
who refuses to give information concerning an event he witnessed. Although such activities would not necessarily fall within Sec. 4505 even if it were not limited to physical interference, the Committee sought to avoid any possibility that
they might result in criminal liability.

The Committee also decided against adoption of a provision,
such as that found in the Model Penal Code and the New York
obstruction sections, that would extend Sec. 4505 to all obstruction by "unlawful acts." This provision would of course
bar such acts of non-physical obstruction as the impersonation
of another in taking a civil service examination on his behalf.
But many such independently unlawful acts are already made illegal by special provisions dealing with the particular subject

1455

matter involved (see e.g., C.L. 1948, Sec. 38.515 (cheating on civil service exam)). Moreover, many others are of minor significance, not befitting a Class B misdemeanor penalty. The failure to file a report required by law, for example, is an unlawful act which may obstruct government operations, but it hardly belongs on a par with obstruction by physical interference. The same can be said for the failure to perform various other legal obligations, including, perhaps, the failure to pay a parking ticket.

Mens rea: purposeful action

Section 4505 requires that the individual intentionally obstruct, impair or hinder government administration. The mens rea required for purposeful action is defined in Sec. 305. It requires in this instance that the individual have a "conscious object" to cause an obstruction of governmental administration. The limitation of Sec. 4505 to intentional obstruction is consistent with the limited purpose of the Title E offenses.

The impact of the Sec. 4505 mens rea requirement on present Michigan law is uncertain. The reference to mens rea in the individual provisions dealing with interference with specific officers varies considerably. Some require that the individuals act willfully (e. g., C.L. 1948, Sec. 289.40), some knowingly (e. g., C.L. 1948, Sec. 409.26), some both (e. g., C.L. 1948, Sec. 750.241) and some neither (e. g., C.L. 1948, Sec. 427.14). The basic obstruction provision, Penal Code Sec. 479 (C.L. 1948, Sec. 750.479) is not much better in this regard. Initially it refers to one who "knowingly and willfully" obstructs, but later it proscribes "resistance" of any officer executing an ordinance and "assault" of an officer serving process without any mention of intent.

Exceptions to the application of section 4505

Current law clearly permits the use of force to resist an illegal arrest and to prevent an illegal attachment. (People v. Krum, 374 Mich. 356, 361, 132 N.W.2d 69 (1965)). The defense of illegality, however, rests solely on the fact of illegality, not on the actor's belief that the arrest or attachment was illegal. If the actor is mistaken in his belief, he must suffer the consequences. Although the Committee believes that the significance of illegality should be altered where peace officers are involved (see commentary to Sec. 4506), present policy seems most appropriate in the case of interference with other governmental officials. Accordingly, subsection (2) (a) makes the section inapplicable to interference with unlawful action by a public servant.

Section 4505 also is not applicable to obstruction of an arrest. This exemption is created because different policies are applicable in that area both as it relates to the degree of force used and the significance of illegality. Obstruction of arrest is covered in other provisions, primarily Sec. 4625.

A third exception to the applicability of Sec. 4505 is the obstruction of a governmental function in connection with a labor dispute involving the government. As previously noted, the physical interference prohibited by Sec. 4505 could include various demonstration techniques, such as sit-ins and mass blockades, which are sometimes used in connection with labor disputes even though they may be statutorily barred as "unfair labor practices" (see e.g., 29 U.S.C. Sec. 141 et seq.). To the degree these activities are criminal they are generally punished under statutes aimed at the protection of life or property (cf. Automobile Workers v. Russel, 78 S.Ct. 932, 356 U.S. 634, 2 L.Ed. 1030 (1958)). A labor dispute involving government employees, however, presents special problems. Without the subsection 2 (c) exemption, activities which might constitute no more than tortious unfair labor practices in the context of normal industrial disputes would take on the added burden of criminal liability when the employer interfered with was the Government. For example, if a group of school employees purposely engaged in mass picketing at the front entrance of a school administration building, they clearly would violate Sec. 4505 by purposely obstructing a government function through physical interference. The Committee feels that while such activity should not necessarily be protected, the appropriate sanctions should be determined by labor legislation, not the Criminal Code; i.e., if normal criminal penalties are to be imposed, this decision should be made after consideration of these activities in the context of general labor policy as reflected in relevant labor legislation.

Penalty

Violation of Sec. 4505 would constitute a Class B misdemeanor, with maximum punishment of three months imprisonment and a fine of $500. Most of the specific provisions under present law dealing with the obstruction of specified administrative officers also impose the basic misdemeanor penalty (see the provisions cited supra). However, the general obstruction provision, present Penal Code Sec. 479, imposes a maximum penalty of two years imprisonment and a $1000 fine. It must be remembered, however, that this provision deals with a wide assortment of obstructive activities and is aimed in large part at illegal interference with peace officers. Section 4506 in dealing with interference with peace officers imposes a penalty more in line with the present Sec. 479. The Committee felt that this more severe penalty was not appropriate in the case of interference with public administrators generally, especially when it is recalled that the more serious forms of interference, such as those involving bodily injury, can also be prosecuted as assaults, etc.

E.   Obstructing a Peace Officer

1. Michigan Compiled Laws (1948)

    C.L. 1948 750.479, supra, page 1435
    C.L. 1948 750.217, supra, page 1436

2. Case Law

People v. Krum
374 Mich. 356

KAVANAGH, C. J. Defendant appeals by leave granted from conviction on jury verdict for a violation of CL 1948, Sec. 750.479 (Stat Ann 1954 Rev Sec 28.747). . . and from sentence thereupon to serve 30 days in the county jail and pay a $1,000 fine and $346.20 in costs.

The criminal proceedings against defendant arose from an altercation which occurred between defendant and a member of the Michigan State police on September 26, 1959. Defendant and two traveling companions were returning from a fishing trip on that date, when the car in which they were riding was stopped at the Mackinac bridge by State police officers. The State police were looking for two prison escapees reported to be traveling by car and had established a blockade at the bridge. Defendant owned the car in which he and his companions were traveling, but someone else was driving it at the time it was stopped. One of the troopers asked the passenger in the back seat of the car to move a duffel bag and some equipment, to which the passenger replied that the trooper could not search the car without a search warrant. The trooper thereupon ordered the car driven to the side of the bridge, out of the line of traffic.

The defendant then got out of the car and advised the troopers that he and his companions were returning from a fishing trip, that there were no escapees in the car, and that there was no need to look into it. This aroused the officers' suspicions, which occasioned a rather loud discussion between the officers and defendant. When defendant was asked to show his driver's license, he refused to do so on the grounds that he had not been driving the automobile, and upon the further request that he show his registration certificate for the automobile, defendant declined so to do. Subsequently, despite his previous refusal to show the certificate, defendant got it from his glove compartment and returned to one of the troopers with the certificate and a pen in hand.

The trooper had, in the meantime, resumed his station near the tollgate where he was engaged in observing cars as they crossed the bridge.

Defendant testified that he asked the trooper his name; that he did nothing but write the name on a slip of paper,

1458

whereupon the trooper arrested him for obstructing the officer in carrying out his duty to inspect other cars as they stopped.

The trooper testified that defendant had asked for his name and badge number; that he told the defendant his name and asserted that the badge number was meaningless; that defendant insisted on seeing his badge, and interposed himself between the trooper and the car to be inspected, finally brushing against the trooper and moving the automatic carbine from the position in which it was held by the trooper; that the trooper told defendant he was under arrest and ordered him to go to the police car; that defendant answered, "I don't have to and you can't make me;" that the trooper then took him by the wrist and, when he wouldn't move, pulled him over to the police car. There defendant was handcuffed and taken to the Mackinac county jail.

Defendant's companions thereupon permitted the remaining troopers to search defendant's car, which search resulted in the finding of nothing incriminating.

These events occurred on September 26, 1959. The day following his arrest defendant was released on bail. Complaint and warrant were issued in February of 1960, during which month a preliminary examination was held. In October of 1960 an amended complaint and warrant were issued, followed by a second examination in November.

In December, 1960, defendant made a motion to quash the complaint and warrant on multiple grounds, which motion was denied. Defendant filed a motion for a speedy trial in March of 1961. The jury trial was then had in April of 1961, with the result noted above.

Defendant claims on appeal that the troopers had no probable cause to stop defendant's car and to search it. His argument is that his arrest was illegal and that he was, therefore, entitled to resist it and to be told the identity of the troopers. He claims errors relating to the alleged illegality of his arrest were committed by the trial court in the denial of his motion for directed verdict at the conclusion of the people's case, in the denial of his motion for new trial, and in the refusal to give instructions, relating to the issue of the legality of his arrest, requested by the defendant.

Defendant also claims that the imposition of a jail sentence in addition to a fine is illegal in view of the statutory provision reproduced in the margin above, which authorizes imprisonment or a fine, the defendant's claim being that the statutory language is in terms alternative. He also suggests that in any event the sentence was grossly excessive under all of the circumstances and taking into account the defendant's past exemplary record.

In addition, defendant claims the delay in bringing the case to trial violated his constitutionally guaranteed right to a speedy trial.

To all of this, the people respond that defendant's conviction was for obstructing an officer in the performance of his

1459

duties and that the legality or illegality of the prior actions by the troopers had nothing whatever to do with the acts upon which conviction was based. The people respond to the claim the sentence was illegal by referring to CL 1948, Sec. 769.5 (Stat. Ann Sec. 28.1077), which provides in part:

"Whenever it is provided that an offender shall be punished by . . . fine or imprisonment, the court may impose both such fine and imprisonment in its discretion."

It is first to be observed that obstructing a public officer is recognized in Michigan as a common-law crime,[2] as well as an offense under the statute quoted above in the margin. This reflects the general rule:

"The obstruction of or resistance to a public officer in the performance of his duties is an offense at common law, and by statute in all jurisdictions." (39 Am.Jur, Obstructing Justice, Sec. 8, p 506.)

While one may use such reasonable force as is necessary to prevent an illegal attachment[3] and to resist an illegal arrest,[4] the basis for such preventive or resistive action is the illegality of an officer's action, to which defendant immediately reacts. In the present case, however, the legality of the actions of the officers is not ruled on since they occurred sometime prior to the exact confrontation on which the complaint is based. It was not necessary to preservation of defendant's rights of personal liberty or property for him to have acted as the jury obviously believed he did, particularly since the officer had left the area and resumed his check of other cars.

Here the question is not whether the previous actions of the officers, aimed at defendant, were illegal or violative of his civil rights; if defendant was aggrieved thereby, he is not without remedy under the law. The question here is merely whether defendant obstructed the "officer, . . . authorized by law to maintain and preserve the peace, in (his) lawful acts, attempts and efforts to maintain, preserve and keep the peace." The jury found that defendant did so obstruct justice, and we find no reason, on the facts or under the law, to disturb that finding.

Defendant's claim that the imposition of a fine and imprisonment is illegal because the statute under which he was charged provided for fine or imprisonment is ineffective in view of the statute, cited by the people and quoted above, which provides that under such an alternative penalty provision, the trial court may impose both alternatives, in its discretion. As to the claim that the sentence was excessive, it is found to be within the limits set by the statute, and that precludes our altering it. People v. Connor, 348 Mich. 456.

The right to speedy trial, claimed by defendant to have been violated here, is guaranteed to the criminally accused by the Michigan Constitution of 1908, art 2, Sec. 19.[5] The right to a speedy trial, as defined by Hicks v. Judge of Recorder's Court of Detroit, 236 Mich 689, and People v. Den Uyl, 320 Mich 477,

means the right to a trial within a reasonable time, under all
attendant circumstances, as will give the people an opportunity
to present its case in court.

It cannot be said that a speedy trial was not given after
requests, since request was made in March and trial was held
in April. See People v. Foster, 261 Mich. 247.

One of the many circumstances to be considered in connection
with reasonable time is whether the accused is free on bail, as
defendant was in this case (People v. Den Uyl, supra p 491) and
the necessity for such ad hoc determination of the question demands that the decision be left largely within the discretion
of the trial judge. (Hicks v. Judge of Recorder's Court of
Detroit, supra.)

In view of the circumstances in this case, as described
above, it cannot be said that the trial judge abused his discretion in finding no violation of the right of defendant to
a speedy trial.

Judgment affirmed.

DETHMERS, KELLY, BLACK, SOURIS, SMITH, O'HARA, and ADAMS,
JJ., concurred.

Footnotes

2. Tryon v. Pingree, 112 Mich. 338 (37 LRA 222, 67 Am St Rep
398).

3. People v. Clements, 68 Mich 655 (13 Am St Rep 373).

4. 5 Am. Jur 2d Arrest, Sec. 94, pp 778-780.

5. The current provision is found at Const 1963, art 1, Sec. 20.

3. Final Draft - Michigan Revised Criminal Code

(Obstructing a Peace Officer)

Sec. 4506. (1) A person commits the crime of obstructing
a peace officer if, by using or threatening to use violence,
force or physical interference or obstacle, he intentionally
obstructs, impairs or hinders the enforcement of the criminal
law or the preservation of the peace by a peace officer recognized to be acting under color of his official authority.

(2) It is no defense to a prosecution under this section
that the peace officer was acting in an illegal manner, provided he was acting under color of his official authority.

(3) This section does not apply to the obstruction, impairment or hindrance of the making of an arrest.

(4) Obstruction of a peace officer is a Class A misdemeanor.

Committee Commentary

This provision is based on the premise that the basic core
of police activity - enforcement of the criminal law and main-

tenance of public order - is more important and needs more
protection from physical interference than governmental functions generally. In large part this follows present practice,
since present Penal Code Sec. 479, which imposes by far the
most severe penalty for obstruction, is aimed primarily at interference with police activity. Like the present section, Sec.
4506 extends to interference with the activities of regular
police officials, although it would not extend to coroners who
are covered by Sec. 479. Under Sec. 4501 (4) a peace officer
must be a public servant who has the duty and not just the
power to make an arrest. This would exclude such non-members
of the regular police force as plant guards, private detectives,
store "police", etc. As any private citizen may, they sometimes
have the power to make an arrest, but unless they are members
of a posse comitatus they do not have a duty to make an arrest.
Moreover, as private rather than governmental employees, they
would not be "public servants" under Sec. 4501 (3) (cf. C.L.
1948, Sec. 28.432 (applying similar standard in defining peace
officers for firearm licensing act)). When the requirements of
Sec. 4501 (4) are considered as a whole, the definition of a
peace officer is essentially limited to sheriffs, deputies,
policemen, constables (1952-54 Mich. Atty. Gen. Biennial Rep.
at 33), and game and fish wardens, insofar as they have a duty
to make and enforce certain criminal provisions of the Conservation Code (see C.L. 1948, Sec. 320.6; 1927-1928 Mich. Atty.
Gen. Biennial Rep. at 250).

Aside from its special application to interference with
peace officers, Sec. 4506 is largely patterned after Sec. 4505.
Like Sec. 4505, it is limited to intentional obstruction of
governmental function through the use, or threat to use, physical force or violence. As with Sec. 4505, it also does not
apply to the area of interference with arrests, since that subject is covered by a special provision. The special exemption
for labor disputes was not included in this provision, however,
because it was felt that typical labor practices in a gover-
ment labor dispute would not, and should not, interfere with
the enforcement of the criminal law or the preservation of
the peace, except possibly in disputes involving peace officers
themselves, and the latter situation is subject to special legislation.

The primary difference between Sec. 4505 and 4506 relates
to the illegality of the activity interfered with. Under Sec.
4506, illegality of the performance that was obstructed is
no defense provided the actor recognized that the person obstructed was (a) a peace officer, and (b) acting under color
of his official authority. In other words, if the actor recognizes that the public servant involved is a peace officer and
that he is seeking to act in that capacity, he cannot use force,
violence or physical interference to obstruct the officer's
action even though he believes that action is illegal. This
probably represents a change in Michigan law. Although Michigan cases justifying the use of force to obstruct unlawful
police action ordinarily relate to resisting an arrest, a

subject not within Sec. 4506 (see, e.g., People v. Krum, 374 Mich. 356, 132 N.W.2d 69 (1965)), it seems likely that the same rule would apply to interference with other law enforcement activities. In proposing a change in this rule, the Committee has followed the basic premise that a private individual should not take the law into his own hands, i.e., he should not seek to remedy what he considers illegal administration of the law by self-help (see Model Penal Code Sec. 3.04 (2)). If he feels that a particular police agency has no jurisdiction to patrol in a certain area, he should not respond by throwing bricks at a patrol car or even by letting the air out of police tires. If he feels that police have no authority, in an attempt to maintain the peace, to direct traffic in a certain manner, he should not respond by blocking traffic. Ordinarily, the use of self help in these situations only leads to escalation of force and in the end to possible injury to the actor. This has frequently been the end result, for example, when an individual has sought to use force to prevent what he considered to be an illegal search of premises. Certainly more adequate legal remedies than self-help can be provided in such instances. It should be remembered, of course, that the foregoing applies only when the actor recognizes that the party on the other side is a peace officer. Moreover, even here the section is not applicable if the actor believes the officer was acting for himself as a private citizen rather than under color of his authority. Since most cases involve uniformed officers, however, there usually will be little difficulty in establishing these elements.

F. Refusing to Aid a Peace Officer

1. Michigan Compiled Laws (1948)

750.483 Neglecting or refusing to aid sheriff, coroner, constable

Sec. 483. NEGLECTING OR REFUSING TO AID SHERIFF, ETC. - Any person who being required by any sheriff, deputy sheriff, coroner or constable, shall neglect or refuse to assist him in the execution of his office, in any criminal case or in the preservation of the peace, or the apprehending or securing of any person for a breach of the peace, or in any case of escape or rescue of persons arrested upon civil process, shall be guilty of a misdemeanor.

750.484 Refusing to apprehend on being required to do so by justice

Sec. 484. REFUSING TO APPREHEND ON BEING REQUIRED TO DO SO BY JUSTICE - Any justice of the peace, upon view of any breach of the peace, or any other offense proper for his recognizance, who shall require any person to apprehend and bring before him the offender, every person so required, who shall refuse to obey such justice, shall be guilty of a misdemeanor.

750.523 Same; refusal to aid officer

Sec. 523. REFUSAL TO AID OFFICER TO DISPERSE OR ARREST RIOTERS - If any person present, being commanded by any of the magistrates or officers aforesaid, to aid and assist in seizing and securing such rioters, or persons so unlawfully assembled, or in suppressing such riot or unlawful assembly, shall refuse or neglect to obey such command, or when required by any such magistrate or officer to depart from the place of such riotous or unlawful assembly, shall refuse or neglect to obey such command, or when required by any such magistrate or officer to depart from the place of such riotous or unlawful assembly, shall refuse or neglect so to do, he shall be deemed to be 1 of the rioters or persons unlawfully assembled, and shall be liable to be prosecuted and punished accordingly.

780.8 Authority of arresting officer

Sec. 8. AUTHORITY OF ARRESTING OFFICER. Every such peace officer or other person empowered to make the arrest, shall have the same authority, in arresting the accused, to command assistance therein, as peace officers have by law in the execution of any criminal process directed to them, with like penalties against those who refuse their assistance.

2. Case Law

There are no Michigan Supreme Court decisions construing the aforesaid statutes. - Ed.

3. Final Draft - Michigan Revised Criminal Code

(Refusing to Aid a Peace Officer)

Sec. 4520. (1) A person commits the crime of refusing to aid a peace officer when, upon command by a person known to him to be a peace officer, he unreasonably refuses or fails to aid such peace officer, in:

    (a) Effectuating or securing an arrest; or
    (b) Preventing the commission by another of any offense.

(2) Refusing to aid a peace officer is a Class C misdemeanor.

Committee Commentary

Summary

This section requires that the actor (1) refuse or fail to aid a "peace officer" (defined in Sec. 4501 (4)) after being commanded to do so, (2) know that the person commanding him to give aid is a peace officer, and (3) have no reasonable excuse for refusing or failing to aid, such as illness or disability. Moreover, the section applies only to commands for assistance in (a) making an arrest or holding a person already arrested and (b) preventing another crime.

Section 4520 is derived primarily from Michigan statutes cited infra, New York Revised Penal Law Sec. 195.10, and Illinois Crim. Code Sec. 31-8. Numerous states have similar provisions (see e.g., Alaska Statutes Ann. Sec. 11.30.200 (1962); Minn. Stat. Sec. 629.403).

Relationship to existing law

Michigan presently has four basic provisions dealing with the refusal to aid a peace officer. The key provision is C.L. 1948, Sec. 750.483, which makes it a misdemeanor for any person, upon request, to "neglect or refuse to assist a sheriff, coroner or constable in the execution of his office, in any criminal case or in the preservation of the peace, or the apprehending or securing of any person for a breach of the pace, (sic) or in any case of escape or rescue of persons arrested upon civil process." C.L. 1948, Sec. 780.8, extends the peace officer's authority to request assistance to cases involving arrests made pursuant to the Uniform Extradition Act. C.L. 1948, Sec. 750.484, authorizes a justice of the peace, upon view of a breach of peace within his jurisdiction, to command aid in apprehending the offender, and makes refusal to obey such a command a misdemeanor. Finally, C.L. 1948, Sec. 750. 523, deals with refusal to assist an officer in quelling a riot, and treats the person who refuses to assist as one of the rioters. Section 4520 is not designed to replace this provisions, which is covered in Chapter 55.

The present provisions extend to requests made by sheriffs, coroners, constables and justices of the peace. Section 4520 is limited to refusals to assist "peace officers." The definition of peace officer has been discussed supra in connection with Sec. 4506. While it clearly encompasses sheriffs and constables, it would not include coroners and justices of the peace (see C.L. 1948, Sec. 52.87 on the authority of coroners). Section 4520 will, on the other hand, include one category of officers not covered by our present law. Game and fish wardens are "peace officers" under the definition of Sec. 4500 (4) since they are public servants who have a duty to make arrests for the commission of specific crimes (see C.L. 1948, Sec. 320.6, 1927-1928 Mich. Atty. Gen. Biennial Rept. at 250). There appears to be no reason why these officers should not be able to command assistance in making arrests within the areas of their authority when constables would have that authority. The conservation crimes involved are primarily misdemeanors, but the authority of constables, deputies, etc. also applies to misdemeanor arrests.

Section 4520 also varies from present law by limiting the areas in which the failure to assist is criminal. C.L. 1948, Sec. 750.483, makes it a misdemeanor to refuse to aid a sheriff in "the execution of his office" in (1) "any criminal case," (2) "the preservation of the peace or the apprehension or securing of any person for a breach of the peace," and (3) "any case of escape or rescue of persons arrested upon civil process." The Committee, including representatives of the police, believe that the present coverage is too broad; a citizen's duty to assist should be emphasized by carefully limiting it to areas of special importance. There are many activities which fall within the "execution of (a sheriff's) office . . . in any criminal case" which ought not be performed if they can only be performed by commandeering the services of private citizens. Read literally, the present law would require a person to serve as a police spy, help search a house, unload contraband from a truck, etc. Section 4520, following the lead of New York, Illinois and other states, limits the citizen's duty to assist to functions which are likely to require assistance in emergency situations - preventing another from committing a crime and effectuating or securing an arrest.

The present provisions make it a crime simply to refuse to obey an officer's command; no mention is made of the defendant's knowledge that the person issuing the command is an officer. Section 4520, however, in accord with the usual policy favoring a mens rea requirement, adds that element. It may be argued that Sec. 4520 goes too far in requiring actual knowledge and that it should be sufficient that the defendant should have known the individual involved was an officer. New York takes this approach, making the defendant liable only when the "peace officer" was either "identifiable" or actually identified himself in making his request. The Committee believes, however, that the knowledge requirement is established easily enough in either situation.

Section 4520 does not apply if the individual's refusal to assist the peace officer was "reasonable." The present Michigan provisions make no reference to this factor. Obviously, assistance cannot be expected from all persons in all situations. The situation may, for example, present great danger to the individual because of some physical illness or other restriction on his activities. To catalogue specifically all such reasonable grounds for refusing to give aid would, however, be impossible. The Committee therefore concluded that on balance, while the phrase "unreasonably refuses or fails" is not as precise as one might desire, it still is preferable to having an absolute requirement to render aid as under the present law.

G. Resisting Arrest

    1. Michigan Compiled Laws (1948)

1466

C.L. 1948, 750.479, supra, page 1435

750.479a Failure to obey direction of police officer to stop
          motor vehicles; assault upon police officer

Sec. 479a. A driver of a motor vehicle, who is given by
hand, voice, emergency light or siren a visual or audible signal by a police officer, acting in the lawful performance of
his duty, directing the driver to bring his motor vehicle to
a stop, and who wilfully fails to obey such direction, by increasing his speed, extinguishing his lights, or otherwise attempting to flee or elude the officer, is guilty of a misdemeanor, punishable by a fine not to exceed $1,000.00 or by im-
prisonment for not more than 1 year, or both. The officer giving the signal shall be in uniform; and a vehicle driven at
night shall be adequately identified as an official police vehicle.
Any person who forcibly assaults or commits a bodily injury
which requires medical care or attention upon a peace or police
officer of this state while the peace or police officer is engaged in making a lawful arrest, knowing him to be a peace or
police officer, is guilty of a misdemeanor, punishable by a
fine not to exceed $1,000.00 or by imprisonment in the state
prison for not more than 2 years, or both. P.A. 1931, No.
328, Sec. 479a, added by P.A. 1966, No. 299, Sec. 1, Eff.
March 10, 1967.

317.165 Unlawful to resist officer

Sec. 5. It shall be unlawful for any person to resist
or obstruct any officer or person empowered to make arrests
under the provisions of this statute.[1]

1. Reference is to P.A. 1927, No. 285, concerning hunting. - Ed.

752.825 Resisting arrest

Sec. 5. It shall be unlawful for any person to resist
or obstruct any officer or person empowered to make arrests
under the provisions of this act.[1]

1. Reference is to P.A. 1951, No. 105, concerning hunting,
fishing, and trespassing. - Ed.

      2. Case Law

                    People v. Haley
                    48 Mich. 495

CAMPBELL, J. Haley was convicted of the offense of resisting an officer. Complaint was first made before a magistrate,

1467

and defendant waived examination and was held to bail to appear at the trial court, which was the Superior Court of Grand Rapids. An information was filed in that court for the statutory offense. . . .

There was testimony introduced by the defence tending to show that the assault which was the officer's excuse for arresting defendant without a warrant was not committed in his presence and was over and the defendant removed before he came to the place where the arrest was made; and that he 'did not make it until he had gained such knowledge as he possessed from inquiries made of third persons.

The doctrine has been repeatedly settled, and has been recognized in this Court, that an officer has no right to arrest without a warrant for any breach of the peace not committed in his presence. Quinn v. Heisel, 40 Mich. 576; Sarah Way's Case 41 Mich. 299. The court below erred in holding differently, and for this error a new trial must be granted.

The judgment below must be reversed, and the defendant discharged from the State House of Correction and Reformatory at Ionia, and remanded to the custody of the sheriff of the county of Kent to be let to bail and if not bailed to be held to be dealt with according to law, and a new trial must be granted unless the prosecution is discontinued.

COOLEY and MARSTON, JJ. concurred.

People v. Burt
51 Mich. 199

(For the opinion in this case see page 420, supra.)

People v. Tompkins
121 Mich. 431

George Tompkins was convicted of assaulting an officer. Reversed.

The following is a copy of the information:

"State of Michigan,
The Circuit Court for the County ss
        of Iosco

"Iosco County - ss
"Albert E. Sharpe, prosecuting attorney for the county of Iosco aforesaid, for and in behalf of the people of the State of Michigan, comes into said court in the August term thereof, A.D. 1898, and gives it here to understand and be informed that George Tompkins and James Hamilton, of the

1468

township of Oscoda, in the county of Iosco and State of Michigan, heretofore, to wit, on the 23d day of July, in the year one thousand eight hundred and ninety-eight, at the village of Oscoda, in said Iosco county, did then and there knowingly and willfully assault, beat, and wound George H. Cosgrove, while, the said George H. Cosgrove, was attempting to serve and execute a warrant for the collection of taxes in and for the said village of Oscoda, in said county, said warrant having been made and executed and attached to the tax roll of said village of Oscoda by Vernon E. Rix, president of said village, on the 20th day of May, 1898, and, by authority of the common council of said village, extended by said president, Vernon E. Rix, on the 8th day of July, 1898, for thirty days thereafter, and the said George H. Cosgrove being then and there the village treasurer of said village of Oscoda, duly elected and qualified as such, it being then and there his duty to levy and collect the village taxes in said village under said warrant, and said tax roll of said village of Oscoda being then and there in the hands of said George H. Cosgrove for collection, contrary to the form of the statute in such cases made and provided, and against the peace and dignity of the people of the State of Michigan.

"Albert E. Sharpe,
"Prosecuting Attorney for the County of Iosco."

Main J. Connine and Crane & Crane, for appellant.

Albert E. Sharpe, Prosecuting Attorney, for the people.

HOOKER, J. The defendant asks that the information in this cause be held insufficient, upon the ground that it fails to allege that he knew that the person assaulted was an officer, or that he knew that he was at the time in the discharge of his duty. It is contended that it states only that the assault was willfully and knowingly made. It seems to me that this is hypercritical, and, moreover, that it is not an accurate interpretation of the language. The law attempts to punish an assault upon an officer while in the discharge of his duty by a penalty more severe than that imposed for other assaults. It requires that the offense shall be committed knowingly and willfully. If an assault is willful, it is intentional; and, if intentional, it must be made knowingly. If, therefore, we are to apply these words as we are asked to do, the word "knowingly" is superfluous. There is no doubt that a knowledge that the person assaulted is an officer in the discharge of his duty was made an element of the offense, and that the insertion of the word "knowingly" in the statute had reference to this, and not to the assault, which could not be willful unless made intentionally, and therefore knowingly. Had this information stated that the defendant willfully, with force and arms, assaulted A. B., knowing him, the said A. B., to be then and there an of-

ficer, etc., it would be held good. Instead of that, the
exact order of language used in the statute (3 Comp. Laws
1897, Sec. 11327) was followed, and, as it could have but
one meaning, it was sufficient.

We think the conviction must be set aside upon the ground
that hearsay evidence of the ownership of the property sought
to be levied upon was admitted.

The conviction must be set aside, and a new trial ordered.

The other Justices concurred.

3.   Final Draft - Michigan Revised Criminal Code

(Resisting Arrest)

Sec. 4625. (1) A person commits the crime of resisting
arrest if he intentionally prevents or attempts to prevent a
peace officer, recognized to be acting under color of his official authority, from effecting an arrest of the actor or another, by:

    (a) Using or threatening to use physical force or vio-
lence against the peace officer or another; or
    (b) Using any other means creating a substantial risk
of causing physical injury to the peace officer or another.

(2) It is no defense to a prosecution under this section
that the police officer was acting unlawfully in making the
arrest, provided he was acting under color of his official
authority.
    (3) Resisting arrest is a Class A misdemeanor.

Committee Commentary

This section is derived from several sources, including
Model Penal Code Sec. 242.2 and existing Michigan law. Until
1966, Michigan had no general provision dealing specifically
with resistance to an arrest. Occasional provisions attached
to specific substantive codes made it a misdemeanor for "any
person to resist or obstruct any officer or person empowered
to make arrests under the provisions of this act" (see, e.g.,
C.L. 1948, Sec. 752.825; C.L. 1948, Sec. 317.165), but there
was no general provision employing similar language. However, C.L. 1948, Sec. 750.479, dealing with obstruction of
peace officers generally, clearly encompasses all such resistance. That section makes it a misdemeanor, punishable
by two years imprisonment, for any person to "knowingly and
willfully obstruct, resist or oppose any sheriff, coroner,
. . . constable . . . or other officer duly authorized in serving or attempting to serve or execute any process," or "resist
any officer in the execution of any local ordinance, or to resist any officer authorized by law to maintain and preserve
the peace." In 1966, a new Penal Code provision, Sec. 479a

1470

(C.L. 1948, Sec. 750.479 (a)), was added dealing specifically with the act of resisting arrest. That provision makes it a misdemeanor, punishable by two years imprisonment, to "forcibly assault or commit a bodily injury which requires medical care or attention upon a peace or police officer . . . while the . . . officer is engaged in making a lawful arrest."

It should be noted that Sec. 4506 is intended to replace C.L. 1948, Sec. 750.479, insofar as that provision deals with the obstruction of police activities other than making an arrest. However, that section is applicable to obstruction by use of any physical force or obstacle. As applied to arrests this would include a person who fled from an arrest, and possibly a person who presented a physical obstruction by passive resistance.

It is not entirely clear whether flight from arrest would constitute a violation of C.L. 1948, Sec. 750.479. Certainly the language of the section, referring merely to knowing obstruction, resistance and opposition, would be broad enough to encompass flight. Also, the section as interpreted in other contexts does not require physical violence (see People v. King, 236 Mich. 405, 210 N.W. 235 (1926); People v. Krum, 374 Mich. 356, 132 N.W.2d 69 (1965) (both involving general obstruction of law enforcement)). On the other hand, all the reported cases on charges of resisting arrest have involved physical violence directed at the officer (see _e.g._, People v. Chesbro, 300 Mich. 720, 2 N.W.2d 895 (1942); People v. Arnett, 239 Mich. 123, 214 N.W. 231 (1927)).

The Committee believes that irrespective of the broad language of C.L. 1948, Sec. 750.479, neither flight from arrest nor passive resistance should be made crimes in themselves. Ordinarily, the officer's authority to use force to effectuate an arrest provides an adequate remedy without any need for additional sanctions. Criminal law reinforcement of the officer's authority to arrest is needed against only that interference that poses a direct threat to the officer's safety. Accordingly, Sec. 4506 was specifically limited so as not to apply to the obstruction of arrest; a specific provision, Sec. 4625, was adopted to deal with that problem.

Section 4625 applies only to resistance by the use or threat of physical force or by other means that might raise a high likelihood of causing physical harm. It thus reflects a policy similar to that expressed in the recently adopted Penal Code Sec. 479 (a), discussed _supra_, except that the key here is an attempt to cause physical injury rather than actually producing injury. This minor change is in keeping with the general emphasis of Chapters 45 and 46 upon interference with law enforcement rather than personal injury to the public servant. Physical injury to an officer as such is covered by Sec. 2102. Thus, Sec. 4625 also proscribes the use of physical force directed against a person other than the officer since this might be an equally effective means of resisting arrest. The section also includes the use of other means than force

1471

directed at the officers or another, that might cause a "substantial risk of physical injury." The term "physical injury" is defined in Sec. 135 (h), while the concept of substantial risk is employed in the definition of recklessness (Sec. 425 (3)). This might include, for example, tampering with an officer's car while in the process of attempting to evade an arrest.

As under the present law (People v. Tompkins, 121 Mich. 431, 80 N.W. 126 (1899)) the defendant must be aware that the person he is resisting is an officer. The requirement that he act "intentionally" includes knowledge of all relevant circumstances (See Sec. 425 (1)). A change has been made, however, in the treatment of the unlawful arrest. Under present law (People v. Haley, 48 Mich. 495, 12 N.W. 671 (1882); People v. De Meaux, 194 Mich. 18, 160 N.W. 634 (1916)) there is no liability if the peace officer was acting without lawful authority. On this issue, however, the defendant must take his chances. He is still liable if he forcibly resists the arrest, believing it to be unlawful, and later finds that it was in fact a legal arrest. The Committee believes, however, that persons should not be encouraged to resort to self-help to resist an arrest which they know is being made by a peace officer in his official capacity. Even if a citizen feels the arrest is unlawful, he should submit and rely upon his legal remedies. The resort to force is an improper remedy that will usually only lead to an escalation of force by the officer and result in far greater injury to the actor than the improper arrest. This same policy is reflected in Sec. 4506 (2) and is discussed in the commentary to that section. It should be emphasized that this provision forbids the use of force to resist the arrest alone; it has no application if the actor apprehends bodily injury, as when the arresting officer uses unnecessary force to make the arrest. At that point, the normal justifications of self defense, etc. (see Chapter 6) are applicable.

Of course this provision also is not applicable to forceful resistance to an arrest made (a) by a person not known to the actor to be a peace officer, or (b) by a person known to be an officer, but believed to be acting on a frolic of his own rather than in his official capacity as an officer.

Section 4625 provides for punishment of resistance of arrest at the level of a Class A misdemeanor. This approximates present provisions. Both C.L. 1948, Sec. 750.479 and present Code Sec. 449a make resistance of an arrest a "misdemeanor" punishable by two years imprisonment in state prison and a fine of $1,000. Under Sec. 1415, violations of Sec. 4625 as a Class A misdemeanor will permit imprisonment not longer than one year.

(Resisting an Order to Stop a Motor Vehicle)

Sec. 4630. (1) A person commits the crime of resisting an order to stop a motor vehicle if he knowingly fails to

1472

obey a recognized direction of a person recognized to be a peace officer to stop his vehicle.

(2) It is no defense to a prosecution under this section that the officer's direction to stop was unlawful, provided he was recognized to be an officer and his direction was recognized as an order to stop.

(3) Resisting an order to stop a motor vehicle is a Class A misdemeanor.

Committee Commentary

Recently adopted Penal Code Sec. 479 (a) (C.L. 1948, Sec. 750.479a) makes it a misdemeanor willfully to fail to obey a peace officer's visual or audible direction to stop a vehicle, "by increasing speed, extinguishing lights, or otherwise attempting to flee." The provision requires that the officer be in uniform and the vehicle be adequately identified when driven at night. Section 4625 restates the substance of this offense without making specific reference to special details. Although it refers to any form of direction, the broad definition of direction employed in present Sec. 479 (a) would, in fact, cover every form of direction. The individual is protected, moreover, by the requirement that the direction be recognized as a signal to stop. Similarly, although the requirement that the officer be in uniform is not restated as such, liability exists only if the driver recognizes that he is being directed by an officer to stop.

The proposed punishment, a Class A misdemeanor, is identical to that under present Sec. 479 (a).

INTERROGATORIES

1. How is treason defined in the Michigan Constitution?
2. Outline the provisions of the Michigan statutes relevant to treason and subversion.
3. What were the elements of treason under the common law?
4. How is treason defined in the United States Constitution?
5. What is the definition of "criminal syndicalism."
6. What was the holding of the United States Supreme Court in Pennsylvania v. Nelson?
7. Has there ever been a treason prosecution under the laws of Michigan?
8. What were the facts, issue and holding of the court in People v. Burman?
9. What were the facts, issue and holding of the court in People v. Immonen?
10. What were the facts, issue and holding of the court in People v. Ruthenberg?
11. Outline the provisions of Sec. 5505, Final Draft, Mich. Rev. Crim. Code.
12. Outline the provisions of the Michigan statutes relevant to the crime of riot.

13. Outline the powers of the Governor to deal with a state of emergency.
14. How is "riot" defined in Sec. 5510, Final Draft, Mich. Rev. Crim. Code? How would this section change the law of Michigan?
15. What are the common law elements of the crime of riot?
16. Do the Michigan riot statutes incorporate the common law tradition?
17. What procedural powers are given to police officers in dealing with riots?
18. What limited immunity is given to police officers who kill during a riot?
19. What are the elements of unlawful assembly under Sec. 5515, Final Draft, Mich. Rev. Crim. Code? How does unlawful assembly differ from common law rout?
20. Outline the provisions of Sec. 5520, Final Draft, Mich. Rev. Crim. Code. What are the purposes of these provisions?
21. Outline the provisions of the Michigan statutes relevant to disorderly conduct.
22. What were the facts, issue and holding of the court in People v. O'Keefe?
23. What were the facts, issue and holding of the court in People v. Kelly?
24. What were the facts, issue and holding of the court in People v. Bartz? What was the actus reus of the offense?
25. What were the facts, issue and holding of the court in People v. Johnson? What was the actus reus of the offense?
26. What were the facts, issue and holding of the court in Davis v. Burgess? What was the actus reus of the offense?
27. What was the holding of the court in In re Robinson v. Miner and Haug? What are the elements of the misdemeanor of "breach of the peace" under the common law?
28. Outline the provisions of Sec. 5525, Final Draft, Mich. Rev. Crim. Code.
29. Was disorderly conduct a crime under the common law?
30. What were the facts and holding of the court in Feiner v. New York?
31. Outline the provisions of the Michigan statutes relevant to obstructing government operations.
32. What were the facts, issue and holding of the court in Tryon v. Pingree? Does the common law offense of obstructing justice extend to all governmental activities? What is the gravamen of the offense?
33. What were the facts, issue and holding of the court in People v. Smith?
34. What were the facts, issue and holding of the court in People v. King? What constitutes an illegal obstruction?
35. What were the facts, issue and holding of the court in People v. Boyd?
36. What was the holding of the court in People v. Ormsby? What constitutes obstruction of justice under the common law? Give some typical examples of the offense.
37. Outline the provisions of Sec. 4501 and 4505, Final Draft, Mich. Rev. Crim. Code.

1474

38. Can threats alone constitute an obstruction of justice?
39. What were the facts, issue and holding of the court in People v. Krum?
40. Outline the provisions of Sec. 4506, Final Draft, Mich. Rev. Crim. Code. Would the adoption of this section make any change in the existing law?
41. Outline the provisions of the Michigan statutes relevant to refusing to aid a peace officer.
42. What are the elements of the offense of refusing to aid a police officer under Sec. 4520, Final Draft, Mich. Rev. Crim. Code? What changes would the adoption of this section make in existing law?
43. Outline the provisions of the Michigan statutes relevant to resisting arrest.
44. What were the facts, issue and holding of the court in People v. Haley?
45. What were the facts, issue and holding of the court in People v. Burt?
46. What were the facts, issue and holding of the court in People v. Tompkins? Must the defendant be aware that the person he is resisting is an officer?
47. Outline the provisions of Sec. 4625, Final Draft, Mich. Rev. Crim. Code. What change would the adoption of this section make in the existing law?
48. Outline the provisions of Sec. 4630, Final Draft, Mich. Rev. Crim. Code. Would the adoption of this section change the existing law?